	LESS		PLUS	EQUALS					
Corporate Profits	Net Interest	Contributions for social insurance	Transfer payments (includes interest and dividends)	Personal Income	Personal tax and nontax payments	Disposable Personal Income	(personal consumption expenditures and interest and transfer payments to foreigners)	Personal Savings	Year
$ 9.2	4.7	$ 0.2	$ 14.2	$ 84.9	$ 2.6	$ 82.3	$ 79.1	$ 3.1	1929
−2.6	4.0	.3	3.3	77.0	2.5	74.5	71.1	3.4	1930
−4.9	2.9	.3	4.5	65.9	1.9	64.0	61.4	2.6	1931
−5.2	1.3	.3	3.8	50.2	1.5	48.7	49.3	−.6	1932
−1.7	4.1	.3	9.7	46.9	1.4	45.5	46.5	−1.0	1933
−1.0	.7	.3	3.9	54.0	1.6	52.4	52.0	.4	1934
−.2	.8	.3	4.1	60.4	1.9	58.5	56.4	2.1	1935
.4	.6	.6	5.2	68.6	2.3	66.3	62.7	3.6	1936
.6	1.4	1.8	4.3	74.1	2.9	71.2	67.4	3.8	1937
−.2	2.0	2.0	4.7	68.3	2.9	65.5	64.8	.7	1938
5.3	3.6	2.1	12.2	72.4	2.4	69.9	67.8	2.1	1939
8.7	3.3	2.3	12.4	77.8	2.6	75.2	72.0	3.3	1940
14.1	3.3	2.8	12.8	95.3	3.3	92.0	81.8	10.2	1941
19.3	3.1	3.5	12.7	122.4	5.9	116.5	89.4	27.0	1942
23.5	2.7	4.5	12.5	150.7	17.8	132.9	100.1	32.7	1943
23.6	2.4	5.2	13.4	164.4	18.9	145.5	109.0	36.5	1944
19.0	2.2	6.1	16.6	169.8	20.8	149.0	120.4	28.5	1945
16.6	1.6	6.1	23.3	177.3	18.7	158.6	145.2	13.4	1946
22.2	2.1	5.8	25.4	189.8	21.4	168.4	163.5	4.9	1947
29.1	2.1	5.4	25.4	208.5	21.0	187.4	176.9	10.6	1948
26.9	2.2	5.9	27.9	205.6	18.5	187.1	180.4	6.7	1949
33.7	2.3	7.1	32.9	226.1	20.6	205.5	194.7	10.8	1950
38.1	2.7	8.5	30.6	253.7	28.9	224.8	210.0	14.8	1951
35.4	3.0	9.0	31.9	270.4	34.0	236.4	220.4	16.0	1952
35.5	3.4	9.1	34.3	286.1	35.5	250.7	233.7	17.0	1953
34.6	4.3	10.1	38.0	288.2	32.5	255.7	240.1	15.6	1954
44.6	4.8	11.5	41.5	308.8	35.4	273.4	258.5	14.9	1955
42.9	5.2	12.9	45.1	330.9	39.7	291.3	271.6	19.7	1956
42.1	6.5	14.9	50.5	349.3	42.4	306.9	286.4	20.6	1957
37.5	8.0	15.2	56.0	359.3	42.1	317.1	295.4	21.7	1958
48.2	8.8	18.0	60.1	382.1	46.0	336.1	317.3	18.8	1959
46.6	9.8	21.1	65.2	399.7	50.4	349.4	332.3	17.1	1960
46.9	11.2	21.9	67.7	415.0	52.1	362.9	342.7	20.2	1961
54.9	12.8	24.3	75.2	440.7	56.8	383.9	363.5	20.4	1962
59.6	14.3	27.3	81.5	463.1	60.3	402.8	384.0	18.8	1963
67.0	15.9	28.7	88.1	495.7	58.6	437.0	410.9	26.1	1964
77.1	18.5	30.0	96.7	537.0	64.9	472.2	441.9	30.3	1965
82.5	21.9	38.8	105.8	584.9	74.5	510.4	477.4	33.0	1966
79.3	24.3	43.4	117.7	626.6	82.1	544.5	503.7	40.9	1967
85.8	26.8	48.1	131.4	685.2	97.1	588.1	550.1	38.1	1968
81.4	30.8	54.9	145.0	745.8	115.4	630.4	595.3	35.1	1969
67.9	37.5	58.7	167.1	801.3	115.3	685.9	635.4	50.6	1970
77.2	42.8	64.8	186.4	859.1	116.3	742.8	685.5	57.3	1971
92.1	47.0	73.6	203.3	942.5	141.2	801.3	751.9	49.4	1972
99.1	52.3	91.5	230.8	1,052.4	150.8	901.7	831.3	70.3	1973
83.6	69.0	103.8	274.8	1,154.9	170.3	984.6	913.0	71.7	1974
95.9	78.6	110.6	325.6	1,255.5	168.8	1,086.7	1,003.0	83.6	1975
127.0	84.3	125.1	328.1	1,380.9	196.5	1,184.4	1,116.3	68.0	1976
144.2	95.4	140.3	393.7	1,529.0	226.0	1,303.0	1,236.1	66.9	1977
159.6	106.3	164.3	434.3	1,708.0	256.2	1,451.8	1,374.9	76.9	1978

Economics

Ron Carmichael   ΣφΔ
302 E. Gregory Dr.
Champaign, Ill. 61820
(217) 337-7511

Please Return
Thank You!

Economics

Third Edition

Lewis C. Solmon

**Higher Education Research Institute
and
University of California, Los Angeles**

Addison-Wesley Publishing Company

Reading, Massachusetts
Menlo Park, California
London
Amsterdam
Don Mills, Ontario
Sydney

This book is in the Addison-Wesley Series in Economics

Sponsoring Editor: Ronald R. Hill
Project Editor: Jane E. Tufts
Production Editor: Barbara H. Pendergast
Designer: Michael Alberghene/Catherine L. Dorin
Illustrator: Phil Carver & Friends
Cover Design: Catherine L. Dorin

Copyright © 1980, 1976, 1972 by
Addison-Wesley Publishing Company, Inc.
Philippines copyright 1980, 1976, 1972 by
Addison-Wesley Publishing Company, Inc.

Second printing, September 1980

All rights reserved.
No part of this publication may be reproduced,
stored in a retrieval system,
or transmitted, in any form or by any means,
electronic, mechanical, photocopying,
recording, or otherwise,
without the prior written permission of the publisher.
Printed in the United States of America. Published
simultaneously in Canada.
Library of Congress Catalog Card No. 79-25514.

ISBN 0-201-07635-7
CDEFGHIJ-HA-8987654321

Library of Congress Cataloging in Publication Data

Solmon, Lewis C
  Economics.

  Includes index.
  1. Economics. I. Title.
HB171.5.S644 1980   330   79-25514
ISBN 0-201-07635-7

This text is also available in split paperback volumes: *Macroeconomics, Third Edition* and *Microeconomics, Third Edition.* The tables of contents for each volume can be found following the Detailed Table of Contents. In addition, each volume is accompanied by its own *Student Learning Guide.*

Contents in Brief

This text is also available in split paperback volumes: *Macroeconomics, Third Edition* and *Microeconomics, Third Edition*. The tables of contents for each volume can be found following the Detailed Table of Contents. In addition, each volume is accompanied by its own *Student Learning Guide*.

PART I
Some basic economic concepts

CHAPTER 1
Introduction to the study of economics   3

Appendix 1
The use of graphs   18

CHAPTER 2
Utilization of economic resources   33

CHAPTER 3
The laws of demand and supply   51
Application 1   Demand and supply: the beef boycott   73

CHAPTER 4
The price system and how it operates   75
DEVELOPMENTS IN ECONOMIC THOUGHT: ADAM SMITH   85
Application 2   Rebates: the price system in operation   93

PART II
The circular flow of expenditures and income

CHAPTER 5
Households in the American economy   99

CHAPTER 6
Businesses in the American economy   109
Application 3   Ford Pintos: a case of corporate responsibility   121

CHAPTER 7
Government in the American economy   123
Application 4   The tax revolt   136

MACROECONOMICS

PART III
National income, economic goals, and fiscal policy

CHAPTER 8
Measuring national income and product   141
Application 5   The underground economy   159

CHAPTER 9
Inflation, unemployment, and business cycles   161
Application 6   The problem of black teenage unemployment   183

CHAPTER 10
Total spending: the consumption and investment components   187

CHAPTER 11
The equilibrium level of output and income   207
DEVELOPMENTS IN ECONOMIC THOUGHT: PAUL SAMUELSON   215

CHAPTER 12
Fiscal policy: government spending and taxation   223

PART IV
Money, monetary policy, and economic stabilization

CHAPTER 13
The importance of money in an economy   245
DEVELOPMENTS IN ECONOMIC THOUGHT: MILTON FRIEDMAN   257

CHAPTER 14
Commercial banks and the creation of money   265
Application 7   Consumer debt   280

CHAPTER 15
The Federal Reserve System and monetary policy   285

CHAPTER 16
Business cycles, fiscal and monetary policies: an overview   305
Application 8   How the recession came about   321

CHAPTER 17
Stabilization: problems and policies   323
DEVELOPMENTS IN ECONOMIC THOUGHT: JOHN MAYNARD KEYNES   329

Appendix 2
Supply side economics   345

PART V
Economic growth

CHAPTER 18
Economic growth theory and the United States' record   355
DEVELOPMENTS IN ECONOMIC THOUGHT: THOMAS MALTHUS   368
Application 9   Productivity: what does it mean?   376

CHAPTER 19
Economic growth in less developed countries   379
Application 10   Mexico: the problems of a developing nation   401

MICROECONOMICS

PART VI
Price and output in the product market

CHAPTER 20
Elasticity of demand and supply   407
Application 11   Elasticity of demand and the pocket calculator   426

CHAPTER 21
Consumer demand   429
DEVELOPMENTS IN ECONOMIC THOUGHT: WILLIAM STANLEY JEVONS   431

CHAPTER 22
The costs of production   443

CHAPTER 23
Price and output under perfect competition   463

CHAPTER 24
The economics of agriculture   487

CHAPTER 25
Price and output under monopoly   505

CHAPTER 26
Price and output under imperfect competition   525

DEVELOPMENTS IN ECONOMIC THOUGHT: JOAN ROBINSON   531

Application 12   Deregulation: the effects on the airlines   542

CHAPTER 27
Big business in the American economy   545

Application 13   Regulating big business: the IBM antitrust case   560

PART VII
Price and employment in the resource market

CHAPTER 28
Demand in the resource market   565

CHAPTER 29
Supply in the resource market   579

CHAPTER 30
General equilibrium   593

Application 14   Supply and demand in the teacher market   604

CHAPTER 31
Labor unions: collective bargaining and wage determination   609

Application 15   Declining memberships in labor unions   627

PART VIII
The economics of current problems

CHAPTER 32
The economics of environmental problems   633

CHAPTER 33
The economics of urban problems   647

CHAPTER 34
The economics of poverty and discrimination   663

CHAPTER 35
The economics of energy   685

PART IX
International economics

CHAPTER 36
Comparative advantage and international trade   705

CHAPTER 37
Barriers to free trade   723

CHAPTER 38
Exchange rates and the balance of payments   737

CHAPTER 39
Current problems in international economics   751

Application 16   The workings of international trade: Japan and the television set   767

PART X
Alternatives to traditional economics

CHAPTER 40
Alternative economic systems   773
DEVELOPMENTS IN ECONOMIC THOUGHT: KARL MARX   779

CHAPTER 41
Radical economics: the old and the new left   793

Appendix 3
A review of formulas used in economics   805

Appendix 4
Nobel prize winning economists   811

Glossary   813

Index   829

Preface

In recent years, economics has taken on an ever more important role in our lives. Steadily climbing prices, the energy crisis, the instability of the dollar—these events and more have touched everyone's lives and have demanded the attention and concern of individuals, businesses, and policymakers at all levels of the national and international economic system. As economics becomes a more noticeable factor in our world, it also becomes increasingly necessary for us as consumers, suppliers, investors, and citizens to attempt to understand the concepts and principles that underlie the economic forces that shape our lives.

This text, now in its third edition, is designed for use in college level introductory economics and attempts to make the basics of economics more accessible to students. As in past editions, current data are included but the timeless elements of economic principles are stressed. The text includes systematic, balanced, and comprehensive coverage of basic principles, the explanation of necessary terminology, the use of simple mathematics, and the application of concepts to some of the almost countless numbers of economic problems facing us.

In revising the second edition, many changes in content and organization have been made in order to help students absorb and understand the often complex study of how we choose to allocate our scarce resources. These changes are outlined below.

FLEXIBLE ORGANIZATION

Macro/Micro

Although most instructors prefer to teach macroeconomic principles first, instructors who want to teach microeconomics first constitute a sizeable minority. In order to accommodate those instructors, the macro and micro sections have been designed as self-contained units, so that the order in which they are studied can be reversed according to the instructor's preference. Outlines for use of this text in one-semester courses emphasizing macroeconomics, microeconomics, or macro- and microeconomic theory follow the detailed table of contents. In addition, this complete text is available in split volumes: *Macroeconomics, Third Edition* and *Microeconomics, Third Edition*. The tables of contents for these volumes are also found after the detailed table of contents, and macro and micro study guides are available.

Theory/Policy

Another important question of organization involves the relationship of economic theory to economic policy. In some cases, the policy chapters follow the appropriate theory chapters—for example, Chapter 19 on less developed countries follows the chapter on growth theory and Chapter 27 (*Big Business in America*) follows the chapter on imperfect competition. In addition, instructors can choose to examine some of our most pressing concerns (e.g., energy and poverty and discrimination) from an economic perspective. Chapters on these and other topics are gathered into one part titled *The Economics of Current Problems*.

Policy chapters have been kept independent and self-contained. Relevant concepts and terminology are briefly defined and reviewed within each policy chapter itself so that students will not have to hunt through other chapters to read necessary background material. Thus, instructors who prefer to delay the detailed examination of policy until students are familiar with basic economic concepts will find it easy to assign the policy chapters in whatever order they choose.

Doctrine

Flexibility has also been extended to another, more subjective area—that of economic doctrine. The author is aware that there are many differing views regarding a number of economic doctrines, and that each of these views has its supporters who can present well-documented studies to back up their cases. Insofar as is possible, this text attempts to let each of these opposing groups speak for itself without editorializing.

READABILITY AND EASE OF COMPREHENSION

The basic function of a textbook is to convey information to the students, but it can perform this function only when the students are willing and able to read it. In the field of economics, which involves the use and understanding of many unfamiliar terms and concepts, students may get bogged down in a tangle of terminology. Therefore, to increase readability and comprehension, a special effort has been made to avoid endless requalification of statement and excessive use of professional jargon while simultaneously avoiding inaccurate oversimplifications. Clear and familiar language is used to explain economic principles, and whenever possible, examples and illustrations of the principles are drawn from the students' own experience in such areas as the exchange of goods and services and the allocation of resources.

As a further aid to better comprehension, the logic of presentation in explaining the basics of economics has been improved. Many chapters have been resequenced and much of the material within chapters has been reorganized. Although it is not possible to point out and discuss all the areas in which such changes have been made, some of the more important changes are discussed in the section on changes in the third edition.

In addition, a number of learning aids (described below) have been included in the text to facilitate student comprehension.

Learning Aids (* indicates features that are new in this edition)

What to look for in this chapter: The opening section of each chapter consists of questions that not only alert the students to the important points of the chapter, but also help students to organize and focus their thoughts for a more effective reading of the chapter.

Recaps: Within the text of each chapter there are one or two boxed-off summaries which briefly condense material covered in extensive sections of a chapter or relate topics covered in different sections.

Definition of terms: When economic terms are introduced, they are boldfaced and associated with an italicized definition. All boldfaced terms are also fully defined in a complete glossary at the end of the book.

Improved section titles: Section titles have been made more descriptive and numerous. Thus, students can glance over the chapter and get a clear overall picture of the chapter coverage before reading the specifics. The titles help students focus on the ideas being discussed and help them to see how the topics within a chapter relate to one another.

Chapter end materials: At the end of every chapter, there is a chapter summary, a list of key terms that have been introduced, and a set of review and discussion questions about topics covered in the chapter. Some of the questions are intended to help students test their comprehension of the material, while others ask them to apply the principles they have learned to their own experiences and to specific situations, both real and imaginary.

Appendix on formulas used in economics: This appendix, found at the end of the text, provides a review of some basic economic formulas (such as those for elasticity and costs) and their definitions. Each entry in this appendix includes a chapter reference so students can review in more depth if they wish. Also included are reviews of some mathematical terms important in economics (such as mean, median, ratio).

Glossary: There is a complete glossary at the end of the text which includes all terms boldfaced in the text. Glossary entries are referenced to the page on which the discussion of the term first appears.

Graphs

An important part of the study of economics is learning to read and understand graphs. For this reason, there is an appendix after Chapter 1 that gives students step-by-step instructions on the use of graphs and explains how to read and interpret the various types of graphs encountered in the text. In addition, all graphs are accompanied by clearly written and informative legends that fully explain the data presented, thus enabling students to study the graph without continually having to turn back to the chapter text for the explanation.

NEW FEATURES AND CHANGES IN THE THIRD EDITION

Among the new features of this edition are eight essays on prominent economists called *Developments in Economic Thought*. While including some biographical information, each essay concentrates primarily on the economist's contribution to the main body of economic knowledge.

The case studies from the second edition have been eliminated and replaced by sixteen new *Applications* which discuss an actual event or situation that illustrates the concepts and principles discussed in the chapter. Graphs and tables are included where necessary, and each application concludes with Questions for Discussion which help the student arrive at an appropriate analysis of the event presented.

The major reorganizations of the third edition involve the coverage of current problems and international economics. The current problems chapters, which were placed throughout the text in the second edition, have now been gathered into one group (Part VIII: *The Economics of Current Problems*). International economics, formerly covered immediately after the macroeconomics chapters, is now placed after microeconomics in Part IX. The placement of these topics was changed because many of the analytical tools useful in these chapters are microeconomic in nature. The placement of the two chapters on alternatives to traditional economics has also changed and these chapters now constitute the final part of the book.

New and updated chapters

In addition to the above, there have been several major and countless minor changes throughout the book. Some of the most important ones are described below.

Chapter 9: Inflation, Unemployment, and Business Cycles discusses two of our most troublesome macroeconomic problems and gives a general introduction to the fluctuations of economic activity.

Chapter 16: Business Cycles, Fiscal and Monetary Policies examines business cycles in more depth (including the roles of consumption, investment, and government spending) and gives an historical overview of economic activity in the United States from the 1930s to the present—what happened, what fiscal and monetary measures were taken, and what the results were.

Chapter 17: Stabilization Problems and Policies replaces Chapter 17 from the second edition and examines our recent economic dilemma of continually high rates of inflation despite recessions and high unemployment. The chapter looks at how the current situation developed, how we have tried to deal with it, why we've failed, and possibilities for the future. In addition, a new appendix has been added to Chapter 17 which examines the effects of shifts in aggregate supply and aggregate demand on the levels of prices and real income.

The chapters on the following topics have been substantially revised to include the most current events and trends: less developed countries; agriculture and big business in the United States; environmental, urban, and energy problems; poverty and discrimination; and problems in international economics.

SUPPLEMENTS

A complete package of learning and teaching supplements is available for use with this text:

The *Student Learning Guide* prepared by Professors Thomas Pierce and Richard Moss of California State College-San Bernardino includes learning objectives; chapter outlines; key terms (with a reminder that the terms are fully defined in the text's glossary); a concepts and definitions review that includes fill-in-the-blank, matching, true/false, and multiple-choice questions; and more thoughtful and involved questions that require students to apply what they have learned to a certain situation or problem. This guide is also available in split volumes to accompany the *Macroeconomics* and *Microeconomics* paperbacks.

A set of *Audio Cassettes on Principles of Economics* accompanied by a *Student Tutor Workbook* (prepared by Dennis Weidenaar and Emmanuel Weiler) is designed to allow students to study the basics of economics independently.

A *Guide to Effective Teaching* includes lecture outlines, additional topics for classroom discussion, essay questions, and a bibliography of the most important current articles and books on the chapter topics.

The *Test Item Bank,* prepared by Professor Terry P. Sutton of Southeast Missouri State University, includes over four thousand true/false, fill-in-the-blank, and multiple-choice test items, and is available in book and computerized formats.

A set of *Transparency Masters* includes most of the graphs found in the text. Also included are graphs (along with legends) that do not appear in the text, thus allowing the instructor to show more than one situation to illustrate a certain principle.

ACKNOWLEDGMENTS

The task of rewriting, revising, and updating a comprehensive text of this scope is truly a monumental one. Without the contributions of the following people, such a thorough revision would not have been possible: James Charkins, California State College-San Bernadino; James Diggins; Richard Moss, California State College-San Bernadino; Timothy Patterson; Thomas Pierce, California State College-San Bernadino; Richard A. Shaffer of *The Wall Street Journal;* and Michael Walker of California State University at Fullerton.

The third edition has benefited greatly from the comments and suggestions of many professors who took the time to carefully review the chapters of this book in varying stages of revision, and I would like to thank them for their efforts:

Kenneth O. Alexander, Michigan Technological University

B. T. Allen, Michigan State University

William A. Bachman, Niagara University

Ronald G. Brandolini, Valencia Community College

John Bungum, Gustavus Adolphus College

R. J. Charkins, California State University-San Bernardino

Ronald J. Gunderson, Northern Arizona University

Robert E. Herman, Nassau Community College

William L. Holahan, University of Wisconsin-Milwaukee

Jack L. Jeppesen, Cerritos College

David P. Lewis, University of Alabama-Birmingham

Richard V. Luchessi, American River College

Carol C. McDonough, University of Lowell

Earl P. Purkhiser, Mt. San Antonio College

Richard Startz, Wharton School-University of Pennsylvania

R. G. Stout, Northwest Missouri State University

Janet M. West, University of Nebraska-Omaha

Robert D. Widmer, Lincoln College

Herbert Scott Young, Miami-Dade Community College

Special thanks for their helpful ideas are due to the following professors who reviewed the final revised manuscript in detail:

John S. Grady, LaSalle College

Michael H. Kupulik, University of Montana

Thomas P. Lantz, Pasadena City College

Terry P. Sutton, Southeast Missouri State University

Finally, I am most grateful to Jane Tufts and Kathe Rhoades of Addison-Wesley. Without their editorial resourcefulness and professional expertise, this third edition would not have been possible.

Los Angeles L. C. S.
October 1979

Suggested Course Outlines

One-semester course emphasizing macroeconomics

1. Introduction to the study of economics
2. Utilization of economic resources
3. The laws of demand and supply
4. The price system and how it operates
5. Households in the American economy
20. Elasticity of demand and supply
21. Consumer demand
6. Businesses in the American economy
22. The costs of production
23. Price and output under perfect competition
25. Price and output under monopoly
7. Government in the American economy
8. Measuring national income and product
9. Inflation, unemployment, and business cycles
10. Total spending: the consumption and investment components
11. The equilibrium level of output and income
12. Fiscal policy: government spending and taxation
13. The importance of money in an economy
14. Commercial banks and the creation of money
15. The Federal Reserve System and monetary policy
16. Business cycles, fiscal and monetary policies: an overview
17. Stabilization: problems and policies
18. Economic growth theory and the United States' record
36. Comparative advantage and international trade
38. Exchange rates and the balance of payments

One-semester course emphasizing microeconomics

1. Introduction to the study of economics
2. Utilization of economic resources
3. The laws of demand and supply

4 The price system and how it operates
5 Households in the American economy
6 Businesses in the American economy
7 Government in the American economy
20 Elasticity of demand and supply
21 Consumer demand
22 The costs of production
23 Price and output under perfect competition
24 The economics of agriculture
25 Price and output under monopoly
26 Price and output under imperfect competition
27 Big business in the American economy
32 The economics of environmental problems
28 Demand in the resource market
34 The economics of poverty and discrimination
29 Supply in the resource market
31 Labor unions: collective bargaining and wage determination
30 General equilibrium
8 Measuring national income and product
9 Inflation, unemployment, and business cycles
10 Total spending: the consumption and investment components
11 The equilibrium level of output and income
12 Fiscal policy: government spending and taxation
35 The economics of energy

One-semester course emphasizing micro and macroeconomic theory

1 Introduction to the study of economics
2 Utilization of economic resources
3 The laws of demand and supply
4 The price system and how it operates
5 Households in the American economy
6 Businesses in the American economy
20 Elasticity of demand and supply
21 Consumer demand

22 The costs of production
23 Price and output under perfect competition
25 Price and output under monopoly
26 Price and output under imperfect competition
28 Demand in the resource market
29 Supply in the resource market
 7 Government in the American economy
 8 Measuring national income and product
 9 Inflation, unemployment, and business cycles
10 Total spending: the consumption and investment components
11 The equilibrium level of output and income
12 Fiscal policy: government spending and taxation
13 The importance of money in an economy
14 Commercial banks and the creation of money
15 The Federal Reserve System and monetary policy
16 Business cycles, fiscal and monetary policies: an overview
17 Stabilization: problems and policies
18 Economic growth theory and the United States' record
35 The economics of energy

Contents

PART I
Some basic economic concepts

CHAPTER 1
Introduction to the study of economics 3
What is economics? 4
Economics as a social science 5
   Applying the scientific method to the study of economics 6
Economics: a not-so-exact science 7
   Differences between our modern economy and the old models 8
   The value of an economic theory 8
Fundamentals of economic study 10
   Empirical data 10
   Concepts 11
   Models 13
Why study economics? 15
Summary 15

Appendix 1
The use of graphs 18

CHAPTER 2
Utilization of economic resources 33
Unlimited desires 34
   Types of consumer desires 34
Scarcity of resources 35
   Land 35
   Labor 36
   Capital 36
   Entrepreneurship 36
   Technology—another productive resource 37
   Interrelationship among productive resources 37
Maximizing output and satisfaction 37
   Full employment of productive resources 37
   Efficiency of production 38
Economic choices 40
   Opportunity costs 40
   Production possibilities 40
   Increasing costs 43
A brief summary 48
Summary 49

CHAPTER 3
The laws of demand and supply 51
The exchange transaction 52
   Conditions for exchange 52
Demand 54
   Law of demand 55
   Demand schedule 55
   Demand curve 55
   Change in demand and change in quantity demanded 56
   Determinants of individual demand 58
   Determinants of market demand 60
Supply 61
   The law of supply 62
   Supply schedule 62
   Supply curve 63
   Change in supply and quantity supplied 64
   Determinants of supply: individual firm 64
   Determinants of market supply 66
Changes in supply and demand and changes in price 66
Market equilibrium of supply and demand 67
   Shortages and surpluses 68
Supply and demand analysis: further uses and applications 68
Summary 70

Application 1 Demand and supply: the beef boycott 73

CHAPTER 4
The price system and how it operates 75
The circular flow 76
   Resource markets and product markets 76
   The circular flow model 76
   Money flows and real flows 76
How the price system answers production questions 78
   A system of "dollar votes" 78
   What to produce 79
   How to produce 82
   For whom to produce 83
Assumptions of a competitive market economy 83
   Self-interest 83
DEVELOPMENTS IN ECONOMIC THOUGHT: ADAM SMITH 85
   Profit motive 87
   Competition 87
The modern American economy: a capitalist system 89
   Imperfect competition 89
   Extensive use of capital 89
   Private ownership 90
   Division of labor and specialization 90
Summary 91

Application 2 Rebates: the price system in operation 93

PART II
The circular flow of expenditures and income

CHAPTER 5
Households in the American economy 99
The household as a production unit 100
   Similarities to businesses 100
Sources of household revenue 101
   Regional variations in income 102
   Determinants of income level 102
   Productivity and inequalities of income 103
Household spending 103
   Taxes on households 104
   Saving by households 104
   Trends in households that affect economic behavior 105
   The importance of households 106
Summary 107

CHAPTER 6
Businesses in the American economy 109
What is a business enterprise? 109
   Firms, plants, and industries 110
Principal forms of business enterprise 111
   Individual proprietorship 111
   Partnership 113
   Corporation 113
Revenues and expenditures of business firms 116
   Expenditures: explicit and implicit costs 116
   Distributing profits 117
Trends in the business sector of the economy 117
Summary 119

Application 3 Ford Pintos: a case of corporate responsibility 121

CHAPTER 7
Government in the American economy 123
Reasons for government intervention 124
   Safeguarding the price system 124
   Correcting inequities of the price system 125
   Providing public goods and services 126
   Stabilizing economic activity 127
Governmental effectiveness and efficiency 128
   Methods of measuring efficiency 128
   Reasons for government inefficiency in producing public goods 128
Government finance 130
   Federal revenue and spending 130
   State revenue and spending 131
   Local revenue and spending 132
Distribution of the tax burden 132
   Benefits-received principle 132
   Ability-to-pay principle 133
   Types of taxes 133
Summary 134

Application 4 The tax revolt 136

MACROECONOMICS

PART III
National income, economic goals, and fiscal policy

CHAPTER 8
Measuring national income and product   141
National accounts   142
Gross national product   142
   Adjusting GNP for price changes   144
   Avoiding double counting   145
   Payments excluded from GNP   145
Calculating GNP   147
   Expenditures approach   148
   Income approach   150
   Components of national income   151
   Nonincome items   152
Measuring economic performance   154
   Problems of GNP system of accounts   154
   Problems in relating GNP and social welfare   155
   Some cautions about comparing GNPs   156
Summary   157

Application 5   The underground economy   159

CHAPTER 9
Inflation, unemployment, and business cycles   161
Economic goals   161
   Full employment and price stability: our two major goals   162
Inflation   163
   Measuring the rate of inflation   163
   Rates of inflation   168
The costs of inflation   169
   Effects on redistribution of income   169
   Effects on productive output   170
Unemployment   170
   Unemployment of labor   170
   How unemployment is measured   171
   Types of unemployment   173
   Level and costs of unemployment   174

Business cycles   177
   A simplified description   177
   Causes of business cycles   179
   Can we forecast business cycles?   180
Summary   181

Application 6   The problem of black teenage unemployment   183

CHAPTER 10
Total spending: the consumption and investment components   187
Consumption   188
   Household saving defined   188
   Consumption and saving schedules   188
   Aggregate consumption schedule   190
   Determinants of aggregate consumption schedules   192
   Concept of permanent income   194
Investment   195
   Business purchases of plant and equipment   195
   Factors influencing business investment decisions   196
   Inventory investment   200
   Investment in residential construction   201
   Stabilizing influences on levels of investment   202
Summary   203

CHAPTER 11
The equilibrium level of output and income   207
Aggregate demand–aggregate supply approach   208
   Aggregate demand   209
   Equilibrium level   210
Savings-equals-investment approach   211
Effect of equilibrium level on planned saving and investment   213
   Reaching saving-investment equilibrium: an illustration   213

Paradox of thrift   213
   Problems and benefits   214
DEVELOPMENTS IN ECONOMIC THOUGHT: PAUL SAMUELSON   215
Multiplier theory: changes in equilibrium NNP   216
   The multiplier effect   216
Achieving full employment: deflationary and inflationary gaps   218
Summary   220

CHAPTER 12
Fiscal policy: government spending and taxation   223
Fiscal policy   224
Stabilizing effect of government   224
   Nondiscretionary fiscal policy: automatic destabilizers   224
   Discretionary fiscal policy   227
The effects of fiscal policy on equilibrium output and income   231
   Government spending   231
   Government taxation   232
   The final effects of spending and taxation on NNP   233
Surpluses and deficits in the federal budget   235
   Disposing of surplus revenue   235
   Financing a deficit   236
Fiscal policy and the public debt   236
   Historical theories of public debt   237
   Effects of the public debt   237
Summary   239

PART IV
Money, monetary policy, and economic stabilization

CHAPTER 13
The importance of money in an economy   245
Functions of money   246
   Medium of exchange   246
   Standard of value   247
   Store of wealth   247
Kinds of money   247
Money in the United States   247
   Currency   247
   Demand deposits   249
   Near-money   249
Money demand   250
   Types of money demand   250
Drawing a demand curve for money   251
   Shifts in the demand curve for money   251
Quantity theory of money   252
   Velocity   253
Quantity theory and full employment: the classical interpretation   254
Quantity theory and unemployment: the Keynesian viewpoint   254
Quantity theory and the "new" new economics   255
Quantiy theory of money: some conclusions   256
Money in the Keynesian model   256
   Money supply and equilibrium interest rate   256
DEVELOPMENTS IN ECONOMIC THOUGHT: MILTON FRIEDMAN   257
   Interest rate and investment spending   259
Summary   262

CHAPTER 14
Commercial banks and the creation of money   265
Components of the commercial banking system   265
   Commercial bank   265
   Central bank   266
Banking business: an overview   267
   Balance sheets   267
Money-creating and money-contracting transactions of commercial banks   270
   Making private loans: money is created   270
   Repayment of loans: money is contracted   274
   Buying government bonds: money is created   275
   Selling government bonds: money is contracted   276

Factors limiting expansion of the money
    supply   276
  Currency leakage   276
  Unwillingness to lend or borrow   277
Summary   277

Application 7   Consumer debt   280

CHAPTER 15
The Federal Reserve System and monetary policy   285
Federal Reserve System   285
  Background of the system   285
  Organization of the system   286
  Board of Governors   286
  Committees   287
  Federal Reserve banks   287
  Member banks   287
Balance sheet of the Federal Reserve banks   287
  Assets   288
  Liabilities   289
Independence of the Federal Reserve
    System   289
  Protection from governmental pressure   290
  Protection from private pressure   290
Functions of the Federal Reserve System   290
  Clearing operations   290
  Distribution of currency   290
  Fiscal agent for the government   291
  Supervisory functions   291
The objectives of Federal Reserve monetary
    policy   291
  Maintaining a high level of employment   291
  Maintaining stable prices   291
Mechanisms for implementing monetary
    policy   293
  Open-market operations   293
  Changing reserve requirements   297
  Changing the discount rate   298
  Selective credit controls   299
  Moral suasion   301
Summary   301

CHAPTER 16
Business cycles, fiscal and monetary policies: an overview   305

Business cycle theory: a synthesis   306
  Recovery   306
  The peak   306
  Recession   307
  The trough   308
The United States' historical record   308
  The 1930s   308
  1940 to 1945   309
  The early postwar years: 1945 to 1950   311
  The 1950s   312
  The 1960s   312
  The 1970s   315
Summary   318

Application 8   How the recession came about   321

CHAPTER 17
Stabilization: problems and policies   323
Goals of stabilization policy   324
  Full employment and stable prices: the impossible dream?   325
  The Phillips curve   325
Achieving stability: traditional theory and
    method   328
  The classical school   328
  The Keynesian viewpoint   329
DEVELOPMENTS IN ECONOMIC THOUGHT: JOHN
MAYNARD KEYNES   329
  The monetarist viewpoint   331
Problems with economic policymaking   332
  Time lags   332
  Public opinion   332
  *Difficulties of reducing government
    spending   333*
  Conflicts between multiple goals   334
Stagflation—the economic dilemma of the
    1970s   334
  The late 1960s: excess aggregate demand   335
  The 1970 recession   335
  New Economic Policy (1971 to 1973)   335
  *The acceleration of inflation in
    1973–1974   336*
  The role of inflationary expectations   336
How can we defeat stagflation?   357

Wage-price control policies 337
Alternatives to traditional fiscal, monetary, and wage-price policies 339
Stabilization problems and policies: an evaluation 342
Summary 342

Appendix 2
Supply side economics 345

PART V
Economic growth

CHAPTER 18
Economic growth theory and the United States' record 355
Measuring economic growth 356
  GNP and growth 356
Factors causing economic growth 359
  Supply factors 359
  Demand factors 360
  Noneconomic factors 361
Growth in the United States 361
  Natural resources 362
  Human resources 362
  Stock of capital goods 363
  Technology 363
  Economies of scale 364
  Entrepreneurship 365
  The importance of demand 365
Theories of economic growth 366
  Classical theory—Adam Smith 366
  Neoclassical theory 367
  Modern growth theory 370

DEVELOPMENTS IN ECONOMIC THOUGHT: THOMAS MALTHUS 368
Costs of economic growth 371
  Inflation, unemployment, and pollution 372
Benefits of economic growth 372
  Achieving growth 373
Summary 374

Application 9 Productivity: what does it mean? 376

CHAPTER 19
Economic growth in less developed countries 379
Defining "less developed" country 382
Barriers to economic development 383
  Low stock of human capital 383
  Low accumulation of physical capital 385
  Problems of using advanced technology 387
  Lack of supporting infrastructure 388
  Cultural and social attitudes 389
  Economic imperialism 389
Paths of economic development 390
  Developing human capital 390
  Accumulating capital goods 391
  Foreign aid 393
  Planning the economy 395
The effect of cartels on less developed nations 396
  OPEC: the effects of the 1973 crisis 396
  Events since 1973 397
Summary 398

Application 10 Mexico: the problems of a developing nation 401

MICROECONOMICS

PART VI
Price and output in the product market

CHAPTER 20
Elasticity of demand and supply 407
Elasticity of demand 408

Calculating elasticity of demand 409
Types of price elasticity 409
Elastic and inelastic portions of the demand curve 412
Elasticity and total revenue 413
Determinants of elasticity 414

Other elasticities of demand 416
Elasticity of supply 417
The market period 417
   The short run 418
   The long run 418
Government actions that affect demand and supply 419
   Price ceilings 419
   Price supports 422
   Sales taxes 422
   Effects of other taxes 422
Summary 423

Application 11 Elasticity of demand and the pocket calculator 426

CHAPTER 21
Consumer demand 429
Theories of consumer demand 429
   Marginal utility theory 430
   Indifference theory 435
Universality of the law of demand 438
   Substitution effect 439
   Income effect 439
   Substitution and income effects from changes in price 439

DEVELOPMENTS IN ECONOMIC THOUGHT: WILLIAM STANLEY JEVONS 431
Summary 440

CHAPTER 22
The costs of production 443
Defining costs 444
   Explicit and implicit costs 444
   Fixed and variable inputs 444
   Short run and long run 445
Product curves 445
   Total product curve 445
   Marginal product curve 446
   Average product curve 448
Short-run costs 449
   Total cost curve 449
   Marginal cost curve 453
   Average cost curve 454
Long-run costs 457
Summary 459

CHAPTER 23
Price and output under perfect competition 463
Characteristics of perfect competition 464
   Function of the market 464
   Assumptions of the perfect competition model 464
   Usefulness of the model 465
The competitive firm in the short run 466
   Price in the perfectly competitive market 466
   Maximizing short-run profits 468
   The firm's short-run supply curve 473
   Minimizing short-run losses 473
Short-run equilibrium 475
   The firm 475
   The industry 476
Long-run equilibrium: the firm and the industry 476
Long-run industry supply curve 480
   Constant-costs industry 480
   Increasing-costs industry 481
   Decreasing-costs industry 482
Evaluating the competitive price system 482
   Benefits 482
   Problems 483
Summary 484

CHAPTER 24
The economics of agriculture 487
The traditional farm problem—an overview 487
   The gap between farm and nonfarm income 488
   Recent developments 488
Causes of the traditional farm problem 489
   The long run 490
   The short run 493
Government farm policy 495
   Parity pricing 495
   Evaluation of government farm policy 499
Agriculture in the 1970s 500
   Increases in foreign demand 500
   Consumer boycotts 500
   Farm legislation in the seventies 501
Summary 502

CHAPTER 25
Price and output under monopoly 505
Characteristics of the monopoly market 506
    No adequate substitutes 506
    Barriers to entry 507
    Long-run situation 510
Price and output under monopoly 510
    Demand in the monopoly model 511
    Maximizing profits: total cost–total revenue 512
    Maximizing profits: marginal cost–marginal revenue 513
Marginal equilibrium: short and long run 515
Defects of monopoly 517
    Inefficiencies 517
    Lack of incentive for innovation 518
Price discrimination 518
    Conditions necessary for price discrimination 518
    Price and output in submarkets—graphic analysis 519
Regulation of the monopoly market 519
    Encouraging competition 519
    Regulating prices and output 520
Summary 522

CHAPTER 26
Price and output under imperfect competition 525
Oligopoly 526
    How does an oligopoly market arise? 526
Price and output under oligopoly 527
    Oligopoly and price inflexibility 527
    Oligopoly and collusion 529
Monopolistic competition 530
    DEVELOPMENTS IN ECONOMIC THOUGHT: JOAN ROBINSON 531
Price and output under monopolistic competition 532
    Demand curve and marginal revenue curve 532
    Short-run equilibrium 533
    Long-run equilibrium 534

Nonprice competition 535
    Product development 536
    Advertising 536
Resource allocation under imperfect competition 538
Summary 539

Application 12   Deregulation: the effects on the airlines 542

CHAPTER 27
Big business in the American economy 545
Bigness in the United States economy 546
    Defining bigness 546
    The trend toward bigness 546
    Attitudes toward bigness 547
Effects of big business on the economy 548
    Restraint of competition 548
    Economies of scale: impact on prices 551
    Product improvement and technological change 551
    Other effects of big business 552
Public policy and big business 553
    The rise of trusts 554
    Other legislation 554
Big business in the 1970s 555
    Future alternatives and directions 556
Summary 557

Application 13   Regulating big business: the IBM antitrust case 560

PART VII
Price and employment in the resource market

CHAPTER 28
Demand in the resource market 565
Calculating resource demand 566
    Marginal revenue product 567
    The demand curve for resources 568
    Resource demand in imperfectly competitive markets 569
Optimum resource mix for the firm 571
Determinants of demand for productive resources 571

Level of product demand 571
Productivity of resources 572
Price of substitutable and complementary resources 572
Elasticity of demand 573
Rate of decline of MRP 573
Elasticity of demand for the final product 574
Resource substitutability 575
Resource cost as a percentage of total production cost 575
Summary 575

CHAPTER 29
Supply in the resource market 579
Supply of labor 579
Supply schedule for a single individual 580
Indifference analysis 580
Plotting the supply curve 581
Wage determination 584
The role of skills 584
The role of job demands 585
Supply of land 586
Economic rent 586
The role of the price system 587
Supply of financial capital 588
The supply schedule 589
Summary 591

CHAPTER 30
General equilibrium 593
General equilibrium analysis 594
General equilibrium: product-market/resource-market approach 595
Input-output approach to general equilibrium analysis 597
Tabular analysis 599
Input coefficients 600
Summary 601

Application 14   Supply and demand in the teacher market 604

CHAPTER 31
Labor unions: collective bargaining and wage determination 609

History of American unionism 610
Early union organization 610
Antilabor activities 611
Prolabor legislation 611
Postwar period 612
The modern labor union 614
Collective bargaining 614
How collective bargaining works 614
Terms of the contract 615
Role of government in collective bargaining 617
Achieving higher union wages 618
Modifying demand 618
Modifying supply 620
Union success in gaining higher wages 620
Unions and resource allocation 621
Arguments of critics of unions 621
Arguments of supporters of unions 621
Inflation: are unions to blame? 621
Unions and the minimum-wage law 622
The future of labor unions 622
Summary 624

Application 15   Declining memberships in labor unions 627

PART VIII
The economics of current problems

CHAPTER 32
The economics of environmental problems 633
Hidden costs—a long-term problem 634
Changing attitudes 635
Economic externalities 635
Effects of divergence between private and social costs 636
External diseconomies: possible remedies 636
Moral persuasion 637
Government regulation 639
Use of the price system 640
How much pollution control? 642
Cost/benefit analysis 643
Summary 644

CHAPTER 33
The economics of urban problems 647
Problems of management and scale 648
   The problem of managerial skill 648
   The problem of scale 648
Urban transportation 648
   Private and social costs of automobile use 649
   Possible solutions 649
The shifting urban population 652
   Problems resulting from middle-class flight 652
   Intracity movement 654
Urban land use 654
   Urban land allocation and the price system 654
   Possible solutions 655
Urban crime 656
   Safety: an economic good 656
   Applying cost/benefit analysis to crime prevention 657
Problems of financing municipal government 658
   Increased demand for services and an eroding tax base 658
   Possible approaches to budgetary problems 658
Summary 661

CHAPTER 34
The economics of poverty and discrimination 663
Poverty: a definition 664
   Advantages and disadvantages of income inequality 664
The poor in America 665
   Distribution of income in the United States 666
Causes of poverty 668
   Low worker productivity 668
   Low level of human capital 669
   Possible solutions 670
   Market imperfections 670
Poverty and discrimination 672
   Effects of discrimination on the economy 672
   Causes of low incomes among minority groups 673
Women in our economic system 674
   Historical background 674
   Factors influencing wage differences 675
   The need for day care 676
Dual labor market theory 676
What can be done about poverty? 677
   Education and legislation 677
   Welfare programs 678
   The negative income tax 679
What can be done about discrimination? 680
   Legislation 680
   Quotas 681
Summary 682

CHAPTER 35
The economics of energy 685
Developments in the 1970s 686
   The energy crisis of 1973–1974 686
   The energy situation since 1974 687
Causes of the energy crisis 688
   Government regulation and control of energy 688
   Demand for energy in the United States 689
   Price controls 690
   Environmental restrictions 691
Proposed solutions to energy problems 692
   The free-market approach 692
   Solutions involving government 693
Fuels of the future 698
Summary 699

PART IX
International economics

CHAPTER 36
Comparative advantage and international trade 705
The basis for international trade 706
   Specialization and interdependence: an illustration 706

Absolute advantage 707
Comparative advantage 707
  A simple model for international trade 708
  Terms of trade 711
  Gains from trade 712
  Why domestic exchange ratios differ 714
Effects of trade 716
  Effect on total world output 716
  Price equalization 717
  Effect on net national product 718
Summary 719

CHAPTER 37
Barriers to free trade 723
Major barriers to trade 724
  Tariffs 724
  Quotas 725
  Other barriers to trade 725
Economic effects of tariffs 725
  An illustration 725
  Inefficiencies caused by tariffs 729
Why are tariffs imposed? 729
  Protection of workers and firms in disadvantaged industries 729
  Stimulation of domestic employment 730
  Protection of developing industries 731
  Protecting industries necessary to national defense 732
  Improving the terms of trade 732
Political uses of tariffs 732
Summary 733

CHAPTER 38
Exchange rates and the balance of payments 737
Financing foreign trade 738
  Exchange rates 738
International balance of payments 743
  Goods-and-services account 744
  Unilateral-transfers account 745
  Capital account 745
  United States balance of payments 746
Summary 747

CHAPTER 39
Current problems in international economics 751
Historical developments in international trade 752
  1914 to 1930 752
  The thirties 752
  World War II 752
  Early postwar years: the European Recovery Program 753
Removal of trade barriers 753
  Reciprocal Trade Agreements Act 753
  General Agreement on Tariffs and Trade 753
  Recent United States tariff policy 754
  The Common Market 755
Historical developments in international finance 755
  Collapse of the gold standard 755
  Development of the postwar monetary system: the Bretton Woods Conference 756
  International monetary developments after Bretton Woods 757
The international monetary system in the 1970s 759
  Adjusting to balance-of-payments disequilibria: the "dirty float" 759
  Providing international liquidity: special drawing rights 759
The ups and downs of the American dollar 760
  Dollar crises 761
The international economic outlook for the 1980s 763
Summary 764

Application 16 The workings of international trade: Japan and the television set 767

PART X
Alternatives to traditional economics

CHAPTER 40
Alternative economic systems 773
Criteria for comparing systems 774
  Plenty 774
  Growth 774

Stability 775
Security 775
Efficiency 775
Equity 775
Economic freedom 775
Classifying economic systems 776
   Problems in comparing economic systems 776
The capitalist market economy 776
   Model 776
   Example 777
The socialist command system 778
   Background 778
DEVELOPMENTS IN ECONOMIC THOUGHT: KARL MARX 779
   Model 780
   Example 783
Other economic systems 786
   Socialist market economy: Yugoslavia 786
   Democratic socialism: Great Britain 787
   The Chinese command economy 788
Summary 789

CHAPTER 41
Radical economics: the old and the new left 793

Marxism: the roots of radical economics 794
   Class struggle 794
   Labor theory of value 794
   The need to accumulate capital 795
   The rise of concentration and imperialism 795
   A proletarian revolution 796
   The Marxist legacy 796
Radical economics today 797
   The radical versus the liberal view 797
   The radical view of capitalism 797
   The radical view of social problems 799
   The radical model of the socialist society 801
Response from the mainstream 801
Summary 803

Appendix 3
A review of formulas used in economics 805

Appendix 4
Nobel prize winning economists 811

Glossary 813

Index 829

Contents for Split Volumes*

MACROECONOMICS
THIRD EDITION

PART I
Some basic economic concepts

CHAPTER 1
Introduction to the study of economics

Appendix 1
The use of graphs

CHAPTER 2
Utilization of economic resources

CHAPTER 3
The laws of demand and supply

CHAPTER 4
The price system and how it operates

PART II
The circular flow of expenditures and income

CHAPTER 5
Households in the American economy

CHAPTER 6
Businesses in the American economy

CHAPTER 7
Government in the American economy

MICROECONOMICS
THIRD EDITION

PART I
Some basic economic concepts

CHAPTER 1
Introduction to the study of economics

Appendix 1
The use of graphs

CHAPTER 2
Utilization of economic resources

CHAPTER 3
The laws of demand and supply

CHAPTER 4
The price system and how it operates

PART II
The circular flow of expenditures and income

CHAPTER 5
Households in the American economy

CHAPTER 6
Businesses in the American economy

CHAPTER 7
Government in the American economy

*Numbers in parentheses indicate chapter numbers in the complete edition; Applications and Developments in Economic Thought that are included in complete edition chapters will also appear in the split volumes.

MACROECONOMICS

PART III
National income, economic goals, and fiscal policy

CHAPTER 8
Measuring national income and product

CHAPTER 9
Inflation, unemployment, and business cycles

CHAPTER 10
Total spending: the consumption and investment components

CHAPTER 11
The equilibrium level of output and income

CHAPTER 12
Fiscal policy: government spending and taxation

PART IV
Money, monetary policy, and economic stabilization

CHAPTER 13
The importance of money in an economy

CHAPTER 14
Commercial banks and the creation of money

CHAPTER 15
The federal reserve and monetary policy

CHAPTER 16
Business cycles, fiscal and monetary policies: an overview

CHAPTER 17
Stabilization: problems and policies

Appendix 2
Supply side economics

MICROECONOMICS

PART III
Price and output in the product market
(Part VI in complete edition)

CHAPTER 8
Elasticity of demand and supply (Ch. 20)

CHAPTER 9
Consumer demand (Ch. 21)

CHAPTER 10
The costs of production (Ch. 22)

CHAPTER 11
Price and output under perfect competition (Ch. 23)

CHAPTER 12
The economics of agriculture (Ch. 24)

CHAPTER 13
Price and output under monopoly (Ch. 25)

CHAPTER 14
Price and output under imperfect competition (Ch. 26)

CHAPTER 15
Big business in the American economy (Ch. 27)

PART IV
Price and employment in the resource market
(Part VII in complete edition)

CHAPTER 16
Demand in the resource market (Ch. 28)

CHAPTER 17
Supply in the resource market (Ch. 29)

CHAPTER 18
General equilibrium (Ch. 30)

CHAPTER 19
Labor unions: collective bargaining and wage determination (Ch. 31)

MACROECONOMICS

PART V
Economic growth

CHAPTER 18
Economic growth theory and the United States' record

CHAPTER 19
Economic growth in less developed countries

PART VI
International economics
(Part IX in complete edition)

CHAPTER 20
Comparative advantage and international trade (Ch. 36)

CHAPTER 21
Barriers to free trade (Ch. 37)

CHAPTER 22
Exchange rates and balance of payments (Ch. 38)

CHAPTER 23
Current problems in international economics (Ch. 39)

Appendix 3
A review of formulas used in economics

Appendix 4
Nobel prize winning economists

Appendix 5
Basic economic data, 1929–1978

Glossary

Index

MICROECONOMICS

PART V
The economics of current problems
(Part VIII in complete edition)

CHAPTER 20
The economics of environmental problems (Ch. 32)

CHAPTER 21
The economics of urban problems (Ch. 33)

CHAPTER 22
The economics of poverty and discrimination (Ch. 34)

CHAPTER 23
The economics of energy (Ch. 35)

PART VI
Alternatives to traditional economics
(Part X in complete edition)

CHAPTER 24
Alternative economic systems (Ch. 40)

CHAPTER 25
Radical economics: the old and the new left (Ch. 41)

Appendix 2
A review of formulas used in economics

Appendix 3
Nobel prize winning economists

Appendix 4
Basic economic data, 1929–1978

Glossary

Index

Part I

Some Basic Economic Concepts

Chapter 1

Introduction to the Study of Economics

What to look for in this chapter

What is economics?

Is economics a science? How is it related to and different from the other social sciences?

Why is economics not a completely exact science? What limitations are imposed on economists by the subject matter, the methods used, value judgments, and politics?

What exactly do economists do? What is the role of data, mathematics, concepts, and models in the study of economics?

How does economics have practical use for you and for the nation?

It is a basic dilemma of human existence that the things we desire are scarce. Our world contains only a certain quantity of materials that can be put to productive or creative uses, only a limited amount of human energy, and perhaps most restricting of all, only a limited amount of time. Since we cannot alter these encompassing circumstances of our lives, we do the next best thing—we learn to make the fullest possible use of the scarce resources we do have.

Many different branches of knowledge help us deal with the problem of scarcity. Philosophy and religion help us establish our system of priorities, so that we can decide which of our desires and goals are most important to us. Technology and the natural sciences extend our knowledge of the way the material resources of the earth can be manipulated and combined to produce a variety of material goods. But the discipline that deals most directly with the problem of scarcity is economics.

✓ **Economics*** is *the study of the way we may choose among alternative uses of scarce resources.*

It is sometimes assumed that the subject of economics is concerned only with the production and the accumulation of material possessions, such as cars and stereo tape decks. Yet economic resources can be used to produce not only the material symbols of the good life but also satisfactions that are less tangible but still valuable. For example, the United States already devotes a significant portion of its resources to providing education for its children, medical care for the aged, and more leisure time for workers. Today many people also want to extend our financial commitment to nonmaterial values—for instance, to surrounding our planet with clean air instead of poisonous chemicals, to saving our remaining wilderness areas protecting our wildlife, and to restoring some measure of quiet and tranquillity to our urban areas. An important part of the economic process is deciding which goals to pursue. Should we make more plastic bags, or protect the American eagle from extinction, or launch two astronauts to explore Mars? Such choices are the very heart of economic study.

WHAT IS ECONOMICS?

The words "economics" and "economical" are already a part of most people's everyday vocabulary. You tell your friend that if he wants to make his money last for the rest of the month, he will have to be more economical; you decide that you should buy an economy car to commute back and forth to your job. But what is the connection between end-of-the-month thrift and the course that is called "Principles of Economics"?

It is easy to understand why, in ordinary usage, economy has come to be synonymous with money saving. Students who must manage economically will attempt to get the most satisfaction, in terms of both material possessions and pleasure, out of their limited resources. They may have to choose between eating three meals a day and staying in at night, or eating only breakfast and dinner and spending the evening at their favorite pub. Or they may discover that they can eat for less money in a diner ten blocks away if they are willing to walk that far. They will have to choose among their various desires—a full stomach, an evening out, a quick and convenient meal—as they try to stretch their scarce resources as far as possible. This maximizing process, getting the most from what resources are available, is a concept fundamental to the study of economics.

Today economics is usually thought of as the study of the ways people try to satisfy their virtually unlimited desires by choosing among the alternative uses of the scarce resources that are available. These resources include a fixed amount of land and raw materials, capital equipment such as machinery and factory buildings, and our own labor and knowledge. Because we can never have everything that we want, we must constantly make choices between different goals and different methods of obtaining those goals, in order to get the most from what we have.

Economics has been described as part of the study of human beings. Exactly which human activities do economists study? Are they interested in learning about the way our sister can get every last cubic millimeter of toothpaste out of her tube of Crest? Or do they want only to know how many tubes of Crest are sold every year?

Economists can detect an economic transaction within almost every human activity; they can attribute economic motives to all kinds of human behavior. For example, they look upon the decision of a young married couple to start a family as a purchase of some amount of satisfaction or utility that the would-be parents hope to get

---
*Terms in boldface are defined in the glossary at the end of the book.

from their children. In a broad sense, economics could be described as a point of view from which one searches for the economic implications of any observable human action. Thus, economists may study exactly the same behaviors as sociologists and psychologists do, but their focus is on the allocation of productive resources.

To illustrate this view of economics, we can select one particular action and examine it through the eyes of scholars in various social sciences. Let us imagine a rising young executive, Ernest Frank, who withdraws $17,265.82 from his savings account in the First National Bank of Podunk, and then splurges on a new, fully equipped Lincoln Continental. A sociologist, looking at this action, would note that in Ernest's middle-class neighborhood in a housing development, an expensive car is the most visible effective status symbol he could buy; the sociologist would view the purchase as Ernest's way of asserting some degree of social superiority over his neighbors. A psychologist might point out that Ernest, now 33 and married more than 12 years, subconsciously views the car as a kind of mistress-substitute, and he would suggest that Ernest bought the car as a means of demonstrating that his virility was undiminished, in response to a common fear of middle-aged men. A political scientist would notice the ways in which Ernest's acquisition of a car changes his demands on the municipal government of Podunk. Now, for example, Ernest may have little interest in inexpensive and reliable public transportation, and therefore he may be quite unwilling to vote for bond issues or increased taxes to extend the metropolitan transit system. Instead, he may want good roads to be built and more places to park in the downtown area.

To the economist, Ernest's purchase represents an individual decision to stop saving and to start spending. It is a decision to use his labor —saved in the form of money—to obtain the particular satisfaction of a new car, rather than the satisfaction derived from some alternative purchase. By buying the new car, Ernest has also made the decision to forgo the yearly interest he earned from his savings account and all the additional pleasure that extra money could buy for him. Because his yearly income will be reduced by the amount of the interest, he faces a greater budget restraint in the future. The economist would be interested in the effect the new car will have on the way Ernest allocates his weekly paycheck. He will save bus fare, but he will have to pay insurance premiums, buy gasoline, and spend money maintaining the car. The economist would also point out other less direct implications of the plumber's action: a decrease in the total amount of savings held in the bank, which subsequently could have been lent out to business for capital investment; increased prosperity for the Lincoln dealer and his employees; and an incentive for the neighbors to increase their rates of saving so that they can be able to buy new cars too.

ECONOMICS AS A SOCIAL SCIENCE

Modern economics is considered a social science. It is social because it deals with an area of human behavior; it is a science because it attempts to apply the principles of the scientific method to its subject matter. Economics is closely related to the other social sciences, and they often share information and discoveries. Economists borrow from the field of sociology as they seek to establish the cultural determinants of an economic system and the social determinants of actions with economic consequences. They turn to history to trace the development of economic systems. Political science offers answers regarding the role that government can play, especially in regard to influencing an economy. Psychology furnishes explanations of the satisfactions people derive from purchasing certain goods and the reasons that some situations can affect public confidence, causing stock prices to rise and fall or depositors to remove their money from a bank all at once.

Applying the scientific method to the study of economics

Like scientists who work in a laboratory, economists try to employ the scientific method by following certain steps that promote accuracy in their observations and in the conclusions they draw from them. Economists gather empirical data, information collected through observation and experience, and tabulate them statistically; they keep careful and complete records of all their observations and their work in progress; they try whenever possible to control the other conditions surrounding the phenomenon they are studying.

Maintaining objectivity

Perhaps the most important part of the scientific method is maintaining an objective and emotionally neutral attitude toward the subject being studied and the conclusions that emerge. Conscientious economists do not condemn a government policy of raising taxes just because they do not agree with the political philosophy of the administration that requests it. Instead, they collect data showing effects of the tax increase on prices, unemployment, and industrial expansion. They may make a study of the effects of similar tax increases that were enacted in earlier times or in other countries, and then they will analyze the evidence to see what conclusions can be drawn from it. As private citizens, they would of course be gratified if the evidence showed that the government they disagree with has made a mistake. But as economists, they would try to prevent their political biases from interfering with an impartial weighing of the objective data. Admittedly, it is often more difficult for social scientists to maintain perfect detachment than it is for physical scientists; increased taxes commonly arouse more emotions than do inorganic crystals.

Limitations of the scientific method

Although economists are committed to the use of the scientific method, it is not possible to apply this method as comprehensively in the study of human behavior as it is in laboratory studies of inanimate chemicals or caged animals. Perfect accuracy requires control of all factors other than the one being studied, and the economist can never hope to achieve this kind of control over the lives and actions of other human beings. For example, government economists cannot arrange to have all workers fully employed, or 10 percent of workers unemployed, so that they can study the effects of either situation on the rate of saving and spending.

Ideally, the scientific method also requires constant repetition of experiment and result. Physical scientists can combine the same chemicals under the same conditions of heat and pressure again and again, until they completely understand the process by which the chemicals combine and can reliably predict the result of the combination. But in economics, as in all social sciences, it is impossible to duplicate the exact conditions of any situation under study. Suppose, for example, that you are an economist who wants to study the effect of a sudden increase in income on a family's pattern of spending and saving. You pick a group of 20 winners of the state lottery in New York and observe in detail the ways they allocate their winnings. How can you repeat this experiment to check your results? If you follow up on the same families, you will be studying people who are already accustomed to their income increase. If you pick new families, your results may be different because the new families as a group may have a different economic outlook and different consumer habits. Moreover, the continued existence of the lottery and the publicity given to the experiences of the previous winners will certainly have some effect on the attitudes of other winners. Changes in the general economy may also have altered the actual value of the prize money, so that it buys more or less than it did before. Your two tests would necessarily differ in significant ways, making exact repetition impossible.

Another limitation on the use of the scientific method in economics is our inability to predict human behavior with complete accuracy. Because economics deals with the actions of human beings, some people believe that guesswork will always be necessary. Human beings never behave completely rationally or predictably; there is always some degree of the unexpected, the whimsical, the irrational in our choices and responses. Economists may predict that a cut in taxes will increase the level of spending, but there will always be some individuals who will decide to save all of the increase in their paychecks. However, although the behavior of a single individual may be difficult to foresee, social scientists find that they are able to predict the behavior of large groups of people with a high degree of accuracy. (All social sciences deal in averages rather than in individual cases.)

Economics and social problems

Recently there has been a growing trend to apply economic principles to many of the practical problems our society faces; the focus of inquiry today is on discovering how economics can help to solve such problems. Some economists believe that a complex economy like that of the United States is so dynamic that economic analysis is always a kind of hindsight that may or may not be applicable to the current situation. They argue that it is not possible for economists to prescribe exactly how to cure an economic problem. We can analyze past problems and evaluate the steps taken at that time to bring about improvement. We can, for instance, discover that certain actions taken by government agencies during a particular recession helped to bring about a period of sustained economic growth. But we cannot be positive that repeating those actions will serve to cure the next recession because the economy will have changed in many important respects; yesterday's solutions may not work on tomorrow's problems.

Nevertheless, this element of uncertainty should not be overemphasized. Since the 1930s, which saw the first large-scale attempt by governments in the West to create economic improvement, economists have been relatively successful in preventing the wide fluctuations that characterized our economy in earlier times.

ECONOMICS: A NOT-SO-EXACT SCIENCE

There is a feeling among some economists that if economics is to be studied as an analytical science, value judgments must be excluded from economic analyses. In other words, they argue that economics should stick to the facts, consider the economy as it is, rather than as it should be; that economics should provide a system of generalizations that would be useful to predict the consequences of changing economic circumstances. As we have said, economic theory is not intended to make the value judgments about economic goals. However, the conclusions obtained in "nonsubjective" economic analysis are relevant to what *should* be done and would help in the formulation of decisions on how to attain various goals or values for the economy.

A difference between economics and other sciences is that most people view themselves as expert practitioners of economics, whereas few laypersons would regard themselves as expert physicists, for example. For the nonprofessional, it is at times very difficult to keep value judgments out of economic considerations. Unfortunately, even the professional economist sometimes finds value-free, objective analysis very difficult. In 1953, economist Milton Friedman stated that most of his fellow economists could agree on a set of goals for an economic system and that a common set of values prevailed. He explained that differences in policy recommendations among economists result from disagreement about predictions of results of various kinds of economic action. The world is now much different, perhaps much more complicated, than it was even 25 years ago. There is disagreement today not only on how the economy works but on the economic goals of the nation as well.

Differences between our modern economy and the old models

Most economists would still agree that the purpose of an economic system is to provide the goods and render the services that people want and that the best economic system is the one that supplies the most of what people want most. However, some economists, including John Kenneth Galbraith, are no longer willing to accept economic models characterized by individual consumers seeking to maximize their satisfaction in consumption and individual producers seeking to maximize their efficiency and profits. Galbraith argues that individuals are not the only ones who have choices to make. In addition, organizations have developed in our economy which have taken over tasks and developed a life and will of their own. Galbraith's perception of our economy is one that includes large organizations operating in socially objectionable ways which cannot be attributed to the interests of any particular individuals. When economists analyze the current state of an economy and make policy recommendations, the differences among their recommendations will depend very much on the particular economists' perceptions of the world. Emphasis on individual action and private motivation leads to very different policies than does a view of the world which stresses the power of large organizations and the interdependencies of our complex world today.

Collective action

Our modern economy is characterized by many examples of collective action, rather than individual action. When a group decides it cannot achieve its objectives unaided, we sometimes observe demands for public provision of goods and services. Aid to the needy aged may be the only effective device by which that portion of the population may be assured of a subsistence level of living; a program to place people on Mars can be visualized only as a collective program. Governments may also be asked to provide education, housing, transportation, and recreation, even though private alternatives exist.

Certain goods, called public goods, have the peculiarity that once they are available, no one can be precluded from enjoying them because of inability or unwillingness to pay. Such goods are provided by the government. An example is national defense, which probably could not be provided by the private market unaided. In some cases, public goods (such as education) might be provided by the private sector, but the characteristics of the privately and publicly produced commodities might differ. We will discuss public goods further in Chapter 7.

Once a political decision is made to provide certain goods (e.g., defense) or prohibit certain goods (e.g., heroin), private individual or corporate choice possibilities are either expanded or limited. As our economy becomes more complicated, more collective decisions and public goods arise, and hence the reality of individual freedom in decision making becomes more of a myth.

The value of an economic theory

The value of an economic theory is measured in part by how well it enables us to understand the implications of policy change. Some very simplistic theories may be more useful in this regard than more complex analyses which seem to better describe the reality of the world.

Why economic theories don't always work

Let us summarize why economics does not always work.

☐ Economists disagree concerning the facts about our current economy. Some important questions include: Do individuals still have the ability to make choices on their own, or are they dominated by the power of huge organizations? Can individuals truly acquire the goods and services they demand by their own efforts, or are collections of individuals needed to provide many of the goods required in our modern economy?

☐ Economists disagree about what will happen if certain changes are implemented. Because they are unable to conduct controlled experiments, economists are unable to define a single theoretical model which would yield universal agreement on outcomes of policy changes. So, even if economists could come to some agreement on the current state of the economy, economics cannot always provide a useful theory to predict how changes in the current situation will affect the economy of the future.

☐ Many modern-day economists, both the professionally certified and the self-proclaimed, have been unable to separate their subjective evaluations of the worthiness of various economic outcomes from their attempts to provide objective analysis. Some of the basic conflicts are outlined in the following paragraphs.

Certain economists emphasize the importance of maintaining individual freedom of choice. Others believe that the government must intervene into the individual's decision process to counterbalance uncontrolled attempts by large organizations to alter individual behavior. Thus those who are concerned about freedom of choice might view advertising as a means of providing information to individuals for their use in making decisions and those who are concerned about the power of large organizations might view advertising as an attempt to manipulate the decision-making process and hence reduce individual autonomy.

Another issue about which economists disagree is inflation. Some economists believe that it is worth living with some inflation to prevent unemployment. Others feel that the damage inflicted on an economy by a continuous inflation is so severe that it would be better to accept unpleasantly high rates of unemployment for short periods in order to get rid of inflation. In later chapters we will see that there is significant disagreement about whether there is a trade-off between unemployment and inflation. The question is, must we accept more unemployment in order to reduce the rate of inflation?

Some economists feel that our major national goal should be to maximize production. Others place more emphasis on the distribution of whatever is produced among the population. Some of these analysts would accept a smaller national pie in order for that smaller pie to be divided up more equally among the population.

Some economists question the acquisitive basis of the capitalist system and contrast it to the self-deprivation that is encouraged in many other cultures. Some economists are disturbed by the discrepency between the standard of living in less developed countries and the affluence of America, as well as the discrepancy between the poverty in American ghettos and the wealth of the suburbs.

As you can see, it is very difficult to develop a consistent and generally acceptable economic policy when goals are so confused and so contradictory in many areas.

Economics versus politics So far the reasons for the failure of economics have been attributable to the economists themselves. However, even if economists could agree on a set of goals and could develop a theory that would enable them to determine how to achieve these goals, one must remember that ultimate economic policy is the responsibility of politicians rather than economists. One might argue that even economists who get into policymaking positions become politicians rather than economists. Certainly economists in government positions are there at the pleasure of some political official or other. This introduces an additional set of conflicts, namely, those between economic policies and political objectives.

One might argue from an economic point of view that an inefficient airplane factory should not be treated to government subsidy but rather should be forced to succeed on its own or go out of business in favor of more efficient competitors. However, if the aircraft company is located in a populous state and if the decision for or against subsidy must be made very near election time, even politicians who understand the economic inefficiency of subsidizing that company might subordinate their desire for efficiency to their desire to get reelected. The result could be a decision for subsidization on noneconomic grounds. Unwillingness to accept the political consequences of economic decisions has probably been the cause of overreaction to periods of inflation and unemployment. Such overreaction sometimes leads to a worsening of the situation that the policy was intended to reverse.

In brief, economics seems to fail because the economists do not agree on the facts, do not agree on the theory that would enable them to predict what would happen if certain policies were implemented, and do not agree on the value of particular economic consequences. Economics also fails because politicians are sometimes unwilling to use what economists do know when the political and economic implications are in conflict. As long as economic policy must be implemented by politicians, it is unrealistic to think that what is in the best *economic* interests of the country will necessarily take precedence over political interests. One of the most important functions of a basic economics course is to enable students to separate economics from politics. Economics will be more effective if voters can understand economic issues which must be decided in the political arena.

In spite of these problems, economics works more often than not, and it does much to explain various aspects of our daily lives as individuals and as a society.

FUNDAMENTALS OF ECONOMIC STUDY

Now that we know the sort of questions that economics seeks to answer, we can find out how economists go about answering them. How do you study the effects of scarcity or the factors involved in a decision about the use of productive resources? How do you really "do" economics?

Empirical data

One important tool of economic study is the collection of empirical, or factual, data about the economic transactions that take place within a given system. Many economists are engaged in gathering figures on the amount and value of goods produced, on the number of hours of labor being used and the wages paid for that labor, and on the prices charged by retailers and wholesalers of goods. Today this function of data collection is performed principally by agencies of the federal government. Both the Department of Commerce and the Bureau of Labor Statistics, for example, maintain large staffs of statisticians for this purpose. Other common sources of the raw data that economists use are studies carried out by national unions, manufacturing associations, private research organizations, and large banks.

The uses of empirical data

Once data have been collected, they can be analyzed and used in various ways. For example, by dividing the total number of hours worked by all employees into the value of goods produced by a factory in one year, economists can determine the average productivity of a factory's workers. Or they can compare the factory's output over a period of years to determine long-range trends and to predict future needs for various types of work skills. By comparing increases in productivity with increases in workers' salaries, economists can estimate the inflation that is taking place. The possibilities of the combination and the comparison of data are limited only by the economist's imagination.

The importance of mathematics and graphs

The examples given above make it clear that the economist needs basic mathematical skills. The use of simple mathematics and graphs is unavoidable in gaining a mastery of economics because it is easier to understand economics through simple mathematical formulae than through verbal descriptions. In this text, we will limit the presentation of statistical data to a level that can be understood by anyone acquainted with high school algebra. The professional economist, however, is often engaged in very sophisticated mathematical operations. In recent years, the computer, which can perform complex mathematical operations with great speed and accuracy, has greatly extended the possibilities of economic analysis. The appendix at the end of this book will help you review some basic mathematics and economic formulas which will be useful in the study of economics.

To aid in the quick comprehension of empirical data, and also to illustrate many theoretical concepts, economists frequently present information in chart or graph form. Students of economics need to know how to read and interpret these graphic presentations, for they are used to illustrate and explain much of the text. The appendix that follows this chapter gives a step-by-step account of the way to read the kinds of visual aids economists use most often.

Concepts

Empirical data alone are of limited usefulness. To help interpret and explain the significance of collected statistics, economists use concepts, generalizations that guide the way information is perceived and understood and that provide a means of relating many seemingly diverse facts. For example, education is a concept—a generalization about one type of human activity. It is a category in which we can place many activities—a child picking up new words from an older brother, a girl learning how to put on makeup effectively at modeling school, or a graduate student doing research on an obscure branch of philosophy. The concept of education helps us to observe certain similarities in these divergent activities; at the same time, it conditions us to expect certain things to happen in any situation that is labeled "educational."

Everyone uses concepts, but in daily usage, the meaning and definition of many concepts are fuzzy and imprecise. In academic disciplines, it is necessary to arrive at some agreement as to the specific meaning of basic concepts, as well as the terminology that will be used to describe them. For economists, precise concepts provide a way to organize their observations, to discover underlying patterns, and to discuss their findings with other researchers in the field. To illustrate the way economists use concepts to develop economic theories, the examples of an economic good and a marginal unit are introduced here; many other concepts will be presented throughout the book.

An economic good

Economics begins with the assumption that many things we value and desire exist in only a limited supply. The concept **economic good** refers to *anything that is both desirable and scarce and for which we are willing to sacrifice some amount of other desirable things*. Our scarce resources are used for the production of economic goods.

The most obvious types of economic goods are the products of factories—a bicycle, a pair of jeans, or a silver teaspoon. Services, such as dancing lessons or hotel accommodations, are also economic goods. But there are many other kinds of economic goods. For some people, money itself has intrinsic value and is therefore an economic good. Leisure is an economic good; only a limited amount of it is available to most people, because of the necessity of working to produce other commodities. Health is an economic good, and so under certain circumstances is freedom: think of the sacrifice of other goods made by the Hungarians who fled their country during the revolution in 1956.

The list of economic goods is not a fixed, unchanging one. Cultural attitudes may shift, causing people to value things differently. Leisure, for example, is an economic good to us, but our Puritan forefathers believed that idle hands did the devil's work and that personal salvation must be earned through diligent labor. Not very long ago, fresh air was considered to be a **free good**, that is, *a good available to everyone in unlimited supply without the sacrifice of any other good*. Now the widespread problems of pollution have changed the situation, and clean air has become an economic good. Businesses incur costs when they install equipment to prevent the emission of harmful gases from the smokestacks of their factories, and this cost is most often passed along to the buyers of their product in the form of higher prices. Privacy, silence, and wilderness have also become economic goods for many people because of the circumstances of life in modern urban society.

It is interesting to note that examples of economic goods can vary, even within a single society. For example, to those who live in crowded cities, population dispersal is an economic good. Apartment-dwellers will sacrifice both money and convenience to move to a house built on an acre of ground in the suburbs. Yet to the people who live on ranches on the lonely Nebraska prairie, the economic good is population density, and some might sacrifice a great deal to be able to move to a house on a 50-foot lot in town, where they can enjoy the presence of close neighbors and convenient shopping.

Opportunity costs Consideration of economic goods becomes even more complex when we realize that time and the ability to consume are also limited. A man who decides that he wants to spend his day working to earn money for the payments on his TV set cannot also spend that day leisurely watching TV, because there is a limit to the number of hours in a day. A woman who chooses to order 10 pieces of chocolate cake at a restaurant cannot decide to have 20 pieces of lemon pie as well; even if she has the money to pay for them and the time to eat them, her stomach simply cannot hold that much dessert.

Therefore, in order to get any economic good, it is necessary to give up some alternative possible goods. Workers can choose to earn extra money by working overtime, but they must give up some amount of leisure. Likewise, General Motors can produce several million more Pontiacs if it is willing to give up the Chevrolets, Buicks, Oldsmobiles, and Cadillacs that its factories could have produced in the same period of time.

Economists use the term opportunity cost to describe all the alternative economic goods that must be sacrificed to gain a chosen good. Usually there is a choice of opportunity costs for an economic good. For example, there are many different ways we could pay for the economic good of clean air. To name just two, we could pay the opportunity cost of higher prices on consumer items (in which case the producers could use the additional revenue to purchase antipollution equipment), or we could pay the opportunity cost of higher taxes (in which case the government might give subsidies to those producers who reduce their level of pollution). One of the values of a knowledge of economics is that it can help us determine the various opportunity costs we must pay for any economic good, so that we can select the least costly alternative. In fact, the concepts of an economic good and its opportunity cost have proven to be such useful tools of analysis that they are sometimes used in noneconomic situations as well. Marriage counselors, psychiatrists, and philosophers have applied these concepts to emotional transactions and personal relationships. We will discuss opportunity costs in greater detail in Chapter 2.

Marginal units and the concept of marginality
To study economics, we must often use very large numbers. The total value of goods and services produced annually in our country now exceeds $2 trillion; there are about 76 million households in the United States. Yet the basic economic decisions deal with much smaller units. The International Business Machines Corporation (IBM), al-

though its total revenue amounts to billions yearly, must decide whether to make 300 new computers or 350; its customers decide whether to buy the most expensive model or one that costs several thousand dollars less. Both in practice and in economic theory, total figures are often less significant than those that deal with the effect of the addition or the subtraction of a few more units.

In order to study such effects, economists look at the **marginal unit,** *a small amount added to or subtracted from the whole.* If IBM is already producing 300 computers, it will have to decide whether or not it wants to add 50 extra units of production. A pipefitter who has just been given a raise of 50¢ an hour will have to decide how to allocate this additional amount of income. A student who sleeps through the alarm when she had planned to get up early and study will have to decide which activities she will give up because of the marginal units of time she lost.

The marginal unit is basic to many ideas about supply and demand, costs and prices, and production rates and yields, and the concept of marginality helps direct the economist's attention to small, easily measured steps in a larger process.

In addition nearly all economic decisions are made in terms of adding or subtracting marginal units—or, as economists say, they are made at the margin. The pipefitter does not have to decide all at once on his entire budget; he has to decide only how to allocate the marginal units of income. IBM does not have to choose between producing no computers and producing 350 computers; it chooses whether to produce 331 or 332.

Models

When economists want to describe the workings of a total economic system or a particular part of that system, they often draw upon empirical data and concepts to formulate a **model,** or theory, which is *a framework for analyzing and predicting the way that a system would work under specified conditions.* For example, economists have constructed a model showing the effect that the unionization of American auto workers has had on the wages paid to them. The model does not tell us what should happen, or what must happen, but what is *most likely* to happen, on the basis of previous experience.

In working out a model, the economist tries to take into account all the probable factors that will be involved in the real situation. But in the real world, some of the expected factors may be absent and other unexpected ones may be present. Thus, in actual practice, the results are often slightly different from those predicted by the model. Nevertheless, models are very useful tools for analyzing and predicting economic processes.

Problems in model building
Models can be misleading if they are taken for ironclad laws when, in actuality, they are only outlines or approximations. They can also sometimes be misleading because of problems encountered in their construction. Three of the problems of model building that can be the cause of inaccuracy are discussed below.

Relevance Economists must make judgments about the factors that are relevant to the situations they are studying. They decide which are important influences on a situation and which are only coincidentally involved. All the factors that they assume to be insignificant or irrelevant will be omitted from the model.

This kind of screening of data is a necessary part of the economist's job. If the model were to include every last factor, it would be so complex and difficult to understand or use that it would be virtually worthless as a tool of study. But sometimes mistakes are made in judging relevance of data, and important elements of the situation are not included. Or the economist may eliminate so many factors that nothing is left but a meaningless abstraction that has almost no relation to reality and therefore yields very inaccurate predictions about actual behavior. The economist must clear away some of the trees in order to see the forest, but must avoid taking away too many or there will no longer be a forest, just a few isolated trees.

Causation and correlation The goal of model building is to indicate the relationship between various sets of data which represent the factors involved in the situation being studied. A common error is to misinterpret the nature of the relationship demonstrated to be present among sets of data by confusing correlation with causation.

Correlation is a statistical term meaning the degree of similarity between two sets of figures. *A and B are positively correlated when it can be shown that every time A increases, B increases. A and B are negatively correlated when it can be shown that every time A increases, B decreases.*

Mistakes creep into model building when an economist who has demonstrated a high degree of positive correlation between two factors assumes that since *A* always accompanies *B*, *A* causes *B*. But there may be no justification for this assumption and no proof of its validity. Correlation is a measure of a statistical relationship, not of causation. The relation of *A* to *B* may be dictated by some other factor not included in the analysis, or it could be an accidental by-product of some other relationship—or it could even be a coincidence. If every time the clock strikes 12 midnight, we observe that it is dark outside, there is certainly no reason to conclude that the striking of the hour has caused the darkness. Causation cannot be proved from correlation; instead, it must be demonstrated in different ways.

The fallacy of composition Economists build models by collecting individual bits of information and assembling them into a pattern. They measure the effects that a wage increase has on Jim, and the effects that a similar increase has on Jean and on Sue. By adding all these individual cases together, they arrive at a conclusion as to the effects of an increase on the whole factory, or the industry, or the economy. But there are cases in which this kind of addition comes up with the wrong answer. A wage increase can be good for Jim, for it increases his buying power in relation to the buying power of other workers. But if everyone gets the raise, the probable result is that prices will rise along with wages, and inflation sets in. Then Jim does not benefit, because his increased salary will not buy any more than his old one did when prices were lower.

The example above illustrates the **fallacy of composition** which is *an incorrect assumption that what is true of the part is also true of the whole.* The relationship between the two basic levels of economic analysis—microeconomics and macroeconomics—is complicated by the problem of the fallacy of composition. Because they deal with the economy on two different levels, a generalization that is true on the microeconomic level is not necessarily true on the macroeconomic level.

Macroeconomics is *the level of economic analysis that deals with the activity of the whole economy and with the interaction between the major sectors (aggregates) of the economy,* such as all households, all businesses, or all government. **Microeconomics** is *the level of economic analysis that deals with the activity of individual*

> **RECAP**
>
> The discipline of ECONOMICS deals with the way people meet the problem of scarce resources, choosing among alternative uses as they attempt to maximize the satisfaction of their desires.
>
> Macroeconomics is the study of the activity of the whole economy and the interaction between the major sectors (aggregates) of the economy.
>
> Microeconomics is the study of the activity of individual agents of the economic system, such as households and business firms.

agents of the economic system, such as a single consumer's demand for a particular good, the price of a single product, or the behavior of a single business.

For example, a microeconomist studies the economic behavior of an individual household, while a macroeconomist studies the aggregate behavior of all households in the nation. Microeconomics is interested in seeing what one individual does with his or her wage increase, while macroeconomics focuses on the effect of a general wage increase on the economy as a whole.

WHY STUDY ECONOMICS?

Empirical data, concepts, and models are tools economists use to arrive at some understanding of the maximization process that enables scarce resources to meet unlimited needs. Economics can be applied to a subject as small and immediate as a student's budget, or as large as an economic system that produces a trillion dollars worth of goods and services every year.

Your study of economics can be useful in helping you understand the causes of many situations you encounter personally, and it can help you determine the reasons for events that occur nationally. For example, do you know how much it really costs for you to take this economics course? how the publisher of this text set the price you paid for it at the bookstore? why the federal government's recent attempt to halt inflation resulted in lowered enrollment on most campuses? and why the president at your college earns a larger salary than your economics professor (who knows the answers to all these questions)? When you have finished this book, you will be able to answer all these questions yourself. A knowledge of the analytical tools of economics can help you find answers to practical questions such as those above and can help you understand the economic principles underlying these answers.

Summary

■ The purpose of this chapter is to give an overview of the study of economics: what it studies, its strengths and limitations as a social science, and the basic tools economists use.

■ Economics is the study of how people meet the problem of scarce resources and how they choose among alternatives to maximize their satisfaction. Economics is simply one part of the total study of human behavior, but from a particular point of view.

■ Because it tries to apply the principles of the scientific method to its subject matter, economics is one of the social sciences. It is related to all the other social sciences, such as psychology, sociology, and history, and borrows from them frequently. Like other social scientists, economists strive to maintain objectivity in their work; but unlike many natural and physical scientists and some social scientists, economists generally cannot run controlled experiments in a laboratory setting.

■ A number of limitations prevent economics from being as exact as the natural sciences. Keeping value judgments completely out of economic analysis is extremely difficult, and economists differ among themselves not only about facts and theories, but also about the goals toward which economic policy should be directed—for example, whether those goals should be individual or collective. Finally, actual economic policy is generally set by politicians, not by economists.

■ Economists do their work on three fundamental levels. First, they collect empirical data and analyze them in mathematical forms, some of which are highly sophisticated. Second, they use concepts, generalizations that provide ways to interpret data and to draw relationships between diverse facts. Finally, they develop models, theories that describe the workings of all or part of an economic system and which predict the results for the economic system under specific conditions. Economic models are never fail-safe and must be examined to see whether the data they employ are relevant, whether they confuse correlation with causation, and whether they mistake a part of a system for the whole.

Key Terms

| economics | free good | model | macroeconomics |
| economic good | marginal unit | fallacy of composition | microeconomics |

Review & Discussion

1. Why is the study of economics important? What are its basic objectives?

2. How is economics related to the other social sciences? How is it different? What aspects of subject matter and method do they all share in common?

3. What kinds of problems are created for economists because they cannot use all the techniques used by all of the natural sciences and some of the other social sciences, such as laboratories, complete control of all variables involved, and repetition of experiments? Are these fatal limitations?

4. The chapter has drawn a distinction between an economic good—something that is both desirable and scarce—and a free good—something that is available in unlimited supply and that therefore does not cost anything. Can you think of any absolutely free goods? What does it mean for society when more and more free goods—clean air, privacy, relaxation—grow scarce and expensive?

5. You have made a decision to purchase a college education. What is the opportunity cost of this decision? How might it affect subsequent economic decisions you make? How might it affect the economic transactions of others?

6. Economists aren't the only people who use models—everybody uses models every day, even if these models are not as precise or conscious as the ones developed by professional social

scientists. A model from physics concerning the properties of solid objects reminds us that we can't walk through walls. A model of what contributes to the success of a football team tells us how to bet on the Superbowl. Think of some everyday models you or other people have used, and find examples that illustrate the dangers discussed in the chapter—the use of irrelevant data, the confusion of correlation and cause, and the fallacy of composition.

7. How can the study of economics help you make choices as a worker, a consumer, and a voter?

Appendix 1

The Use of Graphs

A "good" graph should be able to teach at a glance. The graphs, charts, and diagrams in this text are visual aids that will help explain the different principles of economic theory. The purpose of this appendix is to introduce you to different types of graphs and to explain how to plot, read, and interpret these visual tools of economics.

In everyday experience we often observe that one thing depends on another. The time it takes you to walk into town depends, for one thing, on the distance you must cover. Scientists refer to this type of dependent relationship as a *functional relationship*. How well you do on an exam is a function of the number of hours you spend studying for that exam. In this case, the number of hours spent studying is the *independent variable*—the factor that is free to fluctuate—and your grade is the *dependent variable*—the factor that is determined by (dependent on) the size of the independent variable. We can also say that these two factors—grade and hours of study—are *directly* related; as one increases, so does the other. Thus, other things equal, the more hours you spend studying, the higher the grade you will receive.

Much of introductory economic theory is based on observing and interpreting simple functional relationships. Economists observe that the quantity of a good that buyers are willing and able to purchase is largely a function of the price of that good. They say that an *inverse relationship* exists between price (the independent variable) and quantity purchased (the dependent variable); as the price rises, the quantity purchased declines. This inverse relationship can be observed in *Table A.1,* which indicates the quantity of pineapples a single individual will purchase per month at various prices.

PLOTTING A GRAPH

Functional relationships can be expressed visually as well as verbally. A graph is a visual presentation of some functional relationship. Graphs are

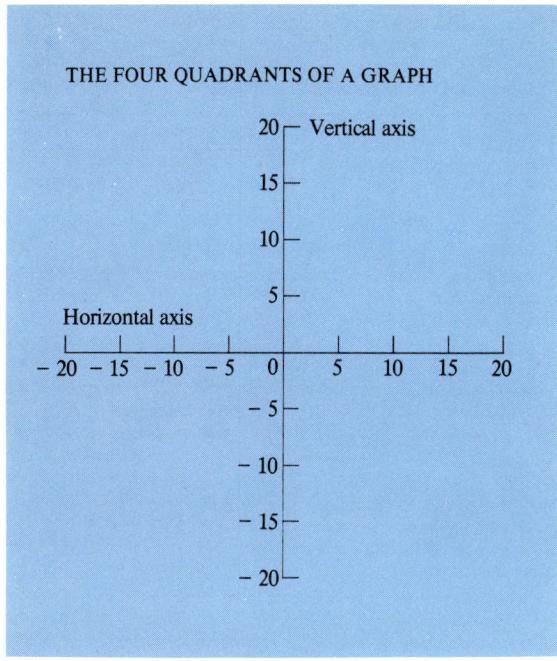

Figure A.1

drawn on squared paper that is divided into four quadrants by horizontal and vertical axes, as shown in *Fig. A.1*. The two axes intersect at a point called the origin, usually denoted by the numerical value of zero (0). The first quadrant, in the upper right portion of the graph, is the only one that has positive values on both the vertical (y) axis and the horizontal (x) axis. This is the quadrant that we will be concerned with in almost all the graphs presented in this text.

Figure A.2 demonstrates how a simple line graph is plotted; it shows the relationship between price and quantity purchased using the data included in *Table A.1*. Price is placed on the vertical axis, and quantity on the horizontal axis. Looking at (a), we see that each of the five price-quantity combinations is plotted by extending perpendicular lines from the appropriate points on the two axes. Thus, by extending a line perpendicular to the vertical axis at a price of $1.00, and another line perpendicular to the horizontal axis at a quantity of 1, we can locate the "$1.00–1 unit" price-quantity combination at the point of intersection. The same process is followed for locating all the other price-quantity combinations. Of course, the final graph shown in (b) does not include the perpendicular lines used to help us locate each combination; it contains only the series of five points. These five points can then be connected by a smooth line, or curve. In doing so, we assume that any intermediate point on the curve is also a tenable alternative or realistic approximation.

INTERPRETING A GRAPH

What does this curve tell us about the relationship between price and quantity? The fact that the curve slopes downward and to the right immediately indicates that the price-quantity relationship is an inverse one: as price decreases, quantity increases. An inverse relationship is always indicated by a curve that slopes downward and to the right; a direct relationship is always indicated by a curve that slopes upward and to the right.

THEORETICAL AND EMPIRICAL GRAPHS

There are many different kinds of graphs. The graphic tools in this text have been carefully selected to clarify meanings, visualize concepts, show time trends, and emphasize basic principles. Essentially, graphs can be divided into two primary categories: graphs that illustrate an economic theory or principle, and graphs that plot empirical data.

Figure A.2 is a theoretical graph. It plots hypothetical data to illustrate a basic principle of economics—the law of demand. The law of demand states that the relationship between the price of a good and the quantity is an inverse one. As we

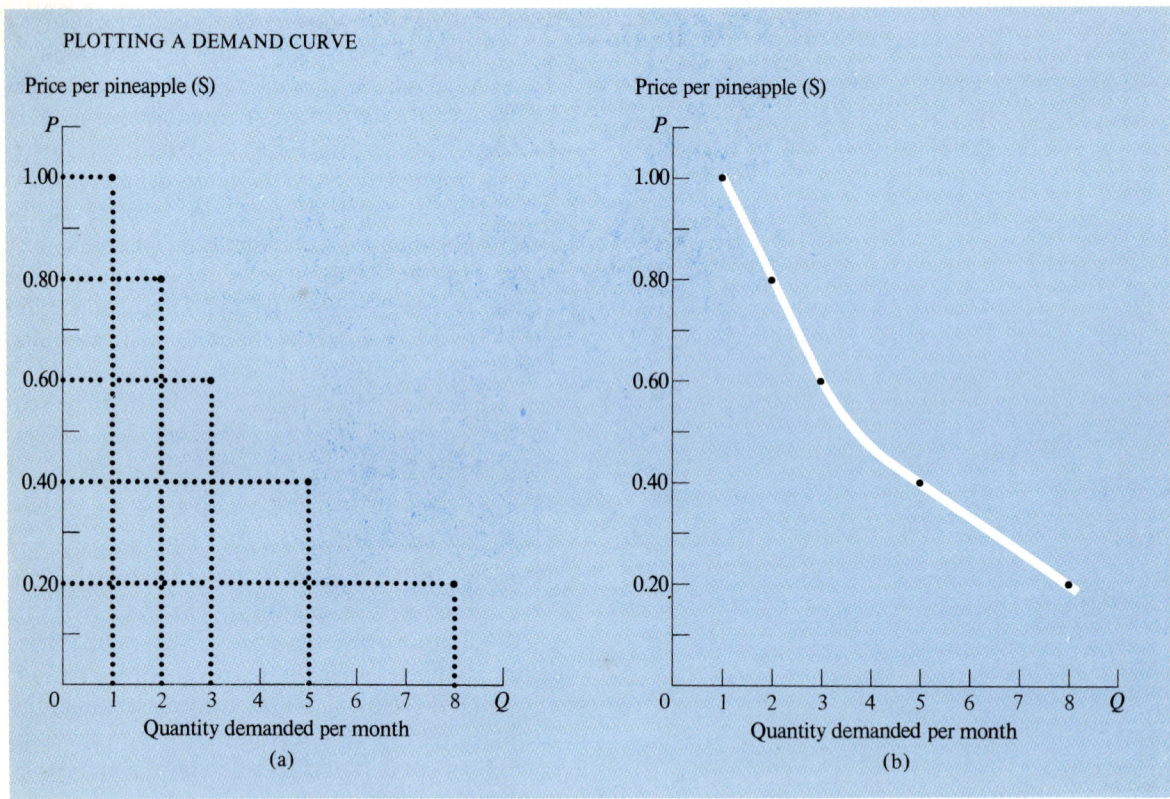

Figure A.2

Table A.1
An individual's demand schedule for pineapples

Price per pineapple	Quantity demanded per month
$1.00	1
.80	2
.60	3
.40	5
.20	8

have learned, this means that as the price of the good declines, the quantity that buyers will be willing and able to purchase increases.

An empirical graph is made by plotting actual or empirical data. We can learn a great deal from empirical graphs—the distribution of income, the concentration of business within certain types of industries, the fluctuations of the prime-interest rate between a period of recession and inflation. Empirical graphs are helpful in observing the changes in economic activity over a period of time. From this type of information, we can better evaluate the performance of a given economy.

DIFFERENT FORMS OF GRAPHS

Both theoretical and empirical graphs can take different forms. The simple line graph drawn in *Fig. A.2* is not the only type of graph economists use. It will be useful to conclude this appendix with a brief description of some of the different forms of graphs you will encounter in this text.

Line graph

☐ A *simple-arithmetic line graph* is a graph that has only one line or curve. It is called an arithmetic line graph because the spaces between each line of the grid always represent the same amount. This type of graph is very often used to show time trends. The horizontal axis denotes passage of time, and the vertical axis denotes some numerical quantity. *Figure A.3*, which shows the average annual rate of unemployment in the United States from 1929 to 1974, is a simple-arithmetic line graph.

When you are interpreting a time trend graph, make sure that you take into account the

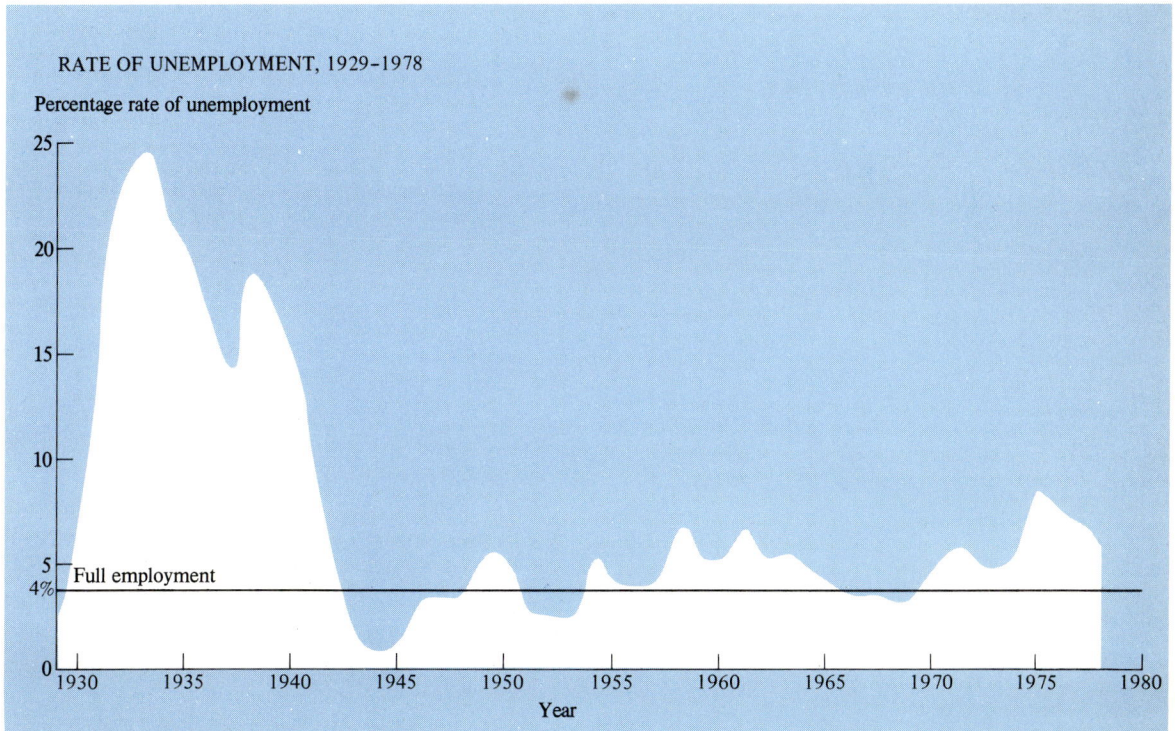

SOURCE: Bureau of Labor Statistics, U.S. Department of Labor.

Figure A.3

22 APPENDIX 1: THE USE OF GRAPHS

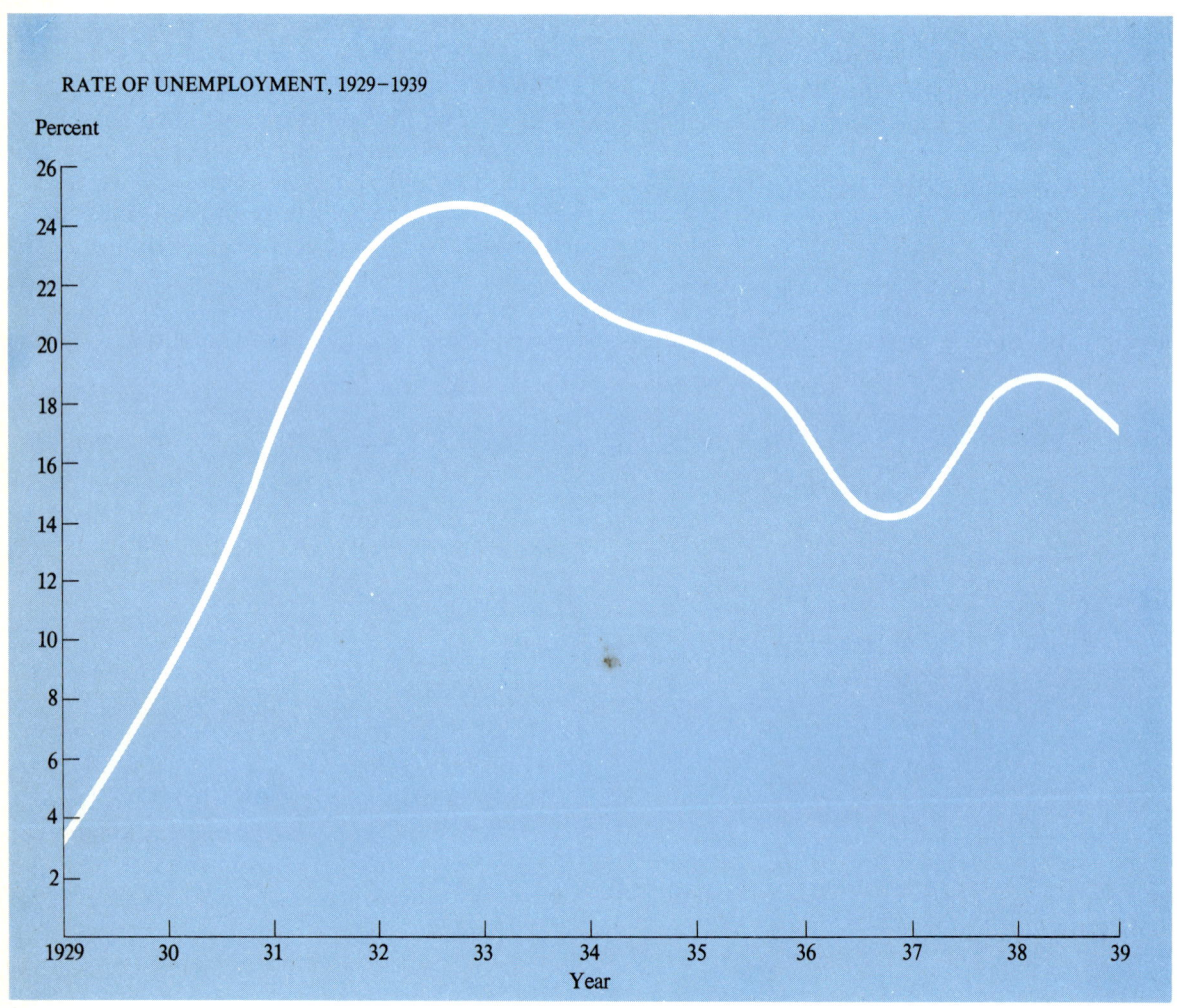

Figure A.4

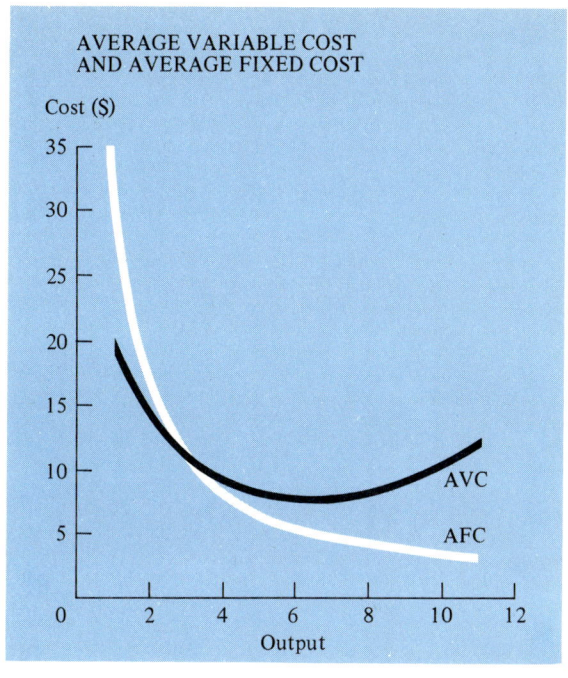

Figure A.5

stability of that particular period of time. If you are using a graph that plots the average annual rate of unemployment in the United States during the years 1929 to 1939 (*Fig. A.4*), you will certainly get a lopsided picture of the overall trend. Those years were not typical years for the United States economy. In general, neither the period of the Depression during the 1930s nor the war years are good indicators of the long-term patterns of economic activity in the United States.

☐ *Multiple-scale arithmetic graphs* must have at least two line curves charted on an arithmetic chart. This type of graph is used to show a comparison. For example, a multiple-scale graph can compare visually how average variable cost and average fixed cost of a firm change as output increases. (See *Fig. A.5.*)

☐ An example of a *surface chart* can be seen in *Fig. A.6*. A surface chart can be easily misread. You should interpret each component by the width of its band and not by the numerical value on the vertical axis. The absolute numerical value should be used only when referring to the total figure.

☐ *Semi-logarithmic* graphs have narrowing intervals along the vertical axis. This type of graph is used for various reasons. For example, in *Fig. A.7* we want equal percentage increases in GNP to be represented by equal distances on the vertical axis. Therefore, equal absolute amounts will be represented by smaller and smaller spaces as we move up the vertical axis. Remember when referring to a graph of this kind that the resulting curve represents rate of change rather than absolute change.

24 APPENDIX 1: THE USE OF GRAPHS

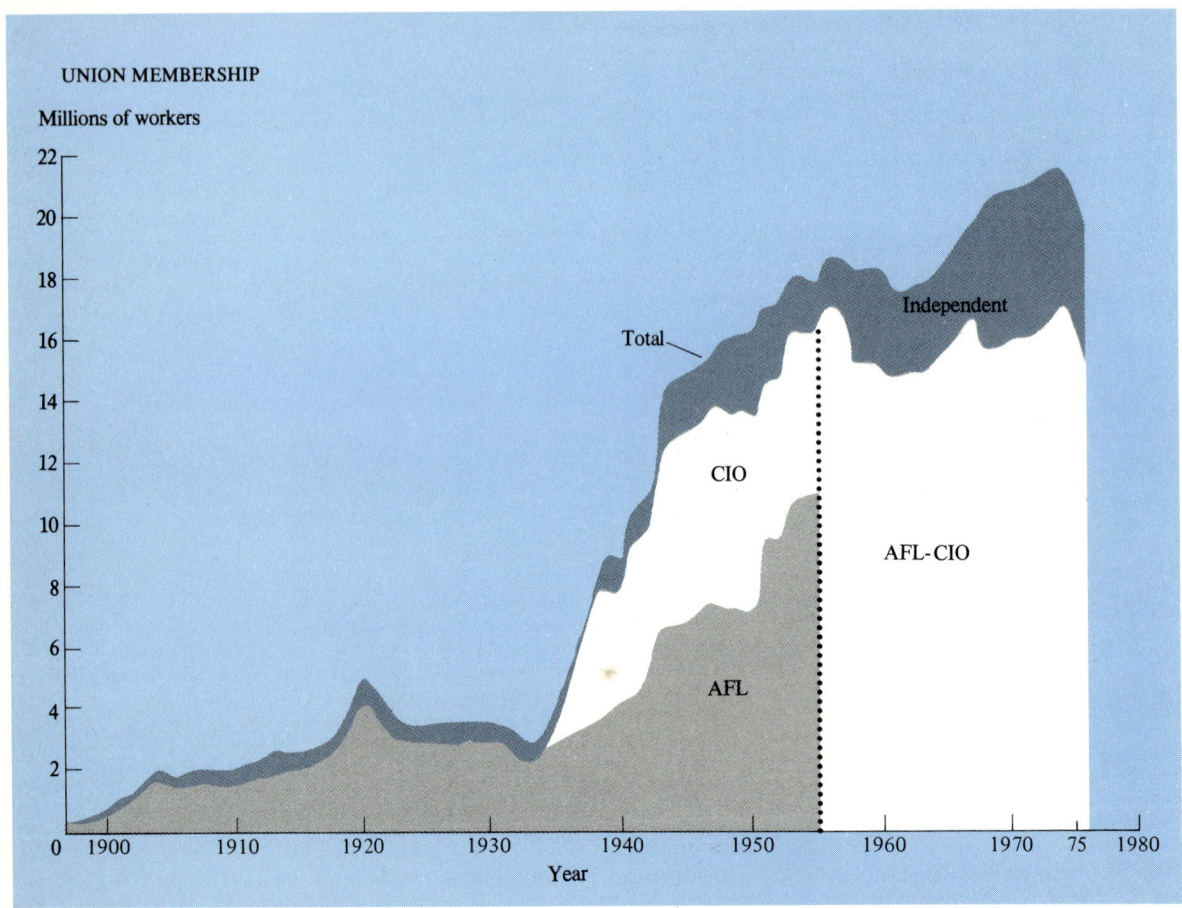

SOURCE: *Historical Statistics of the United States*, and *Handbook of Labor Statistics*, United States Department of Labor.

Figure A.6

DIFFERENT FORMS OF GRAPHS 25

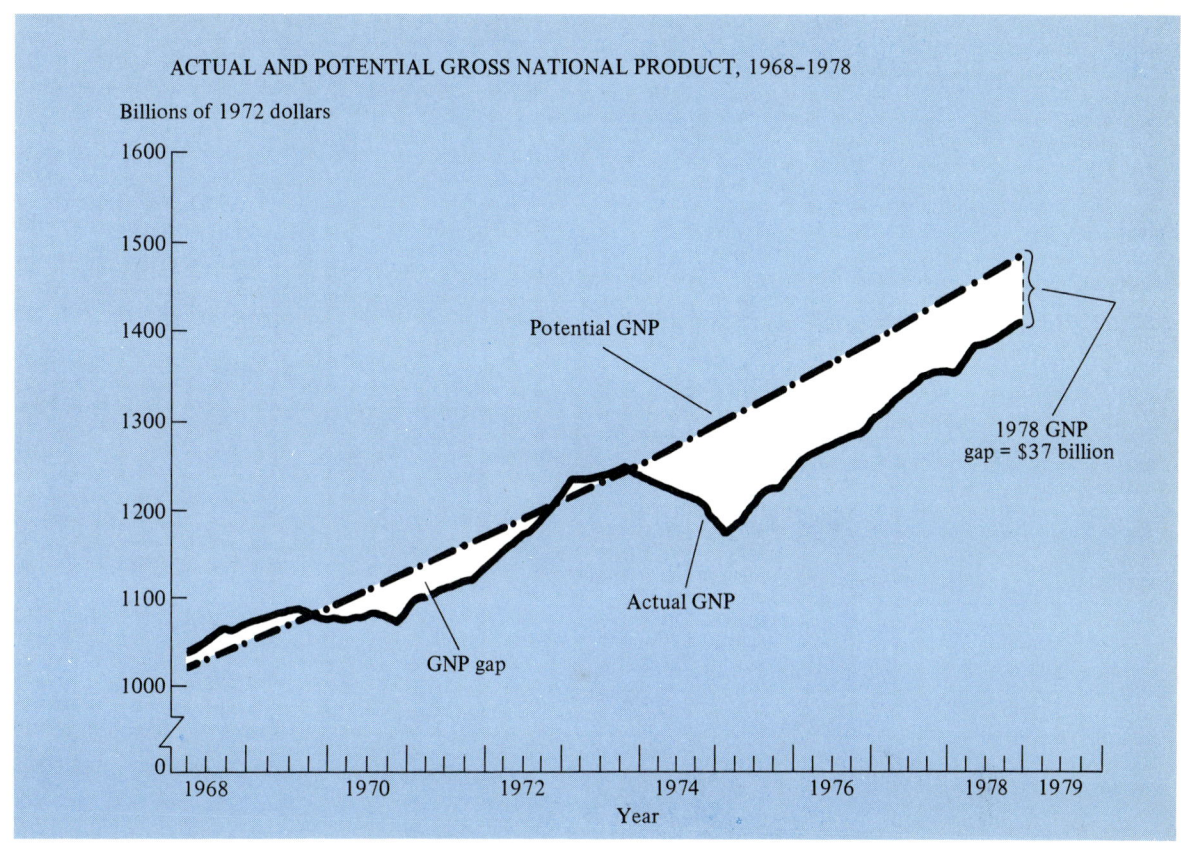

SOURCE: *The Economic Report of the President*, 1979.

Figure A.7

26 APPENDIX 1: THE USE OF GRAPHS

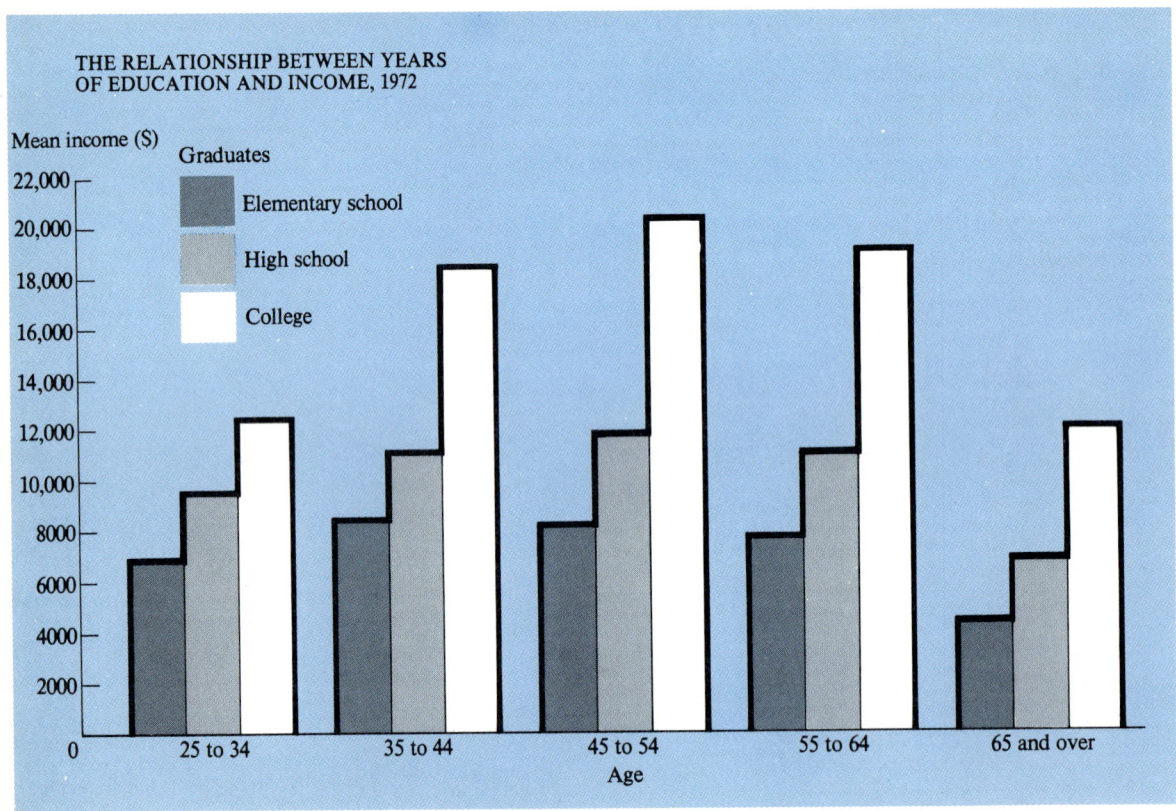

SOURCE: U.S. Bureau of the Census, *Current Population Reports*, Series P-60, No. 92.

Figure A.8

Bar graph

The bar graph is used to show comparisons in magnitude. A single bar may represent a period of time, a certain product, or a particular category. The quantitative or numerical value of the bar will be represented by its length. Bar charts may be presented in clusters, as in *Fig. A.8* showing the average levels of income earned by different age groups, breaking down each age group by years of education. Thus three variables are being shown—age, education, and income. Another technique used in bar graphs is to divide each bar into its component parts. In this way, three different factors can also be shown. In *Fig. A.9* we see time, type of federal government expenditure, and amount of expenditure.

On a 100 percentage bar graph all the bars are of equal length but the divisions are of different sizes. This type of bar graph is used to emphasize percentile differences in a particular category. In *Fig. A.10*, we are taking the same data used in *Fig. A.9*, but expressing each type of expenditure as a percent of total federal government purchases in the given year.

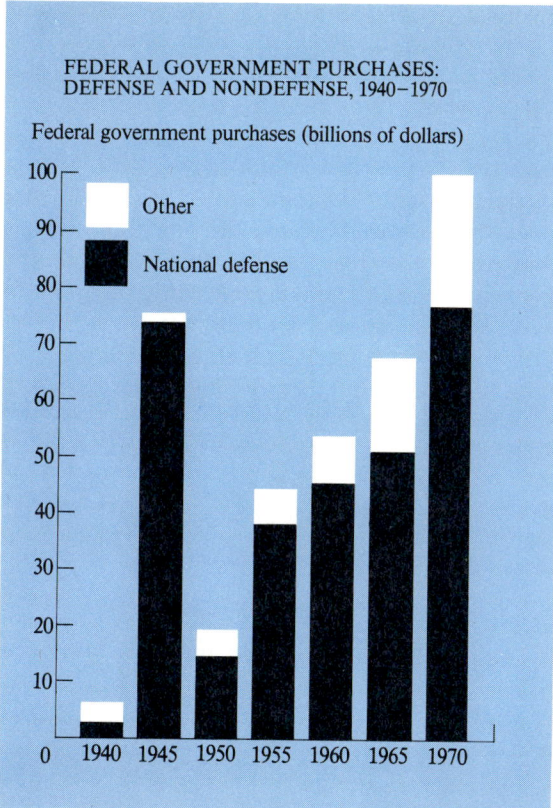

Figure A.9

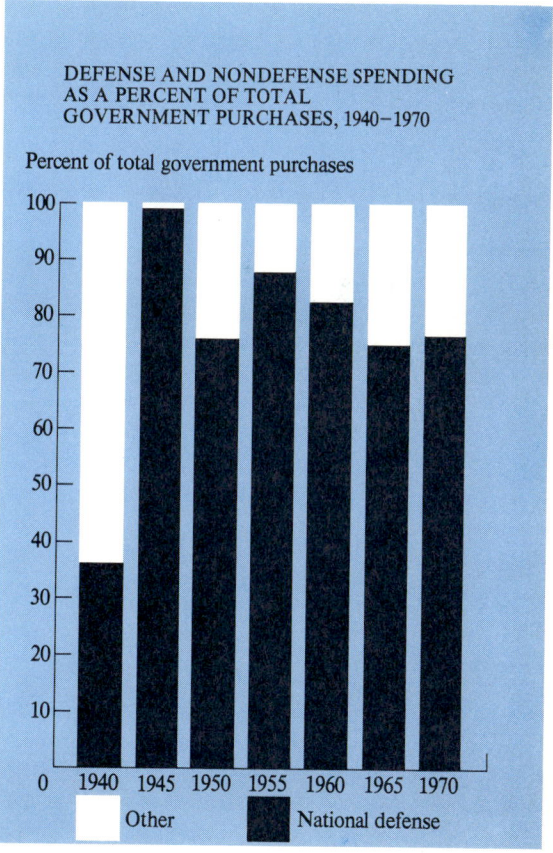

Figure A.10

APPENDIX 1: THE USE OF GRAPHS

Circle graph

A circle graph taken as a whole represents 100 percent of the total. Circle graphs (sometimes called pie charts) are frequently used to show types of expenditures and revenue, but they can be used for any statistical representation of a whole broken up into its parts. As shown in *Fig. A.11,* each section or slice of a circle graph represents a share of the total which is equal to its area.

Flow diagram

A flow diagram is simply a diagram that shows you a step-by-step operation. It shows how some factor—say, money—passes from point to point, finally ending up at the point of origin. A flow diagram of income and expenditure is shown in *Fig. A.12.*

Scatter diagram

A typical scatter diagram shows the relationship between two variables, but the points plotted are scattered across the graph so that no single, unbroken line can be drawn connecting them. However, we can make a kind of visual average by drawing a line that passes through or near the largest possible number of points, as shown in

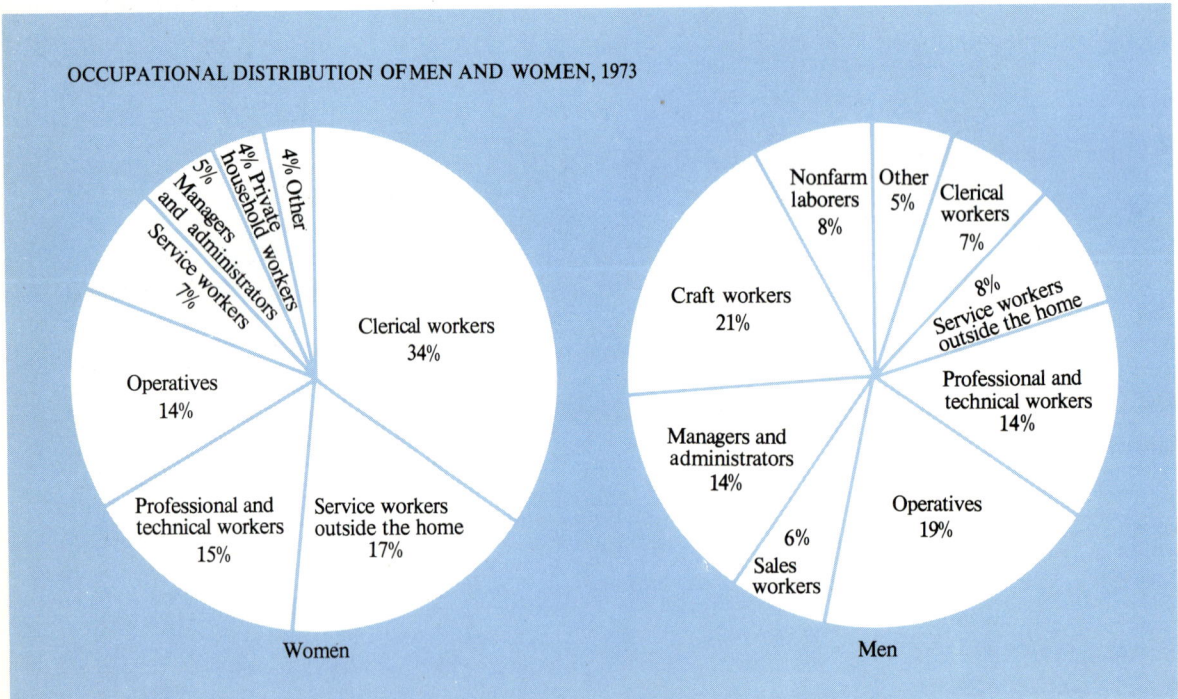

SOURCE: United States Department of Labor, Women's Bureau, *Employment and Earnings,* January 1974.

Figure A.11

DIFFERENT FORMS OF GRAPHS

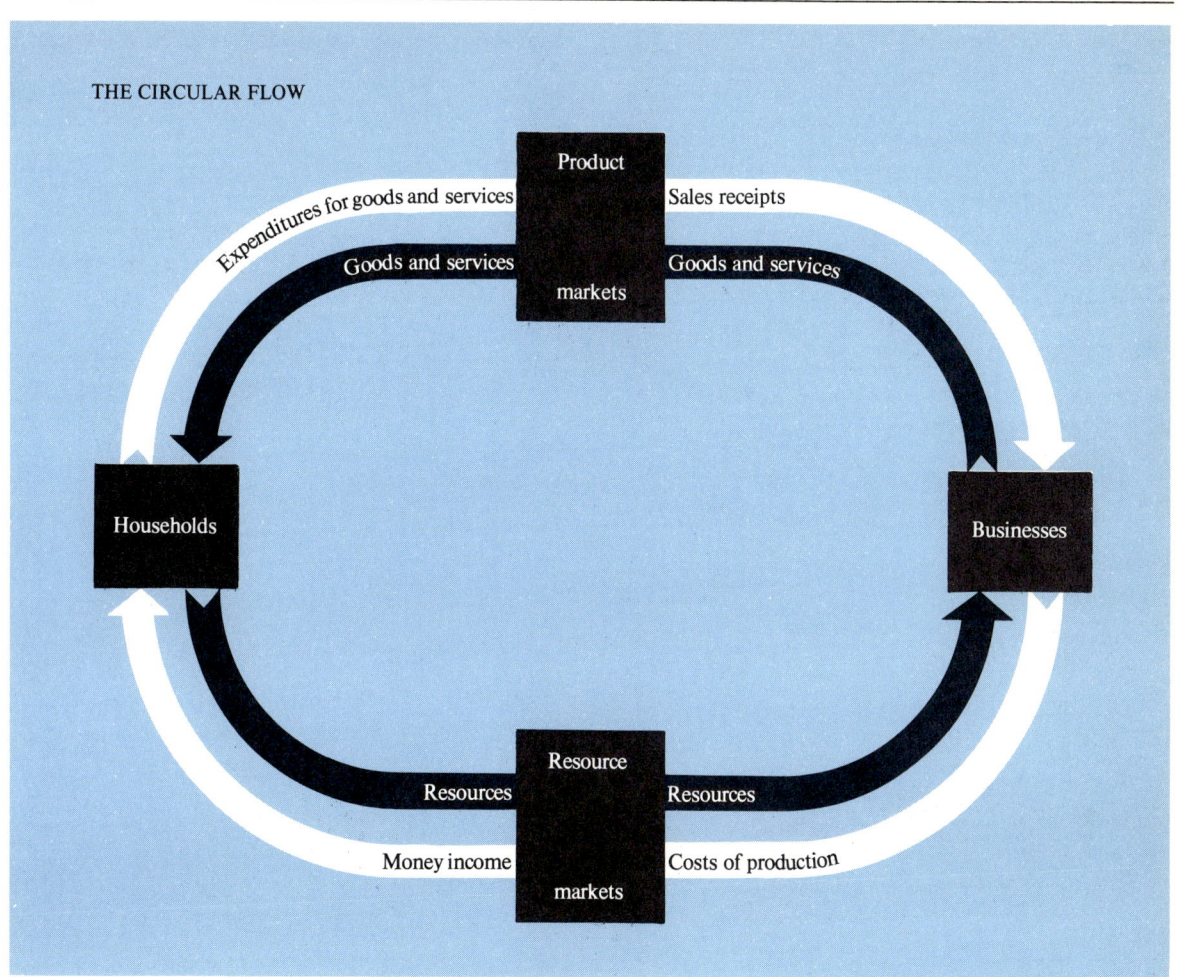

Figure A.12

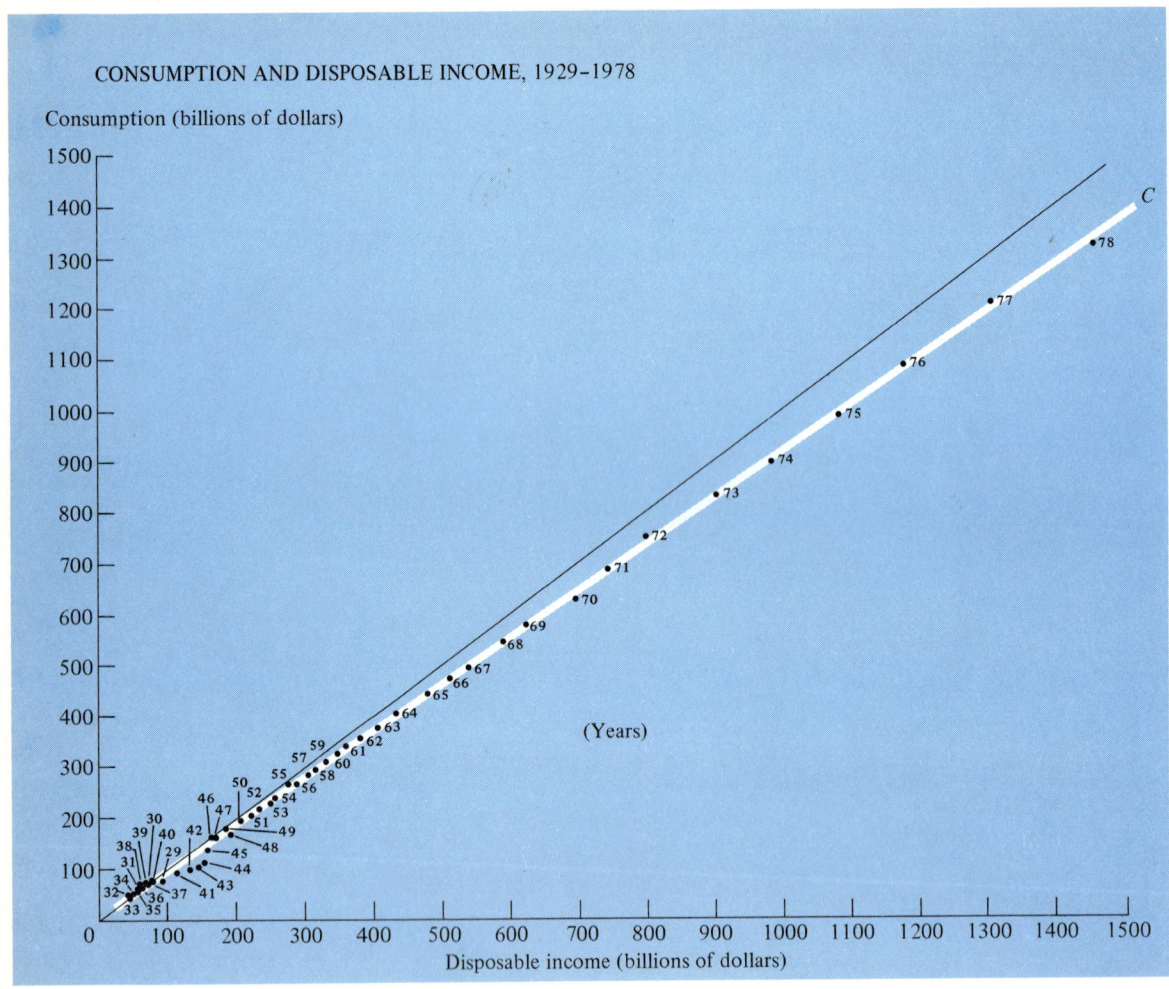

Figure A.13

Fig. A.13. In statistical analysis, this technique is known as drawing the regression line.

In interpreting a scatter diagram, it is important to note the direction and degree of correlation between the two variables included. Graphs showing positive correlations show an overall pattern that slopes upward and to the right. The pattern for a negative correlation slopes downward and to the right. When there is no correlation between two variables, it is impossible to perceive a pattern because the points plotted on the graph take no definite direction. The different directions and degrees of correlation between two variables are summarized in *Fig. A.14.*

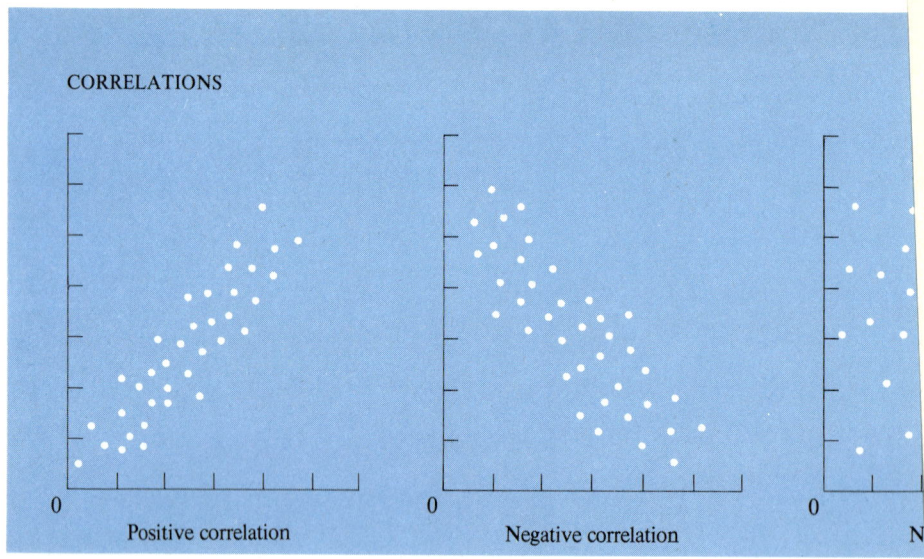

Figure A.14

Chapter 2

Utilization of Economic Resources

What to look for in this chapter

What two basic assumptions do economists make about the extent of consumer desires and the resources available to meet these desires? What are the implications of these assumptions?

What are the basic factors of production, and how can they be combined to maximize output? What conditions maximize both output and satisfaction?

How do the concepts of opportunity costs and production possibilities help a society make its economic choices?

In order to begin to build an understanding of economics, it is important to remind ourselves of two fundamental assumptions: (1) *people have virtually unlimited desires for material goods;* (2) *resources to fulfill these desires are limited or scarce.* Faced with the dilemma of scarce resources and unlimited desires, people try as best they can to get the most satisfaction from the smallest amount of resources. This economic goal sounds both obvious and achievable, but when we get right down to doing it, what exactly does it mean? How do we get the most from the least? With the wants of an entire nation to consider, how can we even know when we have maximized satisfaction? Which goods do we want more of, and which are we willing to sacrifice? It is clearly impossible to get the 200 million people who are a part of the American economic system to agree unanimously on the answers to these questions. Yet somehow the decisions are made and carried out. This chapter and the two following give an account of some of the elements of this decision-making process.

We begin in this chapter with a look at the nature of people's desires and their varying definitions of "the most." Then we will look at the primary condition that limits production—the scarcity of economic resources. From these two starting points, we can deduce the fundamental problem faced by any economy (to produce various goods and services in quantities that will yield the greatest amount of total satisfaction) and some of the conditions necessary to achieve this goal (full employment of resources and maximum efficiency). Next we will introduce the concept of production possibilities—the various combinations of goods that an economy is capable of producing when it is fully and efficiently employing its resources. The chapter concludes with a brief discussion of the various factors involved in the making of economic decisions.

UNLIMITED DESIRES

As we noted above, economists postulate the existence of "unlimited desires," or a never-ending demand for **consumer goods and services**. In economic terms, *consumer goods refer to anything—material or otherwise—that satisfies a human desire*. Thus, services (such as having your TV repaired or your hair styled) are also consumer goods because they satisfy human wants. Some people object that this assumption incorrectly assumes that humans are basically greedy. They also point out that it is quite easy to demonstrate that all desires have some limit: just try offering the family a big turkey dinner the day after Thanksgiving!

It is undeniably true that an individual or a whole economy has only a limited desire for any one kind of good or service. A family may want more than one TV set, but after it has a set for every room of the house, the desire for TV sets disappears. However, the family's desires for goods and services in general are by no means satisfied; they merely shift their focus. The family with five television sets might be very anxious to have a new car. Thus the desire for a single good or service can become satiated, but there are probably countless other commodities, or even different versions of the same commodity, that one will want.

Is it possible than an economy might become so efficient that it is able to satisfy every desire, even with a limited supply of resources? It is doubtful that production can ever catch up with desires. It is generally believed that rising prosperity, both of individuals and of nations, actually leads to multiplying desires: the more money we have, the more ways we can think of to spend it. No matter how much we are able to increase the amount of productive resources available or the efficiency with which they are used, we would be unable to satisfy all desires, for we would continue to be limited by time and by our capacity to consume.

Types of consumer desires

It is helpful to distinguish among different types of consumer desires, such as the desire for physical necessities and the desire for luxuries. Of course all people have a variety of emotional wants as well. To the extent that economic resources must be sacrificed to obtain emotional gratification, this psychological attainment must be regarded as an economic good also. For example, some people believe that you *can* "buy" love or respect.

Physical necessities
All people want the food and water they need to stay alive, the clothes and shelter that will protect them from a potentially hostile environment. These physical necessities represent the most basic level of economic desire and are the first ones that an economy must satisfy. But at some point, the desire for physical necessities will reach its limita-

tions. As incomes go up, families will want better food, a nicer and larger house, more stylish clothes. But they won't want more food than they can eat or more clothes than they can possibly wear. When desires for necessities are satisfied, excess income or productive capacity will be used to satisfy other kinds of desires.

Luxuries

Luxuries are *goods or services which are not absolutely necessary but for which people will spend an increasing proportion of their income as income rises.* A dishwasher, a trip to Europe, and a sports car are luxuries for most American families, but the specific definition of a luxury will vary for each person according to income level and individual needs and tastes.

The desire for greater ease of living is always present, but the demand for a specific luxury item does not appear until the item is on the market. That is, people have always wanted a faster and easier way to wash the dishes, but they have only recently wanted dishwashers. Technology plays an important role in this area of the economy, making possible the development of the specific goods and services that will provide the comfortable living that people desire.

SCARCITY OF RESOURCES

A second fundamental assumption of economics is that *all economic resources—all things that can be used to create the goods and services that we desire—are limited or scarce.* Perhaps this sounds obvious, and yet it is a concept that has, in the past, been difficult for Americans to accept. From the very beginning of our history, we have sought constant expansion. We have thought that there was always more land on the other side of the mountain, land that was available to anyone who could use it. We have expected businesses to grow without stopping, to multiply their total value by 10 or 20 times in one person's life span, and then do the same in their children's. The rapid and sustained growth of our economy for so many years led to the erroneous conclusion that the growth that we had experienced could and would continue indefinitely. All our resources seemed to be unlimited, or infinitely expandable.

Today, the concept of limited resources is easier for us to grasp. The polluted air that hangs over large cities and manufacturing centers, the threatened shortage of oil and other fossil fuels —these have taught us that our natural resources are not inexhaustible. Now we recognize that our planet can offer only a fixed supply of resources, which we must be careful not to waste or destroy.

Economists customarily divide economic resources into four categories referred to as **factors of production** (or productive inputs): *land, labor, capital, and entrepreneurship.*

Land

In the economic sense, **land** refers to *all raw natural resources that might be used to produce goods and services.* Air, soil, minerals, water, timber, and navigable rivers—all fall into this category. Land is the basic material we have to work with, the starting point of all production. It is also the most basic and inescapable of our limitations. For example, with enough labor and capital and with the technological know-how, we can probably produce a silk purse from a sow's ear, but no matter how hard we try, we cannot make it out of nothing.

Natural resources are not distributed evenly throughout the world, which means that people who live in certain areas have a great advantage over others in the struggle to attain prosperity. The classic illustration of the role natural resources have in determining prosperity is the case of Kuwait. Until 1945, this Middle Eastern country seemed to be little more than a sand pile—no rivers, less than 1 percent of the land under cultivation, nearly all of the tiny population illiterate. Today this country has the second highest per capita income of any nation in the world (although the distribution is extremely unequal), free medical care, free education through the college level, and good low-cost housing are available to all citizens. Why? Because it was discovered that underneath all that sand was one-fifth of the entire oil reserves of the world. That one natural resource alone was enough to transform Kuwait from a poor country to a rich one almost overnight.

Labor

Land is only the starting point of production. Unless there is someone to plant and harvest the crops, dig the coal out of the ground, or build pipelines for the oil, these natural resources will have a productive yield of zero. The second productive resource is **labor**, *the human effort needed to turn raw materials into useful goods and services*. The amount of labor available is limited by the size of the population, which in turn is eventually limited by the amount of natural resources available to produce the food, clothing, and shelter needed to sustain it. But it is quite possible for an economic system to increase available labor resources, even though no more people have been added to the population. Programs to provide adequate food and clothing for workers, to immunize them against diseases, or to train or educate them can greatly increase both the number of hours or days that a person can perform a job and the skill or speed with which he or she performs it.

Capital

The term "capital" is commonly used to refer to money, or more specifically, the money invested in a business enterprise. But in economics, money is not considered an ecomonic resource, because it cannot directly produce anything. Instead, in economics **capital** refers to *produced (i.e., man-made) instruments to be used for further production; that is, goods that are used to produce other goods and services*. The machines inside a factory, the factory building, the trucks that transport the finished products are all classified as physical capital. Even the highway that the truck drives over can be considered a kind of capital good, jointly owned by all citizens. Similarly, characteristics of people who are productive, such as knowledge, innate abilities, or skills, can also be classified as capital. These characteristics are often referred to as human capital.

Capital goods versus consumer goods
The decision to acquire more capital goods involves a willingness to sacrifice temporarily the production of a certain amount of consumer goods. This sacrifice is necessary because capital goods are man-made and because their production requires the use of economic resources that might otherwise be used to produce consumer goods. The Acme Balloon Company, with 90 employees, can use its economic profit to hire 10 additional workers, thus producing the maximum number of balloons and the greatest possible profit. Or it may decide to hold the size of its labor force constant at 90 workers and use the money to build an addition to the factory instead. One way to think of the immediate cost of the addition would be in terms of the number of balloons those 10 extra men could have produced. But when the addition is finished, the increase in Acme's capital would allow the company to produce, say, twice as many balloons as it did before.

Entrepreneurship

Entrepreneurship, or **business enterprise**, refers to *a group of skills which include the ability to combine land, labor, and capital in the most efficient way, the willingness to run the risks of business failure, and the creativity required to invent new products and new ways to market them*. Entrepreneurship can be considered a special type of human resource.

In the United States, a number of institutions are designed to train people in the skills that an entrepreneur needs. College courses in business administration, the experience of membership in

Junior Achievement, the activities of Small Business Administration are all meant to teach people entrepreneurial skills. More important, our entire social climate has traditionally encouraged entrepreneurship. As long as profits and income were high for the successful entrepreneur, the incentives were great. There is now, however, a fear that high tax rates may discourage entrepreneurship.

Technology—another productive resource

Technology—*the application of industrial science to production and distribution*—is also sometimes included on the list of basic productive resources. Advances brought about through technology —new types of machines, more efficient methods of combining resources—can lead to increased production from the same amount of input. For example, the assembly line, in which each worker specializes in one small step of the manufacturing process, was a technological advance that allowed a fixed number of workers to produce a larger daily output. Crop rotation can make a single acre produce more food than it does when it is planted with the same crop year after year. The knowledge of how to get the most out of other productive resources can itself be considered an important resource of the economy.

Interrelationship among productive resources

Land, labor, capital, entrepreneurship, and technology are our productive resources—the inputs into the economic system. With our limited supply of these resources, how can we best satisfy our unlimited desires? This is the central question of economics. In order to begin to answer this question, it is essential to recognize that the various productive resources are closely interrelated. Abundant natural resources are of little use unless there are adequate labor and machinery to utilize them. The great oil reserves in Alaska were untapped until people moved in to extract oil and technology was developed to transport it to centers of demand.

Conversely, abundant human resources can sometimes overcome inadequacies of other resources. When Israel became a nation, it contained little more than desert within its boundaries. However, the migrants to Israel were exceptionally well trained; many were scientists and engineers. Developing new seeds and new irrigation methods, they turned deserts into fertile land.

India, on the other hand, with relatively fertile land, has continued to lag in productivity, despite inputs of machinery and personnel, because its labor force is largely unskilled. Success in producing crops is slow and difficult when the laborers are unable to read the instructions on the fertilizer bags or on the ignition button of the plow. However, the gradual reduction of illiteracy there and in other Asian countries has caused productivity to rise somewhat.

In any attempt to alter productivity, all factors of production must be considered, not just the one most easily increased. The relationship between factors of production and economic growth is examined more closely in Chapter 18.

MAXIMIZING OUTPUT AND SATISFACTION

Thus far we have made two basic assumptions: that desires are unlimited and that resources are scarce. From this starting point, it logically follows that in order to supply as many goods and services as possible, an economy must meet two conditions: it must fully employ all of its productive resources, and it must utilize the most efficient methods of production possible. Since these two conditions are so important in any economic system, we shall discuss each in greater detail.

Full employment of productive resources

If an economy is to maximize satisfaction, it must produce at a full-employment level: all workers who seek jobs must be able to find them, all available natural resources must be used (to the extent that the requirements of future consumption have been taken into consideration), and all available capital must be fully utilized. This does not mean that an economy will exploit every productive input to the greatest extent possible, for, as we shall see, this is rarely the best way to maximize satisfaction in the long run. It does mean, however, that none of the economy's productive resources will be *involuntarily* unemployed.

Limitations to full employment of resources
A number of factors limit the extent to which a society can make full use of its productive resources.

Limitations on land One consideration that obviously limits our employment of productive resources is that of conservation. Many natural resources, such as natural gas and oil, are consumed in the production process and can never be replaced or recycled. The use of such inputs is clearly limited by prudence. When deciding how much will be employed in current production, society normally conserves some portion of its irreplaceable natural resources for future consumption.

Labor limitations The employment of labor resources also involves certain considerations that limit their use. For example, most of us prefer to give up at least some of the goods and services we could potentially consume in return for the satisfaction derived from having more leisure time. In our society it is the rare person who chooses to work to the absolute limits of his or her physical or mental capacity; we recognize that time can yield utility as well as any other economic good we might produce. In a full-employment economy, therefore, we expect that people will choose not to work during some part of their waking hours.

The full-employment level of labor resources may also be limited by social factors. Many countries place age or sex restrictions on labor. The United States has child labor laws, which prevent the very young from entering the labor force; it also restricts employment of old people by encouraging retirement at the age of 65. Until quite recently, custom also dictated that married women did not usually enter the industrial labor force except in cases of economic need. These restrictions, though social in origin, can also be viewed as the result of a basic economic choice. We choose to sacrifice a certain number of units of labor input to gain the benefits of retirement for the elderly, a healthy and happy childhood for the young, and, when desired, a family unit with a wife at home full time.

Dangers of involuntary unemployment
The fact that a resource is idle does not necessarily mean that it is nonproductive. For example, it is good farming technique to leave land unplanted every sixth or seventh year; this increases the land's future productivity. Similarly, a person with no regular job may be productive in certain ways; he or she might do odd jobs around the house, or write a poem, or learn accounting. A period of leisure might even be rejuvenating, making the individual more productive in subsequent employment. But in general, involuntary unemployment of resources is of great concern to any society for two reasons: first, it wastes an available resource and thus reduces the output of goods and services that provide utility to society; and second, it causes immediate hardship to those who derive their incomes from the employment of those resources.

Efficiency of production
Unemployment is not the only way in which resources can be wasted. They can also be wasted by underemployment. **Underemployment of resources** refers to *inefficient methods of production which result in waste of resources.* Inefficiency occurs when resources that are unsuited for

> **RECAP**
>
> FACTORS OF PRODUCTION, or productive inputs, are the economic resources used in the production of other goods. They include land, labor, capital, entrepreneurship, and technological advances.
>
> In order for an economy to maximize satisfaction, it must make as full use as possible of its productive inputs. Involuntary unemployment or underemployment of resources results in waste and lessened productivity.

a particular job are used for that job, or when resources are not used in their most efficient manner. For example, a space scientist who is employed carrying bricks at a construction site and who does not have the physical strength to perform this task well represents an inefficient allocation of labor resources. In such a case, it would be possible by merely reallocating resources to produce more of one commodity that society wants without making sacrifices in the output of another. Thus, if the scientist's labor were transferred to an aerospace project, his or her training and talents would contribute to a substantial increase in society's output of successful moon landings, while the simultaneous decrease in the output of new buildings would be negligible.

Underemployment of capital resources can also occur—for example, when tools or machinery are used in a task for which they are unsuited. Suppose that one person sets out to dig the foundation for a large building with a shovel, and a second person uses a back hoe to dig fence posts. It is obvious that with a simple reallocation of capital resources (the manual shovel and the back hoe), the productivity of both people would increase. The original allocation of capital is clearly inefficient.

In general, wages and payments to other productive factors attract resources to their most effective uses. Hence space scientists get more pay in the aerospace industry than for laying bricks.

It is relatively easy to collect statistics on unemployment. We can see the people standing in line to collect unemployment checks; we can count the number of factories that are closed or warehouses that are empty.* Estimating underemployment within the economy is a much harder job. It is difficult to find out how many workers are using inadequate tools, or how many people are not doing their jobs efficiently. This is one reason that underemployment of resources is particularly troublesome in any kind of economic system.

Economies of scale

We have seen how a reallocation of labor or capital can increase the efficiency of production. Another way in which production can be made both more efficient and less costly is through **economies of scale**. Economies of scale refer to *reductions in a business firm's production costs brought about by increasing the scale of production.* This occurs when a business increases in size.

As the business grows, the producer is able to increase the level of specialization of labor, subdividing among a number of employees tasks that were performed before by only one worker. Greater specialization of management tasks is also possible; managers skilled in one area can devote themselves exclusively to that area rather than having to divide their time among a number of functions. In addition, larger firms can often make more efficient use of equipment, since in

---

*Although unemployment is measurable, the loss to society due to unemployment is difficult to gauge. Unemployment is officially defined as the percent of those looking for work who are unable to find work. But certainly a person may be "unemployed" even if he or she is not actively looking for a job. When times are bad, many people become discouraged from seeking work. These people are not included in unemployment statistics, but they do represent lost output.

many areas of production, equipment is available only in large quantities and is best suited to high-volume output. Finally, larger firms are better able to make effective use of by-products than are small firms. A typical example is the meat-packing industry, where large producers make a number of products from the remains of livestock, including pharmaceuticals, glue, and fertilizer.

Economies of scale can be seen very clearly in the automotive industry, where the cost of necessary capital goods is enormous, and the savings of the assembly line, with its standardized units and division of labor, are great. Small auto companies either go bankrupt or are swallowed up by large ones, because their inefficiency puts them in a position where their prices cannot be competitive.

You might wonder how far economies of scale can be realized. The answer is that there is always some point at which the difficulty of coordinating the work, putting together all the various components, and organizing the whole enterprise actually reduces productivity, and output per unit starts to fall. We will discuss how this occurs later in the chapter.

RECAP

A PRODUCTION POSSIBILITIES CURVE represents the various combinations of commodities that an economy is capable of producing at a particular moment in time when it is fully and efficiently employing its resources.

Points inside the curve represent less than maximum uses of resources, since more of one commodity could be produced without reducing the amount of the other. Points outside the curve represent unachievable levels of output given currently available resources and the state of technology.

ECONOMIC CHOICES

Opportunity costs

Regardless of the fact that an economy may be producing at a level of both full employment and maximum efficiency, it can still never satisfy all the desires of all of its members. Because resources are scarce, society is always forced to make choices. To produce more of any one good that society wants necessarily means giving up certain amounts of other goods. *The amount of other goods and services that must be sacrificed to obtain more of any one good is called the* **opportunity cost** *of that good.*

A simple example of opportunity cost involves the economic choices an individual household faces every day. Suppose that a family has only $4000 to spend, and that it decides to spend all of that money on some large purchase. Because its resources are limited to $4000, the household cannot *both* buy a new car and make a down payment on a new home. It is forced to make a choice between one or the other. If it decides to make a down payment on a house, it gains the satisfaction derived from owning that home, but it forgoes the satisfaction that could have been obtained by purchasing the new car.

This simple example clearly demonstrates a fundamental economic condition. *Because our resources are limited, we are always forced to make choices between alternative commodities that will give us satisfaction; in making such choices we are always incurring costs that can be measured in terms of the amounts of other goods and services that we have sacrificed.*

Production possibilities

The economic choices faced by a nation, although on a much larger scale, are quite similar to those faced by an individual household. Even if a nation is using all of its resources—in terms of both full employment and maximum efficiency—its production possibilities are still constrained by the limited supply of those resources. Every nation, therefore, is forced to make choices about which goods and services to produce. To illustrate this basic economic condition, economists have devised the concept of **production possibilities** —*the various combinations of goods that an economy is capable of producing when it is fully and efficiently employing its resources.*

In order to simplify our explanation of the concept of production possibilities, we will begin with several assumptions. First, we will assume that regardless of the commodities a society chooses to produce, it will always fully employ its productive resources in the most efficient way possible. Second, we will assume that the supply of all factors of production is fixed—in both quantity and quality—and that the state of technological knowledge is also constant. Third, we will assume that an economy is producing only two goods or services. For our example, we will imagine a society that produces only shoes and bread. What are the production possibilities available to such an economy?

Production possibilities illustrated

Table 2.1, a production possibilities schedule, summarizes the various combinations of shoes and bread that can be produced in an economy that fully employs all of its resources and uses the most efficient techniques of production possible. At either extreme, it shows the maximum amount of one good obtainable if all resources were directed toward producing that good alone. The combinations of goods listed in the schedule are some of the possible choices available to the society.

By transferring these data to a graph (see *Fig. 2.1*), we can see the production alternatives even more clearly. Output of shoes goes on the horizontal axis, and output of bread goes on the vertical axis. We now have a production possibilities curve. At the ends of the curve, we see the possible extremes of production that would be obtainable if all of the society's resources were devoted to the one product. As we move along the curve from one end to the other, we can see how much of one good would have to be sacrificed to obtain successive units of the other. Each point on the curve tells us one possible combination of the two goods that we could choose to have.

Table 2.1

Production possibilities schedule for shoes and bread

Possibility	Units of shoes produced (in millions)	Units of bread produced (in millions)
A	0	21
B	1	20
C	2	18
D	3	15
E	4	11
F	5	6
G	6	0

In our example of shoes and bread, the choices at either extreme are 21 units of bread and no shoes or six units of shoes and no bread. It can be seen that acquiring each successive unit of shoes requires a larger and larger sacrifice of bread. (The reasons for this will be discussed later.)

This curve cannot tell the members of the economic system which point along the curve would be their best choice. That would depend on the need for the two items and on the value placed on them by that society. All that the curve does is indicate the possible choices.

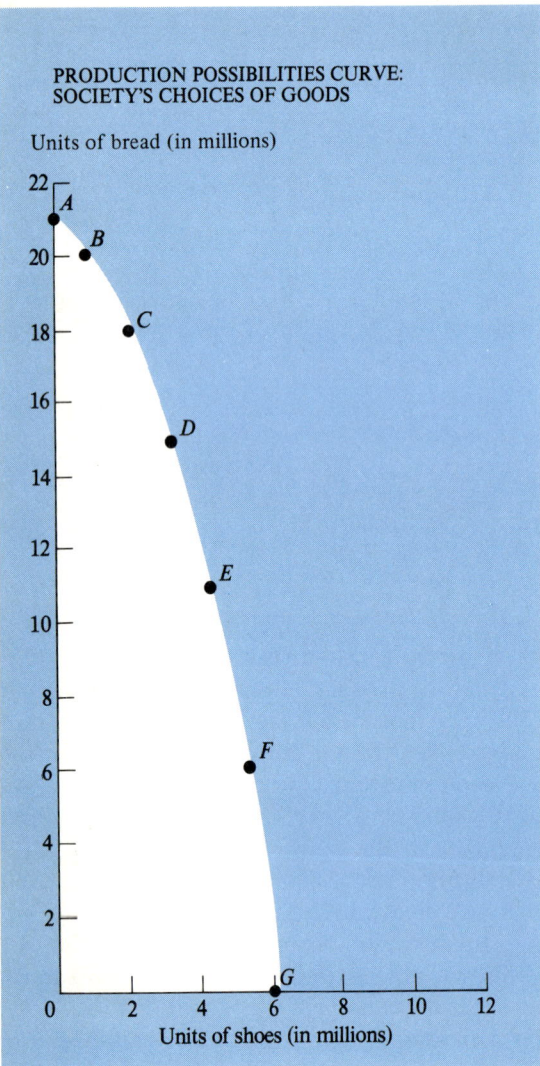

Fig. 2.1
Each point on the production possibilities curve indicates some possible combination of shoes and bread that an economy that employs its resources both fully and efficiently could produce. Depending upon the tastes and the needs of that society, some optimum product mix will be established—the quantities of these two commodities that will yield the greatest amount of satisfaction.

Inefficiency in production
At any level of output that falls on a point inside the curve, shown in *Fig. 2.1,* all available economic resources are not being employed or they are not being employed as efficiently as possible. For example, if we discovered the actual production was 11 units of bread and two units of shoes, we would know that the economy was not reaching its goal of maximizing output. Such a situation is indicated by point U in *Fig. 2.2.* By producing more shoes, or more bread, or more of each, this economy could regain a position on its production possibilities curve. The broken lines in *Fig. 2.2* indicate some of the ways full production could be restored. A point that is outside the production possibilities curve indicates a level of output that is beyond the current productive capacity of the economy. Such a point is point O in *Fig. 2.2.* Given the amounts of resources that exist at this moment and the present state of technological knowledge, it is impossible for the economy to produce both eight units of shoes and 14 units of bread.

But this is not to say that this level of output could never be achieved. The production possibilities curve tells us nothing about the future growth potential of an economy. It is based on present resource limitations, but the amounts of productive resources that are available to any economy are never permanently fixed. The size of the labor force is constantly changing in response to changing population growth rates and certain cultural factors, such as the average retirement age, or the extent to which women are employed outside the home, or the amount of leisure time people expect to have. The supply of available or usable land and capital can also change. A new irrigation project may create more farmland, or a flood can wash topsoil away. New machines can be built, and old ones will wear out.

And it is not only the quantity of resources that can fluctuate. Training programs can improve the quality of labor, and technological

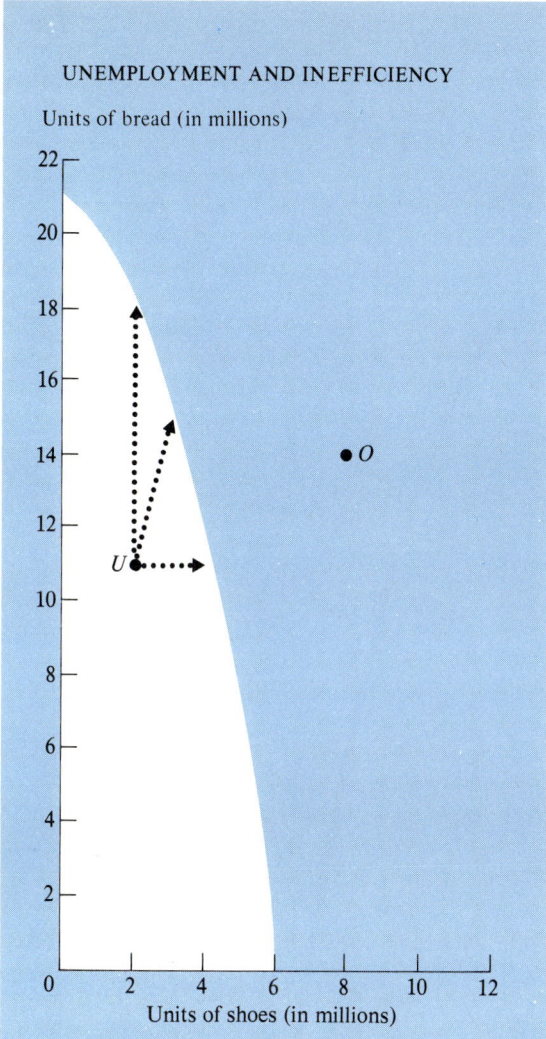

Fig. 2.2
Any point inside the production possibilities curve, such as point U, represents a less than maximum level of production; resources are either being unemployed or inefficiently utilized. By regaining a position on its production possibilities curve, this economy could produce more of either good without sacrificing output in the production of the other; or it could produce more of both goods. (These alternatives are indicated by the broken arrows.) Point O represents a level of output that is beyond the production possibilities of this economy, given its current supply of productive inputs and state of technological knowledge.

Production possibilities curve and economic growth

When there is an increase in the quantity or an improvement in the quality of resources, or if there is an improvement in the methods of production, then the production possibilities curve shifts outward. This shift is a reflection of economic growth. Two possible patterns of economic growth and their causes are presented in *Fig. 2.3*. An outward shift in the production curve means that the economy can produce both more shoes and more bread than was previously possible.

Increasing costs

If you look carefully at the first production possibilities table, you can determine the opportunity cost of producing each equal additional unit of shoes. These calculations are presented in *Table 2.2* and are shown graphically in *Fig. 2.4*. As we move from producing zero units of shoes to producing one unit, we find that we must sacrifice only 1 unit of bread (from 21 units of bread to 20). However, when we increase shoe production by one more unit, we discover that the opportunity cost in terms of bread is not one but two. And if

advances can increase the efficiency with which resources are used. Both circumstances would result in a higher level of output produced from the same quantity of input.

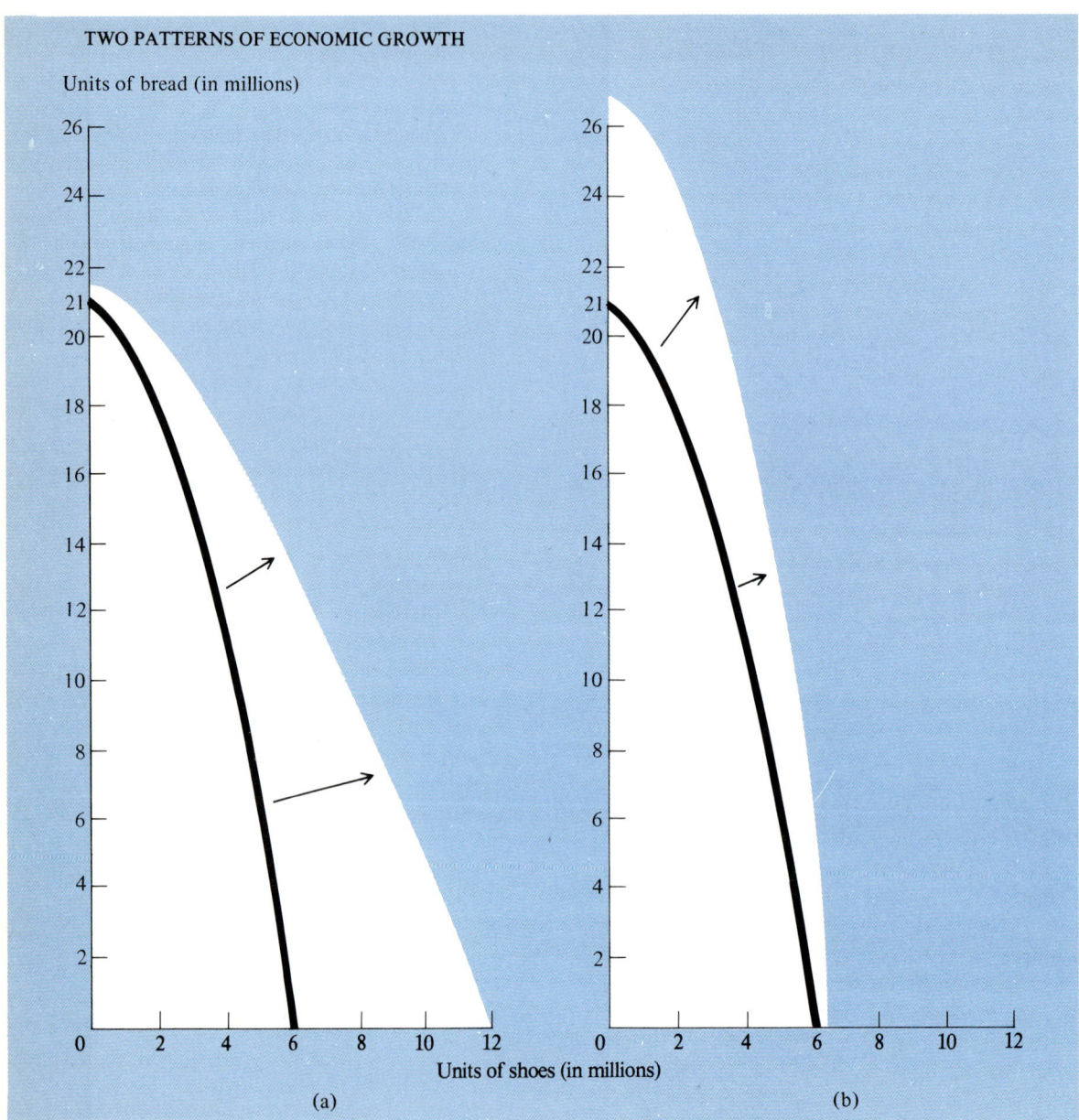

Fig. 2.3
Shown are two possible patterns of economic growth that the hypothetical economy might undergo. Graph (a) shows how growth would look on the production possibilities curve if it were primarily caused by a technological change in the shoe industry or by the discovery of a cheap input for shoe production. Graph (b) shows how growth would appear if it were primarily caused by a technological change in the bread industry or by the discovery of a cheap input for bread production.

Table 2.2
The opportunity cost of producing more shoes

Possibility	Unit of shoes produced (in millions)	Units of bread produced (in millions)	Opportunity cost of additional units of shoes (number of units of bread given up per extra unit of shoes)
A	0	21	1
B	1	20	2
C	2	18	3
D	3	15	4
E	4	11	5
F	5	6	6
G	6	0	

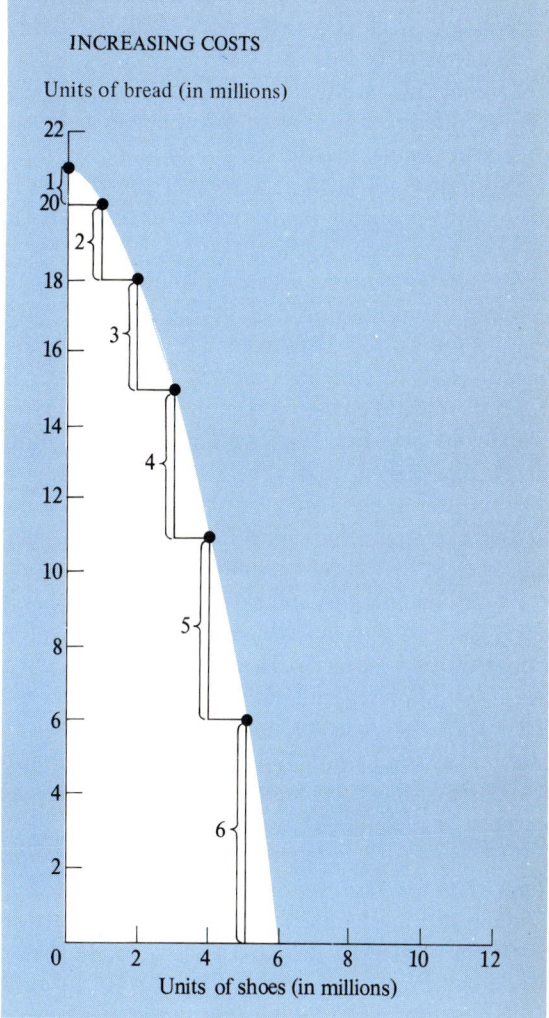

Fig. 2.4
The production possibilities curve we have been discussing is subject to increasing costs. The opportunity cost incurred when the economy moves from the production of zero units of shoes to one unit would be only one unit of bread. As the production of shoes increased, the opportunity cost of shoes would also steadily increase with each additional unit produced. Finally, moving from five units of shoes produced to the maximum of six units would require a sacrifice of six units of vitamins.

we follow the table through to production possibility G, the cost of adding the last possible single unit of shoes involves a sacrifice of 6 units of bread.

Economists refer to this situation as one of **increasing costs**. *Whenever increasing amounts of a product must be sacrificed to get equal additional amounts of another product, the costs involved are said to be increasing.* Let us discuss some of the reasons why increasing costs prevail on the production possibilities curve.

Factor suitability
Imagine that the current output of this hypothetical economy is located midway along the production possibilities curve; it is producing some combination of shoes and bread. What will happen if

the society decides to move up along the curve, increasing production of shoes and decreasing production of bread?

Since full employment already exists, the first step in making this change will involve reallocating input resources from the bread industry to the shoe industry. The first factors of production to switch will probably be those that are not particularly suited to making bread or that can be easily adapted to the manufacture of shoes. But as the economy continues up the curve, more and more highly specialized resources will have to leave bread making. It will become harder and harder to adapt them to the needs of the shoe industry. How could the facilities that were used for making bread be adapted to serve as shoe factories?

As the shoe industry employs more and more of these comparatively unsuitable resources, productivity in that industry will decline. Shoe manufacturers will employ increasingly larger amounts of most inputs to get the same amount of additional output, because the factors of production are not completely adaptable to their new tasks. Therefore the costs of production will show an increase as the economy moves toward the combinations of goods represented at either end of the curve.

Law of diminishing returns

The limitation of some input factor of production also contributes to increasing costs as we move along the production possibilities curve. In agricultural industries, the limiting factor is likely to be land, since good farmland is increasingly expensive and hard to find. In the majority of small businesses, the limiting factor is probably capital. Technologically complex industries, such as those engaged in the manufacture of computers, are frequently unable to find the trained workers they need; here labor is the limiting factor.

What happens when the supply of one factor of production is fixed and unvarying? Does it mean that increases in production are impossible?

The **law of diminishing returns** states that *increases are possible, but that beyond a certain point, the addition of successive equal amounts of one or two variable factors of production (usually labor and land) to a fixed factor of production (usually capital) will result in a smaller and smaller increase in output.* The point at which this begins to occur is said to be the point where diminishing returns set in. Before the point is reached, additional units of the variable input will cause each increase in output to be larger than the preceding one (or at least constant). After the point is reached, additional units of input will cause each increase in output to be smaller than the preceding one.

The law of diminishing returns is based on the concept of marginality (introduced in Chapter 1) which explains what occurs as one unit more is added. *The amount of additional output that is produced when the one extra unit of variable inputs is added* is called the **marginal product.** After the point of diminishing returns is reached, each added unit results in a smaller increase in output (marginal product).

An example may help to make the law of diminishing returns clearer. Imagine a large retail store that sells electrical appliances. It has only one salesclerk. He works at top speed all day, but still he can sell only $8000 worth of goods a week. Many interested customers leave because it takes too long to get waited on, and many fail to buy because the salesclerk is too rushed to do more than merely take orders from people who already know exactly what they want. The owner of the store adds another salesclerk, and weekly sales go up to $17,000 because now most of the potential customers can be waited on. The marginal product of the second salesclerk is $9000 ($17,000 − $8000 = $9000). The owner adds a third salesclerk, and sales jump to $27,000 a week, because every customer can be waited on carefully and because undecided customers can be persuaded to buy. Salesclerk 3 produces a marginal product just short of $10,000. At some point between the addition of the third and the fourth clerk, diminishing returns will set in. Point A in Fig. 2.5 marks this point of maximum marginal product; after this point, diminishing returns will prevail. If the owner adds even more salesclerks, each will give rise to an increasingly smaller marginal product. However, the owner will probably decide to add them anyway. Since she pays them a salary of only $100 a week, she can still afford to buy these extra input units, even though they yield a much lower marginal product than the maximum of $10,000. But finally a point is reached, at the seventeenth clerk, where the marginal cost, $100, is equal to the marginal product. Beyond this point (point B on the graph), there would be no further incentive to add another salesclerk because the clerk would cost more than he or she produces. And if the owner were foolish enough to keep on adding salesclerks, the marginal product might easily drop below zero. By the time she adds the twentieth person, the store would be so crowded with salesclerks that the customers could not even get in the door; she would lose sales instead of gaining them.

The law of diminishing returns is essentially a short-run problem for most producers. By definition, the **short run** refers to *that period of time that is only long enough to allow a firm to alter its variable inputs.* The **long run** is defined as *that period of time sufficient to allow changes in fixed inputs as well.* Thus, *over the long run* all inputs can be increased and the problem of diminishing returns can be avoided.

Diseconomies of scale

The third factor that causes the opportunity cost of producing any one good to rise at an increasing rate as more and more units of the good are produced is called diseconomies of scale. **Diseconomies of scale** refer to *the reduced efficiency and higher costs that occur when a business grows too large.* Usually they are caused by increasing problems of management. In a small firm, the top executive will usually be in touch with all of the

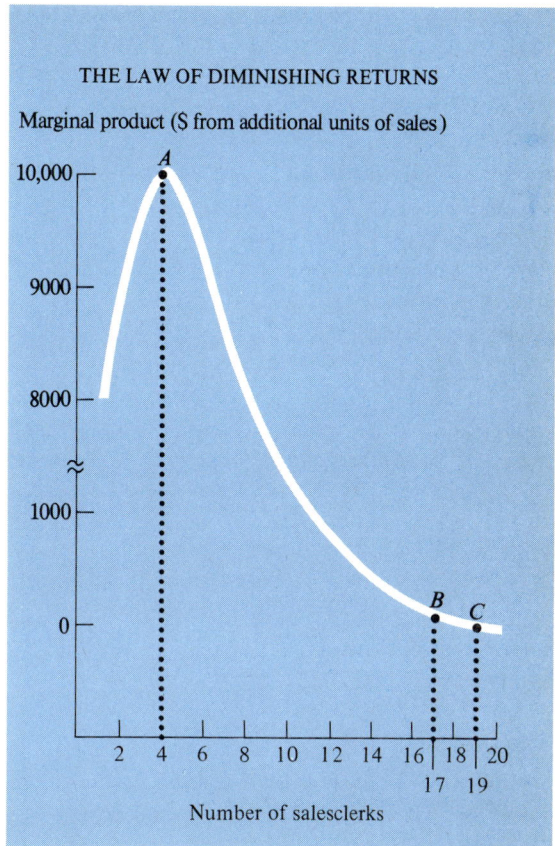

Fig. 2.5
In the appliance store example, beyond the point of diminishing marginal returns (A), each equal unit of variable input (a new salesclerk) added to a fixed resource (the store) will result in a smaller and smaller unit of extra output (sales). At point B (the seventeenth salesclerk), the marginal cost ($100 per week in salary) equals the marginal product ($100 per week in additional sales). After this point there would be no further incentive for the store owner to hire more people, for they would contribute less to sales than they would cost to employ. At point C, the nineteenth salesclerk, the marginal product would have diminished to zero. Beyond 19 salesclerks, therefore, additional employees would actually cause *total* sales to begin to decline.

> **RECAP**
>
> INCREASING COSTS OF PRODUCTION can occur for several reasons:
>
> 1. When input resources must be reallocated for new uses (such as from use in producing bread to use in manufacturing shoes) these resources may not be completely suitable to their new tasks, and costs of production may rise.
>
> 2. A fixed supply of one factor of production (usually capital) can result in smaller and smaller increases in output. This situation is expressed in the law of diminishing returns.
>
> 3. Higher costs can arise when a business firm grows so large that there is great difficulty in organizing and managing its operation. This is the problem of diseconomies of scale.

company's operations and be able to make efficient decisions fairly easily. As a company grows, however, the top executive tends to become further and further removed from daily operations as a hierarchy of managers develops. With more and more levels of management, the problems of smoothly coordinating decision making become increasingly complex. Frequently the result is reduced efficiency and higher costs.

But why not expand output by increasing the total number of firms in an industry, rather than the size of existing firms? Could not increasing costs be avoided in this way? Certainly diseconomies of scale do not set in when an entire industry enlarges, because industrywide coordination is not needed. Still, certain resources used by an entire industry would probably become scarcer and more costly as more firms joined the industry and as the demand for these resources increased. Eventually, expanding output by increasing the number of firms in an industry would lead to increasing costs.

A BRIEF SUMMARY

The production possibilities curve that we have been discussing is of course only hypothetical, since we have never actually devoted all of our resources to the production of only two goods, and it is hard to imagine a real-life situation in which people could exist on two products alone. But every day we all do make choices about which goods we wish to produce or consume and in what relative quantities. The production possibilities concept is useful in considering such choices, for it emphasizes two important facts: *(1) because of the scarcity of resources, there is always a limitation on the total amount of different goods that we can produce or consume; and (2) there is always an opportunity cost attached to any choice that we make.*

The cost involved is an important factor to be weighed in making any decision, but other factors are involved as well. It should be emphasized that all points *on* the production possibilities curve are "best," but the choice of deciding at what point to operate at any particular time is a value judgment. Decisions about how much we want to spend on defense and how much on education, how much on current consumption and how much on investment in capital goods that make possible future growth, whether we want to produce more luxury automobiles for the rich or more low-income housing for the poor—all these and every other decision must be made not only on the basis of cost, but also in accordance with individual values and assessments of utility.

If the fundamental economic goal of any nation is to produce those goods and services that maximize satisfaction, it must have some means of registering the individual wants and needs of all its citizens. The mechanism that a free-market economy employs to accomplish this end is the topic of the following chapter.

Summary

■ The purpose of this chapter is to discuss in detail the two basic assumptions economists make about any economic system: that consumer desires are unlimited, and that the resources available for satisfying these desires are scarce.

■ While economists regard consumer desires as insatiable, they distinguish between two kinds of satisfactions: physical necessities and luxury items. (Emotional gratification is a third category, but it is not generally studied by economists.) The distinction between physical necessities and luxuries is not absolute, but varies according to taste, income, and the level of economic development in a society.

■ The limited resources available are commonly divided into four factors of production: land, in which economists include all raw natural resources; labor; capital; and entrepreneurship. Technology is often included as an additional factor.

■ To maximize both output and satisfactions, an economy must fully employ all of its available productive resources and combine them in the most efficient way. No resources should be involuntarily unemployed, though a decision may be made to use certain resources gradually (for example, such raw materials as oil) rather than all at once.

■ All economic choices involve opportunity costs, the sacrifice of one possible product in order to get another product. Understanding the range of possible combinations of factors of production involves using such concepts as that of increasing costs (where increasing amounts of one product must be sacrificed in order to get equal additional amounts of another) and the law of diminishing returns (which states that after a certain point, equal additional inputs of a factor of production will yield smaller and smaller additional output). Diseconomies of scale may also result when a business grows too large and becomes inefficient.

■ The concept of production possibilities is useful because it emphasizes the limitations on the potential production of goods and recognizes that there are always opportunity costs. These limitations must be taken into account whenever economic choices are made.

Key Terms

consumer goods and services
luxuries
factors of production
land
labor
capital
entrepreneurship (business enterprise)
technology
underemployment of resources
economies of scale
opportunity cost
production possibilities
increasing costs
law of diminishing returns
marginal product
short run
long run
diseconomies of scale

Review & Discussion

1. Consumer desires are affected by many factors, including income, taste, and the range of products available at any given level of economic development. Find examples of consumer desires that exist today that did not exist 50 years ago and examples of products that were once considered luxuries and are now considered basic necessities.

2. Such recent events as the energy crisis have been forceful reminders that natural resources are severely limited. What are the limitations on the other factors of production—labor, capital, entrepreneurship, and technology? How can the limitations on these factors be controlled?

3. Economists say that one condition that must be present for the maximization of output and satisfaction is the full employment of all productive resources. What is meant by full employment? Underemployment? Involuntary unemployment? Is the fact that about one-half of adult women in the United States are not employed in the general economy an example of underemployment of resources?

4. What is the general shape of a production possibilities curve? What does this shape tell us about the relative costs of the two goods at different levels of output? How would growth of an economy affect the production possibilities curve?

5. Think of your economics course as a kind of economic system itself, one which produces knowledge. Apply the concepts of factors of production, marginal product, opportunity costs, increasing costs, the law of diminishing returns, and diseconomies of scale. Then apply these concepts a second time, thinking of the output as grades. Does anything change?

6. This chapter has suggested several considerations that must go into the making of ecomonic choices. How are such choices actually made? For example, when a decision is made to construct a paper mill on a river in a rural area, several opportunity costs are involved. Some other kind of factory will not be built, clean air and water may be sacrificed at least temporarily, the amount of wilderness area available for recreation will be reduced. How are these opportunity costs weighed, and by whom?

Chapter 3

The Laws of Demand and Supply

What to look for in this chapter

How does the United States economy answer the questions of what, how, how much, and for whom to produce?

What is the basis for exchange transactions in the economy?

How do economists understand both individual and market demand? Individual and market supply?

How do market demand and market supply combine to create an equilibrium market price?

We have said that the basic issue in economics is one of choosing among alternative uses of scarce resources. The economy as a whole must make decisions about what goods to produce, how many to produce, and which resources to use in production. On the individual level, there are parallel decisions to make. Individuals have available to them certain resources or economic goods—the ability to do productive work, the consumer goods they have acquired, ownership of productive resources such as land or machinery, and the money they make or save. Each of us must decide how to use these limited resources to bring us the greatest possible pleasure and utility. How many of the economic goods or resources that we currently possess are we willing to sacrifice to obtain other goods we desire?

The way that people decide to use their resources determines both the supply of, and the demand for, the goods and services an economy can produce. This mechanism of supply and demand is the way the American economy works out the answers to the basic production questions of what, how, how much, and for whom to produce.

The system of supply and demand—the market system—is not the only means by which answers could be found for these questions. They could be determined, for example, by a central planning bureau of politicians and economists, which fixes wages and prices, establishes production levels, and rations products. In the future they might be determined by connecting every household to a computer that will register preferences and calculate the amount of everything that can and should be produced from available resources. Here, however, we shall describe the system that is used in the United States—**a market economy,** *in which decisions concerning production, consumption, and resource allocation made by producers and consumers are realized primarily through a system of markets and prices.*

We will begin the chapter with a brief look at the exchange transaction that underlies each decision to buy a product. Then we will analyze both demand and supply, and the relationship between these two market forces. Finally we will consider the concept of the equilibrium level between supply and demand, or the point of stable prices.

THE EXCHANGE TRANSACTION

In order to obtain any desired economic good, individuals must give up some amount of a good that they currently possess. In barter economies, people actually trade one item for another—for instance, a pair of shoes for three dozen eggs. But in an advanced economy like our own, the barter system would be completely unsuitable. Labor is highly specialized; typically people work at producing only one kind of commodity. But they desire to purchase a great variety of goods and services. It would be virtually impossible for a woman who makes shoes in Biloxi, Mississippi, to make direct exchanges for all the goods she might want, because each transaction would require that she find a person who has a shortage of shoes and a surplus of whatever product she needs. Instead of directly exchanging shoes for eggs, she would have to trade her shoes to the people who need them and take in return some quantity of the commodity of which they had a surplus. It might take her four or five trades before she could get the eggs she wanted (see *Fig. 3.1*).

The exchange process becomes much less complicated if we use **money.** By money we mean *any item that is widely accepted by buyers and sellers as a medium for exchange.* Most modern economies, including our own, use paper money; but in the past other commodities have also been used. By using money the shoemaker can sell her shoes to the druggist for cash and then go directly to the farmer and purchase eggs. The farmer can then go and buy a coat; he need not worry that the clothier does not wish to acquire eggs.

Conditions for exchange

Exchange can take place only when two people have differing personal valuations of the economic goods to be traded. People will want to make an exchange when they place a higher value on the additional amount of the good they will receive than on the amount of the good they already possess and must give up. In economic terminology, *the amount of other goods an individual is willing to sacrifice to obtain a desired commodity* is the **price** of that commodity.

Differences in personal taste can account for some differences in valuation; one art collector likes Rembrandt paintings, another prefers the art of Jackson Pollack, and so on. But personal taste alone cannot explain why some people are willing to give up things that other people desire. Bread, for example, has the same nutritive value for

THE EXCHANGE TRANSACTION

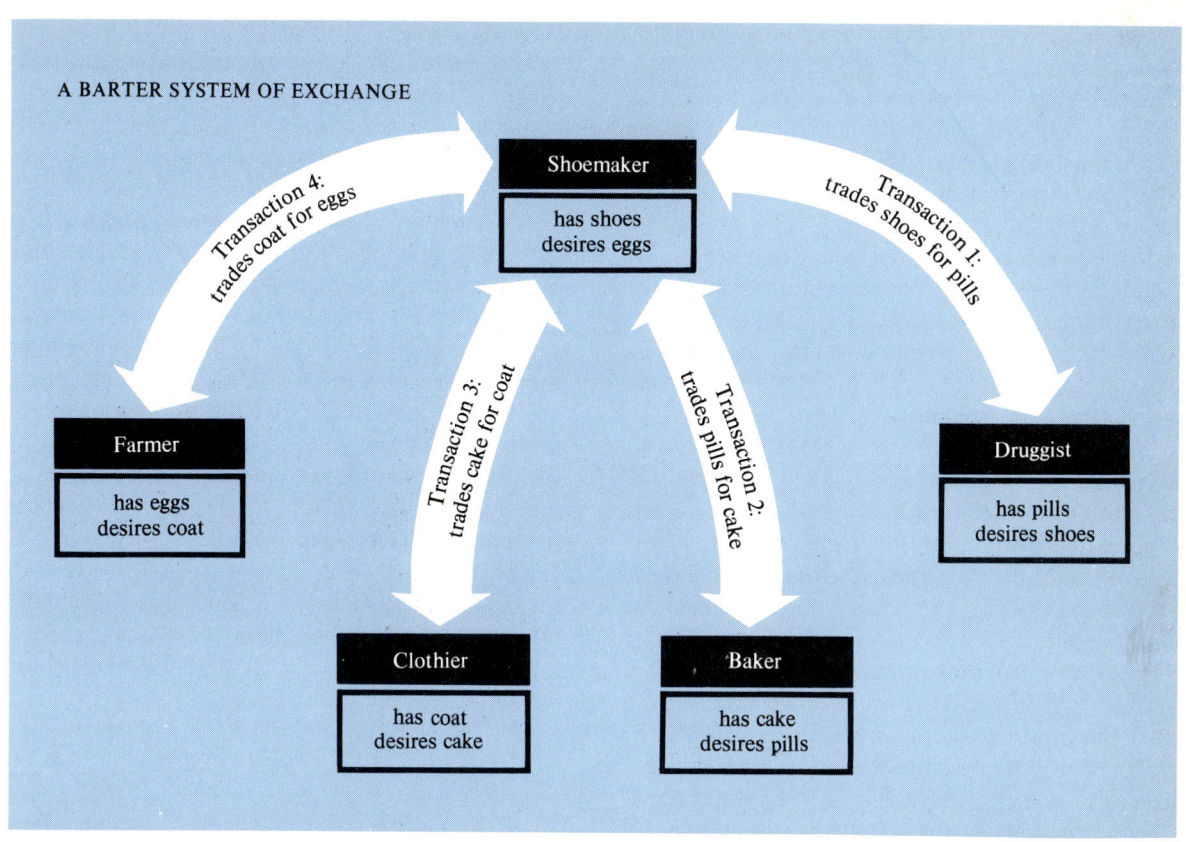

Fig. 3.1
Only the druggist has a demand for the shoes that the Biloxi shoemaker is offering to trade. But the shoemaker's ultimate goal is to obtain eggs, not the pills that the druggist has to exchange. She must therefore make a series of exchanges, successively finding someone desiring shoes, pills, cake, and a coat before she can get the eggs she wants.

everyone. Except for a few bread addicts, personal valuations of a loaf of bread ought to be very similar. If so, why does exchange take place?

The answer lies in a second important factor determining personal valuation of any good, the amount of the good an individual already possesses. If two individuals possess exactly the same number of units of a good *and* the same taste preference for it, they will not trade. Take the example of a woman who has 12 loaves of bread in the breadbox. Like everyone else, she wants bread on the dinner table; therefore, her first loaf of bread is worth just as much to her as it is to anyone else. Since everyone would place the same valuation on that loaf, no exchange would take place. But the woman's family needs only one loaf of bread a day, so the second loaf in her breadbox is worth much less to her. If she keeps it, it may become moldy. She values it at a lower price than does her neighbor who has no bread; therefore, an exchange can be made. The more loaves of bread she has, the less value she places on each additional loaf.

With the second loaf, the woman and her neighbor each put a different personal price on the loaf of bread; this is why the transaction takes place. The woman, wanting to make the greatest possible profit, would like to sell the loaf at the price that it is actually worth to her breadless neighbor. The neighbor, who wants to spend as little money as possible, would like to buy the bread at the lower price it is worth to the owner. They will bargain until they agree on a price satisfactory to both. *The price that the buyer and the seller agree on for a good or service* is called the **market price**.

In our economy, price is usually stated in terms of the medium of exchange, money. We say that the price of a loaf of bread is 65¢. But the actual consumer decision was not to sacrifice 65¢. It was to sacrifice 65¢ worth of some other good. The buyer might drink only two cans of beer on Sunday instead of three, or do without the newspaper for a few days, or give up some leisure time, working longer to increase income. Money is simply the common denominator that expresses exchange rates.

How are prices actually determined? In our example of the loaves of bread, the buyer and the seller bargained over the price of the loaf. In actual practice, prices in our economy are not usually fixed in one-to-one trading of single units. Very rare or costly items—art masterpieces, large blocks of real estate, famous diamonds—may be priced through such bargaining, either at auctions or through experienced dealers. But most prices are fixed impersonally through the action of the market—the place where buyers and sellers of any commodity meet for the purpose of exchange. The individual buyer has only the choice of paying the price already fixed or of refusing to buy.

Actually, market price is usually arrived at through the interaction of the forces of demand and supply. We will explain the process further later in the chapter. But first let us consider the workings of demand and supply.

DEMAND

In economics the word ''demand'' has a very specific and technical meaning. The economist defines **demand** as *the quantities of a product that individuals are willing and able to buy at each and every possible price during some specified period of time*. Demand is expressed as the relationship between the price of a commodity and the quantity, or the number of units, the buyer is willing to purchase. This relationship accurately reflects the economic decisions made by buyers in the market—that is, the quantity of alternative goods and services they are willing to sacrifice in order to obtain each successive unit of the commodity they are demanding.

For demand to be effective in the market, the desire for a commodity must be coupled with the willingness and the *ability* to pay its price. We can say that most American workers show an effective

---

RECAP

DEMAND refers to the various quantities of a product that individuals are willing and able to purchase at each and every possible price during some specific period of time.

Determinants of individual demand include income, the availability of substitute and complementary goods, future expectations, and tastes. An important determinant of market demand is the number of buyers in the market.

demand for automobiles. They want cars; they also have the ability to pay for cars, especially when installment credit is available. But we cannot say that most peasants in India have the same demand. Certainly they may have the same willingness to own a car, but their desire is not backed up by the ability to pay the market price. Their wages are too low for them to be able to afford to pay for the car, no matter how much credit they can get. Thus, at the existing market price, the demand of Indian workers is not effective; the number of units they are willing and able to purchase is zero.

Law of demand

From their observations of the decisions of individual buyers, economists have formulated a **law of demand.** This law states that *as the price of any good decreases, the quantity of the good that buyers are willing and able to purchase will increase. As the price increases, a smaller quantity of the good will be demanded.* This relationship is an inverse one: as one factor increases, the other decreases, and vice versa.

To verify the assertion that there is generally an inverse relationship between price and quantity purchased, we need only turn to everyday experience. From examining our own buying habits, it is clear that if the price of any good is reduced (other things being equal), we do indeed buy more of it, and when the price increases, we buy less. The owners of the retail clothing stores recognize the validity of the law of demand; they typically hold sales at the end of each season to clear their racks of surplus stock.

Demand schedule

We can illustrate demand by constructing a **demand schedule,** *a table that shows the various quantities of any given product that consumers will demand at different price levels during some specified period of time.* Table 3.1 is a demand schedule for strawberries, showing how many

Table 3.1
Demand schedule for strawberries (hypothetical data)

Price per pint	Quantity demanded (pints per month)
69¢	1
59	2
49	4
39	7

pints a given shopper would purchase every month at each price in a series of possible prices. If the price of strawberries is 69¢ a pint, the shopper will buy only one pint a month. If the price drops to 59¢, the shopper will buy two pints; at 49¢ the shopper will buy four, and at 39¢ the shopper will buy seven.

Note that, as the law of demand asserts, the shopper will buy more strawberries at lower prices than at higher prices—just as you will probably buy more LP records when they are marked down than when they are selling at their regular price.

The demand schedule does not tell us what the actual market price will be; like the production possibilities curve, it merely indicates a range of possibilities.

Demand curve

By transferring the data included in the demand schedule from a table to a graph, we can plot the points and arrive at a **demand curve.** *Demand curves express the inverse relationship between price and quantity demanded.* As a matter of convention, we put the price on the vertical axis and the quantity demanded on the horizontal axis. When all the points are entered and connected, the result is a curve that slopes down and to the right (see *Fig. 3.2*).

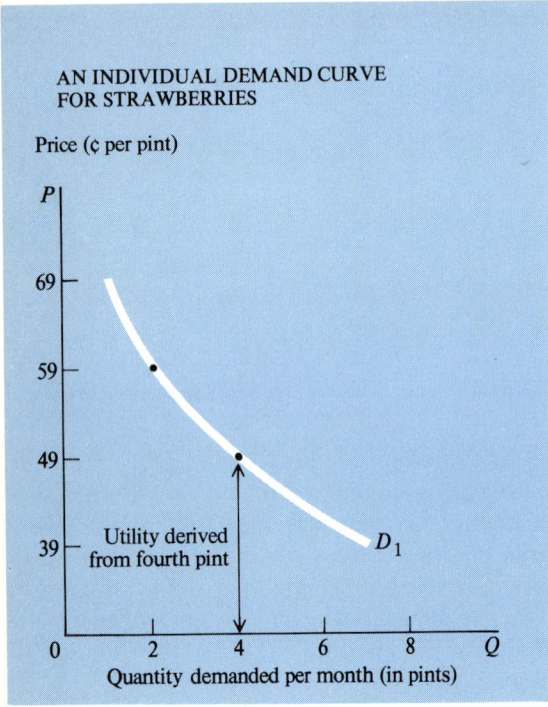

Fig. 3.2
The demand curve expresses the inverse relationship between price and quantity demanded. This relationship is reflected in the slope of the curve, which is always downward and to the right. According to the law of demand, as the price of any good decreases, the quantity of the good that buyers are willing and able to purchase will increase, and vice versa.

Demand curves can be drawn for any good or service in the market, and *the curve will always slope down and to the right*. This configuration reflects the inverse relationship between price and quantity and thus also reflects the law of demand. The shape of the curve will vary from item to item, depending upon the extent to which the quantity demanded changes in response to a given change in price. Some curves drop very quickly; others drop slowly and extend far to the right. But the slope is always down and to the right.

The "all-other-things-equal" assumption
An important assumption of the law of demand is the **"all-other-things-equal" assumption.** This is the assumption that *all other factors that could affect the relationship observed in the demand schedule are held constant.* That is, all the factors except price that might affect the amount of the product purchased remain the same or "equal"; only the price of the good under consideration changes.

Actually, it is logically impossible for price to change and all other things to remain equal. When the price of any good changes, then automatically the price difference between that good and its substitutes has changed; the money income of all those selling the product has changed; the real income (purchasing power) of all those buying the product has changed too. The all-other-things-equal assumption is not a reality, but it is an important analytical tool that allows economists to quantify demand in terms of price.

Change in demand and change in quantity demanded

When illustrating the law of demand on a curve, we are assuming that there will be no shift in that curve. We are merely moving between different price levels on a fixed curve and observing the resulting changes in quantity demanded. Looking at *Fig. 3.3* will help to clarify the difference between a change in demand and a change in the quantity demanded. When curve D shifts to D_1 or D_2, a *change in demand* has occurred because all other factors have *not* been kept constant. The curve itself has shifted to the right or to the left. But a movement from point *a* to point *b* on curve

> **RECAP**
>
> The LAW OF DEMAND expresses the inverse relationship between price and quantity demanded. If the price of any good decreases, the quantity of the good that buyers are willing and able to purchase will increase, assuming that all other factors that determine demand remain constant. As the price increases, a smaller quantity of the good will be demanded.
>
> Movement along a given demand curve due to a change in price is known as a change in quantity demanded. A movement or shift of the entire demand curve due to a change in one of the determinants of demand is known as a change in demand.

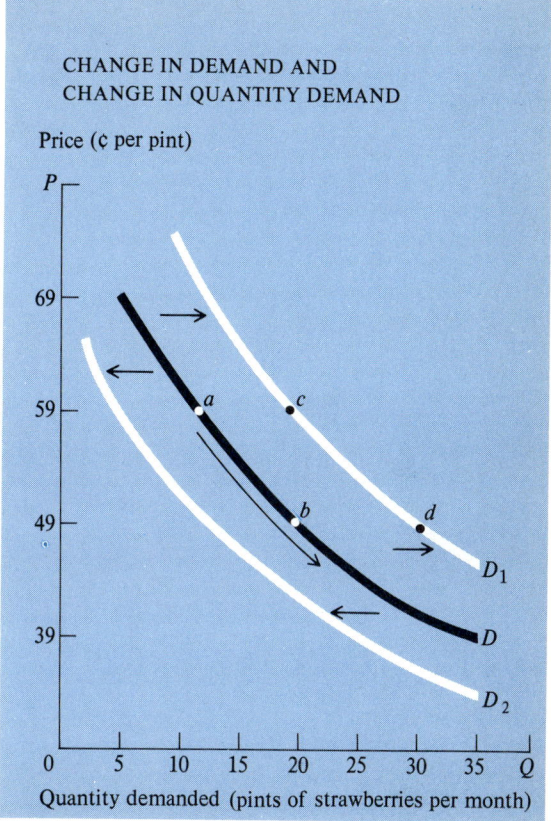

Fig. 3.3
If price falls from 59¢ to 49¢ and if all buyers in the market collectively purchase 20 instead of 11 pints of strawberries, a change in the quantity demanded has occurred, but *not* a change in demand. This change in the quantity demanded is represented by a movement from point *a* to point *b* on demand curve *D*. A movement from point *a* on demand curve *D* to point *c* on D_1, on the other hand, represents a change in demand; at the same price a larger quantity will be purchased. Such a movement is due *not* to the law of demand, but rather to a shift in the entire demand curve. Finally, if we move from point *a* on demand curve *D*, to point *d* on D_1, there has been a change in demand as well as a change in the quantity demanded.

D involves only a *change in the quantity demanded,* because the price of the product has changed, but no other factors have changed.

Failure to hold all other factors constant when observing the effects of price changes on the quantity purchased might lead one to question the validity of the law of demand. For example, in periods of inflation, it sometimes happens that an increase in the price of a good brings no change in the quantity demanded, and at first glance, this might seem to disprove the law of demand. But what has actually happened is that wages have risen in step with prices; that is, dollar incomes have increased. Therefore one of the determinants of demand has changed. On a constant demand curve, a rise in price would have decreased the quantity demanded, but the rise in income acts to increase total demand, shifting the demand curve to the right. The two forces cancel each other out,

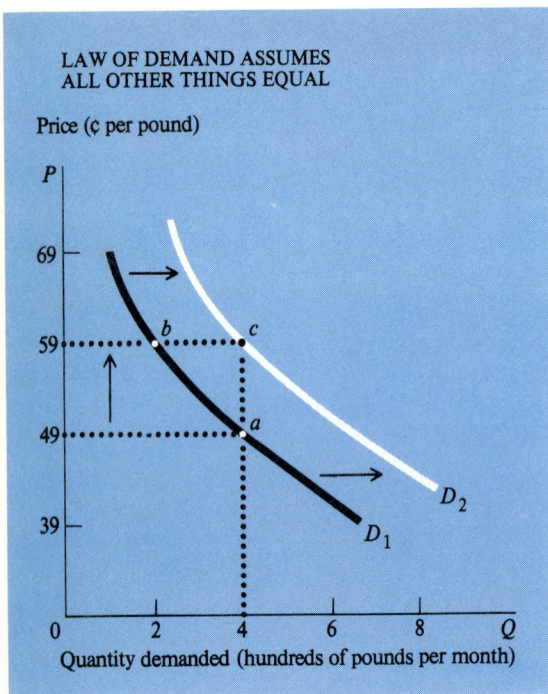

Fig. 3.4
If the price rises from 49¢ to 59¢, a decrease in the quantity demanded will result, as shown by a movement from point *a* to point *b*; this is in keeping with the law of demand. However, if at the same time, money incomes rise just enough to cause the demand curve to shift from D_1 to D_2, more will be demanded at every price. This shift in the demand curve is just sufficient to offset the reduction in quantity due to the change in price. At a price of 59¢, buyers are now willing to purchase the same 400 pounds that they were previously willing to purchase only at 49¢.

with the result that no change in quantity demanded is apparent (see *Fig. 3.4*).

Determinants of individual demand

We have defined demand as the quantities of a product that buyers are willing and able to purchase at various prices during some specified period of time. Demand, therefore, is really a whole schedule of price-quantity combinations. What actually determines a demand schedule? Economists have isolated both individual and market factors that influence demand. When all these factors are weighed together, the exact quantities that would be purchased at every possible price may be established. Any change in one of these factors will cause a change in the entire demand schedule for the commodity considered; a different quantity will be purchased at each possible price. On the demand curve for that product, such a change will be indicated by a shift of the entire curve to the left or to the right. Let us first consider determinants of individual demand.

Income

It is clear that at every possible price a person with a small income demands fewer products and fewer units of any one product than a person with a large income. As personal income rises, so does demand for most products. Additional income enables people to buy more of the goods they already consume and to buy different kinds of goods as well. Poor families do not generally demand sirloin steak for dinner. At their income level, chicken would provide just as much nutritive value and would entail a smaller sacrifice of other essential goods. But once their income is large enough, the same family may begin to include steak in its diet since the sacrifices required to do so are much less vital.

An increase in income means a greater ability and willingness to pay the price of a product—a greater demand. Demand for most goods will rise as income rises, and demand for most goods will fall as income falls. Economists call *goods whose demand varies directly with income* **normal goods.** Most products are normal goods; steak, tennis rackets, perfume, and tailor-made suits are all included in this category. But there are some goods for which demand actually declines as income rises. For example, a poor family whose diet includes large amounts of bread and potatoes will purchase less of these items as their income rises, because they will be buying more expensive substitutes, such as meat and eggs. *Goods whose demand varies inversely with income* are called **inferior goods.** As income increases, people demand less of these goods; as it decreases, they demand more.

Substitute and complementary goods

The demand for a particular good will also be affected by changes in the price of a related good. Whether the demand for the good in question increases or decreases will depend on whether the related good is a substitute for it or a complement to it. Goods are considered **substitutes** when they *can be used in the same way and therefore compete with each other.* As the price of a good increases, the demand for its substitutes will increase. For example, when the price of hamburger rises, many people will decide to switch to a substitute such as chicken, which is now relatively less expensive. The demand for chicken rises because buyers will purchase more units of it at each possible price. Conversely, if the price of chicken increases, more people will switch to hamburger.

It is not only price changes in a substitute good that can affect demand. If demand for one good changes for any reason—changes in tastes, in income levels—then that change will also affect the demand for all substitutes of the good.

The state of technology plays an important part in determining the level of demand for many products. Substitutes have been created for much of what we consume—plastics for leather and glass, saccharin for sugar, synthetic fibers for wool and silk. Each new substitute reduces the total demand for the original product.

Another determinant of demand for a specific commodity is the price of its **complements**—that is, *the commodities that will be used with it.* For example, the demand for film will be directly affected by the price of cameras; the demand for hot-dog buns will be affected by the price of hot dogs. When the price of a good rises, the demand for its complements will decrease.

To summarize: When products are substitutes, the demand for one is directly related to the price of the other; when they are complements, the demand for one is inversely related to the price of the other.

Some goods have no substitutes. Insulin is a good example. Vitamin C and aspirin are cheaper and more readily available, but diabetics cannot substitute them for the insulin they need. Similarly, many products are not complementary: eggs and shoes, telescopes and TV sets, clocks and cashew nuts. In such cases, a change in the price of one good will have little or no effect on the demand for the other.

Future expectations

Decisions about one's willingness and ability to pay for a good must often be made on the basis of future expectations. Expectations of rising prices in the future can increase present demand: if the price of TV sets increases, more sets might be purchased if consumers expect prices to rise even more in the future. Expectations of shortages can also affect demand. When people fear that incomes will drop and that unemployment will spread, they become less willing to buy. Lack of confidence in the economy can actually make a business recession more severe or prolong its duration, because present demand is lowered by the expectation that prices will fall in the future.

Other expectations also can influence demand. When a husband and wife buy a house or a car, or enroll their children in college, they have decided not only what they are willing and able to pay today, but also what they can and will pay for years to come. For example, a young couple may buy a house with mortgage payments so high they must sacrifice some necessities to meet the payments. If they thought that the sacrifice would remain that great throughout the term of the mortgage, they would not be willing to do it. But they expect their income to increase so that in a few years they will be able to meet the payments more easily.

Tastes
Personal tastes are another important determinant of individual demand. Taste includes highly personal preferences, such as a passion for everything that is shocking pink, or a liking for horseradish on eggs. It also includes the shifts in preference created by fads and fashions or successful advertising and marketing campaigns.

When consumer preferences favor a particular product—say straight-legged pants—demand for that product will rise. When tastes shift—for example, if people decide they now prefer wide-legged pants instead—demand for straight-legged pants will decline: fewer pairs will be purchased at each and every price.

Determinants of market demand

A demand schedule can be determined both for individual buyers and for the entire market. The **market demand schedule** for any given commodity is *the sum of all individual demand schedules for that good at each and every price.* Table 3.2 shows the process of calculating the market demand schedule for strawberries when there are four buyers in the market. *Figure 3.5* illustrates this same horizontal addition process when the data are transferred from schedules to demand curves. Of course, when the market demand for any particular product is being considered, there will usually be many more buyers than four. But regardless of whether there are four or four million buyers, deriving the market demand schedule for any given commodity always involves the procedures of adding all individual demand schedules. *The market demand is always equal to the sum of individual demands.*

An individual buyer will reach a point at which she refuses to buy additional units at any price, because her need for more of the good has diminished to zero. Her demand is satiated. But with each decrease in price, new buyers come into the market, so the market curve will show the continued increase in quantity demanded even though some satiated buyers drop out of the market. On the market level, a decrease in price not only

Table 3.2
Market demand schedule for strawberries
(four buyers)
(hypothetical data)

	Quantity demanded (pints per month)									
Price per pint	Buyer 1		Buyer 2		Buyer 3		Buyer 4			Total quantity demanded
69¢	1	+	3	+	1	+	0		=	5
59	2	+	5	+	2	+	2		=	11
49	4	+	8	+	3	+	5		=	20
39	7	+	13	+	5	+	10		=	35

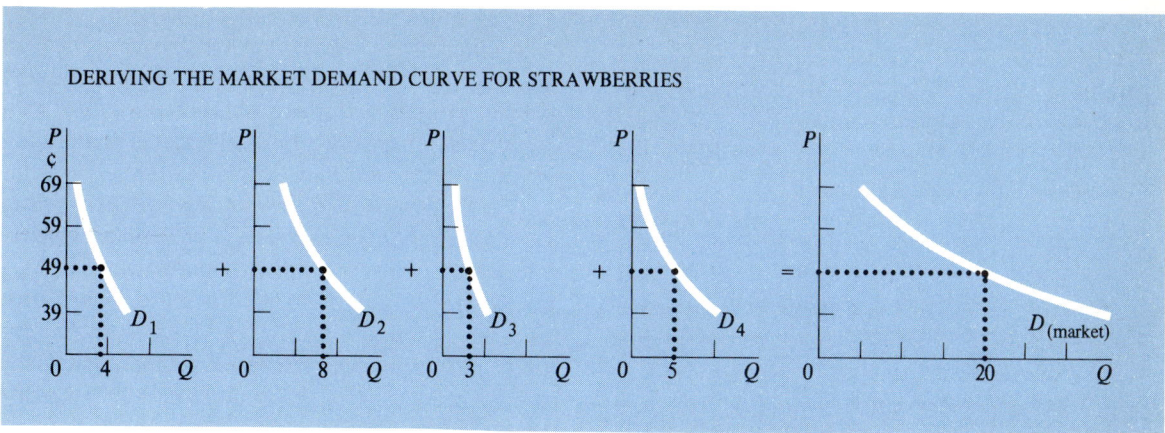

Fig. 3.5
The method of deriving the market demand curve involves adding all the individual quantities demanded by each buyer in the market at a given price. We then plot the total quantity demanded and the corresponding price as a point on the market demand curve. In our example there are only four buyers in the market for strawberries. At a price of 49¢, buyer 1 will demand four pints; buyer 2, eight pints; buyer 3, three pints; and buyer 4, five pints. The sum of these quantities (4 + 8 + 3 + 5 = 20) is the total quantity demanded in the market at a price of 49¢.

encourages most buyers (those whose demand has not been satiated) to take more units; it also attracts additional buyers. People who were not willing or able to buy at the higher price will decide to buy at a lower one.

Number of buyers in the market

When the total demand for a given product is considered the number of buyers in the market is also an important determinant. The number of buyers for a given product is partly dependent on the size of the population. If the population of the country increases, total demand will also increase. Another way to increase the number of buyers is to increase the number of people who are exposed to the product. A man who sells spaghetti sauce to a few of his neighbors can increase demand for the product by bottling the sauce and sending it to supermarkets. Advertising can often create larger total demand by making more people aware of the existence of the product and its uses; the number of buyers in the market has thus increased.

SUPPLY

So far we have been looking at only one side of the exchange transaction, that of the buyer or consumer. Now we will examine the behavior of the seller or producer. In the market situation, he or she is called the supplier.

We have seen in our discussion of the production possibilities curve that an economy's ability to produce goods and services is always limited by the availability of resources. Whenever we produce more of one good, we must pay a price in terms of other goods sacrificed. Thus it is not surprising that economists express supply, as well as demand, as a relationship between price and quantity. **Supply** can be defined as *the various quantities of a product that the supplier is willing and*

> **RECAP**
>
> SUPPLY refers to the various quantities of a product that a supplier is willing and able to offer for sale at each possible price during some specified period of time.
>
> Determinants of supply (individual firm) include cost of production, which is determined by prices of inputs and level of technology; prices and profits obtainable from alternative goods; and future expectations. Total market supply is also influenced by the number of suppliers.

able to offer for sale at each and every possible price during some specified period of time.

It is usual to think of suppliers as the business people who run factories, or the bakers who bake bread. These are the suppliers in the **product market,** *the market for final goods and services.* There is also a **resource market,** *in which the productive resources—for example, an hour of a worker's time or a bushel of wheat to make flour—are sold to producers.* In this market, the suppliers may be the individual workers, the men and women who are the consumers in the product market. The concepts of both demand and supply can be applied to the purchase and sale of input resources such as labor just as accurately as they can to the exchange of productive output such as loaves of bread.

We said that an exchange transaction can take place only when the two parties place different valuations on the items to be exchanged. A producer values the good at the amount it cost to produce it—the total cost of all the productive resources employed. If the consumer places a higher value on the good, an exchange will take place, and the producer will earn a **profit.** By profit we mean *the excess money received by the producer after production costs have been paid.* (A more comprehensive definition will be offered in Chapter 8.)

The law of supply

Economists have studied the behavior of sellers, just as they have studied the behavior of buyers, and as a result of their observations they have arrived at a **law of supply.** It states that *as the price of any good rises, the quantity of the good that suppliers are willing and able to offer for sale increases; as the price drops, a smaller quantity of the good will be supplied.* This relationship is a direct one: as one factor increases, the other increases. (Remember that in the law of demand the relationship between the price of a good and the quantity demanded is inverse; as price rises, the quantity demanded drops, and vice versa.)

Note that, as with the law of demand, the "all-other-things-equal" assumption applies when analyzing supply. With the exception of price, all the factors that determine supply are assumed to remain constant.

It is easy to understand the law of supply when we apply it to an individual business firm. Suppliers want to get at least what it costs them to produce any good. In the previous chapter, we demonstrated through the production possibilities curve that it is generally true that each successive unit costs more to produce. Therefore, only at higher prices will producers be able to meet the cost of producing and offering for sale a larger quantity of goods.

Supply schedule

Economists calculate schedules for supply in much the same way as they do for demand. The **supply schedule** *shows the various quantities of any given product that producers are willing and able to offer for sale at each and every possible price during some specified period of time.* Table 3.3 shows the supply schedule for the Rosebud Sled Company.

It is important to note that the ability to supply is directly linked to the productive capacity of the firm or the individual supplier. Ability to increase the supply of a product is limited and therefore more costly in the short run. But in the

SUPPLY

Table 3.3
Individual producer's supply schedule: the Rosebud Sled Company (hypothetical data)

Price per sled	Quantity supplied per week
$20.00	250
17.50	225
15.00	200
12.50	175
10.00	125
7.50	50

long run, supply can be increased more cheaply by expanding the plant or by adopting new methods of production. In the case of the Rosebud Sled Company, for example, it might be difficult and costly for the firm to supply more than 200 sleds per week.

Looking at *Table 3.3,* you can see that the market price would have to rise above $15 per sled before the firm would be likely to decide to increase its production capacity. In the short run, it might be necessary to pay higher overtime wages or put on a night shift. With more time, it might be possible to buy a factory currently being used for the production of goods that offer a low profit and convert that factory to produce sleds. Or the business might order new machines used in the sled-making process from a producer of capital goods; or a way might be devised to automate certain steps in the manufacturing process that are currently being performed by hand. In the long run, higher prices will continue to call out a response of higher production.

Supply curve

The data included on our supply schedule also can be presented graphically as a **supply curve.** The supply curve *expresses the direct relationship between the price per unit of a good and the quantity of goods offered for sale* (see *Fig. 3.6*). For convenience of comparison, the supply curve is set up on the same kind of diagram as the demand curve, with price on the vertical axis and quantity on the horizontal axis. *The supply curve will*

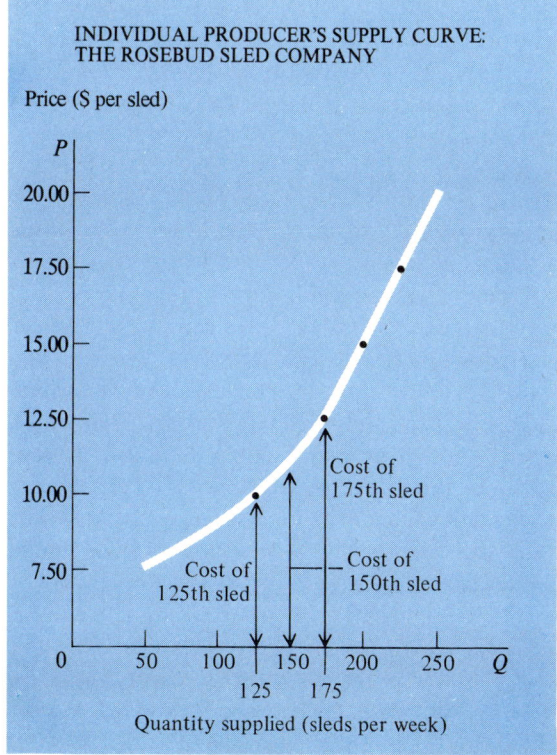

Fig. 3.6
The cost of producing the 125th sled is $10.00; the 150th sled, $11.00; and the 175th sled, $12.50. This means that the *extra* cost of going from 125 sleds to 150 sleds is $1.00 per sled, but the *extra* cost of producing 175 sleds as opposed to 150 sleds is $1.50 per sled. We can conclude that, because of the law of diminishing returns, marginal cost rises with output.

always slope upward and to the right, indicating that as price rises, the quantity offered for sale will also increase.

We can illustrate the direct relationship between price and quantity supplied by looking again at the supply curve for the Rosebud Sled Company (*Fig. 3.6*). When the price of sleds is $5, the company will not be willing to produce and offer for sale any sleds, since that price would not even meet their cost of production. If the market price is $7.50, the company will produce 50 sleds a week. It will not be willing to produce a larger quantity for sale at that price, because each additional sled would be more expensive to manufacture, and it would not make sense to produce extra units costing more than the selling price they would bring. The company will produce 125 sleds only when the market price rises to $10; this increase in price will cover the cost of increasing production, with the cost of unit 125 just equal to the sale price. If the market price is $15, the Rosebud Sled Company will be willing to produce 200 sleds each week, and so on.

Change in supply and in quantity supplied

As we noted earlier, the law of supply, like the law of demand, specifies an "all-other-things-equal" assumption. That is, the law of supply is valid only when all the factors that determine the supply schedule remain constant. A change in any of these factors alters the quantity that will be supplied at each and every price; a change in supply (in the entire supply schedule) has occurred. The law of supply refers only to the changes in quantity of a good supplied that come as a response to changes in that good's price.

Figure 3.7 clarifies the difference between a change in supply and a change in the quantity supplied. When curve S shifts to S_1 or S_2, a *change in supply* has occurred. The curve itself shifts to the right or to the left. But a movement from point *a* to point *b* on curve S involves only a *change in the quantity supplied*.

> **RECAP**
>
> The LAW OF SUPPLY expresses the direct relationship between price and quantity supplied. As the price of any good rises, the quantity of the good that suppliers are willing and able to offer for sale increases, assuming that all other factors that determine supply remain constant. Conversely, if price drops, a smaller quantity of the good will be supplied.
>
> Movement along a given supply curve due to a change in price is known as a change in quantity supplied. A movement or shift of the entire supply curve due to a change in one of the determinants of supply is known as a change in supply.

Determinants of supply: individual firm

As with demand, there are several important factors that determine supply. And as *Fig. 3.7* has shown, a change in any one of these factors will result in a change in the entire supply schedule.

Cost of production

The chief determinant of supply is the cost of production; no business will want to produce goods when the market price is lower than the cost of production. The supply curve can be interpreted as a cost curve. The cost of production is determined by resource costs, the cost of other inputs, and the existing level of technology. Changes in any of these factors will alter the entire supply schedule. When costs go up, fewer units will be supplied at each and every price. If costs go down, producers will be willing to produce and offer for sale more units at every possible price.

Obtainable profits from competitive goods

Producers respond to profits, not directly to prices. Changes in the market price of any good will bring changes in the revenue obtained from the sale of that good and hence changes in profits. As the price of one good rises and the production of that good becomes more profitable, the supply of all competitive goods will decrease, as suppliers switch to producing the good that will earn them the greatest possible total profit. For example, suppose that the demand for wheat rises and the price of wheat goes up. Since the profits obtainable from growing wheat are greater than those from other grains, most grain growers will plant less rye and oats and barley, and more wheat. If the demand for wheat is high enough, the price of scarce land resources will be bid up as more and more farmers try to expand their output of wheat. As a result, growers of hay and alfalfa may also be forced to switch to wheat, even though their land is not well suited to growing that crop and even though they can produce only a small amount. The high price of wheat, coupled with higher production costs, makes wheat the most profitable crop to grow. Theoretically, this process could continue until every square inch of farmland was planted in wheat. Thus increases in the price of wheat will result in an increase in the profits obtainable from growing wheat and hence a decrease in the supplies of other grains. Suppliers alter their production plans in response to the profits obtainable from competitive goods.

Future expectations

Decisions regarding the current supply of a good are also affected by the expected future price of that good. The anticipation of higher oil prices, for example, may lead oil companies to reduce the amount of output currently supplied to the market. That is, currently produced output may be withheld from the market as producers recognize the likelihood of being able to sell this output at a higher price in the future.

In this situation, it is important to distinguish between the concepts of production and supply. Supply refers to the quantities producers are

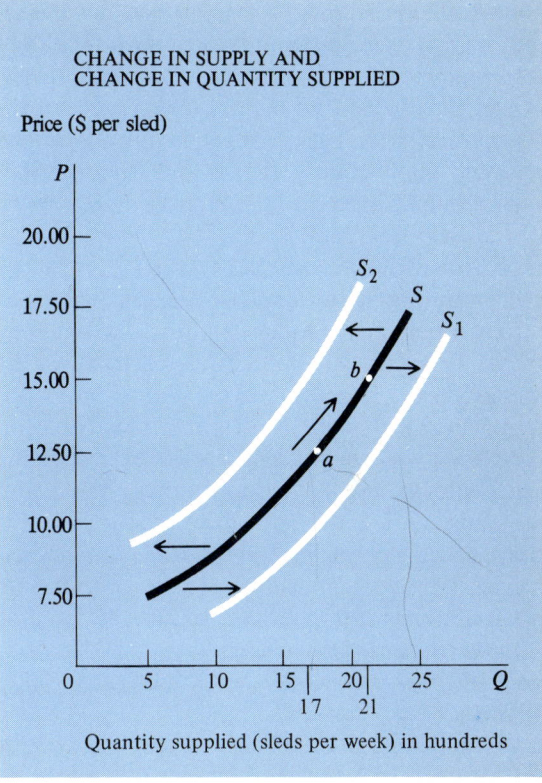

Fig. 3.7
On a fixed supply curve S, a change in price from $12.50 to $15.00 will cause a movement along the curve from a to b and a corresponding change in the quantity supplied from 1700 to 2100 sleds per week. Now suppose that input costs rise, and as a result, the supply curve will shift to the left from S to S_2. This change in supply means that only at a higher price will any given amount be offered for sale. Similarly, a shift of the supply curve to the right, from S to S_1, means that producers will be willing to supply any given quantity to the market at a lower price than previously.

immediately willing to offer for sale at various prices. Production, on the other hand, does not necessarily entail offering output for sale right now. Anticipating higher prices, then, businesses may increase production *now* with the intention of increasing shipments to retailers *later* when they expect the price to be higher. Consequently, the expectation of higher prices may result in decreased supply during the current time period, even though production has increased.

Determinants of market supply

The amount that any single producer is willing to supply is determined largely by the factors already listed. Total market supply is also determined by the number of producers in the market willing to supply goods for sale. Most important, the number of suppliers in a given market over the long run is determined by the obtainable profits. But the number of suppliers is also influenced by the size of the population, the social climate that creates the desire and ability to be an entrepreneur, and the accessibility of the market and ease with which it can be entered.

CHANGES IN SUPPLY AND DEMAND AND CHANGES IN PRICE

In a dynamic economy, it is to be expected that changes in both market supply and market demand will take place. It is always important to remember the difference between a change in the market demand or supply schedules and a change in the total quantity demanded or supplied as prices change.

When we talk about changes in market demand and supply, we are talking about changes in the total quantity of the good that is demanded or supplied at every possible price over a certain period of time. We say that demand has increased when more units are purchased at each and every price level in the whole range. We have already discussed the factors that determine total market demand and supply. Whenever a change in one or more of these factors occurs, the market demand or supply schedule changes; it is then necessary to draw a new curve showing the relationship between price of the goods and the quantity demanded under these new circumstances.

Suppose, for example, that in Altoona, Pennsylvania, there is an increase of $1 in the price of real (as opposed to artificial) Christmas trees. At the higher price, the quantity of real trees that buyers are willing and able to purchase will decrease. But this does not represent a change in the market demand—only a change in the quantity demanded.

Suppose, however, that the market demand for substitutes for Christmas trees does undergo a change. Fifteen families respond to the price increase in real trees by deciding to switch to artificial trees, so the total demand for artificial Christmas trees in Altoona is increased. How could we show that change in graph form? We might think of extending our original curve 15 units to the right, but that would be inaccurate. We do not yet know the number of trees demanded by the new buyers or the prices they are willing to pay for any given quantity of trees. What we must do instead is determine the individual demand schedules of the 15 new demanders and add those to our previous market schedule. The market demand schedule is equal to the sum of the demand schedules of all buyers in the market. If we then plot the new market demand schedule, we arrive at the new demand curve for artificial Christmas trees in Altoona. It will be located to the right of the old curve, showing an increase in total demand. When the total amount demanded or supplied changes at every given price level and when a new market curve is drawn, we say that the curve has *shifted*. There has been a change in demand for artificial trees because of a rise in the price of a substitute, real trees. *Changes in the determinants of supply and demand will shift the curves. But changes in the price of a good will not shift its supply curve or its demand curve.* At the new price, the quantity of a good being either supplied or demanded will change, but the total supply or demand pattern will be unchanged. *Price changes simply cause movements along the existing curve.*

MARKET EQUILIBRIUM OF SUPPLY AND DEMAND

We can now analyze what happens in an actual market situation as the force of demand interacts with the force of supply. In a market economy, it is this interaction that establishes market prices. Exactly how does this mechanism operate?

An example will help to make the process clear. *Figure 3.8* shows the supply and demand curves for sleds, plotted from the figures in *Table 3.4*. Now let us suppose that the price of sleds is $40. At that price, the suppliers will put 10,000 sleds per week on the market, but consumers will be willing and able to buy only 1000. Therefore the suppliers are stuck with a surplus of 9000 sleds that week. They must compete with one another to find customers for the extra sleds. In order to sell these sleds, the suppliers will be forced to lower their prices. The next week, the price may change to $30. At that price, producers will supply 9000 sleds. The market demand schedule shows that consumers will buy only 4000 sleds at that price. Once again a surplus is created, and competition among the suppliers will cause the price to drop again.

If the price drops to $20, suppliers will put 7000 sleds on the market, and at $20 per unit demanders will be willing and able to buy 7000 sleds. The total stock of sleds will be sold. There will be neither a shortage nor a surplus. Therefore there is no pressure on the price to move either up or down. It has reached equilibrium level.

If we look at *Fig. 3.8* we will see that the **equilibrium price**, *the price at which the quantity supplied is equal to the quantity demanded*, occurs at the point at which the supply curve intersects the

Table 3.4
Market supply and demand schedules for sleds

Price per sled	Total quantity demanded per week	Total quantity supplied per week
$40	1,000	10,000
30	4,000	9,000
20	7,000	7,000
10	10,000	4,000

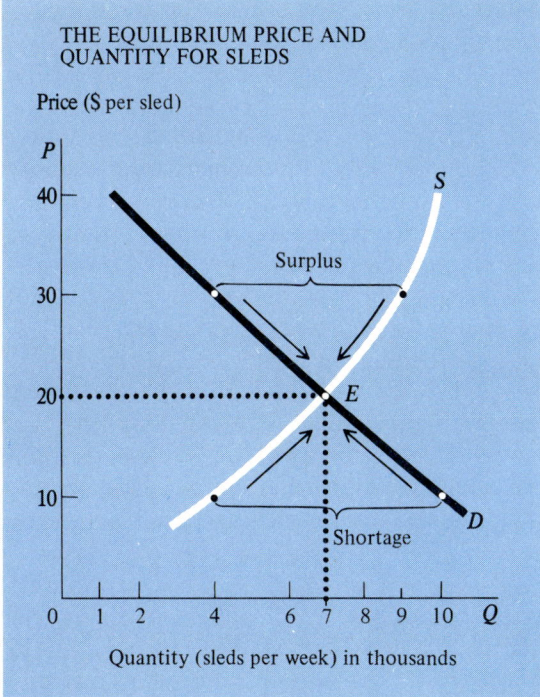

Fig. 3.8
The equilibrium price and quantity occur at the intersection of the supply curve and the demand curve. Only at a price of $20 will the quantity supplied to the market exactly equal the quantity demanded. Any price above $20 cannot be maintained, since the resulting surplus of sleds would cause competition among suppliers for sales, and hence the price would be bid back down to the equilibrium price. Similarly, any price below $20 would cause a shortage of sleds; buyers would bid competitively with one another for the scarce good, causing the price to rise back up to the equilibrium price.

demand curve. So if we know the demand and supply curves, we can locate the equilibrium market price of a commodity.

Shortages and surpluses

In the example above, the first prices were too high, and they created a **surplus** *(an excess of quantity supplied over quantity demanded at a particular price)* that acted to drive prices down. Surpluses create competition among sellers for the few buyers in the market.

Had the sled originally been priced at $10, the problem would have been not an excess of supply but an excess of demand. At a price of $10 suppliers would be willing to put only 4000 sleds on the market, but there would be a demand for 10,000 sleds. After all the sleds had been sold, 6000 buyers would be left without the sleds they wanted. Some of these buyers would be willing and able to pay a slightly higher price for a sled than the market price of $10, and so they would begin to bid up the price of sleds. The price of $10 would not last because it would create a **shortage** *(an excess of quantity demanded over quantity supplied at an existing price)*. Shortages create competition among buyers, who bid up the price of the few goods available in the market.

Since in reality neither production nor consumption actually proceeds on a rigid schedule, sometimes there is a temporary surplus or shortage. For example, it is the practice of many retail stores to delay restocking the shelves and counters for a few weeks after Christmas so that they can take inventory. Although this may create a temporary shortage of some goods, it does not alter prices because the situation is corrected so quickly. But if a shortage or a surplus persists for some time, it is a sign that the market price is not at equilibrium level. This sometimes happens when governments attempt to fix the price of food or other necessities at low levels. Either suppliers withhold their goods from the market altogether, or a **black market** springs up; that is, *an illegal market where goods are traded for more than their fixed legal price.*

To illustrate how this works, one of the problems of the South Vietnamese wartime economy was that farmers would not bring their produce to the government-regulated legal markets, where prices were artificially low. They preferred to take the risk of selling their eggs and vegetables on the black market (where buyers were mostly wealthy Vietnamese and Americans), because the prices there were significantly higher.

If a good is traded freely, neither shortages nor surpluses will last long, because they generate forces of competition that help to readjust prices to the equilibrium level. Those who are willing to pay the most will get what they want, pushing prices up and eliminating shortages. Those who are willing to sell for the least will make the sales, pushing prices down and eliminating surpluses.

The going price of a commodity is not always its equilibrium price. Determinants of supply and demand change constantly, shifting the curves in various directions. A period of trial and error follows, during which prices may be set too low or too high. As shortages or surpluses develop, traders in the market become aware of the problem, and prices are altered. Although prices are not always at equilibrium, in a free-market situation they are constantly moving toward the point where supply and demand will be in balance and equilibrium will be reached.

SUPPLY AND DEMAND ANALYSIS: FURTHER USES AND APPLICATIONS

A thorough understanding of the concepts of supply and demand and their interaction in the marketplace provides us with a particularly useful tool for analyzing a wide range of basic economic issues. The analysis in this chapter has concentrated on the determination of equilibrium prices and quantities in product markets—that is, markets for final goods and services, such as frisbees, hamburgers, and electric can openers. Realizing that the determinants of supply and demand tend to change over time allows us to understand why, for example, consumers have paid higher prices for automobiles and lower prices for pet rocks in recent years. The remainder of the text suggests a variety of other areas to which our supply and demand framework applies. As we will see, resource-market decisions in the private sector as well as economic implications of many government policies can be understood through application of the supply and demand model.

In resource markets the roles of households and businesses are just the opposite of what they are in product markets. Businesses become demanders, while individuals act as suppliers. Land, labor, and capital are demanded and supplied and the prices of these resources are rent, wages, and interest rates, respectively. Despite this reversal of roles and the requirement that we think of wages, for example, as a "price," the laws of supply and demand function in exactly the same manner to determine prices and quantities in resource markets as they did in product markets. If, for instance, entrepreneurs attempt to pay a wage that's less than the equilibrium wage rate, a shortage of labor will result, thereby forcing employers to offer a higher wage. Wage demands in excess of the equilibrium level, on the other hand, produce a surplus of labor at the requested wage. Unless demands moderate, unemployment will result.

Government actions are also subject to the laws of the market. When government regulation sets prices either above or below equilibrium levels, normal market operations are disrupted. In these instances, price is unable to perform its rationing function and the market cannot rid itself of the surplus or shortage that exists. Agricultural price supports and minimum-wage legislation fall into the category of artificially high prices, while rent and interest-rate controls are examples of prices fixed below equilibrium levels. Analyzing minimum-wage legislation from a supply and demand perspective provides a line of reasoning that has led economists to question the wisdom of government price fixing.

The Fair Labor Standards Act of 1938, of which the minimum wage was a part, was passed for the purpose of correcting "labor conditions detrimental to the maintenance of the minimum standard of living necessary for health, efficiency and general well-being of workers." Opponents of the minimum wage contend, however, that this wage exceeds the value of the output produced by some relatively unskilled types of labor. If, for example, the minimum wage is $2.90 per hour but an employee produces only $2.75 worth of output per hour, a layoff will be forthcoming. From the supply and demand perspective, the quantity of labor businesses can profitably hire is less than the quantity of workers seeking employment at the minimum wage. This surplus pool of labor represents unemployment, and those laid off cannot agree to work for, say, $2.50 per hour. It's against the law! Persistently intolerable rates of unemployment among black teenagers, sometimes reaching 40 percent, weaken the contention that the minimum-wage program has improved the lot of unskilled laborers and clearly demonstrate that the mere passage of a law, however well intentioned, will not solve economic problems if the laws of supply and demand are ignored.

In addition to price setting, the government has attempted to deal with a host of other problems, such as air and water pollution and occupational health and safety, by regulating the behavior of businesses in the private sector. Oftentimes, however, the cost of such regulation is exorbitant and progress toward solving the problems a matter of dispute. As an alternative to regulation, utilization of the market system to deal with these problems has been recommended. To illustrate the complexity of regulatory action and the relative simplicity of the market alternative, let's consider past government efforts to control water pollution.*

The Federal Water Pollution Control Act Amendments of 1972 required that the Environmental Protection Agency (EPA) develop specific effluent limits on water pollutants for each type of industrial process. In establishing these limits the EPA was directed to take into account "the age of equipment and facilities involved, the process employed, the engineering aspects of the application of various types of control techniques, nonwater quality environmental impact and such other factors as the Administrator deems appropriate." In addition, the EPA was to consider what was "economically achievable." Since there are 62,000 point sources of water pollution in the United States, the magnitude of this regulatory task is almost beyond comprehension.

Instead of defining effluent limits, it has been suggested that businesses be forced to bear the cost of their polluting activity directly by the establishment of effluent charges for each of the major forms of water pollutants. Polluters would experience increased production costs, as they would be taxed according to the form, and level, of pollution created. In each of these cases, the supply curve shifts to the left, higher market prices and a lower sales volume prevail, and profits fall. Using the market in this fashion, then, provides polluters with an incentive to minimize pollution levels, since doing so reduces production costs and increases profits. This creative use of the supply and demand model appears superior to the bureaucratic boondoggle caused by the regulatory approach to our water-pollution problem.

As the brief discussions of minimum-wage legislation and water-pollution control strategies indicate, the supply and demand framework is extremely useful as both a policy instrument and a tool of understanding. The remaining chapters of this book suggest many other situations in which application of the concepts of supply and demand allows us to better comprehend the nature of real-world economic problems.

Summary

■ Supply and demand is the mechanism used by the market economy of the United States to answer the basic questions of what, how, how much, and for whom to produce.

■ The basis for exchange transactions in the economy is the different valuations people put on goods to be traded. An individual will want to make an exchange when the good that is desired is more valuable to him or her than other goods which must be sacrificed in order to obtain it. The amount which must be sacrificed is the price of the desired good. In our economy prices are expressed in terms of a medium of exchange—money—which represents the power to purchase the other goods that are being sacrificed. The price that buyers and sellers agree on is the market price.

■ The demand for a good in the market is the sum of individual demands for that good. The law of demand states that the relationship between price and demand is an inverse one: as price goes up, quantity demanded will decrease,

---

*This discussion of water pollution control is based on Charles Schultze's *The Public Use of Private Interest* (Washington, D.C.: The Brookings Institution, 1977) pp. 51-54.

and vice versa—assuming that all other factors remain constant. The level of effective demand is also affected by income, taste, the prices of substitute and complementary goods, and the future expectations of buyers. A change in the price of a good will produce a change in the quantity demanded, but sometimes other factors—like a general rise in incomes—will increase the demand at any price level, shifting the demand curve to the right.

■ The market supply of goods is the sum of the supplies of individual firms. The relationship between price and supply is a direct one: as price increases, so will quantity supplied, as producers find it more profitable to expand production. The level of supply is affected by input costs, by the number of producers in the market, by the price of competitive goods, and by future profit expectations. A change in price will affect only the quantity supplied; changes in input costs or in the size of the population of potential buyers may result in a change in the supply curve itself.

■ Changes in the determinants of supply and demand will shift the curves, but changes in the price of a good will not. Price changes simply cause movements along the existing curve.

■ The equilibrium price of a good is that price at which the quantity demanded is equal to the quantity supplied—in other words, the point at which the supply and demand curves intersect. Prices in a market economy are not always at the equilibrium level, but by trial and error price adjustments are made which tend toward the equilibrium price.

Key Terms

market economy	demand curve	market demand schedule	supply schedule
money	"all-other things-equal" assumption	supply	supply curve
price	normal goods	product market	equilibrium price
market price	inferior goods	resource market	surplus
demand	substitutes	profit	shortage
law of demand	complements	law of supply	black market
demand schedule			

Review & Discussion

1. What is the basis for exchange transactions? Why are such transactions more frequent and more necessary in an economy where individuals play very specialized roles in production and

where very few people are self-sufficient in providing for their own needs?

2. How do buyers and sellers agree on a market price? How do they express their disagreement over a current market price? For example, are consumer boycotts of goods, such as the 1973 "beef boycott" organized by shoppers across the country, effective in changing prices?

3. The law of demand states that, assuming all other factors affecting demand are held constant, there is always an inverse relationship between price and quantity demanded—the demand curve always slopes down and to the right. Would this be true of luxury goods, where a high price may actually be part of the attraction?

4. Find examples of substitute and complementary goods you consume or have considered purchasing. How have their prices affected your economic decisions?

5. How would your effective demand for goods and services change if your income doubled? If it dropped by 50 percent?

6. The law of supply, like the law of demand, makes the assumption that all other factors affecting supply stay constant. What are some examples of supply situations where all factors do not remain constant? What are some demand situations?

7. Since profit potential is fundamental to the decisions of business firms about what and how much they will supply, future expectations are extremely important. What kinds of factors influence the future expectations of businesses? As a textile manufacturer, for example, how would your supply decisions be affected by knowing that a drive was starting up to unionize your plant?

8. What factors determine changes in *overall* demand and supply, and not just in the *quantity* demanded or supplied along the existing curves? Can you find some recent examples of goods for which the demand or supply curves have shifted significantly?

9. Over a period of time, the market prices of some goods (such as major household appliances) seem to remain fairly constant. The prices of other goods (such as farm products) fluctuate more dramatically. Why does this happen? How do you account for the fact that some goods settle into an equilibrium price and stay there, while others are constantly seeking a new equilibrium?

Application 1:
Demand and Supply: The Beef Boycott

For years, eating beef in this country was as American as eating apple pie. As the income of citizens went up, so did the amount of red meat they ate even though beef prices were increasing. But in the spring of 1973 consumers finally rebelled against the high price of beef—they began to mix soybean meal with hamburger meat so that it took less meat to feed a family, switched to cheaper cuts, and turned to other sources of protein, such as fish, cheese, and eggs.

The most dramatic signs of outrage at high meat prices, however, was a beef boycott organized by various consumer groups during the first week in April 1973. Homemakers abandoned their kitchens for supermarket parking lots where they carried picket signs urging others not to buy beef. The idea was economic simplicity itself: by cutting demand, the protestors expected to force prices down. As it turned out, however, the beef boycott had the opposite effect: although prices dipped briefly, within a matter of months they were higher than ever. The story of what happened tells us a lot about how supply and demand actually work in the marketplace.

At first, consumers did manage to buy less meat and beef prices did decrease. Supermarkets, finding their meat cases filled with unsold goods, cut back orders to wholesalers, who, in turn, reduced their purchases from slaughterhouses. Within a few days, wholesale beef prices dropped about 4 percent from 72 cents a pound to 69 cents a pound for choice grade beef on the Chicago market.

But the price drop didn't last because the boycott (like most other boycotts before it) attacked the symptom (high prices) of the problem rather than the root cause of the problem—the prices of beef had been rising, not because of a concerted effort by the nation's farmers and ranchers, but because an unusually violent winter had killed thousands of cattle in the plains states. The supply of beef dropped, and therefore prices increased.

Independent of the boycott and in spite of the fact that beef prices were increasing naturally, the federal government imposed ceilings on the price of meat in 1973 as part of a general wage and price control program implemented to fight inflation. This action provoked livestock growers to keep their cattle off the market in hopes of getting more for them once the government restrictions were lifted.

In 1974, when price controls were removed, cattle raisers rushed their overfed animals to slaughter creating a beef surplus, which in turn prompted ranchers to restrict the supply of beef once again by raising smaller herds. The smaller herds meant short supply and higher prices. The end result of this chain of actions and reactions was that beef prices were actually higher a year after the beef boycott than they had been before consumers had protested.

Questions for discussion

☐ Do the laws of supply and demand, in their classic form, assume that producers and consumers act independently of each other rather than in a concerted effort to influence the marketplace? If so, what could consumers have done that would have had a more lasting effect on the price of beef?

☐ Can you trace through this case and cite instances of producer expectation, substitution of goods, determinants of supply?

☐ What effect do you suppose the variations in beef prices had on the price of the grain on which cattle feed?

☐ When beef prices increased, the prices for many alternative sources of protein (substitutes) increased—chicken went from 39 cents per pound to 44 cents per pound; cheese went from 63 cents per pound to 68 cents per pound. Based on your knowledge of supply and demand and substitute goods, does this surprise you? Why? Assuming that all factors that influence the price of the substitute goods stayed the same (except for the price of beef), what explanation can you offer for the increase in the price of substitutes?

Chapter 4

The Price System and How It Operates

What to look for in this chapter

How are choices made about the allocation of scarce resources in our economy?

How does the price system answer the questions of what to produce, what quantity to produce, how to produce, and for whom?

What assumptions are made in analyzing the United States as a competitive market economy? How must these assumptions be qualified?

What are the basic characteristics of the modern American capitalist system?

In an economic system of freely competitive markets, the actions of individual producers and consumers in the market largely determine what goods are produced and how they are distributed. Limited resources force everyone—both producers and consumers—to choose among alternative uses and to employ a variety of substitutes for resources that are scarce or costly. A barrel of oil, for example, can be used to heat a poor family's cabin or a millionaire's mansion; it can lubricate industrial machinery or the engine of a commuter's car; it can be processed to make asphalt for highways or plastic for children's toys. Producers will want to use it in a way that yields the largest value of output and consumers will want to purchase the products that give them the greatest utility and satisfaction. Those who cannot or will not bid a price high enough to buy the oil will have to resort to substitutes or do without the commodity.

THE CIRCULAR FLOW

Individual decisions about the use of resources determine the market supply and demand schedules that exist for every product and service. It is these individual decisions to spend or save, to produce more or less, that underlie the supply and demand curves we studied in Chapter 3; therefore, price is really a reflection of individual choices about how much will be purchased and how much offered for sale. This process of buying and selling takes place in two types of markets: resource markets and product markets.

Resource markets and product markets

In resource markets the principal demanders are business firms. In order to carry on their operations they must purchase the necessary labor, land, and capital resources required to produce their goods and services. The suppliers of these productive resources are households. In product markets the principal demanders are households. They use the money income gained from the sale of productive resources to purchase the goods and services supplied by business firms.* Each round of exchange provides both businesses and households with the money they need to initiate another round, so that the exchange process can continue endlessly.

The circular flow model

Economists call this process the **circular flow.** A circular flow model is shown in *Fig. 4.1*. The lower half of this diagram shows how supply and demand in the resource market determine the prices of factors of production. Households offer the use of their resources—labor, land, capital, and entrepreneurial skills—to businesses in exchange for money incomes. The upper half shows how supply and demand in the product market determine the prices of goods and services. Business firms use the resources they have purchased from households to produce consumer goods. Households, in turn, use the money incomes they have received from businesses—wages and salaries, rent, interest, and profits—to buy the commodities that firms offer for sale.

In each market, price is determined by the existing supply and demand for a product, and the price is either at an equilibrium level or is constantly moving toward that price at which the quantity of a good supplied is equal to the quantity demanded. Price is therefore a kind of summary of all previous decisions regarding resource allocation. However, price also serves to structure future choices and actions. Producers who want to make a profit will try to increase their output of those goods that are high-priced in relation to the cost of producing them, and consumers will choose to buy greater quantities of those goods that are low-priced in relation to the satisfaction they provide. Prices are signals that elicit certain responses from all the individuals—both buyers and sellers—in the market for a particular good.

Money flows and real flows

An alternative to splitting *Fig. 4.1* into its upper and lower portions and examining the resource and output markets is to concentrate on the outer and inner loops in this diagram. This allows us to isolate the two types of flows that occur in the economy. The inner loop depicts the **real flow,** *the flow of resources from households to businesses for use in the production process and the resulting output in the form of goods and services flowing from businesses back to households.* This process deals exclusively with the movement of resources and goods and services. The outer loop, on the other hand, depicts the **money flow,** *money*

---

*Of course, there are also interhousehold as well as interbusiness exchange transactions. But to simplify the relationships between households and businesses at this point, we will consider households to be the suppliers of resources and the purchasers of goods and services, and businesses to be suppliers of consumer goods and services and the purchasers of resources.

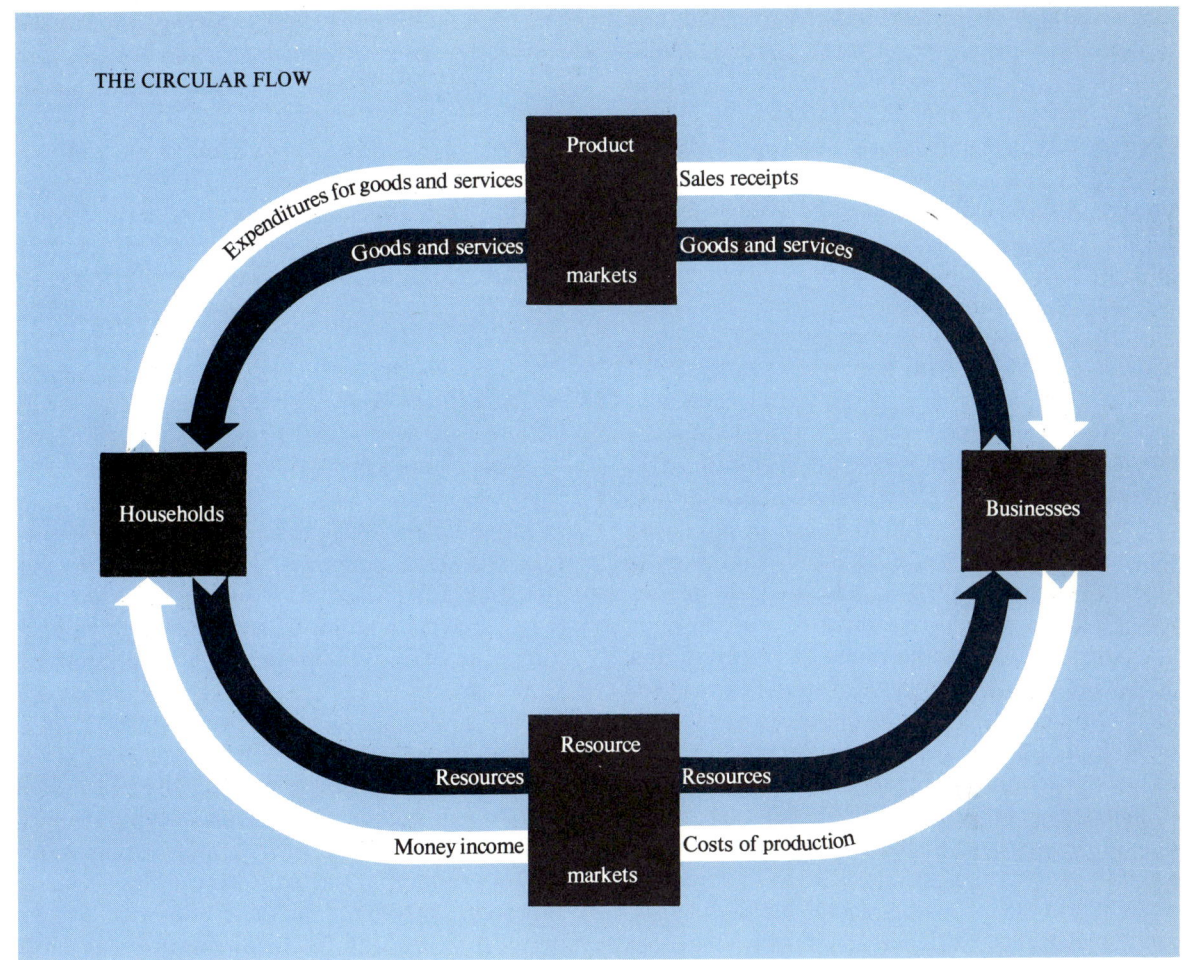

Fig. 4.1
The prices of factors of production are determined in the resource market, shown in the lower portion of this diagram. In the resource market the principal demanders are businesses and the principal suppliers are households. The prices of goods and services are determined in the product market, shown in the upper portion. Here the principal demanders are households and the principal suppliers are businesses.

income being supplied to households and the spending of this income on goods and services. Only the monetary transactions between households and firms are involved in this loop of transactions.

Note that businesses view this outer loop differently than households. Whereas households consider the money payments received for the sale of resources to businesses as income, these payments represent costs of production to the firm.

Likewise, while money expenditures for goods and services flow *out* of households, they flow *into* businesses. Thus household spending becomes sales receipts or revenue for the firm.

The fact that our circular flow model demonstrates both real and money flows indicates that we are dealing with a monetary, rather than a barter, economy. If *Fig. 4.1* depicted only the inner loop, households would receive payment for resources in the form of goods and services instead of money. Consequently, consumers and producers would be faced with the burdensome task of trading goods for goods in this barter economy. Imagine, for example, wanting to purchase eggs, but having only hubcaps to offer in return. You would not only have to seek out a chicken farmer, but one who just happened to want hubcaps. Even if you were fortunate enough to find such a person, you would still be faced with deciding how many hubcaps should be traded for a dozen eggs.

The addition of the outer loop means that people are willing to accept monetary payment for their economic resources as opposed to real payment in the form of goods and services. Similarly, businesses are now willing to accept money in payment for their products. This makes exchange a much easier process. Each good has a money price (in our system, this means a price in terms of dollars) and the difficulties associated with barter are avoided. The existence of monetary flows in the economy makes the buying and selling of goods and services a much more convenient activity.

Omissions from the circular flow

The circular flow diagram in *Fig. 4.1* is the simplest representation of the workings of the market economy, since it contains only households and businesses. We will discuss their participation in more detail in Chapters 5 and 6. The diagram does not take into consideration the role of the government in the economy. Moreover, it assumes that households spend all of their money and does not take into account the money they save. We will explore these aspects of the circular flow in more detail later in the text.

HOW THE PRICE SYSTEM ANSWERS PRODUCTION QUESTIONS

The **price system** is *the mechanism the American economy uses to answer the basic questions of production,* including:

1. *what goods are to be produced and in what quantities;*
2. *how the goods are to be produced; and*
3. *for whom the goods are to be produced.*

In the following sections we will see how the price system operates to answer these questions. We will also look at some of the assumptions underlying the effective operation of a price system and the way it is employed in the American capitalist economy.

A system of "dollar votes"

The price system is sometimes called a system that uses "dollar votes." This means that households, in the act of spending their money to purchase a certain product, are actually registering a vote to allocate resources for the production of that item rather than for any of the alternative uses those resources could be put to. The dollars spent by business firms that are buyers in the resource market are votes for the use of a certain type of input rather than another. For example, if higher wages are paid to taxi drivers than to bus drivers, the price system is signaling that our economy has a relative excess of the latter and an undersupply of the former. The wage differences, which would compensate for training costs, should encourage many bus drivers to learn to drive taxis instead. Transportation firms, through the way they cast their dollar votes, can cause the supply of taxi drivers to increase and the supply of bus drivers to decline. Individuals express their choices in the market by their patterns of spending, thus arriving at answers to production questions.

What to produce

Existing markets

The actual decisions about which goods to produce are made by the managers of business firms, based on an analysis of the expected costs of production relative to sales receipts—that is, profits. Costs depend primarily on the efficiency of the production process being used and the price of needed input resources. Sales receipts can be estimated by multiplying the expected price of the goods by the quantity likely to be sold, both of which are established through the impersonal action of the market.

If predicted costs are greater than predicted receipts, the firm cannot make a profit and the managers will decide against production of that particular good or service. If receipts are expected to be greater than all of the costs involved, there will be a profit in producing the good, and the business firm will be willing to undertake production. The greater the profit margin, compared with that of alternative goods, the greater the incentive to produce. Production decisions are made in response to potential profits, which in turn are determined by the market prices of both resources and products.

Industries can be observed to expand and contract as managers switch their firms into the production of profitable commodities and away from the production of commodities that show little or no profit, although of course, such a switch takes a certain amount of time. At the turn of this century, for example, a number of business firms became involved in the railroad industry. Demand for this transportation service was very great, and costs were much lower than receipts. But in the last 30 years, this industry has been shrinking rapidly. Demand has dropped as many people have switched to substitute means of transportation, such as automobiles and airplanes, and thus receipts have fallen. Costs have risen, especially when railroad labor unions acquired the political power to push the price of the labor input above the equilibrium level. Railroad companies began to cut back their operations, to shut down, to merge with one another. No new firms were attracted into the market, and many of the old ones left. Disgruntled travelers, complaining about the loss of service this industry shrinkage entailed, sometimes were tempted to blame the whole problem on a plot by railroad company executives. But the managers who decided on the service cutbacks and the fare increases were only making the production decisions forced on them by changes in the market supply and demand schedules. They had to reduce greatly the production of train service because a higher level of production was no longer profitable.

In general, we can say that when demand is extremely low, the equilibrium between demand and supply will result in a comparatively low price—perhaps so low that the average cost of buying input resources and producing a unit is higher than its price, and no production will take place. As demand increases, the equilibrium point of supply and demand will fall at higher price levels, thus encouraging production.

New markets: the case of the Super Yo-Yo

This kind of profit-and-loss analysis, based on the prices and costs previously established through the forces of supply and demand, determines the quantity produced of all commodities for which there is an existing market. An interesting and somewhat more complex problem is how the market determines which new products—innovations for which there is yet no market established—will be produced. Each year the Patent Office, a branch of the Department of Commerce, grants more than 50,000 patents on new inventions. How does the economy decide which products, out of this immense number of possibilites, will actually be produced by business firms?

Table 4.1
Supply schedule for Super Yo-Yos

Price per Super Yo-Yo	Quantity supplied per week
$40	38
35	36
30	34
25	30
20	27
15	22
10	12

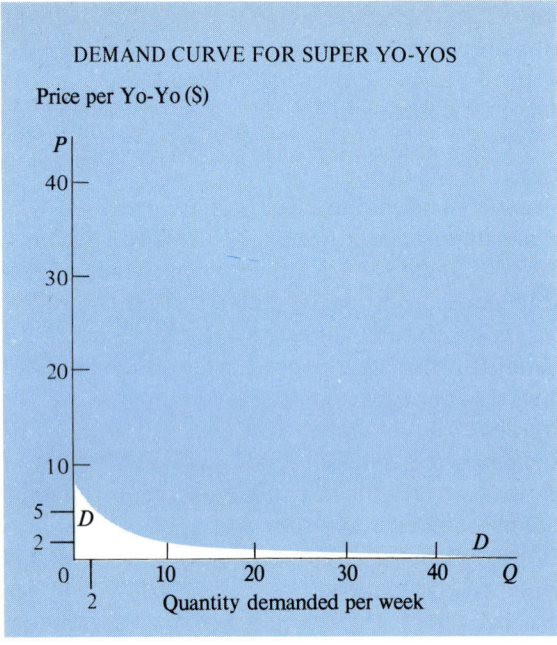

Fig. 4.2
The demand curve for Super Yo-Yos shows that at a price of $5, consumers would be willing to purchase only 2 Yo-Yos a week. In order for buyers to be induced to purchase 10 Yo-Yos per week, the price would have to drop to $2.

Basically, the answer is the same as for products with an existing market: production is determined by the costs of production and the dollar votes of consumers that produce sales receipts for the business firm. An example will enable us to see exactly how this works; it will be a good opportunity to review the concepts of supply and demand and market equilibrium.

Let us suppose that after spending many hours in his damp basement workshop, Norman Ventor comes up with an idea for an improved yo-yo. By putting precision-made tungsten ball bearings in the central shafting and using hollow sides containing molybdenum counterweights, Norman can make a yo-yo that will spin for more than five minutes—practically a perpetual motion machine! Norman is sure that his new, improved yo-yo will drive conventional yo-yos right off the market. So he patents his invention, the Super Yo-Yo, and sets up a company to produce them commercially. Norman determines his supply schedule by analyzing his production costs. Because he is using relatively scarce metals and precision machinery, his input costs turn out to be very high. *Table 4.1* shows his supply schedule.

At this point, he can only guess at the demand schedule for his product, so he decides to begin cautiously, producing only 30 Super Yo-Yos a week. Norman's supply schedule shows that he is willing to sell that quantity at a price of $25 per unit.

The appearance of the Super Yo-Yo on the market is greeted with a great lack of enthusiasm. Most people, after they learn the function and price of the product, decide that it is not worth paying such a large price for a child's toy, when they can buy one the child will enjoy almost as much for 49¢. Only a few people—those who compete in professional yo-yo contests, or who are desperately in need of an idea for a Christmas present for rich Uncle Hubert, or who have very large incomes—will decide that the gain in performance of the Super Yo-Yo is worth the added cost. The demand curve that develops for the product is shown in *Fig. 4.2*. In *Fig. 4.3* we see what happens when we balance demand against supply. There is no point at which the two curves intersect. At any possible price on the schedule, the total revenue (the price of the Super Yo-Yo times the number of Yo-Yos sold) is smaller than the costs of producing that number of Yo-Yos. No matter how high or low he sets his weekly output, Norman cannot possibly balance costs with revenues. He will have to shut down the company, a wiser but poorer man.

What actually happened in this case is that both the producers and the consumers in the market voted with their dollars not to allocate resources for the production of Super Yo-Yos, but to produce other goods that yield greater utility or pleasure per dollar spent. There was a low demand for the product, since few people were willing to give up the equivalent cost of other commodities to obtain the good. At the same time, Norman was forced to buy his resource inputs—labor, machinery, metals, electric power—in competition with other producers of goods that had much greater demand. Those producers were bidding for the use of the same resources, and they could afford to pay more to purchase resources for their products than Norman could for his.

What to produce: a brief summary

The price system thus registers dollar votes regarding use of scarce resources. Consumers buy the products that they consider most desirable and valuable from among the many possible alternative commodities that can be produced from the same input resources. The companies that make these products enjoy the highest profits and are therefore the ones that can afford to pay the most

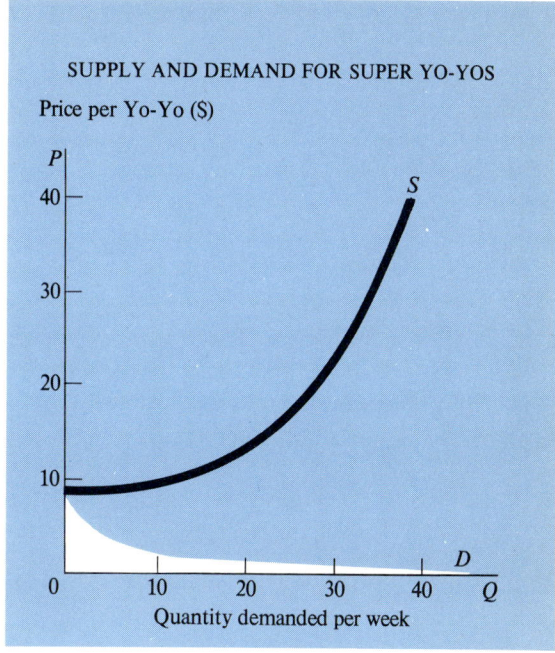

Fig. 4.3
Comparing the supply and demand curves for Super Yo-Yos, we find that there is no point at which the two curves intersect. At any level of output, the per unit cost of producing the Yo-Yos will be greater than the price that buyers are willing to pay.

for resources. Thus resources are automatically allocated to the production of those goods that will provide the greatest amount of satisfaction or utility. If some company tries to manufacture an item (like the Super Yo-Yo) for which the price that consumers are willing and able to pay (which is determined by the amount of satisfaction they derive from it) is less than the price at which the suppliers are willing to sell it (which is determined by the costs of manufacturing the item), the company is soon driven out of business by the competition among producers for input in the

> **RECAP**
>
> The role of the PRICE SYSTEM in production is to determine what goods are to be produced, how the goods are to be produced, and for whom the goods are to be produced.
>
> *What:* A company determines what to produce by weighing predicted costs against predicted profits.
>
> *How:* Producers determine how to produce by analyzing costs of production, especially the cost of input resources and the costs of each step of the production process.
>
> *For whom:* Goods and services will be produced for those people who have the willingness and ability to pay for them.

resource market and for customers in the product market.

How to produce

Price competition in both the resource and the product markets also determines the answer to the second question, how to produce. This decision is freely made by the individual producers, but the price system structures their decisions quite rigidly.

Cost of input resources

In the market, producers must constantly compete with one another on the basis of price. If a producer is able to alter any of the determinants of the firm's supply curve so as to lower costs, he or she can produce more units at a lower price than the competition and can make a larger profit. So each firm is under pressure to produce in as inexpensive a way as possible.

A large part of the cost of production is the cost of needed input resources. To obtain the necessary input resources, a producer must bid against other potential users of the same resource. We already saw how this system works to allocate resources to the producers of items that will earn the greatest profit, thus answering the *what* question. The same system determines *how* resources will be used. The producer who is willing and able to pay the highest price for any given resource is the one who needs it most specifically and uses it most profitably.

The operation of this principle can be seen in the example of an acre of land. A farmer who could grow corn on it would be willing to bid as much as $1400 an acre; the farmer cannot pay more, because then the cost of the land would be greater than the price that can be charged for the corn grown on it. A wealthy executive looking for a lot on which to build a house might be willing to pay as much as $6000 for that same acre, outbidding the farmer. If one's tastes and income are sufficient, one can get that amount of satisfaction from using the land as a building lot. But if the price goes higher, the executive will drop out of the bidding because it is possible to substitute cheaper means of obtaining the same degree of satisfaction, such as by buying a lot outside the city and hiring a chauffeur-driven limousine to go into the city.

The bidding will continue, with potential users dropping out at each price, until at last the acre is sold to the person who can offer the highest price—the person who will employ the land in the way that yields the greatest value of output. In this case, the purchaser is perhaps a corporation that intends to build an apartment house or an office building on the site.

Method of production

Another important element is the method of production chosen. Companies whose production methods are wasteful of resources and are inefficient will not be able to survive the competition of the market. In deciding on the production methods to employ, managers of business firms are guided by careful cost analysis of each step in the production process, and they will try to choose the method with the lowest average cost per unit. For example, cloth is generally manufactured by weaving fibers of cotton, wool, or synthetic materials on a power loom, but it can be produced in other ways. It can be woven by hand, but that is not an efficient method because the cost per yard for the labor is much greater than the cost per yard for the capital goods used by mechanized factories in place of labor.

Government scientists recently announced the discovery of another way to produce cloth. They found that in outer space, in the absence of gravity, it is possible to combine bits of hair and other waste particles and make a kind of cloth. But you can be sure that textile manufacturers are not going to rush out and start building rockets so they can send factories up into outer space. The current costs of that method of production are so high that no company would even consider adopting it.

For whom to produce

The constraints of the price system also shape the answers to the question of for whom goods and services are to be produced. The purchasers of any commodity will be those who have the desire for that item, coupled with the willingness and the ability to pay its price.

Desire for a good is in large part a personal and individual matter, for which sociologists and psychologists can furnish explanations to supplement the work of economists. Willingness to pay the market price of an item is chiefly a function of income level, number of units already possessed, and availability of alternatives.

The third factor, ability to pay, is itself strongly influenced by the working of the price system. A person's income level is dependent on the prices that the factors of production he or she owns or controls can command in the resource market. For most people, the chief resource owned is labor, but one may own other resources as well. At any rate, it is evident that the quantity and the quality of the productive resources one owns determine income level; and the person with the most money to spend will be the one who can purchase the most goods and services, thereby enhancing personal satisfaction. Specifically, this may be the person who earns a large salary or makes a good profit as a producer, who enjoys a high interest return on capital or owns a large amount of high-rent property.

Of course, social rules, customs, and prejudices also influence the ability of an individual to earn money and thus to buy products. Even luck may cause some people to have a larger share of economic resources than do others. But to a large extent, in a market economy the answer to the production question of *for whom* is answered by the prices that labor, land, capital, and entrepreneurial ability can command in the resource market—in short, by the workings of supply and demand.

ASSUMPTIONS OF A COMPETITIVE MARKET ECONOMY

From the preceding discussion of the operation of the price system, it may be noticed that certain basic assumptions regarding economic behavior have already been made. We have assumed that individuals act out of self-interest; we have assumed that producers intend to make a profit; and we have assumed that a condition of free competition exists among buyers and sellers in which no one supplier or demander can influence market price. To understand the functioning of a market economy, we need to know what is meant by each one of these assumptions.

Self-interest

A central assumption of the model of a price system operating within a market economy is that individuals in the market will make economic decisions according to their own self-interest. They will pursue their own goals of maximization in the use of personal resources, hoping to satisfy as many of their desires as possible. When they act, they do not consider society's good, but their own.

Even so, economists who developed the model of the competitive market have pointed out that the price system operates in such a way that, in many instances, the interaction of individual self-interest does actually promote the goals and the welfare of the whole society. A good description of the way a price system serves the general good through individual self-interest was given by Adam Smith in *The Wealth of Nations,* written in 1776. Smith was one of the first to analyze modern economics, and he was especially struck by the order and precision that he found contained within the price system. He said:

> Every individual . . . neither intends to promote the public interest, nor knows how much he is promoting it. He intends only his own security, only his own gain. And he is in this led by an INVISIBLE HAND to promote an end which was no part of his intention. By pursuing his own interest he frequently promotes that of society more effectually than when he really intends to promote it.

The "invisible hand": an example

If we look at the fundamental economic transaction of exchange, we can see how this "invisible hand" works. Sometimes we mistakenly think of an exchange as a transaction in which one person gains something and the other loses it. Even the people who are doing the trading may take this view and understandably so. After all, both know that they got something they really wanted and gave away something they did not want so much. One may therefore conclude that he or she received the advantage of the trade, while the other person did not fare so well. But in actual fact, both individuals received some advantage from the trade, and each is better off afterward than before.

It is easiest to see this in situations that do not involve money but are pure barter. Take the case of two baseball teams that make a trade. When the Red Sox agree to make a trade with the Yankees they are not doing it as a favor to the New York team. Their sole intention is to make their team a stronger contender for the money and fame of the pennant. Yet their trading action has the effect of bringing benefit to the other club. It also has the long-run effect of allocating the resources—good specialized players—to the teams that need them most. It means that resources will be used with greater efficiency; a team with two good third basemen will trade one for the good catcher they need rather than let one of the third basemen sit on the bench half of the season.

Other aspects of self-interest We assume that individuals are constantly motivated by self-interest, but that does not necessarily mean that each economic action a person takes is the one that promotes his or her self-interest most successfully. We must distinguish between motivation and action. For example, a man may buy a washing machine on credit in a local appliance store and pay 18 percent interest a year on the borrowed balance, whereas he could have borrowed the money from the bank at 13 percent. He may buy a cheap washing machine that breaks down and needs constant repairs, instead of selectng a more expensive, sturdier machine that would cost less in the long run. Ignorance, haste, and misinformation can sometimes cause people to act against their own economic self-interest. Nevertheless, the intention of the washing machine buyer was to promote his self-interest, although his actions did not achieve this goal completely or most efficiently. Moreover, in certain instances the self-interest of the consumer is in fact promoted even though to the outside observer it appears not to have been. Suppose, for example, that the washing machine a man purchases costs him $50 in repairs but that it would have taken 10 extra hours to shop for and select a better machine. If the man places a higher value on those 10 hours of his time, he has made a net gain by accepting the $50 in repairs.

Profit motive

Another of the basic assumptions regarding economic behavior is that the producer wants to make a profit from the manufacture and the sale of the goods. This would be true in any economy that permits private ownership of property or that allows individuals and corporations to keep all, or a substantial portion of, the money they earn. Not every type of economy includes a profit motive for producers. For example, in a communist economy, in which the state owns most industries, the government might order the production of certain goods that it judges to be desirable, whether or not they are profitable to make and sell. Or the government may regulate prices of some goods so as to prevent producers and sellers from making a profit.

Does the profit motive always apply?

Although the profit motive lies behind most of the actions that the producer of a product or the supplier of a resource will take, it is not necessarily true that every transaction made in the marketplace has to be profitable. On certain occasions producers may allow themselves the luxury of letting other motives predominate. Even though we must focus our primary attention on the economic aspects of a person's working life, we must remember that profit is not the only motive people may have for working. They may seek self-expression, or desire to help others, or hope to gain recognition and esteem from the community. Thus Picasso sometimes gave to a museum a painting that was worth thousands of dollars because he wanted people to see and appreciate his work; the Ford Motor Company deliberately increased an input cost by starting a program in Detroit to hire and train workers who were previously considered hard-core unemployables. In economic terms, these may well be examples of decisions to secure some emotional satisfaction at the cost of sacrificing some portion of total profits (although some economists argue that Ford's job-training program was merely an effort to expand the market for their automobiles or to develop a new, less costly supply of labor).

There are also instances in which the profit motive leads a producer to sacrifice a small amount of current revenue in order to gain much larger receipts in the future. Paris fashion houses, Dior and St. Laurent, for example, continue to operate their custom dress-making business for a few very wealthy women, even though they are losing money on it, because that is what gives them the prestige that sells scarves, costume jewelry, perfume, and mass-produced dresses—all items on which they make a great profit. Likewise, automobile manufacturers are willing to pay the high price of turning out a luxury model if it increases the demand for their regular models, giving all their cars a more exciting image and making them seem better engineered and more powerful.

Some analysts contend that the profit motive is what actually lies behind what seem to be public-spirited gestures by large corporations. A company that donates $10,000 to help finance public television may actually look on the expenditure as a form of advertising, which can be expected to result in an increased demand for its product and therefore an increased profit for the company; the company also enjoys the benefit of decreased taxes as a result of its gift.

Competition

Another assumption about the operation of the price system is the concept of **competition.** In economics competition refers to *rivalry among buyers and sellers in the purchase of resources and products.* It is competition among suppliers that drives prices down when surpluses occur; it is competition among demanders that pushes prices up toward equilibrium when shortages occur. Allocation of resources depends on the competitive bids from businesses; the competitive bids from consumers determine which commodities are

> **RECAP**
>
> The major ASSUMPTIONS OF A COMPETITIVE MARKET ECONOMY are: (1) individuals act out of self-interest; (2) producers intend to make a profit; (3) a condition of free competition among buyers and sellers exists in which no one supplier is large enough to influence market price. The third assumption is the concept of perfect competition.
>
> Perfect competition also assumes that everyone has full and immediate knowledge of any changes in production or price, and that all productive resources can be switched instantly from one use to another, more profitable use. Perfect competition is not an actuality, but some degree of competition does in fact exist.

produced. The concept of competition underlies the entire system.

Perfect competition

A situation of **perfect competition** *hypothesizes a market in which there are many suppliers producing a uniform product. No one supplier produces a large enough percentage of the total goods on the market to be able to influence the market price of any good by his or her own actions.* This situation also assumes that there would have to be many different demanders. Perfect competition further assumes that everyone in the market has full and immediate knowledge of any changes in production or price, and that all productive resources can be switched instantly from one use to another more profitable use.

Only when economic power is spread among many buyers and sellers does the price system work exactly as we have described it. When one buyer or seller can control a large share of the market, imperfections are introduced, and the system will no longer guide resources to their most efficient uses.

Many economists have written about the virtues of perfect competition, but it is doubtful whether any of them have ever had the opportunity to observe it. In reality some competitive imperfections are nearly always present. Laws may place some restrictions on competition. For example, no one is allowed to dispense prescription medicine without a license; therefore the licensing body has an opportunity to limit the supply of pharmacists and hence increase the prices bid for their services. In an age of complex technology, patent laws also restrict competition, prohibiting some producers from using the most effective production methods available. Both IBM and Xerox owe their prosperity to the fact that they were able to dominate the market for many years while other corporations tried to discover other ways of making computers and duplicators, respectively.

Monopolies

The opposite of perfect competition, called a **monopoly,** occurs when *only one supplier controls a particular good in the market and thus is able to determine price and production levels for that good.* Certain goods and services are said to be natural monopolies, because the quantity of capital goods required in production is so large that it is not feasible for two competitive firms to make the investment and expect to sell enough goods to make a profit. Highways, telephone service, and electricity are examples of natural monopolies. If two or three telephone companies were competing for customers within a single city, no company would have revenues large enough to pay for the enormous cost of creating a communications system.

In every economy, monopolies exist, introducing some degree of imperfection of competition. Usually they are either owned or regulated by the government, but *every* monopoly is still subject to some competitive restraints. Even if electric power companies were not regulated by the government, their prices would have to be competitive with substitute sources of power, such as coal or gas or oil. Monopolies do not completely eliminate competition, although they do affect the workings of the price system.

Today perfect competition is an abstraction rather than an actuality. Yet some degree of competition does exist, both within the market for a single good and between substitute products. Moreover, the competitive model yields predictions which in many cases reflect reality. So economists continue to assume that competitive behavior exists in many markets. This leads to predictions about results of price changes and allocation of resources which for the most part are close to reality.

We will analyze the models of perfect competition and monopoly in detail in Chapters 23 and 25.

THE MODERN AMERICAN ECONOMY: A CAPITALIST SYSTEM

Most of us are aware that the American economy is a capitalist system. The basic aspects of a capitalist economy are that it features the extensive use of capital, that production processes are highly specialized, that it is characterized by competition among buyers and sellers, and that the means of production are owned by private individuals rather than by the government.

Implicit in the concept of private ownership of property is the idea that people in a capitalist economy can make economic choices freely. Thus, entrepreneurs can decide what kind of business they want to set up, and they can obtain the resources they need for production as well as sell their finished products without government interference. Similarly, consumers are free to make choices about what products and services will best suit their needs. By the choices they make (registered through how they spend their dollars) they ultimately determine what the economy will produce.

Other essential features of capitalism are the assumptions of self-interest and the profit motive detailed in the previous section.

How do all these separate elements fit together in one system? Since it is the economy with which we are most familiar, it might be helpful to take a closer look at some of its outstanding characteristics.

Imperfect competition

As we noted in the preceding discussion, the perfect competition that is hypothesized in the model of the free-enterprise economy does not exist in the United States. Instead, the American economy has some elements of competition and some elements of monopoly. We will discuss imperfect competition in greater detail in Chapter 26. For now, the important point to remember is that imperfections of competition usually result in some deviation in the operation of the price system. Prices may be too high or too low, and resources may be wrongly allocated. When such problems occur, it may be necessary for the government to intervene in the workings of the system to try to compensate for the imperfections.

Extensive use of capital

Another marked feature of our economy is the large accumulation of capital goods. This accumulation is possible because individual households and businesses have decided to save money for the purpose of investment. What motivates consumers and producers to give up current utility or profit in order to obtain increased productive capacity for the future by investing in capital goods? People must have a belief in, and a commitment to, the idea of a brighter and better future. American society has always been strongly future-oriented, and therefore it is easy for us to adopt this pattern of present sacrifice for future gain.

The accumulation of capital can lead to economic development, since it increases input resources. Because historically, it has often been the path to growth followed by many currently advanced states, some people have assumed that a high level of capital accumulation is the best road to economic growth and, in fact, many economists actually define an advanced economy as one that has a large stock of capital goods. This assumption is open to question. Extensive use of capital is one way to achieve economic development, but it is not the only way. Growth can also be achieved by developing other productive resources: labor, technological expertise, land, or entrepreneurship. A country like India, for example, with a huge population and little ability to produce capital goods, might expand its economy more efficiently by substituting labor for capital, since the price of labor is much lower in India than the price of acquiring capital. Another country such as Switzerland, which has a relatively small but skilled labor force, might want to develop its resources of technological expertise or entrepreneurship, and substitute those for capital. There is no reason why economic development has to be linked with the development of capital resources alone.

Private ownership

Most of our economy's productive resources are owned privately by individuals rather than controlled by government. Individuals own the productive resources of land, labor, and capital; therefore they collect the rent, wages, interest, and profits that are earned by the resources. This is what adds the incentive of the profit motive to our price system.

The American government does own a certain portion of the capital goods of the nation, for example, the highway system and several large hydroelectric dams. It lends money to small businesses for capital improvement. It regulates certain aspects of private ownership, either through direct restriction of profits, as in the case of public utilities, or through the indirect means of taxation. So while the American economy cannot accurately be described as an example of pure private enterprise, that is the type of ownership that predominates.

Division of labor and specialization

From its earliest days, the United States economy has always shown a high degree of diversification. It has never been purely agricultural, purely industrial, or purely service-oriented, but rather has always produced a wide variety of goods and services. Today the economy also exhibits a high degree of specialization; that is, both companies and individual workers specialize in one specific task. Specialization promotes efficiency because it provides jobs suitable for every imaginable combination of abilities and because it allows the development and learning of vocational skills.

The assembly line is often pointed to as the most efficient example of division of labor. It breaks down the manufacturing process into small steps. Each step is performed by one worker who has learned that specific task and nothing else; for example, a worker tightens a certain set of screws or fits one piece into another. The assembly line permits a small group of workers to turn out a large number of units of a product, perhaps 10, 20, or even 30 times more than if each worker assembled the whole unit from start to finish.

Along with specialization has come a complete interdependence of the various segments of our economy. No worker, company, or industry can be totally self-sufficient today; each depends in some way on hundreds of thousands of other people. This dependence is such an ingrained feature of life in America that most people do not even realize its extent. It is only when some strand of the net of interdependence breaks that people notice its presence. For example, when workers of one company or one industry go out on strike, people suddenly begin to understand how their work was necessary to the operation of the whole system. When General Motors is struck, the whole economy is hurt, profits go down and unemployment goes up; when the mail carriers strike for a few days, all businesses are threatened by crises precipitated by missing checks, orders, contracts, and documents.

American economic interdependence does not stop at the country's national borders. The United States depends on other nations to supply us with needed raw materials (oil from the Middle East, coffee beans from Colombia and Kenya) and to serve as markets for our manufactured products. In recent years, much of our American economic growth has come through finding new buyers abroad and thus expanding demand. So strikes, political changes, and wars in all parts of the globe can have a direct effect on wages, prices, employment rates, and economic growth throughout America.

Summary

■ This chapter describes the general features and working of the price system, the basic mechanism through which supply and demand operate to determine the allocation of scarce resources in the production process.

■ The circular flow in the economy is the continual exchange of both resources and money between households and businesses. Supply and demand in the resource market determine the prices of factors of production; supply and demand in the product market determine the prices of finished goods and services. Prices connect the real flow of goods and resources with the flow of money. Prices summarize the previous choices made about the allocation of resources, but they also help to structure future decisions.

■ The price system is the major mechanism in our economy for answering the basic questions of production. Managers of businesses make decisions concerning what goods to produce and what quantities to produce by estimating the costs of production and potential sales receipts—that is, by estimating profits. Industries expand or contract, start up or fail as they move from production of unprofitable commodities to the production of commodities that are profitable. Prices also determine how goods will be produced, through the bidding among producers for resource inputs and through the pressure of competition to produce in the most efficient and least costly way. The question of for whom goods and services are produced is answered by those with the desire and the ability to pay the prices of the goods, and the incomes of buyers in turn are determined by the prices they can command for their labor or the other resources they can sell in the resource market.

■ The three basic assumptions regarding economic behavior in a competitive market economy are: (1) individuals base their economic decisions on self-interest; (2) producers are motivated by the desire to make a profit from the manufacture and sale of their goods; and (3) suppliers and demanders freely compete with one another in the purchase of resources and products.

■ The major characteristics of the American capitalist economic system are: free competition, although much of it is imperfect competition; the extensive use of capital; private ownership of most productive resources; and a high degree of division of labor, specialization, and interdependence among different individuals and businesses.

Key Terms

circular flow	money flow	competition	monopoly
real flow	price system	perfect competition	

Review & Discussion

1. How does the market price for a given item reflect the past choices of individual producers and consumers? How does it affect their future choices?

2. Describe the circular flow. What are the possible forms of income to a consumer?

3. Under what conditions would a firm decide to produce a given commodity? How does the market price structure its decisions? How else could such decisions be made?

4. How does the market economy determine how a good will be produced? How the resources will be used? The method of production? How does it determine who will get the good? How else could all these decisions be made?

5. Suppose that both a thermometer company and a dye manufacturer are bidding for mercury in the resource market. What factors would determine who gets the mercury? How does this reflect the consumers' evaluation of the utility to be gained from each product?

6. What are the basic assumptions of a competitive market economy? What does the economist mean by competition? Invisible hand? Monopoly? Natural monopoly?

7. Consider this statement: "It is regrettable but true that one of the prices of growth and change in a free-market economy is business failure." What do you think the author means by this? Do some businesses have to fail in order for there to be growth and change?

8. Does self-interest always explain the economic behavior of individuals and businesses? How well does it explain the decision of a highly paid, well-educated New York computer designer to move off into the woods of Vermont and make a living at subsistence farming? How does it apply to the announcement of several large insurance companies in the late 1960s that they would back investments in the nation's ghettos, even though they might lose money in doing so?

9. The major features of the United States economy—extensive use of capital, high degree of specialization, private ownership of productive resources, competition—are so familiar to us that we may forget that they are not universal. How do these features compare with the economies of other countries, such as the Soviet Union, India, or England?

Application 2:
Rebates: The Price System in Operation

At halftime in the 1975 Super Bowl football game, television viewers across the nation were treated to the sight of a well-known former baseball celebrity announcing lower prices on Chrysler automobiles that would go into effect the next day and last for about five weeks. Lower prices? Well, not exactly. Effectively, prices would be lower. But literally what Chrysler was offering was a rebate—a refund of $200 to $400, in cash, to buyers of certain models of Chryslers.

The money-giveaway—a rare tactic in the automobile industry and one never before used by Chrysler Corporation—was designed to bolster new-car sales under the classic theory that demand rises when price falls. As expected, demand did rise, but it rose in a manner that provides a good illustration of the complexities through which the price system operates.

First, this historical background: Federal controls on wages and prices had been in effect from August 1971 to May 1974. During that period, prices of new automobiles were closely regulated by the government, and manufacturers had to obtain official approval for any price increases they sought to impose. When controls were lifted in 1974, major price increases were announced for 1975 model cars. By September, prices on 1975 models at dealer showrooms averaged almost $500 a car higher than prices on comparable 1974 models, an increase of slightly less than 10 percent.

What then developed had all the earmarks of a consumer revolt. The principal target was higher car prices, but other factors involved were the already high and still climbing gasoline prices and the continuing overproduction of large and inefficient "gas guzzlers."

Because this pronounced consumer revolt was accompanied by a precipitous decline in general economic conditions during the final months of 1974, automobile makers in America found themselves at the end of the year with vast inventories of unsold 1975 model cars. Chrysler alone had more than a quarter-million unsold cars, which it stored in rented baseball fields and parking lots in the Detroit area. Chrysler and the other car manufacturers cut production and laid off workers. But while those actions diminished the number of new cars coming off the production lines, they did nothing to promote the sale of cars already on hand. Clearly, a novel strategy was required.

Chrysler, the nation's No. 3 automaker, took the lead with rebates. But instead of spurring Chrysler sales, the cash-back maneuver initially had the reverse effect. It prompted a slowdown not only in demand for Chrysler products, but for cars made by other companies as well. At first glance, this effect would seem to be inconsistent with the law of demand (if the price of a product decreases, all other things being equal, the quantity of the product demanded will increase). But consumers reacted to the rebate according to what they *expected* would happen to car prices in the future: First, would-be car buyers postponed buying Chryslers because word of the rebate leaked out in advance and potential customers wanted to see what it actually would be. When the news did come out, some consumers still delayed making Chrysler purchases, hoping that in another week or so the rebates would be applied to the model they wanted. In addition, some buyers who had their sights set on Ford, General Motors, or American Motors cars delayed buying expecting that if Chrysler had decided rebates were in order, other manufacturers would soon follow suit.

Once these factors of consumer behavior are taken into consideration, it comes as no surprise that, as a consequence of the rebate, dealers in American-made cars sold only about 446,000 automobiles during the month of January 1975 —17 percent fewer than they had sold during the same month in 1974, even though 1974 sales had been badly depressed by concerns over gasoline shortages.

As it happened, consumer expectations were correct. After Chrysler began the rebate program, all the other major automakers in the United States instituted similar price cuts within a couple of weeks. Even the nation's largest producer, General Motors Corporation, usually the industry's price leader, was forced to copy Chrysler, partly because of pressure from GM dealers who feared they were losing the few sales that were available to their competitors.

By mid-February, the rebates began to have their intended effect and new-car sales nearly matched their 1974 level. But then, another complication set in: what to do for a second act. Automakers began to realize that by lowering prices during January and February, they had effectively stolen sales that otherwise would have taken place in March and later months. When they realized their dilemma, the automakers reacted in diverse ways. Some abandoned rebates and boosted sticker prices by modest amounts. At the same time, features such as air conditioning which had been labeled as standard equipment were relabeled as options. Thus, automakers managed to hide the true price increase from some buyers.

Chrysler, however, adopted a second and a third rebate program. The rebates in its second program amounted to about $200 on 1974 models and a few 1975 compacts. When it tried to abandon rebates entirely in April 1975, Chrysler's sales nosedived by 43 percent, and it quickly put rebates back into effect for another couple of months. The final outcome was that Chrysler had applied some sort of rebate to virtually all of its 1975 model cars.

Questions for discussion

☐ Why do you suppose the automobile makers decided to rebate money instead of simply cut prices? What difference is there to the consumer?

☐ Discuss the ways in which anticipation of prices, as well as actual prices, affects demand.

☐ Given that one of the factors behind rebates was the most sluggish year in car sales since the Depression, in what sort of financial condition do you expect United States automakers were left after the combined impact of production cutbacks, layoffs, and consumer rebates in 1975?

☐ What other techniques might have been used to stimulate car sales other than rebates? What, for example, might have been achieved by rewarding dealers with higher sales commissions?

☐ Automobile prices in the United States are traditionally negotiated between the car salesperson and the buyer. Since what the consumer actually pays is usually less than the so-called sticker price, is it likely the car buyers actually saved money during the rebate program or merely thought that they did? In terms of effect on demand, does it really make a difference whether a price cut is real or illusory?

Part II

The Circular Flow of Expenditures and Income

Chapter 5

Households in the American Economy

What to look for in this chapter

What role do households play in the economy?

How do households function as production units?

What are the major sources of household income?

What are the major areas of spending by households?

What trends are currently affecting the economic behavior of households?

We are all familiar with the operation of at least one household, our own, although we may not be used to thinking of it as an economic unit. But in a free enterprise market economy, the household is one of the three major decision-making units, and in many ways it is the most basic. The independent actions of America's 76 million households are the foundation of our whole economic system.

When economists look at a household, they focus on its economic rather than its social unity. For this reason, the **household** in economics is not necessarily the same as a family group. *It is any person or group of people living under the same roof and functioning as an economic unit.* About three out of four households are families, but it is increasingly common for people of all ages to live alone, and young people often live in nonfamily groups; for example, several roommates may live in an apartment or a larger group in a communal arrangement.

The household has two important functions that help maintain the circular flow in our economy. (1) Households own or control most of the input resources (land, labor, capital, and entrepreneurial ability) so it is their willingness to supply these resources to various producers that determines the economy's productive capacity and the price of products. (2) Households also act as consumers of the goods and services offered for sale by producers, so their demand is an important determinant of what and how much will be produced, as well as the price at which it will sell.

This chapter begins with the concept of the household as a production unit and then goes on to examine in detail the sources of household revenue and the way that revenue is allocated. With the help of the United States 1970 census figures, we can then point out some trends in household formation and behavior that affect the modern economy. The chapter closes with a brief summary of the implications for the market economy of decisions made by individual households.

THE HOUSEHOLD AS A PRODUCTION UNIT

The concept of circular flow emphasizes the unique functions of businesses and households, making them appear to be dissimilar in many ways. It is useful, for the purpose of analysis, to look at the ways that households are like businesses, for there are similarities as well as differences.

Similarities to businesses

The household, like a business, can be viewed as a production unit. The final product, or output, of the household is the satisfaction of its members. It will achieve this satisfaction from some combination of economic goods—a car, telephone service, leisure time, community esteem. Its inputs are the resources it owns or controls—the labor of its members, its entrepreneurial ability, and its ownership of capital goods and land. The household may choose to use these resources directly, by building its own home or by growing its own food. But because of the efficiencies that come from specialization and division of labor, the household more commonly chooses to use its resources indirectly, producing its satisfaction through a series of exchanges. It trades the economic goods of which it has a relatively large quantity for those it lacks and desires, using money as the medium of exchange. Those goods acquired either directly or indirectly are combined with other economic goods the household possesses, such as leisure time. The final output of this production process is the ultimate satisfaction of individuals within the household.

Self-sufficiency: dependent on income

The household is concerned with maximizing satisfaction, given its limited input resources. Maximization of satisfaction in households is achieved primarily through skilled and knowledgeable exchange. The extent to which a household is self-sufficient—that is, not dependent on economic exchange with other production units—depends on the income that members can command outside the home. Those who choose to work outside the home will try to find jobs that fully utilize their most valuable skills and talents, so as to earn the largest possible salaries. When the household consumes, it will evaluate the added utility that a proposed purchase will bring, weighing it against the utility of all alternative purchases. The household will try to buy the combination of goods and services that adds the most to its total satisfaction. Members of the household will also decide whether additional income obtained by working more will enable them to purchase goods yielding more satisfaction than they would obtain from the leisure they would thus forgo.

Differences from businesses

One significant difference between the household as a production unit and the business as a production unit is that a household is subject to a much tighter budget constraint. A business that wants to increase its production can sell bonds and stocks to raise the money needed to expand production. But there are very few ways for a household to increase its level of income, especially over a short period of time. A steadily employed worker can get a small bank loan, or a household can borrow a certain amount on the property it owns—a mortgage on the house, a loan with stock certificates as collateral. But the households ability to raise funds is much more limited than is that of a business, since a firm can sell stocks or bonds secured by its assets and prospects of future increased earnings. It is much riskier for investors to lend money secured only by human capital (potential earning power). If the borrower dies, becomes incapacitated, or goes bankrupt, the debt cannot be collected.

Through maximization the household attempts to get the most out of whatever input is available to it, but it has very few ways to increase its quantity of input resources. One such way, however, is **saving**—*the sacrifice of current expenditure in order to be able to purchase more in the future.** We will consider patterns of spending and saving by households later in the chapter.

SOURCES OF HOUSEHOLD REVENUE

Personal income is *the total amount of income actually received by households from all sources.* Personal income is derived from each of six basic sources—wages, rent, interest, proprietors' income,† distributed corporate profits, and transfer

---

*Note that "saving," the act of not consuming, is distinct from "savings," the accumulation of assets that results.

†Proprietors' income refers to income generated from an enterprise that is owned and managed by a single individual; for example, a luggage-repair shop. Transfer payments are payments to an individual by the government for any reason other than productivity; for example, Social Security and welfare payments. We will discuss these types of income as well as corporate profits further in later chapters.

Table 5.1
Sources of personal income, 1978

	Dollars (in billions)	Percent of total
Wages and salaries	1206.7	71
Rental income	23.4	1
Proprietors' income	112.9	7
Dividends	49.3	3
Interest income	158.9	9
Total	1445.3	91
+ Transfer payments	226.0	13
− Social Security contributions	67.7	−4
Total personal income	1705.3	100

Source: Department of Commerce, *Survey of Current Business,* January 1979.
Details in table will not necessarily add up to totals because of rounding.

---

payments from the government. *Table 5.1* presents data on all sources of personal income in 1978.

The largest single source of revenue for American households is the wages and salaries paid by producers to purchase labor input; in fact, labor is the only resource most households can offer for sale. In 1978, wages and salaries made up about 71 percent of total personal income, a proportion that has changed very little over the years.

An additional 7 percent of total personal income was from proprietorships. This includes professional people such as doctors and lawyers, freelance artists, farmers, and the person who opens his or her own lunch counter or beauty salon—where the profits of the business go directly to the single owner/operator. Although the incomes from proprietorships are placed in a separate category in the national income accounts (see Chapter 8), we discuss them together with salaries and wages, since they both represent the money that a household receives in exchange for the labor resources under its control.

Regional variations in income

A household's actual amount of income from wages and salaries depends on the quantity and the quality of the labor it has to sell, and on the current demand in the market for that kind of labor. Today the median* household income in the United States is about $13,600; however, there are marked regional variations, reflecting regional differences in the availability of human resources and the business demand for different types of labor. In selected towns and cities, median household income can be amazingly large. For example, in a small city located near a space center that provides a market for highly trained and skilled labor, the median income of households might be well above $40,000! By sad contrast, the median income of families living on an Indian reservation, where the demand for labor is almost nonexistent, might be only $2000.

We must bear in mind, however, that differences in dollar income do not necessarily reflect equivalent differences in standard of living. In areas where salaries are higher, goods and services tend to be more expensive. A young Manhattan lawyer earning $25,000 may have to pay $5000, or 20 percent of her income, for rent, whereas a law school classmate practicing in a small Kansas town and earning $18,000 may be able to find equally satisfactory housing for half as much, or only 14 percent of his income. If the difference in housing cost is representative of all prices, the Kansan has a higher "real" (purchasing power) income, even though the New Yorker has a higher "monetary" (dollar value) income.

Determinants of income level

Labor

The quantity of labor that the household can supply is an important determinant of income level. The median income for families in which only the husband works is lower than for families in which both husband and wife work. It is a commonsense observation that household incomes will rise if more members of the household sell their labor outside the home.

The quality of labor supplied also influences the income level of the household. Quality is affected by the health, energy, motivation, and training of the worker. Certain valuable productive skills and abilities may be inherited traits, but most are developed by formal education and on-the-job training. And additional education increases potential earning power (see *Table 5.2*).

Other resources

Although labor is the chief resource that households rent or sell, it is not the only one. Through saving or inheritance, the household may have accumulated capital or natural resources. These can later be sold, lent, or rented to create additional income. The household may invest money in corporate stock, becoming the part owner of a business and therefore receiving some portion of the profits; this source of income presently accounts for about 3 percent of total personal income. Money saved or inherited may also be used to buy bonds, maintain a savings account, or purchase real estate. Producers who want to employ capital

---

*The median is a type of average. A median income of $13,600 means that half of all households earn less than that figure and half earn more.

Furthermore, there may be significant differences in the share of nonmarket inputs to the household consumption package in the two locations. If the Kansan has a garden —which is unlikely for the lawyer living in a Manhattan apartment—he may grow at small cost tomatoes that the New Yorker has to spend money to acquire. He may even be able to exchange some of his tomatoes for apples if a neighbor has an apple tree. Less income is needed when self-sufficiency or simple (nonmonetary) exchange is occurring.

or land resources pay the owners a certain sum in rent or interest. Over the years, the interest component of personal income has shown a percentage decline, reflecting a switch to corporate ownership as a form of saving, a more profitable investment in periods of economic growth.

Productivity and inequalities of income

In a market economy based on free enterprise and private ownership of capital, total household income will always be tied to the productivity of the household's members. This does not mean that current income is necessarily a direct measure of an individual's productive ability. Junior executives, for example, have decided to sacrifice some portion of current income in the hope of a future increase, and therefore they earn a low wage while training, since they are actually increasing their productive ability for the future. Or a recession may cut demand and may lower labor wages; that does not mean that the physical productivity of the workers has declined, only that the value of their product is less. Nevertheless, it is roughly true that in the long run, wages and salaries are paid to workers in proportion to their contribution to output.

Distributing income on the basis of productivity usually produces some inequalities of income. A household with one unskilled and uneducated wage earner who must support many children may not earn enough income to provide basic necessities for all its members, whereas a family that consists of two employed persons with advanced degrees will be able to afford many luxuries. Since training and experience increase productivity, young households earn less money than middle-aged households, but it is the young people who often have the heaviest expenses because they are raising families and buying houses.

From the economic point of view, these inequalities cannot be labeled "good" or "bad." But within the framework of the larger society,

Table 5.2

The relationship between years of education and income, 1977

Age and educational attainment		Median money income	
		Women	Men
Elementary:	Less than 8 years	$ 6,074	$ 9,419
	8 years	6,564	12,083
High school:	1 to 3 years	7,387	13,120
	4 years	8,894	15,434
College:	1 to 3 years	10,157	16,235
	4 years or more	12,656	20,625

Source: *Statistical Abstract of the United States,* 1979.

As the table shows, income increases directly with educational level.

At all educational levels men earn more than women, an inequity we will consider further in Chapter 34.

they may lead to questions regarding morality, ethics, and fairness. A society may choose to modify the personal income distribution, so as to provide a minimum income or standard of living for all its citizens. The most productive people, with high incomes, might want to or be required to sacrifice some portion of their income in return for the satisfaction of having done a kind deed or for the security of preventing angry mobs of hungry people from gathering in their city. The question of inequality of income distribution and the modifications of the economic system that are sometimes introduced to combat it will be discussed in more detail in Chapter 34.

HOUSEHOLD SPENDING

The household gets its revenue by exchanging the economic goods it possesses—chiefly labor—for money, in the resource market. It then spends this

Table 5.3
Disposition of personal income, 1978

	Dollars (in billions)	Percent of total
Personal taxes and nontax payments to government	256.1	15
Personal outlays (includes personal consumption expenditures, interest paid by consumers, and personal transfer payments to foreigners)	1375.2	81
Personal savings	76.2	4
Total personal income	1707.6	100

Source: Department of Commerce, *Survey of Current Business,* January 1979.
Details in table will not add up to totals because of rounding.

revenue, with the goal of increasing total satisfaction of its individual members.

What is the pattern of income disposal in the households of the United States? In analyzing expenditures, economists usually divide household spending into three categories: taxes, personal consumption, and saving. Currently, about 15 percent of total personal income goes for taxes; 81 percent is spent for personal consumption; and 4 percent is saved. The disposition of household income in 1978 is summarized in *Table 5.3*.

Taxes on households

All citizens pay a certain amount of their income to the government in the form of taxes, which are the government's source of revenue, enabling it to carry out programs of social and economic benefit. For most households, the largest tax bill is the federal income tax, but it is not the only tax on incomes. Most states and many municipalities have income taxes as well; in addition, there are state and city sales taxes, federal excise taxes on telephone service, cars, and air travel; state taxes in the form of dog, car, and marriage licenses; property taxes; and taxes on inheritance and gifts.

The exact amount of tax paid by a particular household depends on its location, its income level, its source of income, its pattern of individual consumer spending, and its honesty.

Saving by households

Once taxes have been paid, the household must decide how much of its income to spend and how much to save. High-income households have more varied patterns of spending than do low income households. They can afford to buy nonessential goods, and they can accelerate or defer their spending in response to such economic factors as interest rates, changes in price, and inflation. Studies show that in times of prosperity, it is the high-income households that increase their spending; in a recession, it is the high-income group that cuts back. Low-income households maintain about the same level of spending through good times and bad (and they may even **dissave**—that is, *spend more than they earn*), since nearly all of their income is allocated to providing basic necessities.

RECAP

A HOUSEHOLD is any person or group of people living under the same roof and functioning as an economic unit.

Sources of household revenue include wages, rent, interest, proprietors' income, distributed corporate profits, and transfer payments.

Household expenditures are divided into three categories: taxes, personal consumption, and savings.

Patterns of saving and spending at various income levels will be described fully in Chapter 10. For the moment, the important point to remember is that *the amount of income actually available to households to spend or save after personal income taxes have been paid*—the **disposable personal income**—is largely determined by the household's level of income. In looking at spending and saving patterns, economists are interested not only in the total of all personal income in a nation, but also in the way it is distributed in an economy. A country like Argentina has a relatively high total family income, but this total income is very unequally distributed, so that some people have incredibly large incomes, but most have very small incomes. As a result, Argentina has developed different patterns of saving from the United States, where the trend seems to be toward a more equal income distribution.

TRENDS IN HOUSEHOLDS THAT AFFECT ECONOMIC BEHAVIOR

The data of the 1970 census have helped to point up a number of trends in the structure and activities of American households that have far-reaching economic implications. Some of these trends follow.

☐ Households are becoming smaller. There are more single-individual households; married couples are waiting longer to have children; the birthrate is actually dropping. Families with three generations living under one roof are much less common than they used to be.

Since households now have fewer members who are economically unproductive, per capita income within most households is increasing.

☐ The high post–World War II birthrates have affected the age composition of our population, so that there will be many more young households than old ones, at least for the next few years.

Economists have established that young households spend more and save less than older ones (using the traditional definition of saving as that part of disposable personal income that is not spent), so the declining average age will be reflected in both saving and spending.

☐ More women are entering the work force. Today roughly one-half of all women between the ages of 18 and 64 work outside the home, and three-fifths of these women are married. There is also a growing trend toward working mothers. The likelihood of escaping poverty is of course much greater in a family when the wife is an earner than when she is not.

Another important effect is that the household with a working wife or mother buys more goods and services produced outside the home. The household may hire a cleaning service or a babysitter, buy prepared dinners or eat out frequently, or buy curtains and clothing instead of making them. Thus the demand for many products is increased.

☐ The educational level of household members continues to rise. Today the median number of years of schooling completed for all persons over 25 is 12 years; 45 years ago the median was only 8 years.

Since level of education has a direct influence on level of income earned, the trend of increased education is accompanied by a trend of increase in household income level.

☐ Households are increasingly shifting from rural to urban locations. More than two-thirds of all Americans now live in metropolitan areas—cities, plus their surrounding suburban communities. Although many older central cities are losing population, growth in suburban areas shows no sign of stopping.

Statistics show that city households both earn and spend more money than rural households. To some extent, the rural household tends to be more self-sufficient than the urban household. The typical rural family will still employ some portion of its own labor for direct production of some of the goods and services it consumes, although this pattern of self-sufficiency has diminished greatly over the last 40 years. By contrast, the urban household is more likely to take advantage of the efficiency of indirect production, exchanging its own resources for money in order to buy goods and services.

☐ The median income of households is increasing. This trend can be seen in *Fig. 5.1*.

The importance of households

Households are one of the three major elements of the circular flow of our economy. A number of important decisions that affect the entire system of the economy are made within the household. Especially significant are their decisions about saving, about how much to spend and what to purchase, and about how and at what price to employ their productive resources.

Most purchases of stocks and bonds will be made by households, either directly through individual purchases or indirectly through purchases made by insurance companies, banks, and mutual funds in which households have invested their savings. If households are unable or unwilling to save, there will be much less money available for business expansion and capital improvement.

Decisions made in households about how much and what to consume are a major determinant of the goods that will actually be produced.

It is the willingness of members of households to supply labor that makes our system of indirect use of resources possible. Our production capacity depends heavily on our labor supply. A good illustration of this can be seen in the production levels we achieved during World War II. Production exceeded all estimates, largely because people were willing to work longer and harder than they had worked before to meet the national emergency.

When income levels are high and there is no motivating crisis, such as a war, many workers will choose to sacrifice a certain portion of possible earnings in order to obtain leisure, an economic good. Others may choose to sacrifice some of the efficiency of indirect production because

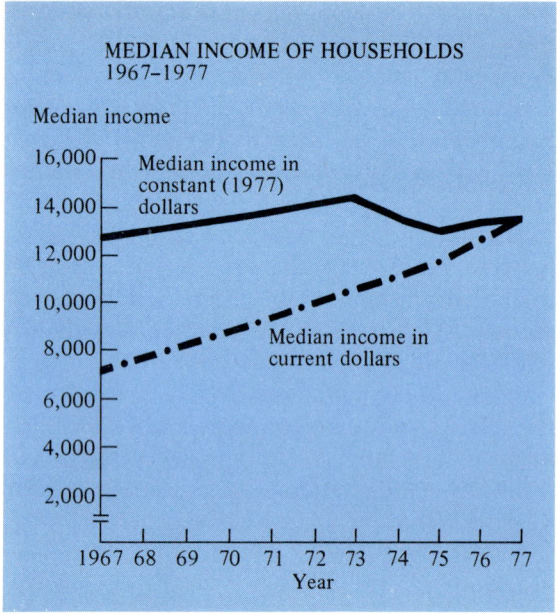

SOURCE: *Statistical Abstract 1978.*

Fig. 5.1
The median household income in the United States has been increasing steadily. During the past decade part of this increase has been due to inflation. Yet even when the figures are measured in constant dollars to take inflation into account, there still has been an increase in the real buying power of most American households.

they want the satisfaction of producing household needs themselves. They take up woodworking or bake their own bread or grow their own vegetables, even though they realize that if they count all materials used and the value of their own time, their onions have cost nearly a dollar apiece —rather more than price of onions at the supermarket!* In the United States today, few people

---

*When President Ford in 1974 suggested victory gardens as a way to "whip inflation now," he was not unaware that homegrown food tends to cost more than food produced on large-scale farms. Rather, his hope was that the decline in market demand would force sellers to lower prices.

are willing to work as long and as hard as they are physically able, and our labor resource in general is subject to a significant degree of voluntary underemployment. This situation influences the supply of labor available, and hence the price for which it is sold.

Summary

■ Households are important as basic units of the economy. They control most of the inputs of resources (land, labor, capital, and entrepreneurial ability), and their consumer demand is significant in determining what and how much is produced and the selling price of finished goods.

■ Households can be viewed as production units. The final product of households is the satisfaction of their members. The inputs of a household are the resources it owns or controls, the most important of which for most households is the labor of its members.

■ Total household income is derived from six basic sources: wages and salaries (the largest source for most households), rent, interest, proprietor's income, distributed corporate profits (dividends), and government transfer payments. Differences in the quantity and quality of resource inputs which a household controls result in income inequalities.

■ Households dispose of their personal income in three ways: taxes, personal consumption, and saving, with personal consumption usually by far the largest expenditure. The percentage of its income that a household will spend or save is largely determined by the size of its disposable income after taxes are paid.

■ Several important trends characterize modern households: they are getting smaller, which means that per capita income within households is rising; they are getting younger, which means they tend to spend more and save less; more women are entering the work force, which increases household income; households are shifting from rural to urban locations, where incomes tend to be higher. As a result of all these factors, median household income is rising. These trends affect the important decisions made by households, which in turn affect the entire economy.

Key Terms

household
saving
personal income
dissave
disposable personal income

Review & Discussion

1. What functions do households have in the economy? How are their functions like and unlike those of businesses?

2. What is the major source of revenue to most households? To your household? What factors influence the amount of revenue available to households?

3. How does the way you and your household dispose of personal income compare with the average figures in *Table 5.3?* Do you spend more or less on taxes, personal consumption, and savings than these percentages? Why?

4. This chapter has suggested a number of changes which have occurred in households in recent years, changes that affect their economic behavior. How would you compare the structure of your household now and 20 years ago? How would you compare your household with your parents' household when they were your age? What changes in economic behavior—saving, spending, and so on—have occurred as a result?

5. For many households today, single-minded devotion to maximizing income no longer seems to be the only way to maximize satisfactions. People are increasingly willing to give up some income in exchange for greater leisure time, a more pleasant living environment, or some other form of enjoyment. Why do you think this is happening? Does it contradict the economist's assumption that households seek to maximize satisfactions?

Chapter 6

Businesses in the American Economy

What to look for in this chapter

What is the nature and purpose of business enterprise in our economy?

What are the principal forms of business organization, and what are their advantages and disadvantages?

What are the major areas of business expenditure?

What are some of the recent trends in the business sector?

The activities of the business enterprise in a modern economy are complementary to those of the household. In the simplest model of the circular flow, businesses buy the input resources owned or controlled by households, paying wages and salaries in return. This money is then used by households to purchase the goods and services produced by business.

WHAT IS A BUSINESS ENTERPRISE?

The oldest form of economic activity was the direct production by a household of all its necessities. But for hundreds of years people have been aware of the advantages of specialization and division of labor, and at least some goods and services have long been produced by a person or group of people outside the household who specialized in one task. Today the majority of commodities are produced in this manner, and the business enterprise is the organized economic unit that carries out the production process.

An interesting debate of modern economics centers around the way the business enterprise is defined. The classic definition, which is still widely accepted today, focuses on the forces that motivate a businessperson to produce; it states that a business is an organization dedicated to the goal of profit maximization, or producing the largest possible profit for its owners.

But some modern observers—both economists and people in business—question the accuracy of this definition. They agree that businesses must unquestionably earn *some* profits; if they do not, they will be forced to shut down. But these observers argue that once a business firm has attained a level of profits that it believes to be "acceptable," the firm will not be strongly motivated to attempt to increase profits beyond this point. In other words, the aim of the business firm will not be to maximize profits, but to "satisfice." This term was coined to express the idea that as long as the target level of profits is achieved, firms will be satisfied to achieve a particular share of the total market for their product, or a certain volume of sales, or a certain annual growth of sales.

Much of the argument over the goals of a business organization—is it maximization of profit? production? sales volume? employee welfare?— arises because of differing definitions of profits. In business accounting, profits mean the excess of receipts over costs in any given year. If we define profits in this narrow short-run sense, then it becomes clear that the typical business enterprise does not always maximize profits. For example, in the first year that a firm is established, or during any year that a particular business begins a large-scale expansion program, it may well be that sales receipts for that year are less than operating costs. But that does not necessarily mean that the firm is a failure. And even if a firm loses money one year because of inefficiency or a decreasing demand for its product, it does not immediately go out of business; instead, it takes steps to improve its long-run profit-earning potential. Therefore, it is more meaningful to define profits in a way that emphasizes the long run rather than the short run. A broad economic definition of **profits** might be *the increase in value of a firm—the amount that a "well-informed and prudent" businessperson would be prepared to pay for ownership of the firm, based on future earning potential—plus the amount of dividends paid out to owners of the company.*

If we agree to use a broad definition of profits, then we can agree with the hypothesis that a business is a profit-maximizing organization.

Firms, plants, and industries

In a market economy, *an organization that produces goods and services* is called a **business firm.** A firm can be any size, from the corner drugstore owned and operated by a single individual, to a mammoth corporation like American Telephone and Telegraph. A **plant** is *an individual producing unit that contains the physical equipment of production*—office equipment, machines, display cases, land under cultivation, and so on. A plant is owned and operated by a business firm. A single firm may have only one plant, or it may have many plants. An **industry** is *a group of producers of the same or similar commodities.* The American automobile industry is an example. In the market automobile firms compete with each other and with foreign automobile manufacturers as well. And it is common for firms to be involved in more than one industry. For example, Ford is also in the home appliance industry and the television industry. *Table 6.1* shows the breakdown of the American business sector by industry, measuring the size of each industry in several different ways.

Table 6.1
Contribution to GNP, number of employees, and employee compensation by major industries, 1977 (current dollars)

Classification of industry	Contribution to GNP (in billions of dollars)		Number of full-time and part-time employees (millions)		Compensation of employees (in millions of dollars)	
Agriculture, forestry, and fisheries	56.3		1.73		11,201	
Mining	49.7		.83		17,354	
Construction	84.0		3.87		60,977	
Manufacturing	451.6		19.72		322,720	
Nondurable goods		179.5		8.10		116,356
Durable goods		272.1		11.62		206,364
Transportation	70.7		2.77		50,590	
Communication	49.4		1.19		25,340	
Electric, gas, and sanitary services	46.9		.75		15,258	
Wholesale and retail trade	325.9		18.67		188,448	
Wholesale trade		138.9		4.73		75,165
Retail trade		187.0		13.94		113,283
Finance, insurance, and real estate	261.5		4.52		61,473	
Services	234.0		17.189		167,394	
Government and government enterprises	235.3		18.39		232,729	
Rest of the world	17.3		−.027		−40	
All industries, totals	1,887.2		89.58		1,153,444	

Source: *Survey of Current Business,* July 1978.
Details do not add up because of rounding.

PRINCIPAL FORMS OF BUSINESS ENTERPRISE

Business firms vary not only in size but also in the way they are organized and in the legal form they take. The three principal forms of business enterprise found in the United States today are the individual proprietorship, the partnership, and the corporation. *Table 6.2* indicates the relative importance of each of these forms in our economy.

Individual proprietorship

The **individual proprietorship** is the simplest form of legal business organization. *One person, the proprietor, owns all the productive property and*

Table 6.2
Proprietorships, partnerships, and corporations

Year	Type of business organization	Number of firms (in millions)	Total receipts (in billions of dollars)	Net profits (in billions of dollars)
1976	Proprietorship	11,358,236	375.0	50.0
1976	Partnership	1,096,379	161.0	9.0
1975	Corporation	2,023,647	3,199.0	146.0

Source: Internal Revenue Service.

legally is solely responsible for the success or failure of the firm. The proprietor may hire salaried employees; may use the services of an advertising agency or a trucking company; may delegate many entrepreneurial decisions to a hired manager, although the final decision-making power belongs to the proprietor. The profits of the business are the proprietor's, to do with as he or she pleases. On the other side of the coin, the risks are also the proprietor's alone. If the firm incurs losses or debts that it cannot pay, the proprietor will be held personally responsible for them and have to dip into his or her savings, sell his or her property, maybe even lose his or her own house.

Disadvantages

The statistics indicate that the rate of business failures for proprietorships is very high; the Department of Commerce figures show that 7 out of 10 individual proprietorships go out of business within five years of opening. And even if a business does not actually fail, income statistics support the conclusion that the typical proprietor earns less than his or her highest possible salary elsewhere.

It is common for a single proprietorship to be at a disadvantage in the market. The only financial resources it has are the savings of the owner and the amount that he or she is able to borrow at a bank (which will probably be very low, since bankers are well aware of the high failure rate for proprietorships). So the typical proprietor is limited in the kinds of business he or she can open. Capital-intensive manufacturing industries are largely ruled out because they require the accumulation of expensive tools and machinery, and perhaps a large inventory as well. The limited financial resources that the typical proprietor has available also means that the business must attract customers and begin to pay its own way quickly, or else the proprietor's small reserves will be exhausted.

In a typical proprietorship, many of the advantages of specialization are lost. It is almost a certainty that the proprietor will not have the training and the knowledge to make the best decisions about all the different operations of the firm alone. And even though a proprietor can hire specialized help, it frequently is too expensive to do so. For example, Pat Murphy, who has worked for some years as a meat cutter for Swift, decides to open a meat market because he is an expert butcher. He knows how to buy meat and how to cut it with the least waste possible. But he might not know how to choose the best location for his store, or how to keep the account books. His competitors at Safeway, however, can afford to employ specialists that are trained to handle each one of these problems, so their chances of success are greater than his.

Advantages

Since government statistics show that the chances of failure are so great, why do so many people continue to open their own proprietorships? One answer lies in the ease with which it can be done. There are few formalities, relatively little red tape, and not too many fees to pay. Another reason is that there will always be people with a gambler's instinct who believe that the chance of success is worth the risk of failure. Everyone has heard some amazing success stories—the man who manufactured toys in his garage and made millions of dollars in a few months when one of his ideas grew into a fad that swept the country; the woman who designed clothes for a neighborhood boutique and was offered a $400,000 contract to design a collection for a major manufacturer.

A third reason is that proprietors can be independent. No one gives them orders, and they do not need to consult anyone before they make decisions. Of course, independence has its cost; the woman who closes her shop every other day will earn little money. But many people are willing to give up some portion of their income in return for the freedom of the proprietor.

Partnership

A **partnership** is essentially *an expanded proprietorship, in which two or more people share direct ownership of, and responsibility for, a firm.* The partnership is the least common form of business organization.

Advantages

A partnership has several advantages over a proprietorship. The firm's available financial resources will probably be larger, since at least two people are contributing to it. There is a good chance that the firm will also have more entrepreneurial resources. Once formed, a partnership allows the various partner-owners to specialize in certain functions, another gain in efficiency.

Disadvantages

There are two major disadvantages to the partnership. One is the need for the partners to reach agreement on many important decisions. They forfeit some of the proprietor's independence, for they must often consult each other.

The other serious drawback is the problem of financial liability. In a proprietorship, the owner is responsible for all the debts of the business; in a partnership, each partner can be held equally liable for business debts. A partnership calls for a great deal of trust among the people involved.

Corporation

The third form of organization, the **corporation,** differs greatly from the two we have already discussed. *Legally, the corporation is created as an entity separate from the persons who established it. It can own property, acquire resources, extend credit, sue persons or other corporations. It can also outlive its creators. Once it is granted its existence, it continues to operate as long as it can balance costs with revenues over the long run.*

By almost any measure, the corporation has the major share of business activity in the American economy. Corporations produce about 60 percent of the output of all private enterprise; they employ more than 60 percent of the labor force; they account for about 66 percent of the total national income produced by private business. Corporations completely dominate the manufacturing, transportation, public utilities, and finance industries. They do slightly more than half of all business in the trade and construction industries. It is only in agricultural and service industries that proprietorships are more numerous and have the major share of business activity.

Advantages

Why has the corporation become so popular as a form of business organization? We can suggest a number of reasons:

☐ The corporate form of organization limits the liability of its owners. If a corporation goes bankrupt, each owner (stockholder) can lose only the amount he or she has invested in the company. Once the corporation's assets are divided up among its creditors, the owners have no further responsibility.

☐ A corporation can raise much more money than can a proprietorship or a partnership. The ownership is divided among stockholders, each of whom puts up some stated percentage of the financial capital that the business requires and receives in return a proportional share of the corporate profits and the appreciation in value, if any. The provision of limited liability encourages people to make this sort of investment.

Corporations can also raise money by selling bonds, just as the government does. A **bond** is a *loan from a private individual or an institution. The lender agrees to lend a fixed amount for a specified time period, during which interest is collected. At the end of the loan period, the person receives exactly the amount lent.*

In addition to selling securities, a corporation usually has an easier time obtaining a bank loan than do most individual proprietorships or partnerships. With loans to a single proprietor, there is always a chance that the proprietor may die before the loan is repaid, thus increasing the risk of default. With a loan to a corportion, there is no direct relationship between the death of the founder and the increased risk. Hence, at the same rate of interest, a bank will be more willing to lend to a corporation than to a proprietor.

☐ A corporation is a more stable organization than the other kinds of business enterprise, and such stability contributes to greater certainty in long-range planning. If the founders die, the corporation still continues to exist. Dividing ownership into a certain number of shares also offers a clear-cut means of making many important decisions about company policy and management. These issues can be decided by vote of the owners, with each share entitling the owner to one vote.

☐ If the business grows large enough to have substantial profits, incorporation is a tax advantage, since the maximum marginal tax rate for a corporation is 46 percent, whereas sole proprietors and partners pay personal income tax rates on profits, rates that go much higher than 46 percent. However, dividends from shares owned are taxed at personal rates, even though the corporate tax has already been paid.

☐ The development of multimillion, and even multibillion, dollar corporations has had many favorable effects on the economy as a whole. The corporation opens up the possibility for large-scale growth in total output. When shares of stock are sold to the public, the firm has gained access to a source of investment funds equal to the amount of all household savings—a huge sum. The result is an enormous increase both in real output and efficiency. The corporation is able to expand in size to take advantage of the possibilities that expansion allows, such as mass production techniques. Also, the large supply of working capital available to the corporation allows it to hire the most highly specialized managers and well-trained workers—another increase in efficiency. For these reasons, many observers list the development of the corporate form of business organization and the potential for growth that accompanies it as one of the chief factors that has contributed to the high standard of living enjoyed in the United States today.

Disadvantages

In spite of the fact that the corporation has made a significant contribution to our record of economic growth over the last 100 years, critics point to some serious shortcomings. Among these are the possible conflict of interest resulting from the separation of ownership and management and the threat of monopoly control.

☐ The first corporations were simply a changed form of accounting, a new legal structure for the old proprietorships and partnerships. People who started businesses just set up a corporation and held most of the stock themselves. But as corporations grew larger, corporate ownership passed from the hands of founding owner-managers into the hands of millions of stockholders. Today only a few of the very large corporations are still privately owned by those who are responsible for their management as well.

When ownership shifted to the public, a new kind of manager began to appear. People who wanted to manage a large business no longer had to inherit or save the money to open a proprietorship; they could work for a salary in a corporation. The new manager was a salaried employee, and was likely to have been trained in business administration.

Because corporate owners and managers are two separate groups of people, their evaluations of what is best for the company do not always coincide. The difficulty of defining and measuring profits can add to this problem. The stockholders of a company may feel that avoiding a costly strike would serve to maximize profits, but the management might contend that the company should accept the costs of the strike and hold out for a lower wage settlement. Judging which recommendation is the best will often involve many subjective criteria.

There are other reasons why the viewpoint of management may be different from that of stockholders. For example, managers of large corporations may be influenced in their decision making by personal self-interest, the demands of labor unions for higher wages, or the request of government for new product features that protect the consumer. Each of these factors may conflict with the desire of owners for greater profits.

In addition, the fact that a highly specialized managerial staff runs the typical corporation does not make for clear-cut channels of responsibility between managers and owners. In a large corporation, responsibility is divided into many segments, and it is not easy to know who is really responsible if inefficiency exists or if profits begin to decline.

Many analysts have suggested that the very diffuse ownership of most large corporations makes it difficult for an individual owner to be heard by the management of the company. In a publicly owned company, the stockholders are scattered all over the country; no one person owns a controlling interest. The government requires all public corporations to send stockholders a balance statement showing them the amount of revenues earned each year and the way those revenues are spent. But the average stockholder is not well enough informed to be able to tell what the balance sheet means about the activities of the company. When matters of policy or personnel changes come before the owners, many stockholders do not even vote; most of those who do simply sign over their voting rights by proxy to the management. In this way, the recommendations of the management are almost always carried out, and as a general rule, the owners of a corporation actually have very little to say about how the firm is operated.

An interesting example of the way management actually does pursue goals that are different from those of owners has been discussed by Milton Friedman.* Friedman points out that managers who dedicate corporation funds and resources to such projects as retraining the unemployed, or cleaning up pollution, or providing community services are actually spending the owners' profits without their consent. Since most people buy stocks not because they want to benefit society but because they want to share in producers' profits, the managers may not be serving the profit-maximizing interests of the owners in making such expenditures. However, the public

---

*Milton Friedman, "The Social Responsibility of Business Is to Increase Its Profits," *The New York Times Magazine,* September 13, 1970.

relations aspect of some of these activities may ultimately increase profits.

Yet in many instances where managers might be tempted to pursue their own goals, the possibility of some action by disgruntled owners is enough of a check to keep management from making decisions that are injurious to owners; and most often, the ultimate ends that owners and managers seek are the same, or at least complementary, even if the means that they propose differ.

☐ Another disadvantage of the corporate form of business organization is the possibility that monopoly control of an industry may arise from the growth of large-scale corporate firms. It sometimes happens that in spite of the efficiencies of large-scale production, the dominance of an entire industry by a single huge firm will mean a very substantial and harmful reduction in competition. Such a firm may be able to earn a much larger than normal share of profits, and economic resources may be wasted. When this kind of monopoly control exists, and businesses are no longer completely responsive to the demands of consumers, society must find an alternative way to allocate resources efficiently.

REVENUES AND EXPENDITURES OF BUSINESS FIRMS

The major source of income for all business firms is the revenue derived from the sale of its product. Some firms also derive a small income from interest or rent of financial capital held by the corporation (businesses also save, just as households do).

Expenditures: explicit and implicit costs

How are these revenues spent? Part of the money goes to the government in the form of taxes. A firm must pay sales taxes and certain excise taxes on the materials it purchases. It must pay payroll taxes for all salaried employees, the firm's contribution to the Social Security program (an item that is frequently included as a part of wages and salaries), and, like individuals, it must pay a tax on its profits. The average corporation exhausts about one-sixth of its revenue in taxes to the government.

The second category of business spending is the purchase of input resources of labor and raw materials. Some revenue must always be allocated for wages and salaries of employees, including such fringe benefits as insurance payments or pension plan deposits. The cost of raw materials varies from one industry to the next; it is relatively high in manufacturing industries and relatively low in service industries.

A separate category of expenditure is the cost of acquiring capital. If the firm has taken out bank loans or issued bonds, it must pay interest on those sums. It must also allocate a certain amount of money to cover the depreciation (loss of value)

> **RECAP**
>
> A BUSINESS FIRM is an organization that produces goods and services usually with the intention of selling those commodities to earn a profit. The three principal forms of business organization in the United States today are the individual proprietorship, the partnership, and the corporation.
>
> The major sources of income for all business firms is the revenue derived from the sale of its product.
>
> Expenditures include explicit costs (taxes, purchase of input resources) and implicit costs (the amount of money that the resources owned by the company and employed in its production process could have earned in some alternative employment).

of its capital goods. Machine parts break, factories need repainting, and offices need redecorating.

The expenditures described above comprise the firm's **explicit costs** (*the costs recorded in a firm's account books*). A portion of the amount left over after these expenditures have been made will be used to cover **implicit costs.** Implicit costs are *the amount of money that the labor and capital resources owned by the company and employed in its production process could have earned in some alternative employment.* Implicit costs are not recorded in the account books; they are the opportunity cost of being in business.

Suppose, for example, that Pat Murphy has finally saved enough money to become the proprietor of his own butcher shop. He resigns from his job at Swift, which pays $200 a week, and uses the $25,000 he has saved to buy a small store. If sales receipts for the first year are $30,000 and the total explicit costs are $22,000, the business will show a profit of $8000. But Pat must also calculate the implicit costs he has incurred by giving up his former job—$10,400 a year—and by forgoing the 5 percent interest the bank paid on his savings account—$1250 a year. When the additional costs are considered, the **economic profit**—*the payments to a business in excess of its explicit and implicit costs*—is negative (−$3650).

A psychological factor might also by considered in calculating the final profits of a business. Suppose that Pat has gained a great deal of personal satisfaction from owning his own business and suppose that the headaches of managing the shop are small. If Pat places a money value on this psychological factor (utility of owning a business minus the disutility of managing it) greater than $3650, it will offset the economic loss, and he will enjoy a "psychological" profit.

Distributing profits
The profits of a firm can be distributed in several different ways. They can be disbursed to owners; they can be used to purchase or produce additional capital goods; they are occasionally distributed to employees as part of a bonus plan or other incentive program. A few companies have even experimented with the idea of distributing some part of profits to their customers, refunding a small percentage of the purchase price. Very young companies will allocate a large portion of profits to acquiring capital goods; established mature corporations pay a relatively larger part of their profits out in dividends to stockholders.

TRENDS IN THE BUSINESS SECTOR OF THE ECONOMY
We can identify several trends within the business sector of the economy that can be expected to hold significance for the future. Some of these trends follow.

☐ Business firms are becoming larger, and larger firms dominate the market. This trend began several decades ago, and it continues today. It is even beginning to affect the agricultural and service industries, in which small proprietorships have long been predominant. Efficient and profitable farming today calls for a heavy investment in capital goods, such as tractors and milking machines. Such a large investment can pay off only if farming operations are carried out on a large scale. More and more small family farms are unable to meet the competition of large ones organized along corporate lines. The most successful small farms are those that have joined together to form a cooperative, in which capital goods and labor resources are shared among the members.

What is causing this trend of bigness? In many instances, it is a desire to reap higher profits. A large diversified corporation may have higher profits than a small one, because it can afford to hire the best managers, to take maximum advantage of tax laws, to be its own supplier of raw materials, or to handle its own products on the retail market. Another reason for growth is the self-interest of the managers of the firm. The larger the firm grows, the more power and prestige the managers will have; and the more their salaries will increase.

☐ There is an increasing number of nonprofit business organizations. Good examples are savings and loan associations, which are giving commercial banks some stiff competition. The savings and loan company's capital comes not from outside stockholders but from the deposits made by members; this money is then lent out to other members.

The same kind of organization is found in consumer cooperatives and in some kinds of insurance firms. Essentially, the nonprofit organization is one that gets its financial capital from the specific segment of the population that uses its services. The owner-customers get lowered prices in place of dividends.

☐ The service sector of the economy (businesses that render services rather than producing tangible goods) is growing in importance. Manufacturing industries still have the largest sales volume and make the greatest total profits. But there is an increasing trend toward allocating productive resources to the service sector. More than half of the labor force is currently employed in service industries, and we can expect to see their sales volume and profits increase.

Economists explain that this trend is part of the maturation process of our economy. They suggest that there is a developmental pattern for economies, just as there is for people. A primitive economy, in which income is low, allocates most of its resources to extractive industries—farming, fishing, hunting, mining, lumbering. The second stage of development emphasizes manufacturing. This occurs when the economy grows wealthy enough to produce all the food it needs, using only a fraction of its resources. When the economy reaches a similar stage of expansion in its production of manufactured goods and when income continues to rise, it moves on to stage three, concentration of resources in the service sector.

☐ There is an increasing trend toward holding firms accountable for the effects of the products they manufacture and sell. Both the government, through regulatory agencies, legislatures, and courts of law, and the consumers, through protests, boycotts, and lawsuits, are beginning to demand that firms take the responsibility for making a safe product in a socially acceptable way.

This is actually a significant change in attitude. Newspapers are full of reports of the effort to hold manufacturers accountable. People sue car manufacturers for designing cars with defects that caused them to get hurt in an accident. None of this could have happened 50 years ago, when the dominant attitude was *caveat emptor,* or "Let the buyer beware."

Sociologists and psychologists might be able to explain why attitudes have changed so much, but economists are concerned primarily with discovering the effects of the change on the way exchanges are made in the market. One effect is certain to be rising prices, since producers have to incur the expense of both providing and proving the safety of their goods. The effect of government regulations demanding certain standards of safety or harmlessness probably restricts competition. For example, it removes the option of selling tuna fish with a high mercury content at a lower price to those buyers who might decide that the risk of eating the fish is worth the saving in price.

Summary

■ Business enterprises in the economy buy the input resources owned or controlled by households and pay wages and salaries in return. Firms produce goods and services, taking advantage of the efficiencies created by indirect use of productive resources. The goal of business is the maximization of profits, especially when we define profits in a long-run, not simply an immediate, sense.

■ The principal forms of business organization today are the individual proprietorship, the partnership, and the corporation. Proprietorships are the most common and partnerships the least common, while corporations are in many ways the most important. Corporations dominate the market, employ most of the labor, and receive most of the profits, making use of their advantages of limited liability, greater ability to raise money, and long-term stability and efficiency. Critics of the modern corporation point to conflict of interest resulting from the separation of ownership and management and the threat of monopoly control by large corporations.

■ The revenues business firms receive from the sale of products are spent on government taxes, the cost of input resources, and the costs of acquiring additional capital. After meeting these explicit costs, a business firm must also calculate how much money its resources could have earned in alternative employment in order to arrive at its economic profit.

■ Some important trends in the business sector today are: businesses are becoming larger, and large firms are increasingly dominant in the market; there are an increasing number of nonprofit business firms (such as savings and loan institutions); the service sector is the most rapidly growing area of business firms; and businesses are being held accountable more and more for the quality and effect of their products.

Key Terms

profits
business firm
plant
industry
individual proprietorship
partnership
corporation
bond
explicit costs
implicit costs
economic profit

Review & Discussion

1. What are the advantages and disadvantages of proprietorships? Partnerships? Corporate organization? How would you explain the fact that the corporate form is so dominant in the market?

2. Although economists generally define a business enterprise as an organization that seeks to maximize profits, it is clear that the definition may have different meaning in different cases. Some businesses seem to try for a quick killing in the market, while some emphasize maintaining a stable share of their market; some businesses are constantly diversifying to find profitable new areas of production, while others are content to stick to their traditional products. How would you account for these differences? Would proprietorships be likely to operate differently from corporations? Would new companies be likely to act differently from established companies? Would different industries behave differently?

3. What are the implications of the "separation of ownership and control" in the modern corporation? Would managers or owners be more likely to do a good job of maximizing profits? Would managers or owners be more likely to pursue the "social responsibilities" of the corporation?

4. What are the major sources of revenue and the major categories of expenditures for business firms? How can profits be disbursed?

5. What are some of the changes taking place in the business sector of the economy? What implications can be drawn from the trend toward bigness, the growth of the service sector, the growing pressure to hold corporations accountable for their products?

Application 3:
Ford Pintos: A Case of Corporate Responsibility

Richard Grimshaw was only 13 years old when the car in which he was riding, a Pinto made by Ford Motor Company, stalled on a freeway in southern California. Another car smashed into the rear of the Pinto, which burst into flames, killing the driver and burning Richard over 90 percent of his body. Despite 60 operations, he was still badly disfigured six years later when his personal-injury lawsuit against Ford came to trial.

In court, the attorneys for Richard contended that Ford's own crash tests showed the gas tanks in Pintos were unsafe and that the location of the tank made even minor rear-end collisions dangerous. Yet Ford, the attorneys said, chose not to protect the tanks or to put them in a less vulnerable spot in order to save about $10 to $15 a car in manufacturing costs. Ford maintained that its Pintos met all applicable federal safety standards and were not defective in construction or design.

After only a day and a half of deliberations, the jury awarded Richard nearly $128 million, the largest sum ever awarded in such a case. "We came up with this high amount so Ford wouldn't design cars this way again," the foreman of the jury explained after the verdict.

The size of the award and the foreman's comments were products of a changing view of the role of corporations in America. The trial, which ended in early 1978, reflected a climate of opinion that questioned whether the pursuit of profit was the only proper goal of business.

There was a time—a decade, or perhaps two, before the Grimshaw verdict—when few doubted that the primary goal of a business was, above all else, to make money for its owners. But gradually, critics of the corporation (sometimes corporate executives themselves) began to take a new look at the need for corporate responsibility. It became clear that, in the name of profit, business often was polluting the earth, turning out shoddy goods, and showing little concern for the effects of their products on consumer health and safety. In recent years the public has come to demand that businesses be held accountable for the goods and services they produce. No corporation, including Ford, the nation's second-largest maker of automobiles, has been exempt from the change in public opinion.

In 1978, for example, Ford was faced with a $10 million bill to repair the engines in certain Ford and Mercury cars because of a design flaw that made them likely to break down in cold weather. It also faced a substantial expense when ordered by a government agency to recall about 640,000 of its cars to fix what the agency said was a defect in their antipollution controls.

The Pinto, however, was among the company's primary concerns. At one point, Henry Ford II, the corporate chairman whose grandfather founded the business, called the Pinto "right now, the biggest problem we've got."

Less than two months after the jury returned its verdict, an appellate court reduced the award to $3.5 million, saying the original amount had been "excessive as a matter of law." The company appealed even that amount to a higher court. In the summer of 1978, the company recalled about 1.5 million of its Pintos and Bobcat model cars for repairs that would reduce the risk of fire in a rear-end collision. Ford said the recall was voluntary.

At an estimated cost of between $30 million and $45 million if all the cars came back for repairs, the recall was also affordable—in 1978, Ford earned $1.67 billion, or 37 times more than the estimated recall expense.

Questions for discussion

☐ Repairing the Pintos in a recall cost Ford an estimated $20 to $30 a car, or roughly twice what critics said it would have cost to have moved the fuel tanks in the first place, or protected them better. Discuss how the company's decision probably affected its profits and the value of its stock.

☐ In what ways might an earlier redesign or recall of the Pintos have increased or decreased the company's overall profit?

☐ Should businesses be held accountable for the effects of their goods on the public, or should the *caveat emptor* principle—"Let the buyer beware"—prevail? What mechanisms can be used by government and by consumers to ensure greater corporate responsibility?

☐ If corporations are held accountable for the effects of their products, how will this affect the price of their products?

Chapter 7

Government in the American Economy

What to look for in this chapter

What is the role of government in the economy?

What are the reasons for government intervention in the economy? What are the controversies about this involvement?

What is the difference between a public good and a private good?

How can we measure the effectiveness of government intervention?

How is government economic activity financed? What are the major sources of revenue and the major areas of expenditure?

How is the tax burden distributed? What are the differences between progressive, proportional, and regressive taxes?

Our original model of a pure market economy included just two elements, businesses and households. In this chapter, we introduce a third element—government. All modern economies include some role for government, which supplements the price system. In the United States, the government collects taxes from both households and businesses. It distributes income to households in the form of wages for government employees and in the form of various benefits—Social Security, Medicare, veterans' benefits, unemployment compensation, and welfare. It also makes resources available to businesses in the form of payments for goods and services from private firms, operating subsidies, research and development grants, and assistance programs, such as low-cost loans to small businesses.

Economists help us to understand the role of government in our economy. For example, they can show how government taxation and spending policies alter our pattern of resource allocation, what long-range effect farm subsidies have on food prices, how the Federal Aviation Administration affects competition among airlines. In other words, economists can tell us how the government actually functions in the roles we currently assign it.

Economists also provide information about the effects of proposed changes in the role of government. What would happen if private fire-fighting firms replaced municipal fire departments? How would demand for specific goods change if we passed legislation guaranteeing every household a certain income level? What would be the total opportunity cost of government sponsorship of wilderness conservation programs? Economists investigate questions like these, so that decisions about government economic activities can be made with relatively full knowledge of the costs and effects of each possible course of action.

REASONS FOR GOVERNMENT INTERVENTION

The United States has chosen to adopt a kind of economy, based on the price system, in which the need for government intervention is relatively low. Most wages and prices are determined in the market, not set by government. Government does not establish "five-year plans" for production and resource allocation. That, too, is decided by the impersonal action of prices in free-market trading. Yet total government expenditures have been increasing enormously. From the mid-1960s to the mid-1970s the Vietnam war accounted for much of the increase in federal expenditures, but in the same period state and local expenditures grew at an even faster rate. The implication seems to be that even in our market economy based on the price system, there is an increasing belief that government should intervene on behalf of the citizens it represents to protect the price system, to modify some of its inequities, or to act as a collective purchasing agent for such things as military hardware or highways. We will examine each of these reasons for intervention in detail.

Safeguarding the price system

Protecting buyers and sellers

On all levels—local, state, and federal—government ensures the continued operation of the price system by seeing that both buyer and seller live up to the rules of market behavior. For instance, the law states that sellers must deliver the merchandise selected by the buyer; they cannot substitute inferior goods at the same price. The law also states that buyers must pay the full price agreed on with the seller. It is illegal to pay for purchases in counterfeit bills, to shoplift, or to ride a train without buying a ticket.

The government also acts to protect both buyers and sellers from coercion. The Coca-Cola Company can try to get you to switch to its product by clever advertising, by a special half-price sale, or by its strategic location on the grocer's shelf. But it cannot send a gang of bullies to your house, threatening to beat you up if you drink Pepsi. Similarly, it is legal for a business firm to engage in a price war with a competitor, but it is illegal for a firm to bomb its rival's factory.

Maintaining competition

Another function of government is to maintain a high level of competition in the market. As we pointed out in Chapter 4, a common danger to competition is the monopoly, in which one company is the sole producer of a good for which there is no close substitute. Legislation has now made this practice illegal except in a few industries, such as telephone service and electric power (the so-called natural monopolies). In these industries monopolies are permitted but are subject to extensive government regulation.

Another danger to competition stems from *secret agreements among business firms in the same industry to maintain artificially high prices or to restrict supply.* This is called **price fixing**, or rigging the market. Recently the producers of breakfast cereals have been accused of this practice.

According to economic theorists, perfect competition exists only where buyers have "perfect knowledge" of the market. This means that when buyers make a purchase of any good, they know the exact price of their purchase and all its specifications—size, weight, color, level of performance—and that they know the same about all the substitutes for the commodity they are purchasing. With the enormous variety of products on the market today, perfect knowledge is rare. Therefore, the government intervenes to aid the buyer in acquiring product knowledge. Laws require manufacturers to label their products with specifications, such as quantity or weight, and laws prohibit false or misleading statements about performance or function of goods offered for sale.

Extent of government intervention in competition: the controversy There is currently an interesting controversy over the extent of government intervention that is desirable in this particular area. You may find that it is difficult to compare prices when you are shopping for food, cosmetics, drugs, and many other items found in supermarkets and drugstores. You may be faced with a choice between one package of 75 paper napkins, priced at two for $1, and another package of 100 napkins, priced at two for 79¢, so that it takes a series of arithmetic computations to figure out which brand offers a lower price per napkin. To help the consumer, some stores have begun to adopt a policy of quoting unit prices. Next to the market price of the napkins, they put the price per napkin (or some reasonable multiple) of each brand. Many states and towns have passed laws requiring producers or retailers to list unit prices for food and for such products as toothpaste and deodorant. In 1975, United States Comptroller General Elmer Staats recommended that the 1966 Fair Packaging and Labeling Act be amended to require nationwide unit pricing of food and health and beauty aids. Sponsors of such legislation suggest that it encourages true competition (that is, competition over price) in the market. However, many manufacturers oppose the measure, claiming that it robs them of an important competitive weapon—the psychological appeal of certain methods of quoting prices—commonly used in marketing products. To change pricing methods also entails an added cost to suppliers, which may be reflected in higher prices to buyers.

Sometimes government action aimed at maintaining stability within an industry may reduce competition and hamper the working of the price system. For example, until 1978, the Civil Aeronautics Board set floors on fares for interstate and international flights to prevent price wars in which stronger firms might drive weaker competitors out of business. Thus prevented from competing over price, airlines resorted to stressing special in-flight services. The control of fares also resulted in loss of business to other nations' airlines and to other forms of transportation in the United States. Residents of areas near the Canadian border were able to fly to Europe at lower cost by leaving from Canada, whose government allowed lower fares. Recently, however, new legislation has provided that airlines can increase rates by 10 percent or decrease them by 50 percent without going to the C.A.B. The result has been a healthy increase in competition among the airlines.

Correcting inequities of the price system
A free-market economy based on the price system has certain inherent inequities. A very small group of people may own most of the land and capital resources, and these same individuals may also have better access to the education and training needed to produce high-quality labor resources. This elite minority will then receive most of the personal income generated in the economy and will therefore be able to cast most of the dollar votes for production. The economy might then produce many goods that are well suited to the

needs of the affluent, but not provide for the needs of poorer people.

Since the action of the price system is impersonal, it does not respond to human problems. The market merely registers dollar votes; it does not make any value judgments about the needs of the voters. Yet the society as a whole may believe that it is important for the economy to provide the basic necessities for all of its members. A more equal distribution of income will certainly be advocated by the poor, who earn a low income; and it may also be supported by those who are better off because of moral or religious principles or because of fear of revolution.

Income redistribution

In the United States during the last several decades, there has been an increasing tendency for people to favor government intervention for income redistribution. The government has taken several steps in this direction. It taxes income progressively, so that those earning more money must pay a larger percentage of their income to the government than those who earn little. In addition, the government imposes taxes on inherited property and on luxury goods (e.g., furs, diamonds) which tend to fall more heavily on the rich. These tax revenues, along with those from the progressive income tax, are redistributed to the poor through welfare payments and unemployment benefits.

The government attempts to bring about income redistribution in other ways as well. Minimum-wage laws are an example of legislation that is intended to boost the income of workers in the lowest income brackets. Preferential hiring of low-income workers for government employment (offering such workers the first chance at government-created jobs) is another technique used to equalize income. Laws forbidding job discrimination against members of minority groups aim to raise the income levels of these groups, as does free public education. In fact, a wide range of government-sponsored programs include the goal of redistributing income, in the hope that most American households will have the income to provide the basic necessities.

There is considerable debate over the effectiveness of many of these income-redistribution policies. For example, many economists feel that the net effect of the minimum-wage laws is to restrict the opportunities of low-income workers. If employers are compelled by law to pay higher than the equilibrium wage rate, they will decrease the quantity of labor they demand.

Providing public goods and services

The price system is geared to respond primarily to the demand of the individual for **private goods** and services. Private goods include *all kinds of products and services people buy from private producers*—milk, bread, cars, clothing. Such products are subject to what economists call the **exclusion principle**. This is *the principle that those who can pay the price can get the benefits of the product, but those who cannot pay are excluded from the benefits of the product.*

The market has no efficient mechanism for responding to the demand for another category of commodities called **public** or **social goods** and services. Public goods include such goods and services as military defense, police and fire services, and highways. *Public goods are not affected by the exclusion principle. These goods are used in common, their benefits cannot be measured in discrete monetary units, and there is no practical way of excluding anyone from using them because of inability or unwillingness to pay.* For example, it would be extremely impractical to try to exclude some people from police protection or from using a highway because they did not wish to pay for it.

Because the exclusion principle cannot be applied to public goods, private producers are unable or unwilling to supply them, since these producers would receive no economic benefit from doing so. For this reason, it is government that provides many of these goods and services by acting either as a collective producer or more commonly, as a collective purchasing agent. Federal, state, and local government serve as the channels through which we determine exactly how much demand there is for various social goods. Although alternative ways of providing for social goods and services are possible, Americans generally agree that government action is the best way to obtain many of these goods. But there is still much public debate about what goods should be considered "social," what quantities of these goods society wants, and what means government should use to obtain them. It is in these areas that the most bitter arguments arise.

Military defense: a case in point

It might be helpful to use a concrete illustration to point out the number of options a government has when it sets out to provide a social good. One good that is indisputably a social good and that is still highly controversial is military defense. It seems safe to say that the majority of people in every country want to purchase some amount of defense so that their nation will not be invaded by an enemy. The first duty of the government is to determine exactly what the demand schedule for defense is. How safe do the citizens want to be? How many other goods are they willing to give up to obtain national security?

The problem is partly an economic one, so it would help to draw up a production possibilities curve for defense goods and civilian goods. We must then decide which position we want to occupy on that curve. How will this decision be made? How can we best measure society's assessment of both the costs and the benefits involved? Should it be decided through a public referendum by all the citizens, or should it be decided by elected representatives in the national legislature? Or perhaps the decision should be made by experts in a country's defense department or in its executive branch. For such an important decision, is a plurality enough or must it be a majority? These are just some of the choices that must be made before we can even complete the first step—determining the quantity of defense goods that a society wants.

Once this quantity is somehow established, the next question is how the goods should be provided. A government can set up its own factories to manufacture airplanes and ships, or it can pay private firms to do the work and buy from them the finished product. The same kind of decision must be made about the labor resources needed for defense. The government can recruit, train, and direct the army itself, or it can rent units of trained fighting men, as has been common in many African countries that use armies of mercenary soldiers.

Another question is how the cost of providing the public good is to be met. The United States government meets much of its defense cost by taxing incomes. Formerly some of the cost was paid indirectly, in the low income received by most soldiers, who made less in the army than they could in civilian life, and by the loss of productivity that accompanies enforced use of highly productive labor resources. Now the government has chosen instead to make the total cost a direct one, by maintaining an all-volunteer army paid competitively with other industries.

This example offers a brief illustration of the options a government has in the production of public goods. It also indicates why there is such disagreement over the role the government should play in the production of public goods.

Stabilizing economic activity

One of the most important functions of government is that of stabilizing economic activity in order to avoid drastic swings in the economy. By altering its levels of spending and taxation, the government can, to some extent, encourage full employment or affect the rate of inflation. It can also try to bolster up specific segments of the economy (an industry, workers belonging to a minority group) by its selection of the suppliers with whom it has contracts and selection of the terms of those contracts. In general, the government attempts to supplement or compensate for the inadequacies or difficulties of private spending. The role of government in stabilizing economic activity is complex, and we will consider it in detail in Chapter 12.

GOVERNMENTAL EFFECTIVENESS AND EFFICIENCY

Just as important as examining possible roles government may play is analyzing the present functions of government. In the United States, the kinds of decisions we outlined in the example of national defense have already been made in one way or another. We have already determined the number of dollars that we are willing to devote to production of defense, and we also know approximately how that money will be spent. The only task that remains is to evaluate the decisions we have made, in terms of both their effectiveness in achieving the goal we desire and their economic efficiency.

Methods of measuring efficiency

Some of the methods of measuring economic efficiency apply primarily to private industry rather than to the government. One such measure of efficiency is the profits earned by a firm; the higher the profit, the greater the efficiency with which resources are being used to produce goods and services. But this measure does not apply to governmental activities since the government is a nonprofit institution. Furthermore, the values of some government-provided goods and services (agricultural manuals, for example) are harder to estimate than their costs, because they do not produce income themselves. Rather, they enable their users to produce income.

Analysis of product cost

Although comparison of profits is not possible, some methods of measuring efficiency in nonprofit organizations have been suggested. One is an analysis of the percentage of product cost that is due to administrative costs, the price paid for input resources, and other cost figures. By this method it might be possible to compare the efficiency of a government bureau with a private firm doing similar work—for example, Medicare and a profit-making insurance company, say, Aetna. If we found that the Medicare office was paying less for paper clips than Aetna, we could rate Medicare as relatively efficient in this respect. On the other hand, suppose that out of every dollar coming into Medicare, 23¢ went for administrative costs, compared with 17¢ at Aetna. We could then classify the government operation as less efficient, and we might recommend that the government buy medical insurance from a private firm.

Ability to reach production goals

Another possible measure of government efficiency is its ability to reach stated production goals. This measure is frequently used in communist countries, where government officials select production and growth goals for a specified period of time. Whether the goals are met determines the government's efficiency rating.

Reasons for government inefficiency in producing public goods

Economists cite many reasons for the likelihood that the federal government will be economically inefficient as a major producer of public goods. One is that government has rules about promotion and tenure that private industry often lacks. Civil servants have considerable job security; procedures for firing or transferring employees are quite complex. These measures were introduced to combat patronage abuses, but they have the obvious effect of potentially reducing efficiency.

Sometimes purely political considerations reduce government efficiency. A newly elected official may award high appointive positions to campaign aides who do not meet the job requirements. Members of Congress may oppose the closing of obsolete naval bases in their districts because this would throw many of their constituents out of work. The latter illustrates another criticism of government—that once started, some programs are difficult to eliminate.

The concept of diseconomies of scale—reduced efficiency and higher costs resulting from bigness—can also explain why it is economically inefficient for the federal government to act as a major producer or purchaser of social goods. The federal government, the largest bureaucracy in the country, has possibly reached the point where diseconomies of scale drive up costs of production. The current interest in decreasing government's role at the federal level is partly due to a recognition of the difficulties that arise when activities of the national government cover such a wide range. Increasing the functions of state and municipal governments might provide a more direct and rapid means of solving such essentially local problems as welfare, housing, and transportation.

Should other alternatives be found?

Many economists suggest that the United States should explore other means of providing public goods rather than acting directly as a collective producer or purchasing agent. The reorganization of the post office in the 1970s as an independent government-owned corporation is one example of this approach. It is doubtful whether this new United States Postal Service has been much more successful than its predecessor. Whether this is because postal services are unmanageable or because the new organization is still subject to many of the old governmental constraints is still a subject for debate. Clearly, private mail delivery services have grown immensely to compete with the Postal Service. Although some of these services charge higher prices than the United States Postal Service, their record of satisfaction has exceeded that of the USPS.

However, even when we can definitely demonstrate that there are some economic inefficiencies involved in the government's providing a certain public good, we cannot necessarily conclude that it would be better for government to withdraw completely. Government participation may be the easiest way to provide many indirect social benefits that accountants do not yet know how to measure monetarily. We do not always choose the option that is the cheapest in terms of dollars and cents; our primary goal is to maximize satisfaction, and in doing so it is necessary to weigh *all* of the costs against all of the benefits.

Suppose, for example, that a study showed that it would cost less for the government to pay each child's tuition at a private school than to operate public schools. Does that mean that we should close the public school system? The answer to that question depends on how we value the social services the public school performs in addition to education or vocational training, and the costs of the substitutes we have available to provide those services.

Public schools do more than simply train or educate children. They serve as a vehicle for important public health programs; through free hot lunches, tutoring programs, and such programs as Head Start and Upward Bound they attempt to compensate the economically deprived; they teach certain attitudes of citizenship; they encourage certain kinds of social adjustment, both through the school curriculum and through the activities of social workers and guidance counselors. By teaching children a common language and certain shared cultural values, they serve as a way of integrating our heterogeneous population so that there is enough national unity to permit easy communication and joint social decisions.

Depending on how we value this extra utility the public school system provides and depending on how cheaply the same services can be provided by other means, we will make our final decision whether to continue operating a public school system.

GOVERNMENT FINANCE

Of all the institutions in an economy, the one least subject to budget constraints is the federal government. It can raise needed funds in a variety of ways. It can, through a vote in Congress, raise taxes and sell bonds; and it can also print money to cover a deficit. Therefore, the federal government (and to a lesser extent the state and local governments, which can sell bonds and raise certain types of taxes but cannot print money) has more freedom than either businesses or households in determining a budget.

Federal revenue and spending

Sources of revenue

As shown in *Table 7.1*, the major source of revenue for the federal government is taxes. The total revenue for 1978 was $402.0 billion, nearly all obtained from some sort of tax. The greatest share came from personal income taxes; that sum is about three times as large as the revenue from corporate taxes. The most rapid rise in revenue has been in social insurance taxes and contributions,* which have gone from $4.6 billion in 1948 to $123.4 billion in 1978. Rates have risen steadily because the benefits are continually expanding, and perhaps the efficiency of government in providing goods and services has simultaneously decreased. Note that in the federal budget, money

---

*Social Security, contributions to federal retirement programs, and the like.

> **RECAP**
>
> GOVERNMENT IN THE ECONOMY
> *Functions:* To safeguard the price system by assuring that both buyers and sellers live up to the terms of their agreements; to maintain a high level of competition by preventing monopolies and price-fixing; to correct inequities of the price system by redistributing income and providing public goods and services.
>
> *Sources of government revenue:* Taxes on households and business.
>
> *Federal expenditures:* Transfer payments and purchases of input resources and finished products.

received through the sale of bonds is not counted as revenue, since the money received is a loan, not income.

*Federal spending:
transfer payments and purchases*

How does the federal government spend this revenue? Economists like to distinguish between two different categories of government expenditure. One is **transfer payments** which are *payments to an individual by government for any reason other than current productivity*. Examples are Social Security and welfare payments. When the government pays an individual for any reason other than productivity, all that really happens is that the government acts as an agent to transfer money from those who have relatively high incomes to those who are in need. Transfer payments are the primary means by which government redistributes income.

The other type of government expenditure is government purchases of both input resources and finished products manufactured by private firms. The government payroll is money spent for the

Table 7.1
Federal government receipts and expenditures, 1978

Receipts	Billions of dollars	Percent of total	Receipts	Billions of dollars	Percent of total
Individual income taxes	181.0	45	Natural resources and environment	10.9	2.4
Corporation income taxes	60.0	15	Agriculture	7.7	1.7
Social insurance taxes and contributions	123.4	30.7	Commerce and housing credit	3.3	.7
Excise taxes	18.4	4.6	Transportation	15.4	3.4
Estate and gift taxes	5.3	1.3	Community and regional development	11.0	2.4
Customs duties	6.6	.8	Education, training, employment and social services	26.5	5.9
Miscellaneous receipts	7.4	1.8	Health	43.7	9.7
Total receipts	402.0	100	Income security	146.2	32.4
			Veterans' benefits and services	19.0	4.2
			Administration of justice	3.8	.8
Expenditures	Billions of dollars	Percent of total	General government	3.8	.8
			General purpose fiscal assistance	9.6	2.1
National defense	105.2	23.3	Interest	44.0	9.8
International affairs	5.9	1.3	Undistributed offsetting receipts	−15.8	−3.5
General science, space, and technology	4.7	1.0	Total expenditures	$450.8	100%
Energy	5.9	1.3			

Source: *Economic Report of the President,* January 1978.
Details do not add up because of rounding.

purchase of labor resources, and a government contract with Boeing, for example, is money spent for the purchase of finished products (jet aircraft).

Through its purchase expenditure, the government contributes to economic growth and expansion, at times also adding to inflation; it is one of the largest single buyers in both the resource and the product market. Transfer payments, on the other hand, do not immediately increase economic growth, but in the long run they may also serve to expand the economy. Since product demand is influenced by income level of buyers in the market, the change in disposable personal income for both the people who are taxed to provide funds for the transfer and the people who receive the benefits of the transfer may affect patterns of demand and cause a shift in the market demand curve for many products.

State revenue and spending

The major source of state government revenue is the sales tax. Most states also tax personal incomes and the profits of corporations. Another major source of state revenue is money granted by the federal government. For a number of years, the federal government has made specific-purpose grants to states for education, transportation, personnel training, and other social programs. Yet most state governments are in serious financial trouble, unable to come up with the funds they need for their basic budgets.

Nevertheless, many of the country's problems can best be identified and dealt with by state or local governments, which are closest to the needs to be served. Education, mass transit, and urban renewal are prime examples. To meet such needs, in 1972 Congress passed the State and Local Fiscal Assistance Act, better known as the Revenue Sharing Act, through which the federal government provides about $9 billion yearly to the various state governments, each of which must pass on two-thirds of its grant to local units of government. The neediest and most populous states receive the largest grants, but each state's own tax efforts are considered as well, in order to encourage them to try to solve their problems themselves and not merely to use the grant as a means of lowering taxes.

A revenue-sharing program helps all state governments, but it cannot be expected to solve the whole problem of state budget deficits. Like the federal government, the state governments can sell bonds to cover the deficit, but in order to compete for public savings with the federal government, which can offer greater security of investment, state governments often have to offer higher interest rates, making their deficit financing more costly.

Local revenue and spending
Municipal budgets vary so widely in structure that it is difficult to make meaningful generalizations in this area. On the one hand, New York City has a budget larger than that of New York State. On the other hand, countless little towns of a few thousand people have budgets smaller than those of some wealthy individuals.

The primary source of local government revenues is the tax on real estate and other personal property. As noted above, local governments also receive revenue-sharing funds, and some now tax their citizens' incomes. Local governments have hesitated to tax corporate profits, largely out of fear that the corporations will simply move to another town, taking away jobs and income for residents. The major expenditures of local governments are for education, police and fire protection, and welfare.

Large budget deficits plague many municipalities, particularly the major cities of the Northeast, where government workers have unionized and demanded rapid salary increases, and where the burden of welfare is great. Many rural communities also have budget problems, because they have such a small tax base—few residents, no industries—and they lack political power to obtain large grants from the state government. Throughout the 1950s and 1960s, the suburban municipalities around our large cities were generally in sound financial shape, but recently even these governments have had problems in raising funds for their budgets. And although municipalities can also sell bonds to cover deficits, they often have to offer high interest rates to attract buyers.

DISTRIBUTION OF THE TAX BURDEN
The way in which the tax burden is distributed among the people is an issue of great importance. Some economists advocate a benefits-received principle, whereas others believe that taxes should be based on a citizen's ability to pay.

Benefits-received principle
The **benefits-received principle** asserts that *people who gain most from goods and services provided by the government should pay most in taxes.* Un-

fortunately, it is impossible to pinpoint the benefits of many kinds of goods and services. For example, John Jackson may never drive on a new interstate highway that enters his town, but if the milk truck that supplies his neighborhood supermarket uses it, he still benefits from its construction. Another problem inherent in the benefits-received principle concerns welfare. Clearly, it would be self-defeating to attempt to finance welfare programs by taxing their beneficiaries.

Ability-to-pay principle

By contrast, the **ability-to-pay principle** suggests that *the amount of taxes an individual pays should be directly related to the individual's income,* that is, those people with the most money should pay the highest taxes. The reasoning behind this principle assumes that an extra $200 has less value for a wealthy family than for a poor family. The wealthy family might use the money to buy an expensive food processor, whereas the poor family would probably spend any additional money on food, clothing, and shelter. According to the ability-to-pay principle, a person earning $4000 a year might pay $100 in income taxes, while a person earning $30,000 might pay $6000.

Types of Taxes

Progressive

In the United States, there has been a tendency (especially on the part of the federal government) to favor the ability-to-pay principle by making taxes progressive with income.

A **progressive tax** is *a tax for which the effective rate of taxation increases as the base amount taxed increases.* For example, the federal income tax is not a fixed amount but an increasing percentage of taxable income. One reason for a progressive tax is to make the burden (in terms of the utility from other goods and services sacrificed) of the tax more equal for all. When taxes are fixed at one amount for everyone—say $1000 a year—the cost is much higher for the poor than it is for the rich. If your income is $5000, the tax will force you to sacrifice many necessities; when your income is $20,000, that same amount of tax will cost the sacrifice of only a few of the many luxuries you can afford.

Proportional and regressive

In actuality, the effect of the progressive income tax is frequently diluted by many proportional taxes and regressive taxes. **Proportional taxes** *(for example, property taxes) use the same tax rate regardless of the base amount taxed.* For **regressive taxes** *(for example, sales taxes) rates decrease as the base amount taxed increases.* These taxes, unlike the progressive tax, take a larger share of income from low-income households than from high-income households. For example, a state sales tax of 5 percent is the same for everyone, rich or poor. But poor people spend a larger proportion of their incomes on consumer goods; thus, the sales taxes they pay take a larger percentage of their total incomes.

Another inequity results from the fact that the tax laws provide many loopholes that permit some wealthy people to pay far less in taxes than might be expected. Rock stars may claim the expensive wardrobes they wear on stage as a business expense, but if they wear the same clothes around the house, they are taking advantage of a tax loophole. Charitable contributions sometimes constitute another loophole. Until recently, political leaders whose private papers were crowding them out of their offices could donate the documents to a university and deduct their appraised value from their taxable income. Even a middle-income citizen who gives a book to the public library or a used sandbox to a local nursery school can take a tax deduction for the value of the item donated.

There is other compelling evidence that in spite of the graduated federal income tax, people at the highest income level pay a somewhat smaller percentage of total income in all taxes than people at the lowest level. This is partly because of the much publicized availability of tax shelters and other types of write-offs to the very rich. However, these so-called loopholes were originally intended to build incentives into the economy. For example, the oil depletion allowance was intended to encourage investment in high-risk drilling for oil, and charitable deductions were intended to stimulate private giving.

Summary

■ This chapter begins the analysis of the role of government in the economy, adding to the previous examination of the roles of business enterprises and households. Government action supplements the price system in a market economy, and an important task of economists is evaluating the impact of existing or potential government involvement.

■ In our market economy, government's role is relatively minimal, though government expenditures have been growing steadily. A major reason for government intervention is safeguarding the operation of the price system, by protecting buyers and sellers and maintaining competition. Government action also aims to correct inequities produced by the operation of the price system, by redistributing income, setting minimum wages, and prohibiting discrimination in employment. When private producers are unwilling or unable to produce certain goods, government also provides public goods and services. Not surprisingly, controversies exist about all these major purposes of government intervention.

■ Two of the ways to measure the efficiency and effectiveness of government economic activity are to analyze product costs and compare them to those in private industry, and to evaluate the performance of government in meeting its stated goals. Such measures should be applied carefully, since many of the benefits of government economic activity are difficult to calculate directly. Among the sources of government inefficiency are the distinctive rules concerning the job security and promotion of government employees, the difficulty in eliminating programs once they have begun, and the diseconomies of scale which result from bureaucratic bigness.

■ By far the largest source of government revenue is money from taxes; the largest single source is income taxes, and the most rapidly growing area is social insurance taxes and contributions. Economists divide government spending into the categories of transfer payments and the purchase of goods and services. Revenues for state government come mainly from sales taxes and federal revenue-sharing programs, and local government revenues come primarily from property taxes.

■ Two different principles have been advanced as the basis for distributing the tax burden. The benefits-received principle asserts that those who gain most from government provision of goods and services should pay the most in taxes. The ability-to-pay principle, on the other hand, argues that those with the highest incomes and most money should pay the highest taxes. In the United States, there has been a tendency to favor the ability-to-pay principle through progressive taxes such as the income tax. However, the effect of the progressive income tax is often diluted by many proportional taxes (such as property taxes) and regressive taxes (such as sales taxes) which tend to take a larger share of income from low-income households than from high-income households.

Key Terms

price fixing

private goods

exclusion principle

public or social goods

transfer payments

benefits-received principle

ability-to-pay principle

progressive tax

proportional taxes

regressive taxes

Review & Discussion

1. What are some of the functions of government in the economy?

2. In what ways does the government safeguard the price system? How good a job do you think the government does in this area?

3. How does the government intervene to correct inequities resulting from the price system? Is this an appropriate area for government action? How good a job does the government do in this area?

4. What is a public or social good? How may the government choose to obtain and finance the production of social goods?

5. What are the benefits you receive from government? Make a list of all the benefits you receive, direct and indirect, federal, state, and local. Considering what you spend in taxes of all kinds, are you getting your money's worth? Why or why not?

6. *Table 7.1* presents a breakdown of the major categories of expenditure by the federal government. What do you think of the priorities shown by the table? What expenditures would you want to increase or decrease? Why?

7. Critics of the progressive income tax—which is based on the ability-to-pay principle—argue that it eliminates or at least reduces one of the major incentives for work and for increasing productivity. Is this true? Are there different effects in the short run and the long run? If you were a government official, what forms of taxation would you advocate? Why?

8. What are some of the present-day functions of government that did not exist 50 years ago? Which of the goods and services that government now provides do you think could be provided more efficiently by the private sector of the economy? Why?

Application 4:
The Tax Revolt

There is an old French saying that taxation is an art, like plucking a goose—the trick is to obtain the largest amount of feathers with the least amount of hissing. In the summer of 1978, a lot of American taxpayers thought they were getting plucked, and their hissing (in the form of a tax protest) may have begun a new direction in government finance. The proponents of tax relief were calling for a reversal of the trend that had persisted for more than three decades, during which more and more taxes had been levied to pay for ever-increasing levels of government services and regulation. The tax protest was intended, among other things, to encourage government efficiency, thereby raising the effectiveness of every dollar spent on government services. Whether it has had that result is debatable, but the tax rebellion certainly reduced the level of some government operations, and had other effects that illuminate the interaction of government and market forces in modern economies.

The wave of tax-cutting was born in California, where citizens voted to give themselves a 57 percent cut in property taxes through an amendment to the state constitution known as Proposition 13. However, tax protests quickly began throughout the rest of the country, and by the end of 1978, voters in eight other states had approved tax reductions or spending limits on government. Income taxes were lowered in 18 states, and a constitutional restriction on federal spending was seriously advocated.

In California the antitax movement resulted in a property-tax roll-back to 1975 levels and prevented assessments from rising to current market levels until a piece of property was sold. The property tax was a natural target because, while larger taxes (such as income taxes) had been reduced to tolerable and less noticeable weekly or monthly deductions from paychecks, property taxes were collected once a year in an often shocking lump sum.

For most homeowners, then, property taxes were the most visible part of the burden, although, at the time the tax movement began, the overall state, local, and federal taxes combined amounted to more than a third of the Gross National Product, or roughly 34 cents of every dollar earned.

The reduction in California's property taxes was quickly reflected in the curtailment of some governmental operations. Libraries and summer schools closed and, in one county, more than 100 staff members were laid off at the only hospital.

From all over the state, representatives of cities, counties, and taxing districts went to Sacramento, the state capital, seeking funds to replace those lost by the property-tax cut. They received more than $5 billion of the nearly $6 billion state-budget surplus to tide them over the crisis.

The California tax protest had several ironic results. One is that by lowering local taxes, proposition 13 reduced the amount of exemptions that Californians were entitled to claim on their federal-income-tax returns, which increased the federal-tax take from that state by $2.3 billion. In addition, homeowners, who provided most of the votes that cut the tax, received the least benefit—while owners of commercial and industrial property in the state saved nearly $3 billion in the first year as a result of Proposition 13, owners of individual homes saved only about $2.3 billion. Moreover, the mechanics of the tax reduction made it likely that the taxes on homes would rise faster in relation to commercial property, because reappraisals became automatic upon sale of property. Since residential property changes hands far more frequently than commercial, its appraisal would be raised more frequently.

Questions for discussion

☐ In some cases, the tax rebellion took the form of demands for ceilings on government spending, rather than maximum tax rates. At various levels, government depends on different types of taxes for its revenue (for example, income tax at the federal level, sales tax at the state level, property tax at the local level). How would limits on government spending differ from limits on taxation in the distribution of the total tax burden? How would these two approaches differ in terms of effects on government services at all levels of government?

☐ How would you decide what programs to eliminate or cut back on if tax revenues were decreased? What are the problems involved in such a decision?

☐ People often want to have their cake and eat it, too. How is this shown in the tax revolt and reactions to cutbacks in government spending? What are some possible solutions to this dilemma?

Part III

National Income, Economic Goals, and Fiscal Policy

Chapter 8

Measuring National Income and Product

What to look for in this chapter

How do economists measure production, income, and performance in the national economy?

What is the difference between nominal GNP and real GNP?

What are the components of the gross national product (GNP)?

What are the expenditures and income approaches to computing GNP? Why do both of these methods reach the same conclusions?

Why are GNP and other national accounts only limited measures? What areas of economic activity do they exclude? Why do they remain useful despite their limitations?

The preceding chapters of this book have introduced the basic tools of economic analysis—the concepts of production possibilities, supply and demand, the price system, and the circular flow. In this chapter and those that follow, we begin to apply those concepts as we look at the overall performance of our economy and embark on our study of macroeconomics, which deals principally with aggregate (national) variables. First, we will investigate the methods economists use to measure income and production. With the aid of such data, macroeconomists construct theoretical models of the economy to explain and predict the performance of our economic system. This performance will be considered in Chapter 9, which deals with our economy's goals, the problems we have achieving them, and the fluctuations that have characterized our economic activity.

In Chapter 10 we will see how total spending (one of the major influences on economic activity) is determined; then, in Chapter 11, we will use the concepts and methods discussed in the preceding chapters to show how our economic system arrives at an equilibrium level of income and output. Chapter 12 will conclude this section by examining the government's affect on economic activity and equilibrium through the use of its spending and taxing powers.

In the remaining macroeconomic chapters, we will examine the role of money and monetary policies, some of our past and present economic problems, and the theories and problems of economic growth.

NATIONAL ACCOUNTS

The system of **national income and product accounts** is *the device that economists use to measure an economy's performance. These accounts can tell us the exact value of the goods and services purchased by households from businesses in the product market, and the exact value of the goods and services that businesses buy from households in the resource market.* According to the simple circular flow chart diagramed in Chapter 4 (*Fig. 4.1*), those two amounts should be equal, but in actual fact they are not. So national income accounting must also trace down the funds that are chaneled into other tracks in the circular flow. Some funds are paid into government and are disbursed again to households and businesses. Some funds are temporarily withdrawn through saving and through the purchase of goods from abroad. The accounts also show certain funds injected, in the form of investment and money received from the sale of goods abroad. With this information, we can draw a more comprehensive chart of the circular flow in our economy (see *Fig. 8.1*).

In certain respects, national accounts are the sum of the accounts of individual households and businesses. But national accounts present special problems that do not usually arise in the less complicated financial accounts of families and business firms. Decisions must be made about which items to include, which statistics to rely on, and how the results should be expressed so that they can be used easily for study, comparison, and ultimately in the policymaking.

Our present system of national accounting is far from perfect, and it includes some irrational aspects. For example, the money spent to improve or to increase physical capital resources (the amount invested in new machines or a bigger office building) is counted as an investment; but money spent to improve human capital resources (the cost of educating children) is not counted as investment. If a woman hires a gardener to cut her grass during the summer, the wages are a part of the national product, but if she pays her own son the same money for the same work, that sum will not appear in the national product. Yet in spite of evident imperfections, our national accounts of income and product continue to be a most valuable tool of economic analysis.

National accounts are an important aid in all types of economic planning. Government officials use them as a guide to policy determination; businesspeople use them in establishing production schedules; investors use them as a clue to the future performance of the stock market. They are the empirical basis of all macroeconomic analysis.

GROSS NATIONAL PRODUCT

Central to all national accounting is the measure of our output of goods and services, or the **gross national product (GNP).** GNP is the *total market value of all goods and services produced for final consumption in the economy during a given year.*

GNP is always expressed in monetary terms, because money is the medium of exchange and serves as a common denominator of value. If accounts were expressed simply as the quantity of goods and services produced (8 million passenger cars, 4.5 billion bushels of corn), we would be faced with the old problem of trying to add apples and oranges, which, as we learned in third grade math, does not work. This approach could also be

GROSS NATIONAL PRODUCT 143

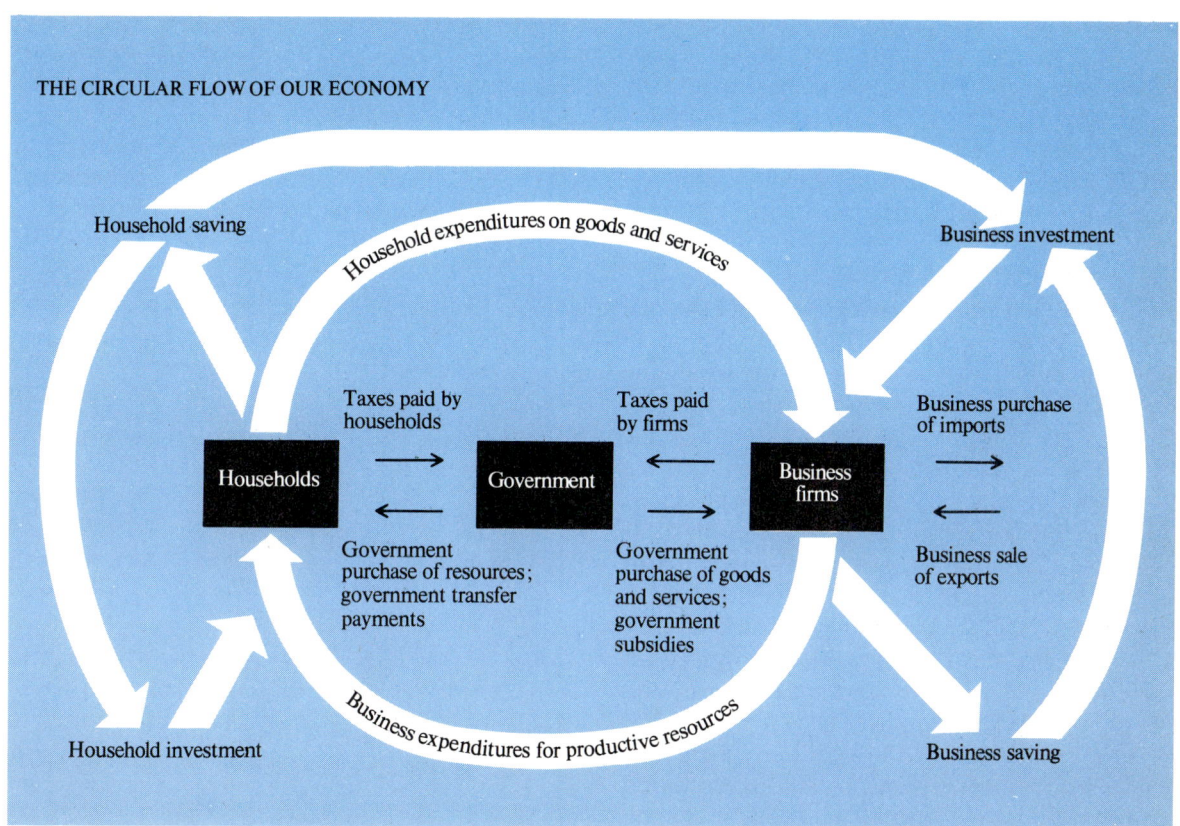

Fig. 8.1
Personal income includes income received by households from business (in the form of wages, rents, and dividends) and from the government (in the form of transfer payments). After taxes are paid to the government, the household is left with its disposable personal income which can then be spent on consumption (flows to business) or saving (flows to business for use as investment). If we add what is spent on consumption and investment to what is spent by the government on goods and services, we have the GNP, the total market value of all goods and services produced for final consumption in the economy. If we subtract from this the capital consumption allowance (depreciation), we are left with the net national product. The net national product is distributed in the form of indirect business taxes (flows to the government) and expenditures from national income to both households and the government. Part of national income is not distributed and instead is directly reinvested in the form of undistributed profits. Expenditures from national income include Social Security contributions, corporate-profit taxes (flows to the government), wages, proprietors' income, rent, interest, and dividends (flows to households). Combining the allowance made for capital consumption (depreciation) and the undistributed profits of the firm, we have gross business investment.

misleading as an economic indicator. Passenger cars, for example, are produced in a wide variety of models, each requiring different amounts of input resources. An output of 8 million Pintos would require much less resource input and would have a lower market value than an output of 8 million Lincoln Continentals.

Adjusting GNP for price changes

By expressing output in dollars rather than in units of goods and services, we are able to place some valuation on our production, but at the same time we encounter a new problem—that of price changes. To arrive at a monetary estimate of the total value of production (GNP), we multiply the number of units of each good or service produced by the market price for that item. For example, if corn sells at $3 a bushel, and if the economy produces 4 billion bushels of corn per year, we add to the GNP $12 billion worth of goods and services ($3 × 4 billion bushels). Now what happens if inflation affects the price of corn the next year, and the price rises to $4 a bushel? Even if the amount of corn produced stayed exactly the same as the year before, the entry in the GNP accounts would still increase to $16 billion ($4 × 4 billion bushels). GNP would show an increase, but there would be no corresponding increase in production.

To make GNP an accurate measure of an economy's level of production, economists must compensate for changes in the value of money by using a **price index,** which *measures the percentage increase or decrease in prices from one year to the next.* Any year can be chosen as the base, or standard; government economists are currently using 1972 (1972 = 100 percent). Using prices for a selected group of commodities, economists calculate the average percentage of increase or decrease in prices for all other years and compile a list called the *implicit price deflators for GNP.* (*Table 8.1* shows the price index now used in national accounting and the adjusted GNP figures in

Table 8.1
Adjusting GNP for price changes

Year	Nominal (unadjusted) GNP	Implicit price deflator (1972 = 100)	Real (adjusted) GNP (1972 = 100)
1929	103.4	32.9	314.6
1933	55.8	25.1	222.1
1939	90.8	28.5	318.8
1941	124.9	31.3	398.5
1946	209.6	44.0	476.9
1950	286.2	53.6	533.5
1954	366.3	59.7	613.7
1958	448.9	66.1	679.5
1962	563.8	70.6	799.1
1966	753.0	76.8	981.1
1970	982.4	91.4	1075.3
1972	1171.1	100.0	1171.1
1974	1412.9	116.0	1217.8
*1978	2106.6	152.1	1385.1

Source: *Economic Report of The President,* January 1979.
*Preliminary

selected years since 1929.) This index allows the statistician to adjust the total value of output for price changes. For example, the index shows that, on the average, 1978 prices were 52.09 percent higher than 1972 prices. Therefore, when we calculate 1978 GNP, the total figure will have to be deflated by that percentage. In 1978 nominal GNP before deflation (in 1978 dollars) was $2106.6 billion; adjusted real GNP (expressed in 1972 dollars) was only $1385.1 billion.

Since unadjusted GNP is expressed in current dollars, we adjust the GNP for a given year—accounting for changes in the value of money—by dividing the implicit price deflator into the unadjusted figure. To calculate the adjusted GNP for 1978, the implicit price deflator we use is a percentage based on the prices of goods in the year 1972; that is, 1972 = 100. In dividing, we move the decimal of the deflator two digits to the left. For example, real 1978 GNP would be calculated as follows:

Unadjusted or nominal GNP = $2106.6
Implicit price deflator = 152.09
Adjusted, or real, GNP = $1385.1
($2106.6 ÷ 1.5209)

That means that about 50 percent, or $721.5 billion, of the increase in unadjusted GNP since 1972 is due to inflation rather than to increased production of the economy. *Figure 8.2* compares GNP in constant (1972) and current dollars from 1929 to 1978.

Avoiding double counting

In our highly specialized economy, it is very rare for one business firm to carry out every step in the manufacturing process; typically the finished product has passed through several different firms to get to the market. Suppose that you go to your local department store and buy a new sweater for $15. The store did not manufacture the sweater it sold you. It bought the good from the Nifty Knits Company, paying them $10. The Nifty Knits Company knitted the sweater, but it bought the synthetic fibers used as raw materials from a chemical company, paying $2 for the fiber used in making your sweater. The chemical company made the fiber by processing petroleum by-products, which it bought from an oil company. The cost of the amount of by-products was 50¢.

If we count each of these intermediate payments made by one business firm to another for the materials needed for production, as well as the amount you paid for the final product, then your sweater, whose total value is only $15, would add $27.50 to the GNP. Here we have made the mistake of double counting; that is, we have counted the value of the input resources more than once, because we have added together all the different forms in which those resources were further processed and then resold. To avoid double counting, we include in GNP only the value of those goods and services classified as final products, meaning that they will not be resold or processed further. All intermediate users' purchases are excluded.

Another way to avoid double counting is to calculate the **value added,** that is, the *increase in value of the good or service added by each step of the manufacturing process.* The value added is equal to the sum of all income payments made during the production process—wages, rent, interest, and profit. Thus, as summarized in *Table 8.2,* we would calculate the cost of the sweater as 50¢ (the cost of the petroleum by-products) + $1.50 (the value added by the chemical company that turned it into a fiber) + $8 (the value added by the Nifty Knits Company that knitted it into a sweater) + $5 (the value added by the department store that merchandised it to consumers), for a total of $15. The resulting GNP will be the same as we would arrive at by totaling the value of final products.

Payments excluded from GNP

Since GNP is supposed to be a measure of the level of productive output, certain kinds of payments and purchases must be excluded from the accounts, so that the accounts will reflect production rather than income transfers. GNP therefore does *not* include the following two transactions.

Money transfers not involving current production

When the government pays money to dependent children under the welfare program, it is not purchasing a productive resource. It is simply transferring money from those who are better off to those who are considered needy. All government transfer payments are excluded from GNP for this reason, as are government subsidies to businesses.

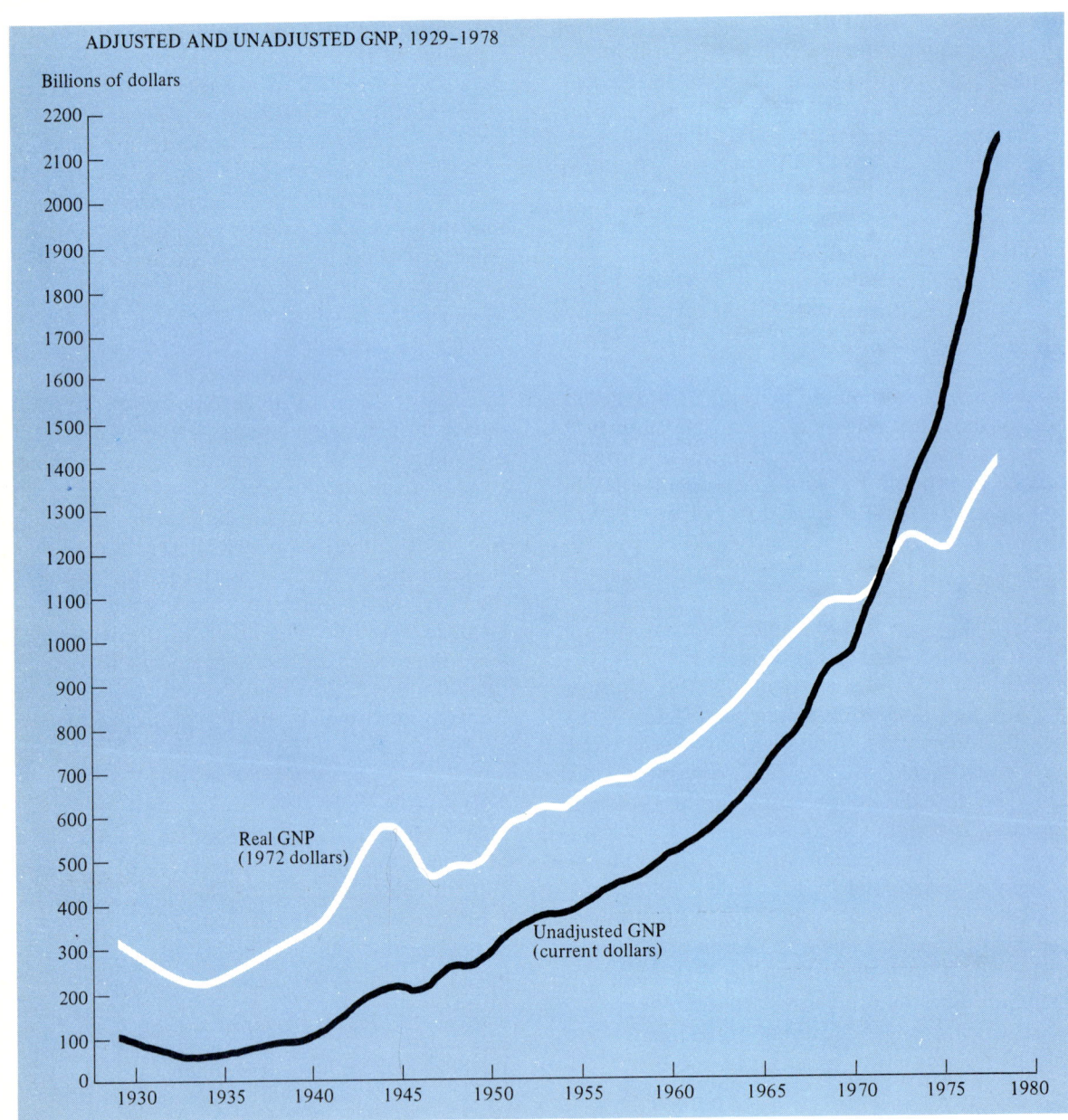

SOURCE: *Economic Report of the President,* January, 1979.

Fig. 8.2
The steady increase of real GNP and GNP in current dollars in approximately the same relationship until the 1960s indicates substantial economic growth with almost no inflation. The diverging pattern after 1960 reflects both the inflationary conditions of more recent years and the recession of the mid-1970s, which brought a significant decline in real GNP in 1974 and 1975 for the first time in many years.

Table 8.2
Sales value and value added at each stage of producing a sweater

(1) Stage of production	(2) Sales value of material or product	(3) Value added (income payments: wages, rent, interest, profits)
Stage 1: oil company	$ .50	$ .50
Stage 2: chemical company	2.00	1.50
Stage 3: Nifty Knits Company	10.00	8.00
Stage 4: retail department store	15.00	5.00
Total sale values	$27.50	
Total value added (=price to final consumer)		$15.00

Gifts from one private individual to another—the $10 your aunt gave you last Christmas—are also excluded, since they are basically a redistirbution of existing income with no productive significance.

Another kind of transaction that does not involve current production is the sale of second-hand goods. We do not count the sale of used cars or the auction of used household goods as a part of our GNP. To do so would be another kind of double counting, since the full value of the car or the television set was already counted when it was sold to the original owner.

In calculating GNP, economists also exclude all sales of securities on the stock exchange. When Mr. Mason pays $10,000 to buy the shares of stock in the Mobil Oil Company that Mr. Dixon is selling, no direct production is involved. Mason just trades one kind of paper asset (money) for another (stock certificates).

CALCULATING GNP

The basic approach to calculating GNP is to measure the expenditures of all buyers in the product market—all the purchases of final goods and services by households, government, and business firms, as well as net purchases made in the export market. We can simply add up the total market prices of all these final commodities sold in one year, and the sum is the year's GNP. This figure can be calculated from the sales receipts of all firms selling to final consumers. In the previous example of the sweater, the amount would be $15, the price at which the final seller sold it to you, the final consumer. And, as we pointed out, the value-added approach is sometimes used as an alternative method for calculating GNP.

But these consumption expenditures are only one-half of the circular flow. Every dollar that consumers spend is received by business firms as sales receipts and is then disbursed again to someone else. It is either used to purchase or to rent input resources of land, labor, and capital, paid out to government as taxes, or distributed to the owners of the business in the form of profits. So a second approach to calculating GNP might be to measure the amount of income generated by the production process. Addition of wages paid to workers, rents, interest, and profits will give us

Table 8.3
Approaches to calculating GNP

Expenditures approach		Income approach
Consumption expenditures by household		Components of national income: wages rent interest profits
+		
Investment expenditures by businesses	Total receipts of all producers of final products = GNP = Total costs of production for all producers of final products	
+		+
Expenditures on exports minus expenditures on imports		Indirect business taxes
+		+
Purchase of goods and services by government		Allowance for capital consumption

total national income; and national income plus nonincome costs incurred by businesses—indirect taxes and capital depreciation—should give us a figure exactly equal to the total of expenditures for final products. Here we are simply looking at different sides of the same coin. One is the total amount spent to purchase final goods and services (business sales receipts); the other is the total amount that businesses pay out again to meet production costs (wages, rents, interest and profits, plus taxes and capital depreciation). These two methods of calculating GNP merely measure the two halves of the circular flow of money in an economy. *Table 8.3* summarizes the expenditures and income approaches to deriving GNP. Let us look further at each approach.

Expenditures approach

The four major components of national expenditure are personal consumption, investment, net exports, and government purchases of goods and services. We will examine each in some detail. *Table 8.4* shows how GNP is calculated using the expenditures approach.

Personal consumption

Personal consumption includes all purchases of goods and services made by households. On many national accounting statements, personal consumption expenditure is broken down into three categories: **durable goods,** *those goods designed to last a year or more* (cars, beds, and refrigerators); **nondurable goods,** *those disposed of within a short period of time* (paper towels, lettuce, and nylon stockings); and **services,** *work or activity of economic value* (haircuts and medical treatment). To aid in economic analysis, government statisticians also prepare more detailed summaries of personal consumption, involving numerous categories—jewelry, magazines and newspapers, foreign travel, and prescription drugs, to name a few.

In the past two decades, personal consumption has accounted for about two-thirds of national expenditures. Before World War II, per-

Table 8.4
Expenditures approach to GNP, 1978
(billions of dollars)

Personal consumption expenditure		$1339.7
Durable goods	$197.6	
Nondurable goods	525.8	
Services	616.3	
Gross private domestic investment		344.5
Producers' durable equipment	144.5	
Changes in business inventories	15.7	
New construction	77.5	
Net exports of goods and services		−11.8
Exports	205.2	
Imports	217.0	
Government purchases of goods and services		434.2
Total gross national product		$2106.6

Source: *Economic Report of the President,* January 1979. Details may not add to totals because of rounding.

and factories (called capital goods or producers' durable equipment).

Another type of investment included in the national income accounts is investment in **inventories**—*the amount of finished goods not yet sold, goods in the process of manufacture, and raw materials held for future production.* This category is included because GNP is a measure of total *output,* not total sales. At the end of the year, a large business firm like Ford might have manufactured many thousands of automobiles that it has not yet sold. It may also have a considerable stock of cars that are not yet finished—bodies with no engines, for example. It may also hold an inventory of raw materials needed for future production, such as steel. These form a part of the year's total output, but they have not yet been registered in the total sales of the year. The value of inventories held by business can either increase or decrease from one year to the next. If it decreases, the loss of inventory is subtracted from GNP, because it means that the economy has consumed more than it has produced in a given year. Gains in the value of inventories are added to GNP.

Another kind of investment included in GNP is the construction of residential housing, which includes both single-family and multiple-family dwellings, for rent or for sale. This kind of investment may be made by individuals or by businesses.

The total value of real productive assets produced in one year is called **gross investment.** However, gross investment alone does not serve to indicate the actual change in value of the economy's stock of productive assets for a given year. Some portion of gross investment is devoted to the replacement of existing capital goods, for capital goods do wear out and need replacing. To determine the annual change in value of the economy's productive assets, then, we must subtract from the year's gross investment the value of depreciation of existing assets. The resulting figure, called **net investment,** is *the actual measure of change in the stock of productive assets.* (Net investment = gross investment − depreciation.)

sonal consumption accounted for an even larger share of GNP (about 75 percent), but this category, as a percent of total expenditures, has declined as government spending has increased.

Investment

The term **investment** has two meanings. (1) *It commonly refers to the purchase of durable goods or financial properties with the intention of receiving income or profit.* (2) For national income accounting, it is defined as *the amount of current output that adds to or replaces the national stock of real productive assets.* It is in the second sense that we use the term here. In our primarily capitalistic economy, investment is the chief path to economic development.

The most familiar kind of investment is the purchase by businesses of new machines, offices,

Investment is a form of spending, and we might expect that investment would fluctuate in response to changes in general economic conditions, just as private consumption does. Comparison of investment statistics over a long-term period shows that indeed this is the case. During the 1930s, gross investment was so low that we probably experienced negative net investment; in the post World War II boom, gross investment increased more rapidly than almost any other indicator of economic activity.

Net exports

Not all of the output of American businesses is actually sold to Americans; some of it is sold to foreign countries. So we must add the value of goods and services exported to other countries into the GNP to measure total output.

However, we must not overlook the possibility that some of the goods sold to final consumers in the United States were actually imported from some other country and therefore do not actually form a part of our productive output. Therefore, in adding the value of exports we must correct for the value of imports. The corrected figure, called **net exports**, is *the value of goods and services exported from the economy minus the value of those imported.* (Net exports = value of exports − value of imports.) The net export figure is the amount that is actually added to GNP. Net exports can be either a positive or negative number.

In recent years, the dollar volume of both imports and exports has increased, but the net export remains a small percentage of total GNP. Although in recent years, imports have exceeded exports, during most of this century our net exports have been a positive number—that is, we have exported more than we have imported. Right after World War II, net exports jumped up to $11 billion, reflecting the great need for the products of American industry in war-damaged Europe. Since then, net exports have consistently remained below the $5 billion mark annually, amounting in 1978 to − $11.8 billion.

Government purchases

The fourth element added to GNP as a measure of total output is the purchase of goods and services by local, state, and federal governments. The percentage of GNP due to government spending is increasing rapidly. In 1929, government spending accounted for about 8 percent of GNP; today it accounts for about 21 percent of GNP. Much of this increase is due to defense spending, but all categories of government expenditure have increased substantially.

Not all government spending is included in GNP. As we noted earlier, transfer payments are not considered part of GNP, because they are not a purchase of any productive capacity or resource. In 1978, total government expenditures (for government at all levels) was about $660.2 billion, but only $434.2 billion of that sum represents government purchases of goods and services to be included in GNP accounts; the rest of government expenditures are transfer payments.

One peculiarity of our present system of national accounting is that portion of government expenditures that goes to purchase government-owned productive assets is not differentiated from the rest of government spending. A highway, for example, is a productive asset that is publicly owned, yet it does not appear in the investment accounts, but in the accounts of government spending. This means that our annual net investment is actually somewhat larger than it appears in GNP accounts, since the category of investment does not include investment by the government.

Income approach

The second way to calculate total national output is to add up the amounts of income generated by the production process plus two nonincome items—indirect business taxes and capital consumption allowances.* This yields the total costs of production for all producers of final products, which in turn is equal to GNP. *Table 8.5* shows that the income method of determining total output results in the same figure arrived at by using the expenditures approach.

Components of national income

National income (NI) is *the amount paid out by businesses in wages, salaries, interest, rents, and profits to purchase or to rent productive services.* National income accounts include five smaller categories of income. Let us consider each of them.

Wages and salaries

The **wage and salary** category includes *all kinds of compensation paid to any business employee.* It covers not only wages but also bonuses, tips, and fringe benefits, such as stock options or paid holidays. The employer's share of Social Security contributions is also included in this category, since it is a necessary expense of obtaining labor resources in our economy.

Wages and salaries constitute the largest single element of national income. When we compare national income statistics (in constant dollars) over a long period, we discover that the proportion of national income generated by wages and salaries has remained remarkably constant, never changing by more than one or two percentage points.

Proprietors' income

Proprietor's income is *the income generated by unincorporated business enterprises, including the incomes of all proprietorships and partnerships, and the income of farmers (including the value of the food that the household consumes personally).* The income statement of a successful proprietor-

---
*Certain miscellaneous adjustments are also necessary (see Table 8.5).

Table 8.5
Income approach to GNP, 1978 (billions of dollars)

Income payments	
Wages and salaries, including supplements	$1301.2
Proprietors' income (business, professional, farm)	112.9
Rental income	23.4
Corporate profits before taxes (adjusted for inventory valuation)	160.0
Interest	106.1
Nonincome items	
Indirect business taxes	178.2
Capital consumption allowance	216.9
Miscellaneous adjustments*	15.3
Total gross national product	$2106.6

Source: *Economic Report of the President,* January 1979.
*Includes business transfer payments, subsidies less surplus of government enterprises, and statistical discrepancy.

---

ship might bear a very close resemblance to that of a small corporation, but for accounting purposes proprietors' income is kept separate from corporate profits, largely because of the important difference in the way income is distributed in the two types of organization.

In 1978, proprietors' income amounted to $112.9 billion. It produces a decreasing share of national income. Although present earnings are about six times greater than the earnings in 1929, corporate profits, in contrast, have increased by about ten times.

Rental income

Rent refers to *income earned by persons for the use of real property (houses, stores) or income from royalties received from copyrights, rights to natural resources, and the like.* Rental income is the smallest element of national income, amounting to about $23.4 billion in 1978.

Corporate profits

Corporate profits refer to *the residual accruing to a corporation after all payments of interest, rent, salaries, and wages have been made to the owners of capital, land, and labor.* A certain portion of profits must be paid to the government as corporate taxes; the rest can be distributed as the managers of the corporation see fit. To help attract investors to the company, the directors may pay out some portion of profits in dividends to shareholders. Profits may also be used by the company to incraease its real assets by purchasing capital goods, such as new machines or additional trucks; or the company may save, by depositing the money in a bank or by purchasing stock in other corporations. Profits allocated in this way are called undistributed profits, but that does not mean that they are held out of the circular flow. Purchase of capital goods creates sales and income for business firms that manufacture the goods; money deposited in banks can be lent to other spenders. Undistributed profits are also a source of indirect profit to owners. They serve to increase the total value of the firm, and therefore the value of the shares of the firm held by individual stockholders will also increase. Thus undistributed profits, as well as distributed profits are counted.

Corporate profits are the fastest growing element of national income; the total in 1978 (adjusted for inventory valuation) was $160.1 billion.

Interest

Interest includes *all payments by businesses to the suppliers of borrowed money capital.* Payments may be made to banks or to holders of corporate bonds. The share of national income produced by interest has overtaken the share contributed by rental income, both in dollar amounts and in percentages.

Nonincome items

As we indicated earlier, national income is added to two nonincome items in the income approach to calculating GNP. These are indirect taxes and capital consumption allowance.

Indirect business taxes

Government levies certain *taxes—primarily sales, excise, and business property taxes—that are often treated by business as part of the costs of manufacturing and therefore added to the price of the products the business sells.* These are called **indirect business taxes** because the burden of payment does not fall directly on the business but is shifted to the consumer in the form of higher prices. It would be misleading to include these costs as income items, since they do not represent earnings of a factor of production (the government contributes nothing to the production of the product in return for the tax). Therefore, indirect business taxes constitute a separate category of total income accounting.

In 1978, the total amount of indirect taxes paid was $117.9 billion. Less than a quarter of this amount was paid to the federal government; most was paid to state and local governments as sales taxes, property taxes, and license fees. The federal government's share is acquired largely by excise taxes, taxes levied on only limited types of items, such as cigarettes and gasoline.

Capital consumption allowance

When we add indirect business taxes to national income, we arrive at the **net national product (NNP)**. *NNP measures the value of a year's production after it has been adjusted for the consumption of capital goods during the period.* So to arrive at GNP through the income route, we must add to NNP the value of depreciation that has taken place.

The measurement of depreciation presents certain accounting difficulties. The moment a

RECAP

The two major approaches to CALCULATING GNP are the expenditures approach and the income approach. Both approaches arrive at the same GNP figure.

The expenditures approach measures all expenditures for final goods and services by households, government, and business firms, as well as expenditures for exports.

The income approach measures the income generated by the production process (wages, rent, interest, and profits) plus two nonincome items: indirect business taxes and capital consumption allowance.

Table 8.6
Relation of GNP, NNP, PI, and DI

1. Gross national product (GNP)
    − Capital consumption allowance (depreciation)
    = Net national product (NNP)

2. Net national product (NNP)
    − Indirect business taxes
    = National income (NI)

3. National income (NI)
    − Income not received by households
      (Corporate income taxes
       Undistributed corporate profits
       Social Security contributions)
    + Income not earned in production of GNP
      (Transfer payments
       Income paid by consumers)
    = Personal income (PI)

4. Personal income (PI)
    − Personal taxes
    = Disposable income (DI)

business firm starts using a new machine, the machine begins to depreciate; yet it may take years before it actually requires replacement. If we count depreciation only at the time that the machine is replaced, the recorded costs of production for all the years between the time of purchase and the time of replacement will be too low, since they do not account for the depreciation that is taking place but has not yet resulted in major replacement expenditure. On the other hand, it is very difficult to create an exact measure of the depreciation of an office building or a typewriter.

The solution for this accounting problem is the **capital consumption allowance,** a *system for charging for depreciation of capital goods. The government specifies that a firm should add a certain percentage of the purchase price of capital goods to its costs of production each year for a specified number of years.* This system is convenient for accountants and helpful for long-range business planning, but it also has certain drawbacks. A business may have fully depreciated a machine—that is, it may have deducted the full price of the machine—and the machine may still be in good working order, because it did not wear out in the arbitrary five- or ten-year period.

When we add capital consumption allowances to the net national product, we get GNP; this should be exactly the same figure that we arrived at by using the expenditures approach.

In order to summarize all the national income and product components we have discussed, and to help you understand how GNP and NI relate to the components of Personal Income (PI) we discussed in Chapter 5, we have summarized the relationships in *Table 8.6*. It would be helpful to review this table to get the full picture of how all these separate elements fit into each other.

MEASURING ECONOMIC PERFORMANCE

Our system of national accounts is designed to act as a means of quantitatively measuring economic performance. How well is it performing this function?

Problems of GNP system of accounts

GNP is often called an index of economic health. Some economists feel that it does not perform as well as it should, but there has been little change in practice—possibly because no one thought that the results would really look very different if the accounts were adjusted to reflect various suggested changes, and partly because many of the suggestions could not be implemented empirically.

Concentration on market transactions

One limitation of GNP as a measure of economic performance is that it concentrates solely on market transactions, even though not all economically productive activity is channeled through the market. The classic example is the work done by women inside the home. It has been pointed out that if a man were to divorce his wife and then hire her as a cleaning lady, a babysitter, and a cook, GNP would increase, although she would be providing exactly the same service she had provided before the divorce. The work that college students do in school is not counted as productive work either, since it does not go through the market, but it is clearly of value to the economy. The current trend, especially noticeable among younger people, to seek the satisfaction of producing one's own household goods rather than buying them readymade (baking bread, knotting macrame belts, planting gardens, building furniture), would show up as a reduction of GNP, since these items would no longer be purchased through the market; yet they still constitute a part of the total output of goods and services. If people use their leisure time to consume, GNP will go up; if they use it to produce, for themselves, GNP will go down—an obvious inaccuracy.

Classification of output

Another problem with our present system of national accounts lies in the way output is classified as consumption and investment. As we have already noted, the government's investment in capital goods (for example, highways) is not counted as an investment. Neither are household goods, such as automobiles and refrigerators, which yield utility throughout a number of years after the initial purchase and therefore are in many senses a form of investment rather than a consumption item. The money that a business spends in its research and development program is counted as part of wages and salaries, yet it is clearly an investment in knowledge that will yield increased productivity in the future. Individual investment in knowledge (a college education, for example) is also treated as consumption (the spending of money for tuition fees) rather than an investment in future productivity.

Measuring value of public services

Special problems arise from the system devised to measure the value of public services provided by the government. For example, the output of a steel plant is measured in terms of its market value to purchasers. However, the output of a police department, since it is a nonprofit activity, is measured strictly in terms of costs of input. The accounts measure the cost of salaries of patrol officers uniforms, police cars, and two-way radios, and this is entered as the value of the police department output. Yet if police protection were to be sold to the public, as it sometimes is by private companies such as the Pinkerton Agency, buyers would probably have to pay more than the price that the police department pays to purchase its productive inputs. The real value added by the police force in providing protection service would also include a normal profit return. If many of the functions of government were to be performed instead by private enterprise, we would probably see an increase in GNP, even though there would be no corresponding increase in productivity (unless the private firm proved to be a far more efficient producer than the government).

Problems in relating GNP and social welfare

GNP was specifically designed to act as a measure of economic performance, rather than social welfare. Yet there is a widespread assumption that there is some positive correlation between GNP and social welfare. Such an assumption is open to question. In fact, social welfare in some ways may fall as GNP climbs. For example, a new factory's output may raise GNP by a million dollars a year, but if the factory has inadequate filters on its smokestacks, the nearby air will be polluted. Cars must be washed more often, and, of more serious concern, citizens in the area may contract lung disease. The additional carwashes and medical treatments will boost the GNP figure still higher, but the increase will be based on a decline in social and physical welfare rather than an improvement.

Omission of some goods

Another basic problem in relating GNP and social welfare is that GNP measures only certain categories of economic goods—those produced and sold by business firms. Yet as we know, there are many other economic goods. Leisure is an economic good; so is a healthy physical or social environment. Yet neither of these is measured in GNP. Free goods are not measured either. For example, in some countries the natural climate makes heating and cooling of houses unnecessary, so a 70-degree temperature is a free good. In most parts of the United States, we have to buy this comfort, thereby increasing the GNP. Yet we are no better off—no more comfortable—than those who get it free.

Because it is difficult to devise an accurate measure of such economic goods as leisure or tranquillity, such goods were deliberately omitted from GNP. Yet they are a part of our total output, and a part that contributes greatly to social welfare.

Still another problem is that GNP really concentrates on what happened during one year, not on national potential for the future. If a huge new oil reserve is discovered but not drilled, there is no effect on GNP. Similarly, if oil reserves are greatly depleted in a particular year, the decline in national economic health will not be reflected in GNP. GNP may be thought of as similar to your annual income tax statement but *not* to the statement of all your assets and liabilities. Even if your income is low for a year, you may be well off because of previously acquired assets.

Distribution not reflected

Even if we were able to include all economic goods in our measurement of GNP, we would still have no indication of the way the output of economic goods and services are *distributed,* and that is a vital part of the general social welfare. GNP tells us only the value of total output; it says nothing about who benefits from that output.

The size of a nation's population is an important consideration in evaluating the meaning of GNP in social-welfare terms. A GNP of $1 billion sounds small, but it would be a tremendous accomplishment for a nation of 1 million people. To indicate the relationship between GNP and the number of people in the economy, statisticians calculate the **per capita GNP,** *the average distribution per individual of the goods and services produced in a given year.* Per capita GNP is calculated by dividing a country's GNP by the number of people in the country.

But per capita GNP still does not tell us anything about actual distribution. Our national output is not divided up equally; it is distributed in proportion to the income earned by each household, which in turn depends on the productive resources that an individual household owns or controls. It is possible for a country to have a large GNP and a high per capita GNP, yet for the majority of people in that country to be facing starvation and to be living in deepest poverty. We can gauge general social welfare only when we know how an economy's output is distributed to its members.

Some cautions about comparing GNPs

One of the reasons for devising a system of national accounting is to establish quantitative measures of production for the purpose of comparison. The performances of one economy can be compared over a long-range period, and different economies can be compared with one another. How valid are such comparisons?

Comparisons of annual GNP for countries or regions of the world should not be interpreted too rigidly. GNP may be calculated differently in the various countries; the populations of the countries may be widely disparate; agricultural economies will appear to be much less successful than industrial ones, even though they may have an equally high rate of productivity, because nonmarket transactions are much more frequent in an agricultural economy. GNP may give a vague indication of a country's economic development, but it is certainly not a conclusive statement.

Even within a single economy, comparisons of GNP have to be qualified extensively. The price index allows such comparisons to be made, but it is not a perfect tool of adjustment, only a rough average. One of the difficulties in making long-range comparisons arises from changes that are made in accounting procedures; for example, many elements in national accounts were handled differently before World War II than they have been in the postwar period, so that figures are not really comparable; too many guesses have to be made about how they should be adjusted.

Another consideration that makes comparisons difficult is the possible change in quality of output that might take place over a period of years. For example, we might want to compare investment in residential housing over several decades. Statistics show that our output in this area is increasing. Yet both builders and homeowners agree that, despite their higher costs, the houses built today are inferior in quality to the houses built before World War II. Hardware that used to be solid brass is now only brass-plated; hardwood floors have given way to less durable pine; lath and plaster walls have been replaced by plasterboard. GNP accounts do not reflect this qualitative change.

Another problem in making comparisons is deciding which statistics to use. GNP is the basic measure today, because it can be estimated most objectively. Its comprehensiveness eliminates the problem of deciding how to determine depreciation or deciding how to classify consumption and investment.

GNP is not a perfect measure. It fails to show what portion of production is being used to replace—and what portion is adding to—productive assets. An increase in sales taxes will show up as an increase in GNP, even though productivity does not increase. Net national product (NNP) is useful as an indicator of the rate at which productive assets are being replaced, yet there are accounting problems that undermine the accuracy of its depreciation estimates. National income is a fairly good indicator of net production, since it is not affected by changes in indirect taxes. National income is often used in making international comparisons, in preference to GNP.

National accounts do not really provide any means of instant comparison or analysis. No one figure can be used as a total index of economic performance or economic welfare. National accounts are a useful tool for the economist, but all of them must be studied in order to arrive at any thorough understanding of the economy.

Summary

■ This chapter begins the study of macroeconomics by examining the major national variables of income and production. National product and income accounts tell us the value of goods and services purchased from business by households in the product market and the value of goods and services purchased from households by business in the resource market.

■ Gross national product (GNP) measures the dollar value of all goods and services produced for final consumption during a given year. GNP calculations take into account price increases or decreases by means of a price index. Double counting is avoided by including only final products or by measuring only the value added during intermediate stages of production.

■ The expenditures and income approaches to GNP both achieve the same final result. The expenditures approach is based on the four major components of national expenditures: personal consumption, investment, net exports, and government purchases of goods and services. The income approach consists of totaling the amounts paid out by businesses in the form of wages, salaries, interest, rents, and profits, and then adding indirect business taxes and capital consumption allowances.

■ As a measure of national economic performance, GNP has several limitations. Nonmarket transactions are excluded, and public services provided by government are undervalued. There is also a questionable relationship between GNP and social welfare. Some economic goods (such as leisure) and some free goods (such as climate in certain areas) are left out, and GNP does not take into account how goods and incomes are distributed. GNP comparisons of different countries' economies or the same economy at different times also present difficulties. Economists can compensate for the weaknesses of each of the various national income and product measures by examining all of them in reaching an understanding of economic performance.

Key Terms

national income and product accounts

gross national product (GNP)

price index

value added

durable goods

nondurable goods

services

investment

inventories

gross investment

net investment

net exports

national income (NI)

wage and salary

proprietor's income

rent

corporate profits

interest

indirect business taxes

net national product (NNP)

capital consumption allowance

per capita GNP

Review & Discussion

1. Define GNP. What is included in GNP when measured in terms of expenditures? Since GNP is based on reporting of market transactions, many kinds of expenditures are not counted. How significantly does this undervalue GNP overall? What part of your own expenditures end up uncounted in the GNP?

2. What is included in GNP when measured in terms of income? How is GNP related to national income? Personal income? Disposable income? Net national product?

3. How do economists correct the national accounts for changes in prices? What does it mean to say that the base year for a price index is 1972 (1972 = 100)? Is the necessity for price indexing always reflected in popular reporting of national accounts—for example, in press reports of GNP growth, or per capita GNP growth?

4. How would you rate GNP as an indicator of social welfare? How would you rate per capita GNP? Why would you have difficulty in comparing income in the United States and Nigeria?

5. Suppose most of California drops into the sea. Because of advance warning, however, the entire population is miraculously saved. The entire country joins in the effort to rebuild, and thousands of volunteers hitchhike west to help. The government provides massive emergency relief funds. If all this happened, the GNP would increase enormously. Which of the separate components of GNP would contribute to this increase? Would GNP reflect the work of the volunteers? How accurately would capital consumption be measured? How accurately would the rise in GNP reflect the actual state of social welfare?

6. You are the owner of a pet shop, buying tropical birds and fish at wholesale prices and selling them at retail prices on the market. If you buy a macaw for $60 and sell it for $80, have you added value to the macaw? If so, how much, and why?

Application 5:
The Underground Economy

One of the problems in measuring GNP is that it does not account for a great number of the money and service transactions that occur in the United States. For example, on his days off, a fireman who lives near Dallas works as a bricklayer, building patios and barbecue pits. Although he does not advertise, he is so busy that would-be customers must call weeks in advance to get him. The reason for his popularity is that he is not only good but also cheap; he charges 20 to 30 percent less for his brick work than most contractors charge. His only condition is that he be paid in cash.

Similarly, an artist in Los Angeles works freelance for several graphics design firms which have agreed to pay him in cash.

These individuals are members of what has been called the underground economy, a hidden but rapidly growing sector of most highly developed economies. Theirs is a secret world in which checks, credit cards, W-2 forms, and the other trappings of what has been called today's cashless society have no place. They work only for cash, and tell no one what they earn—particularly not the government tax collectors—and they keep all of what they earn.

Although no one really knows the extent of the underground economy, recent evidence suggests that it has been growing. According to one estimate, in the late 1970s it approached $200 billion a year in the United States, or nearly a tenth of the Gross National Product, although federal government calculations put the level in the $100 billion range. And in other countries, the amount of unreported and untaxed income may be even higher. In France for example, where the activity is known as *travail au noir* (moonlighting), as many as a fourth of the nation's workers may be involved, according to government estimates. In Italy, the practice, known as *lavoro negro* (black labor), has apparently affected even high-income professional groups such as doctors and dentists. In one recent year, more than eight out of every ten such professionals reported incomes of less than $2400.

Whatever its size, for the most part this subterranean economy involves ordinary workers rather than people who routinely engage in illegal activity, such as narcotics dealers and racketeers. Salaried workers, outside their regular jobs, are probably involved, as are vast numbers of the self-employed: carpenters, plumbers, electricians, consultants of various sorts, writers, artists.

What seems to prompt all this activity outside the normal economic channels is the combined effect of inflation and taxation. Look for a moment at the basic economic data found on the endpapers of this book and notice the impact of rising prices on disposable personal income.

In 1948, disposable income—income remaining after personal taxes and nontax payments—amounted to nearly 90 percent of personal income. By 1958, the level had declined to 88 percent, by 1968, to 86 percent; and by 1978, to 85 percent. The change resulted from a tax system that has not adjusted for inflation. The same inflation that has reduced the purchasing power of the dollar over those 30 years has also pushed families into higher income-tax brackets. So it is hardly surprising that more and more people are apparently avoiding taxes to make ends meet.

One sign of the increased effort to avoid paying taxes, according to some economists, can be seen in the statistics for the basic money supply (M_1) found in the tables of Basic Economic Data on the inside covers of this book. In 1948, currency accounted for about 20 percent of M_1. In 1958, the proportion was 21 percent; in 1978, 27 percent. Indeed, by tracing the proportion of currency to demand deposits in the money supply, some economists believe they can demonstrate the underground economy to be almost equivalent to the levels that followed World War II, when black market activity was at a peak.

Question for discussion
☐ How does the underground economy affect our measure of GNP? Why might this be important?

Chapter 9

Inflation, Unemployment, and Business Cycles

What to look for in this chapter

What are the two major goals of current macroeconomic policy?

What are the causes and costs of inflation?

What are the causes and costs of unemployment?

What are the phases of the business cycle? Why do business cycles occur?

ECONOMIC GOALS

The primary goal of any economy is implicit in the very definition of the term "economy." As we have emphasized in previous chapters, the goal of all economies is maximization—getting the most satisfaction from the scarce resources possessed by society. In order to achieve the ultimate goal of maximization, a number of economic goals must be considered, such as a reasonable rate of economic growth, a favorable position in international trade, equitable income distribution, and efficiency in resource allocation. Perhaps most important, an economy should operate under reasonably stable economic conditions and at the level of full employment.

Stable prices and full employment have been the major concerns of economic policymakers in recent years because of the tremendous impact they have on economic activity and on our everyday lives. In this chapter we will discuss inflation

Table 9.1
Economic goals, 1979–1983, as outlined in the Humphrey-Hawkins Act of 1978

Item	1979	1980	1981	1982	1983
	\multicolumn{5}{c}{Level, fourth quarter}				
Employment (millions)	97.5	99.5	102.6	105.5	108.3
Unemployment (percent)	6.2	6.2	5.4	4.6	4.0
	Percent change, fourth quarter to fourth quarter				
Consumer prices	7.5	6.4	5.2	4.1	3.0
Real GNP	2.2	3.2	4.6	4.6	4.2

Source: *Economic Report of the President,* January 1979.

and unemployment in detail and we will also discuss the fluctuations in all types of economic activity (including employment and prices) that occur in the "business cycle."

Full employment and price stability: our two major goals

The achievement of full employment and price stability is one of the main objectives of current macroeconomic policy, and policymakers are continually trying to discover the means by which we can achieve both goals. The United States Congress placed a statutory responsibility on the federal government to pursue full employment and price stability policies in the Employment Act of 1946. Part of this act reads:

> The Congress declares that it is the continuing policy and responsibility of the Federal Government to use all practicable means . . . for the purpose of creating and maintaining . . . conditions under which there will be afforded useful employment opportunities . . . for those able, willing, and seeking to work, and to promote maximum employment, production, and purchasing power.

The responsibility of the federal government was more clearly defined with the passage of the Humphrey-Hawkins Full Employment and Balanced Growth Act of 1978. This act is directed toward the *longer range* national economic objectives of the federal government, including lower rates of unemployment and inflation, an improved competitive position for the United States economy in the world, a reduction in the federal government's share of national output, and a balanced federal budget. *Table 9.1* shows the goals established by the act for employment, price stability, and growth of real gross national product (GNP).

According to the *Economic Report of the President* (1979), the numerous goals outlined in the Humphrey-Hawkins Act are "very ambitious goals,"[*] and the path to their achievement will be

---
[*]*Economic Report of the President,* January 1979, p. 110.

extremely difficult. As the *Economic Report* also states, "the most difficult obstacle to achieving the 1983 goals arises from the potential inconsistencies between the objective for growth and unemployment and the need to reduce inflation."*

In spite of the optimism of the act's economic goals, many believe it to be little more than a gesture which lacks the necessary force to ensure the establishment of policies necessary to achieve the goals. In order to make any decisions or recommendations for any policies aimed at achieving stable prices and full employment, policymakers need to understand the causes, types, and costs of inflation and unemployment.

INFLATION

As we have mentioned, one major goal of the economy is to maintain a relatively stable price level. In recent years, however, this has been extremely difficult, and many economists feel that price instability is the most serious problem facing our economy today.

There are two directions of price instability. **Inflation** *occurs when the general level of prices rises.* **Deflation** *occurs when the general level of prices drops.* As the price indexes shown in *Table 9.2* and *Fig. 9.1* indicate, over the past several decades, the United States—like many nations—has been troubled by inflation. Deflation, a problem potentially as serious in its consequences for general economic health, is rarely seen today. Our discussion of price instability will focus on inflation, since it is currently the more relevant issue.

During inflation, the prices of most goods and services in the product market rise, although prices of some individual commodities may stay the same or even drop. This general price rise in the product market is accompanied by a rise in

*Ibid., p. 123.

Table 9.2
Percent change per year in consumer prices, United States, 1965–1977

Year(s)	Percent increase
1965–1970	4.2 (5-year average)
1970–1975	6.7 (5-year average)
1975–1977	6.1 (2-year average)
1970	5.9
1971	4.3
1972	3.3
1973	6.2
1974	11.0
1975	9.1
1976	5.8
1977	6.5
1978	8.7

Source: *Statistical Abstract of the United States,* 1978.

prices on the resource market, which means that wages, salaries, rents, and profits will also be higher. At first glance, it might appear that since prices increase in all markets, inflation is not a real problem. If it costs more to buy a new vacuum cleaner, the worker can meet the increased cost out of an increase in salary or wages, and the basic rate of exchange is not altered. The problem with this reasoning, however, is that it does not take into consideration the uneven progress of inflation. Although the general level of prices rises in all markets, the rise is never exactly synchronized.

Measuring the rate of inflation

Currently, there are many indexes used to monitor the behavior of the general price level. The three most commonly quoted indexes are: the Con-

164 CHAPTER 9: INFLATION, UNEMPLOYMENT, AND BUSINESS CYCLES

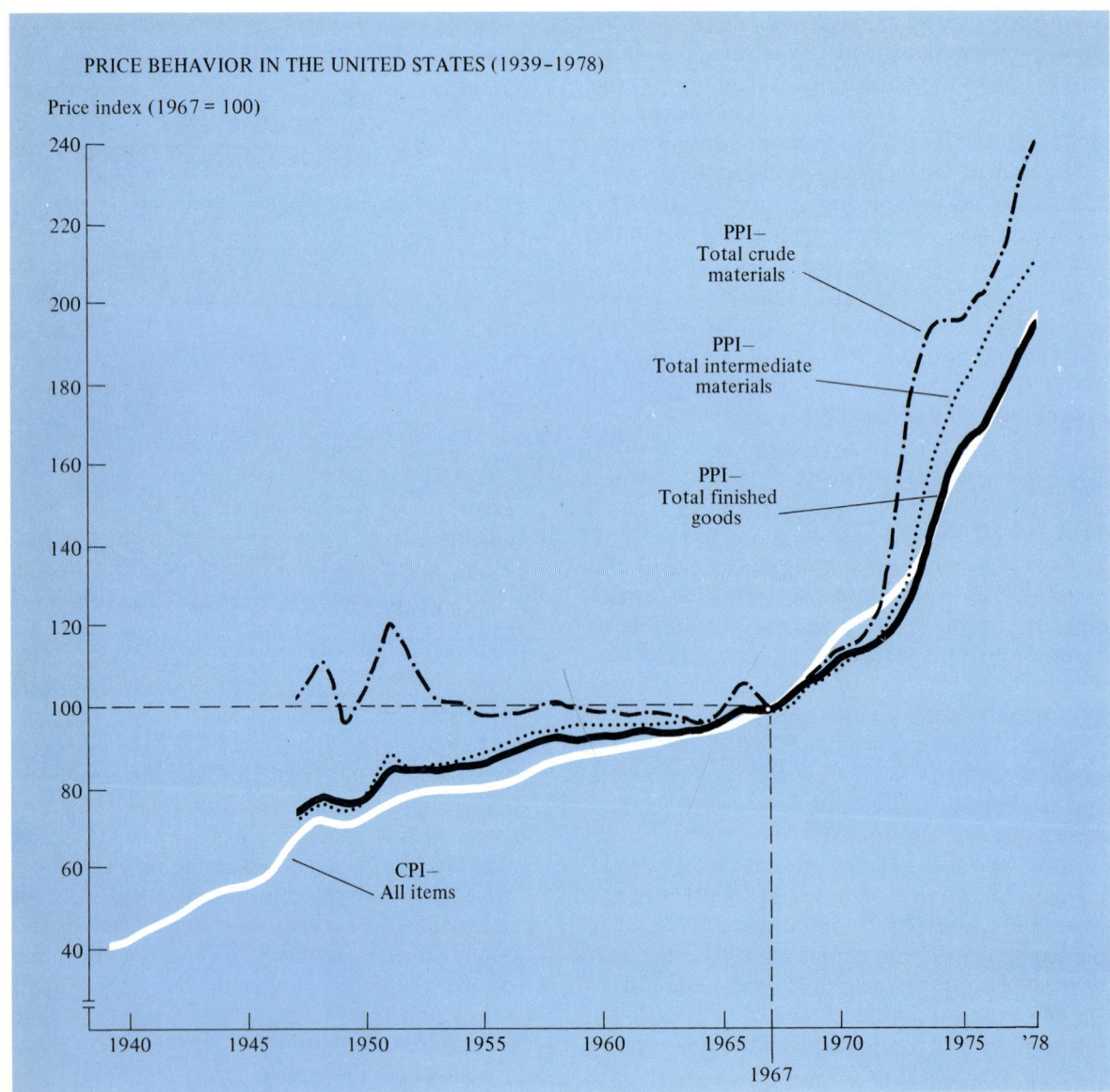

SOURCE: *Economic Report of the President*, January 1979.

Fig. 9.1
This graph illustrates the general trend of increasing prices over the past five decades as measured by the changes in the CPI and PPIs (for finished and intermediate goods, and crude materials). Two periods of sharp increase can be observed: one in the postwar period of 1945 to 1950, and the second from 1966 to the present. All price changes are measured in relation to the base year 1967, where the index is equal to 100.

sumer Price Index (CPI), the Producer Price Index (PPI, formerly called the Wholesale Price Index), and the implicit price deflator.

The Consumer Price Index

The intent of the **Consumer Price Index** is to *measure the price level of the goods and services purchased by an average American household unit*. The method employed to measure the price level is to select a "market basket" of goods and services typical of the average household purchases for a base year. This base year market basket is then priced each year in order to give an approximate measure of the price level of consumer purchases for that year. In the base year (1967 in *Fig. 9.1*) the index is set to 100, and the cost of the market basket in other years is calculated and expressed as a percentage of its cost in the base year. For example, the 1978 index of 195.4 indicates that the market basket cost 195.4 percent of what it would have cost in 1967. The cost had increased by 95.4 percent, or almost doubled.

Problems with the CPI One problem with the CPI is that it measures the price changes of a historically selected basket of goods that may not reflect current household purchases. Indeed, households would reduce their purchases, over time, of goods whose prices have risen more than average and increase their purchases of goods whose prices have increased less or perhaps even declined. The more drastic and uneven price increases are, the greater the substitutions within the market basket. To deal with this problem, the Bureau of Labor Statistics, which computes the CPI, tries to keep the base year within ten years of the current year to avoid the basket becoming too old. Further, very uneven price increases will stimulate the BLS to update the base year.

Another problem is that although estimates are made, it is difficult to account for changes in quality. If the reliability, performance, and price go up on a television, is it correct to say that televisions now cost more, and if so, how much more does it cost after accounting for the other changes?

In spite of its flaws, the CPI is extremely influential in both shaping government economic policy and adjusting incomes. The wages of more than 8.5 million workers covered by collective bargaining are tied to the CPI, as are pensions and other benefits for about 50 million Social Security recipients, retired Federal Civil Service and military employees, and food stamp recipients. Altogether a portion of the income of about half the population of the United States is based on the CPI.

The Producer Prices Indexes

The Producer Price Indexes (PPI, formerly the Wholesale Price Index) *measure average changes in prices of goods at various stages of processing*. PPIs are calculated by groups of commodities and by the stage of processing. For example, PPIs measure price changes in (1) finished goods (goods that do not require further processing and are ready for sale to consumers or business firms—a cotton shirt, for example); (2) intermediate materials (goods that have been processed, but require further processing before they become finished goods—cotton fabric, for example); (3) crude (raw) materials (unprocessed products entering the market for the first time—raw cotton, for example).

PPIs are often used to predict what will happen in the CPI. For instance, if the price of raw cotton increases in August, this may lead to an increase in the price of a cotton shirt by December which will be reflected in an increased CPI. See *Fig. 9.1* for an illustration of the behavior of the PPIs by stages of production.

One major flaw of the PPI is that it overlooks a number of important inputs into production. For example, many types of office equipment, such as computers, are not used in constructing the index.

The implicit price deflator

A third index of inflation, traditionally preferred by economists, is the **implicit price deflator** of the Gross National Product (the GNP deflator), *the price index for gross national product.* Briefly, it is constructed by adjusting various subcategories of goods and services into constant dollar (base year) amounts. These subcategories are then added together to provide a deflated or real GNP figure. The ratio of GNP in current dollars to GNP in constant dollars is the GNP deflator.

The advantage of this measure of inflation over the CPI and PPI is that it covers so many goods and services and can thus measure broad price movements in the economy as a whole.

Causes of inflation

Economists distinguish several different types of inflation, depending on the conditions that appear to have caused prices to rise.

Demand-pull inflation

Demand-pull inflation is *an increase in the general price level caused by an increase in demand at a time when an economy cannot increase production because it is at full employment or is unable to increase production fast enough to keep pace with the increase in demand.* Because businesses cannot increase the supply of goods to meet the increased demand, buyers bid up the prices of the limited output. This situation is illustrated in *Fig. 9.2.*

Our economy experienced demand-pull inflation right after World War II. During the war, few consumer goods had been produced. Families postponed many purchases because goods were unavailable and because the uncertainties of the war led them to prefer saving. But in the first several years after the war, people were actually dissaving—spending all of their annual income and some part of their accumulated savings as well. Demand shot up, but production still lagged, especially since many factories had to undergo a time-consuming and costly reconversion before they

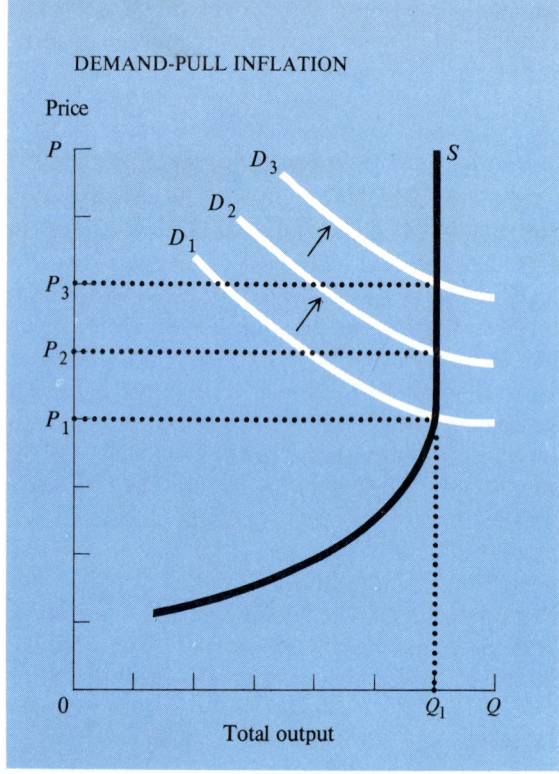

Fig. 9.2
The aggregate demand line D_1 is full-employment demand. Below that line, any increase in demand will be met by an expansion of output. But after output reaches the point of full employment (Q_1), increases in demand, such as those represented by D_2 and D_3, will only cause prices to rise to P_2 and P_3, since supply cannot increase beyond Q_1 in the short run.

were able to produce civilian goods again. So eager buyers bid up the prices on the limited quantity of goods available, and inflation began.

Cost-push inflation

Cost-push inflation is *an increase in the general price level due to increased costs of production* *(increased profits and/or increased resource prices)*. For example, business firms may raise prices in order to increase their profit margin, as when coffee producers, witnessing the sky-rocketing prices paid for manipulated commodities such as oil or sugar, decide to withhold coffee from the market until prices rise and they can increase their revenue and profits.

Another type of cost-push inflation occurs when industries are faced with higher resource prices (usually because of wage hikes or the limited supply of the resource). If the price increases are greater than the increases in productivity warrant, the costs of production go up. This increase is passed along to consumers by increasing the price of the finished product. This type of cost-push inflation is commonly called "wage-push inflation."

An example will best illustrate how this wage-push occurs. Suppose the steelworkers' union negotiates a new contract, calling for a significant wage increase over a two-year period. As soon as the contract goes into effect, steelworkers have an increase in real buying power. Soon, however, the effects of this increase begin to spread throughout the economy. The steel companies are unable or unwilling to absorb the additional resource costs caused by the wage increase, and so they pass the costs along to buyers of steel in the form of higher prices. Buyers, such as automobile and appliance manufacturers, who now have higher resource costs, pass this increase along in turn to consumers and the price of cars and refrigerators rises. Workers in other factories begin to feel a financial pinch because the cost of goods they want to purchase has risen, but their wages have stayed the same. They lose buying power.

When their contracts expire, these other workers ask for more money—at least enough to compensate for their lost buying power, and perhaps a little more, to give them a real increase. There is another round of price increases on the product market, and eventually almost everybody rises to the next price level—salaried workers renegotiate their salaries, landlords ask for higher rents when leases are renewed. In the meantime, the process may be starting all over again in another key industry.

Whether the cost-push inflation is caused by increased wages or increased profits, the effect on the supply curve is the same: the supply curve shifts to the left, reflecting a decrease in supply. In the absence of any change in demand, output will decrease and prices will increase (see *Fig. 9.3*).

Some economists believe that much of the inflation that we have been experiencing recently is due to a self-generating cycle of demand-pull and wage-push/profit-push inflation. Therefore it should be noted that while *in theory* we can divide inflation into neat categories of demand-pull and cost-push, the distinctions are not that clear in reality. Both types of inflation can and do operate simultaneously.

Government-induced inflation

Inflation can also be a result of government action. For example, the federal government can induce inflation by increasing the money supply or by increasing its spending. In both cases, more money is available for spending by households, businesses, and government sectors. This increased spending may, in turn, lead to increased demand for scarce goods and services and demand-pull inflation as described above.

In addition, the federal government can influence prices through direct or indirect regulation. For example, independent commissions, such as the Civil Aeronautics Board and the Security and Exchange Commission, directly regulate pricing methods of a specific industry (airlines, stock exchanges). Indirectly, the government can influence prices by requiring businesses to conform to certain federal regulations concerning pollution (air, noise, water), safety (cars, nuclear-power plants), and health (improved working conditions). Such regulations cause increases in a business's production costs, which are passed along to consumers through higher prices.

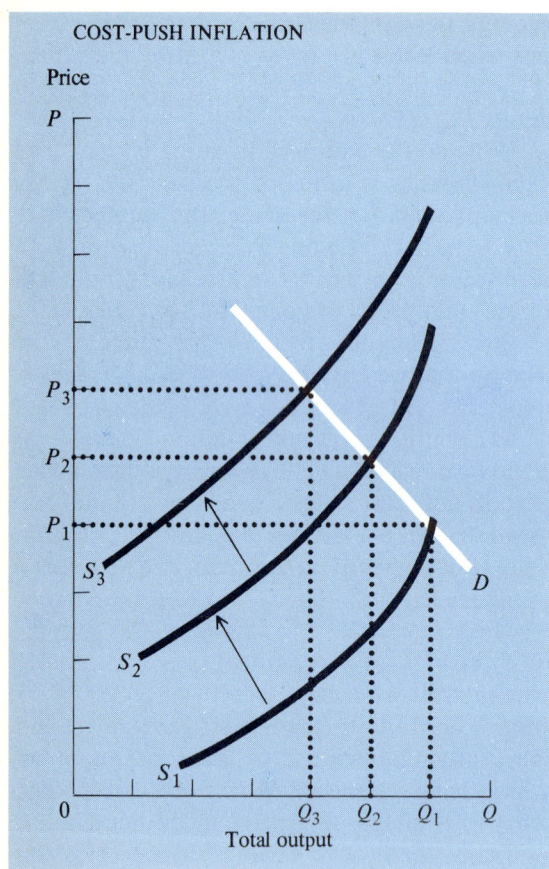

Fig. 9.3
An increase in the price that business must pay to obtain productive factors will cause the supply curve to shift to the left, from S_1 to S_2. Since demand (D) remains constant, the effect of this shift in supply is to raise prices (from P_1 to P_2 to P_3) and to restrict output (from Q_1 to Q_2 to Q_3).

Consequently, the government can be an important source of cost-push inflation.

The role of expectations

Inflation can also have its roots in future expectations of inflation. Fearing that inflation will continue at ever-increasing rates, people accelerate spending in order to buy the commodities they want before the prices increase. They are less willing to save, because savers are among those most hurt by inflation. They borrow money and buy on credit, since they assume that they can spend the money now, before prices rise, and pay it back later in dollars that are "cheaper"—that is, have less real buying power. All of these actions are in themselves inflationary pressures. As we will see in Chapter 17, this is one reason that a spiral of inflation (regardless of its initial cause) is so hard to halt; the actions taken by people who expect inflation to continue serve to fuel a continuing process of inflation.

Rates of inflation

Hyperinflation
Hyperinflation is the most rapid type of inflation. *In hyperinflation daily increases in wages and prices are noticeable. Hyperinflation is also characterized by a snowballing effect—instead of steady increases in prices, the percentage rise in the price level multiplies rapidly.* A few skillful speculators can become rich, while the majority of wage earners struggle for food, clothing, and shelter. A classic case of hyperinflation occurred in Germany after World War I when, between December 1919 and December 1923, Germany's wholesale price index rose from 8.03 to 1,200,400,000,000.00. Hyperinflation is often accompanied by other forms of social instability and is most often linked to wartime disruption of the society and the economy.

Creeping inflation
The type of inflation that we have experienced until very recently in the United States is called **creeping inflation,** which *usually refers to an annual rate of inflation of less than 5 percent.* While most economists agree on the adverse effects of hyperinflation, some feel that a low rate of inflation may stimulate economic expansion. They point out that the tendency for inflation to

discourage excessive saving and encourage spending may have positive effects, since it serves to increase the total market demand for many products. Moreover, since product prices tend to increase faster than resource prices, businesses are able to make large profits, which in turn stimulates all kinds of business activity, and the economy is brought closer to full employment. As long as the rate of inflation is lower than the rate of interest paid on savings, there will be an incentive for people to save, thereby ensuring that the stock of capital goods can be replaced or perhaps increased.

Not all economists agree with this optimistic view that the benefits of a low rate of inflation outweigh the costs. One of the arguments against economic policies that allow creeping inflation is the fear of possible cumulative effects. A yearly rise in prices of 3 percent may sound insignificant, but in only 23 years, prices will have doubled. Another concern is that it may create conditions that lead to an acceleration in the rate of price increases, as each segment of the economy attempts to exert pressure to ensure that its income rises faster than the general level of increase. The result is that the rate of inflation increases, and eventually hyperinflation sets in.

Both sides of this debate agree that inflation always involves some cost to society, even at low rates. Their disagreement is over the extent of the harm done when this process is allowed to continue indefinitely, as measured against the value of the benefits thought to be derived from the existence of a slight degree of inflation. We will examine some of the costs that inflation imposes on an economy in the following section.

THE COSTS OF INFLATION

While it is relatively easy to determine the current rate of inflation, its costs are much more difficult to determine. Before we begin our discussion of the effects of inflation on such areas as redistribution of income, production, and resource allocation, however, we must make a distinction between inflation that is fully anticipated and inflation that is unanticipated.

> **RECAP**
> Inflation and unemployment are two of the major problems faced by our economy today. INFLATION, a rise in the general price level, can have a number of causes, such as excess demand, wage or profit increases, government actions, or consumer expectations. Since it is usually unanticipated, inflation involves some costs to society by affecting productive output and the distribution of income.

Most economists agree that when inflation can be anticipated, its costs can be minimized. Individuals can switch their savings from inflation-threatened bank accounts into other holdings, such as real estate or corporate stocks, which will benefit from inflated prices. Workers can ask for cost-of-living raises in their contracts. Banks can raise interest rates, so that an adequate amount of saving will continue. Theoretically if everyone accurately anticipated the rate of inflation, all wages and prices would rise at the same rate and there would be little effect on any individual's purchasing power. However, inflation is never fully anticipated, and because the adjustments mentioned above are not made, unanticipated inflation is always more costly to individuals.

Effects on redistribution of income

Because inflation never proceeds at a uniform and predictable pace throughout every sector in the economy, it causes some groups to lose some of their buying power. The people most hurt are those who have fixed incomes (pensions, annuities, long-range contractual income) because they will lose buying power as prices increase and their incomes remain the same. For instance, the size of a retired person's pension is fixed and unchanging, but what seemed like a generous retirement income 15 years ago is not even a subsistence income today because prices have increased so much. Since many groups that lose income are those that already have small incomes, inflation often makes the least affluent members of our society relatively poorer. Thus, the redistribution of income caused by inflation can often work in opposition to social policies which are often aimed at making the distribution of income more equal. Other groups that suffer from the redistribution effects of inflation include savers, who are hurt because the dollars they save lose some fraction of their buying power before being spent, and people who lend money, because the real purchasing power of any amount of money loaned (a fixed sum) has decreased by the time it is repaid.

Effects on productive output

In the long run, inflation can also cause a decrease in total production output. In a capitalist economy, saving is a necessary condition for future economic growth. Without saving, we cannot replace depreciating capital goods or expand our stock of them. Thus, if people cut back on or withdraw their savings because of unpredictable rates of inflation, savings may drop below the level required for capital accumulation, and economic expansion will slow down or stop—with fewer capital resources, we will not be able to continue to produce as large an output as before the amount of savings decreased.

Another way in which inflation may reduce output is by making it profitable for people to channel much of their economic activity into nonproductive trading and speculation. For example, because prices of commodities rise at different rates, it is possible to make a profit by buying and selling commodities whose prices are rising the fastest. Capital, labor, and entrepreneurial resources are channeled into this activity, which is profitable but not productive in the same sense as producing an automobile or building a house because it does not increase the number of goods and services on the market.

UNEMPLOYMENT

The second major goal of an economy is to operate at full employment, which, as you will recall from Chapter 2, means that none of the economy's productive resources will be involuntarily unemployed. When all existing resources are fully and efficiently employed, output will be maximized.

Our economy, however, does not always operate at the full-employment level. As we have seen with price stability and inflation, some resources *are* involuntarily unemployed.

Unemployment of labor

Unemployment can refer to any unused resource; a drill press or a copper mine can be unemployed, as can a pipefitter or a philosophy professor. In each case, there is a cost to the economy. On the production side of the national accounts, the cost of unemployment is the value of the unproduced commodities; on the income side of the accounts, the cost is the loss of wages and salaries when labor is unemployed and the loss of rent, interest, and profits when land or capital resources are unemployed.

It is on the unemployment of labor that most attention is concentrated. One reason that economists focus on this resource is that the statistics on unemployed labor serve as a fairly reliable indicator of total unemployment. In addition, the costs of human unemployment are usually more obvious and dramatic than the costs of other kinds of unemployment. An unemployed machine does not show signs of malnutrition; it does not picket or demonstrate or riot; nor does it have a family to support.

Because labor is usually the sole productive resource that a household has to sell, loss of income is most apt to occur when labor resources are unemployed. But for many families, loss of income may be just as great when a land or capital resource is unemployed. An elderly couple who derive all of their income from rents on a building they own will suffer loss of income if they are unable to find tenants.

In addition, when labor resources are unemployed, there is loss of total future output. If a copper mine is shut down for ten years, there will be a loss of current output, but not of the total production capacity of the mine. To a lesser degree, the same is true of many capital goods. A drill press can be left idle for several years during a recession, forfeiting current production. But the remaining hours of its total productive life can still be realized at a later date when economic conditions improve, providing that the machine has not been allowed to deteriorate and that it has not become obsolete.

Human capital, however, depreciates much more quickly and steadily than other kinds of capital or natural resources. When people are unemployed there is virtually no way to recover the loss of total output, because they are capable of working only a limited number of hours per day for a given number of days of their life spans. They may put in some overtime hours upon reemployment, but it is unlikely that they will be able to compensate for the work hours lost during unemployment. These hours are lost forever, as are the additional skills or knowledge they might have gained by on-the-job training if they had been employed.

These are some of the reasons that studies of unemployment usually focus on labor resources. From now on, when we speak of unemployment in this chapter, we will be referring to workers without jobs, just as government statistics on unemployment do. But the reader should bear in mind that there are other aspects to the problem of unemployment, and that "full employment" actually means maximizing use of all productive resources—land, capital, and labor.

Table 9.3

Civilian labor force 1947–1978 (does not include Armed Forces)

Year	Total civilian labor force (millions)	Employed (millions)	Unemployed (millions)	Not in labor force (millions)
1947	59.4	57.0	2.3	42.5
1950	62.2	58.9	3.3	42.8
1955	65.0	62.2	2.9	44.7
1960	69.6	65.8	3.9	47.6
1965	74.5	71.1	3.4	52.1
1966	75.8	72.9	2.9	52.3
1967	77.3	74.4	3.0	52.5
1968	78.7	75.9	2.8	53.3
1969	80.7	77.9	2.8	53.6
1970	82.7	78.6	4.1	54.3
1971	84.1	79.1	5.0	55.7
1972	86.5	81.7	4.8	56.8
1973	88.7	84.4	4.3	57.2
1974	91.0	85.9	5.1	57.6
1975	92.6	84.8	7.8	58.7
1976	94.8	87.5	7.3	59.1
1977	97.4	90.5	6.9	59.0
1978	100.4	94.4	6.0	58.7*

Source: *Statistical Abstract of the United States,* 1978.
*Preliminary figure

How unemployment is measured

The United States Bureau of Census periodically collects a household survey to obtain information on the levels of employment and unemployment. These household surveys, based on a sample of 55,000 households, classify every civilian aged 16 years or older as employed, unemployed, or not in the labor force (that is, does not have and is not looking for a job). See *Table 9.3* for a breakdown of the civilian labor force.

Individuals are classified as *employed* if they have a job, whether it is part-time, temporary work, or full-time employment. They are counted as *unemployed* if they meet all of the following criteria: they must have looked for work some time within the past four weeks; they must be currently available for work; and they do not have a job. The employed and unemployed constitute the civilian labor force.

A number of useful statistics that reflect the current employment situation are computed from the household survey. The most commonly used statistic is the **unemployment rate,** *the fraction of the total civilian labor force that is classified as unemployed.* Historically, this statistic has been highly influential as a measure of economic health, and today it is the most frequently quoted labor-market statistic.

Problems in measuring unemployment
Serious questions have recently arisen concerning the validity of the unemployment rate as a measure of the well-being of an economy. Some believe that this statistic underestimates the unemployment problem. Because of the way it is compiled, it overlooks discouraged workers— those who are not currently working and who are not looking for a job because of previous disappointment in the job market. Discouraged workers have had difficulties finding work for any of a number of reasons (for example, discrimination or lack of experience). After a while, they begin to feel that they could not find any work even if they were looking. Because they are not working and not looking, such individuals are classified as "not in the labor force," and therefore are not counted as unemployed even though they would accept a job if it were available. These individuals are sometimes referred to as the *hidden unemployed*. Hidden unemployment may cause a serious understatement of unemployment, both during periods of slow business activity and among the disadvantaged (the young, the old, females, and nonwhites).

Another reason the unemployment rate may underestimate unemployment is that it makes no provision for workers who are *underemployed* and, therefore, not being used as efficiently as possible. A physicist driving a taxi is part of the unemployment problem, even though he is not unemployed in terms of the official definition. In order for the reported unemployment statistics to show a real improvement, then, many believe that an economy's production must increase enough to provide additional jobs not only for those who are officially classified as unemployed, but also for those who will be encouraged to reenter the labor force to seek a job and for those who are underemployed.

On the other side of the debate on unemployment statistics are those who argue that the unemployment rate overestimates the actual unemployment problem because it does not distinguish between those who are actually unable to find work and those who have simply decided to leave the labor market for a period of time. In addition, many people feel that the recent high unemployment rates reflect the shifts in the composition of the labor force caused by the entrance of women and young people, both of whom enter and leave the labor force frequently.

Such problems in measuring the numbers of employed and unemployed people need to be considered because unemployment statistics are used when businesses make production decisions (how many people will be working and consuming? how much should be produced?) and when the govern-

---

RECAP

UNEMPLOYMENT refers to the situation in which people who are available and able to work do not have a job. Economists distinguish three types of unemployment (frictional, structural, and cyclical), all of which result in economic and social costs.

ment establishes economic policies. Some people have recommended that two or three different statistics be used to give a more accurate, helpful, and reliable picture of the American employment situation, and economists and statisticians at the Department of Labor have been working to develop a new way to measure unemployment. It does not seem likely, however, that such new methods will soon replace the old unemployment rate.

Types of unemployment

Even in an economy operating at maximum output and full employment, there are bound to be some people who are out of work. The United States Department of Labor cites various sources of the unemployment experienced in any one year, which include demographic differences (race, sex, age, location) as well as differences in reasons for unemployment (job turnover, first entry, and reentry into the labor force).

For our purposes, we will divide unemployment into three major types—frictional, structural, and cyclical. However, in an analysis of reasons for unemployment, we may find that some types of unemployment reflect all three situations. The categories, like those of demand-pull and cost-push inflation, do not always operate independently of one another.

Frictional and structural unemployment

Because it is probably not possible for every worker to be employed every single working day of his or her life, there is always some level of **frictional unemployment,** *unemployment caused by functional imperfections in the labor market,* such as the lack of mobility of labor resources and the lack of complete knowledge of all job opportunities. For instance, a worker who voluntarily changes jobs may be unemployed for a period of several weeks, and workers in seasonal industries, such as construction and agriculture, will be temporarily laid off in bad weather. A certain level of frictional unemployment (economists advance the figure of 1 to 2 percent of the labor force) seems to be an inevitable cost of having a large and highly specialized economy operating through the price mechanism. It is an inconvenience to the unemployed individuals, but their unemployment generally does not last long enough to cause them serious economic hardship. In addition, although the percentage remains constant, it is not always the same people who are without work.

Another kind of unemployment is **structural unemployment,** which is *the result of some structural change in the economy,* such as a decreased demand for a certain skill or a change in the technology of a certain industry. Workers are structurally unemployed who do not have jobs because the industry in which they want to work is decreasing output or has become obsolete; because they are looking for work in a location that has no industry that can use their skills; or because they have too few or the wrong kind of skills to offer available employers.

The decline of the shoe industry in the New England states, for example, produced a number of structurally unemployed workers. Many who lost their jobs were reluctant to move to new locations or to enter retraining programs. These men and women were potentially employable, but no firm in their area was willing to pay the salaries they were asking for the type of skills that they had.

A low level of structural unemployment (1 to 2 percent of the labor force) is usually considered tolerable, and many economists believe that it is an inescapable cost of necessary market adjustments. The demand schedules for different products will always be changing, and, as industries expand and contract in response to these changes, some workers will lose their jobs. In order to help reduce structural unemployment, the government sponsors programs to retrain some workers for other jobs.

Because of frictional and structural unemployment, a realistic definition of full employment is employment of about 96 percent of our labor force.* The appropriate level will depend to a large degree on programs such as unemployment compensation which allow workers to search more easily (and longer) for the "right" job. When employment drops below 96 percent, economists say that there is "real" unemployment, and people begin to worry about the health of the economy.

Cyclical unemployment

Cyclical unemployment is *unemployment that is linked to changes in the level of economic activity*. Today, cyclical fluctuations in economic activity are the main targets of the federal government's unemployment policies.

In order to trace the sources of cyclical unemployment, economists sometimes look at supply elements for an explanation of why business firms do not operate at a full-employment level of production. They may suggest lowering wages or relaxing government restrictions on business activities to induce businesses, through the profit motive, to increase production to the full-employment level. Most often, however, economists link the level of employment directly to the level of total spending (demand). When spending is high, business firms can produce and sell a large volume of goods and services at a profit. Therefore, they can afford to buy nearly all of the productive resources offered on the resource market, including labor, and unemployment is low. When spending decreases, business firms must cut back production, and are consequently unable to buy as many resources as are offered for sale. The result is a rise in unemployment.

Level and costs of unemployment

The unemployment rate in the United States from 1929 to 1978 is illustrated in *Fig. 9.4*. The fluctua-

---

*Although many economists currently disagree that 4 percent is a realistic level of unavoidable unemployment, for the sake of simplicity in our discussion, we will accept this level. Dramatic exceptions should be noted, such as times of war, when a high level of labor in employed in war-related industry and in an expanded armed forces effort.

tions in employment that can be observed in this graph are due mainly to changes in the level of cylical unemployment. Unemployment levels during the Depression in the early 1930s were incredibly high—in 1933, one out of every four people in the labor force was unable to find a job. In contrast, the start of World War II brought a sudden rise in employment until by 1944 only 1.2 percent of the labor force was unemployed, probably the all-time record for full employment in the United States. Although the unemployment rate has not fluctuated drastically during the last four decades, unemployment has been a constant concern. When relatively small percentage changes are translated into numbers of workers, the reason for the concern becomes clearer. With a total labor force of over 100 million, each full percentage point of increase in the unemployment figure means that over a million additional workers have lost their jobs.

Furthermore, increases in production or demand do not automatically trigger a corresponding change in employment. We have learned from experience that a given percentage increase in GNP does not necessarily lead to an equal percentage increase in employment. For example, real GNP (in 1958 dollars) increased about 12 percent from the low point of the 1958 recession to the high point of the recovery in 1960, but employment rose only 1.2 percent—from 93.7 percent to 94.9 percent—in the same period.

The economic costs

Economists generally measure the economic costs of unemployment in one of two ways. One approach is to measure the loss of output due to unemployment. The potential GNP for the year is calculated and then compared with the actual GNP. The difference, called the **GNP gap**, *reflects the cost of unemployment in terms of production loss*. *Figure 9.5* shows the fluctuating GNP gap in the United States from 1968 to 1978.

Another economic measure of the cost of unemployment is the loss of national income. This

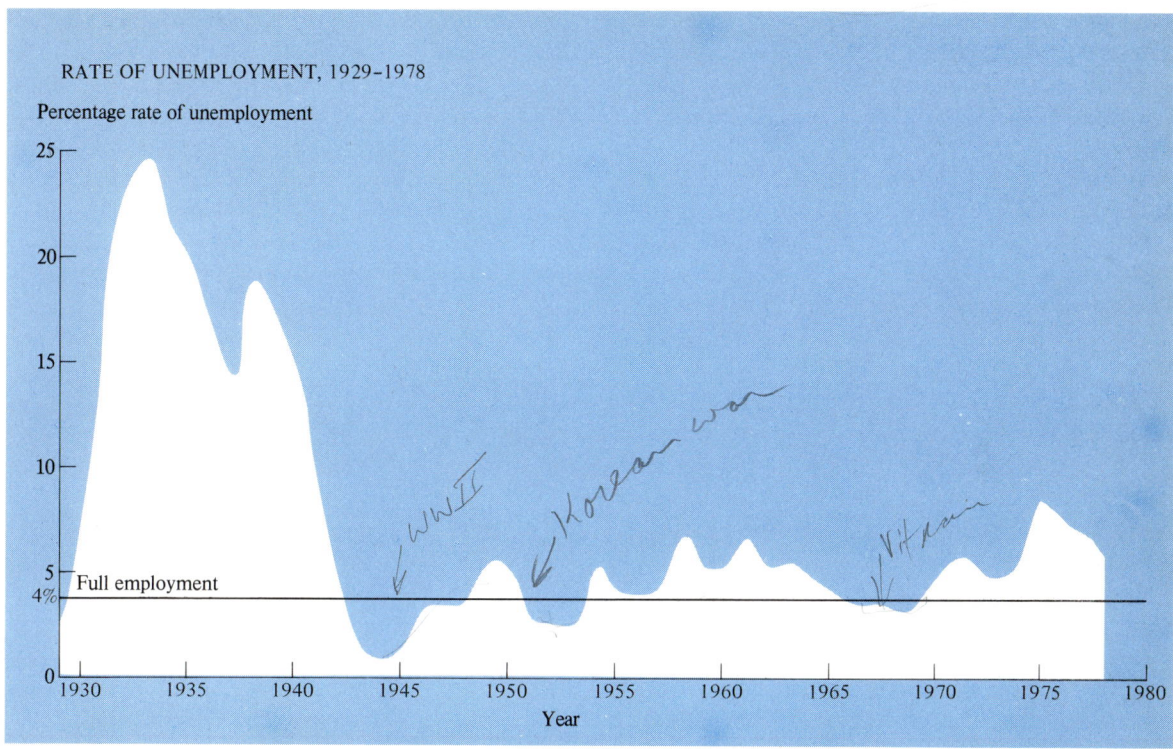

SOURCE: Bureau of Labor Statistics, U.S. Department of Labor.

Fig. 9.4
This chart traces the level of unemployment in the United States from 1929 to 1978, and shows how serious the problem of unemployment was during the Depression of the 1930s. If we define full employment as 96 percent employment, we can see that since 1930, we have had only three periods of full employment or better. They occurred during World War II (1942 to 1946), during the Korean war (1951 to 1953), and during the buildup of the Vietnam war (1965 to 1969).

can be calculated by multiplying the number of unemployed workers by the average annual wage. The actual loss of personal income will be somewhat lower than this figure, since many unemployed persons receive some kind of transfer payment, such as government unemployment compensation or union unemployment insurance, and because those unemployed were often earning below-average wages. Transfer payments or use of personal savings may cushion the problems of the unemployed, but they do not compensate for the loss of total national income for the economy.

The methods of measuring the costs of unemployment described above provide only a rough indication of the total cost. To arrive at a true economic account of the costs of unemployment, we would also have to add in the productivity lost due to underemployed or discouraged workers.

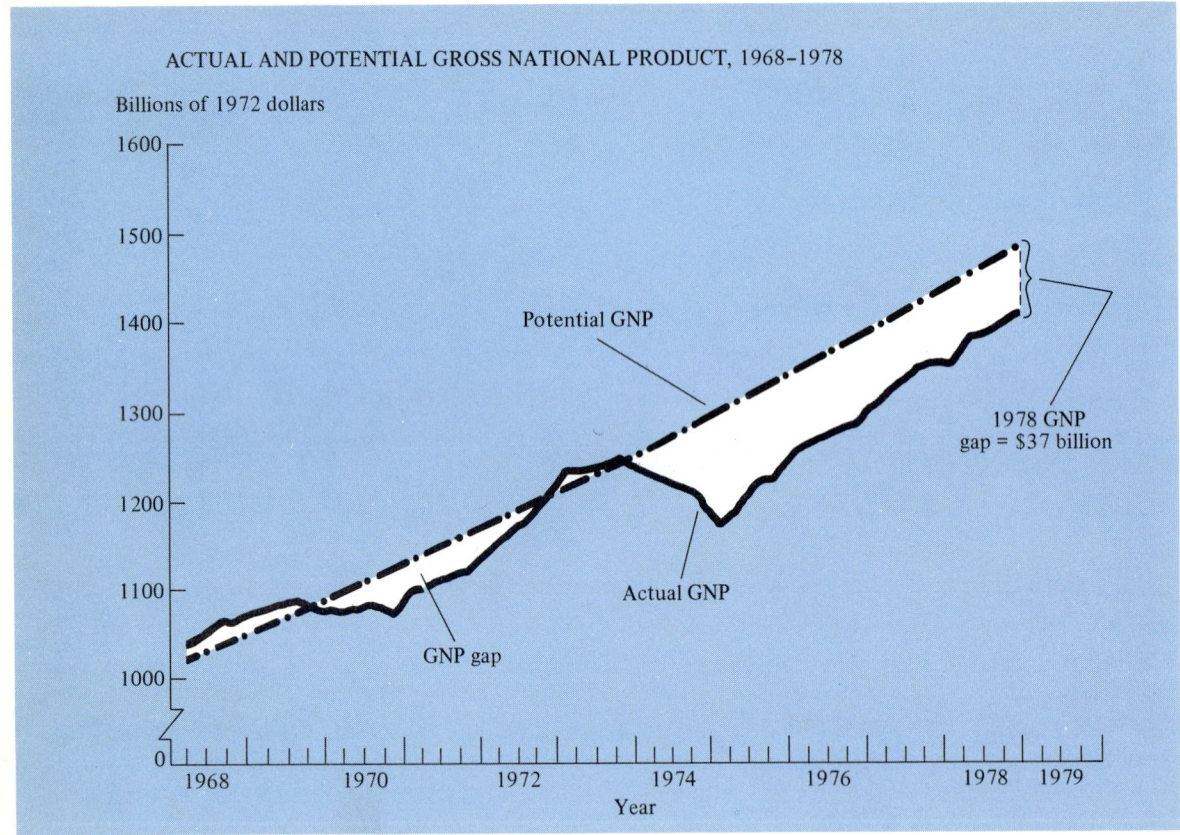

SOURCE: *The Economic Report of the President*, 1979.

Fig. 9.5
The straight line is a measure of potential GNP, the GNP we would achieve if there were full employment (96 percent employment, 4 percent unemployment) and if GNP continued to grow at an average rate. When actual GNP is below potential GNP, as it has been for the years between 1973 and 1978, productive resources are being wasted because of unemployment. This loss of potential output is referred to as the GNP gap. In 1968 and 1969 and at the beginning of 1972, the United States economy actually exceeded the full-employment level, indicated by the fact that the actual GNP line lies above the potential GNP line. In 1978, potential GNP was estimated at $1,423 billion. Actual real GNP in 1978 ($1,386 billion) was only about 2.5 percent below the potential level. This indicates a GNP gap of $37 billion.

The social costs

In order to arrive at a true picture of the *total* costs of unemployment, we should also examine the social costs exacted by the loss of jobs: the loss of skills and training; the disruption of family life; the loss of hope and self-esteem; the costs of the damage resulting from riots, demonstrations, fights, robberies, or other antisocial expressions of the anger and frustration of people who need jobs; the health costs that may be incurred by families of unemployed workers because of inadequate nutrition; and many other costs of resultant social, economic, and political disruption. Some of the programs that have been used to combat unemployment and limit its costs will be discussed in Chapter 17.

BUSINESS CYCLES

In the previous sections we have examined the concepts of unemployment and inflation and some of their effects on our economy. We will now discuss how unemployment and inflation and other economic activities tend to fluctuate over a period of time to form a cycle of business activity. We will also briefly discuss how economists attempt to discover the causes of business cycles.

The long-term trend of economic activity in the United States unquestionably has been upward, but this long-term growth, although constant, has not occurred in a smooth progression. Instead there have been sharp spurts of growth, periods of limited growth, and periods of actual downturn in growth. In order to get an accurate picture of such economic fluctuations, economists look at changes in aggregates such as industrial production, income, employment, prices, and many other factors. The changes we observe from these data are commonly called **business cycles**, *recurrent fluctuations in economic activity that vary in length and severity*. The term "cycle" is somewhat misleading because it implies a regularity in length and frequency, whereas the fluctuations in the United States economy have been erratic in occurrence and varying in size and duration. As a matter of convenience, however, we will use the term "business cycle" to refer to these economic fluctuations.

A simplified description

In its simplest form, a business cycle consists of a period of economic expansion, followed by a period of contraction. For descriptive purposes, the cycle is often divided into four phases, as

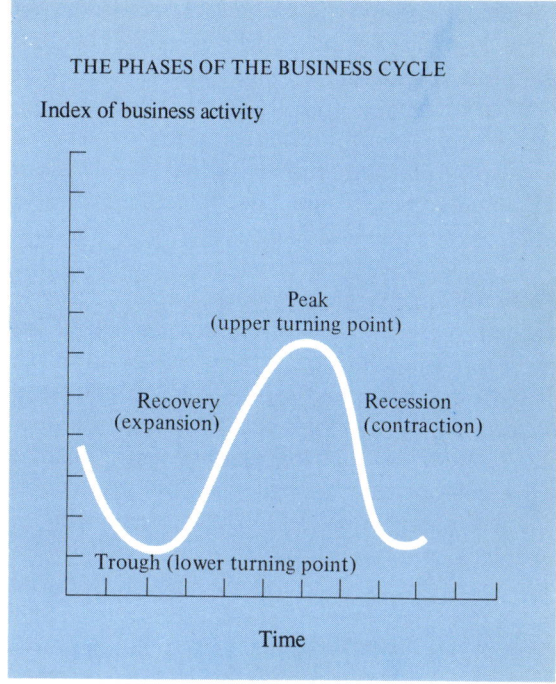

Fig. 9.6
This graph shows a simplified picture of the variations in business activity that occur throughout the business cycle. At the trough, there is substantial unemployment and unused capacity. When a change in any of the determinants of demand causes demand to increase, a turning point is reached and the recovery begins. Employment, income, and profits increase until full employment is achieved (the peak). Further increases in demand can only result in higher prices. Consumption and investment spending will begin to decline and the employment level drops as economic activity contracts during the recession. When the recession bottoms out (the trough), the cycle begins again.

shown in *Fig. 9.6:* (1) recovery or expansion; (2) peak or upper turning point; (3) recession or contraction; and (4) trough or lower turning point. During **recovery**, *employment, income, and profits begin to advance as business activity increases.*

Investment spending is particularly active during an expansionary period; interest rates are high and optimism is widespread. Since idle capacity and labor are available (the economy is just coming out of a recession) businesses find it easy to increase production without having to pay more for inputs. They do not have to raise prices, so inflation generally does not occur.

The recovery progresses, and eventually, the upper turning point or **peak** of the cycle is reached—*capacity is fully utilized, and full employment is achieved.* After a while, however, shortages of labor and capital develop and soon all factors of production become scarce. Because the economy is at full employment, further increases in demand for the factors of production will result only in higher prices, which will, in turn, lead to a fall in demand.

The peak is then followed by a **recession** —*consumption spending slows down and investment shows a sharp decline.* Profits fall as businesses are squeezed between rising costs of production and falling demand. Businesses begin to fail, and the level of employment drops. Economists differ in their precise definitions of recession and depression. Many claim that a depression is merely a more serious recession, and this is the definition we will use in this book. Harry Truman put it another way—a recession is when your neighbor is out of work; a depression is when you are out of work.

When the **trough** of the recession is reached, *there is substantial unemployment and unused capacity, little investment spending, low profits, little confidence, and downward pressure on some prices.*

When some change in any of the determinants of demand—a renewal of confidence, increased government spending, a war, depreciation of existing goods or depletion of inventories —causes demand to increase, a turning point is reached. Spending and business activity begin to pick up and once again a period of recovery occurs.

Seasonal variations

In studying fluctuations in business activity, we must be careful not to confuse seasonal variations with longer-term trends. Department-store sales figures provide an obvious example of the importance of making this distinction: a high sales volume for October, November, and December does not necessarily mean that retail trade is improving or that there is an upturn in the economy—department store sales always go up as Christmas approaches. In order to establish a meaningful trend, we would have to compare one year's seasonal figures with those for the comparable months in the preceding year.

To avoid such problems in identifying long-term cyclical patterns, economists adjust data on sales and production for seasonal variations. Adjusted figures, usually stated in terms of "an annual seasonally adjusted rate" or "an index number," are more reliable guides to cyclical fluctuation than are the raw data.

Variations in sales of durable and nondurable goods

When looking at business cycles, we must also keep in mind that within a given cycle, some parts of the economy fluctuate much more than others. For example, during contraction periods, a household's purchases of durable goods, such as cars or refrigerators, can be postponed, whereas the quantities of toothpaste and bread that the household buys are not likely to change very much. Similarly, when business is bad, a firm will defer construction of a new plant or replacement of its old welding machine. When business activity picks up, the businesses and families that postponed their durable purchases will feel confident enough to order them, and they also will have enough income to pay for them. In sales of nondurable goods, however, no similar surge will occur. No matter how much our income increases, we will not normally increase our use of products such as toothpaste. In other words, the sales of consumer durable goods and capital equipment tend to fluc-

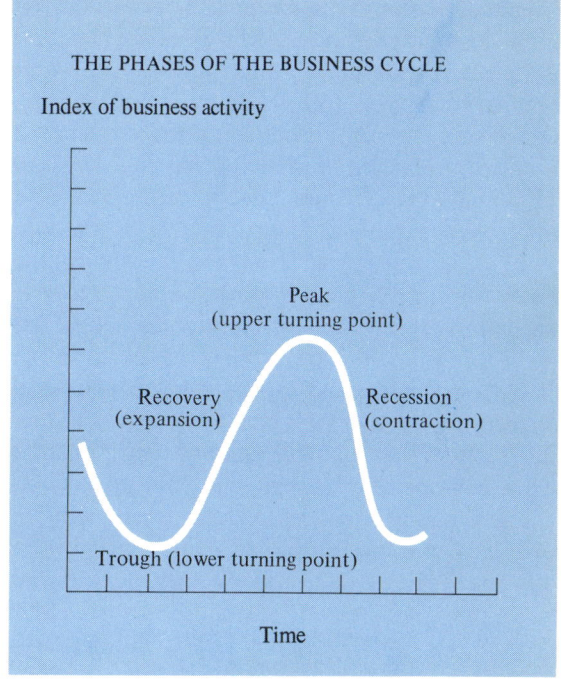

> **RECAP**
>
> Although the overall trend of economic growth in the United States has been steady, it is characterized by fluctuations in economic activity known as BUSINESS CYCLES. These cycles can vary in length and generally have four stages: recovery, peak, recession, and trough.
>
> Although many different theories have been proposed to explain how business cycles begin (money supply variations, random events, rational expectations) economists are not in agreement on the question of whether or not business cycles can be predicted.

tuate in very wide cycles, and industries that supply these goods and their raw materials—such as the steel industry—also show pronounced cyclical patterns.

Causes of business cycles

In general, economists have agreed that once a business cycle starts, certain internal factors take over, and each cycle then more or less follows a pattern of expansion and contraction. However, disagreement remains concerning what starts a cycle moving in the first place. Many different explanations have been proposed.

Nineteenth-century theories

Some nineteenth-century economists believed there was a relationship between business cycles and certain unusual phenomena, such as sunspots or phases of the planet Venus. In brief, the argument was that sunspots, for example, caused or signaled favorable weather conditions that led to abundant crops, which in turn increased rail traffic and stimulated new capital-equipment purchases, increased production of coal, and so on. Although such a theory may strike us as naive, we cannot ignore the real economic implications of the weather-crop relationship. For example, abnormally low rainfall in India in 1972 and late frost in the United States corn belt in 1974 caused widespread economic repercussions.

Another nineteenth-century theory held that business cycles are due to overproduction and underconsumption. During periods of prosperity, this theory argued, the quantity of goods supplied to the market tends to increase, but because of maladjustments in the distribution of wealth, the amount spent on consumer goods does not increase to the same extent. The wealthy don't buy the excess goods because they spend a relatively small proportion of their total incomes on consumer goods, and the poor don't have the money to buy the excess goods. Therefore, available goods exceed the quantity demanded, production slows down, unemployment increases, prices fall, and a recession occurs. According to this theory, the contraction would continue until population growth caused the demand for consumer goods to catch up with productive capacity, but, because of maldistribution of income, the cycle would then repeat itself.

This theory is also inadequate: first, in reality, the wealthy spend more of their incomes than the theory suggests; moreover, the progressive income- and estate-taxing policies of the United States government have helped to redistribute wealth in ways unknown in earlier periods.

Twentieth-century theories

Milton Friedman is the latest in a long line of economists who have claimed that it is disturbances in the money supply and bank credit that cause business cycles. He maintains that any abrupt and drastic change in the money supply can initiate a cycle. R. G. Hawtrey, a British economist of an earlier period, also believed that sharp changes in the supply of money constitute the main source of fluctuations in economic activity.

Other theories about the causes of the business cycle have attributed major fluctuations to technological change brought on by new inventions like the spinning jenny, the vacuum tube, or the transistor. One such theory was proposed by the Russian economist, Kondratieff, who believed that the economy moved in cycles of 40 to 50 years, triggered by significant technological innovations such as the invention of the railroad, electricity, and the vacuum tube. In an elaboration on this theme, Alvin Hansen suggested in the 1930s that the United States had repeatedly been able to pull out of recessions in the past because of the existence of a "frontier" of one kind or another—a new horizon to explore, whether geographical or technical—that provided the stimulus for a new round of expansion.

According to still another school of thought, many business cycles are initiated by random events, such as wars or important political developments. Adherents of this theory point out that the United States did not recover from the Depression of the 1930s until it experienced the surge in demand that accompanied World War II. A recent example of economic change triggered by a random event was the Arab states' oil embargo in late 1973, which was followed by sharp rises in fuel prices and extensive repercussions in all sectors of international economic activity.

Recently, another approach to understanding changes in economic activity has been suggested by members of the "rational-expectations" school of thought. They contend that by observing the economy over time, society as a whole is able to rationally predict the effects of government policy. In doing this, their changing expectations cause them to adjust their behavior, weakening or even eliminating the government's desired effect. This will be discussed further when we explore the policies that the government has at its disposal.

Can we forecast business cycles?

The difficult question of which techniques, if any, are the most useful in predicting changes in the business cycle is unresolved. Some economists believe that indicators of economic activity such as the growth rate of the money supply, the level of government spending, the number of housing starts, or many other factors can provide a hint of the economy's direction. Take, for example, housing starts. As the level of housing construction increases, we usually expect an increased demand for skilled labor (equipment operators, carpenters), raw materials, and tools. We also expect that expenditures on consumer goods will increase and that such an increase in aggregate demand will be felt throughout the economy. Consequently, the number of housing starts has the potential to predict future economic activity. Other indicators that are used to gauge where we are in the business cycle are the size of inventories, consumer debt, and the level of unemployment. Which of these or the other numerous economic indicators are the most informative and/or how they should be interpreted are far from settled issues. As we study further in the area of macroeconomics, we will better understand the difficulty in predicting or forecasting economic events.

Whatever the cause or causes of a business cycle may be, it appears that economists and government planners should direct their efforts to developing efficient, fast-acting techniques for controlling the effects. Thus, once a cycle starts, the most dangerous element of the expansion phase—inflation—and of the contraction period—unemployment—can be limited. In the next few chapters we will see what tools the government can use to affect the level of economic activity, and will discuss the problems the government has had in moderating recent fluctuations in the United States.

Summary

■ Two of the major objectives of current macroeconomic policy are the full employment of resources and the maintenance of relatively stable prices. This chapter examines the causes and consequences of the two major dangers to these goals—inflation and labor unemployment—and introduces the basic outlines of business cycles.

■ Inflation (a general rise in the level of prices) in the product market is usually accompanied by a rise in prices in the resource market, although the actual process tends to be very uneven. The rate of inflation is measured by the Consumer Price Index and by the various Producer Price Indexes, although each of these has limitations; economists prefer the implicit price deflator for measuring real GNP as the most comprehensive indicator. Demand-pull inflation occurs when consumer demand is greater than the current productive capacity of the economy; cost-push inflation occurs when the costs of production (profits and/or resource prices) increase. Both types of inflation may happen simultaneously, and government activity may contribute to both types. While all economists agree that extreme hyperinflation can be disastrous for an economy, some economists think that a relatively low level of inflation may actually stimulate economic growth.

■ The costs of inflation, especially when inflation is not correctly anticipated, include the redistribution of income upward from the relatively poor to the relatively affluent, the curtailment of production through decreased saving, and the channeling of resources into such nonproductive activities as speculation.

■ A certain amount of frictional unemployment (resulting from functional imperfections in the labor market) and structural unemployment (resulting from technological change and other developments in the structure of the economy) is seen by economists as almost inevitable. Cyclical unemployment, linked to changes in the level of economic activity, is a more serious concern. Measurements of the unemployment rate may overlook those who have become discouraged from seeking jobs and not take into account those who are underemployed. The costs of unemployment go beyond the economic loss in reduced production, income, and GNP; there are also important social costs, which may range from lowered self-esteem to poor health to antisocial expressions of anger and frustration.

■ Business cycles—recurrent fluctuations in economic activity—are described as occurring in four phases: recovery, peak recession, and trough, followed by renewed recovery. In such cycles, the durable goods sector shows wider variations than the nondurable goods sector. Economists currently offer a number of explanations for the persistence of business cycles: abrupt changes in the money supply, major technological changes, random (noneconomic) events, and people's expectations of future government policy.

Key Terms

inflation
deflation
Consumer Price Index
Producer Price Indexes
implicit price deflator (GNP deflator)
demand-pull inflation
cost-push inflation
hyperinflation
creeping inflation
unemployment rate
frictional unemployment
structural unemployment
cyclical unemployment
GNP gap
business cycles
recovery
peak
recession
trough

Review & Discussion

1. Why are full employment and price stability the two major goals for our economy? Why is it sometimes difficult to achieve both goals simultaneously?

2. What are the limitations of the CPI as a measure of the rate of inflation? What are the limitations of the various Producer Price Indexes? Why would economists prefer the GNP deflator as an index?

3. Explain the difference between demand-pull and cost-push inflation. How might government economic activity contribute to each type of inflation?

4. Why do some economists argue that a low level of "creeping inflation" may actually be beneficial to an economy? What are the objectives to this view?

5. How does inflation have the effect of redistributing income upwards?

6. Economists generally assume that a certain amount of frictional and structural unemployment is inevitable, and that 96 percent employment is a realistic figure for "full" employment. Is this an acceptable assumption? What steps might be taken to reduce the impact of these types of unemployment?

7. Official unemployment figures do not measure the underemployment rate—the number of workers who are employed in jobs significantly below their potential skill or income level. How widespread do you think underemployment is?

8. What are some of the social costs of unemployment? How important are they compared to the direct economic costs?

9. Describe the phases of the business cycle. In what phase of the cycle do you think the United States economy is at this time? Why?

Application 6:
The Problem of Black Teenage Unemployment

When it comes to dealing with real people or groups of people (as opposed to textbook examples) who need jobs but do not have them, the causes of unemployment are not always easy to distinguish, and treatments to alleviate the problem are not always easy to prescribe. Consider, for example, the plight of the black teenage American.

As you can see from Fig. 1, unemployment among black youths in the United States has run considerably above that of white youths for the last 25 years, and it has been persistently high through good times as well as bad. During the economic downturns in 1960, 1970, and 1974, black teenagers on the unemployment lines outnumbered whites by about 2 to 1, but during the economic expansions in 1955, 1965-1966, and 1968-1969, the ratio was about the same.

About 25 years ago, the fraction of unemployed black youths was only 1 to 6. In the late 1970s, however, more than 1 young black person in every 3 was unemployed, compared with about 1 in 7 among whites, and over all, the ratio of

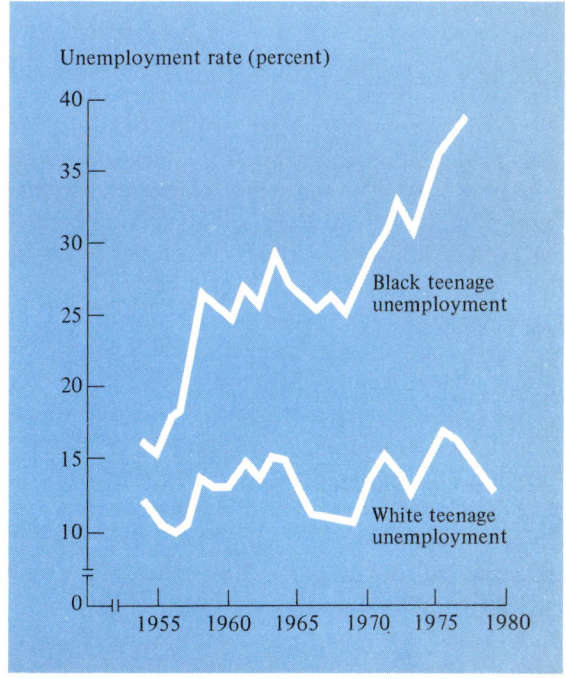

Figure 1

black unemployment to white has been rising fairly steadily from about 1.4 to 1 in 1954 to a record 2.6 to 1 in 1978.

That the problem has become more severe is not surprising in itself, but it *is* surprising that it has done so over the course of decades in which organized protest, court rulings, and new legislation have significantly reduced the discrimination to which black workers once were subjected. It has also become more severe in spite of a number of programs designed to remedy the situation.

Possible explanations for worsening black unemployment are numerous. One cause may be the swelling numbers of aliens, both legal and illegal, who are competing for the low-paid, unskilled jobs once held by blacks. In some cases, jobs are moving away from the blacks as more and more employers move out of the highly taxed central cities, where most urban blacks live, and into the suburbs where tax rates, and the numbers of black workers, are lower. There is also less need for unskilled workers in today's economy—particularly at the wages they would have to be paid—and, although the average educational level of blacks has been rising, test scores indicate that many who hold high school diplomas cannot read well or do simple business arithmetic. Some blacks feel that discrimination is still a factor. "Many black persons automatically do not apply for jobs in many companies because they feel they will be discriminated against," according to the director of an antipoverty agency in the Northeast. In addition, inflation and changing life-styles have brought other groups, once discriminated against, into the labor force. One such group is women, some of whom are displacing black teenagers in jobs that require no particular skills.

In addition, many economists feel that minimum-wage legislation is a most important cause of teenage unemployment. As Milton Friedman said in 1966:

> The shockingly high rate of unemployment among teenage Negro boys is largely a result of the present Federal minimum wage rate. And unemployment will be boosted still higher by the rise just enacted. Before 1956, unemployment among Negro boys aged 14 to 19 was around 8 to 11 percent, about the same as for white boys. Within two years after the legal minimum was raised from 75 cents to $1.00 an hour in 1956, unemployment among Negro boys shot up to 24 percent and among white boys to 14 percent. Both figures have remained roughly the same ever since. But I am convinced that, when it becomes effective, the $1.60 minimum will increase unemployment among Negro boys to 30 percent or more.*

As you can see in *Table 1,* the actual rate did exceed 20 percent in early 1971, and has climbed higher in the years since. The reason that minimum-wage legislation has aggravated the problem for black teenagers (as well as other workers with few skills) is that in the free market, people are paid wages according to the value of their contribution to a firm's income (revenue). Since workers with little or no skill add little to a firm's revenue, they should be paid little for their efforts. Increases in minimum wage make it unprofitable to hire unskilled black workers whose productivity is low at a wage higher than the value of their marginal product. Thus, since minimum wage laws prevent hiring low skilled workers at wages that truly reflect their contribution, a firm will not hire these workers at all, with the result that the unemployment rate among low skilled workers rises.

In the early 1960s, President John F. Kennedy noted that, "The trend in youth unemployment demands special concern and action. . . . Both lack of work opportunity and lack of suitable preparation are involved in this situation—and are combining to spread frustration among large numbers of young people." Since then, government spending on employment and training programs, most of them aimed at black

---

*Milton Friedman, "Minimum-Wage Rates," *Newsweek,* Sept. 26, 1966.

Table 1
Teenage employment history (1954–1978)*

	White teenage employment	White teenage unemployment	Percent unemployed	Black teenage employment	Black teenage unemployment	Percent unemployed	Ratio of black unemployment to white unemployment	Rate of change in prices
1954	3,079	422	12.1	396	78	16.5	1.4	1.4%
1955	3,226	371	10.3	417	78	15.8	1.5	2.2
1956	3,387	384	10.3	431	96	18.2	1.8	3.2
1957	3,373	401	10.6	407	96	19.1	1.8	3.4
1958	3,217	542	14.4	366	138	27.4	1.9	1.6
1959	3,475	525	13.1	363	128	26.1	2.0	2.2
1960	3,701	575	13.4	428	138	24.4	1.8	1.7
1961	3,692	669	15.3	414	158	27.6	1.8	0.9
1962	3,774	580	13.3	420	141	25.1	1.9	1.8
1963	3,850	708	15.5	403	176	30.4	2.0	1.5
1964	4,076	708	14.8	441	165	27.2	1.8	1.6
1965	4,562	703	13.4	475	169	26.2	2.0	2.2
1966	5,176	651	11.2	544	185	25.4	2.3	3.3
1967	5,113	635	11.0	569	204	26.5	2.4	2.9
1968	5,195	644	11.0	585	195	25.0	2.3	4.5
1969	5,508	660	10.7	609	193	24.0	2.2	5.0
1970	5,568	871	13.5	573	235	29.1	2.2	5.4
1971	5,662	1,010	15.1	533	248	31.7	2.1	5.1
1972	6,158	1,017	14.2	564	284	33.5	2.4	4.1
1973	6,602	950	12.6	634	275	30.2	2.4	5.8
1974	6,768	1,099	14.0	635	311	32.9	2.4	9.7
1975	6,452	1,406	17.9	594	347	36.9	2.1	9.6
1976	6,683	1,356	16.9	586	345	37.1	2.2	5.2
1977	7,020	1,275	15.4	590	367	38.3	2.5	5.9
1978	7,312	1,178	13.9	669	381	36.3	2.6	7.4

*Employment and unemployment totals are in thousands. The measure of rate of change in prices is the GNP implicit price deflator.

youths, has risen to an annual level of about $1.5 billion, and yet the situation today is worse than ever.

Some argue that the lack of progress is a matter of too little aid too late and that only greatly expanded training programs can reverse the trend of rising unemployment among black youths. Others call for better management and supervision of existing programs, contending that all too often the job-training funds are not spent on teenagers who need work, or are not properly managed. Some critics have suggested that future funding for employment and training programs be tied to their effectiveness. Only those programs whose graduates actually find jobs and keep them would be given money to continue.

APPLICATION 6: THE PROBLEM OF BLACK TEENAGE UNEMPLOYMENT

The problem of black teenage unemployment is a severe and difficult one which deserves the attention of those who establish economic policies. The costs to American society are high, not only in terms of lost economic production and increased welfare and social service expenditures, but also in terms of social disruptions including loss of self-esteem, discouragement and hopelessness, disruption of family life, and higher crime rates.

Questions for discussion

☐ The year 1972 was a relatively mild one for inflation—the general level of prices climbed only 4.1 percent, the slowest rate since 1967. Yet black teenage unemployment was at a peak that year. How can you account for that?

☐ What are the social and economic implications of high unemployment among black teenagers?

☐ Government training and employment programs to improve the level of black teenage unemployment have, for the most part, failed. What possible explanations can you think of for this failure? What types of programs might be more effective? Why?

Chapter 10

Total Spending: The Consumption and Investment Components

What to look for in this chapter

What determines the level of consumption and investment spending?

How is the spending and saving of households related to income? To other factors?

What factors influence business investment in plant and equipment? In inventories? In residential construction?

What is the accelerator theory?

What factors tend to stabilize the level of investment?

How are investment decisions related to the level of income?

In Chapter 9, we found that an important goal of a capitalist economy is to achieve full employment of its resources in a way that is compatible with a reasonable degree of price stability and with maintenance of the natural-resource base. In this chapter we will look at some of the mechanisms that determine the levels of output and employment in the American economy. Much of our discussion will focus on the theories of John Maynard Keynes, and where appropriate, we will compare Keynes's theories to those of classical economists.

In any market economy, it is the amount of total spending that determines output and therefore employment. This statement, which might be phrased "Demand creates its own supply," forms the basis of Keynesian theory, which focuses on the adequacy of demand as the factor determining a nation's economic health. Business firms will continue to operate at their long-run optimum output levels as long as they can sell their entire output at prices that allow them to earn a satisfactory profit. But if buyers will not purchase the entire output, then competition among suppliers will lead (at least in theory) to a lowered price. The change in price means that suppliers will cut back production, and the economy will move toward a new equilibrium level. And as production is reduced, the level of employment drops.

National income accounts break down GNP into four components: consumption, investment, government spending, and net exports. Here we will deal with the two components of private spending—consumption and investment. We will postpone our discussions of government spending and international trade for later chapters. The reason for doing so is to simplify our analysis and allow us to gain a basic understanding of total spending before we encounter the complications that arise when we consider the roles of government spending and international trade.

CONSUMPTION

Economists sometimes call the United States a consumption economy, and with good reason. The largest single component of GNP is household consumption.

Assuming that there are no governmental transactions whatsoever in our economy and that the business sector does not save, the net national product (NNP) would necessarily be equal to national income and, for that matter, to personal income and disposable income as well. (Review these terms in Chapter 8 to understand why this is true.) Or to put it another way, output always generates an equal value of income. Why, then, does not every level of output give rise to a level of spending sufficient to purchase all the goods and services produced? The answer lies in the fact that households may choose to save some money, rather than to spend their entire income. Remember that disposable income (DI) is composed of consumption (C) plus saving (S). $C + S$ always totals 100 percent of DI. Therefore, any saving is done at the cost of additional spending. Of course, the savings of households may eventually be utilized by businesses for investment purposes. But savers and investors are two different groups, each motivated by different factors. There is no reason to assume, therefore, that the amount that households wish to save will equal the amount that businesses wish to invest.

Household saving defined

In our analysis of the way household income is disposed of, it is necessary to use a very narrow definition of saving. We are interested only in the household saving that does not involve current expenditures. The purchase of durable goods, real estate, and valuable objects, such as paintings, might also be considered forms of household saving, because in each case the household sacrifices some measure of current expenditure to achieve an increased ability to spend or gain utility at a later date. But these forms of saving also involve current expenditures. Moreover, they are not available for business investment. There is no mechanism that enables the Eastman Kodak Company to borrow Elizabeth Taylor's diamond ring and use it to expand their business. Therefore, *in the context of income analysis,* **saving** *refers only to that portion of disposable income which is left over after current expenditures. It includes the cash reserves held by individuals in checking and savings accounts, the amount of insurance equity they own, and the corporate bonds they have purchased.*

Consumption and saving schedules

How does a household decide on its level of spending? Many factors influence this decision. For example, a household of 20 will spend more than a household of 2; a family with children that need braces will spend more than a family of the same size in which all the children have straight teeth. Although many factors help to determine the level of spending in a household, the most

Table 10.1
Consumption and saving schedule for a United States household (hypothetical data)

(1) Disposable income (DI)	(2) Consumption (C)	(3) Saving (S) DI−C	(4) Average propensity to consume (APC) $\frac{C}{DI}$	(5) Average propensity to save (APS) $\frac{S}{DI}$	(6) Marginal propensity to consume (MPC) $\frac{\text{change in } C}{\text{change in DI}}$	(7) Marginal propensity to save (MPS) $\frac{\text{change in } S}{\text{change in DI}}$
$ 2,000	$ 3,600	$ −1600	1.80	−.80	.60	.40
3,000	4,200	−1200	1.40	−.40	.60	.40
4,000	4,800	− 800	1.20	−.20	.60	.40
5,000	5,400	− 400	1.08	−.08	.60	.40
6,000	6,000	0	1.00	.00	.60	.40
7,000	6,600	400	.94	.06	.60	.40
8,000	7,200	800	.90	.10	.60	.40
9,000	7,800	1200	.87	.13	.60	.40
10,000	8,400	1600	.84	.16	.60	.40
11,000	9,000	2000	.82	.18	.60	.40
12,000	9,600	2400	.80	.20	.60	.40
13,000	10,200	2800	.78	.22	.60	.40
14,000	10,800	3200	.77	.23		

important is the size of its disposable income. A family committed to a savings program may spend somewhat less than its entire DI; a family that dissaves may spend more. But common sense and the available statistics tell us that spending is always closely linked to income and that the amount saved or dissaved is usually only a small part (5 to 10 percent) of DI.

The data that we have on the relationship between consumption and DI show a clear and persistent pattern. From statistics of the last decade, we can draw up a hypothetical **consumption schedule** for a typical household. *A consumption schedule shows the amounts a household plans to consume at each possible disposable income level at a specific point in time.* Such a schedule is shown in *Table 10.1*. As we have pointed out,

there are many factors influencing how much of its income a given household will actually decide to spend. But a consumption schedule assumes that all these other determinants of consumption remain unchanged; the only change is in the level of DI.

As you might expect, the relationship between disposable income and consumption is a direct one: as disposable income increases, consumption increases. Note, too, that households with a smaller disposable income spend proportionally more of that income than households with a larger disposable income.

Once we know the extent of consumption at each income level, we can calculate a number of other variables. A **saving schedule** *shows the amounts a household plans to save at each pos-*

sible disposable income level at a specific point in time. A saving schedule (shown in column 3 of *Table 10.1*) is easily figured by deducting consumption from disposable income; the difference is the amount saved.

Average and marginal propensities
By dividing consumption by DI, we get a fraction that represents *the percentage of a given total income that is consumed.* This is called the **average propensity to consume** (C/DI = APC). For example, when a family's income is $6000, it will, on the average, consume 100 percent of its DI. At the level of $14,000 annual income, the average household will consume only 77 percent of its income. The **average propensity to save**—*the percentage of a given total income that is saved*—can be calculated in a similar way, by dividing savings by DI: (S/DI = APS).

Although the average household consumes a certain percentage of its disposable income at any given point in time, it will not necessarily spend that same percentage of any future increase in income. *The proportion of new income devoted to consumption* is called the **marginal propensity to consume** (MPC). Expressed as a fraction,

$$\text{MPC} = \frac{\text{change in consumption}}{\text{change in income}}.$$

The fraction of new income saved is called the **marginal propensity to save** (MPS):

$$\text{MPS} = \frac{\text{change in saving}}{\text{change in income}}.$$

Because any increase in disposable income must go either to consumption or to saving, we know that

$$\text{MPC} + \text{MPS} = 1.$$

Thus the marginal propensity figures tell us how each additional dollar of income will be distributed between spending and saving.

If we look at column 4 of *Table 10.1* showing average propensity to consume, we can see that as income increases, the APC decreases; in other words, the larger a family's income, the smaller the percentage of total income that is devoted to consumption as income rises. But when we look at column 6 showing MPC, it appears that this household consumes about the same percentage of each income increment. When income increases from $2000 to $3000, the household consumes 60 percent of the increase. When income increases from $9000 to $10,000, the family still consumes 60 percent of the extra $1000.

It should be noted, however, that economists disagree as to whether MPC remains the same as income rises. The argument is that a poor household tends to spend all extra money on necessities and save none, whereas a more prosperous household may save some of their extra income. However, aggregate statistics show that the MPC and MPS remain about the same at all levels of income.

The consumption schedule leads us to two important conclusions. First, consumption varies directly with income level. Second, when income changes, the change in consumption is less than the change in income. Each of these facts has important implications for economic policy.

Aggregate consumption schedule
By using data from the national accounts of income and expenditure, we can construct a consumption schedule showing how much households *actually consumed and saved* at various levels of disposable income over a period of years. Although this aggregate schedule differs from the hypothetical consumption schedule for a typical household at a specific point in time, the basic relationships between consumption, saving, and disposable income remain much the same. As total disposable income goes up, so does the total amount of consumption. However, the *rate* of consumption begins to drop as the level of income increases.

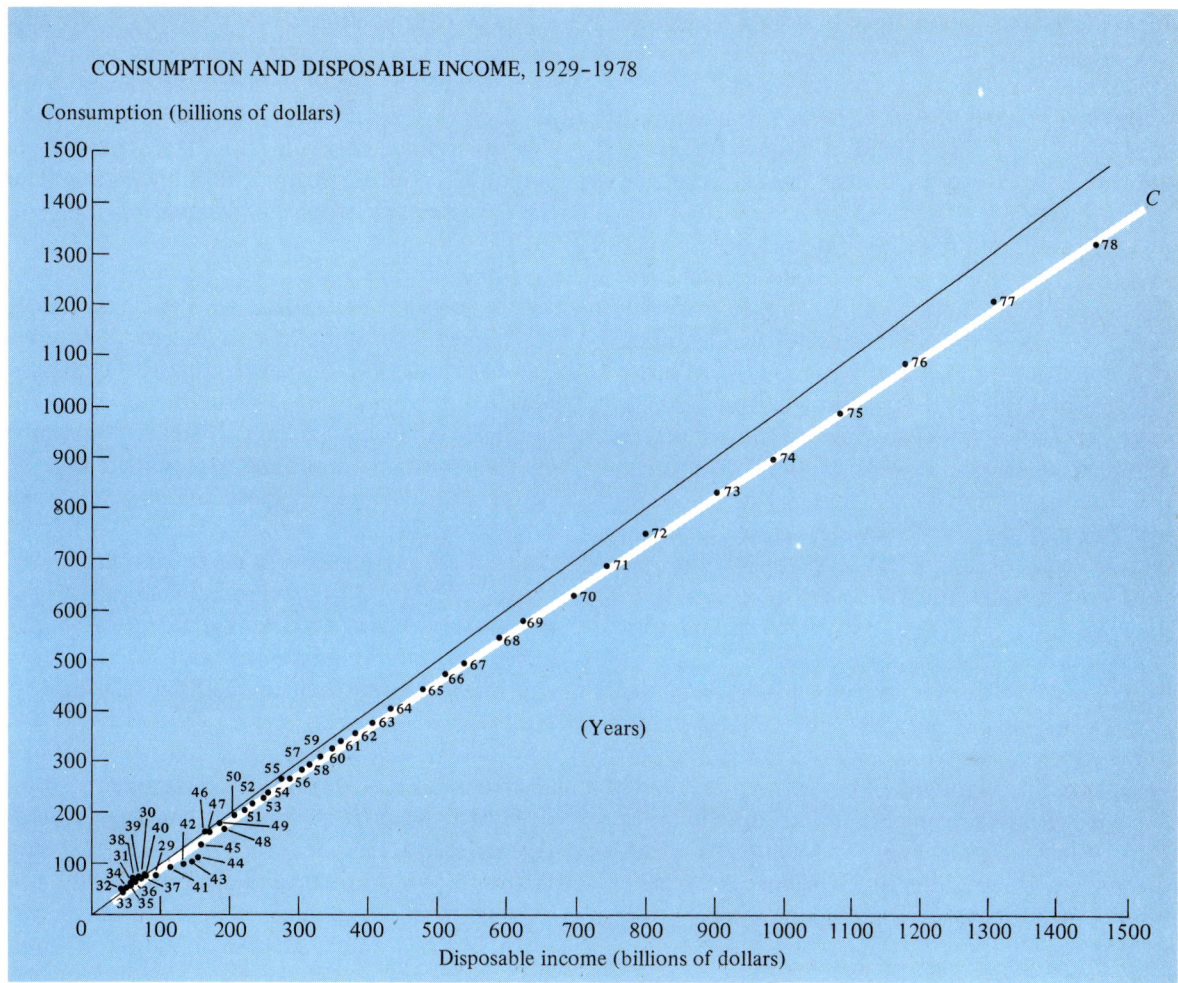

SOURCE: *Economic Report of the President,* January 1979.

Fig. 10.1
The black line is the 45-degree line, which is what we would get if consumption were to increase by the same absolute amount as the increases in disposable income. The white line is the actual consumption line based on real data; it is drawn through or near as many points on the graph as possible. At very low income levels, the consumption line is higher than the 45-degree line, whereas at higher income levels, it drops below the 45-degree line, demonstrating that the average propensity to consume declines as income increases.

In a two-sector economy (with government temporarily excluded) disposable income is exactly equal in value to the net national product, the measure of total production (before adding the capital consumption allowance). Therefore we can also say that as NNP rises, the rate of consumption decreases.

The long-run aggregate consumption schedule for our economy can also be expressed graphically (see *Fig. 10.1*). We plot consumption on the vertical axis and disposable income on the horizontal axis. Each point on the graph represents consumption and disposable income for the year indicated. The points are scattered and cannot actually be connected with a single unbroken line, but we can determine a kind of visual average by drawing a line that passes through or near the largest possible number of points.

If consumption at all income levels were equal to 100 percent of disposable income, the consumption function would go straight out at a 45-degree angle, the same distance at all points from the income (horizontal) axis as it is from the consumption (vertical) axis. But when we draw in this hypothetical 45-degree line, we can see that it differs from the actual consumption line plotted from our statistical data. Consumption expenditures are not always equal to DI. Instead, we see that dissaving occurs at low levels of DI, whereas saving takes place when DI is higher.

The distance between the actual consumption line, called a consumption-function, and the hypothetical 45-degree line is a measure of the extent of saving or dissaving. When the consumption function is above the 45-degree line, households have spent more than they earned; they have dissaved. When the consumption function lies below the 45-degree line, households have not spent all of their disposable income; they have saved.

Determinants of aggregate consumption schedules

As we have seen, the consumption schedule shows the relationship between level of income and the amount of money spent consuming the goods and services produced by business firms. Economists have isolated a number of factors that determine this schedule. A change in any of these determinants will mean a change in the entire schedule.

In a sense, aggregate consumption is the sum of all individual consumption. Whereas a market demand curve shows the relationship between quantity consumed and price, the aggregate consumption function relates quantity consumed and national income. For both market demand and aggregate consumption, the relationships assume that other factors are constant. Hence many of the determinants of aggregate consumption resemble the determinants of market demand.

Average size and age of households

The average age of households is one determinant of aggregate consumption. A household that has just been established—newlyweds, for example—will tend to spend more on durable goods than a household unit that has been in existence for many years. The young family must accumulate a supply of furniture, dishes, appliances, and other household goods, whereas the older family has already made these purchases and needs only to replace things as they break or wear out. That is why businesses are so interested in appealing to what is called the "young adult" market; it is the group that does the most spending for many kinds of goods.

The average size of households is significant as well. The average size of households has been declining and in recent years it has dipped below three. Several reasons can be cited: a falling birthrate; a rising divorce rate; and the fact that as average personal income rises, more people can afford to live alone. One result is that a larger fraction of the breadwinner's income is left over after necessities are purchased, and therefore it may be saved rather than spent.

Stocks of durable goods

When the level of spending has been high for a period of several years, there is a tendency for the average propensity to consume to fall. Once families have already purchased many of the large items they want to own, they no longer seek to purchase certain durable goods. At every income level, more of disposable income will be allocated to saving. So prolonged prosperity in an economy may generate a trend away from high levels of consumption, and thus away from high levels of employment.

At the end of World War II, we saw the reverse situation. Production of many goods had been cut back or eliminated to allow for greater production of military goods; for example, during the war automobile factories were producing only tanks and other military vehicles. The stocks of consumer goods on hand were low, and as soon as the war was over, the market for durable goods was flooded with buyers. People consumed a much higher proportion of their income than they had consumed during the war, or than they would consume under normal circumstances.

Stocks of liquid assets

Statistical studies have shown that, other things being equal, rate of consumption is positively correlated with the amount of **liquid assets** owned by households. *Liquid assets include those assets—stocks, bonds, bank accounts, etc.—that can be converted relatively easily into cash*. One way to interpret this correlation between consumption and assets is to say that the ownership of these assets makes consumers feel more secure financially. Another interpretation is that much of the demand for savings has already been satisfied—that is, consumers have already saved as much as they want to save.

Level of private debt

When households have already borrowed substantial amounts of money, so that a significant portion of current income is going toward installment payments and other contractual obligations, consumers become less willing to spend. If the level of private indebtedness is very high, households may prefer to reduce current consumption so they can repay existing loans. Conversely, if the level of private indebtedness is low, households may feel free to increase consumption by purchasing on credit.

Consumer expectations

If consumers expect that inflation or shortages will occur, they may decide to accelerate their spending to take advantage of current low prices or large supplies. They will make purchases of durable goods, such as television sets and dishwashers, immediately, rather than postponing them until later, when they fear they will have to pay more or do without. Similarly, an expectation of dropping prices, or available surpluses in many consumer goods will cause buyers to delay their purchases.

However, the observation that demand sometimes *declines* when prices are expected to rise may demonstrate a new sophistication in many households. Rising prices not only make goods more expensive but may reduce real incomes (dollar income adjusted for reduced purchasing power of the dollar) as well. Hence, even though a household realizes that things may cost more next year, they may fear lower real incomes if money salary does not rise as quickly as the price level. In this case, expectation of lower income may result in *lower* demands, despite expectations of price increases.

Cultural attitudes

In a society that attaches a high value to the personal quality of thrift, people will be motivated to save a significant portion of their income. Some cultures equate money in the bank with religious virtue. Throughout much of America's history, savings have been considered evidence of personal respectability and sound judgment. When saving is surrounded by so many favorable connotations, the act of saving serves not only to increase future ability to consume, but also to "purchase" current satisfaction.

Many people believe that contemporary American values encourage consumption rather than saving. For instance, many Americans would assign a higher social status to a person who buys a $15,000 car than to a person with a $15,000 savings account. Young men believe that they will become popular with girls if they buy the right suit, wear the right cologne, and drive the right car. They do not attempt to impress a date by telling her how much of last year's salary they were able to save. In a classic book on the subject, *The Theory of the Leisure Class,* written in 1899, economist and social critic Thorstein Veblen pointed out that Americans rely on "conspicuous consumption" to demonstrate their personal value to others. Such a social climate encourages households to allocate a large portion of their incomes to consumption, particularly to the consumption of goods having snob appeal.

Concept of permanent income

The discussion of the relationship between consumption and income that we have outlined here is based largely on the work of John Maynard Keynes. He demonstrated the relationship by comparing income with expenditure in a given calendar year. According to Keynes's findings, the relationship between income and expenditure is based on current income.

In the years since Keynes published his findings, other economists have made empirical studies of the relationship between consumption and income. Some of these studies suggest that it might be more meaningful to relate consumption to **permanent income.** Permanent income *refers to a worker's average income level throughout his or her life.* Presumably, it could be calculated exactly by dividing the number of years worked into lifetime income, adjusted for changes in the price level. But of course, no worker who is currently employed knows exactly what his or her permanent income will be; we can only make an informed guess as to what we will be earning in the years to come.

Nevertheless, most people are able to judge whether their current income is greater than, smaller than, or about the same as the income they will receive in the foreseeable future. For example,

> **RECAP**
>
> The first major component of total private spending is HOUSEHOLD CONSUMPTION.
>
> The most important determinant of individual household consumption is the size of disposable income. The relationship between disposable income and consumption is a direct one.
>
> The major determinants of aggregate consumption are average size and age of households, availability of durable goods, amount of liquid assets held, level of private indebtedness, consumer expectations, and cultural attitudes.

a college-educated young woman of 24 who works as an administrative assistant to the personnel manager of a large corporation and earns $10,000 a year can reasonably expect that her salary will increase significantly in the future. Hence she may decide to consume as if she were already at a higher income level—buying a condominium, purchasing an expensive car on credit, taking out a bank loan for a vacation in Europe. On the other hand, a salesman of construction equipment who gets a $7000 bonus because he finally landed the huge account he has been after for five years, knows that he cannot expect to get a bonus that large every year. Therefore he may decide to save a very large percentage of the bonus rather than spend it in immediate consumption.

Consuming on the basis of permanent income is the way that individuals average out their incomes. In years when their income is unusually low, they consume at a higher-than-normal rate, and may even dissave. When their income is higher than usual, they save a large percentage of the additional income. This kind of averaging prevents extreme fluctuations in the household's standard of living and avoids the consequent social and emotional disorientation.

Many economists feel that the marginal propensity to consume permanent income is the same at all income levels. If this is really true, about 80¢ of each additional dollar of permanent income will be allocated to consumption and 20¢ to saving at each and every level of permanent income.

Permanent income may also account for another phenomenon that economists have noticed about the consumption function. When aggregate consumption schedules are compared over a long period of time (say 30 or 40 years), it can be seen that they are actually very stable. The rates of saving and spending were about the same 10 years ago as they are today, and they will probably be the same 10 years hence. Only World War II and the Depression have caused any noticeable change in consumption and saving schedules. The reason for this marked stability of the consumption function may well be that the long-range concept of permanent income is more influential regarding decisions to save and spend than is the more volatile and short-run current income.

INVESTMENT

The second major component of private spending is investment. Recall from Chapter 8 that investment has two definitions. We are referring here to the more common meaning: the purchase of durable goods or financial properties.

The classical economists of the eighteenth century, including Adam Smith, believed that the amount of investment would always be equal to the amount of savings. Although they recognized tendencies toward imbalance, they theorized that interest rates served as the mechanism that would ensure that all private savings would be used by businesses for investment. Keynes argued that this hypothesis was fallacious; savings does not automatically equal investment because savers and investors are essentially two different groups, motivated by different factors, and will therefore respond differently to a given set of economic conditions. In this section, we will discuss some of the determinants of capital investment in our economy.

If we compare GNP statistics over a period of years, we will notice that investment is the most volatile component of GNP. There is a recurrent pattern of sudden, rapid increases in investment for a few years and then a marked decline for a few years. As we look at some of the various factors that affect business investment, we will see some of the reasons for this instability. On the other hand, certain factors help to smooth out the extremes of fluctuation, and we must be careful not to overstate the degree of instability found in investment spending.

The three major kinds of investment are business purchases of new plant and equipment, changes in business inventories, and residential construction. We shall discuss each item in turn.

Business purchases of plant and equipment

Business purchases of new plant and equipment constitute by far the largest category of investment spending.

Calculating profitability

How do business firms decide on their capital investment commitments? As a starting point, we can assume that businesses invest whenever it seems likely that their investment will be profitable. This means that a business firm will estimate the additional revenue that it can expect to receive as a result of any investment expenditure. If the firm then divides this figure by the estimated cost of the investment project, it can calculate its prospective rate of return. By comparing the rate of return on any proposed capital investment with the current rate of interest (the rate of return the firm would receive by lending funds in the market instead of investing them on additional plant and

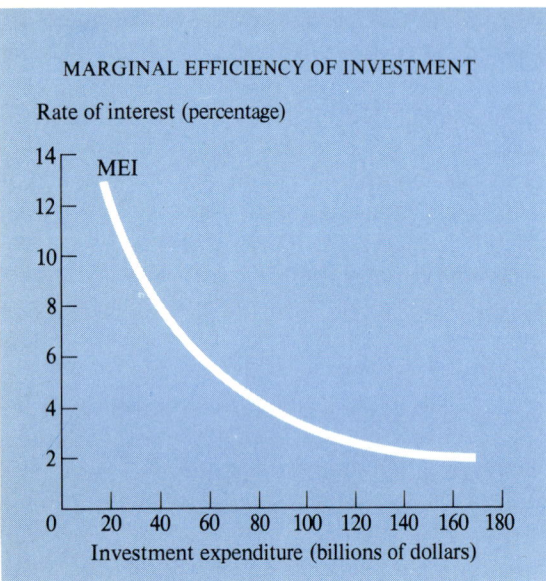

Fig. 10.2
We can expect more investment to occur when the interest rates drop, because the costs of acquiring capital for expansion are lower, and therefore potential profits are higher. In addition, low interest rates mean that there is less incentive to invest in financial securities rather than real capital goods, since the rate of return in the financial market is low.

equipment), it can decide whether the investment will be profitable or unprofitable.

In general, we can see that a business firm will invest if the estimated rate of return on the capital good is greater than the present market rate of interest. Thus, as the market rate of interest declines, other things being equal, total investment spending throughout the economy will increase. This inverse relationship between the interest rate (the opportunity cost of investment spending) and the aggregate level of investment demand can be presented graphically as a marginal efficiency of investment (MEI) curve (see Fig. 10.2).

Raising funds

To some extent, businesses face a budget constraint in deciding how much investment spending they can undertake at any given time. No firm has unlimited credit or borrowing power; yet businesses have many ways to raise investment funds when a good opportunity to invest presents itself. They can issue more stock in the company; they can sell bonds; they can borrow from banks. As long as the executives of the company can convince savers and bank managers that the investment program is sound and profitable, they can probably raise the money. Of course, there are always costs attached to any external means of raising money for an investment project—usually the rate of interest that must be paid on the borrowed funds. If a business is forced to borrow money to finance an investment project, the cost of the project will become greater, and thus its prospective rate of return will decline as interest rates rise.

We have said that the size of investment expenditures is determined by its estimated profitability; the higher the prospective rate of return on investment projects, the greater investment spending will be. But this explanation really begs the question of what factors influence a business firm's calculation of the prospective rate of return on any capital investment. Let us now explore some of these factors to understand the considerations that actually underlie business investment decisions.

Factors influencing business investment decisions

Innovation and technological advance

Businesses searching for ways to cut down their costs of production are quick to adopt technological advances in production methods. If the same output can be produced from a smaller quantity of raw materials, or produced from cheaper materials, or assembled faster, the business firm will save money. So investment in the most up-to-date equipment always looks very profitable to the business firm.

An even more important stimulus to business investment is the invention or discovery that creates a whole new product or industry. The invention of the steam engine, coupled of course with the demand for transportation services, started the railroad industry and stimulated enormous investment activity. Ambitious entrepreneurs organized railroad companies; they also set up companies to make the steel rails, to cut the wooden ties, to manufacture the passenger cars, to build the freight yards and passenger terminals, and to provide meals for hungry passengers. Some of America's largest corporations today owe their start (and much of their prosperity) to the spurt of investment spending which the innovation of the steam engine helped to stimulate.

The invention of the automobile stimulated another boom in investment. In recent years the creation of several new industries, such as the plastics industry and the computer industry, has also stimulated investment.

When there is substantial innovational investment, the forces of economic expansion are very strong. The thrust of the new industry (which creates new jobs and new profits) sweeps much of the economy along in its wake. Even industries unrelated to the new one invest and expand. But eventually, the new industry is established, its rate of growth drops back to a more normal level, and most of the initial investment is over. Then investment by all industries shows a decline, directly attributable to the decreasing growth rate in the new industry, and expansion is either slowed or reversed. The rise and fall of innovation investment is probably the major cause of fluctuation in the level of total investment.

Stocks of fixed business capital

In determining its methods of production, a firm will carefully consider the various ways it can combine input resources to manufacture its product. If labor is very cheap, it may be less costly to use only a few simple machines and many workers. When labor costs are high, the firm will choose to substitute machines for workers where possible.

Once a production method has been chosen, managers of the business will know approximately how much fixed capital they need for each unit of output. Therefore they will invest only until they reach the point at which they have enough capital goods to produce the amount of output they are planning to supply to the market. Once this investment has been made, they will no longer buy capital goods, except when they need to replace the existing stock or when they want to change their methods of production. Of course, the company might decide at a future date to supply a larger quantity of goods to the market; at that time, it would once again begin to invest.

Expectations of future market behavior

Investment involves expectations about the future. We have said that businesses invest because they believe that the venture will be profitable. Investment is essentially a long-range action. A business may plan its expansion in 1980, raise the necessary funds in 1981, issue the contracts and start building in 1982, and have its new building operating at full production by the middle of 1984. So executives must rely on estimates—their own and those of professional trendwatchers—of future market performance, to decide when and how much to invest.

By and large, a business's expectations are not subject to wide fluctuations between optimism and pessimism. Yet it is certainly true that expectations can change suddenly in response to certain kinds of events. A slowdown in new residential construction, a sharp rise in medical costs, an increase in the rate of business failures—any of these can cause a business to lose confidence in the long-range prospects for economic expansion.

It is important to remember that much investment is based on the hope of economic *growth*. A healthy economy (that is, one that is operating at full production without significant price instability) is not enough in itself to stimulate new investment. Business executives usually invest only to take advantage of new cost-cutting methods of production, or when they believe that the economy, or their particular segment of it, is going to expand. They hope for more buyers in the markets and more items demanded at each price level. Since growth is a future-oriented activity, it is clear that future expectations will greatly influence the actions of investors.

Current business profits
The current profit rate of a business firm is a factor in its decisions about investment. One reason for this is that profits can serve as investment funds. Most firms retain some part of current profits, rather than distribute every last penny as dividends to investors. In a strongly growth-oriented company, in fact, management may retain all profits for investment. There are a number of benefits to a firm that is providing all or most of its investment capital from saved profits. There will not be any new issue of stock to dilute the value of stock outstanding; also, the company does not have to disclose its plans for achieving a more competitive position to any outsiders, so there is less danger of other firms jumping in to pursue similar ventures. Most important, the firm does not have to borrow money from banks and bondholders, and it thus has no interest to pay. This lowers the cost of investment, increasing the possible margin of profit on the intended investment. Of course, there is also a cost involved when a company retains some of its profits. That cost is the potential income forgone by not investing that money in interest-earning assets.

Profits play yet another role in investment, in that the rate of current profit may influence future expectations of profitability. It is the expectation of future profits, not current profits, that, in the final analysis, stimulates investment spending. There are times when current profits may be low, yet expectations of future profitability may be high, and vice versa. But on the whole, current profits are frequently a fairly reliable indicator of the potential for future profits.

If the firm is presently selling its entire output at a good profit, it has reason to believe that the costs of expansion could be readily justified by the extra revenue from the additional production. A high rate of profit throughout an entire industry will encourage the formation of new companies in that field. This is one of the ways in which the price system acts to allocate resources for the production of goods and services that get the most dollar votes. A sustained record of high profits may also give a company the financial cushion that makes risk taking seem permissible. Moreover, it has a psychological effect, giving both the firm's management and the potential investors a feeling of optimism and confidence.

Level of business activity: accelerator theory
Substantial increases in investment spending occur only when the level of business activity is *growing*, whether the actual level is high or low. A leveling off of growth, even at a very high level, will bring a decline in investment spending. The following illustration explains why this is so.

The Victory Hosiery Company: a case in point The Victory Hosiery Company requires one knitting machine costing $10,000 in order to produce $100,000 worth of pantyhose a year. In year 1 the company has sales of $2 million and owns 20 machines, purchased at the rate of two a year over the last 10 years. Since machines wear out in 10 years, there is a steady replacement demand for two new machines a year. In year 2, however, demand for Victory pantyhose increases by 10 percent to $2.2 million. To supply the additional $200,000 worth of merchandise, Victory will need two extra machines, or a total of four—two for replacement and two for the new business (see *Table 10.2*). In other words, although demand for

Table 10.2
The accelerator principle

| | | | Machines purchased | | | |
Year	Sales (millions of dollars)	Total machines needed	Replacement demand	New demand	Total	Gross investment
1	$2.0	20	2	0	2	$20,000
2	2.2	22	2	2	4	40,000
3	2.4	24	2	2	4	40,000
4	2.4	24	2	0	2	20,000
5	2.2	22	0	0	0	0

its pantyhose has increased only 10 percent, the company's investment spending must double!

If sales in year 3 again increase by $200,000, Victory will once again need four new machines. But in year 4, sales remain constant at the year 3 level of $2.4 million. Observe that Victory is not having a disastrous year, because sales continue at an all-time high; growth has merely leveled off. Nevertheless, Victory's need for new machines drops from four to two, because the company now needs only to replace worn-out machines, not to build new capacity.

New let us suppose that Victory's sales in year 5 decline by $200,000, or back to a total of $2.2 million. In earlier years Victory required two new machines each year to replace those that had worn out. In year 5, however, the company starts off with excess capacity. It owns 24 machines but needs only 22 to fill its orders for $2.2 million of pantyhose. Therefore it will buy no new machines at all.

This example illustrates the **accelerator theory** of business investment. *This is the concept that investment spending is closely related to changes in consumption. An increase or decrease in consumption spending will induce a change in investment that is proportionally even greater than the change in consumption.* In our example, new orders for pantyhose must keep growing if investment—purchases of new machines—is merely to remain constant. (Note that in year 3 Victory bought the same number of machines as in year 2, although sales had increased by $200,000.) As soon as sales level off—as they did for Victory in year 4—new investment drops off precipitously. From the point of view of the supplier of the machinery involved, a recession took place in year 4, since the supplier's sales (if Victory's activity for that year was representative) were reduced by 50 percent merely because pantyhose sales stopped growing.

The accelerator theory explains why investment spending fluctuates so greatly within business cycles. During expansionary periods, a small increase in consumption demand results in a substantial increase in investment demand and investment spending. As long as consumption is growing, investment spending will continue. However, once consumption levels off, investment will drop sharply, and the seeds of a recession are sown.

> **RECAP**
>
> The second major component of private spending is INVESTMENT. The three major kinds of investment are business purchases of new plant and equipment, changes in business inventories, and residential construction.
>
> Determinants of business investment include analysis of expected profitability, money-saving technological discoveries, stocks of available capital, expectations of market behavior, and level of current profits.

Accelerator theory and business cycles The accelerator theory tells us that investment spending will decline substantially as soon as consumption spending stops growing. But we are left with another question to answer. What causes consumption spending to level off? The economy—particularly one starting out from a low level with underutilized labor and capacity—will expand until productive resources are fully employed, and then production, national income, and consumption will stabilize (stop growing). Once consumption growth slows, investment spending drops, and a downturn is under way.

The accelerator theory explains the end of a boom and the beginning of a recession in terms of the slowdown in consumption growth that comes with full employment, and the sharp decline in investment spending in which it results. The accelerator theory can also be used to explain turnarounds at the bottom of an economic decline. We saw how the Victory Hosiery Company stopped *all* investment spending when consumption spending declined only slightly, because it needed neither new capacity to meet expanding demand, nor replacement capacity. This state of affairs will continue for some time, but eventually consumption will stabilize, equipment will begin to wear out, and Victory will be forced to buy *some* new machines if only to meet replacement demand. Thus investment spending will start once again; employment and income will rise, consumption spending will increase, and a new cycle of expansion will begin.

Inventory investment

Most producers of goods and services find it necessary to maintain some kind of inventory. Firms often buy resources in large quantities when prices are low, and manufacturers must keep on hand a stock of raw materials to ensure a smooth flow of these needed resources. It is also necessary to maintain an inventory of finished goods which can be sent out readily to fill orders, so that customers are not inconvenienced or discouraged by long waiting periods.

There are, however, certain costs involved in carrying an inventory. There must be warehouses to keep it in and clerks to keep track of it. If the inventory is too large, goods may deteriorate or become obsolete before they are sold or used. And of course, the firm's funds are tied up in the value of the inventory—funds that could otherwise be used for expansion or to purchase other interest-earning assets.

Generally speaking, businesses will tend to try to increase the size of their inventories when sales are rising or when a rise is expected. The more rapidly sales increase, the larger the inventory that business firms will try to build up. When sales are constant or are decreasing, businesses may try to cut back the level of their inventory investment. Inventory investment, then, also operates on the accelerator principle.

Not all changes in investment are voluntary. If sales suddenly decline, a company may be *forced* to retain much of its production, an involuntary increase in inventory. And in times of rising sales volume, a firm that is trying to increase its inventory may find that the great demand for its product has caused an unintended decline in its inventory.

Many firms rely on changes in inventory to maintain financial flexibility. They respond to any slowing down of the sales rate by lowering their inventory levels. This releases the funds locked up in the inventory form of investment for use in meeting expenses. For many companies, inventories are an asset more liquid than most kinds of business savings would be. Therefore inventory investment is extremely volatile, and it responds quickly to a great number of economic indicators.

Investment in residential construction

Many economists consider residential construction one of the most important indicators of future trends of the economy. When construction increases, the outlook for a period of general expansion is considered to be good; a sustained decline in housing construction often heralds the beginning of a recession.

Determinants of residential construction

On first analysis, it might seem that the most important determinant of change in residential construction would be the size of the population. If it was growing, more houses and apartments would be needed; it if was static, no new houses would be needed.

Population is certainly one determinant of residential construction, but there can be a great demand for new housing construction even when population growth is at a standstill. Changes in the level of personal income and in the way that income is distributed can alter the demand for housing. For example, when most people are very poor, large groups of people will live in cramped quarters; this is often the case in inner-city slums, with families of seven, eight, or ten people living in a two-room apartment. If incomes were to go up, those people would spread out, perhaps occupying three or four rooms, or even separate apartments.

When income levels are high, many people also buy second houses. They want a cabin in the mountains, a summer house at the seashore, a place in California or Florida for winter vacations. Shelter is a basic necessity, but that does not mean that desires for houses are narrowly limited.

Also important to changes in the demand for residential construction is the availability of credit. Investors in construction are usually individuals, not businesses, and they do not have the varied means of financing an investment that businesses have. Most commonly, individuals borrow from a bank or credit union. When money is "tight"—that is, when interest rates are high and the supply of funds for lending is low—individuals may find it very hard to borrow at all. Even families who are willing and able to pay the interest (rates for individual borrowers have been as high as 12 percent in recent years) may find that banks will refuse them a loan, preferring to lend the money to established commercial accounts instead.

Another cause of changing demand for housing is migration. In many small towns there is little demand for housing and some houses are usually available. In suburban areas of larger cities, however, there are few vacancies, since there is great demand in these areas for housing. Migration causes some of our stock of residential housing to be abandoned, while it creates demand for more housing in other areas.

Cycles in housing construction

There appear to be rather lengthy cycles in housing construction, with periods of heavy construction alternating with periods of almost complete inactivity. Economists believe that this is largely due to the difficulty of measuring demand. Unlike most products, a house or an apartment is not a uniform commodity. Houses tend to differ in location, style, floor plan, and utility. When a new apartment building shows a high vacancy rate, the owner may attribute the problem to a bad choice of location or to the lack of a swimming pool and other conveniences. It takes some time before it becomes evident that many different kinds of apartments are unrented and that the problem is a surplus of housing. People respond to this discovery by halting all plans for new building, and for a while construction activity is negligible. After a period of some years, demand for housing will exceed supply, and the market will finally register a housing shortage. Then a new wave of building begins.

Stabilizing influences on levels of investment

So far the emphasis of this discussion of investment has been on its volatility and fluctuation. Theoretically, when sales volume stops expanding, investment, acting through the acceleration principle, declines substantially.

If everything worked exactly as we have outlined it so far, the American economy would be subject to wild swings in business activity from boom to bust. In reality, this does not happen. Major depressions have been few and far between; there have been many mild recessions that have never deepened into depressions. It is clear that there must be certain factors that serve to stabilize the level of investment.

Long-range planning

One of these factors is the long-range nature of investment planning. A wise investment program is often formulated to take place in a number of distinct stages. This allows the firm to test each new addition and to incorporate the addition into its existing operation before it begins the next one. Problems can be worked out; and there is less danger of disorganizing the already profitable operations of the company, as all the managers concentrate on the new expansion.

Large corporations like Minnesota Mining and Manufacturing usually plan five to ten years in advance, breaking their expansion program down into separate small steps. When sales, profits, and GNP rates of growth fall, 3M might decide to cancel or postpone some of its projects, but it may very well decide that its long-range plans require continuing investment even during periods when economic conditions seem unfavorable.

Suppose, for example, that the company has already spent the money for research and development of a new kind of copying machine. The results of a pilot program of manufacturing and test marketing indicate that the copier has definite sales appeal. Even though most factors influencing investment currently seem unfavorable, the firm may decide to continue with its plan to bring out the new product, because it expects sales to be good in the long run, and it hopes to profit by being the first on the market with the copier. Postponing the new expansion would mean losing its competitive advantage by allowing other companies time to develop a similar machine. It would also mean that test production and marketing would have to be repeated, since market conditions might change later on, driving up the total cost of the expansion.

Fluctuating interest rates

Another factor that serves to stabilize levels of investment is fluctuating interest rates. In times of prosperity, interest rates will be high, thus driving up the opportunity cost of investment. During a recession, interest rates usually fall. This means that certain investment projects that would have a

Table 10.3
Investment schedule (billions of dollars)

Level of income	Investment
$750	$25
790	25
830	25
870	25
910	25
950	25

comparatively low rate of return when interest rates are at 12 percent suddenly become attractive when the rate drops to 8 percent. If a company feels that the long-range prospects for its product are good and that the company is in a secure position, it may prefer to do invest during periods of slackening GNP and sales growth.

Investment decisions and level of income

We have seen that the aggregate consumption and savings schedules are primarily a function of the level of disposable income, but we have not discussed how investment spending is related to income. In other words, to what extent does the level of income influence business investment plans? The answer is that at any single point in time, the level of investment is fairly fixed in relation to current income. Although aggregate consumption may influence the investment decisions of businesses, these decisions are essentially based on long-range profit expectations rather than on the level of current income. We will therefore assume that businesses will invest exactly the same amount, regardless of the level of national income or output. Admittedly, this assumption is a bit oversimplified, since substantial changes in national income would probably evoke some change in investment demand. But our analysis in Chapter 11 will be greatly facilitated if we assume that the same amount of investment spending will occur at every level of income. In this way, we can readily compare business investment plans with household consumption and savings plans. *Table 10.3* is a hypothetical aggregate investment schedule for an economy; these data can also be presented graphically, as shown in *Fig. 10.3*.

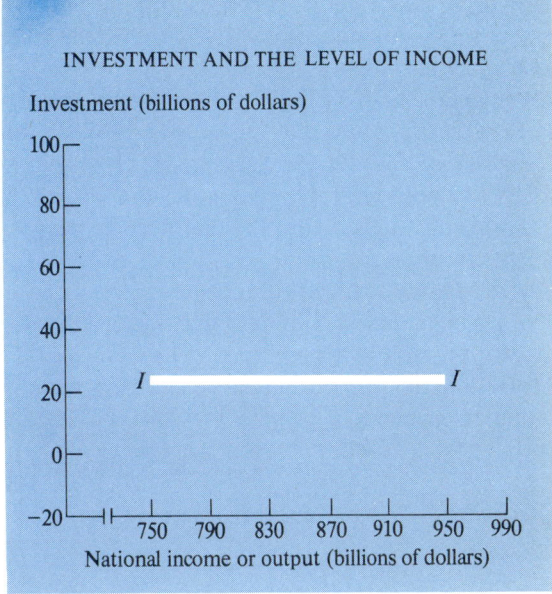

Fig. 10.3
To facilitate economic analysis, we assume that in the short-run period, investment spending is determined independently from the level of income or output. Thus investment (I) can be shown as a straight horizontal line.

Summary

■ The goal of a capitalist economy is full employment of resources, with a reasonable degree of price stability and maintenance of the natural-resource base. This chapter examines some of the mechanisms that determine the level of output and employment, specifically, two of the components of total spending, consumption and investment.

■ Household spending on consumption is the largest single component of GNP, but households may also choose to save some money rather than spend it all. Household saving is not necessarily translated into business investment. The levels of spending and saving are closely linked to the level of disposable income. Aggregate statistics suggest that the marginal propensity to consume and the marginal propensity to save remain the same at all income levels. Consumption spending varies directly with income, but since not all income is spent, the change in spending on consumption will be less than the change in income.

■ Aggregate consumption schedules are determined by many factors: the average size and age of households; their stock of durable goods; their stock of liquid assets; the level of private debt; consumer expectations about the future; and cultural attitudes about thrift and conspicuous consumption. The concept of permanent income—the average income for a worker over a working lifetime—helps explain how consumers make spending and saving decisions and why extreme fluctuations in the standard of living do not occur.

■ Investment is the second major component of private spending, one which is relatively volatile. The principal area of investment is business purchases of new plant and equipment, and these investment decisions are based largely on estimated profitability and on the ability of business to raise funds. Underlying factors in business investment decisions are the stimulus of innovation and technological advance, the existing and potential stocks of fixed capital, expectations about the future behavior of the market, and the current rate of profits.

■ The growth in the overall level of business activity is important for potential increases in investment. The accelerator theory states that an increase or decrease in consumption spending will induce a change in investment that is proportionally greater than the change in consumption. A small increase in consumpton may trigger a flurry of investment, while a small decrease in consumption will set off a precipitous decline in new investment. This is an underlying cause of the pattern of business cycles.

■ The size of inventories is another category of investment. Businesses increase inventories when sales are rising or are expected to rise. Investment in inventories also operates according to the accelerator principle.

■ Investment in residential construction is another key area which economists often see as an indicator of future economic growth or recession. Investment in residential construction is determined by such factors as the size of the population, changes in personal income and income distribution, the availability of credit, and migration patterns.

■ Two factors which tend to stabilize the level of investment are the general practice of long-range planning on investment by major businesses and fluctuations in interest rates which run counter to the fluctuations in investment. While dramatic changes in the level of income will be reflected in changes in the level of investment, investment is more or less fixed in relation to income at any point in time in the short run.

Key Terms

saving

consumption schedule

saving schedule

average propensity to consume

average propensity to save

marginal propensity to consume (MPC)

marginal propensity to save (MPS)

liquid assets

permanent income

accelerator theory

Review & Discussion

1. What is the largest component of aggregate spending? What is meant by the average propensity to consume? The marginal propensity to consume? The average propensity to save? The marginal propensity to save?

2. What factors affect the level of consumption? Which of these factors has been most important in determining your own level of spending and saving in the past?

3. Describe the concept of permanent income. How does the permanent-income theory explain continued consumption even in the face of a drop in income?

4. What factors affect the level of spending for new plant and equipment? For inventory investment? For residential construction?

5. What is the accelerator theory? How does this principle explain the volatility of the investment sector? How would this principle have to be taken into account in estimating the effects of a government decision to raise or lower the level of income taxation?

6. What features of investment expenditure tend to reduce the magnitude of swings in this type of spending?

7. Many economists have noted that people may feel richer even though they are not. A person receiving a large salary may feel that his or her income has risen even though there have been comparable increases in prices. This effect is often called "money illusion." Suppose that a large percentage of households experience this money illusion. What might happen to total consumption if money income doubled?

8. Economist James S. Dusenberry has postulated a close relationship between one's consumption habits and the consumption habits of those one sees—that is, a strong tendency to try and "keep up with the Joneses." What does such a theory suggest about the consumption behavior of relatively poor Americans who are constantly exposed to higher consumption levels through the mass media and the advertising industry?

Chapter 11

The Equilibrium Level of Output and Income

What to look for in this chapter

How is the equilibrium level of income and output determined?

How do the two methods of determining the equilibrium point—the aggregate demand–aggregate supply method and the saving-equals-investment method—arrive at the same conclusion?

How is the equilibrium level related to planned saving and investment?

What is the paradox of thrift?

What is the multiplier effect?

What is the relationship between the equilibrium level and the full employment of resources?

Although classical economists believed that the price system would stimulate an economy to achieve a level of full employment, Keynes argued that a market economy has no mechanism that automatically ensures that full employment will be maintained. Today in the post-Keynesian era, most economists agree that there is no built-in stimulus that will always cause real GNP to reach its highest possible level; it can easily come to rest at a point below full employment. Why is this so?

In the Keynesian model, this phenomenon is explained by the fact that equilibrium in the product market—that level of total output which, once achieved, will tend to be maintained—is a condition unrelated to the full employment of resources. A fundamental assumption of Keynesian theory is that the level of output and employment depends on the level of total spending in the economy. Thus, if a given level of spending evokes a level of national output that is insufficient to employ all available resources, unemployment obviously results. Conversely, if total spending is more than sufficient to fully employ all available resources, full employment will be accompanied by inflation. But even if the level of total spending is "insufficient" or "excessive" in terms of the unemployment or inflation it may cause, equilibrium may still exist in the market for goods and services.

The question then arises, how *is* the equilibrium level of output determined? Why does GNP change from year to year? What causes it to increase? To simplify our analysis, we will not be concerned at this point with whether a given equilibrium level of output gives rise to the unemployment or inflation we discussed in Chapter 9. Our discussion will focus only on the theory of how the equilibrium level of income and output is determined. In the discussion, we will be using many of the concepts developed in Chapters 8 and 10.

There are two ways to determine which of all possible levels of output and income marks the level of equilibrium in the market for goods and services. One method is to compare the economy's schedule of aggregate demand with its schedule of aggregate supply. The equilibrium level of output is that output that will generate sufficient income to produce the exact level of total spending needed to purchase all available goods and services. Or, more simply, equilibrium in the product market occurs when the quantity of all goods and services demanded equals the quantity supplied. The other method is to calculate the amount of investment and to balance that against the amount of saving; the level of output and income where saving equals investment is the point of equilibrium. By either method we obtain the same level of output and income: the equilibrium net national product (NNP).

The models proposed in this chapter will be simplified by omitting the role of government. This means that we are for the moment assuming that national income is not subject to taxes but is all classified as disposable income. It also means that we can equate national income with NNP, since the difference between them is due to business taxes. As an additional convenience for discussion and analysis, we will use NNP rather than GNP, temporarily ignoring the value of capital consumption allowances.

AGGREGATE DEMAND–AGGREGATE SUPPLY APPROACH

In Chapter 3, we discussed demand and supply in the market for a single commodity, and we introduced the concept of market equilibrium—the point at which the quantity demanded and the quantity supplied are equal. Now we can expand these concepts—demand, supply, and equilibrium—to include the entire economy.

In determining aggregates of demand and supply, we want to measure the totals demanded and supplied for all goods and services on the market. Since we are dealing with an enormous number of products, all bearing different price tags, the results will have to be expressed in terms of dollar value rather than quantity of units (as used in market demand and supply curves for a single item). In other words, we want to find out *the total amount of money (expressed in current dollars) that all buyers are willing and able to spend on all goods and services at a given time,* or the level of **aggregate demand** in the economy. And we also want to know *the total value (in current dollars) of all goods and services produced or available for purchase at a given time,* or the level of **aggregate supply.**

Since we have omitted government from our discussion, we are left with only two kinds of spending. There is the spending of households to buy the products of business firms, and there is the spending of business firms, who buy from manufacturers of capital goods and the owners of productive resources.

Table 11.1
Determining the equilibrium level of output and income

(1) Aggregate supply (output and income) NNP = DI (in billions)	(2) Consumption (in billions)	(3) Savings (in billions)	(4) Investment (in billions)	(5) Aggregate demand C+I (in billions)	(6) Resulting tendency of output and income	(7) Level of employment (millions of workers)
$750	$760	$ –10	$25	$785	Expand	50
770	775	– 5	25	800	Expand	55
790	790	0	25	815	Expand	60
810	805	5	25	830	Expand	65
830	820	10	25	845	Expand	70
850	835	15	25	860	Expand	75
870	850	20	25	875	Expand	80
890	865	25	25	890	Equilibrium	85
910	880	30	25	905	Contract	90
930	895	35	25	920	Contract	95
950	910	40	25	935	Contract	100

Equilibrium will occur at the level of $890 billion output. Note that there is no mechanism that ensures that this equilibrium level of supply and demand will be a full-employment economy. We can see that at equilibrium, 85 million workers will be employed; nothing in the table tells us whether that figure represents full employment. If, for example, the labor force consists of 90 million workers, then at equilibrium there will be approximately 5½ percent unemployment.

Aggregate demand

The amount of consumption spending at each possible level of NNP (which, given our simplifying assumptions, is equal to DI) is set out in *Table 11.1*. To find aggregate demand at every level of income, all we need to do is add the value of scheduled investment spending for the year (column 4) to consumption (column 2), or C + I. Since the level of investment is determined independently from the level of income, scheduled investment will be constant at all income levels—in this case $25 billion. The result of adding consumption and investment can be seen in *Fig. 11.1;* it is called the aggregate demand line, or C + I. The line C + I tells us the level of total spending that will take place at each possible level of NNP. However, it alone does not tell us which of the possible levels will actually be produced by businesses.

Keynesian theory, assumes that businesses will be willing to supply exactly as many goods and services as spenders are willing to buy. In other words, the level of aggregate demand creates its own supply. A production level that is higher than the total spending level will not be maintained, since it would leave suppliers with unsold

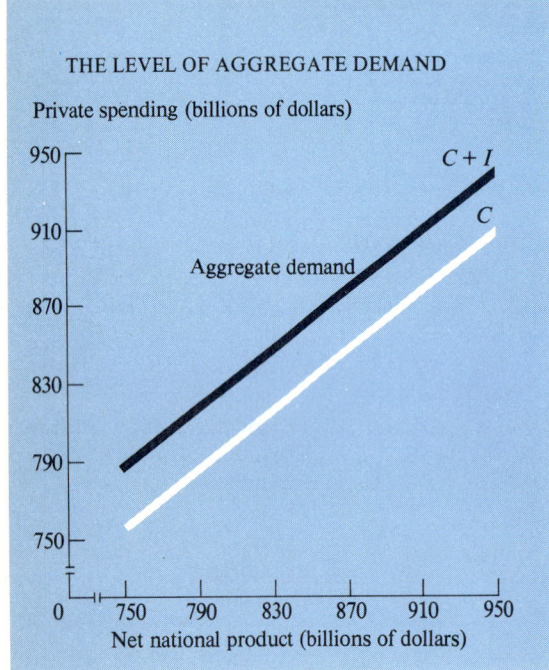

Fig. 11.1
We calculate aggregate private demand by adding consumption and investment (C + I). Since we assume that I is not a function of NNP but is determined independently and remains the same whatever the level of NNP, the line representing C + I is parallel to the line representing C; it is shifted up by an equal amount at all points. Note that the aggregate demand line rises with NNP, but that it does not rise as fast as total NNP. If the increase in demand were exactly proportional to the increase in NNP, the C + I line would be a 45-degree line.

goods on their hands. A production level that is lower than the total spending level will stimulate business expansion, in order to meet the excess of demand. So according to Keynesian theory, supply can be viewed simply as a reaction to demand for the economy as a whole.

Aggregate demand: tabular analysis
We assume that businesses will be willing to supply exactly the dollar value of output that spenders are willing to buy. If spending increases by a given amount, new production will increase by exactly the same amount. Column 1 of *Table 11.1* lists a number of hypothetical levels of NNP. Column 2, taken from consumption schedules for the entire economy, shows the amount of personal consumption expenditures expected at each level of NNP (which is the same as total DI for all households in this simplified model). Column 3, derived by subtracting consumption from total DI, shows the amount of saving that is taking place at each level of NNP. (Remember our assumption that households are responsible for all saving in the economy.) Note that column 3 reflects the pattern outlined in Chapter 10, with dissaving at the lowest income levels, and the rate of saving increasing as income rises. Column 4 shows the amount of investment that will take place. As noted earlier, by adding investment and consumption, we get the aggregate demand (column 5).

Equilibrium level
Equilibrium is reached when aggregate demand equals aggregate supply. At the lower levels of NNP listed in *Table 11.1*, aggregate demand exceeds aggregate supply, so employment, income, and output will all increase as business firms attempt to meet the excess demand. In other words, when NNP is $750 billion, C is $760 billion (because of $10 billion in dissaving), and C + I totals $785 billion. Thus the supply of goods and services is $35 billion less than aggregate demand warrants, and the economy will expand until NNP reaches $890 billion, where aggregate demand (C + I) is also $890 billion, and equilibrium results. But if NNP rises still more to $950 billion, C + I climbs only to $935 billion. Now the level of national output exceeds the expected level of spending. Businesses have stocks of unsold goods. The economy must contract, and employment, output, and incomes must fall.

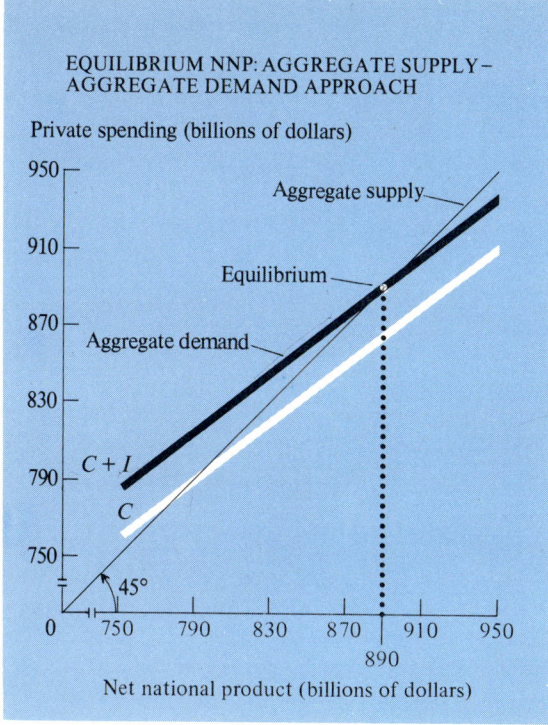

Fig. 11.2
The 45-degree line is halfway between each axis; therefore, at any point on that line, NNP would be exactly equal to aggregate demand. To the left of the equilibrium point, demand is greater than supply, which will cause production and NNP to expand. To the right of the equilibrium point, aggregate supply is greater than aggregate demand, which will cause production and NNP to contract.

Equilibrium level: graphic analysis

Figure 11.2 shows the equilibrium relationship in graph form. If we plot all the points where the value of NNP (supply) equals the expected level of spending (demand), we get the aggregate supply schedule, which is a 45-degree line. Why is it a 45-degree line? We know that each point on the aggregate supply schedule represents (on the vertical axis) the amount people must demand to induce businesses to supply a similar level of NNP (measured on the horizontal axis). Naturally they want to produce only as much as they can sell. Therefore the supply schedule is a line of points equidistant from the output axis measuring NNP and the total spending axis measuring demand. Because the line is equidistant from the two axes, it is by definition a 45-degree line.

If at a given level of supply, such as $950 billion, aggregate demand falls below the 45-degree line, businesses have overproduced and must cut production until it equals aggregate demand ($C + I$) at a point on the 45-degree line. The equilibrium level of output and income is that point where the aggregate demand line ($C + I$) crosses the 45-degree aggregate supply line.

SAVING-EQUALS-INVESTMENT APPROACH

A careful look at *Table 11.1* reveals an additional pertinent fact. We have said that the equilibrium level will be reached when aggregate supply equals

---

RECAP

THE EQUILIBRIUM LEVEL OF NNP is reached when aggregate demand equals aggregate supply. When aggregate demand exceeds aggregate supply, the economy will expand until demand and supply are in equilibrium. When aggregate supply exceeds aggregate demand, the economy will contract until equilibrium is reached once again.

Alternatively, the equilibrium level of NNP is established at the point at which saving equals investment. Equilibrium will be established when investment spending (an injection into the circular flow) exactly equals the amount households wish to save (a withdrawal from the circular flow).

aggregate demand, or at the $890 billion level of NNP. Note that at this level, and only at this level, the figures in the savings and investment columns (columns 3 and 4) are exactly the same—$25 billion. This suggests that a second approach to determining the equilibrium level of NNP would be to find the point at which saving equals investment.

Why is a balance of saving and investment necessary for equilibrium in the product market to occur? If personal consumption were the only type of spending in our economy and if no saving occurred, the level of spending would always be exactly enough to purchase all the goods and services on the market. But saving does take place in all economies, and saving represents a temporary withdrawal from the circular flow. It is logical to conclude, therefore, that when investment spending (an injection into the circular flow) exactly equals the amount households wish to save, equilibrium will be established.

Now let us suppose that households desire to save $35 billion, but businesses want to invest only $25 billion. The result of this imbalance will be that $10 billion is temporarily withdrawn from the circular flow; this will cause total spending to fall $10 billion short of total output. Businesses, left with stocks of unsold goods, will cut back production to the equilibrium point, where saving again equals investment.

When businesses want to invest more than households want to save, the economy is again in a state of disequilibrium; households and businesses will want to spend more than the total value of output, so business firms will respond by increasing levels of production, until they reach the level of NNP that will call forth saving exactly equal to the amount they desire to invest.

Equilibrium: graphic analysis

The saving-equals-investment approach to determining the equilibrium level of output and income can also be shown graphically, as in *Fig. 11.3*.

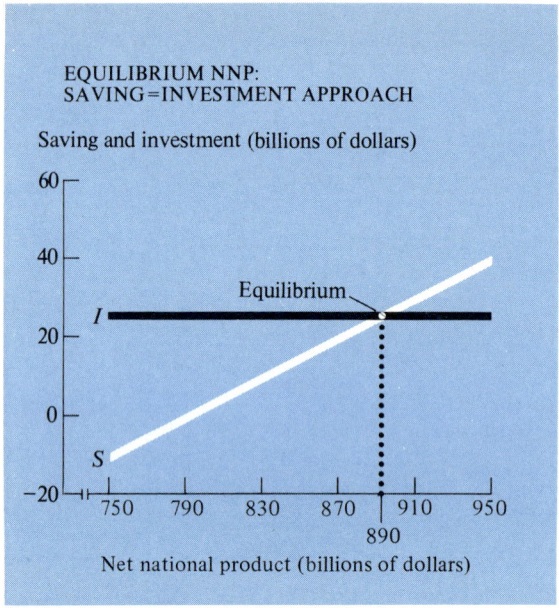

Fig. 11.3
The equilibrium level of output is here defined in terms of saving and investment. Equilibrium NNP occurs when $S = I$. In the $C + I$ approach (*Fig. 11.1*) aggregate supply was a passive factor, and aggregate demand defined NNP; here I is the constant factor, and NNP is defined by the variable S.

NNP is shown on the horizontal axis, and the value of saving and investment is on the vertical axis. Using the data from *Table 11.1*, we see that the line showing investment will be a straight line parallel with the horizonal axis; in other words, changes in NNP will not lead to changes in investment. However, the saving line has a marked upward slope, with the desire and the ability to save increasing as NNP goes up. The point at which the two lines cross will be the point of economic equilibrium—that level of actual NNP which, once achieved, will tend to be maintained.

EFFECT OF EQUILIBRIUM LEVEL ON PLANNED SAVING AND INVESTMENT

In our discussion of saving and investment, we have been talking about the intentions, or plans, of businesses and households. When an economy is at its equilibrium point, households will actually be able to save exactly the amount they had intended to save, and businesses will be able to invest the amount they had intended to invest. However, if intended saving and intended investment are not equal, the disequilibrium will keep businesses and households from being able to realize their intentions. An example will help explain the way this mechanism works.

Reaching saving-investment equilibrium: an illustration

Let us hypothesize that businesses decide to invest $25 billion in 1978, but that households, concerned over the rising level of unemployment, save $30 billion. When there is this sort of imbalance between intended investment and intended saving, what will happen? When households save more, they must spend less; the extra $5 billion they save will mean a corresponding decrease of $5 billion in consumption. But this increased saving will probably not be utilized as investment funds, since businesses do not plan to spend that much for the purchase of capital goods and additional input resources. What actually occurs is that $5 billion of the total output of business firms remains unsold. That inventory is held in warehouses and thus becomes an involuntary investment made by businesses. They have been forced to invest $5 billion in inventory during the year.

When this forced investment becomes evident, businesses will respond by lowering production for the next year. Suppose that they decide to lower total output by $10 billion—$5 billion because they want to sell their inventory overstock and another $5 billion because they want to make sure the same thing does not happen again the next year. The decrease in NNP will soon make itself felt by a corresponding decrease in the levels of employment and income. When national income drops, households find themselves unable to save as much as they had intended to, since their incomes are smaller. This adjustment process will continue, until the amount that households intend to save will be equal to the amount that businesses intend to invest.

When intended investment is greater than intended saving, businesses are forced to sell stocks of inventory they had planned to hold, so that they can meet the demand for their goods and services. In order to compensate for this situation, they will plan to increase production the following year, so that they can replace their inventory and meet current demand. The increase in NNP will bring a similar increase in NI, which will in turn stimulate households to save more. The process will continue until the economy reaches the level of NNP at which intended saving will be equal to intended investment.

PARADOX OF THRIFT

The examples we have just discussed, illustrating the way in which equilibrium will be reached when there is a difference between the amount that households intend to save and businesses intend to invest, point up a curious result of thrift. When households all decide to try to save more money, their plans for saving set in motion a process of adjustment, as the economy seeks a new equilibrium level of production. Eventually this adjustment will result in a reduction in the actual amount that households are able to save. *This reduction in the actual amount of aggregate savings that follows a period of widespread planned increases in saving* is referred to as the **paradox of thrift.**

One of the ways a household can increase its future income is by saving some portion of current income in the hope of increasing its ability to con-

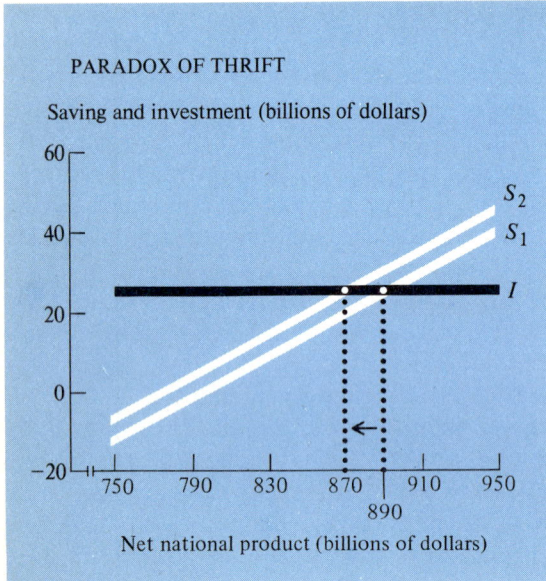

Fig. 11.4
If households begin to save more, saving will move from S_1 to S_2; desired S now exceeds desired I by $5 billion. The increase in S will be matched by a decline in consumption and hence a decline in aggregate demand and income. As income declines, S will decline, a process that will continue until S is once again equal to I. If the economy is to remain at equilibrium, increases in saving must be matched by increases in NNP.

sume at a later date. A basic motive of all households that save is to attempt to build up a larger stock of productive resources, which will increase income in the future. For the individual household unit, saving is an effective way to achieve the goal of maximizing satisfaction.

However, if all households attempt to save large portions of current income, the economy will suffer serious problems. Because the increase in saving must come out of current consumption, the rise in saving will be offset by an equal decline in household spending. Since the investment plans of businesses are determined independently from the saving decisions of households, the increase in saving will not affect the level of investment. Thus the amount saved in the economy will be greater than the amount that businesses want to invest, and the excess savings will be idle. Aggregate demand will decline, calling out a matching decline in aggregate supply, with resultant cutbacks in employment and lowered income for households.

Paradox of thrift: graphic analysis
The paradox of thrift is shown graphically in *Fig. 11.4*. Note that when the economy finally comes to rest at the new, lower level of NNP, households are saving exactly the same amount—$40 billion—as before the shift in the saving schedule occurred. For the individual household, increased saving brings increased wealth, but for the whole community, increased saving may bring declining incomes. This is a good example of the logical fallacy of composition discussed in Chapter 1: what is true for the individual acting alone is not necessarily true for all individuals acting simultaneously.

The paradox of thrift poses difficult problems for economic policymakers. Individual self-interest motivates households to attempt to save. Cultural values teach that saving is a valuable goal; most parents urge even very young children to save part of their allowance, or to deposit in a savings account the checks they get at Christmas.

Problems and benefits
When the economy is operating at less than full employment, the paradox of thrift poses difficult problems, for it is during times of high unemployment and economic recession, when the economy most needs additional spending, that people feel the greatest urge to save. They fear they may lose their jobs, or they want to increase their rate of saving so that they will have some sort of financial cushion.

DEVELOPMENTS IN ECONOMIC THOUGHT:

Paul Samuelson

Wide World Photos

Paul Samuelson (b. 1915) has carried on a dual career as an economist, gaining recognition both for his theoretical advances and for his tireless attempts to make the concepts of economics accessible to the general public. In the latter role, Samuelson has written for magazines and newspapers, given countless interviews, delivered testimony to congressional committees, advised Democratic presidential administrations, and written a principles of economics textbook which has gone through ten editions. Of all professional economists, he is probably the best-known proponent of liberal policies, including active government intervention in economic affairs.

However, as an economic theorist and the first American to receive the Nobel Prize in Economic Science, Samuelson uses methods of analysis and concentrates on subjects that are more difficult for the general public to understand than the economic concepts he has helped to popularize. For example, Samuelson's ambitious Harvard dissertation of 1947, *Foundations of Economic Analysis,* was an attempt to describe the new thinking of twentieth-century neoclassical economists like John Maynard Keynes in rigorous mathematical form.

Largely through Samuelson's continuing efforts, economics comes closer than any other social science to employing mathematics as it is used in the natural sciences. By working to put key economic concepts on a precise mathematical basis, Samuelson has greatly expanded the potential power of economic theory to explain and predict the behavior of the economy. In addition, he has turned his attention to many other areas of economics, such as international trade, consumer behavior, and welfare economics.

Samuelson has also done substantial work on the central economic problem of equilibrium and stability in economic systems. John Maynard Keynes (see Chapter 17) demonstrated that a variety of factors could disrupt the general equilibrium between supply and demand, and that when a new state of equilibrium was reached, it might be far from ideal, with unacceptably high rates of unemployment or inflation. Samuelson has done a great deal of research on the relationships between states of equilibrium by studying such mechanisms as the multiplier effect, the accelerator (see Chapter 10), and the interaction between the two.

Samuelson has consistently advocated federal government intervention as the most effective way of restoring and modifying equilibrium in the economy. His advice was instrumental in influencing the Kennedy administration to consider a tax cut as a stimulus to overcome the recession of the early 1960s. He was a vocal opponent of the Nixon-Ford antiinflation policies which, he claimed, increased the chances of a recession. More recently he has maintained that the tax-reduction proposals of the Carter administration are not bold enough. Despite his expertise and public prominence, Samuelson has always declined invitations to serve on the President's Council of Economic Advisors, preferring to conduct both his theoretical and policy work from his post on the faculty of the Massachusetts Institute of Technology.

On the other hand, when all productive resources are fully employed, any additional spending will only serve to create demand-pull inflation. At the level of full employment, increased aggregate saving not only avoids inflation but also makes funds available that are needed for expansion of productive capacity. In such a situation, saving is beneficial both to the individual and to the economy as a whole.

MULTIPLIER THEORY: CHANGES IN EQUILIBRIUM NNP

At the outset of this chapter, we asked the question, why does the equilibrium level of output and income change? We can now answer that a change in the equilibrium level of NNP will occur as a result of shifts in the aggregate consumption saving schedules, or a shift in the investment schedule. What could cause such shifts? Two factors can be singled out: a change in the average propensities to save and consume, or a change in the amount that businesses decide to invest.

In Chapter 10, we said that the marginal propensity to save and the marginal propensity to consume have remained constant for a long period of time. However, investment is much more volatile. Therefore, we can conclude that most changes in the level of NNP are due to changes in investment spending by business. An increase in private investment will cause both output and income to expand; a decrease in investment will cause output and income to decline.

The multiplier effect

Economists have studied the relationship between changes in investment and changes in income, and they have discovered that any change in investment leads to a greater change in income. An example will help to explain why this happens.

RECAP

MULTIPLIER THEORY helps to explain the relationship between changes in investment and changes in income. Specifically, any change in investment leads to a greater change in income.

The ultimate change in income that will result from an initial change in consumption or investment is called the multiplier effect (the multiplier is a ratio that indicates this change).

Let us imagine that the Polyphonic Musical Instrument Company decides to increase its investment spending by $1,000,000, so that it can build a new factory for the production of pibgorns and cash in on the national craze for pibgorn music. The immediate result of this investment spending is that employees of the company that builds the factory will get an additional $1,000,000 in income. Assuming that the marginal propensity to consume (MPC) is about ¾, we know that $750,000 of that additional household income will be spent in the purchase of new consumer goods and services. That $750,000 will be paid back in wages, salaries, and profits to the employees and owners of the business firms that make the sales. These households will also allocate 75 percent of the increase to consumption spending, so another $562,500 will be spent to purchase goods and services.

Table 11.2 shows how the process will continue. Each time the increased income is returned to households, they will save 25 percent and spend 75 percent of the increase. The result is that the $1,000,000 of increased investment generates $4,000,000 of increased income. This is called the **multiplier effect**. We can define the multiplier effect as *the ultimate change in income that will result from an initial change in consumption or investment.*

The **multiplier** is *a ratio which indicates the ultimate change in income that will result from an initial change in investment.* The multiplier can be calculated easily if we know either the marginal propensity to save (MPS) or the MPC. *The multiplier is the reciprocal of the MPS.* In the example we have used, the MPS is ¼; therefore the multiplier is 4/1, or 4. Since the MPS plus the MPC must always equal 1, the multiplier can also be calculated as 1/(1 − MPC);

$$\frac{1}{1 - ¾} = \frac{1}{¼} = 4.$$

Table 11.2
The multiplier effect

	(1) Change in income	(2) Change in consumption MPC = ¾	(3) Change in savings MPS = ¼
Increase in investment	$1,000,000	$ 750,000	$ 250,000
Round 2	750,000	562,500	187,500
Round 3	562,500	421,875	140,625
Round 4	421,875	316,406	105,469
All other rounds	1,265,625	949,219	316,406
Total	$4,000,000	$3,000,000	$1,000,000

Multiplier effect: graphic analysis

The multiplier theory is another confirmation of the necessity for a balance between saving and investment. Note that the effect of the multiplier is to create saving exactly equal to the initial increase in investment. (See column 3 of *Table 11.2*.) The process stops here, because equilibrium has once again been established. *Figure 11.5* illustrates the multiplier effect graphically. It shows the changes in NNP resulting from both a $10 billion decrease and $10 billion increase in aggregate demand. *Figure 11.6* verifies that in either case, the new equilibrium level of NNP will be one at which saving exactly equals the new level of investment spending.

We have given an example of an increase in investment. The multiplier effect will also occur when there is a decrease. Suppose, for example, that the aggregate level of investment throughout the economy drops by $10 billion; the effect will

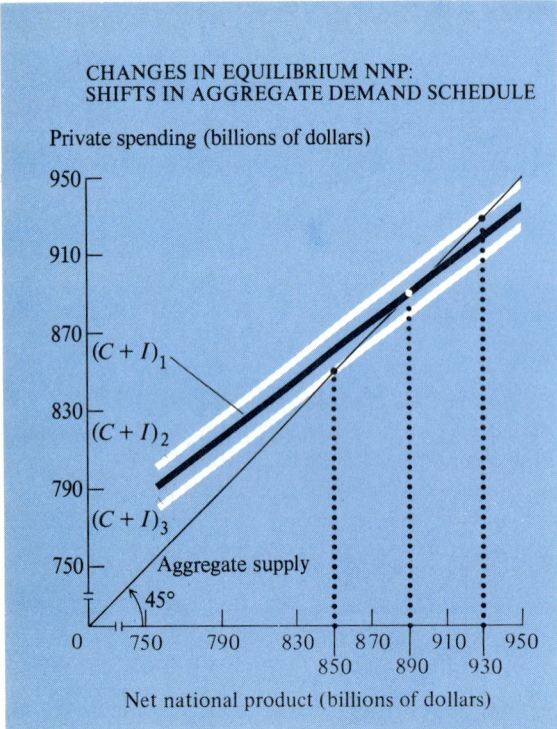

CHANGES IN EQUILIBRIUM NNP: SHIFTS IN AGGREGATE DEMAND SCHEDULE

Fig. 11.5
As investment increases by $10 billion, shifting the aggregate demand line from $(C + I)_1$ to $(C + I)_2$, NNP goes from $890 billion to $930 billion, an increase of $40 billion. Similarly, a $10 billion decrease in investment will shift the aggregate demand line from $(C + I)_1$ to $(C + I)_3$, causing a decline in NNP from $890 billion to $850 billion. In either case, the horizontal movement of NNP is four times the vertical shift in investment; this is due to the action of the multiplier.

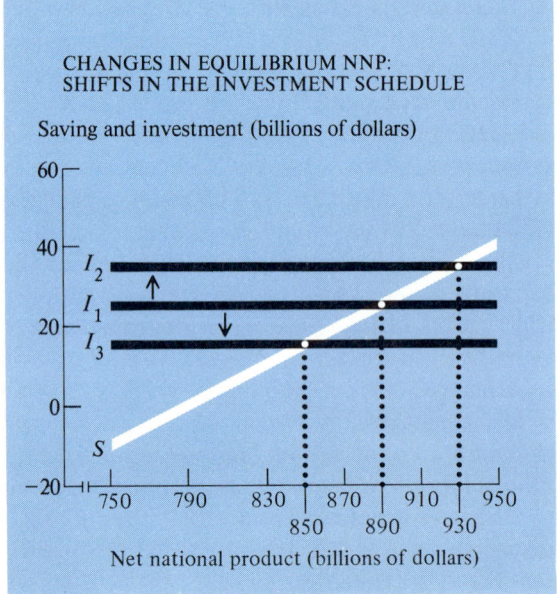

CHANGES IN EQUILIBRIUM NNP: SHIFTS IN THE INVESTMENT SCHEDULE

be to cut income by $40 billion. Some economists call the multiplier a "two-edged sword," meaning that its ability to expand the economy is matched by its ability to contract it.

ACHIEVING FULL EMPLOYMENT: DEFLATIONARY AND INFLATIONARY GAPS

Many modern economists agree with Keynes's view that it is merely an accident if the equilibrium level of the economy happens to coincide with full employment. Referring to *Table 11.1* (column 7), suppose the full-employment level of NNP is $910 billion, whereas the equilibrium NNP is $890 bil-

Fig. 11.6
Suppose that investment increases from I_1 to I_2. Desired I will now be greater than desired S at the $890 billion level of NNP. Since the relationship between S and NNP is assumed to remain constant, the only way to increase S so that it is once again equal to I is to increase NNP to the level of $930 billion, the new equilibrium level of output.

lion. In general, the national accounts show that this supposition reflects reality, for most often our economy comes to rest somewhere short of full-employment NNP.

If the equilibrium level of saving and investment happens to fall at a point below full employment, the result will be a **deflationary gap**. A deflationary gap is *the amount by which aggregate demand falls short of the full-employment level of NNP.* To put it another way, a deflationary gap is a gap in total spending, since total spending is not great enough to maintain a level of production sufficient to employ all available resources. (*Figure 11.7* provides a graphic measurement of a deflationary gap.) Remember that this spending gap will be subject to the effects of the multiplier. If the gap is $5 million, the total loss of income will be $20 million.

What happens if equilibrium NNP is higher than the full-employment level of NNP? In terms of the level of employment, there is an excess of demand. *The amount by which aggregate demand exceeds the full-employment level of NNP* is called an **inflationary gap** (see *Figure 11.7*). Like a deflationary gap, an inflationary gap is subject to the effects of the multiplier, so an increase of $5 million in total spending would mean an increase of $20 million in income. Yet it is clear that the increase in income cannot possibly be due to an increase in production, since the economy was already operating at the full-employment level in the first place. What has happened is that consumers are spending a larger amount of money to buy the same amount of output; in other words, prices have become inflated.

The price system itself has no automatic mechanism to avoid either inflationary or deflationary gaps. Often these problems can be solved through directed efforts to alter rates of spending or saving. In our economy, we tend to rely directly on government to initiate and supervise such action. For example, the government may itself spend more or less; it may try to increase private spending by increasing the money supply or by

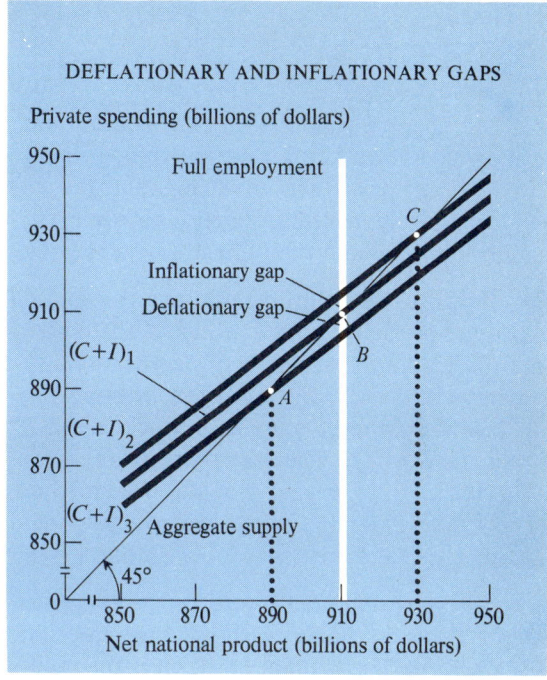

Fig. 11.7
If the equilibrium level of NNP is at $890 billion, and is therefore smaller than the full-employment level of NNP ($910 billion), we have a deflationary gap—aggregate demand is too low. The economy needs to increase its $C + I$ from $(C + I)_3$ to $(C + I)_1$ to raise the equilibrium level of NNP to full employment (from point A to point B). If the equilibrium level of NNP falls at $930 billion, a point above the level of full-employment NNP, we have an inflationary gap, and aggregate demand is too high. $(C + I)_2$ must be moved back to $(C + I)_1$, and equilibrium will change from point C to point B.

waging a campaign to change attitudes toward saving. Chapters 12 and 15, on government fiscal and monetary policy, discuss these and other ways that government can intervene to try to ensure that the equilibrium level of NNP will be at or near the level of full employment.

Summary

■ This chapter examines how the equilibrium level of income and output is determined, the two methods for arriving at the equilibrium point, and the potential difference between the equilibrium level and the full-employment level.

■ The first method of determining the equilibrium level of total output and income is to compare the economy's schedule of aggregate demand with its schedule of aggregate supply. The equilibrium level is the level at which the money value of aggregate supply equals the money value of aggregate demand. This method reflects the Keynesian concept that the level of aggregate demand creates its own supply.

■ The second method is to compare the aggregate investment schedule with the aggregate savings schedule. The equilibrium level is the point at which investment equals saving.

■ When intended saving is greater than intended investment, equilibrium does not occur. Business cuts down on future production, leading to a decline in employment and income, which results in a decrease in saving, thus restoring equilibrium. When intended investment is greater than intended saving, business has to sell stocks of inventory and increase production, leading to a rise in national income and thus a rise in saving, until equilibrium is once again established.

■ The paradox of thrift—where the attempt to increase savings causes an automatic downward adjustment of NNP, which eventually results in a *reduction* of the actual amount that households are able to save—has harmful effects when the economy is operating below full employment. At the full-employment level, however, increased aggregate saving helps avoid inflation and also makes funds available for expansion of productive capacity.

■ A change in the equilibrium level can occur if there is a shift in the aggregate consumption and saving schedules, or a shift in the investment schedule. A change in business investment is the more likely of these two possibilities. An increase in investment will cause both output and income to rise, whereas a decrease in investment will cause a corresponding decline in both output and income. In either case, the change in NNP will be greater than the initial change in investment—a phenomenon known as the multiplier effect. The multiplier is a ratio which can be expressed as the reciprocal of the marginal propensity to save—thus, 1/MPS.

■ According to Keynesian theory, the actual equilibrium NNP is not necessarily the full-employment, noninflationary NNP. The price system itself contains no automatic mechanism to avoid either deflationary or inflationary gaps. A deflationary gap occurs when aggregate demand is below the full-employment level of NNP, causing a multiplied decline in real output and income. An inflationary gap occurs when aggregate demand exceeds the full-employment level of NNP, which causes prices to rise—not an increase in real productive output.

Key Terms

aggregate demand
aggregate supply
paradox of thrift
multiplier effect
multiplier
deflationary gap
inflationary gap

Review & Discussion

1. Draw hypothetical aggregate demand and aggregate supply curves for an economy. Identify the equilibrium level of income and output. What would happen above the equilibrium point? What would happen below the equilibrium point?

2. Draw hypothetical saving and investment curves for the economy. Identify the equilibrium level. What happens above and below the equilibrium point?

3. How is it possible for increased efforts to save actually to cause a lower level of saving? How does this effect tend to aggravate a recession?

4. Suppose that a business invests $2000 by buying new equipment. Assume the marginal propensity to consume is 0.8. Work through at least the first three exchanges to verify that income rises by more than $2000. By what amount will income rise?

5. What is the value of the multiplier if MPC = 0.6? If MPS = 0.2? If there is a decrease in investment by $1000 and MPC = .75, what will be the change in national income?

6. As real income rises, what would you expect to happen to the value of the multiplier? Why? What might happen to the slope of the aggregate spending line?

7. What is an inflationary gap? A deflationary gap? How would you show them graphically?

8. Why, according to the Keynesian model accepted by most contemporary economists, is the equilibrium level reached through the operation of the price system not necessarily equal to the full-employment level?

Chapter 12

Fiscal Policy: Government Spending and Taxation

What to look for in this chapter

What is the role of government spending and taxation in the economy?

What are the potential effects of the various discretionary and nondiscretionary fiscal policies available to government?

How does fiscal policy affect the equilibrium level of net national product (NNP)?

What is the economic significance of government budget deficits and surpluses?

What are the advantages and disadvantages of the public debt in the United States?

In the previous chapters, we have discussed the roles of consumption, saving, and investment in determining aggregate demand and have examined how the equilibrium level of output and income is determined. In both discussions, we simplified the models by omitting the role of government and assumed that national income equaled net national product. In this chapter, we are going to add government spending to the aggregate demand schedules of households and businesses and subtract the taxes paid to the government from national income.

In the first part of the chapter, we will discuss the various fiscal tools that government uses to influence economic activity. We will then examine what happens to the equilibrium level of output and income (studied in Chapter 11) when we include government spending and taxation. Finally, we will consider how the government manages budget surpluses and deficits.

FISCAL POLICY

You will recall from Chapter 7 that one of the main functions of the government is to stabilize swings in economic activity. This goal is accomplished through the use of **fiscal policy,** *actions taken by the government to alter the level of its taxes and expenditures in order to bring about desired changes in economic activity.* By changing its rate of spending or taxation, the government can adjust the economy and help stimulate it to achieve a full-employment noninflationary level of production. On the other hand, ill-advised government action can cause unemployment, inflation, or even both simultaneously.

The ultimate goal of much macroeconomic study is to understand the behavior of aggregate economic variables such as national income and employment. Because the government has such a significant influence on these variables, macroeconomists are interested in determining the probable results of different government programs. However, when establishing and evaluating fiscal policy, economists must be especially careful not to fall into the fallacy of composition. For example, we should not assume that the effects of a government budget deficit will be a magnified version of the effects of a budget deficit on a single household. In the following sections, we will discuss how the government employs two types of fiscal policy (nondiscretionary and discretionary) to affect economic activity.

STABILIZING EFFECT OF GOVERNMENT

We have frequently referred to some of the economic factors that can cause rapid change in the real equilibrium level of net national product (NNP). Investment schedules are altered in response to technological innovation or changes in consumer tastes and spending patterns; inventories are extremely volatile, and the amount of total saving fluctuates from one year to the next. Mechanisms such as the accelerator and the multiplier can cause these initial changes to reverberate throughout the entire economic system, magnifying the degree of change.

Yet even though the multiplier is always at work, transforming small shifts in investment or spending into a much larger change in the equilibrium level of NNP, we rarely see the swings from boom to bust that this might lead us to expect. This is because our economy has certain mechanisms that counteract these effects. In addition, the government can attempt to stabilize fluctuations in economic activity either through the operation of automatic stabilizers or by deliberately altering its rate of spending and taxation.

Nondiscretionary fiscal policy: automatic stabilizers

Not all of the government's stabilizing effect is the result of deliberate measures taken in response to existing problems. The United States government's economic policies contain what are called **nondiscretionary fiscal policy** or **automatic stabilizers.** These are *built-in stabilizers that automatically diminish or cushion any fluctuations in economic activity that occur.* These built-in stabilizers were *initially* established by government action. However, once they became part of the economic system by way of legislation, they were (and continue to be) left to operate automatically in the manner described below.

Stabilizing effect of the tax structure
Perhaps the easiest way to explain the automatic stabilizers of our tax structure is to illustrate the way the process works. Suppose that for one reason or another the rate of business investment drops. As we saw in Chapter 11, the multiplier will cause this drop to show up as an even larger drop in NNP, and there will be a corresponding drop in national income (NI).

As we discussed in Chapter 7, personal and corporate income taxes in the United States are levied *progressively* in relation to the amount of national income (wages, salaries, and profits).

Therefore, when NI drops, the amount of taxes paid on NI, in both percentage and absolute terms, will also drop. This will occur automatically, because the taxes we pay are based on the amount of our income.

What will the effect of this decrease in taxes be? *Table 12.1* shows the answer. If NI drops by $50 billion (9 percent), taxes will drop by $37.5 billion (27 percent). The percentage decline in taxes collected is greater than the percentage decline in NI. Because spending is a function of the level of disposable income (DI—income received by households after taxes are paid), spending will not decline in proportion to the drop in NI because the taxes collected are less. Thus the effects of the decline in NI are partially counteracted.

When NNP increases, taxes perform the same automatic stabilizing function. NI will rise, but taxes will rise at the same time. Therefore the increase in DI will be smaller than the increase in NI. Taxes thus act as a brake on excessively rapid economic expansion.

The effects of tax revenues on government spending In our example, we have assumed that government does not alter its intended rate of spending in response to the fluctuations in amount of tax collected. For a number of reasons, both political and economic, government is usually reluctant to cut spending when tax revenues decrease. Instead, it will meet the **budget deficit** (*an excess of expenditures over revenues*) by selling government bonds or by printing money. On the other hand, if revenues increase, government can readily find ways to increase its spending correspondingly.

When NNP rises and tax revenues increase, the government receives an unexpected **budget surplus** (*an excess of revenues over expenditures*). It has several options regarding the allocation of this money. It can increase its own rate of spending and by so doing attempt to accelerate economic expansion; it can redeem bonds; or it can hold the money. If the economy is bothered by an inflationary gap, holding onto a surplus will help to stabilize the economy and fight demand-pull inflation. (Government spending under these circumstances would probably cause an additional inflationary increase in NNP.) However, if the economy is operating at a high rate of employment without any inflationary gap, the government's decision to hold the extra tax revenues will have a contractionary effect because the money is temporarily removed from the circular flow. Spending will decline, and thanks to the action of the multiplier, there will soon be an even greater decline in NNP. *The contractionary effect of increased tax revenues produced by increases in net national product is* called **fiscal drag.** Fiscal drag will occur automatically whenever NNP increases in a healthy economy; its effect must be offset by other expansionary fiscal policy measures, such as increased spending or decreased taxes, in order to maintain a stable level of economic activity.

Table 12.1
Stabilizing effect of progressive taxation

	(1) Year 1	(2) Year 2	(3) Percentage decline in NI and in taxes collected
National income	$550 billion	$500 billion	9%
Average rate of taxation	25%	20%	
Taxes collected	$137.5 billion	$100 billion	27%

Table 12.2
Stabilizing effects of various tax structures

	National income		
	$300 billion	$500 billion	$700 billion
Regressive tax structure			
Tax rate	25%	20%	15%
Amount of taxes collected	$75 billion	$100 billion	$105 billion
Proportional tax structure			
Tax rate	20%	20%	20%
Amount of taxes collected	$60 billion	$100 billion	$140 billion
Progressive tax structure			
Tax rate	15%	20%	25%
Amount of taxes collected	$45 billion	$100 billion	$175 billion

The effects of other types of tax structures on economic activity It is important to note that not all types of tax structures are as effective in stabilizing the economy as our progressive system of taxes. *Table 12.2* shows a hypothetical example in which the amount of taxes collected rises with a rise in NI and falls with a decrease in NI for three types of tax structures—progressive, proportional, and regressive. As we can see, when taxes are proportional, the percentage increase in taxes collected, given a $200 billion increase in NI (from $500 to $700 billion), will be less than when the tax structure is progressive. When taxes are regressive, the percentage increase in taxes collected will be even smaller than for a proportional tax. In *Table 12.2,* all taxes provide some degree of stabilization, but a progressive tax structure is the most effective in this role.

If we consider the way the three types of tax structures work through the multiplier, we can understand why a progressive tax is the best stabilizer. Assume for the moment that the marginal propensity to consume (MPC) is the same at all income levels. With a regressive tax, we find that households will consume a *larger* portion of each additional dollar of income. The total tax revenue will rise as income rises, but taxes will represent an increasingly smaller percentage of personal income.

With a proportional tax, the percentage of personal income retained by households after taxes are paid will be unchanged with a rise in NI. With a progressive tax, the percentage of personal income retained by households actually falls. In all three cases, total tax revenue will increase, but the greatest rise occurs under the progressive tax system. If, as some economists believe, MPC actually decreases as income rises, the effects of the progressive tax will be magnified by the changes in MPC.

Stabilizing effect of
government transfer payments
Transfer payments and various types of subsidies paid by the federal government also provide some degree of stability and dampen the effects of changes in NNP. When NNP drops for any reason, businesses will respond by cutting back their level of employment, and NI will drop as well. But because of increases in government transfer payments in the form of unemployment compensation and welfare payments, workers who are laid off their jobs will still have a source of income, so their spending will not decline in proportion to the drop in NI. Government welfare benefits also help to cushion the decline in NI.

When NNP rises, there will be less need for government transfer payments to unemployed or impoverished families. The amount paid in transfer payments will drop, but taxes will increase because of the increase in NI. Thus there is an automatic adjustment of spending and revenues that serves to guard against the dangers of excessive spending when NNP rises.

Subsidies paid to farmers also are subject to the same kind of automatic adjustment. When NNP drops, a greater number of farmers need a larger amount of subsidizing, so government spending increases, compensating for the loss of NI. When NNP rises, there is less need for all kinds of subsidies, so government spending drops and tax revenues increase, helping to prevent an inflationary gap.

Limitations of nondiscretionary fiscal policy

The stabilizing effects of taxation and transfer payments are built into our economy. No government officials need to decide to employ these mechanisms, they go into effect automatically whenever there are changes in investment or consumption. But taxation and transfer payments serve only to minimize the effects of these changes—they do not eliminate fluctuations completely. These built-in stabilizers are not completely effective and disturbances in our economy—such as recessions and demand-pull inflation—remain.

In addition, stabilization of upswings by built-in stabilizers can have certain undesirable side effects. Fiscal drag (the deflationary effect of increased tax revenues produced by increases in NNP) is one of these. There may also be times when automatic stabilization is too slow to meet the needs of the economy. For example, at the end of a long and severe recession, it might be desirable for NNP to increase as fast as possible, at least for the short-run period. A sudden sharp upswing might create the necessary public confidence that would stimulate a voluntary increase in spending and investment, whereas a slow and gradual rise in NNP would be less effective.

Because of these limitations, our economy cannot run itself and the government must often step in and take measures to prevent a full-scale recession or runaway inflation. Although its actions are not always effective, the government does have a number of discretionary fiscal policy tools with which it tries to stabilize economic activity. These tools, discussed in the following section, may be supplemented by various adjustments in the money supply and the interest rate as we will see in the next chapters.

Discretionary fiscal policy

Discretionary fiscal policy is *the purposeful alteration of the rate of taxation or government spending to help adjust equilibrium NNP to a full-employment level while also maintaining price stability*. Since the automatic economic stabilizers cannot adequately achieve this goal, government supplements their effects with a variety of discretionary measures, all of which require political action in order to be changed. For example, any change in tax rates requires the agreement of Congress, perhaps acting on the suggestion of the executive branch and the advice of the Congressional Joint Economic Committee.

Altering government expenditures

One way the government may attempt to stabilize the economy is by altering its level of spending to purchase goods and services. Government buys a variety of products of American industry—highways and dams, moon rockets, aircraft carriers—and this amount can be increased or decreased as a part of discretionary fiscal policy.

Let us imagine a situation in which the growth rate of NNP begins to decline. Through the mechanism of the acceleration principle, this will evoke an even greater percentage decline in business investment. If government does not intervene, income will continue to decline until households are forced to reduce saving by an amount equal to the decline in investment. Equilibrium will then fall at a point below the level of full employment and the economy will suffer a recession that may last for several years. Built-in stabilizers will slow down the rate at which NNP drops, but it will still drop.

One solution would be for the government to increase its spending by building a new dam or a supersonic transport. Suppose the government decides to spend an extra $5 billion. The money will go to business firms from whom the government purchases additional goods and services. The business firms will pay it back to households as wages and profits, and then it will enter a second round. The $5 billion will be subject to the multiplier effect, so that the final increase in NNP will be $5 billion times the multiplier (4), or $20 billion.

In terms of fiscal policy, it would be best if the additional government spending injected into the economy could be removed as the rate of private investment and consumer spending begins to pick up once again. However, other considerations may make such a removal undesirable.

Changes in govenment expenditures can also be helpful when the economy is faced with an inflationary gap. Government can reduce its level of spending by canceling or postponing public-works projects—for instance, it can cut down on or postpone for a year or two expenditures for new recreational facilities for our national parks. The effect of cuts in government spending (assuming no accompanying cut in taxes) will be a reduction of aggregate demand that will cause the equilibrium level of NNP to decrease to a noninflationary level.

Increasing the effectiveness of automatic stabilizers

Economic stabilization can also be accomplished by purposeful alteration of government expenditures on transfer payments. This increases the effectiveness of the built-in stabilizer that the payments represent.

When NNP and national income decrease, increased government transfer payments can partially compensate for the loss of NI and can keep DI from dropping as severely as NI. Although this change in the level of transfer payments happens automatically, there are limits to its effectiveness. If unemployment is prolonged, workers may use up their allotted amount of compensation. When that situation occurs or threatens to occur, further action can be taken to extend the stabilizing mechanism. For example, in response to sharply rising unemployment rates in 1974, two new unemployment-insurance laws were enacted to prolong the period during which unemployed workers could receive compensation and to extend the program's coverage. The Emergency Unemployment Compensation Act extended each state's coverage to a maximum of 52 weeks when the jobless rate exceeds 4 percent either nationwide or in that state. Title II of the Emergency Jobs and Unemployment Assistance Act of 1974 provided benefits to citizens not covered by other state or federal programs.

As a part of its discretionary fiscal policy, therefore, government may decide to increase its transfer payments during periods of falling NNP or slackening growth rate. It can alter unemployment-compensation policies as above; it can alter the official definitions of poverty, so more people are able to receive more money in welfare benefits; it can also increase the level of Social Security benefits, extend veterans' benefits, or increase agricultural price supports. Any of these measures will inject additional money into the circular flow and will thereby help to stabilize the economy.

Increasing government spending on transfer payments (as opposed to increasing government expenditures) has the advantage of providing immediate help. As soon as the political decision is made to adopt this fiscal policy, the transfer payments can begin. Moreover, the money will be paid to those households that need it most, the households with low income levels.

Changes in government transfer payments are usually more effective in stabilizing declines in the NNP than in combating inflationary increases. In the first place, there is much more political resistance to a policy of cutting welfare benefits than there is to a policy of increasing them. In addition, a cut in transfer payments with no corresponding decrease in taxes could result in a large, idle surplus held by the government, which might present a tempting invitation to increase spending in some other area, thus defeating the entire program.

Altering rates of taxation

Another way government can stabilize the economy is by raising or lowering the rates of taxation. It can also levy a temporary surcharge or change the tax laws so that more or less of a household's total income will be subject to taxation (for example, it can change the size of exemptions or allowable medical deductions).

When NNP falls or when its rate of growth slows, government may choose to supplement the built-in stabilizing effect of taxes with a cut in the tax rate. This minimizes the drop in DI, and spending will not fall of in proportion to the decrease in NI. When a rapidly rising NNP creates an inflationary gap, taxes can be increased as a contractionary measure. The tax increase will make DI rise more slowly than NI, thus dampening spending and its resultant demand-pull inflation.

Changes in taxation are an effective tool of discretionary fiscal policy because they can be applied immediately. For example, when Congress passes an income-tax cut, taxes are immediately withheld from paychecks at the new lower level of taxation and an individual's disposable income (DI) is increased with the first paycheck that follows. Unlike changes in spending, changes in taxation do not require extensive planning; they only require that new tax forms be printed.

Limitations of discretionary fiscal policy

Politics versus economics The ability to influence the economy through changes in discretionary fiscal policy is complicated by political considerations. Discretionary fiscal measures approved by politicians and voted into law are often compromise versions of the policies originally suggested by economic advisers.

Although economists may recommend certain actions, the votes of the members of Congress on such measures such as tax increases or spending cuts are based not only on what seems best for the entire country, but also on what is best for their respective home districts and for their own self-interest in terms of reelection. Although senators from the oil-producing states may agree with

---

RECAP

The achievement of the economic goals of a high level of employment and reasonably stable prices can be encouraged through the government's use of nondiscretionary and/or discretionary FISCAL POLICY.

Nondiscretionary fiscal tools (the tax and transfer-payments systems) *automatically* counteract swings in economic activity. As NNP increases, taxes increase and transfer payments decrease thus slowing down the growth in NNP. Conversely, as NNP decreases, taxes decrease and transfer payments increase and limit the decline in economic activity.

The government can also affect economic activity by actually changing the rates of taxation and government spending (discretionary fiscal policy). If NNP increases, the government will cut back its expenditures and increase the tax rate in order to slow down the growth in economic activity. If, on the other hand, NNP decreases, the government will increase its spending and decrease the tax rate in order to stimulate economic activity.

economists who say that demand-pull inflation should be halted by raising income taxes, they may find it difficult to support increased tax rates for the oil interests in their states. Similarly, those who owe their election to the support of organized labor will be reluctant to vote for fiscal measures that will increase the workers' tax burden.

Congress may resist the idea of a tax cut, as well as a tax increase. A tax cut is most effective during a recession, when incomes have dropped. The drop in NI will also cause a drop in the amount of taxes collected through the automatic stabilizers and many legislators (few of whom are professional economists) feel that when the budget already faces an unexpected deficit because of lower tax collections, cutting the tax rate will only aggravate the problem. It can be hard to convince people in Congress and their constituents that a tax cut may actually increase the total tax collection by stimulating consumer spending and investment, both of which are subject to the multiplier effect in raising NNP. Another problem is that once taxes have been lowered, it is difficult to raise them again when the economic situation improves.

Some economists stress the role of future expectations in determining rates of spending and saving. They suggest that a tax surcharge, or any tax change that is known to be temporary, will lose some of its effectiveness. Households may continue to spend at their former levels even when their DI drops, because they expect the drop to be temporary.

Time lags Another problem with discretionary fiscal policy is time lag, that period of time between recognition of the problem and the time the policy change has its effect. There is first a decision lag, the period between recognition of the problem and the time remedial action begins. For example, tax bills must go through the House Ways and Means Committee and must be approved by both House and Senate—a time-consuming procedure at best.

Next comes the impact lag, the period between the time the policy decision is made and the time it begins to affect the economy. The impact lag is relatively short for some fiscal measures. For example, once a new tax bill is passed and new withholding schedules are prepared, there is an almost immediate change in the after-tax take-home pay of most employed persons. Changes in government transfer-payment programs also have a fast impact.

Changes in government expenditures, however, take longer because public-works spending programs often require years of planning before the actual hiring of the unemployed can begin. For example, the Tennessee Valley Authority (TVA) was set up in 1932 during the depths of the Depression to build a giant hydroelectric installation on the Tennessee River. This project was to inject much-needed government spending into the economy, and ultimately, the plant would create electric power and a source of irrigation for residents of the valley. But because the project required extensive planning, the TVA didn't begin to hire many workers or to purchase large amounts of construction materials and machines until two years after its establishment.

In a major depression, the old saying "Better late than never" is probably true. Yet sometimes belated spending is worse than none at all. For example, what would have happened if the government had decided to inaugurate a TVA-type project in 1964, when the economy was threatened by recession? The government's spending would not have poured into the economy until 1966 and 1967, when the recession was already over. The result would have been a large inflationary gap.

This kind of timing problem probably could be minimized. The federal government could keep on file plans for possible public-works programs. When a need for increased public spending arose, it could initiate a project without any long delay for planning, although there would still be a time lag in obtaining congressional approval. During the Depression, for example, when the need for government spending was immediate, many hastily conceived programs were pressed into action. Workers were sometimes hired to repaint a building that was then torn down to make way for a new construction project. It was even rumored that some people were hired to dig holes in the morning and fill them again in the afternoon! These projects served the underlying purpose of injecting federal funds into the economy to bolster aggregate demand, but the initial purchase of social goods yielded very little value. Good planning can minimize the timing problems of government expenditures, but there will always be some irreducible delay.

Thus, the government-expenditure approach is not completely satisfactory when the economic situation calls for rapid action. In addition, it is often difficult to stop additional spending once the original economic problem has been resolved. Long-range projects are especially apt to become institutionalized. Government bureaus are formed to handle them, and private business firms often come to expect an annual contract. The decision to terminate or cut back a project, since it involves political as well as economic considerations, can be hard to carry out. Therefore, increasing the level of government spending often proves to be an irreversible process.

One last limitation of discretionary fiscal policies should be mentioned: such policies are generally more effective in stimulating an economy in recession than they are in restraining an economy suffering from inflation. People do not change their consumption habits overnight, and if the government raises taxes to curb inflation, citizens may spend their savings to keep consuming at the level they previously enjoyed.

THE EFFECTS OF FISCAL POLICY ON EQUILIBRIUM OUTPUT AND INCOME

Government spending

You will recall that the aggregate spending schedule proposed in Chapter 11 consisted of personal consumption spending and business investment ($C + I$). But the government, acting as a collective purchasing agent for social goods, also spends money for goods and services produced by the economy (G). Therefore, a complete aggregate spending schedule consists of $C + I + G$.

Figure 12.1 shows how G is added to aggregate demand. Our $C + I$ line intersects the aggregate supply line at the level of $890 billion NNP.

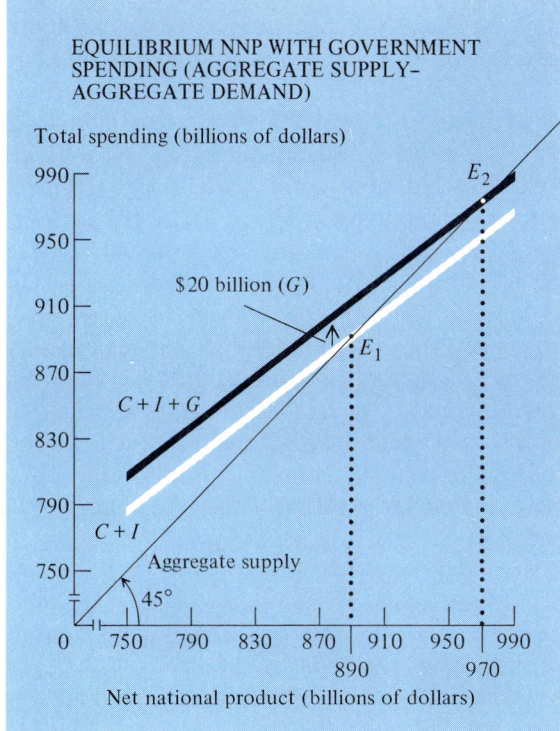

Fig. 12.1
When we add $20 billion of government spending (G) to $C + I$, it is subject to the multiplier. Thus, the increase in NNP caused by the government spending is $20 billion times the multiplier, 4, or $80 billion. Equilibrium NNP for the $C + I + G$ aggregate demand moves from E_1 to E_2 ($890 billion + $80 billion = $970 billion).

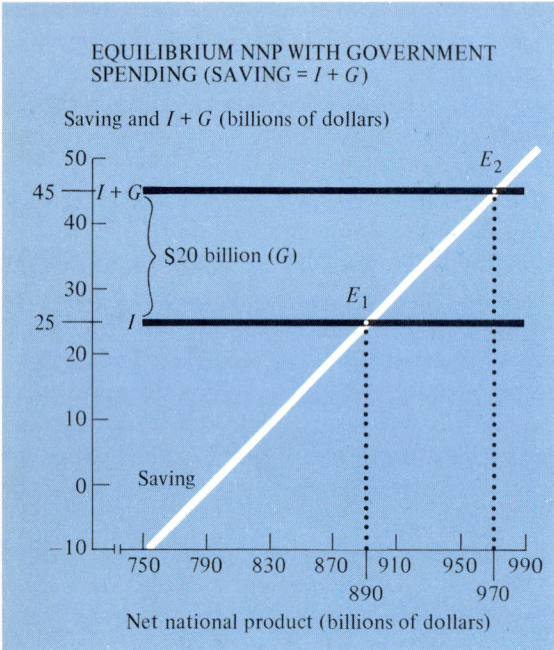

Fig. 12.2
When we add the effects of $20 billion of government spending to the line showing investment (I), we get a second horizontal line at a higher level ($I + G$). If there is no change in saving, NNP will rise by $80 billion (the multiplier, 4, times the government spending of $20 billion) from the equilibrium level of $890 billion ($E_1$) to $970 billion ($E_2$).

Let us assume that the government intends to spend $20 billion, regardless of the level of NNP. By adding this amount to the previous demand line, we get a new higher level of aggregate demand. However, the equilibrium level of NNP will not increase by just $20 billion; instead, it will increase by $80 billion because government spending is subject to the multiplier effect, just as investment is. Thus, NNP will increase by the amount of government spending ($20 billion) times the multiplier (4).

Using the saving-and-investment approach to calculate this new equilibrium NNP, we classify government spending—funds that flow from government to businesses and households—as an injection into the circular flow, since it has the same stimulating effect on the economy as does investment. So, G is added to the amount of investment, as is shown in *Fig. 12.2*. Again, we see the multiplier effect of government spending.

Government taxation

In order to pay for the purchase of social goods and its own administrative costs, the government must have a source of revenue. To simplify our example, we will assume that government revenue comes solely from personal income taxes, although in reality the government also taxes businesses and pays for some of its expenditures by selling bonds and by printing money. Our previous aggregate demand schedule assumed that households would be able to dispose of their total income in spending and saving. But in reality NI is not equal to DI. To find the true amount of DI, we must subtract the money households pay in government taxes from NI.

In our example, we will assume that the total amount of taxes paid by households is $20 billion, regardless of the level of NNP. So from each possible level of NI we must subtract $20 billion. How will this affect the aggregate demand line? If we assume that the MPC is 0.75 and that the marginal propensity to save (MPS) is 0.25, each of the lost dollars of disposable income would have been divided between 75¢ of consumption and 25¢ of saving. Therefore the total decline in consumption will be $15 billion and the accompanying decline in saving will be $5 billion.

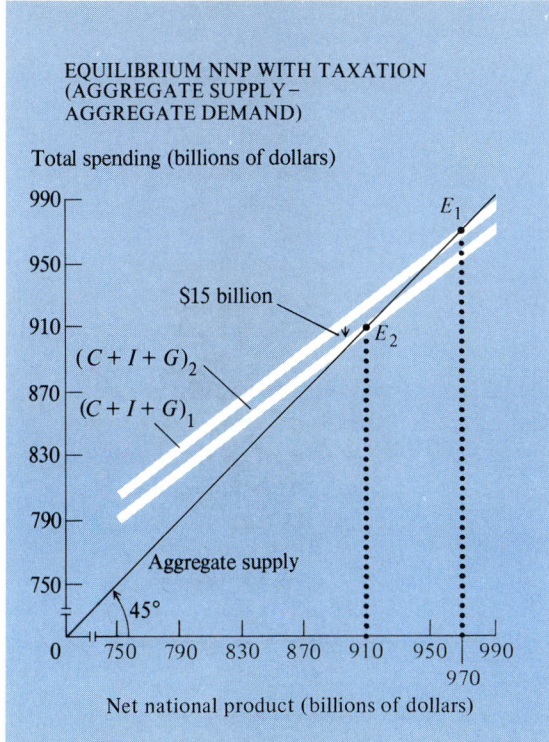

Fig. 12.3
Line $(C + I + G)_1$ represents the equilibrium level of aggregate demand at the level of $970 billion ($E_1$) before the effect of taxes. If the government levies $20 billion of taxes, household income will decrease by $20 billion. If the MPC is ¾, consumption will decline by $15 billion, and saving will decline by $5 billion. To represent the decline in consumption, we draw a new line, $(C + I + G)_2$, exactly parallel to the first but lower by $15 billion. Through the action of the multiplier, the $15 billion drop in consumption will bring a $60 billion drop in NNP to the new equilibrium level (E_2) of $910 billion ($970 billion minus $60 billion).

Figure 12.3 shows the aggregate demand line adjusted for the effects of taxation. Consumption drops by $15 billion, so the aggregate demand line $(C + I + G)$ drops by that amount. This drop causes the equilibrium level of NNP to decrease by $60 billion (due to the multiplier effect) to $910 billion.

When equilibrium NNP is calculated by the saving-and-investment approach, we must first subtract from total saving the amount lost through taxation, or $5 billion. Then, we add the total amount of taxes collected to the new saving figure. To find the new equilibrium level, we then add the amount of government spending to investment. The equation now reads $I + G = S + T$. This approach to calculating the new equilibrium level of NNP is shown in *Fig. 12.4*.

The final effects of spending and taxation on NNP

What is the final effect of equal amounts of government spending and taxation? NNP will rise in the long run. For example, if taxes are $20 billion and MPC is 0.75, taxpayers will decrease consumption by $15 billion and saving by $5 billion. Thus, when the government spends the entire $20 billion, the net effect on aggregate demand will be an increase of $5 billion ($20 billion spent minus the $15 billion decrease in consumption). Given a multiplier of 4, NNP will rise $20 billion.

Table 12.3 is similar to *Table 11.1*, except that now $20 billion in taxes has been withdrawn from the circular flow at each level of NNP, and there is a consequent $20 billion decline in DI and in the sum of consumption and saving at each level. However, the $20 billion in government spending creates a new, higher equilibrium of $910 billion. This situation has important implications for government fiscal policy, as we shall discuss later.

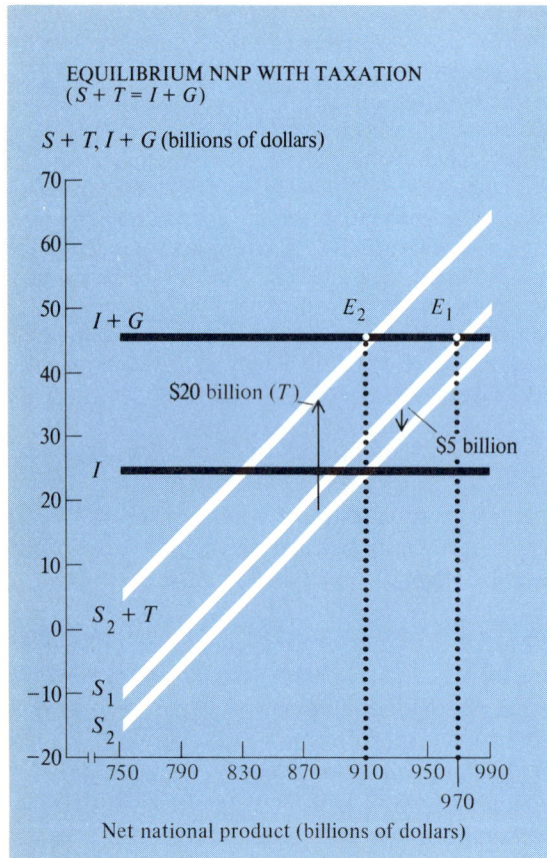

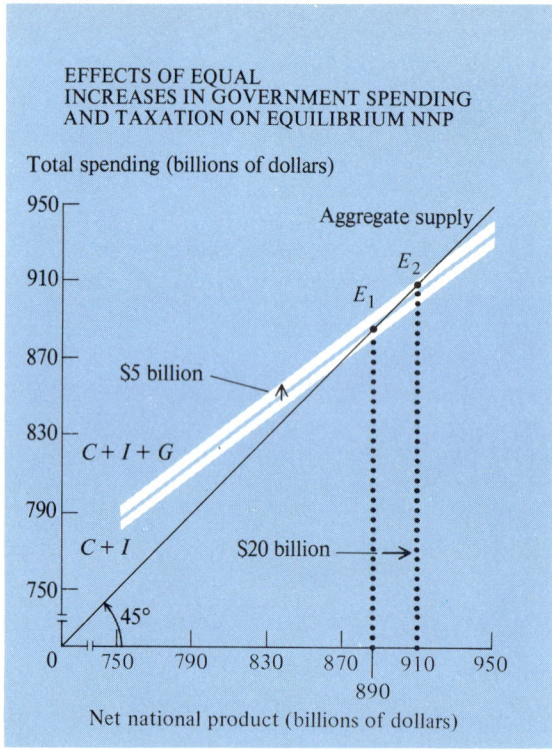

Fig. 12.4
Before the effect of taxes, the equilibrium level of S_1 and $I + G$ falls at $970 billion ($E_1$). If the government imposes a tax of $20 billion ($T$) to finance that spending, saving will decrease by $5 billion (from S_1 to S_2) given an MPS of ¼. To S_2, we now add the $20 billion collected in taxes, since both S and T are deducted from aggregate demand and are used to finance I and G. The new line, $S_2 + T$, intersects line $I + G$ at the NNP level of $910 billion ($E_2$). The *net* increase in saving of $15 billion (the $20 billion added in taxes minus the initial $5 billion drop in saving from S_1 to S_2) causes a decline of $60 billion in NNP due to the action of the multiplier.

Fig. 12.5
If taxation increases by $20 billion to finance an increase of $20 billion in government spending, consumption will fall by $15 billion, given an MPC of ¾. This decline in consumption (and therefore in aggregate demand) only partially offsets the $20 billion increase in aggregate demand due to the increase in government spending. Thus, the *net* effect of equal increases in government spending and taxes is a $5 billion increase in aggregate demand ($20 billion increase in government spending minus $15 billion decrease in consumer spending due to increased taxes). Due to the action of the multiplier, NNP will increase by $20 billion (the $5 billion net increase times 4). The new equilibrium level for NNP will rise from $890 billion ($E_1$) to $910 billion ($E_2$).

Table 12.3
Equilibrium level of output and income with government taxation and spending

(1) Aggregate supply (in billions)	(2) Taxes T (in billions)	(3) Disposable income DI (in billions)	(4) Consumption C (in billions)	(5) Saving S (in billions)	(6) Investment I (in billions)	(7) Government expenditures G (in billions)	(8) Aggregate demand C+I+G (in billions)	(9) Employment (millions of workers)	(10) Tendency of output, income, and employment
$750	$20	$730	$745	$−15	$25	$20	$790	50	Expand
770	20	750	760	−10	25	20	805	55	Expand
790	20	770	775	−5	25	20	820	60	Expand
810	20	790	790	0	25	20	835	65	Expand
830	20	810	805	5	25	20	850	70	Expand
850	20	830	820	10	25	20	865	75	Expand
870	20	850	835	15	25	20	880	80	Expand
890	20	870	850	20	25	20	895	85	Expand
910	20	890	865	25	25	20	910	90	Equilibrium
930	20	910	880	30	25	20	925	95	Contract
950	20	930	895	35	25	20	940	100	Contract

Figure 12.5 also shows the effects of government taxing and spending. It compares equilibrium NNP before the addition of an equal amount of government taxation and spending with equilibrium NNP after the addition.

SURPLUSES AND DEFICITS IN THE FEDERAL BUDGET

When the government raises or lowers tax rates or alters its intended schedule of expenditures, the government budget changes. For example, if the government starts the year with a balanced budget and then decides to increase spending to offset a decline in NNP, it will be left with a budget deficit. When the government incurs a deficit, this has an expansionary effect on the economy. If taxes are increased to fight inflation, there will be a budget surplus. When the government incurs a surplus, the effect on economic activity is contractionary. We will now examine how the government handles these induced surpluses and deficits.

Disposing of surplus revenue

When discretionary fiscal policy creates a surplus because of increased tax revenues or decreased spending, the government must be careful to handle this surplus in a way that will not offset the intended deflationary effect. It must withdraw the money from the circular flow and not allow it to creep back in disguised as some other form of expenditure.

One way to accomplish this goal is to hold the money idle by depositing it with the United States Treasury. Another solution is to use the money to retire some portion of the national debt. Ordinarily, when holders of government bonds cash in their holdings, the government simply issues new bonds to pay off the old ones. It then sells new bonds equal to the amount of the cashed-in bonds to a different bondholder, and the amount of our national debt remains constant. But when the government has a surplus, it can elect to pay off the old bondholders without selling new bonds, thus retiring the debt. Of course, there is a risk that some of this money will find its way back into the circular flow. But for the most part, the money that households and businesses have invested in government bonds is intended for saving. Receivers of the money are therefore most likely to reinvest it in other forms of saving—stocks in private industry, savings accounts, and other securities.

Financing a deficit
If NNP falls, the government may decide to increase its spending at the same time that its tax revenues are falling. This use of discretionary fiscal policy will serve to increase NI and help restore full employment, but in addition, it will almost certainly create a deficit in the government budget. How can this deficit be financed? Government may choose to meet the deficit by increasing the supply of money. That is, it will simply print up new bills in an amount equal to the deficit. Under certain circumstances, this is a satisfactory solution, but sometimes it can lead to inflation. The relationship between money supply and the level of economic activity is discussed in more detail in Chapter 15, which deals with government monetary policy

The other way that government can finance a budget deficit is to borrow money from households and businesses by selling them bonds. One possible drawback to this method is that it may take money from households that would otherwise be spent, or money from businesses that would otherwise be invested in capital goods. Any such decline in spending or investment would, of course, offset the basic goal of an expansionary fiscal policy. Again, however, economists generally agree that most of the money spent to buy government bonds has already been earmarked for saving rather than spending or investment.

FISCAL POLICY AND THE PUBLIC DEBT
When the federal government finances a budget deficit by borrowing from the citizens and institutions of the nation, as discussed above, it increases the **public debt,** *the part of the total of all past budget deficits that has not been eliminated by the total of those portions of all past budget surpluses applied to retire existing budget deficits.* This raises a fundamental macroeconomic issue: How does the public debt affect the economy?

Many people tend to equate the effect of a large public debt with that of a large household debt. But there are significant differences. Unlike the household debt, the public debt never needs to be fully repaid. As long as the government holds the confidence of the public, it can refinance its debt by selling new bonds to repay those that come due. Lending to the government constitutes a safe investment opportunity for citizens with assets to invest, and in this sense, the public debt is at the same time a public credit. Taxpayers, who ultimately pay the cost of maintaining the debt, are also lenders who receive those payments in the form of interest. In other words, United States citizens owe the public debt to themselves. Economists maintain that there is little cause for concern about money we owe to ourselves.

While some budget deficits have resulted from various governmental fiscal policies, the principal sources of the public debt have been the costly wars we have fought in this century. A large proportion of the current debt came into existence during World War II, and the two subsequent wars (Korea and Vietnam) added substantial amounts to the continuing debt. To place the debt in perspective, however, it is important to note that since 1945, though growing steadily, the public debt has been decreasing as a percentage of GNP.

Historical theories of public debt

Classical economists believed that any amount of public debt was harmful to the economy. They insisted that the government budget should always be balanced, implying that it was somehow sinful for a country to be in debt to its citizens. A balanced budget was considered a necessity right up until the 1930s.

During the 1930s, however, the experiences of the Depression and the conclusions John Maynard Keynes drew from them changed many economists' attitudes toward the balanced budget. They began to see a difference between private and public finance and to realize that while a balanced budget was desirable for a household, it was not necessarily desirable for the government, on an annual basis.

Keynes demonstrated that efforts to balance the budget when NNP is changing rapidly in either direction will intensify economic instability. If NNP is falling, government can balance the budget only by increasing taxes or by reducing expenditures; either of these fiscal policies will aggravate a recession. If NNP is rising, the government will have to cut taxes or increase spending to achieve a balanced budget; such a policy would add to the inflationary pressures.

It is currently accepted that an annually balanced budget may do more harm than good to a dynamic economy, depending on how close the economy is to operating at full employment. But economists are much less certain whether or not some sort of long-run balance is desirable. Some believe that over a period of years government deficits and surpluses should be in some sort of balance; the debt incurred during years when NNP sags should be paid off by the surplus that accrues when NNP rises. Others believe that even this degree of balance is unnecessary. They suggest that the only way for a modern mixed economy to achieve full employment without accompanying inflation or fiscal drag is for the government to incur an annual deficit. Theoretically, according to this view, any magnitude of national debt is acceptable as long as the rate of growth of the debt is less than the rate of growth of NNP.

Effects of the public debt

The debate over whether or not a recurrent budget deficit is acceptable centers around the effects of the public debt on the economy. How harmful is it to have a large public debt? The United States government currently has a bonded debt of about $600 billion. Is this an acceptable cost of an expansionary fiscal policy or is it a national disaster?

Effects on future generations

One argument frequently advanced against the existence of a large public debt is that the debt shifts the burden of repayment to a later generation, which will have to make sacrifices to pay for current excesses of consumption. If this current consumption serves to provide social goods and services, future generations will be able to utilize them as well as the present population. If, on the other hand, government borrows money that would otherwise have been used for business investment, it does place a burden on future generations because it has taken from them some portion of their possible production by reducing net formation of capital. If government borrows money from other countries and agrees to pay it back at a later date, that will also place a burden on subsequent generations.

If the government borrows from its citizens only the money they had already planned to save, its borrowing does not interfere with consumption or investment. As long as the amount borrowed is less than the amount of growth in NNP, the only real effect of the debt on future generations will be the way the public debt acts to redistribute income.

Bondholders are paid an annual rate of interest for the use of their money, and the money to pay this interest comes from current tax revenues. In effect, the government taxes one group of people to pay another, just as in a transfer payment—the population as a whole contributes the money to pay interest to bondholders. But bondholders are usually persons with relatively high incomes, since they can afford to save in this form. Therefore the income redistribution caused by the public debt works in the opposite direction to most transfer payments; bond interest goes to the rich at the expense of the general public, whereas welfare and unemployment payments go to the poor.

Other problems

There are a few other problems with the public debt. First, as we will see in Chapter 15, the desire to carry the public debt at the lowest cost to the nation (low interest rates) may conflict with the objectives of monetary policy in times of inflation. The monetary authorities, in order to decrease the rate of inflation, would wish to increase interest rates in order to discourage investment and spending. Such increased interest rates would have the effect of increasing the cost of carrying the public debt.

Another problem is that the acceptability of a public debt encourages Congress to spend more freely than it might if all the government's money had to come from taxes.

Some people also believe that the public debt causes inflation. If the government tries to make money tight to fight inflation, bondholders can still cash their bonds and put their money back into circulation, thus worsening inflation. However, this fairly common argument against the public debt is not well founded. The economy expands not when the debt is repaid, but when the government spends the money it borrows. Since repayment is only a transfer mechanism, no new money enters the economy.

One other complication with the public debt lies in the emotional attitudes it generates. Rates of spending and of investment are partly determined by people's expectations about the future development of the economy. If most people are convinced that a rising public debt is a sign of economic ill health (largely because they equate it with the debt of a household or a business), the existence of the public debt may have negative effects because of its emotional impact on the citizens.

As long as people feel that a large public debt is somehow dangerous economically, they will respond by reducing their spending and their investment in order to prepare themselves for the trouble they believe is lying ahead. Because of this fear and the decreased spending and investment that result from it, the economy slows down and the trouble people have been expecting can actually occur. To avoid this problem, many countries do not release computations of the "public debt"; they simply list the value of redeemed and outstanding bonds (the same thing, but by a different name).

Benefits of the public debt

Against the problems and costs of the public debt discussed above, we must weigh the benefits. It allows us to use deficit financing when that is the best discretionary fiscal policy to help achieve stabilization. It offers an excellent, virtually risk-free way for households to save money—government bonds are highly liquid assets and give their owners feelings of wealth and economic security. In addition a large public debt can sometimes act as a cushion against declines in NNP, since the interest payments are a government expenditure that will continue to inject money into the circular flow.

Not all economists believe that an annual deficit must accompany our future economic expansion, but most economists do agree that a deficit budget and an increase in the public debt are acceptable opportunity costs of a policy of economic expansion achieved through discretionary fiscal measures.

Summary

■ This chapter adds government spending and taxation to our model of aggregate demand and national income in the economy and examines the range of government fiscal tools, the impact of government economic activity on the equilibrium level of net national product (NNP), and how government handles budget surpluses and deficits.

■ Through fiscal policy, government has the ability to change its level of spending and taxation in order to influence the level of economic activity.

■ Some of the automatic stabilizers—nondiscretionary fiscal policy—that operate in our economy are the progressive tax structure (taxes act to cushion any declines in NNP as well as to brake excessively rapid economic expansion) and government transfer payments. Because there are limitations to the actions of these automatic stabilizers, they do not completely eliminate disturbances in the economy and may act too slowly to meet the immediate needs of the economy. Discretionary fiscal policies, which usually require substantial political action, include enlarging or extending the automatic stabilizers and raising or lowering the rates of spending and taxation. Questions of political feasibility and timing must always be considered in determining and enacting discretionary fiscal policy.

■ Changes in government spending and taxation are subject to the multiplier effect, which means that NNP will change by a greater amount than the spending or taxation changes. However, if spending and taxation are altered in equal amounts (for example, if spending and taxes are both increased by equal amounts), the net result will be a rise in NNP.

■ Changes in fiscal policies may result in deficits or surpluses in the federal government's budget. Government surpluses must be handled in such a manner that they do not cancel out their intended deflationary effect. Government budget deficits can be financed either by simply printing money, or by borrowing money through the mechanism of bond sales.

■ A number of controversies surround the issue of the public debt that results from deficit financing. Many economists believe that an annually balanced budget may do more harm than good to a dynamic economy—that some degree of public debt is necessary. Classical economists generally held that a public debt should be avoided since it was essentially sinful, but most contemporary economists believe that a public debt is acceptable as long as it does not increase at a faster rate than NNP. Among the objections to the public debt are that it is passed on to future generations, that the interest paid on bonds to finance the deficit goes primarily to the rich, and that deficit financing may encourage Congress to spend too freely. Among the benefits of the public debt are the flexibility it allows in fiscal policy and the creation of a safe form (government bonds) of household saving.

Key Terms

fiscal policy

nondiscretionary fiscal policy (automatic stabilizers)

budget deficit

budget surplus

fiscal drag

discretionary fiscal policy

public debt

Review & Discussion

1. What are automatic stabilizers? Give examples. How does the progressive tax act as a stabilizer?

2. What discretionary measures can the government take to increase or reduce the equilibrium level of national income? What special difficulties arise in the consideration of discretionary policy?

3. How is government spending of $10 billion represented in the aggregate spending line? How would taxation of $10 billion be represented? What is the net change in national income, given equal amounts ($10 billion) of government spending and taxation?

4. In 1965, government expenditures increased rapidly as a result of increases in the defense (Vietnam) budget. Congressional elections were to be held in 1966. Congress did not act to increase taxes until 1968. What specific problems associated with discretionary policy are illustrated here?

5. Why is a balanced budget considered expansionary? What would be a "neutral" budget—that is, a budget that would not change national income?

6. What choices does the government have in handling surpluses? Which of these are nonexpansionary?

7. How can a public debt be financed?

8. Discuss the advantages of the public national debt. In recent months, the idea of a Constitutional requirement of a balanced federal budget has been widely discussed. What makes such a proposal politically attractive to many people, and how would such a requirement affect public confidence in the government? What would be the economic consequences of such a requirement, both in terms of its effect on NNP and its effect on major current areas of government spending?

Part IV

Money, Monetary Policy, and Economic Stabilization

Chapter 13

The Importance of Money in an Economy

What to look for in this chapter

What are the functions of money in the economy?

What kinds of money are included in the concept of the money supply?

What factors determine the demand for money?

What is the quantity theory of money? How is the relationship between money and NNP seen in the classical, Keynesian, and Chicago School economic theories?

Imagine the difficulties our economy would face if we had no money! When you came to enroll in college, you would bring with you trunks of goods —blankets, wheat germ, lampshades—and use them to bargain with the Treasurer. If you wanted to save for a new stereo, you would have to pile your accumulated bushels of wheat germ in the corners of your room. An evening at the movies would entail carrying along a sack of goods that might interest the ticket seller.

Money—its use, value, and supply—is a very important subject of economic study. In Chapter 10, we discussed the major determinants of consumption and investment spending. Changes in the consumption and investment components of aggregate demand play an important role in establishing the levels of national income, employment, and prices. However, if these levels are determined by total spending in the economy and if spending necessarily involves money transactions, it follows that changes in the supply of money will in turn have some effect on the levels of investment and consumption.

Monetary theory is *the study of the way changes in the money supply and the interest rate can affect levels of income, employment, and prices.* It is of great interest to economists, social scientists, and politicians alike. An understanding of monetary theory will help us to understand why fluctuations in employment and prices occur in our economy—a necessary first step in determining practical solutions to the problems of inflation and unemployment.

In this chapter, we will try to show what money is, what its functions are, and why it is so important. In the next chapter, we will show how the commercial banking system increases and decreases the supply of money. Governments find money a powerful device in the control of economic and social conditions, and the roles that various government and financial institutions play in establishing and implementing monetary policy will be covered in Chapter 15.

FUNCTIONS OF MONEY

In Chapter 3 we defined money as any item that is widely accepted by buyers and sellers as a medium for exchange. Here we will extend our definition to include three functions of money. In addition to serving as a medium for exchange, money is also a standard by which the value of goods and services is expressed, and it serves as a convenient form in which we can store income. Let us now look more closely at each of these functions of money.

Medium of exchange

Money serves as a medium of exchange and facilitates any exchange transaction. Theoretically, it is possible to conceive of economic transactions being carried out through the direct exchange of goods for goods (barter), but as we pointed out in Chapter 3, this process would be a slow and cumbersome way of obtaining the many commodities we need. In addition, the use of barter would inevitably destroy the division or specialization of labor that is directly responsible for the tremendous variety of goods and services our advanced society enjoys.

For example, a window washer who had to exchange his services for bread, housing, shoes, and piano lessons would be hard-pressed to find a seller with the goods he wanted who had windows that needed washing. Each transaction would involve a time-consuming bargaining process until an appropriate exchange rate was established (for example, a certain number of piano lessons in return for a certain number of windows washed). The window washer would probably have to resort to producing these goods himself; others would have to turn out whatever goods they wanted, too. Thus specialization of labor, where each person develops skills to produce a particular item or service, would not exist.

The introduction of money into the exchange process obviously facilitates and speeds up economic transactions. The use of money is absolutely essential to the successful functioning of all but the most primitive economies. Whichever articles societies choose to use as money usually have certain characteristics in common: they are not cumbersome, they are divisible (so that a transaction can be made even when the goods involved have a low value), their supply can be effectively regulated, and they are relatively difficult to duplicate. When any form of money becomes inoperative—as when the total issues of paper currency in Germany rose from 50,065 million marks in December 1919 to 496,585,345,900,000 million marks in December 1923—it must eventually be replaced by another form. It is worth noting, however, that even after such extreme inflation, the replacement again took the familiar form of money—a dramatic indication of the benefits of money as a medium of exchange.

Standard of value

Money is the unit in which the value of goods and services is expressed—as a price. Because we have a workable money system, the value of this economics textbook does not have to expressed in terms of eggs (15 dozen?), or movie tickets (four admissions?). Obviously, it would be impossible to list *all* equivalent trade values and to have such a list available whenever it is needed. Instead, a bookstore merely states the value of a book in terms of dollars and cents, the monetary units currently used in our society. This not only simplifies the pricing procedure but also speeds up the decision-making process of buying. You need to consider only your need for a book, the money cost of the book, and your available funds.

Store of wealth

Money also serves as a convenient form in which we can store our income. It makes saving easier and facilitates long-term planning and projects. This function of money obviously widens the range of choices available to us in deciding what we are going to purchase. We can spend part of a week's pay to buy a surfboard; or we can save for a number of years, accumulating enough money to buy a yacht. In our complex society, where most people possess highly specialized labor skills, an individual could not save without money, the one commodity valued by all. In addition, because it is such a liquid asset, money can be used immediately by households or businesses to pay bills and meet other debts.

KINDS OF MONEY

What commodities can actually be used as money? An incredible variety of items has been used for this purpose in various times and cultures: cattle, sheep, seashells, sharks' teeth. It is clear that commodities will vary in the efficiency with which they fulfill the different functions of money. A rancher whose herd of cattle was struck by disease would find his or her store of wealth quickly eroded in a cattle-money economy.

Clearly there are disadvantages to using such commodities as cattle as money. Are there also disadvantages in the use of paper currency? The most obvious are that it burns, it can be rather easily stolen, and there is more temptation to counterfeit paper currency than metal coins.

No commodity can adequately fulfill *all* the functions of money *all* the time. In every exchange transaction, the success with which a commodity serves as money is always dependent on the willingness of the individuals involved to accept it as money (try paying your landlord in pennies). In certain circumstances, it may be more convenient or efficient for a person to refuse a standard unit of money and to accept instead only some other specified commodity. However, this kind of situation must be considered exceptional. It is clear that what we use as money in the United States *does* meet our working definition: it is widely accepted in our society in exchange for goods and services. In the next section, we will examine the items that make up our money supply.

MONEY IN THE UNITED STATES

There are two major kinds of money in the United States—*currency (coins and paper money) and demand deposits (checking accounts).* These items constitute the narrowest definition of the money supply, which is referred to as M_1. To gain some idea of the relative importance of currency and demand deposits, consider that in 1978 the total money supply (M_1) was about $353 billion, of which $93.2 billion was currency and $259.8 billion was demand deposits.

Currency

Coins

Coins, our fractional currency, constitute a very small proportion, usually less than 5 percent, of the value of all currency in circulation. At one time, the value of coins was linked to the actual value of the metal (gold or silver) in the coins: The coins were said to have a monetary value equal to their commodity value; that is, equal to the value of the materials contained in the coins. Unfortunately, both governments and individuals were constantly tempted to debase the coins—by clipping off the edges or by alloying them surreptitiously with cheaper metals. As a result, such coins became unreliable as a form of money. Today, our coinage is a token money; its stated value is considerably higher than the commodity value of the metal. The use of token money is a deliberate effort on the part of the government to discourage people from melting down coins; the coins are thereby kept in circulation.

A case in which the commodity value of money exceeded its money value occurred in the mid-1960s. The price of silver on the world market almost doubled; consequently, the value of silver in American quarters exceeded 25¢ and American dimes were worth more than 10¢. Although it is illegal for private citizens to melt down silver coins, the temptation to do so became great. At that point, the Treasury started producing new nickel and copper-alloy dimes and quarters, thus maintaining the quantity of fractional currency at a level sufficient to carry on transactions in the marketplace. Had the Treasury not taken this action, quarters and dimes undoubtedly would have disappeared from circulation.

Paper money

Paper money is the other portion of our currency. Today paper money consists almost exclusively of Federal Reserve notes that have been issued by the Federal Reserve banks under circumstances that will be described in greater detail in Chapter 15.

History of paper currency Many people believe that the paper dollars in circulation are backed by a stock of gold in Fort Knox, and that no more dollars can be printed than there is gold to back them. This is not true today, although it has been true in the past. The custom of backing paper money with gold began when English goldsmiths, as a convenience for neighborhood merchants, retained the merchants' gold in their safes, giving them paper receipts in return. When the merchants had bills to pay, they could retrieve the gold they needed by surrendering their receipts to the goldsmith. It became accepted practice to pay one's bills simply by endorsing, or signing over, the paper receipts that stood for the gold. Eventually, the original receipts were written as "payable to bearer," thus making a new endorsement unnecessary for each exchange that took place thereafter. These receipts were an early form of paper money.

Paper currency in the United States: the gold reserve Until 1933, United States paper currency was legally convertible into gold and silver. The Treasury kept a substantial amount of these metals available so that people could exchange their paper money for precious metals. Beginning in the 1930s, however, United States citizens were not permitted to convert paper money into gold, and the Treasury no longer had to keep a stock of gold on hand against possible domestic requests. Subsequent legislation freed the Treasury for the most part from having to convert paper money into gold (except for a few intergovernmental conversions) and eliminated the requirement for gold reserve as a backing against the paper money in circulation.

Although late in 1974, legislation was passed to permit United States citizens to purchase and hold gold bullion for the first time in more than 40 years, it is important to recognize that this action was not a return to "free conversion" as it had applied earlier. A special offer by the Treasury of 2 million troy ounces of gold for sale in January 1975 had its intended effect of cooling somewhat the spiraling price of gold on the world market, but to the surprise of many, the demand for gold in the United States proved to be limited.

What we have now is a **"fiat" money system** *in which paper money need not be backed by any set amount of precious metal*. Paper money is money only because the federal government says it is. The Agricultural Adjustment Act of 1933 decreed our paper currency to be legal tender for the payment of all public and private debts. And most important of all, currency is money because we all accept and use it as money, just as people in other cultures have accepted and used flints, beads, goats, tiger claws, or even wives.

Demand deposits

Demand deposits are *deposits of money in banks against which checks can be written. The bank promises to pay at once (on demand) money in the amount specified by the customer who owns the deposit.* Checks are the means of transferring the ownership of the monies.

Demand deposits constitute almost 75 percent of our money supply; yet they are even more important than this statistic indicates because checks are involved as payment in approximately 90 percent of all transactions. As paychecks have generally replaced pay envelopes filled with dollar bills and coins, and as banks continue to popularize the convenience of personal checking accounts, economists believe that the relative importance of the role that demand deposits assume in our money supply will increase even further.

Checks as money

Checks qualify as money in our society because they are widely accepted as a medium for paying bills. In some circumstances, however, checks are not so effective a medium of exchange as currency. It would be inconvenient (and somewhat embarrassing) to write a check at your local newsstand as payment for a newspaper. Proprietors of smaller stores may refuse to accept a check because they have no way of knowing whether the individual has enough money in his or her account to cover it. Nevertheless, a check in your pocket is practically as good as money because you can con-

> **RECAP**
>
> The narrowest definition of the MONEY SUPPLY, represented by M_1, consists of currency (coins and paper money) and demand deposits (checking accounts).
>
> A broader definition, represented by M_2, defines the money supply as currency and demand deposits plus the money from savings deposits and time accounts.

vert it immediately into currency by going to your bank and cashing it.

Near-money

There are other categories of liquid assets, collectively termed **near-monies,** *that share some of the basic properties of money. Like money, near-monies can be converted easily into currency or demand deposits, but unlike money, they are not widely accepted as a medium of exchange.*

One category of near-monies is savings accounts—money held in interest-earning accounts at commercial banks, mutual savings banks, savings and loan associations, and credit unions. These accounts are often referred to as time deposits, meaning that a bank could legally require you to give it 30 to 90 days' notice of withdrawal (as compared with demand deposits from which withdrawals can be made at once). In practice, however, you can usually withdraw your time deposit immediately. Short-term (less than one year) United States Treasury securities and government bonds, such as the Series E savings bonds, are another category of near-money. Like time deposits, they are liquid—that is, they can be converted quickly and cheaply into a predetermined amount of currency or a deposit in a checking account.

Money supply: a broader definition

Earlier we defined the money supply narrowly as consisting of currency and demand deposits (M_1).

Some economists argue that the money supply should be defined more broadly to include the *money from savings deposits and time accounts in addition to currency and demand deposits*. This enlarged definition of the money supply is labeled M_2. However, as noted above, near-monies do not function directly as a medium of exchange. For this reason, in the following analysis, we will define the supply of money in the United States as including only currency and demand deposits, even though we recognize that a broader definition can sometimes be useful.

MONEY DEMAND

The supply of money is influenced by the day-to-day transactions of commercial banks. However, the actual power to set limits on the money supply in this country lies with the central-bank authorities. Consequently, most economists treat the supply of money as a given quantity that can be predetermined or established by these institutions. We will discuss how or why the central-bank authorities implement changes in the supply of money in the following chapters; here we will look at the demand for money in our economy.

Types of money demand

Why do people hold *any* part of their assets in money? After all, there is an "opportunity cost" in holding money, since dollars in your wallet or checking account* earn no additional dollars. If holding money costs you potential income, why hold it?

Keynes theorized that people hold money in its most liquid form—demand deposits or cash—to satisfy three types of demand: transactions demand, precautionary demand, and speculative demand.

---

*A special form of checking account—called the NOW account—is permitted to earn interest at banks in a limited number of states.

Transactions demand

Everyone needs to have some money readily available to pay day-to-day living costs. Suppose you are paid on the first of each month by your employer. In deciding what portion of your income to hold as money—either as cash in hand or as a deposit in your checking account—you first must consider the cost of goods and services you plan to purchase in the month ahead. Most people have to hold a very large portion of their income as money to be able to pay the grocer, the gasoline-station operator, the druggist. While cash in pocket is a nonearning asset, the various day-to-day demands for money make holding some money an unavoidable necessity.

Businesses have a similar **transactions demand** for money. That is, *they must keep a certain amount of money readily available to carry out day-to-day transactions* such as meeting payrolls, and paying bills, taxes, and dividends. In recent years, astute corporation managers have paid increasing attention to curtailing the high cost of the transactions demand for money. For example, a major retailer handling billions of dollars a year in sales distributes weekly employee checks just before noon every Thursday. Because banks compute interest on large industrial and business accounts by the half-day, the company can save several millions of dollars a year by not transferring funds from an earning account until noon on the day its employees will be cashing their checks in the lunch hour. Of course, this kind of financial transaction is practical only where very large sums are involved; most businesses have few alternatives to meeting the transactions demand for money other than continuing to hold money.

Precautionary demand

Precautionary demand is *the tendency of most people to hold more money than is actually required for everyday transactions.* The fear of unexpected contingencies—minor problems such as a broken carburetor or a leaking roof, or major emergencies such as a serious illness—leads people to keep extra money available.

The amount of money held for precautionary reasons increases in times of general uncertainty. If your next-door neighbor is fired in a layoff at a nearby factory, you may regard this as an economic danger signal and start spending less and saving more. The precautionary demand for money, therefore, is partly a function of psychological factors—levels of optimism, pessimism, and uncertainty—regarding economic conditions.

Speculative demand
If you feel that the price of any commodity will soon drop, you may want to keep your money in the bank temporarily, waiting until the price drops before you buy the desired commodity. If a business that manufactures pots and pans believes that the price of copper (an important input in the production process) will decline, its executives may decide to hold money rather than to buy copper at its current market price. In periods of economic unrest or panic, the **speculative demand** for money becomes especially great. *Households and businesses, anticipating lower prices, convert assets into money and decide merely to hold onto the money until conditions are more predictable.* Here, too, psychological factors are at work.

DRAWING A DEMAND CURVE FOR MONEY

Economists have found it useful to show the demand for holding money graphically in a demand curve or **liquidity preference curve.** The liquidity preference curve is like any other demand curve; it expresses the demand for money in terms of the relationship between the price of holding money and the quantity of money held, assuming that all other factors influencing the demand for money remain constant. In this case, the price of holding money is the potential income that could be gained if the money were invested in interest-earning assets. The price of money is therefore the current rate of interest.

The liquidity preference curve, then, shows the relationship between changes in the interest rate and the amount of liquid assets a person is willing to hold. We plot the liquidity preference curve like any demand curve, by placing the price of money (the interest rate) on the vertical axis and the quantity of money held on the horizontal axis (see *Fig. 13.1*). *The quantity of money held will vary inversely with changes in the interest rate.*

For example, when interest rates are high, individuals and businesses are reluctant to leave money on deposit in checking accounts; interest-earning bonds or time deposits become more attractive, even though these bonds or deposits may pose certain inconveniences when the investor wishes to use the money as payment in a transaction. The higher the available interest rates, the more likely such transfers become. On the other hand, when interest rates are low, as they were during the 1930s and early 1940s, the opportunity cost of leaving money in a demand deposit is also low, and more money is held in that form.

We can plot the demand schedule for money balances of an entire economy. At a rate of interest of 8 percent, the money balances held are apt to be quite small, because the opportunity cost of holding money is high. As the interest rate decreases, the amount of money held will steadily increase, as more people will be willing to forgo the lower interest paid on bonds. Finally, when the interest rate is only 2 percent, hardly anyone will bother to buy bonds or keep their money in savings accounts, since there is such a small price to pay for holding money. *Figure 13.1* plots our hypothetical economy's demand schedule for money.

Shifts in the demand curve for money
As noted above, the liquidity preference curve assumes that only price and quantity are changing;

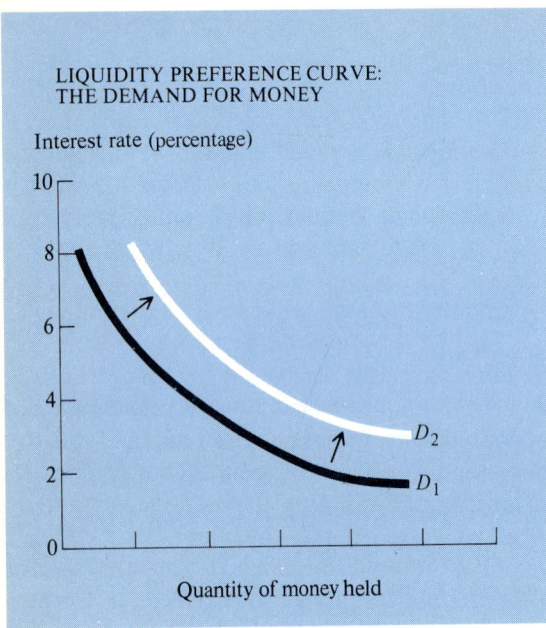

Fig. 13.1
Line D_1 shows the demand for holding money, given the present level of income. As interest rates decrease, more money will be held, since this alternative becomes relatively cheaper. D_2 shows how the demand schedule might shift if household income rises. Alternatively, D_2 might also represent a change in demand if households expect a future rise of interest rates; they would want to remain more liquid so that they could buy higher-yielding securities after the rates rise. In either case, more money will be held at all interest levels than on demand curve D_1.

income and expectations concerning future economic conditions.

Level of income

As income rises, a larger quantity of money will be held, whatever the interest rate is. As income falls, the reverse happens. Fluctuations in income levels are the primary cause of any shift in the demand curve for money. An increase in the level of income will result in a shift of the entire demand curve to the right, whereas a decline in income will cause the curve to shift to the left. (Line D_2 in *Fig. 13.1* shows how the demand curve might shift if income rises.) Why is this so? One reason is that a household with a larger income will make more transactions and so must keep larger money balances on hand to cover these transactions. In addition, such a household will hold more money on a precautionary basis, because it is protecting a higher standard of living against unexpected disasters.

Psychological expectations

The demand curve for money can also shift as a result of changes in public expectations about future economic conditions. If people are pessimistic about the future health of the economy, they may want to hold larger money balances, whatever the level of interest being paid, as a precaution against a sudden decline in income. On the other hand, if people are optimistic about the economic future, the demand curve for money may shift to the left as people start converting part of their money balances into other types of assets.

QUANTITY THEORY OF MONEY

We have examined some of the ways in which the demand for money may change. Now let us consider how the effects of changing demands for money are linked to the money supply itself and to prices and production level. The **quantity theory**

all other factors influencing the demand for money are assumed to remain constant. In fact, however, a change in any of these other determinants of demand will cause a shift in the entire curve. Over the years, studies of economic behavior have shown that changes in the demand for money are caused largely by changes in the level of

of money *deals with the relationship of price level to money supply.*

Velocity

To understand the quantity theory, we must begin by examining the concept of **velocity**—another way of looking at the demand for money. Velocity is defined as *the number of times each dollar is spent or turned over within a stated period of time.*

We can illustrate the concept of velocity by applying it to the spending pattern of a single household. Imagine a family that spends $10,000 over a year. The household does not need to have the total amount available for the entire year. At any one time it holds on the average approximately $1000 in currency and demand deposits. Thus the family is spending or turning over its money supply about 10 times a year. This is described as a velocity rate of 10.

Velocity formulas

What would happen if the family decided to spend less and maintain a larger money balance? Suppose that the family increases its average money balance to $1200. If we employ the formula below, money velocity in the family is at a rate of $8\frac{1}{3}$:

$$\frac{\text{annual income}}{\text{average money balance}} = \text{velocity};$$

or

$$\frac{\$10,000}{\$1,200} = 8\frac{1}{3}.$$

We can apply the concept of velocity to our whole economy. In 1978, the GNP was about $2106.9 billion a year, and the money supply was approximately $353 billion, giving the United States an annual income velocity rate of about 6 ($2106.9/$353 = 6). *Figure 13.2* shows income velocity in the United States since 1900.

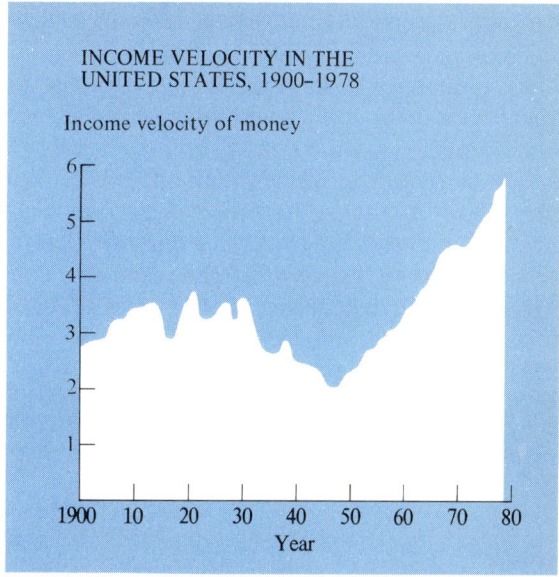

SOURCE: Board of Governors of the Federal Reserve.

Fig. 13.2
Income velocity showed a general trend toward decline from 1930 to 1945. This reflects the general pessimism that prevailed during the Depression and World War II; people wanted to hold large money balances until the future seemed more certain. Since the end of World War II, velocity has been rising steadily.

We can also define velocity (V) as the dollar value of GNP divided by the money supply (M), or $V = (GNP/M)$. By multiplying both sides of the equation by M, we see that $MV = GNP$.

This equation is even more useful when we express GNP as price times quantity. We know that the dollar value of GNP is derived by multiplying the quantity of all final goods and services produced by the prices of these items (for example, $100,000 worth of automobile production can be expressed as 20 cars × $5000). Substituting quantity (Q) and price (P) for GNP, we can express our equation in a very useful way: $MV = PQ$ (money supply × velocity = average price per unit × quantity of units of output). This is the usual form in which the quantity theory of money is expressed.

What does this equation tell us? *Changes in the supply of money or the velocity rate must cause corresponding changes in either price levels, or quantities of goods produced, or both.* This suggests that changes in supply of money (M) can be used to affect the price level (P) or production levels (Q), assuming V is constant.

QUANTITY THEORY AND FULL EMPLOYMENT: THE CLASSICAL INTERPRETATION

When classical economists interpreted the quantity theory of money, they made two fundamental assumptions. First, they believed that an economy always tended to operate at full capacity. In conditions of free competition, the prices of labor and other production costs would always stabilize at the level at which all labor and all productive resources were fully utilized. Second, they assumed that velocity (V) was a constant. According to the classical viewpoint, if the money supply suddenly doubled, people would have twice as much money as they needed for transaction purposes. (The classical economists focused primarily on the *transactions* demand for money.) Presumably, individuals would spend this additional money, directly increasing aggregate demand. But since the economy was assumed to be operating at full capacity already, the quantity of goods produced (Q) could not change greatly no matter how much demand increased. If V is a constant and Q is essentially a constant, the possibility of change in either of these factors is virtually eliminated; therefore, changes in M could only affect P—a given increase in the money supply must cause a proportional increase in the price level.

As evidence, the classical economists pointed to long-term inflation in Spain in the 1500s after gold was discovered in the New World. The huge increase in the money supply in the form of gold coins led to an increase in price levels, supposedly because V remained constant and Q could not increase.

$$\overset{\uparrow}{M}\underset{\leftrightarrow}{V} = \overset{\uparrow}{P}\underset{\leftrightarrow}{Q}$$

This interpretation of the quantity theory emphasizes the effects that changes in money supply have on changes in price levels. Because they predicted such effects, classical economists were reluctant to permit increases in money supply; according to their theory, the result would be inflation.

To summarize, *the classical view of the quantity theory of money asserts that with both velocity and quantity of goods assumed to be relatively stable, an increase in the supply of money must cause an increase in prices.*

QUANTITY THEORY AND UNEMPLOYMENT: THE KEYNESIAN VIEWPOINT

By the 1930s it became obvious that classical economic theory could not account for some of the new problems that were disturbing the economy. According to the classical model, unemployment was supposed to be only temporary until adjustments in the price of resources reestablished full employment. But unemployment had been persistent in England since the mid-1920s and was increasing. Some economists suggested that since the economy was obviously not operating at full capacity, Q should no longer be considered a constant. Therefore, an increase in M could lead to an increase in Q. Increasing the money supply might increase production and hence solve the unemployment problem.

Although John Maynard Keynes was initially a strong advocate of such action, he soon changed his mind. Although a number of governments (particularly the United States) increased their money supplies during the Depression of the 1930s, this had no appreciable effect on the level of unemployment.* In spite of the fact that there was a great deal of unused capacity (unemployment in the United States reached approximately 25 percent in 1933), output (Q) was not reacting proportionately to increases in M, even though prices were stable or actually declining. Keynes therefore reasoned that certain forces must be at work causing V to decline.

$$M\overset{\uparrow}{V} = P Q$$

Keynes focused on the *precautionary* and *speculative* demands for money to explain the large increases in money balances that had precipitated the decline in velocity. He believed that fear of worsening conditions and pessimism concerning the economy were causing people to hold as much money as possible for precautionary reasons. Moreover, the interest rate was so low that the public was certain that it could only rise in the future. Therefore, the amount of money held for speculative purposes also increased; people wanted to hold money so that when interest rates rose they would have cash to put into interest-earning assets.

In Keynes's model, increases in the money supply would be hoarded in ever larger amounts of idle cash; velocity would decrease even further. *Keynes concluded that under the particular circumstances facing England at the time, increases in the supply of money could lead neither to higher production nor to higher prices.*

Keynes concluded—as do Keynesians now—that if you want to stimulate production during a recession, it is not enough merely to increase the money supply. You must make certain that such

---

*Some economists, however, argue that money supply was not increased sufficiently during the early 1930s to influence the level of output, and that the tight money policy of the 1920s was still having an effect on the economy.

> **RECAP**
>
> QUANTITY THEORY ($MV = PQ$)
>
> *Classical view:* V and Q are relatively stable; an increase in M causes an increase in P.
>
> *Keynesian view:* Increases in M are counteracted by decreases in V; neither P nor Q increases.
>
> *"New" new economics:* Changes in V are small; any increase in M in a less than full-employment situation will increase aggregate demand and, therefore, output and employment.

increases in M are not counteracted by a decline in V; in other words, the money must actually be spent, not held as idle cash or idle bank balances. Thus, instead of advocating principally monetary actions to stimulate an economy, Keynesians emphasize government spending—direct welfare payments, work projects, increases in Social Security and unemployment benefits, and the like—as the basic cure for economic recessions. These activities could be financed by printing new money; hence, the money supply rises *as* the new money is spent. (Recall that according to the classical model, M would rise and *then* spending would rise.)

QUANTITY THEORY AND THE "NEW" NEW ECONOMICS

The Keynesian reinterpretation of the quantity theory became known as the "new economics," and was widely accepted throughout the post–World War II period. Many governments, including the United States, have based their economic policies on the Keynesian point of view. In the 1960s, however, a new approach based largely on the work of Milton Friedman at the University of

Chicago, was developed. It has been called by some the "new" new economics. In a way, this title is a misnomer, because the Chicago School reemphasizes some of the concepts of the classical economists. It assigns only a minor role to V, assuming that velocity will undergo only small fluctuations over the years and that such fluctuations are fairly predictable.*

The Chicago School differs from the classical economic point of view, however, in emphasizing that changes in the money supply have an important effect on the level of real output. *Since changes in V are small, any increase in M in a less than full-employment situation will give rise to more spending (increase the level of aggregate demand) and will cause output, and hence employment, to increase as well.*

QUANTITY THEORY OF MONEY: SOME CONCLUSIONS

As we have seen, economists differ greatly in their interpretations and applications of the quantity theory of money. However the theory is interpreted, it does make clear some fundamental truths.

First, huge long-term increases in the supply of money must be inflationary—if M zooms skyward, output (Q) cannot increase as quickly, and prices will rise. In times of full employment, even moderate increases in M are inflationary. In the mid-1960s, the United States economy was operating at virtually full capacity (unemployment was down to 3.2 percent). At that time, the money supply was increased because of the additional spending involved in escalating the Vietnam war. The result was a spurt of inflation from an annual rate of less than 2 percent in 1967–1968 to almost 6 percent in 1970. Similarly, the double-digit inflation of recent years can be traced at least in part to the rapid increase in the money supply from January 1971 to June 1974, when M_1 grew at an average rate of 7 percent a year, the highest growth rate since the end of World War II. Although mid-1974 saw a return to restrictive monetary policy, the reversal failed to slow the rate of inflation. In 1974, the Consumer Price Index rose 11 percent, the largest yearly increase since 1947. One reason for this is that there is a time lag between a change in monetary policy and the realization of its effects.

On the other hand, it appears logical that in a nation with a large number of unemployed or underemployed resources, an increase in the supply of money will lead to an increase in spending and hence an increase in output, other things being equal. We might assume that prices either would not increase or would increase relatively little, since there would be competition for jobs, resources, and productive facilities. In short, a larger money supply would result in a higher level of production and increased employment, rather than in higher prices.

MONEY IN THE KEYNESIAN MODEL

Money supply and equilibrium interest rate

It is clear that changes in the supply of money in a situation of unemployment must have some influence on the level of NNP. But exactly how do changes in the money supply (MS) fit into the Keynesian income model? Our discussion of the demand curve for money suggested that there must necessarily be some interest rate at which the

---

*Apparently, Friedman's research indicates that the multiplier is more variable and unpredictable over the business cycle than is velocity. If this is true, the change in the level of spending that results from a change in the money supply is more predictable than the change in spending that results from, say, a tax cut. At least part of the uncertainty about the extent to which velocity fluctuates arises from the fact that different economists define "money" differently; the stability of velocity over the years depends on how money is defined.

DEVELOPMENTS IN ECONOMIC THOUGHT:

Milton Friedman

Pictorial Parade, Inc.

Although the ideas of the dominant liberal economists are his favorite targets, Milton Friedman (b. 1912) manages to make many of his fellow conservatives uncomfortable as well. Like most conservatives, Friedman opposes extensive government intervention in the economy and argues for the free exercise of individual economic rights in the marketplace. His conservative principles often extend in some surprising directions, however, as illustrated by his early criticism of the compulsory military draft and his suggestion that state licensing requirements for medical doctors are unwarranted.

After obtaining his master's degree in economics at the University of Chicago and his Ph.D. at Columbia University, Friedman began to teach at Chicago and became a guiding force in the development of the "Chicago School" of economic thought—the major influence on contemporary conservative economic thinking. Through his training of students, his research and publications, and his regular column in *Newsweek* magazine, Friedman has established himself as a formidable economist, even among his detractors. Accordingly, he was awarded the Nobel Prize in Economics in 1976 for his work in consumption analysis and monetary history and theory, and for his demonstration of the complexity of stabilization policy.

Friedman's major work has focused on the history, theory, and application of monetary policy, a counterweight to the liberal economists' concentration on fiscal policy. The main empirical evidence for Friedman's views on monetary policy is contained in *A Monetary History of the United States,* coauthored in 1963 with Anna Schwartz. In addition to providing a definitive and detailed account of the evolution of monetary practice, the book also provides historical evidence for his theoretical assertion that the money supply is the key factor in determining the level of economic activity.

Friedman's focus on the critical role of money challenges two basic Keynesian assumptions: that an unregulated market economy is basically unstable and that large-scale government economic activity is efficient and necessary. For conservatives, the advantage of concentrating on monetary policy is that it requires less massive involvement of government in the economy and places less economic control in the hands of Washington policymakers. Friedman would like to limit government involvement even further by discouraging the Federal Reserve Board from constantly increasing and decreasing the money supply. Instead, Friedman encourages the use of a formula whereby the money supply is increased steadily at a rate that reflects the growth in real GNP.

More than many contemporary economists, Friedman agrees with Adam Smith's belief (see Chapter 4) that a truly unregulated economic system is not only freer and simpler, but also more productive than any centrally planned or regulated system. As Friedman wrote in 1964, "the so-called uncontrolled economy is in fact a far more efficient system than the so-called controlled economy for harnessing the knowledge, the energy, and the will of the people of a society for achieving their own separate objectives. The so-called uncontrolled economy is controlled, too; by the right people, by the millions of separate individuals who make up the society, and whose separate aims and objectives collectively make up the true goal of society."

In writings like *Capitalism and Freedom* (1962), Friedman extended his philosophical convictions to other economic and non-economic areas. He has opposed tariff barriers to free international trade, called for the abolition of Social Security and the graduated income tax, and suggested that private individuals, not the government, should pay for and manage national parks. On the other hand, Friedman has strongly endorsed the idea of a "negative income tax"—money grants to people below a certain minimum income level—as a replacement for welfare and the present elaborate system of social-service agencies and programs. Although he has never held a government post, Friedman was an economic advisor to the Goldwater presidential campaign in 1964.

amount of money the public wishes to hold in cash balances exactly equals the quantity of money supplied by the central-bank authorities, working through the commercial-banking system. Such an interest rate is i_2 in *Fig. 13.3*. Any interest rate above or below i_2—such as i_1 or i_3—cannot be maintained, assuming that the existing demand for, and the supply of, money remain constant. Point E then marks the equilibrium point in the money market, that point at which the demand curve for money intersects the supply curve.

Any change in the total supply of money would result in the establishment of a new equilibrium interest rate, as shown in *Fig. 13.4*. If the supply curve for money shifts to the right (from MS_2 to MS_3), the public would find itself holding more money than it would actually want to hold, given an interest rate of i_2. If people use this "surplus" of money balances to purchase bonds and other interest-earning assets, the price of bonds will be bid up, which is the same as saying that the interest rate will fall. Eventually, the interest rate (the price of money) will decline until it reaches i_3, where equilibrium is restored.

The reverse process would occur if the supply of money shifted to the left (from MS_2 to MS_1). At

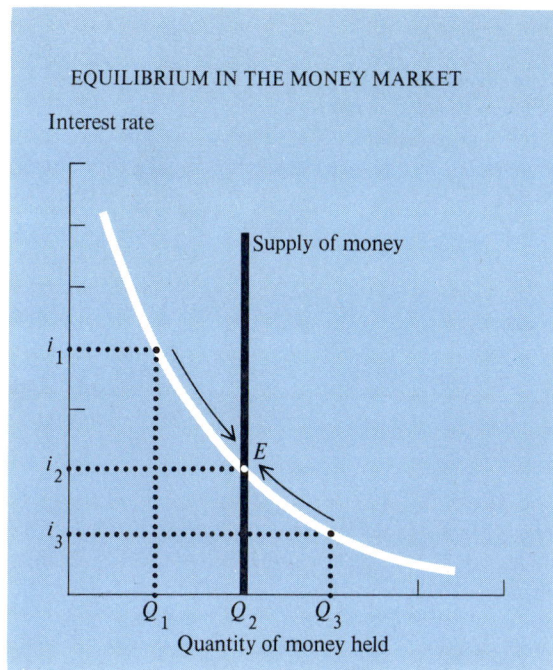

Fig. 13.3
The point of equilibrium, at which the amount of money the public wishes to hold in cash balances exactly equals the quantity of money supplied by the central banking authorities, falls at point E. That means the interest rate will be i_2. If the rate were either i_1 or i_3, demand and supply would not be equal.

the former equilibrium rate of interest i_2, people will wish to hold more money than is actually available after the cut in MS, thus giving rise to a shortage of cash balances. The result would be a tendency for the interest rate to be bid up to i_1, where equilibrium is restored.

Interest rate and investment spending

The interest rate is one of the determinants of investment spending. When interest rates are high, business spending on new plant and equipment declines because the expected rate of return is less than could be obtained through, say, the purchase of bonds. High interest rates also mean a high cost for borrowed funds, which can make investment spending more expensive and decrease its profitability. The opposite holds true when the rate of interest is low. *The relationship between the inter-*

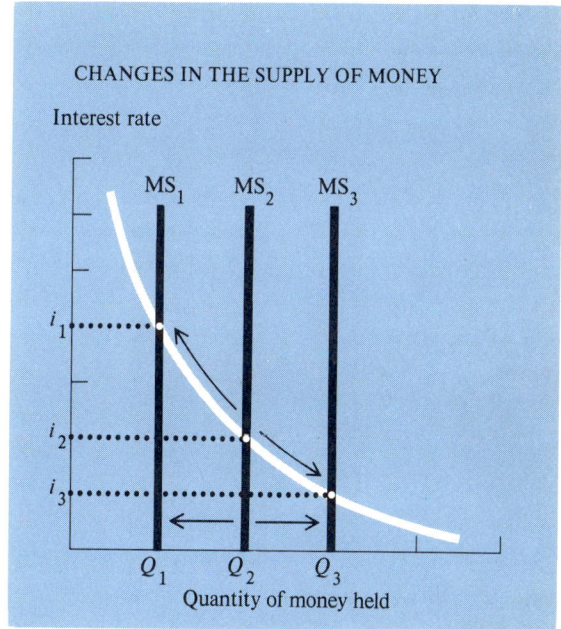

Fig. 13.4
This figure shows how equilibrium interest rates will change in response to changes in the money supply. If the central bank authorities increase the money supply from MS_2 to MS_3, the public finds itself holding more money than it wants to hold. As households invest this cash surplus, they will drive up the price of bonds and other interest-earning securities; the new equilibrium interest rate will fall at the lower level of i_3. If the money supply is decreased from MS_2 to MS_1, interest rates will rise to i_1.

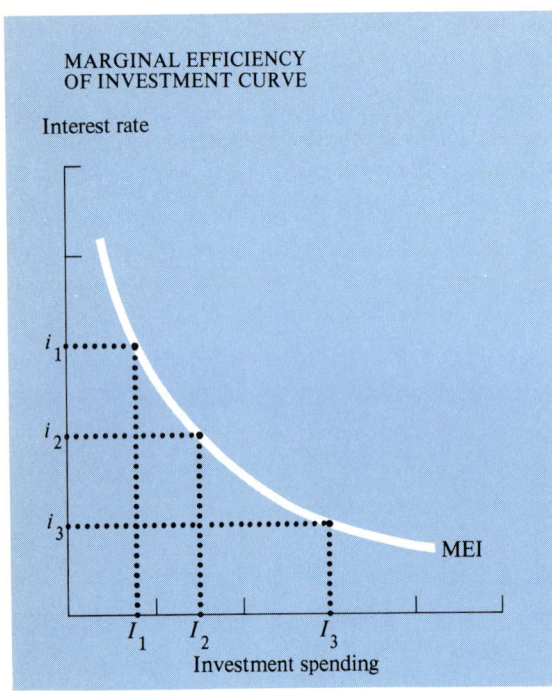

Fig. 13.5
The marginal efficiency of investment curve shows that more investment spending will occur when interest rates are lower. As rates go down, the costs of borrowing also decrease, as does the opportunity cost of investing in a physical plant rather than in interest-earning assets.

Fig. 13.6
These graphs show a situation in which monetary policy could be expected to have very little effect in changing the level of investment. The flat liquidity preference curve indicates that the interest rate is not very sensitive to changes in the supply of money; the steep MEI curve indicates that investment spending is very insensitive to changes in the interest rate.

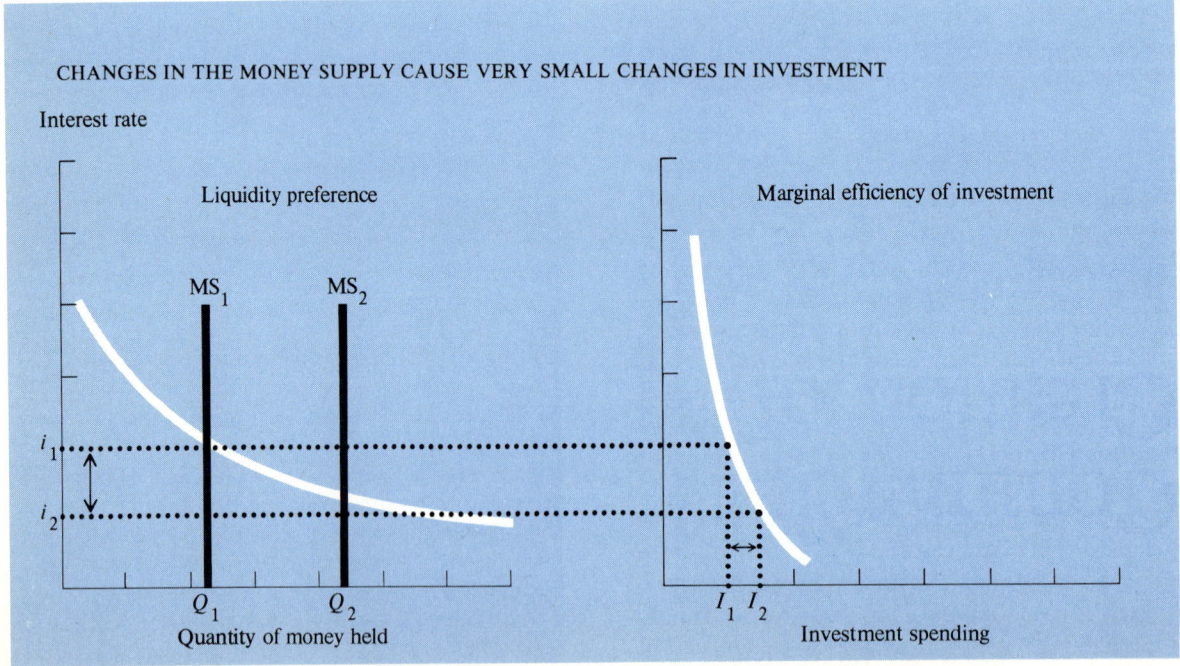

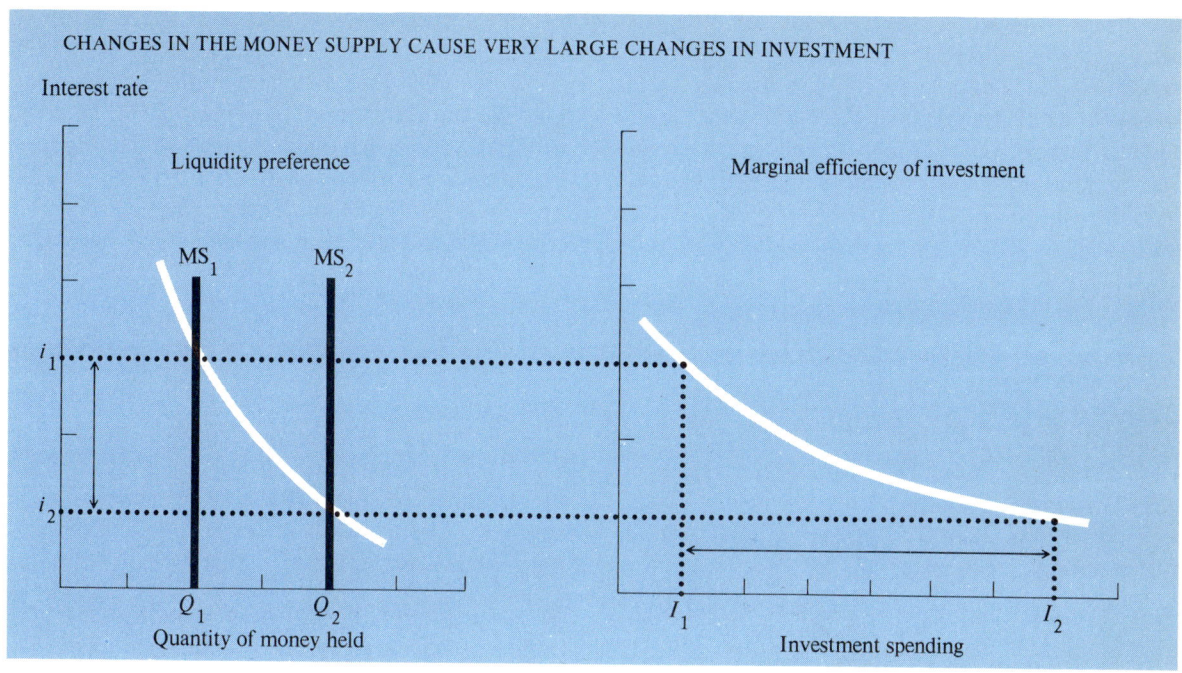

Fig. 13.7
In an economy with these liquidity preference and marginal efficiency of investment curves, we could expect monetary policy to be quite effective in changing the level of investment. The interest rate is very sensitive to changes in the money supply, and investment spending is quite sensitive to changes in the interest rate.

est rate and the level of investment, called the **marginal efficiency of investment (MEI),** is shown in *Fig. 13.5.*

We now know that the rate of interest will vary with changes in the supply of money. As i changes, the level of investment will also vary and so will the level of NNP. This important sequence of events can be summarized as follows:

$M\uparrow \rightarrow i\downarrow \rightarrow I\uparrow \rightarrow$ aggregate demand$\uparrow \rightarrow$ NNP$\uparrow$
$M\downarrow \rightarrow i\uparrow \rightarrow I\downarrow \rightarrow$ aggregate demand$\downarrow \rightarrow$ NNP$\downarrow$.

As M increases, the interest rate is bid down and investment spending rises; because of the multiplier, NNP rises even more than the increase in aggregate demand. As M decreases, the interest rate is bid up and investment spending declines, with NNP declining by a multiplied amount.

One important question remains. How great a change in NNP will a given change in M cause? This depends largely on the shapes of the liquidity preference curve and the MEI curve (see *Figs. 13.6* and *13.7*). If the liquidity preference curve is very flat, as in *Fig. 13.6,* it will take very large changes in M to affect i at all. On the other hand, if the liquidity preference curve is very steep, as in *Fig. 13.7,* small changes in the money supply will cause substantial changes in the rate of interest.

But merely knowing the responsiveness of the interest rate to changes in M is not enough to tell us what the final change in NNP will be. We must also know how responsive business investment demand is to changes in the interest rate. Thus the steeper the MEI curve, like the one in *Fig. 13.6,* the less responsive investment spending will be to fluctuations in *i*; and the flatter the MEI curve, like the one in *Fig. 13.7,* the more responsive investment will be.

Throughout this chapter we have assumed that the size of the money supply was essentially fixed by federal-government authorities working through the commercial banking system. Now we will look at the mechanism through which this control process is carried out. In the following chapter we will discuss in detail the ways that commercial banks increase and decrease the money supply.

Summary

■ This chapter examines what money is, what its functions are, and why it is so important in our economy.

■ Money is anything that is widely accepted in a community in exchange for other things. It serves as a medium of exchange, a standard of value, and a way of storing income.

■ A number of different commodities have been used historically as money, but currency and paper money have the advantages of being convenient to handle and not easily subject to spoilage and destruction.

■ In the United States today, the money supply (narrowly defined) includes currency (coins and paper money) and demand deposits (checking accounts), with demand deposits by far the largest portion. More broadly defined, the money supply also includes near-monies, such as savings accounts and other time deposits and short-term United States Treasury notes.

■ We view the supply of money as a fixed amount, determined by quasi-government authorities. The demand for money includes transactions demand (for day-to-day purchases), precautionary demand (for contingencies) and speculative demand (in the expectation of changing economic conditions).

■ A demand curve for money—a liquidity preference curve—expresses the inverse relationship between the price of money (the interest rate) and the quantity of money held. A given demand curve for money will shift with changes in the level of income or changes in expectations about economic conditions.

■ The velocity of money is the number of times each dollar is spent within a stated period. The quantity theory of money ($MV = PQ$) tells us that the total dollar value of goods and services (price times quantity) in a given period must equal the number of dollars in the money supply (M) times the velocity (V). Therefore, changes in either M or V must result in changes in P, or in Q, or both.

■ Classical economists assumed that the economy would be operating at a full-employment level and, consequently, that increases in the money supply would always be inflationary, resulting only in higher prices.

■ Keynes argued that when an economy was operating at less than full employment (as in the Depression), an increase in the money supply could lead to an increase in production, but that this effect could be negated if velocity was dropping at the same time.

■ The Chicago School economists of the 1960s have argued that changes in velocity are likely to be small; in a less than full-employment situation, therefore, an increase in the money supply will cause an increase in output and employment.

■ It is clear to all economists that a huge and sudden increase in the money supply will be inflationary, raising prices rather than output. In a full-employment situation, even a modest increase in the money supply will have an inflationary effect.

■ In the Keynesian model, an increase in the money supply will cause a decrease in the interest rate, resulting in an increase in investment, an increase in aggregate demand, and therefore a multiplied increase in NNP. Similarly, a decrease in the money supply leads to a decline in NNP. The amount of the final increase or decrease in NNP depends primarily on the relationship between the money supply and the interest rate (expressed in the liquidity preference curve) and the relationship between the interest rate and investment (expressed as the marginal efficiency of investment).

Key Terms

monetary theory
M_1
"fiat" money system
demand deposits
near-monies
M_2
transactions demand
precautionary demand
speculative demand
liquidity preference curve
quantity theory of money
velocity
marginal efficiency of investment (MEI)

Review & Discussion

1. What is included in the nation's money supply? Why do some economists consider time deposits to be money? Describe near-money.

2. How well would a commodity such as light bulbs serve as money? How well would it perform the various functions of money? What would happen to the specialization of labor in the economy if food were used as money?

3. Describe the types of demand for money. Why might people choose to hold large amounts of money in addition to that required to pay bills?

4. Write the equation for the quantity theory of money. According to the quantity theory, what happens to output if the money supply contracts, velocity falls, and prices remain constant?

5. What is the effect of an increase in the money supply in a full-employment economy? What would have to happen if the increase is to cause no change in prices?

6. How is it possible for a wave of pessimism to be antiinflationary? What does it do to the demand for money? To velocity?

7. What is liquidity preference? Marginal efficiency of investment? Draw typical curves to express these relationships.

8. What are the aims of a tight money policy? What response in the economy would a classical economist predict if changes in the money supply occurred? What would a follower of the "new" new economics predict?

9. Suppose that in a given economy the demand curve for money balance shifts to the right because people are pessimistic about the future of the economy. What effect will this have on the level of aggregate demand? What changes in the money supply would tend to counteract this effect?

Chapter 14

Commercial Banks and the Creation of Money

What to look for in this chapter

What is the role of commercial banks in the economy?

How are commercial banks related to the Federal Reserve System?

How do the various common bank transactions show up on a balance sheet?

How do the ways in which commercial banks use their excess reserves operate to expand or contract the amount of money in the economy? What are the limitations on such expansion?

One of the principal economic functions of commercial banks is to provide the opportunity to hold demand deposits. The activities of banks in managing these deposits can actually create and contract money, and therefore banks play an important role in any monetary policy the government may decide to adopt.

COMPONENTS OF THE COMMERCIAL BANKING SYSTEM

Commercial bank

The **commercial bank** is the primary unit of the United States banking system. *It is a business firm chartered by a state government or the federal government to serve a variety of financial functions, the most important of which is creating demand deposits by lending money.* Banks extend credit to individuals and businesses, and they also

THE NATION'S TEN LARGEST COMMERCIAL BANKS AND THEIR DEPOSITS	
Bank of America NT & SA, San Francisco	$71,010,269,000
Citibank NA, New York	$60,889,533,000
Chase Manhattan Bank NA, New York	$43,497,466,000
Manufacturers Hanover Trust Co., New York	$30,092,798,000
Morgan Guaranty Trust Co., New York	$25,765,063,000
Chemical Bank, New York	$23,262,673,000
Continental Illinois NB & T Co., Chicago	$18,353,150,000
Bankers Trust Co., New York	$17,948,812,000
First National Bank, Chicago	$16,714,313,000
Security Pacific National Bank, Los Angeles	$16,218,520,148

Source: The World Almanac & Book of Facts, 1979, Newspaper Enterprise Assn., Inc., 1978, p. 105 - from 300 Largest Commercial Banks in U.S., compiled by American Banker, New York, 1978.
*Based on deposits June 30, 1978.

grant loans to the federal and municipal governments by purchasing their bonds. Other services provided by commercial banks include savings accounts (also offered by savings banks); investment advice; home mortgages (also a primary function of savings banks and savings and loan associations); and various specialized services, such as credit cards, tax guidance, the rental of computer time, and foreign currency exchange.

Great Britain and Canada have banking systems that are dominated by a few very large commercial banks, each of which has hundreds of branches. The United States banking system, by contrast, comprises many commercial banks, numbering more than 14,700 today. Recent changes in state banking laws have facilitated mergers of many independent banks into statewide banking systems. Nonetheless, the relatively small one-town bank, with deep roots in the community it serves, is still a healthy part of the American banking structure.

Central bank

Commercial banks are only one part of the commercial banking system; the other is the **central bank.** *The central bank comprises the principal banking authorities of a nation. Its primary function is to provide a means of controlling the size of the total money supply. In the United States, the central bank is the Federal Reserve System, which consists of a Board of Governors and 12 regional Federal Reserve banks.* Together these are commonly referred to as the Fed. (These central bank authorities and their functions will be discussed in detail in Chapter 15.)

The central bank authorities supervise the operation of the Federal Reserve System, which consists of the central bank plus several thousand privately owned commercial banks. All commercial banks in this country must be chartered (a charter grants the bank the authority to operate) by the federal or the state government. Nationally chartered banks become members of the Federal Reserve System automatically, and they must observe the requirements. Banks chartered by state governments may join the system if they choose. In 1978 less than half of all United States banks were members of the Federal Reserve System. But these banks included the largest and most important ones in the country, and together they held about three-quarters of all United States bank deposits. By regulating the everyday operations of these individual commercial banks, therefore, the Fed is able to control the flow of most of the money and credit in the United States economy.

BANKING BUSINESS: AN OVERVIEW

Why does anyone go into the banking business? Why do groups of people decide to invest their money in opening a bank? Bankers are in business to make money; their overall operations are aimed at maximizing profits. However, the profit-seeking transactions of commercial banks result in an extremely important by-product—the creation and contraction of money. We will consider shortly the transactions of commercial banks that result in expansion and contraction of the money supply. But let us look first at a bank's balance sheet as a convenient means of understanding some general aspects of banking.

Balance sheets

The easiest way to show what happens at a bank each time a financial transaction occurs is to use a simplified **balance sheet.** *A balance sheet summarizes a firm's financial position at any given time.* The term "balance sheet" is used because the two sides—assets and claims—will always be equal, or balanced.

A balance sheet can be drawn up for a bank the same way that it is prepared for any other type of firm. The left side shows **assets**—*things of value that the bank owns*—either outright or in the form of debts owed to it. The right side of the balance, called the liabilities and net worth side, shows what the bank owes—the claims against its assets. **Liabilities** are *things of value, such as cash or property, that the bank owes to its creditors,* for example, customers' deposits that the bank is obliged to pay back on demand. The bank's **net worth** is *the value of the capital stock owned by the bank's stockholders (investors).* Net worth is equal to assets minus liabilities.

Assets − Liabilities = Net Worth

The following is a simplified balance sheet of a bank. Note that when they are added up, the total assets of the bank exactly equal its liabilities plus net worth.

Glendower National Bank Balance Sheet

Assets		Liabilities and net worth	
Cash and cash equivalents	$20,000	Demand deposits	$80,000
Loans	50,000	Capital stock	20,000
Government bonds	20,000		
Property	10,000		

Forming a new bank

Now suppose that we want to form a new bank (one that, incidentally, will be a member of the Federal Reserve System). The first thing we must do, as owners, is to invest an initial amount of money. Part of this money will be used to buy or rent a building and capital equipment; the rest is left as cash. The balance sheet below shows the First National Bank of Hotspur's financial position after we have invested $10,000 and spent $9000 of it on facilities.

First National Bank of Hotspur Balance Sheet

Assets		Liabilities and net worth	
Cash	$1,000	Capital stock	$10,000
Property	9,000		

Making a deposit

Now that we've established our bank, let us see how the day-to-day business affects the balance sheet. When Mr. Guildenstern deposits $1200 in cash in a checking account, the amount of one of our assets (cash on hand) increases by $1200. But the balance sheet must also reflect the source of the cash—in short, that Mr. Guildenstern has a claim for $1200 against the bank. This new demand deposit account of $1200 therefore appears on our balance sheet as an increase in both assets and liabilities. This is how it will look.

First National Bank of Hotspur Balance Sheet

Assets		Liabilities and net worth	
Cash	$2,200	Demand deposits	$ 1,200
Property	9,000	Capital stock	10,000

Reserve requirements

In Chapter 13 we noted that the earliest banking establishments were those of the English goldsmiths, who held gold deposits in their safes as a convenience for neighboring merchants. The gold was simply locked away until the depositors called for it. But the goldsmith quickly realized that only a small number of depositors were liable to request their money at any given time. The same is true today in the United States, where it is estimated that a bank could handle the relatively few cash-withdrawal requests of depositors with only 2 percent of the bank's total deposits available in cash. Therefore, bankers feel that it is safe to keep on hand only *part* of the money deposited by customers. (This is known technically as a fractional reserve against deposit.)

The banks use the balance of the money to earn profits by making loans to private individuals and businesses or buying government securities. Astute bankers want to lend out as much money as possible and to keep as little of their depositors' cash on reserve as is prudent. But exactly how large should reserves be? In an unregulated banking system, this decision is made by the banker. However, those United States banks that are members of the Federal Reserve System have no choice in determining the fractional reserve they will hold against deposits. The system sets *a minimum amount that its member banks must keep in the form of cash or cash equivalents against its deposit liabilities. The percentage that must be held in reserves is known as the* **reserve ratio,** or the **reserve requirement.** The upper and lower limits are set by Congress, and within these limits, the Federal Reserve sets the reserve requirements for member banks on a graduated scale based on the size of their total demand deposits. In the illustrative examples in the remainder of this chapter, we will make the simplifying assumption that the banks involved are required to hold reserves of 10 percent. Bear in mind also that the balance sheets given in the calculations will show only those assets and liabilities we are concerned with here rather than the totals that place the banks in the 10 percent classification.

What does 10 percent actually mean in terms of bank operations? It means that when a bank receives a $1000 deposit, it must keep at least $100 on reserve. The most it can lend out is $900.

$$\text{reserve requirement} = \frac{\text{cash or cash equivalent}}{\text{demand deposits}}$$

$$= \frac{\$100}{\$1000} = 10\%$$

Purpose of reserve requirements Earlier we said that it has been estimated that a bank could handle the relatively few cash-withdrawal requests of depositors with only a 2 percent reserve against deposits. Why, then, would the Fed require a reserve ratio as high as, say, 10 percent? Certainly not for the protection of banks and their investors; the government has protective systems far more effective than the reserve requirement. The most significant of these is the *Federal Deposit*

Insurance Corporation. Established in 1933, the FDIC insures depositors' accounts up to a certain amount and guarantees to provide depositors immediately with the money they wish to withdraw from their accounts if a bank, for any reason, should lack the cash to do so.

The primary purpose of the ratio of, for example, 10 percent, then, is not protection but control. *Through the reserve requirements, the Fed can control the amount of money commercial banks have available for lending purposes. This control over the amount of credit that can be extended by the commercial banks enables the Fed to counteract overstimulation or overcontraction of the economy.* Therefore the range between the upper and lower limits of reserve requirements is wide enough to allow the Fed to implement its policies.

Transfers to reserve account at the Fed

Cash held in the vaults of commercial banks is legally considered reserves. But since only a small amount of vault cash is needed for day-to-day transactions, each local bank sends almost all of its required reserves to its regional Federal Reserve bank, where they are placed on deposit in a non-interest-earning account for the local bank.

Let us return to our First National Bank of Hotspur. The bank now has $2200 in cash—the initial $1000 in cash assets, plus the $1200 Mr. Guildenstern brought in to deposit. Ordinarily, we would probably keep 1 or 2 percent of this cash as currency in the teller's drawer, and send the rest to the regional Federal Reserve bank to be credited to our reserve account. For the sake of simplicity, however, let us assume that we send all $2200 to the Fed. This transfer of $2200 in cash from our vault to our reserve account at the Fed must be recorded on the asset side of our balance sheet. Note that the liabilities side of the balance sheet does not change when this transfer is made. The *changes* in the balance sheet of the Hotspur bank can now be summarized as follows.

Assets		Liabilities
Cash	− $2,200	
Reserves	+ 2,200	

The new bank balance sheet will look like this.

Assets		Liabilities and net worth	
Cash	$ 0	Demand	
Property	9,000	deposits	$ 1,200
Reserves	2,200	Capital stock	10,000

Clearing a check

What happens when Mr. Guildenstern eventually writes a check against his account in our bank? Such a transaction is accomplished easily if the check is made out to another one of our depositors. We would simply increase the other customer's balance and decrease Mr. Guildenstern's, and the total amount of deposits in the bank would remain unchanged. However, with more than 14,700 banks in the United States, most checks are written to people who have accounts in banks other than the checkwriter's bank.

Let us suppose that Mr. Guildenstern writes a check for $200 and gives it to his landlady, Mrs. Fortinbras, who deposits it in her bank, Nordic National. Nordic adds $200 to Mrs. Fortinbras's account, and sends the check to the regional Federal Reserve bank for collection. The Fed credits the check to the Nordic bank, increasing the balance in Nordic's reserve account; Nordic now has $200 more on reserve at the Fed. Next the Fed *subtracts* $200 from Hotspur's reserve account, then sends the check back to the Hotspur bank, where the $200 is subtracted from Mr. Guildenstern's account. This process is called *clearing a check*. Note how the existence of individual reserve accounts at the Fed simplifies the entire clearing process, permitting money to be transferred from one bank to another merely by changing the balances in their reserve accounts.

What will our bank's balance sheet look like after Mr. Guildenstern's check has cleared? One of our assets (our reserve account at the Federal Reserve bank) has declined. But so has one of our liabilities because Mr. Guildenstern's demand-deposit claim on our bank is only $1000, instead of $1200. Here is a summary of the changes.

Assets		Liabilities	
Reserves	−$200	Demand deposits	−$200

The balance sheet for our Hotspur bank now looks like this:

Assets		Liabilities and net worth	
Cash	$ 0	Demand deposits	$ 1,000
Property	9,000		
Reserves	2,000	Capital stock	10,000

To summarize, when a check is drawn against one bank and deposited in another, the original bank's reserves, as well as its demand deposits, diminish.

Excess reserves

Assuming that the reserve requirements of the Federal Reserve are 10 percent against demand deposits, the First National Bank of Hotspur is now required to keep $100 in reserves to cover its total demand deposits of $1000. As we can see, however, our bank has $2000 in reserves, many times more than the amount legally required. **Excess reserves** are *that amount by which a bank's actual reserves exceed its required reserves*. The situation of the Hotspur bank can be summarized as follows.

Actual reserves	$2,000
Required reserves (10% of $1,000 in demand deposits)	− 100
Excess reserves	$1,900

What do these excess reserves mean to the president of our bank? They mean lost profits, since these deposits are not earning any money for the bank (not even interest, since the Federal Reserve Board pays no interest to member banks on their deposits). Our president would undoubtedly like to put these excess reserves to work, either lending them out to individuals or businesses, or buying government bonds with them. And since a bank may profit more by making loans than by buying government bonds, excess reserves tend to encourage bankers to make loans.

MONEY-CREATING AND MONEY-CONTRACTING TRANSACTIONS OF COMMERCIAL BANKS

Making private loans: money is created

Transaction 1: Dr. Yorick is granted a loan

What happens to a bank's balance sheet and its reserve position when it lends money to a borrower? Dr. Abigail Yorick requests a loan of $2000 from our bank to help pay for medical equipment she has purchased for her office. The Hotspur bank's loan officer knows that Dr. Yorick, an established local doctor, is a good credit risk. He is therefore willing to lend her money, but he can lend her only $1900, the amount of the banks excess reserves. The doctor agrees to the loan of $1900 and signs a note, or loan agreement.

Since Dr. Yorick, like most borrowers, pays her bills with checks rather than currency, she wants her loan in the form of a checking account at the Hotspur bank, instead of in cash. Therefore, the bank establishes a checking account for her, with a balance of $1900. The bank now has a new asset (Dr. Yorick's signed note, which represents money she owes to the bank) and a new liability (the $1900 balance in Dr. Yorick's demand-deposit account). Changes in the balance sheet of the First National Bank of Hotspur are as follows.

Assets		Liabilities	
Loans	+$1,900	Demand deposits	+$1,900

The new balance sheet looks like this.

Assets		Liabilities and net worth	
Cash	$ 0	Demand deposits	$ 2,900
Loans	1,900	Capital stock	10,000
Property	9,000		
Reserves	2,000		

The bank also has an additional demand deposit of $1900 that it did not have before, resulting in total demand deposits of $2900 (Mr. Guildenstern's $1000 and Dr. Yorick's $1900). In other words, $1900 of additional money has been created as a result of this loan; the bank has taken a piece of paper from Dr. Yorick (her signed loan agreement) and, in exchange, has created money for her. This process of converting a borrower's note is often called *monetizing a loan*—another way of saying that money has been created in granting the loan.

Perhaps you are wondering why the bank lent the doctor only $1900 when the balance sheet shows reserves of $2000. Since reserves need to equal only 10 percent of the total demand deposits, it seems logical that the bank might have granted Dr. Yorick a loan of as much as $19,000 had she asked for it. (A demand deposit of $19,000 for her, plus Mr. Guildenstern's deposit of $1000 would equal $20,000, or the maximum amount of demand deposits a reserve of $2000 could legally support.) Fortunately for us, however, our loan officer knows his business. In setting $1900 as the maximum, he was simply anticipating the transactions he knew would follow the granting of the loan. Let us now examine these transactions.

Transaction 2: Dr. Yorick writes a check

The first thing Dr. Yorick does with the $1900 in her demand deposit is to write a check to the Bent Bone X-Ray Equipment Corporation. The Bent Bone Corporation deposits Dr. Yorick's check in its own account at the Richman Bank and Trust. When the check reaches the regional Federal Reserve bank to be cleared, the Fed subtracts $1900 from the Hotspur reserve account. When the Fed has returned the check to Hotspur, Hotspur reduces Dr. Yorick's account by $1900. The following changes have been made in the balance sheet of the Hotspur bank.

Assets		Liabilities	
Reserves	−$1,900	Demand deposits	−$1,900

Effect on Hotspur's reserve position Let us look now at the new balance sheet of the Hotspur bank, paying particular attention to the bank's reserve position.

Assets		Liabilities and net worth	
Loans	$1,900	Demand	
Property	9,000	deposits	$ 1,000
Reserves	100	Capital stock	10,000

All of a sudden Hotspur bank is just meeting its reserve requirements! The $100 in reserves is exactly the amount the bank must hold against its $1000 in demand deposits. This illustrates a very important fact of banking: *Individuals (and businesses) generally borrow money in order to use it immediately.* Deposits created through loans, such as the loan made to Dr. Yorick, are apt to leave the bank very quickly. When they leave, the bank's reserve account at the Fed must be reduced accordingly. Thus sensible bankers never lend an amount greater than their excess reserves at the Fed, because they could rapidly find themselves short of the required reserves.

Let us see what the result would have been had the financial officer loaned Dr. Yorick the amount she requested—$2000. She probably would have spent the full sum. The check would gave gone to the Fed, and the Fed would have taken $2000 from Hotspur bank's reserves (our total reserve is only $2000), leaving us with Mr. Guildenstern's demand deposit of $1000 and no reserve whatever to cover it. In other words, we would now be violating federal law. The moral of this episode is clear: Bankers should not lend an amount greater than the amount they have in excess reserves.

Effect on the system Thus far, we have examined only the changes that occurred in Hotspur bank's balance sheet as a result of the loan to Dr. Yorick and the payment she subsequently made to the Bent Bone X-Ray Corporation. Now let us see what happens when the Bent Bone Corporation deposits the doctor's check in its account at Richman Bank and Trust. Richman sends the check to the Fed for clearing, and the Fed increases Richman's reserve account by $1900. Richman's balance sheet shows both a $1900 increase in demand deposits, since $1900 has been added to the Bent Bone Corporation's account, and a corresponding $1900 increase in its reserves account at the Fed. The following changes are made in the Richman Bank and Trust balance sheet.

Assets		Liabilities	
Reserves	+$1,900	Demand deposits	+$1,900

Assume that Richman's reserve position had been exactly 10 percent of its demand deposits before the Bent Bone deposit. As a result of the deposit, Richman has $1900 in additional demand deposits, requiring an additional $190 (10 percent) in reserves. However, it has just gained $1900 in new reserves. Therefore it has $1710 in excess reserves, and it may now grant loans up to $1710 of new money.

What happens when we add Richman's money-creating activities to those of our bank in Hotspur? Hotspur bank, with $1900 of excess reserves, created $1900 of new demand-deposit money by granting Dr. Yorick's loan. After Dr. Yorick used the loan to pay her bill, the process of fund transfer gave Richman excess reserves of $1710, with which that bank can create an addi-

Table 14.1
Expansion of the money supply by the commercial banking system

Bank	A New deposit received	B Reserve required (10% of A)	C Excess reserve (A—B)	D New loans bank can make
Hotspur (initial Yorick loan)				$ 1,900.00
Richman	$1,900.00	190.00	1,710.00	1,710.00
Rosencrantz	1,710.00	171.00	1,539.00	1,539.00
Bank 4	1,539.00	153.90	1,385.10	1,385.10
Bank 5	1,385.10	138.51	1,246.59	1,246.59
Bank 6	1,246.59	124.66	1,121.93	1,121.93
All other banks*				10,097.38
Total new loans granted				$19,000.00

*This category refers to all the other banks in the banking system that would be able to expand their loans as a result of the initial Hotspur loan.

tional $1710 of new loans (or new money). So far, the original $1900 of excess reserves has made possible the creation of $3610 in new money ($1900 + $1710).

Transaction 3: Richman lends excess reserves

Suppose Richman Bank and Trust lends $1710 to the Bottom Appliance Company. The company's checking account is therefore increased by this amount, and Bottom then uses its new demand deposit to pay bills it owes to the Short-Circuit Electric Corporation. Short-Circuit receives Bottom's check and deposits it in its own bank, the Rosencrantz Trust Company. This increases both Rosencrantz's demand deposits and its reserve account at the Fed by $1710. Since the Rosencrantz Trust Company is required to have only 10 percent of the $1710, or $171, as reserve against the new demand deposit, it has $1539 of excess reserves. It therefore can grant an additional loan (create new money) of $1539.

Summary: money-creation through private loans

Hotspur bank's original excess reserves of $1900 have led to the creation of $1900 + $1710 + $1539 of new money. This money-creating process can be expressed in percentages as well. Each demand deposit that a bank receives also creates for the bank an equal amount of new reserves. However, if only 10 percent of the new reserves must actually be held as required reserves, this leaves the bank with excess reserves that amount to 90 percent of the demand deposit. *Table 14.1* summarizes the money-creating transactions that take place when a bank uses its reserve funds to make a loan. Note that the overall effect is very similar to the effect of the multiplier on any increase in consumption spending.

Multiple expansion

Although any one bank can create new money in an amount equal only to its own excess reserves, *the banking system as a whole can expand loans by ten times the amount of excess reserves* (given a reserve ratio of 10 percent). This is so because reserves do not disappear within the system as a whole. The reserves that Hotspur lost were gained by Richman; when Richman lost reserves, Rosencrantz acquired them. Put technically, the banking system as a whole can increase loans by the reciprocal (the inverse) of the fractional reserve requirement. If the fractional reserve requirement is 1/10 (10 percent), the reciprocal is 10/1. Remember, however, that we have been using 10 percent as the reserve requirement for the sake of simplicity in our calculations. Since the Federal Reserve establishes reserve requirements according to a graduated scale based on size of demand deposits, there is no single percentage rate for all banks and all loans. It therefore follows that at any given time the reciprocal by which loans can be expanded is a figure that must be calculated on the basis of total loans granted against actual excess reserves of all banks in the system.

Repayment of loans: money is contracted

We have seen how money is created at the inception of a loan by examining what happened when Hotspur bank loaned Dr. Yorick her money. Now let us see what happens when the loan comes due for payment. Dr. Yorick was given six months before she was required to repay her loan. During this period she receives checks from her patients and deposits them in her checking account at the bank, building up her balance against the note's due date. (Incidentally, each time our bank receives one of these checks from the doctor, presumably drawn on other banks, we send them to the Fed for clearing and thus continue to build up our reserve account.) At the end of the six months, the Hotspur bank's balance sheet looks like this.

Assets		Liabilities and net worth	
Loans	$1,900	Demand deposits	$ 2,900*
Property	9,000	Capital stock	10,000
Reserves	2,000*		

*(original $100 + $1,900 from checks deposited by Dr. Yorick)

*(Mr. Guildenstern's $1,000 and Dr. Yorick's $1,900)

When Dr. Yorick's note comes due, she will repay the loan by writing a check for $1900 on her account, payable to Hotspur bank. (We will ignore the interest she pays—the bank's profit on the transaction—so that we can continue to focus on the economic effect of such transactions.) In exchange for Dr. Yorick's check, Hotspur bank returns her signed note, thus eliminating from the bank's balance sheet both Dr. Yorick's demand deposit account and her loan. The balance sheet looks like this.

Assets		Liabilities and net worth	
Property	$9,000	Demand deposits	$ 1,000
Reserves	2,000	Capital stock	10,000

Comparing the new balance sheet with the one for the day before Dr. Yorick repaid her loan, we see that demand deposits have declined from $2900 to only $1000; the money supply has been reduced by $1900. Since money is created when banks make loans, it is only logical that money is contracted when the loans are paid off.

Buying government bonds: money is created

Let us look again at the present balance sheet of First National Bank of Hotspur. With a demand deposit of $1000 (requiring a reserve of $100) and actual reserves of $2000, Hotspur bank now has excess reserves of $1900. We have said that bankers would prefer to employ excess reserves to grant loans rather than to purchase government bonds because the profits from loans are greater than the profits that result from purchasing government bonds.* The greater profits are due to the fact that there is usually more risk involved in making private loans. Banks will therefore request a higher rate of interest from private borrowers than they do from the government. Nevertheless, banks like to keep a certain portion of their excess reserves in the form of government bonds. Because bonds are both safer and more liquid than private loans they protect the bank's reserve position at the Fed from being jeopardized in the event of a sudden surge of withdrawals.

Let us suppose that the Hotspur bank proposes to use its excess reserves to purchase government securities. It decides to buy $1900 of United States Treasury bonds held by the First Bardolph Corporation, and it pays First Bardolph with its own check (we will assume for our example that First Bardolph uses the check to open an account at the Hotspur bank). Note again that the Hotspur bank could purchase securities only in an amount equal to the total size of its excess reserves. As a result of this transaction, the bank has acquired both a new asset ($1900 in United States government securities) and a new demand-deposit account of $1900. Here is what the Hotspur balance sheet looks like now.

Assets		Liabilities and net worth	
U.S. government securities	$1,900	Demand deposits	$ 2,900*
Property	9,000	Capital stock	10,000
Reserves	2,000		
		*(Mr. Guildenstern's $1,000 and First Bardolph's $1,900)	

Extending a loan creates money in the form of new demand deposits. Whether the bank makes a loan or purchases bonds, the effect on the demand-deposit part of our money supply is the same; it increases. Before long, First Bardolph will probably write checks for $1900 against its balance. When these checks are cleared at the Fed, Hotspur's reserves will be decreased by $1900; once again it will just be meeting the required reserve ratio. The balance sheet will look like this.

Assets		Liabilities and net worth	
U.S. government securities	$1,900	Demand deposits	$ 1,000
Property	9,000	Capital stock	10,000
Reserves	100		

Just as Hotspur lost reserves after its loan transaction, it also lost reserves after purchasing the bonds. However, the reserves are not lost to the banking system as a whole because First Bar-

---

*In general, banks are restricted by law from major investments other than United States government securities and municipal bonds.

dolph's check will almost certainly be placed on deposit in another bank. Thus, as deposits are transferred from one bank to another, the demand deposit created as a result of Hotspur's purchase of a bond from First Bardolph has a multiple effect on the money supply. The total money supply will be increased not merely by the $1900 demand deposit created by Hotspur to pay for its new bond, but by a multiple of the purchase (again, ten times if the reserve ratio happens to be 10 percent).

In terms of the total money supply, it does not matter what a bank does with its excess reserves. Whether it uses them to expand its loans or to increase its investments, the final effect of using the reserves will be to increase the money supply by a multiple, the reciprocal of the reserve ratio of the bank's initial excess reserves.

Selling government bonds: money is contracted

When a bank disposes of the United States government securities it holds by selling them to the public, the total money supply contracts, because each purchaser pays for the bond by reducing his or her demand deposit. The bank's balance sheet will show a reduction in assets (the sold government bond) and a corresponding reduction in liabilities (the amount subtracted from demand deposits used to pay for the bond). Even if the purchaser of the bond maintains his or her demand deposit account at another bank, the effect on the overall money supply will still be the same.

FACTORS LIMITING EXPANSION OF THE MONEY SUPPLY

In this chapter, we have examined the way that such bank transactions as lending or bond purchases affect the total money supply. The commercial banking system expands the demand-deposit component of the money supply by a multiple of its total excess reserves. It is entirely possible for $1000 of excess reserves to result ultimately in an increase of $5000 in the demand-deposit part of the money supply. However, two situations often occur in real life that tend to keep the money supply from increasing to the full extent theoretically possible.

Currency leakage

So far, commercial banking has been presented as a closed system from which no real money actually leaves. But this is not true; money frequently does leave the system. Suppose that Dr. Yorick, on being granted her $1900 loan, had asked us for the money in cash, rather than as a checking account. The First National Bank of Hotspur would have obtained this currency for her from the Federal Reserve bank by writing its own check against its reserve account at the Fed. In other words, the Hotspur bank would be exchanging its reserves at the Fed for vault cash, because Dr. Yorick has asked for cash. Hotspur loses reserves at the Fed, but there is no immediate corresponding increase in the reserves of another bank because Dr. Yorick has taken the money home. If she pays her employees with the currency the next day, there is a

> **RECAP**
>
> The transactions of COMMERCIAL BANKS—specifically, money-lending activities and buying and selling bonds—result in the creation and contraction of money. It is through their impact on the money supply that commercial banks play an important role in monetary policy.
>
> The commercial banking system as a whole can have a significant effect on expanding the money supply, since it can expand loans by a multiple of the amount of excess reserves. This is the multiple-expansion effect.

good chance that some of the cash will soon be redeposited in the banking system. But suppose that Dr. Yorick's receptionist converts the $100 in her weekly pay envelope into silver dollars to give to her nieces and nephews; it will be a long time before that money finds its way back into the banking system. As long as some of the withdrawn currency remains outside the banking system, the money supply is prevented from expanding to its full potential.

How important is this "leakage," as we have described it? Overall, it is not significant, because demand deposits are becoming an increasingly popular form of money. More and more transactions are paid for with checks, and most people feel safer with a healthy bank balance than they do with substantial amounts of cash in their pockets. Nevertheless, at a time when business is expanding and more transactions are taking place (for example, around Christmastime, or in times of economic boom), there tends to be a need for more cash, and the currency leak increases, thereby limiting the expansion of the money supply to some extent.

Unwillingness to lend or borrow

Besides currency leakage, there are two other factors that limit the extent to which the money supply will be expanded: the occasional unwillingness, for one reason or another, of bankers to lend money or buy bonds, and the occasional unwillingness of individuals and businesses to borrow even if banks are eager to lend.

We have assumed throughout this chapter that a commercial bank uses its excess reserves immediately in order to maximize profits. This is not inevitably so. During the worst years of the Depression, for example, nervous bankers were very reluctant to write new loans, and interest rates on government bonds dropped so low (to $\frac{1}{8}$ of 1 percent) that many banks held their excess reserves rather than using them to acquire new earning assets.

When the excess reserves are immobilized so that they do not pass from bank to bank, they cannot cause the multiple expansion of the money supply. Bankers are not always willing to lend an amount equal to excess reserves merely because excess reserves exist. Similarly, the public is not always willing to borrow, even if banks are willing to lend. If the commercial bankers think that most loans are too risky; if they are frightened of the possibility of mass withdrawal, if interest rates on government bonds are very low, or if the public's expectations about future economic conditions are so pessimistic that business firms and households are reluctant to borrow, a large part of excess reserves may lie idle at the banks, and the maximum possible expansion of the money supply will not be achieved.

Summary

■ This chapter examines the basic role of commercial banks and their ability to influence the expansion and contraction of money in the economy.

■ The United States banking system has two major components: commercial banks, which seek to make a profit and which have the major functions of holding demand deposits and making loans to individuals and businesses; and the central bank authority, the Federal Reserve System, consisting of 12 regional banks, a Board of Governors, and the affiliated commercial banks across the country.

■ The Fed requires a certain percentage of demand deposits to be held in cash—not to protect the banks or depositors, but to control credit and the expansion and contraction of the economy. Commercial banks deposit almost all of their cash reserves at the regional Federal Reserve banks, through which checks are cleared. Excess reserves—the difference between actual reserves and required reserves—stimulate banks to loan money and to purchase government securities.

■ By lending out their excess reserves, banks create money in the economy. Since each creation of money leads to further banking transactions and further potential for lending, the maximum expansion of money can be expressed as the reciprocal of the reserve ratio. Purchases of government securities have the same potential for expansion of money. While most banks choose to put some of their reserves in government securities, loans are in general preferable because the interest gained for the individual bank will tend to be higher.

■ The potential expansion of money through banking activity is limited by two major factors. Some amount of the new money created is lost through currency leakage, taking it outside the banking system. For a number of reasons, banks may also be unwilling to lend money up to their excess reserves, and individuals and businesses may be unwilling to borrow all the money available from banks.

Key Terms

commercial bank
central bank
balance sheet
assets
liabilities

net worth
reserve ratio
reserve requirement
excess reserves

Review & Discussion

1. What are the functions of commercial banks? Which of the services they offer are most important for the economy? Which are most important to banking customers?

2. What services does the Federal Reserve System provide for commercial banks? Why do you think some banks would choose not to affiliate with the Fed?

3. Why would it be an unwise policy for a bank to lend out more money than it currently holds in excess reserves?

4. How does a bank's decision to loan money to an individual or business "create" money?

5. On a balance sheet, why do transactions generally result in changes in the balances on both the left (assets) and right (liabilities) sides? Why must the two sides always show equal balances?

6. What is the upper limit on the ability of bank loans and purchases of government securities to result in new money in the economy? Why is that upper limit not likely to be reached?

7. What factors might account for currency leakage? Why is such leakage less and less significant in the United States economy?

8. What might account for a bank's unwillingness to loan out all of its excess reserves and thereby give up potential profits from interest on more loans? What might account for the unwillingness of individuals and businesses to borrow all the money banks make available at any given time?

Application 7:
Consumer Debt

A young couple owed about $5500 when they married. On top of that, they borrowed more money to furnish a new home and to give themselves a vacation. Then came unexpectedly high fuel bills and a baby. And with these additional bills came trips to the banks and finance companies and higher charge-account balances. Within two years, the couple was in trouble and receiving calls from creditors every day. To pay off their bills, they went on a budget so tight that it allowed only $60 a month of their $1480 take-home pay for such extras as a night at the movies or eating out.

Over the last several decades, many Americans have been borrowing at a record pace. The amount of money owed by families and individuals has risen almost half-again as fast as their assets, with consumer debt amounting to just under $300 billion in the late 1970s. Nearly a third of consumer-credit (that is, nonmortgage) borrowing goes to pay for cars; credit cards issued by banks, such as Visa and Master Charge, account for about 5 percent of the borrowings; and loans for the purchase of mobile homes and for home improvement represent another 5 percent each. Although most people are able to pay what they owe, many cannot, and their troubles raise the question: How much borrowing is too much? Given the role of banks and borrowing in the creation of money (and in making possible many of the purchases that help fuel the economy), the question is an important one.

By some estimates, as many as five or six Americans in every hundred may be in serious financial trouble as a result of excess borrowing. The trouble often seems to develop in periods of high inflation, such as the late 1970s, when prices rise faster than incomes, or when people expect that they will. In the latter part of 1978, for example, the Bureau of Labor Statistics estimated that the spendable weekly earnings of the typical worker with a spouse and two children dropped about 3 percent. At the same time, the ratio of total new borrowing (outstanding debt minus amounts repaid on previous loans) to take-home pay rose to a peak of 3.1 percent. Installment-debt delinquencies reached 2.7 percent, the highest level since just before the 1974–1975 recession, and personal bankruptcies also increased, after declining for the three previous years.

"It's a good thing we've done away with debtors' prisons," one economist remarked, "because a lot of people are borrowing so irresponsibly that's where they'd end up, for sure. Too many people are taking the credit plunge and finding they can't swim."

As a result of the plunge, about 20 cents of every dollar Americans earn goes to repay debt, an average of about $4400 for the typical person.

Not everyone views this debt burden with alarm, however. One reason is that it has changed little in recent years, as *Fig. 1* demonstrates. Although consumer borrowing increased nearly three-fold between the mid-1960s and the late 1970s, borrowing as a fraction of disposable personal income stayed roughly the same, hovering between 18 percent and 19-plus percent. The greatest increase in consumer debt came between 1945 and 1965. In that period, consumer borrowings rose from less than 4 percent of net earnings to the present level of just under 20 percent. Demonstrating the relation of borrowing to the creation of money, the ratio of consumer debt to M_1, or the narrow money supply, went from about 6 percent in 1945 to about 50 percent in 1964. (Outstanding consumer debt now amounts to more than three-fourths of M_1).

Although economists disagree on precisely why consumers began to borrow so much more following World War II, a few explanations have been advanced: one probable reason, some believe, is that the economy started growing much faster than it had been and that, with a general shortage of capital following the Depression, consumer borrowing was one of the few ways to finance the growth. There also was a considerable influx of mortgage money into the economy to finance construction of homes for the returning veterans. And in part, at least, the credit expansion was due to people's willingness to take on more debt—having been through a war and a depression, many consumers reasoned that nothing worse could happen and, with faith in their ability to handle it, were willing to risk an increase in debt.

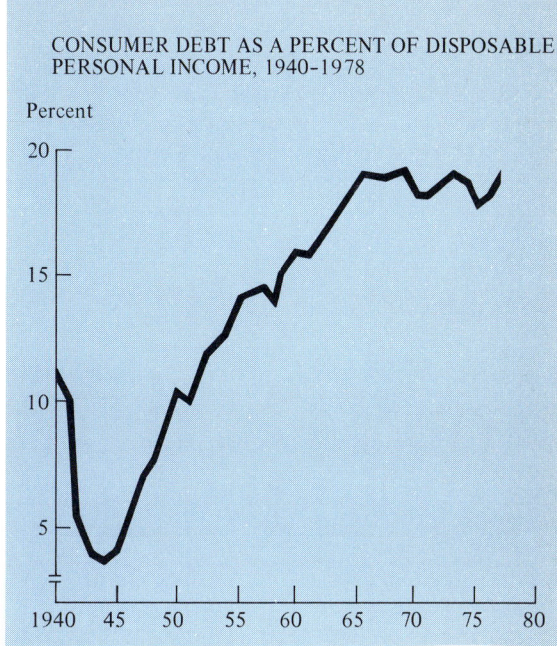

SOURCE: *Historical Statistics, Colonial Times to 1970;* and *Statistical Abstract of the United States,* 1978.

Figure 1

Questions for discussion

☐ Why do you think some people borrow more than they should? What responsibility, if any, do you think bankers, finance companies, and other lenders have to prevent such excesses?

☐ Notice that while the pattern of borrowing has been generally upward, there are downturns,

APPLICATION 7: CONSUMER DEBT

Table 1

Year	Consumer debt outstanding (billions of dollars)	Debt as a percent of disposable personal income	Debt as a percent of money supply (M_1)	Change in consumer debt (%)	Change in prices (%)	Change in GNP (%)
1939	7.2	10.2	21.4	12.5		7.6
1940	8.3	11.0	21.3	15.3		7.7
1941	9.2	9.9	20.3	10.8		16.1
1942	6.0	5.1	10.9	<34.8>		15.5
1943	4.9	3.7	6.8	<18.3>		15.3
1944	5.1	3.5	5.9	4.1		7.1
1945	5.7	3.8	5.7	11.8		<1.5>
1946	8.4	5.3	7.9	47.4		<14.8>
1947	11.6	6.8	10.3	38.1		<1.8>
1948	14.4	7.6	12.9	24.1	7.8	4.1
1949	17.4	9.2	15.6	20.8	<1.0>	0.6
1950	21.5	10.4	18.5	23.6	1.0	8.7
1951	22.7	10.0	18.5	5.6	7.9	8.1
1952	27.5	11.5	21.6	21.1	2.2	3.8
1953	31.4	12.4	24.4	14.2	0.8	3.9
1954	32.5	12.6	24.6	3.5	0.5	<1.3>
1955	38.8	14.1	28.3	19.4	<0.4>	6.7
1956	42.3	14.4	30.9	9.0	1.5	2.1
1957	45.0	14.6	33.1	6.4	3.6	1.8
1958	45.1	14.1	32.0	0.2	2.7	<0.2>
1959	51.5	15.3	35.9	14.2	0.8	6.0
1960	56.1	16.0	38.9	8.9	1.6	2.3
1961	58.0	15.9	39.0	3.4	1.0	2.5
1962	63.8	16.6	42.3	10.0	1.1	5.8
1963	71.7	17.7	45.8	12.4	1.2	4.0
1964	80.3	18.3	49.1	12.0	1.3	5.3
1965	90.3	19.1	52.7	12.5	1.7	5.9
1966	97.5	19.0	55.6	8.0	2.9	5.9
1967	102.1	18.7	54.6	4.7	2.9	2.7
1968	113.2	19.2	56.1	10.9	4.2	4.4
1969	122.5	19.3	58.7	8.2	5.4	2.6
1970	126.8	18.3	57.3	3.5	5.9	<0.3>
1971	139.4	18.4	59.2	9.9	4.3	3.0
1972	157.3	18.8	61.5	12.8	3.3	5.7
1973	181.1	19.3	66.7	15.1	6.2	5.5
1974	191.3	18.8	67.5	5.6	11.0	<1.4>
1975	200.7	17.9	68.0	4.9	9.1	<1.3>
1976	224.2	18.3	71.5	11.7	5.8	5.7
1977	260.8	19.1	77.0	16.3	6.5	4.9
1978					7.6	3.9

many of which come at about the same time as declines in the Gross National Product. In your view, what may account for this phenomenon?

☐ Look at the columns in *Table 1* that show the change in debt levels and the change in price levels. Do consumers seem to increase or decrease their borrowings in times of rapidly escalating prices? Why do you think this pattern occurs?

☐ What would happen to the level of economic activity if, all of a sudden, banks decreased the number of loans they made?

☐ Do you think a high level of consumer debt is good or bad? Why?

Chapter 15

The Federal Reserve System and Monetary Policy

What to look for in this chapter

What is the role of the Federal Reserve System?

How is the Federal Reserve System structured? What are its duties?

What are the objectives of the Fed's monetary policy?

What are the chief mechanisms for implementing monetary policy? How do they work?

Changes in the quantity of money in an economy can affect prices, production, and employment. Therefore, by manipulating the supply of available money, the government can check inflation, stimulate production, reduce unemployment, or achieve other economic goals. All such monetary policies are carried out through the agency of the Federal Reserve System. In this chapter, we will examine those techniques that the central bank uses to control the money-creating and money-contracting activities of commercial banks; in addition, we will consider the various objectives of monetary policy.

FEDERAL RESERVE SYSTEM

Background of the system

The Federal Reserve System was established by Congress under the Federal Reserve Act of 1913.

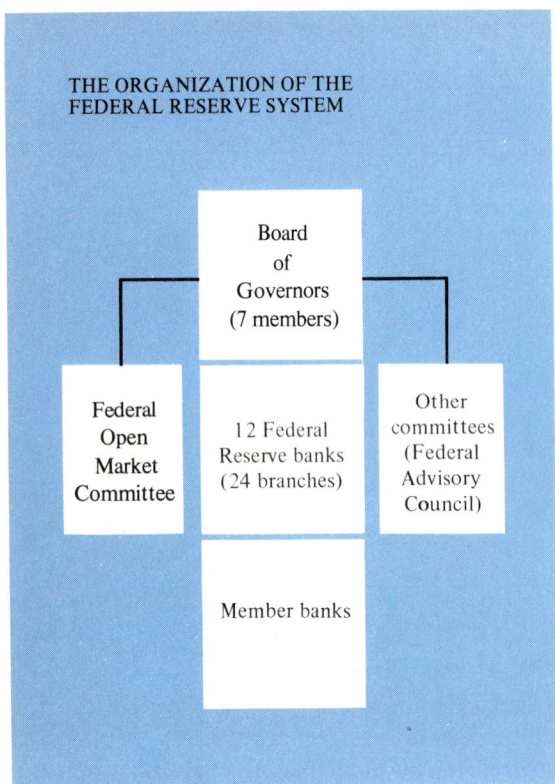

Fig. 15.1
The Board of Governors is the decision-making body of the Federal Reserve System. The 12 Federal Reserve banks act to execute policy, through their transactions with the member banks of the system. The Open Market Committee has the responsibility for buying and selling bonds; their activity helps to determine interest rates and can thus create either an expansionary or a contractionary effect. The Federal Advisory Council advises the Board of Governors on developments that affect banking policy.

The principal reason for the establishment of the system was the growing need for a centralized banking system that would ensure flexible money supply, achieve a uniform currency, and supervise activities of banks. Before the passage of the act, the problem of an inflexible money supply was especially severe. With no centralized system to coordinate banking activity, inflationary and deflationary crises occurred frequently, creating severe economic pressures. The creation of a central banking system was intended to forestall such crises and ensure that the money supply would be flexible enough to respond to changing economic conditions.

Organization of the system

Over the years, the structure and functioning of the Federal Reserve System have been modified by amendments to the original Federal Reserve Act. Today there are 12 **Federal Reserve banks.** *These banks share the responsibility for implementing monetary policy.* Although these banks are scattered throughout the country, they operate under the close guidance of a Board of Governors in Washington, D.C. *The board, together with the 12 regional reserve banks and their branches and any commercial banks that have chosen to join them, make up the* **Federal Reserve System,** *the central banking system of the United States.* The organization of the Federal Reserve System is diagrammed in *Fig. 15.1.*

Board of Governors

The Board of Governors has the responsibility of supervising the overall operation of the Federal Reserve System and deciding which kind of monetary policy will be implemented. It consists of seven full-time employees of the Federal Reserve System, usually prominent bankers, economists, or business executives. Each member of the board is appointed by the president of the United States and is confirmed by the Senate for a 14-year term. Because their terms of service are arranged to overlap in such a way that every two years one governor's term expires and a new member must be appointed, and because members do not always serve their full 14-year terms, the composition of the board does not remain exactly the same for long periods of time.

Committees

In addition to the Board of Governors, there are several important committees within the Federal Reserve System. The Open Market Committee, a 12-member group composed of 7 members of the Board of Governors and 5 presidents of the district Federal Reserve banks, plays a significant role in policymaking. This committee has the responsibility for buying and selling bonds. Their activity helps to determine interest rates and can thus create either an expansionary or a contractionary effect on the money supply. We will discuss the activities of the Open Market Committee in detail later in the chapter.

The Federal Advisory Council, although not a policymaking body, meets periodically with the Board of Governors to advise its members on developments that affect banking policy. The council comprises 12 prominent commercial bankers selected yearly by each of the 12 Federal Reserve banks.

Federal Reserve banks

Under the Federal Reserve Act, the country is divided into 12 Federal Reserve districts (shown in *Fig. 15.2*), with a Federal Reserve bank located in each. The New England states, for example, are included in District 1, whose Federal Reserve bank is located in Boston. In some districts the regional Federal Reserve bank has one or more branch offices, so that transactions between the Federal Reserve banks and member banks can be carried out more speedily.

Generally speaking, the 12 banks act in a coordinated fashion to implement overall national policies established by the Board of Governors. However, any of the 12 banks may be permitted to adopt policies designed to deal with special economic conditions existing within its district.

The Federal Reserve banks deal only with commercial banks, not directly with the public. You cannot open a personal savings or checking account in any of them. These banks instead regulate the deposits and the loan accounts of the commercial banks; they are actually "bankers' banks."

Nominally, the Federal Reserve banks are private organizations, owned by the member commercial banks in their districts, which on joining the Federal Reserve System, must buy a stated amount of stock in their district bank. However, the Federal Reserve banks are not run as private organizations, in that private profit making is not their primary objective. The primary objective of the Federal Reserve banks is to carry out the monetary policies established in the public interest by the Board of Governors.

Member banks

All nationally chartered commercial banks *must* join the Federal Reserve System; state chartered banks *may* join if they wish. In 1979 fewer than one-half of all United States banks were members of the system. However, this included practically all the larger banks in the country, accounting for approximately three-fourths of all demand deposits.

BALANCE SHEET OF THE FEDERAL RESERVE BANKS

We can better understand how the Federal Reserve System, or the Fed, performs its main job of managing the money supply if we look at the combined balance sheet of the 12 Federal Reserve

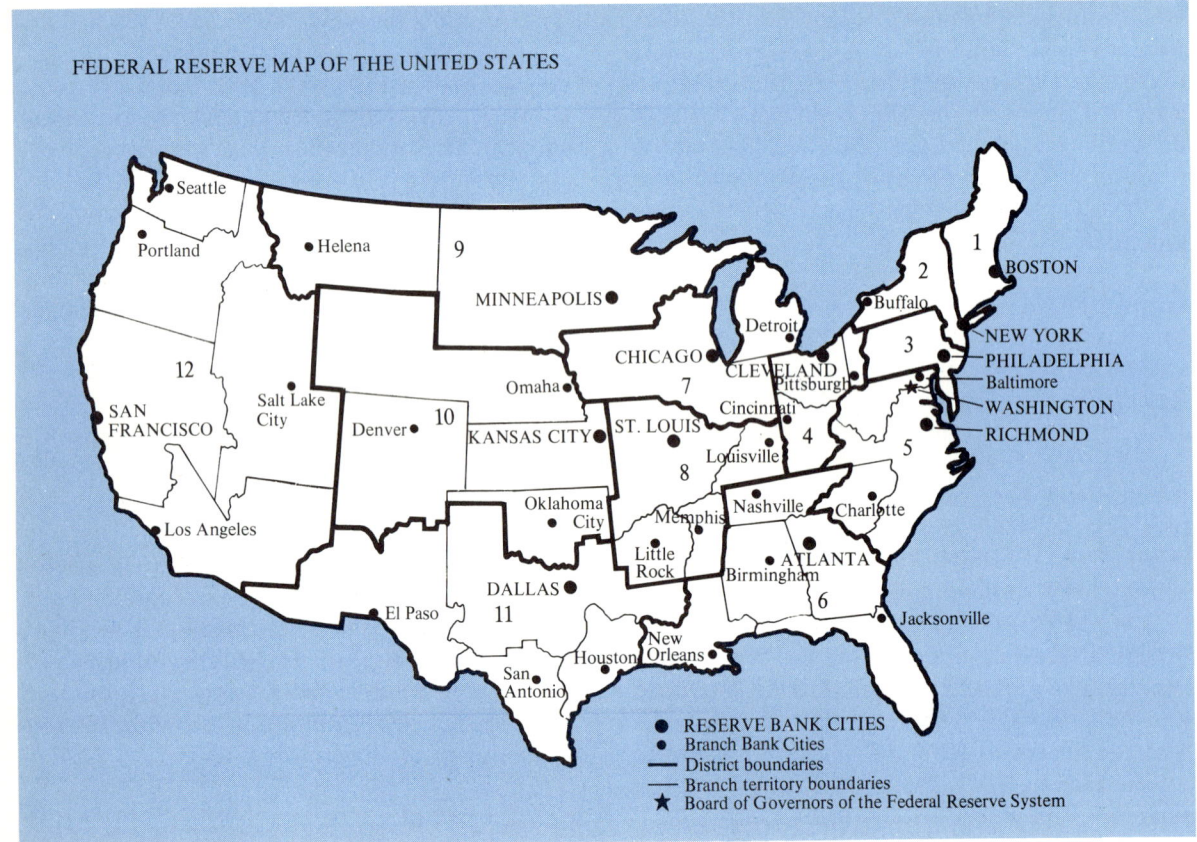

Fig. 15.2
Each of the 12 Federal Reserve banks serves a different section of the country. In some districts, the regional Federal Reserve bank has one or more branch offices, so that transactions between the Reserve banks and member banks need not be delayed by the need for long-distance communication. Two-thirds of the Federal Reserve banks are in the more heavily populated eastern half of the country. Alaska and Hawaii are both included in the twelfth district.

banks (*Table 15.1*). The balance sheet also gives us an overall idea of the different functions of the central banks.

Assets

The following items are the Fed's assets.

☐ **Gold certificates** are *"warehouse receipts" given by the Treasury to the Fed for gold held by the Treasury.* Gold deposits originally were important in that the Fed was required to maintain a 25 percent gold backing for the paper currency it printed. Gold deposits now have significance only in terms of their use in transactions with foreign governments.

☐ **Special Drawing Rights** (SDRs) are *a form of international reserves credited to the accounts of*

Table 15.1
Consolidated balance sheet of all Federal Reserve banks, January 17, 1979 (millions of dollars)

Assets		Liabilities and net worth	
Gold certificates	$ 11,608	Federal Reserve notes	$100,952
Special Drawing Rights	1,300	Member banks reserves	35,900
U.S. government securities	102,373	Treasury deposits	3,061
Loans to commercial banks	2,043	Capital accounts	2,556
All other assets	36,344	All other liabilities	11,199
Totals	$153,668		$153,668

members of the International Monetary Fund that can be used to settle international balances. Sometimes called "paper gold," SDRs represent account entries on the books of the IMF and can be used by governments to finance balance-of-payments deficits.

☐ As a tool for monetary control, United States Government securities, specifically Treasury bonds, are the most important assets that the Federal Reserve banks own. It is through increasing and decreasing its holdings of government bonds that the Fed is able to effect changes in the reserve positions of the commercial banks; these changes enable the Fed to control the size of the demand deposits created by the banks.

☐ Another asset is loans that the Federal Reserve banks have issued to individual commercial banks. They are extended primarily on a short-term basis—borrowed by member banks that have a temporary need for extra reserves.

Liabilities

The following items are the Fed's liabilities.

☐ **Federal Reserve notes** are *paper dollars that the Federal Reserve banks print for member banks and their customers on request.*

☐ As we pointed out in Chapter 14, member-bank reserves are funds that the commercial banks are required to keep on deposit at regional Federal Reserve banks. These are of great importance in the Fed's attempts to regulate the size of demand deposits created by commercial banks, since the amount of excess reserves that a member bank has on deposit at the Fed determines the extent to which it can expand loans.

☐ **Treasury deposits** *are the funds that the United States Treasury deposits in Federal Reserve banks.* The source of the funds is federal government tax receipts. The Treasury writes checks against these deposits to pay for its expenditures, just as individuals do with their accounts in commercial banks.

☐ The **capital accounts** of the Federal Reserve System consist of *the original sums of money that commercial banks pay to purchase stock in their regional Federal Reserve bank*—a purchase that they are required to make when they join the Fed—*plus the accumulated profits that have not yet been returned to the Treasury.*

INDEPENDENCE OF THE FEDERAL RESERVE SYSTEM

The framers of the Federal Reserve Act sought to establish an independent central banking system that could operate in the public interest. For this reason, the act provides workable safeguards against political pressure from governmental agencies and from private groups.

Protection from governmental pressure

Although the president of the United States appoints the members of the Board of Governors, the board is relatively immune to presidential pressure. The lengthy terms of the governors, the overlapping of their terms, and their ineligibility for reappointment all serve to prevent any president from creating a rubber-stamp board that would pursue exclusively the policies most politically advantageous to an individual president or party.

The board is also protected from congressional pressure. Although the Senate must approve the president's nomination of governors and the board must report annually to Congress, giving a full account of all recent policy decisions, Congress has no direct supervisory authority over either the board or the Federal Reserve banks.

Cooperation with government

As a practical matter, the governors are extremely conscious of the importance of keeping both the chief executive and Congress informed of their monetary-policy decisions; cooperation from other branches of government is essential if the nation is to accomplish its economic goals. For example, if the board believes that the level of inflation is too high and if it is pursuing contractionary monetary policies, it will be very eager to explain its convictions to the members of Congress, in order to encourage them to vote against fiscal policies that might add to inflation—deficit budgets, tax cuts, or increases in Social Security payments, for example.

Protection from private pressure

Although the commercial banks own the Federal Reserve banks, they do not possess the usual rights of stock ownership—the ultimate veto power over policy decisions. As further protection from private pressure, the Federal Reserve Act specifies that only three of the nine directors of each Reserve bank may be bankers. The other six directors must not be employed by commercial banks at all, whether as officers, directors, or other employees. In addition, all profits from the operations of Reserve banks in excess of a 6 percent dividend on their stock are paid back to the Treasury. Finally, the Federal Reserve Board appoints three of the directors of each bank, approves the choice of president and first vice-president, and has the authority to suspend or remove any officer or director of any Federal Reserve bank.

FUNCTIONS OF THE FEDERAL RESERVE SYSTEM

The most important duties of the Federal Reserve Board and banks are establishing and implementing monetary policy. Before we consider these activities, however, let us consider some of the more routine administrative and supervisory functions the Fed performs that help our banking system run smoothly and efficiently.

Clearing operations

Commercial banks must keep reserve accounts on deposit at the Federal Reserve banks. Through use of these reserve accounts, the speedy and dependable clearing of checks, essential to the successful operation of our economy, can be accomplished. Therefore, as part of its function as a public service organization, the Fed also provides clearing services at no charge to member banks.

Distribution of currency

It is the responsibility of the Federal Reserve banks to see that there is an appropriate supply of currency in circulation. The amount of paper currency in circulation in the United States today is determined by the public's demand for that currency. The Fed permits the public to have that quantity of paper money it wants. For example, at certain times of the year (right before Christmas or Easter) individuals and businesses generally find it convenient to hold larger cash balances; gifts have to be bought, new clothes are purchases, more dollar bills are needed in cash-register tills. This additional paper money is obtained by cashing checks at commercial banks. When the banks run out of bills, they request a new supply of currency from the Federal Reserve banks. The banks obligingly print as much paper money (Federal Reserve notes) as necessary, ship it to the cashiers' drawers at the commercial banks, and subtract a corresponding sum from the reserve accounts of the banks.

At other periods of the year (for example, after Christmas) the situation is reversed; the banks have a big cash inflow. They ship this cash to the Fed, which either destroys it or stores it and enters the sum on the balance sheets of the commercial banks as increases in their reserve accounts. Instead of trying to limit the amount of currency in circulation, the Fed adjusts the demand-deposit portion of the money supply. In effect, therefore, it stabilizes the economy by controlling the total money supply.

Fiscal agent for the government

The Federal Reserve banks act as bankers for the United States Treasury. The Treasury keeps its checking accounts at the Fed very much the way you keep a personal checking account at your neighborhood bank. Checks for income-tax refunds, Social Security payments, or other government disbursements are written against these deposits. In addition, when the Treasury sells new bonds to raise money, the Fed accepts orders, makes allocations if the demand is greater than the amount offered, receives the payments, and distributes the bonds. The Federal Reserve banks also make the periodic interest payments on government securities and redeem the securities for the Treasury when they come due.

Supervisory functions

The Fed performs various supervisory functions intended to ensure that the loans and investments at member banks are sound and that their books are in order. For example, the Fed periodically examines member banks to see if they are in compliance with central bank standards. If they are not, they may be denied the privilege of borrowing from the Federal Reserve banks.

THE OBJECTIVES OF FEDERAL RESERVE MONETARY POLICY

We have said that the primary job of the Federal Reserve is to control the money supply. What goals do these central-bank authorities seek in determining what monetary policy should be pursued at any time? Most economists would agree that the Fed has the same primary objectives in determining its monetary policy as has the federal government in determining fiscal policies—to maintain both a high level of employment and reasonably stable prices.

Maintaining a high level of employment

In Chapter 13 we explained how changes in the size of the money supply can affect employment. Recall from our discussion of quantity theory that, assuming everything else remains constant, an increase in the supply of money can lead to more consumer spending, as well as to lower interest rates and more investment spending. The general result will be a higher level of aggregate demand, greater net national product, and thus a higher level of employment. Recognizing this sequence of events, the Board of Governors can control the size of the money supply to stimulate the economy toward the full-employment goal.

Maintaining stable prices

The price level also responds to changes in the money supply. In an economy where all resources are fully employed, further increases in the money supply can lead only to rising prices. By reducing the money supply and raising interest rates, the monetary authorities can depress investment spending, aggregate demand, and net national product, thus creating a business climate in which further price increases are less likely.

Difficulty of meeting both objectives simultaneously

This explanation of the relationship between monetary policy and its objectives is, in some ways, an oversimplification. Although the Federal Reserve Board does have at its disposal many of the tools required to achieve both full employment and stable prices, it often finds that these two objectives prove to be mutually inconsistent—at least in the short run. For example, the Fed may feel that it is desirable to decrease the supply of money in order to restrain inflation, but such contractionary activities can simultaneously result in a rise in unemployment. Or being worried about a high level of unemployment, the board may order an expansion of the money supply and then find that the cost of living rises significantly. Achieving more of one goal may require a sacrifice of some portion of the other; there may be an opportunity cost that must be paid if we are to have either higher rates of employment or lower rates of inflation. Economists, politicians, and citizens in general will often find themselves disagreeing with the particular policy mix the Fed has elected to provide.

Problems in forecasting investment spending

The choice of short-term objectives is just one of the problems facing the central-bank authorities. Another problem lies in attempting to determine the real-world relationship between changes in the supply of money and changes in investment spending. We said in Chapter 13 that, theoretically, increases in the supply of money lead to lower interest rates and to higher investment spending, and vice versa. However, experience has shown that it is difficult to forecast with certainty whether investment spending will actually expand or contract with changes in interest rates. For example, if business people are very pessimistic about current economic conditions, it is often impossible to get them to borrow and invest, regardless of how low interest rates are. Conversely, even very high rates will not stop investment spending in a wildly optimistic boom period. The result is that monetary policymakers often find that things do not work out as they are "supposed" to; in theory, monetary policymakers should be able to influence aggregate demand and net national product by changing the supply of money and the interest rates, but investment spending refuses to follow the "rules."

The effect of velocity

Monetary policymakers may also run into trouble because velocity (the rate at which the money turns over) has a habit of changing at inconvenient times. When we first looked at the quantity theory of money ($MV = PQ$), we interpreted it to mean that any increase in the supply of money would affect prices and production levels—*assuming no change in velocity*. However, there is evidence that velocity *does* change. In periods of great business activity, businesses and individuals use their dollars more efficiently; that is, they turn over their money more frequently and reduce nonworking cash balances, and V increases. As a result, the monetary authorities may attempt to dampen an inflationary boom by reducing the money supply (M), only to find that MV remains at a high or even increasing level because V is rising. The reverse is also possible during recessionary periods, when attempts to expand the total supply of money by increasing M may be frustrated by declines in V.

Summary

To summarize, the primary objectives of the Fed in formulating monetary policy are those of most other economic policymakers in the United States—stable prices and high employment. Changes in the supply of money are assumed to result in changes in the level of aggregate demand, which then affects the levels of national income and employment. Some problems arise when investment demand fails to respond to changes in interest rates and when changes in the supply of money are offset by changes in velocity. Moreover, the Fed also finds that it is often impossible to achieve both of its objectives simultaneously; it must choose which objective to emphasize under current conditions. Despite these limitations, however, most economists would agree that monetary policy can provide a very effective method for managing the economy.

MECHANISMS FOR IMPLEMENTING MONETARY POLICY

Now that we have examined the objectives of Federal Reserve Board monetary policy, let us see how the Fed goes about implementing its decisions to expand or contract the money supply. The Fed's attention is primarily concentrated on bank demand deposits. Since the level of demand deposits is directly related to the reserve position of the banks, the Fed's efforts mainly involve increasing or decreasing the amount of excess reserves held by commercial banks.

Open-market operations

The most effective way the Fed has of changing the amount of excess reserves held by commercial banks is through **open-market operations**—*the purchase and sale of United States government securities by the Fed in the open market.* These transactions are carried out by the Open Market Committee. Once the Board of Governors decides on its current monetary policy (whether to increase the money supply in order to stimulate the economy or to decrease the money supply in order to combat an inflationary spiral), this information is conveyed to the Open Market Committee. Then, acting on the advice of its money-market specialists and consulting economists, the committee attempts to implement the board's decision through its activities in the government-bond market. Orders to buy or sell bonds are then placed through the Federal Reserve Bank of New York. However, the purchases or sales are actually distributed among the accounts of all 12 Federal Reserve banks.

Open-market purchases
The excess-reserve position of the commercial-bank system determines, to a large degree, the extent of demand-deposit creation. Let us now examine the effect of Open Market Committee purchases of government bonds on the reserve position of a bank.

Assume that the Open Market Committee buys $100 million worth of bonds. We will see shortly that it makes very little difference from whom the bonds are bought. Let us say that $50 million worth of bonds come from commercial banks and the remainder from other public holders—individuals, government-bond dealers, and business corporations.

Purchases from commercial banks When the Fed buys $50 million of government bonds from the Continental Bank and Trust Co., what effect does this have on the bank's balance sheet, on its reserve position, and eventually on the money supply? First of all, Continental's investment account (bond holdings) decreases by $50 million. Second, since the Fed pays for the bonds by crediting $50 million to Continental's reserve account at the Fed, the transaction results in an increase in Continental's reserves. The following changes are made in the balance sheet of Continental Bank and Trust as a result of the Fed's purchase of $50 million of Continental's bonds.

Assets	Liabilities
Bonds − $50 million	
Reserves + $50 million	

Assets	Liabilities
Reserves + $50 million	Demand deposits (First Boston account) + $50 million

If we assume that prior to this transaction, Continental was just meeting its reserve requirement, the bank now finds itself with $50 million of excess reserves. With these excess reserves, it is free to create new demand deposits (probably through new loans) of $50 million. Moreover, because of the multiple expansion of bank credit that occurs as excess reserves move from one bank to another, the final consequence of the Fed's purchase of $50 million of Continental's bonds may be to increase demand deposits throughout the banking system by several times that amount, with the multiple dependent on the particular reserve requirement then in effect.

Purchases from nonbank sources What happens to bank reserves when the Fed buys bonds from customers other than banks? Let us assume that the Fed buys $50 million of bonds from First Boston Corporation, a bond dealer. The Fed pays for these bonds by sending First Boston a check for $50 million, which the bond dealer promptly deposits in the corporation's account at the Chase Manhattan Bank. Chase sends the check to the Federal Reserve bank for clearing, a process that involves the crediting of $50 million to Chase's reserve account. Thus, as a result of the Fed's purchase of First Boston's $50 million of bonds, Chase has acquired $50 million of additional demand deposits (the increase in First Boston's account), which also are $50 million of additional reserves. These are the changes in Chase Manhattan's balance sheet as a result of the Fed's purchase of $50 million of bonds from First Boston.

We will again make the simplifying assumption that the reserve requirement is 10 percent. If the Chase was just meeting its reserve requirement before this transaction, we can see it now has excess reserves of $45 million—with $5 million of the new reserves held against the new demand deposits of $50 million. Chase can use this $45 million in excess reserves to expand its demand deposits through new loans or investments. Whichever alternative it selects, of course, the ultimate influence on the entire money supply will be significantly higher than $45 million because of the potential multiplier effect of any change in reserves on total demand deposits.

To summarize, we can say that open-market purchases of bonds by the Federal Reserve System, whether from commercial banks or from nonbank sources, result in an increase in member-bank reserves. These purchases tend to create new money, with the ultimate possibility of increasing the money supply by a multiple (the reciprocal of the reserve ratio) of its excess reserves.

Open-market sales
Open-market sales have precisely the opposite effect of open-market purchases. They lead to a contraction in the money supply and to a reduction in bank lending activities.

Sales to banks Let us see how this works by considering what happens when the Fed sells $50 million of bonds to the Bank of America. The bank pays for its newly acquired bonds by sending the

Fed its check for $50 million. The Fed collects this check by deducting the amount from the bank's reserve account. The result is an increase in the Bank of America's bond account and a decrease in its reserves. The changes in the Bank of America's balance sheet as a result of the Fed's sales of $50 million of United States government bonds are as follows.

Assets		Liabilities
Bonds	+$50 million	
Reserves	−$50 million	

If we assume that the Bank of America had only $50 million of excess reserves before this transaction, we see that the Fed has eliminated these excess reserves by its sale of bonds. In other words, the Fed has *prevented* Bank of America from expanding the money supply by extending new loans and thus creating new demand deposits. Moreover, Bank of America will now be under great pressure to improve its reserve position immediately because it has lost all its excess reserves, with no change in demand deposits. Of course, banks cannot cancel mortgages and other long-term loan commitments in an attempt to do this. But many loans extended by banks are short-term. Thus, when the Bank of America's short-term loans come due, it will be reluctant to renew them.

Sales to the public We get a similar result when the Fed sells bonds to the public rather than to a commercial bank. Let us trace the transaction when the Fed sells $5 million of bonds in the open market to the United States Steel Pension Fund. The Pension Fund pays for its bonds by sending the Fed a check written against its account at the Mellon Bank. The Fed collects this check by subtracting $5 million from Mellon's reserve account.

After the check clears, the Mellon Bank finds that it has lost $5 million of demand deposits (from the United States Steel Pension Fund account) and $5 million of reserves. The changes in the Mellon Bank's balance sheet as a result of the Fed's sales of $5 million of bonds to the United States Steel Pension Fund are as follows.

Assets		Liabilities	
Reserves	−$5 million	Demand deposits (U.S. Steel Pension Fund account)	−$5 million

Let us say that the bank's reserve account was at its minimum required level before its customer bought these bonds, with demand deposits of $100 million and reserves of $10 million. As a result of the transaction, however, demand deposits are now $95 million, requiring reserves of $9.5 million to meet the 10 percent minimum-reserve requirement. However, in addition to a $5 million reduction in demand deposits, reserves are also $5 million lower, standing now at only $5 million. We see that the bank must take steps to bring its reserves back up to the required minimum. One effective way would be to reduce demand deposits by refusing to make or renew loans.

To summarize, sales of government bonds by the Federal Reserve System, whether to commercial banks directly or to their customers, reduce bank reserves, thereby encouraging commercial banks to reduce their demand deposits in order to build up their reserve position. The overall effect of these sales is to contract the money supply.

It is important to note that monetary measures are often more effective in contracting economic activity than they are in expanding it. A contraction of reserves is usually quite effective in forcing the banking system to reduce loans, but an increase in the availability of reserves may not necessarily result in an *expansion* of the money supply. The public may not want to borrow, or the banks may be reluctant to make many loans. This problem was illustrated in the early 1930s. Despite the fact that the banking system had substantial excess reserves during most of the period, commercial banks preferred to maintain a very liquid position, and they did not stimulate the economy by increasing loans.

Effect of open-market transactions on investment
We have just seen that the Open Market Committee can change the reserve positions of the commercial bank system by either buying or selling its government bonds. Let us now see what effect these transactions have on investment.

When the Fed wishes to purchase large quantities of government bonds, it bids aggressively for them and thus drives up their prices. The higher prices attract sellers into the market and enable the Fed to acquire their bonds.

When the Fed adopts a contractionary position and wishes to sell bonds, the Open Market Committee permits the price of its bonds to fall until it reaches that level at which customers feel that the bonds are a good investment.

Changes in the market price of government bonds, which allow the Fed to carry out buying and selling transactions, result in changes in the yield (or interest return) that the bonds provide to investors. At a price of $1000, a 5 percent bond (which pays $50 a year in interest) provides a yield of 5 percent (50/1000). If investors pay $800 for the bond, their current yield is considerably better than 5 percent, because they are laying out only $800 in order to obtain the same $50 in annual interest (50/800 = 6.25 percent). Conversely, if the bond is selling at $1200, the yield is less than 5 percent (50/1200 = 4.25 percent).

Effect when the Fed purchases bonds When the Federal Open Market Committee decides to purchase bonds in order to stimulate the economy, such purchases have a double-edged effect. First, they increase the reserve position of the commercial bank system. Second, the higher bond prices *lower* the yield that the bonds provide to investors. Thus, individuals and businesses are more likely to spend their money on other things rather than on bonds. This may stimulate the economy by encouraging home building, factory construction, inventory accumulation, or many other forms of investment.

Effect when the Fed sells bonds The reverse happens when the Fed is selling bonds to contract the money supply and slow down the economy (see *Fig. 15.3*). In order to sell bonds, the Fed depresses bond prices which increases the yield on the bonds. As the bond yield rises, investment in bonds becomes more attractive and draws money away from other types of investments. The net result is to discourage further expansionary activity.

RECAP

The most important function of the FEDERAL RESERVE SYSTEM is to establish and implement monetary policy, with the goal of maintaining a high level of employment and reasonably stable prices.

By increasing the money supply, the Fed can lower interest rates and encourage investment spending, leading to expanded economic activity and a higher level of employment. By decreasing the money supply, the Fed can raise interest rates and discourage investment spending, thereby slowing down the economy and helping to keep prices stable.

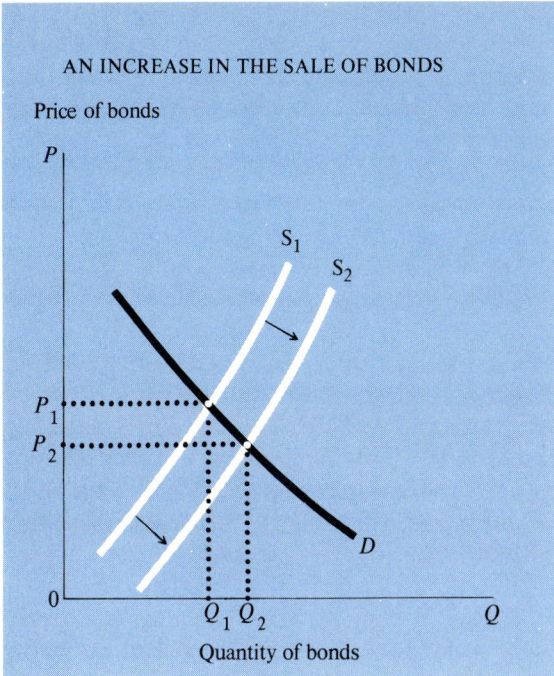

Fig. 15.3
When the Federal Reserve decides to pursue a contractionary policy and orders the Open Market Committee to sell bonds, the demand schedule for bonds remains unchanged, but the Fed's actions shift the supply schedule to the right. The price at equilibrium level drops from P_1 to P_2, and the quantity traded in the market increases from Q_1 to Q_2, since buyers will demand more bonds as the price drops. The drop in bond prices means that the yield of the bonds will now be higher, and more people will feel that they are a good investment. Thus money that might otherwise have been allocated to consumer spending is saved, and aggregate demand decreases.

Open-market transactions and public debt A side effect of open-market transactions is to increase or decrease the cost of carrying the public debt. In times of inflation the Fed wants to increase yield on government bonds in order to discourage other types of investment and spending. This is done in an effort to cause a decline in aggregate demand which should in turn slow down the rate of inflation. Thus, the Treasury has to pay higher rates when it borrows additional money from the Fed to carry the public debt. Prior to 1951, the Fed was unable to sell bonds below certain price levels, because it had an agreement with the Treasury dating back to World War II to maintain prices on government bonds at current high levels. It was committed to keeping yields low so that interest costs involved in increasing the public debt would not be excessive.

By 1951, however, it had become abundantly clear that the Federal Reserve Board could not eliminate excess bank reserves and thus control the Korean war inflation without selling bonds freely, regardless of the effect that such sales might have on the future costs of carrying the public debt. An accord was reached at that time with the Treasury, under which the Fed was no longer obligated to maintain the prices of government bonds at fixed levels. Since then most open-market operations have been conducted solely on the basis of the requirements of sound monetary policy, and the consequent effect of such policy on Treasury interest costs has been largely ignored.

Changing reserve requirements

Thus far we have seen how open-market operations affect the reserve positions of member banks and influence the supply of money in the economy. Another way in which the Federal Reserve Board can accomplish its monetary objectives is by changing reserve requirements. The consequence of such changes can be seen in the following example.

The Saundersville National Bank just meets its 10 percent reserve requirements with $1 milion of reserves and $10 million of demand deposits. Should its reserve requirements be reduced to 8 percent, however, the bank would be able to carry $12.5 million of demand deposits with the same $1 million of reserves. Thus a cut in reserve requirements could lead to expansion of the money supply. On the other hand, if the Fed raised reserve requirements from 10 percent to 12.5 percent, Saundersville would be allowed to carry only $8 million of demand deposits with its current $1 million of reserves. It would be forced to reduce its demand deposits, and it would probably accomplish this by refusing to renew some loans as they came due.

Generally speaking, the power to change reserve ratios has been used by the Fed only sparingly, because even relatively minor changes of 1 or 2 percent in reserve requirements can result in tremendous changes in the reserve positions of the member banks. Moreover, the changes in member-bank reserves created by open-market operations can be adjusted on a day-to-day basis, depending on small fluctuations of economic conditions, but a change in the reserve ratio, once it has been initiated, is fixed in amount. Rather than use this "blunt-hammer" weapon of publicly announced changes in reserve requirements, the Fed appears to be more eager to employ the "fine-tuning" possibilities of open-market operations.

It is interesting to observe that a cut in reserve requirements merely gives member banks the *opportunity* to expand loans if they so desire. On the other hand, an increase in reserve requirements, if instituted at a time when the banking system has no excess reserves (is "all loaned up"), *forces* the commercial banks to reduce lending activity. This is true of many of the central bank monetary weapons; if wielded aggressively enough, they are very effective in reducing the money supply and slowing down an overheated economy. Their effect in stimulating the economy is less certain. Open-market operations and cuts in reserve requirements can only provide excess reserves for the banks; they cannot ensure that the banks will actually use them to create more loans and demand deposits.

Changing the discount rate

Another method by which the Fed can implement monetary policy is through changes in the **discount rate**—*the interest that the Federal Reserve banks charge commercial banks on funds they borrow from the Fed*. The discount rate is so named because the interest on the loan is discounted when the loan is made rather than collected when the loan is repaid.

A bank borrows from the Fed when it finds that its reserves have fallen below the required level, or if it needs to build up reserves temporarily in order to support new loans or demand deposits. When the Federal Reserve Act was originally passed in 1913, the monetary authorities believed that the discount rate would be one of the most powerful and widely used tools in implementing monetary decisions. However, in recent years, the Fed has adopted a policy that strongly discourages borrowing by member banks; member banks may use such loans only for the purpose of providing themselves temporarily with necessary reserves. For this reason, most bankers hesitate to borrow regularly from the Fed, regardless of the current discount rate. Instead, banks that require extra reserves will borrow from outside sources, often from other banks that temporarily find themselves with excess reserves. They may sell investments (United States government bonds) or reduce loans as well.

Effects of changes in the discount rate

Despite the small overall volume of loans made to member banks, the discount rate charged on these loans is of some significance. A higher discount rate discourages borrowing by making it very expensive. A much lower rate (like the 1 percent rate that existed from 1942 to 1945) can encourage some banks to borrow.* Even more important is

---

*During World War II, the discount rate was purposely kept low in order to encourage banks to borrow from the Fed and to buy government bonds. In this way, the Treasury was provided with some of the funds necessary to finance the war.

the psychological effect of changes in the discount rate on the entire financial community. Bankers, businesspeople, and investors consider the discount rate to be the keystone on which all other interest rates are based, as well as an indicator of overall Federal Reserve Board monetary policy. Changes in the discount rate, either up or down, are closely related to changes in other money rates, such as the **prime rate** *(the interest charge that commercial banks make on loans to their best customers),* commercial loan rates, and yields on Treasury notes. Therefore, any change in the discount rate is considered an indication that other interest costs will soon change accordingly.

On the other hand, some economists think that the role of the discount rate as an active tool of monetary policy is overplayed, and that changes in the discount rate usually represent a passive response to changing levels of interest rates in the money market.

The financial community tends to view a cut in the discount rate as a sign that the Fed is embarking on expansionary policies; money will be easier to borrow, and investment spending will increase. For this reason, the stock market frequently rallies whenever a cut in the discount rate is announced. For example, a strong upturn of the stock market in early 1975 occurred partly in response to the fact that the discount rate was lowered three times in close succession, dropping from the all-time high of 8 percent to 6¼ percent.

Conversely, a series of discount-rate increases is an obvious indication that the Fed is seriously interested in restraining business activity.

Selective credit controls

In addition to the major tools of monetary policy used to increase or decrease the *overall* money supply (open-market operations, changes in reserve requirements, changes in the discount rate), the Fed has an assortment of minor tools it can employ to encourage or discourage particular types of loans or deposits.

Stock-market credit

The Federal Reserve Board can set **margin requirements** on stocks; that is, it can specify *the minimum percentage down payment required from customers to purchase stocks.* A margin requirement of 50 percent means that a customer has to put up half of the price in cash and is able to borrow only the other half.

The Fed acts to change margin requirements when it looks as though speculation in stocks may create economic problems. If the Fed is concerned about rampant speculation in the stock market, it can restrain this speculation by raising margin requirements. On the other hand, if it fears that a rapidly declining stock market is spreading unnecessary apprehension throughout the country, it may cut margin requirements to encourage stock purchases.

Installment credit

At various times in the past (during World War II and the Korean war, for example) Congress has given the Board of Governors the power to specify down-payment requirements on installment purchases and repayment periods on consumer loans. With these powers, the Fed was able to accomplish two objectives. It could follow a generally expansionary monetary policy in order to encourage business investment in facilities for producing war goods. At the same time, it could restrain the inflationary pressures that would have developed had the public been permitted to bid aggressively for goods with its usual amount of installment credit.

Interest rates on deposits

Under a mechanism known as Regulation Q, the Fed sets the maximum interest rate that commercial banks may pay on various kinds of time deposits. Since other regulatory agencies have the power to set interest rates too—on such items as savings accounts at mutual savings banks and at savings and loan associations—the monetary au-

Table 15.2
Expansionary and contractionary monetary measures

Mechanisms	Expansionary monetary activities	Contractionary monetary activities
Open-market operations	Buying government securities in the open market	Selling government securities in the open market
Reserve requirements	Reducing reserve-ratio requirements	Raising reserve-ratio requirements
Discount rate	Reducing the discount rate	Raising the discount rate
Selective credit controls		
Stock-market credit	Reducing margin requirements on stock-market purchases	Raising margin requirements
Installment credit	Reducing down payments on installment purchases, and lengthening the repayment period	Increasing required down payment on installment purchases, and shortening permitted repayment period
Interest rates on deposits	Increasing interest rates at those institutions that provide funds for the areas in which additional investment is desired (at savings banks if more home building is required), and cutting interest rates at institutions through which funds are channeled into nondesirable investment media (at commercial banks if a decline in business expansion is required)	
Moral suasion	Has limited usefulness during both expansionary and contractionary periods.	

thorities can often channel money into particular institutions through coordination of effort.

During the late 1960s, for example, an attempt was made to attract funds away from commercial banks and into savings banks, since savings banks are more likely to invest in home mortgages than are commercial banks, and the Fed wanted to stimulate investment in residential construction. Thus interest rates on most time deposits at commercial banks were purposely kept at lower levels (4½ percent maximum) than interest rates at savings institutions (5 percent or higher).

In a similar development during that period, the Fed encouraged the Treasury to set a $10,000 minimum on orders for new issues of certain short-term Treasury bonds. The issues, paying over 8 percent, were formerly available in $1000 units and were consequently attracting withdrawal from the savings accounts of small depositors; this was reducing the supply of mortgage money available from savings banks.

One of the oddities resulting from interest-rate ceilings has been a mushrooming of premium offers by banks to induce savers to open new accounts or increase existing ones. Unable to raise their interest rates to attract new funds, the banks began offering electric blankets and toasters as special inducements. The result was that the purpose of the ceilings was at least partly defeated.

Moral suasion

Moral suasion, or various types of pressure from the Fed, is often listed among the powers that the board can use in effecting changes in monetary policy. Moral suasion can involve asking member banks to refrain from "unnecessary" or "speculative" loans; making public announcements about the dangers of an overheated economy; putting pressure on the banks by having bank examiners tighten up on acceptable loan standards; or even threatening to close the discount (loan) window at the Fed. In actual practice, however, moral suasion has not proved to be a very effective tool for controlling expansionary bank practices during boom times. Commercial bankers are private businesspeople who are eager to take advantage of profitable loan opportunities during good times, regardless of the Fed's desire to restrain the money supply.

Moral suasion is even more ineffective during recessions. Although the Fed would like to see the banks pursue vigorous expansionary policies during bad times (that is, lending money aggressively), it appears that no amount of prodding from the board can make conservative bankers lend money when they are really pessimistic about the health of the economy. And it is equally difficult during a recession to convince a pessimistic businessperson to borrow money and embark on new projects, regardless of how low the interest rate is and how readily available funds are.

Table 15.2 provides a summary of the various mechanisms that the Federal Reserve can use to expand or contract economic activity.

Summary

■ This chapter examines the objectives of federal monetary policy and the techniques used by the Federal Reserve System to control the monetary activities of commercial banks.

■ The Federal Reserve System consists of a seven-member Board of Governors, appointed by the president and confirmed by the Senate; an Open Market Committee and a Federal Advisory Council (composed of private bankers); 12 regional Reserve banks; and affiliated commercial banks.

■ Assets on the balance sheet of the Federal Reserve banks include gold certificates, Special Drawing Rights with the International Monetary Fund, Treasury bonds, and loans to commercial banks. Liabilities include Federal Reserve notes (paper dollars), the reserves of member banks, deposits from the United States Treasury, and the money paid by commercial banks to purchase stock in the Federal Reserve banks.

■ The Fed's independence from government pressure is protected by the long, staggered terms of its Board of Governors, though close cooperation with the government is essential. Independence from private banking pressure is protected by the fact that member banks which own the Reserve banks do not directly control the actions of the Fed and by the limits on the number of bankers who may serve as directors of the Reserve banks.

■ The routine duties of the Fed include clearing checks at no charge to private banks, printing and destruction of paper money, acting as the fiscal agent for the United States Treasury, and supervising the operation of member banks.

■ The general objectives of monetary policy are to maintain a high level of employment as well as relatively stable prices. Increasing the money supply tends to promote full employment, while contraction of the money supply tends to counteract inflation. Difficulties arise in pursuing both goals simultaneously, since it is sometimes difficult to forecast the actual effect on investment of a change in monetary policy and since changes in the velocity of money may undercut the impact of a change in the money supply.

■ The major mechanism for implementing monetary policy is open-market purchases and sales of government securities. Buying bonds from banks or other sources increases bank reserves and thus increases the ability of banks to loan money, thereby stimulating investment; sales of bonds by the Fed decrease bank reserves and contract money available for loans. Bond transactions also affect the interest yield on bonds, which influences other types of investment. Raising bond interest rates raises the costs of maintaining the national debt.

■ Reserves can also be controlled directly by changing reserve requirements; this mechanism is used sparingly because of its enormous potential effect on the reserve position of banks. Both bond transactions and changes in reserve requirements are more effective in contracting money than in expanding it, since banks will not necessarily choose to employ greater reserves in making more loans.

■ The Fed can change the discount rate at which it loans money to member banks; the discount rate itself is not a major tool of policy, but changes in the discount rate are generally regarded as an important indicator of Fed policy intentions.

■ Monetary policy can also be furthered by changing the margin requirements on stock purchases, by regulating consumer credit, by limiting the maximum interest rates for time deposits in commercial banks, and by attempts at moral suasion.

Key Terms

Federal Reserve banks
Federal Reserve System
gold certificates
Special Drawing Rights
Federal Reserve notes
Treasury deposits
capital accounts
open-market operations
discount rate
prime rate
margin requirements

Review & Discussion

1. Describe the structure of the Federal Reserve System. Does the structure provide the right balance of public (governmental) and private (banking) input? Are the safeguards of the independence of the Federal Reserve System adequate?

2. How does the demand for money affect the actions of the Fed in printing, storing, and destroying paper currency? Why does the Fed choose to exercise control over the money supply through changes in demand deposits, not through control of currency?

3. What are the general objectives of monetary policy? Why are the goals of promoting full employment and counteracting inflation difficult to achieve at the same time?

4. In recent years, the United States economy has suffered from what some economists have called "stagflation"—a combination of relatively high unemployment of resources coupled with high rates of inflation. For the most part, the monetary policy of the Federal Reserve System has been a "tight-money" policy, aimed primarily at controlling inflation. Some critics have argued that this is prolonging stagnation and unemployment by discouraging new investment. Are the priorities of the Fed correct? Why or why not?

5. How do sales or purchases of government bonds by the Federal Reserve banks affect the economy? How do they affect bank reserves? How do they affect interest rates?

6. What are the dangers of an overreliance on direct regulation of reserve requirements?

7. Why are the actions of the Fed more likely to be effective in contracting the money supply than in expanding it?

8. Why do you think that moral suasion is a relatively ineffective method of advancing monetary policy?

Chapter 16

Business Cycles, Fiscal and Monetary Policies: An Overview

What to look for in this chapter

What kinds of developments usually characterize the four phases of the business cycle?

What was the role of fiscal and monetary policy in the Depression of the 1930s and the eventual recovery?

What were the general outlines of fiscal and monetary policy in the 1950s?

What changes were brought about by the Kennedy-Johnson "new economics" of the 1960s?

How successful has fiscal and monetary policy been in dealing with the simultaneous problems of unemployment and inflation of the 1970s?

Chapters 8–15 provided an introduction to the macroeconomy. In those chapters, we discussed the measurement of several economic aggregates such as gross national product and the rates of inflation and unemployment, examined the phases of the business cycle, investigated the behavior of consumption and investment spending, and considered the influence of the money supply on economic activity. In addition, we examined the role of government in macroeconomic matters, as evidenced through the employment of monetary and fiscal policy.

At this point, it is appropriate to review the phases of the business cycle and relate the concepts learned in the previous chapters to the macroeconomic experience of the United States over the past 50 years.

BUSINESS CYCLE THEORY: A SYNTHESIS

Let us now take each phase of the business cycle in turn and observe how consumption, investment, and the money supply fluctuate and interact within it.

Recovery

To recover from a recession, the economy needs some kind of stimulus to national income. To some extent, eventual replacement demand for worn-out equipment will lead to a round of investment spending, but government can speed up the process by stimulating consumption spending, either by putting more money in the hands of consumers—through tax cuts, for example—or by spending more on public works. Some other factors leading to recovery are the lower interest rates that result from an increase in the money supply; an increase in confidence in the economy; and in particular cases, revival of both investment and consumption demand triggered by a random event.

Once national income starts growing, the accompanying rise in consumption spending helps to maintain the momentum. Consumption spending grows rapidly, not only because people have more dollars, but also because the multiplier remains at a high rate. There is a pent-up demand for durable goods that has been building up throughout the recession. Furthermore, as confidence grows, consumer credit increases, because households are more willing to take on debts and lenders are more willing to extend loans.

During the early part of an expansionary period, prices are stable. The excess capacity and readily available resources provide the means for meeting higher demand by increasing production.

As consumption spending grows during the recovery period, businesses will need more plant and equipment and more inventory to handle the higher level of sales. If industry in general has very little unused capacity because capital stock was depleted during the recession, the accelerator effect will take over *at once,* and even small increases in consumption will require increases in investment spending. But if the preceding recession was a severe one, industry may find itself with large amounts of idle capacity, and it will then take a while for the accelerator effect to appear. In any event, if the revival in consumer spending continues, heavy investment spending will begin, and the recovery will proceed at a rapid pace.

With economic activity increasing as both consumption and investment spending expand, the demand for money will also increase. At the bottom of a recession it is typical for banks to have excess reserves, so initially the increased demand for money can be met easily as banks expand loans and demand deposits. Moreover, velocity may increase, so the dollars already in circulation will turn over faster than they did before. After a while, however, the existing supply of money will no longer be adequate for the higher level of business activity. If nothing is done by the monetary authorities (that is, the Federal Reserve) to expand the money supply, the recovery may stop at this time. The shortage of money will lead to credit rationing at the banks and high interest rates. Both individuals and businesses will therefore find it difficult to activate their new spending plans. However, the Fed usually responds during the earlier stages of a recovery by supplying the banking system with the needed additional reserves.

The peak

Increased consumption demand is satisfied in the initial stages of the recovery period by increased production. Eventually, however, the economy will achieve full employment of resources, and shortages will begin to develop, forcing up the costs of production and prices. In the short run, the shortages can be met by the formation of additional capital through business investment to increase the productivity of existing resources. But eventually, no more input resources are available in the short run, and competition among buyers drives product prices up even more. Thus, at the peak of a cycle, inflation becomes a serious problem.

In an effort to check inflation, monetary policy tends to be tight during a boom. Since the 1950s, the Federal Reserve Board has been concerned about the rising price levels that have characterized the later stages of expansionary periods and has attempted to restrain these inflationary pressures through monetary means. Generally by using open-market operations and higher discount rates, the Fed has tried to discourage the banks from granting new loans. As a result, money has been especially tight at the tops of recent booms. With the high level of business activity and the large amount of investment in plant and inventory, there is a heavy demand for money and interest rates are high. Nevertheless, because optimism about the future is widespread, businesses compete with one another to borrow funds, regardless of the cost.

Recession

As we suggested earlier, the seeds of a downturn in economic activity are found in the behavior of consumption and investment demand during the last stages of a boom period.

After a long period of expansion, consumption, though at a high level, is no longer growing at the same rate as earlier in the cycle. The slowdown or cessation of growth can be attributed to several factors.

1. Consumers have acquired large stocks of durable goods, and they are consequently in no hurry to buy more.
2. Consumer resistance to higher prices appears.
3. Because income is at a higher level, the marginal propensity to save may increase, thus causing the multiplier to decline.

Consumer demand
This initial stabilization of consumption demand results immediately in a sharp drop in investment demand (the accelerator effect) that leads to another decline in consumption (the multiplier effect), and a recession is under way. As consumption and investment fall, production schedules are cut back, and unemployment spreads. This affects the general level of confidence in the economy, and individuals, fearful of losing their jobs, may increase their saving rate significantly, thus contributing to an additional decline in income and employment as consumption declines further.

Investment demand
During a recession, investment demand initially drops because consumption *growth* ends. The drop may be especially precipitous if business has seriously overexpanded its capacity and inventory during the preceding boom, because even normal replacement demand will be postponed. Investment demand will continue at a low level as the recession continues, because of the interaction of multiplier and accelerator.

New investment is also discouraged because business profits are dropping. Businesspeople who counted on continued consumption growth to justify their earlier outlays on new facilities now find themselves with declining demand for their products, although they must still pay the high interest costs assumed earlier. Hence profits are squeezed, and business confidence sags, making additional investment spending even less likely.

Money supply
Prior to the establishment of the Federal Deposit Insurance Corporation (FDIC) to insure bank deposits, the business problems of a recession were compounded by the behavior of the banks. Individuals tended to panic when business worsened, and they rushed to withdraw savings from banks because they feared the banks would go out

of business and they would lose their deposits. Bankers reacted by refusing to make new loans and calling in old ones. Borrowers unable to repay their loans were forced into bankruptcy or into selling their assets at distress prices. Today, however, the protection offered by the FDIC acts as a brake on the old-fashioned bank run and the financial panic it created.

Nevertheless, money does play a role during a recession. There is a natural tendency for the money supply to contract, both because businesses are less eager to borrow (investment opportunities are fewer in a declining economy) and because bankers are reluctant to lend money during bad times. During recent years, the Federal Reserve Board has attempted to control recessions by aggressively expanding the monetary base (providing the banks with substantial excess reserves) and by forcing interest rates down. In this way, the monetary authorities hope to encourage the banks to write new loans, and their customers to borrow funds and proceed with new investment programs. However, these attempts frequently meet with only limited success, because it is difficult to encourage pessimistic businesspeople to borrow during bad times, despite low interest rates.

The trough

At the bottom or trough of the downswing, consumption spending stabilizes at a relatively low level, and investment spending is minimal. If consumption demand falls enough so that there is substantial overcapacity, there may actually be disinvestment, as businesses fail to replace their worn-out plant and equipment. Prices in some areas of the economy may continue to drop, although today they are likely to remain stable in those industries where strong industry-wide unions or monopolistic pricing-policies, or both, prevail. Profits are low, unemployment is widespread, and there is little confidence in the economy. Although interest rates are low and money is plentiful, pessimism is widespread and borrowers are scarce.

THE UNITED STATES' HISTORICAL RECORD

If it is true that those who do not remember the past are condemned to repeat it, a study of business cycles in the United States since the 1930s should be of interest. The business conditions under which our economy operates today provide fiscal and monetary authorities with opportunities to use a wide range of tools—monetary controls, tax changes, transfer payments, built-in stabilizers—most of which were developed after the Great Depression of the 1930s in order to ensure that there would be no repetition.

This brief overview will show how the government and central-bank authorities have met the challenge of business cycle fluctuations since 1930 and will enable us to see whether monetary and fiscal policies have been effective tools for economic stabilization.

The 1930s

Monetary policy

During the 1930s the United States experienced the longest and deepest depression in its history. The first signs of the crisis that lay ahead appeared in 1928 in the midst of an otherwise booming economy, when construction contracted and housing starts began to drop sharply. This problem was undoubtedly compounded by the actions of the Federal Reserve Board, which had earlier decided to fight the speculative excesses in the stock market through a tight money policy, and had gradually raised the discount rate from 3.5 percent in 1927 to 6 percent by mid-1929.

Late in 1929 the stock market crashed, and in 1930 the nation was reeling. Construction activity continued to decline, and unemployment reached more than 10 percent by the end of the year. The Fed, reversing its previous policy, began to reduce the discount rate, and short-term rates on business loans followed the discount rates down. By 1931, although unemployment was still growing, many economists believed that the worst of the 1929–1930 recession was over and that, given further expansionary encouragement from the Fed, a recovery would begin.

At this point, however, the European financial crises of 1931 brought a worldwide loss of confidence in paper money and an increase in the hoarding of gold. When the United States Treasury found itself facing a massive reduction in its gold supply, the Federal Reserve Board again raised the discount rate, hoping that the resulting increase in interest rates would encourage people to keep their American dollars on deposit. Unfortunately, the higher interest rates also discouraged investment, and the decline of economic activity grew worse. Although the Fed subsequently reduced interest rates somewhat, the damage had already been done.

During 1933, 1934, and 1935, the Fed followed generally expansionary policies as far as bank reserves were concerned, and by 1937 there were many signs of economic recovery: the unemployment rate had fallen from the depression high of nearly 25 percent to 14.3 percent; the stock market had rallied significantly; and industrial activity had been climbing steadily for two or three years.

Confident in the promise of these signs of increasing prosperity and concerned by increasing consumer prices, the Fed again moved to tighten money by raising reserve requirements, which led to a decline in excess reserves and to increases in interest rates. Shortly thereafter the economy once again turned down sharply; unemployment zoomed up again, and by 1938 production levels had fallen almost a quarter from their 1937 highs. The Fed then abandoned any notion of tightening monetary policy. The discount rate was cut to 1 percent, and the banking system was provided with huge amounts of excess reserves. There was some gradual improvement in production and some decline in unemployment, but it is debatable whether the economy was actually on its way out of the depression by late 1939, despite all the expansionary activities of the monetary authorities.

Fiscal policy

What were fiscal policymakers doing during the depression? The popular view is that during the first two Roosevelt administrations (1932 to 1940) the government was pursuing aggressively expansionary activities—injecting huge amounts of money into the economy through spending on public-works projects and paying the cost by deficit financing rather than by taxes. Because the country did not snap out of the depression more quickly many people have cited that period as an example of the failure of fiscal policy.

In recent years, however, economists have taken a new and careful look at the *total* government spending and taxing programs of the 1930s and have come up with some very different conclusions. Although federal government purchases did increase significantly during most of that decade, two other factors, both deflationary, tended in part to offset the expansionary effects of federal spending programs. First, states began to use sales, excise, and income taxes as major revenue-producing devices, and many of them at the same time reduced their spending programs. Second, the federal government felt obliged to raise taxes to help meet its increased expenditures because it was still under the influence of the political and economic view that favored a balanced budget. As a result, most economists now believe that *overall* fiscal policy was actually much less expansionary than had formerly been believed.

1940 to 1945

From 1940 to 1945 the United States economy was shaped by the demands of World War II. The unemployment rate declined to 1.2 percent in 1944, reflecting not only the fact that 11.5 million men and women were in the armed forces, but also an increase of over 10 million in the civilian labor force—from 46 million to 56 million. At the height of the war effort, industrial production was

Table 16.1
Federal government expenditures as a percent of GNP, 1930–1939, 1940–1949

Year	GNP (billions of dollars)	Federal government expenditures (billions of dollars)	Expenditures as a percent of GNP
1930	$ 90.4	$ 2.8	2.2%
1931	75.8	4.2	5.5
1932	58.0	3.2	5.5
1933	55.6	4.0	7.2
1934	65.1	6.4	9.8
1935	72.2	6.5	9.0
1936	82.5	8.7	10.5
1937	90.4	7.4	8.2
1938	84.7	8.6	10.2
1939	95.5	8.9	9.8
1940	99.7	10.0	10.0
1941	124.5	20.5	16.5
1942	157.9	56.1	35.5
1943	191.6	85.8	44.8
1944	210.1	95.5	45.5
1945	211.9	84.6	39.9
1946	208.5	35.6	17.1
1947	231.3	29.8	12.9
1948	257.6	34.9	13.5
1949	256.5	41.3	16.1

Source: *Economic Report of the President,* February 1975.

running at almost twice the 1940 level. Consumer prices increased only moderately, a remarkable achievement considering the highly expansionary fiscal and monetary policies that were required to pay for the war. This relative stability of consumer prices was largely a result of the imposition of wage and price controls passed by Congress early in the war and stringently enforced by the administration. It is questionable whether inflation could have been restrained without these price controls. In addition, rationing, priorities, and appeals to patriotism all worked to restrain consumers from competing for the small supply of consumer goods that were available, although black markets for many products did develop.

Fiscal policy during World War II
The war forced the federal government to take a more active role in the economic life of the country. *Table 16.1* compares government expenditures from 1930 to 1939 with those of 1940 to 1945. It shows that the government's contribution to aggregate demand increased tremendously. Also, the administration found it impossible, despite imposition of many new taxes, to pay for the war effort without resorting to deficit financing. Because it was wartime, however, Congress and the public were willing to accept huge deficit budgets with none of the outcry that had characterized the annual budget hearings during the 1930s. Federal deficits during the six calendar years 1940 to 1945 totaled $182.7 billion, next to which the $18.4 billion deficits for the 10-year period 1930 to 1939 appear insignificant indeed.

Although the concept of an expansionary fiscal policy had been embraced in principle during the 1930s, it was not until the 1940s (whether inadvertently or not) that it was put into action. The results—full employment, and a high level of production—speak for themselves.

Monetary policy during World War II
The commercial-banking system entered World War II with tremendous excess reserves, permitting the banks to help finance the war by buying government bonds. By 1942, however, the banks had exhausted their excess reserves and, under existing regulations, could buy no more bonds. The Fed then created additional reserves for the banks. In effect, what the Fed did was to provide the federal government with an unlimited source

of demand-deposit money. When a new Treasury loan was required in order to finance the budget deficit, the Fed obligingly created excess reserves at the commercial banks by purchasing "old" bond holdings from them. The banks then purchased "new" government bonds, paying for them by giving the government demand deposits, which it used to pay its bills.

During the war, the Fed cooperated with the Treasury to keep interest rates down, so that the cost of carrying the growing federal debt could be controlled. Thus federal monetary policy complemented federal fiscal policy during the war years to finance victory. This success showed that fiscal and monetary policy, in large enough doses, could be effective tools.

The early postwar years: 1945 to 1950

After a brief decline in production and employment as government spending fell off at the end of the war, individuals and businesses rushed to fill the backlog of demand for consumer goods and capital equipment that had built up because of the depression and the war. Consequently, business activity stabilized at a relatively high level. The most serious problem was inflation. Price controls had been removed shortly after the war ended, and the huge postwar demands caused prices to rise almost 35 percent from the end of 1945 to 1948, or at a compounded rate of about 10 percent a year.

Fiscal policy

Immediately after the war, federal fiscal policy was deflationary. High wartime tax rates were maintained until mid-1948, expenditures declined steadily, and substantial surpluses characterized the 1946, 1947, and 1948 budgets. However, state and local budgets in the same period were showing deficits because of spending programs to build long-postponed facilities, and the deflationary effects of the federal budget surpluses were not adequate to control the inflationary forces at work.

President Truman, believing that budget surpluses were the only effective antiinflationary weapon available, was reluctant to accept the tax cuts urged by Congress, but in May 1948, Congress passed a 10 percent tax-cut bill over his veto. By coincidence, the tax cut was ideally timed, because a recession set in shortly after it was passed. The budget deficit that resulted in 1949, together with the expansionary monetary policies of the Fed at that time, helped to make the 1948–1949 recession a relatively mild one.

Monetary policy

Theoretically, monetary policy during the early postwar years should have been directed at controlling inflation. The Fed should have been selling government bonds in the open market to reduce commercial-bank reserves and restrain the growth of the money supply. But a decline in the price of government bonds and an increase in bond yields are an unavoidable by-product of open-market sales, and these consequences were unacceptable to the Treasury.

The Treasury had financed World War II in large part by selling bonds to commercial banks. A sizable proportion of the $90 billion in bonds held by the commercial banks at the end of the war were short-term securities that came due annually. Therefore, each year the Treasury had to sell tremendous amounts of new bonds on the open market in order to pay off its old debt obligations. The Treasury argued that if the Fed drove interest rates up by selling government bonds, it would be forced to offer comparably high interest rates on any new financing, and the cost of carrying the federal debt would skyrocket.

The Fed went along with this line of reasoning until 1951. Throughout the early postwar years, the Open Market Committee purchased bonds from the banks, interest rates remained low, the Treasury happily refinanced its maturing debt at low cost—and inflation, unchecked by tight money policies, grew by leaps and bounds.

The 1950s

On the whole, the United States enjoyed considerable prosperity during the 1950s. Gross national product increased, consumer prices were reasonably steady, and unemployment remained at manageable levels.

There were some major problems, however. The Korean war lasted from mid-1950 to mid-1953, and there were recessions in 1953–1954 and 1957–1958. As the decade ended, there was some concern about the relatively high rate of unemployment that persisted well into the recovery that followed the 1958 downturn. Moreover, overall United States growth rates were averaging 3 to 4 percent a year, compared with the Soviet Union's 7 to 10 percent rate.

Fiscal policy

At the onset of the Korean war, Congress imposed higher taxes, but military spending did not equal the higher tax revenue. The resulting surplus in the 1951 budget helped to restrain the inflation caused by heavy consumer purchasing in anticipation of shortages similar to those of World War II. However, price stability was reasonably well restored by early 1952.

With the end of the war in 1953, a downturn in economic activity became apparent. However, the expiration of certain wartime taxes and the enactment of excise and income-tax cuts contributed to budget deficits in 1953 and 1954; unemployment began to decline, industrial production turned around, and the recession was over.

An expansionary period followed from 1954 to 1957. Government receipts picked up sharply, and the federal budget showed surpluses in both 1956 and 1957. The surpluses, together with a restrictive monetary policy, helped to brake the inflation that was once again picking up speed.

When business turned downward again in 1957, the Eisenhower administration, reflecting philosophical distaste for deficit budgets and concern over inflation, was reluctant to propose any tax cuts. However, budget deficits did develop in 1958 and 1959, because active fiscal policy during the 1957–1958 recession included increased expenditures on highway construction and other public works, as well as extension of unemployment benefits. The recession ended in the spring of 1959. Production climbed sharply, but employment picked up more slowly, and despite the general prosperity enjoyed by the nation as the 1950s drew to a close, unemployment remained at a troublesome 6 percent.

Monetary policy

In 1951 the Fed and the Treasury reached an accord under which the Fed would no longer be obligated to support the price of Treasury securities but could buy and sell government bonds freely, regardless of the effect on bond yields and Treasury financing costs. When the Fed thus regained its flexibility in open-market operations, its first action was to move immediately toward a tight money policy by selling government bonds, driving interest rates up, and restraining the growth of member bank reserves. On the whole, this was to be the story throughout the 1950s. The Fed, worried about inflation and—toward the end of the decade—about the outflow of gold abroad, generally followed a tight money policy. As the decade ended, most interest rates were at their highest levels in 30 years. Some economists were questioning whether the Fed's overwhelming concern with inflation had perhaps resulted in overly restrictive monetary policies that had prevented the economy from growing rapidly enough to reach a full-employment level.

The 1960s

In early 1960, *Fortune* magazine coined the phrase "The Soaring Sixties." In retrospect, it proved to be an apt description of the American economy during most of that decade. Production and employment were at all-time high levels, with real

GNP growing as much as 6 or 7 percent in some years, and unemployment stabilizing for an unprecedented four years at acceptable peacetime rates of under 4 percent. Unfortunately, production and employment were not the only indicators that soared; prices did too, and inflation, a relatively small nagging problem in the early 1960s, reached a 5 to 6 percent rate by 1969–1970, becoming the major concern of policymakers.

The Kennedy-Johnson "new economics"

Despite a gain of almost 25 percent in industrial production from the low point in first quarter 1958 to the top of the 1960 recovery, unemployment remained at about 6 percent. Economists were faced with a new and vexing problem: a seemingly prosperous and growing economy was still unable to achieve full employment. The Kennedy-Johnson "new economics" was a bold attempt to deal with this situation. Measures to stimulate demand were no longer taken only to avoid or correct recession. Instead of merely reacting to cyclical downturns, policymakers now accepted responsibility for stimulating a growing economy to ensure full employment. The "new economics" was also based on two other assumptions.

☐ Budget deficits were no longer to be viewed as extraordinary and potentially dangerous, acceptable only as a temporary expedient during recessions. They were to be viewed as just another tool of economic policy—as a routine way of compensating for insufficient investment in the private sector.

Moreover, the belief that the budget should be balanced at least in the long run was also challenged. Before the 1960s it was generally accepted that sound economic practice involved incurring deficits in recession periods, but compensating for these by accumulating surpluses in good times, thus balancing the budget over the long run. The "new economists," however, suggested that perhaps annual deficits in *most* years might be required as the price of economic growth.

☐ The Kennedy advisers realized that attempts to accumulate budget surpluses during an economic recovery exerted a contractionary impact on the economy. With a higher level of business activity accompanying recovery, more tax revenue was generated for government. When tax receipts exceeded the amount of government spending reinjected into the system, the overall impact of government action was to reduce economic activity. As noted in Chapter 12, this diminished level of economic activity, resulting from the excess of tax receipts over expenditures, is called fiscal drag.

Recognizing that fiscal policy is responsible for slower economic growth, the Kennedy administration proposed the judicious application of either increased expenditures or reduced tax rates as business begins to pick up during the recovery phase of the business cycle. They argued that additional expenditures or tax cuts must be forthcoming in order to offset the deflationary influence of a potential budget surplus.

The implications of the "new economics" are quite revolutionary when compared with the conventional economics of the postwar period. Before the 1960s, it was considered a sign of great economic sophistication that Congress and administration leaders were finally willing to accept temporary budget deficits in times of economic distress, and then only with the understanding that the budget would move to a compensating surplus as soon as times got better. Now they were being asked to approve budget deficits in good times as well, and to initiate such deficits deliberately, by introducing tax cuts or spending programs into a healthy economy.

The result was spectacular. By the end of 1965, the unemployment rate had dropped below 4 percent, and GNP grew at a rate of 6.3 percent in 1965 and 6.5 percent in 1966. In addition, the newly found prosperity led to sharply higher tax collections, so that despite the cut in tax rates, actual tax revenues were almost $10 billion more in the calendar year 1965 than they were in 1963, and federal government receipts and expenditures in calendar year 1965 showed a surplus.*

In 1966, the expanding Vietnam war led to an increase of nearly $11 billion in defense spending alone, and other government expenditures (primarily Medicare) had also increased significantly. By 1965, unemployment had declined to 4.5 percent and stayed below 4 percent through 1969, so the growing rate of inflation became the main concern of policymakers. The administration felt that the expansionary consequences of the increases in government spending should be balanced by some increase in tax receipts. Congress did agree to some boosts in excise taxes, but—in an election year—refused to go along with income-tax hikes. As a result, the budget showed a substantial deficit for the year, and inflation continued.

It was not until July 1967 that Congress finally passed the 10 percent surtax recommended a year earlier by President Johnson. However, military expenditures had accelerated, the budget still showed substantial deficits in 1967 and 1968, and inflation was becoming ever more serious. Employment and production continued at very high rates, although real GNP growth slowed down. Finally, late in 1969, with both a surplus budget and severe monetary restraints at work to stop rising prices, the long boom (1961 to 1969) came to an end.

Monetary policy

Throughout most of the 1960s, the policies of the Federal Reserve were consistent with the expansionary fiscal policies introduced by the "new economists." In the eight-year period from 1961 to 1969, the total money supply increased at an average annual compounded rate of about 4.3 percent, whereas in the preceding eight-year period, 1953 to 1961, the average rate of increase had been only 1.4 percent!

Some economists attribute the extended period of prosperity that the country enjoyed from 1961 to 1969 to the fiscal measures taken (tax cuts, deficit budgets); others attribute it to the increased growth rate of the money supply. According to the monetarists, the stimulation provided by the steady infusion of new money was the single most important factor in producing the steady growth in GNP and the full employment enjoyed for so many years. As confirmation of the important role of money, they refer to the events of 1969, when the Fed imposed strict controls on the money supply to fight inflation. The money supply, which had been permitted to grow by about 7 percent in 1967 and over 7 percent in 1968, increased only 2.8 percent in 1969; during the second half of that year, it was practically unchanged. The monetarists point to the slowdown in business activity of 1970 and the accompanying increase in unemployment as direct consequences of this drastic reversal of monetary policy.

In addition to using changes in the money supply as a policy tool, the Fed continued to employ sharp variations in interest rates as a means of stimulating or contracting the economy. As the pace of inflation accelerated through 1966, 1967, and 1968, the Fed was in a particularly difficult position. Prices were rising, but the fiscal tools to control such price increases were virtually unavailable to the administration. Because the war in southeast Asia had escalated, federal military spending could not be restrained, and the budget was showing big deficits. It was left to the Fed to try to restrain the very strong demand forces in the economy—particularly business investment demand—that were competing for goods and services in a full-employment economy, driving prices ever higher.

The Fed relied almost completely on high interest rates in its attempt to control inflation,

---

*This was exactly what President Kennedy had in mind when he first proposed the tax cuts. The following is a quotation from an address by the president to the Economics Club of New York on December 14, 1962: "It is a paradoxical truth that . . . the soundest way to raise revenues in the long run is to cut rates now."

while continuing to permit the money supply to grow. In a series of moves beginning in 1966, the discount rate was raised to 5½ percent in 1968 and 6 percent in 1969, the highest rates since the 1929 boom. Short-term business borrowing costs (the prime interest rate) reached 6¾ precent in 1968 and 8½ percent in 1969.

Fiscal policy

In retrospect, it appears that the fiscal drag accompanying the recovery of 1959–1960 was probably the primary cause of the recession of 1960–1961. As a result of the higher tax collections forthcoming from a rising level of national income, there was an unplanned and highly contractionary budget surplus in 1960. The recession was a mild one, and the outgoing Eisenhower administration felt it was unnecessary, in mid-1960, to propose any fiscal remedies other than quickening the pace of certain government expenditures. However, the budget went from a surplus basis in early 1960 to a deficit basis in early 1961, thus providing the initial impetus for a turn-around. The Kennedy administration acted to speed up various spending programs even further and reduced business taxes by introducing new depreciation schedules; and Congress passed a 7 percent tax-credit allowance for purchases of new plant and equipment. Recovery began in early 1961, and by 1962 industrial production was hitting new all-time highs, unemployment had declined to 5.5 percent, and real GNP was growing at a 7 percent rate.

At this point, the dangers of fiscal drag became obvious once more. The economy was growing, but the rate of growth had slowed down, and unemployment was beginning to rise. In January 1963, President Kennedy asked Congress for a major cut in individual and corporate income-tax rates, in an attempt to forestall another recession. Because these tax cuts would lead to a budget deficit, there was considerable congressional opposition, and it was not until the spring of 1964, after Lyndon Johnson had assumed the presidency, that the tax cut was finally passed.

The 1970s

The decade of the 1970s began badly and continued to plummet downhill. The inflationary spiral inherited from the 1960s grew increasingly burdensome, and the first half of the decade was characterized by recession and steadily increasing unemployment as well. Skyrocketing food and energy prices took their toll on consumers, who were forced to pay more and more for basic necessities.

During the first half of the 1970s, GNP in current dollars continued to rise, passing the $1 trillion mark in 1971 and reaching $1.3 trillion in 1974. However, adjustment of the figures for the effects of inflation shows that real GNP (in 1958 dollars) not only made less spectacular gains but actually declined by 2.2 percent from 1973 to 1974. Unemployment climbed steadily, reaching 7.2 percent at the end of 1974 and 9 percent in 1975.

Inflation and unemployment persisted to varying degrees in the second half of the 1970s as well. Having reached a post–Great Depression peak of 9 percent in 1975, the unemployment rate declined gradually to 5.7 percent early in 1979. This improvement, however, was at the expense of an accelerating rate of inflation. Stimulative monetary and fiscal policies throughout 1976 and 1977 expanded employment opportunities, but also served to intensify inflationary pressures in the economy. A 9 percent rate of inflation in 1978 was followed by an even more rapid increase in prices during the first quarter of 1979. Double-digit inflation again loomed on the horizon with surging gasoline and beef prices leading the way.

Rising prices were also largely responsible for a 1978 current dollar GNP in excess of $2 trillion. Even after adjusting for inflation, however, economic growth during the recent upswing has been impressive. Between the first quarter of 1975 and the fourth quarter of 1978, real GNP increased more than 20 percent.

Fiscal policy—first half

Wage and price controls The simultaneous occurrence of inflation and recession presented policymakers of the early 1970s with a cruel dilemma. Since action to curb recession by stimulating demand and thereby boosting output and employment tends to feed the fires of inflation, the Nixon administration was at first reluctant to stimulate the economy to any great extent. However, in August 1971 it embarked on a far-reaching economic policy intended to cope with both problems. The program included a $7 to $8 billion tax cut to bolster aggregate demand, repeal of the 7 percent excise tax on cars, a tax credit for new investment, and the acceleration of some already scheduled income-tax adjustments. Because these steps would raise consumers' purchasing power and threaten further inflation, Nixon used powers given him by the Economic Stabilization Act of 1970 to freeze rents, wages, and prices for a 90-day period. The freeze was followed by a phased program of controls that lasted until April 30, 1974. Not since World War II had the government laid such a strong hand on the economy, but not since World War II had the economy been in such serious trouble.

The effectiveness of the wage-price controls between 1971 and 1974 continues to be debated, and a clear conclusion may never by reached. No economic measure takes effect in a vacuum, and this one coexisted with a particularly complex set of circumstances. Because unemployment remained high, there is disagreement about whether the slowing rates of increase in wages and prices in 1972 can be attributed entirely to the effect of the controls. Conversely, even the surges of inflation after each removal or relaxation of the controls were at least in part the result of other influences.

Serious disruptions in world agriculture forced food prices up rapidly in 1973, and the oil embargo of the same year was followed by massive increases in the cost of oil. Inflation was in fact worldwide, not limited to the United States.

Other fiscal actions Other major elements of fiscal policy during the first half of the 1970s were heavy spending on defense and such social programs as Social Security, unemployment compensation, veterans' benefits, and aid to families with dependent children. Cash income-maintenance programs, which had cost $20 billion in 1960, reached $47 billion in 1970 and grew to $74 billion in 1973. The expensive Southeast Asian war worsened the inflationary spiral as the Defense Department competed with the rest of the country for limited supplies of raw materials.

Fiscal policy—second half

When Gerald Ford assumed the presidency in 1974, the United States was in the midst of the worst recession since the 1930s. Not only was real output falling and the unemployment rate on the rise, but inflationary pressures were also acute. The appropriate path for fiscal policy was by no means evident, but the rising rate of unemployment was given precedence in policy decisions since it was felt that inflationary pressures might be abating. In essence, two of the main causes of rising prices in the economy, the oil embargo and worldwide crop failure in 1973, were past history and it was not expected that similar shocks would recur in the foreseeable future.

Emphasizing the unemployment problem, the Tax Reduction Act of 1975 was passed in March of that year to stimulate aggregate demand and production. This legislation slashed personal and corporate income taxes by $12 billion, provided rebates on 1974 income taxes totaling $10 billion, and authorized a special payment of $50 to all Social Security beneficiaries. Additionally, the time period over which one might receive unemployment compensation was lengthened from 13 to 65 weeks.

The revenue-reducing effects of the tax cut in combination with a sharply increased level of transfer payments resulted in the largest federal government deficit since World War II—a whopping $71 billion. However, the surge in the unemployment rate from 5.5 percent in the third quarter of 1974 to 9 percent by the second quarter of 1975 seemed to justify this massive economic stimulus.

Although an increase in real output in the second quarter of 1975 signaled the beginning of the recovery phase of the business cycle, the unemployment problem lingered. Higher levels of production generated more jobs, but the labor force expanded so rapidly that little immediate progress was made in reducing the rate of joblessness. Consequently, fiscal policy remained expansionary during 1976 and 1977 with budgetary deficits approximating $50 billion in both years, and with annual increases in federal government expenditures measuring 8.7 percent and 9.5 percent, respectively. In addition, a small tax cut was approved in 1977. These actions, in conjunction with healthy increases in business expenditures for plant and equipment, were successful in bringing the unemployment figure down to 6.4 percent by December 1977.

As might be expected, however, brightening the unemployment picture was not without cost. The implementation of policies designed to bolster aggregate demand also resulted in upward pressure on prices. After registering a relatively moderate 4.8 percent increase in 1976, consumer prices rose by 6.8 percent the following year. In an attempt both to avoid another episode of spiraling prices and to sustain the economic expansion, federal government expenditures were increased at a much slower rate in 1978 than in the three previous years and the budgetary deficit was trimmed to $30 billion. The economic trend, nonetheless, appeared undisturbed by these measures, as the unemployment rate continued its decline while prices jumped by 9 percent.

Monetary policy—first half

The relative harmony that characterized monetary and fiscal policy during the 1960s dissolved early in the 1970s as the economic situation worsened and the Fed faced problems that could not easily be solved simultaneously.

Concentrating on stemming the recession, the Fed expanded the money supply (M_1) at an average rate of 7 percent yearly from January 1971 to June 1974, thus making inflation much worse. In mid-1974, however, the Fed reversed its policy, and through April 1975 allowed the money supply to increase at a rate of less than 2 percent. In a further move to stimulate the lagging economy, the Fed lowered the reserve requirement three times between September 1974 and January 1975 to release $2.5 billion in reserves back into the banking system. Because there had been a sharp drop in member bank borrowing, the discount rate was also cut from its all-time high of 8 percent in mid-1974 to 7.25 percent in January 1975 and then to 6.25 percent three months later. The intended goal of these actions was not accomplished, however, because banks used most of their increased borrowing power to repay outstanding obligations to the government. The banks hesitated to lend money, and few businesses wanted to borrow for expansion when the economy was so slack. Most of the money injected into the economy by lowering the discount rate therefore merely returned to the Federal Reserve. Member banks had all the liquid assets they needed.

Monetary policy—second half

As the recovery progressed, however, the banking and business communities as well as the general public became more optimistic about future economic conditions. Businesses and households displayed a desire to borrow and banks exhibited an increased willingness to lend. After declining 12 percent in real terms in 1975, real business investment expenditures grew about 8.5 percent annually from 1976 to 1978, home-mortgage loans mushroomed, and consumer installment borrowing for big-ticket items reached record levels.

Besides furnishing additional reserves to the banking system to support this higher level of economic activity, the Fed further promoted economic expansion by lowering reserve requirements on demand deposits and cutting the discount rate to 5.25 percent late in 1976. These easy money policies permitted M_1 to grow at an annual rate of 8 percent during 1977 and the first three quarters of 1978.

Unfortunately this spurt in the money supply aggravated the inflationary situation in addition to spurring real output, and when price hikes proved even steeper than anticipated, the Fed again found itself on the economic stabilization see-saw, forced to alter its game plan radically. A restrictive monetary strategy, instituted in mid-1978, halted money-supply growth for the remainder of the year and established 1.5 to 4.25 percent as the desired range for M_1 growth in 1979. Price pressure will likely recede somewhat as a result of this tight policy, but now the Fed must worry about the prospect of a policy-induced recession.

As we enter the decade of the 1980s, the Fed is under increasing criticism for not solving the country's economic problems, for being too independent of Congress and the president, and for not coordinating its actions with fiscal policy. Its defenders respond that fiscal policy takes so long to put into effect that it cannot be well coordinated with monetary policy, and that too few members of Congress adequately understand economics. Finding an element of truth in each of these arguments, Congress passed the Full Employment and Balanced Growth Act of 1978 directing the Federal Reserve to relate its plans for monetary growth to the short-run economic goals of the administration as outlined in the *Economic Report of the President*. In addition, the House has established a budget committee whose members are trained in economics. The committee's goals are to screen out the least practical economic proposals currently before Congress, to attempt to reduce fiscal lag, and to try to boost stability by focusing attention on specific markets, such as energy, rather than on the economy as a whole. The emphasis on particular markets as opposed to the macroeconomy seems to reflect a growing realization that the problems plaguing today's economy cannot easily be rectified through use of the traditional tools of monetary and fiscal policy.

Summary

■ This chapter reviews the phases of the business cycle and relates the basic concepts from earlier chapters to the macroeconomic performance of the United States economy in the last 50 years.

■ In the recovery phase of the business cycle, consumer spending rises and the multiplier effect induces further stimulation. Idle productive capacity will be brought into use and further business investment in plant and equipment will be made; the demand for money will increase and the Fed will generally encourage this. At the peak phase, when full employment is reached, inflation becomes a threat, and the Fed will move to a tight money policy. Consumer demand, especially for durable goods, eventually tails off because of satiated demand and higher prices; increased saving may also diminish consumption. As a recessionary phase begins, declining consumer demand leads to decreased investment, which results in unemployment. As confidence and the demand for money drop, the Fed will attempt to counter the downswing with an expansionary monetary policy. Eventually the economy stabilizes in a trough, with relatively high unemployment and relatively low consumer spending, investment, and confidence, until new developments again trigger a recovery phase.

■ In the Depression of the 1930s, monetary policy tended to backfire and fiscal expansion was very timid. During World War II, a strongly expansionary monetary and fiscal policy with extensive deficit spending was accompanied by a major recovery.

■ In the late 1940s, pent-up consumer demand created a high level of business activity and rising inflation, only partially countered by a deflationary monetary policy.

■ The 1950s was a period of general prosperity, marked by mild recessions. By the end of the decade, unemployment was at a troublesome 6 percent.

■ The economy soared in the 1960s, with record production, employment, and real GNP growth. The Kennedy-Johnson "new economics" accepted budget deficits as a normal way to ensure growth and employment, and this approach seemed to work well in the mid-1960s. But by the end of the decade, the large budgets of the Vietnam war era were producing low unemployment but high inflation.

■ In the first half of the 1970s, the economy suffered from both high unemployment and high inflation rates, and real GNP actually declined slightly between 1973 and 1974. In the second half of the decade, unemployment was brought down but inflation proved harder to control. The Nixon, Ford, and Carter administrations frequently shifted gears in fiscal or monetary policy or both without ever achieving a clear success. The record of fiscal and monetary policy from the 1970s indicates the lack of clear coordination between the two major areas of government economic policy, and the pattern of simultaneous inflationary and recessionary trends has proven resistent to traditional measures.

Review & Discussion

1. What are the four phases of a business cycle? Briefly describe the behavior of consumption, investment, money, and output during the different phases. What, in general, will be the likely response of government monetary and fiscal policy in each phase?

2. Briefly describe government fiscal and monetary policies during the 1930s. Why were they so unsuccessful in reversing the Depression? What was the prevailing attitude toward deficit spending in this period?

3. Federal government spending increased tremendously during World War II. How did the government finance its expenditures? What was the Fed's relationship to the Treasury during that period?

4. Why did the federal government pass a bill to cut taxes in 1948? What was its effect?

5. How would you characterize the economy during the 1950s? What was the government attitude toward deficit spending in this period?

6. Describe the major departures in economic philosophy of the "new economics" of the Kennedy and Johnson administrations.

7. What dilemmas face policymakers in a period of simultaneous recession and inflation? What actions did the Nixon administration take to try to solve this dilemma? How successful were these steps?

8. How well do you think the federal government is succeeding at the moment in combating inflation and unemployment? How does the situation now compare with the early years of the 1970s?

Application 8: How the Recession Came About

We are pleased to be able to include the following work* of a guest application writer, Art Buchwald.

The recession hit so fast that nobody knows exactly how it happened. One day we were the land of milk and honey and the next day we were the land of sour cream and food stamps.

This is one explanation.

Hofberger, the Chevy salesman in Tomcat, Va., a suburb of Washington, called up Littleton, of Littleton Menswear & Haberdashery, and said, "Good news, the '75 Impalas have just come in and I've put one aside for you and your wife."

Littleton said, "I can't, Hofberger. My wife and I are getting a divorce."

Hofberger said, "That's too bad. Then take the car for yourself. I'll give you $100 extra on a trade-in because of the divorce."

"I'm sorry," Littleton said, "but I can't afford a new car this year. After I settle with my wife, I'll be lucky to buy a bicycle."

Hofberger hung up. His phone rang a few minutes later.

"This is Bedcheck the painter," the voice on the other end said. "When do you want us to start painting your house?"

"I changed my mind," said Hofberger. "I'm not going to paint the house." "But I ordered the paint," Bedcheck said. "Why did you change your mind?"

"Because Littleton is getting a divorce and he can't afford a new car."

That evening when Bedcheck came home his wife said, "The new color television set arrived from Gladstone's TV Shop."

"Take it back," Bedcheck told his wife.

"Why?" she demanded.

"Because Hofberger isn't going to have his house painted now that the Littletons are getting a divorce."

---

*Copyright 1975. Reprinted with permission of the author.

The next day Mrs. Bedcheck dragged the TV set in its carton back to Gladstone. "We don't want it."

Gladstone's face dropped. He immediately called his travel agent, Sandstorm. "You know that trip you had scheduled for me to the Virgin Islands?"

"Right, the tickets are all written up."

"Cancel it. I can't go. Bedcheck just sent back the color TV set because Hofberger didn't sell a car to Littleton because they're going to get a divorce and she wants all his money."

Sandstorm tore up the airline tickets and went over to see his banker, Gripsholm. "I can't pay back the loan this month because Gladstone isn't going to the Virgin Islands."

Gripsholm was furious. When Rudemaker came in to borrow money for a new kitchen he needed for his restaurant, Gripsholm turned him down cold. "How can I loan you money when Sandstorm hasn't repaid the money he borrowed?"

Rudemaker called up the contractor, Eagleton, and said he couldn't put in a new kitchen. Eagleton laid off eight men.

Meanwhile, General Motors announced it was giving a rebate on its '75 models. Hofberger called up Littleton immediately. "Good news," he said, "even if you are getting a divorce, you can afford a new car."

"I'm not getting a divorce," Littleton said. "It was all a misunderstanding and we've made up."

"That's great," Hofberger said. "Now you can buy the Impala."

"No way," said Littleton. "My business has been so lousy I don't know why I keep the doors open."

"I didn't know that," Hofberger said.

"Do you realize I haven't seen Bedcheck, Gladstone, Sandstorm, Gripsholm, Rudemaker, or Eagleton for more than a month? How can I stay in business if they don't patronize my store?"

Chapter 17

Stabilization: Problems and Policies

What to look for in this chapter

How have economists traditionally viewed the relationship between unemployment and inflation? What are some of the schools of thought concerning the achievement of economic stability?

What are some of the problems in designing and implementing economic policy to achieve stability?

What do economists mean by "stagflation"? What policies have been tried to counteract it in the 1970s?

How well have we met our national economic goals of keeping both unemployment and inflation rates down since World War II? What obstacles and problems have we encountered?

This chapter is concerned with recent problems faced by economic policymakers in their attempts to use fiscal and monetary policies to control high rates of inflation and unemployment. When economists refer to economic policy, they include more than just the decisions made by the government in response, presumably, to the desires of its citizens. In the United States, for example, the power to determine economic policy is not held by any one institution—it can be made by executives of commercial banks, the owners and managers of large corporations, and the elected officials of labor unions as well as by the government. No one person or institution can simply decree the adoption of one policy and the discontinuance of all others. For this reason, policies that are being carried out simultaneously may conflict with one another, as when, for example, the federal government decides to attempt to reduce inflation while labor unions attempt to secure wage increases or busi-

Table 17.1
Inflation and unemployment, 1954–1978

Year	Rate of inflation	Rate of inflation (five-year average)	Unemployment rate	Unemployment rate (five-year average)
1954	−0.5%		5.5%	
1955	0.4		4.4	
1956	2.9	1.5%	4.1	5.0%
1957	3.0		4.3	
1958	1.8		6.8	
1959	1.5		5.5	
1960	1.5		5.5	
1961	0.7	1.3%	6.7	5.8%
1962	1.2		5.5	
1963	1.6		5.7	
1964	1.2		5.2	
1965	1.9		4.5	
1966	3.4	2.8%	3.8	4.2%
1967	3.0		3.8	
1968	4.7		3.6	
1969	6.1		3.5	
1970	5.5		4.9	
1971	3.4	5.4%	5.9	5.0%
1972	3.4		5.6	
1973	8.8		4.9	
1974	12.2		5.6	
1975	7.0		8.5	
1976	4.8	8.0%	7.7	7.0%
1977	6.8		7.0	
1978	9.0		6.0	

Source: *Economic Report of the President,* 1979.

nesses pursue increased profits even at the cost of increased inflation. Therefore, as we discuss and evaluate the recent experiences of the United States economy, we must keep in mind that there are rarely any simple and instant policy solutions to the problems of our complex economic system.

GOALS OF STABILIZATION POLICY

As we discussed in Chapter 9, the primary goal of an economy is to get the most satisfaction from its scarce resources by operating at full employment under stable economic conditions. Current macroeconomic policy is primarily concerned with attempting to achieve both goals simultaneously, but many economists have begun to wonder if this is possible. For example, the Employment Act of 1946 stated a major objective of our national economic policy: the government assumes a responsibility to maintain both "full employment" (generally considered to be an unemployment rate of 4 percent or less) and stable price levels. The 1979 *Economic Report of the President,* however, shows that in the last 25 years unemployment has been less than 4 percent only four times (in the years 1966–1969, during the Vietnam war).

As far as price stability is concerned, during the same 25 years, the Consumer Price Index (CPI) declined only once, and that was in 1954! For over a decade, the annual rate of inflation has been in excess of the 2 percent that most economists and most of the public think is tolerable. Everyone agrees that a low unemployment rate and a low inflation rate are desirable, but it is clear that either or both are not easily obtained (see *Table 17.1*).

Full employment and stable prices: the impossible dream?

Traditional economics postulated a clear relationship between unemployment and inflation. Prices would remain stable as long as there was some unemployment; they would rise only when demand exceeded supply and there were no more resources available to increase output (demand-pull inflation). In the traditional view, an economy would have to pass the full-employment mark before inflation became a problem. Today, however, we are aware that even when there is substantial unemployment, inflation can occur due to cost (wage or profit) pushes or demand pulls. (It might be useful at this point to review the concepts of demand-pull and cost-push inflation covered in Chapter 9.) If inflation can thus occur with high unemployment, it is apparent that in a full-employment economy, the added pressures of cost-push and demand-pull inflation will cause prices to increase even faster. A relationship then develops where the price level increases before full employment is realized, creating a trade-off in which unemployment is the cost of price stability.

The Phillips curve

The **Phillips curve** *illustrates the relationship between the level of unemployment and the level of inflation.* The inverse relationship between inflation and unemployment was first charted by A. W. Phillips, an English economist, in 1958. He contended that during periods of low unemployment when demand for labor is high, wages are forced up, with a subsequent increase in production costs and selling prices. Conversely, when unemployment rises, wage increases are not won, and production costs remain relatively stable. *Fig. 17.1(a)* plots the rate of inflation and the unemployment rate from 1961–1978, using the data from *Table 17.1*. The data from the 1961–1969 period produce a curve (highlighted in *Fig. 17.1a*) that is similar to the way a hypothetical Phillips curve is usually drawn; that is, the data illustrate the belief that as unemployment increases the rate of inflation decreases.

Has the Phillips curve trade-off worsened?

In *Fig. 17.1(b)* we see that the Phillips curve relation between the unemployment and inflation rates that existed from 1961 to 1969 seemed to, worsen during the 1970s. This is represented by the shift from A to B in the early 1970s, and then from B to C in the later 1970s. This indicates the following: (1) For any given inflation rate, the corresponding unemployment rate is now much higher. It has been suggested that a major reason for this is that more teenagers and women are now in the labor force, and that, for reasons discussed later in this chapter, they experience higher unemployment rates. (2) For any given unemployment rate, the corresponding inflation rate is now much higher due to increased inflationary expectations,

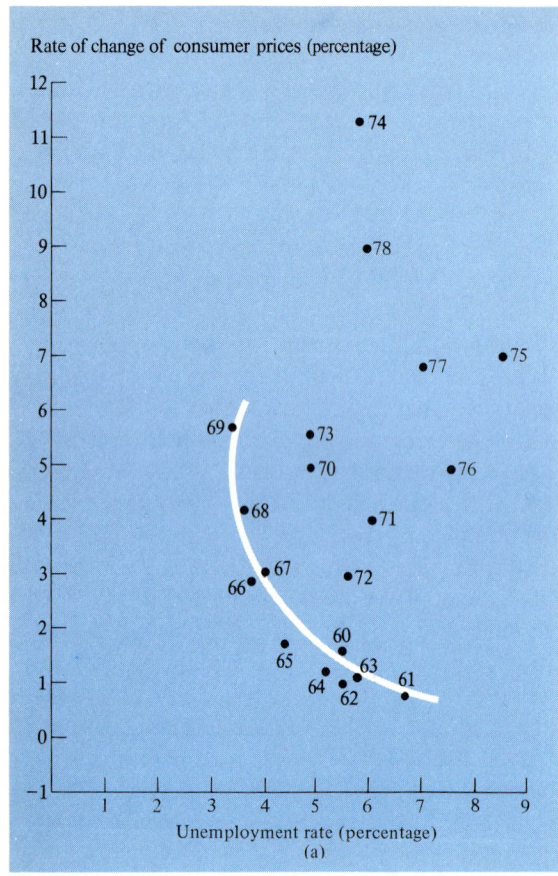

SOURCE: *Economic Report of the President*, January 1979.

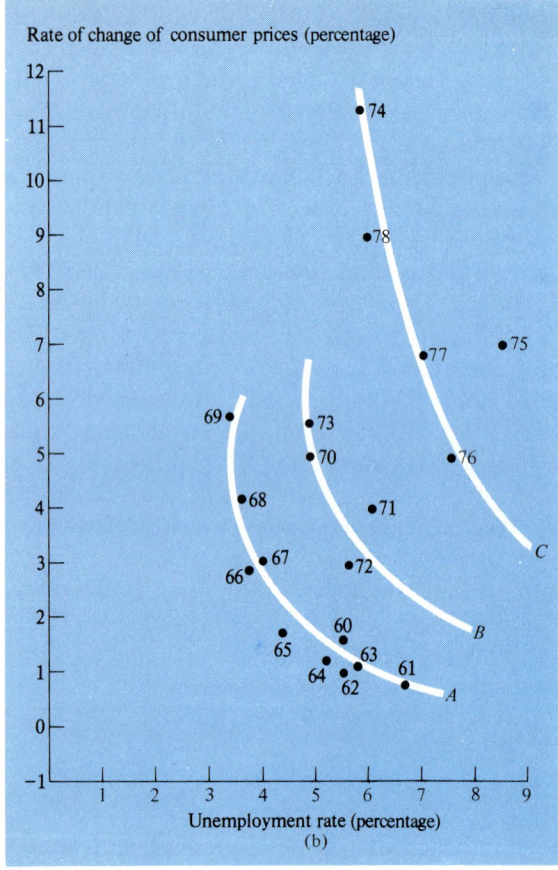

SOURCE: *Economic Report of the President*, January 1979.

which arose from the accelerated inflation of the late 1960s and the 1970s. When people expect higher prices in the future, they continue to buy things at current (cheaper) prices regardless of what the unemployment rate is. We will discuss the problem of expectations in more detail later in this chapter.

Does the Phillips curve really exist?
Some people believe that much of the inflation that occurred in the 1970s was a consequence of events that are unlikely to repeat themselves. An example of this is the 1973-1974 food and oil price increases which accounted for nearly two-thirds of the 12.2 inflation rate in 1974. This explanation suggests that the presence of the United States economy on Phillips curve *C* is temporary and that it will eventually drift back down to curve *B* or maybe even to curve *A*. However, the actions of the Organization of Petroleum Exporting Countries (OPEC) to raise oil prices in 1979 seem to make this possibility remote.

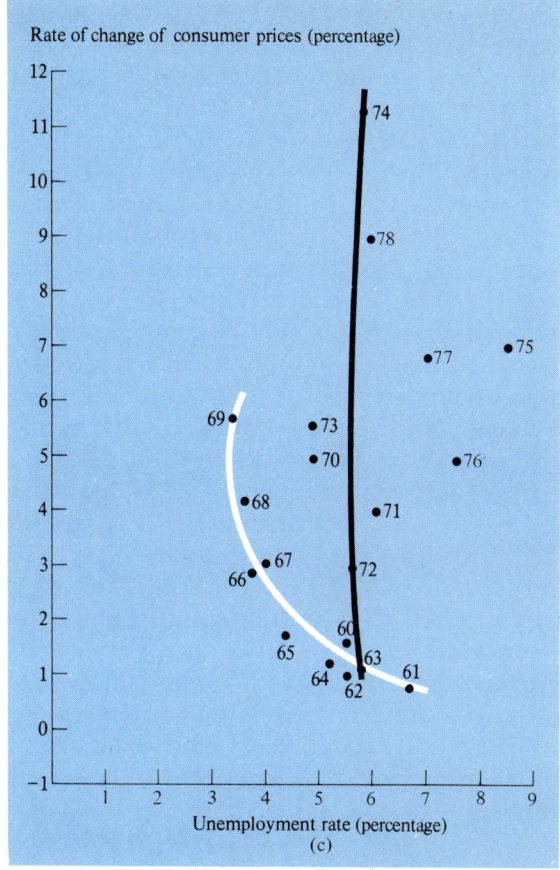

Fig. 17.1
(a) This graph plots actual rates of unemployment and price change for the United States for 1960-1978. The highlighted curve (drawn through the data for 1960-1969) comes closest to illustrating the hypothetical Phillips curve relationship: that in order to have a lower unemployment rate, a higher rate of inflation must be tolerated and vice versa. (b) Curves *B* and *C* have been drawn to pass close to or through as many points as possible for 1960-1978. The upward shift in the curves from *A* to *B* to *C* seems to indicate that the Phillips curve trade-off has worsened—that is, for any given inflation or unemployment rate on curve *A*, the corresponding unemployment and inflation rates on curves *B* and *C* are much higher. For example, on curve *A*, a 5 percent inflation rate would call for approximately 4 percent unemployment. On curve *B*, a 5 percent inflation rate would call for approximately 5.5 percent unemployment, and on curve *C*, the unemployment rate would be 7 percent. (c) This graph illustrates the belief that the Phillips curve trade-off between inflation and unemployment may not exist. In 1963, 1972, and 1974, the unemployment rate was nearly the same, but the rates of inflation were radically different.

SOURCE: *Economic Report of the President*, January 1979.

An alternative explanation is that a long-run Phillips curve doesn't exist. Many economists claim that at any given level of unemployment, there can exist a number of inflation rates. For example, the unemployment rate was 5.7 percent in 1963 and 5.6 percent in 1972 and 1974. But the corresponding inflation rates were 1.6 percent, 3.4 percent, and 12.2 percent, respectively. If you connect these three points, as shown in *Fig. 17.1(c)*, the line doesn't bear any resemblance to a hypothetical Phillips curve!

Many economists believe that it may be possible to decrease the unemployment rate through expansionary monetary and fiscal policies without causing much inflation but that once the unemployment rate approaches 5.5 percent (nearly full employment), the only result from further stimulation is an increased rate of inflation.

The question of the true shape or existence of the Phillips curve has not been resolved, so the effects of monetary and fiscal policy on the trade-off between inflation ad unemployment are uncertain. It is probably safe to say that we can use monetary and fiscal policies to lower the unemployment rate to around 6 percent on the hypothetical Phillips curve without accelerating the inflation rate very much. However, to get the unemployment rate lower than 6 percent without stimulating inflation would require other policies to deal directly with various labor-market problems. The establishment of such policies, some of which will be discussed later on in this chapter, would actually *shift* the whole Phillips curve down to the left, thus making available to economic policymakers a new menu of lower inflation rates *and* lower unemployment rates.

ACHIEVING STABILITY: TRADITIONAL THEORY AND METHOD

Because stability has always been a concern for economists, a number of schools of thought have developed on how best to achieve and maintain a stable economy.

The classical school

The **classical school** consisted of *a group of late eighteenth- and early nineteenth-century political economists* (including Adam Smith) *who believed that an economy functions best if left to itself. They believed that competition alone determined prices, wages, profits, and rents, but that some investments that would benefit society as a whole should be undertaken by the government.*

To the classical theorists, the most limiting factor of an economy was its ability to produce needed goods and services. **Say's law**, a law attributed to J. B. Say, a French economist of the nineteenth century, *states that the act of producing goods generates an income exactly equal to the value of goods produced; therefore supply generates its own demand.* Households would offer their productive resources for sale when they wanted to earn the money needed to buy goods and services produced by the economy. Since the amount that businesses spend in the resource market is exactly equal to the value of the goods at market price, consumers would always have exactly the income needed to purchase all goods produced.

One flaw is evident in this argument. The fact that households earned the income did not necessarily mean that they would spend it. Classical economists had an answer to this objection. They believed that the money saved by households would eventually be made available to businesses, who would then use it to invest in capital goods. However, one question remained: What ensures that businesses will *want* to invest an amount of money equal to the amount of income that households save—that is, what ensures that savings will be pulled right back into the income-expenditure flow? The answer, according to classical theory, is in the interest rate, based on the assumption that the interest rate is the factor that motivates the economic behavior of both savers and investors alike. Investors, wanting to borrow money (demand) to purchase capital goods, would offer a price (interest rate) high enough to lure savers into offering an amount of money (supply) that would meet the demand. If the volume of saving should exceed the amounts that businesses want to invest, or in other words, if the supply of money were to exceed the demand, the price of money would drop automatically. Businesses would therefore want to take advantage of the lower interest rate and would invest more, thus eventually using up the excess savings until an equilibrium between money supplied and money demanded was again achieved.

Classical economists suggested that price changes could act as a fail-safe mechanism if by any chance saving did not exactly equal investment. If spending decreased and aggregate demand dropped, competition among suppliers would cause prices to drop, and the inevitable response would be an increase in the quantity of goods and services demanded. The economy would continue operating at full employment, and the buying power of spenders' money incomes would increase.

The classical economists were confident that a capitalist economy was capable of regulating itself. Since they assumed a more or less closed system, in which no money was permitted to escape, they did not devote much attention to the problem of inflation or deflation. They attributed the occurrence of inflation to the economically disruptive effects of wars and assumed that once an economy was restored to normal functioning in the postwar period, inflation would disappear.

The Keynesian viewpoint

Despite the classical theory, problems did occur in the economy, as shown by the Great Depression of the 1930s. In his *General Theory of Employment, Interest and Money* (1936) John Maynard Keynes recognized that supply did *not* create its own demand—that is, the fact that a few thousand houses were built did not guarantee that anyone would buy them. Keynes also stated that if the homes were not bought, national income would fall by a multiple of this shortfall of demand.

Keynes recognized that problems in the economy would not always correct themselves, and in general he believed that a full-employment econ-

The Bettmann Archive

DEVELOPMENTS IN ECONOMIC THOUGHT:

John Maynard Keynes

If economic theorists were evaluated by their personal financial success as well as their academic contributions, the reputation of John Maynard Keynes (1883–1946) would be even more impressive than it is.

The son of an economist, Keynes was educated at Eton and Cambridge University and went on to excel in nearly everything he did, from mountain climbing, to advising government officials, to socializing with Britain's avant-garde Bloomsbury literary group (which included Virginia Woolf). Once the prize pupil of the noted economist Alfred Marshall, Keynes eventually joined and then overshadowed him on the Cambridge faculty. Keynes was also Bursar (treasurer) of King's College at Cambridge and managed to increase the college's endowment ten times over. In his spare time, Keynes also managed to accumulate a $2 million fortune by investing in the international commodities and currency market.

Classical economists in the early twentieth century generally held to some form of the law proposed by Jean Baptiste Say (1767–1832)—that demand would always rise to absorb supply and that savings would always find its way into investment, thus restoring equilibrium through the natural movement of prices and interest rates on the free market. Temporary hoarding of money or weakness in demand might occur, but price mechanisms would ensure that full production and employment would be restored in short order—as long, that is, as government interference was kept to a minimum.

In *The General Theory of Employment, Interest and Money* (1936), Keynes painted a gloomier picture. In a time of economic uncertainty, Keynes believed, lenders with little confidence in future profts might keep interest rates high, thus channeling savings into uninvested, unproductive forms, such as bank deposits. Furthermore, Keynes stated, in a period of unemployment, the natural lowering of wages may not always lead to more hiring and eventual full employment. In fact, depressed wages may reduce consumer demand even further and lead to production cutbacks and more unemployment. These processes might ultimately restore the general equilibrium, but at a lower level, with high unemployment and unused productive capacity.

In 1936, many of Keynes's beliefs were becoming realities as a severe depression gripped western Europe and the United States, and his advice was sought by both the British government and President Franklin Roosevelt. Keynes proposed that government should step in when a large amount of savings was not being invested. Specifically, the government should borrow that savings and spend it on socially useful projects. Ideally, this would inject money into the spending stream to help renew economic activity. While Keynes preferred such projects as constructing schools, hospitals, and parks, he wrote that, if necessary, the treasury could "fill old bottles with banknotes, bury them at suitable depths in disused coal-mines which are then filled up to the surface with town rubbish, and leave it to private enterprise on well-tried principles of laissez-faire to dig the notes up again. . . . The above would be better than nothing."

The practical demonstration of Keynesian principles, however, did not come in the building of schools or in the various work projects instituted by Roosevelt. It was the huge military expenditures for World War II which finally lifted the Western economies out of the Depression.

Despite continuing controversy over aspects of his work, the impact of Keynes's call for government activism is hard to overestimate. Government intervention (through taxes and spending) is a standard policy of contemporary liberal economists, as opposed to the conservative concentration on monetary policy (regulating the money supply). The conventional response to unemployment and recession (low demand and investment) is to lower taxes and increase spending. Inflation (created by too much aggregate demand) is countered by raising taxes and cutting spending. These post-Keynesian formulas are currently undergoing their hardest test as the simultaneous persistence of unemployment and inflation casts doubts on the adequacy of any single solution.

omy could be achieved only by means of government intervention and regulation. In circumstances where private demand fell below supply, for example, Keynes recommended that the government make up for the lack of demand through increased government spending, lower taxes, and/or increases in the money supply. In the United States few such active stabilization policies have been undertaken by the government because the taxation and transfer-payments systems have usually provided an important degree of automatic stabilization to the economy. (The specific measures the government can take were discussed in greater detail in Chapters 12 and 15 which deal with government fiscal and monetary policy.)

The monetarist viewpoint

Monetarism is a school of thought led by Milton Friedman (see biography in Chapter 13). While monetarism, like any school of economic thought, includes many viewpoints, one idea is basic to all monetarists: the emphasis on the money supply as the key factor affecting the well-being of the economy.

In order to promote a steady growth rate, Friedman believes that the money supply should grow at a fixed rate instead of being regulated and altered by the Federal Reserve. An example will illustrate Friedman's reasoning. Suppose in early 1980 we forecast a recession in late 1980. If we step up the rate of growth of the money supply early in 1980 it will have a strong effect on income, but we don't know how strong the effect will be or when it will occur. If the effect is strong, but doesn't occur until 1981, it may accompany a recovery that would have occurred anyway. The increase in the money supply would cause too much expansion and thus lead to inflation. Friedman therefore recommends a steady and moderate rate of monetary growth to avoid such problems and to ensure a steady and moderate rate of income growth.

Monetarists sometimes claim that Keynesians ignore the money supply, but in reality they do not. (Keynes was a monetary economist first, last, and always. His three major books were *A Tract on Monetary Reform, A Treatise on Money,* and *The General Theory of Employment, Interest and Money*). Since the money supply does matter to Keynesians, there must be something else that causes debate between Keynesians and monetarists. That "something" is whether or not fiscal policy counts. Monetarists claim that without changes in the size of the money supply, changes in government expenditures and/or taxes do not affect the economy. Such fiscal changes without monetary changes will only affect how much the private sector (households and businesses) gets to spend versus how much the government gets to spend. That is, fiscal policies alone will only affect the *distribution* of expenditures rather than the *level* of expenditures.

The politics of Keynesianism and monetarism

Since American economic policy is always planned and undertaken in a political setting, it is important to understand the political distinctions between Keynesians and monetarists. On the one hand, Keynesians ("liberals") approve of planned and continued government involvement, both monetary and fiscal, with the economy, and seem to be more concerned about unemployment than inflation. They also believe that there is a short-run and, to a lesser extent, a long-run trade-off between inflation and unemployment, that to achieve these trade-offs we need government involvement, and that the government sector should be large enough to accomplish these and other goals.

Monetarists ("conservatives"), on the other hand, oppose continued government interference in the economy (thus they recommend a legislated growth rate), do not believe in a long-run trade-off between inflation and unemployment, and prefer a reduction in the role of government in the economy.

PROBLEMS WITH ECONOMIC POLICYMAKING

Most economists agree that if we are to reach a condition of economic stability, choices will have to be made between the "devil" of inflation and the "deep blue sea" of unemployment. The greatest differences among economists arise not about the objectives of economic policy (full employment, stable prices), but about the means—fiscal or monetary—that should be used to accomplish these basic stabilization goals. Regardless of their political or theoretical orientation on policymaking, however, policymakers face a variety of problems in trying to deal with the happenings in our economic system.

Time lags

Although monetarists emphasize the long delay between changes in the money supply and their effects on income, all policymakers must deal with time lags, which are generally divided into the following stages:

☐ The recognition lag—the time it takes for policymakers to realize that action is required. It usually takes about six months to recognize that a disturbance has occurred that needs offsetting by policy.

☐ The administrative (decision and action) lags—these, unlike the recognition lag, differ for monetary and fiscal policy. The Federal Reserve, at least in principle, can take action monthly or more frequently, while fiscal policies like tax cuts and major expenditure changes require long negotiations between the president and Congress. (Remember, however, that the automatic stabilizers of taxes and transfer payments are always at work).

☐ The operational lag—the time it takes a policy decision to affect the economy. Both monetary and fiscal policy have modest initial effects on income and employment, but the effects accumulate over time.

In combination, we can see that the various types of time lags guarantee that it takes a long time before policy actions initiated to offset economic disturbances such as high inflation rates have any effect.

Public opinion

All government stabilization policy is ultimately subject to the scrutiny of public opinion. Even our monetary authorities, who in principle operate outside the day-to-day influence of either public opinion or political pressure, must ultimately be responsive to the desires of the people. For example, the Federal Reserve Board, primarily concerned with stabilizing prices, has traditionally adopted restrictive monetary measures when it felt that inflation was becoming a problem. However, if the Fed were to pursue extremely tight monetary policies to curb inflation while the economy was also facing a severe unemployment problem, public disapproval would be difficult to overcome.

Public opinion can also influence the choice of whether fiscal or monetary tools should be employed. To stimulate the economy through fiscal means, an administration must gauge public sentiment to determine which of two alternatives—a tax cut to stimulate private spending or an increase in public spending—is preferred by the majority of people. Suppose, for example, that most people felt that too much of our GNP was going toward frivolous consumer goods and not enough toward more socially desirable goods such as protecting the environment or expanding education. An administration that wanted to reflect the feelings of the American voter in its programs would choose to increase public spending rather than use a tax cut to stabilize a downturn.

Recently, the American public has been growing increasingly dissatisfied with federal, state, and local government about the relation between what is delivered in public services and what is taken in taxes (see Application 4). The desire for tax cuts, as exemplified by Proposition 13 in California which cut property taxes, is beginning to spread to all levels of government. If this tax-cut fever spreads to the national level, discretionary fiscal policy may become a thing of the past.

Expectations
Although policymakers must consider public opinion, it is often difficult to do so because of the effects of the public's expectations which often change as policy changes. Three monetarists, Robert Lucas of Chicago, and Neil Wallace and Thomas Sargent of the University of Minnesota, believe that policy works only if it comes as a surprise and that expectations can actually defeat economic policy.

Two examples will illustrate how this so-called "rational-expectations" view applies in fiscal and monetary situations.

☐ Fiscal policy: Suppose each time the economy starts to slow down, the government gives a tax credit to those who invest. The first time they do this, it works—investment spending increases and a recession is avoided. But if businesspeople come to *expect* a tax credit on investment each time the economy slows, they will hold off investing as the economy slows, thinking "Why should I invest now when I can wait a few months and get the tax credit?" This causes the economy to slow down even more. When the tax credit is given, delayed investments are made but the increase in investment comes too late to avoid a recession.

☐ Monetary policy: Monetarists have developed similar arguments concerning how monetary policy can intensify a downturn or upturn in economic activity once expectations are taken into account. Suppose the Federal Reserve expects a recession six months from now despite rapid current economic growth. They plan to increase the money supply gradually over the next few months in order to reduce interest rates and thus increase investment spending. The ultimate effect of all these actions will be to offset the expected recession. At the same time, everyone else expects a recession and they also expect that the Fed will soon act to reduce interest rates to encourage investment spending. Rather than buy bonds at lower interest rates in the months ahead (after the Fed has lowered the interest rates), many people will buy bonds now. The competition for the bonds drives the price of the bonds up (that is, lowers the interest rate). Thus, instead of having lower interest rates later in the year, we have them immediately, which encourages investment spending and causes the current expansion to continue at even a faster rate.

Although the rational-expectations issue is still a relatively new idea and no decision has been reached on its validity, it is worth noting that Milton Friedman is not completely convinced—he feels that it *is* possible to fool people for a long time, which implies that policy can still work.

Difficulties of reducing government spending
Another problem policymakers face is that it is often difficult to postpone or cancel long-term government spending projects which are already under way or for which funds have been allocated and plans made. Despite the fact that the immediate economic situation may call for reductions in government spending, they are usually resisted on many fronts because of vested interests and are often legally impossible to implement. For example, during the 1967–1968 boom in economic activity, President Johnson tried to cut back on various federal building projects, and encouraged the states to do likewise. Such cuts in building programs, however, would probably meet with strong resistance not only by elected officials whose constituents are employed in the programs, but also by people who administer the programs and who may fear losing their jobs.

Thus, although a government can, theoretically, use a two-pronged fiscal tool (higher taxes, lower spending) to control inflationary pressures, it often finds, in reality, that due to previous commitments there are only a few areas in which government spending can be cut. Consequently, government must place most of its emphasis on increasing taxes.

Conflicts between multiple goals
Economic policymakers are also hampered in dealing with employment and price problems by the need to consider other goals that a society might want to achieve.

Economic growth
We have seen how monetary and fiscal policy affect economic activity by encouraging or discouraging investment spending. If we adopt policies of low interest rates and tax credits to investors to stimulate investment, we will increase the supply of capital and thereby increase the supply of available goods for future generations. On the other hand, when policy tools are used to restrain economic expansion, the immediate effect is to reduce private business investment, which affects the development of capital goods and, consequently, the level of long-term economic growth. Many economists attribute the relatively slow growth rate exhibited by the United States during the post-World War II period (compared with the growth rates of Germany and Japan) to the effects of domestic stabilization measures. These economists suggest that tight monetary policy is incompatible with sustained long-term growth. Instead, they argue, fiscal measures such as higher taxes should be used to restrain consumer spending and curb inflation.

Balance of trade
Another goal that competes with high prices and unemployment for the attention of policymakers is the import/export balance of payments with foreign nations. A consistently high rate of inflation such as we have had in the United States recently, increases the costs of goods made in the United States relative to Japanese, German, and other foreign goods. "We" then purchase more foreign goods (because they are relatively cheaper than goods made in the United States) and "they" purchase fewer American goods because the prices are higher. Thus, if a country's balance of payments is considered a serious problem, another restriction is placed on policymakers. For example, consider the following dilemma: In mid-1971, the total amount of gold in Fort Knox was less than $10 billion, and the Germans *alone* held more than $20 billion in American dollars. In the light of this foreign balance-of-payments problem, an important part of our overall economic policy in early 1971 was directed at maintaining reasonably high short-term interest rates to encourage foreigners to deposit their dollars in United States banks rather than to exchange them for gold.

However, during the recessionary period 1970–1971, low interest rates were called for in order to stimulate domestic business activity. If interest rates in the United States had been permitted to fall below rates abroad, foreigners would have withdrawn their dollars from United States banks and exchanged them for gold in order to invest elsewhere. The fear of such a serious gold drain made it impossible—or at best, very uncomfortable—for the Fed to use its monetary tools as aggressively as it might have preferred during that economic downturn.

Noneconomic goals
When it comes to establishing policy to achieve a nation's goals, noneconomic goals frequently take precedence over economic goals. The policies implemented during the late 1960s are perfect examples of the dominance of noneconomic motives. The Vietnam war (national-security motives?), Medicare and Medicaid (national-health motive?), environmental programs (clean-air motive?), minority and other social programs (social motive?) were all enacted simultaneously, with little consideration for the inflationary consequences.

STAGFLATION—THE ECONOMIC DILEMMA OF THE 1970s
Even when policymakers account for all the factors discussed in the previous section, they are sometimes faced with a situation that requires a

complete reexamination of the theories and concepts they have traditionally used to analyze and deal with variations in economic activity. This has been the case for the past ten years, when our country has been faced with an economic situation in which the rates of unemployment and inflation have been increasing at the same time.

Stagflation is *the simultaneous occurrence of a maintained unsatisfactory growth rate (stagnation) and a maintained increase in the general level of prices (inflation).* Stagflation is often accompanied by unusually and consistently high unemployment rates. Prior to the 1970s, an inflation rate above 2 percent was usually accompanied by rapid economic growth and low unemployment rates of 4 percent or less. As outlined in the following section, however, the delayed effects of the Vietnam war-induced inflation of the late 1960s plus a series of unusual events in the 1970s have changed this relationship.

Table 17.2
Economic activity, 1969–1978

Year	Rate of inflation	Unemployment rate	General level of economic activity
1969	6.1%	3.5%	Decline
1970	5.5	4.9	Recession
1971	3.4	5.9	Recession-recovery
1972	3.4	5.6	Recovery-boom
1973	8.8	4.9	Boom-decline
1974	12.2	5.6	Decline-recession
1975	7.0	8.5	Recession-recovery
1976	4.8	7.7	Recovery
1977	6.8	7.0	Continued recovery
1978	9.0	6.0	Recovery-pause?

The late 1960s: excess aggregate demand

The increases in production caused by the Vietnam war lowered the unemployment rate below the target of 4 percent set by the 1946 Employment Act for four straight years (1966–1969). However, Vietnam war spending, imposed upon an economy already approaching full employment, set in motion an inflationary process that eventually became part of the 1970s stagflation. An average inflation rate of about 4 percent (1966–1969) laid the foundation for increased inflationary expectations—for the first time in the post–World War II period, the United States economy experienced, *and began to expect,* a steady and significantly higher rate of inflation than it had been accustomed to experiencing. *Table 17.2* shows the economic history over the last ten years, characterized by persistently high inflation and unemployment.

The 1970 recession

The 1970 recession rapidly undid all of the unemployment reduction achieved in the late 1960s. From a low of 3.5 percent in 1969, unemployment was over 6 percent by the end of 1970. There was a deliberate tightening of monetary and fiscal policy in an attempt to slow the rate of inflation. The tight policies did not halt inflation, but they did have the unplanned effect of inducing a recession. This result was a surprise to traditional economists: for the first time, a recession did little to stop inflation and the traditional Phillips curve relationship no longer seemed valid as the unemployment rate rose substantially and the inflation rate barely fell. As often happens when traditional theory and policy seem to fail, nontraditional policies were implemented in the form of a New Economic Policy (NEP).

New Economic Policy (1971 to 1973)

NEP combined wage and price controls to slow inflation with expansionary monetary and fiscal policy to reduce unemployment. A 90-day wage and price freeze was announced on August 15, 1971 and was followed by mandatory wage and price controls. By 1972–1973, NEP had lowered the unemployment rate below 5 percent due to an extremely high rate of growth of real GNP (5.6 percent). Normally, one would expect inflationary pressure to increase during such a period of strong and steady growth of demand. But the wage and price controls temporarily reduced inflation back to its 1966 rate of 3.4 percent.

Two aspects of this statement are worth noting: (1) almost everyone agrees that the reduction of unemployment and interest rates due to controls was temporary; and (2) the controls reduced the inflation rate only to the level of the period where the current inflation problem began. They *did not* reduce inflation to its post–World War II rate of less than 2 percent, which had been considered a "normal" rate for 15 years.

Beginning in 1973, the controls were relaxed due to complaints of inequities and distortions that developed because of the controls. For instance, wages were more effectively controlled than prices and shortages of some critical materials began to develop. By mid-1973 the softening of wage and price controls and the accompanying release of inflationary tensions returned the United States economy to its biggest long-run problem—inflation.

The acceleration of inflation in 1973–1974

Two factors were primarily responsible for the acceleration of inflation in 1973–1974. First, starting in 1972, poor worldwide food harvests caused food prices to rise in 1973 and 1974. Second, the OPEC oil embargo led to a four-fold increase in the price of oil. From the end of 1972 to the beginning of 1975, oil costs had increased by nearly 60 percent. Two important lessons were learned during the period following the oil embargo: (1) prices do not adjust downward very well during recession; and (2) price increases in a single market (i.e., oil) can affect the entire economy dramatically.

Regardless of one's theoretical orientation, the facts are clear. The food and fuel shocks not only helped to produce our worst inflation, they also helped to produce our worst post–World War II recession. All through 1974, real GNP declined and unemployment drifted upward. Since the 12.2 percent inflation rate was considered the main enemy, monetary and fiscal policies were enacted to reduce inflation, thus promoting further recession. By late 1974 and early 1975, the economy was in its deepest postwar recession: unemployment rose to nearly 9 percent as the inflation rate fell well below its double-digit level of early 1974.

As we have seen, each of the two major episodes of accelerating inflation (in 1968–1969 and 1973–1974) was preceded by relatively stimulative monetary and fiscal policy and was followed by recession and an accompanying increase in unemployment. The unusual aspect of both recessions was that they failed to drive down the inflation rate below the 2 percent level that preceded the 1966–1969 acceleration of inflation. A possible explanation for this failure is explored in the following section.

The role of inflationary expectations

During the past 25 years, the underlying rate of inflation has increased to a point where it has been noticed by an increasing number of individuals and institutions who have, as a result, come to expect a higher level of inflation. In previous years (1958–1964), most people were probably unaware of the 1–1.5 percent inflation rate. However, once a high and widely recognized rate of inflation was under way, individuals and firms adapted and responded to it in ways that perpetuated the inflation even during recessions. When inflation continues at a steady and noticeable rate, individuals and institutions begin to expect that prices and wages will continue to increase and they adjust their own positions accordingly, for example, through union contracts.

The process occurs as follows: workers who receive pay increases of 2 percent each year while the cost of living rises over 4 percent per year will eventually notice that it's harder for them to maintain their standard of living. Even if they don't notice, their unions probably will, and some type of cost-of-living escalator clause will be built into contracts with employers. Employers then pass part or all of the wage increases along to consumers in the form of higher prices. This, in turn, raises the cost of living for other workers and the process continues as each group acts to protect its own position. In effect, this is like the chain reaction that occurs when one person stands up to get a better view at a football game. One by one, more people stand up so they can see, and eventually everyone is standing. A few people might see better, but most will not, and nearly all will be less comfortable. This is the current situation in the United States, due to the wage-price spiral: nearly all of us are less comfortable.

This spiral, induced by expectations of continued high rates of inflation, has kept the inflation rate high during the past four years, even though unemployment has remained high as well. Thus, we can see that expectations and the resulting wage-price spiral can sustain inflation long after the initial causes (such as the demand pressures created by an increased money supply) are gone.

HOW CAN WE DEFEAT STAGFLATION?

The standard method of using restrictive monetary and fiscal policies to create a recession and thus slow the rate of inflation has proved to be ineffective and, in addition, exacts too high a cost in terms of lost output in goods and services. (It is estimated that to reduce the rate of inflation by 1 percent we must cut back output by $100 billion.) Thus, we must search for new methods to solve the stagflation problem of high prices and high unemployment. First, we will review some of the unconventional methods that have been tried in the past and their results. Then we will discuss other programs that have been advocated recently.

Wage-price control policies

Wage and price controls have been tried by the United States government at times when it was considered necessary to maintain strong growth of demand without causing much inflation. In their strongest form, wage and price controls are mandatory and attempt to freeze wages and prices at their current levels. In their intermediate form, the government tried to persuade ("jawbone") firms and workers to increase prices and wages only by a certain percent suggested by the government. In their weakest form, the president merely suggests that inflation must be brought under control and occasionally jawbones when large firms raise prices by great amounts. Wage and price controls were used in the United States during World War II and during the Korean war, and periodic jawboning occurred during the Kennedy administration. From 1971 through 1978, three versions of wage and price controls were tried in the United States. It should be noted that in any form in an economy as large as that of the United States, controls are difficult to enforce. Whether the government asks or orders all soft-drink manufacturers to freeze their prices for quarts of soda, some manufacturers will comply no matter what. Others will not comply no matter what. Still others will comply by selling 28-ounce "quarts" at the same price as a true (32-ounce) quart, and will get around the controls that way.

The Nixon controls

It is often forgotten that initially the Nixon administration was strongly against wage-price controls even in their weakest forms. Why, then, did the Nixon administration announce the New Economic Policy with its wage-price controls in August 1971? The reasons were primarily political: the 1972 presidential election was coming up and the economic news was not good. During the period 1969–1971 the administration's policies had increased the unemployment rate by 2.5 percent while reducing inflation by less than 1 percent. That would have been a hard record on which to run!

Thus, a full, mandatory wage-price freeze of 90 days was announced. The freeze attempted to break the wage-price spiral by reducing the inflationary expectations that had been built up during the previous years. In addition, since the freeze was imposed quickly and by surprise, the usual problem of firms and unions increasing prices and wages just ahead of an announced freeze was prevented.

The initial 90-day freeze, known as Phase I, was followed by Phase II, which was more flexible and allowed wages to increase by 5.5 percent per year and prices to be raised enough to pass along cost increases. Phase III continued through June 1973, and since it was even more flexible, the rate of inflation reached 10 percent by mid-1973. Another freeze was then imposed which lasted until August 1973, at which time it was replaced by Phase IV. By April 1974, the controls had ended.

Did Nixon's controls work? During the year and a half from July 1971 through December 1972, the quarterly inflation rate was less than 3 percent three times and over 4 percent only once, even though the economy was expanding rapidly throughout the entire period. The unemployment rate gradually dropped to 5.1 percent by December 1972. In the 1973 *Economic Report of the President,* it seemed that President Nixon had a right to say that 1972 was "a very good year for the American economy."

Nevertheless, it is difficult to determine if the controls actually worked. First, the imposition of wage-price controls during rapid expansion caused an accumulation of inflationary tensions that exploded after the controls were lifted—the rate of inflation averaged over 8 percent during the first two quarters of 1973. Second, some economists claim that controls were responsible for only part of the reduction of inflation—the rate of inflation was already lower during the first half of 1971

> **RECAP**
>
> In recent years, economic policymakers have been struggling with the problem of having high rates of unemployment and high rates of inflation simultaneously. The sources of this dilemma, known as stagflation, can be traced back to the 1960s but it has continued due to inflationary expectations, outside events (such as the OPEC oil-price increases), and other factors. While some nontraditional methods such as wage and price controls and training programs have been instituted in an attempt to deal with stagflation, they have not been successful, and policymakers are still trying to devise an economic policy that encourages full employment and stable prices.

(prior to controls) than it was in 1970. Because the evidence is hard to evaluate, it can be said that the controls, at least temporarily, may have worked moderately well in slowing inflation, but at the expense of the many distortions and inequities they created by interfering with the supply/demand and price/quantity signals relayed by the price system.

Ford's WIN program
In early 1974 inflation (at a rate of 12.2 percent) was the biggest enemy, and Gerald Ford in his *Economic Report of the President* concentrated on deregulation to tackle the price problem. By deregulating the private sector (for example, the airlines), the reasoning went, the forces of supply and demand would operate to lower prices. However, Ford's program to *W*hip *I*nflation *N*ow ran into a major problem—a rising unemployment rate that hit 8.5 percent by 1975. While inflation can seriously alter a person's financial condition,

unemployment directly affects the lives of the population in the form of lost jobs, disrupted family life, and so on. In the face of such high unemployment, inflation programs quickly took a back seat, and policies were enacted to stimulate growth in the economy in order to lower the unemployment rate. Tax cuts and other stimulative programs characterized Ford's *Economic Report of the President* in 1975 and 1976. In 1977, when he left office, the inflation and unemployment rates had dropped, although inflation had by no means been whipped.

Carter's wage-price guidelines
In 1978, Jimmy Carter suggested wage-price guidelines that were thought of as "jawboning-plus." "Jawboning" since the guidelines were legally voluntary, "plus" since the Government both (1) threatened to take steps against organizations that do business with them but do not comply, and (2) implied that mandatory controls would be forthcoming should the guidelines not work. Carter's guidelines proposed wage increases of about 7 percent per year or less, while a more complicated system for price deceleration was proposed for firms. Carter also proposed "real-wage insurance" in the form of a tax rebate for workers who, while holding to the 7 percent wage increase, were hurt by an inflation rate of more than 7 percent. Although the details of how this program would work were unclear, congressional approval would probably be required for its implementation, and the approval by Congress was not at all certain. Nevertheless, the concept of "insurance" against inflation was innovative for this nation.

As of early 1979, it was too early to see if the Carter voluntary program would work, but there seemed to be a great deal of skepticism among economists and the public.

Alternatives to traditional fiscal, monetary, and wage-price policies
Although wage-price controls have been the main nonmonetary and nonfiscal attempt at regulating the rates of inflation and unemployment, other programs have been proposed.

Changes in government programs
The various taxes, regulations, and subsidies controlled by federal and state governments are responsible for much of our inflation. For example, if state sales taxes were reduced by as much as 2 percent, it is estimated that the price level would be reduced by about 1.6 percent. (It should be noted that Proposition 13 in California, by reducing that state's *property* taxes (not sales taxes) reduced the cost of living in the *United States* by 0.2 percent in 1978).

Some possibilities for changes in the government programs were calculated in 1978 by Robert Crandall, a noted economist of the Brookings Institution (a nonprofit organization for scholastic research). If all 12 Crandall programs (such as changes in federal excise taxes) were adopted, the price level would decrease by nearly 7 percent. While new programs and changes would face serious political and economic debate, it is clear that some of our current inflation could be reduced by changes in the pattern of government taxation, regulation, and subsidies. To be convinced of this, one has only to look at the much lower air fares that occurred after the deregulation of the airlines. The deregulation made the airline market more competitive and thus led to reduced prices. It is important to note that each of these measures has a "one-shot" effect: for example, the elimination of all sales taxes this year would reduce the price level and the inflation rate *this* year, but would have little or no effect on the rate of inflation in future years. As yet, little empirical work has been done to estimate the effect of the loss of tax revenue of the goods and services provided by the government.

Indexing
It has been suggested that the tax system be altered so that taxes do not rise just because the price level

has increased. With the current progressive system, workers who received a wage increase of 7 percent to cover a 7 percent increase in the cost of living (due to inflation) would seem to have the same buying power as before. However, if their 7 percent raise puts them into a higher tax bracket, they will have less buying power, because the progressive income-tax schedule is based on nominal, not real, dollars earned.

Assume, for example, that workers were initially making $10,000 per year and paying 10 percent of their income ($1000) in income taxes. The 7 percent pay raise gives them a new income of $10,700. The progressive federal income-tax schedule indicates that, due to this higher income, they have to pay 12 percent ($1284) in taxes, instead of 10 percent ($1000). So, out of the $700 raise workers will take home only $416 ($700 raise minus the $284 increase in taxes). Thus, after taxes, they have effectively received a raise of only 4.17 percent—because the cost of living rose by 7 percent, the workers actually lose about 40 percent of their apparently increased buying power (that is, they lose 2.84 percent out of the 7 percent wage increase).

An indexed system would allow tax brackets to change proportionately to the price level, so that changes in the price level would not affect the taxes that workers pay—that is, they wouldn't have to pay $284 more just due to inflation. One argument against indexing taxes is that it would destroy the powerful automatic-stabilization tool we have in the progressive tax system as it is now structured.

Monetarist Milton Friedman has advocated some "inflation-proofing" indexing programs that would ensure that purchasing power would be protected against rising prices and costs. For example, the Acme Stroller Company sells Oliver T. Cranston a bond with an interest rate of 10 percent—2 percent plus an 8 percent expected rate of inflation. If the inflation rate turns out to be 12 percent, Acme would pay Cranston 14 percent interest on the bond (2 percent plus 12 percent inflation). In that way, Cranston is protected against unexpected inflation. If, on the other hand, inflation turned out to be only 6 percent, Acme would need to pay only 8 percent on the bond. Friedman also recommends that tax adjustments such as exemptions, capital gains, and depreciation of assets be calculated in relation to the Consumer Price Index.

Precedents for such anticipatory actions already exist in wage-escalator clauses of union contractors and in the cost-of-living adjustments in Social Security payments. But, a general fear, if only partly justified, is that indexing would really mean "throwing in the towel" in the fight against inflation. By making inflation more tolerable, it may lower the will to fight it forever, thus institutionalizing a permanent wage-price inflation spiral. In addition, total indexing to protect all buyers, sellers, and taxpayers against inflation would be legally complex and nearly impossible to administer and control. Even at current inflation rates, we are unlikely to see it soon.

Problems in lowering unemployment rates
We have seen that monetary and fiscal policies rarely succeed in stopping inflation because the size of the recession necessary to accomplish this is costly in terms of lost output and high unemployment. It is also true that monetary and fiscal policies cannot reduce unemployment to desirable levels without setting off more inflation.

In order to understand the difficulty of designing special policies that directly reduce unemployment, one must first understand some of the characteristics of those who are unemployed that make the task of lowering unemployment so hard. Teenagers account for only about 10 percent of the labor force, but they account for nearly 25 percent of all unemployment. Teenagers enter and leave the labor force more frequently than adults because they change jobs often before settling down in a career. The proportion of teenagers leaving the labor force in an average month is about 20 times the proportion of adults doing the same. It is the constant entrance and reentrance into the labor force, and not an excessive loss of jobs, that makes the teenage unemployment rate so high.

Minority teenagers share not only the overall teenage pattern of participation in the labor force, but they face, in addition, more difficulty in finding a job once they begin to look. This problem has actually become worse during the past five years of economic expansion and the extremely high unemployment rate of minority youths has become a major—and not yet well-explained—unemployment problem (see Application 6).

Women also have a high unemployment rate due to their widely fluctuating participation rates. A large proportion of working women who still have families at home are considered to be less attached to their careers. (The labor-market behavior of single women and their attachment to jobs are very similar to those of single men.) Other factors in the high unemployment rate of women include the lack of flexible part-time work and the fact that women have often been regarded as temporary or secondary earners in the family. For black women, as with black teenagers, the unemployment rates are much higher than those of their white counterparts, despite much higher participation rates and job attachment for black women than for black teenagers.

Special policies to reduce unemployment

Policies designed to reduce hardcore or long-term unemployment usually involve training programs, public-service jobs, labor-market information, incentives to hire the disadvantaged, and incentives to reduce discriminatory hiring practices. The United States has generally concentrated on training and public-service jobs.

Training programs in basic skills such as reading and writing have had only a limited effect on the unemployment rate. Such programs do produce a rate of return comparable to most types of investments (that is, the money spent on training produces many dollars earned by the trainee), but their coverage is limited.

Since 1971, there has been less emphasis on training and more on public-service jobs through state and local government programs such as CETA (Comprehensive Employment and Training Act) although CETA also includes a stipulation that the job encompass some training. The success of the public-service jobs program remains to be seen. The programs work best if the jobs are given to people (especially youths) with less than average skills whose wage rates are not competitive with private-sector jobs (so the programs will not attract labor out of private jobs). There have been many complaints that neither of these conditions has been fulfilled, but in general at this time, the CETA program is too new and is undergoing too many changes to give it a fair overall evaluation.

Long-run policy, planning, and the Humphrey-Hawkins Full Employment and Balanced Growth Act

As we discussed in Chapter 9, it is currently the official policy of the United States Government to establish short-term policy within the context of longer-term objectives. This is the result of the recent enactment of the Humphrey-Hawkins Full Employment and Balanced Growth Act, which requires five-year economic policy goals to be set by the president.

A major goal of the Humphrey-Hawkins Act is to increase the rate of private and public capital formation which would simultaneously increase productivity and economic growth (thereby reducing unemployment) and reduce inflationary pressures. Another goal is to improve the coordination between monetary and fiscal policy by requiring the Fed to specify its own goals and objectives and to indicate how these relate to the president's goals.

The Humphrey-Hawkins Act itself sets 1983 goals of 3–4 percent unemployment and 3 percent inflation, but does not outline, require, or authorize any new programs to achieve these results. One must be skeptical concerning our ability to achieve these results by 1983, since in the past 25 years, the only time we have achieved 3 percent inflation and less than 4 percent unemployment has been during the Vietnam war.

STABILIZATION PROBLEMS AND POLICIES: AN EVALUATION

We have covered a lot of difficult material in this chapter, and we should briefly review it in order to have a better understanding and perspective on our complicated current economic situation. The facts are that we have not been able to reduce the unemployment rate to the goal of 4 percent or less set by the Employment Act of 1946 (and reaffirmed by the Humphrey-Hawkins Act) without driving the rate of inflation up to intolerable levels.

Keynes's idea that government policy could and should act to avoid another great depression remains intact and believable, but the facts of economic reality have called into question the government's ability to balance the inflation/unemployment trade-off proposed by the Phillips curve. Time lags, political problems, public opinion, expectations, and many other considerations agitate and frustrate monetary and fiscal policymakers, and the optimism of the 1960s seems innocent and naive in retrospect.

Currently we face the problem of stagflation where wage and price increases feed on each other in spite of the amount of slack in the economy as evidenced by high unemployment rates. Various attempts at wage and price controls have not produced convincing long-term results, and other unconventional measures such as training programs have not been applied long enough or with sufficient force to permit an evaluation of their possible effects.

If all of this sounds pessimistic, refer again to the first sentence in the second paragraph of this summary. Keynes's theory is still viable, and our economic monetary and fiscal policies will probably avoid deep depressions and may even limit the size and length of major recessions. To a young person looking at the past decade of economic history, this may not seem impressive. But anyone who was alive during the Great Depression of the 1930s (when unemployment reached nearly 25 percent in 1933) would realize that this is indeed an accomplishment.

Summary

■ This chapter surveys recent efforts to deal with the problems of high rates of unemployment and inflation through economic policy.

■ Traditional economics assumed an inverse relationship between unemployment and inflation; only at or near full employment (i.e., a low unemployment rate) would a high inflation rate be likely to occur. This relationship, however, expressed in a Phillips curve, has been cast into doubt by the simultaneous appearance of high unemployment and high inflation rates in recent years.

■ Many schools of thought have developed on the question of how price stability and full employment are maintained. Economists of the classical school maintained that as long as the market was left alone, Say's law would operate: the creation of supply would automatically create an equal demand. Price competition (including competition in interest rates) would guarantee that any money taken out of demand by saving would be put back in the form of investment. Keynesian economists argued that these mechanisms were not automatic at all, and that government intervention would be necessary to promote stability. Economists of the monetarist school emphasize the steady growth of the money supply as the key to stability and claim that Keynesian fiscal policies merely redistribute income from the private sector to the government sector.

■ A number of problems arise in connection with attempts to promote stability through the use of economic policies. Time lags can delay the impact of new policies; public opinion may reject certain policies; expectations of changing policies may actually undercut their effect; and government spending programs, once they are in effect, are hard to curtail. Stabilization policies may also result in the slowing of economic growth, an unfavorable balance of trade, and difficulties in meeting noneconomic goals.

■ In the 1970s, two periods of recession did not bring down the rate of inflation as they were expected to, and our economy experienced a paradoxical situation which economists refer to as "stagflation" a situation characterized by lack of growth and inflation. One possible explanation of this dilemma is that people now expect inflation to continue and therefore plan for it in ways (such as automatic cost-of-living increases in wage contracts) which continue to produce it.

■ Successive administrations in the 1970s have experimented with wage and price controls, both voluntary and mandatory, with only limited success. Other proposals to alter the current patterns of inflation and unemployment have included a reduction and change in government taxation and regulation policies; indexing, so that taxes and other payments would be based on real, not inflated dollars; and special programs to reduce unemployment, especially among such hard-core unemployed groups as minorities, young people, and women.

■ In general, since World War II, the United States has not been able to keep unemployment down to an acceptable rate (under 4 percent) without having inflation soar to an unacceptable level. On the other hand, Keynesian policies have demonstrated their ability to prevent the recurrence of a severe depression, like that of the 1930s.

Key Terms

Phillips curve   Say's law
classical school   stagflation

Review & Discussion

1. What relationship is expressed by a Phillips curve? Why would traditional economists expect this relationship to hold? How well has the Phillips curve described reality in recent years?

2. How would economic stability (full employment without serious inflation) be achieved according to the classical school of economics? According to Keynesians? According to monetarists?

3. Why does it make sense to refer to Keynesians as "liberals" and monetarists as "conservatives"? What are the implications for social policy of their different views toward government economic policymaking?

4. What are some of the problems encountered in implementing effective economic policy? How can measures to achieve stability sometimes conflict with other economic and noneconomic goals?

5. Describe the symptoms of stagflation. Why is this situation so perplexing for traditional economic theory?

6. What policies have been tried in the 1970s to deal with the simultaneous problems of inflation and unemployment? How successful have they been?

7. In early 1979, the Carter administration announced that its policy was to encourage a mild economic slowdown to fight inflation, even though this would certainly create somewhat greater unemployment. How would you defend such a policy? How would you criticize it?

8. Although since World War II traditional measures to maintain stability have generally failed to meet the official goals of keeping unemployment under 4 percent and inflation under 2 percent, economists still insist that Keynesian fiscal policies are sufficient to prevent the kind of depression that occurred in the 1930s. What is the evidence to support this confidence?

Appendix 2

Supply Side Economics

In Chapter 17, we discussed the thorny problems that economic policymakers have faced in the past few years in attempting to deal with stabilization of employment and price levels. We described the recent state of the United States' economy, characterized by simultaneous increases in inflation and unemployment, and examined the historical roots of this situation. In addition, we discussed some possible legal and institutional solutions to the problem of rapidly rising prices and persistent levels of unemployment. In this appendix, we will use the aggregate demand analysis first established by John Maynard Keynes and post–Keynesian aggregate supply analysis to examine the mechanics behind the inflation/unemployment problem in more depth.

Because there is no well-developed and tested aggregate supply theory to match the Keynesian aggregate demand theory, this section may be difficult and confusing. However, because supply problems are dominating the economics scene in the current decade, these supply issues must be faced despite the lack of a sound theoretical foundation. As is often the case in economics, an extended period of new realities will probably eventually lead to a theoretical model to analyze such supply problems.

SIMPLE KEYNESIAN AGGREGATE REAL DEMAND ANALYSIS

The Keynesian approach to the analysis of macroeconomic activity has been the dominant theoretical approach in the twentieth century. Until recently, Keynesian economics meant that the government should use fiscal and monetary policies to increase the level of aggregate demand until a society reaches its full capacity to produce (supply) all goods and services demanded.*

Underlying the simple Keynesian aggregate demand model is the assumption that no matter how high the level of aggregate demand is, there will always be enough idle land, labor, and capital available to produce the additional goods and services *at an unchanged price*. In other words, the aggregate supply curve will be a straight horizontal line at a given price level (see *Fig. A.1),* and, at

---

*You will recall from Chapter 11 that aggregate supply and aggregate demand are two sides of the same coin: aggregate demand is the total amount (in current dollars) of goods and services demanded by all buyers at a given time. Aggregate supply, on the other side, is the total value (in current dollars) of all goods and services produced by all suppliers at a given time. Aggregate *real* demand and aggregate *real* supply would be the same amounts and values described above, but this time, the values would be adjusted for inflation (measured in *constant* dollars).

that price level, producers will supply as many goods and services as are demanded. As we will see later, this assumption is not always valid.

Aggregate supply in the simple Keynesian model

It may seem naive or ridiculous to us that Keynes would make the assumption we just described. However, we must keep in mind that when Keynes was developing his aggregate demand analysis during the Great Depression of the 1930s, he had little concern for supply shortages since there was substantial unemployment and idle capital. Businesses (suppliers) with warehouses of unsold goods would not raise prices just because the demand for the goods increased—they would sell as many units as were demanded at the same price.

Figure A.1 illustrates a simple Keynesian aggregate demand/aggregate supply model for an economy. P represents the general price level and Y represents real income.* The solid Y_F line represents the level of real income generated when the economy is at full employment.

Initially, a low level of aggregate real demand (D_1) results in a low level of real income (Y_1). This is similar to the position of the United States' economy in the 1930s. Keynes's demand analysis showed that government could raise the level of demand (for instance, to D_2) through tax cuts, increased government spending, or other measures, in order to get nearer to the full-employment level of the economy. Although D_2 represents a higher level of aggregate real demand and of real income (Y_2), it is still far less than the level of aggregate real demand necessary to reach full employment. Because the economy is not yet at full employment, the price level does not rise even though demand is rising. However, if the level of aggregate

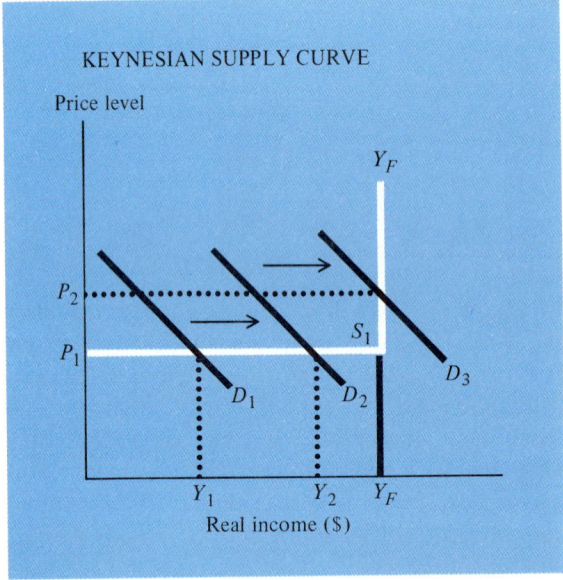

Fig. A.1
This graph illustrates a simple Keynesian aggregate demand/aggregate supply model for an economy. The aggregate supply curve (S_1) is horizontal to the point of full employment (Y_F) at which point it becomes vertical. If aggregate demand increases from D_1 to D_2, real income also increases (from Y_1 to Y_2) but there will be no change in the price level. If demand increases from D_2 to D_3, real income increases (to Y_F) but the price level also rises. Since the economy cannot produce any more goods past the full-employment point any increase in aggregate demand results in bidding up the prices of scarce goods.

---

*Real income is the sum of wages, rents, interest, and profits measured in constant dollars (that is, adjusted for inflation). Recall that in an equilibrium situation, real income is equal to real output (the value in constant dollars of all goods and services produced).

real demand were to increase to D_3, the price level would then rise to P_2. Because the economy *cannot* produce any more goods past the full-employment point, any increase in aggregate real demand results in bidding up the prices of the goods that are available.

Aggregate real supply shifts in the simple Keynesian model

While *Fig. A.1* is useful in analyzing the effects of changes in aggregate real demand on the level of real income, this model of an economy does not accurately represent a real situation because it does not take into consideration the fact that prices may rise when the economy is operating at less than full employment. In reality, reductions in aggregate real supply can occur and do result in increased prices of goods even when an economy is operating at less than full employment. For example, in 1973–1974, the Organization of Petroleum Exporting Countries (OPEC) reduced oil supplies, thus raising the price of oil substantially and permanently to non-OPEC countries. The increase in the price of oil in turn increased the costs of production of many goods in the American economy and therefore increased the price of those goods and the general price level.*

The end result of the OPEC actions was an upward shift of the aggregate real supply curve such as that shown in *Fig. A.2*. It is important to note that due to the shift to S_2, any given aggregate real demand (such as D_1 or D_2) is now associated with a higher price level (P_2) and a lower level of real income (Y_{1*} or Y_{2*}, respectively). But also note that an increase in aggregate real demand from D_1 to D_2 does not raise the price level *above* P_2. When the aggregate real supply curve is flat,

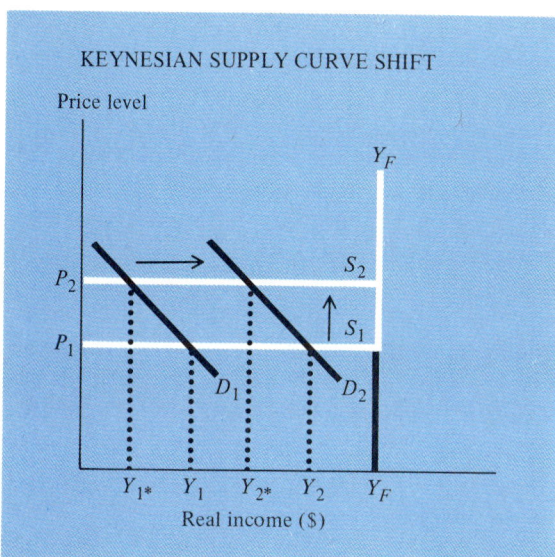

Fig. A.2
Reductions in aggregate supply (such as from S_1 to S_2) can occur even in a simple Keynesian model. As a result of this shift, any given aggregate real demand (such as D_1 or D_2) is now associated with a lower level of real income (Y_{1*} and Y_{2*} respectively) *and* a higher price level (P_2).

---

*Remember that *inflation* is defined as a rise in the general level of prices of most goods and services in an economy. *In principle*, a supply shift such as that shown in *Fig. A.2* will, all else being equal, produce inflation for just a short time. There should be no continuing rise in the price level. As we will see later, this is not always the case.

only decreases in aggregate real supply will raise prices. Thus, when aggregate real supply shifts occur in a Keynesian model, it is possible to have aggregate real demand far to the left of full employment (Y_F) and still have price increases. This occurred in 1974–1975 when we experienced both low real income and rapid inflation.

The appropriate fiscal policy in the above situation would be as follows. When the price level increases due to an upward shift in aggregate real supply, thus causing a reduction in real income (for example, to Y_{1*}), the government should increase spending and cut taxes in order to increase the level of aggregate real demand to D_2 or beyond. This action would increase the level of real income to Y_{2*} or beyond. The economy should not suffer a lower real income when the price level remains at P_2 regardless of the level of aggregate real demand.

As we progress through this appendix, we will continue to examine supply shifts similar to the one just discussed, but the aggregate real supply curve will have a more realistic shape (that is, similar to the upward sloping supply curves we studied in Chapter 3). This will allow us to interpret recent economic developments, such as stagflation, with greater realism and, unfortunately, less optimism.

AGGREGATE SUPPLY IN AN EXPANDED OR "MODERN" KEYNESIAN MODEL

As we saw in the previous section, aggregate real supply reductions can raise prices and reduce real income even when the aggregate real supply curve is perfectly flat. In reality, however, economists have come to realize that the aggregate real supply curve has an upward slope similar to that of the supply curve we studied in Chapter 3. The derivation of this upward sloping aggregate real supply curve and its implications for an economy are discussed in the following sections.

Deriving the sloped aggregate real supply curve

In order to show that the aggregate supply curve is not the straight horizontal line that Keynes assumed it was, we must establish a positive relationship between real income and the price level. That is, to get an upward sloping aggregate supply curve, we need to show that as real income increases, the price level also increases. This can be done by using the relationship illustrated by the Phillips curve: as the unemployment rate drops, the inflation rate consistently rises and vice versa. Since we can assume that a drop in the unemployment rate can be produced by an increase in aggregate real demand (the demand for the labor to produce the goods would increase), *we can expect that increases in aggregate real demand will reduce the unemployment rate and at the same time increase the rate of inflation* (cause the price level to rise at an ever-increasing rate). Since we also know (as shown in *Fig. A.1*) that increases in aggregate real demand lead to an increase in real income, we can then conclude that an increase in real income will be accompanied by an increase in the price level.

Increase in aggregate demand →

    Increase in real income →
    Decrease in unemployment

        Increase in price level

This positive relationship between changes in real income and changes in the price level results in an aggregate real supply curve that slopes up and to the right. This slope shows that as real income (recall that the supply counterpart of real income is real output) increases, the price level will also increase.

Implications of the sloped aggregate supply curve

The net result of all the complicated interrelationships discussed above is that an economy cannot continue to increase the level of aggregate real demand without risking driving up the price level at an ever-increasing rate (that is, without increasing the rate of inflation). *Figure A.3* illustrates the situation. When aggregate real demand is very low (at D_1, for example) or low (at D_2, for example), increases in aggregate real demand raise the price level very little (P_1 to P_2). The inflation problem arises when aggregate real demand shifts occur in the area between Y_2 and Y_3. Because the positive relationship between real income and price level has caused our flat Keynesian supply curve to bend gradually and then rapidly upward at high levels of real income,* increases in aggregate real demand in that bending area will cause the price level to increase greatly.

The right angle in our original Keynesian supply curve (*Figs. A.1* and *A.2*) was a convenient analytical tool and the full-employment level was of little importance when aggregate real demand was D_1 (as it was in Keynes's time) and the supply of goods and resources to satisfy an increase in aggregate real demand was plentiful. Keynes demonstrated how to maintain aggregate real demand in the D_2–D_3 range through fiscal policy which solved the problem of prolonged and deep recession. However, Keynes's theory also helped to produce the following dilemmas: (1) As aggregate real demand *approaches* the maximum ability of the economy to supply goods (the full-employment level) some industries will approach their supply potential more rapidly than others, so they begin to raise prices. Thus, since some but not all industries are at full employment it becomes evident that Y_F for the economy is a *range* (for instance, Y_2–Y_3) and not a fixed number of real dollars of income or output. (2) Although Y_F is difficult to define, policymakers do want to increase aggregate real demand to get close to it, in order to achieve the highest level of real income possible. However, in the "modern" model, unlike in the simple Keynesian model, we risk driving up the price level as we increase aggregate real demand beyond D_2. If we increase aggregate real demand beyond D_3, there is no risk—we simply drive up the price level!

To summarize, when aggregate real demand increases from D_2 to D_3 (an increase which greatly increases the price level to P_3), real income approaches its maximum possible value of Y_3—the economy's full capacity to supply. Thus, in many practical circumstances there exists a trade-off between increasing real income (a good thing only if it is still less than our maximum ability to produce) and price level increases (never a good thing). This situation is unlike the cases of the Keynesian aggregate supply curve (*Fig. A.1*) and Keynesian aggregate supply curve shifts (*Fig. A.2*), and we now admit that increases in aggregate demand *alone* may cause increases in the price level since the aggregate supply curve, in the higher real income range, has an upward slope.

SUPPLY SHIFTS IN THE EXPANDED OR MODERN KEYNESIAN MODEL

We have explored two supply problems that the simple Keynesian demand model ignored: (1) Supply shifts do occur. In *Fig. A.2* we noted that decreases in supply can raise the price level even in a simple flat supply curve Keynesian mode. (2) Any given supply curve is upward sloping. In *Fig. A.3* we illustrated that aggregate demand increases

---

*As real income increases *rapidly,* the unemployment rate will decline rapidly *and* (according to the Phillips curve) the inflation rate (increases in the price level) will also increase rapidly.

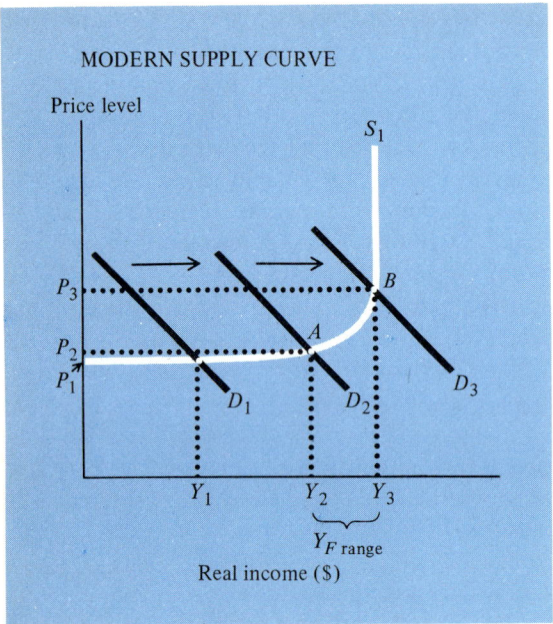

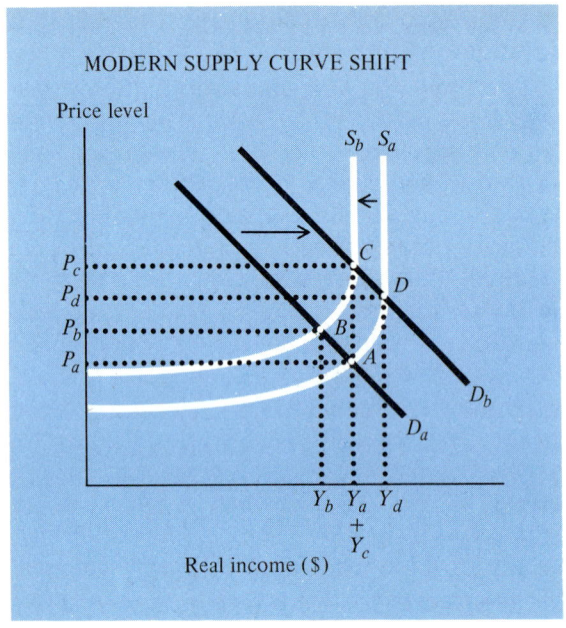

Fig. A.3
In reality, the aggregate real supply curve slopes up to the right (S_1) in the full-employment range of real income (Y_2–Y_3). When aggregate real demand increases from D_1 to D_2, the price level barely increases from P_1 to P_2. As real income approaches its maximum possible value (Y_3), increases in aggregate real demand (such as from D_2 to D_3) greatly increase the price level to P_3. Thus in many circumstances, there is a tradeoff between increases in real income and price level increases. The difference between this graph and *Figs. A.1* and *A.2* is that in this situation (the sloped supply curve), increases in aggregate demand *alone* can cause the price level to increase.

Fig. A.4
In this graph we examine what happens to real income when an upward sloping aggregate real supply curve shifts. At point A (the intersection of D_a and S_a) real income is near the full employment level (Y_a). An aggregate real supply shift from S_a to S_b results in a new equilibrium (point B)—note that at point B, real income (Y_b) is less than it was and the price level is higher than it was (P_b). If at the same time the supply shift occurs, aggregate real demand also shifts up (from D_a to D_b), the resulting equilibrium is point C. At this point, the price level is even higher (P_c) *but* real income has returned to its former level (Y_a/Y_c). If for some reason aggregate real supply shifts back to S_a, the economy would then experience the best of both worlds—a decrease in price level (to P_d) and higher real income (Y_d).

can also cause price increases because the supply curve is upward sloping at levels of real income approaching the maximum ability of an economy to supply.

Together these two facts mean that an economy can face possible price increases from both the demand *and* the supply sides of the economy. In *Fig. A.4* we will now combine these two supply problems and examine their effects on real income in the expanded Keynesian aggregate demand model. To make this very complicated diagram clearer, we will relate it to recent economic events.

☐ At point A, the intersection of D_a and S_a, the level of real income (Y_a) is near the full-employment level of income and output Y_d. We can tell this is near full employment because beyond point A the price level rises rapidly. This point represents the position of the United States' economy in late 1978—near full employment, with an acceptable unemployment rate, but also with a rising price level.

☐ Point B, the intersection of D_a and S_b, represents the equilibrium position of the United States' economy in early 1979 when aggregate real supply was reduced as a result of restricted oil exports and price increases of 60 percent by OPEC. The increased oil prices alone caused a 6 percent rise in the general price level in the United States. Notice that the shift of aggregate real supply from S_a to S_b simultaneously *increases* prices from P_a to P_b and *reduces* real income from Y_a to Y_b. The economy thus experiences more inflation *and* more unemployment (as reflected in the decrease in real income) due to the aggregate real supply shift. The facts of mid–late 1979 confirm this—the price level has risen rapidly (at 13 percent or more)—and the growth of real income has slowed considerably (about zero growth for the average of the last two quarters of 1979). Essentially, all forecasters are predicting a 1980 recession; i.e., an actual drop in the level of real income.

☐ Given the new level of aggregate real supply (S_b), policymakers could accept aggregate real demand at D_a, thus accepting less real income (more unemployment) and somewhat higher prices (P_b). Or, on the other hand, the government could stimulate aggregate real demand to D_b. This action would raise the level of income back to Y_a and lower unemployment, but it would also raise the price level even further to P_c. Since the Federal Reserve in October 1979 renounced any monetary policy that would allow aggregate real demand to expand in 1980, the resulting equilibrium will probably be at point B. It is possible, however, that the government may induce aggregate real demand to increase from D_a to D_b in order to prevent possible high levels of unemployment in 1980 (an election year). If this were to happen, the economy would be at point C.

☐ With a lot of luck, the economy could face oil price decreases in the 1980s. Such decreases would return the aggregate real supply curve to S_a with point D being the new equilibrium. At this point, the price level is not as high, real income rises even further, and therefore unemployment falls further. Alternatively, if the government does not stimulate aggregate real demand to D_b, the economy would return to point A on its own due to the increase in aggregate real supply. Either way, the president would get the best of both worlds if supply shifted back to the right—lower price level, higher real income. However, because at this time such a shift would require OPEC cooperation or some other event and not policy action on the part of the government, economists are searching for feasible domestic policies that would shift the supply curve to the right.

POLICIES TO SHIFT THE SUPPLY CURVE

Since the United States does not want to be at the mercy of aggregate supply shifts due to OPEC or other supply price increases that raise the price level, and since there is a limit to how far aggregate demand stimulation can go without itself causing price increases along an upward sloping aggregate supply curve, the United States needs to establish supply policies to shift the real supply curve. Note that we have now come full circle. Until recently, economists ignored aggregate real supply and concentrated on aggregate real demand. Now they realize the limitations of aggregate real demand management, so many economists are focusing on policies that would shift the aggregate real supply curve to the right. For a given new leftward aggregate real supply shift due to OPEC price increases, any or all of the policies described below should potentially shift the aggregate supply curve to the right and therefore reverse the price increases and income reductions. Among such suggested policies are:

☐ To reduce or eliminate the required Social Security contributions paid by employers. This would reduce their production costs and, presumably, all else being equal, would lead to a price reduction. The major drawback to this policy would be that the Social Security system would not be able to continue operation since one of its major means of support would be cut off.

☐ To increase tax breaks for technological research and development. This would encourage businesses to engage in more R and D and, eventually, technological progress would reduce production costs (and prices).

☐ To allow accelerated tax depreciation on business plant and equipment. If businesses were allowed to deduct from their taxes a larger amount of the nonlabor items they buy, their net costs of production would be reduced and so would their prices.

☐ To reduce government regulation. If the government had less stringent rules concerning air pollution or safety equipment for cars, for example, business costs, and therefore prices, would fall.

Each of these solutions has both supporters and opponents, and there is no easy solution in sight because, as yet, economists and policymakers do not have enough knowledge of how to manage the supply side of the economy.

A FINAL PROBLEM WITH THE SUPPLY SIDE: EXPECTATIONS

In addition to all the above complications with respect to the supply side of the economy, there is one other problem: expectations. In Chapter 17, we indicated that if people expect prices to increase, this expectation by itself will cause more inflation. In our modern aggregate demand/aggregate supply diagram (*Fig. A.4*), this effect works in the same manner. If price increases in the last year lead workers to expect price increases in the coming year (whether such increases occur or not), then workers will insist on wage increases to catch up on their expected cost-of-living increases for the coming year. Business costs will rise accordingly for the coming year and so will prices. Therefore, a one-shot OPEC price increase may have long-lasting inflationary effects on the general price level even though, in principle, a one-shot change should be just that—an action whose effect disappears the next year.

CONCLUSION

In this appendix, we have shown that, contrary to the Keynesian model of the economy, aggregate real supply curves *do* shift (due to changes in supply factors such as OPEC price increases) and aggregate real supply curves are *upward sloping* in the relevant full-employment range of real income. Keynes showed how to keep aggregate real demand in that range through the use of fiscal policy, but the dilemma of shifts in aggregate real supply *and* aggregate real demand causing increases in the price level has created our current economic problem: that of continuing inflation whether the economy is operating at a low level of real income (high unemployment) or at a high level of real income (low unemployment).

Part V

Economic Growth

Chapter 18

Economic Growth Theory and the United States' Record

What to look for in this chapter

How is economic growth measured?

What are the major factors in determining economic growth?

How have classical, neoclassical, Keynesian, and post-Keynesian theorists viewed the question of economic growth?

What are the costs and benefits of growth?

All of economic theory springs from the basic fact of scarce resources. If all goods were so abundant that excesses would remain after all demands were satisfied, all goods would be free and much economic analysis would be unnecessary. As it is, most of the goods and services we desire have their price, and we are forced to earn the money to afford the necessities and luxuries of life.

Thus it is no wonder that from the beginning of time people have searched for the formula to improve their material condition—first to banish the specter of mass starvation, and later to spend less time producing goods and more time enjoying them. Such ambitions still underlie all theories of economic growth, for without growth no nation can hope to ease the basic scarcity of resources, let alone overcome it.

If we want to describe the total economic productivity of a nation, we refer to its gross national product and the rate at which GNP is growing. If we want to determine the living standard of a nation, we divide its GNP by its population and come up with its per capita (per person) GNP. Thus we can say that the Soviet Union is economically much more powerful than Switzerland because its GNP is larger, but that Switzerland has a higher standard of living because it has a larger per capita GNP.

In modern economies, **economic growth** is defined as *an increase in real gross national product*. The term "real" is used because when we measure a country's GNP in terms of current dollars we must adjust it for whatever inflation its currency may have suffered. Growth can also be measured as the increase in GNP per capita. Both scales have useful application, depending on the comparison that interests us.

In many cases the health of a nation's economy is not so much reflected in the volume of production as in changes in that volume. For instance, no economist in the United States, which has the largest GNP in the world, would have described the United States economy in the second half of the 1970s as healthy, since increases in GNP during those years were quite small as compared to previous years (see *Table 18.1*).

Growth theory is concerned with bringing about and maintaining expansion of a nation's economy. It is as applicable to advanced economies such as the United States and western European countries as it is to India and China, whose people live largely at a subsistence level. But modern growth theory cannot yet provide all the answers. In fact, it remains one of the most challenging fields of economic analysis.

Most societies were expanding their economic activity in some way long before economists formulated a theory of growth. With increases in population, the number of goods produced and services performed increased, and thus so did total output. Slowly, scientific discoveries led to changes in productivity, or output per person. When Adam Smith attempted to analyze the wealth of nations in the eighteenth century, he could already discern a process of economic development, which he tried to explain. Later economists found that in order to explain growth they had to be able to measure it first.

Table 18.1
Rates of economic growth, 1970–1978 (measured as rates of change in real GNP, expressed in 1972 dollars)

Year	Real GNP (in billions)	Rate of real GNP growth
1970	1,075.3	−.3 (from 1969)
1971	1,107.5	+3.0
1972	1,171.1	+5.7
1973	1,235.0	+5.5
1974	1,217.8	−1.4
1975	1,202.1	−1.3
1976	1,274.7	+6.0
1977	1,332.7	+4.6
1978	1,385.3	+3.9

Source: *Statistical Abstract*, 1978.

MEASURING ECONOMIC GROWTH

GNP and growth

The problem of measurement is tied to our definition of growth as an increase in GNP. Before the introduction of monetary systems for national economies, no realistic attempt at measurement could take place. To assess the total of goods and services that make up the GNP, we must agree on the value of these goods and services. In barter economies, this is virtually impossible. Even in economies with monetary systems, the sheer task of counting all goods produced and services rendered remains formidable. Because of recurring periods of inflation in the twentieth century, there is a need in a given period to adjust the "money" value of GNP to its "real" value, in order to make meaningful comparisons with other periods and between different nations. To see the importance of using real GNP, consider an economy that is not growing but whose price level is increasing at 10 percent per year. If we look at the dollar value of total output as a measure of well-being, we will incorrectly conclude that their situation is improving by 10 percent, when in fact the country is no better off because this increase is due only to increased prices and not to growth in output.

The measurement of long-term growth is further complicated by the often cyclical nature of economic expansion. No economy has ever managed to maintain an even growth rate. In the contractionary phase of a business cycle the rate of GNP growth slows down, and real GNP may actually decline. During the recovery period, GNP usually increases at a faster rate than before the cycle began. But can such growth be fairly compared to the steadier growth of an economy that is unaffected by such cycles? After all, much of this accelerated growth rate merely serves to have the economy catch up to where it would have been had there not been a recession.

Today, with the introduction of price indexes, real GNP is measured every quarter and adjusted for seasonal variations in output. Such adjustment is helpful if we consider that certain sectors of the economy expand or contract with changes in climate. Construction and tourism burgeon in the summer; gas and electricity consumption are high in the winter. For this reason it is also more meaningful to compare quarterly output figures with the output in *corresponding* quarters of previous years, rather than with output in the immediately preceding quarter. If, for instance, even after a seasonal adjustment a nation's output fell in the autumn of 1979 from the summer of that year but rose from the level of autumn 1978, we could assume that its economy was expanding, not contracting.

To summarize, real GNP usually grows in a cyclical fashion. During each year, there are some periods when GNP rises quickly and some times when it rises very slowly, or even declines. From year to year, there are cycles during which GNP per capita will rise quickly or may not rise at all. However, in a successful economy, real GNP per capita will grow so that it is greater at least every few years.

Rate of growth

The health of an economy cannot be measured by its volume of production alone; equally important is its rate of growth. And the United States, despite the Great Depression and several slowdowns since 1945, can still point to a favorable growth record. Although other nations, notably Japan, Germany, Italy, and France, have accelerated their progress in the post–World War II years and their growth rates have actually surpassed those of the United States for the comparable period, historically the United States has been among the pacesetters.

Other factors to consider

In measuring economic growth, the welfare of a people is sometimes reflected in factors other than indexes of production. Such factors as cultural activity and leisure time may be highly valued in a society, but they cannot be adequately measured in money terms. A longer work week results in higher output, but what if we prefer more leisure to an increase in output? On the scale of GNP per capita, increased leisure causes our living standard to decline, yet we will consider our well-being to have improved.

Of course, if increased leisure results in more market goods (tennis rackets, bicycles) being produced, this will add to GNP. However, if people spend leisure time staying home with their families

> **RECAP**
>
> Determining a country's long-term economic growth is not simply a matter of using price indexes and other measures of production. Among other important considerations are:
>
> 1. Adjusting the money value of GNP to its real value in order to make meaningful comparisons with other periods and between different nations.
> 2. Accounting for nonmarket (barter) transactions.
> 3. Differentiating long-term growth from cyclical fluctuations.
> 4. Considering factors that affect a nation's social well-being, such as leisure time.

or watching their old TV sets, there will be no increase in market transactions and GNP will not rise. It is also possible that more leisure for some will create new market demands and jobs for others. Nevertheless, if all workers work less and take more leisure time, GNP will decline.

Another factor to consider is that some valuable services are not included in GNP, for instance, those produced within the household. To see the importance of this problem, consider a woman who cares for children, prepares meals, and maintains the home. Her work of course is not included in GNP. Contrast this to a woman doing the same tasks but who receives a wage for her services. This becomes a part of GNP. In both cases the same services are performed, but in the second case our measure of well-being, GNP, is greater.

Standard of living Another factor to keep in mind in addition to the size of the GNP is the standard of living that it roughly measures. As mentioned earlier, while GNP describes the total value of produced goods and services, it ignores economic goods such as leisure, a clean environment, and household services. In comparing diverse cultures, failure to take these economic goods into consideration can lead to inaccurate conclusions.

For example, consider Japan where a standard work week consists of six or seven days. Can the GNP of such a nation be directly compared to GNP in the United States where the average work week is only 35.8 hours (see *Table 18.2*)? Also consider the less industrialized nations where it is not uncommon for a family to grow much of its own food, prepare all its meals, and even make much of its own clothing. Can such an economy's GNP accurately be compared to that of the United States where such goods commonly pass through the marketplace? It really is not a valid comparison since many of the goods and services in the less industrialized economy are not bought or sold in the market and so are not counted in GNP.

One way of comparing the well-being of people in different countries might be to determine how many hours a person must work in order to acquire a certain bundle of goods. In a less developed country, individuals might have to

Table 18.2
United States average work week, 1909–1974

Year	Average work week (hours)
1909	51.0
1919	47.3
1929	44.2
1939	37.7
1949	39.4
1959	39.0
1969	37.7
1978	35.8

Source: Bureau of Labor Statistics.

spend ten hours a day for 300 days a year to grow their food, make their clothes, build their homes, and take care of their animals. Yet in highly developed nations, most workers spend only a fraction of their annual salary on food, clothing, shelter, and transportation. The remaining part of their salaries can be saved or spent. The amount of time spent working to provide the basic necessities of life might be a good way to measure a nation's well-being.

FACTORS CAUSING ECONOMIC GROWTH

Analysts generally agree on the basic factors causing growth. They may be considered in three groups:

1. supply factors,
2. demand factors,
3. noneconomic factors.

A favorable interaction of all these factors is required for prolonged, steady economic growth, but changes in a single factor sometimes trigger the growth process.

Supply factors

Supply factors can be broken down into five categories: human resources, natural resources, capital stock, entrepreneurship, and level of technology. Human resources determine the size and quality of the labor force. Natural resources are the economic goods—oil and timber, for example—which a nation can extract from its environment. Capital stock (the total of plants, equipment, and tools accumulated in an economy) helps humans in exploiting their natural resources. Entrepreneurship relates to making innovations which help to resolve inefficiencies, thereby facilitating reduced costs and increased production. Technology represents the productive techniques our labor force uses to create its goods and services.

Each of these factors is important in encouraging economic growth. Later in the chapter, under the heading "Sources of growth," we will discuss in detail how they relate to the American economy.

Supply factors and the production possibilities curve

To illustrate the limitations of these factors of supply at any one point in time, a nation's production possibilities curve is shown in *Fig. 18.1.* (It might be useful at this time to review the discussion of production possibilities in Chapter 2.) As we saw in Chapter 2, if for some reason productive capacity is not fully utilized, the actual level of production will be at a point inside the curve. If output is at capacity level, it will be represented by a point along the curve. The exact location of that point will depend on whether the society desires to produce more locomotives or more ballpoint pens.

Over time the economy can increase its capacity to produce through an expansion in its population, capital accumulation, and/or the supply of other productive factors. The production possibilities curve will shift outward, as shown by the dotted line in the diagram, and the society will be able to produce both more locomotives *and* more pens. In this way, the production possibilities curve, without the use of detailed statistics, demonstrates the process of economic growth.

The following example illustrates the way the production possibilities curve works. As more capital is accumulated, producers can build the most modern machinery and plants, and this causes the production possibilities curve to shift outward. For example, Germany and Japan experienced a period of rapid economic growth after World War II. Economists believe that this occurred because most of their plants and equipment were destroyed in the war and they were forced to build modern replacements. In the United States, on the other hand, the production facilities in many industries (such as steel) are outmoded, so it is difficult to produce as efficiently

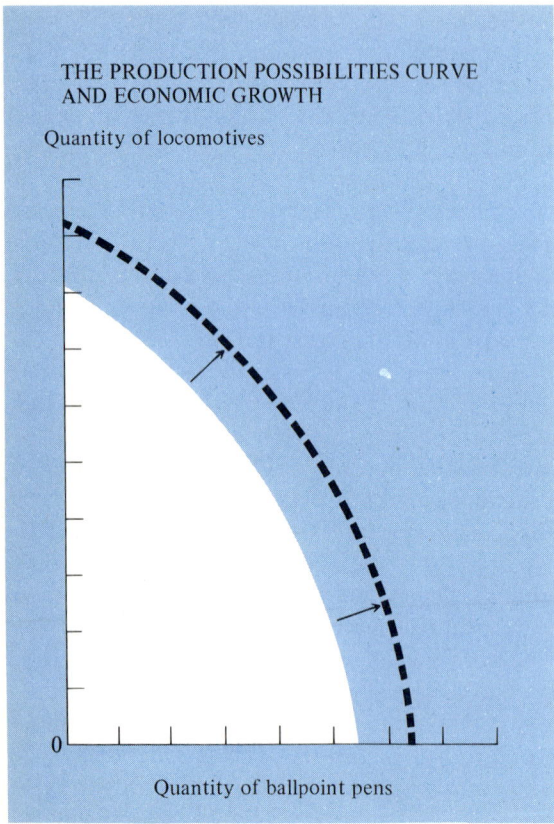

Fig. 18.1
The economy can produce any of the combinations of locomotives and pens located on the line that marks the production possibilities curve. By moving along this curve the economy can have either more locomotives or more pens, but not more of both. In order to increase its output of both goods, the economy must shift the production possibilities curve to the right, through an increase in productive resources or an advance in the efficiency of production techniques.

as the Germans or Japanese can. Thus, rate of growth in those economies has been greater than that of the United States because they have more modern capital goods.

Demand factors

In any consideration of the supply side of growth, emphasis is necessarily on factors that determine how much an economy is *able* to produce. But as we know, a free-market economy will not expand unless there is also a *demand* for the additional goods it can produce. If demand falls short of supply, investment will decline, diminishing the effect of other factors of growth. Unemployment will result, reducing the incentive for technological progress, and ultimately resulting in economic stagnation.

Changes in supply factors thus must be accompanied by changes in demand to result in an adequate stimulus for growth. Demand itself, of course, depends on the size of the market, the income level of consumers, and their tastes and needs.

The continuing breakdown of barriers to world trade is expanding the markets for industries of many nations. Italy, for instance, in the last few years, has produced more shoes for export to the United States than for domestic consumption. The United States, on the other hand, has traditionally exported vast amounts of machinery and farm products to overseas markets.

Expanding markets, whether through population growth at home or through increased trade with other countries, stimulate investment and in turn lead to increases in production, employment, and income. They also allow economies of scale to take effect, raising productivity and the standard of living. When Henry Ford pioneered the mass production of automobiles in the United States early in this century, he deliberately paid his workers more than was customary, thus giving them an incentive to buy the cars they were producing. Such creation of demand helped build the market for the early Ford models and made economies of scale possible.

In the United States today, there is certainly little fear of inadequate demand. Not only do most people spend as much as they earn, but many people spend *more,* by going into debt. The use of credit cards and other means of obtaining credit has made this easier than in the past. Some early growth theorists thought that inadequate demand would lead to stagnation, but this is not the belief today. Slowdowns in the growth rate appear to be caused by limitations in supply and the factors of production (such as fuels) and by less than optimum production techniques dictated by old capital equipment and a labor force that prefers more leisure and less work compared to earlier times.

Some people in the United States today still argue that spending on defense and military equipment is necessary to generate adequate demand for capitalism to survive. Certainly, a great many bicycles must be purchased in order to generate the same dollar demand as does one B-1 bomber. However, if supplies of energy and raw materials are limited, as they are, military demands may do more to heat up inflation than to raise *real* GNP in the United States. Today, less demand for military hardware would probably enable greater production of other types of goods.

Noneconomic factors

Economists have long been aware of the effect that a nation's culture can have on its tendency to grow economically. Religion and social customs promote or restrain the willingness of a people to make the initial sacrifices to trigger growth. As long as the Hindu faith prohibits the slaughtering of cows because these animals are regarded as sacred, India will not be able to develop a beef-processing industry.

Social organization is often crucial to growth. The feudal states of medieval Europe resisted economic progress because it threatened the existing power structure. After the social and political revolutions of the eighteenth and nineteenth centuries, a powerful middle class dominated by commercial interests emerged and the industrial revolution soon followed.

In the United States, the early influence of the Puritan ethic has traditionally been regarded as responsible for developing a cultural orientation toward achievement and thrift, both of which are important attitudes for economic progress. Some economists argue that a class of entrepreneurs is the one element that really makes all other growth factors work. Unless a spirit of enterprise emerges from the culture of a nation, they say, all efforts at economic development will collapse.

This argument has been contradicted to some extent by recent experience. Rubber-planting peoples in Indonesia showed a response to the price mechanism and produced more rubber when traders supplied them with simple industrial goods, such as clothing and bicycles.

Thus a measure of response to certain growth stimulants can be observed in diverse cultures, and contemporary economists believe that growth theory can be adapted to very different cultural conditions.

GROWTH IN THE UNITED STATES

What are the factors that have caused the American economy to grow to its present magnitude? Perhaps it was an advantage of scale that helped the United States achieve economic leadership from the beginning of its industrialization in the middle of the nineteenth century. Americans tend to think that theirs is a big, populous, and by and large well-educated country; but the Soviet Union is larger, China more populous, and many European countries were historically more advanced in technological knowledge than was the United States.

Traditionally, economists have identified five main factors that contribute to a nation's output. They are natural resources, human resources, capital stock, entrepreneurship, and technology. Growth or improvement of any of these input factors should—all other things being equal—logically result in a growth of total output.

Natural resources

In the nineteenth century the natural resources available to the United States seemed unlimited. As the nation expanded westward, more and more of these resources were exploited, thus contributing to its rapid economic growth.

In recent years people have become increasingly aware that the supply of natural resources is not inexhaustible. Fortunately, however, discoveries of new reserves and better ways to employ resources have enabled Americans to use the limited supply more efficiently. For example, the development of offshore drilling techniques has enabled the United States to exploit additional oil deposits in our territorial waters. And the United States has increased its total land resources by filling in many marshy areas along the coastline.

Human resources

The effect of a population increase on economic growth depends on several factors. Basically, a larger population will result in a larger work force and greater production and therefore an increase in GNP. But a larger population also means additional consumers of total output, and GNP per capita may decline.

In the short run, a population increase is usually disadvantageous, because it immediately raises the number of consumers but does not increase the work force until the younger generation enters it. Even in the long run, the contribution of a population increase to output may be limited by the law of diminishing returns (see Chapter 2) unless other supply factors, such as natural resources or capital equipment, increase also.

Labor

In terms of growth, the most significant element within the population is the labor force. Not only its size, but its skills, education, motivation, and willingness to risk investments are worthy of attention. The American labor force has grown in proportion to population (see *Fig. 18.2*), but there are also some changes in the composition of that force that result from social changes in an advancing economy.

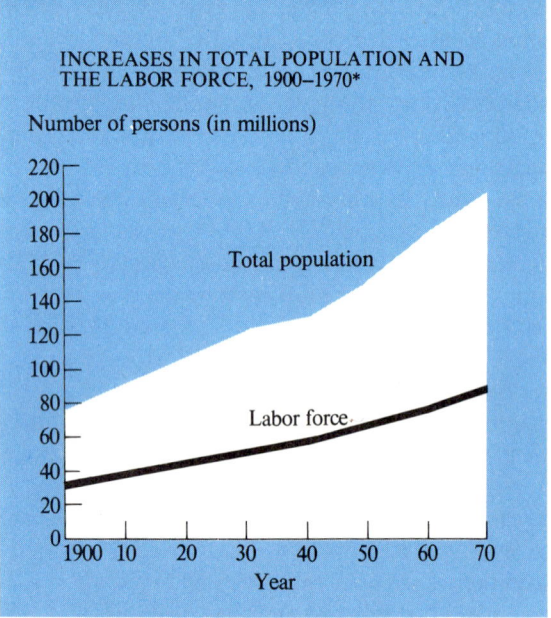

*Data are plotted only at 10-year intervals to show main trends.
SOURCE: Bureau of the Census data.

Fig. 18.2
The labor force has grown in exact proportion to the growth in the total population; the percentage of the population in the labor force has remained constant. Both total labor force and total population have almost tripled since 1900.

Education Young Americans today stay in school longer, thus entering the work force at a later age than ever before. Sixty years ago only 15 percent of the nation's youth graduated from high school. Today about 70 percent of all adolescents graduate from high school, and about 60 percent of those continue their education. Clearly, if people decide to prolong their education by four or six years to train for a certain position in the work force, their training will improve their performance once they start working. They cannot make up the four or six years they had not worked because they stayed in school, but they do bring to work the particular skills they have acquired or the benefits of a higher intellectual development. This prolonged education reflects the demands of a more sophisticated economy, which has less need for the unskilled. But the need to train longer also shrinks the labor force.

Women and ethnic minorities Prolonged education reduces the number of available workers, yet the United States has maintained a steady increase in the labor force because segments of American society, such as women and ethnic minorities, whom custom or prejudice prohibited from participating in the kind of production that is measured by GNP, have made strides to attain social and economic equality. Their inclusion in the labor force has compensated for the drain caused by longer training periods.

Shorter work week Although the American work force has grown along with the population, its composition has changed, and its contribution to output has not grown proportionately with the increase in the number of people working. The reason is the trend toward a shorter work week, as shown in *Table 18.2*. This trend not only reflects the efforts of unions to improve working conditions but also indicates a willingness to sacrifice additional output for a certain amount of leisure. As we learned in previous chapters, leisure itself is an economic good. The value of leisure is not counted in GNP, but we may assume that shorter working hours have a beneficial effect on the quality of work performed. Long job hours with little or no interruption are physically and mentally tiring. If working hours are shortened, people have more energy and their concentration is better. Thus there may be no decrease in output per worker.

Stock of capital goods

In an industrial society, another significant factor in growth is the stock of physical capital—all the plants and equipment that aid people in making use of the resources of the environment. Capital goods differ from other goods in that they satisfy no immediate wants and cannot be consumed. Their value is that they help people to produce goods that can be consumed. Using capital goods simplifies the production process by saving time and energy, or by enabling people to produce things they could not efficiently make by hand.

Saving and capital formation
Usually an increase in capital stock implies a subsequent increase in production. Growth in an advanced economy like that of the United States depends in part on the formation of capital. If Americans were completely satisfied by their present level of consumption, they would not feel a need to grow in excess of the requirements of satisfying population growth. They would spend all of their current income and live happily. However, most Americans at some time in their lives have decided not to spend all their money but to save toward a purchase that at some future date will give them even more satisfaction. This decision to save is the basis of all capital formation.

Saving today takes place not under mattresses but in bank accounts, and the money that accumulates in banks is lent in turn to individuals or companies who want to expand their business by increasing their capital stock. The dependence of investment on saving is immediately clear. The more people save, the more money will be available for investment, or capital formation.

Technology

If we compare the growth of the GNP in the United States in this century with the growth of

> THE TEN MOST SERIOUS TECHNOLOGICAL PROBLEMS CONFRONTING THE UNITED STATES
> (Drawn up by the Congressional Office of Technology Assessment in 1978)
> 1. Alternative energy supplies
> 2. Alternative global food sources
> 3. National water supply and demand
> 4. Health promotion and disease prevention
> 5. Productivity of United States croplands, forests, and wetlands
> 6. Regulations and technological innovation
> 7. The impact of nuclear war
> 8. The impact of changing telecommunication policy
> 9. Technology and world population
> 10. The potential economic effects of federal research and development spending

improved technology is not always easy to measure. In general, we can say that it represents a more efficient use of resources, a better combination of the input factors resulting in higher output. Usually we think of technological advance in terms of capital equipment: more sophisticated machines, faster and bigger airplanes, safer or more energy efficient cars.

Technological improvement also includes the advances made in more intangible areas of the production process—for example, management of human resources, division of labor, and utilization of time and energies available. The development of such skills has become a subject of scientific study.

Economies of scale

In Chapter 2, we learned that mass production can often reduce the cost of production by making it more efficient. Thus an entrepreneur has an incentive to enlarge his or her business by putting to work ever larger amounts of inputs because it reduces the costs of production and increases profits. Of course, there is a point when such economies of scale turn into diseconomies of scale—when the task of coordinating vast amounts of inputs adds to the cost of production

the input factors that we have already discussed, we find that the combined increase in the quantity and quality of labor and of capital stock still does not account for all of the increase in total output. United States GNP has risen faster proportionately than its capital and labor inputs combined. What other factor has caused the difference between the growth rate of American inputs and that of total American output? One answer is technological improvement.

Just as the increasing education and experience of the labor force added something beyond increase in numbers, advances in technology make a qualitative addition to capital investment. And like the increasing quality of the labor force,

> **RECAP**
>
> FACTORS AND SOURCES OF GROWTH
>
> *Demand factors:* size of market, income and needs of consumers, international market situations
>
> *Supply factors:* human resources, natural resources, capital stock, entrepreneurship, level of technology
>
> *Noneconomic factors:* culture and values, social organization

and wipes out the savings that might be realized from increasing the quantities of inputs. But up to that point, the inducement to raise the scale of production must be considered a contribution to the growth of output, and it is a reasonable assumption that economies of scale account for most of the growth that has not already been traced to the increases in labor and capital, and to educational and technological improvements.

Entrepreneurship

It should be remembered that economic growth as increased *productive capacity* (an outward shift in the production possibilities curve) and economic growth as an increase in *actual production* (a rise in real GNP) are not always the same. For an economy to utilize its productive capabilities fully it must combine its resources in the most efficient manner. As you will recall from Chapter 2, inefficiencies will place a nation at a point within the production possibilities curve reflecting a situation in which more of some or all goods can be obtained without reducing the production of any others.

To eliminate inefficiencies is not always a simple task, particularly in an advanced economy in which the tastes of consumers, the supply of productive factors, and the state of technology are continually changing. Traditionally the difficult task of eliminating inefficiencies has been in the hands of the entrepreneur. In the search for new ways to increase profits, entrepreneurs are constantly making innovations which help to identify and resolve inefficiencies. By their efforts they help to reduce costs and hence can make more profit as they produce and sell goods and services.

Joseph Schumpeter, a well-known economist of this century, believed that the obsolescence of the entrepreneur would be a central feature in the decay of capitalism. He asserted that entrepreneurs would eventually be absorbed by large industries or government so that these individuals would no longer be able to be effective in carrying out their creative role. Has this actually occurred?

A look at the high enrollments in business programs in American colleges and universities today suggests strongly that there are still large numbers of individuals who are eager to learn the skills required for successful entrepreneurship. Whether colleges are turning out entrepreneurs of the caliber of Henry Ford or Andrew Carnegie is unclear. Many regulations have been passed in an attempt to avoid the evils of unchecked entrepreneurship such as occurred earlier in this century. Today entrepreneurs can no longer wheel and deal with abandon. Nevertheless, there are still many individuals who have proved that they can work efficiently and profitably within limitations to create new products and build new companies. To date Schumpeter's fears have not been realized in America.

The importance of demand

Strictly speaking, factors of supply have only *enabled* countries to grow. But unless we accept Say's law (that supply creates its own demand), we are left with a list of input categories and not with an explanation of the dynamics of growth. Does the *ability* to produce more and a greater variety of goods explain the fact that the United States has actually *produced* more and better goods? Or did the impetus for output growth come from elsewhere?

Keynes's answer was that demand was the key force in the economics of national growth. A business firm will produce only what it knows it can sell—and sell for a profit. Thus, if there is a great demand for a product, it will step up production of that product; when demand falls off, it will cut back.

Demand and level of output

Keynes's argument seems plausible enough. GNP rises or declines according to changes in aggregate demand. But this occurs only within certain limits. Suppose that demand increased faster than our ability to produce the goods to satisfy that demand. Consumers would bid up the prices of the goods they desired, but our real output would increase very slowly, and in some industries not at all. This would cause a demand-pull inflation which would make the United States GNP appear to grow, because it is measured in dollars and cents. But its *real* GNP—the actual output of goods and services—may have grown not as fast or not at all because supply factors have limited real growth. We consequently arrive at the conclusion that both supply and demand affect economic growth, though in different ways. In a mature economy, the primary function of demand is to stimulate production, whereas supply tends to limit it; but at times the roles of demand and supply can be reversed.

Supply factors and growth of demand
Some economists believe that technological advance, a supply factor, results in better products that will create their own demand. The thinking goes that consumers will prefer to buy an improved version of a given product rather than an outdated one, and indeed they do. Much of the annual demand for automobiles in the United States is stimulated by the constant change in the new models. Thus technological development is more a cause than an effect of consumer demand.

Similarly, we must remember the enormous effect that inventions, such as the steam engine or the radio, have had on economic growth. These inventions are factors that must be counted on the supply side of output and have been essential to rapid American growth. Keynes might have argued that the inventions themselves came in response to an underlying demand. People have always wanted such conveniences as mass transportation or mass communication. But since their demand was for things that did not exist, it could not be reflected in consumer spending and an increase in production. Once inventions enabled entrepreneurs to supply these things, the economy could grow. In this sense, therefore, certain supply factors can stimulate an increase in demand—a modern-day application of Say's law.

THEORIES OF ECONOMIC GROWTH

Classical theory—Adam Smith
Classical theorists, beginning with the eighteenth-century thinker Adam Smith, recognized the importance of only three variables in the growth process: labor, capital, and natural resources. Smith was the first to point out the advantages of division of labor, expanding markets, and capital accumulation. He argued that once markets were large enough to allow division of labor, growth would sustain itself because it would raise both income of workers and profits of capitalists, thereby causing a further expansion of markets and capital accumulation. An end to growth would occur when dwindling natural resources slowed expansion. Smith, however, could not foresee the impact of technology.

Adam Smith was also a leading advocate of free markets and of an economy unfettered by government regulation. He believed that if people were allowed to act in their own self-interest, the public welfare would be maximized and maximum economic growth would be achieved. Today Smith's idea of "the invisible hand" has given way to the very visible hand of government regulation, and some economists blame the dissolution of Smith's formula for the slowdown in American growth.

Ricardo
It was David Ricardo, a contemporary of Smith's, who contributed to economic theory the concept of diminishing returns, which helped to explain how growth slows down. Ricardo based his theory primarily on the fixed supply of land and the ever-increasing population. He reasoned that when additional units of labor are added to a fixed amount of land, beyond some point the extra or marginal output of each successive worker will begin to decline. Marginal output may even become negative, and total output will fall off. The eventual declining level of total output, due to the law of

Table 18.3
Classical growth theory: the law of diminishing returns

(1) Population (millions of workers)	(2) Total output (millions of units of food)	(3) Average output (output per worker)	(4) Marginal output
10	20	2.00	
20	85	4.25	+ 65
30	225	7.50	+ 140
40	350	8.75	+ 125
50	400	8.00	+ 50
60	425	7.08	+ 25
70	375	5.36	− 50
80	275	3.44	− 100

diminishing returns, is shown in column 2 of Table 18.3. Ricardo's growth model distinguished between landlords, workers, and capitalists. The last, he thought, were the moving force in the economy because they reaped profits which in turn they invested, causing the economy to grow. Landlords received rents, workers received wages, and both groups spent all their income. A growing population would cause output per worker (or wages) to drop steadily, as shown in column 3 of Table 18.3. Eventually, a subsistence level of income would be reached. An ever-increasing population would also result in higher and higher rents, shrinking the profits of the capitalists until the incentive to invest was gone and economic stagnation had occurred.

Malthus

Ricardo acknowledged that technological advance could delay stagnation for a while, but in the end he thought it was inevitable. His pessimism resembled that of Thomas Malthus, a nineteenth-century economist who believed that the major obstacle to economic growth was unchecked population expansion. Malthus's observations of the object poverty brought on by population growth in London led him to conclude that it was the destiny of humankind to live perpetually near starvation level. Starvation, resulting from the limited supply of land and food, was a major force that could check population growth. As long as they live above the starvation level, people tend to multiply. Malthus believed that the rate of increase in population would be much more rapid than the rate of increase in food production. Eventually, widespread famines would cause population growth to halt, but the standard of living would remain at bare subsistence level.

Neoclassical theory

Malthus, of course, could not foresee that population growth tends to slow as nations advance economically. And he could not calculate the sweeping force of technological progress. It was left up to *a group of late nineteenth-century economists* known as the **neoclassical school** to incorporate technology into the classical growth models. When it became obvious after the advent of the industrial revolution that income levels were rising rather than declining and that capital investment was also accelerating, the neoclassicists *suggested that technological development not only could alleviate the scarcity of natural resources, but could also create more and more opportunities for profitable investment*. Population increases notwithstanding, income levels would rise because capital accumulation made possible by technological progress was able to match and even exceed the growth of the labor force. Neoclassical economists, notably Alfred Marshall, thus rejected the inevitability of the dismal final outcome predicted by the law of diminishing returns.

Neoclassicists also refined the theory of investment in other ways. By the early twentieth century, with the development of financial institutions, it had become clear that it was not only business owners who made investments with the profits they realized. Consumers, too, saved

DEVELOPMENTS IN ECONOMIC THOUGHT:

Thomas Robert Malthus

For most of the nineteenth century, economics was known by the unfortunate nickname "the dismal science." The man most responsible for this gloomy image was an obscure English minister, Parson Thomas Robert Malthus (1766–1834). Overshadowing all his other work in economics is one depressing prediction for which he became famous: population growth, when unchecked, will inevitably outstrip the ability of an economy to feed its people.

While many other observers were optimistic about the expansion of the western European economies in the early years of the Industrial Revolution, economists from Adam Smith on were already pondering the limits of growth. For Smith, the only theoretical limit to expansion lay in the distant future—the eventual exhaustion of the world's natural resources. For David Ricardo, the finite supply of land was a more pressing problem: demand for land would drive rents up, thus diminishing returns on investment to the point at which no incentive to growth remained. But for Malthus, population growth was the main problem. In the late 1700s the threat of overpopulation and consequent starvation was already being realized in the slums of London, where the evidence of grinding poverty was highly visible. Malthus believed that population tended to expand at a geometric rate (2, 4, 8, 16, 32) while the food supply could only increase arithmetically (1, 2, 3, 4, 5). In *An Essay on the Principle of Population, as It Affects the Future Improvement of Society* (1798), Malthus argued that there were only two kinds of possible solutions. On the other hand, preventive remedies such as sexual abstinence, birth control, and vice (by which Parson Malthus meant practices like homosexuality) could lower the birthrate and thus control population. Although sexual restraint was his preferred choice, Malthus felt that this was an unlikely remedy, since he believed the lower classes were incapable of self-control. On the other hand, what Malthus called "positive" checks were bound to occur eventually: war, famine, plague, and, finally, starvation. If the people themselves did not lower the birthrate, natural forces would operate to raise the death rate. (This stress on the balance between resources and population was later seen in Charles Darwin's evolutionary theory of natural selection, which assumed that only the fittest members of a species would survive).

Malthus, like other classical economists, opposed state interference in the market. He regarded the effort of the British government to better the lives of the poor as particularly misguided. Malthus believed that interfering with the workings of the market simply prolonged and spread the agony by artificially supporting the surplus humanity which was the source of the problem. In a grim passage, he argued that a thoroughly consistent policy would encourage "the operation of nature in producing this mortality. . . . Instead of recommending cleanliness to the poor, we should encourage contrary habits. In our towns we should make the streets narrower, crowd more people into the houses, and court the return of the plague. In the country, we should build our villages near stagnant pools, and particularly encourage settlements in all marshy and unwholesome situations." Malthus did not actually propose that such steps be taken, but he was convinced that efforts to prevent the "natural" remedy of starvation were futile.

Another way in which Malthus questioned the limits of growth was in his formulation of the principle that competition among the ever-growing number of workers would always drive wages down to the subsistence level. He suggested that the economy was in danger of stagnating from underconsumption, because low wages would produce little consumer demand. John Maynard Keynes (see Chapter 10) later expanded upon this idea to explain how a depression might result in capitalist economies because of inadequate aggregate demand.

Malthus's dire warnings about population growth have been challenged most effectively by actual historical developments. Today population pressure remains a controversial problem both in the less developed countries (with high birth-rates and inadequate production of food and other basic survival necessities) and in industrial nations (with much lower birthrates but with extremely high levels of consumption of limited resources). What has changed is the assumption that little can be done to avoid the consequences Malthus predicted. Of course, he never considered the possibility that the practice of birth control would become so widespread. More importantly, he did not foresee that technological advances and economic restructuring would vastly increase a society's productive potential. It has become clear that the problems of population and food are not a matter of rigid geometric and arithmetic rates, and few people today would share Malthus's "dismal" judgment that we are entirely helpless to solve them.

money that became indirectly available for investment. The mechanism of the interest rate affected both savings and investment. The rate of saving was further determined by the level of income, and the rate of investment, of course, by the expected rate of profit. The interaction of these three factors—the rate of saving, the interest rate, and the rate of profit—can stimulate or retard economic growth. This led neoclassical economists to conclude that growth is a harmonious process in which workers and businesspeople equally share the benefits. The rate of growth, they contended, would remain steady. Whenever a temporary disequilibrium of the three factors occurred, it was automatically corrected through their interaction.

This model survived the disruptions of the First World War but was ultimately invalidated by the Great Crash of 1929 and the ensuing depression. Economists once again had to reassess their theories of growth.

Modern growth theory

John Maynard Keynes

In 1936, John Maynard Keynes published *The General Theory of Employment, Interest and Money*. The main objective of this book was to explain the conditions of prolonged unemployment that occurred during the Great Depression. According to neoclassical growth theory, the problem should have already cured itself. Keynes argued that consumers' propensity to save was affected primarily by their level of income, and not by the interest rate. Thus, if investment temporarily fell off and reduced income by causing unemployment, saving would decline, making funds for investment scarce. Investment, Keynes argued, is crucial for maintaining full employment; but there is no automatic mechanism that keeps saving and investment in equilibrium.

His prescription was to increase the role of government, which might stimulate investment through deficit financing. Once investment picked up again, employment would increase and so would aggregate demand. Therefore growth could resume. Government would then recoup its expenditures through increased tax revenues. Of course, there was no guarantee that another slowdown would not occur sooner or later, but with government intervention, such fluctuations could be minimized.

Post-Keynesians

Post-Keynesian economists such as Harrod and Domar tried to find a formula for growth that would describe a healthy and stable economy. Discounting the necessity of government action, they tried to determine the exact rate of investment that would result in both full employment and a level of income and saving that would not cause the investment rate to change. They introduced the concept of the **capital/output ratio,** which *holds that increases in output, and therefore in income, are a function of capital accumulation, or the investment rate.* In the United States, for instance, the ratio of capital investment to increases in output has traditionally been about 3; that is, to increase output (O) by $1, investment in new capital equipment (K) has had to rise by $3. In turn, the increased output means a higher national income, greater savings, and—to complete the cycle—increased investment.

Table 18.4 charts a hypothetical version of this process. (The role of government is ignored.) Column 2 gives the full-employment output, which, without government, equals national income; column 3 gives the investment rate, based on a propensity to save of 10 percent; and column 4 gives the resultant increase in output based on a capital/output ratio (K/O) of 3.

Output increases by a larger amount each year, as does investment, because our capacity to produce expands as we accumulate capital through investment. In absolute amounts, growth accelerates but the *rate* of growth remains the

Table 18.4
Simplified Keynesian growth model

(1) Year	(2) Full-employment output (national income)	(3) Saving-investment increase in capital (APS = .10)	(4) Increase in total output due to increase in capital (K/O ratio = 3/1)
1	$500.00	$50.00	$16.67
2	516.67	51.67	17.22
3	533.89	53.39	17.80
4	551.69	55.17	18.39
5	570.08	57.01	19.00

same. The annual rate of growth we observe in *Table 18.4* is 3.3 percent because each year we are increasing output by the amount of savings or investment in that period (which is 1/10 the year's national income) divided by the capital/output ratio (which is 3/1). We can therefore say that

$$\text{full-employment growth rate} = \frac{\text{average propensity to save}}{\text{capital-output ratio}}$$

or

$$\frac{.10}{3} = 3.3\%.$$

But what if instead of 3.3 percent the growth in the labor supply is 4 percent? The 3.3 percent growth in the economy would not be sufficient to ensure a high and stable standard of living. Similarly, if the growth in the supply of labor were less than 3.3 percent the rate of investment would be too great to allow a stable economy. These peculiar implications have been described as "the razor's edge."

Later these theories were expanded by Robert Solow to allow greater flexibility. Instead of a fixed capital-output ratio, the output of an economy was assumed to be related to the capital stock, the quantity of labor, and their relative proportions. With this more complete model additional insights into the growth process were obtained.

Although they are informative, these modern theories are deficient in several important respects. First, in each of these theories the supply of labor and the population are assumed to grow at a rate determined outside of the economic system. Labor economists are not finding this to be true. Instead, it has been shown that the decision to have children and the decision to participate in the work force are closely related to economic factors. Also, recent theories that assume a fixed relationship between inputs and output in the production process are suspect in discussions of economic growth. Since technology is constantly changing, so are production techniques and so too is reliance on certain natural and human resources.

COSTS OF ECONOMIC GROWTH

We have said that a society may choose the economic good of leisure over the economic good of increased output. Other factors may also dissuade a country from seeking economic growth. There are costs to economic development. Under certain circumstances these costs may offset the benefits of growth; moreover, the opportunity cost of growth may be more than people are willing to pay. A person who spends all her income on necessities finds that to afford some of the luxuries, she has to spend less today, even if it means hardship, to enjoy more tomorrow.

In part this is why a growing tide of serious opinion today holds that current growth in the United States is adequate or even too rapid. This view is based on the realization that growth requires sacrifices. Even if the benefits are greater than the costs, these benefits will only be realized in the long run, whereas the costs must be met now—and, opponents of rapid growth ask, Why should we work harder now so that a future generation will live more easily? Why should we work longer hours rather than enjoy our leisure time, just because labor shows up in production statistics and leisure does not?

Inflation, unemployment, and pollution
Opponents of a more rapid growth also see the specter of inflation around every corner—and with some justification. We found that full employment is a fundamental condition of fast growth. But we also know that consumer demand at full employment may exceed the supply of goods, resulting in upward pressure on prices.

Furthermore, unless effective training programs and improved education accompany rapid growth, structural unemployment may indeed increase. And even if it does not, growth critics assert that a certain amount of social dislocation is inevitable in a changing economy and that the hardships it entails are too high an opportunity cost to pay for in the additional units of output.

The threat to the environment through rapid increases in production is also a cost. Historically in the United States and other countries, industrialization has come at the expense of the environment; and this has usually been accepted as a necessary evil. But the recent swelling of the ranks of conservationists due to the severity of the ecological crisis is perhaps an indication that the United States has actually reached a stage where further growth may not be worth the cost. Some experts, however, contend that pollution control and economic growth are not mutually exclusive. They say that cleaning up and preserving the environment is not so much a macroeconomic problem as a microeconomic one, insofar as pollution control would represent added costs to businesses that are sources of pollution. In Chapter 33, we will take a closer look at these issues.

BENEFITS OF ECONOMIC GROWTH
There are also persuasive arguments in favor of increased economic growth. One benefit of economic growth is that it seems to be the most viable solution to poverty. Obviously, unless incomes are identical for everyone, there will always be some poor people. Yet if GNP per capita rises, even the poorest may have more goods and services at their disposal. Economic growth has the potential to reduce absolute levels of poverty.

A growing economy probably will also be more receptive to socially desirable goals like equal opportunity, environmental safety, and product safety. These programs were instituted during the relatively prosperous 1960s and resistence has developed only when economic growth has slowed in recent years.

Its long-run rate of growth is one important reason that the United States is regarded today as the most powerful nation in the world. Much of the prestige that the nation has traditionally enjoyed abroad is probably linked to its economic accomplishments. Yet in recent years, the growth rates of other countries—notably Japan and the Soviet Union—have surpassed that of the United States. Some politicians and economists say this situation cannot be allowed to continue too long or the American position of international dominance will be threatened. Of course, they are assuming that international dominance is a good thing—an assumption that is open to question.

Other social scientists say that apart from international considerations there are pressing domestic needs that cannot be met unless Americans raise national production and income. Millions of people still live below the official poverty level; some American cities are having serious financial and social problems; adequate education or medical care is still not available to all. The argument is that a redistribution of income is not enough to solve these problems. But if growth is stepped up, the added income generated could be channeled into these areas without taking anything away from anyone.

Achieving growth

What are the policies that might accomplish overall growth? First, the United States can strive to achieve full employment, for as long as there is unemployment, part of the reservoir of human capital will be wasted and output will be lost.

A more long-range policy for increasing growth would be to upgrade the quality of the labor force by instituting widespread training programs, by improving education, and by making improved education more widely available.

Capital formation

Benefits from an increase in the quality of the labor force, however, would be limited by the law of diminishing returns unless capital formation is also increased. To increase investment in a free market economy, however, is not always easy. The level of investment is directly linked to the level of aggregate demand, and the best way to stimulate investment is to stimulate demand. The government can help through tax cuts, increased government spending to purchase goods and services, and general increases in the money supply. It can also stimulate investment by lowering the cost of investment through tax credits and rebates—a step taken in 1975 to help the economy recover from recession.

It may sometimes be helpful to lower interest rates in order to stimulate investment. But the level of investment is often relatively unresponsive to the interest rate. Moreover, lowering interest rates has the side effect of reducing the incentive to save, which may reduce the funds available for investment. A more effective monetary approach is to increase the money supply. However, investment will not take place unless businesses are hopeful enough about the future to believe that the return from their investment will be greater than the amount spent to make the investment.

Technology

Another long-range policy for raising the United States growth rate is to increase expenditures on research and development, an area in which government contributions are already substantial. Research and development add to knowledge in general and to technological progress in particular. The benefits derived from a higher level of research activity are generally not realized quickly, but when the increasing contribution that improved technology has made to overall growth is considered, Americans can hardly afford to forgo efforts in that direction.

Although we have looked at the beneficial effects of American growth and the ways in which policy can be used to stimulate growth, we must constantly weigh the costs of growth—which are often difficult to measure—against the increases in GNP.

On balance, growth is probably desirable, particularly if the United States continues to be responsive to the costs that accompany growth. In the next chapter, we will examine one of the most prevalent problem areas in economic growth: the economic development of emerging nations.

Summary

■ This chapter summarizes the major theories of economic growth, how growth is measured, and some of the factors involved in the growth record of the United States economy.

■ The basic measure of growth is the change in real GNP, adjusted for inflation. GNP figures are adjusted for seasonal variations, and GNP in a given quarter of the year is best compared with the same quarter from previous years. The limitations on GNP as a measurement make simple country-to-country comparisons unreliable, and a better approach would emphasize the comparison of how many hours must be spent working in different societies in order to obtain the same goods.

■ Growth is determined by supply factors, demand factors, and noneconomic factors. Supply factors include human resources, natural resources, capital stock, and technology; increases in any of these factors may lead to an outward expansion of the production possibilities curve. Demand factors include the size of the market, the income level of consumers, and their tastes and needs. Noneconomic factors such as social organization may significantly increase or reduce the potential for growth.

■ In the United States, abundant natural resources have been a major factor contributing to the record of growth. Human resources in the United States in recent years have been affected by a later age of entry into the labor force, more education, higher participation of women and minorities, and a shorter work week. Technological advances, including economies of scale, account for a major share of the increase in output in the United States. Entrepreneurial activity continues to be important, despite the emergence of large, impersonal business structures.

■ Unless demand increases, increases in supply factors alone will not induce growth. Keynes argued that demand is key, since businesses will only expand supply if potential profits are in sight. But demand without supply, on the other hand, simply leads to inflation. Certain changes in supply factors, such as improvements in products, also tend to create demand, not simply respond to it.

■ Adam Smith saw the increasing division of labor as a stimulus to natural expansion of the economy which would continue until resources were exhausted. David Ricardo introduced the concept of diminishing returns, arguing that the addition of more and more labor to fixed land resources would lead to a slowdown of growth. Malthus claimed that population pressure would inevitably keep most of the population at or below a subsistence level. The neoclassical economists of the late nineteenth century emphasized the role of technology in making growth possible and saw both capital and labor benefiting from a harmonious growth process. Keynes argued that since there was no automatic equality of saving and investment, growth was not inevitable, and government stimulation would be necessary. Some post-Keynesian economists have seen increases in production as a function of increases in capital accumulation and in the investment rate.

■ Critics of unrestrained growth have pointed out that the opportunity costs may be excessively high, that rapid growth is likely to produce inflation and increased structural unemployment, and that further destruction of the natural environment is a serious danger.

■ The benefits of growth include a better potential for a solution to the problem of poverty, a better climate for the implementation of important social programs (in such areas as safety, environmental protection, and affirmative action), and increased international prestige. A long-range policy to encourage growth would include measures to reduce unemployment, promote manpower training, stimulate investment by stimulating demand, low interest rates, and encourage technological research and development.

Key Terms

economic growth   neoclassical school   capital/output ratio

Review & Discussion

1. What is meant by economic growth? Why is the measurement of growth something of a problem?

2. What are some of the factors that contribute to economic growth? What factors might impede growth?

3. Is the potential for growth in the United States limited primarily by supply factors, demand factors, or noneconomic factors? Why?

4. If you were a classical economist, would you be likely to attribute growth to increases in supply or increases in demand? Why? What changes in the economy of industrialized nations since the classical economists wrote have undermined their theories?

5. Describe some of the policies that would encourage a more rapid growth rate in an advanced capitalist economy.

6. What are the arguments made by critics of growth? Do you agree with these arguments? How can a balance be struck between the potential benefits of growth and the potential drawbacks?

Application 9:
Productivity:
What Does It Mean?

One important measure of a country's economic growth is labor productivity, usually referred to simply as productivity. It is a gauge of how well average workers are doing their jobs, whether they assemble cars in a factory, type letters in an office, or dig ditches. The more productive they are, the greater the real growth in an economy. When gains in the United States' productivity began to lessen in the 1970s, there was reason for concern, and the Council of Economic Advisers called the slowdown "one of the most significant economic problems of recent years."

Productivity is a measure of the hourly output of goods and services (called output per man-hour). Government statisticians obtain this index by dividing the real gross domestic product of the private sector of the economy by the total hours worked by all private employees.

Throughout the 1960s, productivity rose at a rate of about 3 percent a year. In the 1970s, however, the increases were only half as much, or less.

Changes in productivity are cyclical, because productivity reflects not only the efficiency of workers but also employment rates, the length of the work week, capital investment, and the utilization of manufacturing capacity, all of which fluctuate with the short-term ups and downs of an economy. However, a general trend can be seen by combining changes in productivity over a period of several years into an annual average rate. From 1948 to 1955, for example, labor productivity growth in the private United States economy averaged about 3.4 percent a year. The average dropped to 3.1 percent from 1955 to 1965, and to 2.3 percent from 1965 to 1973. During the next four years, however, the average increase in productivity was only 1 percent a year, and in 1978, the figure was 0.4 percent.

Declining productivity is a cause for concern because of its effect on a nation's standard of living. When each worker produces more goods or services, the wage increases for that worker can be spread out over a greater number of goods and manufacturers can recoup the added payroll cost without raising prices. Thus, assuming for the sake of simplicity that the worker is also a buyer of what he or she produces, the wage increases actually increase the quantity of goods or services that can be purchased. That is, a worker's standard of living, in real terms, rises. On the other hand, when productivity slackens, wage increases are more likely to be passed on to the consumer in the form of higher prices. And, while the dollar value of the worker's wages may be the same in both cases, much of the dollar increase in the latter instance is due to inflation and does not represent any genuine improvement in a worker's economic position.

To be sure, not all parts of the United States economy became less efficient in the 1970s. Productivity in aluminum rolling and drawing, for example, increased by an average of 7.1 percent from 1970 to 1975, and gains in the synthetic fiber, corn milling, and candy industries were even greater. But examples of diminished productivity are more numerous. Productivity is mining, for instance, fell at more than 6 percent annually from 1973 to 1977.

The explanations for the decline are as numerous as the examples of it. One explanation centers on broad social changes in the nation, such as the more casual attitude of younger workers toward their jobs, and the general movement from an industrial to a service economy. In addition, the number of experienced workers as a percentage of the labor force (the "experience level") declined as the children of the post–World War II baby boom and women entered the work force in increasing numbers.

Increasing governmental regulation is another important factor. According to one private study, compliance with environmental, health, and safety regulations may have cut productivity by as much as 0.3 percentage points from 1973 to 1978. Some economists also blame the decline in productivity on reductions in research and development by the nation's industries. In the mid-1960s, research and development amounted to 3 percent of Gross National Product; by the late 1970s, the level was down to nearly 2 percent, and much of what was going toward improvements on existing products instead of basic research into new methods of production or new products. At first, spending for basic research usually decreases productivity because research dollars contribute to the cost of doing business without immediately raising output. But in the long run, the most significant gains in productivity have come from breakthroughs in manufacturing technology and processes. Thus, many people believe that because research spending has been reduced, the number of such breakthroughs has declined, which has led in turn, to lower productivity gains.

Another factor that some economists believe has contributed to decreased productivity is the effects of union practices such as strikes, rigid rules that restrict worker productivity, and high wages that are not linked to productivity. In addition, a shorter work week and longer vacations for some American workers, and the problem of old or worn out capital equipment are other possible contributors to decreased production.

Overall, the Council of Economic Advisers predicted that the annual gains in productivity until the early 1980s would average only 1.5 percent, considerably below the nation's traditional level, and that this rate would significantly affect American growth.

Questions for discussion

☐ In mining, productivity fell from average annual gains of 4.3 percent in the 1950s and early 1960s to 6 percent annual losses in the 1970s, about the time that strict mine-safety laws began to take effect. In addition, at about the same time, mining companies engaged in strip mining were required to protect and restore the environment by returning the land to close to its original condition when mining was finished. Discuss the ways in which concern over productivity statistics may ignore benefits that cannot easily be measured, such as the so-called quality of life.

☐ What steps could be taken to improve productivity in the United States?

☐ While productivity in the United States has been slowing, productivity in German and Japanese industries has been rising sharply. What effect might the different rates of productivity have on the standard of living in those countries? On their growth rates?

Chapter 19

Economic Growth in Less Developed Countries

What to look for in this chapter

What are the patterns and problems of economic growth in less developed countries?

What are the common characteristics of less developed countries?

What are the major barriers to growth in the less developed countries?

What are some of the paths toward development taken by these countries? What are the drawbacks of these approaches to development?

A major concern of many economists is with growth of income and output in countries of the world which are poor—as judged by the income and standards of living in other, predominantly Western nations. A related concern is with economic development in these and other countries. As we pointed out in Chapter 18, economic growth occurs when the production (GNP) of a country increases over time at a rate in excess of population growth. **Economic development** *takes place when economic growth is accompanied by favorable changes in the economic and social structure and institutions of a country such that continuing economic growth is not only possible but also encouraged.*

The United States has promoted economic growth for many decades, with the result that it has a very high level of per capita GNP—one of the highest in the world. Yet today its growth rate is only moderate. A comparison of international

Table 19.1
Per capita GNP, 1972, and average annual growth rate, 1965–1972, for countries with populations of 1 million or more

Country	Per capita GNP Amount (U.S. $)	Growth rate (%)	Country	Per capita GNP Amount (U.S. $)	Growth rate (%)	Country	Per capita GNP Amount (U.S. $)	Growth rate (%)
United States	5,590	2.0	Czechoslovakia[1]	2,180	4.5	Trinidad and Tobago	970	3.6
Sweden	4,480	2.5	German Dem. Rep.[1]	2,100	3.5	Panama	880	4.5
Canada	4,440	3.2	Puerto Rico	2,050	5.7	South Africa	850	2.1
Switzerland	3,940	2.9	Italy	1,960	4.3	Romania[1]	810	6.7
Denmark	3,670	3.7	Libyan Arab Rep.	1,830	8.1	Yugoslavia	810	5.5
France	3,620	4.8	Ireland	1,580	3.7	Jamaica	810	3.9
Germany, Fed. Rep. of	3,390	4.1	USSR[1]	1,530	5.9	Chile	800	2.2
Norway	3,340	3.8	Hungary	1,520	4.2	Portugal	780	5.3
Belgium	3,210	4.6	Poland[1]	1,500	4.0	Uruguay	760	0.4
Australia	2,980	3.1	Greece	1,460	7.3	Mexico	750	2.8
Netherlands	2,840	4.3	Bulgaria[1]	1,420	5.9	Lebanon	700	1.4
Finland	2,810	4.9	Singapore	1,300	10.3	Costa Rica	630	4.1
Israel	2,610	7.1	Argentina	1,290	2.8	Saudi Arabia[2]	550	6.8
United Kingdom	2,600	2.0	Venezuela	1,240	1.1	Brazil	530	5.6
New Zealand	2,560	1.8	Spain	1,210	5.0	Albania[1]	530	5.7
Austria	2,410	5.0	Hong Kong	980	5.7	Peru	520	1.1
Japan	2,320	9.7				China, Rep. of	490	6.9
						Iran	490	7.2

Source: World Bank, *World Bank Atlas*, 1974.
[1] Estimates of GNP for centrally planned (Communist) economies may differ widely because of problems involved in deriving GNP at market prices from net material cost and converting into U.S. dollars.
[2] Estimates of GNP per capita and growth rate.

statistics on rates of economic growth (see *Table 19.1*) shows that many countries whose economies are in a low state of development actually have faster growth rates than United States. Statistics like these indicate, and common sense confirms that in the future, economic growth will be more marked in less developed countries than in countries with relatively highly developed economies. This stands to reason, since we could expect that less developed countries would have smaller current output and more unsatisfied wants. Thus they have a stronger incentive to increase their output

Table 19.1
(continued)

Country	Per capita GNP Amount (U.S. $)	Growth rate (%)	Country	Per capita GNP Amount (U.S. $)	Growth rate (%)	Country	Per capita GNP Amount (U.S. $)	Growth rate (%)
Dominican Rep.	480	5.0	Papua New Guinea	290	7.5	Khmer Rep.[2]	120	−3.8
Nicaragua	470	1.5	Jordan	270	−2.8	Sudan[2]	120	−1.1
Cuba[1]	450	−1.0	Morocco	270	3.0	Tanzania	120	2.9
Malaysia	430	2.9	Senegal	260	−0.7	India	110	1.4
Algeria	430	3.5	Liberia	250	4.0	Dahomey	110	1.7
Guatemala	420	2.2	Egypt, Arab Rep. of	240	0.6	Sri Lanka	110	2.0
Colombia	400	2.4	Philippines	220	2.4	Viet-Nam, Dem. Rep. of[1]	110	−0.1
Angola	390	5.5	Thailand	220	4.2	Zaire[2]	100	3.9
Mongolia[1]	380	0.6	Cameroon	200	3.8	Yemen, People's Dem. Rep. of	100	−7.2
Zambia	380	−0.1	Bolivia	200	1.4	Malawi	100	2.9
Tunisia	380	3.7	Sierra Leone	190	1.8	Niger	90	−5.1
Iraq	370	1.8	Mauritania	180	2.0	Indonesia	90	4.3
Turkey	370	4.3	Viet-Nam, Rep. of	170	−0.7	Yemen Arab Rep.[2]	90	2.4
Ecuador	360	3.8	China, People's Rep. of[1]	170	2.6	Burma	90	1.0
El Salvador	340	1.2	Kenya	170	4.1	Guinea	90	−0.3
Ivory Coast	340	4.1	Togo	160	3.3	Chad	80	1.6
Rhodesia	340	2.9	Central African Rep.	160	2.3	Ethiopia	80	1.2
Korea, Dem. Rep. of[1]	320	4.0	Uganda	150	2.0	Nepal	80	0.1
Honduras	320	1.7	Malagasy Rep.	140	1.4	Afghanistan[2]	80	0.8
Paraguay	320	2.1	Nigeria	130	5.4	Somalia[2]	80	1.1
Syrian Arab Rep.	320	3.8	Pakistan	130	1.7	Mali	80	1.3
Korea, Rep. of	310	8.5	Laos[2]	130	3.1	Upper Volta	70	0.6
Mozambique	300	5.6	Haiti	130	1.3	Burundi[2]	70	1.1
Ghana	300	1.0				Bangladesh	70	−1.6
Congo, People's Rep. of	300	1.4				Rwanda[2]	60	2.1

above current levels than do the more developed countries, and the gains they make will be noticeable.

At one time, it was assumed by both economists and politicians that the process of economic growth and development would be much the same wherever it occurred. Thus the pattern of economic growth that was successful in the United States and Western Europe was prescribed for all less developed nations. Since 1945, however, a whole branch of economic study that focuses on economic growth and development of poor nations has arisen. It is now understood that these countries have special problems with regard to economic growth, and that the problems differ from country to country. There is no single path to economic development and growth; they may be achieved in a variety of ways, depending on existing conditions within each country. Some conditions, such as the recent turmoil in Iran, may make economic growth and development difficult or impossible to achieve.

In this chapter, we will identify the characteristics which are shared by the less developed countries, look at the most common barriers to economic growth that they face, and consider some solutions which may help surmount the barriers.

DEFINING "LESS DEVELOPED" COUNTRY

The label "less developed" is used by economists and others to designate the poor countries of the world. While experts disagree on precisely which countries of the world are poor, statistics reveal that most of the people living in Africa, Asia, and Latin America have incomes and standards of living which are incredibly low when compared with those of people living in the United States and Western Europe. If we define a poor or less developed country as one with a per capita GNP of 10 percent or less than that in the United States, nearly 100 countries meet this definition of poor (see *Table 19.1*).

The group of less developed countries is large and diverse. Nonetheless, in addition to poverty, they share many other characteristics.

☐ In most poor nations, a large fraction of the population lives in rural areas and engages in small-scale, subsistence-level agriculture. Typically, little capital is available to workers in the agricultural sector and traditional rather than modern farming methods are used.

☐ For a variety of cultural and economic reasons, population growth in most developing countries remains unchecked. In many ways this is one of the most serious problems faced by the less developed countries, since even when overall output and income increase, per capita GNP grows slowly if at all.

☐ To a large extent, the population in poor countries has had little formal schooling. Opportunities for the young to acquire education, vocational training, or even literacy are limited to the upper, wealthy, and landed social classes.

☐ Political and economic power in these countries is concentrated in the hands of the wealthy; military power and authoritarian rule tend to go hand in hand in determining the political and economic fate of the population.

☐ Many of the less developed countries have only rudimentary industry, and attempts to expand industrial production and output are thwarted by a limited capability for generating savings and by meager amounts of physical and human capital.

☐ Since domestic production capabilities are often limited, most manufactured goods must be imported. This may result in balance-of-payments problems, since the amount of foreign exchange available for purchase of exports is often limited.

☐ Production for export is often limited to one or two primary commodities whose prices may fluctuate considerably based upon changing world conditions of demand and supply.

☐ Since production for export frequently is foreign owned or controlled, the influence of multinational corporations and big business on domestic policy may be substantial and may result in political decisions which fail to reflect the true needs of the native population, particularly those pertaining to economic growth.

While the foregoing discussion provides some notion of how a less developed country might appear to outsiders, the differences between less developed countries are dramatic. Some nations, such as Brazil and India, cover vast land areas; other poor nations in Africa and Oceania are tiny by comparison. Population pressures vary enormously. Among the less developed countries are densely populated nations such as China and India and those with little population pressure on the land such as Chile and the sparsely settled nations in central Africa. Some of these countries have few resources and little arable land while other countries, such as those in the Middle East, have vast amounts of only one resource (oil) that may be exploited.

In short, there is no typical less developed country. More important, there is no single strategy or prescription for development that is universally applicable. Although this is now well recognized by those concerned with assisting the less developed countries, as recently as 20 years ago it was not. As a result of both limited success and frequent frustrations encountered in trying to apply simple models and theories of development to countries with vastly different political institutions, cultural traditions, and resource endowments, there has been a gradual recognition that finding the key to development is as much an art as it is a science. Only as we have become more informed about the true dimensions of the problems faced by the less developed countries have we recognized the extent of our ignorance and how little we actually know about finding the keys to success for any country to achieve economic growth.

BARRIERS TO ECONOMIC DEVELOPMENT

Low stock of human capital

Although the specific problems that hinder economic development vary from country to country, economists have identified certain barriers to growth that are common to many less developed nations. Chief among these is a low stock of human capital.

As we have pointed out, some of the world's less developed countries are underpopulated, so it is not surprising that these nations would lack adequate human capital. But it is also true that even the nations that are overpopulated often suffer from a shortage of human capital. Let us analyze the causes of this shortage and what it means to an economy.

Low level of education

A major cause is low level of education that generally prevails. In many countries, the average worker can neither read nor write; *Fig. 19.1* shows the correlation between the percent of the population that is literate and per capita GNP in a selected group of countries. Illiteracy is closely identified with low productivity of workers, and the problem is especially acute if the less developed country attempts to adopt advanced technology, which demands a higher level of skilled labor than the country possesses.

Lack of managerial skill

Less developed countries are likely to lack the human capital resources to fill specific managerial and entrepreneurial positions. This is due not only to the relatively low level of education, but also the limited opportunities for on-the-job training and experience. In highly developed economies, such as those of the United States or West Germany, large corporations are willing to spend considerable sums for the recruiting and training of executives who will one day fill the top-level managerial positions. In less developed economies, few if any firms can afford to make that sort of long-range investment in the development of human capital. Often the major industries are run by foreign-owned firms. These firms provide many jobs for native workers, but their executives are frequently European or American, and there is little or no provision for teaching managerial skills to native employees.

Health problems

Health problems also contribute to low stocks of human capital. Although the population may be large, many of the people may not be physically able to perform sustained labor. Often the reason

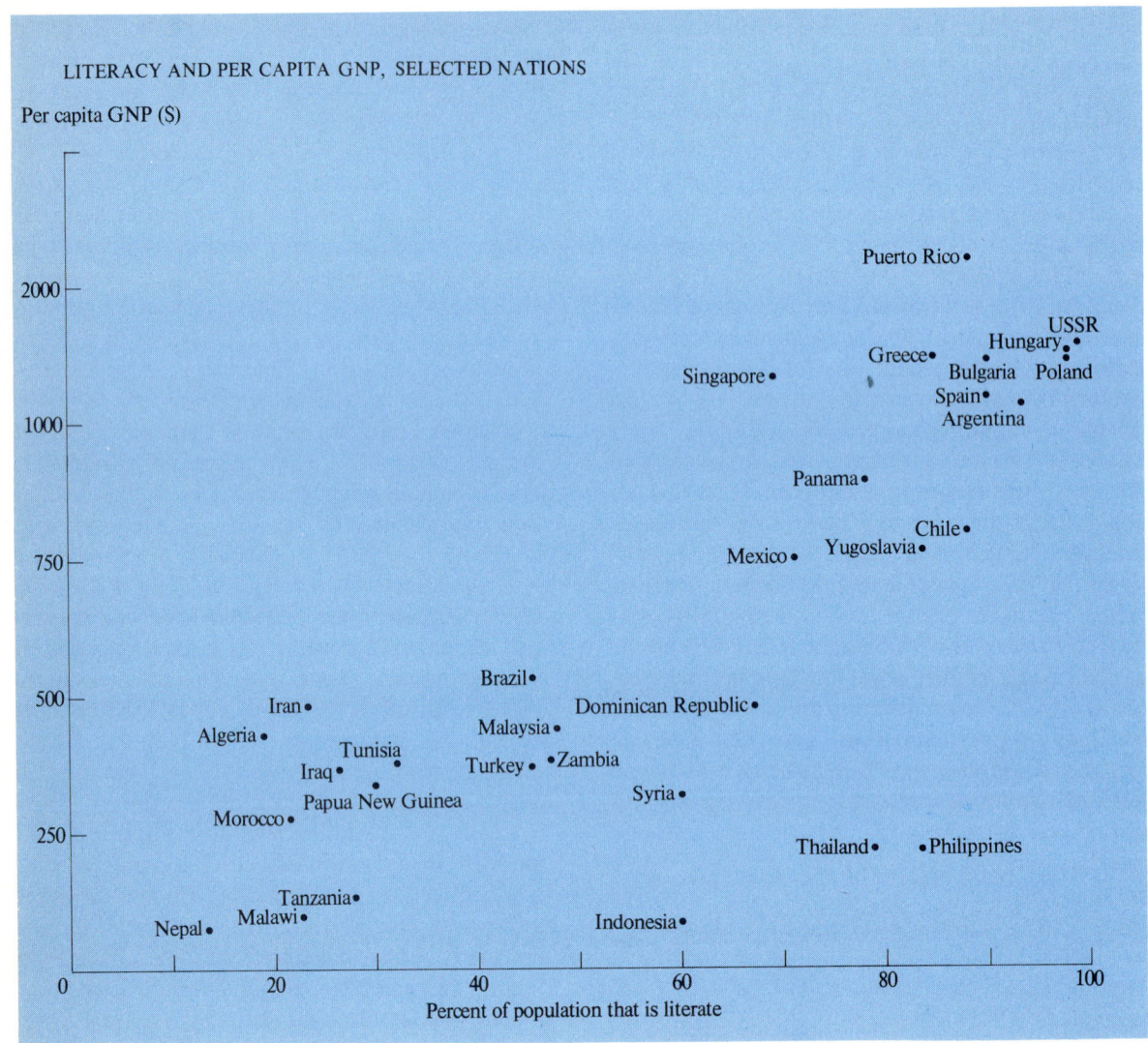

Fig. 19.1
The correlation between high literacy rates and per capita GNP is fairly close.

is inadequate diet. Either people do not get enough to eat or what they do eat is lacking in necessary proteins, minerals, and vitamins. For example, most Asian nations produce enough rice to keep people from going hungry, but a diet of rice alone is not sufficient to provide all the necessary nutrition.

What much of the less developed world faces is a double-headed specter, famine and chronic malnutrition. The Food and Agriculture Organization (FAO) estimates that 61 out of 97 developing nations produced or imported substantially less food in 1970 than was necessary to feed their populations. In 1972, world cereal production fell for the first time in two decades, as bad weather hit Africa, Australia, China, India, the Soviet Union and Southeast Asia all at once.

The FAO estimates conservatively that 460 million people suffer from malnutrition, with its symptoms of bad teeth and stunted growth and its diseases of rickets and beriberi. A drop in United States agricultural production in 1974 and sharp rises in fuel and fertilizer prices further aggravated the world hunger crisis and the problems of less developed countries.

Many less developed countries also lack adequate sanitation systems. Raw sewage runs through cities of India, the Middle East, and North Africa in open trenches and some of the latrines in Latin American villages drain into the local water supply. Doctors and hospitals are scarce, so that many serious cases of disease are never treated. Infant mortality rates are high, epidemics are frequent, and life expectancy is short. (*Table 19.2* shows some indicators of health conditions in selected nations.) All this means that many workers are often too ill to be productive, or must spend working hours caring for sick relatives or burying the dead.

Low accumulation of physical capital

Another major barrier to growth for many less developed nations is a relatively small stock of physical capital (such as productive machinery). Indeed, some economists define a less developed nation as one in which the ratio of capital to other resources is low.

Inability to save

The principal reason for the very low rate of capital formation in less developed countries is that there are few people who are capable of saving. Like low-income households in the United States, households in less developed countries spend most of their income on basic needs. They need to spend because their incomes are not large enough to provide even basic necessities, and they want to spend because they want to achieve a standard of living comparable to that of wealthier people in their own country or elsewhere. Thus the problem of a low level of capital accumulation seems circular: a very small stock of capital means low output per worker, which in turn means low per capita incomes, low rates of saving, and little possibility for capital investment in the future.

Of course, a small percentage of the population is able to save. Less developed nations characteristically display a highly unequal income distribution. A few households have multimillion-dollar incomes, even though the average household income is very low. It is clear that the high-income households can afford to save, and judging by the data on saving in the United States, we would expect these households to show a very high average propensity to save. Yet the savings of these high-income households are usually not made available as investment capital within the less developed country.

Limited investment opportunities

The reason that those with savings do not make this money available to local businesses is that investment opportunities are generally limited and profit rates tend to be low. There are many causes of this lack of investment incentive. One is that the low level of per capita incomes means that there are few potential consumers for manufactured goods within the country itself. If goods are exported, firms must compete with large corporations in highly industrialized nations, and the chances of success are very low. Imagine how difficult it would be for a new firm in Pakistan or Ghana to compete in the international car market with Volkswagen, Toyota, or Ford!

Another obstacle to investment is the instability of the government and the social structure. Nations that are developing economically are also developing politically and socially, and many

Table 19.2
Some indicators of health conditions, selected nations

Country	Expectation of life at birth (years)[1]	Thousands of inhabitants per physician[2]	Percentage average dietary energy supply requirements available[3]	Country	Expectation of life at birth (years)[1]	Thousands of inhabitants per physician[2]	Percentage average dietary energy supply requirements available[3]
Less developed countries				Less developed countries			
Western Hemisphere				Asia			
Bolivia	50–55	2.3	79	Burma	48	9.0	102
Chile	60–66	2.0	109	India	42–41	4.8	94
El Salvador	57–60	4.0	84	Indonesia	48–48	27.6	83
Haiti	45	13.2	77	Pakistan	54–49	3.8	93
Nicaragua	50	2.0	109	Saudi Arabia	42	10.1	94
Panama	58–61	1.6	112				
Peru	53–55	1.9	99	Developed countries			
Africa							
Algeria	51	7.9	72				
Chad	29–35	62.9	89	Canada	69–75	0.7	129
Ethiopia	39	74.6	93	England and			
Ghana	46	13.0	101	Wales	68–74	0.8	126
Guinea	25–28	49.7	88	France	69–76	0.8	127
Ivory Coast	41	12.1	105	Germany			
Kenya	50–51	7.8	102	(West)	67–72	0.6	121
Liberia	46–44	10.5	94	Japan	70–74	0.9	107
Morocco	51	13.3	92	Sweden	72–77	0.7	104
Nigeria	56–62	20.5	96	United States	67–75	0.6	126
Rwanda	41	57.9	84	USSR	70	0.4	131
Tanzania	40–41	21.6	98				

Source: United Nations, *Demographic Yearbook 1974;* World Health Organization, *World Health Statistics Annual 1970; United Nations Assessment of the World Food Situation, Present and Future,* Item 8 of the Provisional Agenda, United Nations World Food Conference, Rome, November 5–16, 1974.
[1]Estimates based on mortality experience in various segments of the 1960s and 1970s. Age for males on left, females on right.
[2]Estimates for period around 1970. Figures rounded.
[3]The dietary energy supply requirements for 1969–1971 are based on the average requirement of a moderately active reference man whose body weight is supposedly the prevailing norm for the particular region.

COUNTRIES WITH THE TEN LOWEST PER CAPITA INCOMES (1976)* Current United States dollars	
1. Bhutan	$ 80
2. Laotian People's Democratic Republic Bangladesh	90
3. Mali Ethiopia Upper Volta	100
4. Nepal Somalia	110
5. Rhwanda Chad Burundi Burma	120
6. Zaire Malawi	130
7. India	140
8. Mozambique Niger	150
9. Vietnam	160
10. Benin Afghanistan Tanzania Pakistan	180

*Only countries with a population of 1 million or more are included.

COUNTRIES WITH THE TEN HIGHEST PER CAPITA INCOMES (1976)*	Current United States dollars
1. Kuwait	$13,960
2. Switzerland	9,160
3. Sweden	9,030
4. Canada	7,930
5. United States	7,880
6. Norway	7,800
7. Denmark	7,690
8. West Germany	7,510
9. Belgium	7,020
10. Australia	6,990

*Only countries with a population of 1 million or more are included.
Source: 1978 World Bank Atlas.

changes may result. Industries may be nationalized, tax rates raised abruptly, and workers drafted for new government public projects of high priority. As we noted in Chapter 10, investment takes place only when potential investors have confidence in the future of the enterprise, and that confidence is very often lacking in less developed nations.

Limitation of investment opportunity is also due to the lack of trained and experienced entrepreneurs who are willing to take the risk of starting new businesses. Joseph Schumpeter identified entrepreneurial willingness to take the risk of business investment as the most essential incentive to investment, and this incentive is almost entirely absent in many less developed countries.

Problems of using advanced technology

A high level of technological research and development is a luxury that only highly developed economies can afford. Training and equipping technologists requires a heavy investment in both time and money that most less developed nations cannot afford. Typically, these countries use inefficient production processes and turn out goods that are generally less desirable to consumers than the goods produced by more advanced technologies.

Expense of using technology

To develop technological knowledge is expensive, but the fact that a developing nation cannot produce its own technology domestically is not an insurmountable barrier. Discoveries made in some countries can be passed along to other countries. Patents can be rented, trained technicians can be hired, and production processes used in advanced nations can be adopted.

However, using technology is expensive. It often calls for sophisticated and complex machines, such as computers and lasers, and these in turn call for specially designed plants. The cost of providing these technological devices and their accessories is very high. The price of oil to run equipment has also risen dramatically in recent years, and this increase presents a large burden to less developed countries that have to import fuel. Only a very large volume of production and sales can make their investment in technology profitable. Therefore, much of the technology of developed economies is not suited for less developed nations because it is meant to solve problems that these economies have not yet encountered.

Lack of skilled work force

Another problem that arises in the use of advanced technology by less developed countries is that it requires a work force with a relatively high level of training and skill. It may be inefficient to dig a building foundation by manual labor because it takes so many hours of hard work, but an able-bodied person can learn to use a shovel in a few minutes. A bulldozer may be a much more efficient tool, but it takes weeks to learn how to operate, repair, and maintain it. In addition, the training will probably take even longer and be more costly if the workers are illiterate and cannot read printed instruction manuals. Most less developed nations lack the necessary human capital to use advanced technology.

Lack of supporting infrastructure

In order to function efficiently, developed economies require an **infrastructure**—*a stock of public goods necessary to facilitate modern production*. For example, different firms need to be able to communicate with one another, so there must be telephone service and a quick and reliable postal service. Raw materials, partly finished goods, and final goods must be transported, so there must be a network of highways that are kept in good repair. For the sake of convenient exchange transactions, there must be some kind of banking system in which the people have confidence and there must be a portable and widely accepted medium of exchange.

In a country such as the United States, where there is a sophisticated highway system, it is difficult for Americans to remember that in many nations transportation systems are an expensive luxury. In Colombia and Peru, for example, few roads are paved, and even those are often made impassable by floods in the spring, snow in the winter, and rock slides from the mountains in all seasons.

Most less developed countries also lack other kinds of public goods as well. Public health facilities may be inadequate or absent altogether, power facilities may be limited, and communications systems may be lacking. This lack of public goods makes extensive industrialization virtually impossible.

The United Nations estimates that advanced nations in Western Europe allocate about 50 percent of investment capital for public goods, such as housing, public utilities, and various public works programs. This level of public investment is required simply to maintain an already large amount of public capital. The investment required of less developed nations that must accumulate this capital would be even higher. And of course, in nations with relatively low annual GNP, such an investment would carry a high opportunity cost.

Cultural and social attitudes

Cultural and social attitudes play an important role in motivating people to do certain kinds of work and to accept certain working conditions. But in many developing countries, basic social and cultural values are not really compatible with the actions and attitudes that seem to be demanded by an advanced economy. A highly developed economy must be future-oriented; it must be based on impersonal relationships between buyers and sellers in the various markets. These requirements may be in direct conflict with existing values, and people are therefore faced with a difficult choice between the old way of doing things and the new.

A few examples will help to illustrate the problems sometimes posed by cultural and social attitudes. In the Moslem countries of North Africa and the Middle East, the religious duties and obligations of workers limit the number of hours they can work. For example, during the 28-day month of Ramadan, Moslems fast all day and are too tired and hungry to work with any degree of efficiency in the afternoons. In the same countries, the social conventions that keep women secluded at home also serve to keep them out of the labor force, thus restricting available labor resources. In Thailand, Burma, and even the advanced economy of Japan, social traditions of the ancient feudal system still influence the relationship between employee and employer. One of the only acceptable grounds for firing a worker is disloyalty, and it is very rare for workers to switch jobs voluntarily, even when they are offered better positions or more pay.

The desire of developing nations to gain international prestige and to play a role in world power politics beyond their national security requirements can create questionable development priorities at times. A number of observers have pointed to poverty-stricken India's expenditures on the nuclear device they exploded in 1974 as an example of such a questionable priority.

Another social phenomenon detrimental to economic growth and development is bribery and other forms of political corruption which may be found in many less developed nations. Of course, as people in the United States have become increasingly aware, political corruption is by no means limited to Africa, Asia, and Latin America. But in those areas, its impact seems more devastating than when it occurs elsewhere.

Economic imperialism

Millions of people throughout Asia, Africa, and Latin America resent **economic imperialism,** which is *the overt or implicit control over the territory, resources, or destiny of a nation by foreigners.* Some people regard this as the greatest barrier to social and economic development. In their view, imperialism distorts development by subordinating the country's interests to those of North American or European businesses in their quest for profit. Activities that some regard as imperialistic may be undertaken for foreign governments concerned with assuring an uninterrupted flow of various resources such as petroleum or copper, or wishing to influence political affairs and attitudes for reasons of national security or ideology.

Among possible distortions of development, we have already mentioned the failure to provide managerial training for native employees and the making of illicit payments to public officials. Imperialism, thus, is seen as a force that makes problems of low stock of capital (human and physical), lack of advanced technology, and supporting infrastructure more severe than they otherwise would be, as well as promoting harmful cultural and social attitudes. Those supporting this antiimperialist critique point out that when corporations of a developed nation, particularly the United States, invest heavily in a less developed country, they may seek to influence political decisions, especially when their interests are threatened by policies which may result in **nationalization**. *Nationalization occurs when a government assumes control (and ownership) of a firm which previously was privately owned.* The previous owners may or may not be compensated for their loss when nationalization occurs.

Chile: A case in point

A frequently cited example of the operations of imperialism occurred in Chile during the early 1970s. When newly elected President Allende, heading a Socialist and Communist coalition, moved to nationalize the holdings of a number of American corporations, he cited evidence that top officials of the International Telephone and Telegraph Corporation had urged government intervention in Chilean affairs to prevent Allende's coming to power. United States officials denied acting on these and other ITT proposals that came to light later, but lines of credit to Chile were cut by United States private banks and by international banks in which United States influence is strong.

Economic chaos engulfed Chile, and President Allende died in a military coup that overthrew his government in 1973. Shortly afterward a number of large United States corporations (including ITT) whose properties had been seized, indicated willingness to resume operations in Chile if the new government proved receptive. Holdings of the corporations were denationalized, and credit lines were restored to Chile. In 1974, the head of the Central Intelligence Agency, testifying before a congressional committee, denied United States involvement in the 1973 coup but acknowledged that his agency had expended more than $8 million in covert "destabilization" activities in Chile between 1970 and 1973.

The other side of the argument, however, is that the nations in which the foreign investment is made *do* benefit. People are employed, taxes are received, goods are available. Surely the foreign investor gains also. It is very difficult to argue that in the absence of foreign investment, the less developed nations could have been as well off economically.

PATHS OF ECONOMIC DEVELOPMENT

Nations that decide to undertake a program of economic development face many problems, some of which we have outlined in the preceding section of this chapter. Because the problems vary so widely, there are no across-the-board solutions. Generally, development programs in less developed nations have been aimed at accumulating either human or financial capital, since these factors are usually more limited than land resources.

Developing human capital

Education

Education is the chief means of developing human capital. Nations can invest in the long-range development of their country by establishing a system of public schools that provide free education for all children. This solution is not so simple as it sounds, since the cost of building, equipping, and operating the schools will be large, and the existing shortage of human capital may make it very difficult to find teachers. A more compelling problem is that people may be taken away from traditional tasks, which means that the opportunity cost of attending school may be less production. Also funds invested in education take away resources that might be used for other purposes, clearly an economic trade-off.

Although most developing nations are establishing public school systems, they also allocate a significant portion of available resources to a variety of short-run human capital development programs. Either the government or private business

> **RECAP**
>
> Less developed nations that seek to undertake a program of economic development generally face a number of problems, including the following:
>
> - low stock of human capital (education, managerial skill, health)
> - low accumulation of capital (few investors and little investment opportunity)
> - lack of advanced technology
> - lack of a supporting infrastructure
> - unfavorable cultural or social attitudes
> - economic imperialism
>
> Development programs generally seek to build up human or financial capital. In addition to domestic programs for acquiring investment funds, aid from foreign sources is a significant factor in helping less developed nations in their quest for economic growth.

firms may set up classes to teach already-employed workers the basic skills of reading and writing. In India, Taiwan, and Mozambique, the government will pay travel expenses and tuition for any student who is accepted at a foreign university—on the condition that once the student obtains a degree, he or she will return to work for the government for a stipulated number of years. When oil was discovered in Venezuela's Lake Maracaibo, the government required foreign oil companies that participated in the profitable development of the deposits to recruit, train, and hire Venezuelans for all phases of construction and operation.

Improved health

Another way to develop human capital is through programs to improve workers' health. Citizens may be offered free vaccinations and inoculations; public clinics may provide basic health care as well as health education; the government or United Nations agencies may distribute free seeds for new varieties of grain with higher protein content. Birth-control programs are also a method of developing human capital. If effective contraceptives are easily available and socially approved, parents can limit the size of their families. Thus, although there may be a decrease in numbers of people in the total work force, there may also be a significant increase in the quality of the work force, since by having fewer children parents will be better able to provide for them. This likelihood is supported by the fact that in advanced economies, such as the United States, it has been shown that families with fewer children also tend to be those with higher incomes.

Moreover, if population growth is limited, per capita increase in GNP will be more rapid. *Figure 19.2* shows how much of the average annual growth in low-income countries is offset by a relatively rapid growth in population. These comparisons for 47 developing and 22 developed noncommunist countries indicate that the average annual rate of growth of GNP is similar in less developed and developed countries. The significant difference is that developed countries tend to have a much lower rate of population growth, and therefore they have a larger rate of per capita GNP growth. In less developed countries, the population increase offsets the gains in total GNP.

Accumulating capital goods

Most developing nations concentrate their efforts on the accumulation of capital goods which are likely to be the scarcest of available input resources. Capital goods have the advantage of yielding a quick return compared to the return from developing human capital. A factory may be

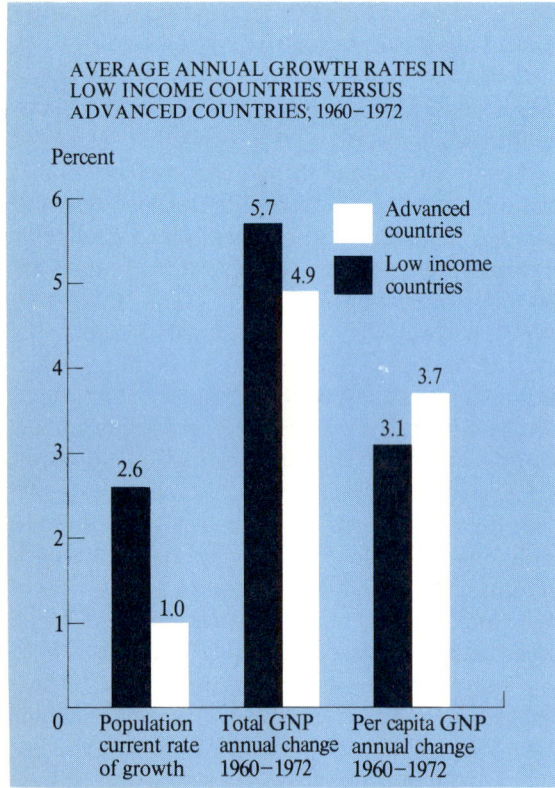

Fig. 19.2
Average annual growth rates in low income countries versus advanced countries, 1960–1972.

built and producing at full capacity in a relatively short period of time. Capital goods are also visible symbols of progress. People can watch the factory being constructed, they can see the machines at work, and they are reassured that their country is indeed advancing toward industrialization. If less developed countries choose to invest in impressive projects—steel mills, automobile factories, airlines—the impact may be smaller than if funds were used in areas which are physically less impressive but have a greater payoff in terms of economic growth.

Encouraging investment
To encourage domestic investment by those households with incomes large enough to permit saving, the government may adopt a variety of taxes and regulations. It is common practice to tax dividends from foreign firms at a higher rate than those from companies at home. Governments may also try to regulate the amount of money that people can take out of the country, so as to make large-scale foreign investment very difficult. Unfortunately, these measures are usually not very effective because the people at whom such policies are aimed have the resources to evade the regulations. They may keep their money in Swiss bank accounts, where their native governments can neither regulate their investments nor tax their incomes. These people will invest in businesses at home only when it becomes profitable to do so.

As noted earlier, most households in less developed nations cannot afford to save. Since total GNP is low, the government's tax base is small and its revenues are characteristically limited, so it does not have the means to make extensive investments in public goods or to stimulate investment in private goods through preferential taxation. However, one means of capital accumulation is still open. If a community wants to have a clinic, it does not necessarily have to raise the funds to have a contractor come in and build it; the members of the community can build it themselves. The same is true of factories, roads, and many other public and private goods. This method of accumulating capital is quite common in communist-governed countries, where the labor can simply be allocated for such purposes by the government, but it can also be adapted to the free-enterprise system. Those who invest their labor to help accumulate private capital could receive some share of corporate ownership; those who help build the social infrastructure could be given tax credits. Of course, this solution will not work for all kinds of needed capital goods; villagers cannot build a tractor or a computer. But this system of paying taxes in kind rather than in money can greatly reduce the amount of financial capital that the nation needs to begin its industrialization.

Foreign aid

An alternative to acquiring investment funds domestically is to borrow from foreign sources. More highly developed countries and many private, national, and international organizations are willing to invest or provide funds and equipment to assist developing countries in their quest for economic growth. In addition to loans, grants, and capital goods, other types of foreign aid include technical assistance, commodities, foodstuffs, and weapons. This variety of types and sources is complemented by a wide array of motives by the donors who provide aid. Because of its complexity, the subject of foreign aid is highly controversial. In this section, we take a closer look at that controversy and its origins.

An historical perspective

Historically, nations have borrowed from one another and from private sources to finance investment projects. With the breakdown of organized capital markets during the depression of the 1930s, however, the amount of money available from private sources dwindled to a trickle and the more highly developed countries, with massive internal financial problems, had few resources from which to make assistance available to others.

Various forms of military aid emerged during World War II, but the array of programs and sources of aid now available to the less developed countries did not materialize until after World War II. In large part, the creation of specific aid programs for the less developed countries coincided with the emergence of many independent nations which previously had been colonies and territorial extensions of the more developed nations.

After the war, programs to provide aid to these and other less developed countries grew. Humanitarian concerns provided and continue to provide the impetus for various aid programs, particularly those that involve disaster relief. More important, however, particularly in the 1950s and 1960s, was the desire by the United States and nations in Western Europe to curb the spread of communism, to create military alliances with the developing countries, and to secure economic and political influence consistent with the interests of the free world.

The United States aid programs in the 1950s, for example, placed heavy emphasis on providing technical and military assistance to the nonaligned or Western-leaning countries, reflecting not only our concerns with national security, but also the feeling at that time that the key to development in the poorer parts of the world rested with technical assistance. These programs were supplemented by the distribution of agricultural commodities to many of the world's poor countries. Under provisions of Public Law 480 (The Agricultural Trade and Development Assistance Act of 1954), the United States expanded assistance to countries regarded as important both for national security reasons and to create a market for surplus farm production. More recently, funds administered by the United States Agency for International Development (AID) have been made available for loans, grants, and special projects, but the recipient countries remain within what is regarded as the Western sphere of influence.

International agencies

Although the United States has played a central role in making aid available to the less developed countries, it has not been the sole source. Other countries as well as international agencies such as the World Bank, regional development banks (including the Inter-American Development Bank, Asian Development Bank, and African Development Bank), the United Nations, and the Organization of Petroleum Exporting Countries (OPEC) have made funds and assistance available to capital-starved countries of the world. Of these, the World Bank has been the most important source of multinational finance. Established in 1944 to provide financing for the reconstruction of Western Europe following World War II, the World Bank and its subsidiary organizations provide not only technical assistance and project aid, but also more general program aid, grants, low-interest loans, financial assistance to deal with balance-of-payments problems, and loan guarantees for private foreign investment.

Aid to the less developed countries from the United Nations has emphasized assistance, in large part because of the notable success achieved by similar programs undertaken by the United States in helping to rebuild Europe after World War II. Although the results of technical assistance have been less dramatic in the poor countries of the world than they were in rebuilding a strong European economy (which had greater human capital), the United Nations continues to stress technical assistance. Several subsidiary organizations such as the World Health Organization (WHO), the Food and Agricultural Organization (FAO), and the International Labor Organization (ILO) carry out the bulk of the United Nations effort to assist the less developed countries.

The political motives which have shaped the assistance programs of the United States and those of multinational organizations have been equally important in influencing the distribution of aid from the Soviet Union and China. Cuba, Egypt, North Korea, North Vietnam and other recipients of non-Western aid have undoubtedly been selected for their strategic and political importance rather than solely for reasons of need.

Private foreign investment

In addition to the aid and assistance provided to the world's poor countries by foreign governments and nonprofit organizations, substantial amounts of capital have been channeled to the less developed countries from private sources. The impact of private foreign investment in the less developed countries has been most evident in those nations whose resources consist of or include primary commodities and raw materials, such as petroleum, which are sought by the more highly developed areas of the world. In addition to direct investment, private capital reaches the less developed countries via private loans and the purchase of securities sold by the less developed countries. Although the need for capital is acute, capital available from private sources is not universally regarded as beneficial to the host country. Private foreign investment can provide funding for projects which would not be financed from other sources. In addition, foreign investment may generate needed jobs and training opportunities for the local labor force as well as revenues for the host government. On the other hand, it has been suggested that large-scale investment in a country may result in reduced domestic savings, balance-of-payments problems, and foreign interference in the internal affairs of the nation.

Issues in foreign aid

Despite the urgent need for external funds, the response to foreign aid (exclusive of private capital flows) is mixed. To some countries, reliance on aid represents a dependency relationship which is regarded as undesirable, as well as being a reminder of earlier colonial status. More serious complaints have been made about the amount and types of aid available from the more developed countries, the conditions under which certain kinds of aid may be used, and the provisions for repayment of foreign loans. Notwithstanding these concerns, the poor countries still seek aid from foreign sources. The issues associated with each of these concerns are identified below.

The flow of funds to the poor countries of the world has never been large, and since the 1950s, the commitment of funds by the United States to aid programs has dwindled in both absolute and relative terms. In most Western European nations in 1977, the amount of aid provided as a percent of GNP was higher than that provided by the United States, but none of these countries provided as much as 1 percent of GNP for purposes of assisting the less-developed countries.

Whether a commitment of this magnitude represents too little or too much is, of course, a subjective matter. From a humanitarian perspective, some people have argued that the amount of aid is inadequate. Others contend that, based upon the limited successes from various aid programs and upon evidence of waste and mismanagement, the amount being spent is too large. It is further suggested that since effective utilization of capital frequently requires trained, literate, and skilled workers, the less developed countries may only be capable of effectively using a limited amount of funds in the short run. Finally, regardless of the actual amount of aid available, some countries, because of political instability and social unrest, have been unable to make beneficial use of whatever resources are provided from foreign sources.

From the perspective of the recipients, the most desirable forms of aid are general development grants coupled with technical assistance. The advantage of grants is that there is no need for repayment; further, the recipient may exercise independent judgment in determining how the funds are spent. In addition, technical and managerial personnel and expertise may help to assure the success of aid-supported projects and programs. Most donors, on the other hand, tend to favor aid for specific projects because they feel a greater sense of control over the uses to which aid funds are put. One criticism of project aid is that it may not be available for programs which the recipient governments regard as most important.

Loans to the less developed countries may pose particularly serious problems for those nations where large amounts of debt have been incurred in a short period of time or where the expected benefits from the expenditure of the loan proceeds do not materialize. Repayment of debt, even at extremely low rates of interest, often imposes serious financial hardships on the poor countries and may result in money being diverted from essential activities to pay off the debt. If the aid-supported projects do not yield the expected benefits, imports may have to be reduced to provide sufficient funds to service the debt. In some cases, under the threat of default, loans have been renegotiated. In these situations, however, it is often necessary for the borrower to take unpopular political actions such as raising taxes to pay off the debt.

In light of worldwide inflation and sharply higher petroleum prices, many of the developing countries have encountered greater and greater difficulty in meeting their obligations. As a result, pressure for debt relief for the poor countries has been increasing and can be expected to grow unless worldwide inflation abates and primary commodity prices become more stable.

Although the needs of the poor countries of the world loom large, the prospects for increasing the amount of aid flowing in their direction seem dim. After years of assistance, the prospect for rapid economic growth in most of the nations of the world seems as elusive as ever. Moreover, the more developed nations, confronted with serious domestic problems such as pollution and poverty, are directing more resources toward these problems and fewer toward the problems of others. Finally, in view of the considerations which have influenced the amount of United States aid and in light of increasing criticism of United States foreign policy by many of the less developed countries, it is likely that larger requests for foreign aid will become increasingly difficult to justify.

Planning the economy

A feature of most nations that are trying to develop an advanced economy is centralized economic planning. With the help of experts in the field of economic development, the government establishes a program of economic goals, with a time schedule for their achievement. Such programs are somewhat less difficult to carry out in socialist nations, where most of the productive resources are owned by the government, but they are also found in developing capitalist economies. The tools of fiscal and monetary policy, plus the regulation of key industries, can implement centralized planning even when productive resources are privately owned.

Centralized planning is especially valuable in helping to maintain a desirable balance between growth in the public and the private sectors of the economy. The profit motive acts as a stimulus to investment in the private sector, and so its growth is likely to be rapid. Yet growth in the private sector is limited by the need for a supporting infrastructure of public goods. For long-range steady growth to take place, development of the public sector of the economy must keep pace with that of the private sector.

THE EFFECT OF CARTELS ON LESS DEVELOPED NATIONS

Economists define a **cartel** as *a group of producers (or countries) who formally agree to control price and output of a commodity or commodities.* In many ways, a cartel may act like a single firm—a monopoly—in limiting the supply and thus raising the price above the competitive price. A cartel differs from a monopoly inasmuch as the activities of each member of the cartel must be regulated so that the goals of the organization may be realized. In addition to decisions about production and price, the cartel also may initiate agreements to share profits.

For the less developed countries whose major source of foreign exchange and government revenue is derived from the sale of primary commodities, participation in a cartel may be advantageous. If successful, the actions taken by the cartel may reduce commodity price fluctuations and, consequently, fluctuations in revenues derived from exports. Perhaps more important, the cartel may serve to increase the income and wealth of member nations.

OPEC: the effects of the 1973 crisis

The Organization of Petroleum Exporting Countries (OPEC) was formed in 1960 but was scarcely visible in the world economy until 1973. At that time, in response to political and military support provided by various Western nations to Israel in her war effort against the Arab states, OPEC brought dramatic change to the world economic order by temporarily reducing or ending oil shipments to a number of countries and, subsequently, quadrupling oil prices. Economic growth in both highly developed and less developed countries is dependent on oil for fuel, fertilizer, and other goods such as plastics. Since the 13 OPEC nations (Abu Dhabi, Algeria, Ecuador, Gabon, Indonesia, Iran, Iraq, Kuwait, the Libyan Arab Republic, Nigeria, Qatar, Saudi Arabia, and Venezuela) produce just over half of the world's current daily production of crude oil, a world economic crisis ensued. Countries scrambled to conserve oil and find new sources of fuel. Increased fuel costs intensified inflationary spirals.

These actions resulted in a rapid increase in the proportion of world income held by the OPEC nations, most of which have generally low levels of economic development. The transfer of income to the OPEC countries from the rest of the world created strains on the international financial structure. Ironically, some people in developed countries began to fear "imperialism in reverse," the possibility that OPEC nations might use their newly acquired revenues to make large-scale investments in and obtain control over vital industries of the developed world. For the less developed nations without oil reserves, the improved economic condition of the OPEC nations meant potential catastrophe. The Organization of African States, for example, reported in mid-1974 that 33 of its 42 members had been hard hit by the oil crisis.

The success of OPEC in controlling supply and raising prices stimulated other commodity-exporting nations in attempts to form cartellike associations for their products. Chile, Peru, Zaire, and Zambia formed the Intergovernmental Council of Copper Exporting Countries. The seven countries that produce 63 percent of the world's bauxite formed the International Association of Producers of Bauxite. Members of the 42-nation World Coffee Producers Group agreed to limit exports in an attempt to reverse the decline of coffee prices on the world market. At a conference of 110 developing nations in 1975, one country's commerce minister proposed that producers form cartels for all raw materials such as bauxite and iron ore and for certain foodstuffs, including bananas, coffee, cocoa, and peanuts. The trend toward more commodity cartels created intense concern among highly developed nations that such actions would have severe worldwide economic consequences.

Events since 1973

Following the sharp increase in oil prices in 1973 and the ensuing worldwide economic problems in 1974 and 1975, concern with future shortages abated. With gasoline, fuel oil, and other forms of petroleum readily available, economic growth resumed in the more developed countries and the energy-related financial difficulties faced by the less developed countries were eased somewhat by aid from the OPEC nations. Although government officials in the West spoke about the need for developing a comprehensive energy policy to deal with increasing dependence on oil from the Middle East, little popular support could be mustered for such a task. Rather, as memories of the 1973 crisis receded, the public's attention turned to more visible problems such as inflation.

After 1974, increased production by individual members of OPEC, augmented by new supplies of oil from sources such as Alaska's North Slope and the North Sea, made it impossible to maintain the "official" OPEC price. In real terms, oil-product prices dropped from 1974 levels and, for a time, a glut existed on world markets. In 1977, official prices rose by 10 percent, but attempts by some members of the cartel to seek an even higher price were thwarted by the Saudi Arabians who, with idle capacity, threatened to increase supply as necessary to keep oil prices relatively stable.

The complacent attitude in the more developed countries regarding oil supplies and prices was severely shaken late in December 1978, when after months of internal strife, violence, and strikes, the supply of oil from Iran reaching world markets dwindled quickly to less than 1 million barrels (bbl) per day and then to a virtual trickle by year's end from an earlier daily average production of 6 million bbl. As Iranian exports to foreign countries were halted and refineries shut down, the spot (cash) price for oil on world markets quickly rose. Since Iran was the second largest of the OPEC suppliers, accounting for nearly 20 percent of the cartel's production, the possibility for worldwide economic problems comparable to those in 1973 and 1974 were evident.

From the point of view of many of the less developed countries, the impending crisis was potentially more severe than in 1973. Not only had the rate of inflation increased since that time, but also, many of these countries had accumulated large deficits to pay for imports including oil. For some countries particularly dependent on Iranian oil (South Africa, for example, imported 90 percent of its oil from Iran), the need to find replacement sources of oil in a world market where the spot price reached over $25/bbl in some transactions has created the prospect of immediate economic chaos.

Although oil production has been increased somewhat by other producing nations, including Saudi Arabia, in response to the current crisis, prices have remained high and are expected to continue increasing. For many of the less developed countries, a new round of unanticipated price increases and accompanying inflation will worsen trade deficits and pose the distinct threat of eroding any gains in real per capita GNP which have been obtained since the 1973 crisis. Moreover, the prospects for rapid economic growth in the less developed countries slip further away as these countries now must work harder simply to try to maintain their current, unenviable economic positions.

For years, economists have argued that cartels are basically unstable because individual members of the cartel, while receiving benefits from collective action, have an incentive to increase production beyond their assigned quotas. Although the OPEC cartel seems to be more cohesive than most similar organizations, from time to time it has shown the strains of conflict among its members. Following the crisis in Iran, member nations attached various surcharges to the official OPEC price in order to obtain extra revenues. These independent actions suggest that the economists' generalization about cartels may have some validity in the case of OPEC.

A more important issue than the long-term stability of cartels is the short-term effect that OPEC has had throughout the world. The strength demonstrated by OPEC and its ability to influence world commodity prices have provided a model for other nations, particularly those with resources in great demand in the industrialized countries. As long as the more developed nations need the raw materials of the less developed nations to maintain their level of development it seems likely that additional producer commodity agreements will be forthcoming. Although these actions may prove beneficial to some, there is no reason to believe that there will be a narrowing of income differences among countries of the world as cartels and producer groups exploit their monopoly power. Indeed, as has been seen recently, the actions of one group of countries to improve its economic condition may seriously worsen the relative income position of other, less favorably endowed nations.

Summary

■ This chapter surveys the problems of and possibilities for economic growth and development in the less developed countries of the world.

■ Among the characteristics frequently found in less developed countries are agriculture-based economies with little agricultural capital; few checks on population growth; a low level of education; concentration of political and economic power in a tiny minority of the population; little industry; dependence on importation of manufactured goods; dependence on one or two primary export commodities; and a high degree of political influence exerted by multinational corporations. From country to country, however, conditions vary considerably.

■ Barriers to development in less developed countries generally include a low stock of human capital, which is a result of inadequate education, lack of managerial skills, and severe health problems in the work force; a low rate of capital accumulation, stemming from a low rate of saving and few investment opportunities; problems in making use of advanced technology; the lack of a well-developed infrastructure to support industrial development; culturally imposed restraints; and the adverse effects of economic imperialism.

■ Less developed countries generally approach the problem of growth by increasing the factors on the supply side, such as by implementing programs to improve the health and education of the work force. The intensive use of labor can help to make up for the relative absence of capital. Nations can also make use of foreign aid from individual countries or international agencies, and private investment can also bring in needed capital from outside. Such infusions of aid and investment from other countries, however, often create problems of indebtedness and dependence. Developing countries generally rely on centralized government economic planning.

■ Since the OPEC oil boycott of 1973, developing countries have increasingly turned to the formation of international cartels to control and gain more income from their export commodities. This approach has achieved limited success, with one major drawback being that higher prices for such basic commodities as oil may be particularly damaging to the economies of the other less developed countries.

Key Terms

economic development

infrastructure

economic imperialism

nationalization

cartel

Review & Discussion

1. What are some of the ways in which economists define "less developed"? Why might less developed nations tend to value growth more highly than developed countries?

2. Even though some less developed countries have a problem with overpopulation, they nevertheless also have a shortage of human capital. Why?

3. Why is it difficult for less developed countries to retain the savings that are generated within the economy? Why are foreign investors often discouraged from investing?

4. What is a supporting infrastructure? How does an inadequate infrastructure tend to undermine development? Why is investment in an adequate infrastructure particularly difficult for less developed countries?

5. Economists have observed that the economies of less developed countries are particularly vulnerable to external influences, such as the international market for primary export products. Why would this be true?

6. What are some of the general policies of developing countries designed to stimulate the

improvement of human capital? The accumulation of physical capital? Why do most developing countries rely on some form of centralized planning?

7. Are producer commodity cartels likely to increase or decrease in the future? Why? What are some of the advantages and disadvantages of this strategy?

8. A cynic once observed that he did not believe that there was any such thing as an "aid" program, only buying and selling between countries. What is the price of aid to many less developed countries? Why might these countries be reluctant to accept foreign aid?

9. Why have some less developed countries moved to nationalize their basic industries? What are the advantages of nationalization for a developing country? What does the case of Chile indicate about the response of multinational corporations to the threat of nationalization?

Application 10:
Mexico: The Problems of a Developing Nation

In per capita income, Mexico ranks about midway between such wealthy nations as the United States and Sweden and such poor ones as Afghanistan and Rwanda. With the modern steel mills of Monterrey, the international playground beaches of Cancun, and the chic cafés of the capital city's Zona Rosa, Mexico is in many ways an affluent nation. Yet millions of Mexicans also live in severe poverty, a problem aggravated by an unequal distribution of income and unchecked population growth. While Mexican executives typically earn half again as much as their counterparts in Argentina, ordinary Mexican workers are paid less than half as much as workers in Argentina. And the Mexican rate of population growth, between 3.2 percent and 3.5 percent a year, is among the most rapid in the world.

With its national mixture of wealth and poverty, Mexico presents a good example of the problems faced by less developed nations in their efforts to achieve economic growth and development. Of particular interest are Mexico's recent difficulties in converting an abundant natural resource—hydrocarbons—into economic advances.

In recent years, Mexico has made a number of strides forward. During the early 1970s, for example, the country achieved an annual growth rate of about 6 percent, doubled its capacity for electricity, iron, and steel production, more than doubled the minimum wage, and improved the general quality of agriculture, education, and health care. But the nation borrowed heavily overseas to finance these activities, which were accomplished primarily through government programs. By late 1975 the debt had become large enough to impair the nation's international credit standing. Interest on the debt alone placed a strain on the economy, which was already suffering from a double-digit inflation that was curtailing demand for Mexican exports and beginning to price the nation's principal source of foreign exchange, its tourist industry, out of the market.

In 1976, in an effort to solve its trade problems, Mexico devalued its currency, the peso, which had remained unchanged in relation to the United States dollar for 22 years. The peso dropped from eight cents to a nickel in the first devaluation, and then to four cents in a second. But instead of improving, the nation's international trade position worsened; moreover, inflation turned sharply upward, rising to an annual rate of more than 43 percent a few months after the second devaluation, compared to about 13 percent for the same period in the previous year.

Many American companies, which had invested some $3.2 billion in Mexican affiliates, lost money because their Mexican assets were worth less in relation to the dollar. These losses, coupled with what private investors perceived as an ultra-liberal attitude on the part of the Mexican government, further reduced much-needed private investment in the economy. To many observers Mexico seemed headed for a serious backward slide, if not economic ruin, despite the best efforts of a new administration which had come into office promising to get all segments of the economy working together again.

Then suddenly the outlook began to brighten. During 1977 and 1978, vast pools of hydrocarbons were discovered in the Gulf of Mexico and the tropical swamps of Tabasco and Chiapas. One area, known as the Reforma field, was estimated to hold almost as much oil as the North Slope of Alaska, about 7 billion barrels of crude. According to *Petroleos Mexicanos* (Pemex), the government oil monopoly, proven reserves of hydrocarbons—both oil and natural gas—totaled 40 billion barrels, a figure nearly twice the previous Pemex estimates and higher than proven oil reserves in the United States. Before long, people began to include Mexico when they talked of major oil producers and Mexicans themselves began to look to oil to turn their economy around. But Mexican officials and others soon realized that they would have to move carefully in exploiting this resource.

For example, one question facing government officials was how quickly to produce the oil. According to estimates made in the oil-thirsty United States, Mexico could be pumping as much as 5 million barrels of oil a day by 1985 and twice that amount by 1990. But how was Mexico to spend the revenue from such a torrent of crude without dangerously overheating its economy? After all, the Mexican government estimated that by producing only 2.3 million barrels of oil daily, and exporting about half of it, the nation would bring in about $11 billion in foreign exchange annually by 1983, or enough to service its $22 billion long-term foreign public debt as well as greatly increase its imports of capital goods and raw materials.

Moreover, it became clear that to some degree the oil boom would be diminished by the need to pay for imports of food. Since 1971 Mexico had not been growing enough to feed itself, and the situation had been steadily worsening. Mexico's agricultural system, burdened with farmland that is split into tiny, unproductive but politically popular plots known as *ejidos,* is so inefficient that more than 45 percent of the labor force works the land but produces less than a tenth of the Gross National Product. The nation is not even able to produce enough of such staples as corn, of which it had to import almost 2 million tons in 1979.

Finally, revenues from the sale of oil are not likely to help raise the level of human capital in Mexico for many years. Today, two-thirds of Mexico's workers have not completed elementary school, and one-fourth cannot read. A great deal of attention will have to be focused on educational programs to develop skilled workers and managers in order for Mexico to realize truly significant gains in economic development.

Questions for discussion

☐ Identify and discuss the barriers to Mexico's economic development.

☐ The Mexican labor force is growing at the rate of 800,000 workers, or potential workers, a year. Half the population of working age is either unemployed or marginally employed in very low-paying and uncertain jobs. One of the principal sources of employment is not in the nation itself but in its northern neighbor, the United States, which attracts countless Mexicans every year. Given this situation, on what sorts of industries would you suggest the Mexican government should concentrate its developmental resources?

☐ With the sensitivity that many less developed nations feel toward what they view as economic imperialism by more highly developed countries, what sort of attitude would you expect Mexico to have toward the desires of the United States for increased imports of Mexican oil and natural gas?

Part VI

Price and Output in the Product Market

Chapter 20

Elasticity of Demand and Supply

What to look for in this chapter

What is elasticity of demand?

How is price elasticity of demand calculated? What factors affect price elasticity?

What are the other forms of elasticities of demand?

What is elasticity of supply? What factors affect elasticity of supply?

How can government actions affect the workings of supply and demand? Why are demand and supply elasticities important to consider in designing such policies?

With this section we begin our study of microeconomics, the level of economic analysis that deals with individual agents of the economic system, such as a single consumer's demand for a particular good, the price of a single product, the behavior of a single business. Using the skills we will develop, we will be better able to focus on such issues as consumer response to changes in prices or income or the response of workers to variations in their wages.

Much of this section of the text will rely heavily on an understanding of the laws of demand and supply presented in Chapter 3. (We urge you to review that chapter at this time.) Briefly, the law of demand states that as the price of any good decreases, the quantity of the good that buyers are willing and able to purchase will increase. As the price increases, then a smaller quantity of the good will be demanded. The law of demand expresses an *inverse* relationship between price of a good and quantity demanded.

Similarly, the law of supply states that as the price of any good rises, the quantity of the good that suppliers are willing and able to offer for sale increases; as the price drops, a smaller quantity of the good will be supplied. The law of supply expresses a *direct* relationship between the price and the quantity supplied.

Recall, too, that the laws of demand and supply both operate under the "all-others-things-equal" assumption, the assumption that all other factors that could affect the amount of the product purchased or supplied remain constant. Together the laws of supply and demand enable us to study the workings of markets.

In this chapter we will examine demand and supply in greater detail and will develop the concept of elasticity to help us understand the degree to which price changes affect quantities demanded and supplied. We will also consider the effect of government economic policy on the workings of demand and supply.

Let us turn now to demand. In the following analysis we will deal with both individual and market demand. You will recall from Chapter 3 that market demand is always equal to the sum of the quantities demanded by individual consumers at each price. In other words, the market demand curve is the horizontal sum of all individual demand curves (see *Table 3.2* and *Fig. 3.5* for a quick review).

ELASTICITY OF DEMAND

The law of demand is based on the observation that consumers will respond to changes in price of any given item by making adjustments in the amounts they purchase: as price rises, the quantity of the good demanded will decrease, and as price falls, the quantity demanded will increase.* But

---

*Some economists believe that certain goods known as Giffen goods are an exception to this rule. A Giffen good is one for which the quantity demanded increases as price increases. For example, when the price of potatoes went up in Ireland during the famine of 1845, poor families bought *more* potatoes rather than fewer. However, this phenomenon can be explained within the framework of the income and substitution effects (Chapter 3).

although the relationship between change in price and change in quantity demanded is always an inverse one, the *extent* to which the quantity demanded is responsive to price changes is not always the same. For example, if a retail liquor store lowers the price of a bottle of red wine from $3.29 to $2.88 it may be able to increase sales by about 75 percent. We can say that over this price range, the quantity of wine demanded is very sensitive to price changes. But other commodities may be much less responsive to price changes. Lowering the price of a tube of cortisone ointment—a treatment for skin allergies that is available only by prescription—from $4.00 to $2.00 would not appreciably increase the demand for the ointment.

Elasticity of demand (E) is *the term used to describe the responsiveness (in percentage terms) of the quantity demanded to changes in price*. If a certain percentage price change creates a larger percentage change in the quantity of the good demanded, the demand for that good is said to be *elastic*. If the percentage price change results in a smaller percentage change in the quantity of the good demanded, the demand for that good is said to be *inelastic*. Returning to our example, we may conclude that the demand for red wine is elastic, whereas the demand for cortisone ointment is inelastic.

Reason for using percentage changes

It is important to remember that elasticity must be calculated on the basis of *percentage* changes in price and quantity demanded. It is not possible to estimate the degree of elasticity of demand for a good by simply examining the shape of the demand curve. The slope of a demand curve is a function of the size of the units of measure used on the graph. *Figure 20.1* demonstrates that it is

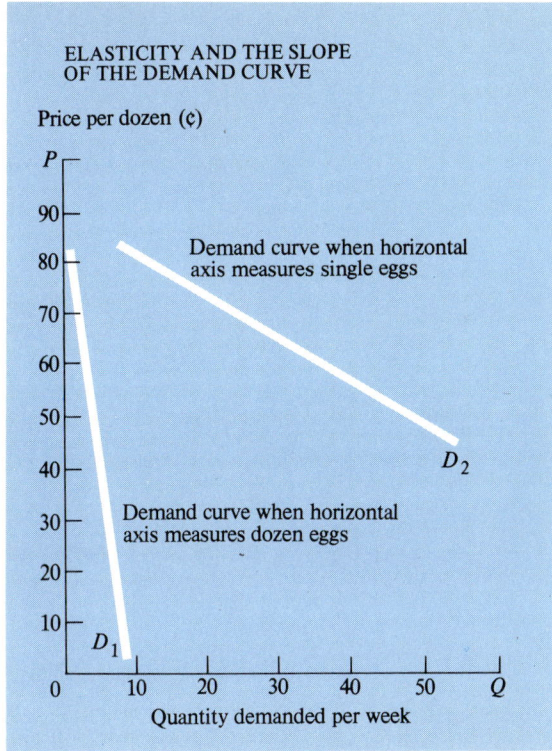

Fig. 20.1
The horizontal axis measures the quantity of eggs. When the quantity demanded is expressed in terms of dozens of eggs, we get the steep curve shown in D_1. When the quantity demanded is expressed in terms of single eggs, we get the less steep curve shown in D_2. Both curves are derived from the same data and have the same elasticity, but their slopes look very different.

possible to derive two very differently sloped demand curves from exactly the same data, simply by changing the size of the measurement unit. When the quantity of eggs demanded is expressed in terms of number of single eggs, the resulting curve has a different slope than when the same quantity demanded is expressed in terms of dozens of eggs. However, between any two corresponding points on these two curves, elasticity is identical. Thus the only way to measure elasticity accurately is to compare percentage changes in price and percentage changes in quantity.

Calculating elasticity of demand

By using a known demand schedule for any commodity, we can calculate elasticity over any price range on that schedule. *To determine the degree of elasticity (also called the **elasticity coefficient**), we divide the percentage change in quantity demanded by the percentage change in price for any good.* The formula is stated this way:

$$E_D = \frac{\% \text{ change } Q}{\% \text{ change } P}$$
$$= \frac{\text{change } Q}{Q} \div \frac{\text{change } P}{P}$$
$$= \frac{\Delta Q}{Q} \div \frac{\Delta P}{P}.$$

Types of price elasticity

The demand for most goods is either price elastic or price inelastic. However, there are other types of elasticity that are less common: unitary elasticity, perfect elasticity, and perfect inelasticity. We will now examine each of these cases in detail.

Price elastic

Demand is **price elastic** when *the percentage change in quantity is larger than the percentage change in price.* In the case of price elastic demand the elasticity coefficient is greater than 1.* Figure

---

*It is worth noting that all price elasticities of demand are negative numbers. This is because either the change in price *or* the change in quantity is negative (that is, either price or quantity decreases). However, in economics, the elasticity coefficients are usually expressed as positive numbers.

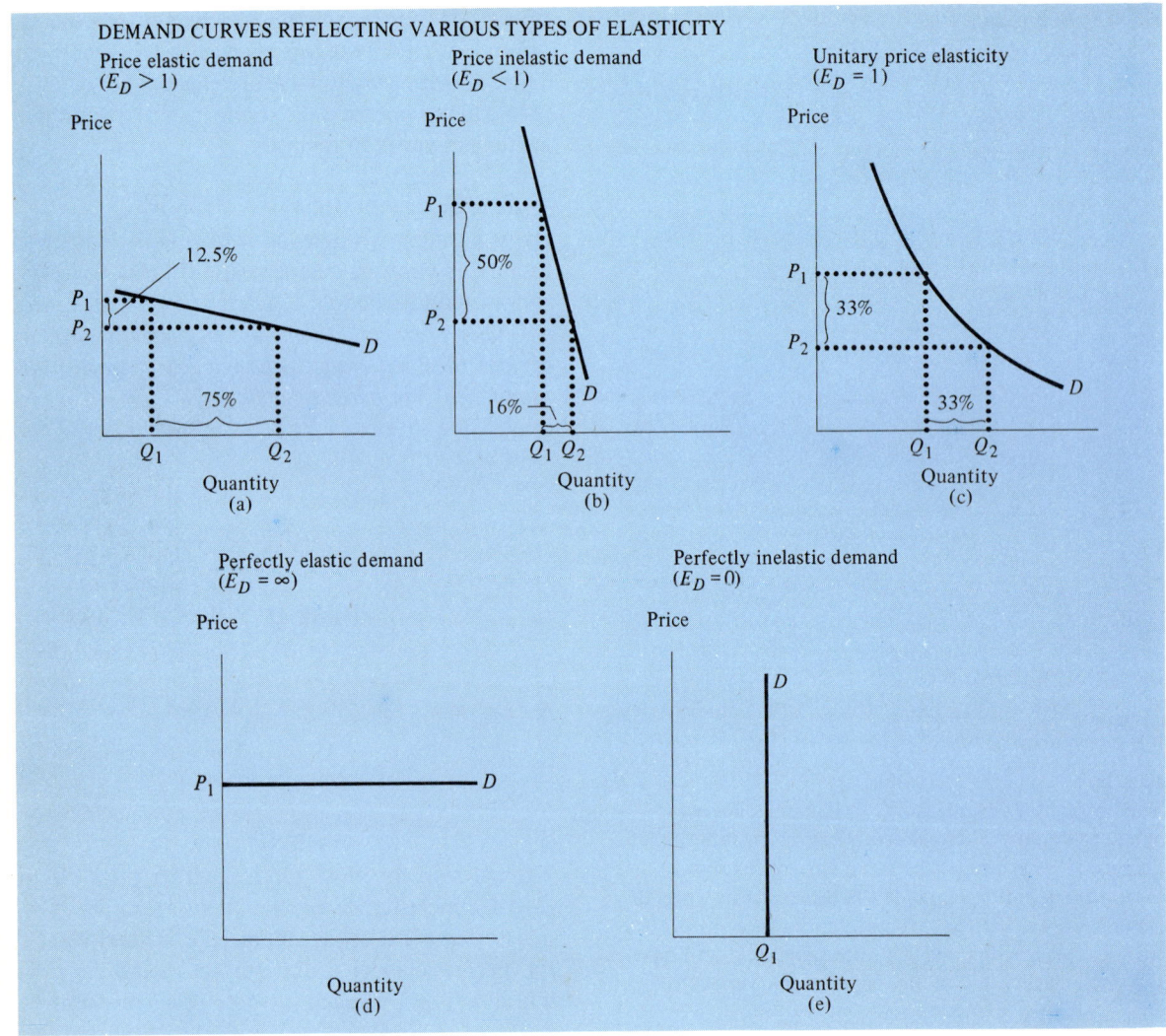

Fig. 20.2 E_D is the elasticity coefficient
< is the mathematical symbol for "less than"
> is the mathematical symbol for "greater than"
∞ is the mathematical symbol for infinity

(a) When demand is price elastic, a small percentage change in price (here, a 12.5 percent decrease from P_1 to P_2) will result in a greater percentage change in quantity demanded (here, a 75 percent increase from Q_1 to Q_2). (b) When demand is price inelastic, a large percentage change in price (here, a 50 percent decrease from P_1 to P_2) results in a smaller percentage change in quantity demanded (here, a 16 percent increase from Q_1 to Q_2). (c) When demand is of unitary price elasticity, the percentage change in price (here, a 33 percent decrease from P_1 to P_2) results in an equal change in quantity demanded (here, a 33 percent increase from Q_1 to Q_2). (d) When demand is perfectly elastic, the quantity demanded will be infinite at price P_1 or less. Above P_1, no quantity of the good will be demanded. (e) When demand for a good is perfectly inelastic, the quantity demanded will not vary from Q_1 in spite of changes in the price of the good.

20.2(a) illustrates the demand curve for a good whose demand is price elastic: a slight decrease in price from P_1 to P_2 will induce consumers to buy many more units of the good and the quantity demanded will increase by a much greater percentage than the percentage decrease in price.

Example: Suppose the price of red wine decreases from \$3.29 to \$2.88 per bottle (a 12.5 percent decrease). This decrease in price causes the quantity of red wine demanded to increase from 100 million to 175 million bottles (a 75 percent increase). The percentage change in quantity (75 percent) is larger than the percentage change in price (12.5 percent); therefore, the demand for red wine is elastic.

Price inelastic
Demand is **price inelastic** when *the percentage change in quantity is smaller than the percentage change in price*. When the demand is price inelastic, *the elasticity coefficient is less than 1*. An inelastic demand curve for a good is illustrated in *Fig. 20.2(b)*: if the price of a good decreases by a large amount (from P_1 to P_2), the demand (which increases from Q_1 to Q_2) does not increase by as large an amount. Consumers will buy more of the good when the price falls, but the change in the quantity they demand is relatively small compared to the decrease in price.

Example: Suppose the price of a tube of cortisone ointment decreases by 50 percent from \$4.00 to \$2.00. This decrease induces an increase in the quantity demanded from 3 million to 3.5 million tubes (an increase of 16 percent). The percentage change in price (50 percent) is greater than the percentage change in quantity (16 percent); therefore, the demand for the good is inelastic.

Unitary elasticity
The demand for some goods may be of **unitary price elasticity,** that is, *the percentage change in quantity is equal to the percentage change in price*. When demand is of unit elasticity, *the elasticity coefficient is equal to 1*. A demand curve reflecting unit elasticity is illustrated in *Fig. 20.2(c)*: here, a 10 percent decrease in price from P_1 to P_2 is reflected by a 10 percent increase in quantity demanded from Q_1 to Q_2.

Example: The 33 percent decrease in the price of a candy bar from 30¢ to 20¢ leads the consumers to increase the quantity of candy bars demanded from 10 million to 13.3 million, an increase of 33 percent. Because the price and quantity both change by 33 percent, the demand for candy bars can be said to be of unitary price elasticity.

Perfectly elastic and perfectly inelastic demands
Two special cases of elasticity are found at the extremes of the spectrum of elasticity. One special case is that of **perfectly elastic demand** when *any given percentage change in price will lead to an infinite change in the quantity purchased* (see *Fig. 20.2d*). In other words, at price P_1 (or less), consumers will buy an unlimited amount of the good. At any price above P_1, however, consumers will not purchase any amount of the good. In the case of perfect elasticity, *the elasticity coefficient is equal to infinity(∞)*. Although actual examples of goods for which the demand is perfectly elastic are rare, we will use the example of chewing gum. If the demand for chewing gum were perfectly elastic, at a price of 20¢ a pack or less, consumers would buy as many packs of gum as they could. If, however, the price increased to 21¢, consumers would not buy any gum at all.

The second extreme case, (illustrated in *Fig. 20.2e*), is that of **perfectly inelastic demand,** when, *regardless of any percentage change in price, there is no change in the amount purchased*. The elasticity coefficient is 0.

Real-life examples of goods with a perfectly inelastic demand are relatively rare. For our example, we will use insulin, a drug used in the treatment of diabetes. As shown in *Fig. 20.2e*, diabetics will demand quantity Q_1 of insulin no

Table 20.1
A single household's demand schedule for eggs

Price per dozen	Quantity demanded per week (dozens)	Elasticity coefficient (E_D)
80¢	1	
70	2	5.00*
60	3	2.60
50	4	1.57
40	5	1.00
30	6	.64
20	7	.38
10	8	.20

*Over the 40¢–50¢ price range, for example, the elasticity coefficient is calculated as follows.

$$E_D = \frac{1}{(5+4)/2} \div \frac{.10}{(.40+.50)/2}$$
$$= \frac{1}{4.5} \div \frac{.10}{.45} = \frac{1}{4.5} \times \frac{.45}{.10} = 1.$$

matter how high or how low the price goes. If they do not take a certain amount they will die. If they take more, it does them no good. Hence, the quantity of insulin demanded will be the same regardless of its price.

Midpoint price elasticity of demand formula
Table 20.1 shows how elasticity is determined from a demand schedule for eggs. One small problem arises when we attempt to calculate the percentage changes in price and quantity. Which price-quantity combination should we use as a starting point? Take, for example, the 40¢–50¢ price range. If we start with the 40¢–five dozen price-quantity combination as a point of reference, the percentage *increase* in price (from 40¢ to 50¢) will be 25 percent and the percentage *decrease* in quantity (from 5 dozen to 4 dozen) will be 20 percent. The elasticity coefficient, therefore, is .8, slightly inelastic. However, if we take the same 40¢–50¢ price range but calculate the elasticity when price decreases, we will come out with a different elasticity coefficient. Starting with the 50¢–four dozen price-quantity combination as a point of reference, we find that the percentage *decrease* in price is 20 percent, while the percentage *increase* in quantity is 25 percent. Over exactly the same price range the elasticity coefficient is now 1.25, or slightly elastic. Therefore the increase in price has produced one elasticity coefficient while the decrease in price over the same range has produced a different elasticity.

This problem is handled by taking the average of the two prices and the average of the two quantities as points of reference. Thus over the 40¢–50¢ price range in our demand schedule for eggs, we calculate the elasticity coefficient using 45¢ (the average of 40¢ and 50¢) and four and one-half dozen (the average of four dozen and five dozen) as points of reference. Using the midpoint formula for elasticity, we find that the percentage changes in price and quantity are now both 22 percent, indicating that elasticity is unitary. Thus our elasticity formula should be restated as follows:

$$E_D = \frac{\text{change } Q}{(Q_1 + Q_2)/2} \div \frac{\text{change } P}{(P_1 + P_2)/2}.$$

Elastic and inelastic portions of the demand curve
Most demand curves have elastic and inelastic portions. Look at the example of a single household's demand for eggs (*Table 20.1* and the resulting demand curve drawn in *Figure 20.3*.) Over the 70¢–80¢ price range the household's demand is very elastic—a 67 percent change in quantity, as

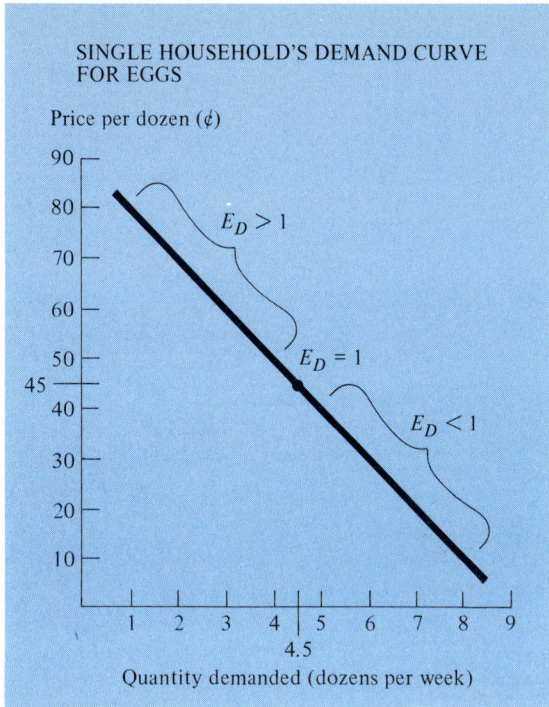

Fig. 20.3
This demand curve illustrates the demand schedule for eggs presented in *Table 20.1*. Here, we see that the degree of elasticity varies along the curve. Between the price range of 40¢–50¢, the elasticity of demand for eggs is unitary ($E_D = 1$). At higher price levels, the demand for eggs is elastic ($E_D > 1$); at lower price levels, the demand is inelastic ($E_D < 1$).

compared with a 13 percent change in price. The elasticity coefficient over this price range is 5.0.

As we continue to move down the demand curve, the percentage change in quantity will decline as the percentage change in price increases. Note that as we move down the demand curve, price gets lower and quantity demanded gets higher. Hence, a given change in price represents a larger percentage and a given change in quantity represents a smaller percentage. The elasticity co-efficient, therefore, will become smaller, indicating a diminishing degree of elasticity. Eventually, the percentage change in quantity will be equal to the percentage change in price, and the elasticity coefficient will be 1.

In our demand schedule for eggs, this situation occurs between the price of 50¢ and 40¢; over this price range, the elasticity of demand is said to be unitary. If we move even further down our demand curve, to the 40¢ to 30¢ price range, we find that the elasticity coefficient is now less than 1, or inelastic. This means that the percentage change in price range has become greater than the percentage change in quantity. The further down the curve we move, the more inelastic the demand will be. That is, this household's demand for eggs will be elastic over the upper portion of the curve, unitary over the middle range, and inelastic over the lower portion.

Elasticity and total revenue

Market demand curves show the same variations in elasticity as do the curves of individual households. This fact carries important implications for businesspeople and for the makers of economic policy. A business decision to increase product prices or a city's decision to increase the price of bus fares cannot be made without an understanding of the elasticity of demand for these commodities over the relevant price ranges. Suppose, for example, that Eggs Extraordinaire, Inc. (EEI) wants to increase its monthly revenues. The president's son-in-law suggests raising the price of a dozen eggs from 60¢ to 80¢. This suggestion confirms the president's belief that his daughter has married an oaf. He points out to the young man that over the relevant price range for eggs (60¢–80¢) the demand is quite elastic. If the price is increased by a given percentage, the quantity demanded will decrease by an even greater percentage. As we shall see, the proposed 20¢ increase in price would result in a drop in the total sales revenue from $600 to $800 since many people would buy fewer eggs and more cheese or other sources of protein. Thus, instead of raising the price, the president lowers it to 40¢. This decreases the profit the company makes on each dozen eggs but it also leads to a large increase in the number of dozens sold, so that the net result is an increase in total revenue.

Under certain circumstances, the son-in-law's proposal could have been the best solution. For example, this type of proposal worked well when, several years ago, New York taxi companies decided to increase fares by about 50 percent. As was expected, the number of taxi riders immediately decreased. But the decrease in number of riders was only about 20 percent, and the increased revenue from the higher fares more than made up for the revenue lost as the quantity of rides demanded fell off. The fare increase did lead to an increase in revenue for the companies (although the taxi drivers were generally unhappy—they said their incomes had decreased, because passengers were less willing to tip generously when they had to pay the higher fares). On the other hand, when the New York City Transit Authority raised the subway and bus fare from 20¢ to 30¢, opponents of the increase claimed that total revenue fell off. However, because the percentage change in the price of bus and subway rides was 40 percent,

$$\frac{10}{(20 + 30)/2},$$

it would have required a decrease of greater than 40 percent in the number of riders to cause a decline in total revenue. It is very unlikely that such a large percentage decrease in the volume of passengers really occurred; probably what the critics of the fare increase meant was that revenues did not rise by the full 40 percent of the price increase. We could conclude, therefore, that although the demand for both subway and taxi services appears to be inelastic, the demand for taxi rides is probably less inelastic (the elasticity coeffcient is closer to 1).

These examples indicate how important it is for a business firm to be aware of its position on

Table 20.2
Elasticity and total revenue for Eggs Extraordinaire, Inc.

(1) Price per dozen	(2) Quantity demanded per week (market demand)	(3) Elasticity coefficient	(4) Total revenue
80¢	1000		$ 800
		5.00	
70	2000		1400
		2.60	
60	3000		1800
		1.57	
50	4000		2000
		1.00	
40	5000		2000
		.64	
30	6000		1800
		.38	
20	7000		1400
		.20	
10	8000		800

demand curves and the degree of elasticity over the relevant range of prices. When the elasticity coefficient is greater than 1 (that is, when the demand is elastic), total sales receipts will rise as price falls. If the coefficient is exactly 1 (if the elasticity of demand is unitary), receipts will be unchanged as the price falls. If the elasticity coefficient is less than 1 (if demand is inelastic), total sales receipts will fall as the price falls. *Table 20.2* shows the changes in total revenue (number of units demanded times price per unit) that would accompany changes in the price of a dozen eggs.

Determinants of elasticity

In the preceding discussion, there have been examples in which factors other than price changes have helped to determine the degree of elasticity of demand for a product. We will now explore some of the determinants of elasticity in more detail.

Availability of substitutes

The more substitutes there are for any one good, the more elastic the demand for that good will be. (You will recall from Chapter 3 that goods are substitutes for each other when they can be used in the same way and therefore compete for the buyer's dollar.)

The demand for a certain brand of red wine over the typical price range tends to be quite elastic, because consumers can switch to other brands of wine, other types of wine, and other beverages. When your favorite French vintage wine shoots up to $10 a bottle, you may decide to switch to California wine in half-gallon jugs, or you may choose to drink nothing but water with your meals. There are many acceptable substitutes for the particular bottle of wine you are considering buying. But as we have noted, the demand for cortisone ointment is relatively inelastic throughout the relevant ranges of the demand curve, because it has a low degree of substitutability. The patient who is suffering from a serious skin allergy cannot switch to another method of treatment when the price of the ointment goes up, because nothing else would be as effective in curing the rash.

Substitutability is a factor in the responsiveness of a commodity to price cuts as well as to price increases. When the price of milk goes down, people begin to substitute it for water, soft drinks, or fruit juices. A commodity such as a refrigerator, on the other hand, has relatively fewer alternative uses over the relevant price range.

Number of uses of the product

Closely related to the substitutability factor is the number of uses the product has. Milk can be used to drink, to cook with, and even to bathe in, but insulin has only one use, the treatment of diabetes. If a good has many uses, the demand for it will tend to be relatively elastic over the relevant part of the demand curve, since people will buy more of it to use in more different ways as the price declines. If a good has few alternative uses, the demand for it will tend to be relatively inelastic.

Degree of necessity

The demand for a good that is a necessity tends to be more inelastic than the demand for one that is not. If the price of electrical power rises, it is unlikely that a household will greatly reduce its consumption of this good. A certain amount of electricity is necessary as a source of lighting and as a means of running essential appliances. A good that is a necessity will have a relatively inelastic demand over the relevant part of its demand schedule; the demand for a good that is not a necessity will be much more elastic.

Cost relative to income

The demand for a good whose cost represents a large share of a household's income will be quite responsive to price. The cost of a color television set represents about 2.5 percent of the median household income in the United States today. If the cost of a color television set increases by 10 percent, the quantity demanded might decline by 20 or even 30 percent. But when the price of baking soda goes from 30¢ to 40¢, there is little effect on the quantity of baking soda demanded, since the price of baking soda represents such a minute fraction of total household income. In general, it is safe to say that the larger the percentage of one's total income the expenditure on a good entails, the more elastic the demand for that good will be.

The relevant time period

When discussing any demand curve, we must specify the time period to which it pertains. Given a price change, we would not expect consumers to adjust instantaneously. Instead, we would expect a gradual change; therefore, the longer the time period the more elastic the demand for a good.

Among the reasons for this phenomenon is the fact that the longer period of time makes possible the development of new uses of the product if the price falls, or development of substitutes for it if the price rises. For example, in the short run, the demand for soybeans, like that for most other agricultural products, is fairly inelastic. But because soybeans have been relatively cheap for a long time, there has been an incentive to undertake research on additional uses of soybeans. Companies have learned to process soybeans and extract from them a protein fiber that can be spun out to make a meat subsitute. When the beans are pressed, they yield a milk that can be used to make cheese and butter. With the discovery of these new uses, the demand for soybeans increases over the relevant price range, since soybeans can be substituted for beef or milk if their price is low in comparison with the price of these products.

Similarly, a rise in price will cause a larger reaction over a longer period of time. Take, for example, a rise in the price of gasoline. Within the first few weeks, consumers will probably do little more than cancel a few Sunday drives. Given a period of months, and a large enough increase in the price of gas, those who can afford to may move closer to where they work so that they will consume less gas. And, over time (as we have been seeing over the past several years), larger cars will be replaced with smaller, more fuel-efficient ones.

Other elasticities of demand

Income elasticity

Fundamental to the law of demand is the "all-other-things-equal" assumption. Such important factors as income, tastes, and prices of other economic goods are assumed not to change. In Chapter 3 we found that when we relax this assumption for one factor at a time, the result is a shift in the demand curve.

To measure the effect of a change in income on the quantity demanded of a certain good, we can calculate the **income elasticity of demand**—*the*

> **RECAP**
> ELASTICITY OF DEMAND refers to the responsiveness (in percentage terms) of the quantity of a good demanded to changes in the price of that good, all other things equal. There are various degrees of responsiveness: perfect elasticity, elasticity, unitary elasticity, inelasticity, and perfect inelasticity. The degree of elasticity of demand for goods is determined by the following factors: the availability of substitutes, the number of uses of the product, the degree of necessity, the cost relative to income, and the relevant time period. Elasticity of demand for a good can also be calculated for the responsiveness (in percentage terms) of the quantity of a good demanded to changes in income and to changes in the prices of other goods.

responsiveness (in percentage terms) of changes in quantity demanded to change in income. The formula for income elasticity of demand is:

$$E_D^Y = \frac{\% \text{ change quantity}}{\% \text{ change income}}$$

$$= \frac{\text{change } Q}{Q} \div \frac{\text{change } Y}{Y}$$

where Y is consumer income.

We say that the demand for a good is **income elastic** when *the percentage change in the amount of a good demanded is larger that the percentage change in income. The elasticity coefficient is greater than 1.* Luxury goods are income elastic. For example, if a person's income rises by 10 percent, but his or her purchase of diamond necklaces increased by 30 percent, we could assume that the demand for diamond necklaces was income elastic. *If the percentage change in the amount of* a good purchased is smaller than the percentage change in income (elasticity is less than 1) demand for this good is said to be **income inelastic.** Necessities such as food are often said to be income inelastic. As consumer income rises, expenditures on most foods will also rise up to a point, but the percentage rise is smaller than the percentage increase in income.

Cross elasticity
Another factor that determines the position of the demand curve is the prices of other economic goods. Recall from Chapter 3 that as the price of substitutes rises, the demand curve for each good shifts to the right. In order to measure *the effect of price changes of one good on the quantity demanded of another good,* we calculate the **cross elasticity of demand,** *the percentage change in the quantity demanded of a good divided by the percentage change in the price of another good.*

$$E_{AB} = \frac{\% \text{ change } Q \text{ of good A}}{\% \text{ change } P \text{ of good B}}$$

ELASTICITY OF SUPPLY

Just as elasticity of demand refers to percentage changes in quantity demanded as the price changes, **elasticity of supply** deals with *the responsiveness (in percentage terms) of the quantity of a good supplied to changes in price.* Supply elasticity reflects producer reactions to a price change.

$$E_s = \frac{\% \text{ change in quantity supplied}}{\% \text{ change in price}}$$

If producers are highly responsive to price changes (percentage change in quantity is greater than percentage change in price), supply is elastic. If they are relatively unresponsive (percentage change in quantity is less than percentage change in price), supply is inelastic.

The major factor in determining the elasticity of supply is the amount of *time* the producer has to respond to a given change in product price. In general, the greater the time for response, the more elastic supply will be. A longer adjustment period allows resources to be shifted into production of higher priced goods, new techniques to be developed, new resources to be uncovered, and new producers to enter into the production process.

The production process can be divided into three time horizons: the market period, the short run, and the long run.

The market period
The market period is that time period in which a fixed number of goods is available. This period is so brief that producers generally cannot respond to changes in demand and price. For example, poultry farmers who have a limited number of chickens available to sell in the marketplace cannot increase that number in the market period to take advantage of an increased price. In order to increase supply, they would have to further expand their stocks, which would necessitate another growing season. Since their goods are per-

---

RECAP
ELASTICITY OF SUPPLY refers to the responsiveness (in percentage terms) of the quantity supplied of a good to changes in the price of the good. The major factor in determining elasticity of supply is the amount of time the producer has to respond to a given change in the product price. In the market period, supply is generally perfectly inelastic; in the short run, when the suppliers can vary some of their resources, it is relatively more elastic; and in the long run, when all resources are variable, supply is even more elastic, and can be perfectly elastic.

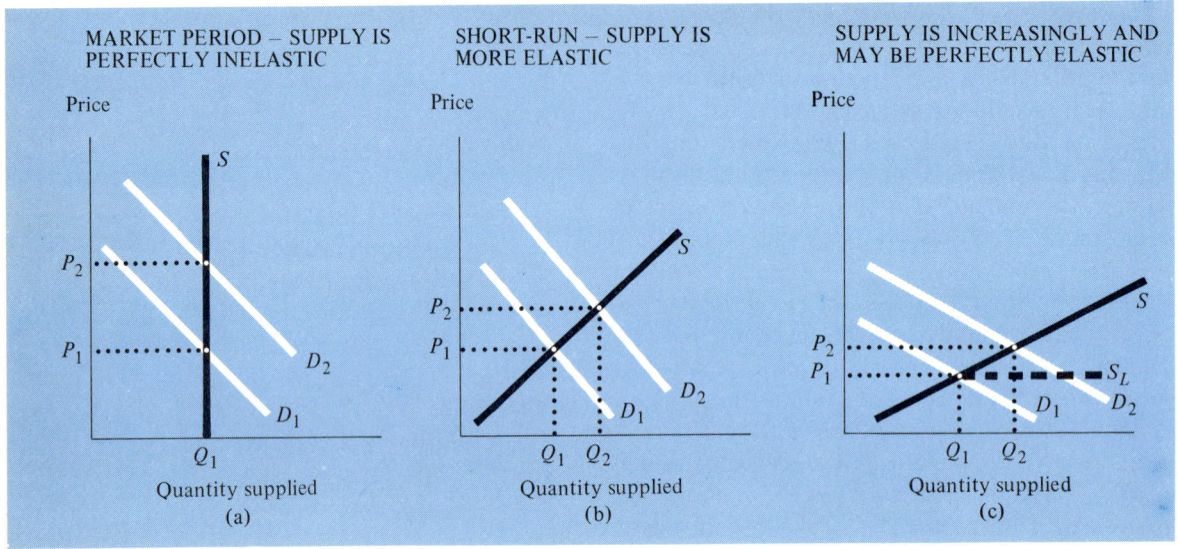

Fig. 20.4
(a) Even though a shift in the demand curve from D_1 to D_2 has caused the equilibrium price to increase from P_1 to P_2, the supplier cannot respond to these changes with an increase in the quantity supplied in such a short period of time. Therefore, the market period supply is perfectly inelastic. (b) In the short run, because certain resources can be varied, supply is more elastic. The supplier can respond to changes in demand (from D_1 to D_2) by increasing output from Q_1 to Q_2. (c) In the long run, all inputs in the production process become variable, and supply becomes more elastic (the percentage change from Q_1 to Q_2 is relatively larger than the change from P_1 to P_2). Eventually, supply may reach perfect elasticity (S_L) when the supplier will supply an unlimited amount at a given price (here, P_1).

ishable, farmers tend to sell all their goods at the prevailing price. *Figure 20.4(a)* illustrates this relationship between supply and demand in the market period with a supply curve that is perfectly price inelastic.

The short run
In the short run, producers have more flexibility to respond to changes in demand because certain of their resources are now variable. Although the short run does not allow for changes in plant size (the farm in this case), for example, producers do have time to make more or less efficient use of that plant. In the short run, poultry farmers can increase the number of chickens they raise, if, indeed, they have not yet reached plant capacity, or they can decrease that number in response to changing prices and/or demand. They might also crowd the chickens in the coop more or feed them more to get more pounds of chicken. The supply curve, illustrated by *Fig. 20.4(b)* is, as a result, more elastic. An increase in demand from D_1 to D_2 results in an increased supply, Q_1 to Q_2.

The long run
The long run is that time period that allows for all inputs in the production process to become variable. Individual plants can be enlarged or reduced

in size; existing firms may leave the industry while new firms may enter. In the long run, price elasticity of supply is thus at its greatest, reflecting the most flexible supply response to shifting demand. The poultry farmers cited in the examples above have sufficient time in the long run to increase or decrease their plant size, which may necessitate the acquisition or depletion of land and equipment, or they may even choose to leave the industry. In addition, they may experience new competition from entering chicken farmers.

In response to increased demand and higher prices for chickens, as illustrated by the shift from D_1 to D_2 in *Fig. 20.4(c)*, the long-run effect on output is relatively large and the price change is relatively small. The new long-run equilibrium price (P_2) reflects the increased cost of producing chickens for an expanded market—poultry farmers will pay more for their feed, machinery, land, etc., which will probably be in greater demand as the industry expands.

If, however, the farmers' expansion costs remain relatively constant, the price they need to make a profit will also remain constant in the expanding market. The "constant-cost" situation is reflected by the infinitely elastic supply curve S_L in *Fig. 20.4(c)*.

GOVERNMENT ACTIONS THAT AFFECT DEMAND AND SUPPLY

The model of the equilibrium level of demand and supply described in Chapter 3 assumed that trading was taking place under free-market conditions, with perfect competition. But sometimes the government intervenes in the trading of the marketplace to bolster the operation of the price system or to compensate for some of its shortcomings in terms of social policy.

The mechanisms of government action may vary widely, from offering a tax advantage to firms engaged in certain kinds of endeavors (oil exploration, for example) to the outright rationing of sales or fixing of prices. We shall now look at the ways that these various actions affect the workings of demand and supply.

Price ceilings

It sometimes happens that there is a sudden decline in the supply of some staple commodity. This may be the result of wartime shifts in production goals, an embargo of a foreign product such as oil, or a bad growing season that killed most of a crop. During World War II, for example, the United States experienced serious shortages of sugar, gasoline, rubber tires, and nylon stockings. And in 1973 the Arabs temporarily cut off their shipments of oil to the United States. If shown graphically, the supply curves for these goods would have shifted to the left.

If the price system is left to itself, it will adjust to such a shortage by causing prospective buyers to bid up the price of the good. Buyers will move back (upward to the left) along their demand curves to a new, higher equilibrium price. In a free-market situation, this might have the long-run effect of increasing supply (shifting the supply curve back to the right), since the new higher price of the good would allow producers to increase their production and still make a profit on the sale of the goods.

However, in the situations noted above, price increases cannot lead to an immediate increase in production. If most of the year's crop of grain is destroyed by a drought, no amount of price increase can supply more grain until the following fall. Similarly, it takes time to find and develop new sources of oil. In such cases the government may step in and establish **price ceilings**—*enforced maximum prices which can legally be charged for a good*—to keep the prices of such products as bread and gasoline from rising to exorbitant levels.

Figure 20.5 illustrates a price ceiling in the wheat market where both demand and supply pertain to a one-year period. The supply curve S_1 represents the output from a normal crop, while S_2 represents the supply of wheat during a drought

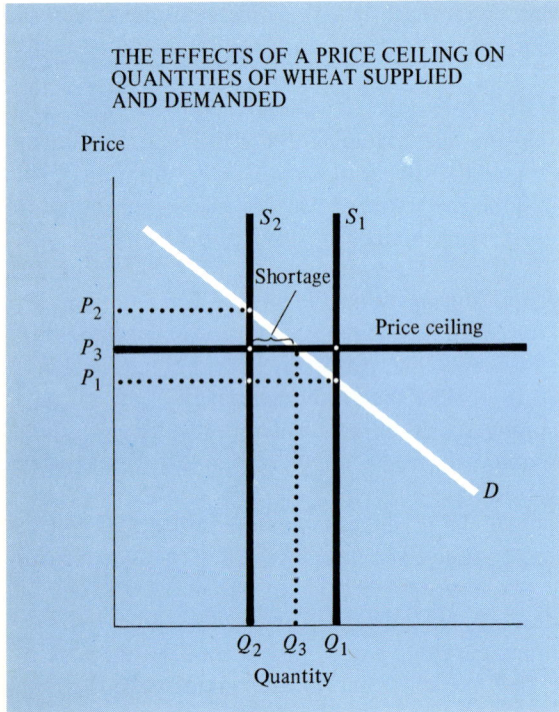

Fig. 20.5
In a drought year, the supply of wheat will shift from S_1 to S_2. Under normal conditions and given demand curve D, the quantity demanded at the new, higher price (P_2) will decrease from Q_1 to Q_2. If, however, the government imposes a price ceiling at P_3, consumers will demand Q_3 and a shortage of $Q_3 - Q_2$ will result because suppliers cannot produce any more wheat due to the drought.

year. Without government intererence, we know from Chapter 3 that the drought will simply cause the price of wheat to rise from its normal level of P_1 to the higher price of P_2. At P_2 the market will be in equilibrium and all who wish to purchase wheat at this price can readily do so.

If, instead, the government enforces a price ceiling of P_3, the result will be substantially different. At this price, consumers will wish to purchase Q_3, and since there is only Q_2 available, there will be a shortage of $Q_3 - Q_2$. Hence, some mechanism for allocating wheat, perhaps ration coupons, might be required.

The elasticity of demand for this commodity is an important determinant of both the amount that the price rises when the supply is reduced and the size of the shortage if in fact a price ceiling is enforced.

If demand is relatively inelastic, as shown by D_1 in *Fig. 20.6*, the price will rise substantially (from P_1 to P_2) without regulation when supply decreases by a relatively small amount (from S_1 to S_2). The shortage caused by the price ceiling at P_3 will be substantial ($Q_3 - Q_2$). On the other hand, if demand is relatively elastic, as shown by D_2, the opposite will hold true. A reduction in supply from S_1 to S_2 will cause a smaller rise in the free-market price (P_1 to P_2) and a price ceiling at P_3 will create a smaller shortage ($Q_4 - Q_2$). These implications are important to consider when deciding whether or not to implement such policies as price ceilings.

Effects of price ceilings
The usual effect of establishing price ceilings is to shift the competition among buyers into some area other than price. For example, in the early months of 1974, before the Arabs ended the oil embargo, gasoline stations shortened their hours because their limited supplies were inadequate for normal operations, and drivers arrived before dawn and waited hours in line to purchase what the operators could sell.

Black markets Another common result of establishing a maximum price is the development of a black market—since it is profitable for an individual to buy at the ceiling price and resell at the higher black-market price (which is equivalent to the free-market equilibrium price, plus a premium for the risk of being caught). In a black-market situation, the price system is once more allocating the scarce commodity. Often the government will decide to intervene by deciding who gets how much of the good. It determines the amount of the good available and issues ration tickets that will give each person a fair share.

Interestingly enough, the use of ration tickets may actually restore the working of the price system if the tickets can be bought and sold. Those who want the good most and are willing and able to afford a high price can buy other people's ration tickets. Others may shift to substitutes. In this situation, those who do not use the scarce product are given extra income rights, since when they sell their tickets they can keep the amount of money they receive. When selling is outlawed, a black market develops.

Effects of price ceilings on freely produced commodities Shortages due to wars or to crop failures are really beyond the ability of the price system to cure, since there is no way that the quantity supplied to the market can increase in response to a higher price for the good. But a very different situation prevails when the government puts a price ceiling on commodities that can be freely produced. From time to time, governments have attempted to give economic aid to the poor by fixing the prices of certain kinds of necessities—food, housing, medical care. This kind of interference with the working of the price system almost always creates more problems than it solves.

An example can be seen in the rent-control laws of New York City. Passed shortly after World War II, they were intended as protection for residents against great postwar rent increases on existing housing units because of a temporary housing shortage. One of the results has been a lack of incentive for suppliers to keep up the quality of apartments. Unable to raise rents, landlords cut corners on maintenance and repairs, allowing the apartments to become run down. Moreover, the rent-control laws have turned a temporary

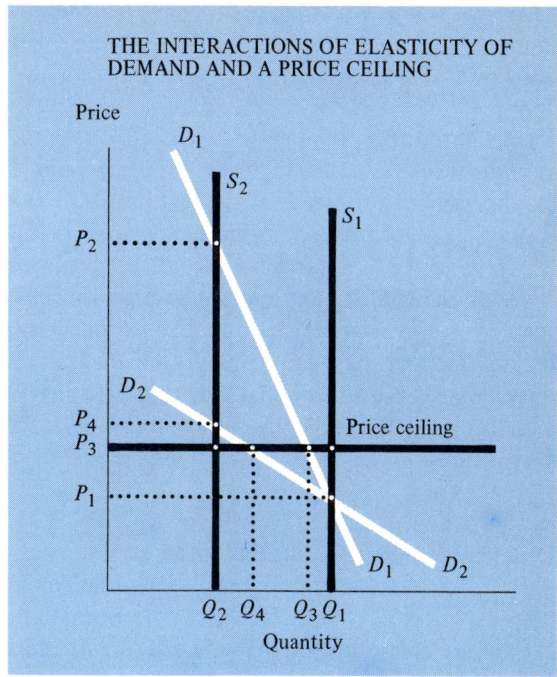

Fig. 20.6
If demand is relatively inelastic (D_1), the price of wheat will rise substantially (P_1 to P_2) when the supply drops from S_1 to S_2 due to the drought. If a price ceiling is set at P_3, consumers would demand Q_3 (given demand curve D_1). But if, due to the drought, suppliers can only supply Q_2, the resulting shortage is substantial: $Q_3 - Q_2$. If, however, demand is relatively elastic (D_2), the price would only increase from P_1 to P_4 as a result of the shift to S_2. At price ceiling P_3, consumers will demand Q_4 (given demand curve D_2), but producers can still only produce Q_2. Because of the more elastic demand, the shortage will be much less ($Q_4 - Q_2$) than it was with an inelastic demand.

shortage into a permanent one by discouraging the construction of new units for fear that they also would eventually become subject to rent control. Another effect has been an increase in the practice of giving bribes to owners for better service and maintenance—in effect, another example of a black market.

Price supports

Results similar to those caused by price ceilings can be found in the case of price supports. Price supports are enforced minimum prices below which the price of a good cannot fall. If this floor is above the equilibrium level, the result will be a surplus. At such prices the quantity supplied will be greater than the quantity that consumers wish to purchase. We will discuss this topic further in Chapter 24 when we consider the economics of agriculture.

Sales taxes

Other government actions that influence the workings of demand and supply include the implementation of sales taxes. In *Fig. 20.7* we see that the conditions of supply and demand for sassafras tea imply a stable market price of $3.00 a pound at which five pounds of tea will be demanded and supplied. What happens to the equilibrium price when we add to it a government-imposed sales tax of $1.00 a pound? The demand schedule remains unchanged, since the addition of the tax in no way changes consumers' desire, willingness, and ability to purchase certain amounts of tea at specific levels of price. What will change is the supply schedule, since it is the suppliers who must pay the tax to the government, which has the effect of raising the costs of production by $1.00 per pound. Thus, the tax shifts the supply schedule upward by the amount of the tax (from S_1 to S_2).

The change in the supply schedule means that there will be a new equilibrium level of demand and supply. As shown in *Fig. 20.7,* equilibrium is reached when a smaller volume of tea (4.5 pounds) is traded at a slightly higher price ($3.50 per pound). Part of the cost of the tax falls on the supplier, who must accept a slightly lower after-tax price for each pound of tea sold ($2.50), the other part falls on consumers who are willing to pay a

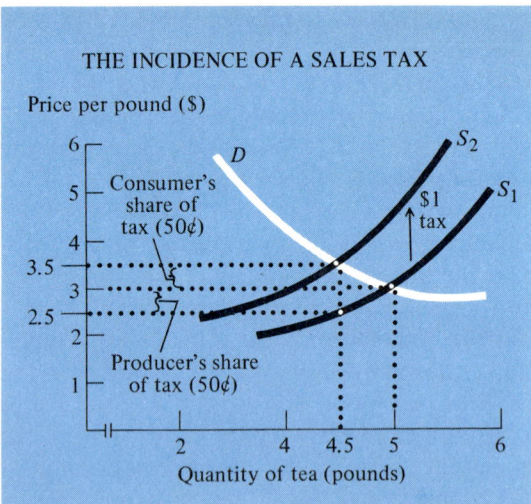

Fig. 20.7
A $1.00 tax on tea (which in effect increases the cost of production) shifts the supply curve upward by the amount of the tax shown S_1 to S_2. In this case, we see that consumers assume half of the burden of the tax, since they must now pay $3.50 per pound of tea instead of the previous $3.00. Producers, too, are assuming half of the burden of the tax; after the tax is paid, they now receive only $2.50 per pound of tea sold, in contrast to the $3.00 they received formerly.

little more money for the fewer units of tea they consume.

The exact division of the tax burden between supplier and demander will depend in part on the degree of elasticity of demand and supply. If demand is relatively inelastic, suppliers will shift more of the tax burden to the consumer. If demand is quite elastic, suppliers will assume more of the burden themselves.

Effects of other taxes

Similar effects will be observed from certain other kinds of taxes. For instance, excise taxes imposed on manufacturers will affect the equilibrium level of demand and supply in the same way that sales taxes do; so will import duties on goods brought to the United States from other countries to be sold here. Real estate taxes imposed on owners of rental properties will serve to increase rents and decrease the number of rental units on the market.

This effect of certain kinds of taxes is one that policymakers must keep in mind when deciding on tax schedules. A large sales tax suddenly imposed on a commodity for which demand is quite elastic would substantially decrease the quantity purchased. This would necessitate a cutback in production, with perhaps a resultant significant increase in unemployment.

Summary

■ This chapter begins our study of microeconomics by examining demand and supply in greater detail, developing the concept of elasticity, and considering the effects of government policies on the workings of demand and supply.

■ The elasticity of demand is a measure of the responsiveness (in percentage terms) of changes in quantity demanded to changes in price. Elasticity is computed as:

$$E_D = \frac{\% \text{ change in quantity}}{\% \text{ change in price}}.$$

If E_D is greater than 1 (percent change in quantity is greater than the percent change in price), demand is elastic; if E_D is less than 1 (percent change in quantity is less than percent change in price), demand is inelastic. Less frequently, demand for a particular good may be of unitary elasticity (when percentage changes in quantity exactly match percentage changes in price), perfectly elastic (when any given change in price produces an infinite change in quantity demanded), or perfectly inelastic (when changes in price do not affect quantity demanded at all). Generally, demand will be elastic in the upper portion of a demand curve, unitary in the middle range, and inelastic in the lower portion. Business firms have to consider price elasticity in order to estimate the effect of price changes on their total revenue.

■ Elasticity is affected by many factors, including the availability of substitute goods, the number of uses for particular product, the cost of a good relative to a household's income, the degree of necessity of the good, and the relevant time period in which a price change may have its full impact. In addition to price elasticity of demand, economists also make use of the concepts of income elasticity (the responsiveness in percentage terms of changes in quantity demanded to changes in income) and the cross elasticity of demand (the responsiveness of changes in quantity of one good demanded to changes in the price of another good).

■ Elasticity of supply is a measure of the responsiveness in percentage terms of changes in quantity supplied to changes in price. Supply is elastic when the change in quantity supplied is greater than the change in price, inelastic when it is less. The major factor in determining supply elasticity is the amount of time a producer has to respond to the price change. In the immediate market period, supply tends to be perfectly inelastic; in the short run, supply is more elastic;

and in the long run, supply is even more elastic, and may tend toward becoming perfectly elastic.

■ Many government actions can affect the workings of demand and supply in the market place. For example, government action to impose price ceilings on certain goods may perpetuate shortages and foster the growth of black markets. The more elastic the demand, the smaller the shortage created by such price ceilings; the more inelastic the demand, the more severe the shortages. Government sales taxes cause the supply curve to shift upward by the amount of the tax. If demand is inelastic, most of the burden of the tax will be shifted to the consumer; and if demand is elastic, most of the burden will be borne by suppliers. Excise taxes, price supports, and other policies may also affect the workings of demand and supply, and consideration of elasticities must always be taken into account in evaluating such policies.

Key Terms

elasticity of demand

elasticity coefficient

price elastic

price inelastic

unitary price elasticity

perfectly elastic demand

perfectly inelastic demand

income elasticity of demand

income elastic

income inelastic

cross elasticity of demand

elasticity of supply

price ceilings

Review & Discussion

1. What is elasticity of demand? What is the difference between price elasticity, income elasticity, and cross elasticity of demand?

2. Suppose the demand for a particular product is very elastic. What characteristics might you expect of the product?

3. For each of the products below, decide whether you would expect demand to be elastic or inelastic. Why?

new furniture

a degree from a private college

sculpture

postage stamps

cigarettes

record albums

4. How does the relative elasticity of demand faced by a business firm figure in its calculations about a potential price change? Under what circumstances would a price increase lead to reduced total revenues?

5. The demand curve for breakfast cereal is shown in the left column on the next page.

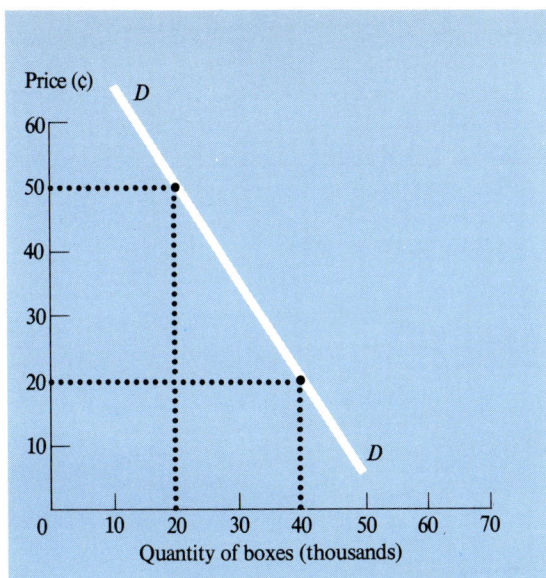

What would be the total revenue to the industry if the market price were 50¢? 20¢? How would you characterize the elasticity of demand for breakfast cereal?

6. How does time affect the elasticity of supply? What possible responses to a price change are available to businesses in the immediate market period, the short run, and the long run?

7. What are the consequences of imposing price ceilings? Critics of the rent-control programs in New York and other cities contend that such a price ceiling discourages new construction and maintenance and thus perpetuates a housing shortage. On the other hand, what are the possible consequences of *not* controlling rents in a city with hundreds of thousands of low-income families? What alternatives are there?

8. Suppose the demand and supply curves for tropical fish are those shown below. The government levies a tax on tropical fish of 15¢ per fish. What will happen to the price? Are fish sellers or fish buyers more likely to bear the burden of this tax? Why?

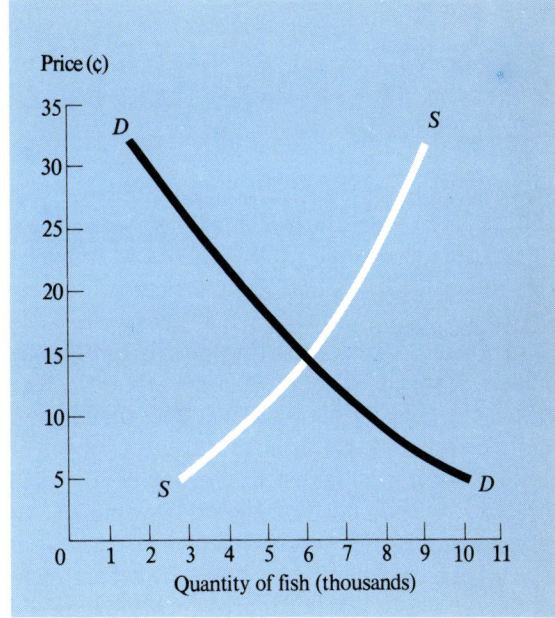

Application 11:
Elasticity of Demand and the Pocket Calculator

The cost of living doubled between the late 1960s and the late 1970s. But while most goods and services cost twice as much at the end of the decade as they did at the beginning, the prices of some were less than half of what they had been. One such good is the pocket calculator—the price of some models dropped by more than 40 percent a year during the ten-year period. The effect on demand of that decline in price illustrates the concept of elasticity of demand; that is, the degree to which the quantity demanded of a good is responsive to changes in the price of that good.

Introduced in the late 1960s, the hand-held calculator was at first far more expensive than the widely used slide rule or adding machine. One of the earliest hand-held calculators sold for about $300, or about ten times the price of a good slide rule and about five times the price of an adding machine.

But the calculator's price handicap soon disappeared. In the summer of 1972, Texas Instruments, Inc., which was to become one of the nation's largest calculator suppliers, introduced its first commercial model, the TI-2500, at a suggested retail price of $149.95. Five years later, the direct descendant of that model, the TI-1000, had a list price of only $8.95.

The market responded and calculator sales swelled from about 3 million calculators in the United States in 1972 to more than 26.1 million in 1977. Of course, in the long-run situation many other variables may have affected the increase in the numbers of calculators demanded by consumers. However, the effect of price decline was clearly an important one.

The decline in the price of calculators was made possible by many factors. In part, increased competition helped to lower calculator prices. The battle for a share of the rapidly growing calculator market was fierce enough that the number of manufacturers based in the United States dropped from a few dozen in the early days to just two in the late 1970s. But the major factor was technological advances—not only did manufacturers reap the usual economics of scale, which make each item cheaper to produce as more are produced, but the companies also found new ways to squeeze the essential electronic components into less space, thus reducing the cost per calculator.

As its price came down, the electronic calculator began to take the place of the adding machine for many uses, and some suppliers of the traditional machine, such as SCM Corporation and Singer, abandoned the business. In other cases, the pocket calculator supplanted the slide rule, and companies such as Keuffel & Esser Co., which had been major manufacturers of slide rules, stopped making the product and became distributors of calculators.

As calculators became more accessible to the general public, many people found a use for them. People who once had been content to use mental arithmetic or a pencil and scratch pad began using pocket-size calculators at the grocery store and to balance their checkbooks. And students were permitted and often encouraged to use calculators in school, even during mathematical examinations. As the elasticity concept would predict, by the late 1970s manufacturers found that price decreases had ceased to make much of a difference in sales of the least expensive calculators. Many calculator models seemed to sell about as well at $10 apiece as at $5, sometimes even better. Thus in the relation between the price and the demand for calculators, we are able to see the operation of elasticity in the marketplace.

Questions for discussion

☐ Describe the substitution effect as it relates to the history of electronic pocket calculators.

☐ Using the formula for calculating the elasticity of demand

$$E_D = \frac{\text{Change } Q}{(Q_1 + Q_2)/2} \div \frac{\text{Change } P}{(P_1 + P_2)/2}$$

calculate the elasticity of demand for calculators using the data given for the years 1972 and 1977. Is the demand elastic or inelastic? Why? What does this reflect about the demand for calculators?

☐ Although the demand for calculators is slightly inelastic, manufacturers found in the late 1970s that the demand for this became more inelastic. What are some possible explanations considering the determinants of the elasticity of demand?

Chapter 21

Consumer Demand

What to look for in this chapter

What assumptions do economists make about consumer behavior?

What is the significance of the concept of marginal utility? What is the law of diminishing marginal utility?

How do consumers maximize the total utility of all their purchases?

What is indifference theory?

How do the substitution effect and the income effect indicate that the law of demand is universal?

In the last chapter, we developed the concepts of elasticity of demand and supply and considered the effect of government economic policy on the workings of demand and supply. In this chapter we will consider demand further, focusing especially on theories of consumer behavior in an attempt to discover how consumers make their purchasing decisions.

THEORIES OF CONSUMER DEMAND

As we have noted, a market demand curve is the sum of individual household decisions about how many units of a good to purchase at varying price levels. The actual data can be collected simply by observing the way people act in the marketplace. A question of great interest to economists and to industry as well is why people make the choices they do. When paperback mystery novels are priced at 75¢ in the drugstore, why does Ms. Gardner buy only one book, whereas Mr. Doyle buys four?

To try to answer such questions, economists have formulated several theories of consumer demand. The practical applications of these theories are useful both to households, as they make their maximizing decisions, and to businesses, which must plan ahead to meet consumer demand promptly and efficiently.

Marginal utility theory

All theories of consumer behavior begin with the assumption that consumers are making rational choices concerning the allocation of their resources, with the ultimate goal of maximizing their own satisfaction. Economists speak of this goal as the desire to purchase the largest possible amount of consumer utility. In this sense, **utility** means *the ability to satisfy a particular want*. It does not refer to a good's actual usefulness. The consumer who spends $300 on a string of pearls may be buying just as much consumer utility as the consumer who spends the same amount on insulation for the attic; one person buys a few extra degrees of warmth and lower heating bills, while the other gets the pleasure of owning a beautiful ornament. Both goods have satisfied a particular want.

Total utility

The concept of total utility measures the sum of utility of all units of a good consumed. For example, the total utility of paperback mysteries to Mr. Doyle is the utility he derives from his first book plus the utility of the second book, and so on, right down to the utility of the book he is currently purchasing at the drug store.

It seems safe to conclude that the total utility of a necessity, like water or salt, is greater than the total utility of a nonnecessity, such as coffee or steak sauce or a TV set. Faced with the choice of giving up all water or giving up all television sets, everyone would choose to sacrifice the television sets. A woman with no water at all would gladly pay all that she had to get that first glass of water, whereas she would not pay more than several hundred dollars to acquire her first television set.

In actual fact, however, we pay much less for water and air than we do for television sets and other nonnecessities. Adam Smith first pointed out this curious fact in what he called the "diamond-water paradox." He asked why water, so necessary to sustain life, should have such a low price, while diamonds, merely an attractive kind of decoration, should be so expensive. The total value of water is much greater than the total value of diamonds; why, then, do diamonds cost more?

Marginal utility

The answer to Smith's question, provided by William Stanley Jevons (see biography), lies in the **marginal utility** of additional units of diamonds and water. Marginal utility is *the additional satisfaction derived from one additional unit of a good*. The first unit of water is very valuable, but since additional units of water are abundant and easy to obtain, by the time the last unit obtainable is used, it is yielding very little utility. But each diamond, scarce and costly to obtain, yields almost as much satisfaction as every other diamond previously purchased. Few people have so many diamonds that additional ones yield little utility. Diamonds have a much higher marginal utility than water, given the amounts of each that a typical person possesses.

Consumer demand for a commodity is not based on its total utility, because the choice facing each consumer is not whether to buy all of that commodity or none. The consumers are deciding whether or not they want to acquire an additional unit; therefore, they are willing to pay only the value of the marginal utility of the last unit they are getting. In the market, all trading is done in terms of marginal units, or at the margin.

More specifically, economists often think in terms of Jevons's **law of diminishing marginal utility.** This law states that, *in a given time period,*

DEVELOPMENTS IN ECONOMIC THOUGHT:

William Stanley Jevons

The decade of the 1870s marked an important turning point in the development of economic theory. Economics became a distinct academic discipline, taught primarily in university departments by a new breed of professionals. In contrast to an earlier era in which economic theory was advanced by philosophers (like Adam Smith) or ministers (like Malthus), economics increasingly became the concern of technicians, statisticians, and empirical researchers who were much less committed to grand social vision. The turning point in economic analysis in the 1870s involved the emergence of marginal utility theory, which was put forward independently but simultaneously by Karl Menger in Austria, Leon Walras in Switzerland, and William Stanley Jevons in England.

Jevons (1832–1882), probably the most influential representative of this entire generation of economists, was trained in mathematics and chemistry and taught economics at the University of Manchester and London University. His statement that "about politics I confess myself in a fog," suggests that Jevons was typical of the new economists who were not primarily concerned with social reform. Although he wrote widely on such topics in applied economics as labor relations, the British coal industry, and Australian gold mining, his major contributions were in pure theory.

Jevons's *Theory of Political Economy* (1871) was a strong statement of his belief in the necessity of applying mathematical principles to economic analysis. "It is clear," he wrote, "that Economics, if it is to be a science at all, must be a mathematical science.... The theory consists in applying the differential calculus to the familiar notions of wealth, utility, value, demand, supply, capital, interest, labour, and all the other quantitative notions belonging to the daily operations of industry. As the complete theory of almost every other science involves the use of that calculus, so we cannot have a true theory of Economics without its aid." Jevons's goal was to express fundamental economic principles in a relatively small number of basic equations.

A particular philosophical position, however, served as a starting point for Jevons's mathematical theorizing; this was the principle of utility, which states that individuals always act to maximize pleasure and minimize pain. The principle of utility assumes that all the participants in the economy are not only hedonistic (pleasure seeking) but are also completely rational in making choices among their various alternatives. Unlike classical economists who had concentrated on objective, social factors (such as price or population), Jevons emphasized the personal, subjective factors, and the concept of utility was the basis of his theory of value, exchange, and consumption.

Jevons paid particular attention to marginal utility, the additional satisfaction derived from one additional unit of a good. Since consumers are rational, according to Jevons, they weigh the advantages of one more unit of this good against one more unit of that good and make their decisions about various purchases in order to obtain the greatest utility or satisfaction. For the economy as a whole, Jevons concluded that in equilibrium, marginal utilities would be proportional to prices.

Critics of Jevons point out an historical irony about his work. In the 1870s, while he was developing a theory which focused on independent individuals making rational choices in a perfectly competitive market, the economies of the industrial nations were in fact becoming increasingly characterized by large concentrations of economic power, particularly monopolies and oligopolies. Nevertheless, although many of the particulars of Jevons's theories are no longer accepted, marginal utility analysis and its counterpart, marginal productivity analysis, remain central to modern economic theory.

---

as an individual acquires additional units of an economic good a point will be reached beyond which each additional unit provides less marginal utility than the previous one. It is especially easy to see this principle working in the case of water, where the first few units appear priceless.

Consumer surplus

The fact that prices are based on marginal rather than total utility has interesting implications for the consumer. The total amount Mr. Doyle spends for any good is the dollar value he places on the utility derived from the last unit purchased times the number of units purchased, since he generally pays the same price for every unit of an item, and he would not pay more for any one of the units than it is worth to him in utility. But the value of total utility to him, calculated by adding the utility value of the first unit to the value of the second, and so on, will be greater than the price he pays. Table 21.1 shows the marginal value of paperback books to Mr. Doyle. (This schedule is exactly the same as Doyle's demand schedule for paperback books.) Mr. Doyle buys only four books because, in terms of the marginal utility he derives from the fifth book, he values it at only 50¢—less than the market price of 75¢. His purchases of four books cost him $3, but if we add the total utility of his four books, we see that he has acquired $4.50 worth of total utility for his $3 expenditure.

The extra value for the consumer in excess of the price of the good is called a **consumer surplus**; it is shown in *Fig. 21.1*. The more units that are traded in the market, the greater the consumer surplus will probably be. This is one of the efficiencies of modern mass production. For example, in the fourteenth century, when books were handwritten, so few books were traded that a buyer had to pay for the total utility of each book. Today, millions of books are traded, so book buyers get the benefit of a large consumer surplus.

If a seller found herself in the relatively unusual position of being able to charge the consumer different prices for each unit, she might be able to reduce consumer surplus to zero. As an example, let us assume that the books were sold at auction. Mr. Doyle might bid $1.50 for the first book, $1.25 for the second, $1.00 for the third, and 75¢ for the fourth book. He would then be getting *no* surplus.

When only one unit is purchased at a time (such as an automobile), the seller is more likely to get the consumer to pay full value. However, if the seller is desperate to make a sale and the buyer can bluff the appearance of valuing the item less than he actually does, he may get a lower price and still keep some consumer surplus.

Maximizing utility

The goal of consumers is to maximize their total utility by the careful allocation of their income. They will choose the combination of purchases that adds most to their total utility. They will try to make sure that the last dollar they spend to buy any good obtains the greatest possible marginal utility.

Suppose, for example, that a young Yoga instructor has just received her weekly check for her take-home pay, $85.69. On the way home she passes the Mother Nature Health Food Center and

Table 21.1
The marginal value of paperback books to Mr. Doyle

Quantity of books consumed	Marginal value of each book
1	$1.50
2	1.25
3	1.00
4	.75
5	.50
6	.25

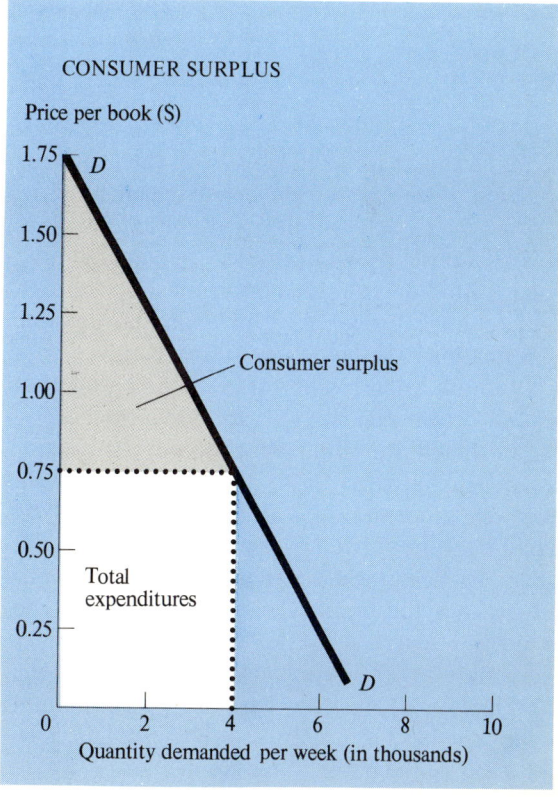

Fig. 21.1
At a market price of 75¢ per book, Mr. Doyle will buy four books, since 75¢ is the marginal value to him of the fourth book. Yet the first three books he bought were worth more to him than the price he paid for them; the shaded area represents this consumer surplus. The more units that are traded in the market, the larger the consumer surplus will be.

Table 21.2
Consumption possibilities of yogurt and rice with expenditures of $10

Quantity of yogurt ($1.00 per pint)	Quantity of rice (50¢ per pound)
10	0
9	2
8	4
7	6
6	8
5	10
4	12
3	14
2	16
1	18
0	20

decides to purchase a few staples for the following week. She determines that her budget will allow her to spend $10 on the two foods she likes most—natural brown Zen rice and goat's milk yogurt. But how will she choose how much of each item to buy? *Table 21.2* shows all the possible combinations she could buy for $10, given that goat's milk yogurt sells for $1 a pint and that natural brown Zen rice sells for 50¢ a pound.

Although she could afford to buy 10 pints of yogurt, she chooses not to allocate her money in that way, since she could derive greater utility by spending some portion of her $10 on rice. She will keep sacrificing additional units of yogurt until she reaches the point where the last dollar she spends on yogurt yields the same marginal utility as the last dollar she spends on rice. This is the combination that gives her the greatest total utility; she has no incentive to shift a dollar from one good to the other.

Equal marginal utility principle Economists call the attempt to balance marginal utility per last dollar spent the **equal marginal utility principle.** In our example, it can be expressed as the formula:

$$\frac{\text{MU of rice}}{\text{price of rice}} = \frac{\text{MU of yogurt}}{\text{price of yogurt}}$$

or

$$\frac{MU_1}{P_1} = \frac{MU_2}{P_2}.$$

When

$$\frac{MU_1}{P_1} = \frac{MU_2}{P_2} = \frac{MU_3}{P_3} = \frac{MU_4}{P_4} = \frac{MU_n}{P_n},$$

the consumer has achieved an equilibrium condition in which no changes in the way she allocates her income could yield any increase in total utility.

Now suppose that there is an increase in the price of good 1. If the consumer has previously divided her purchases to be in the optimum condition, the rise in P_1 will cause

$$\frac{MU_1}{P_1}$$

to be less than

$$\frac{MU_2}{P_2}.$$

RECAP

The THEORY OF MARGINAL UTILITY explains consumer demand as deriving from the desire to obtain the greatest amount of utility (satisfaction) from a good. According to this theory, in order to maximize total utility a consumer will allocate income so that the last dollar spent on each good is equal to the amount of satisfaction received from the additional unit of the good.

The consumer can increase her total utility by buying less of good 1 (as is predicted by the law of demand) and more of good 2. As the quantity purchased of good 1 declines, the utility derived from an extra unit (MU_1) will increase since each additional unit obtained is worth less. Similarly, as the quantity purchased of good 2 increases, the utility derived from an extra unit (MU_2) will diminish. This reallocation of expenditures will continue until the consumer is eventually in equilibrium again, with

$$\frac{MU_1}{P_1}$$

equal to

$$\frac{MU_2}{P_2}.$$

Criticisms of marginal utility theory

Of course, people do not explicitly make this calculation for each expenditure. There is no objective yardstick by which we can measure marginal utility right down to the last drop of satisfaction, and we do not actually perform all those computations each time we set foot in a store. But we all do have some conception of the value to us of additional units of various commodities, and we do allocate our incomes in a way roughly corresponding to the equal marginal utility principle. A household's budget is based on an estimate of the marginal utility yielded by additional units of various categories of expenditure. Similarly, a student's schedule, allocating certain times for study and others for socializing, applies the equal marginal utility principle to the scarce resource of time.

Indifference theory

The equal marginal utility principle is a useful concept, but as we have pointed out, it is difficult to apply when more precise statistical data are needed. The utility theory assumes that we can somehow measure amounts of satisfaction—10

Table 21.3
Indifference schedule for beer and cigarettes

Combinations		Marginal rate of substitution (cans of beer sacrificed to obtain one more pack of cigarettes)
Beer	Cigarettes	
48	1	8/1
40	2	7/1
33	3	6/1
27	4	5/1
22	5	4/1
18	6	3/1
15	7	2/1
13	8	1/1
12	9	

units of satisfaction derived from a tube of toothpaste and $7\frac{1}{2}$ units from a hamburger. Actually, however, no workable method of quantifying degrees of satisfaction has ever been devised. An alternative approach to explaining consumer behavior, which avoids the problem of measuring utility, is the use of *indifference theory*, specifically, the use of the **indifference curve**. The indifference curve is *a graphic representation of the various combinations of two goods which yield the same level of satisfaction to the consumer.*

Table 21.3 shows nine different combinations of beer and cigarettes that yield equal satisfaction to a single individual, Wilfred White. The combination of five packs of cigarettes and 22 cans of beer will give Wilfred just as much satisfaction as the combination of six packs of cigarettes and 18 cans of beer. He has no rational reason for choosing one combination over the other; in economic terms, he is *indifferent* to choosing between these two combinations of goods. If we plot these nine combinations of goods and draw a line

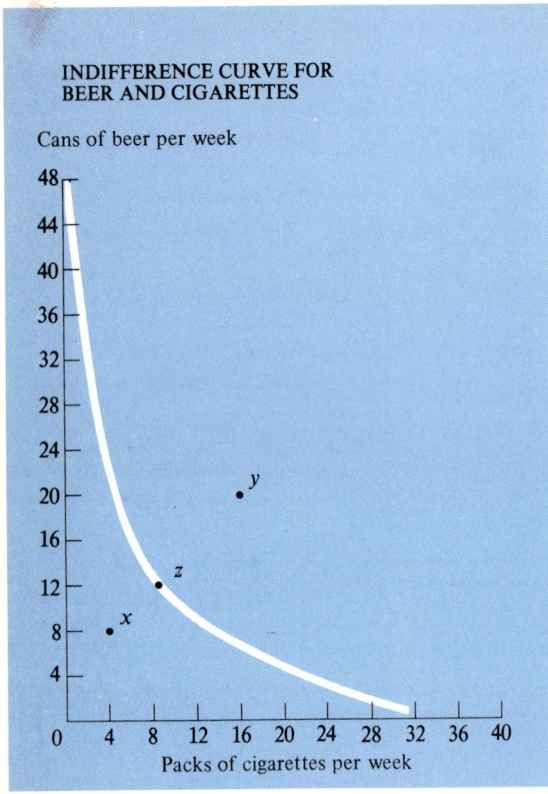

Fig. 21.2
This indifference curve shows all the combinations of beer and cigarettes that offer Wilfred White the same amount of satisfaction. Every point on the curve offers him exactly the same satisfaction as every other point, so he is indifferent to choosing between any of these combinations of goods. The curve slopes downward and to the right, indicating that in order to obtain the same utility from each combination of goods, Wilfred must compensate for a decrease in the quantity of beer consumed by increasing his consumption of cigarettes.

through the points (see *Fig. 21.2*), the resulting curve shows all the combinations of beer and cigarettes that offer Wilfred the same amount of satisfaction. The curve slopes downward and to the right, showing that in order to obtain the same total utility from each combination of goods, Wilfred must compensate for a reduction in the quantity of beer consumed by an increase in his consumption of cigarettes. The indifference curve gets flatter as we move downward, because as Wilfred continues to consume fewer cans of beer and more packs of cigarettes, he becomes willing to sacrifice fewer and fewer cans of beer to obtain one additional pack of cigarettes. This relationship, called a decreasing **marginal rate of substitution,** is shown in the right-hand column of *Table 21.3*. The marginal rate of substitution is *the number of units of one good that a consumer is willing to sacrifice to obtain an additional unit of another good, with total satisfaction remaining the same.*

The data given here do not carry Wilfred's rate of substitution beyond the ratio of one can of beer to one pack of cigarettes. But eventually it will take more than one pack of cigarettes to compensate for each additional can of beer that Wilfred gives up.

If Wilfred moves from one point to another on his indifference curve, he has changed the amount of beer and cigarettes consumed, but he has *not* changed his total satisfaction in any way. If he moves off the indifference curve to the left—for example, to point *x*—his level of satisfaction will decrease, since at *x* he has less beer *and* fewer cigarettes than at point *z*. If he moves to the right of the curve, for instance to point *y*, his satisfaction will increase.

Indifference maps
By changing the magnitude of the combinations offered to Wilfred, we can derive many other indifference curves, to the left and right of our first one (see *Fig. 21.3*). Since it is assumed that more is always preferred to less, Wilfred will prefer to be located on the indifference curve farthest to the right. But once on that curve, he is indifferent to the various combinations of beer and cigarettes located on that curve.

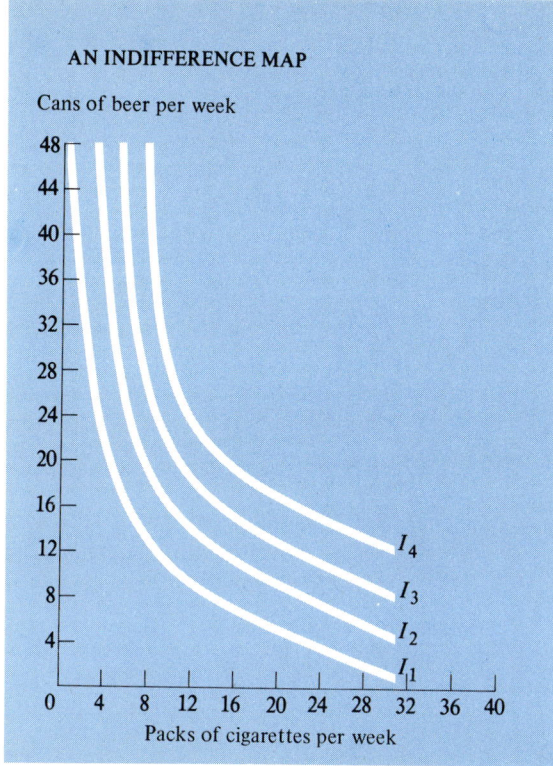

Fig. 21.3
On Wilfred's indifference map, I_4 will yield him greater satisfaction than I_3, and I_3 will yield greater satisfaction than I_2. Since we assume that more is always preferred to less, we know that Wilfred would prefer to be located on I_4. But once on that curve, he is indifferent to the various possible combinations of beer and cigarettes it shows.

This set of indifference curves, called an **indifference map,** *describes the range of consumer preferences.* But the indifference map alone cannot tell us which combination of the two goods a consumer will actually buy. To discover this, we have to investigate the individual's ability to consume. In this case, we need to know the amount of Wilfred's income and the prices of beer and

RECAP
An alternative way of describing consumer demand is to employ an INDIFFERENCE CURVE, which represents graphically the various combinations of two goods that yield the same level of satisfaction to the consumer. The indifference curve enables us to determine how many units of one good a consumer will have to sacrifice in order to obtain more units of another good.

cigarettes. From this information we can draw up a schedule of consumption possibilities.

Consumption possibilities: beer versus cigarettes
Let us imagine that Wilfred's daily income is $20, that beer costs 50¢ a can, and that cigarettes cost $1 a pack. From this information we can construct a consumption schedule such as the one shown in *Table 21.4*. It shows some of the various combinations of beer and cigarettes that Wilfred could purchase if he spent all of one day's income on these two goods. This consumption schedule is very much like the schedule of production possibilities we discussed in Chapter 2. It indicates a range of possibilities but says nothing about their relative desirability.

In *Fig. 21.4* the data from the consumption schedule are drawn on the indifference map. This gives us the **line of budget constraint,** or price line. This line *indicates the combinations of goods that a consumer may purchase, given the price of each good and the consumer's level of income.* Wilfred is able to purchase any combination of cigarettes and beer that falls on or to the left of the budget constraint line; he cannot afford the combinations that fall to the right of the line.

The budget constraint line does not at any point intersect the indifference curve farthest to the right; that means that Wilfred cannot afford

Table 21.4
Consumption possibilities for beer and cigarettes with an income of $20 per day

Quantity of beer (50¢ per can)	Quantity of cigarettes ($1 per pack)
40	0
36	2
32	4
28	6
24	8
20	10
16	12
12	14
8	16
4	18
0	20

any of the combinations on that curve. Wilfred can achieve the highest possible satisfaction level, given his tastes, his income, and current market prices of the goods he is buying, by purchasing the combination of goods located at point C (20 cans of beer and 10 packs of cigarettes). The combinations of goods represented by points A, B, D, and E are also possible for Wilfred to buy, but he will achieve greater satisfaction by moving to the highest possible indifference curve.

UNIVERSALITY OF THE LAW OF DEMAND

Economists formulated the law of demand by observing the behavior of buyers in the market. The data thus collected are supported by two theoretical concepts that help to explain why the law of demand is so universally applicable.

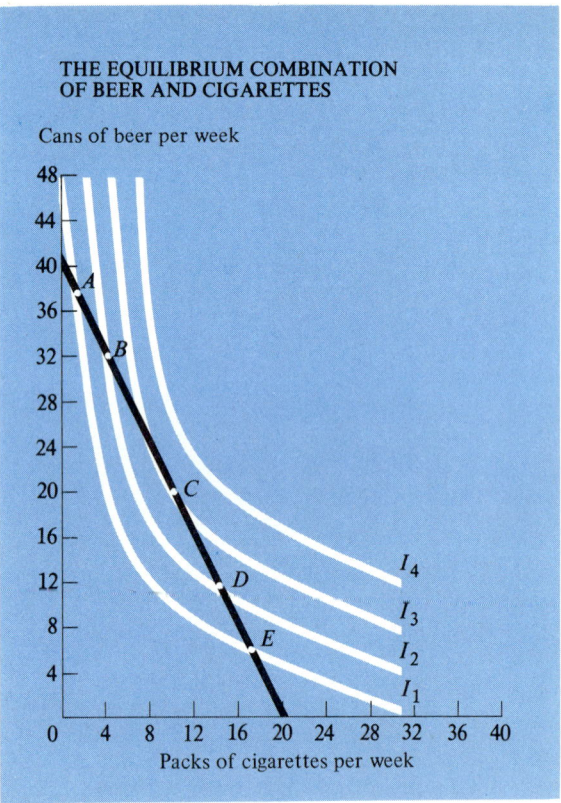

Fig. 21.4
By adding a budget constraint line to Wilfred's indifference map, we can determine the maximum satisfaction that he can actually afford to buy. Wilfred's daily income of $20 can buy either 40 cans of beer at 50¢ a can or 20 packs of cigarettes at $1 a pack. By joining these two extremes, we get his budget constraint line. Wilfred cannot afford to consume on I_4 because his budget line does not touch that curve. However, he can afford to consume on I_3, since the budget line touches it at point C. Although he could consume more beer at points A and B or more cigarettes at points D and E, his indifference map shows that these are less desirable bundles of goods to Wilfred, since they are located on lower indifference curves.

Substitution effect

The **substitution effect** states that *as the price of any commodity declines, consumers turn to that good as a substitute for other similar goods whose prices have remained the same.* Similarly, if the price of one good goes up, consumers will turn to other goods as substitutes. For example, when the price of hamburger goes up, many consumers will substitute chicken, which is relatively less expensive. When the relative prices of goods change, this substitution effect always holds true for any type of good.

Income effect

The effect of a change in prices is to alter the real purchasing power of the consumer. This is referred to as the **income effect.** For example, suppose that your laundry raises the price of washing and ironing a shirt from 50¢ to 60¢. Your weekly laundry of five shirts will now cost $3.00 instead of only $2.50. In effect, you have lost 50¢ of your weekly income. With a lower real income, you will now have to buy less of most goods; the total combination of goods you will be able to purchase is of less value in the marketplace, and so is the level of satisfaction it yields.

Substitution and income effects from changes in price

Let us return to our consumer, Wilfred White, to reinforce our understanding of the income and substitution effects. Suppose that the price of beer rises from 50¢ to $1 a can. With the same income of $20, Wilfred can now purchase a maximum of 20 cans, instead of the 40 cans he could purchase previously. This shift in Wilfred's consumption possibilities line is shown in *Fig. 21.5.* (Here we are assuming that Wilfred's consumption choice is no longer limited to beer and cigarettes alone; Wilfred can now choose between beer and all other goods.) The optimum consumption choice Wilfred can now make is 12 cans of beer and $8

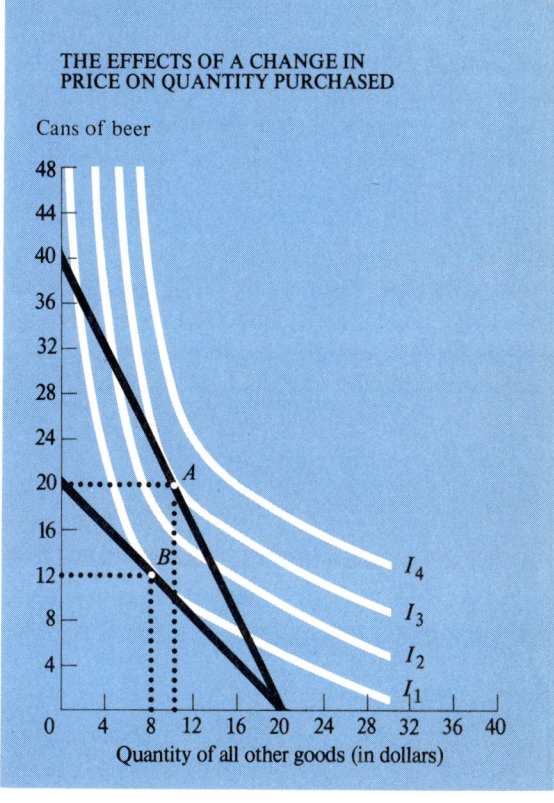

Fig. 21.5
An increase in the price of beer from 50¢ to $1 causes Wilfred to consume both fewer cans of beer and fewer of all other goods. His reduction in the quantity of beer consumed is due to both the substitution and the income effects, while his reduction in consumption of all other goods is due to the income effect alone.

worth of other goods—or point *B,* where his new budget line is tangent to the lower indifference curve I_1.

Wilfred is purchasing *both* fewer cans of beer *and* fewer units of all other goods than before, although the reduction in beer is greater than the reduction in other goods. These changes in Wilfred's consumption pattern can be explained by the income and substitution effects. Because the price of beer has risen, beer has become relatively more expensive when compared with all other reasonable substitutes for beer. Wilfred will therefore begin to substitute other goods for beer in his daily expenditure pattern. This is the substitution effect. However, the increase in the price of beer has now made Wilfred relatively poorer, in the sense that the overall purchasing power of his $20 income has declined. Because of this reduction in real income, Wilfred will buy fewer cans of beer and fewer units of other commodities, even though the prices of all other goods remained the same. This is the income effect.

We can conclude that Wilfred's reduction in his consumption of beer will be greater than his reduction in consumption of all other goods because for beer, both the income and substitution effects are at work, whereas for all other goods, only the income effect is influencing the level of consumption.

The income and substitution effects help to explain why the demand curve always slopes downward and to the right, and they give theoretical support to the observation that changes in quantity demanded are inversely related to changes in price.

Summary

■ This chapter continues our study of demand by examining theories of consumer behavior, in order to discover how consumers make their purchasing decisions.

■ Theories of consumer demand begin with the assumption that the consumer seeks to maximize satisfaction or utility. Total utility is a sum of all the utilities derived from each unit of a good that the consumer obtains; marginal utility (a more important concept in economic analysis) is the utility derived from the last unit obtained.

■ The law of diminishing marginal utility states that, in a given time period, as an individual acquires more units of an economic good, a point will be reached beyond which each additional unit provides less marginal utility than the previous unit. The price the consumer pays represents the value to him or her of the final unit purchased, the marginal utility. Hence total utility is greater than the total amount spent, and the difference between total utility of the good and total utility of the dollars spent is called a consumer surplus.

■ To maximize utility, the consumer will continue to adjust expenditures so that the last dollar spent for each good yields the same amount of additional utility from each good. This condition is represented as:

$$\frac{MU_1}{P_1} = \frac{MU_2}{P_2} = \frac{MU_3}{P_3} = \frac{MU_4}{P_4} = \frac{MU_n}{P_n}.$$

■ In analyzing the choices of consumers, economists make use of indifference curves. An indifference curve represents all the combinations of two goods that would yield the same amount of satisfaction—that is, the consumer is indifferent as to whether he or she is at one point on the curve or another. We can predict the choice that a consumer will make in purchasing the two goods by drawing a budget constraint line on the consumer's indifference map. The budget constraint line shows the various combinations that the consumer could purchase with a given amount of money and the specific prices for the two goods. The equilibrium point for the consumer is the point at which the budget line touches the highest possible indifference curve; this point represents the greatest satisfaction available to the consumer.

■ The law of demand states that as the price of a good rises, the quantity of the good demanded will fall. This relationship is confirmed by the substitution effect, in which an increase in price encourages consumers to switch to the purchase of relatively lower-priced substitutes, and by the income effect, in which a rise in price represents a decrease in real income to the consumer.

Key Terms

utility

marginal utility

law of diminishing marginal utility

consumer surplus

equal marginal utility principle

indifference curve

marginal rate of substitution

indifference map

line of budget constraint

substitution effect

income effect

Review & Discussion

1. Why do economists assume that consumers act rationally to maximize satisfaction? Is this a realistic assumption? For the assumption to be true, is it necessary for consumers to be conscious and explicit about calculating the utilities to be gained from different purchases?

2. What is the difference between marginal utility and total utility? What is the law of diminishing marginal utility? The consumer surplus? The equal marginal utility principle?

3. What is an indifference curve? An indifference map? How would you determine the combination of goods to be purchased with a given sum of money?

4. What is the substitution effect? The income effect? How do they support the economists' belief in the universality of the law of demand?

5. Consider your own behavior as a consumer. How do you determine your choice of purchases? Do you approach this decision making as a process of maximizing utility or as a process of acquiring necessities? Why would an economist say that there is no contradiction between these two approaches?

Chapter 22

The Costs of Production

What to look for in this chapter

How are the various costs of production defined?

What are the different product curves used by firms and economists to show the relationship between inputs and outputs? How are these curves related to each other?

What are the different cost curves used to represent the relationship between costs and output? How are these curves related to each other?

How does the information contained in product and cost curves influence a firm's short-run and long-run decision making?

In a market economy, product prices are arrived at through the interaction of the forces of demand and supply. In the previous chapter, we looked at the microeconomics of demand. Although many of the technical terms and concepts used to explain demand are unfamiliar to people outside the field of economics, the basis of demand—the consumer's decision to buy a certain number of goods at certain prices—is a part of everyone's daily life.

In studying supply, we are dealing with decisions that depend on production techniques and costs—matters that are unfamiliar to most people. In any large corporation, decisions about how and how much to produce are made by the business's management, not by consumers. Therefore, the mechanics of supply are much less familiar to us than the mechanics of demand.

What is the basic reason for a firm's decision to produce and supply to the market a certain quantity of goods? The quantity of goods that a firm is willing to supply at any given market price is determined by the cost of producing the goods; this link between production costs and supply is found in all kinds of markets—perfect competition, monopoly, and the range of market structures between these two extremes. In this chapter, we will look at the costs of production. The following chapters will examine how price and output are determined under different market conditions.

DEFINING COSTS

It will be helpful at this point to review and elaborate on some concepts that were covered earlier in the text. In particular, we will focus on the types of costs incurred by an individual firm.

Explicit and implicit costs

As we learned in Chapter 6, an important goal of any business firm is to make a profit. Simply defined, profit equals total revenue minus total costs. However, in calculating total costs, firm managers will add to the basic costs of buying and processing productive resources—their so-called explicit costs—the implicit costs incurred by the firm. Implicit costs, you will recall, can also be thought of as the opportunity cost of staying in business—the amount of money needed to bid all necessary resources away from alternative uses. In a proprietorship, implicit costs would include the salary that the owner could earn if she worked for someone else, the rental income the owner could receive if she leased her store to another businessperson, and the interest she could earn if the funds she has invested in the business were put into stocks or bonds or a savings account. In a corporation, the implicit costs would be the amount of income the firm's capital could earn if it were invested elsewhere. Stockholders who have invested in one particular corporation have sacrificed the opportunity cost of a reasonable return on the same amount of money invested in some other way.

It is important to emphasize that throughout our analysis, when we refer to "total costs," we mean both explicit and implicit costs. Therefore, when revenues are exactly equal to total costs, the business firm is making a **normal profit,** *a profit equal to what the same resources would earn elsewhere;* that is, the resources it employs are earning as much as they could in any alternative use. If total revenues are greater than total costs, the firm is actually earning an economic profit, a situation that encourages supply to increase since more profits can be made here than elsewhere.

Fixed and variable inputs

To determine a firm's production costs, we need to understand the relation between its input and its output. An important cost of any product is the cost of purchasing the resources of land, labor, and capital that it needs for production. In order to estimate the per-unit cost of any level of output, the firm must first know the quantity of inputs needed to produce that output.

All firms, whatever their size, are faced with some limitations of input possibilities in the short run. A common limitation is the size of the factory. For example, American Cyanamid has only a fixed number of machines that can make Formica counter tops. To expand, it would have to build a new factory and buy more machines, a process that might take several years. In most industries, the firm's capital goods and plant facilities are **fixed inputs** of production—*those productive resources that the firm cannot change in the short run.* Of course, fixed factors can be increased or decreased in the long run.

Variable inputs are *input factors that can be increased or decreased in the short run.* Labor inputs are usually quite variable, except where employees need highly specialized training and experience. The raw materials that manufacturers process are usually a variable input also; they can order a larger quantity (or use their inventory), or they can stop ordering raw materials. The real difference between a fixed input and a variable input is the length of time it takes to alter the amount of input the firm purchases. The exact classification of input as fixed or variable will depend on the individual situation of the firm.

Short run and long run

How do we distinguish between the concepts of short run and long run? It is impossible to define the short run in terms of a specific time, because it varies from industry to industry. In an industry where the costs of obtaining needed capital goods—the so-called "set-up" costs—are high, the short run may be two or three years. It would take at least that long, for example, for General Motors to build new factories or introduce a new model on the market. For a barber shop, though, the short run may be only three to six months; that is the length of time it might take to rent a new and larger building or buy some additional barber chairs.

As defined in Chapter 2, the short run is that period of time that is long enough to allow a firm to alter its variable inputs (usually labor and natural resources), but not its fixed inputs. For example, in the short run, a firm can add more workers, buy more raw materials, or add a night shift to increase its production. The firm can also decide to produce less in the short run. It can cut back production or lay off workers, thus underutilizing its existing capacity. Such a situation occurred in 1975, when automobile companies cut back production. However, in the short run, a firm cannot alter its total productive capacity.

The long run is the length of time sufficient to allow changes in fixed inputs as well. Thus, over time a firm can increase its total capacity by adding to its physical plant. In the long run, a firm can expand its productive capacity indefinitely, as long as operating at that new capacity will be profitable. A firm can also contract over the long run by selling some of its plant and equipment to other businesses, or by not replacing machines as they wear out. All inputs can be altered in the long run.

PRODUCT CURVES

As pointed out in the introduction to this chapter, the basic factor that determines the quantity of goods that a firm is willing to supply at any given price is the cost to the firm of producing the goods. In this section, we will present a general analysis of product curves that show how much of a single variable input (in our example, labor) a firm would need to use to produce various levels of output.

Total product curve

A **total product curve** *shows the total amount of output that can be produced from increasing levels of a variable input, holding all other inputs constant.* Figure 22.1 shows such a curve for the Delicious Doughnut Company; the curve is drawn from the data given in columns 1 and 2 of *Table 22.1*. The vertical axis shows the number of boxes of doughnuts produced, given a fixed amount of capital (the doughnut factory and the doughnut-making machines owned by the company). The horizontal axis shows the number of units of variable inputs that are added to the fixed factor; for simplicity of analysis, we will assume that labor is the only variable input.

At the start of the curve, the increase in output per added unit of labor is slight, because there are too few workers for the amount of capital equipment—an inefficient ratio. As we add more workers, the slope of the curve increases for a time, until it tapers off and eventually shows a downward movement. Between the origin of the curve and point *A*, each additional unit of labor yields a greater increase in output than the preceding unit. This range of the total product curve is called the *range of increasing returns*. From point *A* to point *B* the output continues to increase as

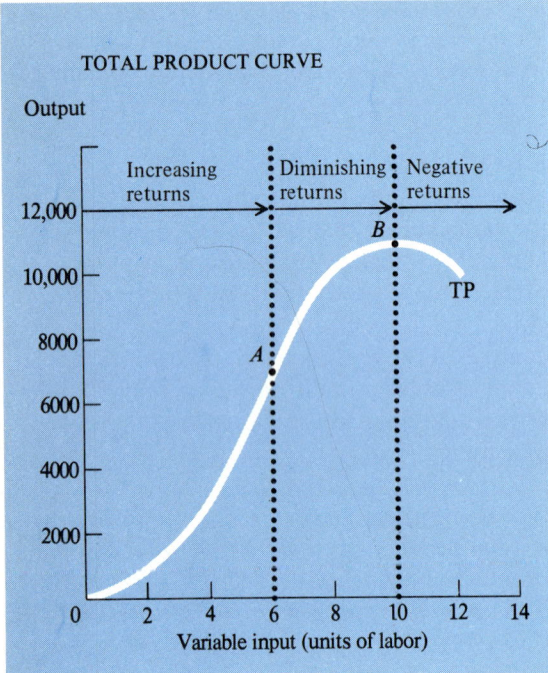

Fig. 22.1
Delicious Doughnut's total product curve shows the number of units of doughnuts it can produce by adding units of variable input (labor) to its fixed inputs of plant and machinery. Between points 0 and A, the company experiences increasing returns as it adds workers; between points A and B, it experiences diminishing returns (but the returns are still positive). Beyond point B, total product falls off, and returns are negative.

Table 22.1
Total, marginal, and average product curves for Delicious Doughnut Company

(1) Units of variable input (labor) (VI)	(2) Total product (TP)	(3) Marginal product $\left(MP = \dfrac{\text{change in TP}}{\text{change in VI}}\right)$	(4) Average product $\left(AP = \dfrac{TP}{VI}\right)$
1	200	600	200
2	800	1000	400
3	1,800	1200	600
4	3,000	1800	750
5	4,800	2200	960
6	7,000	2000	1170
7	9,000	1200	1290
8	10,200	600	1290
9	10,800	200	1200
10	11,000	−200	1100
11	10,800	−800	980
12	10,000		830

extra labor is added, but each additional unit of labor yields a smaller increase in output than the previous unit; this is called the *range of diminishing returns*. After point B, the yield is negative, as each unit of added labor actually decreases the size of output.

This shape of the total product curve—a range of increasing returns, followed by diminishing returns, followed by negative returns—is approximately the same for all kinds of products. Its characteristic slope between points A and B is due primarily to the law of diminishing returns, which, you will recall, states that beyond a certain point the addition of successive units of a variable input to some fixed factor of production will eventually result in a smaller and smaller amount of extra output.

Marginal product curve

Using our original total product data, we can derive the **marginal product (MP)** of each new worker. *The marginal product is the additional (or marginal) output obtained by adding each extra unit of variable input,* in this case, labor. The

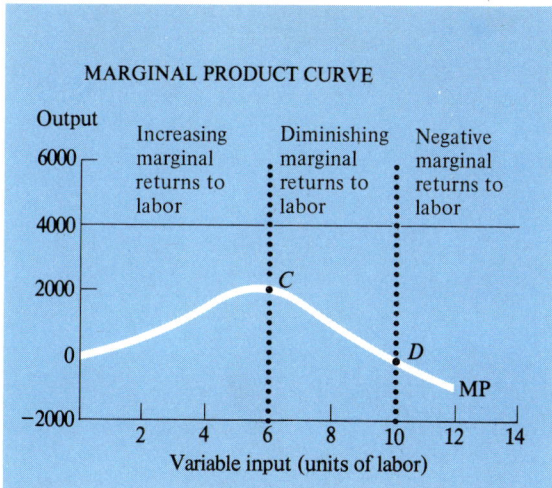

Fig. 22.2
We calculate the marginal product by dividing change in total product by the change in variable input. In other words, marginal product is equal to the slope of the total product curve. The MP curve shows increasing marginal returns to labor up to point C, diminishing marginal returns from C to D, and negative marginal returns beyond point D.

marginal product data for the Delicious Doughnut Company are given in column 3 of *Table 22.1*. To calculate marginal product, divide the change in total product by the change in variable input:

$$MP = \frac{\text{change in TP}}{\text{change in VI}}.$$

In other words, marginal product is equal to the slope of the total product curve, since the slope of a curve between any two points on it is the change in the vertical distance divided by the change in the horizontal distance. If we plot the marginal product data for the Delicious Doughnut Company (see *Fig. 22.2*), the resulting curve shows a steady rise until point C, and then a swift decline until point D, where the marginal product becomes negative, meaning that additional units of variable input will cause total output to decline. Again, this characteristic shape of the marginal product curve is the effect of the law of diminishing returns.

When we compare the marginal product curve and the total product curve (see *Fig. 22.3*), we see that total product continues to increase even after marginal product is declining. What is

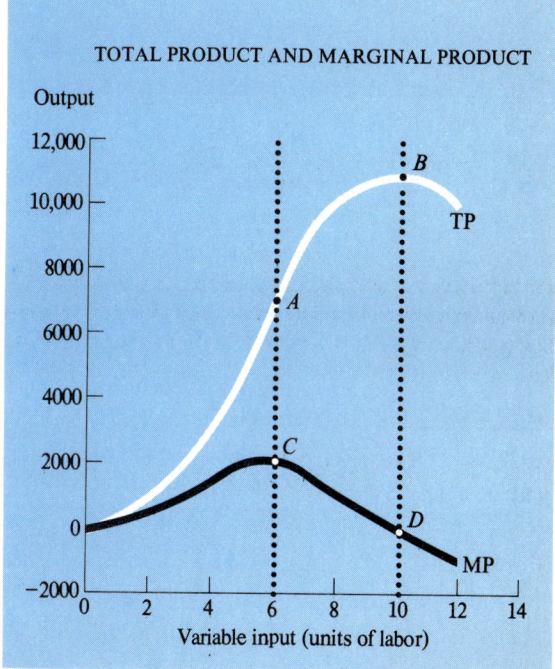

Fig. 22.3
Comparison of TP and MP curves shows that TP is still rising while MP is starting to fall. This means that beyond six units of labor, additional workers will still contribute to an increase in TP, but the amount of increase will be smaller as each worker is added. Beyond ten units of labor, extra workers will cause TP to decrease, since the workers' MP is negative.

the reason for this? Beyond point *A* on the total product curve, each additional worker still increases total production, but the amount by which production is increased—the marginal product—diminishes. Thus six workers is the point at which diminishing returns sets in, and it also represents the highest point on the MP curve (point *C* on *Fig. 22.3*). Total product does not decline until somewhere between the tenth and eleventh worker (point *B*)—the same number of workers at which the marginal product becomes negative (point *D*). Obviously, it would be unprofitable for any company to use any more units of variable input beyond this point, since adding costly labor would only decrease output.

Average product curve

With the original total product data for Delicious Doughnuts, we can also determine the **average product**, shown in column 4 of *Table 22.1*. The *average product is the ratio of total product to the*

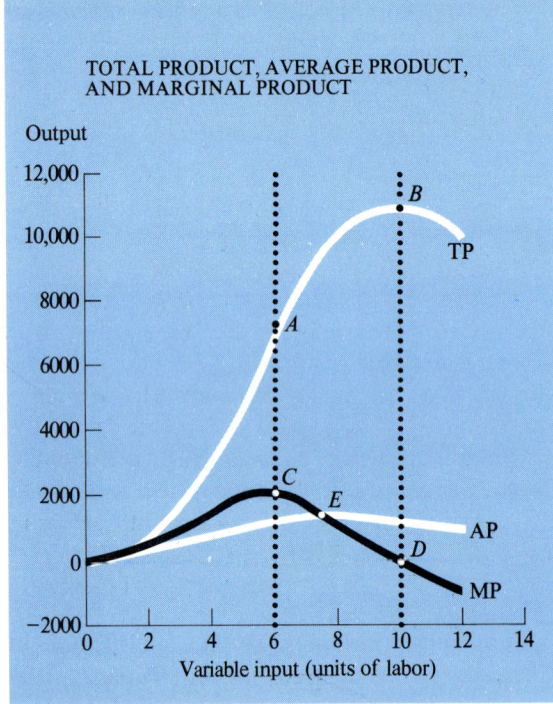

Fig. 22.4
The average product curve is derived by dividing the total product by the variable input at each level of production. The AP curve continues to rise even after the MP curve declines; the MP curve intersects the AP curve at point *E*, the highest point on the AP curve. For most companies, the actual production level will be somewhere between points *E* and *D*.

quantity of variable input resources used to produce that product. The formula for calculating the average product is

$$AP = \frac{TP}{\text{total VI}}.$$

If we plot the average product curve for Delicious Doughnuts and compare it with the total product and marginal product curves (as shown in *Fig.*

RECAP

Product curves represent graphically how much of a single variable input a firm would need to use to produce various levels of output. The various types of product curves include:

TOTAL PRODUCT CURVE—shows the total amount of output that can be produced from increasing levels of a variable input, holding all other inputs constant.

MARGINAL PRODUCT CURVE—shows the additional output obtained by adding each extra unit of variable input.

AVERAGE PRODUCT CURVE—shows the ratio of total product to the quantity of variable input resources used to produce that product.

22.4), we see that the AP curve reaches its peak while the TP curve is still rising. We also see that the MP curve intersects the AP curve at the latter's highest point, point *E*. This relationship will always be the same. As long as MP is greater than AP, each additional worker will be adding more to the total product than the average of all workers up to that point, and therefore the AP curve is still rising. As soon as an extra worker adds less to total product than the average up to that point, the MP curve will be below the AP curve, and the AP curve will fall.

As long as the AP curve is still rising, most companies will have an incentive to continue to increase production; any level of production that uses fewer units of variable input is not making full use of available fixed input and is therefore inefficient and more costly. On the other hand, the company will not want to produce beyond the point where MP is negative and TP is declining. In most cases, actual production levels will fall somewhere between the top of the AP curve and the point at which MP becomes negative. The exact output is determined by costs and demand (price), as well as by the production situation.

In the short run, the product curves of the Delicious Doughnut Company are fixed. But in the long run, if demand is large and if the industry in general is experiencing excess profits, the company can shift its TP curve upward, by adding more units of fixed input.

SHORT-RUN COSTS

The product curves we have developed show us how much of a single variable input—labor—the firm would need to use to produce each level of output. By attaching prices to all variable inputs, as well as to fixed inputs, we are able to derive a schedule that shows various costs of production at various levels of output. *Table 22.2* is a cost schedule for the Delicious Doughnut Company. The total product data presented in *Table 22.1* now appear in column 1 of the cost schedule as the quantity of output. To simplify our analysis, we have assumed that one unit of output equals 1000 doughnuts. Through the use of graphs we will examine how each of the cost concepts presented in *Table 22.2* is related to the level of output.

Our discussion will focus on the short-run costs, since we will continue to assume that it is not presently possible to increase certain factors of production (the doughnut factory and its machines). Of course, in the long run a firm can increase both variable and fixed factors. We will consider long-run costs in the last section of the chapter.

Total cost curve

The **total cost** to the firm of producing any quantity of goods is *the sum of the costs of its fixed inputs and the costs of its variable inputs.* The formula reads TC = TFC + TVC.

Variable costs

Variable costs include *the costs of labor, raw materials, electricity needed to operate the plant, and all other expenses connected with production that can be increased or decreased in the short run.* To make a curve showing total variable costs, we need to know how much of each unit of input is needed for every unit of output and how much those inputs will cost the firm.

Part of the information regarding the input-output relationship is already contained in the total product curve. *Figure 22.5(a)* shows again the TP curve for the Delicious Doughnut Company. In this graph, output is on the vertical axis, so the height of the curve measures the quantity of output. Now we are focusing our attention on costs rather than productivity, so it would be more useful to have the height of the curve measure quantity of input, or labor. We can do this by reversing the axes of the graph (see *Fig. 22.5b*). The vertical axis now shows units of variable labor input per unit of fixed output; the horizontal axis shows units of output per unit of fixed input. The new figure contains the same data as the figure

Table 22.2
Cost schedule for Delicious Doughnut Company

(1) Quantity of output (Q)*	(2) Total fixed cost (TFC)	(3) Total variable cost (TVC)	(4) Total cost (TC) TC = TFC + TVC	(5) Average fixed cost (AFC) AFC = $\frac{TFC}{Q}$	(6) Average variable cost (AVC) AVC = $\frac{TVC}{Q}$	(7) Average total cost (ATC) ATC = $\frac{TC}{Q}$	(8) Marginal cost (MC) MC = $\frac{\text{change in TC}}{\text{change in Q}}$
1	$35	$ 20.00	$ 55.00	$35.00	$20.00	$55.00	$ 8.00
2	35	28.00	63.00	17.50	14.00	31.50	6.00
3	35	34.00	69.00	11.67	11.33	23.00	4.00
4	35	38.00	73.00	8.75	9.50	18.25	4.00
5	35	42.00	77.00	7.00	8.40	15.40	5.00
6	35	47.00	82.00	5.83	7.83	13.67	7.00
7	35	54.00	89.00	5.00	7.71	12.71	10.00
8	35	64.00	99.00	4.38	8.00	12.38	16.00
9	35	80.00	115.00	3.89	8.89	12.78	23.00
10	35	103.00	138.00	3.50	10.30	13.80	31.00
11	35	134.00	169.00	3.18	12.18	15.36	

*1 unit = 1000 doughnuts

preceding it, but it presents the input-output relationship from a different viewpoint. Costs and productivity are actually opposite sides of the same relationship.

Figure 22.5(b) shows the relationship between the quantity of variable labor input and units of output. To turn this into a cost curve, we need only change the units on the vertical axis from numbers of inputs into dollar costs of the same number of inputs. For example, the first line on the vertical axis in Fig. 22.5(b) represents one worker; in Fig. 22.5(c) it represents the hourly wage of one worker, or $4. (We will assume for the moment that all firms pay the same prices for labor in a perfectly competitive market.) Figure 22.5(c), then, is the cost-of-labor curve. But labor is only one of the variable costs that a firm incurs. Column 3 of Table 22.2 shows Delicious Doughnut's total variable costs at each level of output. If we plot total variable costs, putting output on the horizontal axis and costs on the vertical axis, the result is a curve similar in shape to the cost-of-

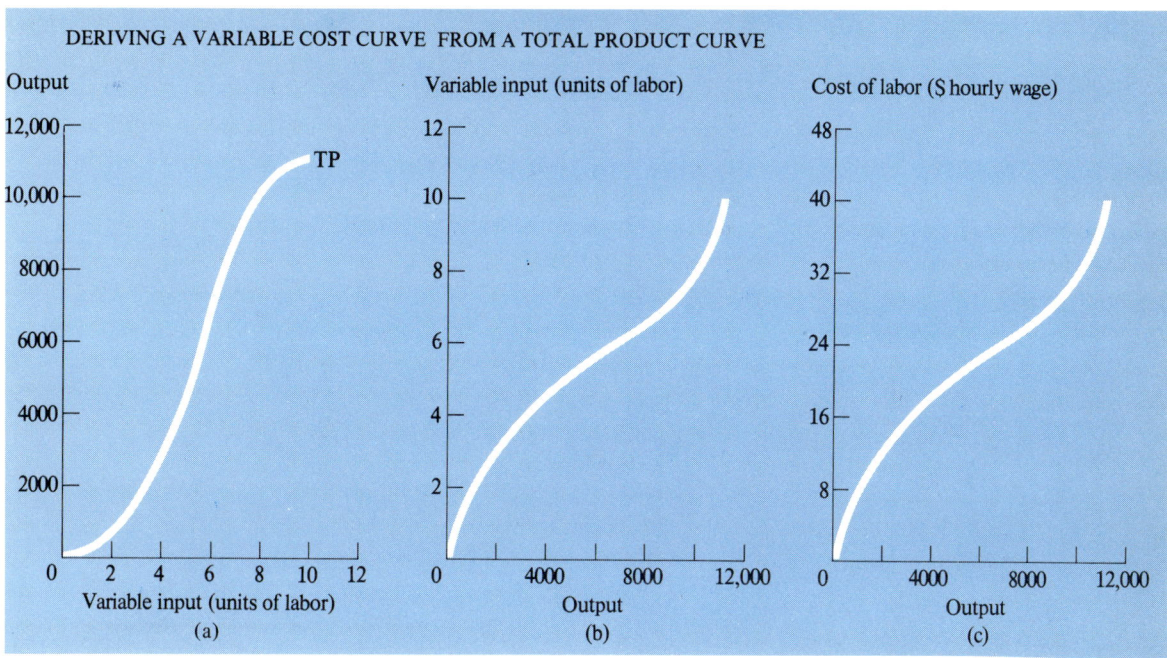

Fig. 22.5
The graph in (a) is the TP curve we have previously drawn for Delicious Doughnut; the vertical axis shows output and the horizontal axis shows variable input. In graph (b), we have simply reversed the two axes, putting input on the vertical axis and output on the horizontal axis. Both graphs show the same data. In graph (c), we change the measurement unit of the vertical axis. Instead of showing quantity of workers, it shows the cost of those workers' wages.

labor curve we just derived. *Figure 22.6* is the total variable cost (TVC) curve for Delicious Doughnuts.

Fixed costs

We have said that total costs are the sum of total variable costs plus total fixed costs. So to derive a total cost curve we must add to *Fig.* 22.6 the amount of total **fixed costs**. *Fixed costs are costs that cannot be increased or decreased in the short run, no matter what the size of the firm's output is.* These costs include the rental of the factory site, the interest on any bonds or loans, and the depreciation expense on plant and manufacturing equipment. Another name for the fixed costs of a business is overhead. The total fixed costs for Delicious Doughnut are $35 (shown in column 2 of *Table 22.2*).

Variable costs increase as the number of units of output increases, but as we have said, fixed costs do not change in the short run. Therefore, while total variable costs are represented by a

452 CHAPTER 22: THE COSTS OF PRODUCTION

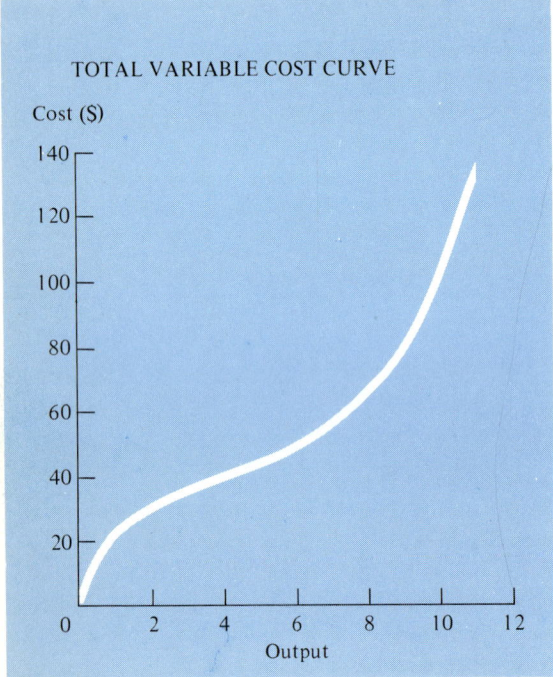

Fig. 22.6
This graph shows the cost to the company of obtaining variable inputs. It is like *Fig. 22.5(c)*, except that it adds the cost of all variable inputs—not labor alone.

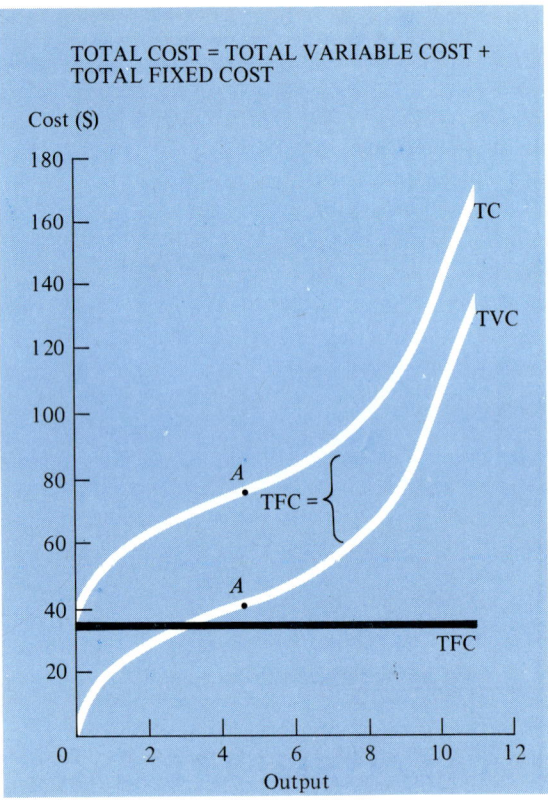

Fig. 22.7
To find total costs, we add to our TVC curve the amount of total fixed costs: TC = TVC + TFC. Since TFC is constant no matter what the level of production, we can show it by a straight horizontal line. The TC curve looks like the TVC curve, but it is located higher up the graph. Note that both the TC and TVC curves, like the total product curve, are governed by the law of diminishing returns. From the origin to point A, total costs and total variable costs are increasing, but at a decreasing rate. This area corresponds to the area of increasing returns on a total product curve. After point A, total costs and total variable costs both begin to increase at an increasing rate; this area corresponds to the area of diminishing returns on a total product curve.

curve that rises upward as it moves to the right (TVC rises as quantity rises), fixed costs will be represented by a horizontal line, since TFC is constant.

Total costs—graphic analysis

To arrive at the total costs for each level of output, add the amount of total variable costs and the amount of total fixed costs for each level of production. Since fixed costs are always the same, total costs will be greater than variable costs by exactly the same amount at every point on the curve. Therefore the TC curve will look exactly like the TVC curve, except that it will be located higher up on the graph—the distance between the two being equal to TFC. *Figure 22.7* shows the TC curve for Delicious Doughnuts, as well as the TVC and TFC curves from which it is derived.

The **total cost curve** *shows the total dollar costs for each different level of production.* Note that the curve slopes up and to the right. Like the total product curve, the total cost curve is governed by the law of diminishing returns. From the point of origin to point A, total costs are increasing but at a decreasing rate, whereas after point A, total costs are increasing at an increasing rate.

Marginal cost curve

A **marginal cost curve** *shows the additional cost of producing each additional unit of a product.* This curve is another way of looking at the same data presented in the total cost curve. However, the decision most firms must make is not whether to produce at all, but whether to produce additional units of their product. For this reason, the marginal cost curve is an important tool of analysis.

The TC curve already contains all the information we need in order to develop a marginal cost curve. The TC curve tells us that the cost of producing one unit of doughnuts is $55; the cost of producing two units is $63. The first unit costs $55 to produce, whereas the cost of producing an extra or marginal unit is only $8. The formula for calculating marginal cost is

$$MC = \frac{\text{change in TC}}{\text{change in output}}.$$

In other words, marginal cost is the slope of the total cost curve.

Figure 22.8 shows the MC curve for the Delicious Doughnut Company. It first declines and then rises, showing that marginal costs of the first several units drop rapidly, but after a while, marginal costs begin to increase. All MC curves have this characteristic shape that reflects the law of in-

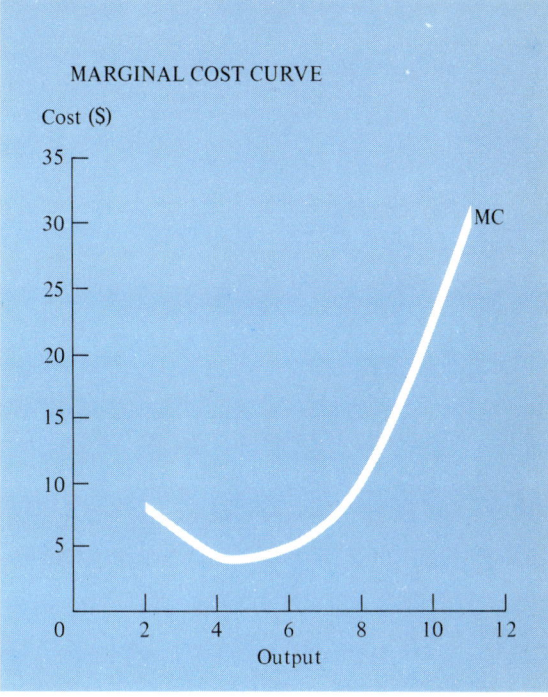

Fig. 22.8
The MC curve drops at the outset, but then it begins to climb as production expands to the point where the law of diminishing returns sets in. This curve shows that between the fifth and sixth units of output, marginal costs begin to rise; after this point, each additional unit will cost successively more.

creasing returns early in the production process, and then diminishing returns that set in as production expands. When we compare the MC curve with the TC curve (*Fig. 22.9*), we see that the point where MC begins to rise corresponds to the point where total costs begin to increase at an increasing rate.

The MC curve has a number of uses. As we will see later, a portion of it is actually the firm's short-run supply curve. It is also used by the firm

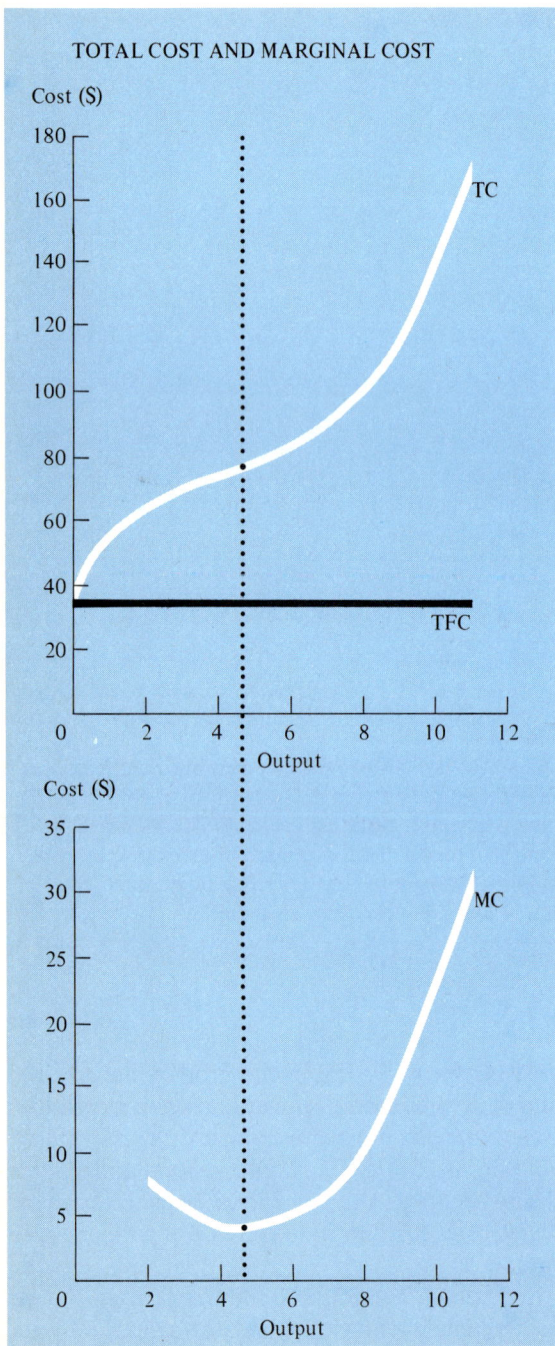

Fig. 22.9
This comparison of the TC and MC curves shows that TC begins to rise at an increasing rate at the same point at which the MC curve turns upward. This is the point at which diminishing returns set in.

to determine the level of production that will bring maximum profits, or in less advantageous circumstances, minimum losses.

Average cost curve

Let us now look at one other short-run cost concept—that of average or per-unit costs. Since product prices are always quoted on the basis of unit averages—the competitive businessperson must charge one single price for all units, even though some cost more to produce than others—it is necessary for the firm to know its average cost per unit.

Again, we need to distinguish between fixed, variable, and total costs. **Average fixed costs** are *the total fixed costs for any level of production divided by the number of units produced:*

$$\text{AFC} = \frac{\text{TFC}}{Q}.$$

We have seen that total fixed costs remain the same whatever the level of production (*Fig. 22.7*). When we divide that fixed amount of costs by an ever-increasing denominator (the number of units produced), the resulting average fixed cost will be smaller and smaller as more units are produced. This information (given in column 5 of *Table 22.2*) is shown in *Fig. 22.10* as a downward-sloping curve; this shape is characteristic of all AFC curves.

Average variable costs are *the total variable costs at each level of production divided by the total number of units produced:*

$$\text{AVC} = \frac{\text{TVC}}{Q}.$$

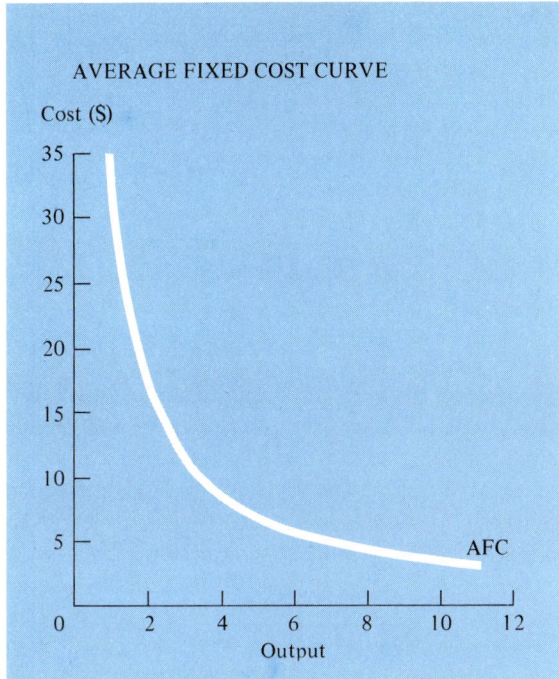

Fig. 22.10
We calculate average fixed costs by dividing total fixed costs by the quantity of units produced at any level of production. The AFC curve is always a downward-sloping curve; we have a fixed numerator divided by an ever-increasing denominator.

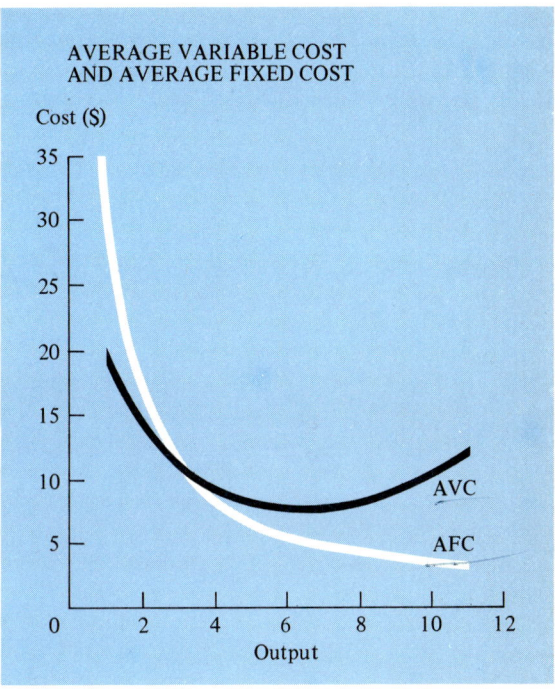

Fig. 22.11
We calculate average variable cost by dividing total variable costs at each level of production by the total number of units produced. The AVC curve shows a slight initial decline and then a steady increase beyond the level of seven units of output.

Plotting the AVC information (given in column 6, *Table 22.2*) results in the curve shown in *Fig. 22.11*. At first, the curve slopes down because of the increasing returns that the initial levels of variable inputs yield. But soon the law of diminishing returns takes effect, and the cost curve slopes upward.

The **average total cost** (ATC) is *the total cost to the firm at any level of output divided by the total quantity of output*. To find ATC we add AFC and AVC for each level output (see column 7, *Table 22.2*). Average total cost also can be calculated directly by dividing total cost at each level of production by the total number of units produced. The formula is

$$ATC = \frac{TC}{Q},$$

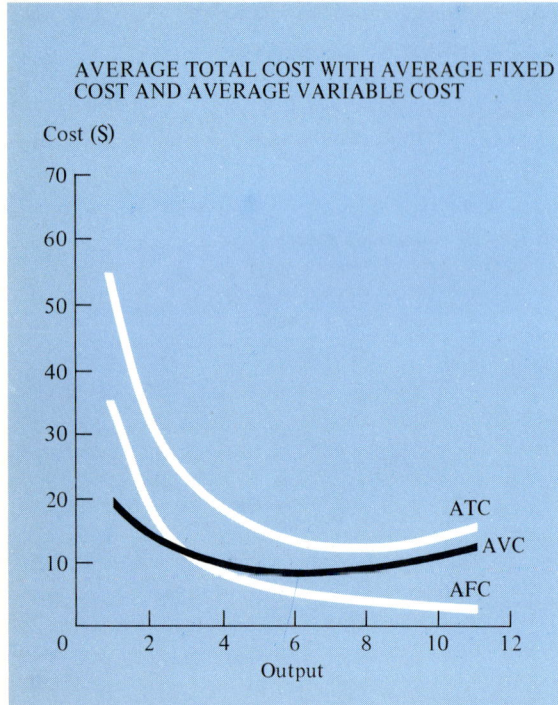

Fig. 22.12
To find the average total cost, we add the AVC and the AFC at every production level. The ATC curve shows the characteristic shape, due to initial increasing returns as the AFC curve drops and subsequent diminishing returns as the AVC curve climbs.

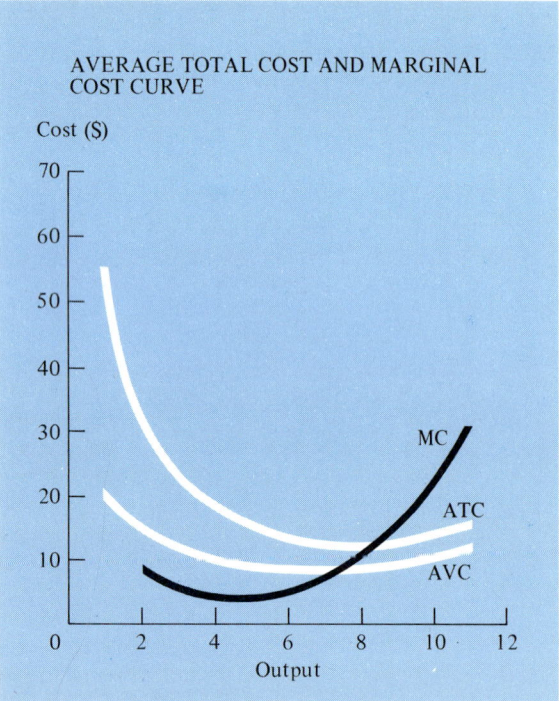

Fig. 22.13
Note that the MC curve intersects both average curves at their lowest points. This relationship between MC and AC curves will always hold true; it shows the relationship between marginal values and the average of all values.

or average total cost equals total cost divided by total quantity of output. *Figure 22.12* shows the ATC curve. Like the AVC curve, it falls initially and continues to fall even after the AVC starts to climb; this reflects the influence of the steadily declining AFC curve. Eventually, however, the ATC curve also starts to rise. By this time the effect of the law of diminishing returns overpowers the effect of diminishing average fixed cost. The ATC curve is always U-shaped. When AFC is greater than AVC, the ATC will go down.

Figure 22.13 plots the ATC and AVC curves on a graph containing the MC curve. Note that the MC curve intersects both the ATC and AVC curves at their lowest points. This is not a coincidence; it always happens with these curves because of their special relationship. This tells us that whenever the marginal cost of adding an extra

> **RECAP**
>
> Cost curves represent graphically the various costs of production at various levels of output. The various types of cost curves include:
>
> TOTAL COST CURVE—shows the total dollar costs for each different level of production. Total costs are arrived at by adding total variable costs and total fixed costs.
>
> MARGINAL COST CURVE—shows the additional cost of producing each additional unit of a product.
>
> AVERAGE COST CURVES—show the average or per-unit costs. There are three types of average cost curves: average fixed costs, average variable costs, and average total costs.

unit is less than the previous average cost, the average cost of the increased level of production will be pulled down. If marginal cost is above average cost, the average will be pulled up.

LONG-RUN COSTS

So far our analysis has focused only on the short-run costs. We have assumed that certain factors of production are limited and that it is not presently possible to increase them. But in the long run, a firm can choose any productive capacity it wants. Because of the firm's desire for profit maximization, it will want to choose the plant that will allow it to produce at the lowest possible cost per unit whatever quantity of goods it plans to offer to the market. How can the firm determine where that point of minimum costs will fall?

Once a plant is built, no matter what its size, it will be subject to the limitations of the short run. Its average total costs will be those we have already described in *Fig. 22.12*. The choice of plant size will be made by comparing the short-run average total cost curves for each size plant. For example, *Fig. 22.14* shows the short-run ATC curves for a number of different possible plant sizes. Let us assume that Q_2 is being produced; hence Delicious Doughnut's existing plant size is shown as ATC_3. If Delicious Doughnut wanted to

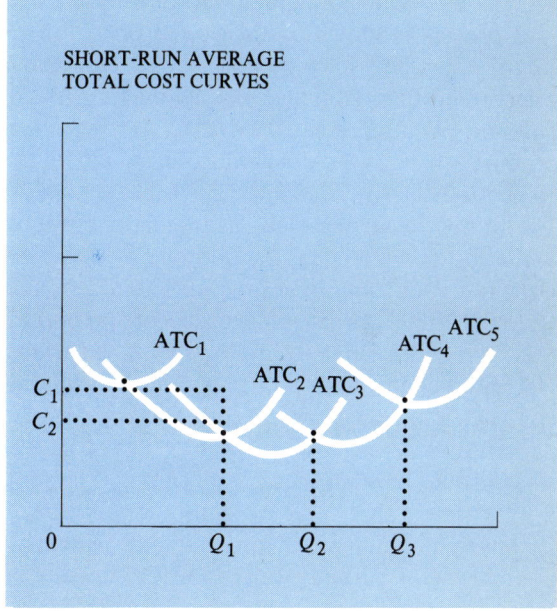

Fig. 22.14
This graph shows the ATC for plants of various sizes. The plant now occupied by Delicious Doughnut is represented by ATC_3; this is the optimum plant for producing at the level of Q_2. Suppose, however, that Delicious Doughnut decided to cut production back to Q_1. Delicious Doughnut could reduce costs from C_1 to C_2 by switching to the plant size represented by ATC_2.

make a long-run reduction in its level of production to Q_1, it would want to switch to the smaller plant shown as ATC_2, in order to lower per unit costs from C_1 to C_2. If it wanted to expand production in the long run, it would switch to a larger plant, such as ATC_4 or ATC_5, depending on the level of output it intended to produce.

The first decision the firm must make is the choice of the quantity it desires to produce in the long run. Once that is known, the firm simply compares ATC curves for different plant sizes and chooses the one with the lowest possible per-unit cost. Graphically this point can be found by drawing a vertical line straight up at the desired level of production and locating the point of intersection. This process is shown by the dotted lines in *Fig. 22.14*. If in the long run Delicious Doughnut wants to produce Q_2 units of doughnuts, it should build the plant represented by ATC_3; if it wants to produce Q_3 units of doughnuts, it should build plant ATC_4.

In one sense, the plant size that corresponds to the cost curve ATC_3 is the "optimum" scale for Delicious Doughnut, because on this curve the lowest possible average total cost occurs (at output Q_2). It is interesting to note that if Delicious Doughnut chooses to produce at a level of output less than Q_2, it will be cheaper for the firm to underutilize a plant rather than to overutilize a smaller one. In other words, the firm will be producing below that level of output which corresponds to minimum costs for that plant. Similarly, at any level of output greater than Q_2, it will pay Delicious Doughnut to overutilize a smaller plant, rather than underutilize a larger one. This means that the firm will be producing above that level of output at which minimum costs are achieved for a given plant.

By referring again to *Fig. 22.14*, we can verify the validity of these rules. From this we can conclude that a firm seeks to minimize costs, *given* output; it does not *select* output according to the minimum ATC of its existing plant. A firm does

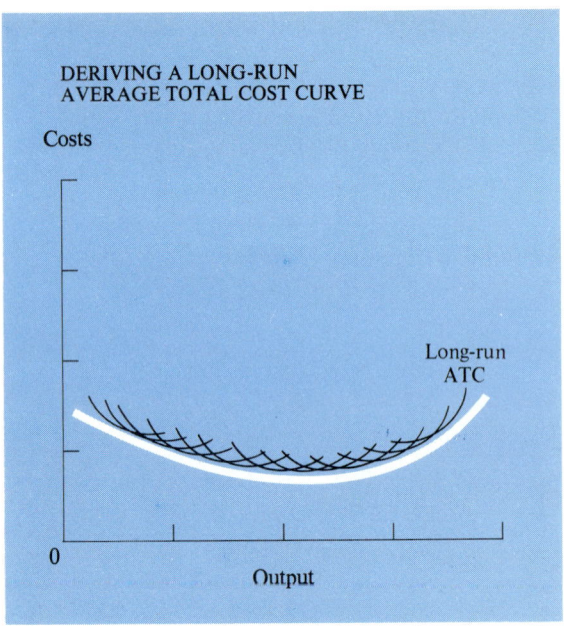

Fig. 22.15
To derive the long-run ATC curve, we connect the relevant points on the short-run ATC curve in a large envelope curve. The long-run ATC curve shows the lowest per-unit cost at which any level of output can be produced in the long run.

not build a plant and then select the output that achieves minimum average total costs. Rather, it selects an output and then builds the plant in which that output can be produced at the lowest cost.

In theory, there are an infinite number of possible plant sizes, not just the four we have shown in our example. To derive the long-run cost curve, we draw a curve connecting the relevant points on all short-run ATC curves—those points that represent the levels of output for the various plant sizes. This is shown in *Fig. 22.15*. The long-run ATC curve is a smooth U-shaped curve that touches all the short-run curves. Note, however, that the long-run curve does not touch the lowest point on each short-run ATC curve. The long-run ATC curve does *not* show the series of outputs that can be produced at minimum cost from each plant size. What the long-run ATC curve does show is the lowest per-unit cost at which any output can be produced in the long run. The shape of the long-run curve is due to the initial effect of economies of scale, with eventual diseconomies of scale setting in as production capacity continues to expand. The long-run average total cost curve is not subject to the law of diminishing returns, since we assume that in the long run any limiting factor can be increased.

Summary

■ This chapter examines the microeconomics of supply, specifically the links between the costs of production and supply.

■ In calculating the total costs of production, managers include both explicit and implicit costs. Explicit costs are the costs to the firm of buying and processing resources. Implicit costs are the opportunity costs of staying in business. When total revenue to the firm equals the total costs, the firm is making a normal profit. If total revenue is greater than total cost, the firm is making an economic profit.

■ The inputs that a firm must buy can be classified as fixed or variable. Fixed inputs are those productive resources that the firm cannot change in the short run, such as the basic plant facilities. Variable inputs are those resources that the firm can either increase or decrease in the short run, such as labor and raw materials.

■ The short run is the period of time that is too short for the firm to change its fixed inputs but within which the firm can nevertheless change its variable inputs. The long run is the period of time that the firm requires to change its fixed inputs. The short run and long run vary from industry to industry, depending on the amount of time needed to change variable and fixed inputs.

■ The total product curve for a firm shows the amount of output that the firm can produce with a given plant by changing the quantity of a variable input, such as labor. The total product curve slopes upward to the right, representing increases in output as the firm increases the amount of variable input. Eventually, however, the firm encounters diminishing returns, and the slope of the curve levels off and will eventually drop as the large quantity of variable input now interferes with the production process. The average product curve represents the ratio of total product to total variable input at each level of production. The marginal product curve intersects the average product curve at the latter's highest point. Actual production by a firm will occur somewhere between this point and the point at which marginal product becomes negative.

■ The marginal product curve shows the amount of added output produced by the firm when it adds one unit of variable input. The marginal product curve drops off more sharply and sooner than the total product curve and becomes negative at the point where the total product curve reaches its peak.

■ The total costs to the firm are the total fixed costs plus total variable costs. Marginal cost is the change in total cost brought about by a change in total output. Marginal cost is therefore the cost to the firm of adding one more unit of total output. The average cost curve is the total cost to the firm for a given amount of output divided by the total amount of output. The marginal cost curve intersects the average cost curve at the lowest point on the average cost curve.

■ The short-run average total cost curves for different sizes of plant appear as a series of U-shaped curves. The long-run average total cost curve touches all the short-run curves and represents the lowest average cost of production of any output in the long run. The slight U-shape of the long-run cost curve is due to initial economies of scale and eventual diseconomies of scale as the plant size continues to increase.

Key Terms

normal profit

fixed inputs

variable inputs

total product curve

marginal product

average product

total cost

variable costs

fixed costs

total cost curve

marginal cost curve

average fixed costs

average variable costs

average total cost

Review & Discussion

1. What are some of the explicit costs of production for a firm? What do managers include in their estimates of implicit costs? Under what conditions would the firm be making normal profits?

2. What are the firm's fixed and variable inputs? Why are the short run and the long run not specified as a given length of time?

3. What is the general shape of a total product curve? Why does the curve rise more slowly as it moves to the right?

4. What is the relationship between the marginal product curve and the total product curve? What does it mean when the marginal product curve becomes negative?

5. What are the components of total cost? How would you draw the total cost curve?

6. How is marginal cost computed? What is the general shape of a marginal cost curve? Why? What is the shape of an average cost curve? How are the marginal and average cost curves related?

7. How is the long-run average total cost curve related to the short-run average cost curve of the firm? Why does the long-run average total cost curve have the shape of a "U"?

8. A hypothetical firm, Handkerchief of America, Inc., can produce the total output for each number of workers shown in the schedule in the column to the left. Draw a total product curve from this schedule.

Number of workers	Output of handkerchiefs per week
1	40
2	75
3	110
4	135
5	155
6	170
7	180
8	185
9	186
10	185
11	180
12	170

9. Now draw the marginal product curve for Handkerchief of America. Why is it that the last few handkerchief workers actually reduce the number of handkerchiefs being produced?

10. Suppose that Handkerchief of America has the following costs for each level of production.

Number of units produced per day	Total cost of production
20	$100
30	120
40	130
50	135
60	150
70	170
80	190

Assume that the firm has fixed costs amounting to $60 per day. Draw the fixed, variable, and total cost curves for the firm. From the same schedule, draw the marginal cost curve.

Chapter 23

Price and Output under Perfect Competition

What to look for in this chapter

What are the characteristics of a perfectly competitive market?

How does a competitive firm maximize profits in the short run? How does such a firm reach its short-run equilibrium point?

How does an industry reach long-run equilibrium in a perfectly competitive market?

What are the benefits and drawbacks of perfectly competitive markets?

The previous chapters in this section have focused on a microeconomic analysis of the forces of demand and supply. The concepts presented in them are the tools that help us understand the workings of the market, where goods are sold by suppliers and purchased by demanders.

Economists have formulated two basic models for use in the study of markets: one for a perfectly competitive market, and the other for a monopoly market. Perfect competition and perfect monopoly represent opposite ends of the market spectrum. It is only rarely that we find either of these extreme models in an actual market situation. The American economy, for example, contains a mixture of both market types. Public utilities are nearly always monopolies; certain agricultural industries, such as the growing of roses, are almost perfectly competitive. The markets of most industries combine some of the features of perfect competition with some of the features of monopoly. To understand how the market works in a more realistic context—that is, in situations of imperfect competition—economists have developed two additional intermediate models, oligopoly and monopolistic competition.

This chapter, the first of three that will look at product markets, deals with price and output decisions under perfect competition. Perfect monopoly will be presented in Chapter 25, and oligopoly and monopolistic competition will be covered in Chapter 26.

CHARACTERISTICS OF PERFECT COMPETITION

Function of the market

The primary functon of the market is to bring together suppliers and demanders so that they can trade with one another. Buyers and sellers do not necessarily have to be in face-to-face contact; they can signal their desires and intentions through various intermediaries. For example, the demand for green beans in California is not expressed directly by the green bean consumers to the green bean growers. People who want green beans buy them at the grocery store; the store orders them from a vegetable wholesaler; the wholesaler buys them from a bean cooperative, whose manager tells local farmers of the size of current demand for green beans. The demanders of green beans are able to signal their demand schedule to the original suppliers, the farmers who raise the beans, without any personal communication between the two parties.

Suppliers may be located in a precise geographic area, and demanders may be specific groups of individuals. For example, in large cities, there is generally a warehouse area where fruit and vegetable wholesalers sell their fresh produce every morning to stores, hotels, and restaurants. But markets can also be diffuse and unspecific. We know how many pounds of green beans are sold annually to consumers in California, but we do not know who those consumers are. A woman who buys a pound of green beans does not think of herself as being in the green bean market, and she usually has no idea who else is in the market with her. But no matter how scattered the demanders may be or how many intermediaries are involved in the transaction between buyer and seller, a definite market is in operation as long as there is some mechanism by which buyers and sellers can signal to each other.

Assumptions of the perfect competition model

What does it mean when we say that a market is perfectly competitive? It means that we assume that certain basic conditions exist within the market.

☐ *There are many demanders and many suppliers in the market.* Every buyer has a wide choice of sellers with whom to make an exchange, and he or she can choose freely among them. If the price of one supplier is too high, the buyer will simply go to another supplier; therefore, all suppliers will charge the same price. This condition also assumes that all buyers and sellers have equal access to one another. Under perfect competition, no buyer would have to choose between paying a low price at a discount store 25 miles away or paying $5 more for the same product at a small neighborhood store. We assume that he or she can buy at one store just as easily as at another, and at exactly the same price.

☐ *No single buyer or seller is able to influence the price of the good.* Under perfect competition, each supplier's share of the market is an insignificant fraction of the whole. If one supplier raises prices, he or she does not have the power to coerce other firms into doing likewise, therefore the supplier loses customers, as buyers switch to lower-priced sellers. If the supplier cuts back production, the market will not experience a sudden shortage; if he or she increases production, there will not be any noticeable surplus of goods on the market. Similarly, no buyer makes large enough purchases to influence the position of the market demand curve. If one buyer drops out of the market (decides not to purchase anything), the market demand curve does not shift enough to cause a price decline. Prices will be determined solely by the equilibrium point of total market supply and demand; no one firm and no one buyer can significantly manipulate either of the curves.

☐ *The good being traded is a standardized, uniform product.* It is assumed that buyers cannot tell the difference between the goods produced by firm A and those produced by firm B. It is obvious that we could not expect to find perfect competition in any industry that deals with a specialized service, such as preparing food. The daily menu differs from restaurant to restaurant, as does the skill of the chef; so the product of the restaurant industry is by no means uniform. An example of a uniform product would be bushels of wheat or ingots of steel (although steel is not produced in a perfectly competitive market for other reasons, which we will discuss later).

☐ *All buyers and sellers have perfect knowledge of the market.* The model of perfect competition assumes that no supplier has any secret knowledge. As soon as one supplier discovers a new and cheaper way to produce the commodity, every other supplier has immediate access to the process. Under perfect competition, there would be no patents, no copyrights, and no trade secrets. It is also assumed that every buyer knows the price charged by all suppliers, as well as the function and utility value of the product.

☐ *All input resources are perfectly mobile and adaptable.* Under perfect competition, any firm that finds itself engaged in an industry where profits are low can switch immediately to another type of manufacturing. We assume that a factory's machinery can be quickly adjusted to produce soda crackers instead of diesel engines, that workers who have been packing sardines in tins will be able to operate jigsaws with the same degree of skill and speed. A firm can enter an industry overnight when it sees that costs are low and revenues high; if costs suddenly increase and the industry is no longer profitable, firms can leave the industry as quickly as they came into it. The only actual market that approaches this ideal flexibility is the market for financial capital. For example, one can easily sell shares in United States Steel and invest in the Nabisco Company on the same day.

Usefulness of the model

Perfect competition is not a description of an actual existing market. There is no perfectly competitive market in the United States. The various agricultural commodity industries are among the most competitive of our industries, and they are frequently used to illustrate the workings of a perfectly competitive market. In agricultural industries there are many suppliers; they are the small farmers. The products are standardized; we cannot tell the difference between oats grown by farmer McDonald in Nebraska and oats grown by farmer Grey in South Dakota. In addition, the farmer can generally adapt from one agricultural product to another. If oats are not profitable, either farmer can plant rye; if grain is not profitable, the farmer can plant alfalfa and keep cows, or plant feed corn and raise hogs. Finally, no single farmer supplies a large enough portion of the market to be able to affect the price of the product.

But even in these markets there are many competitive imperfections. Not all farmers use the most efficient methods of cultivation. To switch from growing oats to raising cows does take some time; the farmer would have to build a barn, buy milking machines and a hay baler, visit stock auctions all over the state to look for good dairy cows. It would take several years to learn to be as efficient at dairy farming as one was at growing oats. Moreover, most farmers sell their produce through a marketing cooperative, which can sometimes behave like monopoly since it controls large amounts of output.

You may wonder why, then, if the model of perfect competition is not very realistic, we should

> **RECAP**
>
> PERFECT COMPETITION is a basic model formulated by economists for use in analyzing the working of markets. The model of perfect competition assumes the following conditions: a large number of demanders and suppliers, none of whom is able to influence the price of the standardized, uniform product being traded; perfect knowledge of the market on the part of all buyers and sellers; and perfect mobility of resources used in the production process.

spend time analyzing it. It is important at this time to recall what we pointed out in Chapter 1: a model is an analytical tool; its purpose is to help us understand the economic principles underlying an actual market situation. We do not judge a model on the basis of its realism; a model is not necessarily good because it describes reality or bad because it assumes conditions that are rarely found in actual market situations. A model should be evaluated by looking at the results of analyses made with its help. Does the model give us a way to understand and to predict the behavior of real markets? Does it help us isolate causes and results of economic actions? Does it show us how to look at a complex chain of economic events and break it down into small steps that can be studied easily?

The model of perfect competition is the basis for many important economic principles, such as the laws of demand and supply, the way to determine the point of maximum profits for a firm or an industry, and the effects of disequilibrium on price and production levels. Thus the model of perfect competition is an extremely important analytical tool of the economist. Let us examine how the model helps to explain the operation of price and output.

THE COMPETITIVE FIRM IN THE SHORT RUN

In Chapter 22, we saw that the lowest point on a firm's short-run ATC curve is the level of production at which total per-unit costs are the lowest. However, we cannot therefore conclude that a firm will produce at that level of output. It might be more profitable for the firm to produce at some other production level; we cannot determine profitability by looking at costs alone. Profits are revenues minus costs; therefore, to discover the point of maximum profitability, we must introduce the factor of price.

Price in the perfectly competitive market

In a perfectly competitive market, the ruling market price is determined by the equilibrium point of the market demand and market supply curves. Recall that the market demand curve is the sum of all individual demand curves; the market supply curve is roughly the sum of all supply curves of all firms in the market (although we shall see that costs will rise more rapidly as the whole market expands than they will for the expansion of any one firm). A stable market price will be reached at the point where the amount demanded in the market is exactly equal to the amount supplied. *Figure 23.1* shows this equilibrium point in the trout-fly industry.

As we have said, under perfect competition, no individual firm can affect the market price of the good. Trout Fishing in America, Inc., can double its output and at the going market price sell all of it, it can double its price and sell zero, or it can leave the market altogether without any change in market price taking place. In this market situation, TFIA is a "price taker"; that is, the firm can sell any amount it wants to as long as it asks the going market price. Under perfect competition, the demand curve faced by any one firm appears perfectly elastic. The demand curve that TFIA faces is shown in *Fig. 23.2;* it is a straight, horizontal line drawn at 50¢—the market price of

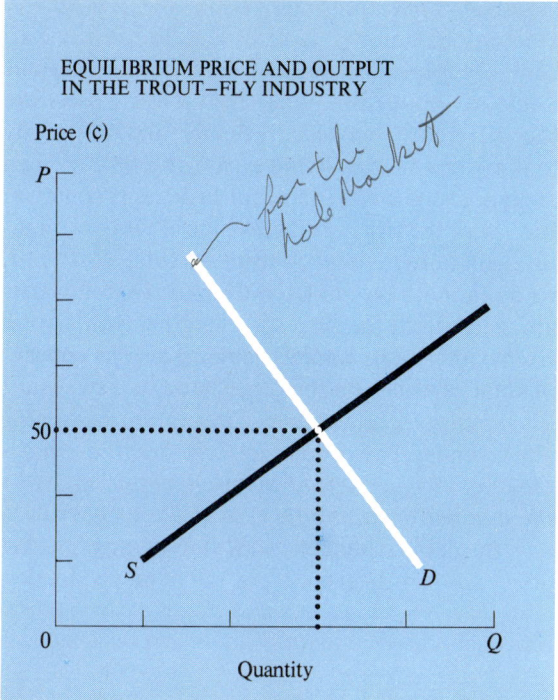

Fig. 23.1
The trout-fly industry as a whole faces a downward-sloping demand curve; for the whole industry to be able to sell a larger quantity of trout flies, the price of flies must be lowered. In the market, equilibrium between supply and demand will occur at the price level of 50¢.

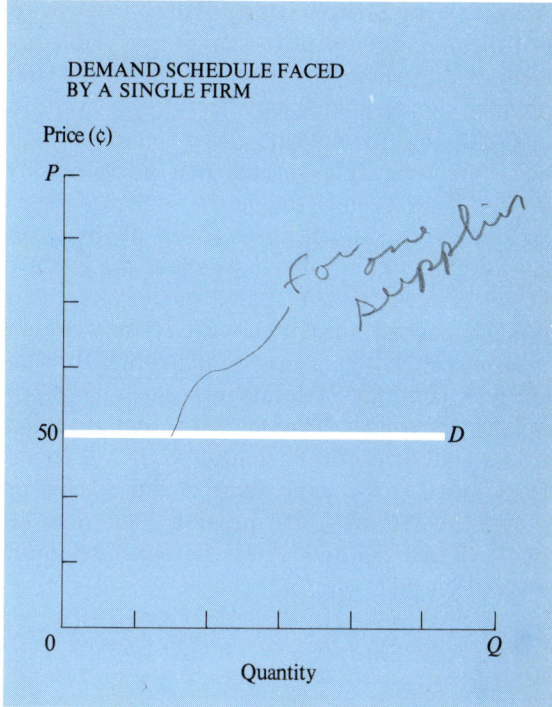

Fig. 23.2
The market forces of supply and demand establish the going price for trout flies. At that market price, under perfect competition, any single trout-fly firm can sell as large or small a quantity of trout flies as it desires to produce. The individual firm is thus faced with a horizontal, or perfectly elastic, demand curve; no matter what quantity it chooses to supply, the price it receives for each unit sold remains the same.

trout flies. This demand curve differs from the demand curve which an individual consumer has for a product; the consumer's demand curve is downward sloping since each successive unit of the good is less valuable.

It is interesting to note that TFIA has little incentive to lower its prices or to create a better product. At the going price, it can sell all the trout flies it can produce; therefore, there is no advantage to the firm in lowering its price in an effort to sell more trout flies. Nor is there any advantage in improving the product in order to increase demand for it, since from the standpoint of the firm, demand is already perfectly elastic; this means that the firm can sell any amount it produces at the current price. Under perfect competition, no supplier has any reason to try to undersell the going market price.

Maximizing short-run profits

For the purely competitive market as a whole, the level of output is determined by the equilibrium point of supply and demand. In the case of the individual firm, the demand curve it faces is virtually horizontal. This means that all additional units of a good can be sold at the same price as the previous units. This leads us to the obvious conclusion that a firm's decisions about the quantity it will produce are not based on the amount it thinks it can sell, since it is able to sell any amount it wants. How, then, does an individual firm under pure competition decide how much of its product it will produce? The answer is that given that firm's goal of profit maximization, it will choose to produce at the level where it will receive the greatest total profits. The question that remains to be answered is, how does the firm determine where that point will fall?

Total costs and total revenue

One way to find the point of greatest profits is to compare total revenues with total costs at various levels of production, since profits (or losses) are the difference between revenues and costs. By looking at columns 4 and 6 of *Table 23.1* we can compare total costs for Trout Fishing in America, Inc., with the firm's total revenue at various quantities of output. The concept of total cost is already familiar to you from Chapter 22; total costs are derived by adding together the firm's total fixed costs and its total variable costs. The concept of **total revenue**, on the other hand, is new, but it is very easy to calculate a firm's total revenue for any given level of production. *The total revenue is the price of each unit of the product multiplied by the number of units sold* ($TR = P \times Q$).

By comparing TR with TC at any market price, we can determine the range of production

Table 23.1
Total cost and revenue schedule for TFIA

(1) Quantity output per day (Q)	(2) Total fixed cost (TFC)	(3) Total variable cost (TVC)	(4) Total cost (TC) TC = TFC + TVC	(5) Price per unit (P)	(6) Total revenue (TR) TR = P × Q	(7) Net revenue (NR) NR = TR − TC
100	$100	$ 25	$125	$.50	$ 50	− $ 75
200	100	45	145	.50	100	− 45
300	100	60	160	.50	150	− 10
400	100	70	170	.50	200	+ 30
500	100	85	185	.50	250	+ 65
600	100	120	220	.50	300	+ 80
700	100	165	265	.50	350	+ 85
800	100	225	325	.50	400	+ 75
900	100	315	415	.50	450	+ 35
1000	100	420	520	.50	500	− 20
1100	100	560	660	.50	550	− 110
1200	100	730	830	.50	600	− 230

levels at which the firm would be able to make a profit, and the point of profit maximization. Given a market price of 50¢ in the trout-fly industry, the difference between TFIA's total cost and total revenue at each level of output is calculated in column 7 of *Table 23.1,* the net revenue column. Clearly, only when the difference between total revenue and total cost is positive will the firm be earning a profit. Remember that this profit will actually be an *economic profit,* since a normal profit is already included as an implicit part of total costs. From the table we can see that profits are maximized at the production level of 700 units.

Graphic analysis A graphic comparison of total costs (TC) and total revenues (TR) is presented in *Fig. 23.3.* It shows that the TC curve for TFIA has a shape similar to the TC curve presented in Chapter 22; it also shows that the TR curve is a straight line from the point of origin. In other words, the slope of the TR curve is constant. (This makes sense, since we know that the slope of the TR curve is equal to the change in total revenue divided by the change in quantity,

$$\frac{\Delta Q \times P}{\Delta Q} = P,$$

and price for the perfect competitor is the same for every level of output.) Clearly, when TR is above TC, the firm is making a profit. If the firm produced at any level to the left of point *A*, it

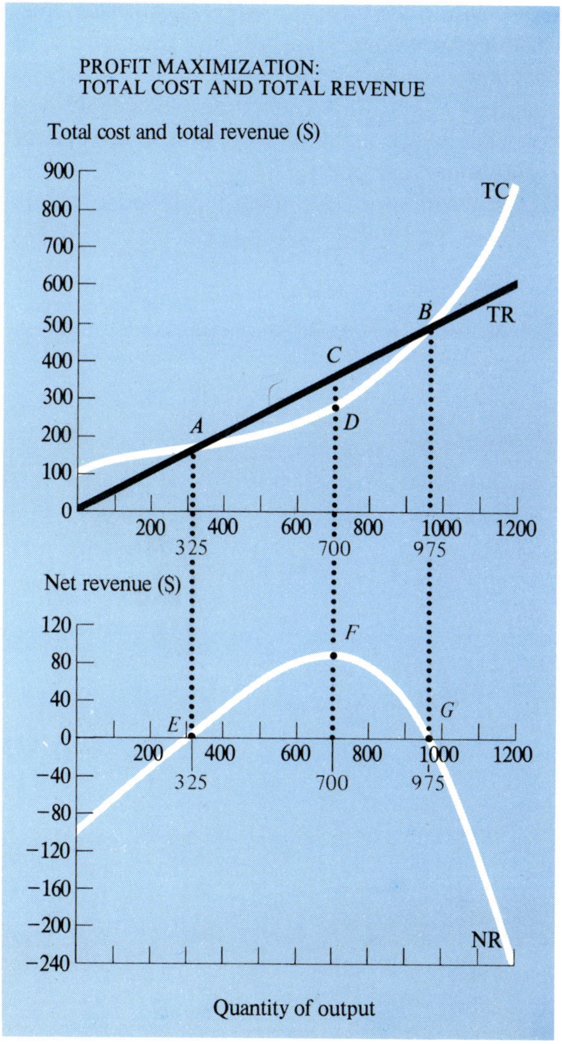

Fig. 23.3
The total cost curve for TFIA shows the familiar upward-sloping shape. Since price for the perfect competitor is the same at every level of production, the total revenue curve is actually a straight line with a constant slope. In order to show a profit, the total revenues of TFIA must be greater than the total costs. Therefore we can be certain that TFIA will produce only between points *A* and *B*. If it produces fewer than 325 units or more than 975, TC will be greater than TR. The production level at which the firm will enjoy maximum profits comes at 700 units, where the TR line is farthest above the TC curve (the distance *CD*). In terms of net revenue, we can see in the bottom graph that TFIA will only produce between points *E* and *G* (where its net revenue is positive). The production level at which the firm enjoys its greatest net revenue is at 700 units where the NR curve is farthest above the zero level of net revenue (point *F*).

would incur a loss, since costs would be greater than revenues. The same thing would be true if the firm were to produce at any level to the right of point B. If the firm is to earn a profit, it must produce somewhere between A and B, the two break-even points.

The production level at which the firm will enjoy maximum profits comes at 700 units, where the TR line is farthest above the TC curve, as represented by the distance CD. At this level of output, the slope of the TR curve is equal to the slope of the TC curve. To produce any more or any less than 700 units would mean a smaller gap between total cost and total revenue, and therefore less total profit.

We can verify our conclusions by comparing our total cost-total revenue graph to a graph that plots net revenue (as shown in the bottom portion of *Fig. 23.3*). We find that the output of 700 units corresponds to the top of the net revenue curve. This level of production is the one at which profits are maximized.

Marginal cost and marginal revenue
Another method for calculating the point of maximum profits, the marginal cost-marginal revenue approach, should help to enhance our understanding of a firm's production decisions.

Table 23.2 presents a complete cost and revenue schedule for Trout Fishing in America, Inc. The only new concept in this schedule is that of marginal revenue, which, you will recall from Chapter 20, is the increase in total revenue derived from the sale of one more unit. (Marginal revenue is shown in column 7.)

How do we derive marginal revenue? Since

Table 23.2
Average and marginal cost and revenue schedule for TFIA

(1) Quantity (Q) output per day	(2) Price per unit (P)	(3) Average fixed cost (AFC) $AFC = \frac{TFC}{Q}$	(4) Average variable cost (AVC) $AVC = \frac{TVC}{Q}$	(5) Marginal total cost (ATC) $ATC = \frac{TC}{Q}$	(6) Marginal cost (MC) $MC = \frac{\Delta TC}{\Delta Q}$	(7) Marginal revenue (MR) $MR = \frac{\Delta TR}{\Delta Q}$
100	$.50	$1.00	$.25	$1.25	$ .20	$.50
200	.50	.50	.23	.73	.15	.50
300	.50	.33	.20	.53	.10	.50
400	.50	.25	.17	.43	.15	.50
500	.50	.20	.17	.38	.35	.50
600	.50	.17	.20	.37	.45	.50
700	.50	.14	.24	.38	.60	.50
800	.50	.13	.28	.41	.90	.50
900	.50	.11	.35	.46	1.05	.50
1000	.50	.10	.42	.52	1.40	.50
1100	.50	.09	.51	.60	1.70	.50
1200	.50	.08	.61	.69		

the price of each unit is the same, the marginal revenue for each additional unit will simply be the price of the unit. We can prove this mathematically:

$$MR = \frac{\Delta TR}{\Delta Q}$$

or

$$\frac{\Delta Q \times P}{\Delta Q} = P.$$

Graphic analysis Figure 23.4 plots marginal revenue, average total costs, and average variable costs on the same graph. Marginal revenue is represented by a straight line parallel to the horizontal axis, drawn at the price level of 50¢ (the existing market price of trout flies). That is, the extra revenue is the price per unit, which is the same regardless of how many units the individual firm sells. Thus, under perfect competition, the MR curve represents the demand curve faced by the individual firm. The ATC and AVC curves are already familiar to us from Chapter 22. By looking at this graph, we see that if TFIA produces fewer than 325 units of trout flies (point A), its total costs per unit will be greater than the per-unit price (50¢). Therefore, it will not earn a profit below this level of production. Since the ATC curve is U-shaped, it again rises above the marginal revenue line at the production level of 975 units (point B). TFIA will not be able to earn a profit at any level above that one. Note that points A and B correspond to the two break-even points we located by comparing the total cost curve with the total revenue curve.

If Trout Fishing in America, Inc., produces anywhere between 325 and 975 trout flies, it will make some profit. However, since the goal of TFIA is profit maximization, it will want to produce at the level that brings in the maximum profit. How do we locate that level?

It might appear as if the firm could make the maximum profit by producing at point C, the low-

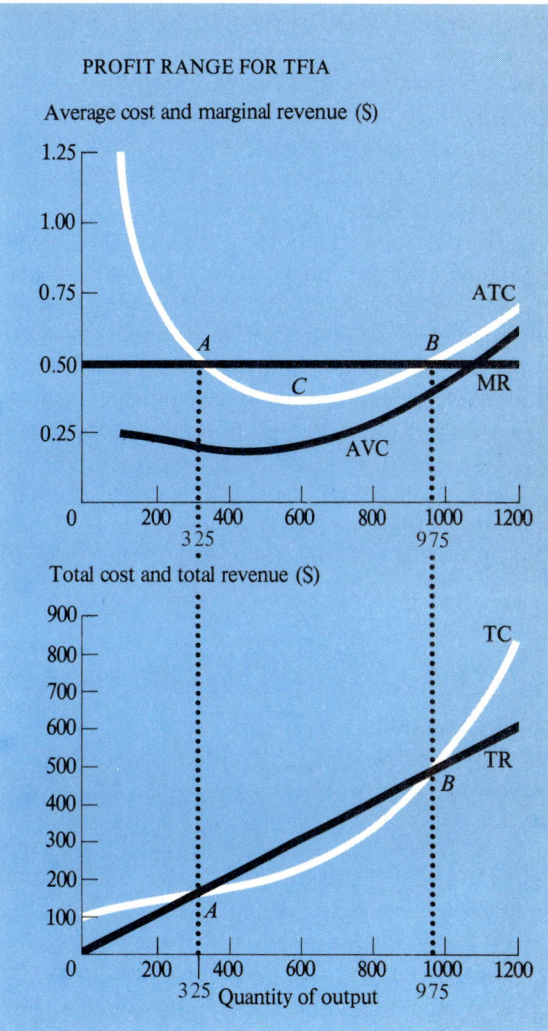

Fig. 23.4
For a single, perfectly competitive firm, the MR curve will be a straight horizontal line at the level of the going market price. The MR curve will intersect the ATC curve at the same levels of production—325 units and 975 units—as the TC curve intersects the TR curve.

est point of the ATC curve. This is where the firm's *average* or per-unit profit is the greatest. But the president of TFIA, Mr. Brautigan, is interested in *total* profits. He will continue to produce past the point of greatest average profit as long as the production results in some additional profit to the firm.

To determine the point at which producing an extra unit will no longer result in an increase in profits, we need to add to the graph the marginal cost curve, showing the cost of producing each additional unit. *Figure 23.5* shows this addition. Now we can see the results of producing extra units. Suppose that TFIA is presently producing at the lowest point on its ATC curve (600 units), and decides to expand production by another 50 units. The gain in revenue from the sale of those 50 units would be 50¢ per unit sold; that is the marginal revenue of each unit (MR is the same for every additional unit, since in a competitive market the price of each and every unit is the same). The MC curve shows that the marginal cost of producing each of the 50 extra units will be less than the marginal revenue obtained from the sale of that unit. Therefore, it would pay TFIA to increase production at least up to 650 units.

As long as the cost of producing an extra unit of trout flies is smaller than the increase in revenue that the extra unit will bring, TFIA will expand its production because it can add to its profits. For the individual firm, the point of maximum profit will be the point at which its marginal cost curve intersects with the marginal revenue curve (which also represents the demand curve). *Figure 23.5* shows that point *D* is the point of maximum profits for TFIA. If the firm produced one more unit over 700, the cost of making that unit would be greater than the additional revenue that the sale of the unit would bring (that is, the price); therefore, the firm's total profit would be diminished. If the firm produced one less unit, the reduction in revenue would be greater than the reduction in cost; total revenue then would decline, and the company would be making less than the maximum

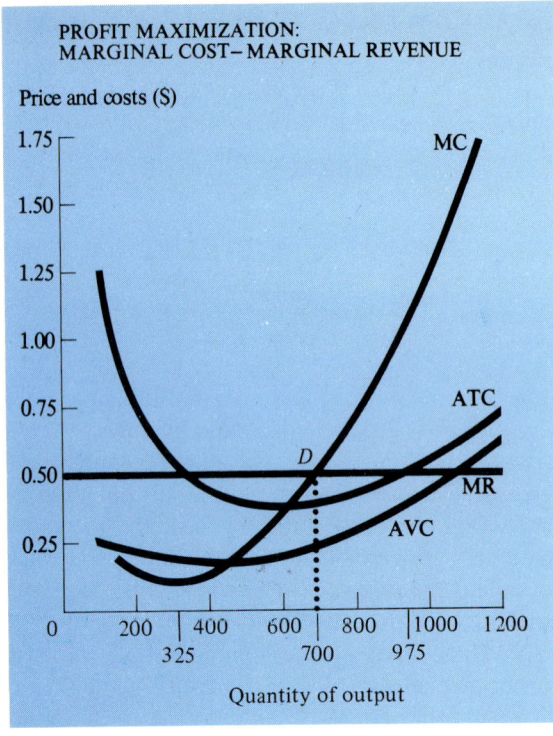

Fig. 23.5
We know by looking at the MR and ATC curves that the firm will show a profit if it produces anywhere between 325 and 975 units. To find the point of profit maximization, we add the MC curve. It intersects the MR curve at the production level of 700 units (point *D*); that is the quantity of output that will maximize TFIA's total profits.

possible profit. Only at the intersection of the MR and MC curves, where marginal revenue or price is the same as marginal cost, will the firm be making the greatest possible total profit. The basic profit-maximizing condition is MR = MC. This is true not only for a firm under perfect competition but for all business firms.

THE COMPETITIVE FIRM IN THE SHORT RUN 473

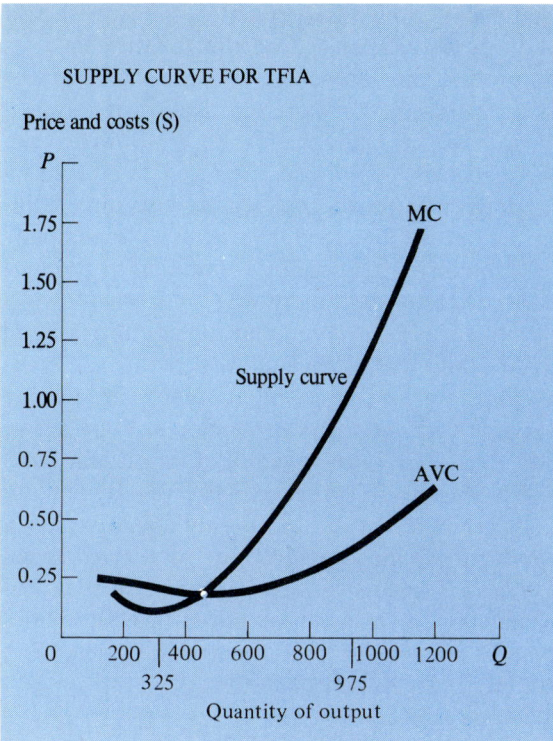

Fig. 23.6
In effect, the MC curve is the supply curve for the single firm. However, the firm would not be willing to produce, where MR is less than AVC, since the revenue received would not be sufficient to cover even the variable costs of production. This means that only the portion of the MC curve that lies above the AVC curve is the supply curve for the firm.

The firm's short-run supply curve

Using the formula MC = MR, we can now easily calculate the amount that TFIA is willing to supply at any given price. The firm will supply at the level of production where the marginal cost curve intersects the marginal revenue curve.

Since in a perfectly competitive market, the MR curve for a single firm is a straight line at the market price, the point of intersection with MC will be determined solely by the location of the MC curve. The portion of the MC curve that lies above the AVC curve is the supply curve. This is in keeping with our earlier interpretation of a supply curve as showing the minimum price needed to induce the firm to produce each level of output. *Figure 23.6* shows the supply curve for TFIA. Like all supply curves, it slopes upward and to the right, reflecting the law of diminishing returns and increasing costs.

Minimizing short-run losses

Let us now hypothesize a situation in which the market price of trout flies drops from 50¢ to 25¢. What should TFIA do in response to this change in the going market price?

Figure 23.7 plots MR at the new price level on the same graph with the firm's average total, average variable, and marginal cost curves. If TFIA were to continue to produce at its previous level of 700 units, its MC would be higher than its MR. Fortunately, the firm's president, Mr. Brautigan, took an economics course in college, so he knows what he should do. He immediately orders production cut back to the point where the new MR line, drawn at the lower price level, intersects with TFIA's MC curve.

Brautigan notifies his Board of Directors of his action, assuring them that the company is once more producing at the optimum short-run level. But one old grouch on the Board (who obviously did not have the benefits of a knowledge of economic principles) criticizes Brautigan's decision, claiming that he should have shut the trout-fly factory down entirely. The grouch points out that the average total cost of the units produced is now larger than the per-unit price at which they can be sold; therefore, the firm is losing money on each unit it produces and sells.

Brautigan is able to defend his decision by showing the Board of Directors the graph in *Fig.*

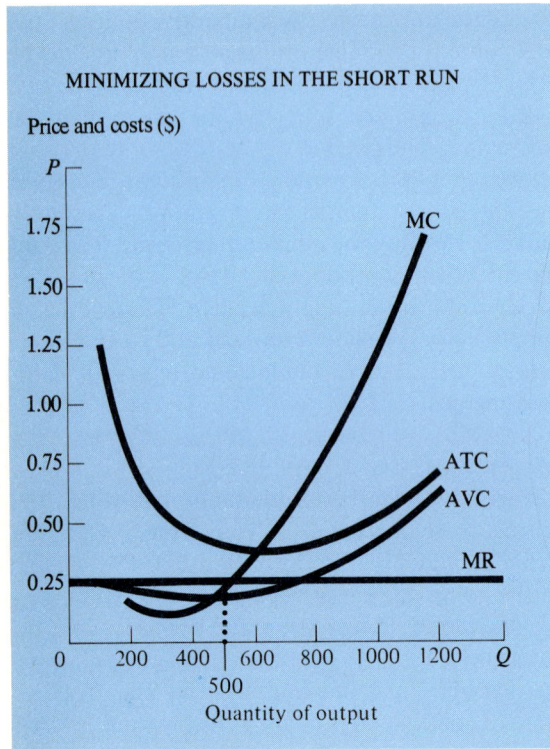

MINIMIZING LOSSES IN THE SHORT RUN

Fig. 23.7
When the market price of trout flies drops from 50¢ to 25¢, the firm can minimize its losses by cutting back production to the point at which the new MR line intersects the MC curve; that would be at the production level of 500 units. Although the price per unit is lower than the ATC per unit, it is more profitable for the firm to continue production than for it to close its doors. Since the MR line is above the AVC curve, the firm will be able to pay for all the variable inputs it uses in production, and also pay some portion of its fixed costs.

would not eliminate these costs, the firm should make its decision on the basis of the *variable* costs of production. These are the costs of the raw materials used, the wages or salaries of the production workers, and the bills for the power to run the machines. As long as the revenues created by production can cover the variable costs directly incurred by the production process, the company will minimize its losses by continuing to produce rather than by shutting down.

In *Fig. 23.7*, we see that the new intersection of MC and MR is located at a point below the average total cost curve, but it is *above* the average variable cost curve. By producing at this level of 500 units, TFIA can cover all of its variable costs and pay a part of its fixed costs as well. By remaining open, the firm will lose only $60 a day. If it closed, it would lose $100, the total fixed costs. *Table 23.3* calculates total losses for each level of production, given a market price of 25¢; it verifies that 500 units is the level of output at which TFIA will minimize its short-run losses.

Table 23.3
Short-run minimum loss position

Quantity (Q)	Price per unit (P)	Total revenue (TR)	Total cost (TC)	Loss
100	$.25	$ 25	$125	−$100
200	.25	50	145	− 95
300	.25	75	160	− 85
400	.25	100	170	− 70
500	.25	125	185	− 60
600	.25	150	220	− 70
700	.25	175	265	− 90
800	.25	200	325	− 125
900	.25	225	415	− 190
1000	.25	250	520	− 270
1100	.25	275	660	− 385
1200	.25	300	830	− 530

23.3. He reminds the Board that the firm already has certain fixed costs that will continue whether the factory is open or closed. These fixed costs amount to $100 a day. Since closing the plant

SHORT-RUN EQUILIBRIUM

The firm

Short-run equilibrium is the level of output toward which the firm will move in seeking its goal of profit maximization with a given fixed-sized plant. Once equilibrium is achieved, it will tend to be maintained, provided that all of the factors affecting output decisions remain constant. When will a firm be in short-run equilibrium? Obviously when it is either maximizing its profits or minimizing its losses, given its fixed costs of production (which are impossible to change in the short run) and the market price it faces. Let us review the various short-run equilibrium conditions in which a competitive firm might find itself. These conditions are summarized in *Fig. 23.8*.

First, a firm can make an economic profit when market price (P_1) is greater than the lowest point on its average total cost curve; in this case, the firm can maximize profits by producing where $MC = MR_1$ (at E_1). Second, if price (P_2) is equal to the lowest average total cost of production (at E_2), the firm will be earning a normal profit, but no economic profit. Third, if price (P_3) drops below the firm's ATC curve, losses can be minimized in the short run by continuation of production where $MC = MR_3$ (at point E_3) provided that the price is greater than the average variable cost. And finally, the firm should shut down when the price of the unit (P_4) is less than the average variable cost of producing that unit.

It is important to remember that these situations represent different short-run equilibrium positions for the firm, optimum choices given its costs and the market price it faces. These are equilibrium positions because the firm is doing all it can to maximize profits or minimize losses in the short run.

In the long run, of course, the firm will try to make further adjustments to the new price level. It will try to cut back its fixed costs; it may be able to reduce costs by shifting to a smaller plant size if it was previously located on the rising part of the

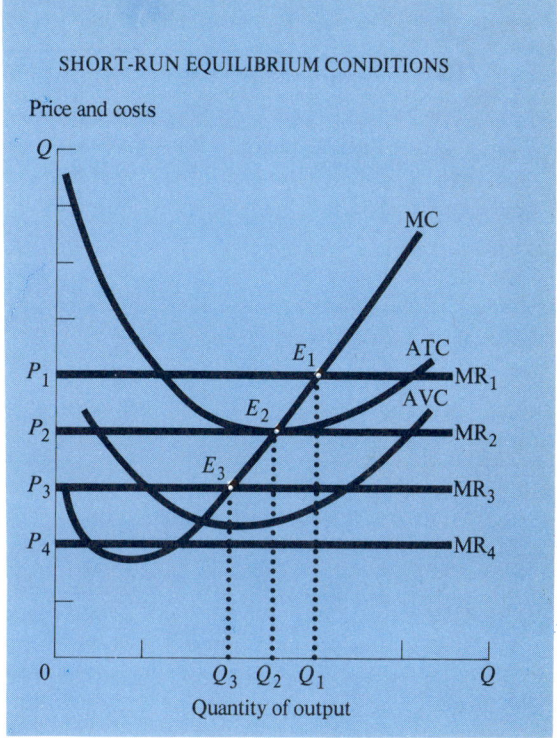

Fig. 23.8
This graph shows the various optimum choices of production level that the firm will make in response to changes in the market price of trout flies. If the market price is at level P_1, the firm will produce Q_1 and enjoy an economic profit. At price level P_2, the firm will produce Q_2, achieving a normal profit. At price level P_3, the firm can continue to produce, operating at an output of Q_3; this is the point at which losses are minimized. And at price P_4, the company should shut down production, since it would not be able to recover the variable costs of production.

long-run average cost curve. If there seems to be no way for the firm to reach a position where the average cost of its product is equal to, or smaller than, the price of the product, TFIA will leave the

> **RECAP**
>
> SHORT-RUN EQUILIBRIUM is the level of output toward which the firm will move in seeking its goal of profit maximization with a given fixed-sized plant. A firm will be in short-run equilibrium when it is either maximizing its profits or minimizing its losses, given its fixed costs of production and the market price it faces. The short-run equilibrium is achieved where MR = MC.

trout-fly industry and perhaps switch to manufacturing garbage cans.

We know that under perfect competition, no one firm can affect price; but the equilibrium price level is determined by the point at which the market demand curve intersects the market supply curve, which is determined by all individual supply curves taken together. Each individual firm in the trout-fly industry must accept the market price as a given factor over which it can exercise no control. In the short run, Trout Fishing in America, Inc., like all other firms in that industry, can respond to changes in prices only by altering its level of production along a single MC curve. The MC curve of each firm in the industry is derived, given its package of fixed inputs, which can only be altered in the long run. Therefore, in the short run, the market supply curve cannot shift either to the left or to the right; we can only move along the same curve to a higher or lower level of output.

The industry

In Chapter 3, we demonstrated that, given a shift in the market demand curve for a good, a new equilibrium price would be reached, at which the quantity demanded is exactly equal to the quantity supplied. We can now qualify this explanation by adding that we were then referring to a short-run equilibrium position for that particular industry.

Figure 23.9(a) shows short-run equilibrium for the trout-fly industry in the year 1—the time at which trout fishing was declared our national sport. Since trout fishing had become a popular fad, the demand for flies increased greatly; the demand curve shifted to the right. Because of short-run limitations of small plants and the scarcity of firms in the industry, the market supply curve rose steeply. Attempts to increase output by adding more workers or other variable inputs yielded a relatively small marginal product, due to the law of diminishing returns. So for that year, the market price was P_1 and the level of output was Q_1.

Figure 23.9(b) shows the profits of a typical firm in the industry at that particular equilibrium level. The point at which MC = MR, which is the production level at which the firm will enjoy maximum profits, happens to fall well above the average cost per unit for that level. TFIA will receive not only the normal profit, which is a part of the cost of production, but an economic profit as well. This will be true of most of the firms that manufacture trout flies, since all firms face approximately the same market situation and sell their product at the same price. We may say, then, that in this short-run period the trout-fly industry is enjoying substantial economic profits.

LONG-RUN EQUILIBRIUM: THE FIRM AND THE INDUSTRY

In the long run, it will not be possible for the industry to continue to enjoy excess rates of profit. Paradoxically, the desire of business firms to maximixe their profits will eventually lead to a lower rate of profit. We can see why by looking at the long-run plans of a single firm.

The goal of TFIA is to achieve the largest possible *total* profit. Therefore, when President Brautigan observes that the current market price is significantly higher than the average cost of pro-

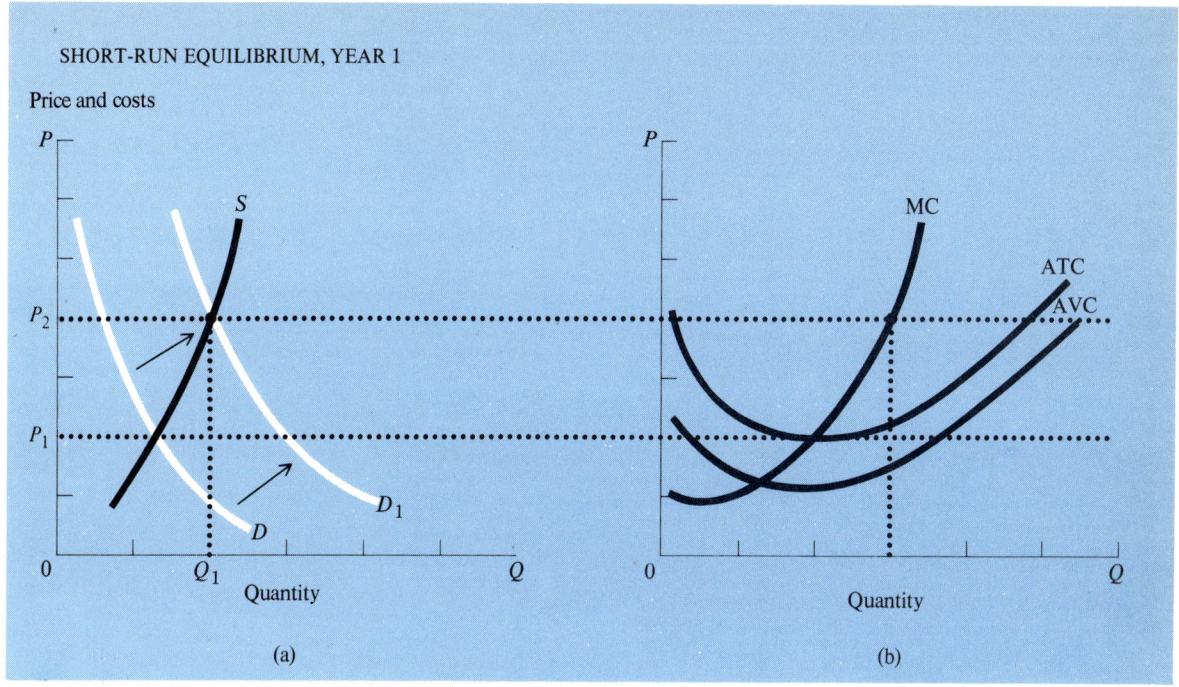

Fig. 23.9
Part (a) shows the effect on market equilibrium of supply and demand when the demand for trout flies increases from D to D_1. In the short run, the market price of flies will rise to P_2 as the level of output increases. Part (b) shows the individual firm's profits at the old and new price levels. At P_1—the old price—the company enjoyed only a normal profit; at P_2, it enjoys a sizable economic profit.

duction, he will plan to expand his total productive capacity. By building another factory right beside the original one, TFIA can double its output by year 2. This is a profit-maximizing decision for the firm, increasing total profits.

Since most of the firms in the industry will behave in the same way, we find that an entirely new market supply curve will have to be drawn. Many existing firms have increased their output; moreover, new firms attracted by the reports of high profit rates have entered the field. So for the short-run period of year 2, we must draw a new supply curve, which gives us a new short-run equilibrium level (see *Fig. 23.10a*).

Because of this shift in the supply curve, the new short-run equilibrium of supply and demand will be reached when the price of trout flies is P_2 and the total quantity supplied is Q_2. To adapt to the new market conditions, all firms will have to lower their price to that new market level; otherwise they will be unable to sell all that they produce. Any attempt to maintain prices at the former high level would result in excess supply that would require firms to bid against one another for the existing customers. This would force prices down once again.

As *Fig. 23.10(b)* indicates, the new price level is barely higher than the average cost of produc-

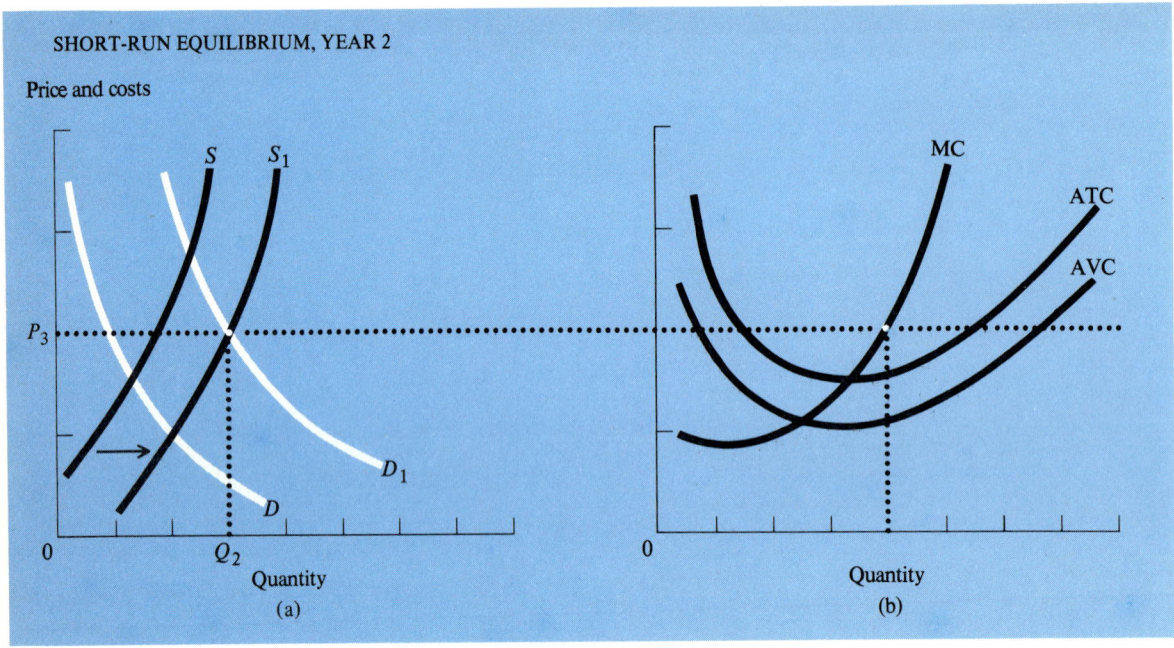

Fig. 23.10
This figure shows the long-run adjustments that will be made in the trout-fly industry. The lure of economic profits has attracted more suppliers into the market, and so the supply curve is shifted from S to S_1. This causes another increase in output, but it is accompanied by a decrease in equilibrium market price. Part (b) shows the position of the individual firm. It still enjoys a small economic profit.

tion at the firm's level of output. The firm has lost most of the economic profit it enjoyed the previous year.

Since there is still a small amount of economic profit, the process of expansion in the trout-fly industry will continue the next year. The industry will keep making these adjustments until the long-run equilibrium point is reached. This point falls at a level of production where the price of the good is exactly equal to the minimum average total cost of all firms in the industry. No further shift in the industry supply curve will occur; since there are no economic profits included in ATC, there is no incentive for further expansion, or for entry for new firms seeking higher profits.

Figure 23.11 shows the long-run equilibrium position for the trout-fly industry and for a single firm within that industry. In comparing the new market price and output with those that existed

RECAP
LONG-RUN EQUILIBRIUM—in the long run, it will not be possible for an industry to continue to enjoy excess rates of profit if the industry is perfectly competitive. Long-run equilibrium is achieved where P = MR = MC = SRATC = LRATC.

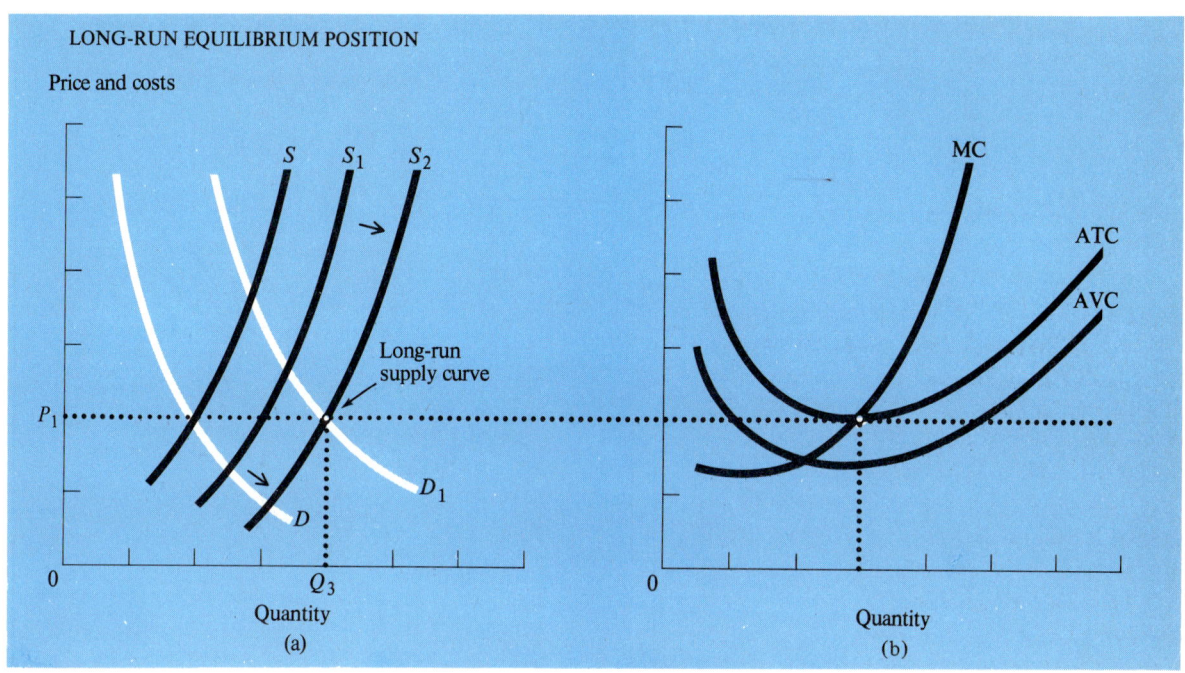

Fig. 23.11
The long-run equilibrium position will be reached in the trout-fly market. The supply curve has shifted to S_2; market price has once again dropped, so that it is now at the original level P_1; the equilibrium level of output has increased significantly. As part (b) shows, the individual firm in the industry once again enjoys only the normal rate of profit.

before the shift in demand occurred, we notice that output has increased substantially but that equilibrium price is the same as before. For the individual firm, the new marginal revenue curve intersects the marginal cost curve at the lowest point on the firm's ATC curve. This long-run equilibrium position for a single firm can be upset only by a shift in the market demand curve for trout flies or a change in the costs of producing trout flies. When this long-run equilibrium condition prevails for every firm, the entire industry is said to be in long-run equilibrium.

Both economic profits and excessive losses are only short-run conditions. The existence of economic profits will cause expansion of the industry as new firms enter the field and old ones increase their capacity in the long run; this expansion will shift the supply curve, causing price to fall until it reaches the level of minimum ATC. The existence of losses would cause the industry to contract, as some firms leave the field and others decrease their capacity in the long run. This contraction will shift the supply curve, causing price to rise until it is equal to the minimum ATC.

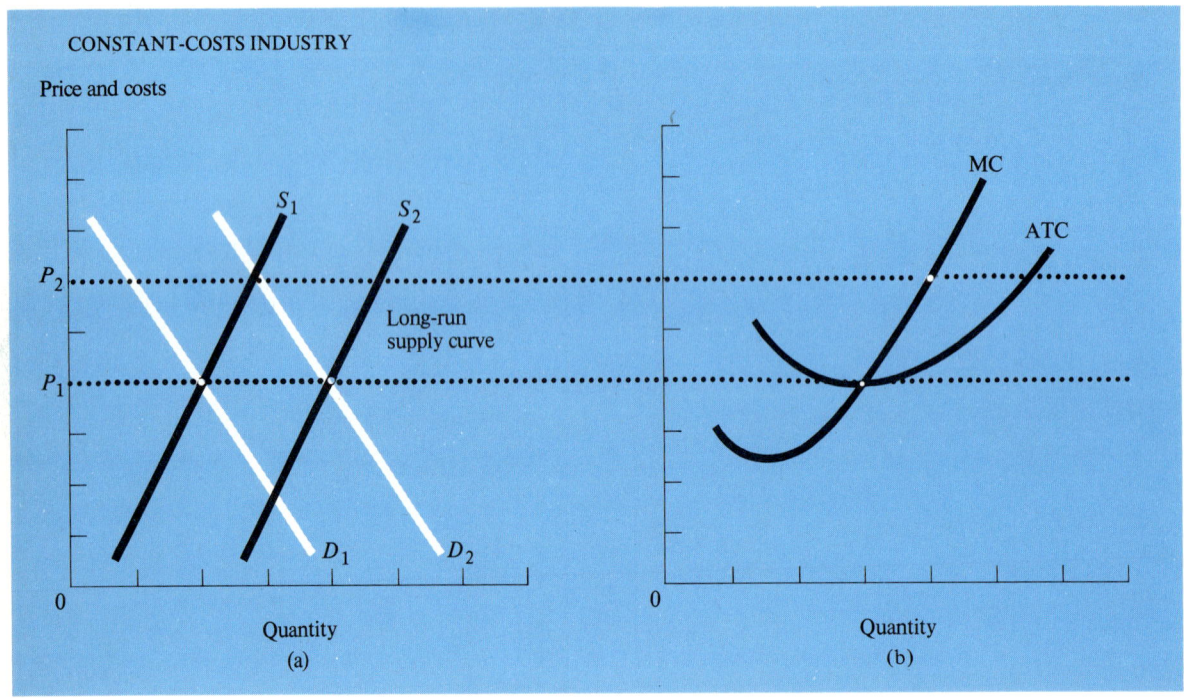

Fig. 23.12
In a constant-costs industry, an increase in demand from D_1 to D_2 will initially cause a price increase from P_1 to P_2. But the economic profits created by the price rise cause the industry to expand, and the supply curve will shift from S_1 to S_2. However, the ATC curve of the individual firm remains at the same level, even though the supply curve has shifted. Therefore the equilibrium market price will eventually return to its original level, where price equals ATC.

LONG-RUN INDUSTRY SUPPLY CURVE

We are now ready to introduce one final concept—that of the long-run industry supply curve. Figures 23.12 and 23.13 present the long-run supply adjustments in two different industries. In each case we will assume that the industry is responding to an increase in demand (a shift in the demand curve to the right).

Constant-costs industry

Figure 23.12 shows the long-run supply curve for a **constant-costs industry,** *an industry in which the expansion of existing firms and the entry into the market of new firms will have no effect on the prices of input resources.* Although this does not occur often, it is possible to imagine such a situation. An industry that uses unskilled or unspecialized labor or an abundantly available raw material might expand almost indefinitely without causing resource prices to rise. Imagine, for example, an adobe brick industry. The raw material needed is dirt, of which we have millions of square miles; the production process by which the dirt is turned into brick uses sunlight, a free good; the only skill needed by most production workers is the ability

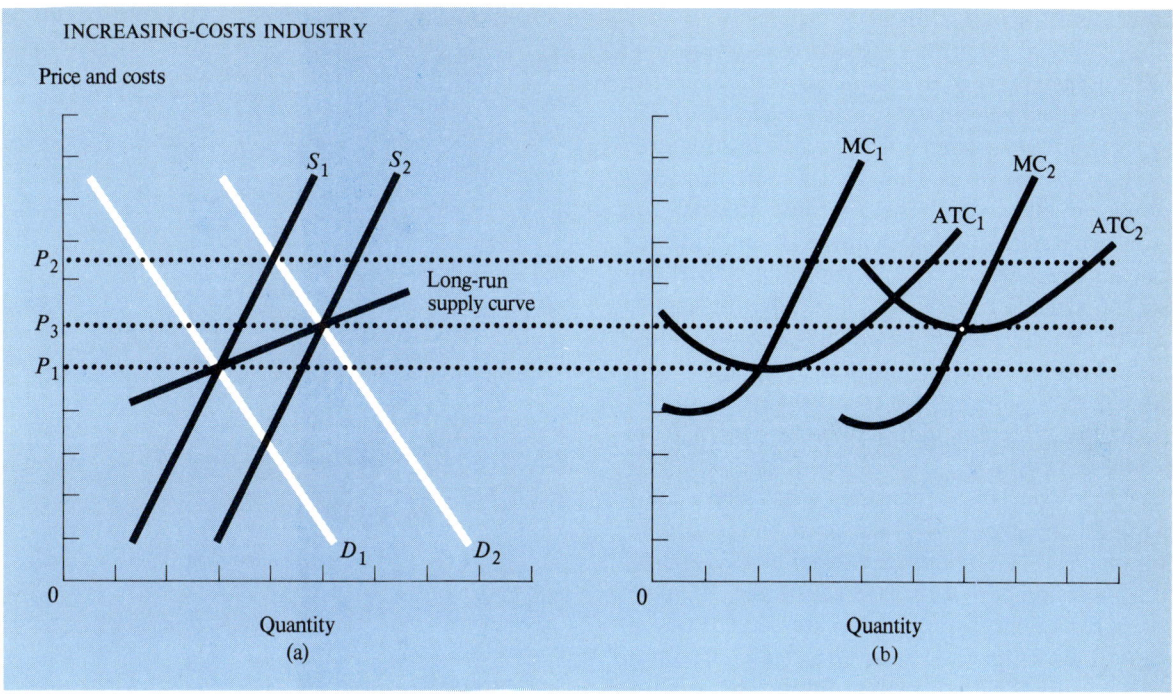

Fig. 23.13
As shown in (a), in an increasing-costs industry, as in a constant-costs industry, an increase in demand from D_1 to D_2 will cause a price increase from P_1 to P_2. The economic profits created by the price rise cause the industry to expand, and the supply curve will shift from S_1 to S_2. However, in this case, the increase in supply will cause corresponding upward shifts in the ATC curve and the MC curve as reflected in (b). Therefore the new equilibrium market price will be at a higher level than the original market price; it will occur at P_3 where MC_2 intersects ATC_2.

to pour mud into a mold and to dump bricks out of the mold. Even during a period of rapid expansion, costs should be constant in the adobe brick industry.

In a constant-costs industry, supply would be perfectly elastic. Every increase in demand would be met with a matching increase in supply but with no alteration in price. In terms of the single firm, its ATC curve would not shift upward as existing firms increased output simultaneously and new firms entered the industry. The long-run supply curve of the typical firm in the industry would be virtually horizontal over a wide range of output.

Increasing-costs industry

In most industries, the situation of constant costs does not prevail. An **increasing-costs industry** is *one in which the entry of new firms and the expansion of old ones usually result in increased competition for the factors of production.* This causes the ATC curve and MC curve of the typical firm in the industry to shift upward as industry-wide output increases; therefore, supply will increase only if prices go up. In general, higher prices are required to induce more production, since costs increase as an industry expands. *Figure 23.13* gives the picture for the increasing-costs industry.

Decreasing-costs industry

A very special situation is that of the **decreasing-costs industry.** *This is an industry in which the entry of new firms and expansion might result for a time in lower resource prices and therefore lower costs of production.* That is, as more resource inputs are demanded, they become cheaper for firms to purchase. For example, if an industry uses an input which was previously produced by small firms using inefficient methods, the expansion of this industry might enable the input industry to adopt mass-production techniques and supply the input at lower costs. If this input is a major one, the user industry might benefit from decreasing costs.

Decreasing-costs industries today are usually involved in activities which have huge capital equipment requirements (the telephone company, the power company). Even to get started, a power company requires huge generators and power plants. As output expands the fixed generator costs can be divided over more units of production; hence average cost per unit of power declines. In this situation the marginal and average cost curves would fall as supply increased, and a negatively sloped long-run supply curve would result.

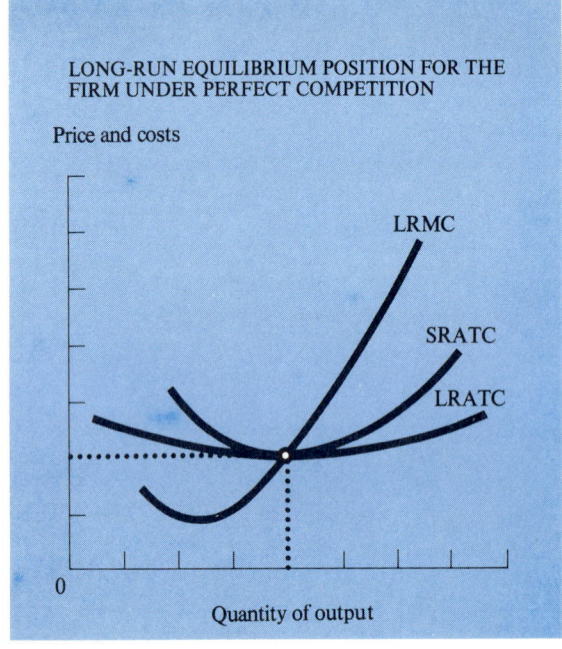

Fig. 23.14
This graph shows the long-run equilibrium position in the trout-fly market. Under perfect competition, this equilibrium is reached when marginal cost = marginal revenue = short-run average total cost = long-run average total cost.

EVALUATING THE COMPETITIVE PRICE SYSTEM

Our analysis of long-run market equilibrium has shown that under perfect competition, the marginal revenue curve (price) for each individual firm will intersect the marginal cost curve at the lowest point on the ATC curve. Moreover, as *Fig. 23.14* indicates, in the long run each firm will be forced to utilize the "optimum" plant size; that is, it will end up producing at the lowest point on its long-run average cost curve. So we can say that long-run equilibrium for the competitive firm is reached when MR = MC = SRATC = LRATC. This four-part equation has significant implications regarding resource allocation within the society.

Benefits

Economists speak of the competitive system of pricing as "ideal," by which they mean that it achieves optimum allocation of scarce resources.

Under perfect competition, the price of a good in the long run wil be equal to the minimum average cost of production. No firm will be able to stay in business if it is not using the most efficient possible methods of production. As a result, firms will plan ahead carefully to select the optimum plant size for their production level; they will not use productive resources wastefully and they will not allocate any of their money or resource budget for unnecessary activities. This is clearly beneficial to the consumer as well, since it guarantees that in the long run the price of any good will be at the lowest possible level.

Under conditions of perfect competition, the price of a good will also be exactly equal to the marginal cost of producing the good. This means that scarce resources will be allocated in a way that corresponds exactly with the desires of consumers. The market will cause the production of those goods that are most valued by consumers. Remember that the marginal cost is a reflection of the price the firm must pay to acquire the needed input resources and that the firm must bid competitively against other users. The producer who obtains the resource will be the one who can pay the most for it, and his or her ability to pay depends directly on the willingness of buyers of the product to pay higher prices. Marginal cost will be equal to price only when consumers as a whole value the added unit of that good more highly than they value an added unit of some alternative good.

Problems

The price system is an efficient way of allocating scarce resources; it eliminates waste. But many economists have pointed out that efficiency is not necessarily identical to social welfare. Under perfect competition, the price system does have some shortcomings.

One problem has already been touched on in this chapter. Under perfect competition, there is little incentive for any firm in the industry to look for new products. If a firm can sell an infinite number of pizza cutters at a fixed market price of $1.59, there is no need to search for a new improved pizza cutter. In the short run, of course, there is an incentive to reduce costs in order to enjoy the resulting economic profits. But since the model of perfect competition assumes that any new cost-saving method of production introduced by one firm will be copied immediately by all other firms in the industry, these economic profits will be short-lived. In the long run, we can conclude that perfect competition might tend to hamper the development of technology and keep us from discovering new efficiencies. It might also restrict the number of products on the market, thus limiting the opportunity of some consumers to satisfy their desires.

A second problem is that the price system considers only the cost incurred by the firm in the process of production; it does not account for the social costs and benefits that may arise in the course of the production, use, or disposal of the good. For example, under our price system, the cost of an aluminum beer can is considered to be only the cost of actually producing the can. But once the can has been used, there is a social cost involved in disposing of it. At present, we pay this cost separately, through the taxes that support the city sanitation department. But in a very real sense, it is part of the cost of using the can. The same is true of the water pollution caused by many chemical and paper plants. The chemical firm's costs end after the waste has been dumped into the nearest river, but the social cost of cleaning up the river must somehow be paid.

Actually, the core of this problem lies more in the accounting system used than in the price system itself. As long as the marginal cost reflects *all* of the sacrifices entailed by the production, use, and disposal of any good, and its price reflects all of the satisfactions, the price system will work to allocate resources in the most efficient way possible. But if social costs and benefits are not included, the allocation may be less than optimal.

Another drawback of the competitive price system is one we have mentioned in previous chapters. The price system does not register the needs of all consumers equally. If dollar votes are not distributed equitably, the needs of consumers will not be weighed equally. Some consumers will have the power to vote for luxuries, while others are unable to vote for the production of an adequate supply of necessities. The price system does not always provide the greatest good for the largest number of people. If we desire to achieve the goal of equal distribution of economic power, regardless of individual differences in productivity, we need some regulation of the price system. But regulation of the price system will, of course, impose its own problems.

Summary

■ This chapter examines the workings of the market under conditions of perfect competition.

■ The function of the market is to bring sellers and buyers together, allowing them to signal each other about price and quantity either directly or indirectly. In a perfectly competitive market, there are a large number of buyers and sellers, no one of which is able to influence prices. The goods being sold on a particular market are uniform and standardized. All buyers and sellers have perfect knowledge of the market, and all input resources are perfectly mobile and adaptable. There are no perfectly competitive markets in the United States economy, although the market for some agricultural goods does have many of these characteristics. Economists find the model of perfect competition useful, however, because it does help to predict the behavior of real, imperfect markets.

■ The market price for a good occurs at the intersection of the market demand and supply curves. The demand curve faced by an individual firm is perfectly elastic—a horizontal line at the market price.

■ The point of maximum profit for the firm can be determined by examining the total cost and total revenue curves and by selecting that point at which total revenues exceed total costs by the greatest amount. However, economists prefer to identify the point of maximum profit by examining the marginal cost and marginal revenue curves of the firm. The marginal revenue curve is a straight, horizontal line at the level of the market price. The firm will maximize profits if it produces at the point at which the marginal cost and marginal revenue curves intersect.

■ The MC = MR method also applies to imperfect markets and to the best strategy for a firm to minimize losses. The firm's short-run supply curve will be its marginal cost curve (above its average variable cost curve) since the intersection point for every possible price will be along the marginal cost curve. As price drops, the firm will cut back production to the new intersection of the marginal cost and marginal revenue curves. The firm will continue to operate as long as it is able to cover its variable costs (thus minimizing losses), but will shut down when the price is so low that the firm cannot cover variable costs.

■ In the short run, the firm will produce at the point where MC = MR. At this short-run equilibrium point, the firm may be making economic profits, normal profits, or incurring losses. The long-run equilibrium for the industry occurs when all firms are making normal profits. If firms are making economic profits, existing firms will be encouraged to expand fixed capital and new firms will be encouraged to enter the market. The supply curve for the industry will therefore shift to the right, and the price will drop until all firms are making only normal profits. If firms in the industry are incurring a loss, production will be cut back and some firms will leave the industry; the market supply curve will shift to the left, and prices will rise until all firms are once again making normal profits. In either case, a new long-run equilibrium for the industry is reached.

■ The long-run supply curve for most industries slopes upward to the right, reflecting the tendency for firms to bid up the prices of inputs as production expands. This type of industry is called an increasing-costs industry. The supply curve for a constant-costs industry in the long run is a straight, horizontal line; firms are able to expand output without bidding up prices. Economists also recognize the special case of the decreasing-costs industry, where expansion might for a period of time actually lead to a decrease in resource costs.

■ Under perfect competition, equilibrium for a firm is reached at the point where MR = MC = short-run average total cost = long-run average total cost. The benefits of this are that price in the long run will be equal to the minimum average cost of production, which promotes the most efficient use of resources and production techniques. Price will also be equal to the marginal cost of production, which means that the goods consumers demand will be supplied in an efficient way.

■ Some of the problems with the perfectly competitive system include the lack of incentives for the development of new products or significantly more efficient means of production, the failure to include some of the social costs of production in decision making, and a failure to register the wishes and needs of all consumers equally because of the unequal distribution of income.

Key Terms

total revenue

constant-costs industry

increasing-costs industry

decreasing-costs industry

Review & Discussion

1. What are the assumptions of the model of perfect competition? What actual markets in the United States resemble this model? Why? How well would the markets for the following goods

fit this model? Why?

aluminum wheat
refrigerators lettuce
radios clothing

2. The model of perfect competition assumes the perfect mobility of input resources. What does the phenomenon of frictional unemployment say about the mobility of labor as a resource input?

3. How would you identify the point of maximum profit for a firm by using total revenue and total cost curves? How would the curves appear if the firm were making economic rather than normal profits?

4. How would you identify the point of maximum profit by using marginal cost and marginal revenue curves? What is the shape of the marginal revenue curve for a perfect competitor? Why?

5. What cost curve is also the firm's short-run supply curve? Why? Under what conditions would the firm make economic profits? Normal profits? Minimize its losses? Under what conditions will the firm decide to shut down?

6. At what point would the firm with the curves shown to the right be in short-run equilibrium? Will it be making a profit or a loss? What is its short-run supply curve?

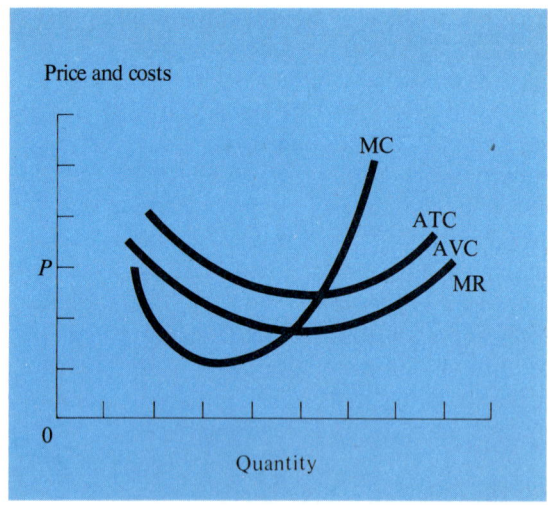

7. What is the condition of long-run equilibrium for the perfectly competitive firm? What happens if there are losses or economic profits in a perfectly competitive industry?

8. What is the difference between a constant-costs and an increasing-costs industry? How would their long-run supply curves differ? Under what circumstances might an industry be in a situation of decreasing costs?

9. Describe some of the benefits of perfect competition. Why does it tend toward a condition of optimum resource allocation? What are some of the major problems of the competitive price system? Can you suggest an alternative?

Chapter 24

The Economics of Agriculture

What to look for in this chapter

What is the traditional farm problem in the United States?

What are the causes of the long-run problem of declining farm prices and the short-run problem of extreme income fluctuations? How does inelasticity of demand for agricultural goods affect farm income?

How is the situation different for large-scale and small-scale farmers? Why have more farmers not given up farming and moved into other areas?

What has been the direction of government policy to deal with the farm problem, and how successful have government measures been?

THE TRADITIONAL FARM PROBLEM—AN OVERVIEW

For more than 50 years, an American "agricultural problem" has aroused the concern of farmers and rural dwellers and challenged the imaginations of economists and politicians. Traditionally, the problem has taken the form of great agricultural abundance but relatively low incomes for those who produced the abundance. The irony of this situation was intensified by the fact that the agricultural sector was praised as being the best—and last—example of the perfectly competitive market in our economy.

Because of the great abundance of essentially undifferentiated agricultural products and the competition in the industry, no one farmer was able to influence the price of the goods produced. Farmers could not simply raise their prices to increase their incomes. Dependent on the parity concept and other forms of government sup-

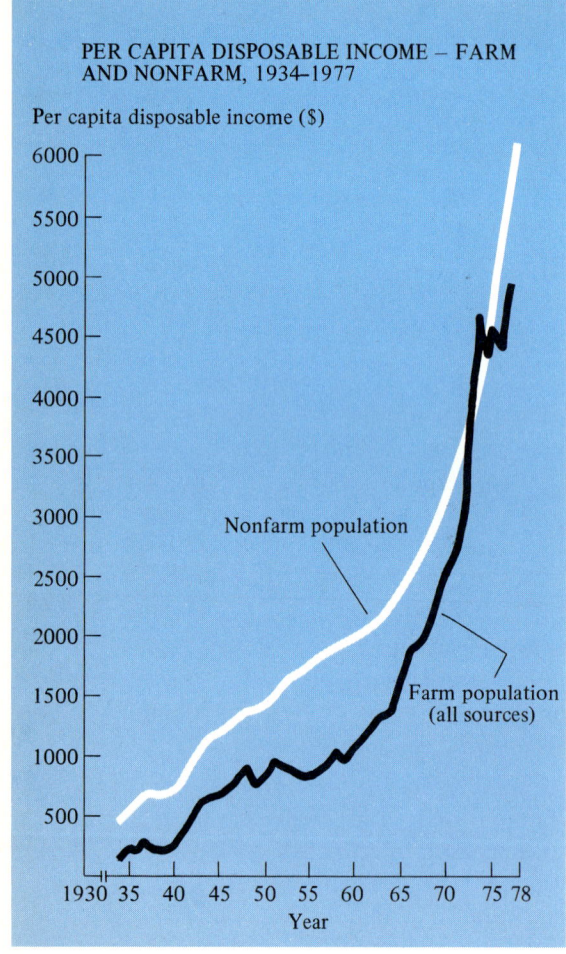

Fig. 24.1
Despite government subsidies, the discrepancy between farm and nonfarm disposable personal income persisted for many years. Although 1973 produced a reversal, the familiar pattern resumed in 1974 and continued through 1977.

SOURCE: United States Department of Agriculture, *Farm Income Statistics*, July 1978.

port—some given in exchange for not growing crops—they constituted an economically handicapped minority in America's predominantly urban-industrial society.

The gap between farm and nonfarm income

Figure 24.1 shows that between 1934 and 1977 per capita income of farmers consistently lagged behind that of other workers. Although in 1973 there was a dramatic reversal of this pattern it was short-lived and between 1974 and 1977 per capita farm income was again below nonfarm income. *Figure 24.2* illustrates a major reason for the gap between farm and nonfarm incomes. Except for brief periods, notably during wartime, the prices that farmers have had to pay for the goods they need to live and to produce their crops have been far higher than the prices they receive for their products. This difference between prices paid by farmers and prices received by farmers causes the discrepancy between farm and nonfarm incomes.

Another reason for low farm incomes is advanced technology. Because of better farming technology, farmers have been able to raise the productivity of their existing acreage. But greatly increasing the supply of farm commodities has also caused the lowering of prices on agricultural goods, so farmers have therefore received lower incomes themselves.

Recent developments

Many economists traditionally described the American agricultural sector as part of a gross misallocation of resources on a national scale. Because there was more demand for manufactured goods than for farm goods, economists reasoned that shifting resources of land, labor, and capital from agriculture (with its chronic problem of overproduction) to other sectors of the economy would increase efficiency throughout the economic system. The result, more efficient use of re-

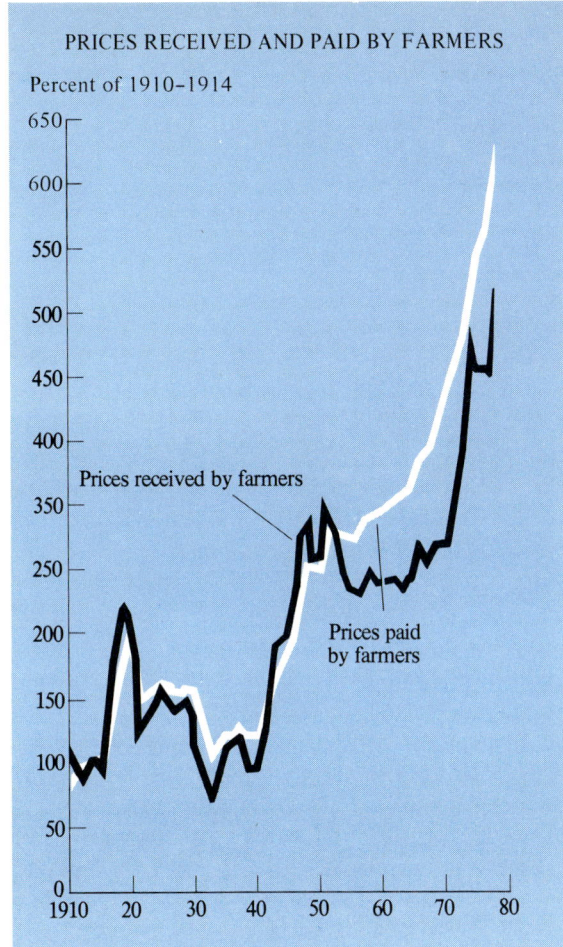

SOURCE: *Survey of Current Business,* January 1979.

Fig. 24.2
Except during the two world wars and the Korean war, the prices farmers pay for their goods and services have been consistently higher than the prices they receive for the goods they produce. This price differential causes the discrepancy between farm and nonfarm incomes shown in *Fig. 24.1.*

sources, would make everyone, including those who remained on the farms, better off.

Dramatic changes on the national and world scene in the past ten years have caused this traditional definition of and solution to the farm problem to undergo examination. These years have seen a massive surge in demand from abroad for American farm products accompanied by increases in domestic per capita food consumption. At the same time, small farms have begun to disappear as they are absorbed into larger agricultural corporations. Because significant economies of scale exist in agriculture, such large-scale units are more productive and more profitable than the "family farm," as *Table 24.1* shows. If such units combine in states or regions, they can become powerful enough to manipulate output in order to restrict supplies and thereby raise prices. In 1973, these factors brought about an end to the traditional agricultural surplus problem—food prices soared and, in 1973, farmers' income exceeded nonfarm income for a brief time. In the remainder of this chapter, we will examine in further detail the causes of the traditional farm problem and the policies that have been established to deal with it. We will also take a brief look at some of the developments of the past decade.

CAUSES OF THE TRADITIONAL FARM PROBLEM

In addition to the long-term decline in agricultural income relative to earnings in the remaining sectors of the economy, there is another dimension to the farm problem. Agricultural prices tend to fluctuate dramatically in the short run, thereby causing significant variability in farmer income from one year to the next. Although increases as well as decreases occur, this erratic behavior of income represents a source of instability in the agricultural

Table 24.1
Farms, cash receipts, and net farm income by value of sales classes, 1977

Farms with sales of:	Cash receipts		Net farm income, before inventory adjustments		Farms	
	Amount (in millions)	Percentage	Amount (in millions)	Percentage	Number (in thousands)	Percentage
$20,000 & over	88,782	89.3	15,853	78.8	831	30.8
$10,000–$19,999	5,409	5.4	1,551	7.7	311	11.5
$ 5,000–$ 9,999	2,697	2.7	814	4.0	302	11.2
Under $4,999	2,562	2.6	1,913	9.5	1,262	46.5
All farms	99,450	100.0	20,131	100.0	2,706	100.0

Source: United States Department of Agriculture, *Farm Income Statistics*, July 1978.

sector. Our immediate task is to identify and explain the factors underlying these long- and short-run problems.

The long run

Income inelasticity of demand

How could abundance backfire on the very producers of that abundance? Why did increased productivity and growth benefit most other industries but depress agriculture? The answer is that, agricultural demand is income inelastic (see Chapter 20 for a review of elasticity). Most agricultural products are normal goods; when income rises, the percentage increase in expenditure for these goods is less than the percentage increase in income. Some farm products, such as potatoes, are actually inferior goods in many households. Expenditures for these goods decline as income increases. Thus demand for agricultural products has not increased proportionately with the general rise in incomes.

Table 24.2
Total number of persons supplied farm products by one United States farm worker, 1820–1977 (selected years)

Year	Persons supplied per farm worker*
1820	4
1870	5
1920	8
1930	10
1940	11
1950	16
1960	26
1970	47
1977	59

Source: United States Department of Agriculture, *Agricultural Statistics*.
*Persons supplied included the farm workers. Thus in 1820 the average farm worker supplied himself and 3 other persons.

Table 24.3
Production assets used in agriculture

Year	Total production assets (in billions)	Production assets per farm worker
1940	$ 37.7	$ 3,326
1950	$ 95.0	$ 9,529
1960	$156.4	$ 21,304
1970	$247.0	$ 53,800
1975	$426.4	$ 96,800
1978*	$597.0	$143,300

Source: United States Department of Agriculture, *Agricultural Statistics*, 1978.
*preliminary

Shifts in supply due to technological advances

The modest outward shift of the demand curve for agricultural goods (primarily due to increases in the size of population) has been insignificant in relation to the dramatic shift of the supply curve. Enormous gains in productivity have resulted from technological advances embodied in new machinery and hybrid seeds, the accumulation of a greater stock of human capital among farm workers, and efficiencies made possible by large-scale production. *Table 24.2* indicates that the total number of persons supplied with farm products by one farm worker increased about sixfold from 1930 to 1978. In addition, *Table 24.3* shows that better technology and capital accumulation (combined with a reduction in the farm work force) have resulted in there being an average of $143,300 worth of capital equipment at the disposal of every farm worker in 1978. In 1940, by comparison (when one farm worker could feed only 11 people) the average farm worker was aided by only $3326 in capital equipment.

The overall impact of long-term changes in the supply and demand for agricultural goods is depicted in *Fig. 24.3*. The income inelastic demand in combination with the remarkable increase in productivity has resulted in a much greater outward shift in the supply curve than in the demand curve. Consequently, prices have fallen.

Price inelasticity of demand

Another element of the traditional farm problem is the price inelasticity of demand for agricultural products. Consumers may applaud a drop in the price of onions, but that does not necessarily mean they will buy five pounds more of them each week. The marginal utility derived from eating additional onions drops off very quickly. Moreover, most food items have very few alternative uses. Therefore, as farm prices have fallen over time, the corresponding increase in quantity demanded has not been sufficient to prevent incomes from declining.

Uneven effects of technology

Although technological improvements have been an important factor contributing to the substantial overall increases in productivity in the farm sector, this does not mean that change has occurred evenly throughout agriculture. Many farmers still lack the resources and the knowledge to become efficient producers. Government-sponsored research undertaken by land-grant colleges, experimental stations, and the Agricultural Extension Service has been fruitful, but most of the gains have been in the area of improving methods of large-scale production. Consequently, large farmers have benefited most. The small farmers in Kentucky and Maine, on the other hand, have often been unable to take advantage of new seeds, fertilizers, and pesticides; of improved breeds and feeds for livestock; and of mechanization. For them, changing technology has meant a deterioration of their competitive position. And yet, they

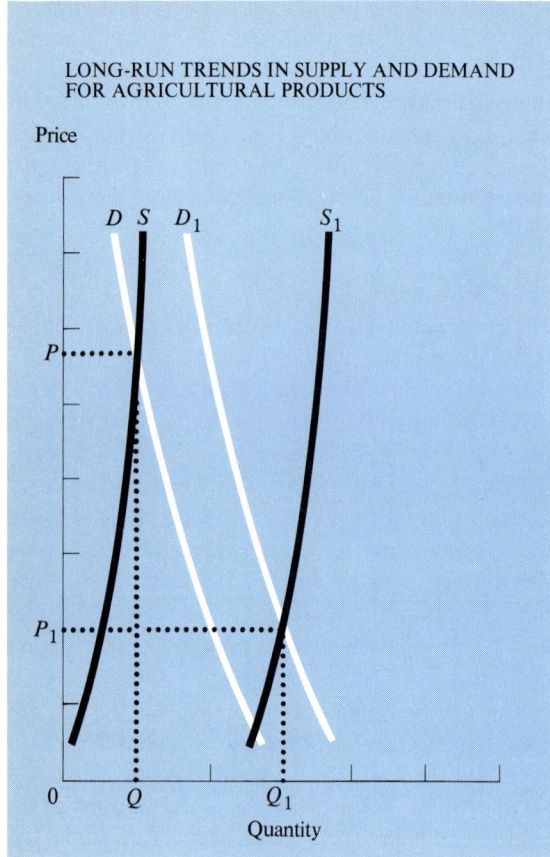

LONG-RUN TRENDS IN SUPPLY AND DEMAND FOR AGRICULTURAL PRODUCTS

Fig. 24.3
The long-run trends in supply and demand for agricultural products have shown a much greater outward shift of the supply curve than of the demand curve. The increase in demand is primarily due to population growth, which in the United States is relatively slow. The substantial increase in supply is due to dramatic gains in productivity caused by technological advance, the accumulation of a greater stock of human capital among farm workers, and the efficiencies of large-scale production.

are still the majority among United States farmers. As shown in *Table 24.1*, in 1973 more than one-half of domestic farm output was produced by small farmers—those with sales of less than $10,000.

The traditional farm problem—excess production under highly competitive market conditions—affects mainly these marginal, low-income farmers. There is little they can do to improve their market position. Since farm goods are so uniform, attempts at product differentiation that might lead to a better competitive position in the market are unlikely to succeed. The development of new or improved products, such as turkeys that have a larger percentage of white meat, requires a large investment—larger than any marginal farmer can afford. Thus small farmers tend to be relatively inefficient, and their meager earnings reflect this fact.

Why don't more farmers quit?
Under the circumstances outlined above, we might wonder why more farmers have not been able to see the writing on the wall. *Figure 24.4* shows that, in fact, the number of people engaged in farm production has decreased drastically.

Nevertheless, it is less easy to abandon farming for some other enterprise than it might at first seem. One reason is cultural: farms tend to be handed down from generation to generation, and those who have tilled the soil for generations are reluctant to give up their familiar way of life, even though it may have long since ceased to be profitable. In many cases, farmers seem to prefer the nonmonetary rewards of rural life over the increased income they might earn in an urban setting.

In addition, the cost of relocating in an urban area and undergoing job retraining is, of course, quite high. Moreover, in many cases farm life has left the farmer relatively unequipped to cope with the adjustment to urban life. Finally, isolated in

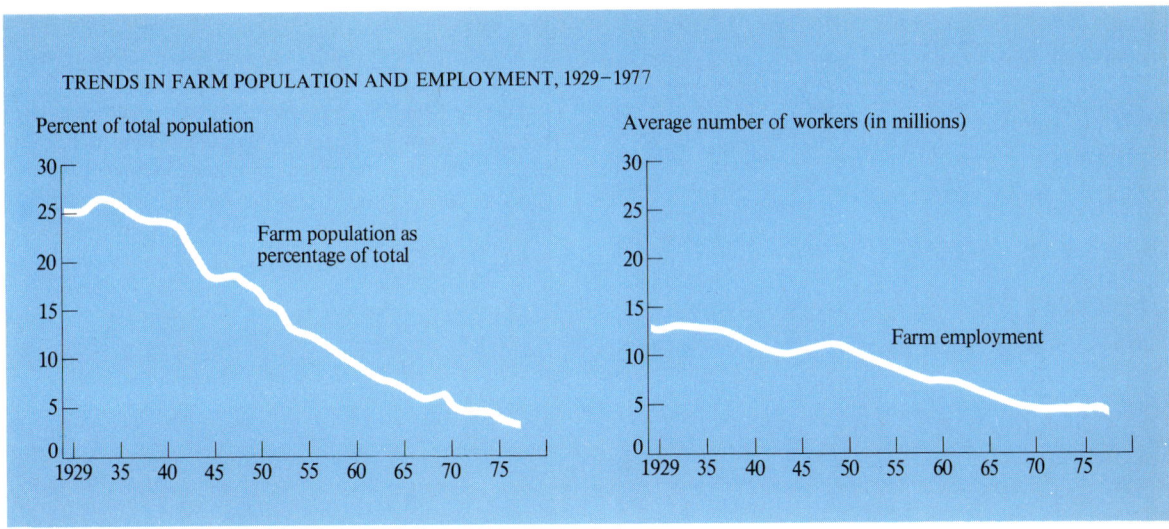

Fig. 24.4
The significant long-run increase in the supply of farm commodities is not due to an overall expansion of the agricultural sector. On the contrary, both the percentage of the population living on farms and the number of workers employed in agriculture have declined steadily since 1929.

the country, the farm population may lack information about other job opportunities. As a consequence, although the exodus from the agricultural sector has been significant, it has not occurred to the degree dictated by economic efficiency.

The short run
While the inability of agricultural income to keep pace with the growth of earnings in the rest of the economy is a persistent problem, uncertainty regarding the level of income from year to year also haunts the farmer. Variability in annual income is due primarily to the price inelasticity of demand for agricultural products and is triggered by changing supply and demand conditions for particular commodities.

As noted in our discussion of long-run issues above, the responsiveness of consumers to changing food prices is limited. Therefore, if agricultural prices fall by 10 percent, quantity demanded increases by less than 10 percent. This less-than-proportionate buyer response results in reduced farmer income. Conversely, when agricultural prices rise by 10 percent the farmer's income increases because the number of units purchased declines less than 10 percent. *Figure 24.5* further explains the relationship between price inelastic demand and farmer income.

Effect of supply on income: graphic analysis
How often do these price-income changes occur in agricultural markets? Whenever supply conditions change. And they tend to change frequently, since agricultural production processes are subject to the whims of nature. Floods, droughts, and unexpected cold spells are common examples of

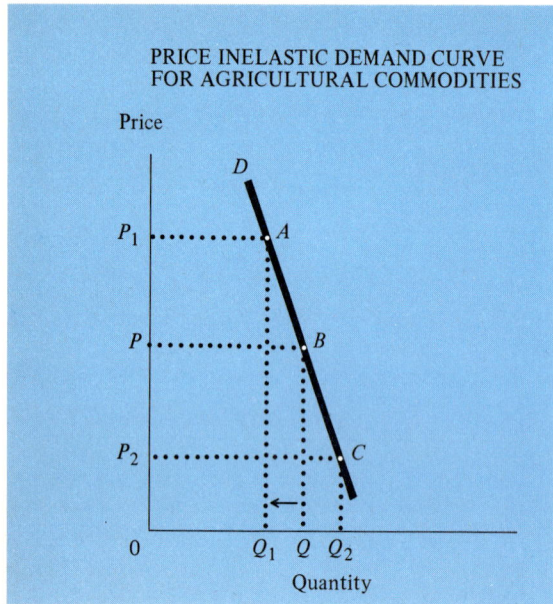

Fig. 24.5
If price increases from P to P_1, quantity demanded declines from Q to Q_1 and we move from point B to point A on the demand curve. Since the decrease in quantity is smaller in percentage terms than the increase in price, farm sector income increases from the area $0PBQ$ (price times number of units sold) to $0P_1AQ_1$.

natural phenomena which disrupt production and reduce market supply. To assist us in illustrating how supply changes affect income, let's use *Fig. 24.6* which considers the interaction of our demand curve from *Fig. 24.5* with three different short-run supply curves.

Assuming that S represents the initial output plans of producers, the effect of a drought, for example, is to reduce supply from S to S_1 and create a shortage equal to the distance QQ_1 at the original equilibrium price of P. In order to rid the market of this shortage, a particularly steep price increase is necessary because consumers are relatively insensitive to changing food prices. Equilibrium is ultimately reestablished at point A where price is P_1 and quantity is Q_1. This substantially higher price more than compensates for the fact that fewer units are purchased, so the reduction in supply in combination with the inelastic demand curve results in greater income for farmers. Graph-

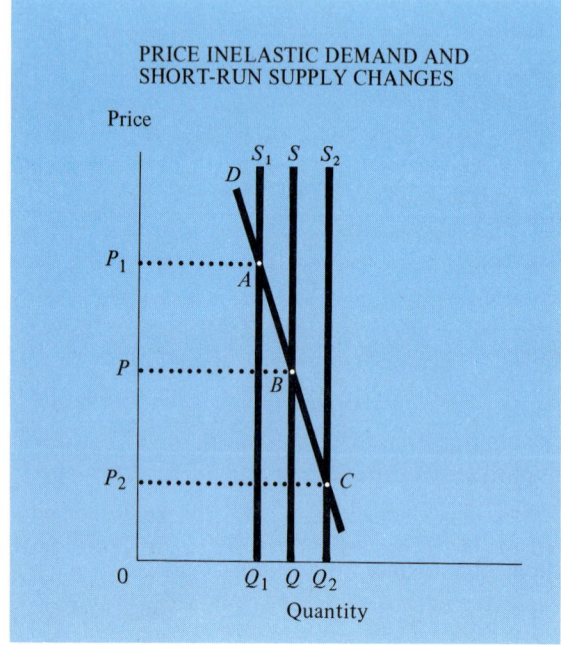

Fig. 24.6
If favorable weather conditions increase supply from S to S_2, price will decline sharply to restore equilibrium between the quantity supplied and demanded. This price cut from P to P_2 is accompanied by only a slight increase in units sold (Q to Q_2) so farm sector income falls. (*Note:* The short-run supply curve is vertical because once the growing season begins, production plans cannot be altered in response to a changing price.)

ically this is indicated by the fact that the area $0P_1AQ_1$, corresponding to the income generated by the newly established price and quantity, exceeds $0PBQ$, the original level of income.

An unexpectedly plentiful harvest, on the other hand, causes a shift in the supply curve from S to S_2. A surplus equal to the horizontal distance QQ_2 exerts downward pressure on price. Initial price cuts, however, affect consumer behavior only slightly and surpluses remain until the price is whittled all the way down to P_2. The increase in quantity sold, QQ_2, is not sufficient to fully offset the fact that each unit now sells for less, so income declines. Graphically, the decline in income is illustrated by the fact that $0P_2CQ_2$ represents a smaller area than $0PBQ$.

Since the demand for agricultural products is price inelastic and weather conditions, which vary from year to year, play such an integral role in determining the actual level of production, the farmer does not enjoy the comfort a stable level of income affords. Furthermore, farmers as a group find themselves in a paradoxical position. More production means less income, and less production means more income.

Effect of demand on income

In addition to changing supply conditions, altered demand circumstances also affect farmer income. If our price inelastic demand curve shifts to the right, as it did in 1972 in response to crop failures in many foreign countries, a shortage arises at the original equilibrium price. Again, since consumers react stubbornly to higher food prices, a stiff price increase is required to restore equilibrium to the market. Selling more output at significantly higher prices boosts farmer income considerably. By contrast, decreases in demand result in drastically reduced prices and earnings.

Having specified and explained both the long- and short-run problems confronting the farmer, we now turn to a discussion of government policies intended to alleviate these difficulties.

GOVERNMENT FARM POLICY

After World War I, government aid was first provided to farms in the form of information about agricultural methods and conservation, and by making farm land available to settlers. (At that time, the problem of overproduction had not yet become apparent.) In 1929, the Federal Farm Board was set up, and the era of direct subsidies to farmers began. The following areas were officially identified as needing immediate attention:

1. Farmers, particularly, suffer from business fluctuations, and the onslaught of the Great Depression was causing them special hardship.
2. The unpredictability of weather and natural disasters, such as plant disease epidemics or insect infestation, required a stabilizing counterforce.
3. Existing legislation gave favored treatment to other groups by permitting imperfect competition, sometimes providing tariff protection and tax advantages—all of which handicapped farmers, who had to operate under rigidly competitive conditions.
4. Fertile soil, like forests and mineral deposits, is a national resource that should be conserved through federal government action and not be allowed to be depleted by farmers who cannot afford to let land lie fallow.

Parity pricing

Once these conditions were officially acknowledged, government moved swiftly—if not always effectively—to correct them. At the heart of its aid program was interference with the forces of supply and demand in order to establish prices for farm goods above their equilibrium level. To arrive at the new level, the concept of **parity pricing** was developed. *In agriculture, parity means that year after year there should be an equivalence between farmers' current purchasing power and their purchasing power to a selected base period.*

This equivalence is maintained by government support of agricultural commodity prices. Let us see how the parity concept was developed and implemented.

The years 1909 to 1914 are often described as the golden age of United States agriculture. Prices were stable, and farm income was comparable to that in other economic sectors. Soon after World War I, however, the farmers' position began to deteriorate. When government assistance was formulated in the 1930s, it was argued that it would be fair to reestablish the level of parity between farm and nonfarm prices that existed from 1909 to 1914. If a bushel of wheat gave farmers enough income in 1914 to buy a certain amount of goods and services, it should get them the same amount in 1935 and in 1975.

The parity concept was enacted, but in practice it did not always have the expected results. In spite of the implementation of parity pricing, the prices received by farmers did not keep pace with the prices paid by farmers.

Part of the reason is that parity did not always apply to *all* farm products; rather, it applied primarily to those that could be stored. When consumers demanded more perishable products, such as strawberries, and fewer products that could be stored, such as grain, overall farm prices fell below parity, because the government left most perishables unsupported. Prices of supported products were generally kept too high and those of unsupported products too low.

The parity pricing formula

In 1948, to remedy this difficulty, Congress enacted an adjustment in the parity formula. Previously, the price of a farm commodity in a given year was calculated by dividing the index of prices paid by farmers that year by 100 (the index of farm prices from 1909 to 1914) and multiplying it by the price of the commodity in the base period. Thus, if the index of prices paid by farmers in 1950 stood at 256, the parity coefficient in that year was 2.56. To arrive at the parity price of any farm product in 1950, we multiply the price of the product in the 1909-1914 base period by 2.56. Thus if a bushel of wheat sold for 86.8¢ in 1914, it should sell in 1950 for 86.8¢ times 2.56, or for $2.22.

When Congress modernized this formula, it declared that parity based on 1909–1914 prices should be maintained as a *goal* for agricultural commodities as a whole, but that parity prices for individual goods should also reflect their average price in the most recent ten years. That average differed from the parity price because the government's support price was often set at less than parity.

Thus parity remained the goal of the law, but actual market conditions were to be taken into account. What is evident from the revised formula is the importance of the base period in calculating parity prices in subsequent years. If the base period had been a prosperous one for farmers, as the years 1909 to 1914 were, parity would work to maintain that level of prosperity. If the base period had been a poor one for farmers, parity would perpetuate that poverty. By combining the 1909–1914 period with a ten-year period immediately preceding the parity year in question, a compromise was struck.

A serious drawback of the parity concept was its relative rigidity in the face of constantly changing market conditions. Perhaps if the parity formula had been regularly reviewed, its effect would have been fairer. But as it was, inefficiencies and distortions of some prices and incomes persisted.

Once the parity formula was settled upon, however, how did government go about maintaining parity prices? The two main programs were the purchase of surplus production and the imposition of production controls.

Purchase of surpluses

If the government guaranteed a price for farm products at or near parity, farmers were induced to produce a certain amount of output. Demand at that price, however, fell far short of supply because the parity price was set artificially above the equilibrium price. If farmers tried to sell this entire output in the free market, the price would drop from the support level to the equilibrium level. *Figure 24.7* illustrates the situation.

The line P_1 is the support price guaranteed by government to farmers, who at that price will produce quantity Q_2. Consumer demand, however, will be at Q_1, and the government ends up buying the surplus production designated by the distance between Q_1 and Q_2. If it did not do that, the market price would fall to E, the free-market equilibrium point.

Therefore, what has taken place in effect is an artificial shift in the demand curve to intersect the supply curve at point G. Farmers are able to produce more and receive higher prices for it. Consumers are paying a higher price, but buying less. And through taxes they are footing the bill for the government purchase of surpluses.

Such purchases were usually made under a loan support program, whereby the government lent farmers money and kept their excess output as collateral. If market conditions changed and farmers were able to sell some of the surplus production stored by the government, they repaid the government with the proceeds. If after a certain time they were still unable to sell the surplus, it became the property of the government.

The disposal problem What did the government do with the surplus? Long storage made some food inedible, and there was no alternative but to destroy it. If it was still in marketable condition, the government might decide to "dump" it abroad—that is, sell it abroad at a lower price than it cost to produce at home. Dumping is usually prohibited by international trade rules, but because the prices of United States farm goods were kept artificially high, the dumping price was not always low enough to undercut producers in other countries, and therefore our sale of surplus food did not provoke charges of unfair competition.

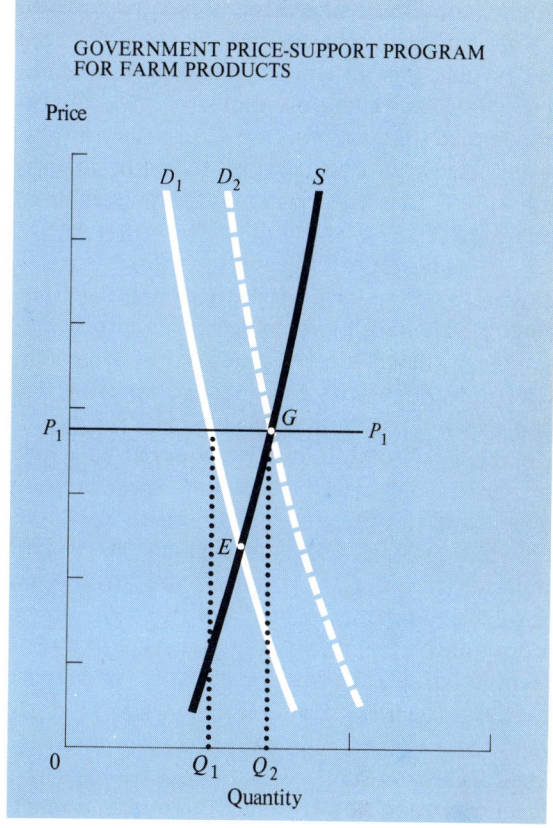

Fig. 24.7
Suppose the government guarantees farmers the price P_1 for their products. At this above-equilibrium price, the quantity supplied will be Q_2, but the quantity demanded by consumers will be only Q_1. To maintain the support price, therefore, the government must purchase the surplus represented by the distance from Q_1 to Q_2. In effect, what has occurred is an artificial shift of the demand curve from D_1 to D_2. Farmers are now producing more and receiving higher prices, while consumers are buying fewer agricultural goods and paying higher prices.

Under the Food for Peace program, some of the United States surplus farm output was channeled to underdeveloped countries as a form of foreign aid. Domestic use for surplus farm output has traditionally been limited. Although some of the surplus was distributed to needy households under various welfare programs, political opposition tended to restrict this use of our food surplus. Also the costs of transporting the surplus and distributing it to needy households were sometimes very high.

A great deal of time and money was spent to find ways to use farm products in industrial production. The results were not encouraging, and it would probably have required even greater government subsidies for the type of research to make such a program viable.

That left the alternative of destroying farm surpluses. Sometimes farmers took such action on their own, and the government did its part, too. Between 1943 and 1950, for example, in order to support the price of potatoes, the government burned millions of bushels, and it dyed millions more blue to keep them off the market and resell them to farmers at a fraction of their original price for use as feed and fertilizer.

Production controls

It is not hard to see why under these circumstances government moved to tackle the problem of surpluses at the supply end instead by imposing production controls. For as long as an extensive price support program was in effect, farmers had no incentive to reduce their output voluntarily and, in fact, may have been tempted to expand it. The problem of surplus disposal or storage was then created, requiring additional expenditures. A program requiring farmers to restrict their production to begin with would have been less costly.

Since demand for agricultural goods is usually rather inelastic, a program of crop reduction results in higher receipts by farmers. And since they also reduce their costs by producing less, their net income will go up by an even greater percent than their gross revenues.

Government used two approaches to bring about such a result: (1) restrictions on acreage to be planted; and (2) the establishment of *voluntary* marketing quotas. The latter, while sensible in conception, ran counter to the marketing psychology of farmers and was generally ineffective.

Curtailing planted acreage The main means of output control, therefore, was the curtailment of planted acreage. How well did this method work? Surprisingly, acreage reductions resulted in less than proportionate decreases in production and sometimes even in increases in output. The apparent paradox can be explained easily. One reason is that when farmers agreed to set aside some of their land, they usually gave up their poorest soil and retained the most fertile. Thus the output reduction was not proportionate. Another reason is that land is only one of the factors of production needed in farming. Farmers still had their supply of labor and capital, and when they employed them more intensively on reduced acreage, productivity rose. The intensified application of these resources to the smaller land area may actually have increased total output.

Such results were especially likely when we consider that the main government incentive to farmers to set aside land was an outright payment for land left unplanted. Thus, if farmers could maintain their level of output on the reduced acreage, their market revenues would remain steady, and in addition they would receive government funds for the unused acreage.

For this reason, it was suggested that marketing quotas based on physical units be imposed to control production. Farmers would be allowed to sell a certain amount of a commodity at its support price and be taxed punitively if they sold more. Such quotas existed for tobacco, cotton, and potatoes under the Agricultural Adjustment Act of 1933, which was later declared unconstitutional. A general plan of this type was proposed by President Kennedy in 1961, but it was rejected by Congress under the pressure of middle- and upper-income farmers, who would have lost income through its adoption.

Evaluation of government farm policy

How well did government intervention work toward a solution of the farm problem in the United States? Recall that farmers were partly victimized by the relative advantage that other sectors enjoyed in our market economy. Government programs helped the farmer, at the expense of taxpaying businesses and households Thus the burden was shifted from the few to the many, but the basic misallocation of resources continued. The surplus purchase program did not work to reduce inefficient farm employment, and acreage restrictions did not drastically reduce overproduction.

The government program did little to solve the problem of poverty in the agricultural sector. Because of the uneven distribution of farm output, most of the government support went to the large farms that sold the largest quantities of output. But those were the farmers that already enjoyed relatively high incomes. Poor farmers who made their livelihood from a few acres of inefficiently cultivated soil were hardly better off in 1970 than they were in 1920. It was they who suffered most from the farm problem, which in a way could be blamed on the abundant output of the large, modern farms. Yet the attempted solution to the program did not help them so much as those farmers whose incomes were relatively high to begin with.

On the positive side, the United States farm program, especially the output controls, resulted in increased productivity. It also encouraged agricultural research to discover new products and methods of production.

Proposals to revamp the program centered on two extremes: a return to free markets, and direct *income* subsidies for farmers.

A return to free markets?

Proponents of a return to free markets asserted that government programs, by treating symptoms rather than causes, delayed, rather than hastened, the solution to the farm problem. They argued that if the government had instead permitted the free play of supply and demand, the reallocation of resources from the farm to the nonfarm sectors of the economy would have been speeded. Critics of this proposal, however, said that because of the specialized nature of farm resources, their flow to the nonfarm sector would be too slow to benefit industry. They would remain tied up in farming until they became obsolete. Furthermore, in the absence of government price supports, the return on capital in agriculture would decrease, slowing technological development and causing inefficiencies to reoccur. Several studies concluded that a return to free markets would not bring about resource adjustment fast enough and would result in a prolonged period of low incomes for farmers.

A direct income subsidy?

A direct income subsidy for farmers was first proposed by President Truman's secretary of Agriculture, Charles F. Brannan. The Brannan Plan, as it is commonly called, would replace parity price payments to farmers with direct payments to farmers. It would preserve a free market for farm goods. The compensation to farmers would be based on the difference between the free-market price of their products and some higher target price which would result in income equity. Under the plan, farmers would be assured of adequate incomes, and consumers would enjoy low prices. The plan would also do away with the costs of storage and the wastes of destruction and spoilage, and it would discourage dumping abroad. Most of all, however, it would make the farm subsidy visible to taxpayers and probably cause pressure for frequent adjustments as economic conditions changed.

It is precisely this visibility of farm subsidies to which farming interests objected. Their fear was that subsidies might gradually be reduced or that stricter controls would be demanded.

These issues became political ones and in retrospect it is fairly accurate to say that America's approach to the farm problem was guided as much by political considerations as by purely economic considerations. At the beginning of the 1970s a lasting solution was not evident.

AGRICULTURE IN THE 1970s

In the 1970s the American farmer has been at the center of an array of interrelated developments that pose both new and old problems while holding out promises and questions for the future. Early in the decade demand for and prices of agricultural products rose to such an extent that concerns about how to increase production replaced concerns about how to deal with overproduction. The farming community continued to live up to its reputation as a sector plagued by erratic swings in earnings, however, and farm income shriveled in the mid-1970s, only to rebound sharply as we move into the 1980s.

Increases in foreign demand

At the outset of the 1970s, crop failures in many countries, the desire of foreign nations to improve their living standards and change their dietary habits, and policy decisions regarding economic growth and structure led to a sharp increase in foreign demand for American agricultural products. In July and August 1972, for example, the Soviet Union purchased about 441 million bushels of American wheat for approximately $700 million. This amount was equivalent to 30 percent of average annual American wheat production during the previous five years and more than 80 percent of the wheat used for domestic food during that period. The unprecedented export boom was also stimulated by the devaluations of the dollar that occurred in 1971 and 1973. Dollars became less expensive relative to other currencies, and American agricultural products thus became cheaper for foreign countries to buy. By 1973 the export boom had eliminated much of the excess productive capacity that had become the chronic problem of agriculture in the United States. The increasing role of foreign markets became central to American agriculture in the 1970s.

As a citizen of an interdependent world economy, the American farmer is subject to climatic, political, and economic developments around the globe, not just in the United States. American farmers face the important question of whether the increased demand for exports is traceable primarily to abnormally poor weather conditions in other countries or to a long-term rise in world demand. They also face the problem of obtaining from foreign suppliers certain goods they need for production of their own goods—goods that they may hope to sell to foreign countries. For example, it takes enormous quantities of oil to operate farm machinery, run irrigation pumps, and produce fertilizer. In 1974, in the wake of the oil embargo and price increases by OPEC, costs of production for farmers rose steeply; fertilizer prices alone increased 75 percent. American farmers of the 1970s therefore found themselves operating on an economic seesaw with such assorted companions as Soviet bureaucrats and Arab sheiks.

In addition, farmers are always on the supply-demand seesaw with their fellow citizens, the American consumers. The export boom has been accompanied by increasing domestic demand for food. Per capita food consumption in the United States increased every year but one from 1965 through 1974, with the consumption index in the latter year more than 6 percent higher than in the former. Increases in the incomes of Americans in this period apparently led them to improve their diets, particularly by buying more meat. However, because of the income inelasticity of demand for agricultural products, the percentage increase in consumption was small and the percentage increase in incomes large. Nonetheless, a 6 percent increase in a country with more than 200 million people is a lot of food.

Consumer boycotts

In 1973, consumer resistance—including a week-long nationwide meat boycott—to higher prices and limited supplies caused a decline in per capita food consumption. Fear of consumer protests also led the Ford administration in 1974 to pressure exporters to cancel contracts for more grain sales to the Soviet Union, sales that might otherwise have contributed to price rises, as the 1972 sales did. The year 1974 also saw inflation-conscious consumers rebel against soaring prices for dairy products and sugar. Some ranchers and dairy farmers slaughtered cattle in response to consumer resistance, and some hatchery operators in 1973 killed chicks to protest a government freeze on meat prices while the cost of feed rose.

Although per capita income of farmers surpassed nonfarm income in 1973, the individual farmer still was not becoming rich. Returns to farm resources were sufficiently high in the 1970s to encourage the expansion of productive potential, but year-to-year changes in incomes emphasized the increased uncertainty of earnings. In 1974, farm income declined and once again was lower than nonfarm income. Crop yields were off because of bad weather, costs increased for such necessities as fuel and fertilizer, and government payments were reduced. By 1977, annual farm income was just 62 percent of what it had been four years earlier, and the American Agriculture Movement reacted by dispatching angry farmers, in their tractors, to the nation's capitol to protest their economic plight.

More recently, market conditions have improved. In September 1978, the prices received by farmers were 23 percent higher than they had been 12 months before, and record corn, soybean, hay, and fall potato crops were expected. Yet despite this resurgence, the real income of farmers was no higher in 1978 than it was in 1969. Viewed from this perspective, the period of the seventies was not a prosperous one for the farmer.

Farm legislation in the seventies

In 1973, as demand for food was increasing and food stocks were being depleted, Congress enacted important new farm legislation, the Agriculture and Consumer Protection Act. The new law marked a break with long-standing restrictive policies, such as the parity-pricing concept, and encouraged all-out production. Restrictions on the planting of most crops were ended, and the system of payments and price supports being used to persuade farmers to reduce plantings was replaced with a new system of **target prices**, *which are essentially guaranteed minimum prices on basic agricultural products*. The target prices are expressed in specific dollar figures rather than as a percentage of parity. If market prices fall below target prices, the government will pay farmers the difference based on normal yields on allotment acreages. If market prices remain above target prices, no payments are made. Price-support loans would be available only at price levels lower than the target prices. Previously legislated authority to set aside certain acreages from production was continued but at the discretion of the Secretary of Agriculture. In 1974, Secretary of Agriculture Earl Butz announced that he would not exercise this authority, and farmers were free to produce as much as they chose.

This increased reliance on market forces in the agricultural sector was initially tolerated by farmers because prices were so high in 1973 that government assistance was largely unnecessary. However, when prices fell precipitously around the time that President Carter took office, farmers became painfully aware of the free-market elements of the new legislation.

At the urging of farm lobbyists, the Carter administration raised target prices and encouraged farmer participation in set-aside programs. As a result, government outlays to support farm programs quadrupled, to an estimated $7.9 billion, between the 1976 and 1978 fiscal years.

More recent legislative efforts, in the form of the Food and Agriculture Act of 1977 and the Emergency Asistance Act of 1978, appear as attempts to strike a compromise between the free-market and government-dominated approaches to the farm problem. Recognition of the desirability of allowing farmers the freedom to produce and the emphasis on target prices (as opposed to use of parity pricing) characterize the spirit of the 1973 legislation, while maintenance of *authority* to restrict production and the observed willingness to *increase* target prices indicate that the farm sector will not be regulated solely by the forces of supply and demand in the eighties.

A radical proposal
Finally, during the gasoline shortage of 1979, it was suggested that the agricultural sector be used as a tool to combat reductions in the supply of oil from the Middle East and increases in the price of crude oil. Since many oil-exporting countries depend upon American agriculture for some essential foodstuffs, such as wheat, it was proposed that quantities and prices of United States agricultural exports to be tied to quantities and prices of oil imports. Although this quite radical proposal may turn out to be little more than a songwriter's fantasy—"Give us crude or no more food"—its implications for the income and power of the agricultural sector in America might be staggering, and, if any such action is undertaken, this will be an interesting situation to watch.

Summary

■ This chapter examines the particular problems of the market for agricultural goods in the United States and surveys the history of government policies to deal with these problems.

■ The traditional farm problem in the United States is the paradox of great abundance of production accompanied by low incomes for farmers. Ironically, this has occurred in the sector of the economy which most closely resembles the model of perfect competition. Per capita income for farmers has consistently been below per capita income for nonfarm families for the past 50 years. The prices farmers pay for goods and services they purchase tend to be higher than the prices they receive for their products. Technological development in farming has greatly increased supply, leading to lower prices. Increased demand in recent years, both internationally and domestically, has brought some changes in this traditional problem.

■ The demand for agricultural products is income inelastic, with only limited expansion of demand as consumer income rises. Many agricultural products are actually inferior goods, the demand for which decreases as income rises. Increase in demand in the past few decades has come primarily from population expansion. Technological development in farming has greatly shifted the supply curve, but the demand curve has shifted only slightly in comparison. Technological development has also primarily benefited large-scale farmers, even though small farmers constitute the majority and are responsible for about half of agricultural output. Many farmers have moved to other employment, but cultural factors make many farmers reluctant to give up.

■ The demand for agricultural goods is also price inelastic. As prices drop, consumption goes up only slightly, resulting in a substantial drop in income; as prices rise, consumption goes down only slightly, resulting in a significant rise in income. Thus the income for farmers may fluctuate dramatically from year to year, dependent on such unpredictable factors as the weather.

■ From the Depression of the 1930s on, government policy recognized the special problems of farmers in several ways. The concept of parity pricing committed the government to supporting agricultural prices in order to maintain the purchasing power of farmers from year to year at the level of the relatively prosperous years 1909–1914. Initially this resulted in keeping the prices of supported goods too high and the prices of nonsupported goods (like perishables) too low, and so in 1948 parity pricing began to take the level of prices from the preceding ten years into account as well. The parity goal was accomplished through a combination of government purchases (to keep demand up) and production controls (to keep supply down). Government purchases of farm surpluses mean that consumers pay higher prices as well as paying the costs of government purchases through their taxes. The government could then dispose of the surplus goods by dumping them on international markets, destroying them, or distributing them through social welfare programs. Production controls on acreage generally have not resulted in a decrease in actual output, and direct control of output has not been politically acceptable when tried or proposed. The effect of all these policies has been to shift the burden from farmers to larger and more affluent sectors of the population, but the basic problem of resource misallocation has not changed. More radical proposals for a return to a free market or for direct income subsidies to farmers have been made but have encountered stiff political opposition.

■ In the 1970s, international demand for agricultural goods from the United States has increased sharply, along with the costs of certain input resources (such as oil) which also come from international sources. Domestic demand has also increased somewhat. On the whole, the 1970s were not a prosperous decade for farmers; real income for farmers in 1978 was the same as in 1969. In 1973, Congress instituted a new approach in setting target prices, essentially guaranteeing minimum prices for basic agricultural products while encouraging high levels of production. Although this approach satisfied many farmers in the boom year of 1973, the subsequent drop in farm prices made farmers aware of the free-market character of the new policies, and they demanded higher target prices. The 1970s have also witnessed organized boycotts by consumers and greater political pressure by farmers on government officials.

Key Terms

parity pricing

target prices

Review & Discussion

1. What was the nature of the traditional farm problem? Explain what is meant by the statement that farmers were victimized by perfect competition.

2. Why does the persistence of the farm problems suggest that there has been and continues to be a misallocation of resources? Why has farm income generally remained below non-farm income? What would normally happen if an industry suffers below-normal profits for an extended period of time? Why was the farm problem not resolved in this way?

3. Why is the demand for farm products relatively stable? What consequences does the price inelasticity of demand have for the income of the agricultural sector?

4. What have been the consequences of technological change in farming? How have these changes affected the supply curve? How have these changes affected large-scale and small-scale farmers?

5. Describe the concept of parity. What policies has the United States government pursued in order to maintain parity? What have been the effects?

6. What difficulties have been associated with government action to control farm production?

7. What factors have shaped agriculture in the past decade? In what ways are farmers more integrated into the international economy? What changes have there been in government policies? What is the significance of the greater political organization of farmers and consumers of agricultural products?

Chapter 25

Price and Output under Monopoly

What to look for in this chapter

What are the characteristics of the monopoly market model?

How does a monopoly market differ from a perfectly competitive market?

How does a monopoly producer maximize profits and reach short-run and long-run equilibrium?

How does monopoly control over price and output misallocate resources?

In what ways can monopolies be regulated?

We previously defined a perfectly competitive market as a market model in which no one buyer or seller has the power to influence price or significantly change total production. At the opposite end of the spectrum from the perfectly competitive market is the monopoly market. You will recall from our discussion in Chapter 4 that a monopoly exists when a single firm is the only producer in an entire industry of a product or service for which there is no close substitute. As a result of this situation, a monopoly has significant power to influence price and output.

Despite popular political and journalistic claims to the contrary, monopolists who are aiming to maximize their profits are not free to set *any* price and sell *any* quantity they wish. We shall see in this chapter that for any level of market demand and for any costs of production, there is a profit-maximizing price to be charged and quantity to be sold that will be chosen by the monopolist. Keep in mind that in our discussion we will be analyzing a market model, much as we did in Chapter 23. Monopoly in its pure form, like perfect competition, is rarely encountered in an actual market situation.

CHARACTERISTICS OF THE MONOPOLY MARKET

As we learned in Chapter 23, when a market is perfectly competitive, the market supply curve is the sum of the individual supply curves of the many small firms, or a slightly steeper curve when the industry is one of increasing resource costs. No one supplier sells a large enough percentage of total market volume to be able to influence price or output through his or her own actions. Each producer faces a horizontal market demand curve at the market price. In the monopoly market model, we find exactly the opposite situation. There is only one supplier; one single firm faces the entire market demand curve, which is negatively sloped. And of course, being the only supplier, the monopolist is able to set the price at which to sell output. (Note once again, however, that the pricing and output decisions are determined by the level of demand and production costs.)

No adequate substitutes

A pure monopoly can exist only when there is no near substitute for the product traded in that market. Ohio Bell is a pure monopoly in that it controls the telephone service market in northern Ohio; not only does the company have no direct competitors selling phone service, but its product has no adequate substitutes. No other means of communication—writing a letter, paying a personal visit, sending a carrier pigeon—allows the quick, convenient, and lengthy exchange of information that is possible in a telephone call. If a good substitute for the product is available, even a firm that is the only supplier in the market does not have a pure monopoly. For example, there is only one newspaper in Jefferson City, Missouri, but the paper's publisher does not really have a market monopoly. Jefferson City residents can get local news from radio and television stations in the area; they can read the national news in the Kansas City or the St. Louis papers or in news magazines; they can call the government weather bureau to find out if it is going to rain; and they can buy the latest Beetle Bailey comic book at the drugstore instead of following the strip in the paper.

It is interesting to note that the existence of a monopoly may depend on the way the market is defined. The motor vehicle market consists of many competitive firms selling cars, trucks, dune buggies, snowmobiles, and power boats. If we narrow the market down to the automobile market, we have all foreign and domestic producers of automobiles; if we further narrow the market to the market for American autos, then we have only four American firms competing in that market. And if we talk about the Mustang market, we have narrowed the market down to a monopoly possessed by Ford (although the monopoly is not a perfect one, since there are many substitutes for Mustangs).

One of the basic goals of advertising, especially the type of advertising that tries to create some strong product image, is to narrow the public's definition of the market and thus create a monopolistic market. If Ford can convince buyers in the automobile market that their Mustang is so different from other small sporty cars that there could be no adequate Mustang substitute, then it has formed a Mustang market in which it is the only supplier. By differentiating its product, Ford can monopolize a segment of the huge demand for automobiles—creating a demand for Mustangs by customers who will accept no substitutes. This differentiation of demand gives the supplier much more market power than he or she could have in a competitive market, where a price change might make Mustang buyers switch to Camaros.

Another way a monopoly might arise is through the use of political barriers to trade. Suppose, for example, that the state legislature of Alabama passed a law making it illegal for any Alabama resident to buy dust mops in another state; anyone caught sneaking back over the Alabama border with a mop purchased in Mississippi would be fined $100. The effect would be a fragmentation of the national demand for mops and the establishment of a smaller monopoly market, the Alabama mop market. In this smaller market, it would be possible for one or two large firms to hold a great deal of economic power and to influence levels of price and output.

No state has ever passed a law that specifically prohibits the purchase of goods in another state, since this would be unconstitutional, but it is common for our national government to give American firms greater control over the domestic market by imposing taxes, duties, and tariffs. The import duties charged by the United States on Japanese-made color television sets serves to fragment the vast international demand for sets and to establish a United States market, in which a few large American electronics firms can enjoy some degree of market power.

It is important to note that even theoretically there can be no pure monopoly. Although there may be no good substitutes for a product, there are usually several poor ones. For example, let us assume that automobiles are produced by only one company. We may then be tempted to define the auto industry as a pure monopoly. However, there are still substitutes for cars—bicycles, buses, even feet! But let us assume further that there is only one way to get from one point to another, namely, cars. Walking, biking, and busing are ruled out. There is still the option of not going, not using transportation at all. Any good competes with others for part of one's budget. We might define television sets as alternatives to travel from *A* to *B,* because instead of leaving *A,* one might stay there and watch TV. In other words, no one product or service has exclusive claim to a share of the budget.

Barriers to entry

In a monopoly market, there is only one supplier, and that firm can therefore determine total industry output, influence price, and often earn economic profits. Such a situation is obviously desirable from the firm's point of view; why, then, do not other firms enter the market?

The major reason is that barriers exist to entry by new firms. The barriers may be the natural result of the needs of large-scale industry, or they may be artificially created by circumstance or law. Let us look in more detail at some of these barriers.

High set-up costs

Certain industries, especially capital-intensive industries, require a heavy investment before production can begin. Scarce resources are wasted if a number of competitive firms duplicate the needed capital goods—for example, if several sets of electric power lines are constructed side by side.

In industries where set-up costs are high, full efficiency (the lowest possible point on the ATC curve) can be reached only at a very high level of production. The reason for this is shown graphically in *Fig. 25.1,* using the cost curves of an electric power company. Because set-up costs are so high, the company has a very large fixed cost. (Remember that fixed costs per unit decline as volume of production increases.) Variable costs, which increase with output, represent a relatively small percentage of total costs. Therefore the long-run average total cost curve shows a long, slow decline. The company can reach the point of greatest efficiency, meaning that it is operating at

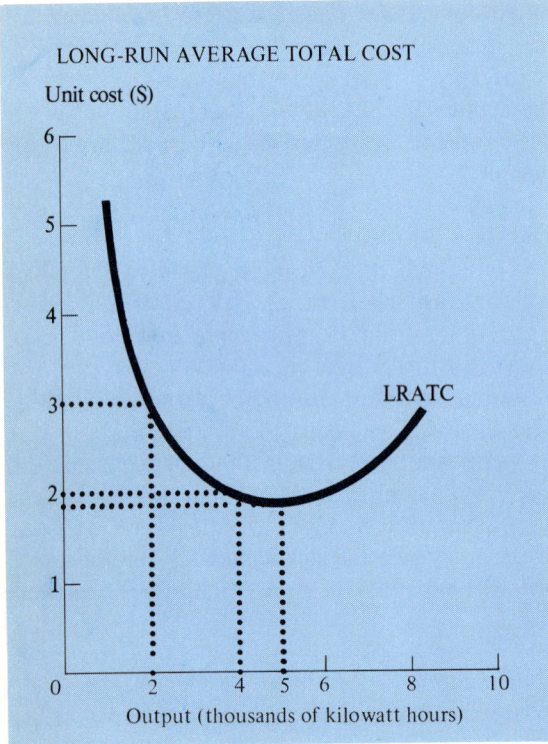

Fig. 25.1
The lowest point on the LRATC curve is at the production level of 5000 kilowatt hours; if the company can expand to that level of output, it will have the lowest possible per-unit cost. Suppose, however, that the total kilowatt hours demanded is only 4000. If one firm produces the entire supply, the per-unit cost will be 2; if there are two competitive firms in the power market, each producing half of the total supply, then the per-unit cost will be 3.

the lowest point on the long-run average total cost curve, only when it is producing a very large quantity of electric power. In *Fig. 25.1,* we assume that maximum efficiency is achieved at an output of 5000 kilowatt hours.

Since capital-intensive industries require such a high volume of production to be really efficient, firms are reluctant to commit themselves to the large expenditures needed to establish such a business unless they can be sure of a secure market position. At times, the government will intervene and guarantee a monopoly for certain industries. In this way, it attempts to prevent wasteful duplication and to effect low costs. In general, however, when the government guarantees a monopoly, it also regulates price and profits to ensure that the company does not use its monopoly position to exploit consumers of its product.

Indivisibility of the product

Under perfect competition, the suppliers are turning out identical units of a uniform product. This assumes that the product is one that can be produced in small units, with each unit being sold separately. But some goods and many services are indivisible. Phone service is a good example. It is not practical to buy phone service in tiny units—to buy a new line each time you want to make a call. Phone service is really useful only when it is a total system, so that you can pick up your phone and make a call immediately, without the inconvenience of having to wait for the phone company to install a line between your house and that of the person with whom you wish to speak.

When a product is indivisible, it is inefficient and confusing for a number of firms to compete with one another to produce it. If there were three telephone companies in your city, you would probably have to have three different phones, and you would have to remember which phone could be used to call different friends. Even more annoying, you would probably have to pay three different bills every month.

Ownership of essential materials

Some products require very specific resource inputs for which there are no substitutes. For example, aluminum can be made only through processing bauxite ore. This ore is not scattered in equal amounts all over the earth but is contained in several intensive deposits. If one company can buy the land containing all these deposits, it will have a monopoly in the aluminum industry (except for the possibility of reprocessing scrap aluminum). This is what the government accused Alcoa of doing in a famous antitrust case. Only after new bauxite deposits were discovered and the recycling of scrap was perfected did new companies develop.

Diamonds, nickel, copper, oil, and other natural resources might be subject to this same type of monopoly control, and in various times and places there have been monopolies in all of these industries. It is not only land resources that can be monopolized through exclusive ownership. Through exclusive contracts, labor resources can also be monopolized. For example, for many years the Metropolitan Opera had a virtual monopoly in the American opera industry, because all the trained and experienced opera singers in the United States were under contract to the Met. The professional baseball and football organizations have a similar monopoly today, since they sign up all the talented players for their teams. Before any would-be competitor could hope to attract fans, it would have to spend years scouting for likely young players, signing them up and teaching them how to play professional ball, or it would have to pay huge bonuses to lure professional players away from the existing major leagues.

Legal restraints

Some of our existing laws actually confer monopolistic power on certain firms. Most significant are the **patent laws.** *By issuing a patent, which gives a firm the exclusive right to produce, use, transfer, or withhold a product or process for a limited period of time, the government in effect enables the firm to exercise a temporary monopoly.* Perfect competition assumes that whenever one firm discovers an improvement in the production process or the final product, all firms can immediately adopt that improvement. Patent laws introduce a competitive imperfection because they allow one firm to enjoy the advantage of an improvement while denying it to other firms.

Rationale for creating patent monopolies It may seem as if this form of government intervention in the competitive market works against society's best interests; why should the government help create a monopoly? Basically, the government's intention is to promote and reward innovation and product improvement. We mentioned earlier that under perfect competition, firms have little incentive to lower their prices or improve their products. Since each firm can already sell an unlimited amount of its product at the going market price, there is no reason for the firm to try to cut its prices or improve the product in order to increase sales. Moreover, although lower costs will lead to higher profits in the short run, any improvement in process or product will immediately be copied throughout the entire industry;

RECAP

MONOPOLY, like perfect competition, is a basic model developed by economists for use in analyzing the workings of markets. Pure monopoly assumes the opposite situation from perfect competition. In a pure monopoly one firm is the sole producer of a good for which there is no close substitute. Other firms do not enter the monopoly market and thus create competition because a variety of barriers prevent their doing so. Some of these barriers are: high set-up costs, indivisibility of the product, ownership of essential materials by the monopolist, and legal restraints.

any cost reduction will eventually lead to a reduction in the market price of one good rather than permanent economic profits for the innovating firm. The government, therefore, grants the temporary market power of monopoly as a reward for innovation. The financial gain that this market power brings is intended to serve as an inducement to the invention of new products and processes. Society as a whole is helped because we learn new and more efficient ways to use our limited resources, and we discover substitute means of satisfying our many desires.

Granting a patent creates only a short-term monopoly. After a period of 17 years, the innovation is available to all firms in the industry. But the innovating firm has benefited from the extra profit during that period. If the firm has used part of its profit for continued research and development, it might be able to enjoy a new patent advantage when the old one expires. This has been the secret of IBM's dominance in the computer industry; the profits from its initial patent advantage have been used to develop more innovations that can be patented, so that the company continually creates a monopolistic market.

Copyright laws also create a type of monopoly. For example, when a new John Updike novel is published, only Updike's publisher can market the book. The writer of a hit song or play enjoys a similar legally created monopoly, as does the record company that sells a new album. However, since any one book, song, or play often has many close substitutes, it is very difficult to exploit a copyright (for instance, by charging $40 for a best seller) in the same way that a firm can exploit a monopoly on computer production.

Long-run situation

Most of the barriers to entry we have mentioned are essentially a short-run problem for would-be competitors. In the long run, it is possible to overcome most barriers. Reynolds and Kaiser were eventually able to enter the aluminum market and break Alcoa's monopoly, because these firms continued to prospect for bauxite mines and were encouraged to develop them by the government's prosecution of Alcoa. There is now a flourishing New York City Opera, because that organization was willing to invest many years and a great deal of money in training young unknown singers. By adopting an intensive long-term research and development program, Honeywell has been able to develop new computer systems of its own, and thereby to challenge IBM's position of dominance in the computer market.

Many monopolies, therefore, are only temporary acquisitions of market power. In the long run, other firms attracted by the higher rates of profit can overcome the barriers to entry and become suppliers in the market. Some observers have commented on the fact that our present high level of technological development has reduced the period of time needed to surmount the barriers. When Xerox comes out with a new copying machine, it takes Minnesota Mining and Manufacturing only a year or so to devise an alternative method of producing a copier with the same features; when one company found oil in the Arctic, it did not take long for other companies to send teams of geologists to make a scientific search for similar deposits in nearby areas. Thus in most cases today, monopolies are short-lived. Many economists feel that even "natural" monopolies, such as water and telephone service, would in the long run be threatened by competing firms, if it were not for government regulations that protect existing monopolies.

PRICE AND OUTPUT UNDER MONOPOLY

The market situation of the monopolist is quite different from that of the perfect competitor, because the monopolist is the only supplier in the market. Yet the monopolist, too, must make decisions about the levels of price and production that

Table 25.1
Cost and revenue schedule for a monopolist

(1) Quantity (Q)	(2) Price (P)	(3) Total revenue (TR) TR = P × Q	(4) Total cost (TC)	(5) Average total cost (ATC) ATC = $\frac{TC}{Q}$	(6) Marginal cost (MC) MC = $\frac{\Delta TC}{\Delta Q}$	(7) Marginal revenue (MR) MR = $\frac{\Delta TR}{\Delta Q}$	(8) Net revenue (NR) NR = TR − TC
0	$6.00	$ 0	$ 4.35	—	$ .90	$5.40	$ −4.35
1	5.40	5.40	5.25	$5.25	.75	4.20	.15
2	4.80	9.60	6.00	3.00	.60	3.00	3.60
3	4.20	12.60	6.60	2.20	.90 } 1.20	1.80 } 1.20	6.00
4	3.60	14.40	7.50	1.88	1.50	.60	6.90
5	3.00	15.00	9.00	1.80	2.10	− .60	6.00
6	2.40	14.40	11.10	1.85	2.70	−1.80	3.30
7	1.80	12.60	13.80	1.97	3.30	−3.00	−1.20
8	1.20	9.60	17.10	2.14	5.40	−4.20	−7.50
9	.60	5.40	22.50	2.50			−17.10

Note: Some figures have been rounded.

will maximize profit. The same tools of analysis that we developed in Chapters 22 and 23—total, average, and marginal cost and revenue concepts—are applied to analysis of monopolies.

Table 25.1 presents the cost and revenue data for a monopolist. It is clear that the monopolist is subject to cost constraints similar to those any firm must face. But given the costs of production and the nature of market demand, it is the decisions of the monopolist (rather than some "invisible hand" of market forces) that determine what the market equilibrium will be.

Demand in the monopoly model

The monopolistic firm faces a different demand curve than does the perfectly competitive firm. Under perfect competition, the individual firm supplies only a very small percentage of total industry output. Because total demand is so great in relation to a single firm's output, the perfect competitor, in theory, can sell at the going market price any quantity of goods he or she wants to produce. The demand curve faced by any one firm is perfectly elastic. If a firm wants to sell more units, all it needs to do is produce them and offer them for sale at the same market price asked for previous units; the perfect competitor does not have to lower prices to bring about an increase in the quantity of units sold. As we have seen, the demand curve faced by a single firm under perfect competition is a straight horizontal line at the level of the going market price.

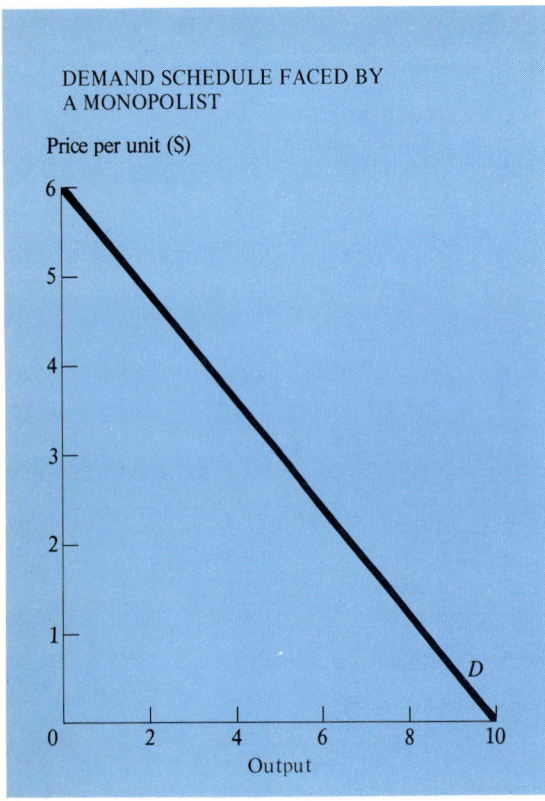

Fig. 25.2
The demand curve faced by the monopolist requires a price decrease in order to sell a larger quantity of goods. This is in contrast to the demand curve faced by perfect competitors; they can sell all they want at the going market price.

Graphic analysis

For the monopolist, the market demand curve and the demand curve faced by the firm are identical. The first two columns of *Table 25.1* show quantity of output and price per unit for a monopolist; these columns obviously constitute the market demand schedule that the firm faces. *We can see that price and quantity are inversely related; for the monopolist firm to sell a larger quantity of its product, it must lower the price of all units traded.*

Figure 25.2 plots the demand schedule faced by the monopolist. The resulting demand curve has the characteristic downward slope found in all market demand curves, indicating that demand for the monopolist is not perfectly elastic—as it is for the firm under perfect competition.

Note, however, that the monopolist firm does not determine the demand. It may affect demand by advertising or by changing the nature of the product, but ultimately it faces a demand curve determined by consumer tastes, incomes, expectations, and all the factors discussed in earlier chapters.

Maximizing profits: total cost— total revenue

The problem faced by the monopolist is the same as that faced by any firm—to find the most profitable level of output. A look at column 8 of *Table 25.1* (the net revenue column) indicates that the monopolist will not want to produce as many as seven units of output, since to do so would incur losses for the firm. The difference between total costs and total revenues is greatest at the production level of four units; that would be the point of profit maximization. Although this is not the level at which per-unit profits are greatest, it is the level that will generate the largest possible amount of total profit.

Graphic analysis

This total cost-total revenue analysis also can be presented graphically by plotting the data from columns 3 and 4 of *Table 25.1*, as shown in *Fig. 25.3*. Note that because price decreases with increases in output, the total revenue curve will eventually reach a peak and then decline. The level of output at which profits are maximized is four units—the level at which the distance between the total cost curve and the total revenue curve is greatest. On our graph, maximum net revenue is measured by the distance *AB*.

Note that the monopolistic firm cannot sell any amount it wants. As in a competitive market,

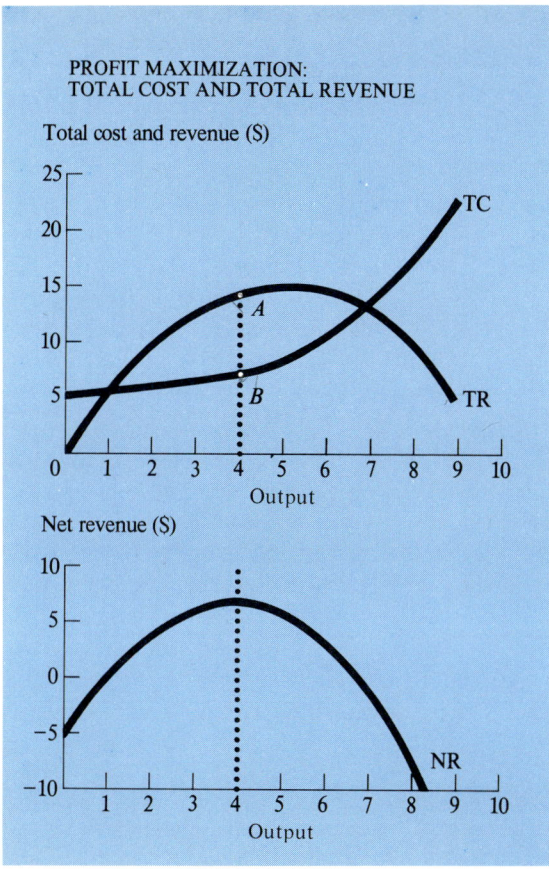

PROFIT MAXIMIZATION: TOTAL COST AND TOTAL REVENUE

Fig. 25.3
Since for monopolists, price must decrease as output increases, their TR curve will reach a peak and then begin to decline. The company will make a profit if its output is anywhere between 1 and 6.8, but the point of profit maximization comes at 4 units of output—that is, where the distance between the TC and TR curves is the greatest (the distance AB).

Monopolists are competing with other firms in different industries to purchase input resources of land, labor, and capital, and they also have fixed factors of production that make them subject to the law of diminishing returns in the short run. Therefore the monopolistic firm has the same kind of rising marginal cost curve as any other firm. However, in many monopoly firms, the MC curve will usually show a much more extended decline than it does in the typical competitive firm; this reflects the high fixed costs that prevail in most monopolistic industries.

Under perfect competition, the marginal revenue line is identical both to the price line and to the demand curve faced by the firm. The competitive firm can sell as many units as it likes at the going market price. Its marginal revenue, therefore, is constant, with each unit adding revenue equal to the going market price.

This is not true for the monopolistic firm. It faces a downward sloping demand curve, and its ability to sell its output is governed by the law of demand: as the price of a good increases, the quantity demanded will decrease. A monopolistic firm can sell a larger quantity of its product only by lowering the market price of the good.

Column 7 of *Table 25.1* shows the marginal revenue at various levels of output for a monopoly. When the firm wants to sell additional units, it must lower the market price, not only of those additional units but of all units traded on the market (including those that could have been sold at a higher price if fewer units were sold). Since the

there is a unique quantity of sales that is consistent with profit maximization, and it is determined by levels of demand and costs.

Maximizing profits: marginal cost—marginal revenue

Under perfect competition, the individual firm's point of profit maximization is reached when marginal costs exactly equal marginal revenues. *This same rule holds true for the monopolistic firm as well. MC = MR is always the point of maximum profits (or minimum losses).*

514 CHAPTER 25: PRICE AND OUTPUT UNDER MONOPOLY

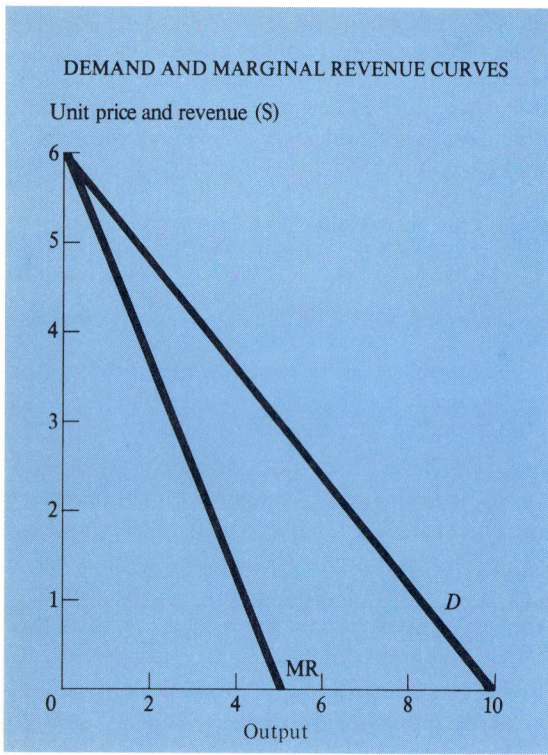

Fig. 25.4
The demand curve faced by the monopolist firm has the characteristic downward slope, as dictated by the law of demand. Since the firm must lower prices to sell more units, its MR curve will also be downward sloping, and it will fall to the left of the demand curve.

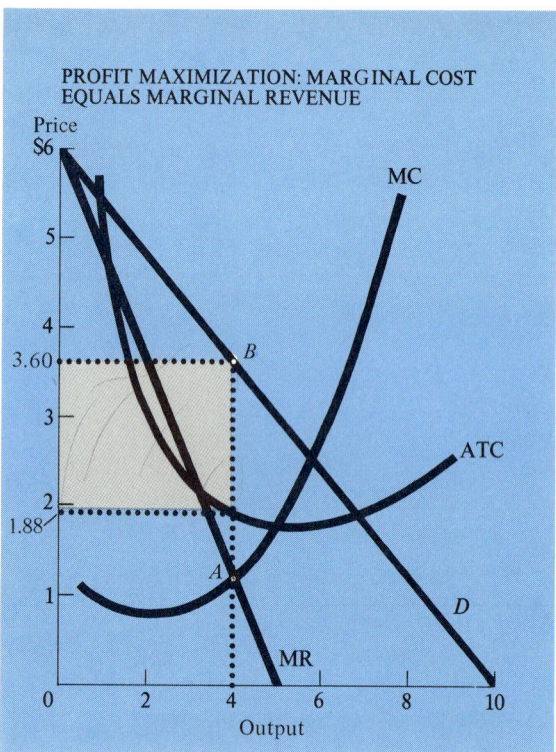

Fig. 25.5
As in any firm, the monopolist's optimum level of output is at the point where MR = MC. In this example, MR and MC intersect at the level of 4 units of output (point A). The point at which the chosen level of production intersects the demand curve (point B) will determine the price that will be charged for the product ($3.60). At this point profits are maximized at $6.88: it costs only $7.52 (4 × $1.88, the ATC) to make the 4 units, but the monopolist receives $14.40 (4 × $3.60) from the sale of that output. The economic profit is indicated by the shaded rectangle.

price of all units must always be lowered to sell more units, we find that eventually total revenue $(P \times Q)$ will decline and marginal revenue will be a negative number as more units are sold. For our monopolist, this occurs when production is increased from five units to six units.

Graphic analysis
The information contained in column 7 can be plotted on a graph to derive the MR curve (see *Fig.*

25.4). When we compare the MR curve with the demand curve, an important relationship becomes apparent. At each and every level of output, marginal revenue lies below price. This relationship between demand and marginal revenue is a crucial factor in many of the monopolist's decisions regarding price and supply.

The monopolistic firm, like any other firm, will choose to produce at the point where marginal costs are exactly equal to marginal revenues. *Figure 25.5* shows this point graphically (point A); the firm's optimum level of output will be four units. If the firm were to produce more units, the extra units would add more to total costs than to total revenues, causing total profits to decline. If the firm were to produce fewer than four units, it could add more to total revenues than to total cost by expanding; therefore, the firm could increase total profits by increasing its output.

To determine the price that the firm will charge, we observe the point at which the chosen level of production (4 units of output) intersects the demand curve (point B). The price per unit at point B is $3.60. This is the best price the company can get at that level of output. Above that price the quantity demanded will fall; below that price the firm will not be maximizing its total profits. Note that this price is considerably higher than the price level at which the intersection of MC and MR occurs.

Figure 25.5 also indicates an important difference between the perfectly competitive firm and the monopolist. In Chapter 23 we showed how, under perfect competition, the section of a firm's curve above its AVC curve is also its supply curve—it shows the minimum price needed to induce the firm to produce each level of output. But for the monopolist, the same output may be produced at different prices, depending on the shape, location, and slope of the demand curve. *We can therefore conclude that in the monopoly model there is no supply curve in the traditional sense; output depends on the relative positions of the firm's cost curves and the demand curve for its product.*

It is sometimes charged that monopolists can ask whatever they want to for their product, but the graph shows that this cannot be true. If the monopolist firm were to ask $4.20 for each unit, it would be able to sell only three units. This means that it would be producing at a point where the MR from additional units would be greater than the MC of producing those units; it is earning less than the maximum possible total profit. The monopolist's ability to set prices is always limited by the effects of the law of demand. If the firm charges more money for each unit, it will not be able to sell as many units.

MARKET EQUILIBRIUM: SHORT AND LONG RUN

Figure 25.6 shows various short-run equilibrium positions that are possible under monopoly. In each of the three cases the firm is producing where MR = MC (at point A). It has no incentive to increase or decrease its level of output, since it is maximizing profits or minimizing losses, given short-run conditions. In (a) the monopolist is earning a large economic profit, shown by the rectangle $P_1 TRS$, because the price per unit of the good is substantially higher than the average total cost. However, the highest price the monopolist can charge under these conditions is P_1, the price at which the firm's total output will be sold. If prices are raised, the firm cannot sell its entire output; if for some reason (government intervention, for example) the price were to be lowered, there would be an excess of demand for the product at that price level, so a shortage would occur. In this equilibrium position, it is evident that the company is not operating at its point of greatest efficiency, since it is producing at a level above the minimum point on the ATC curve.

As we saw in Chapter 23, short-run equilibrium in a perfectly competitive market can sometimes show these same characteristics of economic profit and a production level above the minimum ATC point. In the long run, however, neither of these conditions can persist in a perfectly competitive market. The entry of new firms into the market increases supply; the new market equilibrium

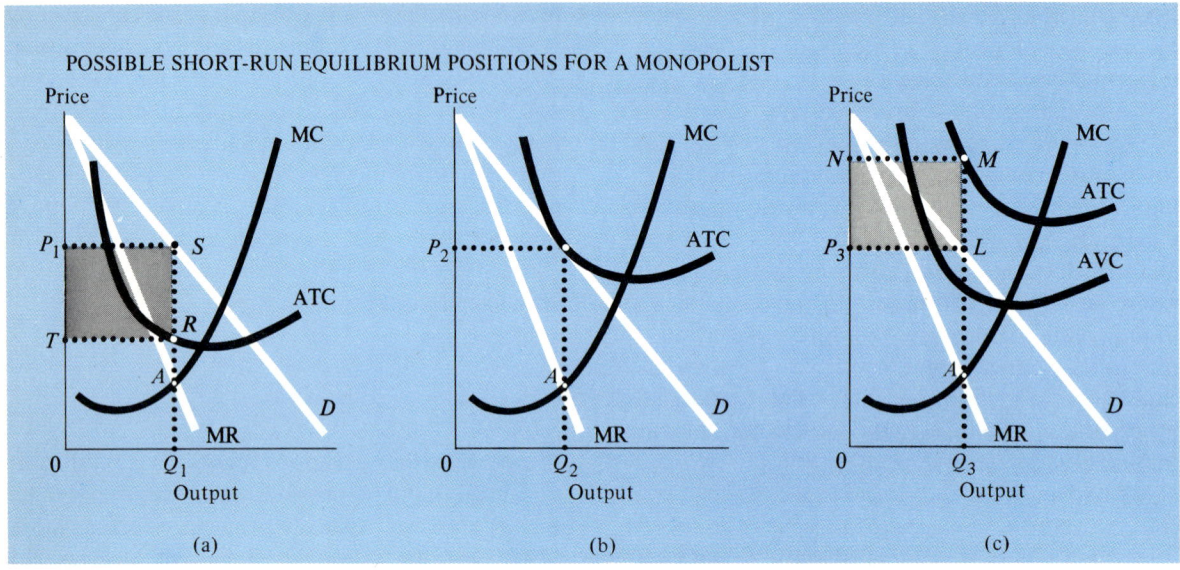

Fig. 25.6
In part (a) we see a monopolist firm that is able to earn economic profits. The per-unit profit is the difference between the price at point S and the average per-unit cost at point R; total profits are indicated by the rectangle P_1TRS. This situation can be maintained in the long run, as long as the monopoly is not broken. In part (b) we see a monopolist firm that is earning only a normal profit level; P_2 is equal to ATC. This situation too can be maintained in the long run. In part (c) we see a monopolist firm that is operating at a loss. Although it is earning enough to cover its AVC, it is not covering its ATC. Its loss is shown by the rectangle NP_3LM. This is a short-run situation; if the monopolist cannot demand or lower costs, the firm will eventually be forced to shut down.

level is set at a lower market price; economic profit disappears; competition forces every firm to operate at a minimum ATC. Under perfect competition, long-run equilibrium is reached when MR = MC = P = minimum ATC.

The monopoly does not automatically achieve these long-run corrections. Since no new firms can enter the industry, supply will not increase, and price will not drop in response to added supply. The firm can continue to operate at a point where price is greater than ATC and where ATC is not at its lowest possible level. In a monopoly, long-run equilibrium can be just the same as short-run equilibrium, because there is no competitive pressure to *force* a change. However, this is not to say that the long-run equilibrium position for the monopolist is static. A shift in the demand curve for the product or a shift in the ATC curve might occur, either of which would alter the firm's profit position.

In *Fig. 25.6(b)*, the monopolist firm's cost curves are higher in relation to its demand curve than we observed in (a). As we have said, this might be due to an increase in the cost of the inputs required in the production process or to a decline in the demand for the product. The monopolist will still maximize profits by producing where MC = MR. But given the short-run conditions shown here, the monopolist firm finds that the per-unit price it can charge at output Q_2 is just sufficient to cover its total per-unit costs (P_2); it is earning only a normal profit. It is important to note, however, that similar to (a), the monopolist is producing at a level above the lowest point on the ATC curve—the point of maximum efficiency.

Finally, in (c), the monopolist is incurring a loss, since the firm's ATC curve is everywhere above the demand curve. But the firm will minimize its losses in the short run by producing where MC = MR (Q_3 units of output), and charging a per-unit price of P_3. At this equilibrium price and output, the firm is incurring as small a loss as possible, given this set of short-run conditions; its total loss is shown by the rectangle P_3LMN. Remember that the equilibrium position shown in (c) is only a short-run situation. In the long run, the monopolist could not continue incurring losses. If the firm could not lower its ATC curve or increase the demand for the product, it would be forced to shut down.

DEFECTS OF MONOPOLY

Inefficiencies

Our analysis shows that a monopoly results in a misallocation of resources by charging a higher price than the same firm would charge under conditions of perfect competition, and by restricting output. This is shown in *Fig. 25.7*. The price (P_1) that the monopolist charges for each unit of a good in the market is always greater than the marginal cost of producing that unit. When price is greater than MC, this indicates that society places a higher value on consuming an additional unit of that good than on the marginal cost of producing that extra unit. Yet the additional unit of the good will not be produced, and the resources will instead be allocated for the production of some alternative good that is less preferred by society. Thus a monopoly imposes an artificial restriction on production of a desired good.

A second way in which a monopoly can restrict output can also be observed in *Fig. 25.7*.

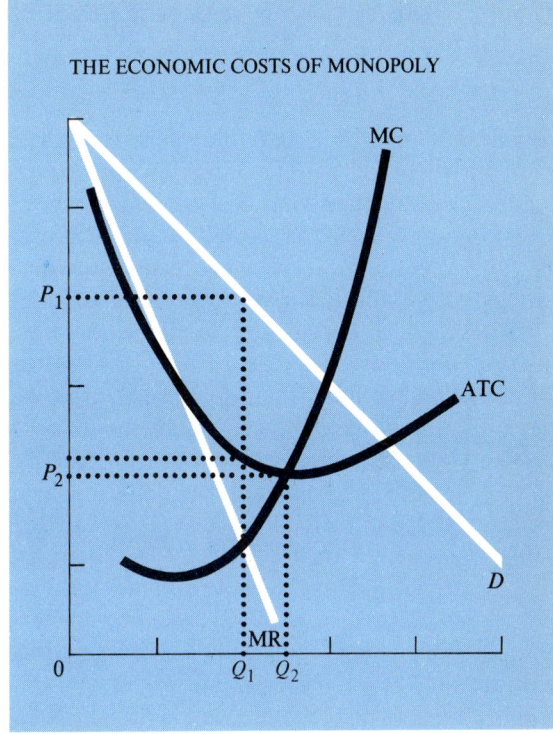

Fig. 25.7
Under monopoly, the price (P_1) charged for the good, which indicates the value placed on that unit by the consumer, is greater than the MC of the good. Society as a whole would benefit by increased production, since the extra benefit from another unit would be more than the extra cost. Another defect of the monopoly market structure is that the firm is not operating efficiently at the lowest point on its ATC curve (Q_2). In both situations described, output is artificially restricted at Q_1—it is less than is desired by consumers or dictated by production conditions.

The monopolistic firm is producing at an output level (Q_1) above the lowest point on its ATC curve. This means that it is producing a smaller output than that which is required for maximum efficiency (Q_2). The monopolist, therefore, restricts output and fails to make the most efficient use of all of its resources.

A problem of greed?
Because monopolies cause output to be restricted, prices to be higher than the marginal cost of production, and average total cost to remain above the minimum, some observers have concluded that the fault lies in the exceptional greed of the monopolist. It is more accurate to say that the monopolist is guided by the same motives in making business decisions as is the perfect competitor. Like the competitor, the monopolist tries to maximize the firm's total profit; both the monopolist and the competitor will choose to produce where MC = MR, since that is the point at which the greatest total profit is achieved.

The economic inefficiencies of a monopoly market are not due to the actions of the individuals who manage the firm but to the inherent characteristics of the monopoly model. Under perfect competition, the combined actions of many individual firms, each seeking to maximize its own self-interest by achieving the greatest possible total profit, result in the most efficient allocation of scarce resources. In a monopoly, the profit motive leads to inefficient resource allocation. No matter how good the intentions of the people running a monopoly may be, an unregulated monopoly market will inevitably lead to misallocation of productive resources.

Lack of incentive for innovation
Some economists feel that another important shortcoming of the monopoly market is that it does not encourage innovation. Since a monopolistic firm can select any level of price and production at which it wants to operate, there is no incentive for the firm to discover ways of lowering its price or increasing its output by means of new technology. In fact, the firm may choose to suppress innovations that would make its existing capital equipment obsolete. However, other economists point out that there is a strong incentive for a monopolist to develop both new products and new production processes, since any cutting of cost will increase total profits, as will any increase in demand.

PRICE DISCRIMINATION
One of the conditions of perfect competition is that the supplier must charge the same price for every unit of goods sold. If suppliers attempt to discriminate among buyers—for example, to make people who are rich pay more than people who are poor, or make people with an inelastic demand pay more than people with an elastic demand—they will simply lose the customers from whom they are asking the higher price, since the customers can buy from another producer.

A monopoly, on the other hand, creates the possibility of successful **price discrimination.** *This is a situation in which the monopolist may charge different prices to the same or to different buyers,* knowing that those who must pay more for the same good or service cannot obtain it from a competitor at a lower price. However, not all products lend themselves to price discrimination, so the existence of a monopoly does not guarantee that price discrimination can be practiced. There are two necessary conditions for successful price discrimination.

Conditions necessary for price discrimination
☐ *The original purchaser is not able to resell the product.* If one purchaser can sell it to another, those who are charged the lowest price will buy many units and sell them to those who are charged higher prices. The additional profit then would go to the customers charged the lowest price rather than to the monopolistic firm.

Suppose, for example, that General Motors achieved a monopoly on automobiles in this country and that it initiated a policy of price discrimination. In large cities, where the combination of good public transportation and crowded city streets lessens the demand for cars, GM could charge its lowest price. In small towns where a car is the only means of transportation, GM could charge more for each car it sells. Let us suppose that GM charged $500 more. This attempt at price discrimination would not be successful, since people from the city would buy cars and then sell them to people in the country, asking perhaps $350 or $400 more than they paid for them. The country people would save some money, the city people would make some money, and GM would be selling all its cars at the lowest price.

Examples of commodities that do lend themselves to successful price discrimination are telephone calls (the same buyers pay more to call during the day than at night), or electricity (different buyers—residential users and industrial users, for example—are charged different rates). Since it is fairly easy to resell goods of any kind, price discrimination is most often practiced by the sellers of services.

☐ *The monopolist must be able to distinguish clearly the different groups of demanders.* The demand schedules of individual households often vary, but it is usually difficult for sellers to identify those households that place the highest value on their products. For example, there are some people who love ice cream and would continue to demand the same quantity even at a price twice as high. But there is no way that the grocer can differentiate these people from the other consumers who would not value ice cream so highly.

Nevertheless, there are a number of ways in which the market can be divided up easily into discrete submarkets. For example, demanders can be differentiated on the basis of sex, income, geographic location, or age, and charged according to the elasticity of demand in the particular group. Thus an individual earning a very high income may be charged more for surgery than a person with a very low income.

Price and output in submarkets—graphic analysis

Figure 25.8 shows the way in which a monopolist firm makes decisions about price and output in the various submarkets. Since the firm is attempting to maximize profits, it will always follow the MC = MR rule. It determines the demand schedule and the resulting marginal revenue line for market 1 and market 2 then adds the two MR lines to get a total MR. Next the firm's officers plot MC and find the output level where MC = total MR (at Q_3). They then select the outputs in each of the two separate markets, where MC = MR_1 (at Q_1) and where MC = MR_2 (at Q_2); that is, MC = MR_1 = MR_2. To market 1 the firm sells Q_1 at P_1, and to market 2 it sells Q_2 at P_2. Thus, instead of charging the same price for all buyers, the monopolist will increase total profits by charging a different price to each group depending on the elasticity of demand in that submarket. In market 1, where demand is relatively inelastic, it is able to charge a higher price than in market 2, where demand is relatively elastic.

REGULATION OF THE MONOPOLY MARKET

Economic analysis indicates that a monopoly market system will always lead to the misallocation of resources. Therefore, it is in the interests of society in general to intervene whenever a monopoly market becomes established. Basically, this intervention can take two forms. The government may pass laws that prevent the formation of monopolies; it may also pass laws that prevent monopolists from operating at the point of profit maximization.

Encouraging competition

One way the government can prevent the formation of monopoly markets is to break down the barriers that keep competitive firms from entering the industry. For example, although we still have

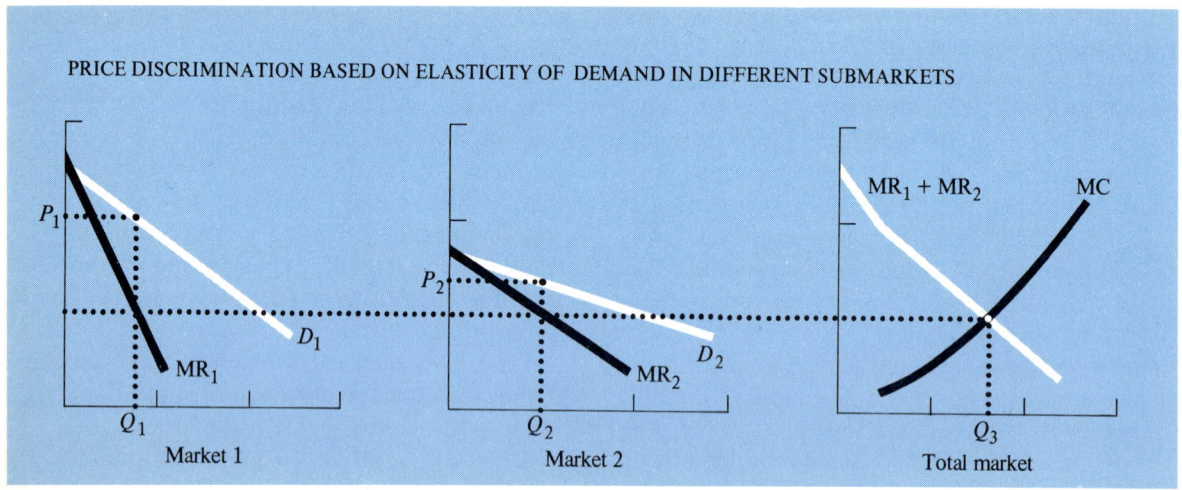

Fig. 25.8
Monopolists determine the demand schedule and the MR curve for two submarkets. They then add MR_1 and MR_2 to get total MR. Next they plot MC to find the profit-maximizing level of output. To determine price, they find the point at which $MC = MR_1 = MR_2$. To market 1, they will sell Q_1 at P_1; to market 2, they will sell Q_2 at P_2.

patent laws, the recent trend is for courts to interpret them rather liberally. A competitor may not use a patented production process, but is free to devise alternative means of developing the same product. Patent laws do not protect a kind of product, but only a specific process of production. The government also encourages competition for ownership of important input resources. For example it offers special tax privileges to firms that search for new deposits of necessary minerals, thus lowering the cost of entering industries that use these resources.

In addition to helping competitors overcome the existing barriers to entry, the government has passed important pieces of legislation designed to prevent deliberate monopolization. We will discuss this legislation in detail in the next chapter.

Regulating prices and output

In certain instances, the government has decided to give legal status to existing monopolies in return for the power to regulate the operation of the monopolist. This is true of most public utility companies. The government supports the firm's monopoly and may actually pass laws that forbid competition; but the government also determines the price that the company can charge for its product, and it may also require the company to produce at a certain level of output.

Government regulation of monopolies is usually handled by special commissions set up for this purpose, such as the Public Utilities Commission or the Interstate Commerce Commission. These commissions determine the prices that a monopolist is allowed to charge for its product.

Fig. 25.9
Faced with this set of demand and cost curves, an unregulated monopoly will decide to produce at Q_1 and charge price P_1. If the firm is prohibited by the government from enjoying economic profits, the firm will have to increase output to Q_2 and lower price to P_2; at this level of price and output, it will enjoy a normal profit but will no longer be able to earn economic profits. But real economic efficiency of resource allocation is not achieved until the firm operates where $P = MC$—which would be at the level of Q_3 output and P_3 price. At this position, the firm would be losing money, since price is less than ATC.

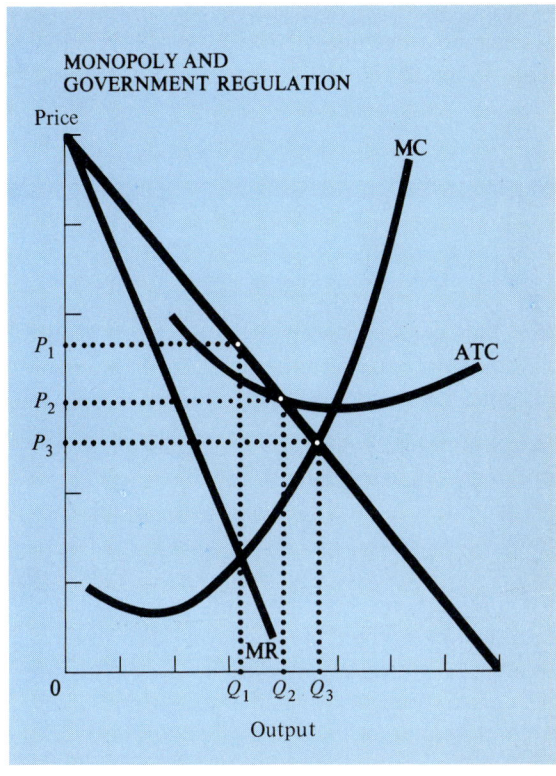

Figure 25.9 shows once again the equilibrium level of price and output (P_1 Q_1) of an unregulated monopoly. The firm is making an economic profit, since at this level of output price is higher than average cost. The figure also shows that the price of the good is greater than the marginal cost of producing another unit, so that resources are not allocated with maximum efficiency.

In order to eliminate the monopolist's economic profit, the government may decide to regulate price. One approach is to impose an excess-profits tax. By imposing such a tax the government can, in effect, raise the ATC curve to the point where it touches but does not intersect the demand curve, as shown in *Fig. 25.6 (b)*, thus eliminating excess profits. Since production costs and demand have not changed, the monopolist will still produce an output of Q_1.

However, if the government wants a lower price rather than the elimination of profits, it can set the price at the point where demand intersects with average cost. At this price level, the monopolist firm can make the same normal profit that a perfect competitor makes, but it loses its economic profit.

This solution allows the monopolist to stay in business, but it is not perfect. The price of the good is still greater than the marginal cost of producing another unit of the good, which indicates that we have not yet achieved optimal resource allocation. In general, consumers would still prefer to have additional units of the monopolistic good rather than additional units of alternative goods that could be produced from the same resources. But this desire is not being satisfied. However, if price is set at the point where demand intersects the marginal cost curve (P_3)—the ideal condition in terms of resource allocation—the monopolistic firm will often lose money. The average cost per unit of the good will be greater than the price per unit of the good (the AC curve passes *above* the point where D intersects MC). If the monopolist operates at the point where P = D = MC, it will incur an annual deficit.

Summary

■ This chapter describes the model of a pure monopoly market and the power over price and output which a monopoly producer can exercise.

■ A monopoly market exists when there is only one supplier facing the entire market demand curve, which is negatively sloped. In a monopoly market, the one producer has the ability to set price. A pure monopoly exists only when there is no near substitute available; in fact, however, there are always at least poor substitutes which buyers can choose. Economic barriers to the entry of new firms into a monopoly market include high set-up costs in certain industries; indivisibility of the product offered (such as telephone service); monopolized ownership of essential materials; and patent laws, which effectively grant a producer a temporary monopoly. In the long run these barriers can be overcome, unless government regulation protects a monopoly producer.

■ The demand curve for the monopolist slopes downward and to the right, and demand is not perfectly elastic. As with any producer, the monopolist maximizes profits at the point where total revenue most greatly exceeds total cost, or the point at which MR = MC. The monopolist also has a rising MC curve, but one which rises more slowly than that for the producer in a perfectly competitive market, since initial set-up costs tend to be high. At every level of output, marginal revenue lies below price. Consequently, when the optimum output point is determined for a monopoly producer, the price charged will be higher than the price at the point where the MR and MC curves intersect. In the monopoly model, there is no supply curve in the traditional sense; output depends on the position of the firm's cost curves and the market demand curve.

■ In the short run, monopoly production at the point where MC = MR may result in an economic profit, and production may be occurring above the minimum average cost. In a monopoly market, there are no competitive pressures to change this situation, and the short-run equilibrium may become the long-run equilibrium. A monopolist may also be making normal profits, or even incurring losses.

■ A monopoly is inefficient because it is able to charge higher prices and maintain lower output than would exist under perfect competition, and because the monopoly does not use all of its resources. Although some people argue that higher pricing and lower output under monopoly are a problem of greed, a more accurate view is that the situation results from the monopoly structure itself, which misallocates resources. Some economists also point to the tendency of monopolies to discourage innovation, while other economists argue that there is always an incentive to lower total costs.

■ Monopolies are also in a position to engage in price discrimination (charging different prices for the same product) under two conditions. The original purchaser must not be able to resell the product; otherwise, the profits will be earned by the reseller and not the monopolist. Monopolists must also be able to distinguish clearly between different groups of consumers with different levels of demand in order to discriminate in pricing.

■ Government can regulate monopoly either by preventing its formation or by prohibiting the monopoly from exercising its power over price and output. Government can encourage competition by reducing some of the barriers to entry. In some cases, such as in the case of public utilities, government may give legal status to a monopoly in return for control over its pricing. Regulation may also include taxes on economic profits or price controls to eliminate economic profits and require the firm to produce at the lowest point on its average total cost curve.

Key Terms

patent laws

price discrimination

Review & Discussion

1. What are the characteristics of a monopoly? What are some of the barriers to entry into a monopoly market? What does it mean to say that a product is indivisible? How can labor become a monopolized resource?

2. Give some examples of the way in which advertising tends to create artificial monopoly markets for products.

3. What is the shape of the demand curve for a monopoly? Why does a monopoly firm not have a traditional supply curve?

4. Draw the demand curve, the marginal revenue curve, and the marginal cost curve for a monopoly. What price would the monopolist charge? How does this position differ from that of a perfect competitor?

5. Now draw the average cost curve and identify the area of excess profit. What allows this short-run equilibrium to remain the long-run equilibrium?

6. Suppose that the marginal cost of producing doorknobs is $1.00. The monopolist in the doorknob business, however, is charging $1.50 for each doorknob. How, then, can it be argued that consumers are not getting as many doorknobs as they want?

7. What are the economic costs of a monopoly? How does the existence of a monopoly affect the allocation of resources?

8. Some experts point out that the large investments required for efficient operation in certain industries will result in monopolization. Can a case be made in favor of monopolies in such industries, as opposed to having a large number of small firms?

9. What are the options for government policy toward monopoly?

Chapter 26

Price and Output under Imperfect Competition

What to look for in this chapter

What is monopolistic competition?

What is oligopoly?

How are price and output determined under market conditions of oligopoly and monopolistic competition?

What is the role of nonprice competition in these markets?

How efficient are these market structures compared to the perfectly competitive and pure monopoly models?

As we have already discussed, perfect competition and perfect monopoly represent opposite ends of the market spectrum. It is only rarely that we find either of these extreme models in an actual market situation. Real-life markets contain some aspects of the competitive market and some of the monopoly.

As an aid to the analysis of real-life markets that have mixed features of perfect competition and monopoly, economists have formulated two models that can be placed along the market spectrum. One is the model of **oligopoly,** *a market structure characterized by a few firms selling either a uniform or a differentiated (similar but not identical) product.* The other is **monopolistic competition,** *a market structure characterized by many small firms selling a differentiated product.*

OLIGOPOLY

The oligopoly market model specifies a "few" suppliers. This can mean as few as two firms, or perhaps as many as a dozen or more; the exact number depends on the size of the firms in an industry and the extent of demand for the industry's product. An oligopoly differs from a situation of perfect competition, in that the actions of individual firms can and do influence levels of price and production in the market; it differs from a monopoly in that each firm has identifiable competitors within the industry.

The product of an oligopoly industry can be uniform or differentiated. The American oil industry, which is an oligopoly, deals in a uniform product, since one barrel of crude oil is virtually indistinguishable from another. The automobile industry, another oligopoly, deals in a differentiated product; even the least car-conscious Americans can see that there is a difference between a Corvette Sting Ray and a Mercury station wagon.

Perhaps the best way to determine whether or not an industry is oligopolistic is to observe how sensitive a firm is to the actions of its competitors. In the model of perfect competition, each firm faces a perfectly elastic demand curve; it is able to sell all it wants at the predetermined market price. In an oligopoly, market price is not determined by the impersonal action of the market, but by the actions taken by the few firms in the market. Moreover, in an oligopoly, each firm is fighting to retain or to enlarge its share of the market; if one competitor sells more, and total demand remains constant, the others must necessarily lose sales. This creates a market situation in which the few suppliers are mutually interdependent, and each firm is intensively aware of the actions and reactions of all of its competitors.

How does an oligopoly market arise?

Oligopolies typically occur in industries that are capital-intensive, with high set-up costs, and in industries that are heavily dependent on advanced technology. Under these conditions, the only viable size for the firm is a large one. Only by investing in a large stock of the necessary capital goods and then producing at a high level of output can a firm reap the economies of scale that will permit profitable operation. A small firm that tried to enter such an industry would have to operate at a point so far up (left side) on the long-run average total cost curve that it could not hope to price its goods competitively with the larger firms, which can operate at the size that affords the lowest possible average total cost or largest possible total profit.

The need for economies of scale, therefore, results in a limitation on the number of firms in the industry. Since the capital required to enter the industry is so large, there is a formidable barrier to entry by new firms. And in order to get the benefit of economies of scale, the few firms in the industry must produce at a very high level of output; each firm's productive capacity is quite large in relation to the total market demand. The need for technological knowledge and the extensive reliance on patented processes also serve as barriers to entry. Under these conditions, it is possible for firms in the industry to make a profit only when their number is few. If too many firms are competing for the limited number of customers, no firm will be able to sell the large quantity it must produce.

Some of the oligopolies in American industry have arisen when a competitor manages to overcome the barriers to entry in a monopoly market. The oil and aluminum industries, for example, were once monopoly markets. Rival firms succeeded in penetrating these markets by developing new sources of raw materials—and by receiving government support in the sense that the monopolist was prevented from barring new entrants by actual or potential prosecution.

Other oligopolies result from a gradual decrease in the number of firms—with small firms being squeezed out, and some of the remaining firms merging with one another. A good example of this process can be seen in the automobile industry. Early in the twentieth century, when cars were first produced, the capital required to enter the industry was not large, and many different suppliers were in the market. With the development of the automated assembly line, the capital required increased, and only a firm with a large output could make a profit. Many small companies were forced to leave the industry. Firms like DeSoto, Oldsmobile, and Pontiac were bought out by, or merged into, even larger firms. Today, the Big Three—General Motors, Ford, and Chrysler—supply well over half of the American car market.

Mergers have been identified as a leading cause of oligopolistic markets. Competing business firms, motivated by the desire both to take advantage of economies of scale and to obtain an additional degree of market power, merge to form one large firm that controls an even larger share of the market.

PRICE AND OUTPUT UNDER OLIGOPOLY

Economists are still in the process of working out all the aspects of the oligopoly model. It is the most complex of all market models, because there are many possible variations. If industry products are differentiated, the market situation will vary from the situation in which all firms produce uniform products. The number of firms in one industry may differ, as may the difficulty of entry. Moreover, in some oligopolistic markets, firms may engage in **collusion;** that is, *they may secretly agree to set a single industry-wide price.* (Collusion is also referred to as price-rigging.) In others there may be no collusion.

Analysis of oligopoly is further complicated by the fact that the interaction of the few suppliers in the market can influence price and output decisions, and perhaps even the shape of the demand curve faced by individual firms. In fact, a whole field of economics, called the theory of games, has been developed to explore the various strategies oligopolists may use to compete in the market situation. The solution to the oligopoly game—the equilibrium output and price—depends on the assumptions made about the market. What do the firms in the market believe competitors will do in response to other actions? What degree of collusion exists?

Oligopoly and price inflexibility

The market situation of the oligopolist is very similar to that of the monopolist. Oligopolists, too, face a downward-sloping demand curve; they cannot sell an unlimited amount since the model assumes that any single oligopolistic firm supplies a significant percentage of the total market demand. Because the demand curve is downward sloping, it follows that the marginal revenue curve will also slope downward, and it will be located below the demand curve. In order to sell a large quantity of units, oligopolists, like monopolists, must lower the per-unit price of their goods. To sell one more unit, the firm must lower the price of all units it places on the market; so the marginal revenue of each successive unit will be smaller than that of the one before it. Like all other businesspeople, the oligopolist will choose to produce at the profit-maximizing point, where marginal cost is equal to marginal revenue.

But the question of price determination under oligopoly is somewhat more complex. If National Standard Uniform, a hypothetical oligopolist in the uniform industry, were instead a monopolist, it could safely set its price at the point where the MC-MR level of output intersected with the demand curve. But the decision is not so simple for an oligopolist. The monopoly price will be NSU's optimum price *only* if all its competitors charge that same price. But what if the Eager Beaver Uniform Company tries to expand its share of the total uniform market by setting its price lower?

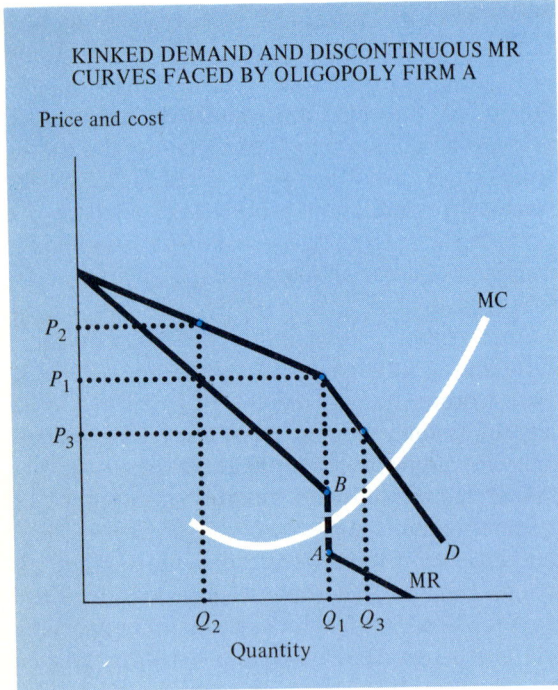

KINKED DEMAND AND DISCONTINUOUS MR CURVES FACED BY OLIGOPOLY FIRM A

Fig. 26.1
This graph represents the demand and marginal revenue (MR) curves faced by a firm in an oligopolistic market. Suppose the market price and quantity are at output level Q_1 at price P_1. If firm A raises its price to P_2, the quantity it sells will decline from Q_1 to Q_2. Other firms will not follow the price increase because they stand to get a larger share of the market sales if they keep their prices at P_1. If, however, firm A cuts its price from P_1 to P_3, other firms will probably follow suit and drop their prices, since they would lose business if they did not. The sales quantity will increase by only a small amount (Q_1 to Q_3). The sales of the good will increase due to the law of demand, but large increases in firm A's sales will not occur because its competitors have also cut their prices. The kinked demand curve causes a similar distortion in the MR curve, and price and output will remain the same if MC intersects MR anywhere between points A and B.

The result is that many buyers, attracted by the lower price, switch from the other firms they have been patronizing and become customers of Eager Beaver.

National Standard Uniform is now faced with a difficult pricing decision. If NSU does nothing in response to its competitor's price cut, it faces a greatly diminished demand curve, since the level of demand the firm faces depends on the price charged by other firms in the industry. Clearly, the firm cannot raise its price to try to make a larger per-unit profit to compensate for the lost sales, since any price increase will inevitably result in an additional decrease in sales, in accordance with the law of demand. NSU's other possible choice of action is to match the price cut of its competitor. This step will restore NSU's original share of the market and reestablish industry equilibrium. But of course all firms in the industry will now make a smaller profit than they did before the price cut.

Since oligopolistic industries tend to enjoy some excess profits, the uniform industry can probably survive several such rounds of competitive price-cutting. However, if one firm continually tries to use the strategy of price-cutting to extend its market, the industry may end up with a market price that is below the average cost per unit of the good. This situation will spell economic disaster for most firms in the market: only firms with very large cash reserves or very good credit can sell at a loss over any extended period of time, and few companies would be foolish enough to take this kind of risk.

Kinked demand curve and discontinuous MR curve
Economists demonstrate the tendency for oligopolists to follow a price reduction but not a price increase by means of a kinked or bent demand curve (shown in *Fig. 26.1*). Because of the unusual shape of the demand curve faced by an

individual firm, there is no advantage to a single firm in either raising or lowering its price. If it raises its price from P_1 to P_2, its sales will decline to Q_2—other firms will not follow the price increase because they stand to gain by holding their own price constant and attracting sales away from the now higher priced NSU. If NSU lowers its price from P_1 to P_3, other firms in the industry will follow its lead or lose sales. Thus, there is little chance that the initiator of the price cut will attract sales away from its competitors, and increases in quantity sold will be small (Q_1 to Q_3). Keep in mind, however, that there *will* be increased sales due to the law of demand. Furthermore, if the portion of the demand curve lying below the kink is less elastic, the initiator of a price cut will suffer decreases in total revenue. It is clear then that all firms can enjoy maximum profit when no firm alters the price of its goods.

The kink in the demand curve of the oligopolist causes a similar distortion of the MR curve; part of it is actually a straight line. This means that the MC curve can move anywhere between points *A* and *B*, and price and output would remain unchanged. Therefore oligopoly markets are characterized by some degree of price rigidity.

Summary The kinked demand and discontinuous MR curves explain the price rigidity characteristic of the oligopolistic market. Under perfect competition, changes in the demand schedule or in the costs of production will bring about rapid changes in the price level of a product. This is not true in an oligopolistic market, where prices tend to be stable. Moreover, once prices are fixed at a certain level, it is in every firm's interest to keep that level unchanged, since this eliminates the need to guess at one another's action. Oligopolists will generally raise their prices only when such a step is dictated by a *large* shift in the cost or demand curve that will affect all firms in the industry equally; then each firm can feel fairly safe that all other firms will follow and that a new equilibrium will be reached at a higher price level.

Oligopoly and collusion

In oligopolistic markets, prices are usually very inflexible, and when a price change does come, it is enacted by all firms in the market at the same time. This characteristic behavior causes observers to suspect that collusion among the firms in an oligopolistic industry is common. As we will see in the next chapter, much of the government's antitrust and antimonopoly legislation is directed toward preventing collusion.

Collusion among oligopolists not only eliminates the uncertainty each firm has about the others' behavior, it also enables the colluding firms to reap most of the advantages of a monopoly. In the long run, however, real price collusion in an oligopolistic market is often difficult to maintain. Moreover, no intentional illegal collusive activity is necessary to induce oligopolistic firms to act in concert with one another. The president of National Standard Uniform does not need to wear a disguise and hold secret meetings with the president of Eager Beaver in order to decide to retain the present price. All that is needed

---

RECAP

While perfect competition and pure monopoly represent extremes of the market spectrum, oligopoly and monopolistic competition are models that more often reflect the situation in real-life markets. An OLIGOPOLY market is characterized by a few firms selling either a uniform product or a differentiated product. MONOPOLISTIC COMPETITION is characterized by many small firms selling a differentiated product.

is the ability to make certain assumptions about the reactions of competitors to any price-changing action. It is not a secret agreement, but rather the structure of the oligopolistic market that makes price rigidity the best policy for all firms in the market.

Price-changing patterns

An oligopolistic market, over a period of time, tends to fall into somewhat ritualistic patterns of pricing behavior. For example, in the automobile industry, it is understood that price changes will occur each year when new models are introduced; usually during the rest of the year changes will not be made by the manufacturers, even though prices may change at the retail level.

In some oligopolistic industries, such as the steel industry, it is accepted practice for one firm to be the **price leader.** As the term suggests, the price leader is *the firm that makes the initial move to set prices and all other firms follow with matching increases or decreases.* The industry price leader is frequently, but not always, the largest firm in the industry. When the price increase is instituted by a smaller firm, there is less likely to be criticism of the abuse of market power. Other industries develop readable signals that one firm can send to the others regarding its intentions. When one copper-mining corporation holds a press conference to announce that increasing costs are hurting the company, it is signaling a desire to raise the market price of copper; and if we read in the paper several days later that the executive director of a competitive company made a speech to the local Chamber of Commerce that also included a reference to the problems of rising costs, we can be fairly certain that a price increase will take place throughout the industry. On the other hand, if the executive director had talked about the need to fight increasing inflation, that would have been understood as a signal that the company was not presently in favor of a price increase.

MONOPOLISTIC COMPETITION

As we noted in the introduction to this chapter, the second model that contains elements of both perfect competition and monopoly is called monopolistic competition. In monopolistic competition, the market has many small firms selling a differentiated (similar but not identical) product. This has the effect of splitting up the large market demand curve into smaller curves for individual products, thereby introducing monopoly elements into the competitive model. Because differentiation splits up the total market demand curve, the individual firms are no longer faced with the perfectly elastic demand curve of the perfect competitor; no firm call sell an infinite quantity of its differentiated product.

Service industries furnish many examples of monopolistic competition. In a large city, there may be several hundred barber shops, all of which offer a similar service, that of cutting hair. Yet the service is not identical at every barber shop. A barber shop that is close to your home or office is more convenient than one that is located on the other side of town. The skills of the various barbers and their ability to handle different types of hair will differ from one shop to another. One shop might be run by a very friendly barber, but another might offer more contemporary styling techniques. These small variations in service and satisfaction break up the total demand curve for haircuts into smaller demand curves—the demand for haircuts that make the most of thinning hair, the demand for haircuts on one particular block of the financial district.

When products are successfully differentiated, we can no longer assume that buyers will automatically select the commodity with the lowest price. Many buyers will be willing to pay a somewhat higher price in order to obtain the specific variation of the product for which their demand is greatest. As we shall see, this has a significant implication for equilibrium price and output.

DEVELOPMENTS IN ECONOMIC THOUGHT:

Joan Robinson

Ramsay & Muspratt Studios, Cambridge, England

Nearly all classical economists and most neoclassical economists accepted the model of perfect competition in the marketplace. This model assumes that no individual seller or buyer can influence market prices and that as a result of the free play on competitive forces, the unregulated economy naturally allocates resources in socially desirable ways, maximizes the benefits to all participants, and stabilizes itself more or less automatically.

Economic developments in industrialized nations prior to the Great Depression and the economic chaos which resulted from that depression led some economists to challenge the earlier optimistic view of the workings of markets. By World War I, instead of reflecting a situation of perfect competition, the economies of the Western industrial nations had developed sizable monopoly and oligopoly sectors. Large corporations gained dominance in various markets and as a result were able to maintain artificially high prices, restrict total supply in order to increase profits, and otherwise distort the free operation of the forces of supply and demand.

Among those who recognized the defects of the model of perfect competition was an English economist Joan Robinson (b. 1903), then a young assistant lecturer at Cambridge University. Robinson, who worked on the drafts of Keynes's *General Theory of Employment, Interest and Money* (1936), explored and refuted the accepted model of perfect competition in her own earlier publication entitled *Economics of Imperfect Competition* (1933). It was her contention that *imperfect* competition (particularly monopoly) was the norm and that perfect competition was the exceptional case.

Robinson focused her attention on a market which was still characterized by a large number of sellers but which nonetheless was marked by monopolistic competition. Along with E. H. Chamberlain (1899–1967), whose *The Theory of Monopolistic Competition* was also published independently in 1933, Robinson helped direct the attention of economic analysts to the shortcomings of the internal logic of the classical model. Subsequent work by many theorists has continued to explore such questions as the role of product differentiation (competition among products of the same general kind which are marketed by emphasizing their "special" features), the effect of advertising on market behavior, and the response of sellers to inelastic demand.

Working with Keynes and extending his critique of classical orthodoxy, Robinson has also made significant contributions to the theory of economic growth and the analysis of the accumulation of capital. Robinson has described herself as a "left-wing Keynesian," and some of her work has served as a bridge between neoclassical and Marxian economics, notably *An Essay on Marxian Economics* (1942).

She has been consistently outspoken on social and public policy issues, focusing her criticism particularly on what she perceives as the abuses and failures of private economic power. Market capitalism, she asserts, has not been able to eliminate poverty in highly developed economies or aid the economic development of the poor countries of the world. According to Robinson, private economic decision making also encourages waste, and lack of regulation leads to destruction of the environment. She is an active proponent of large-scale government intervention as the only available counterweight to corporate power.

Monopolistic competition differs from oligopoly in that it includes many more firms in the market. Moreover, monopolistically competitive firms are not interdependent, and they do not need to react to one another's decisions regarding pricing and output as do firms under oligopoly. Because of product differentiation, a firm may, within limits, charge a higher price for its products and still attract customers.

Another characteristic of monopolistic competition that distinguishes it from oligopoly is that it is relatively easy to enter a monopolistically competitive industry. The necessary capital investment is not high, and so new firms can quickly enter the market when profits are high; by the same token, they will leave if losses are incurred. This is very different from an oligopoly market, where high set-up costs form a barrier to entry and where the large size of its investment in capital goods makes it difficult for the firm to adapt quickly to changes. Monopolistically competitive firms have much more flexibility than oligopolistic firms.

PRICE AND OUTPUT UNDER MONOPOLISTIC COMPETITION

The monopolistic competitor faces a demand curve that is highly but not perfectly elastic. The exact degree of elasticity will depend on the number of firms in the market in addition to the degree of product differentiation they are able to achieve. If there are a large number of firms and their products are only slightly different from one another, each firm will face a very elastic demand curve; any change in price will create a corresponding change in quantity demanded. On the other hand, if the market is clearly differentiated, the demand curve faced by a single firm will be relatively inelastic; the quantity demanded will not be very responsive to changes in price.

Demand curve and marginal revenue curve

Figure 26.2 shows the demand curve faced by the Clip Joint, a neighborhood barber shop. It is slightly downward sloping, but still quite elastic. Since the demand curve slopes downward, the

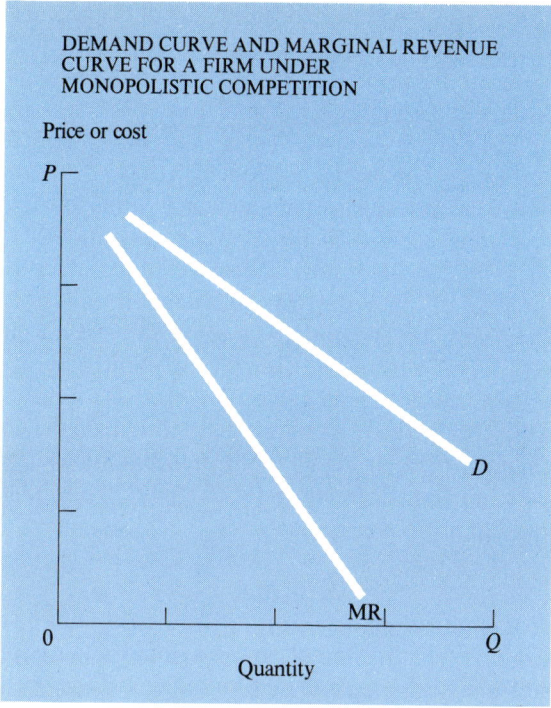

Fig. 26.2
By differentiating its service product, the Clip Joint has become a monopolistic competitor; it therefore faces a downward-sloping demand curve and has an MR curve with a corresponding downward slope.

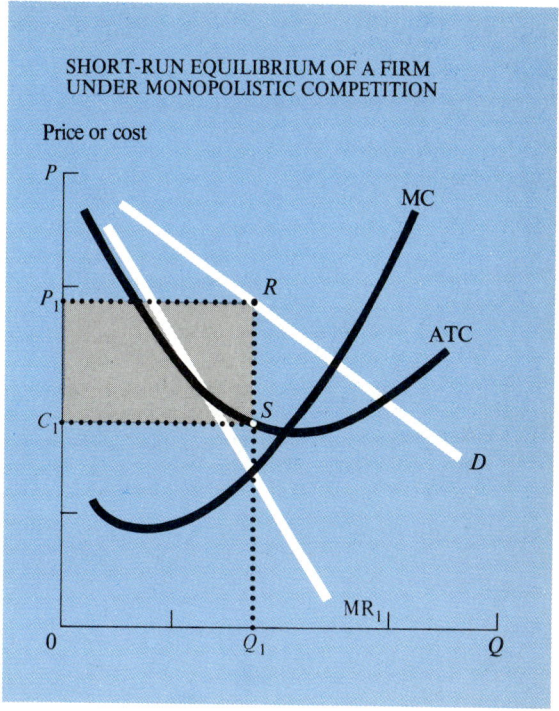

Fig. 26.3
In the short run, the Clip Joint will maximize profits by producing output Q_1 at price P_1 (the cost of producing Q_1 is C_1). At this equilibrium level the Clip Joint can achieve the economic profits shown by rectangle P_1C_1SR.

firm's marginal revenue will also slope downward. The Clip Joint can sell more of its service only by lowering the price of its haircuts (or improving service for the same price, which is another form of a price decrease). Therefore each additional haircut will add a smaller amount to total revenue. *Figure 26.2* also shows the downward-sloping MR curve.

Like all other business firms, monopolistic competitors will choose to produce where marginal cost equals marginal revenue—the point of profit maximization. To determine price, monopolistic competitors will check to see where their chosen level of output intersects the demand curve they face. That will be the price they can safely charge.

Short-run equilibrium

Figure 26.3 shows the short-run equilibrium for a monopolistic competitor. Since the price per unit (P_1) is greater than the average cost per unit (C_1), the competitor is making an economic profit, rep-

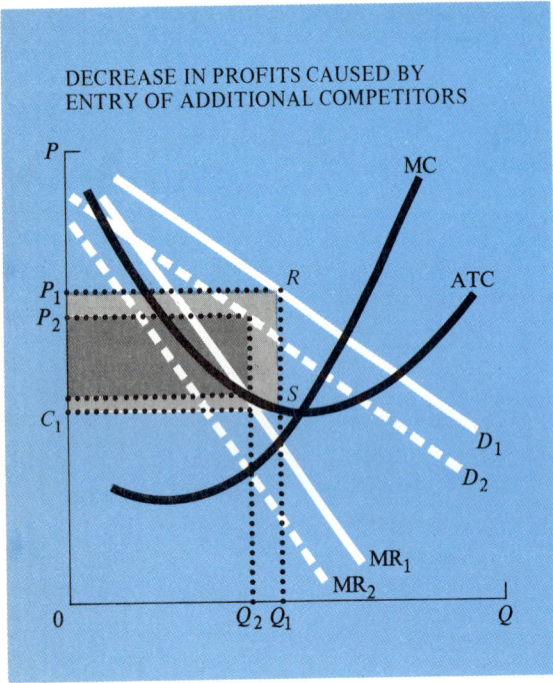

Fig. 26.4
Unlike monopolists, monopolistic competitors cannot maintain economic profits in the long run, since these profits will attract other competitors into the market—a market which can be entered easily. The entry of new competitors will cause the demand curve faced by the Clip Joint to shift from D_1 to D_2 and the MR curve to shift from MR_1 to MR_2. At the new equilibrium level (where MR_2 intersects MC) the Clip Joint will sell fewer haircuts (Q_2) at a lower price (P_2). The profits realized at this equilibrium level are now smaller than they were before other competitors entered the market (represented by the larger rectangle P_1C_1SR).

resented by rectangle $P_1\,C_1\,SR$. This profit will attract new firms into the industry, which is one they can easily enter. For example, a competitor might open another barber shop just two blocks away from the Clip Joint. The effect of this added competition will be to shift the demand curve faced by the Clip Joint down and to the left, since some of its former customers will choose to patronize the new shop because it is closer to home or has a more convivial barber. This is illustrated in *Fig. 26.4* by the shift from D_1 to D_2.

The shift in the demand curve will also cause a downward shift in the MR curve from MR_1 to MR_2. *Figure 26.4* shows these two curves after the entry of a competitor in the neighborhood. MR_2 intersects the MC curve at a lower level of output (Q_2). This will be the firm's new point of profit maximization. Once again, the firm sets its price at the point where its output level intersects the demand curve (P_2). At P_2 the firm is making a slight economic profit (rectangle $P_2\,C_1\,SR$) but a smaller one than it did previously.

Long-run equilibrium

Competition among firms will force a continual process of adjustment, until a long-range equilibrium is reached and all economic profits are eliminated. As long as economic profits exist, new firms will enter the market, and the demand curve faced by each firm in the market will shift down; a new equilibrium will be reached at a lower price level, causing firms to lose their excess profit. If, by chance, too many firms should enter the market, so that the demand curve is below the ATC curve, the resulting losses would cause some firms to leave the market. The elimination of these competitors would then cause the demand curve to shift back up and to the right, until price is equal to average total cost.

Inefficiencies of monopolistic competition

Figure 26.5 shows the long-run equilibrium condition (output Q_1 at price P_1) for a monopolistically competitive firm: MR = MC, and P = D = ATC. This is similar to the perfectly competitive market, but unlike the perfect competitor, a monopolistic competitor's price is not equal to MC. This inequality means that resources are not

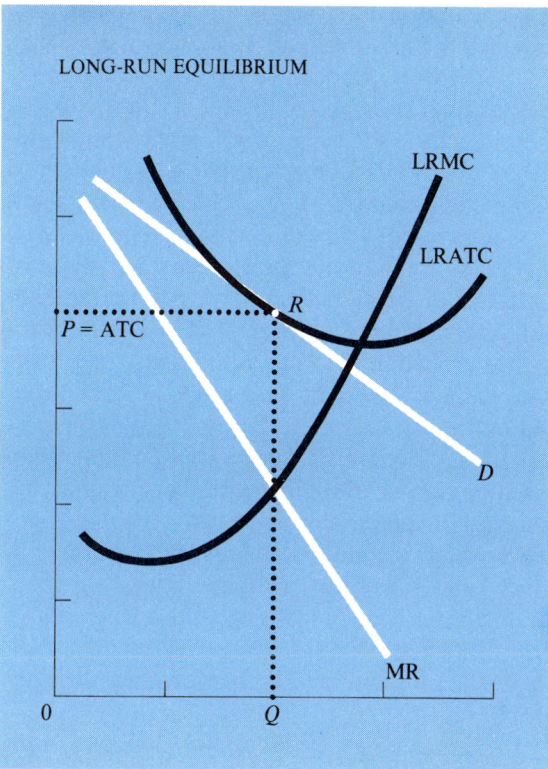

Fig. 26.5
In the long run, enough new competitors will enter the market to reduce profits to a normal level. Price is now equal to long-run ATC. But it is still higher than the long-run MC—a source of economic inefficiency.

being allocated in the most efficient way—the cost of producing an extra unit is less than the price or value of that unit to consumers. Thus society would be better off if the monopolistic competitor increased output.

Monopolistic competitors are also wasteful because they are not producing at the lowest point on the ATC curve. Under perfect competition, firms would be forced to produce as economically as possible, moving toward the lowest point on the long-run ATC curve. But in a monopolistically competitive market, the slight inelasticity of demand, caused by product differentiation, allows the firm to operate inefficiently at a level of output less than the optimum, least-cost level. Because they produce less than optimal output, monopolistically competitive firms usually underutilize plant and equipment in order to earn a normal profit.

NONPRICE COMPETITION

The model of perfect competition assumes that every supplier produces a uniform product that is indistinguishable from the product of other suppliers. Because of product uniformity, the demand curve faced by any one firm is perfectly elastic—perfectly responsive to changes in price. In a

RECAP

OUTPUT decisions are similar under oligopoly and monopolistic competition. In both markets production level will be at the point of profit maximization—where marginal cost equals marginal revenue. Because of their different structures, however, the two types of imperfectly competitive markets make their PRICING decisions differently. Oligopolistic firms are few and interdependent; therefore, they must react to one another's pricing decisions. As a result, the prices they charge for their products tend to be stable. In a monopolistically competitive market there are many more firms which are not interdependent. Therefore there can be greater price differences as each firm sets prices according to its individual demand curve.

perfectly competitive market, competition is based on price and price alone.

Oligopolistic and monopolistic competition, on the other hand, both assume the existence of some degree of price inelasticity of demand—some willingness on the part of the consumer to be less than perfectly responsive to price changes when deciding on how much to purchase. This inelasticity is usually the result of successful product differentiation. In a complete monopoly, the product of the monopolist is so totally differentiated from all others that it has no close substitutes. A firm under monopolistic competition tries to create this same differentiation, so that its demand curve will be as inelastic as possible. (Remember that the greater the inelasticity of the demand curve it faces, the greater the power of the individual firm to determine price and output level.) Oligopolists can also improve their market position by differentiating their product. Moreover, because of the price rigidity that exists in their market, oligopolists have a special interest in nonprice competition, which can be waged by means of strong product differentiation.

There are two major types of nonprice competition used by imperfect competitors. One is the differentiation of products through product development; the other is product differentiation through advertising. The underlying goal of both these competitive strategies is to fragment the total demand curve into smaller demands for products that consumers believe have no adequate substitutes. This will make the demand curve more inelastic and will thus confer on the supplier of the differentiated product some degree of market power.

Product development

Product development refers to the efforts of a firm to create a product with special features that will clearly distinguish it from similar products on the market. A good illustration of nonprice competition through product development can be seen in the laundry detergent industry. Basically, all firms sell the same product—a detergent that helps get your clothes clean. But different firms have developed highly individual products. One detergent contains fabric softeners as well as cleaning ingredients; another has enzymes that are supposed to help in stain removal. Some detergents are meant to be used in hot water, others in all temperatures; detergents come in the form of powders, liquids, tablets, and premeasured envelopes. Because of this great differentiation of products, some consumers are willing to pay slightly more to get the differentiated detergent that meets all their needs and preferences.

Some economists suggest that competition based on product development is beneficial in that this kind of competition is likely to stimulate innovation and technological advance, neither of which is necessary for a firm operating under conditions of perfect competition. Indeed many large firms in oligopoly industries are directly responsible for substantial advances in product development.

Another type of product development is directed toward making similar products different in appearance. The makers of breakfast cereal, for example, try to package their products distinctively, so that the customer will get the impression by looking at the boxes that the cereals are all different. The unique shape of the Coca-Cola bottle is an illustration of packaging that successfully differentiates a product from its competitors. And of course, most of the changes in automobile design from one year's model to the next represent an attempt to create a distinctive package for basically very similar goods.

Advertising

The advertising industry specializes in nonprice competition. Through advertising campaigns, imperfect competitors seek to differentiate their goods by creating a specific product image that is unlike the image of other products in the market.

Competition by image is especially apparent in the cigarette industry, an oligopolistic industry. Cigarette manufacturers do not compete with one another by lowering prices. And although they do compete to some extent through product development—developing low-tar cigarettes, king-sized cigarettes, menthols, and hard or soft packs—the primary basis of competition in the cigarette industry is the image a brand conveys through its advertising. One cigarette has a fresh, outdoor image; another has a strong he-man image, aimed at bolstering the masculinity of its customers. And now that the women's liberation movement has become an accepted part of the American scene, several companies have successfully developed an image that appeals to that market.

Does advertising have any economic value?
Pros American business firms currently spend billions of dollars a year to foster competition through image differentiation. There is a great deal of controversy over the economic value of this expenditure. Some economists defend advertising as an aid to competition in the market and economic health in general. They suggest that advertising is often informative, telling consumers what a product can do for them, what its price is, what its ingredients are. This information helps the customers acquire more knowledge of the market, thus improving the market competition. Some economists also point out that advertising promotions featuring free gifts, box-top bonuses, or trading stamps are actually a means of indirect price competition, since the consumer's cost is the price of the good less the value of the free gift. In an oligopolistic situation, where price changes are very risky, gifts and bonuses are a safe way to lower the true cost of the product.

Supporters of the advertising industry also claim that product image campaigns can actually add to the consumer utility of the product. When a man buys a pack of Marlboro cigarettes, for example, he is getting not only something to smoke but also something to make him feel more virile and aggressive; he is buying the emotional satisfaction of being a "Marlboro man."

Another argument in favor of advertising is that it stimulates spending, thus returning national income to the circular flow and allowing the possibility of continued full employment and economic growth. Finally, supporters of advertising say that advertising expands the market for a product, thereby enabling the firm to increase its level of output and take advantage of economies of scale. They maintain that average total costs will thus be lowered even though the additional costs of advertising have shifted the long-run ATC curve upward. This argument is presented graphically in *Fig. 26.6*. Note that we might also view the gap between the two curves as additional costs of research and development.

Cons Critics of advertising also make some strong points. They suggest that advertising expenditures are relatively unproductive and that to spend billions of dollars a year on building product images is a gross misallocation of productive resources that could be used in other ways. They argue further that through the use of suggestion, half-truths, and occasional misrepresentation, advertising seeks to persuade consumers to buy a product rather than to inform them about the market. Critics of advertising also deny that advertising allows firms to increase output, thereby enjoying economies of scale and lower per-unit costs of production. In their view, advertising actually has very little effect on a firm's share of the market, since it is likely that all rival firms will wage similar ad campaigns. The overall effects of advertising, therefore, tend to be self-canceling. This argument is shown graphically in *Fig. 26.6*.

Critics also suggest that, to the extent that it is successful, advertising works against the general social good by causing people to prefer private goods over public goods and luxury goods over necessities. For example, according to government

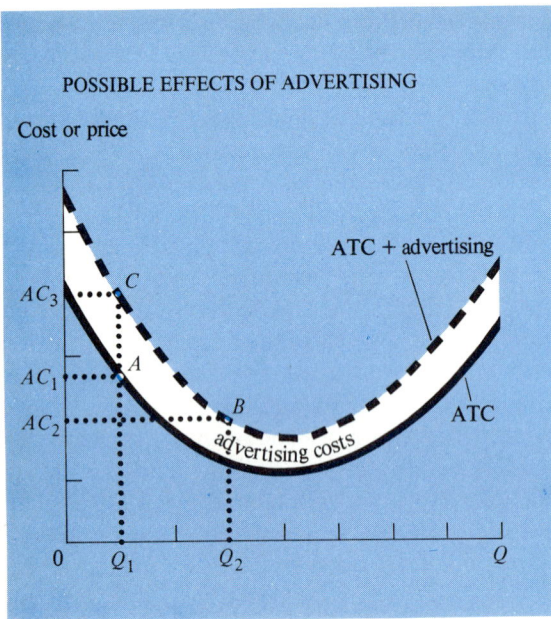

Fig. 26.6
According to the proponents of advertising, the effect of advertising would be to shift the demand curve to the right. Thus, output would expand from point A on the ATC curve to point B on the ATC + advertising cost curve. Cost would then be lowered from AC_1 to AC_2. On the other hand, if critics of advertising are correct in saying that it does not significantly alter demand, the effect of advertising would be to move the cost from the level of point A at AC_1 to the level of point C at AC_3.

statistics, there are more households with television sets than there are with indoor plumbing. The implication, according to critics, is that it is advertising that has led these families to choose entertainment over sanitation. To take another example, advertising attempts to persuade consumers to buy electric carving knives, but not to support better hospital care, better schools, or other public goods.

Some economists have also pointed out that the need for a large advertising budget constitutes a barrier to entry in many markets by greatly raising the initial cost of investment. And finally, they allege that by causing consumers to increase their rate of spending, advertising is either creating or contributing to the problem of inflation.

The few empirical studies that have been made of the economic and social effects of advertising have not been conclusive. They do suggest that the effects of advertising are not so adverse as its critics suggest, nor are its benefits so great as its supporters claim.

RESOURCE ALLOCATION UNDER IMPERFECT COMPETITION

Only under perfect competition are resources automatically allocated in the most efficient way possible. Wherever there are imperfections of competition, the "invisible hand" no longer guides the economy to this optimum solution, and there will be some inefficiencies of resource allocation.

The primary inefficiency of product differentiation is that it results in a less-than-optimum level of output. Suppliers are not operating at the lowest point on the average cost curve; they maximize profit at an output level at which the average cost curve is still falling. Since the goods are not manufactured as efficiently as possible, resources are used wastefully and consumer prices are higher than necessary.

It appears that this inefficiency of resource allocation is the price we pay for the luxury of choosing among differentiated products. If we were willing to settle for one uniform product, we could have it at a lower cost. The government of China, for instance, faced with the dilemma of providing large quantities of consumer goods for a vast population with a low average standard of living, has chosen to restrict consumer choice of dress to only a few alternative patterns. In this way, the government has managed to produce enough cloth for everyone to dress warmly and neatly; by restricting the variety of foods it produces, it has managed to feed its population adequately.

In America, we have opted for greater variety among products, but of course we must pay the price—both in the form of higher consumer prices charged for differentiated products and in the form of the social cost of wasting scarce resources, some of which can never be replaced.

Summary

■ This chapter looks at two models economists have formulated to describe market situations which frequently exist in reality— oligopoly and monopolistic competition.

■ The oligopoly model assumes that there are few suppliers in the market. The products can be either differentiated or uniform. Oligopolies usually occur in industries with high set-up costs. They may also form when a pure monopoly market is broken by the entry of a new firm, or when a number of small firms leave the industry or merge with larger firms.

■ The oligopolist elects to produce at the point at which MR = MC, since this is the point of profit maximization. The demand curve for the oligopolist slopes downward and to the right, with the MR curve below it. The kinked demand curve of the oligopolist reflects the tendency of the oligopolist's competitors to follow price reductions but not to follow price increases. A portion of the MR curve may actually be a straight line (discontinuity), corresponding to the kinked demand curve. In an oligopoly market, prices tend to be rigid, and there is little incentive either to raise or to lower prices. This often gives the appearance of collusion among firms in the industry, but market structure also leads to the same results. Many oligopolistic markets have a ritualized pattern for price changes, often with one firm acting as a price leader.

■ The model of monopolistic competition assumes that there are many firms selling a differentiated product. Market entry is relatively easy. Because of product differentiation, some consumers will be willing to buy a supplier's product even at a higher price, and monopolistic competitors do not need to maintain price equality to the extent required for oligopolists. If products in a monopolistically competitive market are only slightly differentiated, the demand curve for a particular firm will be highly elastic; if the degree of differentiation is great, the demand curve will be relatively inelastic.

■ The point of profit maximization for a monopolistic competitor is the point at which MC = MR. A particular firm will have a slightly downward-sloping demand curve with a downward-sloping MR curve below it. In the short run, there may be an economic profit at equilibrium, but eventually new firms will enter the market and create a new long-run equilibrium with normal profits. The oligopolistic firm also tends to have excess capacity, since it is not operating at the lowest point on the ATC curve, and since the selling price will be above marginal cost.

■ Firms in both of these types of imperfectly competitive markets place considerable reliance on nonprice competition and product differentiation to simulate the advantages of the pure monopoly market model. The two major methods are product development and advertising. Because of product differentiation, consumers may be willing to pay more for a particular product. This can give producers an incentive to improve products and introduce new ones, but critics point out that the changes introduced are often simply new packaging on basically uniform products. Supporters of advertising claim that it conveys useful information to consumers, that free gifts and the creation of product images add to the consumer's utility, and that advertising encourages spending and expands markets, thus lowering average total cost of production. Critics of advertising say that it is an unproductive allocation of resources, that it spreads misinformation, that it encourages the demand for private goods and luxuries rather than public goods and necessities, and that the encouragement of further spending may actually fuel inflation.

■ There are inefficiencies associated with imperfect competition. Resource allocation is less efficient than under conditions of perfect competition. The profit-maximizing point does not occur at the lowest point on the ATC curve, so the firm is not producing at a point of maximum efficiency and has some excess capacity. Some of these inefficiencies are the inevitable cost of providing a high degree of variety and consumer choice.

Key Terms

oligopoly

monopolistic competition

collusion

price leader

Review & Discussion

1. What are the basic assumptions for the oligopoly model? How do oligopolies develop?

2. How does the oligopolist settle on the quantity to produce and the price? Why does the demand curve for an oligopolist have a peculiar "kinked" shape?

3. Why do prices tend to be stable in an oligopoly market? Why is there often the appearance of collusion in an oligopolistic industry?

4. What are the basic assumptions for the model of monopolistic competition? How does the producer decide on price and the quantity to

be produced? Does the producer have to charge the same price as competitors do? Why or why not?

5. What happens in the long run in a monopolistically competitive market?

6. What are the objectives of advertising? What are the major criticisms of advertising?

7. In the 1950s, American-produced automobiles gradually became larger, more powerful, and more luxurious. Some experts have suggested that the costs for model changes from 1956 to 1960 ran about $5 billion a year for the economy as a whole. Economist John Kenneth Galbraith has advanced the idea that much money in today's economy is spent simply making consumers respond to artificial wants. What would automobile companies in the 1950s have been trying to accomplish with their model changes and advertising? Is it possible to accomplish advertising goals without creating artificial wants?

8. How is the allocation of resources affected by imperfect competition? What is the effect on capacity utilization? On price? On costs of production?

9. Think over your own consumer purchases. How much of your buying is done in oligopoly markets? In monopolistically competitive markets? In perfectly competitive or pure monopoly markets?

Application 12:
Deregulation: The Effects on the Airlines

San Francisco is nearly as far from Los Angeles as Boston is from Washington. In mid-1978, however, it cost $30 to fly one way during peak hours between the two California cities, a distance of 450 miles, but twice as much to fly the 399 miles between the two eastern cities.

The difference in fares resulted from a difference in airline regulation. The $60 Boston-Washington tickets were sold by interstate airlines, whose rates as well as routes must be approved by the Civil Aeronautics Board (CAB), the agency established by Congress to oversee airlines operating between states. The $30 tickets were offered by intrastate airlines—those flying only within one state—California, in this case. Airlines flying only within a state are regulated by the state's Public Utilities Commission (PUC), instead of by the federal agency. The PUC gives the airlines under its jurisdiction much greater freedom in setting fares than does the CAB. In fact, the fare structure of the California airlines closely resembles that of a free market.

The rate disparity between *inter*state and *intra*state air carriers began to diminish, however, in late 1978 with the passage of the federal Airline Deregulation Act, which was designed gradually to diminish the authority of the CAB. The act and its impact deserve attention for several reasons. Airline deregulation is a lesson in what actually happens in those rare instances where the government loosens industry reins it has held tightly for decades. And if it works, airline deregulation might serve as a model for reduced federal control of other industries in which demands for greater reliance on free-market forces are growing, such as trucking, oil, and communications.

Deregulation of the nation's airlines was hotly debated long before it actually took place. Proponents argued that regulation merely added to the cost of doing business, and thus to the price of tickets. Without regulation, they said, competition would reduce fares on the most heavily traveled routes, while the freedom to charge whatever rate seemed necessary would ensure enough profit on seldom-traveled routes to guarantee continued operation. Critics of the proposed changes, by contrast, warned that deregulation would bring higher fares, poorer service, and perhaps even financial ruin for the industry. Small communities, the critics said, would be cut off by the major carriers, and increased competition would force a number of airlines out of business, resulting in a loss of shareholder investments and employee jobs.

Like most legislation, the deregulation law, as eventually enacted, was a compromise between the best hopes and the worst fears. In general, it opens the skies to any carrier that is able to convince the CAB that it can transport passengers on scheduled routes reliably and safely. The agency itself would continue to operate, however, until 1985.

Although a complete assessment of the success or failure of the deregulation effort may not be possible for a while, some of its initial effects already are apparent. One of the most visible is that as routes were adjusted by major companies, (the trunk carriers) and the regional, or feeder, airlines, the amount of service to some cities rose, and to others it fell. Seven airlines, for example, started flying to Reno, Nevada, but two of the five major airlines eliminated flights to and from Providence, Rhode Island. In total, more than 75 cities learned within a few months after the deregulation act was passed that at least one carrier no longer would fly there.

On balance, however, according to a CAB study, service increased. For the 12 months ending February 1979, scheduled air service, as measured by aircraft departures, rose 8.4 percent nationwide. The gains came not only at hub airports—those near principal cities—but at smaller airports as well. Air service to such places as Florence, South Carolina, for example, rose 5.2 percent between February 1978 and February 1979, the CAB said. Departures rose 23 percent at Elmira, New York, and at Dubuque, Iowa, the gain was 20 percent.

As another consequence of deregulation, nonscheduled carriers such as World Airways and Capital International Airways began offering scheduled service, sometimes at extraordinarily low fares. Deregulation also enticed at least one fledgling company into the airline business. Running a fleet of second-hand jets from its Seattle, Washington, headquarters, Aeroamerica initiated service between its hometown and Honolulu for just under $100 one way, or almost a third less than the fare charged by the more established carriers for such a trip.

Perhaps most important, fares plunged even before deregulation actually became law, as the airlines, noting the direction of the legislative winds, attempted to woo customers away from competitors by cutting prices instead of offering fancier meals or newer in-flight movies, their former principal means of competition. Airlines adopted so many special discount plans—"We even have a rate for lefthanded Irishmen on rainy Tuesdays," one airline official quipped—that rate changes were difficult to compare with accuracy. But fares on the average were considerably lower.

The decline in prices was not universal, however. In California, which had provided a classic example of how much cheaper air travel could be, the state regulatory law was challenged by intrastate airlines as invalid following the adoption of the federal deregulation act. The California-only carriers sought to charge fares closer to the 18 cents-per-mile average imposed by the state regulatory agency, the PUC. In an initial court ruling the airlines won, raising the possibility that the deregulation which brought lower fares to the rest of America would bring higher ones to California.

Questions for discussion

☐ Identify the segments of the economy to which airline deregulation in its present form is beneficial and those to which it seems detrimental.

☐ If you were a member of Congress, what would you look for in order to determine whether deregulation should be permitted to proceed?

☐ What would you expect the consequences to be if the communications industry—the radio and television stations, the telephone companies—was gradually deregulated?

Chapter 27

Big Business in the American Economy

What to look for in this chapter

What is the role of big business in the American economy?

How is bigness measured?

What are the economic effects of big business? In what ways do large corporations exercise power in the economy and affect the lives of the population?

How has public policy dealt with business concentration in the past? What are the major alternatives for future policy?

With the rise of the corporate form of business organization, American business firms have been getting larger and larger. How big is business? In 1978, General Motors rang up a total sales revenue of more than $63 billion—a sum that is larger than the total national budget of many of the member countries of the United Nations. The three giant corporations that dominate the American automobile industry contributed about $122 billion to the total United States GNP in 1978.

What effect do large corporations have on the American economy? The goal of this chapter is to address this question as well as related issues, including public policy with regard to big business and the state of big business today.

BIGNESS IN THE UNITED STATES ECONOMY

Defining bigness

How do we define "big business"? "Big" may refer either to the absolute size of a firm—total sales revenues, assets, market value—or to the firm's control of the market. If market control is the primary determinant of economic power, the only general store in a town of 100 people may have greater economic power than has the Ford Motor Company, which must compete with other giants, including the even larger General Motors Corporation, for its share of the automobile market. Yet the power of the general store is still small in scale; at the very most, it affects the economic situation of 100 people. The power of Ford, even though it is limited by competition with other auto producers, touches millions of people—the households that buy Ford cars, employees of the company, employees of smaller firms that act as suppliers or distributors for Ford. A considerable proportion of our total population can be economically affected by the decisions Ford makes about price and production.

In this chapter, we will use the term "big business" to refer to those few hundred firms that are large in absolute size, that sell their products in monopolistic or oligopolistic markets and that exercise economic power over a considerable segment of the population.

The trend toward bigness

A simple means of determining whether there is a trend toward bigness is to measure the assets of large corporations. Studies that have done this have shown a continuing growth in corporate assets in the United States. In 1929, the 100 largest corporations in America held 29.7 percent of total manufacturing assets and 38.2 percent of *all* assets; in 1955, they held respectively 44.3 and 43.0 percent; in 1968, they held 49.3 and 48.8 percent. According to this measure, big business is very big indeed.

We can also look at the number of acquisitions of large firms (with assets of $10 million or more)—for example, mergers that have taken place in the manufacturing and mining industries since 1948. As shown in *Fig. 27.1,* there were about 44 times as many such mergers in 1968 as there were in 1948. The late 1960s were peak years for merger activity, but the economically troubled years of the 1970s saw a decline from this record level.

Concentration ratios

Concentration ratios may also be used to measure the trend toward bigness; *they indicate the percentage of total output produced by a certain number (usually four) of the largest firms in any particular industry.* For example, the Big Three—General Motors, Ford, and Chrysler—plus

THE NATION'S TEN LARGEST INDUSTRIAL CORPORATIONS AND THEIR ASSETS, 1979	
	Billions of dollars
Exxon Corporation	$41.5
General Motors Corporation	30.6
Mobil	22.61
Ford Motor Company	22.1
International Business Machines	20.77
Texaco	20.25
Standard Oil of California	16.76
General Electric, Gulf Oil	15.04
Standard Oil	14.11
International Telephone & Telegraph	14.03

Source: *Fortune,* May 7, 1979.

American Motors Co. account for over 90 percent of domestic automobile production. A partial explanation for the dominance of these four firms is the existence of significant economies of large-scale production, which means that a few large firms can produce cars more efficiently than many small ones could. The shoe industry, on the other hand, has a very low concentration ratio. Many firms are able to compete as the shoe-production process tends to require larger amounts of labor than capital and, hence, the economies of scale available are limited. Although there has been little change in the average level of concentration in the United States economy as a whole over the past 70 years, a survey of market-concentration ratios by the Federal Reserve Bank of Cleveland shows that concentration within consumer goods industries has been rising rapidly since the end of World War II.

Attitudes toward bigness

The United States has the largest GNP in the world, and a significant portion of that output comes from large corporations. One study estimated that "oligopolies operating in national markets create almost half of the value of the shipments to all manufacturing industries."* It is undeniable that big business is responsible for much of the productivity and prosperity of the American economy today.

Yet in spite of the importance of big business to prosperity, a number of Americans feel that all large corporations should be forcibly broken up into smaller units. They suggest that the case for the efficiency of big business has been overstated and that the costs actually outweigh the benefits.

Much of the argument between critics and supporters of big business centers on abstract concepts, such as freedom and independence. Critics

---

*Richard Caves, *American Industry: Structure, Conduct, Performance.* Englewood Cliffs, N.J.: Prentice-Hall, 1967, p. 11.

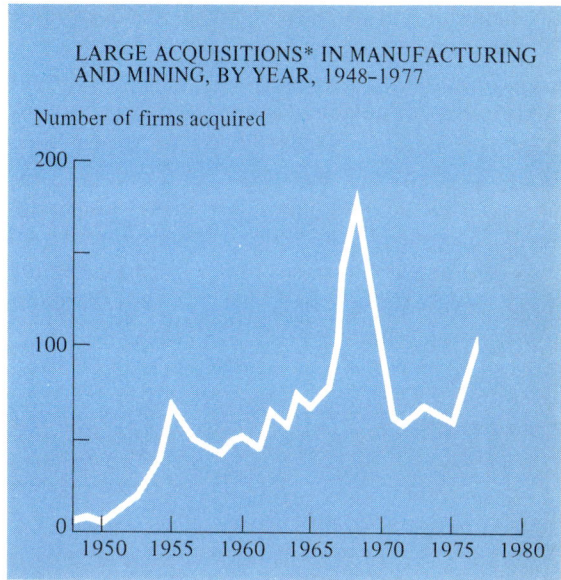

*Acquired firms with assets of $10 million or more.
SOURCE: Federal Trade Commission, *Statistical Report on Mergers and Acquisitions,* December 1978.

Fig. 27.1
From 1948 to the late 1960s there was a pronounced upward trend in the number of large manufacturing and mining firms acquired in the United States, but a sharp drop occurred following the peak reached in 1968.

say that heavy concentration of power in any one firm curtails the freedom of other firms to enter that industry; supporters reply that the concept of freedom includes the freedom to grow to the most efficient and profitable size. Critics say that monopolies and oligopolies limit the consumer's freedom of choice; supporters reply that only large corporations can afford the cost of developing and the risk of marketing new products. Critics say that big business restricts market competition; supporters reply that such restriction is a small opportunity lost in view of the great gain in efficiency and productivity brought about by large corporations.

Many of these arguments result from conflicting value judgments—or as the economist might put it, different preferences for the satisfactions of freedom, individual initiative, variety, and efficiency. Many feel that such value judgments are outside the scope of economic study. The economist, however, can help to clarify the debate by analyzing the impact of large corporations on the economy.

EFFECTS OF BIG BUSINESS ON THE ECONOMY

Restraint of competition

A major effect of big business on the economy is the restraint of competition. Let us examine a number of ways in which this can occur.

Monopsony power

A resource market in which there is only one buyer is called a **monopsony.** More generally, if there are only a few important buyers of a particular factor of production, these purchasers are said to possess a degree of monopsony power. One of the chief ways a large corporation can restrain competition is by exploiting its position as the only, or most important, customer for suppliers of certain raw materials, capital goods, and highly specialized or skilled labor. For example, a large corporation can insist on discount prices as a condition for purchasing large orders. This lowers the firm's production costs, but it does not necessarily mean that the price the consumer pays for the product will be lowered, although it may be. Monopsony power in the resource market also serves as a barrier to entry into the field by smaller firms who would not buy enough to get the discount. The large corporations can also set delivery dates and contract terms with their suppliers to gain the best advantage. Suppliers may not be happy about the concession they must make, but since there are few or no other possible customers to bargain with, they must either accept the terms of the large corporation or go into some other business.

Vertical integration

Another way in which a large corporation may reduce competition is by buying or establishing a company that would normally supply it with an input into its production or marketing process. By eliminating intermediate transactions, production costs are lowered. *The process through which a firm eventually acquires control over all of the resources necessary to produce and market a particular product* is called **vertical integration.** For example, a manufacturer of cast-iron pipe might purchase an ore mine or a processing plant. It might also buy a trucking company to provide quick and cheap transportation of its pipes to customers.

Vertical integration may also lead to a situation in which one large corporation acts as supplier to its competitors. Such a situation might occur, for example, in the television industry, where one large company that manufactures parts and television sets might sell many of the parts used by competing companies that also produce television sets. Thus, vertical integration is another way in which competition within an industry is weakened. (Of course, the costs of reduced competition must always be weighed against the possible benefits of lower manufacturing costs and lower consumer prices which vertical integration may also encourage.)

Horizontal integration

A large corporation may also restrain competition through **horizontal integration**—*the purchase of competing companies in the same industry, or companies that produce substitutable products.* As railroads began to encounter high operating costs and excess capacity, rail companies merged with one another to try to achieve greater economies of scale and minimize the pressures of competition. The merger movement has spread to airlines as well—Eastern Airlines has linked with Caribbean-Atlantic, and Mohawk with Allegheny. A more subtle kind of horizontal integration can be seen in the attempt made several decades ago by certain aluminum companies to acquire interests in the magnesium industry. Since aluminum and magnesium are substitutable in many of their uses, any such merger would greatly extend the market power of aluminum companies.

Most mergers in recent decades have been **conglomerate mergers**—that is, *mergers between firms that produce unrelated products*. The process of acquiring firms in a variety of unrelated industries is also referred to as diversification. Diversification helps a large corporation add to its economic power. Because a heavily diversified corporation participates in many different markets it may record a profit even when one (or more) of the markets in which it sells its goods is badly depressed or economically unhealthy. Those smaller competitors who are limited to that one depressed market may be forced out of business.

The record of one conglomerate, Gulf & Western Industries, Inc., will illustrate the process of diversification. In 1957, Gulf & Western was solely a manufacturer of bumpers and bumper parts for trucks and passenger cars, but in 1968 it was dubbed by a Federal Trade Commission report "the most active acquiring company of the 1960s."* During the period 1961–1968, Gulf & Western acquired at least 67 other companies and an aggregation of assets of approximately $2.8 billion. It diversified far beyond its initial field, automobile parts, into such industries as motion pictures, sugar, cigars, zinc, fertilizer, wire and cable, publishing, paper, musical instruments, real estate, insurance, and investments.

---

*Federal Trade Commission, *Economic Report on Corporate Mergers,* 1969.

Control of distributors

Another way in which the large corporation may restrain competition is through control over the distributors of its product. In theory, distributors are independent business firms whose decisions regarding products to carry, retail prices, and type of advertising can act as a balance to the power of the large producer. But in reality, large corporations can enforce their wishes on the small distributor in many ways: by demanding a particular program of advertising; by prohibiting the distributor from carrying a competitor's product; by insisting that a distributor carry their full line, regardless of how poorly some of the products sell in the area; by requiring the distributor to build a certain size and style of building; and by setting the price the distributor must ask for goods.

Large manufacturing firms can exercise control over distributors because the producer can choose among a large number of possible distributors, whereas the would-be distributor must deal with the two or three firms in the industry. Moreover, a large corporation has the resources to set up its own retail outlets if it is dissatisfied with the distributor. Large corporations also use their economic power to transfer costs and risks to distributors by such means as devising contracts that shift to others whatever losses and costs arise from such problems as delays of shipments, damage in transit, and changes in freight rates. Smaller firms that buy from large ones usually accept the provisions of such standard contracts without change.

In fact, much of the apparent efficiency of the large corporation may be a result of its ability to shift to other firms the operations that carry the highest risk and are the least efficient. For example, large clothing manufacturers often contract with small firms to do any necessary hand finishing. Thus the small firm must assume all of the cost and problems of finding or training skilled workers in this field (they are extremely scarce), of turning out handwork under the pressure of a tight schedule, and of accepting the losses caused by errors or substandard work. The small firm must, of course, be earning at least a normal profit to stay in business, but this procedure allows the large firm to operate at a higher profit margin than the small one. Consequently, it appears to be more efficient.

Legal and political advantages
A large corporation may also use legal and political means to restrain competition. Individuals and organizations connected with large corporations have traditionally been in a position to contribute substantial sums to political candidates or to groups backing some specific issue. This does not necessarily mean that a large corporation could blatantly buy a political candidate, but it does mean that the candidate's self-interest might lead him or her to make a special effort to find areas of mutual interest or easy compromise solutions for any differences he or she might have with the corporation. The money the corporation could contribute—for example, to defray the high cost of radio and television advertising—could mean the difference between success and failure in the election.

Although changes in campaign-financing laws have restricted such corporate-related political contributions, the influence of large corporations can be felt in other ways. Their presence in a community, for example, means revenue for the city government and employment for the residents. The financial needs of the community tend to make officials sympathetic toward the problems of the large corporations located there. If a corporation feels that tax increases are too great, pollution laws are enforced too strictly, or other of its special interests are being endangered, it always has available the powerful threat of moving to a more cooperative community.

Another kind of advantage the large corporation has over its smaller rivals and the individual consumer of its goods is its ability and willingness to bear the cost of litigation. Large corporations employ legal staffs and the expense of legal action, including fines or financial restitution if the company loses the case, can be treated like any other kind of operating cost. The actual costs of litigation may be the same for smaller rivals as for large corporations, but such costs are harder for smaller companies to bear because they must pay them out of a smaller income or total revenue. A large corporation is quick to sue a smaller rival for patent infringement or unfair trade practice, whereas the small company—for whom the cost of legal action is relatively greater—is much more reluctant to take such action. A large firm can afford to sue even when the chance of winning seems slight but small firms can afford to take legal action only when their chances of success are great.

Individual consumers are similarly reluctant to undertake the high costs of legal action when they feel they have been treated unfairly by a large corporation. One possible remedy to this problem is the class action suit—a lawsuit initiated on behalf of a group of people (for example, consumers) against another party (such as a corporation). The costs of the suit may be divided among all the participants in the action, but more often they are borne by the agency supporting the suit (a consumer organization, or perhaps the government). On the other side, corporations are not reluctant to proceed against consumers who default on their part of the exchange bargain.

Other means of restraining competition
There are many other ways in which a large corporation can use its immense financial assets to restrain competition. It can lobby for favorable legislation; outbid its competitors to obtain control of scarce resources (buying the most promising patents, hiring the best-known and best-qualified employees); erect psychological barriers to entry in its industry by allocating huge sums for advertising which a smaller company could not hope to match; hire expert public relations firms to make its activities more popular with the public; and even hire private detectives to investigate its critics.

> **RECAP**
>
> One of the major effects of large corporations on the American economy is RESTRAINT OF COMPETITION by the following means:
>
> - Monopsony—becoming the only or most important customer for suppliers of factors of production
> - Vertical integration—acquiring control over all necessary resources for producing and marketing a product
> - Horizontal integration—acquiring other companies that produce substitutable products
> - Controlling distributors of a product
> - Using legal resources and political influence to obtain desired goals.

Economies of scale: impact on prices

Another effect of big business on the economy results from economies of scale that are possible in large corporations. In an industry that requires high set-up costs, the cost of supplying a small number of units of product would be very great. The price can be lowered only when the high fixed costs can be divided by a large quantity of units of goods.

For example, if the American automobile industry were to become a truly competitive industry rather than an oligopolistic one, the price of automobiles might rise. Although perfect competition would dictate that the price of the car would be equal to the marginal cost of production, it might cost more to produce cars made in many small factories than it does under the present oligopolistic arrangement. So even though the big automobile companies today exercise oligopolistic power to charge a price for their product that is higher than the marginal cost of its production, their marginal cost of production is so much lower than it would be if production occurred in smaller plants that it is possible for the price to be lower than it would be under perfect competition.

The basic point here is that in order to take advantage of the economies offered by large-scale production techniques, the individual factory or plant, not necessarily the firm, must be large. Economies of scale are generally realized within a particular plant, not between plants that are part of the same corporation. In order to operate at peak efficiency, it may be necessary to have a large plant, but there is little evidence that justifies the existence of multiplant firms on efficiency grounds. In fact, upon studying the structure of 20 different industries, Joe S. Bain concluded that the "economies of large multiplant firms are left in doubt by this investigation,"* noting that many of the largest firms possessed market shares substantially above those required for maximum efficiency, or lowest costs of production.

Product improvement and technological change

Another economic effect of large corporations lies in the area of product improvement. It is generally only large corporations that can afford the expensive research necessary to determine the many possible uses of a product. For example, a large chemical company can afford to undertake research that might combine a currently effective antibiotic with other drugs that might make it more effective, prevent side effects, extend its shelf life, or control the speed with which it is absorbed. The company can also afford to supply the new formula drug to hospitals and clinics for use in testing, and it also can afford to wait for the five or more years it might take to produce proof of the new drug's safety, so that the Food and

---

*Joe S. Bain, "Economies of Scale, Concentration, and the Condition of Entry in Twenty Manufacturing Industries," *American Economic Review*, 1954. The Bain Study was largely revised by H. Michael Mann, "Sellers Concentration, Barriers to Entry, and Rates of Return in Thirty Industries, 1950–1960," *Review of Economics and Statistics*, 1966.

Drug Administration will permit its sale and use. Large companies also can afford the test-marketing and advertising promotion that is needed to launch new products in the consumer market. Through research, large companies may also develop innovations that will reduce their costs of production. Even the largest firms have an incentive to develop cost-saving innovations—if costs can be reduced, profits can be increased.

Besides possessing the resources necessary to finance product improvement, economist John Kenneth Galbraith* contends that large firms also have an incentive, in the form of greater returns on investment, to undertake expensive research. Whereas small firms may receive only short-lived rewards for research if new firms enter the industry and successfully imitate their product, the sheer size of oligopolistic firms functions as a barrier to the entry of new firms. Therefore, the return on investment in research is potentially much greater, as imitators are essentially barred from the industry.

It is important to realize that product improvement does not necessarily imply technological advance. Many products introduced each year differ from already existing items only in terms of styling, packaging, etc. For example, the 1980 Cadillac may have a "new look" in comparison to the 1979 model, but the engineering techniques used in the production of the two automobiles may be exactly the same. Thus, while large corporations spend a lot of money on product development, whether or not these expenditures represent technological progress remains a controversial issue.

As mentioned above, big business can afford, and appears to have the incentive, to be progressive. A case for technological lethargy, however, can also be made. Critics contend that the reduced degree of competition in concentrated industries results in a complacent attitude toward technological advancement. It has even been suggested that big business may sometimes resist technological advance because it may render existing production processes requiring extensive capital suddenly obsolete. In this situation, the firm is forced to retool at great expense.

Empirical evidence seems to confirm these contentions. A study of 61 important inventions made between 1900 and 1955 disclosed that "... more than half were the product of independent inventors, working alone, unaffiliated with any industrial research laboratories. Among these were such diverse inventions as air conditioning, automatic transmissions, the cotton-picker, the jet engine, and insulin."†

Therefore, when product *improvement* is viewed in terms of product *development,* there is no doubt as to the contribution made by big business. The extent to which product improvement represents technological advance, however, is debatable.

Other effects of big business

Extent of competitive restraint
Some economists feel that large corporations do not always restrain competition to the extent that is usually supposed. Formation of large corporations may also help to retain a competitive balance in an industry that already has one large company in the field. For example, when other companies began to invade what was once a virtual monopoly on the steel-making industry held by United States Steel, it was clear that real competition would be stimulated only if the new firms also were oligopolistic. Small companies could not acquire the economic power needed to offer a real challenge.

---

*John Kenneth Galbraith, *American Capitalism*. Boston: Houghton Mifflin, 1956, pp. 86–88.

†Daniel Hamberg, "Size of Firm, Monopoly, and Technological Progress." In Campbell R. McConnell's *Economic Issues: A Book of Readings.* New York: McGraw-Hill, 1972, p. 250.

> **RECAP**
>
> Galbraith's concept of COUNTERVAILING POWER suggests that the ability of large corporations to restrain competition tends to be offset somewhat by the emergence of a counterreaction by those who are affected by corporate power. For example, labor unions have arisen in order to strengthen the bargaining position of workers, and chain stores have emerged to counter the influence of manufacturing and processing firms.

Countervailing power

Countervailing power, a concept suggested by John Kenneth Galbraith, is another result of big business. Galbraith proposed that *the existence of concentrated economic power in one group tends to stimulate a counterbalancing reaction by another group.* In Galbraith's words:

> Private economic power is held in check by the countervailing power of those who are subject to it. The first begets the second. The long trend toward concentration of industrial enterprise in the hands of a relatively few firms has brought into existence not only strong sellers, as economists have supposed, but also strong buyers.*

Galbraith suggests that countervailing power is most clearly seen in the labor market, where groups of workers are confronted with the economic clout of large corporations. In such situations workers tend to organize for their own protection. Thus strong unions frequently arise where strong corporations serve the markets.

Another example of countervailing power is the relationship of the large retailer to its suppliers. The rise of chain stores in the twentieth century reflects the efforts of retailers to develop power to offset the power of large manufacturing and processing firms with which they must do business. There is further evidence of countervailing power in markets for producers' goods; for example, automobile manufacturers can counterbalance the power of steel suppliers because they are such important purchasers of steel.

Galbraith notes further that the government comes to play a role in this process.

> Without the phenomenon being fully recognized, the provision of state assistance to the development of countervailing power has become a major function of government—perhaps *the* major domestic function of government.†

Countervailing power, then, tends to have the effect of encouraging competition in the economy and thus helps limit the ability of large corporations to restrain competition.

PUBLIC POLICY AND BIG BUSINESS

The question of desirable and effective public policy in regard to the existence and operation of big business has been debated in the United States for a hundred years. It was discussed at the Constitutional Convention of 1787, and it continues to be an issue today. The Constitution gave the government the power to intervene in the operation of private businesses and to establish regulation in the market, if it were deemed necessary. However, for a hundred years after the Constitutional Convention, government intervention in the conduct of business was largely limited to a certain degree of regulation of banks, since banking was the only industry in which large and powerful businesses were to be found.

---

*John Kenneth Galbraith, *American Capitalism: The Concept of Countervailing Power.* Boston: Houghton Mifflin, 1952, p. 118.

†*Ibid.,* p. 133.

The rise of trusts

It was not until the last quarter of the nineteenth century—after the rise of industrialism, the establishment of faster communication and transportation systems, and the invention of the corporate form of business organization—that the federal government began to see a need for broad legislative action to preserve and protect market competition in industries where large corporations had acquired considerable economic power. The immediate target of such legislation was the **trust**, *a combination of firms or corporations under the control of a single individual or group.* The Civil War had stimulated industrial development and the government's laissez-faire attitude—the attitude that government should refrain from interfering in economic affairs—had permitted the development of large trusts. Karl Schriftgiesser, in his book *Business and the American Government,* gives some idea of the magnitude of nineteenth-century trusts:

> In their efforts to control competition from others, without government intervention, the new combinations invented new methods; they set prices and rates among themselves and made production-allocation and profit-pooling agreements. But such practices were puny compared to the methods of John D. Rockefeller's Standard Oil. Created in 1882, Standard Oil drew into one huge company some thirty-nine separate oil-refining concerns, thus almost completely dominating the production, refining, and marketing of oil in the United States. In 1892, forty independent sugar refining companies merged into one firm, the American Sugar Refining Company. Other trusts were formed in tobacco, leather, meat-packing, and the infant electrical goods industry.*

The Sherman Antitrust Act

Although at the time Congress was dominated by a probusiness faction, in 1890 the legislature passed into law a bill sponsored by Senator John Sherman of Ohio, which provided for government regulation of trust activities. The **Sherman Antitrust Act,** as it has come to be called, was aimed at curbing the power of trusts and monopolies. *The act made it illegal to monopolize trade or to conspire to restrain trade.* It stated that "every contract, combination in the form of trust or otherwise, in restraint of commerce among the several states, or with foreign nations, is illegal."

Despite passage of the act, most of the large trusts continued their operation. In part this was because the act was broadly written and therefore difficult to enforce. Moreover, at the time, government officials were disinclined to use the powers that the act granted them. A recession that began three years after the act was passed did rouse public sentiment against some of the trusts, but the basic trend of growth by merger continued. In 1897, there were fewer than a dozen corporations with assets of $10 million; within five years there were over 300. By the turn of the century, 17 firms had assets of more than $100 million.

Other legislation

As time went by, the continuing accumulation of economic power and some glaring instances of its abuse moved the federal government to more vigorous enforcement of the Sherman Antitrust Act. In 1904, a trust that pooled the railroad interests of J. P. Morgan and John D. Rockefeller was ordered dissolved. In 1911, Standard Oil, which controlled 91 percent of the refining industry, and American Tobacco, which controlled about 80 percent of the tobacco industry, were found guilty of unreasonable restraint of trade against smaller rivals and were dissolved. Yet after ruling against these corporations, the Supreme Court continued to define the Sherman Act very narrowly. In 1920 in the case of *U.S. v. U.S. Steel Corp.,* the Court established the "rule of reason" which held that a distinction should be made between "good" trusts and "bad" trusts. In other words, the Court took the view that the size of a corporation was not in

---

*Karl Schriftgiesser, *Business and the American Government.* Washington, D.C.: Robert B. Luce, 1964, p. 32.

itself an offense, and that the act should be applied only to those firms which engaged in unfair practices, such as making predatory attacks on their smaller rivals.

The Sherman Act contained no guidelines distinguishing good from bad behavior. So in 1914, two more acts were passed. The Clayton Antitrust Act outlawed specific activities that were held to result in restraint of trade, and the Federal Trade Commission Act established a federal agency, the Federal Trade Commission (FTC), charged with the responsibility of making and enforcing rules regarding the conduct of business. The goal of both of these pieces of legislation was to end "unfair" competition, which meant specific collusive or predatory acts. At the time, it was felt that this additional legislation was needed to close the loopholes left by the Sherman Act, but legal historians today point out that the problem was not the limitations of the Sherman Act, but the narrow way in which the Supreme Court had defined its application.

These three statutes—the Sherman, the Clayton, and the Federal Trade Commission Acts—comprise the main body of American antitrust policy. In 1936, a section of the Clayton Act was amended by the Robinson–Patman Act, which forbids price discrimination by manufacturers to retailers, unless different prices charged can be justified by actual differences in costs. This amendment was intended to provide protection to small independent stores that were being squeezed out of the retail market by large chain stores that induced manufacturers to give them substantial volume discounts.

In 1950, another amendment to the Clayton Act was passed, the Celler-Kefauver Antimerger Act which prohibits one firm from acquiring the stock and the assets of competitors when the effect of such action is to reduce or weaken competition. The Celler-Kefauver Act was designed to limit horizontal mergers, but it too has been weakened by a narrow interpretation. Mergers that involve only the assets of a firm, and not its stock, are allowed. So it takes only a little legal manipulation to accomplish any desired merger.

Although no major antitrust legislation has been passed for a number of years, the interpretation of existing legislation, most notably the Sherman Act, has changed. As we noted earlier, originally, prosecution for alleged violation of the Sherman Act was limited to "bad" firms observed using unfair practices to drive smaller competitors out of business. However, in a major antitrust suit against the Aluminum Company of America (the Alcoa case of 1945), the previously established "rule of reason" was repealed and the Sherman Act was reinterpreted to mean that monopolies should not exist at all. In Judge Learned Hand's majority opinion " . . . [The Sherman Act] did not condone 'good' trusts and condemn 'bad' ones; it forbade all." The fact that economies of scale, indivisibility of product, or dedicated entrepreneurship may have produced a monopoly was deemed irrelevant. Consequently, long-established monopolies, such as the Bell Telephone System, that were formerly considered largely immune to antitrust legislation, now find their behavior scrutinized.

The evolving nature of antitrust-law interpretation, however, has not always been matched by enthusiastic enforcement. As a result, the traditional emphasis on eliminating "bad," as opposed to "big," business is still very much in evidence.

BIG BUSINESS IN THE 1970s

The social, legal, political, and economic climate of America has tended to be stormy in recent years. Economic troubles have included balance of payments deficits, dollar devaluations, high interest rates, wage and price controls, inflation, and recession. How well did big business cope with the turbulent seventies?

Each year the business magazine *Fortune* publishes a directory of the "*Fortune* 500," the 500 largest industrial corporations in the United States. The performance of these firms provides an indication of how big business is faring in the American economy.

Combined annual sales for this group of corporations rose throughout the decade, but after adjustment for inflation, real sales actually declined in 1975 as the economy was mired in its worst recession since the 1930s. Similarly, profits exceeded previous year levels in all years except 1975. In 1978, just 12 of the 500 operated in the red, the biggest loser being the Chrysler Corporation with a deficit in excess of $204 million.

As always, however, while a few corporations experienced serious difficulties, others prospered. General Motors replaced Exxon at the top of the heap in 1977 and remained there the following year. Its 1978 sales totaled a whopping $63.2 billion with net income equalling $3.5 billion. Despite Exxon's second-place finish, oil companies occupied 8 of the top 15 spots on the 500 list. This strong performance by the oil industry has proved a mixed blessing, however, as in 1979 the Carter administration proposed that an excess-profits tax be levied on these firms should domestic prices be decontrolled. In addition, surging gasoline prices, gasoline shortages, and long lines at the pump in the first half of 1979 led to accusations by consumers that oil companies were purposely creating shortages in an effort to increase profits. At present the available evidence is too sketchy to verify either the consumer or the oil companies on this issue.

Unfavorable public opinion is a matter of concern for all large corporations, as it is at least partially responsible for the ever-increasing government regulation of business and also likely affects the interpretation of antitrust legislation by the courts.

Employee and citizen complaints have played an important role in the government's establishment of industrial health, safety, and pollution-control standards, and this intervention has resulted in a substantial financial burden for big business. For example, the Chrysler Corporation cited rigid government fuel-economy standards as one factor contributing to its poor profit showing in 1978, and while GM's profit picture was much brighter, it still had to spend more than $1 billion to comply with regulations imposed by all levels of government. The plight of the steel industry is even more serious, as producers must comply with some 5600 regulations administered by 26 different federal agencies.

In the antitrust arena, consumer cries of big business "rip-offs" have probably been influential in the introduction of legislation aimed at banning most mergers resulting in corporations with more than $2 billion in assets or annual sales. Although passage of this legislation would by no means guarantee enforcement, the mere consideration of such action has caused distress in the big-business community.

Thus, although big business generally succeeded in weathering the economic crises of the 1970s, changing public attitudes suggest that additional troubles lie ahead.

Future alternatives and directions

Although predicting the future is hazardous, it appears that recent increased concern regarding the possible abuse of economic power by big business is unlikely to wane. There remains, however, much controversy over how best to control economic power. Three diverse proposals on this matter are discussed below.*

The first position holds that more zealous enforcement of existing antitrust laws would significantly enhance the degree of competition in the economy. Since there is little evidence of interplant economies of scale, breaking up large corporations should be considered. Although some feel that the likelihood of successful implementation of antitrust laws in this fashion is minimal, Justice Department officials seem to be moving tentatively in this direction, and, as noted earlier, Congress

---

*These proposals are based on Galbraith's book *American Capitalism: The Concept of Countervailing Power,* cited on p. 544.

has proposed legislation that would ban mergers resulting in corporations with more than $2 billion in assets or annual sales. This action represents a direct attack on expanding industrial concentration. Limiting such legislation to mergers alone, however, indicates that the government has little intention of dissolving the operations of established oligopolists.

A more radical reform proposal is the replacement of antitrust legislation with some form of big-business regulation. The view here is that antitrust laws have not prevented the dominance of large corporations. Since, in the opinion of many, the interests of these firms are inconsistent with the welfare of the general public, some type of government intervention is considered necessary. Nationalization of oil companies, for example, is sometimes urged for precisely this reason. Galbraith suggests, however, that much of the support for such action has been "general and verbal" and that advocates of this approach have often been those "who [don't] quite know where they want to go."

The final perspective is that, despite a general lack of *price* competition, other forms of *workable* competition serve to regulate the behavior of big business. Consequently, no significant changes in either antitrust legislation or its enforcement are necessary. Workable competition exists because large corporations must fight for the consumer's dollar just like other businesses, remain technologically progressive in order to maintain their market shares, and realize that exploitation of their economic power will only serve to incur the wrath of government regulators and trustbusters. In short, advocates of maintaining the status quo feel that the benefits provided the United States economy by big business outweigh the costs by a considerable margin.

Instead of wholly adopting any one of these alternatives, it is likely that the direction taken by Congress and the Justice Department in dealing with monopoly and oligopoly power will reflect a combination of the first and third approaches. Buttressed by public opinion, there appears to be a movement toward more vigorous enforcement of antitrust laws in order to create a more competitive atmosphere in the economy. At the same time, however, there is considerable reluctance to declare full-scale war on big business.

Summary

■ This chapter looks at the role of big business in the American economy, examines some of the effects of business concentration, and surveys public policy in the past and present toward big business.

■ By big business economists generally mean the few hundred large corporations which operate in oligopoly or monopoly markets and which exercise economic control over large segments of the population. The proportion of assets held by the 100 largest corporations had steadily increased in the twentieth century, and the 1960s were a peak period of business merger activity. Concentration ratios—the percentage of a total market controlled by a certain number of firms—are a useful measure of bigness.

■ There are a number of important ways in which large corporations restrain free competition and trade. Large corporations often exercise a degree of monopsony power, as the only buyer or one of few buyers. Vertical integration may mean that a corporation controls all the steps in a production process, thus cutting its own supply costs compared to costs of competitors. Horizontal integration through mergers also reduces competition among producers of a particular product; conglomerate mergers (the acquisition of companies in unrelated fields) help cushion the effect of losses in certain areas of corporate holdings. Large corporations can also control distributors of their products, establish their own distributors, or transfer high-risk and low-efficiency jobs to outside firms. Bigness also provides a capacity for political and legal leverage, public relations work, and other activities which extend corporate power.

■ The economies of scale enjoyed by large corporations may result in lower prices than would result from the activities of many small firms. Even though a firm in an oligopoly market may set its price above marginal cost, the price may still be lower than the price set at marginal cost by a smaller firm. Research indicates that economies of scale are achieved primarily through large plants, not through multi-plant firms. Large corporations can afford to do extensive research and development, testing, and test-marketing to develop products; some critics observe, however, that bigness may induce lethargy instead of real innovation. Economist John Kenneth Galbraith has argued that corporate power is checked in the long run by countervailing powers; that is, the tendency of concentrated economic power to call forth a counterbalancing response from another group or institution.

■ The emergence of huge trusts in the late nineteenth century led to the first government legislation to check big business, the Sherman Antitrust Act of 1890. Although the Sherman Act was the basis for breaking up the Rockefeller-Morgan railroad trust in 1904 and the Standard Oil company a few years later, enforcement of antimonopoly legislation was ineffective. The Clayton Act (1914) forbade specific activities in restraint of trade, and the Federal Trade Commission was established in the same year. The Robinson-Patman Act (1936) forbade price discrimination by manufacturers to retailers. The Celler–Kefauver Antimerger Act (1950) prohibited firms from buying stock in competing companies if the effect would be to reduce competition. Overall, the history of enforcement of antitrust legislation has shown a concentration on prosecuting "badness," not "bigness," and legislation has not reversed the trend toward consolidation.

■ In the 1970s, the *Fortune* 500 top corporations showed increases in sales for every year except 1975, and even in that year, only 28 of the 500 firms actually showed a loss. There has been a high degree of consumer outcry against large corporations, including a widespread belief that the oil companies had rigged the energy shortage of the late seventies. Demands have also been raised for environmental protection, for improved health and safety measures, and for increased antitrust activity. Businesses have pointed to the dangers of overregulation, which they contend imposes significant financial burdens on major corporations.

■ Three major schools of thought exist about the future course of public policy toward big business: an increased attention to prosecuting antitrust violations and the prevention of new concentrations; replacement of antitrust with strong regulation and, if necessary, nationalization of huge corporations which do exist; and acceptance of bigness, with the recognition that even monopoly corporations must still strive to satisfy consumers.

Key Terms

concentration ratios	vertical integration	conglomerate mergers	trust
monopsony	horizontal integration	countervailing power	Sherman Antitrust Act

Review & Discussion

1. What are the characteristics of "big business"? How do economists measure bigness?

2. What are the advantages a big producer has over a small producer?

3. Define vertical, horizontal, and conglomerate mergers. In what ways do mergers tend to restrain competition? In what ways do they allow for lower costs of production?

4. Why might a large corporation tend to be more efficient even though it had monopoly power?

5. Review the history of major antitrust legislation. How successful has this legislation been in curbing business concentration? What has been the effect of focusing on "bad" instead of "big" business practices in the implementation of this legislation?

6. Many experts argue that most economies of scale occur at the level of the individual plant. Yet the large firms operate many plants. How might this situation tend to refute the argument that firms must be large to be efficient?

7. What has been the state of big business in the 1970s? How have big corporations fared overall in terms of sales and profits? What kinds of demands have been placed on large corporations by consumers and workers? What has been the general trend in public attitudes toward big business?

8. Discuss the alternatives which have attracted some support as orientations of public policy toward big business for the future. Which of these approaches seems most practical and realistic? Why? Which seems most likely to solve the problems raised by business concentration and power? Why?

Application 13:
Regulating Big Business: The IBM Antitrust Case

A few years ago, the leading companies in the computer industry were sometimes known as Snow White and the Seven Dwarfs. The number of dwarfs is smaller now; such companies as General Electric and RCA no longer make computers. But Snow White, as the International Business Machines Corporation (IBM) is irreverently called, is alive and well—and its critics view as ironic the purity of the fairy-tale name chosen to represent a very competitive corporation that has proven adept at eliminating competitive threats from its rivals.

IBM, one of the nation's largest corporations, accounts by itself for about two-thirds of the *world's* computer revenues. Put another way, IBM is twice as large as the rest of the computer industry, which includes such major companies as Burroughs and Sperry-Rand. Not surprisingly, its size and its determination to keep growing have made IBM a popular target for antitrust lawsuits. But the unusual nature of the computer industry, and the duration of the legal battles involving IBM, raise interesting questions about the real role of such a mammoth company in the economy and about the validity or effectiveness of attempts to restrict it by enforcing antitrust laws.

In 1979, IBM's revenues reached $21 billion, a 91 percent increase from its $11 billion level in 1974, despite a steady decline in the price of the company's principal product, computer systems. Indeed, while IBM's revenues have risen at a fairly reliable rate of 15 percent a year for decades, the price of computing has fallen faster, with the result that a calculation costing $1.50 to perform in the early 1950s cost less than a penny in the late 1970s.

With the price of computing going down at a time when the price of almost everything else was going up, how could competitors complain that IBM unlawfully monopolized the computer industry, as 20 private companies did in the late 1960s and the 1970s? Some contended that IBM cut prices for the sole purpose of putting smaller competitors out of business. Others focused on new products through which, they said, IBM unfairly damaged their business.

Whatever the case, it is clear that IBM could move swiftly when its market was attacked and that its countermeasures could leave rivals devastated, primarily because its competitors had chosen not only to supply computers that performed as well as those made by IBM, but also to supply actual IBM computers and related equipment, or machines that performed exactly like IBM equipment. In the late 1960s, for example, a number of young companies became overnight successes in the business of leasing IBM computers. They would buy computers from IBM, lease them to customers for less than IBM rental rates, and in so doing make a substantial profit. All went well until 1973, when IBM surprised the leasing companies by introducing a new family of computers, the System 370, which suddenly outdated the System 360s owned by the leasing companies. The unprepared leasing companies lost millions of dollars and some went broke.

A similar situation had occurred a few years earlier with similar effects on makers of accessory equipment (known as peripherals) for IBM computers. These independent companies had enjoyed rapid growth as suppliers of such peripherals as magnetic tape units that performed like those made by IBM (the units "read and write") but usually sold for much less. According to one estimate, by the end of 1970, independent companies had taken perhaps as much as 10 percent of the market for IBM-type computer accessories away from IBM. IBM struck back with equipment of its own that was faster, cheaper, and more difficult to imitate; this action served to severely curtail the growth of independent accessory makers. The price of stock in such accessory makers as California Computer Products and Telex dropped 25 percent in a few days after the new IBM equipment was announced.

Less than a decade later, the giant stirred again when competitors began making imitation IBM computers as well as imitation IBM accessories. IBM responded by cutting product prices at once—10 percent, 15 percent, and more. In addition, the corporation unveiled new computers that not only worked better than earlier models but could be sold for less than the imitation models. And, just as before, computer buyers and investors began moving away from the manufacturers and suppliers of substitute equipment, such as Amdahl Corporation and Itel Corporation and back to IBM.

For all their protests about IBM's maneuvers, none of the antitrust plaintiffs has been able to inhibit them. Although many of the 20 private antitrust cases were still on appeal in the late 1970s, IBM had not lost any, and in a few cases, judges had actually ruled that IBM's activities were legal and justifiable in the name of fair competition. Meanwhile, the most important antitrust case against the company, brought by the federal government, continues to drag on with no end in sight.

This case, which IBM once dubbed "the Methuselah of antitrust cases," was filed in January 1969 on the last day the Johnson administration was in office. The suit accused IBM of trying to monopolize the market for general-purpose computers. Among the illegal means that IBM was alleged to have used to maintain its dominant position were charging different computer users different prices, forcing clients who bought IBM computers to buy IBM computer programs and related equipment as well, and changing the design of its computers so that related equipment built by other manufacturers would not work with IBM computers.

In its defense, IBM countered that competition in the computer industry is not only significant but increasing. As evidence it cited the fact that its competitors had expanded their revenues by 23 percent annually since 1960 while IBM was growing at an average annual rate of 17 percent. IBM also denied the government's charge that its activities were responsible for the withdrawal of General Electric and RCA from the computer market. The defense suggested that the inability of those companies—both giants that wield extensive market power—to develop successful computer lines indicates that size and strength are less important to success in the manufacture and sale of computers than are skill and efficiency.

Ironically, during this long period of time not only were many new computer companies born but new types of computers were created, casting doubt on the validity of a key term in the government case against IBM: the market for general-purpose computers. For in the first decade of the trial, smaller machines known as minicomputers had sprung up to challenge the so-called mainframe computers made by IBM and others. And eventually, minicomputers themselves came under attack from smaller, cheaper, but equally powerful machines called microcomputers, devices smaller than a thumbnail yet capable of arithmetic feats that once would have required room-size computers.

Recently, the *Wall Street Journal* reported that the IBM suit will probably not be settled for three to five more years, and appeals promise to carry the case into the next century. Clearly, by that time the nature of the product and the industry will probably have changed so significantly (as they have already) that any judgment is likely to be of questionable worth.

Thus, as the IBM case illustrates, there are tremendous limitations on the ability of antitrust suits to achieve their objectives—they are often waged at tremendous cost, regardless of the usefulness of the outcome.

This case also suggests that the mere presence of monopoly power in the market may not always be sufficient grounds for government intervention. The costs of intervention must be weighed against the gains that are expected to result from the improved market structure. It may turn out that the costs exceed the benefits, and that the economy would be better off living with the present inefficiency of the monopoly instead of compounding the problem with antitrust actions.

Questions for discussion

☐ What are the critical elements in determining whether a company has monopolized or attempted to monopolize a market?

☐ How important is size alone? Does a dominant position in the market constitute a monopoly?

☐ Classical economic theory holds that monopolists can price goods at any level they choose because they face no effective competition. What does the pricing history of the computer industry tell you about the amount of competition in the industry?

☐ Should a company such as IBM be considered an illegal monopoly if it continues to sell better-quality products more cheaply than it sold less-sophisticated products earlier? If a company is so superior that it naturally dominates the industry, should it automatically be illegal? Why or why not?

Part VII

Price and Employment in the Resource Market

Chapter 28

Demand in the Resource Market

What to look for in this chapter

How is demand calculated in the resource market?

What are the consequences of imperfect competition in the resource market?

How does a firm determine its optimal resource mix?

What are the determinants of resource demand?

How does the concept of elasticity apply to resource demand?

As we saw in Chapter 4, the exchanges made in product markets are only one-half of the mechanism of our circular flow system. Equally important are the exchanges made in the resource, or factor, markets in which factors of production (or input resources) owned by households are sold to businesses. The prices that households can obtain for their productive resources in the resource market determine their incomes and hence their ability to buy the products of business.

In turn, the number of units traded in resource markets and the price of those units determine the costs of production, the level of output, and the price of the final product in the product markets. Because a firm's supply curve is actually the marginal cost of producing various amounts (Chapter 23), we can see that supply is directly affected by prices in the resource market. The ability of a firm to produce is also limited by the amount of input resources it can purchase.

Table 28.1
Resource demand: perfect competition in the product market

(1) Units of resource (labor)	(2) Total product (TP) (output per day)	(3) Marginal physical product MPP = ΔTP	(4) Product price* (P)	(5) Total revenue (TR) TR = TP × P	(6) Marginal revenue product (MRP) MRP = ΔTR
0	0		$10	$ 0	
		20			$200
1	20		10	200	
		19			190
2	39		10	390	
		17			170
3	56		10	560	
		15			150
4	71		10	710	
		13			130
5	84		10	840	
		12			120
6	96		10	960	
		10			100
7	106		10	1060	
		8			80
8	114		10	1140	
		6			60
9	120		10	1200	
		4			40
10	124		10	1240	
		2			20
11	126		10	1260	
		0			0
12	126		10	1260	
		−2			−20
13	124		10	1240	

*Since this is a perfectly competitive product market, the price of each unit sold will always be the same.

In this chapter, we will see that the concepts of demand discussed in Chapter 23 (perfect competition in the product market) are equally applicable to the resource market. Using those concepts, we will calculate a demand schedule that shows the quantities of an input that businesses will be willing and able to purchase at various prices. In addition, we will examine other aspects of resource demand such as the determinants of resource demand, its elasticity, and how business firms determine the optimum resource mix for the production of their particular product.

CALCULATING RESOURCE DEMAND

We will begin our discussion of resource demand by showing how an individual business firm determines its demand for a single factor of production. In our example, the factor will be labor; the business firm will be Super Studs.

Super Studs is a company that manufactures decorative metal studs that can be fastened to clothes, furniture, picture frames, or anything else in need of decoration. The company has already invested in a fixed amount of capital such as a factory, the machinery that stamps out the metal studs, and offices for its executives. We will assume that Super Studs operates under conditions of perfect competition and is therefore unable to influence either the market price of its studs or the market price of workers in its neighborhood.

Marginal revenue product

Super Studs' demand for labor will be determined by two factors:

☐ How many studs each additional worker is able to make (productivity), which is measured by the **marginal physical product (MPP)**, *the change in total output brought about by a change in one unit of a variable factor of production* (in our example, one worker). It is the change in total output divided by the change in the number of units of the variable factor. The MPP of additional workers employed by Super Studs is shown in column 3 of *Table 28.1*.

☐ The value of these additional studs, given the present market price, which is measured by the **marginal revenue product (MRP)**, *the change in total revenue that results from the addition of one unit of a variable factor of production.* It is the change in total revenue divided by the change in the number of units of the variable factor. Column 6 in *Table 28.1* shows the MRP for each additional worker hired by Super Studs.

If the factory has no workers at all, its output, or total product (TP), will be zero. When one worker is hired, the factory can produce 20 units of studs. Therefore, the marginal physical product of the first worker is 20 units. With the addition of this worker, total revenue changes from $0 to $200; therefore, the MRP is $200.

When another worker is hired, the factory can turn out 39 units of studs. The MPP of the second worker is 19 units, and because these 19 units result in a $190 increase in total revenue (from $200 to $390), the MRP of the second worker is $190. When the factory employs a

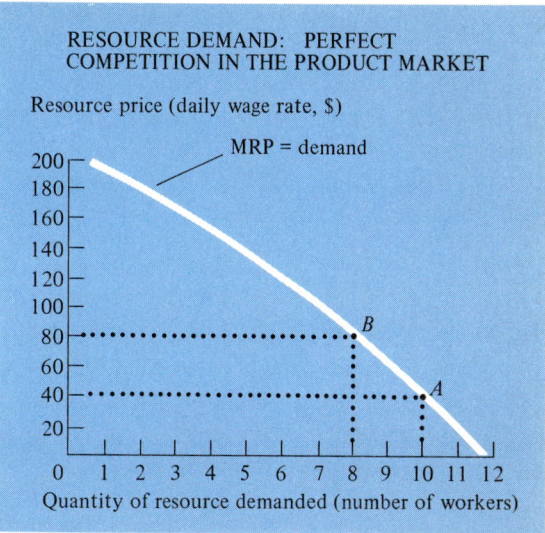

Fig. 28.1
Resource demand is a function of the marginal revenue product (MRP) of the input resources. Due to the law of diminishing marginal returns, the MRP of each additional unit declines; the first worker has an MRP of $200; the MRP of the twelfth worker is zero. The firm will hire workers up to the point where marginal revenue product equals marginal resource cost. For example, if the wage rate (MRC) is $40 a day, Super Studs will hire 10 workers (point *A*). If the wage rate is $80 a day, Super Studs will hire 8 workers, the quantity at which MRC equals MRP (point *B*).

twelfth worker, total product is the same as it is when 11 workers are employed. This means that the MPP of the twelfth worker is zero, and hiring that worker will have no effect on the total revenue of the company. If a thirteenth worker is hired, both the MPP and the MRP will be negative, since the plant will be overflowing with workers who crowd each other, thus impairing their productivity.

When we plot the MRP data in *Table 28.1* we end up with the MRP curve shown in *Fig. 28.1*.

MPP, MRP, and the law of diminishing returns

When we look at column 3 of *Table 28.1* (MPP), we see a constant decline in MPP as more workers are added. This seems to indicate that each new worker hired is less efficient than those already working for the company, but this is not so: marginal physical product is not an evaluation of the efficiency of the individual units of input. MPP declines because of the effect of the law of diminishing returns, which (as you will recall from Chapter 2) states that the addition of successive equal amounts of a variable factor of production to a fixed factor of production will result in a smaller and smaller increase in output. The sixth worker may be as knowledgeable and fast as the first worker. Yet the MPP will inevitably decline when the sixth worker is hired because the amount of fixed resources each worker has to work with will decline. As MPP declines, the MRP of each worker declines as well (see column 6, *Table 28.1*). This is reflected in the MRP curve which slopes downward to the right.

The demand curve for resources

The MRP curve in *Fig. 28.1* which shows the MRP of additional units of labor is actually Super Studs' demand curve for labor. To understand why $D = MRP$ in the resource market, we must recall our discussion of profit maximization in product markets: we noted that in terms of production, the point of profit maximization will be reached when the marginal cost of production equals the marginal revenue. The formula $MC = MR$ can also be applied to a firm's level of resource use.

In order to maximize its total profits, a business firm will continue to add one more unit of a resource as long as the cost of acquiring the resource (marginal resource cost, MRC) is smaller than the additional revenue that the resource can produce (MRP). Profits will be maximized when a firm employs resources to the point where $MRC = MRP$. Since we are dealing with a perfectly competitive resource market, the MRC will be equal to the wage rate, just as marginal revenue equals price in a perfectly competitive product market.

Thus, if the daily wage rate (MRC) at Super Studs is $40 per day, Super Studs will hire ten workers because, according to *Table 28.1*, it is at the tenth worker that the worker's MRC is equal to MRP. This equilibrium point is shown as point A in *Fig. 28.1*. Super Studs will not hire an eleventh worker because this worker's MRP ($20) is less than his or her MRC ($40).

Thus, the MRP curve indicates the firm's demand for a resource (here, labor) because it shows the number of workers the firm is willing and able to hire at various prices (here, wage rates). The demand curve for labor inputs, like all other demand curves, slopes downward and to the right. All other things equal, the company can be induced to hire an additional worker only by a

---

RECAP

RESOURCE DEMAND is determined by that resource's marginal revenue product (MRP). Due to the law of diminishing returns, the MRP curve slopes downward and to the right. The MRP curve of a resource is also the demand curve for that resource—it shows the number of resource units a firm is willing to hire at various prices. In order to maximize profits, a firm will employ units of a resource up to the point where its marginal cost (marginal resource cost, MRC) equal its MRP. A firm will achieve its optimum resource mix when it has hired resources to the point where the $\frac{MRP}{P}$ of one resource equals the $\frac{MRP}{P}$ of all other resources being employed.

Table 28.2
Resource demand: imperfect competition in the product market

(1) Units of resource (labor)	(2) Total product (TP) (output per day)	(3) Marginal physical product MPP = ΔTP	(4) Product price (P)	(5) Total revenue (TR) TR = TP × P	(6) Marginal revenue product (MRP) MRP = ΔTR
0	0		—	$ 0	
		20			$300
1	20		$15	300	
		19			246
2	39		14	546	
		17			182
3	56		13	728	
		15			124
4	71		12	852	
		13			72
5	84		11	924	
		12			36
6	96		10	960	
		10			−6
7	106		9	954	
		8			−42
8	114		8	912	
		6			−72
9	120		7	840	
		4			−96
10	124		6	744	
		2			−114
11	126		5	630	

decrease in the market price of labor resources, just as would be the case in the product market. The quantity of input resources demanded will increase as the price of the resources decreases.

Market demand
To obtain the market demand curve for labor, we add the demand curves established for all individual firms in the market. This gives us an approximate answer. It is not exact, because if all firms in the market buy more resources when the price is low and use them to increase their current production, the total product supply will increase, causing a change in the equilibrium level of price on the product market. The market price of the product will decline; this will mean a change in the MRP and therefore a change in the demand schedule for resources. Thus, industry demand is not exactly equal to the sum of all individual demand curves.

Resource demand in imperfectly competitive markets
Our analysis so far has been based on the assumption of perfect competition in the market for the business firm's product. But what if the firm buying the resources is an imperfect competitor?

Competitive imperfections in the product market will cause the MRP schedule to fall at an even faster rate than it falls in a perfectly competitive market. The schedule shown in *Table 28.1* assumes that product price is constant, that the firm can sell any quantity of goods it desires at the going market price. But in the case of imperfect competition, the quantity of a good sold can be increased only by lowering the price of the good. (As we saw in Chapters 25 and 26, imperfect competitors always have a declining marginal revenue curve.)

Table 28.2 shows the effect of imperfect competition in the product market on a firm's

MRP. Note that each successive unit of the product is sold at a lower price than the previous unit. Thus, when we determine MRP for an imperfect competitor, we are multiplying a declining MPP by a declining price, and MRP will show a much faster decline for an imperfect competitor than it does for a perfect competitor.

Monopsonistic market power

There may also be competitive imperfections in the market for resources similar to those of a monopoly in the product market. If the sellers of a resource acquire enough market power to influence the quantity of resources sold or the market price of the resources, the situation will be similar to the kinds of imperfect competition regarding the product market we discussed in Chapters 25 and 26. An alternative possibility is that resource market power may be held by the buyers of resources—the business firms that purchase land, labor, and capital. This type of market situation, as you will recall from Chapter 27, is called a monopsony.

In the American economy, large business firms often possess some degree of monopsonistic power, especially in towns and small cities, where one firm employs most of the available labor force. Workers are faced with the choice of working for the monopsonistic firm at wages lower than those on the fully competitive resource market, or not working at all. Some economists call this exploitation of labor. In economic usage, a resource is being exploited when its market price is lower than its MRP.

Figure 28.2 shows the effects of monopsony in the labor market. Like all business firms, the monopsonist will determine how many workers to hire by finding the point at which the MRP of workers intersects with the marginal resource cost of their purchase. But monopsonists do not face the perfectly elastic supply curve that the perfect competitor faces. Instead, they face the somewhat inelastic curve of market supply—to attract more workers, they must pay higher wages to all workers, even those who would have worked for less pay. Thus, marginal costs rise with each worker hired.

Monopsonists hire at the level where MRP equals MRC. But they fix wages at the point where

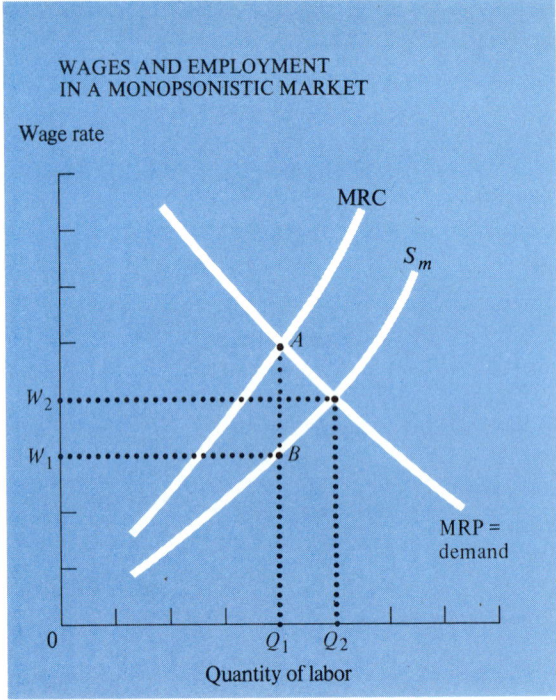

Fig. 28.2
Monopsony in the resource market causes the marginal resource cost line to be upward sloping instead of horizontal as it is in the perfectly competitive market. Monopsonists will hire workers up to the point where MRC equals MRP (point A on the graph); that is, they will hire Q_1 workers, but they will fix wages at W_1, the point where the quantity of workers they demand intersects the market supply curve (point B). Not only is the number of workers hired lower than it would be in perfect competition (Q_1 instead of Q_2), the wage level is lower than the market equilibrium wage rate (W_2). Workers therefore receive a wage lower than the MRP they produce.

the quantity of workers they demand intersects with the supply curve. This exploits the workers, because it means that they receive wages that are lower than the MRP they produce.

OPTIMUM RESOURCE MIX FOR THE FIRM

Because a business firm is interested in maximizing profits, and because of the law of diminishing returns, it is important for a company to use the right proportion of all resources in its production process. The marginal revenue product schedule for each input resource can help the managers of business firms decide on the **optimum resource mix,** *the best combination of input resources to use in the production of a commodity.*

The firm achieves the optimum resource mix when the MRP from the last dollar spent to purchase each resource is exactly equal to the MRP per last dollar spent on every other resource. A business firm purchasing input resources is much like a household purchasing consumer goods, where optimum allocation of funds can be achieved through the equal marginal utility principle (see Chapter 21).

For a business firm, the marginal value of each worker would be expressed as his or her marginal revenue product. The formula would be:

$$\frac{\text{MRP of labor resource}}{\text{Price of labor resource}} = \frac{\text{MRP of land resource}}{\text{Price of land resource}}$$

or

$$\frac{\text{MRP}_1}{P_1} = \frac{\text{MRP}_2}{P_2}.$$

When the last dollar spent to purchase one resource yields the same MRP as the last dollar spent to purchase every other resource, the firm has achieved the best possible allocation of its funds. No change in the quantity of any resource purchased could increase the efficiency of production.

When $\frac{\text{MRP}_1}{P_1}$ is greater than $\frac{\text{MRP}_2}{P_2}$ the company can increase its total MRP by reallocating its funds to buy more of Resource 1 and less of Resource 2. As less money is spent on the purchase of units of Resource 2, its MRP rises. As dollars are added toward the purchase of additional units of Resource 1, its MRP declines. Eventually, the two ratios will be equal, and maximum efficiency of production will be achieved.

DETERMINANTS OF DEMAND FOR PRODUCTIVE RESOURCES

Before we begin our discussion of the determinants of resource demand, it is important to point out that the demand for a resource is a **derived demand**; that is, *resource demand is based on the demand for the finished products that can be manufactured with the resource.* Consolidated Edison does not buy a new generator (productive resource) simply because company executives value its utility, but because the generator enables Consolidated Edison to produce the amount of power demanded by consumers in the product market at the lowest possible cost to the company. The demand for products, on the other hand, is a direct demand. A household demands an electric grill because it values the utility and satisfaction obtained from it more than it values the utility and satisfaction that could be obtained from any alternative purchase made with the same amount of money.

In the following sections, we will examine some of the specific determinants of demand in the factor market. A change in any of these factors will cause a change in the level of demand and therefore a shift in the entire demand curve. (It might be helpful to review the determinants of product demand discussed in Chapter 3.)

Level of product demand

Because resource demand is derived, any change in the demand for a product will bring a change in

> **RECAP**
> The demand for any resource is derived from the demand for the finished products that can be manufactured with the resource. Other DETERMINANTS OF RESOURCE DEMAND include the resource's productivity and the prices of substitutable and complementary resources. The quantity of a resource demanded can also show varying degrees of response to price changes (elasticity). The elasticity of resource demand is influenced by the rate at which the resource's MRP declines, the elasticity of demand for the final product, resource substitutability, and the percent of total cost that is accounted for by the resource.

the demand for the resources needed to produce the product. For example, scientific research regarding possible harmful effects of sugar substitutes could cause a drop in the demand for low-calorie soft drinks. This drop in product demand would then cause a corresponding drop in the demand for the raw materials used by chemical companies to formulate sugar substitutes. Because some consumers would switch to other low-calorie beverages, such as iced tea, there might also be a drop in the demand for aluminum used in the cans in which soft drinks are sold. Demand for soft-drink-producing machines and other capital goods used in the industry would also decline as would the number of workers demanded by soft-drink manufacturers.

Many labor unions are also aware of the implications of the connection between the level of demand for a product and the derived demand for productive resources. If the union can help producers in the market expand the demand for products, then the union can reap the benefits—in new jobs and higher wages—of the corresponding increase in the derived demand for labor resources.

Some labor leaders also recognize that prolonged strikes may lead many demanders to switch to substitute products, and will therefore lead to decreased product demand. This, in turn, will eventually be reflected in decreased derived demand for labor.

Productivity of resources

The quantity of a productive resource demanded will also depend on the productivity of the resource. Generally speaking, the most productive resources are in the greatest demand, since they perform most efficiently and produce the largest addition to total product per dollar spent on the resource. Thus, any change in a resource's productivity will bring a change in the demand for that resource.

Technology plays a key role in introducing changes in productivity, and scientists and engineers are constantly experimenting to discover better ways to use and combine the productive resources we have. Entrepreneurial skills also help determine a resource's productivity, for it is up to the manager to decide on the best and most efficient way to combine resources. For example, a firm that has failed to buy the necessary stock of capital goods may find that its resources of labor and raw materials are relatively unproductive. The productivity of labor increases greatly when well-educated and trained workers are equipped with the proper tools, have enough space in which to work comfortably, and have a steady flow of the necessary raw materials.

Price of substitutable and complementary resources

The business firm, in its effort to maximize total profit, is constantly seeking to cut costs of production and will choose the combination of input resources with the minimum cost. The demand for any one resource, therefore, will be affected not only by the price of other substitutable resources, but also by the prices of other resources which are complementary.

We can see the mechanism of factor substitution at work in automated industries. In most cases, automation comes as a response to the rising prices of labor resources. As wages of workers rise, business managers begin to look into the possibility of developing substitutes for the expensive labor input. By purchasing the capital goods needed for automation, they are able to substitute capital for labor and reduce the total cost of production. This substitution would seem to cause a decrease in the demand for labor, but some people claim that technological progress does not reduce the total demand for labor, since it will be accompanied by an increase in the demand for labor in capital goods industries.

ELASTICITY OF DEMAND

Demand in the resource market may show varying degrees of elasticity, just as demand in the product market does (see Chapter 20). In the following section we will briefly discuss what factors determine the elasticity of demand for a given resource.

Rate of decline of MRP

One factor that influences elasticity of demand for resource inputs is the rate at which MRP declines. If MRP declines sharply with the addition of each worker, resource demand will be relatively inelastic; that is, a percentage change in the price of a resource will result in a smaller percentage change in the quantity demanded. To understand the connection between sharply declining MRP and elasticity of demand, look at *Fig. 28.3(a)*. It shows a situation in which MRP drops sharply. The third worker hired produces an MRP of $20 a day, but a fourth produces only $5 a day. The company faced with this MRP schedule would hire three workers if the cost of labor was $20 a day, but after that point, even a small decline in price (say to $19 or $15) would not alter the company's hiring plans because the MRC (the wage of $19 or $15) would be greater than the worker's MRP ($5).

The wage rate (price of the resource) would have to drop to $5 a day in order to induce the company to hire an additional worker. Thus, a 75 percent decrease in wages (from $20 to $5 a day) would result in an increase of only 33 percent in the quantity of labor demanded (from three to four workers). Because the percentage change in quantity demanded (33 percent) is less than the percent change in price (75 percent), this firm's demand for labor is inelastic.

Figure 28.3(b) shows the MRP schedule of a firm whose demand for inputs is relatively elastic. That is, a percentage change in the price of a resource will lead to a greater percentage change in the quantity of the resource demanded. Here, the rate of decline in MRP is much slower than that shown in *Fig. 28.3(a)*—the addition of one more worker (from 6 to 7), for example, results in only a $1 decline in MRP (as opposed to the $15 decline in MRP caused by the addition of a fourth worker in *Fig. 28.3(a)*.

Thus, a 5 percent decrease in wages (from $20 to $19 a day) will induce the company to hire a seventh worker, an increase in quantity demanded of 17 percent. Because the change in quantity demanded (17 percent) is greater than the change in price (5 percent), this firm's demand for labor is elastic. The principle is the slower the rate of decline in MRP, the more elastic the resource demand will be.

Imperfect competition and the rate of MRP decline

As we discussed earlier, an imperfect competitor's MRP declines at a faster rate than that of a perfect competitor. Therefore, we can conclude that an imperfect competitor's demand for resources will be more inelastic than a perfect competitor's. In other words, when the price of a resource falls, imperfect competitors are reluctant to buy more resources and expand their production. This behavior is in keeping with the general characteristics of imperfect competitors, who always artificially restrict output in some way in order to

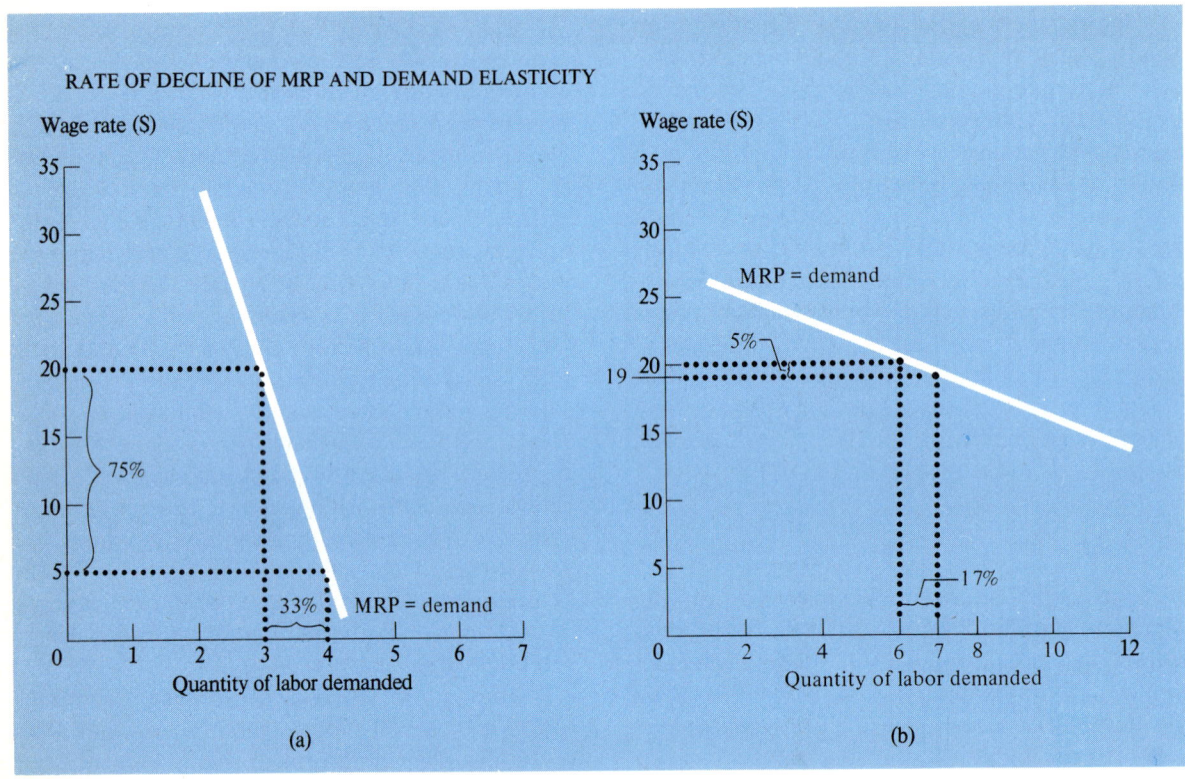

Fig. 28.3
In (a) we see the resource demand curve for a firm with a relatively inelastic demand for labor. The price of labor must drop by 75 percent from $20 to $5 a day before the firm will respond by hiring a fourth worker (a 33 percent increase in quantity demanded). Because the percentage change in price is greater than the percentage change in quantity demanded, demand is inelastic. In (b) we see a firm with a relatively elastic resource demand. A small change in the price of labor (here, a 5 percent decrease from $20 to $19) will bring a larger percentage change in the number of labor units the company will buy (here, a 17 percent increase from six workers to seven workers). Because the percentage change in price is smaller than the percentage change in quantity demanded, demand is elastic.

maximize profits. Inelasticity of resource demand is an aspect of this limitation of output.

Elasticity of demand for the final product

The elasticity of demand for resource inputs is also closely linked to the elasticity of demand for the product for which the resources are used. If demand for the product is very elastic, a small percent change in price will cause a larger percent change in the quantity the company can sell. The level of output will change significantly, and this change will require a change in the demand for productive resources as well. For instance, in Chapter 20, we cited insulin as an example of a good with an inelastic demand; the demand for factors used to produce insulin would therefore be inelastic also.

Resource substitutability

Another factor that determines degree of demand elasticity for a productive resource is the number of adequate substitutes there are for the resource. A cloth manufacturer, for example, may use wool, cotton, linen, or any of the large number of synthetic fibers as raw materials. If the price of cotton suddenly doubled, cloth manufacturers could switch to a synthetic fiber that could be made into a cloth that is an adequate substitute for cotton cloth. Therefore, the resource demand for cotton would be relatively elastic in the cotton industry. On the other hand, the demand for cotton in the gauze-bandage industry is much more inelastic. No other fiber yet known has the softness, the absorptive power, and the fibrous texture that promotes blood clotting; thus, a synthetic-fiber bandage would not be an adequate substitute for a cotton-gauze bandage. Thus, the demand for cotton in the bandage industry will be inelastic—bandage-makers will go on demanding about the same quantity of cotton, in spite of drastic changes in the price of cotton.

Resource cost as a percentage of total production cost

A final factor influencing the elasticity of demand for a resource is the percentage of total costs the purchase of that resource represents. For example, imagine what would happen in a labor-intensive industry if the price of labor went up. Since labor is the largest cost of production, the increase in the price of labor would probably force firms to charge more for their product. As the product price rose, the quantity of product demanded would decrease. The manufacturers would have to cut back their total output and, therefore, also cut back their purchase of input resources. In this instance, the quantity of labor demanded would be highly responsive to the change in the price of labor (demand for labor would be elastic). If, on the other hand, the same industry had been faced with an increase in the price of a particular raw material that represented only a small fraction of their total production costs, it would not have needed such a large increase in product price to afford the additional cost. There would be little change in product demand and, consequently, little change in the demand for input resources other than labor (demand would be inelastic).

Summary

■ This chapter explores aspects of demand in the resource market: how demand is calculated, the optimum mix of resources for an individual firm, the determinants of demand, and elasticity and inelasticity.

■ The number of additional units of output produced by adding one more unit of an input is called the input's marginal physical product (MPP). MPP falls as each additional unit of the input is added because of the law of diminishing returns. The marginal revenue product (MRP) is the amount of revenue obtained from the sale of the output produced by one more unit of input; that is, the change in total revenue due to the addition of one more unit of input. When MRP is plotted on a graph, the resulting curve slopes downward and to the right. The firm will continue to purchase additional units of the input until a resource's MRP is equal to its marginal resource cost (the cost of adding another unit of input). At this point, the firm will be maximizing its profits. Because the MRP curve reflects the number of resource units a firm will hire at various costs, the MRP curve is actually the firm's demand curve for that resource. A firm achieves its optimum resource mix when the MRP of the last dollar spent for each different resource input is equal.

■ Demand in the resource market is said to be derived, not direct, since it is dependent on demand for the firm's output in the product market. A change in the demand curve for resources may occur because of changes in demand in the product market, changes in the productivity of resource inputs, or changes in the prices of substitutable or complementary resources.

■ If the MRP of an input declines rapidly (as it does in an imperfectly competitive market), demand for that input is said to be inelastic; that is, a percentage change in the price of that input will lead to a smaller percentage change in the quantity of the input demanded. The slower the decline, the more elastic the resource demand. Resource demand elasticity is also related directly to elasticity of demand for the final product and to the availability of resource substitutes. For example, if substitutes are readily available, demand for a particular input will be elastic. Finally, elasticity is affected by the proportion of total cost accounted for by the particular input. If the cost of the resource is a large portion of the total cost of production, demand will be relatively elastic. If the cost of the resource is a minor part of total cost, demand will be relatively inelastic.

Key Terms

marginal physical product (MPP)

marginal revenue product (MRP)

optimum resource mix

derived demand

Review & Discussion

1. Define marginal physical product. How is the marginal physical product related to the marginal revenue product?

2. How does the firm decide on the quantity of a particular resource to be purchased?

3. Draw an MRP curve, a supply curve, and an MRC curve for a monopsonist. What price will a monopsonist pay for the input? How does this condition differ from that of a perfect competitor on the resource market? How does an economist define exploitation in a technical sense? Why would a monopsonist tend to exploit inputs to a greater extent if the firm also had monopoly power?

4. How does a firm determine its optimum resource mix?

5. Why is the demand for factors of production considered to be a derived demand? How is it affected by the level of demand for final products? By the productivity of resource inputs? By the price of substitutes?

6. What factors affect elasticity of demand for a particular input? What is the effect of a sharp downward slope in the marginal revenue product curve?

7. Suppose that the marginal physical product for the production of kitchen sinks is shown by the following schedule. If each sink sells for $46, what is the marginal revenue product schedule? What is the company's demand curve for labor?

Number of workers	Sinks produced per week	MPP	Price	Total revenue	MRP
0	0	7	$46		
1	7	6			
2	13	5			
3	18	4			
4	22	3			
5	25	2			
6	27	1			
7	28	0			
8	28				

8. How many workers would the above company hire if the going rate for labor was $100 a week? Why?

9. Suppose now that the sink company is an imperfect competitor in the product market. The first sink can be sold for $55, but the price will drop by 50¢ for each additional sink the firm tries to sell. Using the same schedule for MPP, figure the new MRP schedule, and draw a new demand curve for labor. How does it differ from the previous curve?

10. How does a firm determine its optimum resource mix?

Chapter 29

Supply in the Resource Market

What to look for in this chapter

What factors influence supply in the resource market?

How are wages determined in the resource market for labor?

How does the price system allocate the fixed supply of land? How does land differ from other factors in the resource market?

What determines the supply of financial capital?

In the last chapter, we discussed the various factors that influence and determine the demand for resources. Now we are going to examine how the supply of resources (specifically, labor, land, and financial capital) is determined.

The law of supply governs behavior in the resource market, just as it does in the product market. Households supply businesses with the productive resources of land, labor, and financial capital, and the quantity they are willing to supply depends on the price offered for the resource. In general, we can assume that the higher the market price of resources, the more resources will be supplied to buyers of productive factors.

SUPPLY OF LABOR

Because current national accounts indicate that wages constitute about 65 percent of total national income, we can conclude that the labor market is the largest and most important of the resource markets. There are over 100 million suppliers in the American labor market (the size of the total labor force). In addition, there are millions of other potential suppliers—homemakers, retired people still able to work, people who have incomes from rent, interest, or government transfer payments (such as Social Security) adequate for their needs— who might be induced to enter the market by an increase in wages.

Supply schedule for a single individual

In order to arrive at the market supply of labor, we must first analyze the supply schedule for one individual worker. How does the worker decide how much labor he or she is willing to supply at various market prices?

It is important to realize at this point that the quantity of labor supplied does not necessarily increase as prices increase. This is an important difference between supply in the resource market and supply in the product market.

In the product market, we assume that supplying business firms are motivated by the desire to maximize profit. All supply decisions will therefore be made solely on the basis of prices—the market price of the goods, the price of needed productive resources, the market price of the same inputs if they were devoted to some alternative use. But in the factor market the suppliers are households, and although they make their decisions on the basis of self-interest, they do not necessarily equate self-interest with profit maximization. Because people may value satisfaction in their work or leisure time more highly than they value additional income, they may turn down the opportunity to earn more money for their labor. For example, a corporation executive may turn down a promotion that would mean a move to the home office because the family is so deeply rooted in its present location, or a person with a master's degree in business may turn down lucrative offers from giant corporations and accept a job at a lower salary with a pollution-control firm because she feels that she can make a more valuable contribution to society. Workers are not automatically willing to supply labor to the highest bidder. Nor are they always willing to supply all the labor that they can, whatever the price. They are faced with a choice of economic goods and can choose between income and leisure, or income and independence, or income and job satisfaction.

Indifference analysis

In analyzing the way people decide how much labor to supply, economists have found the concept of indifference curves a useful tool. In Chapter 21, we used indifference curves to plot the choice a consumer makes between one good and another. Indifference curves can also be used to plot the choice a worker makes between income and some other economic good.

Let us look at the hypothetical case of an individual worker, Leroy Faunt, the machinist. To simplify our analysis, we will assume for the moment that Leroy's only choice is between income and leisure. *Figure 29.1(a)* shows Leroy's indifference curve for these two goods. All the points on this curve represent combinations of income and leisure that would yield Leroy equal satisfaction. Fifty dollars of income and three hours of leisure appear just as satisfying to him as $30 of income and seven hours of leisure—he is indifferent to choosing between them.

By offering Leroy choices involving larger quantities of both income and leisure, we can derive other indifference curves for him. *Figure 29.1(b)* shows Leroy's indifference map—a succession of indifference curves. This is just like the consumer indifference map we constructed in Chapter 21.

Line of wage constraint

To determine the combination of goods that a consumer will actually buy, we introduced the line of budget constraint on the indifference map; this

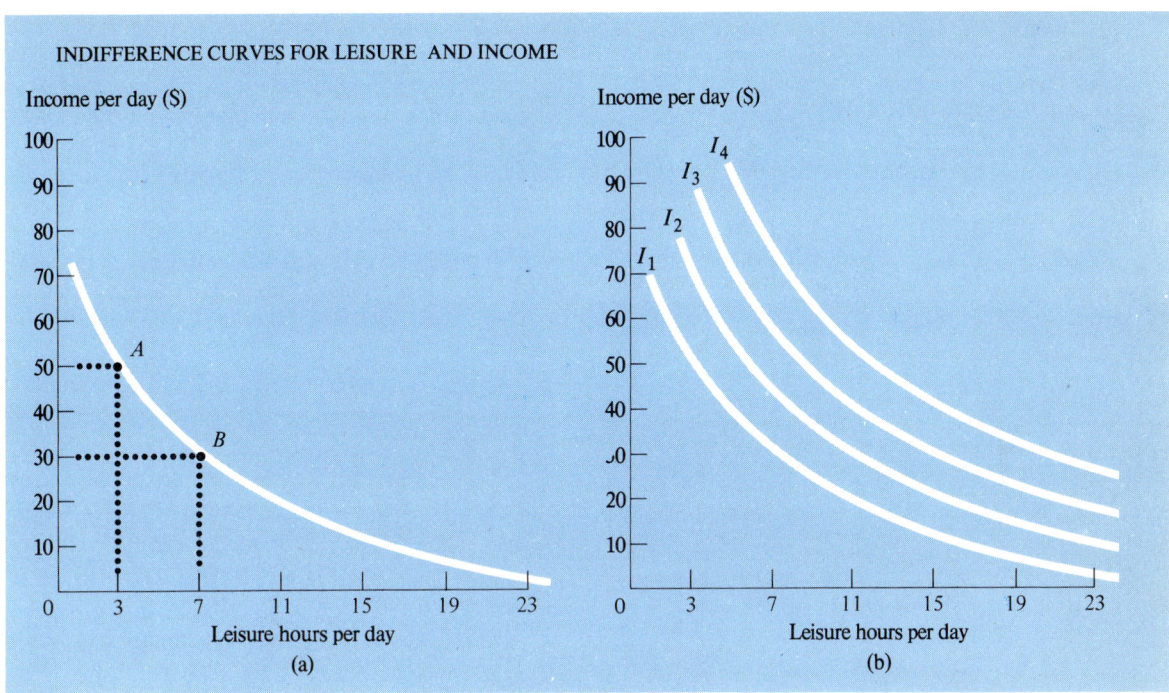

Fig. 29.1
Any combination of the two economic goods of income and leisure that lies on the indifference curve shown in (a) would be as satisfying to Leroy as any other combination. He is indifferent toward the combinations of work and leisure represented by point A ($50 a day, three hours of leisure), point B ($30 a day, seven hours of leisure), and all other points on this indifference curve. Part (b) shows Leroy's indifference map for leisure and income, that is, a succession of indifference curves that offer Leroy larger quantities of both income and leisure.

shows what the actual consumption possibilities are, given a fixed level of income. For the labor supplier's indifference map, the line of constraint is not due to budget but to wages. The wage rate tells us the rate at which Leroy can transform an hour of leisure into money income. Suppose the going wage for machinists is $1 an hour; the resulting wage constraint line is drawn in *Fig. 29.2*. This line shows all the various combinations of leisure or income from labor that Leroy could obtain in a given period (in this case one day). The point at which this wage constraint line is tangent to (that is, touches) the highest possible indifference curve shows the optimum choice for Leroy. This point occurs at point A, at which Leroy chooses $4 of income (4 hours of labor) and 20 hours of leisure.

Plotting the supply curve
Using this information, we can calculate one point on Leroy's supply of labor curve. If the price of labor is $1 an hour, he will be willing to supply 4

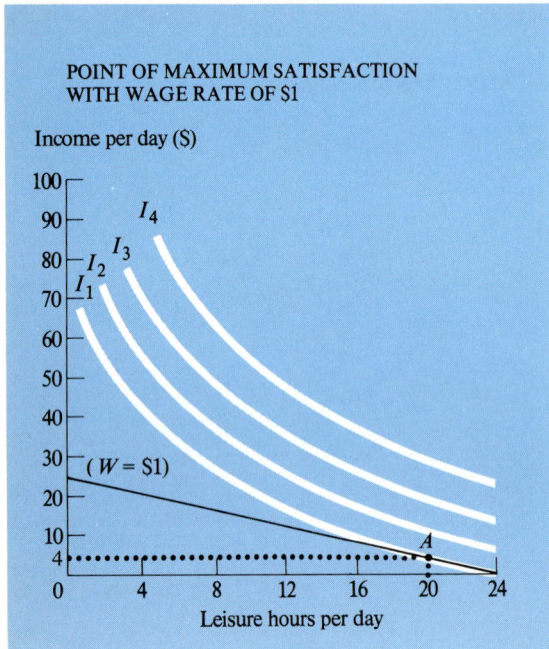

POINT OF MAXIMUM SATISFACTION WITH WAGE RATE OF $1

Fig. 29.2
When we add a line of wage constraint to Leroy's indifference map, we can determine the actual combination of income and leisure that is available to him at a given wage level. If the wage rate is $1 an hour, Leroy will be willing to supply 4 hours of labor for an income of $4 and will enjoy 20 hours of leisure. This combination (4 hours labor, 20 hours leisure) is the point at which Leroy's wage constraint line is tangent to (that is, touches) one of his indifference curves (I_1).

hours (24 hours in a day minus 20 hours of leisure equals 4 hours of labor). By drawing other wage constraint lines at different wage rates and imposing them on his indifference map, as shown in *Fig. 29.3*, we can then determine the amount of labor Leroy will supply at other possible wage rates. When we plot points A, B, C, and D from Leroy's indifference maps on a graph which measures the number of hours Leroy will work at various wage rates, we have derived his supply of labor curve (shown in *Fig. 29.4*).

The backward-bending supply curve
Note that the supply curve we have drawn for Leroy's labor has the standard upward-sloping shape that we have found in all other supply curves. However, economists hypothesize that if we were to extend the schedule to include even

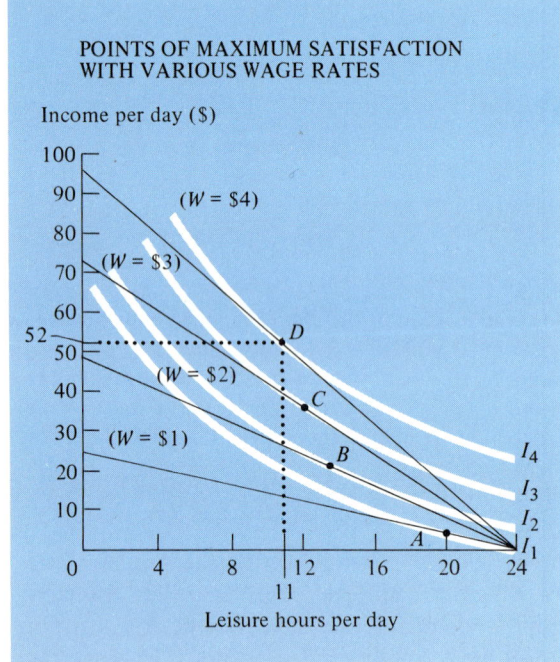

POINTS OF MAXIMUM SATISFACTION WITH VARIOUS WAGE RATES

Fig. 29.3
Other combinations of income and leisure are available to Leroy at a variety of wage levels. If wage levels rise to $4 an hour, Leroy can move to the highest indifference curve shown, I_4; at point D, he will work 13 hours a day, earning $52, and take 11 hours a day in leisure.

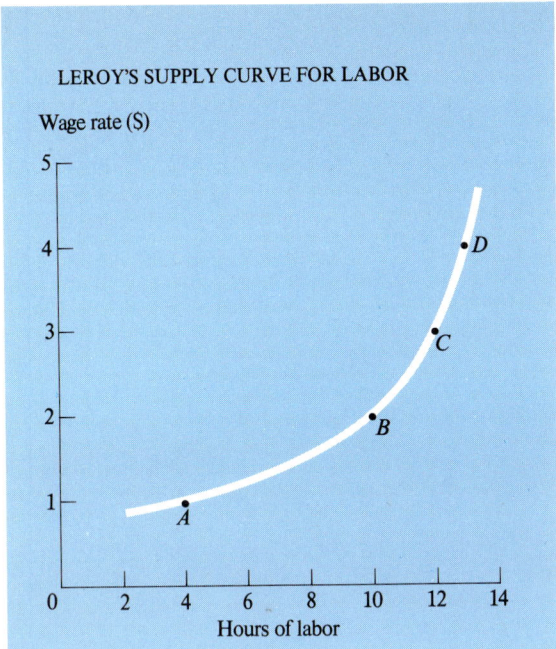

Fig. 29.4
By calculating the number of hours of labor that Leroy is willing to supply at each of the wage rates shown in Fig. 29.3, we can derive his supply curve for labor.

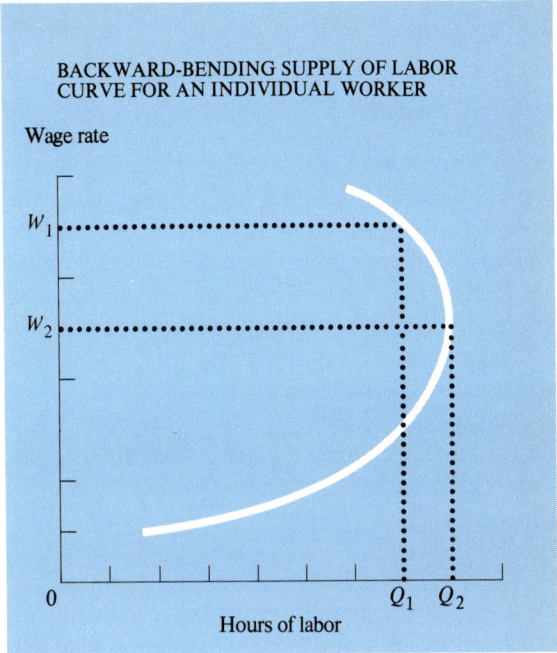

Fig. 29.5
The backward-bending supply curve is shown for an individual worker. If wage rates rise above a certain level (for example, to W_1), the worker will begin to choose more leisure, since the income that can be earned from a small number of hours of work will provide a comfortable standard of living. The number of hours of labor the worker is willing to supply at the higher wage (Q_1 hours at W_1) is fewer than the number of hours he or she is willing to supply at a lower wage (Q_2 hours at W_2).

higher wage levels, we would find that the curve would start to bend back toward the left. This would indicate that after a point, Leroy would not be willing to supply more hours of labor even at higher wages. Suppose, for example, that Leroy could earn $50 an hour. With only a few hours' work a day, he could earn enough to be able to afford a high standard of living for himself and his family. It is likely that he would become less willing to supply a full day's labor and would prefer instead to spend the afternoon splashing around in his swimming pool. His choice can easily be explained in terms of the concept of marginal utility.

When wages are very high, a few hours of work will give Leroy a large income. He has an abundant supply of money, but his free time is still limited. So he values the extra units of relatively scarce leisure more highly than he values the extra units of relatively abundant income.

Figure 29.5 shows the backward-bending supply curve for labor. The shape of this supply curve suggests that, from business's point of view, there is an optimum wage level that should not be exceeded. To raise wages beyond that level would actually decrease the total supply of labor.*

The market supply curve
We can establish the market supply curve for labor by adding all the individual curves that are the result of choices between income and other economic goods. There will be one difference, however: the market supply curve for labor will probably be positively sloped throughout because (1) not all workers' supply curves bend backward at the same time; and (2) while some people will choose to work shorter hours, most people will work more if wages increase.

WAGE DETERMINATION

By imposing the market supply curve onto a market demand curve for labor, we can see what the price (wage) for labor will be and how many hours of work will actually be bought and sold at that wage. This equilibrium level is shown in *Fig. 29.6*.

The market supply and demand concepts imply that all workers will be paid exactly the same wages, but we know from experience that wages vary widely. A student who delivers flowers after school for a florist may earn $2.75 an hour. By contrast, it is not unusual for executives in corporations to earn more than $80,000 a year, which is about $40 an hour. The difference in the wages that workers are able to obtain is determined by the level and quality of their skills.

The role of skills
Many different kinds of skills are needed for the processes of production. Some of these skills, such as the ability to move a series of levers on an as-

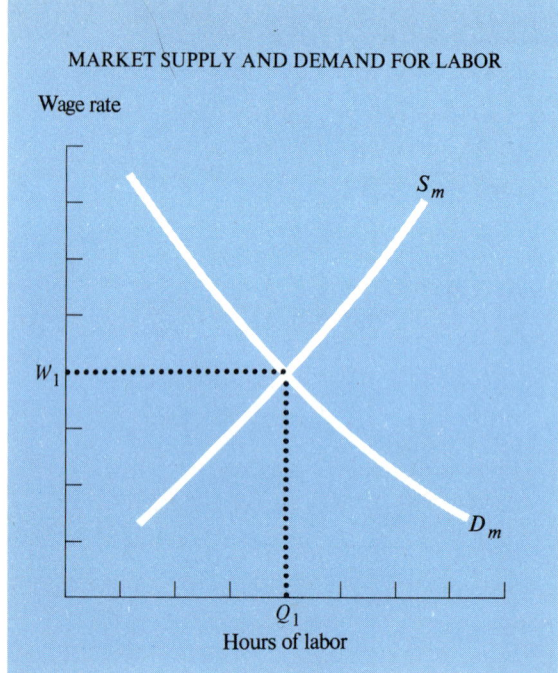

Fig. 29.6
The forces of supply and demand in the labor market determine the quantity of labor exchanged and the price of labor, just as in the product market. Here, the price of labor will fall at wage level W_1; the number of units traded will be Q_1.

sembly line, are possessed by nearly every able-bodied adult, but others require training or on-the-job experience. For example, a baker cannot perform the work of a surgeon. A surgeon needs skills that can be acquired only through years of schooling and more years of on-the-job training. Therefore, the labor of one worker is not a perfect substitute for the labor of every other worker.

If all workers had the same skills, training, and ability, and if all jobs were identical in the demands they made on workers, we would expect

---
*Another way of saying this is that leisure is a luxury good; as income rises, the percentage change in leisure demanded is greater than the percentage change in income demanded.

> **RECAP**
>
> The SUPPLY OF A RESOURCE is governed by the same law that governs product supply. The quantity of a resource that households will supply to businesses depends on the price offered for the resource.
>
> In the labor market, the individual's supply curve can be derived by plotting the points at which various wage constraint lines are tangent to curves on the individual's indifference map. The curve shows us how much (how many hours) labor the individual will supply at various wages (prices). The actual wage that an individual will command in the labor market depends on the level of his or her skills and on the demands that the job places on the worker.

there to be a single market wage that every worker was paid. But because these conditions do not exist, the price system allocates workers with different abilities to jobs for which there are different demands.

In accordance with the principle that the valuation of all units is dependent upon the value placed on the last unit traded, we would expect people (i.e., units of labor) with skills that are in shortest supply to be the most expensive since fewer of these units are traded. Therefore, people with skills that are in abundant supply will be valued at a lower wage. File clerks are paid much less than doctors because there are many more people who have the skills of a file clerk than those of a doctor. This means that the supply curve for file clerks is lower (farther to the right) than that for doctors. The supply of file clerks is large in relation to the demand for them, and so the marginal utility of the last file-clerk skills purchased will be lower than the marginal utility of the last hour of doctors' services purchased.

The fact that scarce skills command high wages guides society to the most efficient use of these scarce resources. Cost-conscious employers will not hire workers with scarce skills unless the job really requires their use. For example, when Ford hires a woman with a graduate degree in business administration, she is not assigned to a job in the assembly line that she could perform adequately without using any of her special training. Ford will give her a job that fully utilizes the scarce skills they are purchasing. This is the most efficient pattern of resource allocation.

The higher wages paid for scarce skills also encourage people to undertake the training and education needed to acquire those skills. Because young people know that a doctor's wage is high, they are willing to make the large investment needed to go to college, attend medical school, and work for several years as an intern at a low salary.

Since the high salary for scarce skills will coax more of those skills onto the market, relatively highly paid skills will become more plentiful, and skills valued at low rates will decline in supply.

The role of job demands

Another reason for the differences in wages paid for various jobs is that the demands of the jobs differ. Some jobs require employees who are willing to work at night; others are unusually stressful. In order to get workers to agree to accept uniquely demanding jobs, a business firm may have to pay them more. This compensation for the differences in working conditions is called the equalizing difference in wages.

An example of an equalizing difference in wages is the higher wage rates paid to those who work on the night shift instead of the more convenient day shift; and some people maintain that doctors are paid higher wages than many other people in part because of the critical life-and-death responsibility they must bear and the emotional distress they must suffer.

SUPPLY OF LAND

Unlike other productive resources, the supply of land is more or less fixed. We can increase our capital resources by deciding to devote a larger proportion of current productivity to the acquisition of capital. We can increase our labor resources by inducing more people to work more hours, and, in the long run, by expanding the population. But in the imaginable future, there is no way that we can increase the supply of land. It is possible, of course, that a new continent may be pushed up from the ocean floor, but that would take several million years—hardly a practical planning period.

While in one sense, the supply of land is fixed, in another sense, it is not—with new discoveries, the *known* quantity of natural resources is continually expanding, and with advances in technology, natural resources are continually becoming more accessible and more productive. By more exploration, for example, we can discover new supplies of coal, oil, or diamonds which are considered part of the land resource because they are natural resources. As prices of these valuable resources rise, the incentive is greater to use and develop new (and often more costly) methods of production and exploration. But for purposes of analysis, we will assume that the supply of land is fixed in the short run. Therefore, the short-run supply curve for land will be perfectly inelastic—no increase in price can coax more land on the market; no decrease can remove it from the face of the earth.

Figure 29.7 shows the supply curve for land resources; it is a straight, vertical line at the quantity Q_1. In such a case, demand alone (represented by curve D) will determine the market equilibrium

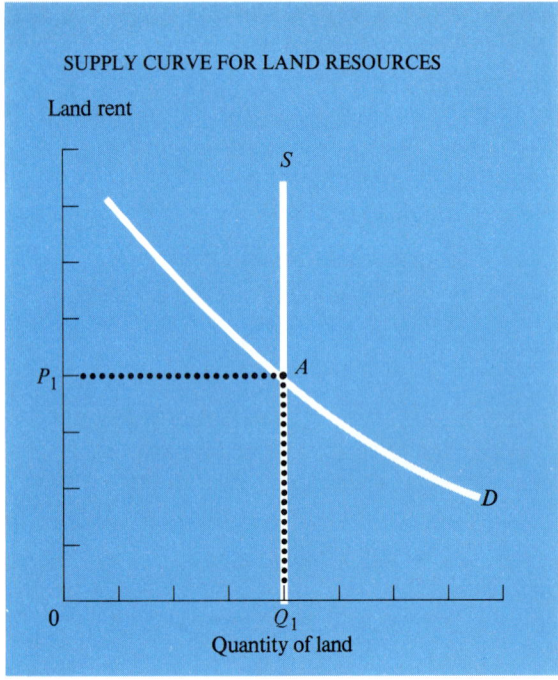

Fig. 29.7
Since the supply of land is considered to be fixed in the short-run period, supply is shown by a straight vertical line. The equilibrium price level is thus determined by the level of demand. Here, equilibrium is at point A (P_1, Q_1).

price and the amount of land that is traded (indicated by point A).

Economic rent

Economists call *the price paid for the use of land or any other resource that is fixed* **economic rent**. (The concept of economic rent should not be confused with the common concept of rent, such as the rent for an apartment.)

There is a major difference between the money businesses spend for land and the money they spend for other resources. The money that businesses pay to purchase labor and capital resources has an incentive function; that is, the price paid for the resources is responsible for their being on the market. If businesses did not pay wages, households would not be willing to offer their labor to them; and if businesses did not pay interest on borrowed funds, households would not be willing to save part of current income for investment in capital resources. The payment of rent, on the other hand, does not serve any incentive function. Whether or not rent is paid, the same amount of land will be in existence. Paying a higher rent does not make land more productive or more useful; failing to pay rent does not make land nonexistent.

Because rent is not connected with productivity, economists call land rent a pure surplus. Unlike other kinds of expenditures in the purchase of resources, rent does not create or encourage productivity; therefore, the price paid to the owner is really a surplus.

This particular feature of the land market has led many people to suggest social and economic reforms in the way land is owned and taxed. Theoretically, a redistribution of land ownership would have no effect on productivity; the only change would be in the distribution of the income from land.

One way to redistribute the pure surplus of economic rent would be to tax it. Indeed, in an enormously successful book on economics, *Progress and Poverty,* published in 1879, Henry George proposed a change in the United States tax structure that would place one large tax on the owners of land and eliminate all other taxes. However, the single tax never became a reality on a national level, and today the American tax structure actually favors the owners of land over the owners of other resources. Wages and salaries are always taxed at the maximum rate within each tax bracket; and the owners of capital resources pay slightly lower tax rates on their income through the use of investment credits and capital-gains allowances. The lowest tax rates are enjoyed by the owners of land resources, due to such loopholes as depreciation allowances. The reason for this protection of landowners' income seems to be more political than economic—landowners can best afford the expensive practice of lobbying to protect their special interests. On the positive side, however, tax incentives for landholders in the past stimulated them to open up land for productive use.

The role of the price system

Some social and economic reformers have suggested that since rent is a pure surplus, rent payments should be abolished altogether. However, by removing land from the effects of the price system, we would lose the benefits of the price system's efficiency of resource allocation, and the total productivity of our land resources might drop.

This drop in total productivity would occur because all units of land are not identical and interchangeable and because the alternative possible uses of land are not all equally productive. Physical differences in the land itself are obvious: some land is fertile loam; other land is hard clay. Some land is located near rivers; other land is made inaccessible by mountains or deserts. Thus, natural differences make certain pieces of land better suited for one use than another, and through the mechanism of the price system, and the resulting variation in rent, land is allocated for the purpose to which it is best suited.

User productivity

The differences in the productive yield of land in alternative possible uses lead to another factor to consider in the land supply. The total supply of land is perfectly inelastic, but the supply of land available for any one use—growing corn, building apartments, establishing parks—is elastic. For example, in an industry where a particular piece of

> **RECAP**
> While the SUPPLY OF LAND, unlike that of other resources, is fixed, it is possible through discovery to increase the known quantity, and through technology to make existing land more accessible and productive. Because the land supply is limited, the price paid for the use of land (economic rent) is determined by the demand for land. Although the price system usually allocates land to achieve the most efficient use, it can create problems since it does not take into account the social costs and benefits and alternative uses of resources.

land would yield a higher marginal revenue product (MRP) than it would in another industry, one firm can afford to outbid potential competitors for the use of the land and can adapt it for its own use. As a result, the available quantity of a particular type of land increases for the industry that can afford to pay a higher price for it, while the quantity available to some other industry (which cannot afford the price) decreases.

Thus, the actual market price of land is directly determined by the productivity of the land user. Landowners will sell to the highest bidder because they want to get the largest possible rent. Among potential bidders, the business that can make the greatest profit from the land will be able to bid the highest price for the land. It is the profit yield to the user of the land that determines the price that is required to obtain it.

A drawback to the price system
Rent, through the mechanism of the price system, helps to allocate land for the most profitable of all alternative uses, and therefore rent serves an economizing function. However, there are certain special problems created by the use of the price system in land allocation.

All our productive resources are scarce, but land is the most limited, and in many cases it is irreplaceable once used. So the question of optimal allocation is especially crucial in this area. It has already been pointed out many times in this book that the price system does not take into account the social costs and benefits of various alternative uses of resources. This leads to serious problems in the allocation of land. For example, at the present time, our resources of aluminum are large enough to permit aluminum cans to be competitively priced with glass, plastic, and waxed-paper containers. But the market price of these various substitutable containers does not reflect all the social costs and benefits of their use. Our supply of paper containers may be renewed by planting new trees, but our supply of aluminum is limited and irreplaceable. This raises the possibility that future generations may face a shortage of aluminum needed for uses for which there are no adequate aluminum substitutes. There are also social costs involved in disposing of these containers. Paper containers can be burned to obtain an ash useful as fertilizer or can be buried in a landfill where they will decompose quickly. Aluminum cans, on the other hand, cost more to dispose of since they cannot be burned and do not decompose. This is one example of the shortcomings of the price system, and some people believe that other forms of social action must supplement the economizing effect of market prices.

SUPPLY OF FINANCIAL CAPITAL

Capital goods are often referred to as an intermediary rather than a primary resource because they must be made from other resources of land and labor. The formation of capital goods requires a sacrifice of current consumption to be invested in building up a stock of tools and machinery for future production. In order to accumulate capital goods, someone must be willing to save some portion of disposable income in the form of money.

This saving can be supplied by all three of the elements in the circular flow. Households save some part of their current income, and government and business save some part of their current revenue for the acquisition of capital goods. In addition, saving may also be an intentional part of the government's fiscal policy to offset inflationary spending in other sectors of the economy.

When we speak of the market for **financial capital,** we are referring to the market for *loanable funds*—that is, *funds that businesses can borrow and use to purchase capital goods*. The financial-capital market is the medium through which savings can be exchanged for real capital goods. Either directly or through the operations of financial intermediaries (such as banks, life insurance companies, or mutual funds), this financial capital becomes available to business firms which invest it in capital goods. Financial capital can be obtained through loans or through the sale of stocks and bonds.

The demand for the financial capital comes from a business firm's desire to increase its stock of capital (this desire in turn comes from the demand for the firm's product). The firm borrows the money, purchases the capital goods, and then repays the loan with interest out of the profits it earns from the sale of final products manufactured through the use of the capital goods.

The supply schedule

Like all other supply schedules we have studied, the supply of financial capital (loanable funds) is responsive to the market price of the resource. *The payments made by a borrower to a lender for the use of the lender's money or loanable funds over a period of time* are called **interest.** It is common to quote interest as the *ratio of the payment for the use of financial capital to the amount borrowed,* such as a 5 percent rate on a loan of $500. This ratio is the **interest rate.** Thus, the interest rate reflects the price of borrowing financial-capital.

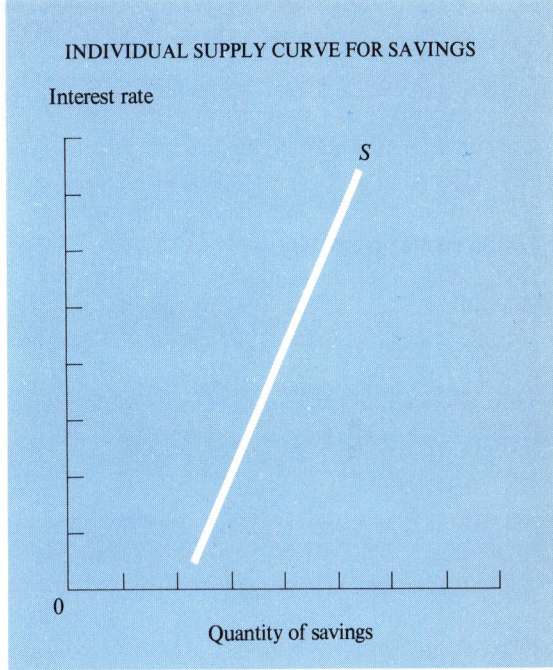

Fig. 29.8
The supply curve for savings of a single individual (Aunt Rhody) will show the characteristic upward slope. As interest rates rise, Aunt Rhody will be willing to save more and more of her income.

We can assume that in accordance with the law of supply, the higher the interest rate is, the more savings will be supplied to the financial-capital market. A high interest rate means that current saving will purchase a significant increase in future income, so there is more of an incentive to save than at a low interest rate. Yet the supply curve will probably be relatively inelastic because saving is determined by the size of income and other factors, as well as by the interest rate.

A supply schedule for savings can easily be constructed for each individual by determining the amount of money he or she is willing to save at each of a range of varying interest rates. *Figure 29.8* shows the supply curve for Aunt Rhody.

RECAP

The quantity of FINANCIAL CAPITAL supplied to businesses depends on the price offered for the funds. As the price (called the interest rate) increases, more people will be willing to loan out their funds and the available supply will increase. In addition, the daily operations of the financial-capital market are influenced by various financial institutions (banks, insurance companies, etc.) and by the Federal Reserve System.

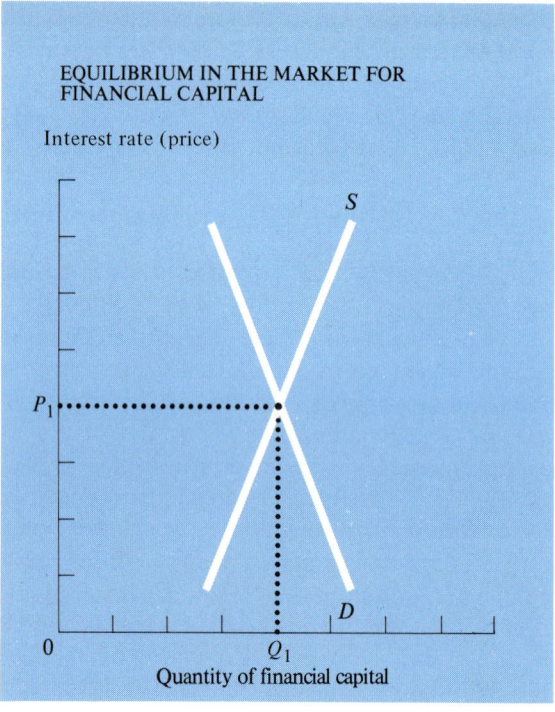

Fig. 29.9
As interest rates (prices) fall, the demand for financial capital will increase. By comparing the demand and supply curves, we can determine the market equilibrium level. This tells us the quantity of financial capital that will be traded in the market, and the price (interest rate) at which it will be bought and sold. Here, Q_1 of financial capital will be purchased and supplied at interest rate P_1.

Note that it slopes upward and to the right, as do all supply curves. As interest rates go higher and higher, Aunt Rhody is willing to sacrifice a larger percentage of her current income to purchase additions to her future income.

The market supply curve in financial capital is calculated by adding together all the individual supply curves in savings, plus the saving curves for the business and government sectors of the economy. We can then determine the equilibrium level of the market in the usual way, by comparing the supply curve for financial capital with the market demand curve. This is shown in *Fig. 29.9*. The point at which two curves intersect will tell us the interest rate (price) of financial capital and the amount of financial capital that will be exchanged on the resource market. (Here, Q_1 financial capital will be supplied and demanded at an interest rate of P_1.)

The day-to-day operations in the market for loanable funds are conducted by the different types of financial institutions we mentioned earlier. These institutions are able, within certain limits, to alter the interest rates charged, thereby ensuring that the amount of financial capital supplied to the market will be equal to the amount demanded. But as we saw in Chapters 13 through 15, the interest rate is not a truly free-market price. The central-banking authority, the Federal Reserve System, influences the supply of loanable funds and hence the interest rate to a sizable degree. Through their open-market operations and variations in the discount rate and the reserve requirement, the Fed can expand and contract the supply of money available for business loans. Regulating the supply of investment funds is, in fact, a basic goal of government monetary policy.

Although we won't go into such detail here, an accurate and detailed analysis of the market for financial capital must take into account the role of government in regulating the activity of the market.

Summary

■ This chapter examines the determinants of the supply of land, labor, and financial capital in the resource market.

■ Labor is the largest and most important of the resource markets. An individual's willingness to supply labor is a function of his or her preference for income versus nonmonetary rewards such as leisure, job satisfaction, or independence. The equal amounts of total satisfaction a worker can derive from different combinations of income and leisure time (for example) can be expressed in an indifference curve. When various lines of wage constraint are imposed on an indifference map, we can determine the actual choices an individual worker will make at different wage rates. In general, the amount of labor a worker is willing to supply to the market will increase as the wage rate rises; but after a certain wage is reached, the supply curve for an individual worker is backward bending—that is, once wages are high enough, the number of hours worked will be reduced instead of increased. The market supply curve for labor, however, will be positively sloped throughout.

■ Wage levels are extremely varied in the American economy. The primary determinants of wage level are the skill level and quality of the labor supplied, with scarce labor resources more highly valued, and the demands of the job, with unpleasant or dangerous or highly responsible jobs paying more as an inducement to workers.

■ The supply of land is a fixed, finite resource, and so the supply curve for land can be expressed as a straight, vertical line (a perfectly inelastic curve). Economic rent is the price paid for land or any other resource that is totally limited. Unlike wages, rent does not call new resources into existence or provide any incentive for the expansion of the supply of land. Land resources are allocated by the price system: owners of land will rent it at the highest possible price, and the highest bidders will be those buyers who can make the most economically productive use of the land. Because it does not take into account the costs and benefits of land use, the price system as a method of allocating land and land use has limitations, such as the lack of adequate protection of resources.

■ Interest rates determine the supply of financial capital (loanable funds) available in the resource market. The supply curve for capital is relatively inelastic because the level of saving in the economy is determined not only by the price offered for it (the interest rate), but also by other factors (such as income). The market supply of financial capital is a combination of capital available from households, businesses, and government, but, because of government intervention (primarily through the Federal Reserve Board), the market for financial capital is not completely free.

Key Terms

economic rent financial capital interest interest rate

Review & Discussion

1. Why is the supply of labor not entirely responsive to the wage level? How would you determine the amount of labor a worker is willing to supply at various wage levels from his or her indifference map?

2. Why do some economists believe that at high wage levels the supply curve for labor will slope backward? What would be the maximum level that business would want to pay for labor if the supply curve sloped backward?

3. Why is there no single equilibrium wage? What accounts for the differences in wage levels?

4. What effect might labor unions have on wage rates in the labor market? Could a union's successful attempt to create a monopoly seller's position in a particular labor market result in higher wages, by eliminating perfect competition among potential workers?

5. What is the shape of the supply curve for land for all uses? What might the supply curve for land for public housing look like? Why?

6. Why did Henry George suggest redistributing income through a single tax on land? Would this tax have had any effect on the allocation of land? Who would bear the burden of the tax?

7. Why is capital considered to be an intermediary rather than a primary resource? How is financial capital formed? What do economists consider to be the price of financial capital?

Chapter 30

General Equilibrium

What to look for in this chapter

What is general equilibrium analysis?

How does general equilibrium analysis tie together microeconomics and macroeconomics?

How are the resource and product markets interrelated?

How can input-output analysis be used to estimate the impact throughout the economy of changes in a particular industry?

In our discussion of microeconomic theory we have concentrated on **partial equilibrium analysis;** that is, *the analysis of the economics* (price and output determination, supply and demand interactions, etc.) *of individual, independent markets for specific goods and services.* For example, we have looked at how prices and output are determined in the markets for doughnuts and trout flies and how supply and demand operate in the resource markets for factory workers, mechanics, and farmland. Each market has been viewed as a closed system, in which supply and demand interact to determine the equilibrium level of price and output. Central to our analysis has been the assumption that although market prices of products and resources may change, all other things remain equal.

We also noted that such an assumption is unrealistic. A change in the price of one good will in itself change many other conditions. It will change the buying power of consumers and, therefore, will change their real income. It will also alter the relationship of that good's price to the price of its substitutes and complements. A price change will reallocate productive resources and may cause some change in the distribution of income throughout the population. The all-other-things-equal assumption is a useful analytical tool, but it is a simplification that may be misleading when we take a broader view of the economy.

Thus, partial equilibrium analysis leaves many questions unanswered. For example, in Chapter 22 we assumed that if the Delicious Doughnut Company wanted to expand, it would readily find the additional productive resources it needed. But where do the new workers come from? What will happen to the companies they left? What if several other firms in the city are also expanding at the same time? Will additional workers move to the city, or will the price of labor be forced up? The model we established for the doughnut industry does not tell us any of these things. To supply the answers, we must turn to general equilibrium analysis.

GENERAL EQUILIBRIUM ANALYSIS

In order to determine the relationships between various product and resource markets within the economy, economists use the concept of **general equilibrium analysis,** which eliminates the all-other-things-equal assumption and *examines the effects of changes in one market on other markets in the determination of a general balance between economic forces.* General equilibrium analysis can be used to study selected markets and to understand the interrelationships between a particular market and other markets or to look at the economy as a whole. It actually provides a connecting link between the microeconomic analysis of individual markets and prices and the macroeconomic analysis of broad aggregates and averages. The relationships between individual product and resource markets help illuminate the mechanism by which changes in aggregate variables, such as consumer spending, business investment, and saving, take place.

General equilibrium analysis is a relatively new field of economic study. The concept was first suggested by a nineteenth-century economist, Leon Walras, but little empirical work was undertaken in the field until the 1930s, and many of the techniques are still in the testing stage. For example, some economists are now beginning to use computers to develop full-scale simulations of our economy. A computer can be programmed with a proposed model of economic interrelationships, and then the data for any given year can be processed according to this pattern. Although a fully accurate model has not yet been established, many models have been used with a significant degree of success in making certain kinds of economic forecasts.

If we carry general equilibrium analysis to its extreme, we might conclude that every single economic event in the world influences every other subsequent economic event. While this idea may be attractive on a philosophical level, it is impractical as a guide to economic research. It may be true that all economic events are related, but the degree of influence many of them exert on the others is negligible. As a practical matter, therefore, economists are not interested in constructing a general equilibrium model that will account for every variable circumstance, but in one that will account for the most influential variables. The model could then be used to understand and to predict consequences of changes in these variables.

By definition, the term "equilibrium" implies an eventual state of rest. Some economists suggest that the constant adaptations made in various independent markets as a result of changes in other markets are working toward such a state of balance. But the concept of some ideal and static outcome is misleading when applied to a complex and dynamic economy. For example, the United States economy is extremely complex: it includes thousands, perhaps millions, of different markets; social and economic programs of the last several decades have attempted to bring about changes in the distribution of income; advanced technology continues to create new products and new methods of production; and enthusiasm for innovation causes consumer tastes to change rapidly and frequently. It is difficult to imagine that such an economy could ever be in a state of rest. But the concept of general equilibrium can help us follow, and perhaps even anticipate, the many changes that occur constantly.

GENERAL EQUILIBRIUM: PRODUCT-MARKET/ RESOURCE-MARKET APPROACH

In order to analyze the effects of change in one individual market, we can set up a very simple two-product economy. Imagine a country that specializes in manufacturing lace and felt-tip pens. Most of the lace must be made by hand, since the process of lace making has not yet been satisfactorily mechanized. Thus, the lace industry will require large amounts of labor. The production of pens, however, calls for a large investment in capital machinery, since it is almost entirely automated.

Figure 30.1 shows the results of partial equilibrium analysis of four different markets in this economy. Two of the markets are product markets: *Fig. 30.1 (a)* shows the long-run equilibrium of the lace market; and *Fig. 30.1(b)* shows the long-run equilibrium of the felt-tip-pen market. The other two markets are resource markets: the equilibrium of the labor market is shown in *Fig. 30.1(c)*, and that of the capital market is shown in *Fig. 30.1(d)*.

We will assume that, for some reason, the tastes of consumers buying pens and lace suddenly change. Lace is considered old-fashioned, dowdy, and impractical. What effect will this single change in the lace market have on the other markets in the economy?

As illustrated in *Fig. 30.2(a)*, the first change will appear in the demand schedule for lace—the change in tastes will cause demand for lace to decrease. This will be reflected in a shift to the left from D_1 to D_2 and with the shift will come a new equilibrium in the lace market. The price of lace will decrease to P_2 and the quantity of lace exchanged on the market will decrease to Q_2.

This change in the equilibrium of the lace market cannot be isolated from the rest of the economy and it will make itself felt in a variety of ways. Lace manufacturers, faced with a lower product price, will find that the marginal revenue product (MRP) has declined. As you will recall from Chapter 28, the MRP curve is also the market demand curve for labor; thus, there will be a downward shift in the labor demand schedule from D_1 to D_2. As a result, the price (that is, the wage) at which it can be purchased and the number of units of labor that are traded in the market will change (to W_2 to Q_2 respectively).

The change in demand for lace and the subsequent change in the price of lace will also affect patterns of consumption. Since consumers are no longer buying as many units of lace, they have more income. Even those who continue to buy lace will have an increase in real income, because they are paying a lower price for their lace. This income effect may cause a further change in the demand for lace (since income is an important determinant of demand). It is also likely that the income effect will cause the demand for pens to increase (from D_1 to D_2 in *Fig. 30.2 b*). This will cause a change in the price of pens (to P_2) and the quantity traded (to Q_2). This, in turn, will lead to a change in the demand for capital (to D_2), with an

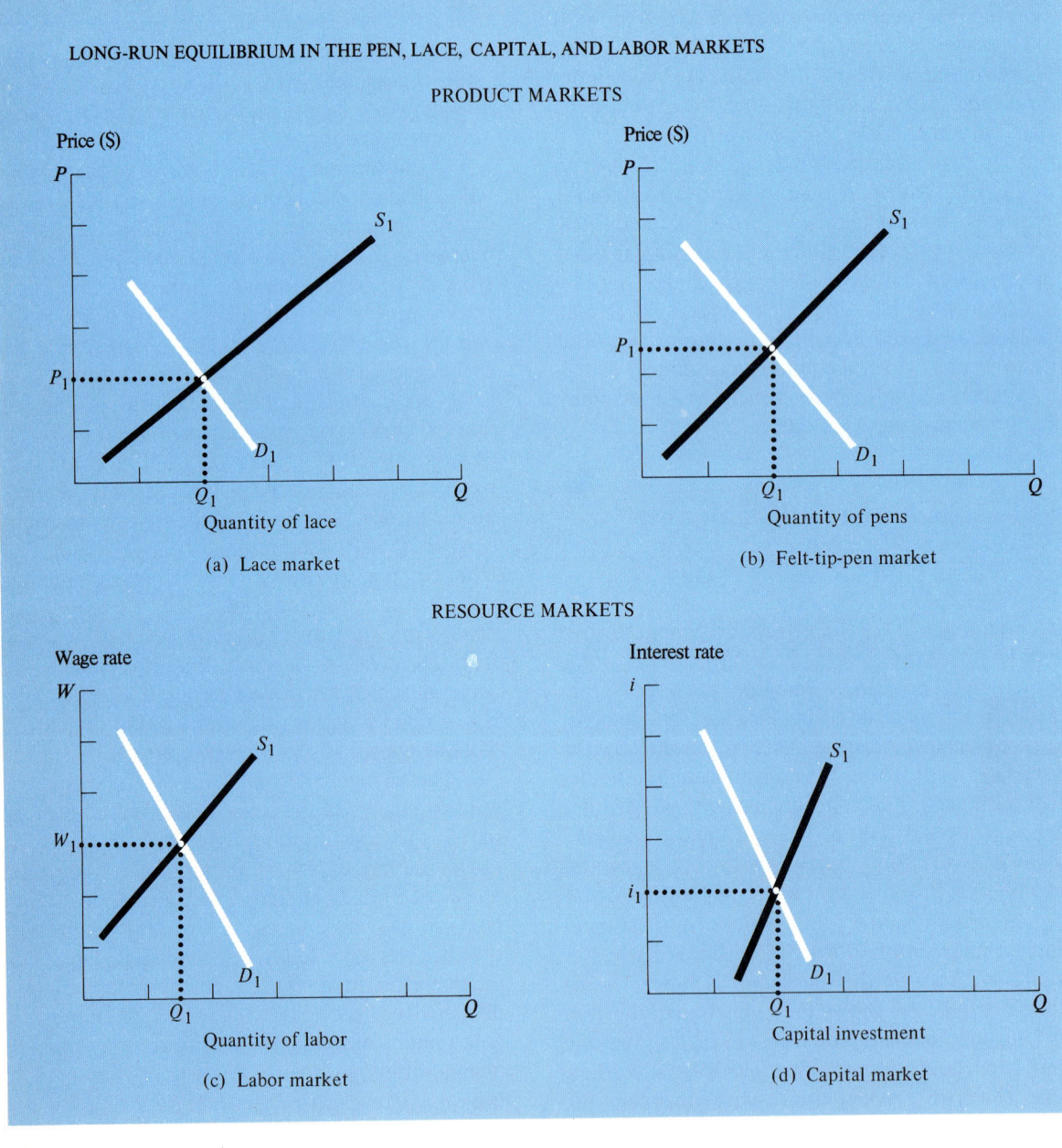

Fig. 30.1
Lace and felt-tip pens are the only two products that are produced in our hypothetical economy, and we are assuming that long-run equilibrium situations exist in the various markets. The supply and demand conditions are shown for the two product markets—lace and felt-tip pens—and two of the resource markets—labor and capital: (a) at price P_1, Q_1 quantity of lace will be demanded by consumers and supplied by producers; (b) at price P_1, Q_1 quantity of felt-tip pens will be demanded by consumers and supplied by producers; (c) at wage W_1, Q_1 workers will be supplied to and demanded by lace manufacturers; (d) at interest rate i_1, quantity of capital will be supplied to and demanded by felt-tip-pen manufacturers.

eventual increase in interest rates to I_2 to attract the needed additional supply into the market. Also, since labor is now cheaper, the pen production process might use relatively more labor and less capital.

The changes in the various markets are shown in *Fig. 30.2*. But the changes will not end in these four markets. The change in equilibrium of the two resource markets will bring a change in the pattern of income distribution: before the change in taste for lace, most income went to laborers; now it will go to the owners of capital. Since income distribution is a major determinant of market demand, we can expect demand curves for the two products to shift again. The direction and extent of these shifts will depend on the workers' and capital owners' (as consumers) preference schedules for lace and pens. This change in income distribution, like the change due to the income effect, will be fed back to the lace industry where the initial change took place and will probably alter the demand schedule of lace once again, thus setting off another chain of adjustments.

As the interest rate climbs in response to the added demand for capital (due to the increased demand for pens), households may decide to save more and spend less.

In the long run, we could expect changes in the long-run supply curves of both pens and lace, because existing lace-making firms would leave that industry and switch to making pens. The supply curve for lace would shift to the left, and the supply curve for pens would shift to the right. These shifts will bring even more adjustments in market price and volume traded.

INPUT-OUTPUT APPROACH TO GENERAL EQUILIBRIUM ANALYSIS

The kind of analysis of general equilibrium presented in *Figs. 30.1* and *30.2* helps us understand the reasons that change in one market will create change in many other markets. But this analysis is not as useful when we attempt to *measure* such changes or to predict the extent of future change. To help solve these problems, economists have developed the **input-output table,** *an economic model that can be used to quantify changes in general equilibrium. The main goal of an input-output table is to show the interrelationships between different industries within a single economy.*

We have often spoken of inputs and outputs as if they were two totally separate categories, but in reality these categories frequently overlap. For example, the output of a corn farmer is, of course, ears of corn. But it is less obvious that some percentage of this output will later become the farmer's input—some of this season's corn will be used as seed for the corn of next season. Some of the corn output that the farmer sells will also become an input to the hog-raising industry and to the makers of corn chips or tortillas.

Another example will help to clarify input-output: we think of steel manufacturers as supplying input resources for the makers of

CHAPTER 30: GENERAL EQUILIBRIUM

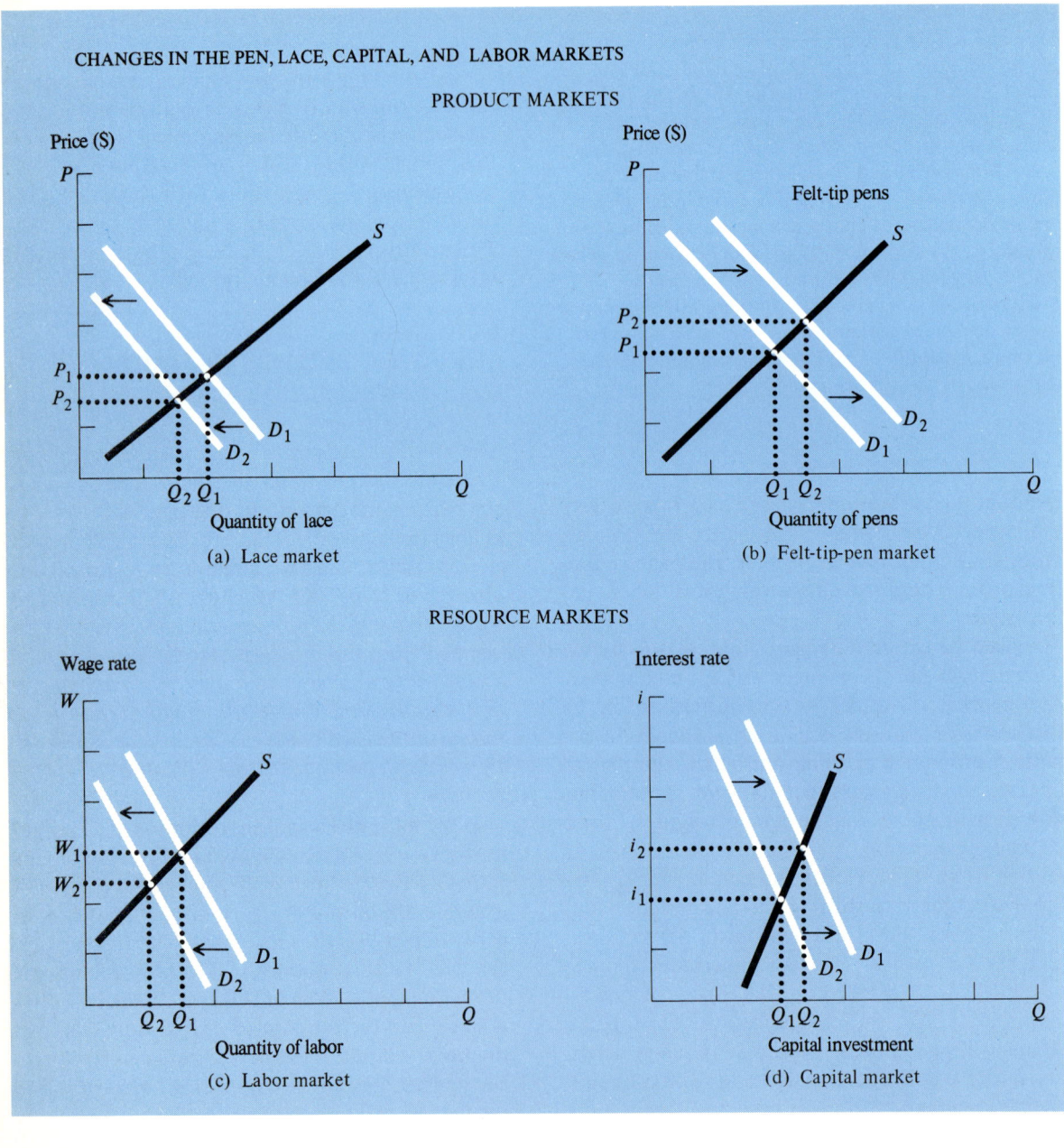

Table 30.1
Simplified input-output table (millions of dollars)

	(1) Primary metals	(2) Machinery	(3) Transportation equipment	(4) Final consumption	(5) Total output
(A) Primary metals	200	300	150	50	700
(B) Machinery	250	200	250	200	900
(C) Transportation equipment	150	250	50	200	650
(D) Labor	100	150	200	(450)	
(E) Total value of inputs	700	900	650		(2250)

trucks, but truck manufacturers also supply inputs to the steel industry. Some of the trucks that are produced will eventually be used to transport raw materials to steel factories and to carry finished steel away to the market. To the steel companies, trucks are capital goods that the steel companies must purchase in order to produce their output. Therefore, some percentage of the truck manufacturers' output must be regarded as an input for steel manufacturers.

Tabular analysis

The tangled web of economic interrelationships must be taken into account before we can determine the effects of a price increase in any one market, and an input-output table shows these relationships. *Table 30.1* is an example of a simple input-output table for three industries. It lists the various industries and measures the value of their total output (column 5). Each horizontal row traces the distribution of this output as it is distributed to the originating industry, to the various other industries that use it as an input resource, and to the final consumption sector.* For example, row A shows us that of the $700 million of output in primary metals, the industry pur-

Fig. 30.2
In (a) a change in consumer tastes causes a decrease in the demand for lace, and thus a downward shift of the demand curve from D_1 to D_2. The lower market price for lace means a decrease in the MRP curve of lace manufacturers and a consequent decrease in both the quantity of workers hired and the market wage rate shown in (c). It is also likely that the increase in real income caused by a decrease in the purchase of lace will result in an increase in the demand for pens (shown in (b) as a shift from D_1 to D_2), which subsequently will bring about an upward shift of the demand curve in the capital market.

---

*In our simplified example, this includes only households, which, we have assumed, spend all of the income earned from the sale of their labor. In reality, however, the final consumption sector would include government, foreign purchasers, and all other final demanders.

RECAP

GENERAL EQUILIBRIUM ANALYSIS is a relatively new area of economic study in which economists investigate the effects that changes in one market may have on other markets. It also provides a link between microeconomic analysis of individual markets and prices and the macroeconomic analysis of aggregates (consumer spending, savings, etc.).

General equilibrium analysis can be approached with two different methods: (1) In the *product-market/resource-market approach,* the effects of a change in one market (for example, a product market) can be traced through the markets for the resource(s) used in the manufacture of the product as well as through the market of another product and in turn, its relevant resource markets. (2) The *input-output approach* shows the interrelationships between different industries in an economy and can be used to analyze and measure the numerous market movements toward equilibrium set off by a change in one market. Thus, input-output analysis helps economists predict the extent of future changes brought on by a single change in one market.

chases $200 million worth of its own output. The remaining $500 million worth of metals is distributed among the other industries as follows: $300 million to machinery, $150 million to transportation equipment, and $50 million to final consumption.

Each vertical column tells us the value of all the different inputs each industry needs to produce its total output. For example, *Table 30.1* shows that in order to produce the $700 million worth of primary metals discussed above, the industry needs input of $200 million worth of primary metals, $250 million worth of machinery, $150 million worth of transportation equipment, and $100 million worth of labor. Adding up column (1), we find that the total value of all inputs used in the primary-metal industry is $700 million—equal to the value of the total output.

Input coefficients

If we take the information about the input requirements in each industry given in the vertical columns of *Table 30.1,* we can calculate the industry's **input coefficient**—*the value of each input needed to produce $1 worth of output. The input coefficient is a ratio determined by dividing each input requirement by the total value of inputs in that industry.* For example, we can determine from the table that the input coefficient for machinery in the primary-metals industry is 250 ÷ 700,

Table 30.2
Input coefficients calculated from Table 30.1

	(1) Primary metals	(2) Machinery	(3) Transportation equipment
(A) Primary metals	.29	.33	.23
(B) Machinery	.36	.22	.38
(C) Transportation equipment	.21	.28	.08
(D) Labor	.14	.17	.31
(E) Total value of inputs	1.00	1.00	1.00

or .36. This indicates that to obtain $1 of primary metal output $.36 worth of machinery input is required. *Table 30.2* lists the input coefficients for the four inputs given in *Table 30.1*.

Using tables similar to *Table 30.2*, economists can calculate what will happen to output in industries if there is a change in the demand for any one of the products used as an input. Suppose, for example, the demand for transportation equipment in the final-consumption sector of the economy increases by 50 percent from $200 million to $300 million. Not only will the transportation-equipment industry have to produce the extra $100 million worth of vehicles to sell to final consumers, but it will also have to produce an additional $8 million worth of goods to use as its own input for the production of this extra output: the input coefficient (.08) times the needed increase in output ($100 million) equals $8 million. In addition, the primary-metals industry will also have to produce an extra $23 million worth of metal to supply the needed input for the increase in vehicle production (.23 × $100 million). The output of machinery must increase as well since the transportation-equipment industry will need an additional $38 million worth of machinery as an input. Finally, the increased output of transportation equipment will require an additional $31 million worth of labor.

To summarize, we find that an increase in production in the transportation-equipment industry stimulates increases in production in all other industries that supply the inputs needed to produce transportation equipment. But the process of expansion does not stop here, because as each of the other industries in our table expands output to meet the new input requirements of the transportation-equipment industry, their inputs, too, will have to be increased. These interactions will continue with round after round of expansion in each industry until eventually all the input requirements are met. Thus, input-output analysis clearly demonstrates how a change in one industry can give rise to an intricate network of changes throughout the economy.

We have used a simple input-output table to demonstrate the way the model works. Every year, there are economists who use actual market data to construct input-output tables for the American economy. Much of the work on input-output tables in our economy has been pioneered by Wassily Leontief. He has used these tables to predict the outcome of various proposed spending changes. For example, in an article entitled, "The Economic Effects of Disarmament," Leontief traced the changes in output of major sectors of our economy that would be the result of adopting a policy of disarmament.

Summary

■ This chapter describes the goals and strategies of general equilibrium analysis, an economic model which attempts to tie together the partial equilibrium analysis of particular markets on which we have been focusing.

■ General equilibrium analysis removes the all-other-things-equal assumption we have been making in previous chapters. This field of analysis is comparatively recent, but it has made considerable strides in developing sophisticated models of economic interrelationships. In these models, economists attempt to account for only the most influential variables. Though the term "general equilibrium" implies a state of rest, there are constant changes in an economy as complex as that of the United States.

■ General equilibrium analysis helps economists to follow and predict the effects that changes in one market may have on other markets. For example, this chapter considered the interrelations between product and resource markets in an economy producing lace and felt-tip pens. A reduction in the demand for lace results in a decrease in the price of lace. Lace manufacturers cut back on production and therefore reduce the demand for the resources used to produce lace. Because of the drop in the price of lace, consumers have more disposable income and may save more. The higher disposable incomes may also mean that consumers will buy more felt-tip pens. There will be a change in the relative demand for capital and labor since lace is labor intensive and felt-tip pens are capital intensive. In addition, some lace firms would leave the industry and enter the felt-tip-pen industry.

■ In order to measure the interrelations between various markets more precisely, the input-output approach is used. The input-output table is an economic model that shows a simplified relationship between real markets. The output of one industry may serve as the input for several industries, including itself. In addition, a table of output coefficients can be derived from an input-output table which shows the value of inputs needed to produce one dollar's worth of output in each industry. If there is a change in the demand and output of a particular industry (for example, transportation equipment), the input coefficients give us a way of estimating the effects on other industries (such as primary metals, machinery, and the transportation-equipment industry itself). The changes required in other industries will set off another round of smaller adjustments within the economy. These interactions will continue with round after round of expansion in each industry, until eventually all the input requirements are met.

From the work pioneered by Wassily Leontief, economists have developed input-output tables from empirical data on the United States economy. These tables may be used to estimate the effects of proposed changes on the economy as a whole as well as on individual sectors.

Key Terms

partial equilibrium analysis

general equilibrium analysis

input-output table

input coefficient

Review & Discussion

1. What happens to the all-other-things-equal assumption in general equilibrium analysis? Why? What are the objectives of the study of general equilibrium? What is partial equilibrium analysis?

2. Consider the following statement. "The economy, in fact the whole universe, is never in equilibrium. It therefore makes little sense to analyze events as though they will reach some sort of stable level." Do you agree or disagree? Why?

3. Suppose an economy produces doorknobs and fireplaces. Due to a new ordinance on pollution control, there is a reduction in the demand for fireplaces. Doorknobs are produced in a large plant using much machinery, while most fireplaces are constructed by a mason and other workers on the site. What changes would you expect to see in this economy?

4. What is an input-output table? Is a given product simply an input or simply an output?

5. What is an input coefficient? How are they used in input-output analysis?

6. Choose one of the industries in *Table 30.1*. Using input coefficients, trace the effect of a 10 percent increase in demand on the industry itself and the other industries associated with it.

Application 14:
Supply and Demand in the Teacher Market

In the early 1970s, the United States education system began to recover from an ailment that had afflicted it for decades, a shortage of teachers, only to fall victim to another woe, a surplus of teachers. In 1966, a survey by the National Education Association, a professional organization found that the nation lacked 72,500 teachers. Just four years later, the federal Office of Education estimated that 100,000 more teachers would graduate from colleges that year than could be placed in teaching jobs. The story of this sudden turnaround in the market for teachers illustrates the often complex forces behind the supply of and demand for labor.

The teacher shortage began to be felt just after World War II with the postwar baby boom. As *Fig. 1* shows, the number of babies born annually in the United States climbed from about 28 million in 1945 to about 38 million just two years later, an increase of more than one-third.

These children began entering school in the early 1950s, and the effect of their numbers can be seen in *Fig. 2;* the line representing pupils in school starts rising at a steeper angle in 1952. With the exception of a brief downturn from 1948 to 1950, the number of babies born annually continued to grow for several more years, swelling school enrollments and increasing the demand for teachers.

The demand was further heightened by government programs that tended to drain the existing pool of teachers. For example, 5400 new teaching jobs were created by the founding of the Peace Corps in the early 1960s. Ironically, new government efforts to aid education also played a role in creating the dearth of instructional staff. For instance, an estimated 60,000 new teaching positions opened as a result of the Elementary and Secondary Education Act of 1965, which tried to improve the situation of poor Americans by,

APPLICATION 14: SUPPLY AND DEMAND IN THE TEACHER MARKET

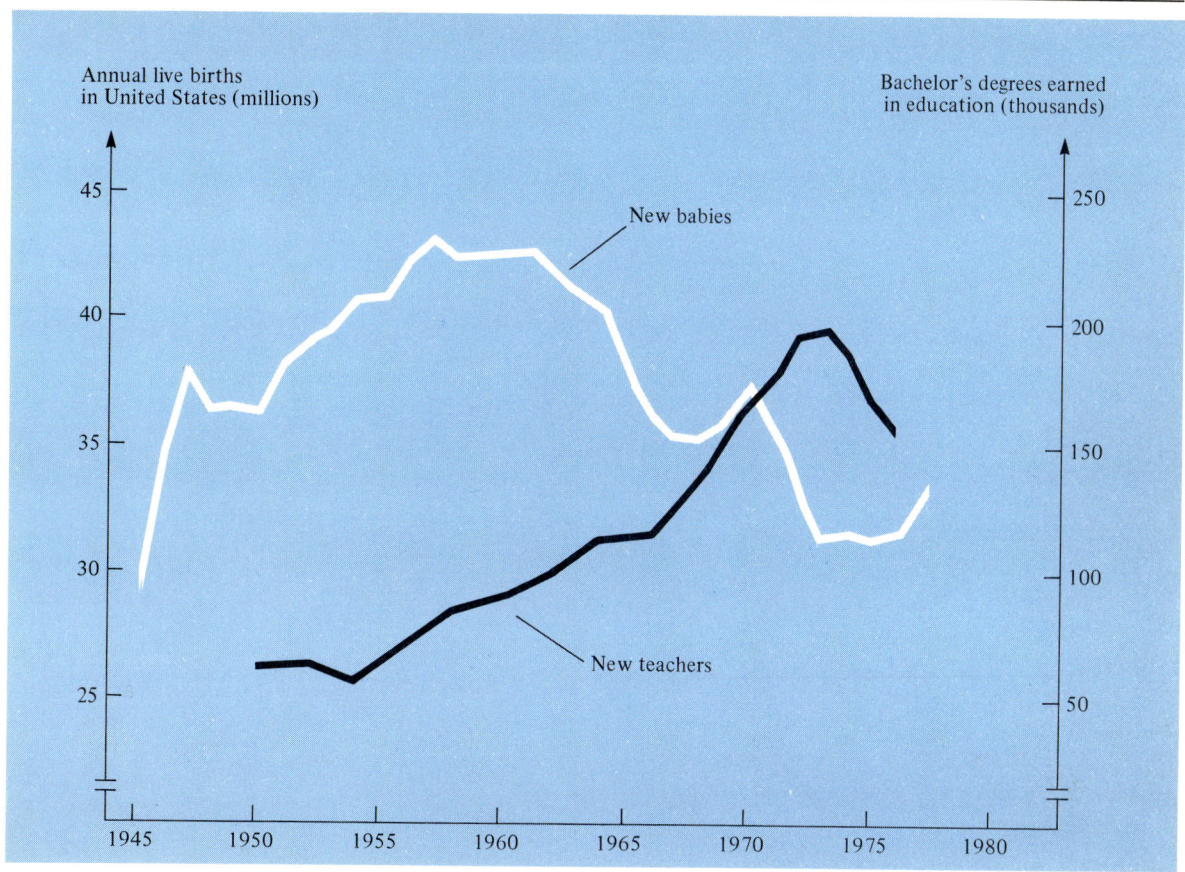

SOURCE: National Center for Education Statistics, and Bureau of Census.

Figure 1

among other things, providing them with additional and earlier tutoring in reading, writing, and other basic skills.

The supply was slow to respond to the higher level of demand for two reasons. The first can be seen in *Fig. 2;* real teacher salaries were not rising as rapidly as school enrollments, reflecting the fact that during those years when the economy was generally expanding, teaching paid less than positions in government and industry requiring similar skills or training. At the same time, there was a rise in the so-called expansion demand for teachers. College graduates who wanted to teach found themselves able to get positions in colleges rather than elementary or secondary schools because of instructional shortages on the campus, and many teachers who might otherwise have gone into high school took positions in junior colleges, where the pay was better. Replacement demand also increased as more women, who accounted for

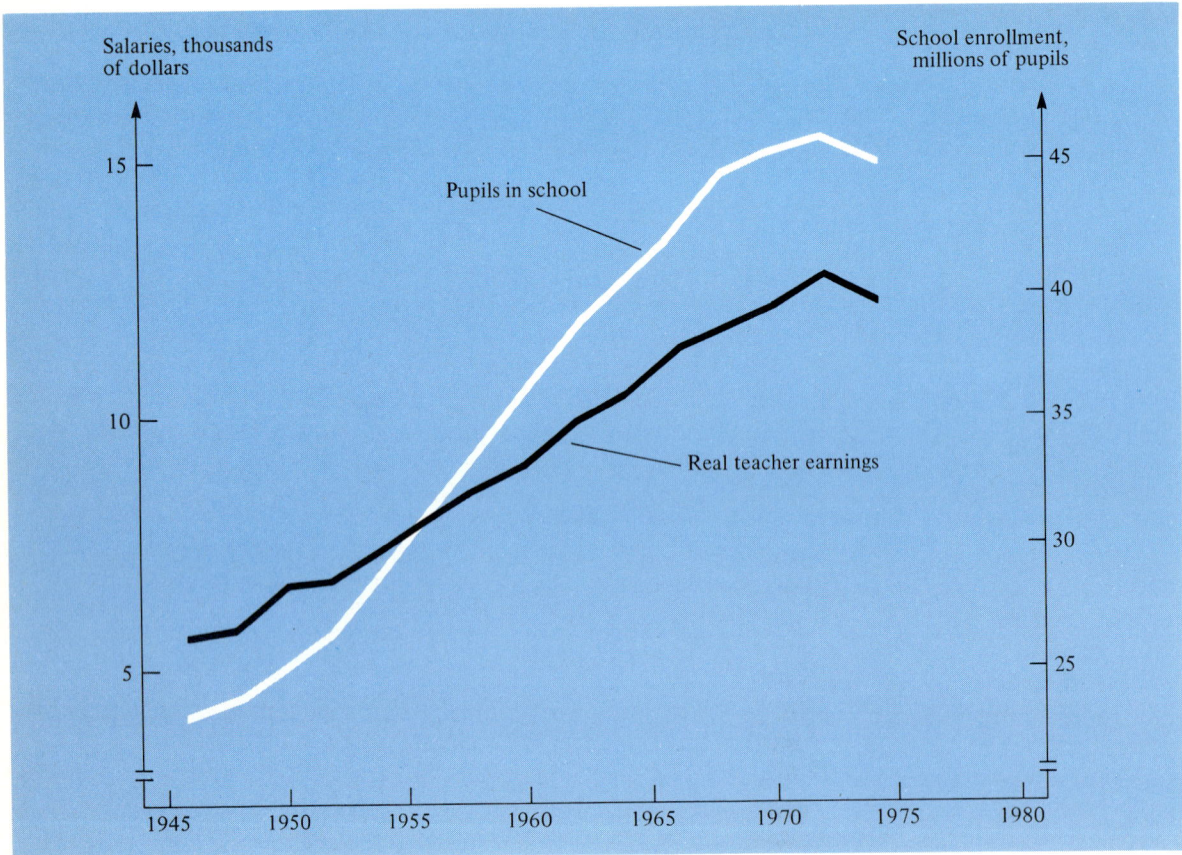

SOURCE: National Center for Education Statistics.

Figure 2

the majority of teachers, began to leave the classroom to raise a family or to take advantage of promising opportunities for women that were just beginning to emerge in other fields.

The shortage of teachers was not uniform. School districts where salaries for teachers were relatively high, such as Hempstead, Long Island, continued to be flooded with applicants. Most school districts, however, felt at least some effect, with consequences ranging from relaxed standards for hiring to intensified recruiting efforts and new staffing patterns. The Cleveland schools, for example, began hiring any college graduate as a teacher, even if he or she was available to teach only one period a day. In the District of Columbia and in Virginia, school boards lowered their professional requirements for teachers, particularly those that specified the number of teacher-training courses that any new teacher must take in college. One district in Maine sought teachers as far afield as Tunisia, Greece, and Turkey. And northern school personnel directors traveled to the South in search of black teachers displaced by the closing of racially segregated schools.

It was not long, however, until what had been a teacher gap became a glut. In the fall of 1970, school districts that had been forced to delay opening the previous year for lack of teachers were deluged with applications. In Grand Rapids, Michigan, for example, 50 teachers, or would-be teachers, applied for each post as a history instructor for the city system.

Behind the change was a mixture of demographic, financial, and other forces. One influence was the tightness of the labor market in general and for Ph.D.s in particular, which allowed school systems to hire candidates with doctoral degrees for positions that formerly had required only bachelor's degrees, thereby displacing holders of the bachelor's degree.

On the financial side, rising costs and the increasing resistance of taxpayers to vote additional levies on themselves in the name of education forced school boards to cut back on the largest single item in their budgets, teacher salaries, which accounted for about eight-tenths of current expenses in the typical school system. As a consequence, there were many layoffs. Teachers responded by staging strikes, walkouts, and rallies, activities that hitherto had been almost unheard of in the profession. But as school finances dwindled, more and more protesting teachers lost their battle. In Seattle, for instance, 550 teachers were dismissed in the 1975–1976 school year, and 715 the following year.

An equally important reason for the layoffs, however, was demographic. The same baby boom that had helped to create the teacher shortage was largely responsible for ending it as young people began to graduate from college, many of them with degrees in education. The trend is visible in *Fig. 1,* which shows births peaking in 1957 and the number of new teachers reaching a high point several years later, in 1973. As the number of children born each year eased downward, so too, eventually, did school enrollments, which in 1972 began to slide for the first time since World War II. This decline not only lessened the demand for teachers, but also decreased the amount of money local school districts had available for instructional salaries, because in most places state aid, a significant proportion of the budget, was closely tied to enrollments, or to similar measures, such as average daily attendance.

Questions for discussion

☐ Using information from this case, illustrate the principles of labor market supply and demand described in the preceding chapters.

☐ Although there was a record number of births in 1957, the number of college graduates with degrees in education peaked only 16 years later, before students in 1957 could have graduated. How do you account for this?

☐ In what ways might the reduced demand for teachers improve the quality of education? What changes, for example, might you expect to see in the ratio of pupils to teachers in the typical classroom?

☐ Discuss the significance of the decline in the earnings of teachers, after adjustments for inflation, that began in 1972 (see *Fig. 2).*

Chapter 31

Labor Unions: Collective Bargaining and Wage Determination

What to look for in this chapter

What is the role of labor unions in the American economy?

What are some of the turning points in the history of organized labor in the United States?

What are the functions of today's unions?

What are the major issues covered in collective-bargaining agreements negotiated by unions and management?

Have unions succeeded in gaining higher wages for their members? Do wage increases for labor lead to inflation?

The effects of unionism in the United States have been widespread. About one-fourth of all workers in the civilian labor force*—over 21 million people—belong to nationally organized labor unions. These unions play an important role in wage and price determination and exert considerable influence in national and international politics. In addition, unions have a strong voice in deciding the goals of the American economy, and of American society in general. For example, the passage of national programs of Social Security, unemployment compensation, and benefits for workers injured on the job was promoted by union efforts to win these benefits for workers.

In order to understand the importance of labor unions in modern America, we will examine the history of the American labor movement and discuss the structure and functions of present-day

---
*Does not include members of the armed forces.

unions. We will then discuss the process of collective bargaining between union and management, which determines union wages and working conditions (and, indirectly, those of many nonunion employees as well). The chapter concludes with an assessment of the impact that unions have on supply and demand in the labor market.

HISTORY OF AMERICAN UNIONISM

In eighteenth- and nineteenth-century America, wages were low and working hours were long in comparison with today's standards. In 1909, the average work week for industrial employees was 51 hours, and the average wage was only 19¢ per hour. Large corporations which were springing up in the industrialized North eliminated close personal relationships that had formerly prevailed between employers and employees, and the resulting estrangement encouraged workers to organize into groups to strengthen their bargaining position with employers. As these groups grew in size and effectiveness, they began to take on more functions—providing benefits for disabled workers and exerting political pressure on government officials.

Early union organization

Many people are surprised to discover how long ago the formation of organized groups of workers in the United States began. Concerted activity among workers on the American continent was recorded as early as 1636 when a group of fishermen in what is now Maine protested their wages being withheld; and in 1799, the first recorded meeting to discuss labor demands took place in Philadelphia, between representatives of a group of local shoemakers and their employers. As a result of these meetings the shoemakers had to appear in court. The court's action, the *Philadelphia Cordwainers Case* of 1806, resulted in the criminal conviction of the shoemakers and established the criminal-conspiracy doctrine which made it a criminal offense even to meet for the purposes of forming a union. This doctrine was not overturned until *Commonwealth* v. *Hunt* in 1842.

One of the first historically documented **strikes,** *organized work stoppages designed to win or enforce certain conditions of employment,* took place in 1741 when the New York Bakers struck to protest a municipal regulation on the price of bread. These early attempts at organization among workers were confined to local areas and included only a fraction of the total workers in any given business. Yet such efforts brought workers together, pioneered the techniques of bargaining, and stimulated interest in a successful labor organization.

The growth of the American labor movement was directly linked to the increasing industrialization that took place during the nineteenth century. In the decade of the 1860s, the additional production demands caused by the Civil War and the accompanying increase in demand for labor, gave the skilled workers in growing industries the opportunity to organize. By 1864, more than 300 local unions had been established throughout the northern states, with a membership total that was soon to reach 300,000.

The Knights of Labor

The Noble Order of the Knights of Labor, established in 1869, was one of the first labor organizations to be organized on a national level. This group began as a secret organization of Philadelphia garment workers, but it rapidly expanded to include workers in other cities and in other crafts as well. By 1886, the Knights of Labor claimed over 700,000 members, both skilled craftsmen and unskilled workers in mines and on railroad gangs. Their main goal was to bring about basic social change by means of improved education for workers and increased political participation. The organization clearly showed the influence of the Utopian social movements of the 1840s that had sought to build a better society for the common person. Although it enjoys little support among American workers today, this philosophy of unionism remains influential in many European countries.

The American Federation of Labor

The Knights of Labor did not succeed in bringing much noticeable improvement to the economic position of workers in America, and it was soon replaced by a new national labor organization, the American Federation of Labor (AFL). The AFL was founded in 1886 by Samuel Gompers, who believed that a union should concentrate on short-range economic goals and bread-and-butter issues. The union's main task was to secure higher wages and better working conditions by using collective bargaining and strikes to increase the power of individual workers in negotiating these issues with employers. Gompers called this narrower economic focus "pure and simple unionism" and summed up the union's goal at the turn of the century in one word—"more."

The AFL was organized by craft, with a separate union representing each type of skilled worker. For example, among railroad employees there was one union for locomotive engineers, another for conductors, firemen, and switchmen, a third for the workers who laid and repaired the tracks, a fourth for signalmen, and a fifth for clerks. The AFL was designed in such a way that the national union maintained great control over the local unions.

Antilabor activities

As the AFL grew steadily, employers began to fear that powerful labor organizations might be able to dictate wages and working hours, so they fought back with all the weapons at their command. They fired workers known to be union members and placed them on an industry-wide blacklist that kept them from finding new jobs elsewhere. When workers started to organize, employers often imposed a **lockout,** *the closing of a plant by an employer to deprive workers of their salaries, usually to dampen enthusiasm for unionization.* They forced workers to sign **yellow-dog contracts** (*agreements made by an employee never to join a union, usually as a condition of employment*). They also hired spies to infiltrate the unions and brought in workers, often from other cities or states, to break strikes. Some employers even raised wages slightly in the hope that workers would be deterred from organizing and demanding still higher wages. When all else failed, they offered the promise of company unions, with limited benefits under strict company control.

In all these measures, the employers had the law on their side for many years. Union activities that were intended to improve the workers' bargaining position—such as striking, picketing, and boycotting—were held by the courts to be unlawful. The Sherman Antitrust Act of 1890, originally designed to restrict business monopolies, was interpreted to restrict union growth as well. Antiunion employers, led by the National Association of Manufacturers, found it easy to obtain a **protective injunction,** *a court order prohibiting a strike or a boycott*, by claiming that they might suffer irreparable damage from such an act.

Prolabor legislation

During the 1930s, unions at last began to enjoy legal protection. The Depression had a major role in bringing about this change. The severe economic problems of the period led to an interest in improving working conditions; at the same time, falling wages stimulated an increased interest in unionism among American workers.

Two different pieces of prolabor legislation were enacted during the depression years. The Norris-La Guardia Act of 1932 limited the use of injunctions in labor disputes and also outlawed yellow-dog contracts. In 1935, the National Labor Relations Act (the Wagner Act) guaranteed all employees the right to organize and to bargain collectively. It also established the National Labor Relations Board, a government agency that hears complaints regarding illegal acts by employers against unions and union members. Additional gains for labor came from the passage of the Fair Labor Standards Act of 1938, which guaranteed a minimum hourly wage and overtime pay for work beyond 40 hours in any week.

The Congress of Industrial Organizations
The favorable attitude of the federal government toward organized labor in the 1930s brought both union growth and change. By 1940, there were nearly 9 million union workers. The AFL, however, no longer completely dominated the labor movement. New industries had sprung up, with jobs—such as assembly-line work in automobile plants—that did not fit any of the traditional AFL craft-based categories. Many workers and the leaders of some local unions felt that they would be in a stronger position if they were organized by industry rather than by craft. For example, under a craft-based system employees in a small clothing factory might belong to three or four different unions— one for cutters, one for tailors, one for unskilled labor—yet they all shared the same working conditions and had to bargain with the same employers. In 1938, a group of industry-based unions broke away from the AFL and formed their own national federation, the Congress of Industrial Organizations (CIO).

Although the AFL and the CIO differed in their approaches to labor organization—the AFL being craft-based and the CIO industry-based— they were similarly committed to the concept of unionism. The rivalry between the two groups acted as a spur to their efforts to enroll new members. The economic boom of the war years was also favorable to union growth, and the War Labor Board strongly supported the unions' rights to organize and bargain collectively during wartime. As shown in *Fig. 31.1*, membership in 1945 was four times larger than it had been only ten years earlier.

Postwar period
After the war was over and government controls on production, prices, and wages were dropped, the unions began to use the new power they had gained as a result of their rapid increase in membership. Strikes increased in frequency and duration, some of them causing serious economic damage throughout an entire industry. These work stoppages, combined with the generally unsettled condition of the postwar economy, led to a call for new legislation regarding unions. The result was the Labor-Management Relations Act (the Taft-Hartley Act), which was passed in 1947 not only over the noisy objections of union leaders and members but also over the veto of President Truman.

The Taft-Hartley Act established a list of unfair labor practices which, if carried out by unions, could be reported by employers to the National Labor Relations Board. One such outlawed practice was the **closed shop** — *a factory or business in which only union members are accepted for employment.* At the same time, legal status was conferred on the **union shop** — *a factory or business in which every employee must join the union within a specified period after being hired if he or she is not a union member when hired.* Restrictions on the use of injunctions against strikes and other union activities were eased, and the president was given the power to intervene in any strike that he judged to be a threat to national health or safety.

In 1959, the Labor-Management Reporting and Disclosure Act (the Landrum-Griffin Act) was passed. This act further regulated union activities by making union leaders accountable to the secretary of labor concerning the fairness of union elections and the handling of union finances.

Weakened by legislation and threatened with government investigation of charges of corruption and communist infiltration within some unions, the labor movement sought strength through increased unity. After several years of negotiations, the AFL and the CIO merged in 1955. In 1976, the

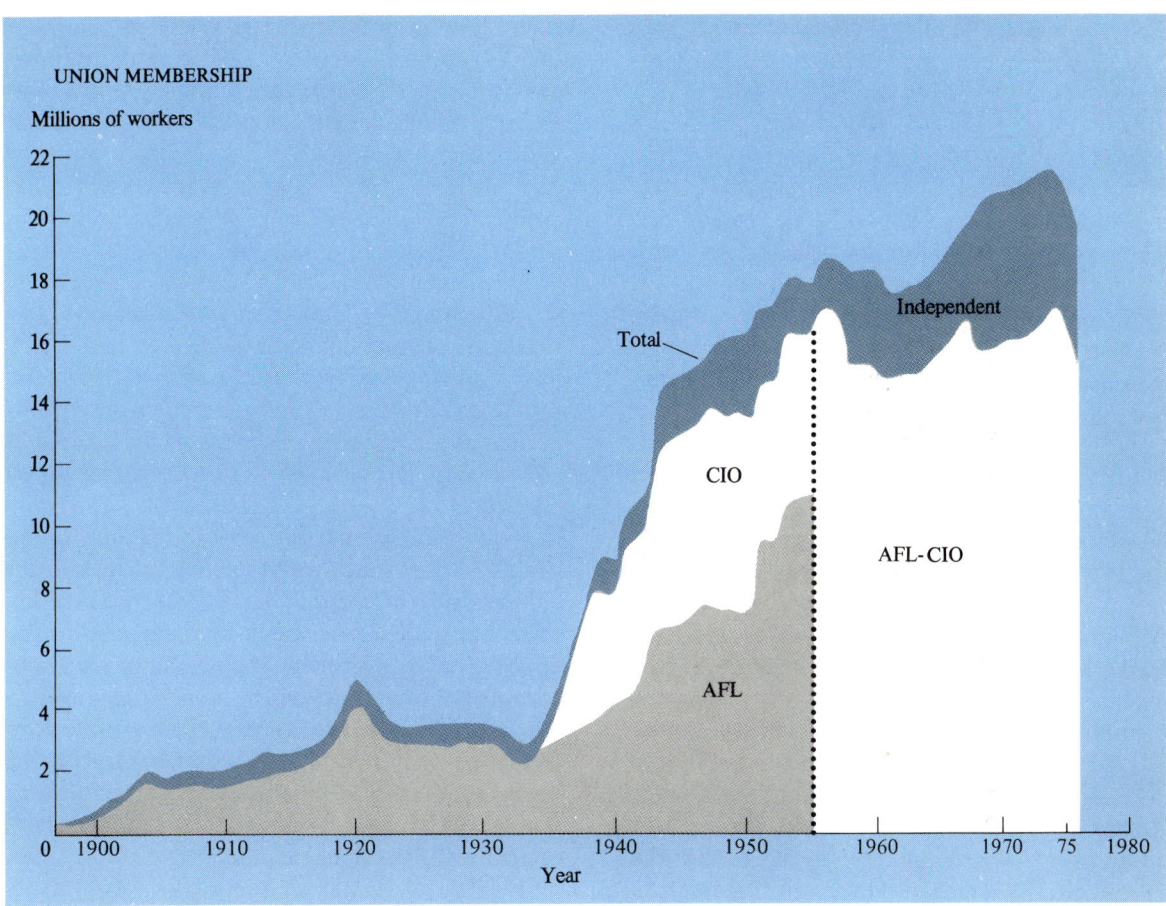

SOURCE: *Historical Statistics of the United States,* and *Handbook of Labor Statistics,* United States Department of Labor.

Fig. 31.1
Since the establishment of organized labor in the United States during the late nineteenth century, total union membership has grown to over 21 million workers, which is about one-fourth of the civilian labor force. Comparing the rate of union growth over the years, we see a dramatic increase after 1935. However, the upward trend has not been constant. During the late 1950s and early 1960s, all unions suffered a period of declining membership. In more recent years membership has remained relatively steady.

AFL-CIO numbered 15.3 million members; another 4.6 million workers belonged to independent unions such as the Teamsters, the United Mine Workers, and the United Auto Workers. About 22 percent of the civilian labor force in the United States is unionized; the percentage is even higher in certain industries, such as transportation and construction, where well over half the workers belong to unions. The labor union is now recognized as a permanent part of the American economic system.

The modern labor union

Structure
There are three levels of union organization. Most basic is the local union, which can consist of a few dozen workers or many thousands of workers. The local enrolls members, collects dues, holds meetings to discuss problems, and negotiates contracts.

The local union is a branch of a national union. The national union, to which the local pays about half of the dues it collects, determines the broad policies within which the locals must operate. The national union is responsible for extending unionization into previously unorganized areas and often provides financial assistance to new or weak locals. The national staff usually includes expert lawyers and negotiators who will assist local officials during contract talks.

The third level of organization is the federation level, which is an association of national unions. The AFL-CIO is the largest organization of this type. The main role of the federation, which depends on the national unions for funds, is to speak for the interests of all unionized workers and to encourage public concern on labor issues.

Functions
In the course of the long history of unionism in America, the functions of the unions have changed in response to the changing needs of workers. Originally, organized groups of workers were mutual-aid societies; then, like the Knights of Labor, they attempted to become agents of social change. With the founding of the AFL—marked by an interest in short-term, pragmatic goals—the functions of the union were narrowed to a few very specific activities regarding wages and hours of workers. The trend in the twentieth century has been toward broader concerns, and the union today has taken on a wider variety of functions than ever before. Among the functions it performs are collective bargaining on economic issues, fraternal and benevolent functions, and educational and political activities.

COLLECTIVE BARGAINING

How collective bargaining works
Collective bargaining is *the process by which union and management arrive at a mutually acceptable contract that spells out the privileges and obligations (such as wages and working hours and conditions) of both parties for an agreed-upon period.*

Long before a contract expires, the union begins to draw up a set of specific proposals for changes to be included in the new contract. During the same period, the company, association, or government agency that employs the union workers formulates its own suggestions for change.

Following a prescribed schedule, the two sides meet to negotiate a new contract. During the bargaining sessions initial positions are modified. Eventually a new agreement may be reached. Union members vote on the proposed contract and if it receives majority approval, a contract is signed. This agreement will govern the employment relationship over the life of the contract (usually one or two years) until changing economic conditions—higher cost of living, larger union membership, new government regulations, increased competition from imports, larger settlements won by other unions—make it desirable to alter the agreement once again.

If collective bargaining breaks down
There are some instances, however, in which the contract terms requested by union and management are vastly different, or in which one side refuses to make concessions in the negotiation process. If an agreement is not reached by the time the old contract expires, the union may use its ulti-

mate weapon against management by calling a strike. Although strikes are always featured prominently in the news, they actually occur relatively infrequently. In 1978, strikes caused the loss of about 27 million work days of labor, which was only about one-seventh of one percent of total working time of the labor force. Since World War II, the loss in work days has only once exceeded one percent of total working time, and that was in 1946, when the labor force was reacting to the restrictions that had existed throughout the war. In the years between, man-days lost have ranged only from one-tenth to one-half of one percent of total working time. Unions employ strikes only as a last resort because a shutdown invariably causes financial hardship not only for the employers but also for the workers who must go without their salaries.

The economic damage a strike can cause an employer varies from industry to industry. In manufacturing industries, where factories normally operate below potential production capacity, production is often increased and larger than normal inventories are accumulated before contract talks begin. Many orders can be filled from excess inventory during one strike, and after the strike is settled, inventories can be rebuilt if industries operate at full capacity for a time.

But the situation is different in, for example, service industries. If the operations personnel of an airline go out on strike, the company loses customers to competing carriers, and it is difficult to make up for this loss of revenue at a later date. A very large or diversified corporation may continue to operate some divisions profitably while others are on strike, thereby softening the economic impact, but a company with only one product loses its entire revenue during a strike. Large corporations can often afford to outwait strikers, but small companies may be ruined by the loss of income.

Terms of the contract

The finished contract usually covers the following basic areas: wages and hours of work, job seniority and security, grievance procedures, and status of the union on the job. It may also cover other issues, such as job safety, supplementary benefits, and penalties for breach of contract.

Wages and hours

The primary purposes of the contract are to determine the wages paid to various kinds of workers, the rate for overtime work, the length of the work week, and the number of paid holidays. Since the end of World War II, wages have been increasing steadily. Even more dramatic has been the growth of nonwage (or fringe) benefits such as paid holidays, vacations, sick leave, health and accident insurance, retirement plans, and so on. Before World War II, the total pay for most workers was for time worked or output produced. Today it is rare that a worker is paid only for hours worked or output produced. It is estimated that from 20 to 25 percent of most payroll costs at present are for fringe benefits.

Some people have argued that growing wage and fringe-benefit demands of union members produce inflationary pressure in the economy. That is, they push wages up in periods of prosperity but do not let them fall when economic conditions are unfavorable. Of course, the wage demands of workers are reinforced by their fear of inflation, and this circular pattern is difficult to break.

How will the amount of the wage increase be determined? Four factors are central to wage negotiations.

The productivity of workers

If productivity has increased, the company can raise workers' wages without having to raise prices or trim profit margins. If productivity has fallen off, employers have good grounds for refusing to make substantial wage increases.

The cost of living

Current union demands for higher wages are often based on the rising cost of living. Many contracts today contain provisions known as **escalator clauses** that *provide for automatic increases in wages and/or other benefits to match any rise that might occur in the cost of living as measured by the Consumer Price Index or another measure.* Tying wages to the cost of living appears to be the only way workers can maintain their purchasing power in the face of rapidly rising prices. But the eventual effect of this link between prices and wages is to keep inflation spiraling upward.

The going rate of wages for similar work The union may point out that in neighboring cities workers performing the same kind of work are better paid, or they may point to a higher-paid job that calls for approximately the same skills, suggesting that the wages ought to be the same for both jobs. For example, striking taxi drivers may ask for a wage increase that would allow them to earn the same weekly pay that city transit (bus and subway) system workers receive. If the wage for a certain type of job is already high compared with the going wage for similar jobs, management can be expected to use this comparison in defending the existing salary level.

The company's ability to pay When the company has had an especially profitable year, the union points to management's increased ability to pay as justification for its wage demands. Likewise, if business is bad, the company will use that as a reason to turn down union demands.

Although these criteria may be based on quantifiable data, it is clear that they cannot provide a scientific formula for objectively determining wage and benefit increases. Statistics on profit margins and productivity can be juggled by each side to strengthen its case. Furthermore, the different criteria may contradict one another to some extent. For example, a company earning less than a normal rate of profit may be paying lower wages for a certain type of work than other employers because it does not have the ability to pay more. The criterion of the "going wage" would suggest an increase, but the criterion of "ability-to-pay" would suggest that no increase was warranted.

Other factors Other, harder-to-measure factors can also influence wage settlements: the political strength of the union, the climate of public opinion regarding the raise the union is requesting, the union's ability to subsidize members during a long strike, and the firm's ability to withstand or compensate for the loss of revenue during a strike are all determinants in wage settlements.

Job security and seniority
Under seniority rules, the workers who have been with the company the longest get first consideration in all job changes—promotions, transfers, and layoffs. The last worker to be hired is the first to be fired when demand drops, the last to be rehired when it picks up again, and the last to be considered for promotion.

The seniority system has provoked criticism from several sources. Some managers, for example, feel that it prevents them from laying off inefficient senior workers. Other critics assert that seniority rules hurt minority workers especially. Because of discriminatory practices by unions, minority workers often have had difficulty in getting hired; as a consequence they have not been able to build up any seniority, and therefore are "last hired, first fired."

On the other hand, it has been argued that seniority is a sensible criterion for promotion, since it is often those with long work experience who are the most competent and most efficient employees. In companies in which on-the-job training is essential, so too is the cooperation of the worker who possesses the skills and must provide the training. Seniority insulates those providing the training from later competition by those whom they have trained. Without such protection for incumbent workers, it becomes much more difficult to provide training on the job.

Grievance procedures
It is to be expected that in actual practice there will be disagreements about the way contract rules regarding the relationship between labor and management are to be interpreted and applied. For example, suppose the Efficiency Manufacturing Company fires old Joe Dodder (who has been with them for 23 years) in a time of suddenly decreased demand for its goods. The boss says that Joe was fired with cause. Joe continually extended his lunch hour an extra 15 minutes. Joe, however, claims that he is the victim of false charges that were invented so that the company could circumvent the seniority rules that forbid laying him off—the contract rules specify that seniority must be observed; however, they also permit firing "for cause."

To determine how these rules should apply to Joe's case, the contract will set up certain grievance procedures. There may be a committee or a union official to whom Joe may make his complaint and ask for an investigation. Or a neutral third party may be appointed to arbitrate the matter. Overseeing the handling of grievances throughout the life of the contract is one of the important obligations of the union toward its members.

Status of the union
The degree of recognition that the union is to receive is an issue in many contracts. The union usually prefers a contract specifying a union shop. This strengthens the size and influence of the union and means that all those who profit from collective bargaining will be dues-paying members. The unions point to certain advantages for the employer in a union shop. They claim that the requirement that workers join the union helps to screen out job applicants who are not interested in or capable of steady employment, and so the rate of employee turnover is cut down. And, the unions argue, they will share some of the employer's responsibilities, such as providing job training and supervising the quality and output of work.

In spite of these arguments, many states have passed **right-to-work laws** *that make it illegal to require membership in a union as a condition of employment.* Supporters of right-to-work laws claim that it is unfair to require employees to join an organization—perhaps one whose goals and ideology they do not support—as a condition of employment. Membership obligations may in some cases be a financial hardship, for the initial cost of joining a union may be very high, in addition to regular dues. Social critics have also pointed out that many unions (skilled construction trades, for example) continue to discriminate against various minorities, particularly nonwhites, so the union shop perpetuates the economic problems of these groups. More than one-third of all states, particularly in the South, where antiunion feeling is strong, now have right-to-work laws.

The union's right to participate in decisions regarding the way work is done or work quotas are assigned may also be spelled out in the contract. Although companies are understandably reluctant to share many of their managerial functions, organized labor has recently been asking for an increased role in the formation of business goals and policy.

Role of government in collective bargaining
In the United States, except in wartime, there has been a strong tradition of resistance to government control of wages and prices. In 1971, however, as part of a concerted action to cope with domestic inflation and the serious international monetary crisis that had developed, the Nixon administration announced a 90-day freeze on wages

and prices that was quickly transformed into a three-year program of controls. Attempts to evaluate the effectiveness of that control program have been complicated by the need to assess the impact of other events that occurred during the same period—notably, the oil embargo and severe problems in world agriculture.

While government intervention in wages and prices occurs infrequently, participation in contract negotiations and various labor disputes is more common. This participation ranges from a few discreet words from government officials regarding the course they would like to see the negotiations take, to the personal intervention of the president. When negotiations are at a standstill, Department of Labor officials may be able to persuade both sides to accept the services of government mediators to act as neutral third parties, thus allowing the negotiations to continue. A strike may also be settled by submitting the differences between the two parties to arbitration by a group of government-appointed experts. Usually, but not always, this procedure is voluntary, although during the railroad strike of 1963, Congress passed a bill decreeing compulsory arbitration of the work-rules dispute that had caused the talks to break down.

Since the passage of the Taft-Hartley Act in 1947, the president has been empowered to intervene in strikes that he judged a threat to national health or safety by calling for a "cooling off" period, during which there could be no strike or lockout. In 1959, for example, the United States Supreme Court upheld an injunction against an industry-wide steel strike on the grounds that the strike's effect on specific defense projects imperiled national safety.* The emergency machinery of the Federal Mediation and Conciliation Service has been used many times in strikes of the steel, coal, and maritime industries, among others.

As our economic system becomes more complex and interdependent, it seems likely that government intervention of all kinds in labor disputes and contract talks will continue.

ACHIEVING HIGHER UNION WAGES

A basic goal of all unions is high wages. In pursuit of that goal, a union may attempt to influence the supply of and demand for labor. As shown in *Fig. 31.2,* if a union can control or restrict the supply of workers available to an employer, it will exert upward pressure on the equilibrium wage. A union also may attempt to raise the wage by changing the demand for labor. Assuming all other factors remain unchanged, an increase in demand for labor will result not only in a higher equilibrium wage but also in greater employment. Some of the ways in which organized labor attempts to modify equilibrium in labor markets are discussed below.

Modifying demand

Increasing productivity
The union may try to shift the demand curve for labor by improving the productivity of its members. Union-shop supervisors, for example, have the responsibility of ensuring that member workers are putting in a full day's work. They may also suggest changes in work procedures to make production more efficient, such as altering the positioning of workers or the sequence of steps in the production process. The union may also increase the marginal revenue product of its members by increasing their stock of human capital. This is one reason that unions have undertaken so many educational functions, training workers in their trade or helping to finance their attendance at a school or college.

---

*Steelworkers v. U.S., U.S. Supreme Court No. 504 (1959) 45 LRRM 2066.

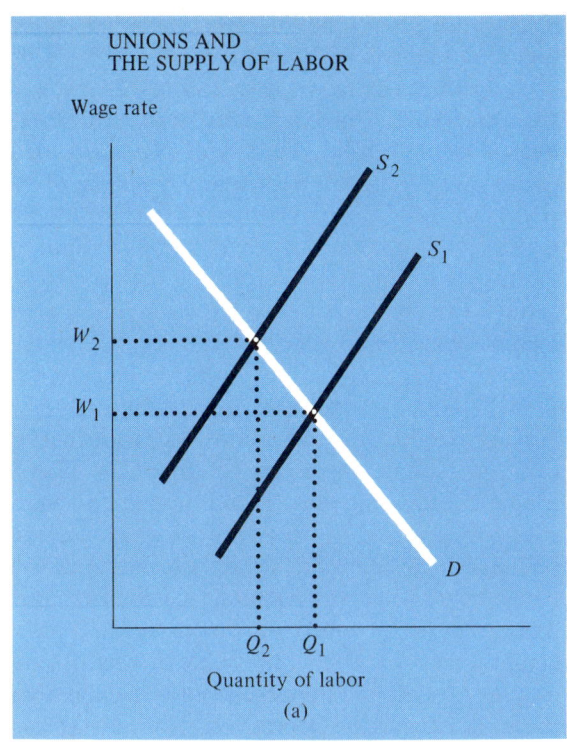 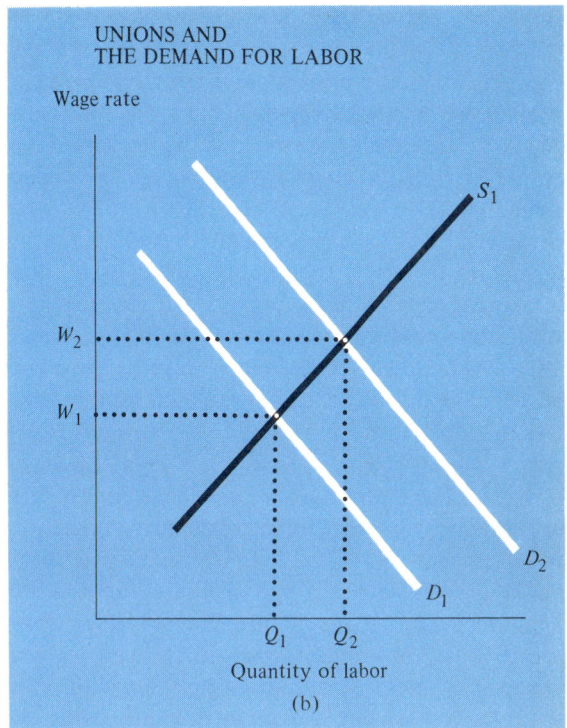

Fig. 31.2
(a) If unions are able to reduce the supply of labor from S_1 to S_2, the equilibrium wage rate will increase from W_1 to W_2. (b) By increasing the demand for labor from D_1 to D_2, unions can obtain a higher wage and additional employment for union workers.

Increasing the demand for union-made products ("look for the union label")

Another way that the union can increase the demand for labor is to increase the demand for the employer's product, since resource demand is derived from product demand. A good example of this can be seen in the advertising campaign for the International Ladies Garment Workers Union, asking consumers to look for and buy only clothes that bear the union label. Unions can also increase product demand by encouraging union members to buy the products of unionized corporations, rather than competitive products made in nonunion shops. Sometimes union members are offered discounts on these products. For example, members of the United Federation of Teachers can buy union-made cars at discount prices; thus they become customers of Ford or Chrysler rather than of Fiat or Toyota.

Featherbedding

Featherbedding, *the imposing by unions of limits on work loads, production quotas, or kinds of equipment to be used on the job,* also serves to increase the demand for labor. For example, the musicians' union requires that whenever any kind of music is played at a public performance—at a play, concert, on a television show—a minimum number of union musicians must be present. This rule is extended to cover cases in which the music is on tape or on a record. In such instances the producer of the entertainment must pay several musicians to sit idly by and listen to the recorded music during the performance. Clearly, such a practice increases the total demand for musicians and therefore helps to keep their wage rate up, but at the same time it wastes resources in nonproductive activity.

The union vs. nonunion workers A strong labor union may also affect the demand curve for labor in another way; it may differentiate the total demand for labor into two separate curves—the demand for union labor and the demand for nonunion labor. By using its bargaining strength, the union may succeed in pushing up the wages paid to union labor, but it may be at the expense of lower wages for nonunion workers. There is probably a limit to the extent of the wage differential, because, if the difference between union and nonunion wages is too great, it may be worthwhile for the employer to move to some other location where the union is not so powerful. This trend did, in fact, become apparent in the 1960s, when many large corporations moved their manufacturing operations to the South, which is still a largely nonunionized section of the country.

Modifying supply

The second general way in which the union can raise the equilibrium wage is to restrict the supply of labor, so that the supply curve shifts upward and to the left, reflecting a decrease in the supply of labor at all prices. The now-illegal closed shop and the union shop are both mechanisms that serve to limit the supply of workers. Another device used for this purpose is to limit union membership in certain industries and professions. It has been suggested that the American Medical Association limits the supply of doctors, thus keeping the earnings of doctors high. The AMA has also resisted transferring certain routine treatment functions from the doctor to a nurse or a paraprofessional. Although many members of the AMA are no doubt motivated by a concern for high quality medical care, their actions in limiting the supply of doctors and resisting the transfer of certain functions also serve to keep the annual income of doctors high.

Union success in gaining higher wages

How successful have the unions been in achieving their goal of higher wages for union members? Studies comparing union and nonunion wages over a long period of time have reached some surprising conclusions. In the last four decades, the percentage wage differential between skilled unionized trade and nonunionized jobs has actually decreased—there is less difference in the wages of union and nonunion workers today than there was during the Depression. This may be partially explained by the rising level of the minimum wage. Workers receiving the minimum wage are not members of unions, therefore as the minimum wage increases the average wage to nonunion workers also rises.

Although figures do show that unionized industries on the average pay a higher wage than nonunionized industries, it is not certain that the credit for this situation should go to the unions. By and large, the industries that have been unionized are those that are operating under conditions of high product demand and oligopolistic profit levels, so it is possible that the higher wages they pay are due to their greater prosperity rather than to the unionization of workers.

Other evidence shows clearly that unions bring about a certain wage rigidity. The model of perfect competition would lead us to expect that in times of economic ill health in any industry or in the entire economy, wage rates might fall, since during these times product demand and thus the demand for factors of production decrease. Yet rarely do we see wages drop. The unionized company that is experiencing financial difficulty will most often lay workers off or close down its plant, but not reduce the wages paid to those union members who are still employed.

UNIONS AND RESOURCE ALLOCATION

Arguments of critics of unions

Workers naturally prefer to move from lowpaying jobs to high-paying jobs, all other conditions being equal. According to the model of the perfectly competitive economy, this desire results in an efficient allocation of labor resources to maximize production. High-wage jobs are assumed to be those with high productivity, and therefore the increasing employment in these areas (due to the desire for the higher wages) will bring an expansion of total output.

Critics of unions say that unions interfere with the workings of this competitive process. Unions may limit the number of people who can actually move into the high-paying jobs, either directly by restricting union membership while insisting on a union shop, or indirectly through work rules or apprenticeship standards.

The same critics also suggest that unions have used their power of collective bargaining to break the link between high wages and high productivity. For example, union house painters receive high wages, but they also work under a set of rules (concerning width of brushes and number of workers on the job) that restricts productivity. Therefore nonunion painters would probably be able to paint a house faster than union painters, and they would get a lower hourly wage, even though their productivity would be greater. This inversion, in which high wages become associated with lowered productivity, is an obvious handicap to efficient allocation of labor resources. Union rules of seniority governing layoffs and promotions are also cited as practices that diminish efficiency.

Arguments of supporters of unions

Union leaders and supporters present a different view of the effect of unions on resouce allocation. They claim that the labor market can never be perfectly competitive, nor labor resources perfectly mobile, whatever the unions may do. They also suggest that union-backed wage increases do indeed serve to increase general productivity and are therefore a sign of efficient resource allocation. The history of many industries shows that rising wages will attract more productive workers. It can also be demonstrated that an increase in wages can serve as a stimulus to a worker's productivity. Workers who feel that they are underpaid may become apathetic and uninterested in the company's progress, whereas those who feel they are well paid are likely to have a stronger sense of involvement with the company.

INFLATION: ARE UNIONS TO BLAME?

Wage increases that are not based on increases in productivity tend to be inflationary. As wages go up, prices keep pace and, in the long run, unit labor costs and prices show a high degree of correlation. The long-lasting inflationary trend in the United States since the end of World War II is often viewed as being the direct result of the power of unions to demand unreasonable wage increases. During the last decade, however, a period characterized by both high inflation and high unemployment, the link between union wage demands and inflation became less clear.

Although union supporters certainly agree that inflation is a major problem, they put most of the blame for inflation on the companies that raise their prices when demand goes up. They contend that inflation is caused by management's unwillingness to share its profits with labor and its decision to pass all costs along to the consumer rather than give up income. Moreover, they claim that the economy is stimulated to real growth by increased wages, because workers have more purchasing power in their role as consumers.

Some economists today feel that the current inflationary trend—although it may have been started when prices were raised in response to increased demand in the postwar period—is now being fueled largely by wage increases. In recent years, wages have increased but the productivity rate has declined.

Of course, union workers are not the only ones who demand and receive wage increases, but union activities have proven to be influential in various ways. Union rhetoric may cause all workers to expect large and regular wage increases. On the other hand, if unions act responsibly in meeting the Carter administration's voluntary guidelines to dampen inflation, public officials may point to unions as a model for others to follow in their wage-determination activities. Some unions have the size and strength to demand and receive excessive wage increases and have succeeded in shifting the criteria for increases from productivity to other factors—such as cost of living and the going wage rate—which may contribute to the inflationary spiral. On balance, it seems as though unions do a better job of protecting their members as wage earners than they do of protecting them as consumers.

UNIONS AND THE MINIMUM-WAGE LAW

The Federal Fair Labor Standards Act, passed in 1937, set a statutory minimum hourly wage, and also decreed that overtime work should be given premium pay. Since then, amendments have increased the federal minimum wage to $2.90 an hour and further changes for 1980 and 1981 are found in the most recent amendments. Moreover, many states have also passed minimum-wage laws to protect those workers not covered by the federal law.

Interestingly, organized labor opposed the minimum-wage law at the time of its passage. Unions feared that once the government guaranteed wage levels for workers, it would be difficult to attract and hold dues-paying members, and they suspected that the drive for minimum wages was actually only a disguised effort to weaken the unions. They also feared that employers would treat the minimum wage as a maximum and that the differential between union and nonunion wages would be wiped out.

By the mid-1960s, when President Johnson, in his "war on poverty," asked for increased minimum-wage protection, the unions had changed their stand and had lined themselves up with supporters of minimum-wage legislation. At that point, the differential between union and nonunion wages had grown so marked that many business firms were leaving the unionized North and building factories in the southern states. This migration meant jobs lost to union workers, a trend that organized labor wanted to see halted. The passage of a uniform minimum wage above the wages paid in the South would dry up the supply of cheap labor that some businesses were finding there, thus protecting the union interests.

THE FUTURE OF LABOR UNIONS

Although union membership has gradually increased in the past few decades, the size of the labor force has increased even more rapidly, so that the percentage of workers who belong to unions has actually declined. Some union leaders blame this decline in the growth of organized labor on the restrictive effects of recent antilabor legislation, but labor economists point to other factors as being more important.

The labor movement in the United States has always been geared to blue-collar workers (such as factory workers and machinists), but in our changing economy the number of blue-collar jobs is decreasing and today more than one-half of all jobs employ white-collar workers (such as office workers). Although these workers traditionally have been less interested in union organizations than blue-collar workers, a number of recent changes suggest the possibility for substantial growth of white-collar unions. As a result of specialization of individual jobs, some white-collar workers find themselves further removed from management than previously; moreover, with rapid inflation and substantial unemployment, many of them now seek to enhance their income and working conditions through professional or union organizations. Among white-collar workers, those in the public sector seem to possess the greatest potential for substantial union gains. Union organizers have been able to stress not only economic benefits, but also improved job security for government workers whose employment may be threatened, for example, by taxpayer groups seeking actions that would trim the size of public payrolls. As a result, interest in collective bargaining has grown among previously unorganized groups who work in the public sector.

At the same time, support by the general public for public-sector unions is mixed, particularly as strikes by public employees disrupt activities traditionally regarded as essential, such as fire, police, and other emergency services. Some people have suggested that the right to strike by public employees be limited to less essential services (such as those provided by park employees, file clerks, etc.), but it is unlikely that such a division of essential and nonessential services could be formulated. More important, public employees have used the strike even where it is illegal to do so, and the threats of reprisals against striking employees have rarely materialized. As a practical matter, there is no easy way to replace all striking employees who normally perform an essential service (such as fire protection). Consequently, mechanisms such as fact finding and binding arbitration will, most likely, become more important as a means to mediate disputes in the public sector than as a means of mediation in unionized companies in the private sector.

Among the other factors that have inhibited union growth, a particularly important one has been a recent trend for population and industry to migrate from the Northeast and Midwest, traditional areas of union strength, to the South or "Sun Belt" where unions historically have been weak. The seeming inability of unions to make significant organizational breakthroughs in large-scale private industry in the South, especially in the garment and textile trades, suggests that union growth in the private sector may remain sluggish. This trend is reinforced by the spread of multinational corporations that possess the ability to shift production operations abroad in response to worker demands for higher wages. Moreover, with substantial public concern about inflation, organized labor is faced with an ever more difficult task in trying to convince Congress to enact legislation and to encourage regulation to stem the tide of relatively inexpensive imports which are threatening many traditional manufacturing jobs.

Unions also have failed to appeal to large segments of the labor force which traditionally have not organized. Since World War II, the proportion of women in the labor force has grown dramatically, yet only a modest segment of this group is affiliated with unions. In part, this is a result of women's traditionally weaker attachment to the labor force than men's, and of a desire to avoid labor conflict which might eliminate employment opportunities. With additional opportunities for employment of women in permanent positions and additional evidence of stronger attachment to the labor force by this group, the opportunities for organizing women's jobs seem to be more promising than in the past. Finally, minority workers who frequently have been excluded from craft unions may regard organized labor as a barrier to advancement, particularly inasmuch as seniority plays an important role in collective-bargaining agreements. Since the seniority provisions of union contracts may represent an impediment to upward mobility by minorities in previously "all-white'' occupations, the appeal of unions to various unrepresented groups seems mixed.

Although traditional blue-collar unions seem to be on the decline in today's economy, the concept of unionism continues to appeal to a broad spectrum of workers. Opportunities abound for increased union activity, and in light of historical evidence of union growth and survival even under particularly adverse conditions, it would be unwise to underestimate the impact that organized labor will likely have on the economy in the future.

Summary

■ This chapter looks at the history, structure, and function of labor unions in the United States and describes the process of collective bargaining and the impact unions have on supply and demand in the labor market.

■ Organized labor activities in the United States date back to the eighteenth century. The Knights of Labor, one of the first national unions, was organized in 1869. The American Federation of Labor (1886) concentrated on "pure and simple" unionism and organized workers according to craft. Antilabor measures in the late nineteenth and early twentieth centuries included lockouts, yellow-dog contracts, blacklists, labor spies, armed guards, and legal prohibition of union tactics. Major pieces of prolabor legislation were enacted in the 1930s, guaranteeing the right to organize, establishing the NLRB, and recognizing the 40-hour week. The CIO organizing drives of the 1930s unionized workers along industrial rather than craft lines, and both the AFL and the CIO grew steadily through and after World War II. The Taft-Hartley Act (1947) prohibited the closed shop but gave legal status to the union shop, and it also authorized the president to intervene if a strike threatened national health and safety. The AFL and CIO merged in 1955, but the major growth in recent years has been in independent unions.

■ Contemporary unions are organized on three levels: local, national, and federation. The major functions are collective bargaining (primarily on economic issues), fraternal and benevolent functions, and educational and political activities.

■ Under a collective-bargaining agreement, labor and management attempt to reach an agreement before an existing contract expires. A union may ultimately resort to a strike to win its demands, but the loss of working days of the total labor force caused by strikes in recent years has been only between one-tenth and one-half of one percent. A contract will usually specify wages and hours of work and fringe benefits, with the bargaining often revolving around issues of productivity, the cost of living, the going rate of pay in the industry, and the company's ability to pay; job security and seniority; grievance procedures; and the status of the union in the shop. Government frequently plays a role in collective bargaining, with involvement ranging from informal advice to presidential invocation of the Taft-Hartley Act, to the use of government mediators and arbitrators.

- Unions attempt to raise wages both through raising the demand for labor and limiting the supply. Demand for labor can be raised by increasing productivity, by increasing the demand for union-made goods, by featherbedding, and by differentiating the price of union and nonunion labor. Supply can be limited by forming a union shop or by limiting union membership. In the past four decades, the wage gap between unionized and nonunionized skilled workers has actually narrowed. Wages in unionized industries exhibit rigidity; in a recessionary period, a company may lay off workers but is unlikely to lower wages. Unionization of workers has tended to occur primarily in the most prosperous industries.

- Critics of unions say that they are inefficient in allocating labor resources, since they reduce competition and break the link between increased productivity and higher wages. Supporters of unions argue, on the other hand, that the market for labor can never achieve perfect competition and mobility, and that higher wages do spur both productivity and consumer demand.

- Some critics of unions argue that wage increases won by unions which are not accompanied by increases in productivity are the major reason for the inflation rates of the past two decades. Unions respond that the inflationary problem is caused by price increases, while wage increases promote real economic growth. In the past few years, unions have done a better job in protecting their members as workers than in protecting them as consumers.

- In the 1930s, unions generally opposed the imposition of minimum-wage laws, fearing that minimum wages would become maximums, close wage differentials, and weaken unions. In the 1960s, however, unions generally supported the extension of minimum wage legislation, since it would help dry up the pool of low-wage labor in the largely nonunion South.

- The percentage of the labor force that is unionized has declined in recent years, along with the decline in the blue-collar proportion of the work force. The growth areas for unionization have been and probably will be in white-collar occupations and especially in public-sector jobs. Since strikes by public employees are politically controversial, it is likely that government mediation and binding arbitration in the public sector will increase. The shift of industrial plants to the nonunion Sun Belt and overseas presents serious difficulties for organized labor, as does the historical difficulty of organizing women and minority workers.

Key Terms

strike
lockout
yellow-dog contracts
protective injunction
closed shop
union shop
collective bargaining
escalator clauses
right-to-work laws
featherbedding

Review & Discussion

1. How did the American Federation of Labor differ from the Knights of Labor, one of the first national unions? What were the limitations of the AFL's strategy of organizing workers along craft lines?

2. Describe the techniques used by businesses to prevent union organization. What conditions during the 1930s changed the public attitude toward unions? What were the major provisions of the Wagner Act and the Norris-LaGuardia Act? How did the Taft-Hartley and Landrum-Griffin Acts restrict the actions of labor?

3. Describe the organizational structure of a modern union. What are the functions of a modern union? Why has the percentage of workers belonging to unions declined in recent years?

4. Briefly describe the process of collective bargaining. What are the major features included in a contract with management? What factors would be considered in settling on a wage increase? How might the various criteria for determining a settlement conflict with each other?

5. What are "right-to-work" laws? How do they affect the position of the union? In what ways may the government intervene in labor disputes?

6. With respect to demand and supply in the labor market, what are the objectives of unions? How do unions attempt to accomplish these objectives?

7. How do unions affect the allocation of resources? Inflation? The profits of large corporations?

8. Do you see any signs that contemporary unions are broadening their functions and taking a more active stance on social and political issues? Do you think they should?

Application 15:
Declining Memberships in Labor Unions

It may soon be all over for organized labor in the United States. That, at least, is what a number of articles in popular magazines have suggested in recent years. In 1972, *U.S. News and World Report* asked in a headline, "Is the Labor Movement Losing Ground?" and then raised the question again four years later with the query, "Are Unions Losing Their Clout?" In 1977, *Newsweek* gave a big spread to "Labor's Creaking House." And the following year, *The Atlantic Monthly* and *Harper's* announced "The Big Squeeze on Labor Unions" and "The Last Days of the Labor Movement." In the *Harper's* article, syndicated columnist Nicholas von Hoffman wrote: "On the teeter-totter with Big Business, the unions find themselves high in the sky with legs flailing. The vaunted labor vote has vanished; the labor lobby has come down with pernicious anemia, and labor itself, this once mighty force in the society, has shrunk to the status of just another special interest group, like consumers or the steel industry or sugar refiners."

The labor movement, of couse, is still with us, having survived its most recent obituaries just as it did those of the past. Nonetheless, there is no lack of evidence that its power and membership are far below the robust levels of its younger days. More workers these days are tossing unions out of their factories in what are known as decertification elections. Unions lost 21,600 members this way in 1977, up from 4800 a decade earlier. Unions that wanted to continue representing workers at a particular plant were able to do so only about a third of the time in 1977, although unions won more than half of the decertification elections held in 1967.

The union record is equally dismal when it comes to recruiting new members. During World War II, unions won about eight of every ten organizing elections. But the proportion dropped to less than two-thirds by the mid-1960s, and to less than half by the late 1970s.

As a consequence, although millions of workers have been entering the labor force every year

APPLICATION 15: DECLINING MEMBERSHIPS IN LABOR UNIONS

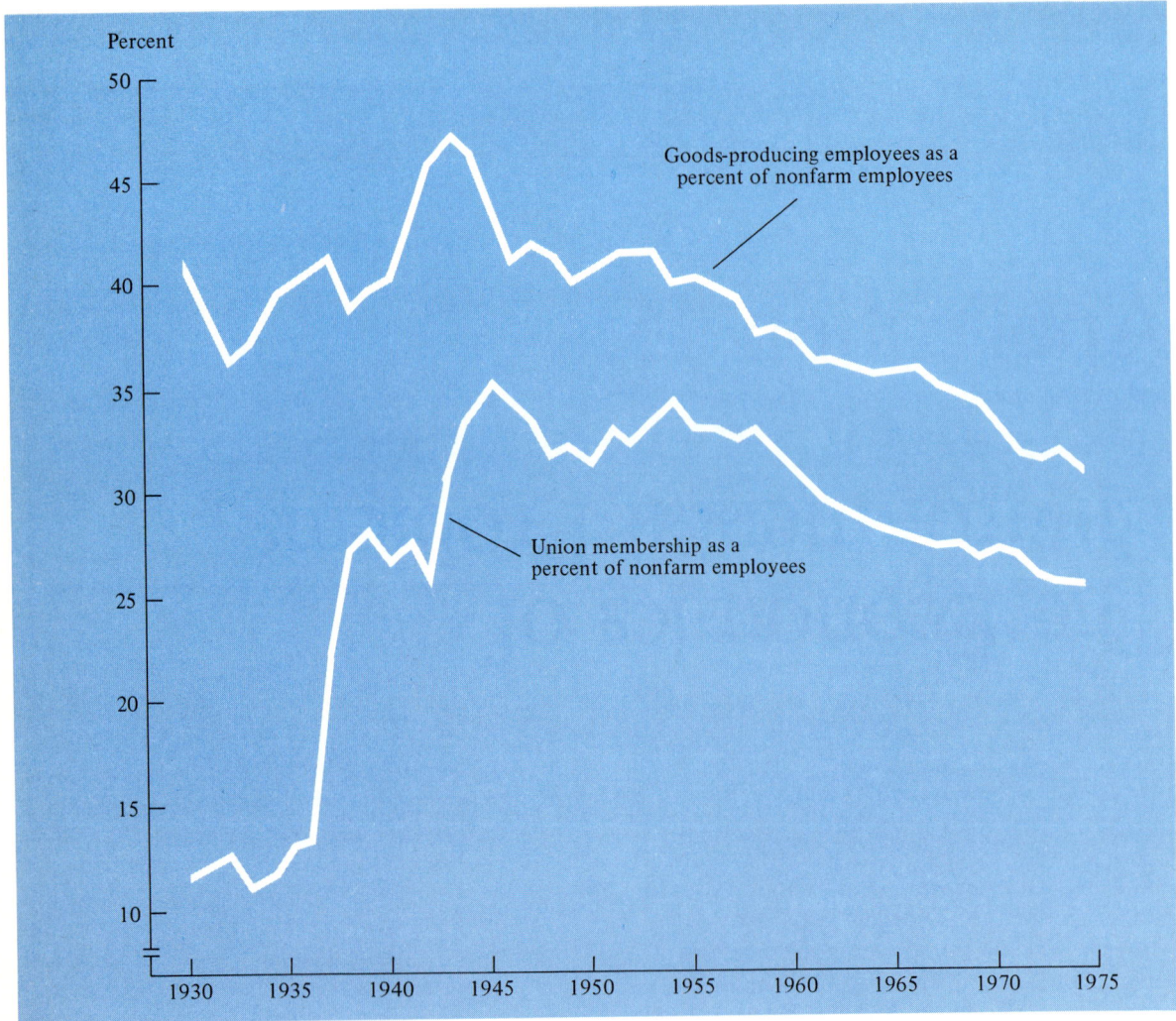

SOURCE: Bureau of Labor Statistics.

Figure 1

since 1974, union membership peaked that year at 22.8 million workers. Indeed, since the end of World War II, the proportion of nonfarm employees who belong to unions has declined, as *Fig. 1* shows, from more than one in every three to about one in four. Even such onetime union strongholds as the construction industry have given way; in 1978, almost half of all new construction in the United States was undertaken by nonunion labor.

The labor movement has been weakened by several social and economic changes. Companies increasingly do business in so many nations that a single union in any one of them is able to affect it to a far lesser degree than would have been the case a generation ago. Companies based in some of these foreign nations have cut into markets once dominated by American firms, costing jobs in such highly unionized industries as textiles, shoes, and steel. There is also the Sun-Belt phenomenon, the gradual movement of people and companies away from the union strongholds of the Northeast and Midwest to other parts of the country, particularly the South, where unions have never had much of a foothold.

In addition, today's workers are, on the average, younger, better educated, more affluent, and less worried than their parents had been about the possibility of unemployment. They tend neither to rally to calls for worker solidarity nor to be stirred by orations on class struggles.

Management, too, has changed. Companies are not only paying more attention to the needs and desires of employees, but also are coming out into the open with antiunion programs in the name of increased management flexibility and efficiency. Many are hiring management consultants who in a simpler time would have been called union busters.

However, the principal cause of the diminished economic role of organized labor has been the nation's gradual shift from a manufacturing to a service economy. Since the early 1940s, factory jobs have dropped from nearly half of all nonfarm employment to about a third, a decline that, as *Fig. 1* demonstrates, closely parallels the change in union membership. The balance was tilting against such industries as construction, mining, transportation, and manufacturing in which unions had traditionally been strong, and in favor of difficult-to-organize, white-collar employers such as insurance companies, banks, publishers, and other service and trade organizations.

Questions for discussion

☐ Between 1936 and 1938, union membership as a fraction of the nonfarm labor force doubled. Another sharp, although smaller, upturn took place between 1942 and 1945, as can be seen from *Fig. 1*. What events can you cite to account for these spurts?

☐ In the automation scare of the 1950s, unions worried that robots would soon replace workers in factories. Although that has not yet happened to a meaningful degree, automation has played a role in the decline of unions. Discuss why automation would affect union membership.

☐ How might unions be able to stop the decline in their memberships?

Part VIII

The Economics of Current Problems

Chapter 32

The Economics of Environmental Problems

What to look for in this chapter

How can economic analysis contribute to our understanding and solution of environmental problems?

What are the hidden costs of production and consumption? What is an economic externality?

What are the major types of remedies which have been proposed for dealing with environmental problems? How successful have they been?

How does cost-benefit analysis provide a means of determining how much pollution control is socially desirable and economically efficient?

In a much earlier, simpler time when population was less dense, the use of the atmosphere and waters to dispose of waste products seemed acceptable, since the volume of waste seemed relatively small. Moreover, when one area became uninhabitable or undesirable as a place to live and work, it was comparatively easy to move to other, unspoiled areas of the country. As we enter the final decades of the twentieth century, however, and face a situation in which much of the land area has already been exploited and the volume of waste products has grown enormously, no longer is it considered acceptable to pollute our air and water with the by-products of production and consumption. The rapid, often drastic changes that have taken place in twentieth-century America have brought about significant material gains for much of the population. But these same developments have concurrently given rise to environmental problems which constitute the focus of this chapter.

Since the 1960s, concern about environmental problems has heightened. Environmental issues hold special interest for economists. Their interest is focused around two central questions: (1) How can the American economy best continue to prosper and grow without, at the same time, permanently damaging or destroying the environment? More fundamentally, is it possible to maintain incomes without seriously, perhaps permanently, damaging the environment? (2) What mechanisms exist to help deal with the devastating effects of pollution? In attempting to answer these questions, economists have looked closely at the trade-offs involved in dealing with environmental problems. They also have analyzed the costs associated with production and consumption. In many instances, production and consumption are accompanied by hidden costs. When these costs are ignored, prices are lower and output is larger than they otherwise would be. And yet, the failure to consider these hidden costs is a major cause of the environmental problems we face today.

HIDDEN COSTS—
A LONG-TERM PROBLEM

Increasing numbers of people in our society are becoming concerned about the hidden costs of the production and the use of a variety of commodities. A good example of these costs is provided by the daily newspaper. The price the consumer pays for the paper (together with advertising and other revenues) covers the cost to the supplier of buying the newsprint, hiring reporters and press operators, and buying machines that print, cut, and fold the paper.

Nevertheless, there are many costs of the paper's production that are not included in the price of the product, but that ultimately have an enormous impact on society. One is the cost of the loss of the trees used for the paper. Cutting down the trees may mean destroying the recreational and aesthetic value of a tract of land. It means that the land loses the natural fertilizer provided by fallen leaves and dead tree trunks. When the trees are cut down, the soil may lose much of its ability to absorb and retain moisture and hard rains will cause erosion of the land.

Another aspect of the hidden cost of the paper is the pollution caused by the production of the newsprint. Most paper mills dump great quantities of a sludge composed of paper pulp, processing chemicals, and inorganic dyes into nearby rivers. These substances contaminate or kill much of the animal and plant life of the river, and they make the water unusable for humans as well.

A third type of hidden cost involved in the production of the newspaper is the cost of disposing of the paper. We speak of the people who buy the paper as the final consumers, but they do not really *consume* the paper. They extract from it a certain amount of consumer utility in the form of information and entertainment, and then discard it. If the paper is left in its solid form, it must be taken to a garbage dump, buried in a landfill, or carried by barge and discarded at sea; if the paper is burned, it is simply translated into another type of waste—gases that will pollute the air.

The hidden costs of pollution and environmental damage incurred by the many processes of production are often cited as a problem specific to modern technological societies, especially capitalist economies. In reality, however, the problem is as old as civilization itself. The irrigation techniques that permitted the ancient Sumerians and Babylonians to produce adequate amounts of food did such severe damage to the ecological balance of the environment that eventually all of Mesopotamia was turned into an infertile desert. Moreover, the same dusky chemical haze that hangs over Gary, Indiana, and Lorain, Ohio, can be found in the air of steel-making cities of communist Russia.

Although the problem of pollution itself is not new, the magnitude of the problem in today's world is. Previously, when population was relatively sparse, the assimilation of wastes caused little damage. But today's waste loads are severely straining the capacity of the atmosphere, rivers, lakes, and land to absorb them.

Changing attitudes

Fortunately, modern attitudes toward pollution are also changing. Contemporary Americans are showing an increasing willingness to pay the opportunity cost of reducing pollution and environmental damage. This willingness is probably due in part to high standards of material prosperity. Americans enjoy such a vast quantity of goods and services that they are willing to sacrifice some portion of them in order to obtain an environment that is healthier, quieter, and more beautiful.

One way to explain this is to classify protection of the environment as a luxury good, with the demand for it increasing as GNP goes up. Or, to put it in terms of the concept of marginal utility, the more goods and services people already have, the less value they place on additional units. For example, a family that already owns three cars might be quite willing to give up an additional car in order to get a 25 percent reduction in air pollution. But a family that has no car at all would attach a much higher value to obtaining that first car and probably would not be willing to sacrifice the car even to achieve a 100 percent reduction in air pollution. For an affluent nation, the opportunity cost of reducing pollution would seem relatively small; for a nation with a low level of production, the cost would be much greater.

ECONOMIC EXTERNALITIES

The hidden costs associated with production, distribution, use, and disposal of a daily newspaper, for example, arise because many activities of both producers and consumers have effects which the market fails to record. This occurs because in many areas of economic activity private property rights are not well established. As long as private property rights are clearly defined, people must pay for benefits received and must be compensated for costs or discomforts incurred. If, for example, an individual wanted to dump waste products in a *private* land fill, he or she must pay the owner to do so. On the other hand, an individual's use of *publicly owned* resources such as the air and water is not, in general, limited. These resources are owned by everyone, and yet no single person has the authority (or ability) to ensure that people pay when they use the air or water for waste disposal. When people drive their private automobiles, the tailpipe emissions add pollutants to the air. At present there is no direct charge levied on individuals specifically for their use of the air in this fashion even though, in combination with the emissions of others, there are costs to society resulting from these pollutants.

When the actions taken by some in using a resource affect others, then an **economic externality** exists. This term refers to *a situation in which the use of resources by some individuals has unintended side effects on the welfare of others, and in which there is no economic mechanism to record the change in welfare.* No one stands ready to charge a fee for the use of the resource, and no one is in a position to compensate individuals for the harm inflicted upon them by the actions of others. The distinguishing feature of externalities is that they are economic activities that do not or cannot involve market relationships or transactions, and thus people may receive benefits without any direct cost and may incur costs or discomfort without compensation.

Externalities may be either harmful or beneficial. *When the actions of a producer have a harmful effect on others and when no compensation is paid to the affected individuals, the outcome is called an* **external diseconomy.** If, for example, a chemical company in the process of making goods for its customers produces toxic or foul-smelling waste products which are then dumped into a river, the company has created an external diseconomy. Other downstream users of the river must cope with the chemical company's pollutants, but in general they, and not the chemical company, must bear the cost of either putting up with a polluted river or of purifying the water. The external diseconomy arises when individuals or communities downstream are not compensated for the harm inflicted upon them.

Conversely, *when a producer's actions have a beneficial effect on others and payment cannot be extracted from those who receive benefits, the outcome is called an* **external economy.** If the chemical company provides landscaping and attractive buildings which enhance the value of adjacent properties, there is no mechanism through which the company can charge others for the unintended benefits which have accrued to them. The external economy arises when the chemical company is not paid for the benefits it provides to others.

An economic externality can also be defined as a divergence between **private costs** of production *(the costs to the producer)* and **social costs** of production *(the costs to society, such as the damage caused by air and water pollution, in addition to private costs).* When suppliers of a product or service calculate costs, they take into account only direct production costs, including the cost of the resources purchased and the opportunity cost of remaining in business. If the supplier does not have to pay for the use of the air, water, or the final disposal of the product after all consumer utility has been extracted, these costs will not be included in pricing the product.

Yet the social costs do exist. They are measurable, and they must eventually be paid by someone. They will be paid in the form of taxes that finance a city sanitation department; as medical bills for the treatment of respiratory and heart diseases, lung cancer, and skin allergies; in loss of productivity and in direct damage to crops, clothing, buildings, and other types of property; in the high cost of boating, fishing, or swimming in special recreational areas rather than in the polluted river; and in the loss of valuable land or the destruction of important ecological systems. The Environmental Protection Agency has estimated the annual damage caused by air pollution alone at over $16 billion. And this includes only the direct monetary cost of damage to human health, vegetation, materials, and property devaluation, not the aesthetic and other more subjective costs as well.

For the individual producer, then, resources such as air and water are free. But society as a whole incurs additional costs to secure air we can safely breathe, water we can safely drink, and viable ecological systems.

Effects of divergence between private and social costs

One of the effects of the divergence between private costs and social costs is that a much larger quantity of a good will be demanded than would be otherwise. Consumers tend to think of the cost of the good as its purchase price, but that price measures only the private cost. The social cost, which the consumers as a group must inevitably pay, is not included in the purchase price. Therefore, for a good with external diseconomies, the quantity demanded is artificially high. This is illustrated in *Fig. 32.1.* If the going market price of a newspaper is 15¢, 1 million will be demanded. But a market price of 15¢ means that suppliers are considering only the private cost of producing the paper. When the social costs are added, the total cost of the paper is 25¢. At that price level, only 300,000 papers would be demanded. Because of this divergence between private and social costs, consumers buy 700,000 more newspapers than they would actually want to consume if they were required to pay the total cost. Resources are thus misallocated in production since the true preferences of consumers are to use those resources for the production of other goods.

EXTERNAL DISECONOMIES: POSSIBLE REMEDIES

There can be no question of the burden that the existence of external diseconomies places on an economic system. We pay vast sums to alleviate

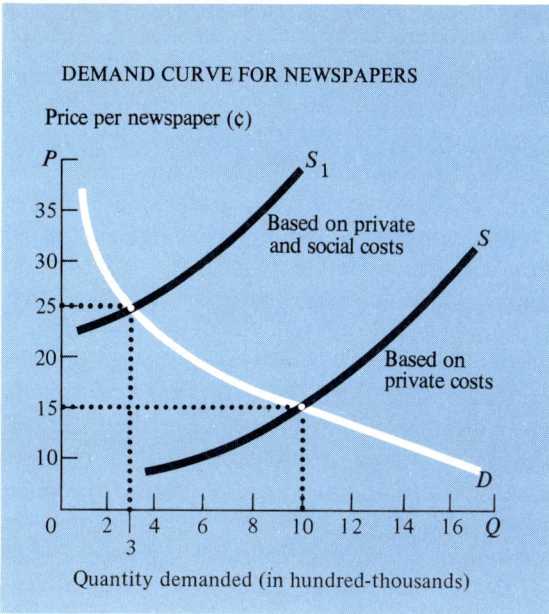

Fig. 32.1
If the supply curve for newspapers is based on private costs alone, the quantity purchased will be 1 million and the market price will be 15¢. However, when the supply curve is based on both private costs and social costs, we see that the quantity traded is only 300,000 papers and that the market price is 25¢. In other words, when product price reflects private costs alone, buyers will demand a larger quantity than they would actually want to consume if they were required to pay the total cost.

the external effects of production processes. We must live with such problems as noise and congestion, externalities that are hard to measure in dollars and cents. Because supply schedules are based on private costs alone, we misallocate our resources, producing more of many goods than would actually be demanded at the true market price—one that reflects both private and social costs. Are there any solutions to these problems?

Most of the solutions that have been proposed for the problem of external diseconomies can be grouped into three categories: (1) moral persuasion, which is used to urge business firms and individuals to respond to the interests of society as a whole and to disregard narrow self-interest; (2) regulation, which seeks to eliminate or curtail the production of goods and the external diseconomies associated with their production and consumption; and (3) use of the price system to limit the volume of external diseconomies that arise in the production and consumption of goods and services. Each of these alternatives is examined in the following sections.

Moral persuasion

A common approach to the problems of external diseconomies is to attempt to persuade both consumers and businesses to act against what they consider to be their own short-run self-interest, in order to promote social welfare. When the price system is operating perfectly, there is no conflict between private self-interest and social welfare. But when there are social costs or benefits that are not included within the price system, externalities arise, and private and social costs diverge by the amount of social costs.

In such cases, households and businesses that continue to make decisions on the basis of self-interest are actually injuring the public welfare. Some people believe that this problem can be solved by urging people to change their basis of decision making to include public as well as private goals. Thus corporations are urged to use their profits not for capital expansion but for the installation of antipollution devices. Workers are asked to voluntarily sacrifice the luxury of riding to work in their own cars, in favor of walking, bicycling, or using public transportation.

This approach to the problem of external diseconomies is currently widespread. Organizations of stockholders have been formed in an attempt to persuade corporations to choose public over private interest. Magazine articles suggest that consumers stop buying colored toilet paper, since the dyes which provide the color are pollutants; buy milk and soft drinks in refillable containers; and return metal hangers to the dry cleaner. All of these substitutions involve time, trouble, and expense to the consumer, and as such may not be justified on the basis of economic self-interest—unless the extra utility to the individual who acts for the public good is worth the cost of doing so.

Although the moral-persuasion approach is popular, it has not been very effective. One reason is that most people continue to put their own self-interest first. An even greater problem is the difficulty of judging what is best for society. If we are to choose the common social interest over self-interest, we must have some way of evaluating that social interest.

Difficulty of evaluating public interest
Is it really better for society if General Motors allocates more of its profits to pollution control than to other activities, including research and development? What would happen to unemployed factory workers in Detroit who could have been given jobs if the money had been used for plant expansion? Of course jobs will be created for workers in firms that specialize in pollution control. But are these workers really more deserving of a salary than the auto workers are? Is a rise in consumer prices worth the risk of increased inflation? How will it change the real income of American consumers?

Another example of the trade-off involved in antipollution efforts occurred in California during the spring of 1979. Among its many effects, the revolution in Iran resulted in a gas shortage in the United States. Some oil companies argued that if the lead content of gasoline could be increased, more gallons of gasoline could be produced from each barrel of crude oil. The choice facing consumers was clear: dirtier air and more gasoline or less gasoline and cleaner air. California's Lieutenant Governor Mike Curb tried to change the rules about lead content, and because the gas shortage was being reflected by long lines at service stations, more public sympathy for the higher lead content argument developed. However, the lead content rules remained the same.

Thus, although many consumers possess the knowledge required to make sound individual economic decisions, they lack the information required to make objective judgments on questions involving social policy such as those outlined above. As a result, attempts to make decisions that will reflect "the public interest" tend to be based on somewhat arbitrary notions of what will best serve the majority, and such decisions frequently fail to appeal to large groups of people.

Evaluation of moral-persuasion approach
Efforts to solve the problem of external diseconomies through moral persuasion have had some beneficial effects. Most important, they have made consumers more aware of the real cost of the products they purchase. The majority of consumers had probably never before stopped to think that the taxes they paid to operate the sanitation department, the money they spent to go on a vacation in some still unspoiled part of the country, and the new shirts they had to buy because their old ones wore out so quickly (the chemical pollutants in air and water cause fabrics to disintegrate) are all part of the price they must inevitably pay for the products they consume. As consumers learn to calculate the costs of externalities as well as the purchase price, they are likely to alter their patterns of consumption. A family may then decide to buy milk and soft drinks in refillable containers or recycle their newspapers, not out of an altruistic desire to benefit society, but out of enlightened self-interest. They will understand that the total cost of throwaway containers, for example, with the diseconomies they create, will actually be greater than the cost of refillable ones.

Moral persuasion may be effective in modifying behavior, but the desired results often fall short of original expectations. Use of this tactic requires not only sufficient time to change people's behavior from existing patterns, but also implicit recognition that full cooperation may never be achieved. Antilitter campaigns, for example, undoubtedly have had some impact in reducing the amount of waste discarded by individuals. Yet the almost universal presence of litter on streets and in other public places indicates that not everyone has taken the problem seriously. The advantages of this approach are that it may be undertaken quickly at nominal cost, and it provides minimal disruption in production and pricing decisions. It places the burden of responsibility on individuals and appeals to their sense of community to take actions which are socially beneficial. The likelihood of achieving success with this approach is enhanced where social and private goals overlap to a large extent.

Government regulation

In the last decade, there has been increasing involvement of government in the affairs of businesses and individuals in an attempt to control external diseconomies. In some cases, government has taken steps to halt production of products or services which are responsible for significant external diseconomies; in other cases, the government role has been one of regulating industry to achieve particular goals regarding environmental quality.

Curtailing production
Curtailing the production of goods that create external diseconomies is an extreme course of action. Nevertheless, it has very persuasive supporters. Calling a halt to production is often urged on the grounds that continued production poses unacceptable dangers to the population. Recent decisions by the Nuclear Regulatory Commission to halt power production by certain nuclear-powered generating facilities is an example of this type of action. Other arguments in favor of halting production are based upon the hypothesis that Americans already possess an excess of material goods and therefore can easily forgo additional ones. Often, this position is supported by claims that expanded industrial production and enhanced social welfare are incompatible and that only by giving up some production can we achieve gains in social welfare. While curtailing production of some goods may be an acceptable means for some individuals to deal with the problem of external diseconomies, it is not a solution that we can expect poor Americans or economically less developed countries to adopt willingly.

Regulation of industry
As society has grown increasingly complex, government has been asked to intervene more and more in matters traditionally handled in the private sector. This intervention has been undertaken in order to achieve national objectives and has been accomplished almost exclusively with detailed laws and regulations. In the area of environmental protection, for example, the federal government has passed legislation requiring new cars to be equipped with emissions-control devices, and some state governments have established requirements beyond those specified in federal law. Many state governments have enacted rules which prohibit or limit the dumping of untreated wastes into rivers and streams and some municipalities have banned the local sale of phosphate detergents which are a serious source of water pollution.

Evaluation of regulation approach
A number of economists have pointed out the inefficiency of this kind of blanket regulation. For example, if every factory must build its own waste-treatment facilities, there may be unnecessary duplication of effort and the creation of large unused capacity. An illustration of this was shown

in a 1967 study of pollution in the Delaware estuary. Researchers estimated that it would cost $106 million to clean up the water if each polluter did so on an individual basis. But one treatment plant placed downstream would cost only $61 million, to obtain the same results.

Even in the case of air pollution, regulation of the pollution level is not necessarily economically efficient. Instead of legislating a uniform 15 percent reduction in pollution emission, it might be cheaper and more effective to permit some firms to continue to pollute at the same level while other firms install equipment that will bring a reduction of 50 or 60 percent; in this way, possible economies of scale could be realized, while the same net reduction in pollution could be achieved.

Another objection to the regulatory approach is the expense and difficulty of enforcement. A number of cities have already passed some sort of legislation against high levels of air pollution, with fines and/or jail sentences for offenders. But the detection of offenses requires a special department of the city government; many workers must be hired and trained in the skills of estimating pollution level by smoke color and density. Once the offense is detected, the offender must be prosecuted—an additional cost to the city government. Enforcement cannot be completely effective, and therefore many companies may find that it is cheaper to pay an occasional fine than it is to install control devices.

One of the most persuasive arguments for government regulation is that it produces immediately visible results. Since control must be undertaken by government and inasmuch as politicians run for election and reelection frequently, the political process itself encourages this form of action. Waiting for markets to adjust to incentives and penalties or for people to respond to moral persuasion may be far too slow to be politically acceptable. In general, when a problem becomes serious, people want immediate action and they demand quick results from politicians.

Although curtailing or regulating production to eliminate or reduce external diseconomies is urged by some, others take a different stand. Many people argue that this approach to the problem of external diseconomies is cumbersome and inequitable. Not only is it necessary to identify the amount of pollution generated by individual firms, it is also essential that a mechanism exist for deciding which firms' production should be regulated or curtailed and by how much. Precise information on the amount of pollution produced by individual firms is scanty at present, and more detailed information is costly and time-consuming to acquire. Even if the necessary data were available, however, it is extremely difficult politically to make decisions of this type.

To the extent that government actions reduce production or raise the cost of goods, pressures are brought to bear on decisionmakers by those affected. Even when decisions have been made, they are frequently postponed or modified as various interest groups attempt to minimize the impact through litigation and appeal. As a result, regulation and control are often weakened and original goals are subverted. Nonetheless, because the political rewards for regulation and legislation are substantial, we can look forward to increased activity at all levels of government in an attempt to control the harmful effects of external diseconomies.

Use of the price system

A solution many economists favor is including externalities in the price system. This means that the government would put some kind of price on pollution. This approach would work within the framework of the existing price system rather than by creating some substitute mechanism. Advocates of this solution believe that putting a price on pollution would to some extent restore the functioning of the "invisible hand," and once the prices were established, the need for government intervention would be minimal. People would be able to continue making their consumption and production decisions on the reliable basis of self-interest, with the difference that product price would reflect social costs as well as private costs.

Charging a fee to industries

One useful suggestion that has been advanced regarding the operation of this extended price system is to charge a fee for wastes discharged into the earth's atmosphere or waters. This would not be a fine for breaking pollution regulations, but rather an operating cost of industry. In accordance with the type of industry, the level of production, and the number of antipollution devices installed in the factory, an annual charge could be established that would become one of the fixed costs of the firm.

This system has several advantages. Producers and consumers are free to determine how they can achieve maximum profits or utility. Some business firms may find it cheaper to pay the charge for their category of pollution than to install additional control devices; others will take steps to cut their pollution down to a minimum.

As one writer has pointed out, under this system it would not be necessary to be able to calculate the exact costs of the various types of pollution; the price levels could be set pragmatically, by observing the resulting change in pollution levels. If the first price level set did not reduce pollution to the level deemed socially acceptable, the prices could be raised.*

Charging producers of goods that create air and water pollution (external diseconomies) would have the effect of altering the supply schedule for the good. The additional cost of using the good would cause some decrease in quantity demanded; the additional costs of production would cause a decrease in the number of units supplied at each price level. The result would be a new level of market equilibrium, with fewer goods being produced.

Would pricing externalities contribute to recession?

It has been suggested that pricing pollution would bring about a recession in the economy, since it would eventually entail significant cutbacks in production and employment. Empirical support for this view was published by economist Robert Anderson. Anderson used a model of the economy that was fairly successful in predicting economic trends and conditions from 1962 to 1964, and he changed the data to reflect the setting of a price on air pollution. He found that according to the model, the rate of GNP growth would be greatly slowed, unemployment would rise, and prices would be higher.

Compensation approach

Another way to include externalities in the price system is to introduce some method of direct compensation between the producer of the externality and the victim. This inevitably requires definition or redefinition of property rights since externalities cannot exist where property rights are clearly defined. On an individual level, the compensation approach is perhaps the most common way in which problems involving externalities are resolved. Many lawsuits, for example, are concerned with situations in which one individual alleges that another person's actions are damaging. By making a ruling, the courts in effect establish property rights which either permit or restrain the action in question. Furthermore, monetary compensation is often provided to the injured parties. On a broader scale, class-action lawsuits are designed to remedy situations where externalities affect large numbers of people.

The economics of the compensation approach are straightforward. Imagine that a large company, in the process of manufacturing tractors, also causes air pollution in the immediate vicinity of its factory. Assume further that every

---

*Larry E. Ruff, "The Economic Common Sense of Pollution," *The Public Interest,* Spring 1970.

family in the immediate vicinity of the factory must spend $10 a month to cope with the effects of the factory's pollution. These expenditures most likely would include *additional* medical bills, painting, dry cleaning, and so on, expenses which would not be incurred by families living some distance from the factory. If a law is passed (or a court judgment rendered) which requires the company to compensate the victims of the air pollution it has caused, the company's production costs will increase. Subsequently, the price of the tractors will increase and sales will probably decrease. This will serve the purpose of reducing the pollution, and it also will have the effect of allocating productive resources away from this polluting industry. The social cost of the pollution is then no longer borne by the victims, but by the producers and consumers of the pollution-producing good.

Evaluation of the price-system approach

Use of the price system to curtail external diseconomies has the inherent defect of being slow to bring forth desired results. In the short run, even in the face of higher costs, business firms will not necessarily be in a position to implement new technology to curtail external diseconomies. As a result, people often are under the impression that this method is ineffective. Another drawback is that many people, including public officials, are genuinely skeptical about the effectiveness of the price system to achieve certain results even though the great bulk of economic activity is regulated by the signals of price and profit. From a standpoint of efficiency, use of the price system is without equal from among the choices discussed. Prices force people to make behavioral adjustments in line with social preferences, and the adjustments which are made reflect the opportunity cost of resources used.

The effectiveness of the price system in achieving social goals is shown in the following example. In many areas, discarded beverage containers constitute the bulk of litter found on public thoroughfares and in public recreation areas. In response to public pressure to deal with this problem, the state of Oregon, a few years ago, implemented a method of control which relies heavily on the price system. By placing a sufficiently high value on used bottles and cans through a system of deposits, the state was able to motivate some people to return empty containers to their supermarket or store for a refund and to induce others, whose opportunity cost of time was low, to collect discarded containers. In essence, the consumers of beverages were being taxed (by forfeiting their deposit) if they discarded the container, and the tax revenue (the deposits) was used to pay people to collect others' discards. After only a few years in operation, this program has been judged to be an unqualified success. In this instance, heavy reliance on the price system coupled with government regulation (limiting the sale of nonreusable containers) and a vigorous campaign of moral persuasion has demonstrated that the problem of external diseconomies can be dealt with effectively.

Through recognition of the economic basis of the environmental problems we face and the judicious use of various methods of control, it is likely that we will see significant progress in dealing with external diseconomies without seriously infringing on free consumer choice or substantially affecting the standard of living in the United States.

HOW MUCH POLLUTION CONTROL?

An important issue today concerns the extent to which pollution control is desirable. We all agree that it is undesirable to breathe toxic gases; does that mean that the most desirable condition occurs when the air is completely free of pollution? Or is there some optimal position short of perfect cleanliness?

Cost/benefit analysis

An economist provides answers to questions concerning pollution by analyzing the marginal costs of reducing external diseconomies and by analyzing the marginal benefits that can be obtained from such a reduction. The optimum position for society is reached when the marginal costs and the marginal benefits are equal.

If perfectly clean air were a free good, no doubt everyone would choose clean air over air with even the slightest degree of pollution, just as any of us would choose to have four radios rather than one if we did not have to pay for them. The hypothesis is that people will always prefer more to less. But clean air is an economic good, and to obtain more of it, we must sacrifice some quantity of alternative goods. We must decide whether we want one more unit of clean air or one more automobile. We probably would not choose perfectly clean air because those last units of cleanliness would not be worth the price.

The optimal position is reached when no change in the way our money is allocated can bring any increase in satisfaction, when the marginal utility from the last dollar spent to purchase one good is equal to the marginal utility from the last dollar spent to purchase every other good (the equal marginal utility principle). In the case of eliminating air pollution or any other external diseconomy, this means that the optimal position is reached when the marginal cost of reducing the pollution is equal to the marginal benefit that the reduction yields. It is a fallacy to believe that since air pollution causes $16 billion worth of damage annually, we should spend $16 billion to get rid of it; it is likely that long before we have spent the whole $16 billion, we will reach the point where we are spending more to remove a unit of pollution than we gain by having it removed.

Economic analysis of the marginal costs and marginal benefits of pollution reduction requires a certain amount of ingenuity. By definition, an external diseconomy is not subject to the price system, so economists must devise some monetary measure of the costs and benefits involved.

Measuring costs of pollution

The benefits derived from reducing pollution are obviously the costs of allowing pollution to continue at its current level. But how do we measure the current costs of pollution? Solutions vary widely. One study measured air-pollution costs in terms of additional laundry bills for residents; another measured it in terms of deterioration in real estate values; a third estimated the cost of the increased decomposition of rubber in automobile tires. The health costs are generally measured in lost value of workers' productivity as well as in actual medical-care costs. Even the cost of death has been estimated, by calculating the lost earnings of the deceased.

Another possible method of figuring the marginal costs of external diseconomies is to ask the victims how much they would pay to have the problem stopped, or how much they would accept to allow it to continue. This tells us the opportunity cost that victims are willing to pay to escape diseconomies. Other economists might compare the salaries paid to workers in the asbestos-manufacturing industry, where there is a high risk of serious and incapacitating lung disease, with the salaries paid to workers with comparable skills and experience in other industries. This tells us the amount of compensation these workers demand for accepting the diseconomy of such a health risk.

Measuring costs of pollution control

Once we have some measure of the damage wrought by current levels of pollution, we also have a measure of the benefits to be gained from reducing pollution. Yet this is only half the information we need to establish a standard of environmental quality; we must also have some measure of the marginal costs of pollution abatement. Just like the costs of damage from pollution, the costs of pollution control are also difficult to calculate, although most cost-of-control estimates are somewhat more precise than damage estimates. Studies indicate that the greater the amount of pollution curtailed, the higher is the cost per unit withheld. In other words, the marginal cost curve for controlling pollution rises quite steeply. For example, the Council on Environmental Quality, reporting on a 1969 study of the greater Kansas City area, gave the following information. To reduce sulfur oxides and particulates 5 percent and 22 percent, respectively, would cost $50,000. To reduce these levels by 42 and 66 percent, respectively, would cost $7.5 million. However, to reduce sulfur oxides by an additional 6 percentage points to 48 percent and particulates by an additional 3 percent to 69 percent would triple the costs to over $26 million.*

Attempts already have been made to set standards of environmental quality by comparing the marginal benefits of pollution abatement with the marginal costs of control programs. The conclusions from one study made about the Delaware estuary offer an example.

That study estimated recreational benefits from $120 to $280 million for a level of water quality that would cost $65 to $140 million to achieve. Somewhat higher expenditures of $85 to $155 million would have yielded benefits of $130 to $310 million, while an even higher expenditure of $215 to $315 million would have yielded benefits of $140 to $320 million. The higher levels of water quality necessitated much higher levels of control costs compared to increased benefits.†

Although such calculations are admittedly rather crude, marginal cost and marginal benefit analysis does provide a useful tool that can help us make decisions about levels of pollution control. The current figures most likely err in underestimating the marginal benefits of pollution reduction, and perhaps the marginal costs of control programs as well. However, they do furnish a guideline in setting standards of environmental quality, and they provide an analytical framework for dealing with a complex and difficult issue.

---

*Second Annual Report of the Council on Environmental Quality, August 1971, p. 118.

†Ibid., p. 120.

Summary

■ This chapter examines the economic aspects of the environmental problems which have gained attention in recent years, including questions of how to reconcile growth and environmental protection and how best to deal with the hidden costs of production and consumption.

■ Environmental problems represent one of the major hidden costs of production and consumption in our economy. Harmful environmental consequences of economic activity have existed for centuries, but these problems have been magnified in the past few decades with rapid industrialization and technological development. There are signs that the public is becoming more concerned and more ready to support steps to remedy problems of pollution.

■ The costs or benefits that occur incidentally in the process of production or consumption, and for which payment cannot be extracted, are called economic externalities. The external costs must be paid by somebody, but they are not usually paid by the producer of the externality. Externalities can also be seen as the difference between the private costs of production and the social costs. Since the social costs are not figured into the market price, demand for goods that produce external diseconomies is artificially high.

■ Three major types of remedies for environmental problems have been proposed. Moral persuasion, which aims at getting businesses and individuals to pursue the social welfare rather than narrow self-interest, is a very popular approach, but not a very successful one. Although such appeals have made people more aware of the problems that exist, it is difficult to convince people to contradict their self-interest and equally difficult to arrive at a commonly accepted definition of the "public interest."

■ Because moral persuasion has been relatively ineffective, there has been increasing pressure for government regulation of pollution-creating industries and products. Outright curtailment of production of goods that create external diseconomies is an extreme remedy and one not likely to appeal to the poor or to the less developed countries. Regulation that requires antipollution equipment and standards can have a rapid and politically visible effect, but it tends to be cumbersome for industry and expensive and difficult for the government to enforce.

■ Many economists favor the third remedy, utilizing the price system itself to curtail external diseconomies. One possibility would be for government to charge industries for their pollution; this would result in higher product prices, but it might also lead to reduced production and recessionary influences. Industries might also be required to pay direct compensation to those victimized by pollution, which would mean that the social costs of pollution would be borne by the producers and consumers of goods. In the long run, use of the price system provides the most efficient means of resource allocation.

■ In considering solutions to environmental problems, economists make use of cost-benefit analysis. Ideally, the marginal costs of reducing pollution should be equal to the marginal benefits derived. Benefits can be calculated by measuring the costs of not reducing pollution, or by finding out what people would pay to have pollution removed or what they would accept to allow it to continue. Costs of pollution control are also hard to calculate, but evidence does indicate that the marginal cost curve for reducing pollution rises sharply—that is, removing additional units of pollution becomes more and more expensive.

Key Terms

economic externality
external diseconomy
external economy
private costs
social costs

Review & Discussion

1. Give some examples of the hidden costs of production and consumption.

2. What is an economic externality? How is it related to private and social costs?

3. How do external diseconomies affect the demand for final products? The level of production? The price?

4. What would be the consequences of halting production in industries that produce substantial external diseconomies? What would be the effect of such a policy if demand were inelastic?

5. What are the limitations of moral persuasion as a remedy for environmental pollution? Why has this approach not been very successful?

6. Why might there be a conflict in goals between those who would eliminate poverty and those who would clean up the environment?

7. How might government use the price system to control external diseconomies?

8. How would you describe the optimum amount of cleanliness in the environment? Why would people be unlikely to demand a completely clean environment? What are some of the problems in determining the costs of external diseconomies?

9. What are the external diseconomies associated with the generation of nuclear power? How effective has government regulation been in dealing with these externalities? How efficient would the price system be as a means of dealing with them?

Chapter 33

The Economics of Urban Problems

What to look for in this chapter

What are some of the major contemporary urban problems? What factors have produced these problems?

How can supply and demand analysis be used to determine the implications of employing user charges to reduce automobile congestion?

What are some typical external diseconomies created by urban land use? What are some possible means of dealing with these diseconomies?

How can cost-benefit analysis be useful in seeking a solution to the social costs of crime?

How have cities been affected by the combination of a shrinking tax base and an increased demand for social services? What are some possible approaches to the budgetary problems created by these conditions?

The problems facing our large cities are a source of serious concern for the nation. About 32 percent of our total population now lives in central metropolitan areas; another 27 percent lives in the suburbs surrounding these cities and is directly dependent on the city for income, goods, and services. Even those who live in rural areas have some stake in the economic health of the cities, since cities provide large markets for agricultural goods and for labor that is no longer needed on the farm.

The term "urban problems" is heard so often that it has become a cliché. Yet most city residents could recite a specific and colorful list of the difficulties they face. Among these are the problem of finding a comfortable and safe place to live at a reasonable cost; air and noise pollution; shortages of water and electric power in the heat of the summer; fear of burglars, muggers, car thieves, and other unsavory fellow residents; and ever-increasing taxes that seem to accompany a steady decline in municipal services.

The goals of this chapter are to consider some of the major urban problems from an economic perspective and to analyze possible economic solutions.

PROBLEMS OF MANAGEMENT AND SCALE

The social and economic problems of large cities are undeniable, and as yet they are largely unsolved. Some economists feel that the basic problem of the cities is a problem of scale. A large city offers considerable economies of scale in the provision of goods and services for its residents. Bus rides, kilowatt hours of electricity, and chemically purified drinking water can all be purchased at lower cost in big cities because of the large demand for these goods and services and the accompanying economies of scale in mass production. But in the last several decades, prices for such services have been rising faster than have prices for comparable services in small towns. Some economic theorists, using cost curves and other empirical data, assert that the solution lies in an even greater expansion in the production of these services. For example, they suggest that the rise in bus fares can be halted if more people switch from taking cars to riding buses. However, the experiences of private companies and city agencies that are facing expanding demand seem to contradict this conclusion. The demand for electrical power is increasing rapidly, as more and more homes and offices rely on electrical equipment; yet at the same time consumers are confronted with rising prices and inadequate service.

The problem of managerial skill

One way to reconcile these persistently rising costs is to look at the input factor of managerial skill. To achieve real economies of scale, all input factors must be increased proportionately. The plans for expansion of city services call for added capital and land resources; they also call for additional workers. But the factor of managerial skill seems to be limited. In part, this may be the consequence of a scarcity of trained and experienced managers in the field of municipal services; but it may also indicate that efficient coordination and management are impossible beyond certain size limits. So in terms of managerial abilities, many city governments and public agencies have grown to an uneconomic size, and when other input resources are increased, they become subject to diminishing returns.

The problem of scale

Another important problem facing modern cities is finding the correct scale of operation. Optimum size can vary with the function to be performed. For instance, it may be most economical to treat sewage on a very large scale but to administer parks on a small scale. Moreover, even within a function, size of the decision-making unit can vary. There may be economies of scale in having a large city's elementary and secondary schools purchase supplies and furniture together because of quantity discounts. Yet decisions concerning curricula, class size, and spending for certain programs (e.g., construction of a swimming pool or meeting the needs of remedial teaching) probably should be made at a school or district level rather than by the entire school system.

While the problems of scale of operation and lack of managerial skill are two of the more general difficulties that face modern cities, there are more specific problem areas that affect city residents. In the following sections, we will examine some of the more difficult ones.

URBAN TRANSPORTATION

If a city is to survive and prosper, it must have a reliable transportation network. Supplies of food and other goods must be brought into the city's stores and markets; the goods it manufactures must be transported to other markets across the country; workers, visitors, and tourists require easy access to the heart of the city; and residents need a high degree of mobility so that they can travel between residential, commercial, and recreational districts with reasonable speed.

Private and social costs of automobile use

Most of the movement in and out of cities today depends on the private automobile. For decades, cars have been the quickest and most comfortable means of urban transportation. In recent years, however, this situation has begun to change. So many people have become car users that the highways in and out of all major cities are badly congested. Rush-hour traffic is certainly not fast, and because of the nervous strain of stop-and-go driving at speeds of 10 or 15 miles an hour, it cannot really be considered comfortable either. Once in the city, people find that parking space is scarce and, therefore, expensive. In addition, the price of gasoline has risen dramatically since the oil embargo of 1973. Yet even though the costs and inconvenience of automobile use are mounting, many people still feel that a car is the best means of transportation, especially when public transportation is usually slow, unreliable, and crowded.

At the same time that congestion has made the private car less convenient, economists and city administrators have begun to point out that the true cost of automobile use—the private cost plus the social cost—is even higher. Automobile use produces many external diseconomies, and most users are not aware of the true social cost of cars. Exhaust fumes from cars pollute the air in central cities (cars are responsible for 60 percent of all air pollution) and create a constant racket of honking horns, racing engines, and squealing tires. In addition there is a high toll in injuries to people and in damage to property from the many accidents that occur in congested areas. Indeed, crossing the street is difficult, even hazardous, for pedestrians.

Possible solutions

User charges: supply and demand analysis

One solution to the urban transportation problem could be to include more of the social costs of automobile use in the price paid by the user. The city might charge tolls to those who enter, with highest tolls charged at rush-hour periods. (This would reverse the current situation in some cities, where access by toll bridges and tunnels is less expensive during periods of heaviest traffic.) Parking permits could be sold, with the fee varied in accordance with the traffic density in the area. Car owners might also pay a pollution tax, based on the amount of exhaust fumes their cars emit.

Economists are not certain about the degree of price elasticity of the demand for commuting by automobile, since elasticity depends on such variables as the availability of substitutes or the percentage of the household budget that automobile operating costs account for. Therefore we cannot predict whether such user charges would significantly reduce the nuber of automobiles driven into urban areas. However, the revenues received from auto users could be used to improve old roads or build new ones, to hire more police for traffic control, or to build more parking structures.

Figures 33.1 and *33.2* consider the impact of private and social costs on automobile use and the implications of employing user charges to reduce congestion.

The demand curve for automobile use, depicted by curve D in *Fig. 33.1,* indicates the benefit associated with any given level of driving. For example, the benefit produced by Q_1 units of driving is indicated by point A. The downward slope of the demand curve suggests that the law of diminishing marginal utility has set in—less addi-

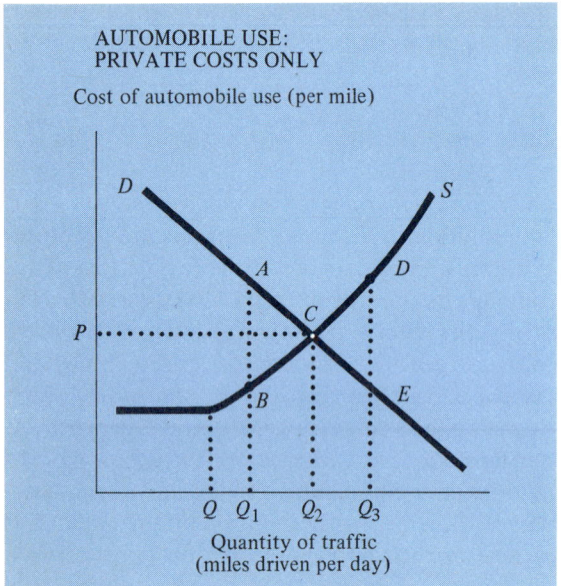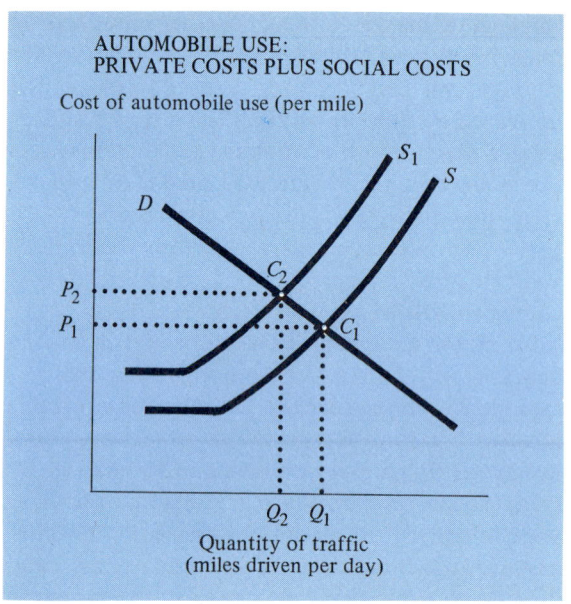

Fig. 33.1
The demand curve for automobile use (D) indicates the benefit associated with any given level of driving. The downward slope of D shows that less additional satisfaction results from each successive mile of driving. The supply curve (S) measures the private costs generated at various levels of driving. The upward slope of S indicates that after a certain point (at quantity Q) the increased traffic volume will result in rising unit costs of automobile use. The point of equilibrium is located at point C (Q_2 miles a day at price P_2 per mile). This is the point at which D and S intersect and at which the private cost and benefit associated with the last mile driven are equal. If drivers are driving Q_3 miles a day, the benefit is less than the cost (point E is below point D) and the drivers would be better off if they decreased their driving from Q_3 to Q_2. If people are driving Q_1 miles a day, however, the benefit is greater than the cost (point A is above point B), and it would make sense for drivers to increase their driving from Q_1 to Q_2.

Fig. 33.2
When social costs are added to the private costs of operating an automobile, the supply curve shifts from S to S_1. Equilibrium shifts from point C_1 to point C_2—that is, when the price of automobile use increases from P_1 to P_2, the costs exceed the benefits and people will decrease the number of miles they drive (from Q_1 to Q_2) until the costs and benefits are equal once again.

tional satisfaction results from each successive mile of driving.

S is the supply curve for automobile use, which measures the private costs generated at various levels of driving. These costs include, for example, gasoline, maintenance, and the value of time lost due to traffic delays. For example, point B represents the cost incurred in driving Q_1 miles. The flat portion of the curve indicates that the unit cost of driving remains relatively constant at lower levels of automobile use. However, when traffic volume exceeds a certain level (in our example, Q), congestion occurs. Time lost due to traffic tie-ups increases and the wear and tear on automobiles caused by bumper-to-bumper traffic necessitates greater maintenance expense. These factors result in a rising unit cost of automobile use and, therefore, the positively sloped portion of S.

The equilibrium volume of automobile use is quantity Q_2 at the unit cost of P. This is shown at point C where the private cost and benefit associated with the last unit of driving are equal. With equilibrium at point C, automobile use will not exceed Q_2 because drivers feel the cost of additional driving will exceed the additional benefits. At Q_3, for example, the costs (indicated by point D on the supply curve) exceed the benefit (point E on the demand curve). At Q_1, on the other hand, the marginal benefit (indicated by point A on the demand curve) outweighs the marginal cost (point B on the supply curve). Therefore, it would make sense for drivers to increase their automobile use toward Q_2.

There is a problem with the market-determined outcome, however, because the price fails to account for all of the costs of driving. Curve S registers only the private costs of automobile use; that is, those costs actually borne by drivers. Automobile use, however, also generates social or external costs, such as air pollution, which all members of the community are forced to bear. Since these external costs are not paid by drivers, the automobile seems like a relatively cheap means of transportation. Consequently, the amount of driving is great.

If individuals could be forced to bear the true cost of their driving (the private plus the social costs), the supply curve would shift upward by the amount of external costs related to each level of automobile use. This is illustrated in *Fig. 33.2* as a shift in the supply curve from S to S_1. Equilibrium (formerly at point C_1) now occurs at C_2. The consideration of social costs increases individuals' driving cost from P_1 to P_2 which in turn reduces the quantity demanded (traffic volume) from Q_1 to Q_2.

One method of curtailing traffic volume is to impose user charges. Levying a pollution tax on car owners based on the amount of exhaust fumes emitted, for example, would also increase the unit cost of automobile use and would induce a shift in the supply curve similar to the shift from S to S_1. Less driving would result and demand for alternative modes of transportation such as mass transit would expand since the rising cost of driving makes these substitutes appear more attractive.

Note that our conclusions rest on the assumption that drivers are, to some extent, responsive to higher automobile use costs. That is, the demand curve is assumed to exhibit some degree of elasticity, as demonstrated by D.

Improved public transportation

Another approach to the urban traffic problem would be to make public transportation more attractive to those traveling into and around the city. Of course, increasing the price of driving a car would probably serve to increase the demand for car substitutes, such as buses and subways or trains. But public transport is not a cure-all, and if drivers switched away from cars, the necessary expansion of public-transportation facilities would offer new and knotty problems.

The fixed costs and capital investment of a public-transportation system are very large, and it will be profitable only if the demand for services is also very large. This cost problem is compounded by the uneven pattern of demand for service. If the company buys enough buses or builds enough tracks to provide all the service that is demanded during rush hour, it must pay for excess capacity during the rest of the day. Again, the solution might be a varied rate schedule, so that it costs more to travel during rush hour than at other times of day. Such a program might encourage those who can switch riding times with a minimum of inconvenience to do so.

Some cities have recently begun to experiment with reduced fares on public transit, and commuter railroads in many cities have introduced special reduced fares for passengers entering and leaving the city in off-peak hours. It has been estimated that as many as 20 percent of rush-hour travelers are on errand and shopping trips that can be taken at other times. However, incentive rates are more commonly applied in the opposite direction. Trains and buses offer commuter plans under which regular travelers (who tend to use the system only during peak hours) pay less than other users. One disadvantage of a rate schedule that discriminates against rush-hour travellers is that private cars are then relatively more attractive to commuting workers.

Some other possible solutions

The imposition of some kind of user charge seems to afford the best hope of changing the pattern of urban transportation, but a number of other solutions have also been suggested. Working hours can be staggered to space rush-hour congestion over a longer period. Such a solution has been attempted in cities with limited public-transportation systems. The success of this measure depends on how closely the individual business firms need to coordinate their working day with one another. For some firms, opening an hour later or closing an hour earlier would have the effect of shortening the business day. Other cities, such as Boston, attempt to relieve rush hour congestion by providing special commuter lanes on major arteries into the city that can be used only by buses or car pools. Another type of solution has been implemented in New York. This city, following the lead of many European cities, is encouraging the use of bicycles in the crowded downtown area. The city has experimented with creating bike lanes and has placed bicycle racks on corners around the city. Other cities have banned cars from the central shopping district, creating a pedestrian mall for shoppers.

THE SHIFTING URBAN POPULATION

From the end of World War II until the mid-1970s, middle-income families moved from the central city to the suburbs and, for the most part, were replaced by low-income households. As *Table 33.1* shows, incomes are now higher outside the central city than they are inside—a reversal of the situation that prevailed before World War II.

More recently, some affluent suburbanites have relocated in central cities, while the nonwhite, poor population, to some degree, has been leaving. "Black migration to the suburbs is now a significant demographic pattern, and for the first time since the inauguration of the Underground Railroad, more blacks are emigrating to the [largely rural] South than are leaving it."*

At this time, it is unclear whether these new developments constitute trends or are merely transitory. Regardless, these events have not yet significantly improved the plight of American cities, and the urban scars left in the wake of a 30-year period of middle-class exodus are still very much in evidence.

Problems resulting from middle-class flight

The years of middle-class flight and the arrival of low-income households had unfortunate results for the central cities, as the latter contributed less in tax revenues to the city budget than they demanded in public goods and services. *Table 33.2*, which summarizes the net migration of white and nonwhite New York City residents between 1950 and 1970, suggests one basis of the financial problems of most urban areas.

---

*T. D. Allman, "The Urban Crisis Leaves Town," *Harper's*, (December 1978), p. 53.

Table 33.1
Money income of families in metropolitan areas, 1977

	Inside central cities		Outside central cities	
Income level	White (11.8 million families)	Nonwhite (3.2 million families)	White (21.0 million families)	Nonwhite (1.2 million families)
Under $3,000	2.9%	8.5%	1.7%	8.8%
$3,000–4,999	5.6	14.9	3.0	7.8
$5,000–6,999	7.4	13.4	5.0	8.8
$7,000–8,999	7.5	10.5	5.5	7.4
$9,000–11,999	10.4	12.5	8.9	13.0
$12,000–14,999	11.3	10.0	10.0	9.7
$15,000–19,999	17.4	12.5	18.5	17.8
$20,000–24,999	14.5	8.2	16.2	11.9
$25,000 and over	23.0	9.6	31.2	14.7
	100.0%	100.0%	100.0%	100.0%
Median income	$16,286	$9,610	$19,210	$13,023

Source: *Statistical Abstract,* 1978.
Details may not add to totals because of rounding.

The fact that the city's population is composed of groups at both extremes of the income spectrum—the very rich and the very poor—creates additional problems for the city. Because the needs and desires of the two groups are very dissimilar, it is costly to provide for both at once. For example, well-to-do households may want libraries, museums, public marinas, and top-flight universities; poor households lack the education to enjoy some of these advantages and the funds to enjoy others. They may want increased welfare benefits, lower-cost public universities or colleges, and free medical clinics. There is no easy compromise between these two sets of desires, so the city may have difficulty trying to provide both types at once.

Table 33.2
Net migration of New York City residents by race, 1950–1970

Years	Net out migration of whites	Net in migration of nonwhites
1950–1960	1,239,000	173,000
1960–1970	955,000	436,000

Source: United States Department of Labor, Bureau of Labor Statistics, Middle Atlantic Regional Office.

The most frequent explanation for the exodus of middle-income households from urban areas is that they are escaping the increasingly heavy tax burdens. Income, property, and sales taxes are all higher in central cities than in most of the suburbs around them. And in order to provide public goods and services for lower-income residents, the city must tax the remaining middle-and upper-income households at an even higher rate. This creates a vicious cycle of tax increases and leads to a departure of middle-income taxpayers.

Another part of the problem is the city's inability to attract middle-income residents by providing the quantity and quality of public goods and services that are in keeping with a middle-income standard of living. For example, urban public education is often low in quality, and parents who hope to send their children to college may feel that the public schools cannot provide an adequate preparation. So they choose to move to a community with a larger tax base and a more homogeneous population. The typical suburb has more money to allocate for education, since it does not need to provide as many other services, such as welfare and a system of mass transportation. It also tends to have less need to offer special educational services, such as bilingual classrooms for non–English-speaking students.

Intracity movement
Not only do people move in and out of cities, but they also move to different locations within cities. Some neighborhoods seem almost deserted; others are overcrowded. Although population density can lead to certain economies of scale, there is an optimum point beyond which additional density creates external diseconomies. Yet new residents may continue to move into overcrowded neighborhoods, since they pay only the private cost of renting or buying a place to live. The cost of the external diseconomies of overcrowding must be paid mostly by other residents and the government, which is asked to provide services for those high-density areas.

One approach to solving the problem of crowd-caused external diseconomies is zoning laws and building codes. For example, by requiring all new houses to be built on a lot of some minimum size, the city can prevent the overcrowding of a neighborhood. The city can also prevent the operation of rooming houses in certain areas that already have too dense a concentration of population.

Some people might prefer to approach the problem by attempting to include the full social cost of moving into a city in the price system. For example, the city might adjust the tax strucures so that rates of property and income taxes are based on number of years of residence in the city, with relatively high rates for newcomers and relatively low rates for long-term residents. Raising the cost of moving into the city would decrease the quantity of housing demanded and thereby prevent overcrowding; those who are still willing to pay the higher price would be contributing extra revenue to the city, so that it could meet the expense of expanding necessary facilities.

URBAN LAND USE
In densely populated urban areas, the scarce productive resource of land becomes even scarcer, and the number of alternative uses for it increases. How can the community determine how best to allocate this scarce resource?

Urban land allocation and the price system
The basis of urban land allocation, like all other resource allocation, is the price system. Prospective users of the land bid against each other to obtain control of the resource. The highest bidder will be the one who can expect the largest revenue from the use he or she has selected. Since revenue is a function of the demand schedule for a commodity, it is logical to assume that the land will be used for the production of whatever good or service yields the greatest profit.

For three decades migration to the suburbs reduced the viability of central-city businesses and depressed the price of once-prime urban land. The incentive of low price, the growth of urban service industries, and several other factors, however, have rekindled interest in urban real estate in recent years. Currently

> corporate investment is flooding American cities, and the influx of American capital into downtown areas is being matched by funds from [abroad]. While automobile money flows into Renaissance Center in downtown Detroit,... developers are sinking $350 million into a real estate package of seven office buildings in New York. Money Market Directories estimates that over the next few years America's 300 largest corporate funds will invest more than $6 billion in [urban] real estate...*

The revival of the urban real estate market will result in a socially and economically desirable pattern of land allocation, as long as the private costs of the land to users were identical to the total social cost of such use. Unfortunately, in many instances, urban land use creates external diseconomies, so that there is a divergence between private and social costs.

External diseconomies: some examples

We can illustrate some of these diseconomies in the example of a real estate developer who buys a wooded tract of land near the edge of a large city and turns it into a housing development. In deciding how many houses to build and where to put them, the developer will consider only the private costs of construction balanced against the profits of selling the house. But the effect of cutting down the trees and covering the land with rows of identical houses is to produce a diseconomy for owners of adjacent property, who lose their beautiful view, experience an increase in the noise level in the neighborhood, and find local roads congested.

---

*Ibid., p. 43.

The builder may leave to the city the task of providing sewage treatment or police protection. In addition, there may be a demand that the state government build a new highway to ease the heavier traffic flow created by the commuting trips of workers from the new development to their jobs in the central city. There may also be a demand that the city government provide bus service.

If, as often happens, a shopping center is built near the development, there will probably be external diseconomies for the central business district. When people stop coming into the central city to shop, they also stop coming in to have dinner in a restaurant or to see a movie or a play. The central business district may begin to decay. Likewise, companies with offices in the central city may find that they need to increase salaries and wages in order to persuade workers to make the time-consuming and often uncomfortable trip between home and work. Some corporations may choose to follow the workers, and move out of the central city, thus creating additional expenses for the company and a loss of tax revenue for the city.

The renewed attraction of the central city to both the affluent and corporate investors has somewhat alleviated these problems, but much of this relief has occurred in very large urban areas as opposed to cities with fewer than 500,000 residents.

Nearly every kind of urban land use creates external diseconomies for some of the residents. Large stores and office buildings create congested highways and sidewalks. New housing can cause adjacent property values to go up or down; high-density housing can create overcrowding, and low-density housing can create unsightly urban sprawl. Airports pollute nearby air with noise and fumes. Restaurants, bars, and movie theaters may attract noisy customers and undesirable loiterers.

Possible solutions

Two common methods of dealing with these external diseconomies are the enactment of zoning codes and the imposition of taxes and license fees.

Zoning codes

Currently, the favored solution for a divergence between the private and social costs of land use seems to be regulation by the municipal government via zoning codes. Based on a brief cost-benefit analysis, a zoning code is adopted that prohibits certain kinds of land use in certain areas of the city. Building codes can be an even more sophisticated regulatory device. For example, the city may require that new office buildings in the central business district use the ground-floor space for shops or restaurants or attractive terraces with fountains and benches, so that people will continue to be drawn to the area for shopping and recreation; such codes are now in effect in New York along Fifth Avenue and in Paris on the Champs Élysées. New Orleans has protected the economic and aesthetic value of its historic French Quarter, which attracts a lucrative tourist trade and makes the city more appealing to potential residents, by prohibiting all new building in the area.

Taxes and license fees

To supplement the effects of regulatory policies, many economists favor including a larger portion of social costs in the private price a user pays for land. Since most land sales are private transactions between two individuals, the most effective way the city government could extend the price system is through the use of taxes or license fees. Including more of the total cost (social plus private costs) in the purchase price would decrease the quantity demanded of land for uses that are high in social cost, and at the same time would bring in revenue that could be used to compensate for diseconomies and inconveniences.

In establishing a price structure for various kinds of land use, the city government needs to devise a monetary measurement not only of social costs but also of social benefits. For example, a garbage dump is a kind of land use that no neighborhood wants to have nearby; it is ugly, unpleasant smelling, generates heavy truck traffic on the roads, and causes property values to decrease. Yet the cost of not collecting the garbage, or not dumping it in some central place, is even greater.

One solution is to raise the price of garbage collection and use the extra money to compensate those who live near the dump for their loss. Some cities have found that it is even cheaper to truck garbage far away to virtually unpopulated areas. San Francisco, for example, transports its garbage a distance of more than 100 miles, where it is used as landfill to build a recreation area. The total cost of the long trip is still lower than the total social cost of using scarce urban land for garbage disposal. By considering the total cost of certain kinds of urban land use a city can encourage the development of this sort of alternative solution.

URBAN CRIME

Statistics show that as population becomes more dense, crime rates of all types go up. So although a high incidence of crime is by no means confined to the cities alone, it does present a greater problem there.

Safety: an economic good

Everyone agrees that it is unpleasant to live in fear of some kind of criminal attack. But safety is not a free good; it is an economic good that must be paid for by sacrificing alternative goods and services. Although politicians like to speak of the need to make our cities safe, in reality the demand for complete safety is almost nonexistent. For example, complete safety might be achieved if every person hired a bodyguard to accompany him or her everywhere. But how many people would be willing to sacrifice other goods and services in order to pay for the bodyguard? Thus, because of the law of diminishing marginal utility, additional units of safety are valued at a continually lower rate. Beyond a certain point, most consumers will decide that they are unwilling to continue buying safety and will spend their money instead on dinner in a good restaurant or a week-end vacation. Because of the equal marginal utility principle, such an allocation of funds will yield greater satisfaction than the same amount spent to purchase additional units of safety. The opportunity cost of complete safety has become too high.

Applying cost/benefit analysis to crime prevention

Crime prevention is costly, but so is crime. Therefore we need to turn once again to a cost-benefit analysis. The public cost of crime is measured in terms of the monetary costs of providing police protection, maintaining courts, public prosecutors, and other legal machinery, building jails and prisons, and feeding, clothing, and rehabilitating prisoners.

There are also large private costs which are somewhat harder to measure. These include the loss of damaged or stolen property, and the cost of the physical and psychological injuries received by some victims of crime. Another part of the private cost is the loss of revenue suffered by movie theaters and restaurants and other recreational businesses when potential customers are afraid to venture out after dark. Finally, there is a cost of higher wages that have to be paid to employees of businesses located in areas with very high crime rates; in fact, some people will stop working altogether rather than have to work in neighborhoods where the crime rates are high.

Cost-benefit analysis can help a city determine how much to spend on crime prevention. If it cost $10,000 to prevent a single $100 robbery, the cost far outweighs the benefit. The current demand for cime prevention is probably artificially low, because the total social costs of crime are not generally included in cost-benefit analyses of crime-prevention programs. As economists develop the tools to measure social costs more precisely, there may be some changes in this situation. For example, a recent study undertaken in New York City indicated that the total cost of setting up city-wide clinics that could dispense medicine to take drug addicts off heroin for a period of 10 to 14 days would be outweighed by the social benefits of even so brief a period of nonaddiction. The addicts could be expected to steal more in the 10-day period than it would cost to administer the treatment.

Another way to register the full social cost of crime is suggested by economists Douglas C. North and Roger Leroy Miller in their book, *The Economics of Public Issues*. They point out:

> Right now in almost all cities and states in the Union, a man beaten up in the streets and left with permanent brain damage has no one to sue for his injuries. If the attacker is caught he will be jailed. That really does not help the victim, who actually ends up paying part of his taxes for the prisoner's room and board! If, on the other hand, the city or state were held liable for all damages sustained, the victim (or his dependents) could sue the city or state for compensation. Unlimited liability on the part of the government for crimes against the populace would certainly alter the present allocation of resources between crime prevention and other public endeavors. Under present laws the private cost of crime is borne by the individual and he has little hope of being compensated.... Hence suboptimal expenditures for crime prevention and control now prevail.*

Another solution might be to require the criminal to reimburse the victim for the private cost of the crime and the government for the costs of crime detection and conviction. Instead of sentencing criminals to enforced idleness or busywork in a prison, the government might send them to some sort of work camp, with the wages for productive labor being turned over to the victims; the length of the criminal's stay would depend on the cost of the crime. Such a program may or may not serve as an additional deterrent to crime, but it would at least produce revenue to compensate victims of crime for their economic loss.

---

*Douglas C. North and Roger Leroy Miller, *The Economics of Public Issues*. New York: Harper & Row, 1971.

PROBLEMS OF FINANCING MUNICIPAL GOVERNMENT

Increased demand for services and an eroding tax base

The typical city spends more to provide basic services for its citizens than it can collect in tax revenue—that is the crux of the problem of financing city government. The demand for many municipal services has increased tremendously in the last several decades. City residents want a rapid and inexpensive public-transportation system, since traffic congestion has made the use of private cars inconvenient. With rising crime rates has come an increased demand for police protection. Because of the high level of technology in most industries today, businesses need highly trained and educated workers; this means that people want their cities to provide more and better schools. Most of all, there is an increasing demand for goods and services for the urban poor. Medical care, welfare payments, medical clinics, employment services—these are just some of the social goods and services that the city is asked to provide for its low-income residents.

While the demand for social goods and services in urban areas has been increasing, the ability to pay for them has declined, primarily because of the changing tax base of the typical American city.

Census figures show that since the great spurt of urban growth that took place around the turn of this century, the population of the older central cities has remained fairly constant. But although the size of the cities has not changed, the income levels of the residents have. As we saw in *Tables 33.1* and *33.2,* for an extended period of time, people with relatively high incomes moved out of the central city, while those with relatively low incomes moved in. Moreover, cities lost some business firms with high levels of income. This reduced both tax revenues and job opportunities, so that there were more unemployed people seeking financial help from the city government.

As low-income households replaced high-income households, the tax revenues of the city shrank. In order to obtain the money needed to keep running, the city raised the tax rate; this had the effect of driving even more households and businesses out of the city. The process became a vicious circle.

A continuing problem stems from groups that use city facilities but pay no taxes. One such group is suburban residents. Many come to the city to work and to shop. They are daytime users of city transportation, water and sewers, and police and fire protection, but may pay little or no tax to help provide the additional services they consume.

A somewhat similar problem arises as a result of tax-exempt property such as that owned by government agencies and religious and charitable organizations. Tax-exempt buildings require sewers, clean water, police and fire protection, transportation facilities, public sidewalks, and garbage removal, yet they do not contribute a cent in property taxes.

Possible approaches to budgetary problems

When budgetary problems appear, the city can either try to increase revenues, or it can cut expenditures. Most cities tend to concentrate on the first approach by raising taxes, altering the tax structure, or by asking state and federal governments for more assistance. They may also extend taxes to new items or to new people and may even sponsor profit-earning corporations such as Off-Track Betting in New York.

Revenue Sharing

One source of federal funding for cities in recent years has been revenue sharing. This program was initiated by passage of the State and Local Fiscal Assistance Act of 1972, which provided $30.2 billion to state and local governments over a five-year period. It was extended in 1976, with $6.65 billion to be shared annually over the ensuing four years. As opposed to conditional grants, which must be used for a purpose specified by the federal government, revenue-sharing funds may be used for a variety of purposes at the discretion of the recipient. States and many forms of local government, such as counties and townships, receive these funds. Therefore, this program is not aimed solely at solving the financial problems of urban America, although one of its goals is to reduce the fiscal disparity between cities and suburbs.

While it is too early to determine the degree of reduction of fiscal imbalance achieved by revenue sharing, cities did receive more funding than outlying areas in 1972. Analysis of data from Standard Metropolitan Statistical Areas (SMSAs)* associated with 19 of the nation's 26 largest cities indicates that on average cities received almost twice as much shared revenue per capita as did the remainder of the SMSA, i.e., the suburbs. Nevertheless, these grants amounted to less than 8 percent of the tax revenue collected by these cities in the 1970-1971 fiscal year. And although a recently introduced counter-cyclical assistance feature, which funnels additional aid to high unemployment areas experiencing tax-base erosion, has been relatively more beneficial to distressed central cities, the overall impact of revenue sharing on the fiscal condition of urban areas has not been of sufficient magnitude to prove a panacea for city problems.

Direct federal aid

In addition to the essentially "no strings attached" revenue-sharing funds, the federal government has been pouring large sums of money, for specific purposes, into central city coffers during the years of the Carter administration. Strangely enough, however, the influx of financial resources documented in Table 33.3 is not the outcome of a marked change in the administration's

---

*A SMSA generally consists of a central city and its surrounding suburbs.

Table 33.3

Accelerating federal aid to cities

Direct federal aid as a percent of city's general revenue, selected cities and fiscal years 1957–1978

City	Fiscal years				Per capita federal aid based on 1975 population	
	1957	1967	1976	1978 (est.)	1976	1978 (est.)
St. Louis	0.6	1.0	23.6	54.7	$ 86	$223
Newark	0.2	1.7	11.4	55.2	47	251
Buffalo	1.3	2.1	55.6	69.2	163	218
Cleveland	2.0	8.3	22.8	68.8	65	217
Boston	*	10.0	31.5	28.0	204	203
Baltimore	1.7	3.8	38.9	53.3	167	258
Philadelphia	0.4	8.8	37.7	51.8	129	196
Detroit	1.3	13.1	50.2	69.6	161	248
Atlanta	4.3	2.0	15.1	36.0	52	150
Denver	0.6	1.2	21.2	24.2	98	140
Los Angeles	0.7	0.7	19.3	35.7	54	120
Dallas	0	*	20.0	17.8	51	54
Houston	0.2	3.1	19.4	22.7	44	68
Phoenix	1.1	10.6	35.0	58.3	57	116

Source: T.D. Allman, "The Urban Crisis Leaves Town," *Harper's* (December 1978), p. 47.
*Less than .05 percent.

---

urban policy. A new urban strategy has been unveiled, but none of the proposals contained therein has yet been adopted. Rather, the federal government's generosity is largely a result of previously enacted programs that possess built-in spending-growth mechanisms. Consequently, "on an annual, virtually self-renewing basis, without any additional new programs, some $80 billion in federal money now goes specifically for urban aid programs, and for social programs aiding people who live in cities."*

Despite the fact that massive federal aid has made possible balanced budgets for many cities that were operating in the red just a few years ago, we cannot infer that the quantity and quality of public services provided are now adequate and that urban problems are largely solved.

Reducing expenditures

While from a political perspective, it is usually desirable to address budgetary problems by increasing revenue, if this can be accomplished without raising local taxes, many economists look at the opposite side of the ledger and consider expenditure reduction.

The question of scale comes up again in this connection. Economists recommend that city administrators exploit all possible economies of scale in providing public services. Wasteful duplication of facilities and services is a common occurrence—especially in cities that are composed of a number of independent political entities. It would be more efficient for these independent units to centralize many operations, such as buying supplies, screening new employees, and making out weekly paychecks. Economist Wilbur R. Thompson speculates that there is a demand for more costly localized government, because it is more personal and open to wider community participation. He says:

> Residents of large metropolitan areas have, in effect, chosen to devote part of their rising incomes to the luxury of buying small local government. And even if they were made fully aware of relevant costs of this choice—knowledge we do not have—we have every reason to believe that urban residents would still elect to have local political entities appreciably smaller than the least-cost local government, although perhaps not quite so small as many now are. Small local governments offer some very high style features,

such as easier political participation by the citizens and greater responsiveness of the public officials to the desires and aspirations of the local residents.†

If Thompson is correct, residents should be willing to vote for bond issues or specific taxes that would allow the city to continue the luxury of providing service on a less than efficient scale.

Some economists feel that a large part of the budgetary problems of local governments (in fact, of governments at all levels) is due to the establishment of artificially high demand schedules for public goods and services. The reason is that there is no clear and direct connection between the price that must be paid and the services and goods that are received. To most residents, the services provided by the city seem to be "free." Although they of course realize that they pay property taxes and perhaps an income tax as well, it is difficult to remember that these taxes are actually the price they pay for having their garbage collected, the snow removed, the block patrolled by police. As a result, people demand more comprehensive medical care, frequent garbage pickup, and more extensive fire protection than they are really willing to pay for.

User taxes

There are a number of ways in which the municipal government can make the cost of public goods and services clear to residents. One is to alter the tax structure, so that more revenues are collected in the form of user taxes. For example, instead of financing the cost of garbage collection from a portion of property taxes, the city could lower those taxes, and every family could be billed semi-annually for the collection service provided by the city. Any improvement in the service—collecting three rather than two times a week, special col-

---

*Allman, p. 47.

†Wilbur R. Thompson, *Preface to Urban Economics*. Baltimore: Published for Resources for the Future by The Johns Hopkins University Press, 1968, p. 259. ©The Johns Hopkins Press.

lection days for large and bulky trash, leaf collection in the fall—would show up as an extra charge on the garbage bill. With the costs of garbage collection made so obvious, many people might decide that they prefer to make do with less frequent collections or that they are willing to take large boxes of trash to the city dump themselves. If the city were to go one step further and differentiate in their rate schedules between garbage that has already been sorted and mixed garbage that is more expensive to process, many people would probably be willing to do the sorting themselves, using one container for trash, another for organic garbage, and a third for bottles and cans.

Most of the current efforts to resolve the financial problem of cities involve trying to increase revenues. Yet many economists believe that as long as city services continue to appear to be "free," the demand for services will outstrip the city's ability to finance them.

Summary

■ This chapter discusses contemporary urban problems from an economic standpoint and looks at some proposed solutions.

■ Some economists believe that the basic problem of the cities is one of scale. Cities should be able to benefit from economies of scale in the services they provide, but this does not seem to be the case today. Among the reasons offered for why these benefits are not realized are the lack of managerial skill and the difficulties in defining a workable scale of operations.

■ Cities have a special problem with transportation. Though cars have provided the most convenient form of transportation in the past, increased congestion and pollution have created serious external diseconomies. One suggested solution to the problems created by too much traffic would be to require that drivers pay more of the social costs, for example, through user taxes. Raising the costs of automobile use would shift the supply curve for driving upward and thereby reduce driving and increase the demand for substitutes such as mass transit. Public transportation can be made more attractive, but the difficulty remains that in order to handle rush-hour loads there must be an investment in very expensive facilities that would not receive heavy use during much of the day.

■ Until the mid-1970s, cities experienced a gradual shift in population, with middle-income families moving to the suburbs and low-income families concentrated in the inner cities. The cities were therefore left with the wealthy and the poor—two groups which have entirely different demands for social goods and services. Intracity population movements have also been significant, emptying some neighborhoods and overcrowding others. Suggested solutions to these problems might include zoning regulations and selective modification of the tax rates.

■ The current rekindling of interest in investment and residence in the central cities of the United States highlights the problems cities face in land use, since many uses of urban land result in external diseconomies. User taxes on land and license fees could help to defray the social costs as well as the private costs.

■ The present demand for safety in urban areas may be artificially low because many of the social costs of crime are not considered; both crime and crime prevention are very expensive. One suggestion for handling the crime problem is to allow the victim to sue the city for damages; another would require the criminal to pay both the victim and the government for the costs.

■ The typical American city is caught in a squeeze between falling tax revenues and increased demand and costs for social services. Cities have a predominantly low-income population; suburbanites make use of city facilities but usually pay no taxes; much valuable real estate is held by the government or religious and charitable organizations that pay no taxes. In recent years, most cities have raised tax rates as one means of overcoming deficits. Federal revenue-sharing and direct-grant programs are another source of increased revenues. Expenses can be cut somewhat by eliminating waste and duplication. Since many municipal services are provided "free," people may not realize the actual costs of the services they demand. User taxes may be one method of making the costs of services clear to consumers of these services, as well as serving to raise revenues.

Review & Discussion

1. Why might it be inefficient to have a large number of local governments within a single metropolitan area? How would you describe the opportunity costs of small governmental units in a large urban area? What are some of the considerations in defining an effective scale of operations for the government of a large city?

2. Examine again the economic effects of a user tax on driving, illustrated graphically in Figs. *33.1* and *33.2*. How would the shape of the demand curve (*D*) be altered if the demand for driving was perfectly inelastic? Given a perfectly inelastic demand, how effectively would a pollution tax reduce traffic congestion?

3. What are the general trends in urban population shifts in recent years? How might the recent dramatic rise in the cost of gasoline affect residence patterns?

4. What are the diseconomies of crowding? How do diseconomies of crowding explain the shift in the population in the cities? How could a city address the problem of crowding?

5. How might economists explain the rise in the crime rate as population density increases in a large city? Would consumers tend to demand perfect safety? Why or why not? Why do some experts believe that the current demand for police protection is artificially low? What are some of the proposed solutions to the problem of the social costs of crime?

6. Suppose that the entire population—urban and rural—was taxed at the same rate. Would this provision help solve the problems of the cities?

7. Faced with a deficit of $120 million in its 1975 budget, New York City found it necessary to discharge thousands of city employees, thus increasing the already severe recession in that period, and to turn over a large amount of the control of city finances to the state of New York, the federal government, and large private banks. What long-run policy alternatives might a city in such a predicament adopt to cope with financial instability? Compare the advantages and disadvantages of different alternatives.

Chapter 34

The Economics of Poverty and Discrimination

What to look for in this chapter

How can poverty be defined, in both absolute and relative terms?

What is the extent of poverty in the United States? What groups in the population are particularly affected by poverty?

What are the causes of poverty?

What are the special problems facing minority and women workers in the economy?

What is the dual labor market theory?

What are the possible solutions to the problems of poverty and discrimination?

Elimination of poverty has become a major goal of American economic policy. In recent decades, people have become increasingly aware of the great differences that exist in the economic and social circumstances of people in the United States, and some Americans have begun to reevaluate whether America really is the "land of opportunity."

Throughout much of American history poverty was regarded as a reflection of personal inadequacy, and people were expected to pull themselves out of poverty "by their bootstraps." Although this attitude still finds support, in recent years most Americans have come to realize that the causes of poverty are complex and that often poverty is tied to discrimination. Today the prevalent attitude is that equality of opportunity ought to be the birthright of all Americans.

In this chapter we will present some of the causes of poverty and discrimination and discuss the implications of these problems for the economy. We will also consider some possible economic solutions.

POVERTY: A DEFINITION

In most definitions of poverty, the major distinguishing characteristic is income. Poverty may be defined in either absolute or relative terms. A family is poor in absolute terms when it cannot afford to purchase the basic necessities of food, clothing, and shelter. In relative terms we can say that some households are poor in comparison with others. Suppose that we rank every person in the United States according to size of income. The people who rank in the bottom fourth or fifth of the group will probably be viewed as poor, by themselves and by the rest of society, no matter what their monetary income. Even if the last person on the list has an income of $25,000, that person will feel poor in comparison with the person at the top, who has an income of $10 million. If we define poverty as the inability to purchase the material comforts that the majority of people in the economy possess, then the minority will always be living in poverty.

Another approach to defining poverty has been advanced by economists at the New School for Social Research in New York City. They developed the concept of bands of poverty, classifying poor families according to the quantity of necessities and comforts their income could purchase. The lowest band of poverty consists of families with an income insufficient to provide minimum subsistence. These are the people who suffer from hunger, cold, and malnutrition. The next band of poverty is that of minimum adequacy. These families can afford a nutritionally sound diet and they can provide for other basic necessities, but they cannot afford any luxuries (an automobile, a washing machine). The third level is minimum comfort. At this level, the family's income is large enough to buy some luxuries. According to the New School definition, we will have eradicated poverty only when all family incomes are above the minimum comfort line.

One drawback to this definition of poverty is that the social definition of an adequate or a comfortable standard of living changes in response to economic development. What seemed a comfortable standard of living to our great-grandfathers might seem to us a primitive existence. Most people today feel that a television set, a telephone, perhaps even a car, are necessary for minimum comfort. Each time the standard of living escalates, many families at low-income levels will once again be unable to purchase what is considered a minimum of comfort.

Although income level is usually a major defining feature of poverty, low income in itself does not always indicate poverty. Examples of people who have low incomes but have available reserves of wealth are business executives who treat themselves to long vacations by using money they have saved in previous years, or farmers whose earnings may be low in a given year because of bad weather but who own many thousands of acres of fertile land. Perhaps in this category we should also include all those to whom other people's wealth is available. Many young couples or students with low incomes cannot be considered poor because if it became really necessary, their parents would be able and willing to help them.

From the preceding discussion then, it is apparent that it is difficult to construct a comprehensive definition of poverty. To simplify matters, we can state in broad terms that a family is poor when its current income is too low to allow the purchase of goods and services that will satisfy its basic needs and when it has no other financial resources stored in the form of accumulated or acquired wealth.

Advantages and disadvantages of income inequality

While few people would argue that income inequality is beneficial to the poor in the short run, some would contend that income inequality may be beneficial to the economy, and to the poor themselves, in the long run. The major argument in favor of income inequality dates back to the theories of Adam Smith. Smith contended that the rich were capable of saving a great deal, providing the funds necessary for investment. If the income were redistributed to the poor, they would surely squander it on consumer goods. Since investment is necessary for growth and saving is necessary for investment, income inequality promotes growth. Thus, Smith argued, by giving the rich a larger share of the pie today, there can be a larger pie for everyone in the future.

It is also argued that income inequality results from the necessity for providing incentives to productivity. Many socialist countries which preach income equality actually provide wage incentives of one type or another to more productive workers because they have found these incentives stimulate productivity. Once again, the advocates of income inequality suggest that their method increases the likelihood of there being a larger pie in the future, making everyone better off.

While the arguments outlined above are based on the assumption that income inequality generates a larger pie for everyone in the long run, some economists assert that the costs in the short run are too great. One of the goals of economic policy is to maximize total satisfaction, or utility. Economists who favor income redistribution argue that taking a dollar away from a very rich family and giving it to a poor family would increase total utility for society. They reason that the poor family would gain more utility from the dollar than the rich would lose. (This is part of the rationale of the progressive income tax system.)

A second argument against income inequality is that inequality impairs rather than promotes productivity. The very poor aren't physically capable of reaching maximum productivity because of such factors as poor diet and lack of medical care. Furthermore, monetary incentives lose their allure for the very rich who no longer need these sorts of rewards.

What you should notice about the arguments concerning income inequality is that they are based on productivity and efficiency, not on emotion or equity. Note too that the arguments lead to completely opposite conclusions because the assumptions on which they are based are very different.

Whether income inequality is good or bad for the economy is largely an academic question, since it has been the stated policy of every administration since Franklin Roosevelt to attempt to eliminate poverty.

THE POOR IN AMERICA

Using our definition of poverty, we will now try to evaluate the extent of poverty in America. The federal government, in order to decide who is eligible for antipoverty aid, measures net income according to family size. For example, as of 1977, a nonfarm family of four with an income of $6191 a year or less was defined as existing below the poverty level. A nonfarm family of six with an income of $8261 was also classified below the poverty level.* *Table 34.1* gives minimum income figures for families of various sizes.

There are several problems with this net-income approach, however. One is the frequent difference between money income and real income. Inflation or deflation can change the buying power of a fixed amount of money. In 1904, sociologist Robert Hunter suggested that a poverty-level income for a family of five was anything below $460 a year; today the figure is almost 16 times as large. Inflation necessitates continual redefinition of poverty levels of income. Moreover,

---

*For purposes of determining the poverty level and of making other comparisons, a distinction is made between farm and nonfarm income, because farmers use more non-market goods. That is, they need less money to buy food at the market because they can eat what they grow.

Table 34.1
Poverty levels for nonfarm families and individuals, 1977

Size of family unit	Money income*
1	$ 3,075
2	3,951
3	4,833
4	6,191
5	7,320
6	8,261
7 or more	10,216

Source: *Statistical Abstract of the U.S.*, 1978.
*Money income is income before the deduction of income taxes and Social Security taxes. It does not include nonmoney items such as wages received in kind, or the net rental value of owner-occupied homes.

even at a fixed point in time, there are regional differences in the cost of living. A person in Wyoming can live relatively comfortably on an income that would create hardship if he or she lived in San Francisco.

In 1977, there were 24.7 million Americans, or just under 12 percent of the total population, living below the poverty level. If we break down the statistical averages by age, geographic location, and race, we find that some groups face especially severe problems. In the nation as a whole, 29 percent of blacks were living in households with incomes below the poverty level as opposed to 8.9 percent of whites. The figure for blacks was even higher in inner-city ghettos.

Other groups that are especially prone to poverty are the young, the elderly, residents of rural areas, and people living in families headed by women. A third of all poor people live in households headed by women, while only 7 percent of the poor population lives in households headed by men. In 1975, 43 percent of the nation's poor were living in the South. Furthermore, although 20 percent of America's poor people are employed, their wages are so low as to be below poverty level and their employment tends to be unstable. These are the working poor. Another especially disturbing statistic is that in 1977 10 million children were living below the poverty level.

In 1963, Michael Harrington's book *The Other America* awakened the nation to the fact that there are a great many more poor people within the boundaries of the United States than Americans realized. Some go unnoticed because on the surface they look like everybody else. Others—the invisible poor—are unnoticed because their lives are isolated from those of most other citizens. Old people who never leave their homes are examples of the invisible poor. So are the hill families of Appalachia. One program that owed some of its inspiration to the general reaction of shock to Harrington's disclosures was President Lyndon Johnson's War on Poverty, a series of economic programs initiated in 1964. A decade later, however, the situation of poor people in America had changed little.

Distribution of income in the United States

How widespread is the problem of poverty in America today? In order to determine the number of poor people in our society and also the extent of their poverty, we must look at the statistics on income distribution.

Since the household is the basic economic unit in our economy, the data on income distribution is usually stated in terms of household income, rather than per capita income. *Table 34.2* shows the way total personal income (income before taxes) was distributed in 1977. While 36.3 percent of all families had incomes greater than $20,000, this group received more than 61.7 percent of total personal income. At the other end of the scale, 16.5 percent of families earned less than

Table 34.2
United States distribution of income, 1977

Total money income	Percentage of families	Percentage of total family income
under $3,000	3.6%	0.2%
$3,000 to $4,999	5.7	1.3
$5,000 to $6,999	7.2	2.4
$7,000 to $9,999	10.9	5.0
$10,000 to $11,999	7.2	4.3
$12,000 to $14,999	11.3	8.3
$15,000 to $19,999	17.8	16.9
$20,000 to $24,999	13.9	16.9
$25,000 to $49,999	19.8	34.9
$50,000 and over	2.6	9.9

Source: United States Department of Commerce, Census Bureau, *Money Income in 1977 of Families and Persons in the United States,* March 1979.

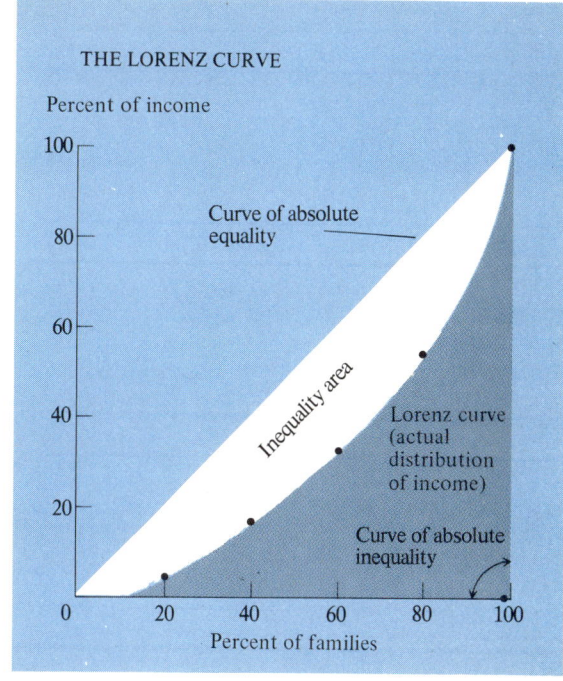

Fig. 34.1
The inequality area represents the difference between a totally equal distribution of income (the 45-degree line) and the actual distribution of income.

$7000 and received only 3.9 percent of total income. Of course, these statistics do not tell us the size of the family. If a family consists of only one member, an income of $4000 will be above the poverty level, and an income of $5000 could represent reasonable comfort, but for a large family, that income would represent real need.

There is unquestionably a significant degree of inequality in the distribution of income in the United States. There is a large differential between the group at the bottom and the group at the top; clearly, there are a number of people who possess great wealth, just as there are many who live in abject poverty. Yet the fact remains that a majority of families are situated in the middle range, earning between $7000 and $25,000 in annual income. Our income structure is not a pyramid with a few people at the top and the masses at the bottom; it is a diamond with most people in the middle and a minority at either extreme.

The Lorenz curve

Economists use a graph called a **Lorenz curve** (Fig. 34.1) to show income distribution. A Lorenz curve is *a diagram that includes curves that illustrate a hypothetical, totally equal distribution of a society's income and the actual distribution of that income; the distance between the two curves indicates the degree of inequality in the distribution of income in a given society*. Percentage of

Table 34.3
Percentage of aggregate income received by families, 1977

Rank of families by income	Percentage of aggregate income	Cumulative percentage
Lowest 20%	5%	5%
Second 20%	12	17
Middle 20%	18	35
Fourth 20%	24	59
Highest 20%	42	100

income received is put on the vertical axis, and percentage of total number of families is put on the horizontal axis. If income were perfectly evenly distributed with everyone receiving the same amount of money, the Lorenz curve would be a 45-degree line. Looking at the 1977 income distribution in *Table 34.3,* we see that the poorest 20 percent of the nation received 5 percent of aggregate income, so we plot 20 on the horizontal axis and 5 on the vertical axis. The next 20 percent of the nation received 12 percent of aggregate income. Adding the wealth of these two lowest groups, we find that the lowest 40 percent of the families received 17 percent of aggregate income. Using this method, we continue to plot the income distribution curve for all families in the nation. The area between the curve and the 45° line is called the "inequality area." It represents the difference between a totally equal distribution of income and the actual distribution of income.

CAUSES OF POVERTY

When America was founded, the Calvinists who settled in New England believed that wealth was a sign of God's favor and that poverty was a manifestation of God's displeasure. The attitude that poverty reflected some personal inadequacy was still reflected well into the twentieth century. At the start of the Depression, President Hoover felt that the federal government should not give aid to the poor but should leave that task to local agencies and private charities. As the Depression deepened, however, it became increasingly obvious that able-bodied people with good work attitudes could be poor because of circumstances beyond their control and that massive government aid was needed. The nation then began to reconsider its attitudes toward poverty, its causes, and its cures.

Today, more and more people have come to accept the idea that poverty can result from various causes beyond the individual's control. These causes may involve the individual alone, or they may involve an entire society. Natural disasters such as floods, low employment or economic growth rates, oversupplies of workers with particular skills, lack of education or opportunity, and discrimination in hiring and wages are examples of the latter.

Low worker productivity

Price-system explanation
Perhaps the greatest cause of poverty is low worker productivity. In Chapter 4, we talked about the way the price system responds to the production questions of what to produce, how, and for whom. The economy produces for those who have the dollar votes to cast; households acquire these dollar votes by renting, selling, or lending the productive resources they own or control. The largest incomes, therefore, go to those who own the most, or the most valuable, productive resources.

Thus the price system creates a link between income and productivity. We can deduce that, as a general rule, those with the largest incomes are the most productive, though not necessarily that they are productive workers; they may own valuable land or capital resources. According to this principle, those with the lowest incomes—people who are really poor—are, in general, the least productive. This is not to say that the poor cannot be as productive as others; rather, it means that for many reasons—lack of education, low prestige associated with a particular job, discrimination—society does not highly value their output.

But measures of productivity are, in fact, somewhat arbitrary. For example, one society might believe that its witch doctor provides a vital service and may grant the doctor a large share of the community's wealth. Another society, on the other hand, would not consider this service productive and would pay little or nothing for it. Thus, different cultures attribute different values to the same job. In American society productive individuals are defined as those who produce more units of something than other persons do; and they are workers who may produce more valuable items.

Resource-demand explanation
The theory of resource demand, which was discussed in Chapter 28, also emphasizes the connection between income and productivity. An employer is theoretically willing to pay each worker a salary equal to the value of the marginal product that worker adds to the firm's output. We must be careful to remember that a worker's marginal revenue product (MRP) is not a measure of the individual's ability or willingness to perform his or her job; rather, it is a monetary measure of the value of output from one additional worker's labor.

A firm might be able to draw up a MRP schedule that shows an average of all kinds of workers in the company, but it is much more realistic to think of MRP in terms of separate job categories. At Procter & Gamble, for instance, there might be one MRP schedule for workers in the factories, another for the supervisory staff there, another for middle management, and a fourth for top executives. Presumably, the work performed by a vice-president in choosing production processes, making marketing decisions, and signing contracts with suppliers will do more to expand the firm's revenues than the work performed by a single operator of the machine that fills up boxes with soap powder.

Low level of human capital

One way to explain inequality of income distribution is in terms of the level of **human capital.** By human capital we mean *the productive skills and degree of knowledge possessed by an individual worker.* Labor is a productive resource, but not all kinds of labor yield the same value of output. For example, making managerial decisions about production processes is considered to be a more productive type of work than performing a small task on the assembly line. However, in order to perform successfully the highly productive job of vice-president, a worker must have a number of specialized skills, which he or she has developed through formal education and on-the-job training. The productive skills and degree of knowledge possessed by an individual worker are part of his or her human capital.

Human capital is obtained by the expenditure of money (frequently, tuition payments for education and training) and time. It also involves income forgone either by delaying entry into the job market to study in school, or by taking lower-paying jobs that offer a chance to learn. For example, a new lawyer earns less by working as a clerk for a judge than by opening an office right after graduation. But the clerkship provides both prestige and valuable experience. The opportunity costs of being a clerk are a form of investment incurred in order to increase the lawyer's rate of return in subsequent years.

It is logical to assume that workers who have the largest amount of human capital will also earn the largest salaries, whereas those who have very little human capital will earn considerably less.

Factors contributing to low level of human capital

One of the chief causes of poverty, then, might be a low level of human capital. Analysis of the data collected on the characteristics of low-income households supports this explanation. On the average, income rises with every year of schooling a person gets and with the quality of schools attended, since this adds to the person's store of human capital. The majority of the poor in America have completed fewer years of school than those who are better off. Consequently, the poor who are employed typically work in low-level or temporary jobs that offer no advancement. In addition, many of the unemployed lack such basic skills as reading simple material, doing simple calculations, filling out a job application, or using common tools. The lack of these skills also is often tied to lower levels of education.

Human capital includes not only skills and knowledge but also good health. There is a high rate of poverty among the chronically ill, the physically handicapped, and the weak and frail. Ill health and a low level of human capital form a vicious circle. People with little human capital cannot earn enough to buy decent food, clothing, and shelter. Therefore they suffer from ill health and malnutrition. This lowers their ability to work, which further lowers their earning power. Their children do not get enough to eat and must often leave school to go to work before they have learned enough to obtain a good job. Thus poverty breeds poverty, and the vicious circle of low human capital continues.

Possible solutions

The theory of human capital points to a possible solution to much of the current problem of poverty. An investment in the human capital of low-income workers might raise their incomes. It is probably unrealistic to expect these workers to make the investment themselves, since their incomes are too low to permit any form of saving. Remember that education and training are both forms of saving—accumulation of human capital. But the government might make the investment, on the grounds that it is in the best interests of society as a whole. A number of antipoverty programs attempt to do just this; they provide job-training programs, special tutorial programs to keep children of low-income families from dropping out of school before they graduate, and low-cost educational loans.

The chief disadvantage of most of these programs is that only the actual purchase price of training—the cost of enrolling in a college or trade school—is taken into account; the high opportunity cost of earnings given up during the training period is not. Even when college tuition is free, many children of low-income families cannot go to college because the family's need for the additional income they might be earning appears too urgent. If programs to increase human capital are to be a success, they will probably have to provide reward (or incentive) in the present. While it cannot be expected that the poor will make a sacrifice in terms of current income (since that could virtually mean starvation), it can be expected that some type of monetary reward over and above their current opportunity cost would interest them in the program. The success of this program would depend upon the ability and willingness of the taxpayers (1) to understand the argument presented above and (2) to pay for the program.

The high unemployment of recent years has sparked several suggestions that would tie unemployment benefits to education and training. While this would work well for those workers whose skills are no longer required, it would be less practical for those who find themselves temporarily out of work. These workers might not be willing to be retrained, or the problem may be one of relocation instead of retraining.

Market imperfections

The theory of resource demand states that under conditions of perfect competition, a worker will be paid a salary equal to the value of his or her marginal revenue product. This leads to the conclusion that the poor are those whose productivity is low. So, as a remedy to poverty, one's first impulse is to prescribe more training, greater motivation, and putting more hard work into the job.

Imperfect mobility

But perfect competition is only a model, and the conditions it assumes are not always present in a real market situation. There are a number of imperfections to be found in most labor markets, so many workers are not actually paid the value of the MRP. Mobility is not perfect; workers who are earning a low wage in a southern factory may not be able to afford the cost of moving to an area where pay rates are higher. Nor may workers be willing to accept the disruption of family and community life that such a move entails; in other words, they may prefer stability over the increased income obtainable from moving.

Sometimes people who would like jobs cannot leave their homes. Mothers of young children must locate sitters or day-care centers to care for their children before they can work. Handicapped persons may find it difficult to get about. These people may have the desire and the human capital necessary to perform a job, but until they can achieve greater mobility, they must remain unemployed.

Imperfect knowledge

The perfect knowledge that is assumed in the model of competition is often missing, too. A young woman who has graduated from college and is ready to accept her first job probably is not sure whether the salary she was offered is low, average, or high by industry standards.* Many workers have no idea what size salary their co-workers are getting, or what their counterparts at another firm earn; finding out what other people in your office are earning often requires considerable tact or excellent connections.

Monopoly and monopsony powers

Monopoly and monopsony powers also can create market imperfections, as we saw in Chapters 25 and 28. Workers at a monopolistic firm may be able to earn more than the value of their MRP, because the firm has the market power to earn excess profits and distribute some portion of these among its employees. A monopsonistic employer may be able to exploit workers by paying them less than their MRP. Workers may have to accept this wage because there are no other jobs available. Nonunionized labor may lack the organization and the financial means to bargain successfully with a large, affluent, well-functioning bureaucracy which has the means of coping with small amounts of worker unrest.

Even a market that is moving toward a long-run equilibrium at which all workers will be paid the value of their MRP will have many short-run irregularities. An overcrowded industry may have to lay off many people and ask others to accept salary cuts. In the long run, this will serve the function of reallocating productive resources into industries producing goods and services that have a higher level of demand, but in the short run, it will mean that many workers will receive low pay for their work.

Inefficient mix of capital and labor

Under perfect competition, each firm will be forced to find its most efficient resource mix; for example, if it uses too many workers and too little capital, it cannot survive the competition. But in the real world, it sometimes happens that a firm operates with an inefficient mix of capital and labor. The labor of each additional worker is subject to the law of diminishing returns, so that marginal physical product is very low; consequently, salaries will be low, too. This inefficiency is not the fault of the workers employed by the firm, nor do these particular workers have any less human

---

*There are organizations that attempt to provide such information, however. For example, the College Placement Council in Bethlehem, Pennsylvania, will send on request information about starting salaries for various jobs.

capital, compared with workers doing the same job in more efficient firms; yet the employees of such a company will have to accept lower salaries for their work. Since job mobility is not really perfect, especially among the poor and uninformed, many will remain with the low-paying situation rather than try to search for a job at a higher wage.

Low employment and/or growth rate
A final market-related cause of poverty is low employment and/or a low economic growth rate. Perhaps the economy is not expanding fast enough to fill the needs of a growing population, to absorb young adults into the labor force, and to keep job holders employed in their current capacities. This was the situation in the mid-1970s, when even the strength of the unions could not prevent the laying off of thousands of auto workers as manufacturers cut production and closed down plants when business slackened.

Possible solutions
The actual distribution of income will be affected by the existence of the market imperfections discussed above. This means that low-income workers cannot always raise their incomes by working harder or by investing in human capital improvement. Many households with low incomes are simply the victims of an imperfectly competitive market structure. In most cases, investment to cover the cost of gaining knowledge and mobility is the solution. This investment, once again, might be made by either the individual concerned or by government.

POVERTY AND DISCRIMINATION
Another major cause of poverty is **discrimination**. In economic terms, *discrimination exists when, between two workers with the same skills and training, one worker is preferred over the other on the basis of some criterion that is not directly related to the worker's ability to perform the job.*

Discrimination can take various forms. It can be by wage, as when a man and a woman do identical work but the woman receives less pay. It can be by job restrictions, as when minority applicants are not considered for higher-paying kinds of jobs. Some groups are victims of more than one type of discrimination.

Demographic studies show that blacks are poorer than whites. The median family income for whites in 1977 was $16,060; for black families, median income was $9485. In urban areas, the unemployment rates are a good deal higher for blacks than for whites. Some of these differences remain even after one takes into consideration differences in human capital, type of job, etc. Other minority groups, most particularly American Indians, suffer from an even greater degree of economic deprivation.

To many people, these economic disparities supply evidence that some minority groups in America do not have economic opportunities equal to those of whites. What can economists tell us about the problem of discrimination?

Effects of discrimination on the economy
Economists generally agree that the fundamental causes of discrimination are beyond the scope of economic analysis. We would probably have to turn to psychology or sociology to explain why discrimination exists in American society. But economics can offer some important insights into the impact which discrimination in employment practices has on the economy as a whole.

Higher prices, lower output
Let us analyze the effects of racial discrimination on the demand schedule for labor resources. If we consider an employer's preference for white workers as a determinant of the demand schedule for labor—in addition to the MRP of the resource—we will get two separate schedules. One schedule is the demand for the more preferred

white workers, a labor unit for which employers are willing to pay higher prices; the other schedule is for the less-preferred nonwhite workers.

Most legislation forbidding discrimination is based on the assumption that such practices are unjust. Are there any economic reasons to support government prohibition of discrimination? There are two economic factors to consider. One is that the cost of indulging this preference for one group of workers over another probably will be reflected in higher consumer prices. If a consumer pays more to purchase the car model which best suits his or her taste, the cost of this indulgence is borne by that individual alone. But when a business executive pays more to indulge a preference for white workers over black workers, the result is an increase in the costs of production, which will cause a shift in the supply schedule, and, therefore, a higher market equilibrium price. A policy of discriminatory hiring increases the costs of production; it also reduces the level of output.

But why would any executive deliberately increase the costs of production and, in so doing, reduce total profits? Clearly, if discriminatory employment practices do raise the price of productive inputs, an employer must be deriving some kind of nonmonetary reward from hiring an all-white work force, and the reward must be sufficient to compensate for the higher monetary costs. In regulated industries (i.e., public utilities) profit levels are set by the government, so there is less incentive to end discrimination than in the unregulated sector. Returns in excess of the allowable rate are taken in the form of such nonmonetary benefits as working with the colleagues one likes.

Higher taxation

The second economic consideration in the prohibition of discrimination is that the social costs of discrimination will be borne by the public in the form of higher taxation. Economist Gary S. Becker explained this in his book, *The Economics of Discrimination*. Discriminatory hiring serves to depress the wage rates of nonwhites while it raises the wage rates of white workers. So discrimination distributes more income to the already more affluent whites and less income to the nonwhites. But since the United States has already adopted a goal of achieving greater equality of income distribution, this means that taxes will have to be increased in order to make more transfer payments to poor nonwhites and to provide needed goods and services for them.

So there are economic costs to a policy of discrimination. It raises consumer prices, reduces productive output, decreases the return on white capital, and necessitates tax increases.

Causes of low incomes among minority groups

It is impossible to deny that discrimination in hiring and in paying wages exists. Many business firms pay lower salaries to blacks, Puerto Ricans, Mexican-Americans, and women than they are willing to pay to white males with the same training and skills. And many businesses hire white male candidates over minority or women candidates. Yet present discrimination is not the sole cause of this difference in hiring practices and incomes.

Differences in human capital

The differential in average salaries can be explained partly in terms of human capital. For example, comparisons of black and white male workers have shown that, on the average, white male workers possess more human capital than do blacks. They have had more years of schooling, they are more likely to have had professional training, and they are more likely to have had valuable on-the-job training in their previous employment. There is statistical evidence that white workers are healthier than black workers —whites have a longer life expectancy, a lower disease rate, and can afford better medical care when they are sick.

So present discrimination is only a part of the problem. As long as blacks and other minority groups have a smaller amount of human capital to offer employers, they will continue to earn less. It is unrealistic to expect businesses to pay high wages to a worker who lacks the necessary skills to produce at a high rate. It is also bad economic policy, since it would require businesses to pay more for a resource input than the value of its MRP; and this increased cost would be passed on as increased prices. A better solution is to make it possible for the disadvantaged groups in our society to acquire the training and education they need to improve their stock of human capital.

It is important to note that while the differences in human capital discussed above are not necessarily the result of present discrimination, they may well be attributed to *past* discrimination in education, health care, and job opportunities.

WOMEN IN OUR ECONOMIC SYSTEM

In recent years there have been growing charges that women have been discriminated against in the job market for no other reason than that they are women. It is certainly true that women have traditionally held lower-level types of jobs and that women are not paid as much as men for doing the same work. In addition, while a woman is not usually paid less for the same *job title* as a man, new job titles are often developed. An "administrative secretary" may do the same job as the "assistant to the director," but guess who makes $20,000 a year and who makes $12,000! How did this situation come about?

Historical background

Historically, women's disadvantage in the working world resulted from their generally smaller size and the assumed limitations of availability because of pregnancy and child rearing. Only in times of emergency did women do the same work as men. Their time was principally devoted to caring for home and children. Because it was believed that these jobs required little education or skill development, there was little effort to train women for the job market. Interestingly, however, it has been shown that more education results in more efficient family operation.

In the 1940s, the situation of women began to change. During World War II, with many men in the armed forces, women filled their places in factories and offices. When the war was over, many women left the work force to return to being homemakers, but a number of factors contributed toward fundamental changes in the pattern that had existed prior to the war emergency. Technological advances and a rising standard of living made many labor-saving devices available and decreased the amount of time and energy it took to complete household chores. At the same time, family-planning measures enabled couples to control the number of children they would produce. Furthermore, many families not only had sufficient income to educate their daughters as well as their sons, but they also saw the social value of doing so. Thus women had more free time and more human capital than ever before, and, not surprisingly, they sought jobs.

In recent years more and more women have begun to enter the job market as a matter of necessity. They are working to *maintain,* not to improve their standard of living. For example, many young couples are postponing having children so that their dual income can provide them with enough money for a down payment on a house. Similarly, many women are seeking jobs to provide a college education for their children, and single and divorced women are working because they must. In addition, a changing sociological climate has made the goal of a career not only acceptable but even desirable for many women. The attitude that "woman's place is in the home" has changed considerably.

Fig. 34.2
The occupational distribution of women is very different from that of men. Women are concentrated in clerical, retail sales, and service jobs and are clearly underrepresented as craft workers, managers, nonretail sales workers, and operatives.

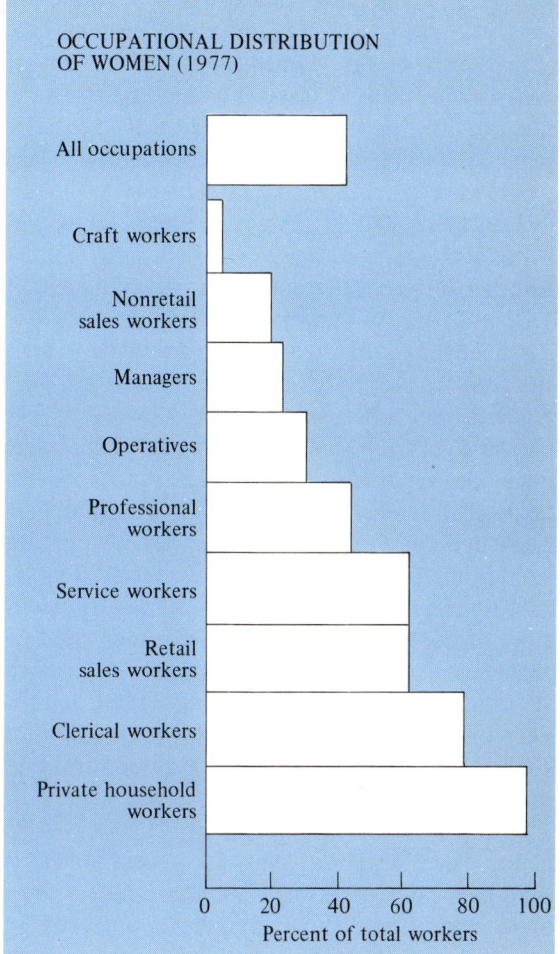

SOURCE: Prepared by the Women's Bureau, Office of the Secretary, from 1977 annual averages data published by the Bureau of Labor Statistics, U.S. Department of Labor, August 1978.

Factors influencing wage differences

In 1977, a full 48 percent of all American women age 16 and over were working. However, statistics compiled by the United States Department of Labor verify that, on the whole, women do not receive a proportion of national income equal to their work efforts.

In 1977, the average income of full-time male workers in America was $15,070, while the average income of full-time female workers was $8,814. Lack of education was not the cause of this discrepancy, since working males and females alike averaged 12.5 years of schooling. Clearly, factors related to a worker's sex are more important than education in predicting income.

What are the reasons for this situation? First is the different nature of the jobs that men and women have traditionally filled. As shown in *Fig. 34.2*, women are concentrated in clerical, retail sales, and service types of jobs; they are clearly underrepresented as craft workers, managers, nonretail sales workers, and operatives. Even though women account for 43 percent of professional workers, they tend to be concentrated in positions such as teaching, library work, and nursing, where salary schedules are lower than in the other professions. Men generally fill the better-paying jobs as engineers, scientists, doctors, and lawyers.

It is commonly believed that at least part of the difference is due to the reluctance of some women to enter the more competitive job areas for fear they will be considered "aggressive" or "unfeminine," but a more pervasive reason is that women are often not considered for the better-paying jobs. Employers have attempted to justify their resistance to hiring women for these jobs by pointing out that many women do not remain in the work force for long periods. Employers are understandably reluctant to fill an important job with someone they believe is not likely to stay with the job.

Clearly, the time women take off from work to raise children has a serious effect on their lifetime earning power. Remember that if we look at the earnings of a man and a woman of the same age, we may be comparing a man who has more years of work experience with a woman who has spent fewer years in the labor force.

Do women take men's jobs?
Another cause of resistance to hiring women is the belief that they will take jobs that would otherwise go to unemployed men. However, there is little evidence to support this fear. As *Fig. 34.2* suggests, men are usually not attracted to the types of jobs generally held by women, particularly since these jobs often pay less well than do traditional men's jobs. And even if the opposite were true—and there are indications that women are attempting to move into positions traditionally held by men—a dynamic labor market provides more of these jobs each month. No man need be pushed out of a job; new jobs need to be opened to both men and women. The argument of efficiency suggests that it is in the company's best interests to hire the person best qualified for a job.

The need for day care
It has been suggested that the development of child-care alternatives will facilitate the entrance of women into the labor market, enable women who have been able to work only part time to select full-time employment, and enable well-educated women to pursue higher-level jobs. The desire of women for child-care facilities is demonstrated by the fact that currently the demand for day care far outstrips the supply.

There are a number of reasons why more day-care centers have not developed. If they are to be privately financed, the poor are unlikely to be able to afford them, and the rich can find more satisfactory alternatives, such as private babysitters, maids, or nursery schools. The value of publicly supported day-care centers has been questioned by those who suggest that the cost to society may be almost as much as the income that can be earned by those who are freed to work. This argument leads some to conclude that it is better to pay poor mothers to look after their own children. However, this attitude ignores the desire of poor women to expand their aspirations and increase their marketable skills, thus adding to their human capital.

DUAL LABOR MARKET THEORY
The problems of poverty and discrimination have been summarized in the dual labor market theory. This model suggests that there are two distinct markets for labor in the United States. The primary sector is characterized by high wages, highly skilled jobs, and good job stability, while the secondary sector is characterized by low wages, unskilled jobs, and poor job stability. Workers in the secondary sector are generally perceived by employers to have some of the following characteristics: low-level skills, poor work habits, lack of creativity or imagination, tardiness, and unreliability. As a result, the workers in the secondary sector tend to conform to these expectations. The jobs are often repetitive; most require little training, so that one worker can easily replace another who doesn't report to work; and chances for advancement are slim. It is not surprising then that workers in the secondary sector tend to stay there, trapped in a vicious circle that is difficult to break.

The dual labor market theory can help explain the situation of many minority and women workers by focusing on the supply and demand factors that tend to generate low wages in the secondary sector. *Figure 34.3* compares the secondary labor market supply and demand conditions with supply and demand conditions in the primary labor market. The low demand shown in *Fig. 34.3(b)* can be accounted for by employers' *perceptions* of the workers' ability to produce. Discrimination in hiring and wages can be viewed as a result of these perceptions. The low supply curve, which represents low labor-force participation

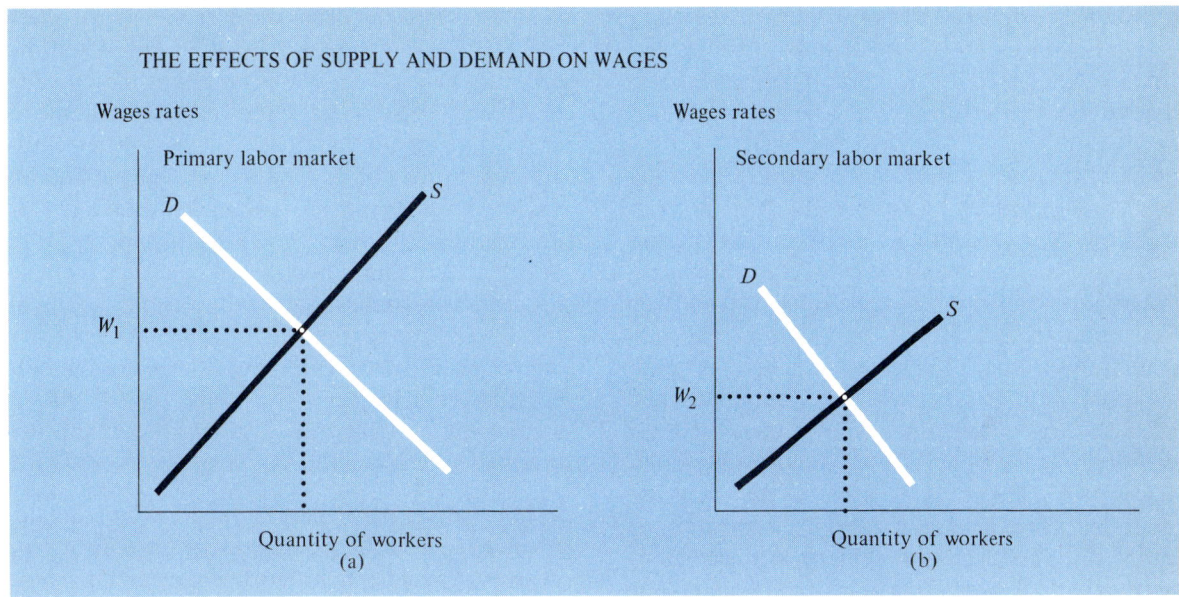

Fig. 34.3
According to the dual labor market theory, high supply and demand in the primary sector (a) tend to generate high wages for workers (W_1). In the secondary sector (b), low supply and demand tend to generate low wages. The lower level of demand in the secondary sector is often due to employers' negative expectations of workers' potential productivity, while the lower supply in this sector may reflect discouragement of workers for whom only low-level, low-paying jobs are available. The lower demand and supply result in a wage level (W_2) lower than that in the primary market.

rates, can be accounted for by factors such as discouraged workers and mothers who cannot find day care. Thus, attempts to solve the poverty problem should include finding ways of shifting the demand and supply curves of secondary workers to the levels of the demand and supply curves of workers in the primary market.

WHAT CAN BE DONE ABOUT POVERTY?

The preceding analysis of some of the complexities of the problem of poverty suggests that the solutions will not be simple and clear-cut. There is no magical solution, no instant program to eradicate poverty.

Education and legislation

Clearly, part of the answer lies in the education and training of the poor to allow them to expand their stock of human capital. This would shift the demand curve for the labor of the poor (shown in *Fig. 34.3b*) to the right as employers' perceptions of their productivity increased. Present legislation that makes job discrimination illegal is another step in the right direction, since it helps to distribute incomes more equitably. However, when the penalties for discrimination are smaller than the benefits employers derive from discriminatory practices, this type of legislation is ineffective. Once again, effective antidiscrimination legislation would shift the demand curve in *Fig. 34.3(b)* to the right.

Legislation that promotes competition among firms and industries is also helpful; it is the existence of such competitive imperfections as monopolies and monopsonies that causes many workers to be paid more or less than the value of the MRP. For example, one study has shown that discriminatory hiring practices were more prevalent in the regulated monopolies, such as public utilities, than in any other type of firm. Because the dollar rate of profit is limited, regulated monopolies have little incentive to eliminate the inefficiencies of discrimination. Concentration of market power also allows many companies to operate with inefficient ratios of capital and labor inputs, which lower the value of a worker's MRP and, therefore, his or her salary.

Welfare programs

Most of this chapter has been devoted to a discussion of income earned through participation in the labor market. Another method of solving the immediate problem of the poor is through income supplements provided under various welfare programs. These programs do not directly increase the "marketability" of their participants, but do help provide them with food, shelter, and health care.

OASDHI Old age, survivors, and disability and health insurance (commonly referred to as Social Security) is the largest of all supplement-income programs. Basically, it is a massive social insurance plan paid for by employers and employees. Employees can begin to draw some benefits at age 62 and full benefits at 65. If the worker should become disabled, payments begin immediately. If he or she should die, the survivors receive payments. As can be seen, the insurance is against loss of income due to disability, death, or old age.

OASDHI has been under close scrutiny over the last few years because the fiscal stability of the program is threatened by changes in the age distribution of the United States' population. Due to these changes, the number of beneficiaries is increasing while the percentage of the population paying into the program is actually declining. This has threatened the system with bankruptcy. More important to some, however, is the fact that the program is mandatory and provides only minimal relief in old age. In fact, critics claim, the system is *not* an insurance program, but a forced income-redistribution scheme. If this is the case, it would seem more suitable to use general taxes and tax revenues to achieve this goal.

SSI Supplementary Security Income is a federally financed and administered program which provides cash payments to aged, blind, and disabled individuals who do not qualify for OASDHI or other programs.

AFDC Aid to Families with Dependent Children is a federal/state/local program designed to aid families whose income-earning parent has died, become disabled, or left the family. The problem with this program (one that is pointed out by opponents of the welfare system) is that it actually promotes the breakup of families. Income earners are in effect encouraged to leave the family so that this aid can be received.

Food stamps The food-stamp program is designed to provide an adequate diet to all Americans. Initially, participants in the program were allowed to buy food stamps at 75–85 percent of the face value of the stamps. The coupons could then be used to purchase certain foods at the grocery store. In 1978, it became apparent that many of those most in need of the stamps could not afford to buy them. As a result, recipients are no longer required to buy the stamps.

Though often criticized because of various abuses, the food-stamps program seems to have gone a long way toward achieving the goal of eliminating starvation in America. The major advantage of the plan seems to lie in its ability to help those most in need of help—the very poor.

Medicare and Medicaid Medicare is a mandatory insurance program that provides hospitalization benefits to the aged. Older people, many of them living on fixed incomes, have an especially difficult time paying for hospital care. Their medical needs grow as they become older, and the costs have increased tremendously. A voluntary portion of the Medicare program will also provide insurance to help defray doctors' costs outside of hospitalization. Medicaid enables recipients of AFDC and SSI to receive help for their medical expenses.

While there can be little doubt that the poor and the elderly need help with their medical expenses, abuses of the system have been widespread. It is claimed that some doctors and hospitals charge for services that have not been performed, or charge for unnecessary services that they have performed, knowing the government will pay. In addition, some doctors refuse to handle Medicare and Medicaid patients because of the extra paperwork involved.

Unemployment compensation The purpose of unemployment compensation is to "tide workers over" a period of temporary unemployment. Employers pay into the fund and workers receive payments up to about half their normal salary while they are out of work. This payment helps them meet basic needs while they are searching for a new job. The results, in some cases, have been to prolong the period of unemployment. In other cases, some workers who have no intention of seeking a job have also been able to collect.

In general, an argument against many of the welfare programs discussed above is that they *promote* idleness, providing little or no incentive to work. While many of those covered are over or under working age, others fall well within the working-age population. Most Americans are not callous enough to want to see people go hungry, but they do believe that those who are capable of work should earn their living. Most economists believe that incentives to work will cause people to work and disincentives to work will cause people not to work.

Table 34.4
Negative income tax (hypothetical data)

Family income	Income tax Negative	Income tax Positive	Net income
$ 0	$2500	—	$2500
1000	2000	—	3000
2000	1500	—	3500
3000	1000	—	4000
4000	500	—	4500
5000	—	—	5000
6000	—	$500	5500

The negative income tax

One program that has been suggested as an alternative to the numerous and proliferating welfare systems in the country involves guaranteeing a minimum annual income for each household. Households earning below the minimum amount would receive money from the government.

Under this system, called the **negative income tax,** *each household would report its total earnings on a tax form, just as it does now. If the total amount was above the level established as the poverty line, the household would have to pay a tax to the government (a progressive tax). But if total income was below the poverty level, the government would pay the household an amount to bring it closer to the minimum income* (a negative income tax). *Table 34.4* shows how the negative income tax plan would work. Any family of four that earned more would pay tax on the additional amount, but the family would be allowed to keep a certain portion of income earned. In other words, it would have an incentive to *earn* an income.

Advantages
There are a number of clear advantages to such a program. It could be administered through the existing Internal Revenue Service, much of which is now automated, and so would cost considerably less than the present caseworker system. It would remove all subjective judgments, such as the morality of the poor person or the degree of one's need for new shoes or medical treatment. Budgeting would be done entirely by the recipient households; no "free" goods would be offered and therefore no artificially high demand schedules would be created.

Incentives to work could be built into the system. If the tax structure was designed so that people at all levels of income would make more money by working than by accepting a dole, incentives to work would exist.

The Office of Economic Opportunity has made several small-scale tests using this approach, asking welfare clients to declare the amount they needed each month, up to a ceiling of $5000. A surprising result of these tests was that under this plan, more households increased their market earnings than a similar group on the traditional welfare system; in fact, by the end of the program, a number of families had declared themselves ineligible for further subsidies.

The debate
Many economists of varying political beliefs agree that the negative income tax offers the best method of effecting needed transfer payments. Yet adoption of this plan is by no means assured. There are vested interests to take into account. People currently employed by the Department of Health, Education and Welfare are afraid of losing their jobs as are local welfare department workers.

Getting the bill passed into law is not within the professional province of economists. They can only tell us that from an economic point of view, the negative income tax, coupled with programs to improve human capital, appears to hold promise as part of the effort to eliminate poverty.

WHAT CAN BE DONE ABOUT DISCRIMINATION?

Legislation
There have been several effective laws and Executive Orders to combat discrimination against minorities and women. Title VII of the 1964 Civil Rights Act prohibits discrimination based on race, color, religion, national origin, or sex where such discrimination affects access to jobs. (The sex provision was added to the bill by a senator who wanted the bill to be defeated, but it passed anyway! Ironically, in the first year of its enforcement by the Equal Opportunities Commission, more than 40 percent of the complaints were based on sex discrimination.)

The Equal Pay Act of 1963 prohibits paying members of one sex less than the other for doing identical work. Under this law, the Supreme Court in 1970 forced the Wheaton Glass Company to pay more than $900,000 in back wages and interest to women who had received 21.5 cents an hour less than men while performing essentially the same task. Three years later, American Telephone and Telegraph agreed to give back pay adjustments to 15,000 employees (87 percent of whom were women) who had had no opportunity for assignment to better positions. In May 1975, the government brought a second action against A.T.T. for failing to live up to its 1973 agreement. This time, some A.T.T. employees were eligible to collect from $125 to $1500, depending on the job and the nature of the discriminatory act.

In 1978, Congress enacted legislation which forbids the practice of forcing workers to retire at age 65. The effect of this law on the labor market is not clear, since statistics seem to show that many workers are ready to leave the labor force at age 65 or even younger. What is clear, however, is that the law does offer the worker a choice. If the firm wishes to fire a worker, it must do so on the basis of productivity, competence, or some other factor, rather than on the basis of age. This may result in many decisions being contested in court. Thus the law prohibits discrimination against older workers. There still remain, however, the problems faced by middle-aged workers seeking new jobs. Discrimination against this group is widespread.

The Equal Rights Amendment (ERA), if passed, will guarantee equal rights to women and presumably help to prevent discrimination against women in the work force. This amendment has aroused a great deal of controversy, and many of the arguments against it are highly emotional. Opponents claim that the amendment would rob women of various privileges they now enjoy. For example, they assert that passage of the ERA would mean an end to alimony payments for divorced women, that it would force women to participate in military combat, and that it would take away sexually segregated restrooms. At present the future of the ERA is in doubt.

Quotas

In an attempt to end discrimination against women and minorities, some businesses and universities are admitting quotas of these groups. Hiring or entrance requirements stipulate that the percentage of minorities employed or enrolled must equal their proportion of the nation's population. Sometimes this has allowed qualified minority members to reach positions they would not otherwise have attained, but at other times, less qualified minority candidates or women have been chosen over better qualified white males. Such favoring of the minority has become known as "reverse discrimination." Some people support quotas in the belief that they help to correct centuries of sexism and racism, but others oppose them on the grounds that discrimination is undemocratic, regardless of which group is favored. Furthermore, it can be argued that productivity suffers when a job is given to other than the most competent person available, regardless of race or sex, and then society in general loses.

A recent Supreme Court decision may have considerable effect on the use of quotas and on antidiscrimination legislation in general. In the well-known "reverse discrimination" case of *Bakke* v. *The University of California,* the Court ruled that Alan Bakke, who is white, could not be denied admission to the University of California Davis Medical School solely on the basis of color. (While his qualifications were superior to those of some minority applicants who were admitted, Bakke was passed over under a minority quota system.) This decision could have serious repercussions on the admissions and hiring practices of many schools and business firms.

As we move into the 1980s, it is clear that progress has been made in increasing the awareness of government and citizens of the problems of poverty and discrimination. It is also clear that these situations will not be easy to solve, because they are deeply engrained in the economic and cultural fabric of our society.

Summary

■ This chapter considers the causes and consequences of poverty and discrimination and looks at some of the possible solutions.

■ Income measures of poverty can be either absolute (an income level insufficient to provide for basic necessities) or relative (the lowest portion of the income scale, regardless of absolute income level). It is possible to describe degrees, or "bands" of poverty, distinguishing between those unable to obtain necessities, those unable to achieve minimum standards of comfort, and those able to achieve only minimum comfort. Broadly, we can say that those whose income is insufficient to satisfy basic needs and who have no other sources of income available are poor.

■ Some people argue that income inequality is a good thing, providing incentives and leading to economic growth for all in the long run; others argue that income redistribution would increase total social satisfaction and remedy the ways in which poverty inhibits productivity.

■ In 1977, the federal government defined poverty for a nonfarm family of four as a net income of less than $6,191; in 1977, 12 percent of families (24.7 million people) were below this poverty line. Poverty is especially prevalent among minorities, young people, elderly people, and households headed by women. Income distribution in the United States is certainly unequal, but incomes are distributed in the shape of a diamond (with a large bulge in the middle), not like a pyramid. Income distribution can be displayed graphically on a Lorenz curve.

■ In the past, poverty has often been explained as the result of individual human failure; more recently, explanations have focused on factors beyond the control of individuals. A major factor is low worker productivity; that is, income will come to those who are productive, according to a particular cultural definition of productivity. The poor also tend to have the lowest stock of human capital. Most low-income families are not able to afford the high opportunity costs of education and vocational training, nor can they afford decent food, clothing, and shelter. Their health suffers, lowering their productivity still more. Poverty can also be aggravated by imperfections in the market. Workers do not have perfect knowledge of the market, nor are they perfectly mobile. Workers in areas dominated by a monopsonist will be paid less than their marginal revenue product. An inefficient capital/labor mix in production, a low rate of economic growth, and high rates of unemployment are also causes of poverty.

■ Economic discrimination takes the form of not hiring certain types of individuals on the basis of some criterion that is not directly related to ability, or paying them lower wages than those received by other individuals for the same work. The practice of discrimination is costly because it creates two demand schedules for labor, which effectively raises wages for some workers and thereby increases the costs of production. Discrimination also is costly because it leads to higher taxes to finance social welfare programs for victims of discrimination.

■ In recent years, more women have been able and willing to enter the labor force, with 48 percent of women over age 16 employed in 1977. In recent years, many of these women have gone to work to maintain, not increase, their family's standard of living. Women workers are concentrated in lower-paying jobs—clerical, retail sales, service occupations, nursing, and teaching—and are underrepresented in higher-paying categories—craft workers, managers, doctors, and lawyers. One major reason for this is that employers have resisted considering women for the better-paying jobs. Increased provision of day care for children could counter the argument that women tend to drop out of the labor force and thereby facilitate the entry of more women into the work force.

■ The dual labor market theory has served as a useful means of summarizing the economics of poverty and discrimination. This model suggests that there are two distinct categories of employment, one characterized by high wages, skilled jobs, and job stability, the other by low wages, unskilled jobs, and job instability. The jobs in the secondary sector tend to reinforce employers' expectations about the workers who hold them, with the result that many workers remain trapped in the secondary labor market. Resolving this problem requires steps to create an upward shift in both the supply and demand curves for labor in the secondary market.

■ Measures to reduce poverty have included programs of education and training to increase human capital, legislation which prohibits discrimination, and an increase in competition among business firms. The government also provides welfare programs and income supplements, such as Social Security and disability payments, SSI, AFDC, food stamps, Medicare and Medicaid, and unemployment compensation. It is sometimes argued that such programs actually reduce incentives to work. A promising alternative to the numerous welfare programs is the negative income tax, which would build in incentives for earning additional income.

■ The 1964 Civil Rights Act and the 1963 Equal Pay Act are important legislative bases for eliminating discrimination. Affirmative-action programs, including the use of quotas, have been undertaken in the past decade, but their future remains in doubt because of the controversial charge that they are "reverse discrimination."

Key Terms

Lorenz curve
human capital
discrimination
negative income tax

Review & Discussion

1. Why is income alone a somewhat inadequate measure of poverty? What are the advantages of absolute and relative measures of poverty? Why do definitions of "necessities" or "minimum comfort" change over time?

2. How would you describe the distribution of income in the United States? What kind of people tend to be represented at the top? At the bottom?

3. What is a Lorenz curve? What would the curve look like for an economy in which there is great inequality of income distribution? How would you represent absolute equality of income distribution on a Lorenz curve?

4. What is the evidence that the poor tend to be less productive? What is human capital? How is it acquired? What is the relationship between human capital and productivity? Between human capital and poverty? What are the difficulties in increasing a poor family's stock of human capital?

5. How do the imperfections of the market add to the problem of poverty?

6. What are the economic costs of discrimination for those discriminated against? For the firm practicing discrimination? For the economy as a whole?

7. Why are minority and women workers primarily concentrated in lower-paying jobs?

8. How does the dual labor market theory explain the economics of poverty and discrimination?

9. What are some of the possible solutions to the problem of poverty? What is the negative income tax concept? Is it possible to eliminate or even significantly reduce poverty in the United States without extensive government intervention in the market economy? Why or why not?

Chapter 35

The Economics of Energy

What to look for in this chapter

How did the energy crisis of the 1970s develop?

What have been the long- and short-run causes of the current energy problems?

What have been the effects of government regulation of energy production?

What are the advantages and disadvantages of the "free market" and "government action" strategies for energy?

What are some of the economic problems involved in developing alternative sources of energy?

The emergence of energy as an issue with worldwide economic, political, and social consequences occurred in late 1973, following a short-lived war between Egypt and Israel. As an outgrowth of that conflict, crude-oil prices soared, and helped trigger worldwide inflation and recession. For several years following the 1973 crisis, energy problems seemed to lessen, and relatively little attention was focused on this topic. Then, in late 1978, political turmoil in oil-rich Iran helped to bring about another crisis. The problems which surfaced in 1973 and 1974 reappeared and revived old concerns about adequate energy supplies as well as energy conservation.

The atmosphere of alarm and shrill political debate surrounding the energy crises of 1973 and 1979 have contributed to confusion about energy and have obscured many fundamental economic issues. Some people believe that the crisis in 1979, as in 1973, was engineered by the oil companies for their own economic gain. These individuals regard the shortage of gasoline as artificial, and consider claims of increasing scarcity of energy resources as deceptive. Others blame the federal government for shortages, long gasoline lines, and higher gasoline and utility prices because of the great number of energy-related government regulations and controls which have been established in response to the energy situation. Still others argue that a combination of private and governmental actions taken over a period of many years brought about the crises.

In this chapter, we will trace the development and history of the energy situation in the 1970s and will examine some relevant economic issues in order to shed light on the current debate. The special attention given to energy in this chapter is warranted because of the influence that energy has on the lives and behavior of all Americans. Unlike changes in other commodity prices, which may have only a negligible macroeconomic effect, changes in energy prices have far-reaching consequences. Not only are prices higher for goods that use petroleum or petroleum derivatives as a direct input to production, but because increased transportation and utility costs (the result of increased oil costs) affect every sector of the American economy *all* commodity prices tend to increase.

At present, the United States obtains about 96 percent of its energy from four sources: oil, natural gas, coal, and uranium. Because of the prominence of oil in the energy picture, it receives primary attention in the discussion that follows. The remaining three sources of energy cannot be ignored, however, since together they meet slightly more than half of the demand for energy in the United States.

DEVELOPMENTS IN THE 1970s

The energy crisis of 1973–1974

Although problems in assuring adequate supplies of energy to American businesses and consumers had been brewing for several years, the general public did not view the situation with alarm. However, the public suddenly became more concerned after the Egyptian military defeat in the 1973 conflict with the Israelis. In retaliation for the political and economic support given to Israel by the United States and the Netherlands, ministers of the seven Arab members of the Organization of Petroleum Exporting Countries (OPEC) met in Kuwait in October 1973 and announced an embargo on the sale of crude oil to those nations.

In addition to the selective embargo, a general production cutback, the effects of which would be widely felt, was announced in order to build support for the Arab cause. The worldwide reaction to this form of economic blackmail was immediate and predictable. Led by Japan, the world's largest petroleum importer, many nations called for Israel's withdrawal from captured Arab territory.

In the United States, a nation heavily dependent on petroleum and petroleum by-products, people's lives were suddenly and severely disrupted. There were power shortages because generating facilities were unable to obtain sufficient quantities of oil or alternative fuels for producing electricity. Schools and factories closed for lack of heating fuel, and motorists suddenly found gasoline difficult to obtain. When service stations were open—and many were not—prices were high, purchases were limited to a few gallons, and lines were long.

The increased scarcity of petroleum products and the shortages of gasoline and petroleum by-products, such as fertilizers (caused by price controls)* triggered an immediate political response. A new energy agency was created by the federal government, and Congress took steps to investigate causes of the crisis as well as ways to deal with it. State governments developed special programs to help ease the conflicts that developed. Outside

---

*Wage and price controls were in effect at this time as part of President Nixon's fight against inflation.

TEN LARGEST OIL-PRODUCING NATIONS (BY MILLIONS OF METRIC TONS), 1975*	
Union of Soviet Socialist Republics	491.0
United States of America	413.1
Saudi Arabia	352.4
Iran	267.6
Venezuela	122.2
Iraq	111.2
Kuwait	105.2
Nigeria	88.4
United Arab Emirates	80.5
Libya	71.5

Source: Information Please Almanac, Atlas, & Yearbook, 1979 *(33rd Edition), New York, Viking Press, 1978, pp. 125–126.*

*Crude petroleum production, including shale oil, but excluding natural gasoline.

The energy situation since 1974

By mid-1974, with an easing of gasoline and other shortages, the public's attention turned to other, more traditional concerns, such as attempting to balance the family budget in the face of sharply higher prices for gasoline, food, and utilities. The energy crisis was no longer a hot political issue, and although public officials in Washington tried to construct an energy policy to deal with the crisis and its aftermath, little support could be mustered. Until early 1979, the energy issue remained largely dormant, notwithstanding warnings by Presidents Ford and Carter that the days of seemingly limitless energy resources had come to an end. Some state officials as well as private groups called for an end to the nationwide 55 mph speed limit and other legislation which had been enacted in a crisis atmosphere to help restrain demand for fuel. Electricity for fountains, lighting outdoor advertising signs, and other "nonessential" purposes, which had been turned off at the height of the crisis, was turned back on. And the public's demand for larger, less energy-efficient automobiles and even larger recreational vehicles soared.

Late in 1978, with only slightly more warning than in 1973, gasoline shortages again became commonplace. First in California, and then across the nation, motorists were once again lining up for hours to obtain a few gallons of gasoline. This second crisis, triggered by political upheaval in Iran, revived emergency allocation measures and reopened debate about the role of the oil companies in the crisis. As gasoline prices approached, and in some cases exceeded, $1 per gallon, politicians were flooded with complaints as well as recommendations on how best to deal with the situation. Proposals for the funding and accelerated development of alternative energy sources again became the subject of intense public debate. Advocates of mass transit systems saw new opportunities to obtain funding for projects which had previously been rejected, and ideas formerly

of government, various groups used the crisis to advance particular causes. Environmentalists urged American consumers to stop their apparent waste of energy and called for an end to unrestrained and "irresponsible" use of energy and other finite natural resources. Others used the crisis to urge an easing of restrictions designed to curb pollution.

The effects of the embargo were equally dramatic abroad. Shortages and rising prices immediately followed the embargo, and industrial production was curtailed. Unemployment rose dramatically, and many countries were hit with the worst recession since the Great Depression of the 1930s.

But the embargo was not the only cause of the ensuing crisis. While it triggered the events that occurred in late 1973 and throughout much of 1974, its primary role was one of worsening problems whose coming had been predicted well before October 1973.

regarded as impractical or unworkable suddenly found a new audience.

In 1979, as in 1973, no single factor was responsible for causing the crisis. Political events in Iran which led to removal of the Shah and interrupted the flow of Iranian oil to world markets were certainly a major cause. But the 1979 crisis was also caused by several domestic factors, including government regulation and control of the oil industry and other energy-providing industries, high and growing levels of energy demand in the United States, domestic price controls, and environmental restrictions. The contribution of each of these factors to the energy situation is examined below.

CAUSES OF THE ENERGY CRISIS

Government regulation and control of energy

Government intervention and control in energy-producing industries has a long history. This involvement has served not only to protect and enhance the position of some suppliers, but to distort market prices for energy, and, in most instances, to inhibit domestic energy production as well.

Oil

Following the embargo in 1973, the American government made changes in its regulations concerning the domestic oil industry for the purpose of counteracting reduced imports from the Middle East. It allowed for increased production from domestic sources at a more rapid rate than had earlier been planned. For nearly 40 years, certain states had limited either the number of days or months that oil wells could operate or the amount they could produce. These limitations were initially justified on the basis that they encouraged conservation. However, many observers believe that the limits on production actually had been established to support the price of domestic oil by inhibiting competition, and that relatively little consideration had actually been given to conservation. In a related development, in 1959, an oil-import quota was established in response to industry pressure. Because foreign oil was much cheaper to produce, and because, since 1947, the United States had been a net importer of oil, producers sought protection from this threat to their profits. They also argued that increasing dependence on foreign sources of oil posed a threat to the defense and security of the United States since the American market could become dominated by foreign oil. By keeping oil prices high, the industry claimed, the quota helped to stimulate domestic production and to protect the United States from potential disruptions in foreign supply lines. In a sense then, government was supporting a cartel of American producers by enabling them to restrict the import of cheap, competing oil from abroad. Since 1973, of course, the price of oil in world markets has generally been above the government-established prices for domestic oil which, some have argued, has inhibited the search for new supplies of this fuel by American oil companies.

Natural gas

Since the development of nationwide markets for natural gas in the 1920s, government has played an active role in pricing and allocating this commodity. In gas-producing states, the amount supplied is regulated. When natural gas is transported in interstate pipelines, the price is set by the federal government. Finally, due to significant economies of scale, most local governments grant to one firm the right to supply natural gas to all residents. In return, the sole producer (a natural monopoly) is subject to price and quantity regulation by the locality.

Although for several years the available supply of natural gas was sufficient to meet demand even at the low regulated price, the limitations on what could be charged for gas moving through *interstate* pipelines inhibited most attempts to increase supply. In addition, because price remained unregulated in *intrastate* markets, many producers found it unprofitable to release natural gas into interstate commerce in quantities sufficient to meet the growing demand. Instead, the tendency was to try to sell the gas in intrastate markets where it commanded a higher price. In the 1960s and 1970s, shortages of natural gas appeared in several nonproducing states. Some public utilities refused to add new customers, and many potential residential and industrial users of natural gas turned to electricity as a source of heat.

Attempts to add to dwindling domestic supplies of natural gas from foreign sources have met with little success. Importing natural gas from abroad was impractical until the 1960s, and even after the technology was developed to liquify natural gas for shipment across the oceans, the potential danger from explosion of liquified-natural-gas storage facilities has limited use of that source. Although natural-gas pipelines from Canada provide some supply to the northern states, political considerations within Canada have restrained the amount that may be exported to the United States. In the future, Mexico may be able to satisfy some of the American demand for natural gas. However, efforts to develop that source of supply have been blocked (at least temporarily) not only by current federal government restrictions on the price which may be paid for imported gas, but also by diplomatic problems in dealing with the Mexican government.

Coal

Coal is a high-energy fuel which is found in enormous quantities in the United States. Throughout the 1800s and until the 1920s coal played a central role in providing energy to American homes and industry. Since that time, however, demand for coal has declined. Presently, only about one-fifth of the energy consumed in the United States comes from coal, and unlike oil and natural gas, coal has remained free from direct governmental control.

Indirectly, however, the government's influence on the demand for coal has been substantial. As a result of growing concerns in the 1960s about the environmental impact of both strip mining and burning coal with a high sulfur content, government restrictions have inhibited the use of this fuel to replace dwindling supplies of alternative energy sources. Moreover, the use of domestic coal to meet a substantial fraction of energy demand seems unlikely unless environmental regulations are relaxed or the cost of converting coal to oil and gas becomes competitive with fuels already available. The last option will become a more realistic possibility if prices of other fuels rise high enough.

Nuclear power

Civilian use of nuclear power for production of energy emerged in the 1950s. Because of the military uses of nuclear material, the potential danger from nuclear radiation, and nuclear-waste-disposal problems, government control in this industry has been substantial. Public concern over nuclear radiation and disposal has limited the development of nuclear power as a major source of energy. Since 1977, for example, only two orders for new nuclear-power-generating plants have been placed, compared with 35 in 1973.

The accident at the Three-Mile Island Power Generating Facility in Middletown, Pennsylvania, in late March 1979, evoked additional concern about the safety of existing nuclear-power-generating facilities and will undoubtedly slow or even halt the construction of additional plants. This event, coupled with environmental concerns and extensive federal regulations, lessens the likelihood that increased reliance on nuclear power will satisfy the growing demand for energy.

Demand for energy in the United States

Excluding the Depression of the 1930s and the energy crisis of 1973–1974, the long-term trend in energy use in the United States since 1900 has been upward and has accelerated since the 1950s, generally following the growth of domestic output and incomes. In other words, as incomes have risen, so has the demand for energy.

Throughout the period from 1950 until 1972, residential and commercial energy use for heating, cooling, lighting, and powering small appliances grew at an average annual rate of between 5 and 6 percent per year. From 1973 to 1975, consumption leveled off, and only in 1975 did it resume its upward course as the economy improved. In the industrial sector of the economy, which accounts for slightly more than one-third of the nation's total energy demand, consumption leveled off in the mid-1970s and actually declined by 0.1 percent from 1976 to 1977 despite a sharp increase in industrial production over the same period. In contrast, industrial energy demand in the 1960s grew by approximately 3.5 percent annually.

Energy use for transportation purposes grew steadily from the mid-1960s through 1973 at an annual rate of more than 4 percent. At the same time, the cost of energy, in constant dollars, actually declined. During the crisis of 1973–1974, energy use in transportation declined absolutely, and barely rose in 1975. Some of the impetus for conservation during this period came, of course, from shorter supplies of petroleum and sharply higher prices. Additional pressure came from governmental programs and legislative policies, including the 55 mph speed limit and gas mileage standards for new automobiles. Since 1973–1975, however, energy demand for transportation has increased sharply.

While it is expected that the 1979 crisis will again force a temporary drop in consumption for transportation purposes, longer-term reductions in energy demand in this sector will depend upon the strength of government policy to induce conservation as well as on the public's response to higher energy prices. Although energy use over the next decade will probably grow more slowly than it has historically, a sharp reduction in the consumption of nonrenewable energy may be necessary to avoid potential economic chaos arising from increasing dependence on foreign sources of supply.

Price controls

In response to political pressures to deal decisively with inflation, President Richard M. Nixon imposed price controls on the American economy in August 1971. These controls contributed substantially to the impending crisis of 1973 and to subsequent developments in 1979.

When controls were enacted in 1971, the price of gasoline was high and the price of fuel oil was low. Thus, even when the demand for gasoline eased at the end of the summer of 1971 and the demand for heating fuel grew, oil producers found it more profitable to continue to produce relatively large amounts of gasoline and comparatively less fuel oil from each barrel of crude. As a result, fuel oil shortages during the winter of 1972 forced the closing of schools and factories for lack of heat. In 1973, gasoline supplies were short as a result of government-controlled prices. The embargo, of course, made the problem worse, and by late in the year, a serious crisis emerged.

Throughout the period of direct price controls from 1971 to 1974, the prices of oil products were fixed at relatively low levels. The oil companies, realizing that prices would eventually rise, had incentive to withhold oil from the market so that more would be available when prices went up. Although Congress ultimately allowed the price of newly discovered oil to reach world-market level, price controls on existing sources of crude remained well below those prevailing outside of the United States, thus inhibiting additional production.

Attempts to increase supply during the period after the embargo were met with frustrations and bottlenecks in supply. Pipe for use in drilling new wells, for example, was hard to get because the control prices for pipe and for flat steel made it more profitable for steel producers to produce flat steel than pipe. In addition, environmental restrictions and regulations inhibited new drilling by limiting where drilling could take place and by raising the cost of any new undertaking through legal delays and court challenges.

Since 1975, price controls and regulations on oil-industry production have continued to create market disruptions. When more than one type of fuel can be produced from a raw material, the producer decides which fuel to produce by looking at potential profits from each. Because profits depend on costs and selling price, less of a fuel will be produced if its costs are higher or if its selling price is set at relatively low levels. For example, although the demand for unleaded fuel for automobiles has increased sharply, government policy has inhibited the production of this fuel. Basically, the cost of production of a gallon of unleaded fuel is greater than that of leaded fuel. To help ensure that consumers will use unleaded in vehicles requiring that fuel, the price of unleaded fuel has been controlled by government action. In this instance, although consumer demand for unleaded fuel is high, production has failed to keep pace with demand since the oil companies find it more profitable to produce regular and premium grades of gasoline containing lead. As a result, spot shortages of unleaded fuel have occurred.

As we noted before, the government has successfully held the price of natural gas below market levels. As a result, shortages have resulted in the natural gas market and attempts to induce larger supplies to meet the growing demand have had only limited success. To deal with fuel shortages during the winter of 1976-1977, emergency legislation was passed to permit prices to be raised for gas in interstate pipelines. But this legislation was only temporary and efforts to provide longer-lasting solutions to the problem of natural gas shortages have generally been frustrated by political considerations.

Environmental restrictions

The environmental movement which surfaced in the 1960s received strong public support following a series of environmentally damaging accidents. In 1966, an oil tanker ran aground off Nantucket Island, Massachusetts, and spilled much of its cargo of crude oil into the water. This accident threatened not only the fishing industry but also the resorts in the Cape Cod area. Later that same year, a second tanker ran aground in the Delaware River, and its cargo contaminated the water for miles downstream. Thousands of miles away, in the North Sea, an oil-drilling platform exploded in early 1967, and oil from the accident spewed into the ocean for several days before the well could finally be capped. Two years later, an oil well in the Santa Barbara Channel off the California coast exploded, releasing vast quantities of crude into the water. The pollution of the water and the nearby beaches, as well as damage to fish and waterfowl, received widespread media coverage.

The environmental damage caused by these accidents and the heightened concern about air and water pollution culminated in passage of the National Environmental Protection Act of 1969. This legislation required an environmental-impact statement to be prepared for any federal project that might affect the environment and provided mechanisms to prohibit or delay projects where the environmental impact was potentially harmful. One example of the effect of this legislation was the postponement of the building of the trans-Alaska pipeline for several years. Only after the energy crisis of 1973 was special legislation enacted which permitted construction of the pipeline.

Other federal legislation quickly followed as the environmental movement gained momentum. For example, the Clean Air Act of 1970 provided specific limitations on the amount of harmful emissions that could be discharged into the atmosphere. Although many benefits are attributed to that legislation, it has also raised the costs of production for industries that pollute the environment. For example, emissions standards for automobiles have helped to reduce air pollution, but at the same time the emission controls in the automobile have caused engines to use more fuel than would be used otherwise.

PROPOSED SOLUTIONS TO ENERGY PROBLEMS

While many alternatives have been proposed to deal with the energy problems faced by the United States and other Western industrial countries, there are only two distinct ways of dealing with the situation. One involves use of the market system and its incentives of price and profit to assure adequate supplies of energy to meet current and projected needs. The other requires some form of government action, either direct—for example, through public ownership of energy resources and energy-production facilities—or indirect—for example, by imposing regulations designed to modify the decisions of individuals and firms regarding the quantity demanded or quantity supplied. The advantages and disadvantages of each approach are discussed below.

The free-market approach

The market approach to the energy problem relies on price and profit signals to restrain consumption and spur production until quantity demanded is equal to quantity supplied. Once a market is in equilibrium, the price will remain stable as long as neither demand nor supply changes. If, however, demand continues to grow over time, as it has in American energy markets, without sufficient increases in supply, the market price must rise to ration available supplies among competing users. If the price fails to rise, shortages result.

On the demand side of the market, higher prices serve to discourage consumption and induce consumers to find alternatives which use fewer of the resources in scarce supply. The increased demand for smaller automobiles in 1974 and again in 1979 that followed rapid and substantial increases in the price of gasoline provides a good indication of the effectiveness of high prices in inhibiting demand. Only when the real cost of gasoline fell after 1974 did the market for large automobiles and low-gas-mileage recreation vehicles rebound to pre-1973 levels.

On the supply side, higher prices and profits provide incentives for producers to expand production from existing facilities as well as to seek new sources of supply. For example, as the price of crude oil rose in world markets following actions by the OPEC cartel, many wells that had ceased to produce were again tapped as a source of supply. With the higher world price, many companies found it feasible to inject water and steam into old wells to help extract crude that previously had been too costly to recover using conventional techniques. In addition, oil from shale or from oil sands can be produced profitably if prices rise enough.

Pros and cons

The advantage of using price as a mechanism for rationing scarce resources as well as for increasing supply has been stressed earlier (see Chapter 32). You will recall that in a market system, prices provide necessary information for rational decision-making by both consumers and producers in an economic and political environment in which free choice is emphasized. Many individuals, however, object to higher prices in energy markets.

Some believe that these higher prices impose a special burden on individuals with low incomes. While it is true that people with low incomes must consume less of *all* goods than those who are more affluent, it is not necessarily true that the poor suffer more from higher energy prices than from high prices of other essential commodities like food and shelter. In essence, the problem is not high prices as such but an unequal distribution of income. To the extent that high prices pose unacceptable hardships on the poor, government may remedy that inequity through programs to redistribute income. Although initially it may seem more equitable to control prices rather than let them rise to market levels, the resulting shortages may in fact impose even greater hardships on the poor than if commodity prices were permitted to reach equilibrium.

A second objection to higher prices is that they add to producer profits. Although higher prices may increase profits, that result isn't always assured. Whether profits grow or decline depends not only on revenues but also on costs. Since the demand for most energy resources is inelastic, we may expect that higher prices will generate larger revenues, at least in the short run. At the same time, since the costs of production for most petroleum products have risen very rapidly, short-run increases in profits may disappear as they did for oil companies following cost adjustments brought about by higher world prices of crude oil following the 1973 embargo.

A related concern is that profits obtained from higher prices will not be used for increasing supply, but rather, will be used for corporate expansion in new fields. While some firms may use their revenues for purposes unrelated to increasing supply, it is unlikely that that situation would prevail generally unless one firm had a monopoly on all sources of energy. Indeed, high prices (and profits) in one area may spur development of alternative technologies. For example, the sharply higher cost of crude oil following the 1973 embargo accelerated developments in solar energy and other nontraditional means of generating electric power and heat. Although, as noted below, most of these alternative sources are still very costly and, for the most part, inefficient compared to oil, gas, and nuclear energy, recent developments hold out the prospect that some of them may soon become competitive with conventional sources of energy.

Finally, central to much of the discussion regarding the free-market approach to the energy situation is the concern that higher energy prices contribute to domestic inflation and a continuing inflationary spiral. While higher energy prices increase the cost of production of most goods and, consequently, the price level, they also serve to increase supply. Some forms of energy that previously were unprofitable suddenly become competitive and appear in the market, and in addition, higher prices and profits create incentives for investment in new technology. These developments, over time, shift the supply curve for energy to the right and, ultimately, may reduce American dependence on petroleum supplies from other countries. As the United States achieves greater independence in meeting energy demand, the extent to which disturbances abroad (such as those in 1973 and 1978) result in increased domestic inflationary pressures will be reduced. If the government attempts to restrain inflation by imposing control, the nation will find itself in the unenviable position that prevailed in 1974 when, particularly as a result of price controls, Americans were confronted with shortages and, at the same time, lacked incentives to conserve or to develop new sources of energy.

Solutions involving government

Instead of relying solely upon the market to meet American energy needs, it has been suggested that government should assume a more active role in assuring adequate supplies of energy as well as in directing how available energy will be used. To some extent, these arguments are simply an extension of the current political reality which, as we have discussed, finds government involved in a substantial way in most energy markets.

Energy supply

On the supply side, government has been active for years in controlling energy prices and, since the 1973 crisis, it has also influenced the allocation of crude-oil supplies among refiners as well as the composition and distribution of refinery output. Some would argue that because of the importance of energy in every facet of the economy, government should become even more actively involved on the supply side of the market, perhaps to the extent of assuming control of the industry. Although nationalizing the assets of private firms has been suggested, that idea has received little political support because of a tradition in the United States of permitting private enterprise to meet consumer demand. A less extreme proposal would have government enforce more vigorously the antitrust laws to encourage greater competition in the production and distribution of energy.

For years, it has been illegal for natural-gas suppliers to own pipeline distribution companies. Some have suggested that a similar policy should extend to the oil industry so that oil production would be separated from refining and distribution operations.

Although it has been argued that certain benefits accompany competition, no definitive studies have been undertaken which show precisely how much benefit would be derived from additional competition in the oil industry. Moreover, economies of scale in refining operations, for example, limit the extent to which competition is actually feasible. Other proposals would restrict companies in one area of energy supply (i.e., oil) from competing in other areas (i.e., coal, nuclear power), thus limiting the extent to which one or a group of firms could actually dominate the energy market. One drawback to these proposals is that any new government involvement would add to overall costs because of additions to the bureaucracy, additional forms to fill out, additional law suits, and so on.

Somewhat more attention has been given to proposals for government funding of basic and applied research aimed at developing new sources of energy and finding ways to conserve existing sources. By allocating large sums of money to research and development activities, the government may accelerate developments which would occur more slowly under privately sponsored research where, because the perceived risk is great and the potential for commercial application may be years away, funding may not be readily available from conventional sources. Furthermore, by placing strong emphasis on the development of alternative energy sources, the government also may encourage additional current production by the OPEC nations while the demand for oil remains strong and the price high, thus tempering potential price increases in the immediate future. If oil prices are expected to continue to increase over time, there is little incentive for the OPEC nations to increase current production. If, on the other hand, developments in the United States indicate that future demand for OPEC oil is likely to taper off, it makes sense for OPEC to increase production now. That, of course, would result in increased supplies of oil on world markets, which would exert downward pressure on prices.

Energy demand
Influencing long-term demand Government may influence energy demand in various ways. At a minimum level, it may take steps to ensure that the true cost of energy is reflected in its price. If energy prices were to cover costs not traditionally considered, such as the external costs incurred in power generation or in fuel production and use, many prices would probably rise above current levels. To the extent that these prices increased, we would anticipate reductions in quantity demanded as consumers responded to higher prices by moving up along their demand curves.

In addition, government may take an active role in restraining demand. By adopting appropriate legislation, it can influence long-term demand by requiring the use of energy-efficient processes and technologies by households and firms. Furthermore, it may dictate that particular products should achieve specified goals for reduced energy use, and may prohibit sale of products that fail to meet standards. For example, the government requires that each automobile manufacturer's product line meet a sales-weighted average-fuel-consumption goal of 27.5 miles per gallon by 1985—if some models fail to meet this standard, then others must exceed it. Moreover, by making automobile manufacturers publicize estimates of gasoline consumption, the government seeks to reduce demand for energy-inefficient automobiles and increase demand for those that use gasoline more sparingly.

There are also federal energy standards that appliance manufacturers must meet. Manufacturers of most appliances are now required to provide product information which specifies relative energy consumption so that consumers may make informed decisions when comparing particular products. In addition, by 1980, major appliances will be subject to minimum efficiency standards set by the Department of Energy, and those appliances that fail to meet these standards may not be sold. Similar requirements are in effect in a few states. In some states, for example, new appliances that use natural gas as a fuel must have an electric ignition system instead of a pilot light. By eliminating continuously burning pilot lights on stoves, water heaters, and furnaces, substantial energy savings are projected.

Another way the government may influence long-term energy demand is by providing tax incentives for efficient energy use. With deductions and tax credits, government effectively lowers the price to homeowners when they purchase items that increase their home's energy efficiency. Such items include storm windows, insulation, solar-heating devices, and other energy-conservation equipment that meets the specified federal or state standards.

Although precise estimates of the impact of energy-conservation programs on demand are difficult to obtain because most such programs have been in effect only a short time, it is expected that they will result in substantial reductions in *long-term* energy demand, particularly as households replace older, less efficient vehicles and appliances with new ones, and as homeowners take steps to conserve energy used domestically.

Influencing short-term demand: gasoline rationing Short-term demand may be restrained by restricting consumption for particular purposes, or through some form of mandatory rationing. An example of the former is found in California, where natural gas may not be used to heat newly installed swimming pools.

Mandatory rationing programs are most frequently associated with the sale of gasoline. To eliminate frivolous use, it has been suggested, for example, that gasoline be allocated to consumers according to need. A major difficulty of rationing proposals lies in the determination of need—any definition would be subjective, and what one person perceives as a need may not be a need for another person. Most gasoline-rationing proposals would establish maximum fuel prices and would, in addition, require that a coupon be presented when making purchases. Without a coupon, it would not be possible to buy gasoline legally. The difficulty with that and most other methods of rationing is in devising a scheme for equitably allocating the available supply. Although several methods have been proposed which would allot an equal number of coupons to each licensed driver or to each vehicle owned, arguments about potential inequities arising under any method of rationing have been sufficiently forceful that, to date, no mandatory rationing plan has received congressional approval.

Under any form of coupon rationing, economic analysis would predict that a black market in coupons would emerge if the number of coupons allocated were insufficient to meet demand at the prevailing price per gallon. Some individuals would attempt to buy additional coupons and, undoubtedly, others would be willing to sell unused coupons. To deal with that situation, it has been proposed that under any coupon-rationing program it would be legal for individuals to buy and sell coupons. If that were the case, the outcome of coupon rationing would be similar to the free-market solution. Those who could afford to purchase additional coupons would get the gasoline.

In addition to paying a premium to consume more, it would also be necessary for consumers to pay more in taxes to support a rationing program since the cost of printing and distributing coupons and of enforcing the program would have to be met from government funds. The major benefit of a coupon-rationing program is that individuals who possessed coupons, whether they were rich or poor, would be assured of a certain allotment at specified prices. For those individuals whose use was low, sale of excess coupons would bring a windfall gain in income.

Another form of gasoline rationing, dubbed the odd-even plan, emerged from the 1973 crisis and was revived on a much broader scale in 1979. Under this program, fuel prices were subject to control, at least one-half tankful of gasoline had to be purchased, and purchases could be made only on odd- or even-numbered days, depending on whether the vehicle license number was odd or even. The purpose of this program was to reduce daily demand for gasoline, given a situation of short supplies and long lines. *As with any form of rationing, it did not make additional gasoline available.* Rather, it attempted to restrain demand, particularly for discretionary driving, by designating those eligible to make purchases, and to minimize situations of panic buying in which people would wait in line for hours to buy only two or three gallons. In California, where the program first appeared in 1979, the odd-even plan was successful within a few weeks, and long lines soon disappeared. Whether this was due solely to the odd-even plan is not certain, however, since additional gasoline was made available in the state at the same time the program was introduced. Moreover, gasoline prices had risen to their legal price ceilings (an increase of 30–45 percent) in the first six months of 1979, a situation which forced many people to reduce driving and to search for substitute modes of transportation independently of the odd-even allocation system.

Current federal energy policy
Energy policy in 1979 was shaped by diverse goals embodied in both old and new legislation, and by political pressures exerted by competing groups in the economy.

Legislative measures As an outgrowth of the crisis of 1973, two major pieces of legislation were passed by Congress, the 1975 Energy Policy and Conservation Act (EPCA) and the 1978 National Energy Act, which, along with the 1978 Energy Conservation and Production Act, placed conservation at the center of federal policy. This body of legislation mandated model-year mileage standards for all new-car manufacturers, efficiency standards for new appliances, energy-performance standards for newly constructed buildings, and tax credits and incentives for households and firms to make purchases that would result in lower energy use. It also provided an elaborate scheme for controlling the price of domestically produced oil and established a timetable for removing price controls, for eliminating the distinction between intrastate and interstate natural gas, and ultimately, for eliminating some of the price controls on that commodity. Although Congress and successive administrations recognized the need for higher prices to encourage domestic production and curb energy use, they moved only tentatively in that direction. This tentativeness was in part because of the inflationary consequences of removing controls, and in part because of the fear of the potential political backlash that was certain to follow if oil and gas prices were suddenly allowed to rise.

Presidential actions: decontrol and windfall-profits proposals As the effects of the crisis of late 1978 were felt throughout the economy, it became obvious that while conservation was important in easing the crisis and slowing the rate at which energy demand would grow in the future, it did not provide a long-term solution. As a result, President Carter took the politically unpopular step in April 1979, of decontrolling domestic crude-oil prices, beginning June 1, 1979. By specifying a gradual timetable for decontrol, the president sought to avoid a sudden shock to the economy which would ensue if prices quickly rose to market levels when the control provisions of the 1975 EPCA expired in October 1981. In addition, allowing oil prices to rise gradually to world levels would encourage consumers to reduce demand for oil through both substitution of alternative fuels and outright conservation, encourage investment in solar energy and synthetic fuels, and stimulate additional supply from existing sources and new discoveries. The expected macroeconomic impact of this action is a slightly higher rate of inflation, a leveling off of economic activity, and a mild increase in unemployment. It may also give oil companies an incentive to hold back supplies in anticipation of higher prices in the future.

In his April message, the president also proposed a windfall-profits tax on oil-company revenues and creation of an Energy Security (trust) Fund from which resources would be channeled into energy research and development, into grants for mass transit, and into assistance for low-income households where the burden of higher energy prices would be felt most severely. By taxing some of the additional revenues expected to accrue to oil companies as a result of decontrol, producer incentives for exploration and development of new sources would be somewhat inhibited. However, it was also felt that the gains after taxes, coupled with federal subsidies when necessary, would provide sufficient inducement for moving closer to the goal of energy self-sufficiency in the United States.

Problems resulting from controls At a microeconomic level, the controls on gasoline and petroleum distillates (primarily heating and diesel fuels) have spawned numerous problems. Current regulations provide that oil companies set aside 5 percent of diesel fuel and gasoline stocks to be used as directed by state governments. These allocations have been used by some states to ease the general incidence of shortages and long lines, to augment supplies of gasoline for sale on weekends, and to bolster industry—particularly tourism—where shortages have resulted in a lower-than-normal level of economic activity. In addition to the 5 percent set aside for states, other priority users (such as farmers, police and fire departments, and other emergency services) receive special allotments according to Department of Energy policy before gasoline and diesel fuel are made available to the public through normal distribution channels. As a result of special allocations of diesel to farmers, shortages of that fuel were common during the first half of 1979. The diesel shortage precipitated a strike by independent truckers in June 1979, as they sought to obtain increased supplies of diesel at lower prices. In the face of this strike, Department of Energy policy was changed to remove farmers from the list of priority users. Although this alteration made more diesel available, the situation remained confused and troublesome. As noted in *Time* magazine,

> the Government has been trying to please everybody in managing the shortage. The Department of Energy has set up a hideously complex allocation system. . . . [In] trying to manipulate this system, allocators resemble a tailor who tries to get cloth to mend a hole in the sleeve of a coat by snipping a piece out of the back and hoping no one will notice. . . . But while it is easy enough to blame the Government, the public's "me first" spirit is fouling up matters too. Truckers are now demanding unrestricted access to diesel fuel. . . . Simultaneously other consumers clamor for exemptions from any gasoline rationing system or demand that heating oil stocks be built up to guard against a cold winter. *There is no way that refiners can give farmers and truckers unlimited supplies, turn out maximum supplies of gasoline and build heating-oil inventories—and the Government has failed to set clear priorities.** (Emphasis added.)

---

*"The Great Energy Mess," *Time,* July 2, 1979, pp. 116.

As government tries to deal with the situation by responding to immediate political pressures, the problems grow more serious. For example, by mid-1979, inventories of fuel oil for heating were below levels historically regarded as adequate. Any attempt to rebuild those stocks in time to prevent fuel shortages during the winter of 1979–1980 would necessarily involve tradeoffs—in this case, reduced gasoline production, which would in turn increase the severity of gasoline shortages during peak summer driving months.

Fundamentally, the dilemma faced by government and the Department of Energy in attempting to deal with the oil shortage is no different from that faced by any economy. In the presence of scarcity, choices must be made to determine what will be produced, how it will be produced, and who will receive what is produced. Until the government and the Department of Energy formulate a clear set of priorities or establish a consistent policy to guide their actions, the energy situation in the United States will remain confused. Moreover, the political pressures which gave rise to many of the current problems will undoubtedly become even stronger as the 1980 congressional and presidential elections draw near and as the effects of recent oil-price boosts by the OPEC nations impose new economic problems for government policymakers to resolve.

FUELS OF THE FUTURE

As supplies of easily accessible oil and natural gas have dwindled in the United States, and as dependence on foreign sources to meet demand for these fuels has grown, the need to develop alternative sources of supply has increased. Although at one time nuclear power appeared to be a viable alternative to conventional fuels, renewed concerns regarding the safety of nuclear generating facilities and the disposal of nuclear waste material have forced Americans to consider other possibilities.

Solar energy

Among the most promising alternative fuel sources is solar power, which has the long-term potential for yielding unlimited quantities of non-polluting energy. At present, because of technological limitations and cost, solar power meets less than 1 percent of America's energy needs. Until technology is refined to make possible the direct conversion of solar power to electricity at a cost competitive with other fuels, use will be limited to thermal units primarily for space- and water-heating systems in houses, apartments, and office buildings.

Enhanced recovery and conversion

Additions to the nation's declining stocks of easily accessible oil may be obtained either directly by enhanced recovery methods or indirectly, by processing coal, shale, or tar sands. Enhanced recovery essentially involves injecting water, steam, or chemicals into an old oil reservoir to increase the flow of more viscous oil and oil trapped in geological formations. Since this process is more costly than obtaining oil by conventional pumping, crude-oil prices must rise if widespread use of this technique is to become economically feasible.

Although the technology for converting coal into coal gas and oil has existed since the nineteenth century, the cost remains high. Furthermore, the environmental damage associated with extensive coal-mining operations poses serious constraints on the use of this alternative. Similarly, extracting oil from tar sands or shale is environmentally damaging as well as extremely costly. Moreover, the feasibility of processing large quantities of either shale or tar sands is limited due to the fact that sufficient water for processing is not available in close proximity to supplies.

Harnessing the sea

For years, scientists have been intrigued by the possibility of tapping the oceans to provide energy and electricity to meet the needs of society. Although the technology to develop electricity from ocean tides exists and is already in use in France and the Soviet Union, the cost is high and the economic potential is limited due to an inability to store power once generated. Other possibilities currently being investigated include using wave motion and the oceans' temperature gradient to drive some form of continuously operating power generators. As with other nontraditional methods of generating electricity, the high cost associated with using known technology has effectively blocked development of large-scale, commercial ventures. Although the possibility of harnessing the sea to provide energy remains a possibility, there is little likelihood at present that commercial exploitation of sea power will replace any but a small fraction of the nation's formidable energy demand unless the cost of obtaining power from traditional sources is increased significantly above current levels.

Wind and geothermal power

Other possibilities currently being examined by scientists include wind and geothermal power. While both of these sources presently provide minute quantities of electricity and energy, their widespread application is limited because only a few places in the United States yield wind or geothermal steam in sufficient quantity to provide an uninterrupted source of supply.

While it is impossible to predict which, if any, of the foregoing sources of power will yield promising results in the near future, the support provided by government for research and development will likely accelerate the pace at which commercially feasible developments surface. In the short run, however, the likelihood is great that the United States will continue to depend on traditional sources to meet its large and growing demand for energy.

Summary

■ This chapter traces the development of the energy situation of the 1970s and examines the economic issues raised in the current debate.

■ The energy crisis of 1973–1974, triggered by the Arab oil embargo, was marked by severe shortages and contributed to worldwide recession. In the following few years, interest in energy subsided, but the renewed crisis in 1979 again highlighted the necessity of dealing with underlying problems and causes.

■ The causes of the energy crisis stem from government regulation, changing levels of demand, and legislation enacted as a result of the demands of environmentalists. In the case of oil, for 40 years some states had limited production, which many observers believe had the effect of inhibiting competition. In addition, since 1959, the United States government has supported American producers by allowing the restriction of imports of once-cheap foreign oil, thus lessening the competitive pressures on domestic producers. Government regulation of natural-gas prices has singled out interstate prices for control, leaving intrastate prices free to rise on the open market. Moreover, the possibility of significant imports of natural gas has not been realized. Coal, once the backbone of American industrialization, has declined in demand in recent decades, and environmental regulations in recent years have further limited its importance as an energy source. The potential of nuclear power is in considerable doubt because of concern about radiation and disposal and because of extensive federal regulation.

■ The long-term demand for energy has risen consistently, only briefly lessening after the 1973 embargo produced dramatically higher prices. The Nixon administration's price controls from 1971 to 1974 kept prices and production down, and attempts to restore production after the embargo were hampered by supply bottlenecks in related industries and by environmental regulations. Price controls continue to be disruptive in the energy market.

■ The two general strategies for long-run solution of energy problems are the "free-market" and "government-action" alternatives. The use of the free-market approach would maximize efficient resource allocations and allow for an equilibrium without shortages or price distortions. Critics of the market approach assert that poor people spend a larger proportion of their income on energy and thus would be especially affected by the higher prices that would result; proponents believe the problem is more one of unequal income distribution, which could be dealt with by income-redistribution programs. Proponents also believe that higher industry profits would encourage expansion of production. Finally, they respond to the argument that the free-market approach would lead to higher prices by stating that although decontrolling prices would have a small inflationary effect in the short run, in the long run it would increase supply and consequently exert a downward pressure on prices.

■ Government action could involve nationalization of energy industries. Less extreme measures would include antitrust actions to increase competition and the funding of research into alternative energy sources. On the demand side, government could make sure that energy prices reflected the real external costs of energy production and could mandate or encourage through tax credits technologies and processes that promote conservation. Rationing of gasoline would be likely to create a black market in ration coupons and would not, in any case, increase supply.

■ As an outgrowth of the 1973 embargo, United States government policy has largely stressed conservation. Gradual steps have also been taken toward decontrol of the prices of both oil and natural gas. In 1979, the Carter administration proposed speeding up decontrol and taxing the windfall profits the oil companies would gain from higher prices. Allocation systems have generally been ineffective since they have usually been undertaken in response to immediate pressures rather than according to carefully set priorities.

■ In view of the dwindling supplies of easily accessible oil and natural gas, the need to develop alternative energy sources is urgent. Solar power, enhanced recovery of oil, conversion of coal to oil and gas, harnessing the sea and wind, and geothermal power are all possible sources of greatly expanded energy supply. But government support of research and development programs is essential if new energy sources are to be developed quickly.

Review & Discussion

1. What were the major developments in the unfolding energy crisis of the 1970s? What were the symptoms of the energy problem? What was the public reaction?

2. What combination of forces created the energy crisis? What were the effects of government regulation of energy industries?

3. What kinds of special treatment has the United States oil industry received over time? What limitations have been placed on the importation of natural gas?

4. Why has the use of coal declined as an energy source?

5. What has happened to the enthusiastic early predictions about the potential of nuclear power?

6. What has been the long-term trend in demand for energy in the United States? What accounts for that trend? What would be required of industry, government, and consumers to reverse the trend?

7. What were the effects on petroleum production of the Nixon administration's price controls in 1971–1974? What difficulties arose when these controls were phased out after the OPEC embargo?

8. Contrast the "free-market" and "government-action" strategies for long-term solution of energy problems. What are the advantages and disadvantages of each? Which do you favor? Why?

9. How do rising prices affect consumers? Producers? Are price rises for fuel necessarily inflationary?

10. Why is it difficult to allocate rations for scarce resources on the basis of need? In what sense does rationing appear to be economically inefficient?

11. What is the potential for new alternative energy sources for the 1980s?

Part IX

International Economics

Chapter 36

Comparative Advantage and International Trade

What to look for in this chapter

What is the basis of international trade?

What are absolute advantage and comparative advantage?

How do economists define the terms of trade?

How are the gains from international trade calculated for each trading partner?

How does the theory of factor endowments help to account for the differences in domestic exchange ratios which influence trading decisions?

What are the economic effects of international trade?

The previous units of this text have focused on the American economy as an isolated unit. But the United States is obviously tied to other nations through an intricate system of international trade and finance. In the following four chapters we will describe and analyze international trade and financial relationships with particular emphasis on the advantages and problems connected with them.

The objectives of this chapter are to examine the reasons that international trade occurs, the terms under which nations will trade, the gains to be made from trade, and the economic effects of international trade.

THE BASIS FOR INTERNATIONAL TRADE

Specialization and interdependence: an illustration

Adam Smith wrote: "It is the maxim of every prudent master of a family, never to attempt to make at home what it will cost him more to make than buy." Households should "employ their whole industry in a way in which they have some advantage over their neighbours, and to purchase with it, whatever else they have occasion for." In other words, they should specialize and then trade their products with other households. Specialization and the mutual dependence that trade implies are at the root of the high standards of living that modern, industrialized economies are able to enjoy.

To illustrate Smith's point, let us imagine a household in eighteenth-century Philadelphia, that of Abner Grey and his family. The Grey family has a high degree of productivity in the work of making shoes. If they specialized and devoted all of their time and resources to shoemaking, they could turn out 100 pairs in a month. Other families in the community find they cannot match this level of productivity. Some find that they lack the necessary talent or skills, others that the investment in tools and raw materials is too great.

Now suppose that Mrs. Grey tells Abner that she needs 20 yards of cloth to satisfy the family's clothing needs. From past experience, he knows that the family will have to devote all their time to cloth making for a month to produce 20 yards at home. During this month they will not be able to produce shoes or any other goods, since all of their time and resources will be tied up in cloth production. Since the Greys would have to forgo the production of 100 pairs of shoes in order to nake 20 yards of cloth, we can say that 20 yards of cloth costs the Grey family 100 pairs of shoes. This is the opportunity cost of cloth in terms of shoes; for every yard of cloth they produce, the Greys must sacrifice a potential 5 pairs of shoes.

Abner, however, discovers another alternative. In Philadelphia, shoes are selling at $1 a pair and cloth at $.25 a yard. At this exchange ratio, one yard of cloth costs only one-quarter the price of a pair of shoes. Evidently, there is at least one producer selling cloth in the marketplace who has a clear advantage over the Grey family in cloth making. Grey quickly realizes that his family needs to sell only 5 pairs of shoes in this market to obtain the $5 needed to purchase 20 yards of cloth. He compares the opportunity costs of the two methods of obtaining the 20 yards of cloth needed. If he trades, the cloth will cost only 5 pairs of shoes; if he produces the cloth at home, it will cost 100 pairs of shoes. The conclusion is clear; the Greys should specialize in shoe production and sell their surplus shoes on the market so that they can buy the other goods they need.

It is important to note that producers should specialize only in the goods in which they have productive advantages. If the Greys specialized in shoemaking, they would have a monthly income of $100; if they specialized in cloth making, they could earn only $5 a month. Because the household's productivity is higher in the manufacture of shoes than in the manufacture of cloth, shoemaking represents a more efficient use of their resources. This is reflected in the higher return they can get from shoe production.

Not only will the Grey family be better off if they specialize in shoe production, but the total income of Philadelphia will also be higher. It is easy to see that economic self-sufficiency is costly and that this cost will be borne not only by the Grey family but by the entire community. When the Greys specialize in making shoes, more shoes will be available in the stores of Philadelphia, and many families can buy them at a reasonable prices.

If, for some reason, the Greys decided to fill all of their economic needs by trying to produce everything at home, they would soon discover that the opportunity cost for each good in which they do not have a production advantage is higher than its price in the market, just as it was for cloth. The returns they would receive for their labor and resources would be much lower if invested in making all of the goods they need than it would be if they specialized in shoes.

To summarize, in order for specialization to succeed, several conditions are necessary. First, as we have clearly noted, the two potential traders must not produce all commodities with the same efficiency. Second, the buyers and sellers must be able to meet with one another in a common marketplace so that the exchange of goods can take place, and all traders must be willing to depend on others to sell the variety of goods and services they need. It is therefore the ability and willingness to trade freely and to depend on other producers that make the gains of specialization possible.

Absolute advantage

It is a simple step to apply the principles of specialization, as illustrated in the case of the Grey family, to the much larger scale of trade between nations. The principle of **absolute advantage** states that *one nation has an absolute advantage over another nation in producing a good or service when it can use fewer resources than the other nation to produce one unit of the good or service.*

To demonstrate the principle of absolute advantage, let's take a hypothetical example in which the United States and the United Kingdom are both producing steel and cloth. Each nation can produce the following units of steel and cloth with the same amount of labor:

	Labor input	Steel output	Cloth output
United States	1000 units	500 units	100 units
United Kingdom	1000 units	200 units	200 units

Comparing these figures, we see that using the same amount of labor, the United States can produce more units of steel than the United Kingdom, and the United Kingdom can produce more units of cloth than the United States. Thus, in the production of steel, the United States has an absolute advantage over the United Kingdom—the United States uses only two units of labor to produce one unit of steel ($1000 \div 500$) while the United Kingdom uses five units of labor to produce one unit of steel ($1000 \div 200$). Similarly, the United Kingdom has an absolute advantage over the United States in the production of cloth because it uses only five units to make one unit of cloth while the United States uses ten units of labor. It follows that if the two countries trade with each other, the United States will benefit by specializing in steel production and exporting its surplus steel to finance cloth imports from the United Kingdom. The United Kingdom will benefit by specializing in cloth production and exporting its excess cloth to finance steel imports from the United States.

COMPARATIVE ADVANTAGE

Although the principle of absolute advantage can account for a good deal of international trade, it does not provide a full explanation. A logical extension of this principle is that if a nation has an absolute advantage in the production of all goods that its potential trading partner produces, it will refuse to trade.

Suppose, for example, the United States can produce both more steel *and* more cloth at lower cost than it can buy them from the United Kingdom. Why should the United States import cloth from the United Kingdom when it can produce it more cheaply at home?

The reason that trade can occur profitably even when, as in our example, one nation has an absolute advantage over its trading partner in the production of all goods is demonstrated by the principle of **comparative advantage,** which was proposed by the English economist David Ricardo. The principle of comparative advantage takes into account the relative efficiency with which a nation uses its scarce resources to make a product. The principle states that *if one country can produce each of two goods at a lower opportunity cost than another country and can produce one of these goods at a lower opportunity cost than the other, it should specialize in the production of the good with the lower opportunity cost and should trade with another country to obtain the other good.* That is, a country should specialize in the production of that good which makes the most efficient use of its resources (for which the opportunity cost is the lowest). If all countries specialize according to such comparative cost advantages, the least amount of resources will be used in the most efficient manner, and total world output will be the greatest. In the following section, we will develop a model for international trade that will help explain the principle of comparative advantage.

A simple model for international trade

This model will be based on production possibilities curves, which were introduced in Chapter 2. In order to simplify our analysis, we will begin with some basic assumptions.

☐ Only two countries are involved—in this case, the United Kingdom and the United States.

☐ Both economies are limited to producing only two goods—steel and cloth.

☐ Both economies are operating at full employment—that is, on their production possibilities curves.

☐ Each nation's production possibilities curve is subject to *constant costs* rather than *increasing costs*. Recall from our discussion of production possibilities in Chapter 2 that the concept of increasing costs would mean that the costs to the United States and the United Kingdom of producing steel and cloth would vary with output and this might affect each country's comparative cost advantage. The assumption of constant costs means that we do not have to correct for the effect of changes in output on costs in order for our analysis to work.

☐ No transportation costs exist to influence the costs of goods exchanged between the two domestic markets.

☐ Competitive product markets exist both domestically and internationally, so that the price mechanism is free to respond to the forces of supply and demand.

Production possibilities curve for the United States

Figure 36.1 shows the production possibilities curve of the United States, based on data from *Table 36.1*. If the United States were to specialize completely in cloth making, it would be able to produce a maximum of 50 units. If, on the other hand, all United States producers were to devote themselves exclusively to the production of steel, the nation would be able to turn out a maximum of 150 units. The limit on output capacity in each industry is set by the input resources possessed by the United States and by the productivity of these resources at the time.

The United States could produce and consume at either of these two extremes, or it could

Table 36.1

Production possibilities schedule for the United States (hypothetical data)

Units of steel produced	Units of cloth produced
150	0
120	10
90	20
60	30
30	40
0	50

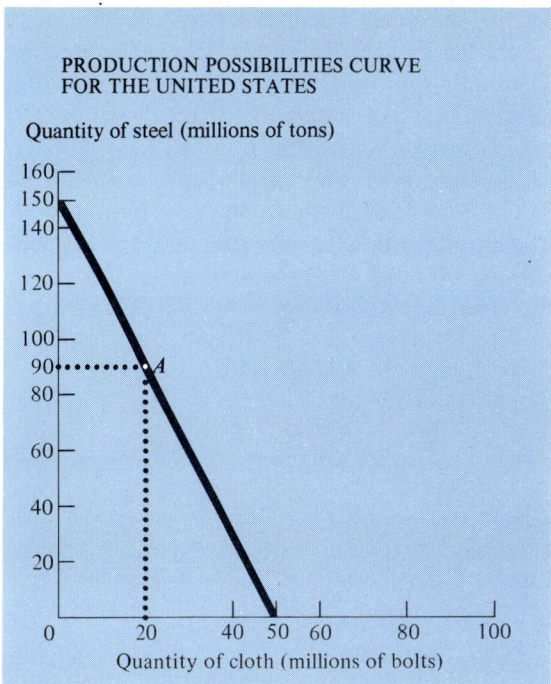

Fig. 36.1
Given its input resources and the productivity of these resources, the United States can produce any combination of goods on the production possibilities curve. We will assume that the choice of actual consumption lies at point A, with 90 units of steel and 20 units of cloth.

produce and consume various combinations of the two goods between the two extremes. The schedule in *Table 36.1* shows some of the possible combinations available to the economy—given that it both fully and efficiently employs all of its available resources. If production and consumption are taking place at the combination of 90 units of steel and 20 units of cloth, and if the production of 30 additional units of steel is desired, the production of 10 units of cloth must be sacrificed to arrive at the combination of 120 steel and 10 cloth. We can therefore say that 30 units of steel costs 10 units of cloth, or that the opportunity cost of 3 units of steel is 1 unit of cloth. This is referred to as the **domestic exchange ratio** *(the opportunity cost of one good relative to the other)* for the United States between two combinations. In economic shorthand, the exchange ratio is written as 3S:1C.

Note that in this example the domestic exchange ratio for the United States is always 3S:1C, no matter what shift is made along the production curve. Try it on the schedule or on the graph, remembering that here we are interested in the ratio of the changes that occur as we move from one combination to another, not in the ratios of any of the absolute quantities. This and the fact that our production possibilities curve is a straight line reflect the assumption of constant costs. (Math students will recognize this as a constant slope.) Thus the shape or slope of the production possibilities curve is a reflection of domestic exchange ratios (or relative costs of steel and cloth) between various points on the curve.

Determining production and consumption in the United States How is the combination of steel and cloth that the American economy will produce and consume determined? Let us consider the alternatives. Operating at full employment the United States can choose any combination along its production possibilities curve. Operating at less than full employment means that the United States must produce and consume some smaller combinations of goods represented by a point inside its curve. Because of the limits on output imposed by the resources possessed by the United States and its level of productivity at this time, it is impossible for the United States to produce a combination of steel and cloth lying beyond its curve. However, as we shall see, through trade the United States will be able to consume larger combinations lying beyond its curve even though it will not be able to produce them at home.

In a competitive market economy operating at full employment, which the United States is in

Table 36.2
Production possibilities schedule for the United Kingdom (hypothetical data)

Units of steel produced	Units of cloth produced
40	0
30	10
20	20
10	30
0	40

our model, consumers will choose, through the operation of the price mechanism, some combination of goods that is on the production possibilities curve. For example, if the United States were producing and consuming 90 units of steel and 20 units of cloth and if the demand for steel were to increase relative to the demand for cloth, the prices offered for steel would rise, and producers would respond by shifting productive resources out of the cloth industry and into the steel industry. Thus the combination desired by consumers would tend to be met by producers, and the economy would move upward along its curve. We will suppose that American consumers choose the combination of 90 units of steel and 20 units of cloth, represented by point A in *Fig. 36.1*.

Production possibilities curve for the United Kingdom

Now we will look at the production possibilities curve of the United Kingdom. The logic behind its construction is the same as that described for the United States. In *Table 36.2* and the resulting curve drawn in *Fig. 36.2,* we see that by complete specialization, a maximum of either 40 units of cloth or 40 units of steel can be produced, given the productivity and input resources of the United Kingdom at this time. The slope of the production possibilities curve is constant at 1:1, which means that the domestic exchange ratio is 1S:1C. Finally, through the price mechanism, consumers in the United Kingdom have chosen the consumption-production combination 20 steel and 20 cloth represented by point *B* on the graph.

It is crucial to note that the domestic exchange ratios, or the relative costs in the United Kingdom and the United States, are different:

| United States | 3S:1C |
| United Kingdom | 1S:1C |

This difference indicates that a basis exists for mutually beneficial trade between the United Kingdom and the United States if they specialize according to comparative advantage—*even though the United States has an absolute advantage in the production of both goods.* Let us look at the significance of these different ratios. As we have seen, in the United Kingdom one unit of steel costs one unit of cloth and one unit of cloth costs one unit of steel. In the United States one unit of steel costs one-third unit of cloth (three units of steel costs one unit of cloth), and one unit of cloth costs three units of steel. Given these exchange ratios, where would you prefer to buy one unit of steel—in the United Kingdom where it would cost you one unit of cloth, or in the United States, where it would cost you one-third unit of cloth?

Most people would prefer to buy steel in the United States at the relatively cheaper price. What about cloth? In the United Kingdom, one unit of cloth costs one unit of steel, and in the United States it costs three units of steel. Cloth is relatively cheaper in the United Kingdom. In our model, therefore, the United States would have a comparative advantage in steel, since, viewing the cost of steel in terms of cloth, the United States can produce steel more cheaply than can the United Kingdom. The United Kingdom, on the

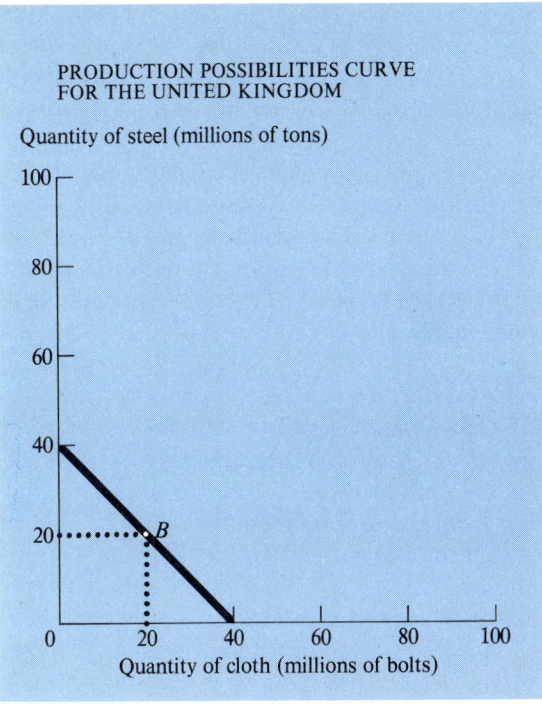

Fig. 36.2
The United Kingdom is also constrained by its production possibilities curve, which is shown in this graph. Let us assume that the actual choice of consumption lies at point B, with 20 units of steel and 20 units of cloth.

other hand, would have a comparative advantage in cloth (even though the United States had an absolute advantage in the production of both steel and cloth) because, viewing the cost of cloth in terms of steel, the United Kingdom can produce cloth more cheaply than can the United States. According to the principle, the United States should specialize in the production of steel and export its surpluses to the United Kingdom to pay for imports of cloth. The United Kingdom, in turn, should specialize in cloth, exporting its surpluses in exchange for imports of steel.

Terms of trade

According to the theory of comparative advantage, the domestic exchange ratios in the United States and the United Kingdom indicate that mutually beneficial trade can take place. However, our model of international trade is still incomplete. We have yet to determine the exchange ratio at which the United States and the United Kingdom will trade with each other in the international market.

The international exchange ratio (or the **terms of trade,** as it is most commonly called) is defined as *the number of units of goods that must be given up in exchange for one unit received by each trading party.* It is not difficult to see that the international exchange ratio will come to rest somewhere between the domestic exchange ratios of two countries—in our example, between 3S:1C and 1S:1C. Clearly, the United Kingdom will have an incentive to export cloth only if it can get more for it (in terms of steel) in the international market than it can in its own domestic market (that is, if it can get more than one unit of steel for one unit of cloth). By the same token, the United States will not be willing to import this cloth unless it can buy it in the international market for less (in terms of steel) than it can buy cloth in its own domestic market (that is, if it can buy one unit of cloth for less than three units of steel). The same type of reasoning can be applied to the import-export requirement for international trade in steel. Therefore, the terms of trade for the two goods must lie somewhere between 3S:1C and 1S:1C. But where will this point fall?

Effects of supply and demand

For a long time international-trade theory simply assumed that the terms of trade would lie exactly at the midpoint between the two domestic exchange ratios. However, John Stuart Mill refined the theory in an important way, by pointing out that the international market is a separate market in its own right. He showed that the terms of trade

> **RECAP**
>
> The principle of COMPARATIVE ADVANTAGE helps to explain why trade can occur profitably even when one nation has an absolute advantage over another in the production of all goods. According to this principle, a nation has a comparative advantage if it can produce each of two goods at a lower opportunity cost in terms of other products sacrificed than can its trading partner. If the country with the comparative advantage specializes in the production of the good it produces more cheaply and leaves production of the other good to the other country, both nations benefit, since total output of both goods will be greater.

are determined by the interaction of the forces of supply and demand in the international market, just as they are in any other market. According to this view (called the law of reciprocal demand), in order to arrive at the terms of trade, we must consider the varying strengths of demand for both steel and cloth in both the United States and the United Kingdom.

For example, suppose that the demand for cloth (the United Kingdom's export) in the United States is relatively higher than the United Kingdom's demand for steel (the United States' export). In other words, suppose that consumers in the United States need cloth more urgently than consumers in the United Kingdom need steel. It is logical to conclude that in such a situation, the international price would lie closer to the United States exchange ratio, thus favoring the United Kingdom, whose export would be more highly valued in the terms of trade.

Once trade has been established, the international market will tend toward an equilibrium exchange ratio, where supply and demand for both goods are balanced in both domestic markets. Exports from the United States will equal imports from the United Kingdom, and exports from the United Kingdom will equal imports from the United States. For the purposes of our model, we will assume that reciprocal demand has set the costs in the international market at 2S:1C—one unit of cloth must be given up for two units of steel. At these terms of trade, both of the domestic markets, as well as the international market, are in equilibrium.

Gains from trade

Now that we know what the terms of trade will be between the United States and the United Kingdom for cloth and steel, we can determine how the gains from specialization and trade will be divided between the two nations. In *Fig. 36.3* the terms of trade 2S:1C are represented by the **terms-of-trade line** *(T),* which *represents the new, possible combinations of goods* (in this case, cloth and steel) *that are now available to a nation as a result of trade.* Now neither country's consumption is limited by its own production possibilities curve (*P*) as it was before trade. Both the United Kingdom and the United States can consume beyond the limitations of their own production curves at any combination allowed by the terms-of-trade line. It is important to note, however, that although both the United Kingdom and the United States can now *consume* larger combinations of cloth and steel, their actual *production* is still limited by their respective resources and levels of productivity. *Total output,* however, has increased as a result of specialization according to comparative advantage. Each nation has a different production mix that uses available resources more efficiently. These production mixes would not have been chosen in the absence of trade, since consumers in the United States did not want to stop consuming cloth and consumers in the United Kingdom did not want to do without steel. But as a result of specialization and trade, each country has more of both goods.

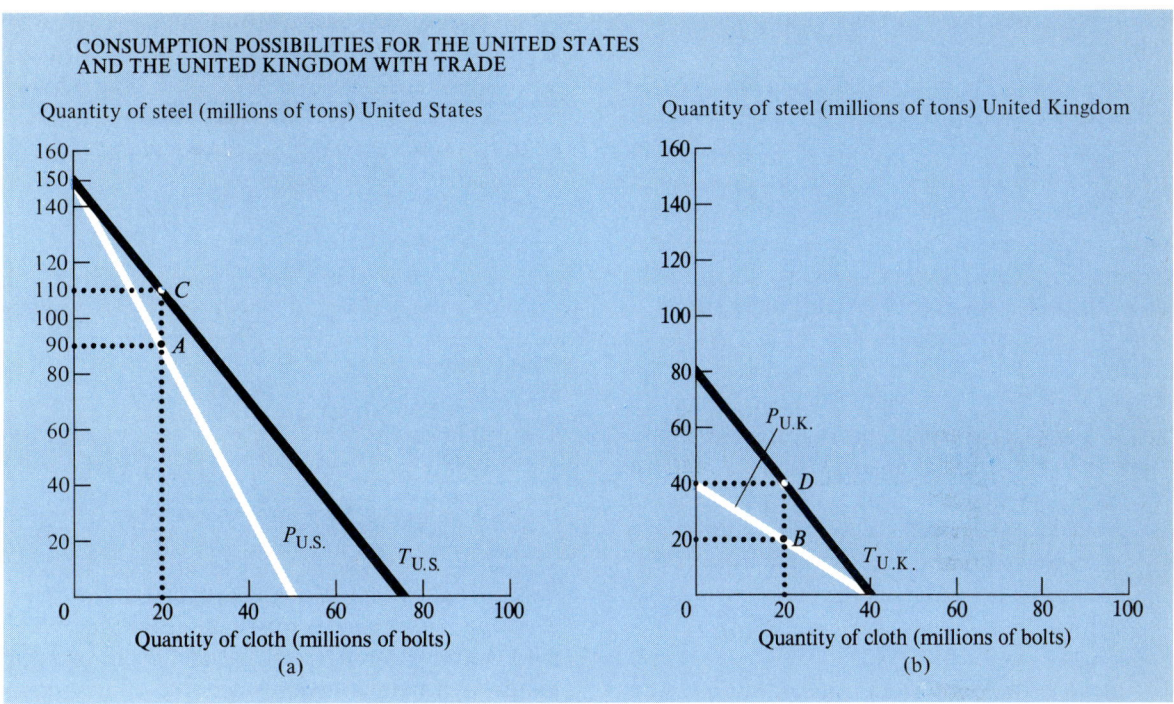

Fig. 36.3
Without trade, the United States would have to consume at point A on its production possibilities curve ($P_{U.S.}$). But with the help of trade, it can actually consume beyond the curve, moving to the new position shown at point C on the terms of trade line $T_{U.S.}$. The United Kingdom will also benefit from the trade, moving from point B on its curve to point D on the terms of trade line $T_{U.K.}$.

Once trade has begun, we will assume that demand in the United States and the United Kingdom is reflected by the choice of consumption combinations along the terms-of-trade lines indicated by points C and D in *Fig. 36.3*. Consumers in the United States choose 110 units of steel and 20 units of cloth, while consumers in the United Kingdom choose 40 units of steel and 20 units of cloth.

Now we can review the trade situation in real terms. Looking again at *Fig. 36.3*, let us assume that the United States is producing 150 units of steel and no cloth on its production possibilities curve, but that it has chosen to consume 110 units of steel and 20 units of cloth, on the terms-of-trade line. Since the United States produces 150 units of steel and selects to consume only 110, the amount of surplus steel it will want to export will be 40 units. Since at point C the United States produces no cloth but wishes to consume 20 units, it will therefore wish to import 20 units of cloth. Because the terms of trade reflect equilibrium prices in all markets at 2S:1C, the United States can export its 40 units of surplus steel and receive in return exactly the 20 units of cloth it wants to import.

Turning to the United Kingdom, we see that domestic production is at 40 units of cloth and no steel; the desired consumption combination along the terms-of-trade line is 40 units of steel and 20 units of cloth. Since 40 units of cloth are produced and only 20 are consumed, there are 20 units of surplus cloth left to export. Again, because the terms of trade reflect equilibrium prices, these 20 units of cloth can be exchanged for exactly the 40 units of steel demanded by consumers in the United Kingdom. Note that the exports from the United States equal the imports from the United Kingdom. If demand changes and if imports demanded do not equal exports offered, the terms of trade will shift to bring about equilibrium at a new price that again balances desired exports and imports.

Calculating gains from trade

To calculate the gains from trade and to see how they are divided between the two nations, we compare production and consumption points before and after trade. First, we look at production.

	United States		United Kingdom	
	Steel	Cloth	Steel	Cloth
Production after trade	150	0	0	40
Production before trade	90	20	20	20
	+60	−20	−20	+20

Total increase in production: 40 units of steel

When we add the changes in steel and cloth production in both countries together, we find that total world output has increased by 40 units of steel. This is the result of the more efficient use of resources involved in specialization according to comparative advantage.

Now we compare consumption before and after trade to learn how the gains from trade have been distributed. Both nations have gained by 20 units of steel, which reflects the fact that the terms of trade in our example happen to lie midway between the two domestic ratios.

	United States		United Kingdom	
	Steel	Cloth	Steel	Cloth
Consumption after trade	110	20	40	20
Consumption before trade	90	20	20	20
Gains from trade	+20	0	+20	0

Why domestic exchange ratios differ

Throughout our discussion of comparative advantage, we have emphasized that there is a basis for mutually beneficial trade whenever domestic exchange ratios, or relative prices, differ among nations. At the root of the matter, why do these different domestic exchange ratios exist?

The theory of factor endowments: the role of supply

At one time, many economists believed that differences in domestic exchange ratios were a reflection of national differences in the productivity of the factors of production. However, two twentieth-century Swedish economists, Heckscher and Ohlin, have advanced another, more compelling explanation. Their **theory of factor endowments** is widely accepted by modern economists as an important explanation of the supply forces that affect international trade.

Heckscher and Ohlin began with the assumption that the productivity of the factors of production is equal in all countries. With productivity held constant—that is, not responsible for differences in a nation's capacity to supply goods—they were able to isolate a crucial reason for domestic price differences among nations. They concluded that *different domestic exchange ratios exist primarily because (1) the distribution of factor endowments is uneven among nations, and (2) the production of different goods requires the use of varying proportions of the factors of production.*

Distribution of factors Nations do indeed possess unequal amounts of the factors of production. Differences in such things as climate, national character, economic history, social and cultural environment, natural resources, and population growth can all contribute to uneven factor endowments among nations.

When a country has a relatively large or abundant supply of a factor, such as capital, we say that it is *capital-abundant*. When it has a relatively small or scarce supply of another factor, such as labor, we refer to it as *labor-scarce*. Thus we can observe that the United States is capital-abundant and labor-scarce, that Japan is labor-abundant and land-scarce, and that Australia is land-abundant and labor-scarce. The basic principles of supply and demand tell us that if a factor is in relatively large supply, its price will be relatively cheap. If, on the other hand, a factor is in relatively small supply, its price can be expected to be relatively high. Applying this to the examples above, we can therefore expect to find interest rates (or the price of capital) to be low in the capital-abundant United States; wages (or the price of labor) to be high in labor-scarce United States and Australia, but low in labor-abundant Japan; and finally, rent (the price of land) to be high in land-scarce Japan and low in land-abundant Australia. This means that the factors of production will have different relative prices in different countries due to their uneven world distribution.

Proportion of factors Now let us consider Heckscher and Ohlin's second conclusion: production processes for different goods require different proportions of the various factors of production. Economists are able to rank goods according to the intensity with which the various factors of production are used in the production processes. If we consider the production of steel, we realize that it involves large investments in capital equipment but relatively little in labor; it is a *capital-intensive good*. To produce wheat, on the other hand, large amounts of land are needed, so wheat is a *land-intensive good*. To produce cloth, relatively large investments in labor are required, so cloth is a *labor-intensive good*. Because the prices of final goods can be expected to reflect their production costs, the costs of the factors used most intensively in producing those goods have an important effect on their prices.

An application of the theory At this point, we will return to our model of international trade and reconsider the reasons behind the different domestic exchange ratios in light of the Hecksher–Ohlin theory. Here we will assume that steel is a capital-intensive good and that cloth is labor-intensive; we will also assume that the economy of the United

> **RECAP**
> The THEORY OF FACTOR ENDOWMENTS is a useful explanation of the supply forces that affect international trade. According to this theory, different domestic exchange ratios exist primarily because (1) the distribution of factors of production is uneven among nations, and (2) the production of different goods requires the use of varying proportions of the factors of production. Nations will have comparative advantages in the production of goods that require a high proportion of the productive factors they have in greatest supply.

States is relatively capital-abundant and labor-scarce, whereas the United Kingdom is relatively capital-scarce and labor-abundant. It follows that the United States will be able to produce steel more cheaply, since this good requires the use of large amounts of its relatively cheap, abundant factor, capital. The United Kingdom will be able to produce cloth more cheaply, because this labor-intensive good requires the use of large amounts of labor, which is relatively abundant and therefore cheaper in the United Kingdom. This is a very plausible explanation for the existence of the different domestic exchange ratios in the United States and the United Kingdom.

From this example, it should be clear how different factor endowments, given the different factor intensity of goods, can influence the shapes and positions of production possibilities curves. Nations will have comparative advantages in the production of goods requiring a high proportion of their relatively abundant factors.

The role of demand

The theory of factor endowments focuses on supply in its explanation of differing exchange ratios. But what is the role of demand in international price differences? Let us imagine a situation in which the production possibilities curves of the United States and the United Kingdom are the same. The productivity of factors and their distribution between the two countries are assumed to be identical. However, because of differences in tastes, the consumers in these two countries place different values on the two goods. Their domestic exchange ratios in the absence of trade would therefore be different, indicating the basis for mutually beneficial trade. If the domestic exchange ratios of the two countries reflect that consumers in the United States value cloth more highly and that consumers in the United Kingdom value steel more highly, the United States would export steel and import cloth, whereas the United Kingdom would import steel and export cloth.

Internal demand

One interesting thesis explaining international trade that is based on demand has been developed by another Swedish economist, Staffan Linder. Linder contends that for manufactured goods, which account for the greatest volume of trade, demand patterns are chiefly responsible for the direction and volume of trade. A nation cannot export any good for which it does not have a healthy internal demand. This demand is essential if the export industry is to develop to a size sufficient to enable it to compete in foreign markets. In this way, the range of a nation's exports is determined by internal demand.

Linder also asserts that trade can be expected to occur in greatest volume between nations of similar levels of economic development and sophistication. Income levels dictate the level of sophistication that consumers will demand in their imports. These ideas are consistent with the trading patterns that actually exist between nations. For example, the United States conducts the largest volume of its trade in manufactures with nations having standards of living closest to its own, such as Canada, Japan, and the countries of Western Europe. The volume of United States trade in manufactures that is conducted with less developed countries is markedly smaller.

EFFECTS OF TRADE

We will conclude this chapter with an examination of some of the economic effects of trade.

Effect on total world output

We have already demonstrated the primary and most obvious effect of international trade—an increase in total world output. This increased output is the direct result of the more efficient use of national productive resources that takes place when nations can specialize according to comparative advantage. Once trade begins, resources shift out of relatively disadvantaged industries and into relatively advantaged industries, where they can be more efficiently employed.

In our model, for instance, resources in the United States were shifted out of the cloth industry and into the steel industry. In the United Kingdom, resources were shifted away from steel production and into cloth production. The subsequent gains in world output were then divided between the United States and the United Kingdom, according to the international terms of trade. Both countries could then consume combinations of cloth and steel that their own limited resource bases were unable to make available in the absence of trade. These gains were made possible by the freedom and willingness of the United States and the United Kingdom to engage in the exchange of goods and services and thus become mutually dependent.

Price equalization

The shift of resources, which is so essential to trade-induced increases in world output, actually occurs in response to new demand situations that are able to develop when opportunities to trade are introduced. This redirection of demand brought about by trade has another major effect: the prices of both the goods traded and the input factors used to produce the goods tend to become equal in the trading countries.

In our model, we saw that the prices of steel in the United States and the United Kingdom tended to equalize in the international market—the international market being simply the sum of the combined domestic markets when trade is occurring. Before trade, steel was relatively cheaper in the United States as a result of domestic supply and demand. When trade began, however, steel producers in the United States experienced what we can refer to as an upward-shifting demand curve for their product. This occurred because consumers in the United Kingdom directed their demand away from relatively more expensive steel made in the United Kingdom to the less expensive steel made in the United States, which trade made available to them. As a result, once trade was established, producers in the United States found that the demand curve they faced consisted of their own domestic demand plus foreign demand of the United Kingdom. Consequently, the price of steel rose in the United States.

In the United Kingdom, the reverse occurred. Steel, being in relatively small supply, was expensive before trade. Once trade had begun, the supply increased; the United Kingdom domestic market then had suppliers from both the United Kingdom and the United States serving it. This is equivalent to a shift in the domestic supply curve for steel in the United Kingdom. This shift in supply brought about a decrease in the price of steel to consumers in the United Kingdom. The price of steel in the United States and the United Kingdom, as a result, tended to equalize. The terms of trade reflect the fact that two units of steel now cost one unit of cloth (or one unit of steel costs one-half unit of cloth) for consumers in both countries. The same reasoning can be applied to show how the prices of cloth would tend to become equal as well. This is due again to the different levels of supply and demand that international trade introduces in domestic markets. In effect, trade created an international market with one new international price which is available to the consumers in both nations.

Equalization of input prices

Hecksher and Ohlin point out that the redirection of demand resulting from international trade also equalizes the prices of the factors of production. It is often said that trade in final products serves as a substitute for the direct international exchange of the factors of production that are generally considered to be less mobile between nations. Instead of trading the less mobile factors of production directly, nations trade them indirectly through

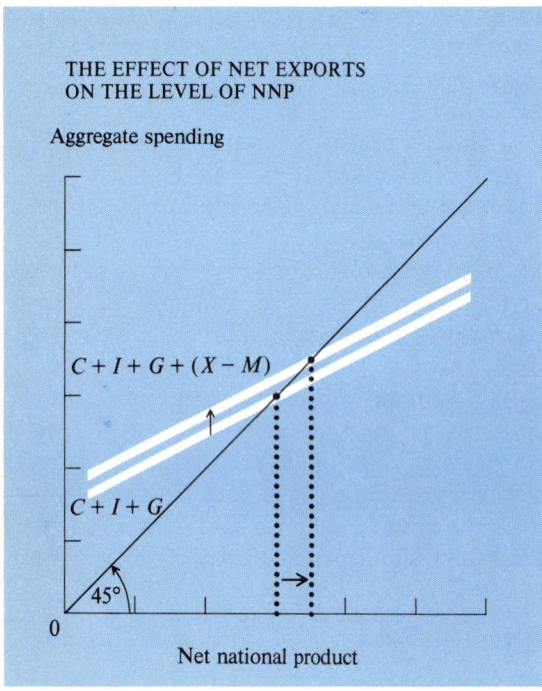

Fig. 36.4
In calculating NNP, we add the total value of net exports; that is, X (exports) minus M (imports). Assuming that $(X - M)$ is a positive number, NNP will show an even greater increase due to the multiplier effect.

trading the goods resources are used to produce. Let us trace this process in our model.

Since the United States is capital-abundant, the cost of capital is relatively cheap there. Once trade begins, however, steel producers in the United States are faced with a higher demand for this product, and therefore the opportunity to sell steel at a higher price. The steel industry in the United States responds to this higher level of demand by increasing production. Since steel is a capital-intensive good producers will demand increased amounts of capital as they increase production. As demand for capital rises in the United States, its price also rises.

At the same time, producers of cloth in the United States find that demand for their product is falling because American consumers prefer the less expensive cloth from the United Kingdom. The cloth industry begins to contract. Since cloth is a labor-intensive good, a greater supply of labor is available in the the American market. Since the available supply of labor has risen and there has been a corresponding decrease in demand for labor, wages will tend to fall in the United States. In summary, capital—the abundant factor in the United States—becomes less abundant with trade, so the price of capital tends to rise. Labor—the scarce factor in the United States—has become less scarce as a result of trade, so the price of labor tends to fall.

While this is happening, precisely the opposite tendencies are at work in the United Kingdom. Demand for labor—the abundant factor—will rise; this will cause its price to rise too. Demand for capital—the scarce factor—will fall. Thus its price will also fall. Since these factor-price movements occur in both nations, the prices of capital and labor in the United States and the United Kingdom will tend to become equal.

Effect on net national product

Finally we will consider the effect of trade on the level of net national product. Earlier in the text we learned that

$$NNP = C + I + G;$$

that is, net national product is the sum of consumption, investment, and government spending. Now we can add the final component of aggregate spending to the right-hand side of this equation. This is $(X - M)$, which is called *net exports*. We now have

$$NNP = C + I + G + (X - M),$$

where X represents exports (foreign spending on domestically produced goods) and M represents imports (domestic spending on foreign-produced goods).

Money received for exports is an addition to the national income stream, and expenditure on imports is a leakage from the income stream. Looking at $(X - M)$, we see that when exports increase with imports remaining fixed, the value of net exports will rise, but when exports decrease with imports remaining fixed, the value of net exports will fall. The reverse is true for imports.

The important point to note is that the net amount here has the same effect on aggregate demand as does any other component of the NNP equation. Any fluctuations in exports or imports are subject to the multiplier (see Chapter 11) and will cause an even larger fluctuation in NNP. This is shown in *Fig. 36.4*. If an increase in NNP occurs when the economy is operating at less than full employment, it can be a healthy stimulus. However, in situations of full employment, an increase in net exports could overheat the economy and result in inflation. Thus increases and decreases in net exports have a significant effect on the economic stability of nations where net exports represent a sizable part of NNP.

Summary

■ This chapter discusses the basis, the terms, and the economic effects of international trade.

■ The basis for international trade is the fact that specialization and interdependence in economic production benefit both nations engaged in trade. Absolute advantage provides the basis for trade between two countries if each produces a good the other needs at a lower price than the other. Comparative advantage is the basis of trade when one country produces all goods at a lower opportunity cost than its trading partner but still finds it more efficient to specialize in the production of the cheapest good.

■ Through the use of production possibilities curves for both nations, domestic exchange ratios can be established to express the opportunity costs of various combinations of goods produced in either country. The terms of trade (the international exchange ratio) are the number of units of goods that must be given up in exchange for one unit of another good by each trading partner. The terms of trade are determined primarily by the strength of demand in each country for the goods to be traded. Once trade is established, the international market will tend toward an equilibrium exchange ratio, where supply and demand for both goods are balanced in both domestic markets. Exports and imports for both countries will tend to balance equally. Both nations gain, with the division of gain reflecting the terms of trade.

■ Differences in domestic exchange ratios are based on the uneven distribution of factors of production and on the different mixes of factors required for the production of different goods. Demand factors are also important; two countries with identical production possibility curves but with different levels of demand will have a basis for specialization and trade. It has been argued that for a nation to have an export trade in manufactured goods it must first have built up its domestic market and thus its productive capacity. It has also been observed that the greatest volume of trade will occur between nations at comparable levels of development.

■ Trade increases total world output. It also tends to create price equalization, by creating essentially one international market; and it tends to equalize input prices.

■ Net exports (exports minus imports) are the final component of NNP, in addition to consumption, investment, and government spending. Net exports have the same economic effects as the other components: changes in export income are subject to the multiplier effect, an increase in net exports can be an economic stimulus when an economy is operating at less than full employment, and an increase in net exports when there is full employment can help to overstimulate the economy and contribute to inflation.

Key Terms

absolute advantage

comparative advantage

domestic exchange ratio

terms of trade

terms-of-trade line

theory of factor endowments

Review & Discussion

1. What is the basis for international trade? Why is trade more efficient than domestic production of all goods?

2. The production capabilities for two countries—given equal inputs of labor—are shown below. Would these countries trade? Would they specialize? How? What would be the effect of trade?

	Lemons	Lawnmowers
Country A	10	2
Country B	5	10

3. How do the principles of absolute advantage and comparative advantage help to explain why it is advantageous for nations to engage in trade?

4. David Ricardo stated that countries would trade if their domestic exchange ratios were different. What is the domestic exchange ratio? Why would it be to the advantage of both countries to trade? What is the relationship between domestic exchange ratios and the terms of trade?

5. In a perfectly competitive international market, what are the long-run effects of trade on product prices? Input prices?

6. What is the theory of factor endowments? How does factor endowment affect the domestic exchange ratios of different countries? In which commodities would a capital-abundant, labor-scarce country most likely have a comparative advantage? How can demand affect domestic exchange ratios?

7. What are net exports? What role do they play in the determination of net national product? Under what circumstances can an increase in net exports be economically undesirable?

Chapter 37

Barriers to Free Trade

What to look for in this chapter

What are the major barriers to free trade?

What are the economic effects of tariffs on the domestic economy?

What are the economic arguments in favor of tariffs? What are the counterarguments?

How do political considerations play a role in tariff policy?

Our discussion of international economics to this point leads us toward a significant conclusion: free trade is a necessary prerequisite in the maximization of world output. When nations specialize in producing those goods in which they enjoy a comparative advantage, and when they trade those goods freely with other nations, the result is a higher total world output. Each country is able to consume beyond the boundary of its own production possibilities curve.

Yet in spite of the evident advantage of free world trade, most nations continue to pursue restrictive policies by imposing tariffs, quotas, and other barriers to free trade. In this chapter, we will try to account for the continuance of restrictive trade policies, and we will examine the effects of such policies on the economies of trading nations.

MAJOR BARRIERS TO TRADE

Tariffs

The most common barrier to international trade is the **tariff,** *a tax levied on commodities imported into a country.* This kind of tax reduces or eliminates the trading partner's comparative advantage because, in effect, it raises the trading partner's production costs. Tariffs may be of two types. A **specific tariff** is *a fixed amount charged per unit of goods imported.* For example, a specific tariff for bananas might be set at $5 for every 100 pounds of bananas brought into the United States. An **ad valorem tariff** (from the Latin meaning "to the value") *is levied according to the value of the goods imported.* A tariff on plywood, for instance, might be set at 10 percent of the total value of the shipment of plywood when it arrives in the United States.

The advantage of the *ad valorem* tariff is that the percentage of tax paid always remains the same, no matter how the price of the good may fluctuate. With a specific tariff, the percentage of tax paid will decline if the price rises. For example, if the value of 100 pounds of bananas is $100, the tariff will be 5 percent of the value of the goods. But if demand for bananas suddenly increases, pushing the price up to $150 per hundred pounds, then the tariff will be only 3.3 percent of the value of the bananas. The specific tariff is least effective as a barrier to trade when, due to increased demand, prices are rising and increased quantities are being imported.

Tariffs are collected from the importers of the taxed goods. The importers usually pass this additional expense along to consumers of the goods; thus the end result is that higher prices are charged for the goods.

Revenue and protective tariffs

Historically, one important purpose of tariffs has been to create revenue for a government. It was for this reason that tariffs were initially adopted in the United States. When the country was founded, there was no tax on the incomes of either businesses or households; instead, the government relied on various excise taxes to produce the needed revenues. Tariffs on imported goods had the advantage of being relatively easy to collect. The government needed only to police the few harbors where the goods were brought in—and if importers were reluctant to pay, the goods could be seized and held until the tariff was paid. Many less-developed economies today still rely on tariffs to raise revenues.

Nations with highly developed economies also continue to impose tariffs, even though they no longer regard them as a principal source of revenue. Today the motives for placing tariffs on imported goods are largely protectionist in nature. For a variety of political and economic reasons, to be discussed shortly, many governments, including that of United States, want to discourage their citizens from buying certain goods imported from certain foreign countries. A tariff increases the cost and, acting through the laws of supply and demand, serves to restrict domestic purchases of an imported good. The increase in consumer price that results from the added tax brings a decrease in the amount of the good demanded.

Tariffs imposed in order to generate revenue are generally levied on products not produced domestically, such as tea, platinum, and tin in the case of the United States. Tariffs of this nature tend to be relatively low. Protective tariffs, on the other hand, tend to be higher than revenue tariffs, since they are designed to restrict the flow of goods. The more effective a tariff is in achieving the goal of restricting imports, the smaller the amount of revenue it will generate, since the quantity and value of taxable imports will dwindle in response to decreased demand. A country that tries to pursue a tariff policy for both revenue and protective purposes will find that the more successful it is in achieving one goal, the less successful it will be in achieving the other—the goals are incompatible.

Quotas

In certain cases, not even the imposition of high tariffs seems to diminish demand for an imported good to the low level desired by a government. An example is the continuing demand in the United States for Japanese television sets in spite of high tariffs that make the consumer price of these sets higher than the price of comparble sets made by domestic manufacturers. Although the tariffs have made it difficult for some Japanese companies to compete with American manufacturers in terms of price, the foreign manufacturers still offer strong competition in terms of quality, so many consumers are willing to pay significantly higher prices to buy the Japanese sets.

In such a case, the failure of a tariff to diminish the demand for an imported good may lead a government to adopt other measures to supplement the action of the tariff. For example, the United States government might set quotas for certain types of sets, imposing a maximum limit on the quantity of sets that could be imported over a specified period of time. Once the quota had been filled, no more sets could be imported, regardless of the price or tariff rate consumers were willing to pay. Quotas do not produce any revenue for a government; they are strictly protectionist instruments.

Other barriers to trade

A government can also impose other barriers to free trade. It may, for instance, require licensing of importers, thereby achieving some degree of control over the number of importing firms and hence the volume of imports. A government may also employ currency restrictions as barriers to trade; for example, importers may be prohibited from sending domestic currency abroad to pay for goods purchased, and may be unable to buy foreign currency through their own government or central banking system.

A barrier to trade that is usually politically rather than economically inspired is the embargo, an absolute cessation of all forms of trade or exchange with one particular country.

ECONOMIC EFFECTS OF TARIFFS

An illustration

The imposition of a tariff will affect the economy of both the importing country and its trade partner. An example will help us to understand the nature and extent of these effects.

Eriador and Mordor establish trade relations

Let us imagine that the countries of Eriador and Mordor decide to enter into trade with one another. In Mordor, there are many deposits of valuable minerals and precious stones; as a result, a large jewelry-making industry has sprung up, leading to the development of efficient techniques of production, a large labor force of skilled jewelers and the existence of significant economies of scale in jewelry production. We will assume, therefore, that Mordor possesses a comparative advantage in the manufacture of rings.

Neighboring Eriador is comparatively disadvantaged in the production of rings, and therefore the price of domestically produced rings is higher than in Mordor. Supply and demand for rings in the two countries, in the absence of trade, are shown in *Fig. 37.1*. Note the difference in equilibrium price between the two countries—$70 in Eriador and $40 in Mordor.

Since rings are much cheaper to produce in Mordor than in Eriador, Eriadorian importers seek to establish trade relations with Mordor. *Figure 37.2* shows the results of a free trade in rings conducted between the two countries. Citizens of Eriador benefit from free trade because they are able to buy rings at a lower price; since the price is lower, they purchase a larger quantity. Citizens of Mordor benefit because net income increases as a result of the increase in domestic ring production. Mordorians will then be able to use the added income to buy goods from Eriador

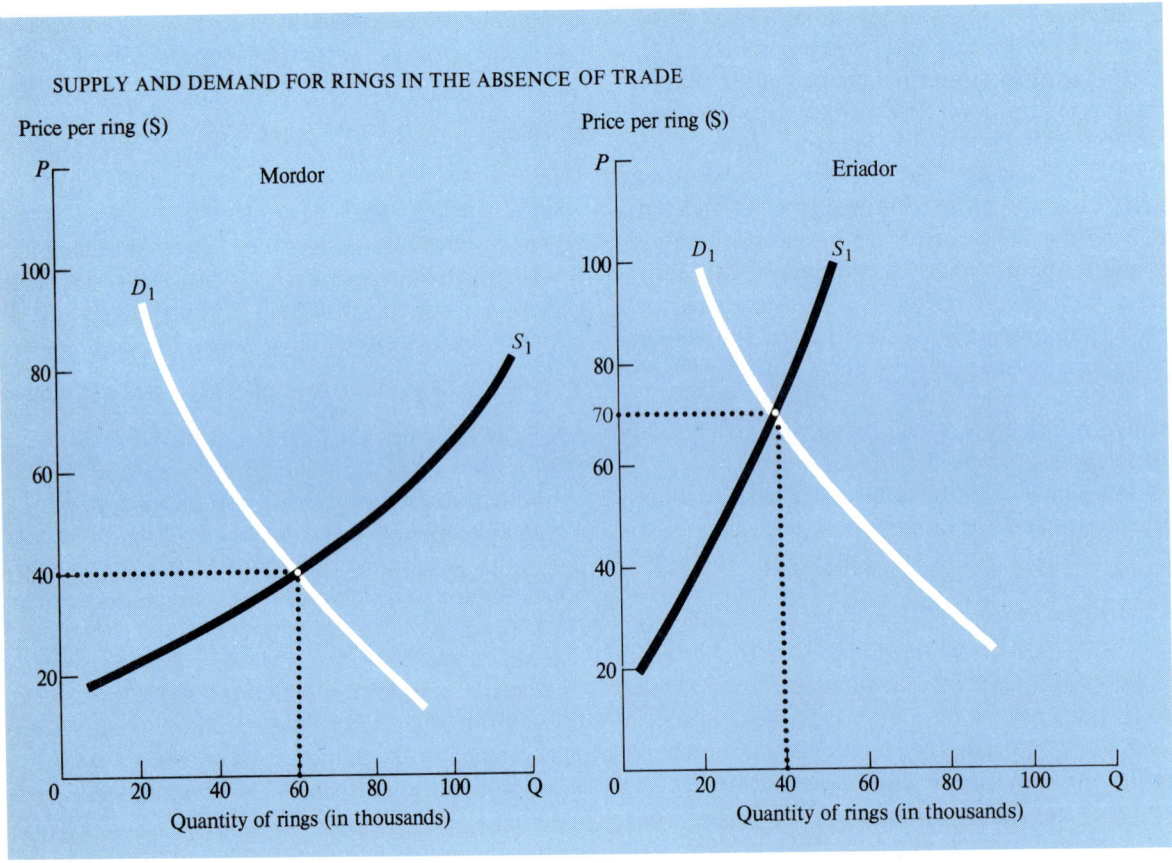

Fig. 37.1
In the absence of trade, the price of rings will be $40 in Mordor and $70 in Eriador. It is clear that Eriadorians would demand a larger quantity of rings if they could buy the rings at a lower price, similar to the price that prevails in Mordor.

—goods for which Eriador has a comparative advantage.

The short-run problem for Eriador

When Mordorian rings are imported into Eriador, most ring buyers will no longer be customers of Eriador's own jewelry-manufacturing firms, but will buy the lower-priced Mordorian rings instead. Economic principles tell us that in the long run this contraction of Eriador's ring industry will be beneficial to that country, for resources that were formerly employed in the relatively inefficient and disadvantaged jewelry industry will be released to work in a more efficient and advantaged industry—that of artificial flowers—causing both gross national product (GNP) and national income (NI) to increase. However, in the short-run, the contraction of the ring industry in Eriador will bring problems: many jewelry-manufacturing firms will go out of business, causing stockholders to lose

ECONOMIC EFFECTS OF TARIFFS

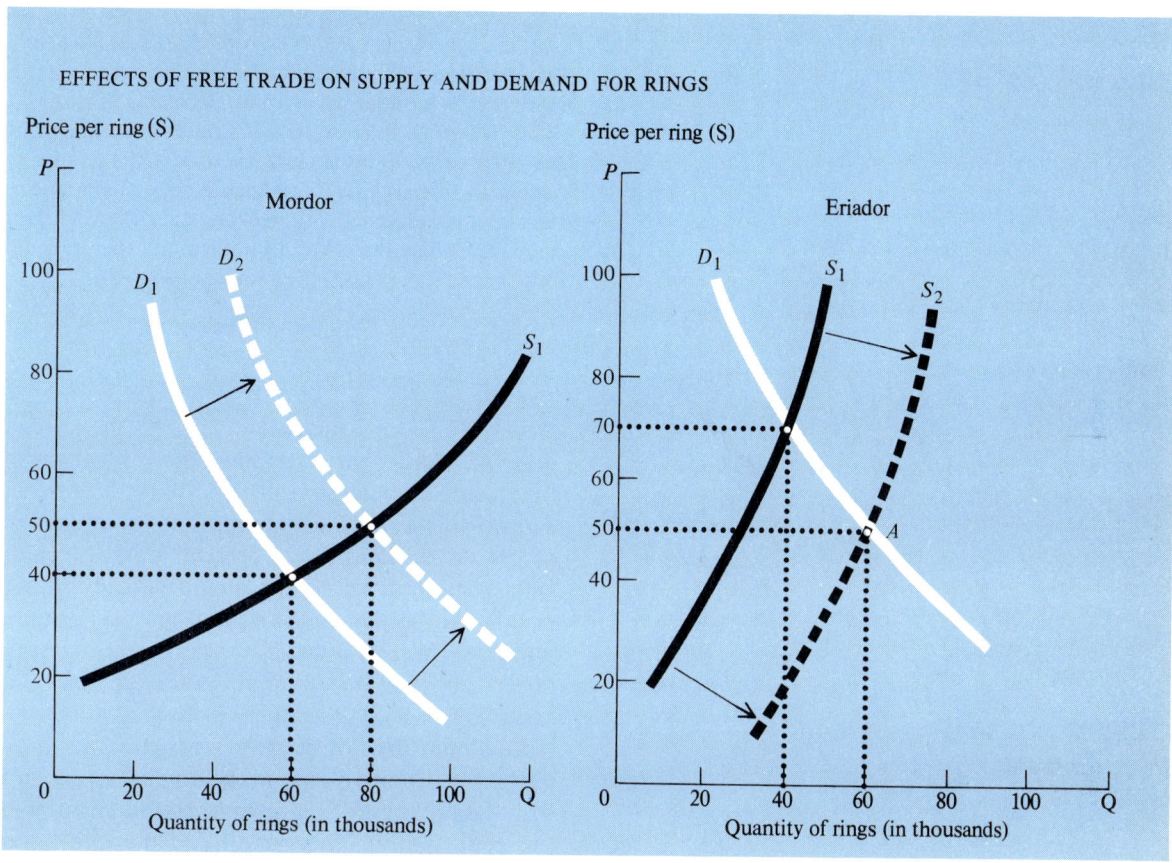

Fig. 37.2
Ring production in Mordor will increase because of the increase in demand caused by the addition of the foreign buyers to the market. This is reflected in the shift from D_1 (domestic demand) to D_2 (domestic plus foreign demand). As a result, new jobs are created and a significant rise in Mordor's NNP occurs. In Eriador, the supply curve for rings shifts outward, from S_1 to S_2, reflecting the addition of foreign suppliers to the domestic market. At the new equilibrium point (point A), domestic producers are supplying 30,000 rings, while foreign producers are also supplying 30,000 rings to the Eriador market. The benefit to Eriador is that consumers can now buy more rings at lower prices.

money and workers to lose jobs. It will take time to adapt all jewelry-producing resources to the production of artificial flowers.

Let us suppose that jewelry workers in Eriador have a very strong union. When the process of resource reallocation is undertaken, union leaders protest the high unemployment rate currently existing in the jewelry industry. The president of the union makes a speech warning that all Eriadorian workers may soon find their jobs threatened by the products of cheap Mordorian labor and asking for support from other labor

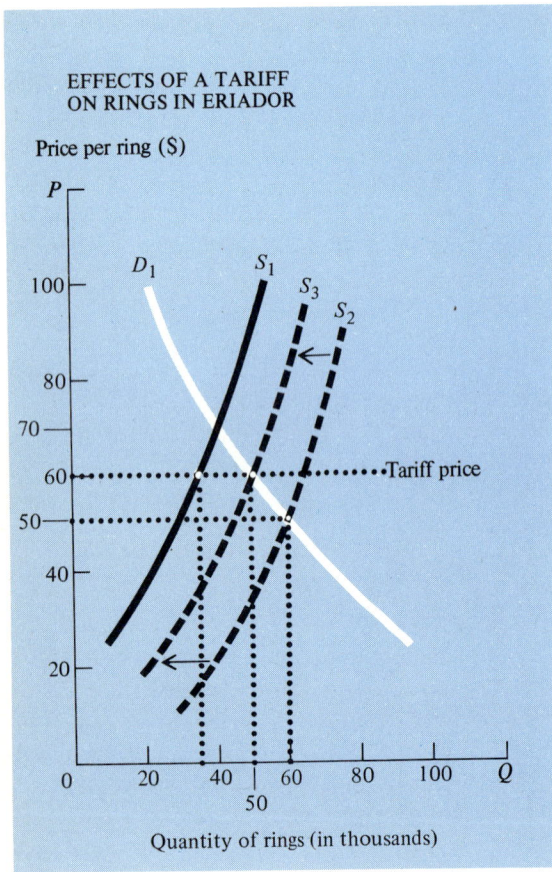

Fig. 37.3
In the absence of trade, the price of rings in Eriador will be set at $70, the point of intersection of D_1 and S_1. With free trade, the price would fall to $50, the point where D_1 intersects S_2. If Eriador then imposes a tariff on rings, the price will rise to $60, the point where D_1 intersects S_3. Note that in spite of the price increase, Eriadorian consumers are still better off than they were when there was no trade at all; they can still buy more rings (50,000) at a lower price ($60).

unions. As a result a 48-hour general strike is scheduled. At the same time, the Eriadorian Association of Jewelrymakers is spending the last of its available funds lobbying in the federal capital, trying to persuade the government to adopt some kind of protectionist measure. The government of Eriador finally responds to this concerted pressure by announcing a 20 percent *ad valorem* tariff on all imported rings.

The imposition of a tariff
Figure 37.3 shows the effects of the new tariff on the economy of Eriador. The tariff will shift the price of Mordorian rings upward, with the result that a smaller quantity of rings will be demanded. The price of a ring in Eriador is now $60 as a result of the tariff ($50 plus 20 percent, or $10, equals $60). As a result, a smaller quantity—only 50,000 rings—will be demanded at the new equilibrium point. At this new price, however, Eriadorian producers now will be willing to increase production to 35,000 rings. At the higher price their goods are more competitive. Resources are therefore shifted to the less productive use in the ring industry. This increased domestic competitiveness, coupled with the reduction in the quantity demanded, also means that fewer rings will be imported. Mordorian exporters must therefore cut back on the quantity they will supply (contributing to the new lower supply curve, S^3 on the graph). Since 50,000 rings are now being consumed and 35,000 are produced domestically, only 15,000 will be imported instead of the 30,000 that free trade made possible. It should be evident that with the tariff, Eriadorians are not as well off as they would be under free trade, since the price is higher. Nevertheless, they are better off than they would be in the absence of trade, or with a higher tariff of 40 percent—which would be equivalent to the absence of trade.

Economic effects of a tariff—summary
We can summarize the economic effects of a tariff under four principal points.

☐ A tariff raises the price of an imported good. Under free trade, the products of a foreign industry that enjoys a comparative advantage will be lower in price than the same goods produced by a disadvantaged domestic industry. The purpose and effect of a protective tariff is to lessen or eliminate that price advantage.

☐ Consumers will be faced with the choice of paying either the higher price of the domestically produced good or the higher price of the imported good with the tariff. In this way, a tariff causes domestic consumers to lose buying power.

☐ Because the price of the good goes up, fewer units of the good will be demanded. A tariff therefore reduces domestic consumption of the good; it also reduces world output.

☐ A tariff causes productive resources to be reallocated to disadvantaged and less efficient industries. Under free trade, a comparatively disadvantaged industry will contract, and the resources once used in that industry will be reallocated to more efficient industries, thus expanding total GNP and NI. But after a tariff is introduced, consumers once more begin to buy from the domestic disadvantaged industry, with the result that resources are reallocated to this use.

Inefficiencies caused by tariffs

The cost of a tariff is borne primarily by domestic consumers. Part of the additional payment made by consumers is distributed to the government as additional revenue; part is distributed to domestic producers of the disadvantaged good, who also enjoy increased revenues; and part is lost to the entire economy through inefficient resource allocation.

The benefit of a tariff accrues to the government, and to employees and stockholders of domestic producers of the good. In both cases, it is an economically inefficient source of revenue. It would be more efficient for the government to obtain its revenue through taxes on income or output, because a tariff acts to constrict GNP, and, therefore, reduces the total tax base available to the government. Moreover, a tariff is basically a regressive tax. Every consumer pays the same additional cost—a cost that represents a greater proportion of total income for low-income households than it does for high-income households (unless the good is a luxury good purchased only by the rich). It becomes apparent, then, that in the United States—or in any other country that has adopted a policy of redistributing income to achieve a greater degree of equality—tariffs counteract other measures of fiscal policy.

As we have seen, a tariff produces revenue for domestic producers of the taxed good; a tariff forces consumers to subsidize the protected industry. Some kind of subsidy may well be desirable, because the short-run adjustments in a contracting industry that produces disadvantaged goods can be very painful. But it would be much more economically efficient for the government to give unemployed workers a direct subsidy until they can be retrained and employed in another industry. The subsidy provided by the tariff is a reward for inefficiency that will serve to preserve the inefficiency. By allowing free trade and by directly subsidizing workers in a disadvantaged industry until they can be relocated, the government can increase total GNP and NI. In so doing, it also can increase total public welfare—it can make everybody a little better off without injuring anybody.

WHY ARE TARIFFS IMPOSED?

Economists are in general agreement regarding the harmful effects of a tariff: higher prices, restricted output, and a pattern of resource allocation that is not optimally efficient. Yet many nations continue to impose tariffs, despite the evidence of their economic inefficiency. What are some of the reasons for this, and how valid are these reasons?

Protection of workers and firms in disadvantaged industries

One argument frequently advanced in favor of a tariff is that it will protect workers and business firms in disadvantaged industries. In a number of industries, especially those that are labor-intensive, the price of goods made in the United States is higher than that of comparable goods imported from other countries. This is true in the textile industry, for example, and in many segments of the electronics industry. These goods are comparatively disadvantaged; that is, the opportunity cost of their production is higher in the United States than it is in other nations. There is no doubt that free trade will contract disadvantaged industries; this is the basis of its economic efficiency. People whose income is derived from disadvantaged industries are motivated by their own interpretation of self-interest to ask for tariff protection.

Supporters of tariffs always point to the dangers of "cheap foreign labor," which they feel will undermine the hard-won wage gains of domestic workers. In part, this fear is based on an incomplete understanding of the link between productivity and wage levels. Workers are generally paid on the basis of what they produce. One reason that wage rates in the United States are high is that American workers are productive—a factor that free trade will not alter. However, if it is true—as some critics of the labor movement suggest—that labor unions artificially restrict the supply of labor in this country, thereby pushing the equilibrium wage rate higher, it is possible that free trade will reduce wage levels for some workers. According to a theory advanced by economists Paul Samuelson and Wolfgang Stopler, free trade serves to make the scarce factors of production more abundant, and this increase in supply may well result in lower prices in the resource markets—in other words, lower wages. However, in the long run, the gains in productivity that come from the reallocation of resources imposed by free trade should more than offset any wage-lowering effects of an increase in the labor supply.

Negative effects of government protection

It is understandable that those who own or work in disadvantaged industries would ask for government protection. Their self-interest causes them to look not at the benefits to the economy in general, but at the costs to their own industry. Until the machines, factories, and work skills of the disadvantaged industry can be adapted for use in an industry that possesses a comparative advantage, these people will suffer a loss of income.

More debatable is the issue of the government's *response* to the requests for assistance in the disadvantaged industry. The imposition of a tariff causes the whole economy to suffer through the loss of potential output and income that would be possible under free trade. A tariff also helps to perpetuate the existing misallocation of resources. If society decides that it is desirable to compensate for the inequities of income distribution that will occur during the reallocation of resources, there are other, more efficient methods of achieving this goal. The government might bear the cost of retraining workers and helping them find new jobs, or it might increase unemployment compensation for workers in selected industries. In the long run, either of these programs would serve not only to compensate the workers in disadvantaged industries but also to expand total output and income.

Stimulation of domestic employment

Another argument often advanced in favor of a tariff is that it will stimulate domestic employment in general. Imported goods, made by workers in other countries, will become relatively more expensive; many buyers will switch to domestic goods, thus creating new jobs for domestic workers. According to this perspective a tariff may be viewed as a sort of cure for recession, stimulating increased domestic output.

Counterarguments

One of the problems with this reasoning is that it overlooks the law of demand, which says that as prices rise the quantity demanded will decrease. Suppose that under free trade, Americans can buy imported bone meal for $100 a ton, as compared to a price of $110 a ton for domestic bone meal. Most purchasers will choose the imported bone meal—and let us assume that at the price of $100, they will demand 500,000 tons. What happens when a tariff of 10 percent is imposed on the imported bone meal? Imported bone meal no longer has any price advantage; therefore, consumers will probably choose on the basis of intangible taste preferences. No matter which kind they buy, however, they must now pay $110 a ton; at that price, a smaller quantity (let's say 300,000 tons) is demanded, as many consumers search for low-cost substitutes or decide to do without. Much of the apparent gain of a tariff vanishes when consumers are faced with higher prices and respond by lowering the quantity they are willing to purchase.

In a complex and highly specialized economy, an increased tariff may cause the prices of many domestic goods to rise as well. For example, the electronics industry in the United States buys many of the small parts it uses in assembling television sets, radios, and phonographs from Japanese manufacturers. The Japanese have a comparative advantage in the production of these goods and can turn them out at a lower price than can domestic producers. Therefore, a tariff on the importation of those parts will raise the costs of manuacturing in electronics industries, with the result that American brands of final goods also will have a higher price tag. Much of the increase in jobs due to increased domestic manufacture of components will be offset by a loss of jobs due to decreased demand for the final products. Hence, it might make more sense to establish a tariff policy that put a tariff on *assembled* products but *not* on parts.

A third problem with the argument that tariffs stimulate domestic employment is that it fails to consider the response of the trading partners. They will probably retaliate by imposing tariffs of their own, in order to compensate for the disadvantages that the tariff creates for their own industries. As we saw in Chapter 36, the contribution of trade to our GNP is arrived at by subtracting the value of imports (M) from the value of exports (X), or $X - M$. It is true that GNP will increase if we lower M. Since the trade component of GNP is also subject to the multiplier, the increase in GNP will be much greater than the increase in the trade component. But when a government lowers M by imposing tariffs, the result is nearly always that X also is lowered, through retaliatory tariffs imposed by trading partners. When both X and M are lowered, there is no net gain to the economy, no increase in GNP, and therefore no creation of new jobs. X also may be lowered because foreigners are unable to obtain the currency they need to buy goods. For example, if a tariff prevents trading partners of the United States from obtaining dollars by selling goods to the United States they have no dollars with which to buy American goods.

Protection of developing industries

Another argument sometimes used to support the imposition of tariffs is that they protect developing industries which cannot yet be fully competitive, and thus they facilitate economic development. An example of this use of tariffs can be seen in Ghana, a less-developed nation has been trying to establish a textile industry so that it can move away from economic dependence on a single crop (cocoa). Because the textile industry in Ghana has not yet matured, most plants are smaller than optimum size, few workers are skilled in the trade, and there is a low degree of specilization. Against Japan or Hong Kong or Great Britain, Ghana has a comparative disadvantage in making textiles, and the price of cloth made there is higher than the price of imported cloth. But the government of Ghana is determined to embark on a program of industrialization, and it is thought that if the infant textile industry can be protected at this stage of its development, it can eventually be established as an industry with a comparative advantage. For this reason, the government imposes high tariffs on all imported textiles.

Drawbacks of tariff protection of developing industries

The primary drawback to this use of tariffs is the difficulty of determining the end of infancy. Once inaugurated, subsidies produced by tariffs have a tendency to become permanent. There is also some debate over whether or not industrialization is the wisest course in circumstances where protective tariffs would be needed. If a comparative advantage exists for agricultural products and raw materials, why should a nation make industrialization its goal? The reasons are likely to be more political than economic.

Protecting industries necessary to national defense

In the past, many countries have used tariffs to protect and develop industries that were necessary to national defense. Prior to World War II, for example, the major powers all began to impose tariffs in order to protect their steel, rubber, and munitions industries, so that domestic supplies of these goods would be adequate if war came and trade was suspended.

Under the conditions of all-out modern warfare, this use of tariffs would be outmoded. A major nuclear war is likely to be fought so quickly that the question of producing additional war material would never arise. The limited wars fought in various areas of the world in recent years often have not substantially disrupted trade for the countries involved. When Egypt and Israel were at war for example, each relied on foreign powers as sources of military hardware, and the existing state of hostility did not stop the flow of tanks, fighter planes, and machine guns to either country.

Improving the terms of trade

Another reason advanced for the use of tariffs is that one country can improve its terms of trade by imposing tariffs on imported goods. Economist Peter B. Kenen comments:

> This resembles the familiar proposition that a monopolist can increase his profits by limiting his sales. By restricting imports with a tax, a country *can* sometimes force down the price at which other countries sell it, and thus improve its terms of trade. If it carries the process too far, the loss it suffers by forgoing the consumption of imported products will exceed the gain it takes by reducing foreign prices. . . . The fact remains, however: a country that enjoys a strategic position in world trade can rearrange the gains from trade in its own favor by a judicious use of import restrictions.*

The terms-of-trade argument is effective only if the trading partner does not retaliate by imposing a similar tariff of its own; if the other country retaliates, all gains are wiped out and both countries are left in a worse position than they were with free trade. Such retaliation would be the expected course of action in most situations. This is especially true when the tariff-imposing nation is, like the United States, a major trading partner of many countries. Unilateral tariff action would cause severe economic damage to the exporting nations; they would certainly move to impose tariffs of their own. However, it is possible that a small country whose trade represents an insignificant amount of the world market might succeed in escaping retaliation and could actually better its terms of trade through the imposition of tariffs.

POLITICAL USES OF TARIFFS

As we examine the arguments advanced in favor of tariffs, it becomes apparent that there are few economically defensible grounds for their imposition. In most cases, tariffs are imposed for reasons of political expediency rather than because they

---

*Peter B. Kenen, *International Economics,* 2nd ed., p. 24. © 1967, Prentice-Hall, Inc., Englewood Cliffs, N.J.

are economically desirable. An example of this is the protection of workers and firms in disadvantaged industries in the United States. It sometimes happens that the president will impose such a tariff through presidential decree, an action that can be taken quickly and that produces quick results. An economically preferable method of helping unemployed workers in disadvantaged industries, that of providing a direct subsidy, would require congressional approval of two measures—one to raise the needed revenue and another to allocate it for the needs of the workers. Similarly, although it would be economically preferable to stimulate economic expansion through a tax cut, this action also requires congressional approval. If the president has reason to believe that the Congress, perhaps from political motivations, will be reluctant to cooperate with such programs, the president may choose to use the less efficient tool of a tariff, simply because imposing it does not require congressional approval.

Tariffs may also be passed in response to public pressure from organized labor or from business associations that want to protect their own self-interest. These groups may wield considerable political power, causing their demands to take precedence over the advice of economic theorists. The harm caused by tariffs in restricting output and limiting the growth of GNP is much more difficult for the average person to observe and understand than is the unemployment and profit decline in a disadvantaged industry that is being forced to contract.

Summary

■ This chapter examines the restrictions frequently placed on free international trade, the reasons for these barriers, and the effects of such policies on the domestic economies of the trading nations.

■ A major barrier to free trade is the tariff. Tariffs may be imposed for the purpose of gaining revenue or for the purpose of protecting domestic industry and employment; it is not generally possible to pursue both goals at once. A tariff may be levied at a specific rate per unit of imported goods, or *ad valorem;* that is, according to the value of the imported goods. Tariffs are collected from importers and are usually passed along to consumers in the form of higher prices. If a tariff is not sufficient to produce the desired effect of limiting imports, quotas may be imposed. Trade can also be controlled by the licensing of importers, by currency restrictions, and by the complete prohibition of trade with a particular country (embargo).

■ The economic effects of tariffs can be summarized under four basic points: (1) A tariff raises the price of the imported good, lessening the comparative advantage enjoyed by the foreign good over the good produced by the disadvantaged domestic industry. (2) Consumers—faced with the choice of buying the higher-priced domestic good or the higher-priced imported good with the tariff—lose some degree of their buying power. (3) Higher prices also mean that fewer units will be sold, domestic consumption will go down and total world output will decrease. (4) Resources will be allocated to less efficient uses, because once the tariff is imposed, consumers will again buy from domestic disadvantaged industries.

■ Two major inefficiencies are caused by tariffs. First, part of the cost of a tariff will be lost to the economy through contraction of GNP. Second, part of the costs of the tariff will go to the government, but this is a less efficient and more regressive means of raising money than direct taxation and is a form of government subsidy for inefficiency.

■ Proponents of tariffs argue that tariffs are beneficial because they protect workers and businesses in disadvantaged industries. While it is true that free trade would lead to the contraction of some industries, it would be better in the long run to reallocate the labor and other resources that would be threatened in more efficient ways. It is also argued that tariffs provide a general economic stimulus by encouraging the purchase of more domestic goods, but the result may in fact be to lessen total demand, not shift it to domestic goods, and a tariff may lead to an increase in domestic prices as well. Tariff retaliation by other countries is also very likely. Tariff supporters claim that tariffs are useful in protecting a nation's newly developing industries, but opponents counter that once they are in place, tariffs often prove difficult to remove. It is further argued that tariffs are essential to protect industries that are vital to national defense, but the experience in modern wartime situations suggests that this is not the case. Finally, some supporters of tariffs claim that by imposing tariffs it is possible to change the terms of trade; however, this argument again ignores the likelihood of retaliation, and has validity only with respect to the trade of small countries.

■ In the final analysis, the strongest arguments in favor of trade tariffs are really political, not economic. In the United States, the imposition of tariffs may reflect the strength of a particular pressure group and have the advantage of quicker implementation and results than the slower but ultimately more efficient move toward an extensive reallocation of resources.

Key Terms

tariff

specific tariff

ad valorem tariff

Review & Discussion

1. What are the basic types of tariffs? What are the different purposes of tariffs? What is the only purpose of a quota? Of an embargo?

2. What are the effects of tariffs on consumer prices for the protected goods? On domestic producers? On the patterns of resource allocation?

3. How does the imposition of a tariff affect the exporting country?

4. Draw demand and supply curves for a product. Assume that a tariff is imposed that shifts the supply curve upward. What happens to the equilibrium price of the good? To the quantity demanded and supplied?

5. Suppose that the demand for rice in a particular country is fixed at a certain quantity, regardless of price. What would be the effects of a tariff on rice imported from other countries? Why?

6. Give as many arguments as you can in favor of protectionism. Which of the arguments do you think are the most persuasive?

7. What must be assumed if tariffs are to improve the importer's terms of trade? How likely is this condition in practice?

8. What arguments would you use to persuade someone who was afraid of the economic adjustments to be made if tariffs were dropped that these adjustments would not be as difficult as he or she supposed?

Chapter 38

Exchange Rates and the Balance of Payments

What to look for in this chapter

How is international trade financed?

How are exchange rates determined under a gold standard? A gold-exchange standard? Floating exchange rates?

What accounts make up a balance-of-payments statement?

What has been the balance-of-payments situation for the United States in recent years?

The principle of comparative advantage suggests that each nation should export those goods that it can produce at the lowest relative cost. If all nations produced according to comparative advantage, total world output would be increased and there would be a wider range of consumption possibilities. It logically follows that it is advantageous to all nations to facilitate free international trade, and to seek out and develop those mechanisms that simplify and encourage the expansion of foreign trade. We will devote most of this chapter to a discussion of exchange rates and the balance of payments—two of the most important considerations in determining the level of international-trade transactions. Chapter 39 will review the development of international-trade arrangements since World War II, with particular emphasis on the problems now facing the United States in this area.

FINANCING FOREIGN TRADE

When a department store in Iowa orders $200 worth of wool sweaters from a textile firm in North Carolina, there is no currency problem involved when the time comes to pay for the merchandise. The company in North Carolina has priced sweaters in dollar amounts; the store in Iowa sells them for dollars, figures its costs and profits in dollars, and pays for the sweaters in dollars. The situation is different, however when a department store in Iowa orders sweaters from a firm in England. The English firm must pay its rent and workers in pounds, and therefore it wants to be paid in pounds. On the other hand, the American store will be selling the sweaters for dollars and will not obtain the pounds required by the British supplier in its day-to-day business transactions. If foreign trade is to be facilitated, there must be a simple, reliable way for businesspeople to exchange one currency for another.

Such a service is routinely provided by most banks, and every day thousands of American firms arrange to pay for German cars by buying German marks with their dollars, or to purchase Norwegian fish by buying kroner. At the same time, foreigners all over the world are using *their* currencies to buy the American dollars they need in order to pay for American washing machines, tobacco, or airplanes.

Exchange rates

The price at which one currency may be traded for another is called the **exchange rate**. Obviously, the exchange rate is of primary importance to foreign traders. If the pound is selling for $2, our American sweater importer will have to pay $200 to acquire the £100 that the English manufacturer is charging for sweaters. If the exchange rate is £1 = $3, the American importer will have to pay $300 for £100 and may decide not to buy sweaters at that price. Alternatively, one can look at the exchange rates from the point of view of a foreign importer seeking to buy goods from the United States. Suppose an English firm wants to buy American electric toasters with a dollar price of $12.00. An exchange rate of £1 = $2 means a cost of £6 per toaster, but at £1 = $3, each toaster will cost only £4. When dollars are cheaper the English firm will probably be much more eager to import American goods; conversely, when dollars are more expensive and the firm's pounds will buy fewer of them the firm will not import as many items from the United States.

It is apparent then that the exchange rate is an important determinant of the level of exports and imports between any two nations. Let us therefore examine how exchange rates are established.

The gold standard

Until the mid-1930s most nations were on the **gold standard,** a mechanism whereby each country defines its monetary unit in terms of gold. *Under the gold standard, every country agrees to convert its paper money to gold on request at a set legal rate and to permit gold to be imported and exported freely.* For example, in 1925 the dollar was set at 23.22 grams of gold and the pound was set at 113 grams of gold, or 4.86 times as much gold as the dollar (113 ÷ 23.22 = 4.86). Thus the exchange rate for pounds in terms of dollars was 1 £ = 4.86. Under these conditions—fixed legal rates and unrestricted importation and exportation of gold—the exchange rate tended to be stable and to fluctuate only within narrow limits.

The actual upper and lower limits within which the exchange rate fluctuated were dependent on the costs of shipping gold between two countries. In the 1920s, for example, the costs of shipping, packing, and insurance for each pound's worth of gold shipped between the United States and England was about 2¢. At that time, then, the lower limit for pounds was $4.84 and the upper limit was $4.88. *The upper and lower limits within which the price of a currency fluctuates under a gold standard* are called **gold points**. To continue with our example, the dollar price of a pound would remain within these limits because of the practice of **arbitrage,** *the process of buying any commodity* (in this case, currency) *in one market and simultaneously selling it in another market in order to profit from the price discrepancy.*

Thus, if the exchange rate rose to $4.89 to the pound, it would be advantageous for American traders to convert $4.86 worth of dollars into gold in New York, ship the gold to London, buy a pound with the gold, and sell it for $4.89. Conversely, if the exchange rate fell to $4.83, it would be profitable for British currency traders to buy pounds, convert them to gold, ship the gold to the United States, buy dollars with the gold, and sell them for $4.86. The practice of arbitrage tends to equalize commodity prices in different markets—in this case, to stabilize exchange rates within the established limits.

Advantages of the gold standard The fact that the gold standard provided stable exchange rates means that it tended to foster the growth of international trade. Stable exchange rates meant that importers and exporters faced fewer risks. Importers could determine their costs, in terms of their own currencies, at the time they placed their orders, regardless of delivery or payment dates. Exporters could accept orders confidently, knowing they would receive enough money—in their own currencies—to cover cost and profits.

Another significant advantage of the gold standard is that it provided an automatic mechanism through which imports and exports always moved toward equilibrium, and through which the foreign trade of each nation tended to stay in balance.

We can understand the automatic balancing mechanism by first considering the effects of gold outflow on a nation whose imports exceed its exports. Under the gold standard, each country has a gold-backed domestic currency. Therefore, if the United States, for example, loses gold because of an excess of imports over exports, the amount of money in the United States will decline, credit will be harder to come by, and interest rates will increase. As a result of this tightening of monetary conditions, business will contract, incomes will decline, and prices will fall. As prices fall, American goods will become increasingly attractive to foreign buyers because of the operation of the law of demand on a worldwide basis, and American exports will increase.

Suppose that at the same time that the United States is experiencing a deflation because of its gold drain, the reverse is occurring in England, which has been acquiring the gold lost by the United States. An increase in gold leads to an increase in the English money supply, more credit, cheaper money, and inflation. Business expands, and incomes, costs, and prices of English goods begin to increase. With English goods now commanding higher prices, Americans are less willing to buy them, and American imports from England drop. To summarize, we see that because of the initial gold drain, American costs and prices decline, and English prices increase. As a consequence, American exports increase and imports drop, the trade between the two nations moves toward a state of equilibrium, and the flow of gold out of the United States stops.

Thus the gold standard has two major advantages. First, it provides stable exchange rates, which foster the growth of international trade. Second, it provides a self-adjusting mechanism through which disequilibria in foreign trade are corrected. Gold flows from one nation to another lead to overall changes in domestic price levels, with prices declining in those countries experiencing a gold drain and increasing in those nations where gold is being acquired. As a result of these price changes, exports tend to increase in those countries that are losing gold and to decrease in those where an increase in the gold supply has caused inflation. Thus equilibrium can be restored automatically, provided that the nations involved permit that result to occur without taking any offsetting actions, such as selective import and export controls, changes in currency values, or tariffs.

Disadvantages The gold standard does have a very serious disadvantage. Any country that imports more than it exports will soon find itself faced with internal deflation. According to basic monetary theory (discussed in Chapter 13), if the money supply (gold) decreases, either prices or the quantity of output must decline too. The supporters of the gold standard assumed that most of this decline would come in the form of a reduction in prices. In practice, however, prices tend to be inflexible downward, so that a decline in the gold supply will probably lead to a decline in quantity of output—and in particular to an increase in unemployment. In other words, under the gold standard, a nation with an excess of imports must be willing to accept the unpleasantness of overall deflation—including a rising level of unemployment—as the opportunity cost of stabilizing its foreign-trade position. Conversely, a country with excess exports must be willing to undergo inflation in order to achieve foreign-trade equilibrium.

The gold-exchange standard
At the end of World War II, most important trading nations adopted a modified version of the gold standard, called the **gold-exchange standard** (see Chapter 39 for the historical developments that led to this mechanism). The gold-exchange standard can be characterized as follows:

☐ *The exchange value of each currency was fixed in terms of both gold and United States dollars,* and international balances could be settled in either gold or dollars, with dollars becoming increasingly important. For example, in common usage, the foreign-exchange value of the Norwegian krone was generally quoted 14¢, rather than as .004 ounces of gold.

☐ Although precise details varied among different countries, *every major currency was convertible for foreign-trade purposes into the stated amount of gold or dollars.* However, very few currencies are domestically convertible into gold on demand. In other words, most nations have eliminated the direct link between the amount of their gold reserves and the domestic money supply.* As a result, under a gold-exchange standard, gold inflows or outflows caused by international imbalances would no longer necessarily affect the domestic money supply as directly as they did under the old gold standard.

Let us see how a gold-exchange standard operates. Consider a Norwegian importer of French wine who placed an order for a dozen bottles of rare champagne. The price of the 12 bottles of rare champagne is quoted as 1000 francs. By consulting a list of the dollar-exchange values of the Norwegian krone and the French franc, the importer can determine the costs of French champagne in terms of kroner. Suppose the exchange values of francs and kroner are:

$$1 \text{ krone} = 14 \text{ cents}$$
$$1 \text{ franc} = 18.003 \text{ cents}$$
$$1 \text{ franc} = 1.285 \text{ kroner}$$
$$1000 \text{ francs} = 1285 \text{ kroner}.$$

The dollar-exchange values of the two currencies are fixed; they are not permitted to fluctuate more than 1 percent in either direction. So the Norwegian importer knows in advance how many kroner will be required to pay the 100 francs at the time the champagne is delivered. In other words, the gold-exchange standard provides stable exchange rates for foreign trade.

Role of the IMF The purpose of the gold-exchange standard was to encourage the growth of international trade by providing the same kind of desirable stable exchange rates that the old gold standard afforded, but without its drawbacks. To accomplish this, a series of mechanisms were de-

---

*For example, there have been no gold-reserve requirements for the U.S. dollar since 1934, so changes in our gold supply no longer directly affect our domestic money supply.

veloped which attempted to provide more flexibility for countries with import or export imbalances. Among the most important of these was the establishment of the **International Monetary Fund (IMF),** *a world monetary body designed to provide a central pool of currencies on which any member nation could draw when its own reserves of gold or dollars became temporarily inadequate to maintain its currency-support operations.*

A nation with an excess of imports could borrow the currency it required, rather than being forced to start shipping scarce gold or dollars abroad. However, the intention was that the IMF would make currency loans to countries with *temporary* export-import imbalance problems —for example, a nation faced with a series of domestic strikes which have cut exports, or one experiencing a temporary increase in imports while domestic industry is tooling up to supply an export market.

Thus, under the gold-exchange standard, nations with long-term foreign-trade disequilibria could not depend indefinitely on the IMF loans. If a trade deficit occurred, the country would be able to pay for its excess imports only as long as its gold or dollar reserves lasted. Eventually, however, it would have to do something to bring its exports and imports into line.

It was just such a long-term balance-of-payments deficit in the United States that signaled the end of the gold-exchange standard. Confronted in 1971 with an increasing buildup of foreign dollar holdings and a dwindling domestic gold supply, the United States announced that it would no longer convert foreign-held dollars into gold. Under IMF rules, other nations were no longer obligated to support the fixed exchange values of their own currencies. In short, the gold-exchange standard, which had been in effect since 1944, was no longer in operation.

Floating exchange rates

We have seen that exchange rates under the gold standard remain stable, regardless of a disequilibrium between total exports and imports. Another method of solving the problem of an imbalance between exports and imports, however, is to allow the exchange rates to fluctuate freely. Under the system of **floating exchange rates** *the price of one currency in terms of another is determined simply by supply and demand,* as exporters and importers compete in the open market to buy the currencies they require. (In the next chapter we will examine the *modified* system of floating exchange rates that has evolved since the United States announced in 1971 that it was suspending the convertibility of the dollar into gold.)

To understand how such a system works, let us assume a situation in which American and English exports and imports are about equal, and the pound is selling for $2. Now assume that the United States begins to step up its imports from England, while exports remain unchanged. American importers of English cloth and Scotch whisky will attempt to buy the pounds they need to pay for these goods. When exports and imports were in equilibrium, American importers could purchase all the pounds they required from the English importers, who in turn needed dollars to pay their American suppliers. Now, however, the demand for pounds has increased, but the supply of pounds has remained constant. As a consequence, the price of pounds rises, let us say to $2.30.

Let us examine the consequences of this change in the price of pounds. The American importer, who formerly could buy a yard of Harris tweed for one pound (or $2), is still billed £1 by the English supplier. However, the importer must now pay $2.30 for this £1. Therefore, in order to make a profit when the fabric is sold in the United States, the importer must raise the retail price. In other words, as a direct result of the higher price of pounds resulting from the import-export disequilibrium, English goods become more expensive (and less attractive) to American consumers. Eventually, American consumers will reduce their purchases of these expensive English goods, and English exports to the United States will decline.

At the same time, consider the effect of the changing exchange rates on English merchants who import wheat from the United States. If wheat is selling at $3 a bushel in the United States, £1 will buy one bushel of wheat when the pound is worth $3. However, with the pound selling at $3.30, it will buy 1 1/10 bushels of wheat. In other words, American goods now become cheaper and more attractive to the English, and as a consequence American exporters should be able to sell more to the English market.

Thus, under floating exchange rates, a state of export-import equilibrium should be maintained as a result of changes in exchange rates. Certain parts of the domestic economy will suffer more than others during the adjustment process—as the price of the pound increases and English exports decline, there will be a loss of income and employment, particularly in those sectors of the English economy devoted to the export business, and to a lesser extent in other sectors as well. But the overall domestic adjustment that was required under the gold standard is no longer necessary. Instead of nationwide deflation or inflation as a response to international trade disequilibrium, there will be only a somewhat smaller adjustment, and its effect will be more limited.

Price uncertainty One disadvantage of freely floating exchange rates is that, because the prices of the various currencies are free to fluctuate, international traders cannot know in advance what the precise costs or revenues will be in their own currencies. For example, suppose an American car dealer orders a Mercedes in January for July delivery at a price of 20,000 marks. The dealer may consider this a good deal in January, when the mark is selling for 50¢. However, when the bill becomes due in July, the dealer finds that the price of the mark is now 75¢. The cost of the car, originally figured at $10,000 (20,000 × 50¢) is now $15,000 (20,000 × 75¢). If the current selling price of a Mercedes in the United States is $13,000, the transaction is no longer attractive for the American car dealer, who at the current price of $13,000 will lose $2,000. Since the dealer would not take this substantial loss, the eventual result of the change in the exchange rate would be an increase in the price of a Mercedes in the United States.

However, there are ways of circumventing the price uncertainties connected with floating exchange rates. For example, an American business firm contracting to buy French wine in March for delivery in September could immediately purchase a **futures contract** under which *the seller promises to sell the buyer a given amount of foreign currency at a stated price some time in the future, regardless of the actual market price of the currency at that future date.* Dealing in "futures" contracts is a common practice among many businesspeople. The cost of such a contract is usually only a small premium, and by purchasing it, the buyer is protected against any increase in the cost of the foreign currency before payment date.

But the problem of uncertainty with freely fluctuating exchange rates becomes more acute for those foreigners contemplating long-term investments. Consider the case of an American who is considering an investment of $300,000 (or £100,000) in English bonds at a time when the exchange rate is $3 = £1. The investor calculates that the investment will yield a return of 10 percent (£10,000, or $30,000) a year. Suppose, however that at the end of the first year the American collects £10,000 but finds that the exchange rate is now £ = $2! The return on the investment has dropped to $20,000 or $6\frac{2}{3}$ percent, and the investor has no assurance of what the actual dollar yield will be in future years.

To summarize, the primary advantage of floating exchange rates is that they permit a country to handle a foreign-trade disequilibrium with

> **RECAP**
>
> Advantages and disadvantages of the gold standard, gold-exchange standard, and floating exchange rates:
>
> GOLD STANDARD
>
> *Advantages:* Fixed legal exchange rates and unrestricted importation and exportation of gold ensure stable exchange rates.
>
> *Disadvantages*: Countries whose imports exceed their exports experience internal deflation, causing decline in output and increase in unemployment. Countries whose exports exceed their imports are faced with internal inflation.
>
> GOLD-EXCHANGE STANDARD
>
> *Advantages*: Stable exchange rates ensured by IMF, which provides loans to correct temporary trade disequilibria.
>
> *Disadvantages*: Does not provide for correcting long-term balance-of-payments disequilibria.
>
> FLOATING EXCHANGE RATES
>
> *Advantages*: Currency prices are determined by market forces of supply and demand; thus export-import equilibrium is maintained as a result of changes in exchange rates with relatively little domestic economic upheaval.
>
> *Disadvantages*: Price uncertainty, which inhibits willingness of investors to make long-term capital investments abroad.

relatively minor domestic economic repercussions; the main disadvantage is that the relatively greater uncertainty that comes with such fluctuating rates may somewhat inhibit the growth of foreign trade and, in particular, long-term capital investments abroad.

INTERNATIONAL BALANCE OF PAYMENTS

Thus far we have discussed some of the problems that a nation must face when its demand for foreign currencies does not equal the amount of its own currency that foreigners demand. For the sake of simplicity, we have confined our examples almost exclusively to currency needs resulting from merchandise exports and imports. Now, however, let us consider the entire range of international transactions in which a country may be involved. We can do this by examining a **balance-of-payments statement.** *A nation's balance-of-payments statement is an attempt to record all of its monetary transactions with the outside world during a given period.* It includes not only exports and imports of merchandise, but purchases of services (hotel rooms, leases of oil tankers), government loans and gifts (contributions to NATO, foreign aid), business investments abroad (construction by an American truck company of a factory in Italy), and such miscellaneous items as money sent to relatives living abroad, or dividends received by domestic residents on their foreign investments. In addition, it notes any shipments of gold or actual currencies to and from any foreign country.

In this section we will describe the components of the international balance-of-payments statement for the United States in 1978. The statement is presented in simplified form in *Table 38.1*. The basic principle underlying this recording system is quite simple. Credit entries (recorded as plus) reflect transactions which ordinarily give rise to a flow of funds into the nation; debit entries (recorded as minus) reflect the flow of funds out of the nation.

There are many different ways of summarizing the items in a balance-of-payments statement. We will divide the total statement into three parts:

Table 38.1
United States balance of payments, 1978 (in billions)

Exports—Goods and services	$ + 218.0	
Imports—Goods and services	− 228.9	
Goods-and-services balance		$ − 10.9
Unilateral transfers		− 5.1
Capital flow		
United States capital outflow (private)	− 55.0	
Foreign capital inflow (private)	+ 29.3	
Net-capital-flow balance		− 25.7
Errors and omissions (statistical discrepancy)		+ 11.4
Balance-of-payments deficit		− 30.3
United States official reserve assets and other United States government assets		− 3.8
Liabilities of foreign official agencies		+ 34.0
Financing the deficit		$ + 30.2

Source: Adapted from *Survey of Current Business*, March 1979 (preliminary figures).
Details may not add exactly because of rounding.

(1) **goods-and-services account**, (2) **unilateral-transfers account**, and (3) **capital account**.

Goods-and-services account

Merchandise

Exports and imports of merchandise constitute the largest items on the balance-of-payments statements, and the expression **balance of trade** is often used to describe *the relationship between a nation's merchandise exports and imports*. A country with more merchandise exports than imports is said to have a "trade surplus" or a "favorable balance of trade," and a country importing more merchandise than it exports is said to have a "trade deficit" or an "unfavorable balance of trade."

In 1978, the United States reported a $34.2 billion excess of merchandise imports over exports. Although in most recent years the United States has had a trade deficit, this was not always the case. A trade deficit of $2.7 billion in 1971 was the first in this century. It is important to keep in mind two factors when attempting to determine the significance of the trade figures. First, although much public attention is focused on the trade figures, they are only one item in the balance-of-payments statement, and there are often significant counterbalancing amounts elsewhere. Second, as a nation develops from its early agricultural condition toward a more mature industrialized condition, the nature of the items on its balance-of-payments statement—and their relative importance—change. However, because the merchandise figures were the most important items during the earlier period (and also because they are more easily understood than the intangible "invisible items" and the complicated capital accounts), it is difficult to switch public attention away from them.

Military transactions

Since the end of World War II, the balance-of-payments position of the United States has been vastly complicated because of the large volume of military transactions that occur. The United States exports military goods abroad and pays military aid to other nations. It also buys military goods and services from foreign countries. All these transactions must be included in a special category in the goods-and-services accounts because appropriate data to distinguish between military transactions involving goods and military transactions involving services have not yet been developed.

Invisible trade

Investment income and transactions involving services are the next items in the goods-and-services account. They are often collectively referred to as "invisible transactions" since they do not involve the exchange of tangible goods. Services include travel expenditures (spending by American tourists) and transportation, as well as other services, such as the purchase of insurance.

Although services are called "invisible," they affect the demand for currency just as physical exports and imports do. An American renting a hotel room in Paris must pay for it in francs, just as an American merchant who imports gloves from France must pay for this purchase in francs. On the other hand, when foreigners buy services from American companies, the result is much the same as if they were buying American computer components or drill presses. An Italian company leasing an American oil tanker pays for this service in dollars, as must a German museum buying insurance on its paintings from an American insurance company.

Investment income is also included in the general category of invisible trade. For many years Americans have invested heavily abroad. Each year, dividends or interest payments are earned on these investments. For example, assume that an American corporation has set up a French subsidiary and has invested $1 million in its plant and equipment. If successful, the French company will pay dividends to its American parent company each year. Since the French subsidiary sells its products for francs and earns its profits in francs, it will have to exchange francs for dollars in order to pay a dividend in dollars to the American owners. In other words, a foreign corporation that sends dividend or interest payments to an American firm requires dollars in much the same way as a foreign buyer who is importing American merchandise.

The situation is reversed of course, when foreigners hold United States securities. Dating from the time when they were financing the early growth of American industry, British interests have held substantial blocks of United States securities. When American firms pay dividends on these securities to British investors, a demand for British currency is created, similar to that resulting from direct imports of British goods into the United States.

Unilateral-transfers account

The unilateral-transfers account records international transfers of resources that involve no exchange or return; they are gifts. Private remittances and transfers include gifts from United States residents to friends and relatives living abroad. For example, an Irish immigrant might send $500 to her mother in Ireland, or an American father might send his daughter $100 while she is spending a year of study in Italy. Government unilateral transfers include all government remittances and grants (excluding military) paid to foreigners.

Government pensions and transfers that appear here include money flows from the United States to foreigners and Americans living abroad who are entitled to Social Security, government-employee retirement programs, and other transfer payments. Also included are money flows for educational exchanges, foreign research programs, and other similar expenditures from which no monetary return is expected. United States government economic grants, part of the American foreign aid program, are also considered unilateral transfers. The balance on unilateral transfers is expected to be negative in economically advanced nations. This means that gifts have flowed out of the United States and as a result have been recorded as debits in United States balance of payments.

Capital account

Private capital flows include the loans and investments that individuals and businesses make abroad. For example, an American company might build a plant in Brazil; or an American individual might deposit dollars in a Swiss bank. This group of accounts is divided into two parts: long-term and short-term capital flows.

Long-term capital flows
Long-term capital flows are expected to remain in the foreign country for more than one year. Private long-term capital flows include direct foreign investments in the United States, purchases of foreign securities, and other investments, which include lending activities. Here the actual investments are listed as debits since such transactions involve money flows out of the United States. Foreign investments in the United States are, of course, recorded as credits.

Short-term flows
Short-term capital flows are expected to remain in a foreign country for less than a year. In the case of flows to the United States, these include purchases of American stocks by foreigners, deposits of foreign funds in American banks, and foreign investment in Treasury bills and other money-market securities. In addition to these more speculative investments, an important portion of the short-term capital flow to the United states consists of dollars held by foreign central banks as part of their reserves.

To a certain extent, official United States government action can regulate the movement of short-term funds; but the government will take such action only when it is deemed desirable in the light of its other economic objectives. If the monetary authorities can be persuaded to maintain high short-term domestic interest rates, foreign funds will flow to the United States. At a time when the domestic economy is overheated, action by the Federal Reserve to keep short-term interest rates high can, in effect, kill two birds with one stone. The high interest rates will help to slow down the economy and will attract foreign depositors, thus reducing the balance-of-payments deficit. On the other hand, at a time when the economy is faltering and facing serious domestic unemployment, high interest rates that might attract foreign deposits would also tend to slow economic recovery.

United States balance of payments
We have now examined the principal accounts under which the international transactions of the United States are recorded, and which together reflect the monetary relationship between the nation and the rest of the world. The completion of the United States balance-of-payments position, by definition, requires that the final result be in balance.

Refer again to *Table 38.1*, which lists the balances of the three accounts, producing a total debit entry of $-41.7 billion for 1978. Correcting for statistical errors and omissions,* we see that in 1978 the United States had a balance-of-payments deficit of $-30.3 billion; that is, more dollars flowed out of the United States in the form of import purchases, grants, investments abroad, and other capital outflows than came into the country as a result of exports, foreign-investment income, and other capital inflows. When the United States has a net debit balance or deficit, the imbalance must be settled by some form of international payment. There are two ways the United States might finance this $30.3 billion deficit. One way would be for the government to sell a portion of either its gold stock or some other form of foreign currency it holds in reserve. In other words, a foreign country would accept gold or a stable currency, such as the German mark, in payment for goods and services it sold to the United States.

---

*The entry for errors and omissions (statisical discrepancy) stands for the net difference between all known debits and all known credits and is included simply for double-entry bookkeeping purposes. Although in *Table 38.1* the entry appears to be very large, it becomes less so when considered in the context of the entire balance of payments. The errors and omissions could have occurred in various parts of all three of the principal accounts, since each represents a highly complicated collection of data over an extensive area of economic activity.

The United States, however, has chosen a second course of action. It has asked foreign countries to hold that amount of dollars that represents the deficit. What this means is that in the eyes of foreign governments, the United States is a good credit risk; they are willing to hold dollars because they know the United States will not renege on the loan. (Furthermore, a foreign country can earn interest on dollars it holds, but not on gold.) Thus *Table 38.1* shows that United States payments were balanced in 1978 because on the one hand, foreign countries held $34 billion, while on the other hand, the United States held $3.8 billion in gold and other reserves and owed the rest ($30.2 billion).

Summary

■ This chapter discusses international-currency exchange rates and the balance of payments, two important determinants of the level of international-trade transactions.

■ The exchange rate is the price at which one currency may be traded for another. Until the 1930s, most countries operated on the gold standard, with their currencies valued in terms of and redeemable in gold. The gold standard had the advantage of creating stable exchange rates and providing an automatic, self-correcting mechanism for any nation in a situation of trade disequilibrium. The major disadvantage of the gold standard was its strong link to the domestic money supply; an excess of imports could lead to deflation and restriction of output, or an excess of exports to inflation. Under the gold-exchange standard, which was adopted by most of the major trading nations after World War II, foreign currencies were exchanged at fixed rates based on their value in gold or dollars, but most currencies were not domestically convertible into gold. Thus gold inflows and outflows caused by international imbalances in most cases did not affect the domestic money supply, and any adverse effects were contained in particular import or export sectors of the economy.

■ Exchange rates may also be set through the market forces of supply and demand. This system, a modified version of which is in current operation, involves floating exchange rates. The advantage of floating exchange rates is that equilibrium between exports and imports can be established without necessitating nationwide inflation or deflation. The disadvantage of floating rates is that prices of imports and exports may change frequently. For short-term transactions, this danger can be compensated for by buying a futures contract for foreign currency, but the instability of exchange rates still poses a problem for long-term capital investment.

■ A nation's balance-of-payments statement may be summarized in three basic categories: the goods-and-services account, the unilateral-transfers account, and the capital account. The goods-and-services account includes the imports and exports of merchandise (the figures for which are frequently called the balance of trade), military transactions, and the "invisible transactions" of service costs and the return on foreign investments. Unilateral transfers include both private gifts to individuals and government grants for which no remuneration is expected. The capital account includes loans and investments that individuals and businesses make abroad. Short-term capital flows (less than one year) for the United States include purchases of American stocks by foreigners, deposits of foreign funds in American banks, foreign investments in Treasury bonds, and dollars held by foreign banks as part of their reserves.

■ The balance-of-payments statement for the United States in 1978 showed a $30.3 billion deficit from all three accounts, the highest ever. Such deficits can be paid off in gold or in a stable currency; the United States has chosen to ask foreign countries to hold an amount of dollars equal to the deficit, and other countries are willing to accept the United States as a good credit risk.

Key Terms

exchange rate

gold standard

gold points

arbitrage

gold-exchange standard

International Monetary Fund (IMF)

floating exchange rates

futures contract

balance-of-payments statement

balance of trade

Review & Discussion

1. If an American wine merchant wishes to import French wine, in what currency will he or she probably pay the French exporter? How would the exchange of United States dollars for French francs normally be handled?

2. What is an exchange rate? How does it influence the level of exports and imports?

3. How would a nation on the gold standard define its currency? What are the advantages of the gold standard? How would imbalances of trade be corrected under the gold standard?

4. What are the advantages and disadvantages of the gold-exchange standard?

5. Describe the workings of floating exchange rates. How would an imbalance of trade be corrected? What are the advantages and disadvantages of floating rates?

6. John Maynard Keynes is reported to have done more to help Britain in World War I than any other single person through his ability to raise enormous sums in currency speculation. How would it be possible to make money specu-

lating in currency under the gold standard? With floating exchange rates?

7. In a balance-of-payments statement, what items are included in the goods-and-services account? What are the "invisible transactions"? How could short-term capital investments keep the demand for dollars up? How can the Fed attract short-term investment from abroad? What will be the effect on the domestic American economy if the Fed follows policies designed to attract short-term foreign investors?

8. What was the balance-of-payments situation in the United States in 1978? Which accounts were primarily responsible for the overall deficit? How did the United States settle its deficit?

Chapter 39

Current Problems in International Economics

What to look for in this chapter

What have been the major developments in international trade and finance since World War II?

What has been the general trend in tariff patterns in the postwar period? Why is there increasing pressure in the United States for protectionist measures now?

What steps have been taken to stabilize international reserves since the end of the gold standard?

How serious is the decline in the value of the United States dollar?

What factors influence the international economic outlook for the 1980s?

As World War II drew to a close and the victorious Allies contemplated the postwar world, they were very much aware of the instabilities which an unsatisfactory foreign-trade situation had contributed to prewar conditions. The growth of aggressive nationalism had been abetted, in part, by the discriminatory controls that almost all nations had instituted during the 1930s; these controls favored domestic production and encouraged exports. Moreover, the collapse of worldwide foreign trade—which declined from $60 billion in 1928 to $25 billion in 1938—had worsened the depressed economic conditions and widespread unemployment. As a result, the nations of the world were now eager to provide a favorable economic climate and to set up the mechanisms needed to foster international trade.

In this chapter, we shall discuss the major developments in world trade and international finance in the postwar world, with special emphasis on those problems still confronting us today.

HISTORICAL DEVELOPMENTS IN INTERNATIONAL TRADE

1914 to 1930

During World War I (1914 to 1918), there was a tremendous demand on the part of the warring European nations for supplies from the United States. Since the world was still on the gold standard and since the European nations had only limited goods to export in exchange, their purchases were paid for by transfers of gold to the United States and by American loans. During the 1920s, world trade continued to be strong. American sales and investments abroad grew, with private American lenders providing dollars for these purchases through loans to foreign governments and businesses.

The thirties

During the 1930s, however, world trade declined significantly. Depressed economic conditions around the world reduced total demand for all goods, both domestic and foreign. And because foreign borrowers were no longer able to obtain loans in the United States, this drop in world demand increased. As a result of massive defaults on the part of both foreign governments and private borrowers during the 1930s, private lending to foreigners from American sources disappeared completely.* Moreover, monetary uncertainties made many businesses unwilling to undertake international transactions. For example, the German mark became completely worthless because of runaway inflation, and the English pound increased in worth. The fear of such currency changes kept many investors and merchants from making long-term commitments when dealing in foreign currencies.

The drop in the level of world trade was accelerated by the actions of individual governments. Each nation was concerned primarily with its own economic problems and looked to changes in foreign trade as a way of expanding the demand for its domestic products. Governments attempted to reduce imports, assuming that this would provide larger domestic markets for home producers. At the same time, they tried to expand exports in the hope that new jobs could be created in exporting industries. In theory, such policies could help any *one* nation increase its domestic production levels; but when practiced simultaneously by all countries, the net effect was further to reduce total international trade.

The Hawley-Smoot Tariff,† passed in 1930 in the United States, is an example of the kind of economic protectionism practiced by most countries during the thirties. With this tariff the ratio of duties collected to imports was the highest in more than 100 years.

World War II

During World War II, the worldwide demand for goods once again increased spectacularly, reflecting military needs and full employment in most of the industrialized world. Since there was now a worldwide shortage of most commodities, attention everywhere was focused on increasing production, rather than on protecting domestic industries. Production efforts were assigned to each Allied nation according to the principle of

---

*In 1928, American capital outflow abroad was over $1.5 billion; by 1931, not only had such foreign investment ended but there was a net *inflow* of $450 million.

†When the Hawley-Smoot Tariff was proposed, almost all United States economists were publicly opposed to it, recognizing that it would be impossible for American exports to expand if foreigners were no longer able to obtain dollars by selling their goods in the United States. They believed that the new tariff, instead of protecting American producers by increasing their markets, would reduce potential sales. In later years, the Hawley-Smoot Tariff, because of its high rates and the economic inconsistencies it embodied, became known to generations of economics students as the "Holy Smoke" tariff.

comparative advantage, with each country turning out what it could produce most cheaply. As a result, total world trade grew.

For the United States, there were two especially important economic consequences of the war years. First, there was a flow of gold to the United States from abroad, as foreigners used gold to pay for purchases or sent gold to the United States for safety. And second, the United States experienced an expansion of total industrial capacity relative to the rest of the world, because, with the exception of Hawaii, production was never interrupted by enemy attacks.

Early postwar years: the European Recovery Program

The immediate postwar goal was to stimulate world trade again. Outside the United States, there was a shortage of productive capacity and consumer goods as a result of the destruction caused by the war, and most foreign nations no longer had significant amounts of gold or dollars that they could use to buy the needed goods or capital equipment from the United States. Moreover, because of their limited productive facilities, they had no way of earning dollars in the near future. This "dollar shortage" presented the postwar economic planners with a serious problem. The Bretton Woods gold-exchange standard had just been approved, and one of the keystones of the plan was stable currency prices. But if no remedial steps had been taken, the worldwide dollar shortage could have resulted in competitive bidding for the few dollars available abroad, thus sabotaging the new monetary system before it had a chance to work.

To prevent this—and also to ensure political stability in Western Europe against aggressive Russian efforts to impose communism throughout Europe—in 1948 the United States government established the European Recovery Program (also known as the "Marshall Plan") to provide foreign nations with vast supplies of the dollars they needed for postwar recovery. Much of the aid was in the form of outright grants and gifts.

The important role of these programs in first restoring and then expanding foreign productive capacity and general economic well-being cannot be overstated. It is estimated that in less than four years after its establishment, the Marshall Plan had provided over $10 billion in aid to the European nations.

REMOVAL OF TRADE BARRIERS

In addition to providing dollars abroad, the United States made a major effort to expand international trade by liberalizing the tariffs and other restrictions that had been imposed during the Depression and the war years.

Reciprocal Trade Agreements Act

An early move in the direction of tariff reduction that laid the groundwork for later agreements was the Reciprocal Trade Agreements Act of 1934. It permitted the president of the United States to recognize tariff cuts with individual foreign nations that were willing, in exchange, to lower their tariffs on American goods. These arrangements were bilateral; they were negotiated separately with each individual trading partner.

General Agreement on Tariffs and Trade

A much more comprehensive postwar arrangement was envisioned and finally came to fruition in 1947, when 23 major nations signed the General Agreement on Tariffs and Trade (GATT). Today, GATT membership includes most of the large trading nations of the world. Unlike the earlier Reciprocal Trade Agreements, it involves a multinational approach through which all members enjoy all benefits; any tariff reduction arrived at between any two members must be extended to all members. Moreover, each signatory agreed to grant to every other signatory any concession it might make in the future to a highly favored non-signatory nation; this is referred to as the "most-favored-nation" clause. The GATT code also attempts to increase the volume of international trade by outlawing the use of import quotas except under special circumstances. In addition, GATT provides channels through which trade disputes can be settled between member nations.

Trade Expansion Act

In 1962, Congress, stimulated by the success of the early GATT tariff reductions, passed the Trade Expansion Act (Kennedy Act), which gave the president new powers to lower or eliminate many tariffs under GATT. The president could reduce all tariffs by at least 50 percent if other nations agreed to similar cuts. Under the authority granted by this act, the "Kennedy Round" of tariff cuts was negotiated in 1967. It involved drastic tariff reductions to be effected in a series of five annual stages, from 1968 to 1972.

Advocates of tariff cuts believe that such reciprocal reductions provide important benefits to many areas of the American economy. American consumers benefit because of lower prices on imports. American business is stimulated in two ways: (1) lower foreign tariffs give American producers access to new foreign markets; and (2) because American manufacturers can buy foreign raw materials at lower costs, they are able to lower the prices of their finished goods and can thus compete more effectively in foreign markets.

However, the creators of the Trade Expansion Act recognized that despite these overall advantages, certain American business enterprises and workers were bound to be hurt by the tariff reductions, at least in the short run. The act therefore provided "trade adjustment assistance" for these groups. Workers who lost their jobs because of increased imports from abroad could request allotments for vocational training or relocation allowances. Businesses could obtain tax relief and loans to modernize their plants so that they could compete with the foreign imports. The shoe industry in New England, for example, used these provisions of the Kennedy Act in response to a surge of shoe imports from Italy, Spain, and the Far East.

Recent United States tariff policy

The primary direction of United States tariff policy since the Hawley-Smoot Tariff of 1930 has been toward reducing trade barriers. In recent years, however, special-interest groups have been lobbying for increasing protection. Requests for protection from foreign imports have poured in from producers of electronics, textiles, automobiles, and steel. While these groups do not dispute the overall advantages of free trade, they claim that foreign governments have subsidized their inefficient domestic industries to make them competitive on the world market. In addition, some companies have been guilty of "dumping" in American markets—that is, deliberately selling goods at artificially low prices in an attempt to capture American customers. Japanese manufacturers of televisions and steel, for example, have been accused by American companies of selling below cost in the United States and making up such losses by raising prices in their own markets. While dumping may mean that Americans can purchase goods at lower costs in the United States marketplace, it also presents a major problem in terms of fewer (or lost) jobs for American workers. Congress has recently taken steps to provide protection for American producers of steel and color television sets through tariffs and other means but the trend is a dangerous one. To the extent that the charges against foreign companies and governments are true, the proper economic move would be to dissuade them from such practices rather than to increase the level of protection in the United States. It has been estimated that "the incremental cost to consumers of a 12 percent quota, or an additional 3.5 percent tariff ... is about $1 billion per year."*

While the economic arguments for freer trade rather than greater protection are clear, political realities may lead to even more restrictive policies by the United States and its trading partners.

The Common Market

A major effort toward liberalizing trade has been the establishment of "trade" or "customs unions" among groups of European nations. One such group is the *European Economic Community* **(EEC)**, or Common Market. The original group was formed in 1957 by Belgium, France, Italy, Luxembourg, West Germany, and the Netherlands. *The objective of the EEC was the gradual elimination of tariffs and quotas among the members, so that goods and capital could move freely from one country to another.*

The EEC has not been without problems, however. Differing growth rates and different rates of inflation among member countries have caused some unevenness in trade flows. Italy's balance of trade within the European community was so disturbing that it actually restricted imports from the EEC in 1974. The "wine wars" occurred when wine-producing members felt their industries were being threatened. The Common Agricultural Policy (CAP) has raised the price of agricultural goods throughout much of the market because it protects inefficient farmers from more efficient external producers. In effect, consumers are subsidizing agriculture by paying higher prices than would be necessary if free trade with non-European countries were allowed.

Despite its problems, the EEC has grown and prospered since its beginning. The admission of

---

*Staff Report on the United States Steel Industry and Its International Rivals: Trends and Factors Determining International Competitiveness, Bureau of Economics, Federal Trade Commission (Washington, D.C.: United States Government Printing Office, 1977), p. 564.

Great Britain was opposed for many years by Charles DeGaulle of France, but entry was offered in the spring of 1971 and formally accepted in 1973, as was the admission of Ireland and Denmark. Greece was admitted in the spring of 1979, and it is probable that several other European countries will eventually join—perhaps Austria, Portugal, Spain, Sweden, Switzerland, and Turkey. A European Parliament was directly elected in 1979, and a single European Party may emerge. Plans are well under way for a single currency called a European Monetary Unit (EMU). All of these events could make the Common Market one of the most powerful free-trade areas in the world with a population larger than that of the United States and a GNP almost as large.

Is the success of the Common Market a threat to the rest of the world? The answer to that question depends on the extent to which the EEC restricts imports from other countries. The Common Agricultural Policy, for instance, which protects European farmers, hurts American agriculture badly. On the other hand, increased trade among the EEC partners and the resultant increased efficiency are to everyone's advantage. World efficiency will improve as long as the Common Market increases internal efficiency and does not retard external efficiency. However, as the income of the Community grows, there will most likely be pressure to import goods and services from abroad: much of the worldwide effect of the EEC will depend upon the willingness of European and non-European nations to negotiate lower tariffs worldwide.

HISTORICAL DEVELOPMENTS IN INTERNATIONAL FINANCE

Collapse of the gold standard

In Chapter 38, we examined the workings of the gold standard, under which international trade operated before World War I. While the gold standard was in effect, balance-of-trade disequilibria between nations were settled by shipments of gold. These gold transfers would, in turn, result in changes in domestic prices, which would then reverse the previous export-import imbalance. In the aftermath of World War I, however, there were growing imbalances among trading nations, and by the 1930s, the international and domestic economic problems of most nations had become so serious that the gold standard was no longer an acceptable mechanism. Inflations, tariffs, import quotas, and changes in domestic production patterns had upset the prewar export-import relationships among trading countries. The traditional remedy for such trade imbalances under the gold standard was internal deflation, and in the pre-World War I days, this could be accomplished, at least in part, by maintaining production levels and merely cutting prices.* However, because of the growing power of unions and the introduction of imperfectly competitive markets, it became increasingly difficult to cut prices in response to a gold outflow. Instead, domestic deflation meant production cuts and unemployment. By the 1930s governments were no longer willing or able to accept such growing unemployment as the solution to a balance-of-payments problem.

Many nations attempted to solve their balance-of-payments problems by devaluing their currencies. **Devaluation** *occurs when a nation declares the official value of its currency to be worth less in terms of gold and other currencies.* In 1932, Britain cut the gold value of the pound by about a third; similar devaluations were announced by the United States in 1934 and by most other major trading nations throughout the 1930s. However, once the public recognized the possibility of continued changes in the relative value of currencies, many opportunities for speculation in international money markets arose, and there were tremendous speculative movements of monies from one country to another, with traders "dumping" those currencies they believed would be devalued and buying the stronger ones.†

As a result, many nations were faced with gold drains resulting not only from their normal trade imbalances but also from these movements of "hot money." The "hot money" drains of the 1930s led the major trading nations to abandon the gold standard, to limit convertibility of currency into gold, and to attempt to restore trade equilibrium by rigid trade controls. However, the net result of these restrictive trade policies was disastrous. Within ten years, worldwide international trade had dropped to less than half its 1928 level.

Development of the postwar monetary system: the Bretton Woods Conference

The international monetary troubles of the thirties led to a strong desire for change. After World War II, the Allied nations agreed that a new system was needed—one that would include fixed exchange rates but at the same time provide a way of solving balance-of-payments problems without internal deflation.

The framework for the postwar gold-exchange system was developed at the Bretton Woods Conference in New Hampshire in 1944. The new monetary system was highlighted by the following four points.

☐ *Gold-exchange standard.* Each participating government agreed to establish a fixed value for its currency in terms of the United States dollar and/or gold. In actuality, each foreign currency

---

*If $MV = PQ$, and if M (gold or money supply) is reduced because of a gold outflow, then either P (price) or Q (quantity) must also fall.

†For example, a speculator who had exchanged British pounds for dollars before the 1932 devaluation, would have received $4.86 for each pound. After devaluation, when the pound was pegged at $2.80, one could buy about 1.7 pounds with his $4.86—for a profit of about 70 percent.

had a **parity value**—*an exchange or equivalency rate*—that was stated in terms of dollars. The United States dollar, in turn, had a fixed gold value. (Thus each dollar was worth 1/35 of an ounce of gold; the pound was pegged at $2.40, or 2.4 × 1/35 of an ounce of gold.) Each government pledged to maintain the stated value of its currency in the open market, and the United States agreed to buy all dollars offered to it for a fixed price of 1/35 of an ounce of gold.

☐ *Free convertibility.* Each government promised to move toward free convertibility of its currency into dollars or gold—at least for foreign-trade purposes. This meant that eventually each government would be willing, on request, to exchange its currency for dollars or gold at the stated parity.

☐ *Devaluation as the preferred method of handling long-term imbalances.* The Bretton Woods program introduced an important new concept in handling long-term basic balance-of-payments imbalances. Formerly, under the gold standard, a country faced with a persistent deficit could either deflate at home or restrict imports by controls. Now a third choice was offered—that of devaluing its currency. The government could change the parity value of its currency by 10 percent without approval of other governments; it could be changed by even more if the International Monetary Fund (IMF) agreed.

☐ *The role of the IMF.* As noted in Chapter 38, the IMF was the world monetary body created at the Bretton Woods Conference to make the new monetary system workable. Short-term, temporary imbalances were to be handled by "support operations" of domestic central banks. The price of a currency would no longer fluctuate in response to a sudden change in demand. Instead, the monetary authorities in the country would buy or sell sufficient amounts of the currency in order to maintain a stable price—within 1 percent of parity. At the time the plan was drawn up, the experts believed that worldwide gold reserves were adequate for this purpose. In addition, the IMF could supply additional backup reserves if required.

The IMF was designed to provide a central pool of currencies on which any member nation could draw when its own reserves of gold or dollars became temporarily inadequate to maintain its currency-support operations. For example, if there was a short-term seasonal or speculative run on the pound, and the Bank of England needed dollars in order to buy pounds at the support level of $2.376, it could obtain dollars from the IMF and need not repay until the crisis was over, or within a maximum of five years.

Each member nation was supplied with a certain quota of foreign currencies (called its "gold tranche") on which it could draw automatically on request. It could obtain additional funds by convincing the IMF that it was taking effective steps at home (such as fighting domestic inflation) to solve its payments imbalance.

International monetary developments after Bretton Woods

It became apparent by the late 1960s that existing gold and dollar reserves of nations were not enough to handle the increased volume of trade. In recent years, therefore, various measures have been taken in order to increase total world reserves.

Elimination of United States gold-backing requirements

Prior to 1968, the gold that the United States had stored at Fort Knox served two purposes. Some of it was required, under United States law, to supply a 25 percent gold backing for the paper dollars that the Federal Reserve printed. The rest was available to serve as international monetary reserves. In 1968, Congress repealed the 25 percent gold-backing requirement, so that all of the gold could be used for international-reserve purposes.

Introduction of the two-tier system

One reason for the inadequacy of monetary reserves was the leakage of gold from the monetary system. Legitimate trade customers (jewelers, dentists, electronics fabricators), as well as speculators and hoarders, accumulated gold supplies by redeeming their paper currencies for gold.* Once in private hands, this gold was no longer available for use as reserves in settling international trade balances. In February 1968 alone, the United States lost about 3 percent of its total gold reserves through such activities, thus further reducing the reserves remaining available to settle routine trade imbalances.

To correct this problem, the IMF members agreed to the introduction in 1968 of a two-tier gold system, a system to keep the world's current monetary gold from being further depleted by speculation and hoarding.

The official tier
All IMF members agreed to keep their present gold reserves for use in settlement of international trade balances only. No longer would they sell gold to outsiders; gold would move only between governments and only at the official IMF parity price. Moreover, IMF members would no longer buy gold from outsiders at guaranteed prices. For example, if the Bank of England accumulated $35 million in the course of its activities in stabilizing the pound, the United States would exchange the dollars for 1 million ounces of gold on request. However, the United States would not sell gold for dollars to private foreign buyers, nor would it buy gold from any seller except as part of an international-reserve transaction. Only one nation was exempted from the selling prohibition. Because of the importance of gold production to its economy, South Africa was permitted to continue to sell gold in the open market.

The outside or free-market tier
All gold not part of the official tier supply and all newly minted gold would be traded in the open market, as would any other commodity. This gold no longer had any potential monetary value, since all IMF members had promised not to buy any of it for their reserves. Its price would depend on nonmonetary factors. For example, a large increase in the demand for gold to be used in jewelry or transistor components could send its price zooming up. On the other hand, the opening of a major new gold mine could result in an oversupply and a drop in price.

What did the proponents of the two-tier system plan to accomplish? First, they hoped that further attrition of world gold monetary reserves would be eliminated, since all participating nations had agreed not to permit any of their gold to leave the system in the future. Second, they assumed that speculation in gold would be discouraged, now that monetary authorities would no longer provide a guaranteed $35 an ounce floor for private sellers.

Problems with the two-tier system
Unfortunately, the installation of the two-tier system solved neither the reserve problem nor the speculation problem. Because of the continuing drain on United States gold reserves caused by the growing United States balance-of-payments deficits from 1969 on, speculators became convinced that the United States would be forced eventually to increase the value of its dwindling gold reserves by increasing the price of gold. There was also a growing temptation for certain small-nation central banks to ignore their IMF two-tier commitment—that is, to exchange dollars for gold at its official price and then to resell the gold in the open-market tier for much more. Such sales

---

*Although private citizens in the United States were unable to redeem paper dollars for gold or to hold gold until 1974, many foreign governments (for example, France) continued to permit their citizens to do so.

represented leakages of gold from the official reserve tier and a further reduction of total world monetary reserves.

THE INTERNATIONAL MONETARY SYSTEM IN THE 1970s

Adjusting to balance-of-payments disequilibria: the "dirty float"

As a result of increased pressure on the dollar, it became apparent that basic changes would have to be made in the international monetary system. Some system for adjusting to fundamental balance-of-payments disequilibria was required. In the spring of 1971, the German government announced that it would no longer sell German marks for United States dollars. By midsummer 1971, waves of speculative selling hit the dollar in Europe and Japan, and as the supply of official United States gold holdings fell, it began to look as if the United States might run out of gold. President Nixon solved the immediate problem on August 15 by announcing that the United States would no longer convert foreign-held dollars into gold. Immediately, under IMF rules, other nations were no longer obligated to use their own reserves to keep their currencies at former fixed par values. The Bretton Woods agreement was dead.

The coffin was nailed shut with the Smithsonian agreement of December 1971. The two major conditions of the agreement were (1) the value of all major currencies would be realigned, resulting in an effective devaluation of the dollar by 7.9 percent, and (2) members of the IMF would reconsider the entire international monetary system at some future date. In January 1973, the new rates had to be abandoned as speculative pressure once again mounted against the dollar. The "dirty float" was initiated whereby the values of currencies were allowed to fluctuate freely against one another while central banks maintained the right to intervene when necessary. This new system was officially accepted as the new international monetary system with the Jamaica agreement of 1976. This document accepted the "dirty float" as the major means of adjusting to balance-of-payments disequilibria.

Providing international liquidity: special drawing rights

With the acceptance of the Jamaica agreement, governments signaled their intention to solve the two basic problems of the international monetary system—adjusting to balance-of-payments disequilibria, and providing sufficient international liquidity to meet the standards of an ever-increasing volume of trade. Thus, most major IMF nations agreed to the creation of **special drawing rights (SDRs),** *a form of international reserves credited to the accounts of IMF members that can be used to settle international balances.* SDRs can be created in any amount approved by 85 percent of the member nations in amounts roughly proportional to each nation's original IMF contribution.

SDRs were designed to be used to settle international balances, just as gold or dollar reserves had been used in the past. For example, consider a situation in which the United States has a balance-of-payments deficit and the German central bank has accumulated extra dollars it wishes to dispose of. The United States could use its SDRs to exchange for the dollars. In theory, such an exchange would be perfectly satisfactory to the Germans, since SDRs are, by agreement, universally acceptable among IMF members in settlement of international balances. This means that the Germans could use these same SDRs in the future for their own settlement purposes.

On paper, the SDR (often called "paper gold") represented an effective new reserve for settlement of international monetary balances. Unlike gold, which cannot be expanded as the volume of world trade increases, SDRs could be created when required. Moreover, being exclusively an international-reserve unit, SDRs did not possess the speculative characteristics of gold. Nonetheless, there was a certain ambivalance toward SDRs, even on the part of sophisticated central bankers, who seemed to prefer gold for international settlements when offered the choice.

In effect, however, that choice became unavailable with the 1971 announcement that the United States would no longer convert dollars into gold. Since then a series of international agreements have brought about changes in the management of the system.

A widening of the basis for calculating the transactions value of SDRs to include the currencies of 16 IMF countries was adopted in July 1974. It was further agreed that the currencies to be included and their relative weights would vary with their importance in world trade. (It is interesting to note that the United States dollar makes up 33 percent of the value of the SDR, and that the currencies of Saudi Arabia and Iran entered the group of 16 in July 1978.)

The Jamaica agreement further enhanced the position of the SDR by institutionalizing the demonetization of gold—governments agreed that gold would no longer be used to settle official international debts. Thus, the IMF became an international central bank with the power to create reserves for the system. As long as central banks are willing to accept SDRs, the liquidity problem will be solved.

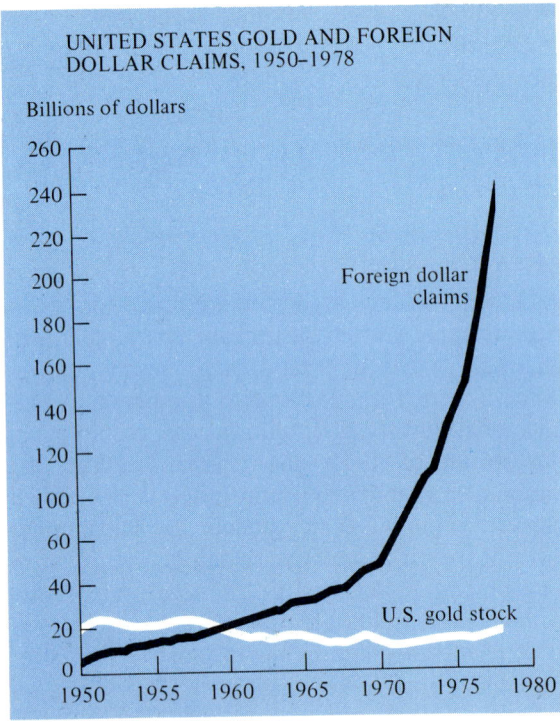

SOURCE: Federal Reserve Bulletin.

Fig. 39.1
Since 1960, serious balance of payments deficits have depleted United States gold reserves and resulted in huge foreign dollar claims. In the past several years alone, foreign dollar claims have risen almost exponentially.

THE UPS AND DOWNS OF THE AMERICAN DOLLAR

In the period since 1945, the American dollar has taken an uncertain course. The early post–World War II era was characterized by a scramble for dollars as foreign buyers attempted to purchase goods and services from the United States, which was one of the few major industrial powers whose economy had not been destroyed by the war. By late 1978, the situation had reversed itself, and foreigners were unloading dollars as fast as possible. What caused the sharp reversal? Should we worry about it? If so, what can we do about it? These are a few of the questions many Americans have been asking themselves about the decline of the dollar.

A declining dollar has both positive and negative effects on the American economy. To the extent that it makes exports more competitive

TEN COUNTRIES WHOSE CURRENCIES HAVE APPRECIATED MOST COMPARED TO THE UNITED STATES DOLLAR SINCE 1970			
Country (currency)	Units per United States dollar—1970	Units per United States dollar—1978	Percentage appreciation
Switzerland	4.3160	1.7020	60.57
Japan	357.6000	188.2000	47.37
West Germany	3.6480	2.0065	45.00
Austria	25.8200	14.6300	43.34
Belgium	49.6800	31.6500	36.29
Denmark	7.4880	5.4945	26.62
Norway	7.1300	5.2850	25.88
Saudi Arabia	4.5000	3.3900	24.67
France	5.5200	4.3637	20.95
Sweden	5.136	4.4515	13.78

abroad and imports less competitive in the United States, the declining dollar should improve the American balance of trade. Thus, a slight devaluation can sometimes be a good thing. However, when the dollar's value beings to plummet, a speculative rush on dollars can have detrimental and far-reaching effects on the American economy. A little historical background will help provide a better insight into these effects.

Dollar crises

In the last 20 years, the dollar has passed through various cycles caused by severe balance-of-payments disequilibria. The United States balance of payments has shown a deficit far more frequently than a surplus during this time period and the transfer of gold to foreigners has covered only a small amount of the deficit. As *Fig. 39.1* shows, most of the deficit has been handled by persuading foreign buyers to hold their surplus dollars. Thus, as the balance-of-payments deficit has worsened, the number of foreign dollar claims has skyrocketed.

Efforts to solve the balance-of-payments problem

The 1971 crisis has been explained above, and, as we mentioned, the dollar was devalued by 7.9 percent at the time. In addition, the band around parity within which a currency is allowed to fluctuate without market intervention was widened. Under the previous Bretton Woods agreement, a country was required to keep its currency within 1 percent of parity—or within a total range of 2 percent. After the 1971 change, exchange rates could shift 2¼ percent above or below the fixed par value without market intervention—an overall range of 4½ percent.

Fundamental as these steps were, however, they by no means solved the United States balance-of-payments problem. In 1971, the United States imported $2.7 billion more than it exported, and the deficit increased still more in the next year, to $6.9 billion. Even with the wider range permitted for fluctuation, the balance of payments continued to run a chronic deficit, forcing heavy intervention by foreign monetary authorities. Therefore, in February 1973, the United States again devalued the dollar—raising the official price of gold to just over $42 an ounce—and other countries again floated their currencies against the dollar.

The second devaluation of the dollar did help to ease the United States balance-of-payments condition. With the dollar devalued, American exports became cheaper, allowing the trade balance to climb to a slight surplus in 1973 and the official-reserve transactions balance to show a smaller deficit. American economic troubles were not over, however. The official-reserve transactions balance began to fall again in 1974, and the trade balance plunged back into a deficit of almost $6 billion.

By 1977, the balance of payments was again in deficit, with a larger deficit in 1978. By mid-1978, the value of the dollar had declined to record lows against most major currencies, and the decline continued through October of that year. Initially, government officials had taken a stance of benign neglect, realizing that some depreciation of the dollar helped the United States to maintain a competitive position in world trade. As the outcry from its trading partners increased, however, and as the oil-producing nations began to make threats about increasing prices for oil to offset the declining value of the dollar, it became clear that some steps would have to be taken. The dollar was declining so rapidly that some people thought it might eventually become worthless.

On November 1, 1978, President Carter announced a "rescue package" for the dollar, which consisted of moves to raise interest rates in the United States in an attempt to attract foreign capital. In addition, the Federal Reserve Bank borrowed foreign currencies from other central banks and the IMF to buy dollars on the world market, thereby raising the price of the dollar. Finally, the Treasury expanded its sales of gold to foreign buyers to reduce the trade deficit. These three moves caused a frantic buying spree, and the dollar skyrocketed against other currencies. In the following months it tended to level off a bit, but, for the time being, the dollar had been saved.

Causes of the 1978 decline

What brought about the need for the rescue operation? Several events and policies influenced the decline. First, the massive American aid program called the Marshall Plan enabled the Western European nations to rebuild their economies, and in the process it also sent billions of United States dollars overseas. The Vietnam war, financed by large increases in the money supply, had a similar effect. In addition, the United States economy was growing more rapidly than were the economies of its major trading partners, causing imports from those countries to grow faster than United States exports to them. Another factor of major importance was the increasing dependence of the United States on imported oil. As the price of oil increased (quadrupling in 1974), the value of imports to the United States also increased.

The above were the major, historical causes of the 1978 decline, but some of the more immediate causes deserve discussion because they illustrate the effect of psychological factors on the value of a currency. In the fall of 1978, the economy was suffering from a difficult coal strike. Americans continued to consume large amounts of foreign oil, and the inflation rate was approaching 9 percent. These situations were viewed by foreign dollar holders as contributing to the weakening of the dollar. In addition, President Carter had experienced little success in persuading foreign governments to use expansionary monetary and fiscal policies to speed up their economies and his attempts to solve the energy crisis and control inflation were seen as too little, too late. Finally, many government officials had indicated their unwillingness to support the dollar. As a result of all these factors, speculators envisioned a continuous dollar decline, and they began to sell. The selling binge gathered force, and the situation quickly reached crisis proportions.

The interesting thing about the "rescue package" of November 1 is that it did very little to solve the underlying problems of rapid inflation, oil imports, uneven growth rates of the world economies, or the huge number of dollars held by foreigners. What President Carter did was convince the market that the United States was committed to a strong dollar, and that the administration was prepared to take strong and difficult steps to defend it. By making this commitment, he reversed the psychology of the speculators. However, while the short-term effect was positive, the long-term effect will depend upon the solution to the more fundamental problems of the American economy.

THE INTERNATIONAL ECONOMIC OUTLOOK FOR THE 1980s

Fundamental changes have occurred in the international economic order since the days of Bretton Woods, and they will have important implications for the world economy of the 1980s. Some of them are summarized below.

Petrodollars

Along with the increasing dependence of much of the industrialized world on oil from OPEC has come tremendous financial clout by oil-producing nations. Accumulations of vast amounts of *dollars from the sale of OPEC oil*—**petrodollars**—have given the OPEC nations a great deal of influence in international financial markets. A major problem has been in recycling these petrodollars. If oil producers were to hold the dollars, rather than spend them, unemployment in oil-importing countries could result. Perhaps more important, a decision by OPEC members to accept some other currency and to sell their dollars could have destabilizing effects on world currency markets. Fortunately, this is not likely to occur since it is in the interests of those who hold dollars to maintain the value of their dollars.

East-West trade

The 1970s saw an emergence of expanded trade between the Western countries and the communist nations. The "spirit of detente" with Russia and the recognition of China by the United States may lead to a new era in United States trade. The potential economic advantages to both groups are significant—Russia and China have huge deposits of natural resources (including oil), and the United States has technology and expertise that are much needed by the communist nations. The political difficulties, of course, are also significant and will have to be surmounted before extensive trade relations can develop.

The emerging nations

In 1945, the world was divided into colonial powers and colonies. Since that time, most of those colonies have attained their independence and are seeking a position of equality with the industrialized world. Rapid industrial expansion, financed to a large extent by foreign aid, is the goal of many of these new nations. For others, the daily survival of their citizens is a more immediate concern. In any event, this group represents a new force in the international economic order that is already emerging as a commercial rival to the advanced economies.

Japan

It is becoming more obvious that the economic miracle that has taken place in Japan since World War II is based largely on its massive volume of exports. This has caused continuous friction between American producers and the Japanese. The main areas of concern are the alleged "unfair" trade practices of Japanese firms and the Japanese government, such as dumping, export subsidies, and tariffs imposed on American products. These problems are likely to come under closer scrutiny as the United States attempts to correct its fundamental balance-of-payments difficulties.

Gold, the dollar, and SDRs
As the 1970s saw the gradual decline of gold as an international currency, it is likely that the 1980s will see the decline of the importance of the dollar. Few financial officials in the United States will regret this. As SDRs and the European Monetary Unit gain acceptance, a great deal of unnecessary pressure will be lifted from American policymakers. Providing the "proper" amount of liquidity in the form of international reserves for the world is a difficult task and a risky business. Many would claim that the disadvantages far outweigh the advantages.

The changes that have occurred offer the potential for long-term political and economic stability on an international level. The necessity and opportunity for cooperation among central banks and governments is greater than at any time since Bretton Woods. The outcome will depend upon the ability of policymakers to exploit those opportunities.

Summary

■ This chapter examines the major developments in international trade and finance since World War II and surveys the problems and prospects facing the United States and other major trading nations today.

■ During the Depression of the 1930s, international trade declined sharply, major currencies suffered from instability, and most nations embarked on a course of extreme protectionism. During World War II, protection and trade increased significantly, particularly for the United States. Immediately after the war, the Marshall Plan aided European recovery with a massive inflow of American dollars, and barriers to trade were reduced. The General Agreement on Tariffs and Trade (1947) provided a multinational arrangement for tariff reduction, expanding "most-favored-nation" status to include all major trading nations. The 1962 Trade Expansion Act gave the president authority to negotiate further reductions, increasing American access to foreign markets and to stocks of lower-priced raw materials. The act also recognized the government's responsibility to assist particular industries and groups of workers adversely affected by increased foreign competition. By the late 1970s, however, pressure mounted in the United States for protectionist measures to benefit certain major industries (electronics, textiles, steel, automobiles) which claimed they were being unfairly victimized by foreign dumping and the subsidizing of inefficient producers by their governments. The growth of the Common Market in Europe promises an increase in world productive efficiency as long as it does not erect barriers to external trade efficiencies.

■ In the 1930s, countries with balance-of-payments deficits frequently devalued their currencies, leading to considerable speculation in international currencies. The rigid trade controls imposed to deal with this problem resulted in a contraction of trade. The 1944 Bretton Woods Conference attempted to stabilize world trade and finance by establishing fixed parity values for all currencies, convertibility in dollars or gold, by stressing devaluation as the preferred method of handling long-term imbalances, and by giving a central role to the International Monetary Fund. By the 1960s, it became clear that the gold and dollar reserves of nations were not sufficient to handle the growing volume of world trade. In 1968, the United States eliminated its gold backing of paper currency so that all of its gold reserves could be used for international purposes. The IMF established a two-tier system for gold: governments pledged to use their gold reserves only for settling international trade balances, and the rest of the privately-held gold supply was allowed to have its price determined on a free market.

■ In 1971, the United States announced that it would no longer convert dollars into gold. As a response to continuing problems in the 1970s, the Jamaica agreement (1976) recognized that currency values should be determined freely on the international market, with national central banks able to intervene if necessary to shore up a particular currency. The IMF created a new category of reserve, Special Drawing Rights, thus taking on an important role as an international central bank with the ability to solve liquidity problems, as long as national central banks universally recognize the SDRs.

■ From its extremely strong position right after World War II, the United States dollar declined steadily in value against other currency, and by 1978 this had become a serious concern both for the United States' major trading partners and the OPEC nations. The "rescue package" instituted by President Carter in 1978 included high interest rates in the United States to attract foreign capital, borrowing of currency from foreign governments in order to buy dollars, and expanded gold sales to reduce the balance-of-payments deficit. These steps helped to counter the negative psychological climate surrounding the decline of the dollar, but the long-run solution requires addressing more fundamental economic problems.

■ The international economic outlook for the 1980s is shaped by several new factors: the large quantities of petrodollars held by the OPEC nations; increased trade with communist countries; the emergence of demands by developing nations; friction between the United States and Japan because of Japan's export-based economy; and the diminished significance of the dollar as an international reserve currency.

Key Terms

European Economic Community (EEC)

devaluation

parity value

Special Drawing Rights (SDRs)

petrodollars

Review & Discussion

1. What were the major international economic problems created during the Depression of the 1930s? What was the state of trade and finance on the eve of World War II?

2. What was the economic position of the United States at the end of World War II? Why did the United States emerge from the war in such a strong position? What steps did it take to encourage international economic recovery?

3. What has been the trend in protectionism since the Hawley-Smoot Tariff? What was an important difference between the Reciprocal Trade Agreement Act and the General Agreement on Tariffs and Trade? Why has there emerged a new pressure in the United States for protectionist measures for certain industries? Do you support these demands for protection? Why or why not?

4. What is the major purpose of the European Economic Community? Why was Britain's admission so significant? What are the potential positive and negative effects of the EEC on world trade?

5. What were the arrangements for international payment under the Bretton Woods gold-exchange standard? What problems developed?

6. Describe the two-tier system for gold established by the IMF. What were the goals of these arrangements? How successful were they?

7. What were the major features of the Smithsonian agreement of 1971? What are the consequences of floating exchange rates? How has the role of the IMF increased with the creation of SDRs?

8. Why is the decline in value of the American dollar regarded as a serious problem by Japan, the nations of Western Europe, and the OPEC countries? What were the aims of the Carter administration's "rescue package" in 1978?

9. What new international economic trends and forces are likely to shape the world economy of the 1980s? Do these factors seem to add up to a prospect of renewed stability or greater instability?

Application 16:
The Workings of International Trade: Japan and the Television Set

In 1975 the Japanese, who had already captured a large share of the American market for radios, small cars, and cameras, invaded another profitable territory that once had been the exclusive domain of American producers: color television. The story of the Japanese televisions points out many of the intricacies and problems involved in international trade today.

With the exception of Sony Corporation, whose products sold at a premium price, Japanese manufacturers had long priced their television sets about 5 percent to 10 percent below the cost of comparable models made in the United States. Then, in 1975, the Japanese widened the price difference to as much as 25 percent in some cases, and began to win over many important private-label marketers, such as Sears, Roebuck & Company and Montgomery Ward. Sears, for example, which sells about one of every ten color television sets in the United States, began switching more of its business to the Japanese and away from American companies that had been making the Sears-brand televisions. Montgomery Ward and other mass merchants quickly followed suit. The American producers tried to avoid a price war, stressing what one advertising campaign called the "handmade quality" of their sets. But the Japanese seemed to gain ground every week, doubling their share of the market in less than a year to nearly 40 percent of all sales.

United States television manufacturers, nearly 80 percent of whose profits were coming from color television sets, were understandably upset, and complained to courts, government agencies, and the press that the competition was unfair. "If I did what the Japanese are doing, I'd be thrown in jail," said an executive of General Telephone & Electronics Corporation, whose Sylvania division made television sets.

Was unfairness the secret of Japanese success, or were they attracting customers by turning out better goods that could be sold at a lower price because of greater production efficiency? The answer is especially important because Japan is second only to Canada in the volume of business ($40 billion in 1978) that it does with the United States. In addition, the Japanese invasion of the American television market, and American attempts to repulse it, exemplify many of the problems of trade that exist between any two nations and also typify the growing misgivings that competitors have concerning Japan's strategy for growth.

After World War II, to resurrect its war damaged economy, Japan began striving to boost exports and hold down imports, a policy that in recent years has met with impressive success. Although the country's growth rate was cut in half as a result of the oil crisis of the early 1970s, it still managed to expand faster than any other industrialized nation. As a side effect, however, its trade surplus with the United States soared from only $1.2 billion at the begining of the decade to $8.1 billion in 1977. In a representative comment on the situation, *Forbes* magazine wrote, "The U.S. trade gap with Japan must be sharply curtailed for their sake as well as ours." The *New York Times* warned, "American consumers have a stake in open trade with Japan. . . . But if Japan does not look inward for future growth, our great Asian ally may become a victim of its success."

To some degree, Americans themselves were to blame for the Japanese success they sought to curtail. In the 1960s, American producers, by failing to enter the market in Japan, allowed Japanese firms to gain valuable experience in television set manufacture. At the time, Japan imposed no restrictions on the import of American TV sets and the American products were not only higher in quality, but were selling for about $150 less than comparable Japanese sets.

The Americans also permitted the Japanese to catch up in television technology. By the mid-1970s, *Consumer Reports* magazine found Japanese and American-made color sets about equal in "overall quality." One reason American producers lost this technological edge is that they were not spending as much money on research and development as, for example, companies that made computers were spending.

The Japanese also employed unfair and sometimes illegal tactics. Some Japanese color sets selling for $300 in the United States carried price tags of more than $450 at home, and although the Japanese contended that they had done nothing wrong, the Treasury Department found in 1971 that they had been "dumping" television sets in the U.S.—that is, selling their exported sets at a low price in order to gain a better marketing position. While dumping is not in itself a crime, it *is* illegal to evade the duties that the federal customs service imposes on dumped products to bring their price up to a fair level. And there was at least some evidence of such evasion. One chain store pleaded guilty to fraud involving illegal rebates of dumping penalties by a Japanese manufacturer, and in mid-1979, grand juries were investigating the possible involvement of large national stores in the kickback scheme.

It is undeniable, however, that to a large extent, the Japanese owed their television marketing triumph to a simple strategy of concentrating on areas where they held an economic edge. Although in comparison to the United States, Japan has many economic handicaps (it must import nearly 90 pecent of its energy needs, nearly two-thirds of its grain, and almost all of its iron ore, copper, and bauxite), Japan is not without advantages. Capital, for example, is more abundant there. The Japanese save about 22 percent of their takehome pay (Americans save 5 percent), and they invest more of their savings in industry. Capital is also more available for productive investment because less of it is needed for defense—about 1 percent of Japan's gross national product goes to defense; the United States spends 6 percent.

The country's principal asset, however, is its human capital. Its workforce is comparable in skill and education to that of the United States, but in 1970 their productivity (output per hour) was higher (an index of 146.5 compared with 101.5 for the United States). In addition, the labor productivity of the Japanese also was growing more rapidly than that of the Americans.

Nonetheless, protectionists in the United States advocated several measures to restrict the importation of Japanese television sets. Some called for high tariffs. Others wanted import quotas. Still others sought to invoke federal antitrust laws. The eventual compromise was an orderly marketing agreement, or voluntary quota system, in which Japan promised to limit its exports of color television sets to the United States to no more than 1.75 million complete and partially complete sets a year from 1977 through mid-1980, or about 30 percent fewer than it had exported in 1976.

The orderly marketing remedy was not a cure-all, however. Indeed, soon after it went into effect, set makers in the United States were complaining that their plight was worse than ever. Some Japanese manufacturers evaded the agreement by moving their production for the American consumer to areas not covered by the agreement, such as Taiwan, Korea, and Singapore. Others formed joint-ventures marketing with United States companies. Most significantly, the Japanese also began building in the United States factories of their own. Sony, Mitsubishi Electric Company, and Hitachi Ltd. started making television sets in California. Sanyo manufactured them in Tennessee, Matsushita Electric Industrial Company in Illinois, and Toshiba Corporation in Pennsylvania.

The move to American soil not only sidestepped customs problems, it also took advantage of American labor rates, which had suddenly become cheaper as the value of the dollar fell relative to the yen. The dollar, worth 357 yen in 1970, declined to 270 yen by 1977, and as a consequence, the unit labor cost, on a United States dollar basis, ended up nearly twice as high in Japan in 1977 as in the United States. According to one estimate, as a result of the manufacturing shift and the orderly marketing agreement, while Japanese color television imports declined by 500,000 units in 1977, Japanese production in the United States climbed by 450,000 units.

Questions for discussion

☐ Discuss the absolute and comparative advantages (Chapter 36) of the Japanese economy and the reasons that such a nation might choose to specialize in the manufacture of high-technology goods, such as television sets, cameras, and computers.

☐ How could foreign manufacturers who dump products in the United States be dissuaded from such practices?

☐ What prevents American corporations from dumping products overseas?

☐ By one estimate, Japanese imports of color television receivers cost 70,000 American jobs. In 1977, for example, Zenith Radio Corporation, the principal set maker in the United States, which had resisted moving its factories abroad, closed a plant in Iowa that employed 2000, and reduced its operations in three other states, increasing them in Mexico and Asia. How could the American jobs have been saved?

Part X

Alternatives to Traditional Economics

Chapter 40

Alternative Economic Systems

What to look for in this chapter

What are the alternatives to the capitalist market economy?

What criteria can be used to compare different economic systems? How can these comparisons be measured?

What are the comparative strengths and weaknesses of the capitalist market system and the socialist command system? How closely do the United States and the USSR fit these models in practice?

What are some of the distinctive characteristics of the socialist market economy of Yugoslavia, the democratic socialist economy of Great Britain, and the command economy of China?

In the United States, when baby needs a new pair of shoes, mommy and daddy go to the shoe store and buy a pair of Cozeetoes shoes, size 4, color white, price $7.98. The shoes are made in a factory hundreds of miles away, by a firm that has never heard of this particular baby or her need for shoes. The firm's decision to produce those shoes was based on a comparison of the cost of making the shoes with the revenue to be expected when the shoes are sold at the going market price. Its motive in undertaking the production of shoes was not to help the baby, but to earn a profit. The parent's decision to buy those shoes was made by balancing the increase in household welfare that the purchase of the shoes would bring against the increase in welfare that the family might obtain by other purchases with the same $7.98. They gave their business to Cozeetoes rather than to its competitors not because they wanted to do Cozeetoes a favor, but because these particular shoes seemed (to them) to offer the greatest degree of consumer satisfaction at the lowest price.

The way that baby gets her new shoes in the United States is characteristic of a capitalist market economy. But as we mentioned at the outset of the book, the capitalist market economy is only one of the possible systems that human beings have devised for meeting the economic goal of maximization of satisfaction from scarce resources. In some societies, the baby's mother might make her shoes out of the hide of an animal. In the society envisioned by Karl Marx, the baby's parents would simply go down to the Shoe Bureau and be given a pair of shoes that were designed by a panel of experts to be the most practical and safe baby shoes imaginable. In modern-day Russia, the parents would go to the state-owned department store and buy a pair of shoes produced in the state-owned factory, which has to meet a certain quota of shoe production every month. In Yugoslavia, the parents might buy the shoes in a privately owned shoe store, but the shoes would have been produced by a factory that was owned either by the state or by a workers' collective.

As we compare alternative economic systems, we inevitably end up asking the question, "Which system is best?" Economist Gregory Grossman points out that this question is by nature highly subjective:

> It is difficult enough to tell which of several automobiles is best. Some of the criteria we apply to cars—purchase price, credit terms, operating cost, resale value—can be brought to the same denominator, dollars and cents, discounted to the same point in time, and combined into a single figure for each car, which can then be compared with corresponding figures for other car. But other criteria—appearance, comfort, ease of handling, safety, snob appeal—cannot be reduced to a common denominator; and insofar as they enter our decision, they do so through our subjective preferences. The preferences of different persons need not be alike; which is why there are so many different cars on the road.

Even more than evaluating cars, evaluating economic systems involves subjective preferences as well as rational appraisal. But unlike the criteria that apply to cars, the criteria that apply to economic systems include many of the basic philosophical issues—welfare, progress, freedom, security, efficiency—on which reasonable men have disagreed for centuries and no doubt will continue to disagree for many more. Only the dogmatic will insist on applying a single yardstick to measure the performance of all economic systems.*

CRITERIA FOR COMPARING SYSTEMS

What are the criteria that we use in comparing alternative economic systems? A good basis of comparison would include the following factors.

Plenty

One of the basic goals of any economic system is providing the largest possible number of goods and services; this is the maximizing function. To measure plenty, economists use real GNP per capita. Although comparisons of real GNP are not always completely accurate measures of comparative plenty, since many kinds of nonmarket transactions may not show in GNP accounting, they are nevertheless useful as a rough basis of comparison. But we must remember that a country's per capita production depends not only on its economic system, but also on a number of geographical and social circumstances. A large real GNP per capita is not by itself conclusive proof of economic superiority; it may be due to the way resources are distributed rather than to the way they are maximized.

Growth

Another way to compare the performance of an economy is through its rate of growth. Even in a

---

*Gregory Grossman, *Economic Systems,* 2nd ed., pp. 3–4. © 1974, Prentice-Hall, Inc., Englewood Cliffs, N.J.

highly developed economy like the United States, that of growth continues to be a national objective, and of course in less-developed nations, it is an even more important economic goal. Comparisons of growth are usually made on the basis of annual percentage changes in real GNP.

Stability
It is generally agreed that stability is a desirable feature of an economy. A stable economy is one in which the swings of business cycles are minimized and in which the level of prices is more or less constant, without marked inflation or deflation. A perfectly stable economy is probably an impossibility, since some sectors of the economy will always be in the process of adjusting to some change in production processes, or consumer demand, or resource availability. We can judge performance by the extent to which the economic system minimizes fluctuations of this sort. This comparison can be made on the basis of changes in price level and changes in the level of real GNP.

Security
Existence is a risky condition; one of the primary goals of all social and economic activity is to lessen that risk. No economic system can prevent all economic hazard. Some people will lose their jobs, fall sick, have their savings stolen by a burglar, or see their houses destroyed by an earthquake. But the economic system can provide some way to minimize the effects of losses through disasters over which the individual has no control. Such protection of the individual is one of the main distinguishing features of many modern economic systems. And by providing economic stability, the system can also to a large extent avert many individual losses.

Efficiency
An economy can be said to be using its productive resources efficiently when no reallocation of resources can bring about an increase in production. Efficient resource use is the primary means of obtaining the goal of maximizing satisfaction. Yet an economic system might succeed in allocating its resources with considerable efficiency and still be judged unsatisfactory by the majority of its members. It may sometimes be desirable to sacrifice a certain measure of efficiency in order to gain some other value, such as stability or equity.

Equity
Another way that we can compare economic systems is by looking at the way the gains of production are distributed. Most people agree that a very unequal distribution of income and wealth is undesirable. That does not necessarily mean that the most desirable condition is perfect equality of income distribution; in fact, many economists believe that a certain degree of inequality is a necessary motivation for productivity. But extreme inequity strikes most people as unfair, even when they are among those who reap the advantage.

Economic freedom
When we speak of freedom in an economic context, we generally mean a breadth of choice in regard to economic activity. When a household is free to purchase any goods available, within the limits of its purchasing power, this is called freedom of consumer choice. When a household is also free to choose how much labor it will supply and to whom it will supply the labor, this is called freedom of job choice. When a business firm is free to choose what and how much to produce, in any way it wants, with any resources it can afford to buy, this is called freedom of enterprise. Economic freedom may be valued by itself, as part of the general concept of individual freedom. It may also be valued as a means of enabling each household to maximize its own satisfaction, and as a means of efficient resource allocation.

CLASSIFYING ECONOMIC SYSTEMS

There are various ways in which economic systems can be classified. For example, they are often classified according to the type of mechanism that coordinates the activities of the various sectors of the economy. As we have seen earlier in the text, a market economy is a decentralized system of decision making. Decisions concerning production, consumption, and resource allocation are made by large numbers of individuals acting independently. There are also *centralized economies in which the economic decisions of what and how much to produce and sometimes for whom to produce are the responsibility of agencies of a central government.* These are called **command economies.**

Another way of classifying economies is according to the ownership of productive resources. We can distinguish between *systems in which most resources are privately owned*—called **capitalist economies**—and *systems in which most productive resources are owned publicly by the government,* called **socialist economies.**

In comparing alternative economic systems, we must also be careful to differentiate between real examples and hypothetical models of systems. For example, although the United States can be classified as a market economy, there are many ways in which the actual markets of the United States differ from the pure model of the market system. So, too, the model of the command economy differs from the examples we shall look at here—the economy of the Soviet Union—in many significant ways. Let us analyze these models and the real economies that illustrate them.

Problems in comparing economic systems

We should caution that any attempt to compare different economic systems poses certain inherent problems. Chief among these is the difficulty of obtaining reliable and complete statistics. A country like China, for example, does not take an accurate census; under such circumstances, it would be unrealistic to expect the figures on unemployment or median household income to be as accurate as similar statistics for the United States. Definitions of such important categories as unemployed workers or households below the poverty level may also differ from country to country. In addition, variables for which no reliable statistics exist—underemployment, for example—may actually be more significant than the variables used here for comparison. Therefore, our ability to assess the relative economic positions of various nations is somewhat limited by the lack of uniform international data collection practices.

THE CAPITALIST MARKET ECONOMY

Model

The model of the capitalist market economy specifies that one price system will answer all production questions through the decentralized actions of households and businesses. The questions of *what* and *how much* to produce are ultimately answered by the independent decisions of a large number of buyers and sellers in the marketplace. Since consumers are actually the final decision makers—the ones who cast their dollar votes for the production of various goods and services—a market economy may be said to be characterized by **consumer sovereignty.** *This means not only that the consumer has the freedom to choose between possible purchases, but also that consumer choices in the marketplace have some consequences for production decisions and the allocation of resources.*

The question of *how* to produce is also answered in the marketplace. Firms able to produce a particular good most efficiently will be able to outbid other firms, which must then look for substitute inputs, turn to producing other goods, or drop out of the market altogether.

Relative success of the capitalist market model

By and large, the capitalist market mechanism has succeeded remarkably well in achieving an equilibrium between supply and demand. Its decentralization disperses the power of decision making, thus avoiding bureaucratic bottlenecks and allowing each economic unit to achieve its maximization goals in its own way. When judged by the criterion of efficiency, this system merits a high rating.

The market mechanism can also be judged successful in terms of economic freedom. Households and businesses are essentially free to make a wide variety of economic decisions without any restraint other than their income, tastes, and preferences. Many political scientists believe that the capitalist market system also promotes political freedom. By decentralizing most economic decisions, it removes some of the power that might otherwise accumulate in the central government. It also builds up counterbalancing centers of power. Large corporations, wealthy individuals, unions, and various well-organized groups can sometimes challenge the power of government. If we agree that plurality is the best guarantee of political freedom, then we would probably agree that the decentralized economic system of the market is likely to bring more political freedom than the centralized command system.

The capitalist market system can be given a relatively high rating on the criterion of plenty. The incentives to productivity in this system are self-interest and the profit motive, both of which have a proven record of being able to induce people to work hard and well.

When judged by the other criteria, however, the capitalist market economy is less successful. In itself, it contains no mechanism to ensure equity of income distribution. Any attempts to secure equitable distribution must stem from government intervention. It also lacks the mechanism to provide security. Equity and security must be secured by political means because they are not a part of the economic system.

When judged by the criterion of stability, the capitalist market economy is again found wanting. The mechanisms of the capitalist economy for reaching and maintaining full employment and price stability have many flaws. Indeed, periods of unemployment, inflation, sluggish growth, and recession are all characteristic of capitalist systems.

Fundamentally, the fluctuations stem from the decentralized and uncoordinated nature of decision making, rather than from private ownership of the means of production. For example, malfunctioning of the market economy as a whole may arise from the way individual consumers and businesses assess their economic prospects. If people are uncertain about the future—as they often are—firms will make the wrong investment decisions, slowing or overheating economic activity and causing unemployment or inflation. If consumers expect inflation, they will seek to make their purchases immediately, when prices are still relatively low, thereby actually accelerating the rate of inflation.

The capitalist market economy also may have difficulty in encouraging economic growth, which does not result automatically from the mechanisms of a market economy. Even government planning and action are not always successful in stimulating growth or reaching a desired growth rate. The difficulty in encouraging growth again derives from the basic decentralization of capitalism. Private owners tend to ignore long-term benefits that might accrue to society as a whole if they do not result in profits to the firm. Since all people eventually die, self-interest dictates that we enjoy the fruits of our efforts while we are alive. If, as an extreme example, everyone decided to live for today only, saving would be senseless, investment impossible, and economic stagnation a certainty.

Example

The economy of the United States is not as efficient as the model suggests. In many markets, competition is far from perfect, and therefore resource allocation is not optimal. Problems also arise because the price system has not been extended to cover certain social costs of economic activity. The production and consumption of many goods create external diseconomies that also result in less than optimal resource allocation.

Also, there is probably less economic freedom in the real economy of the United States than there is in the ideal model of the system. The American government has passed a number of laws regulating and restricting economic choices of both households and businesses. For instance, a bank cannot choose to extend its business by lending money to poor credit risks at high interest rates, because the laws against usury prohibit that; by the same token, the household that is a poor credit risk is thus deprived of the choice of borrowing money. In addition, monetary and fiscal policies resulting in tax incentives and changes in the money supply and credit conditions have stimulated private-sector investment and are partially responsible for a long-term American growth rate of about 3 percent a year. In addition, racial and sexual discrimination tend to artificially restrict the mobility of certain groups in the labor force. And, some individuals contend that small business ventures are stifled by the inability to afford expensive advertising campaigns. Consequently, freedom of enterprise is constrained and consumer choice is limited to the range of goods and services produced by large corporations able to devote significant financial resources to product promotion.

The real United States economy shows several changes made in the model. By adopting a progressive tax structure, the government has taken steps to redistribute income in the direction of greater equity. Programs of social insurance, such as Social Security and unemployment compensation, have greatly increased the ability of the economic system to protect the individual against economic loss. Much of the American monetary and fiscal policy is intended to prevent or minimize business fluctuations and the attendant unemployment and rapid changes in the level of prices. Although the United States' record of success in preventing unemployment and inflation leaves a great deal to be desired, most economists agree that the likelihood of experiencing another widespread and deep depression has been significantly reduced.

Thus, while resource allocation is somewhat inefficient and economic freedom is constrained, government intervention in the marketplace has resulted in improvements in the areas of equity, security, stability, and growth in the American economy. Naturally, debate continues regarding both the nature and desired degree of government involvement. Should we sacrifice some current growth and abundance in order to obtain greater efficiency of resource allocation through the regulation of pollution? Is additional security worth the sacrifice of more of our economic freedom? Should more extensive redistributive programs be undertaken in order to reduce the income gap between wealthy and poor? These are the questions that our system will have to answer in the future.

THE SOCIALIST COMMAND SYSTEM

Background

The development of complex, capitalist market economies accompanied the Industrial Revolution in Europe. By the nineteenth century, the Industrial Revolution was causing serious social disruption. Discrepancies of wealth and poverty, exploitation of workers, and child labor—all these conditions became targets of anger and protest. One of the most influential protestors was Karl Marx, a German social philosopher who had traveled over the European continent and finally settled in London. In 1848, Marx, together with his col-

DEVELOPMENTS IN ECONOMIC THOUGHT:

Karl Marx

Culver Pictures

Karl Marx (1818-1883), the intellectual founder and foremost theorist of socialism, devoted almost all his attention to the critique of capitalism. His reputation, both now and at the time he wrote, owes more to his radical political beliefs and his active role as a socialist leader than to his work as an economist. Marx's political views were responsible for his expulsion from Germany in the 1840s, and he spent his most productive years in London researching at the library of the British Museum and developing an economic theory of capitalism which was central to his other writings on politics and history.

Marx was trained in philosophy, but soon decided that the arguments of philosophers were simply ideal reflections of more substantial developments in the political economy of capitalist societies. Although he drew extensively on the work of the classical economists, he argued that they, too, were distracted by surface appearances and by their own idealized picture of a perfect natural economic order. Marx claimed that the classical economists mistakenly viewed prices, money, markets, profits, and wages as things in themselves, rather than as manifestations of basic social relationships between people. He argued that, in the final analysis, all these economic factors were determined by the struggle between the two major classes in capitalist society—the bourgeoisie (the owners of capital) and the proletariat (wage workers). *Das Kapital (Capital)* (1867), Marx's major work on economic theory, combines a systematic review of classical economics, an attack against social injustice, and his own alternative theory of capitalism.

The starting point of Marx's analysis was the labor theory of value. According to this theory, all economic value was produced by labor, and labor alone. After the worker was paid a subsistence wage, however, a portion of the value produced was kept by the capitalist as profit, even though the capitalist had done nothing to produce this value. Marx believed that the system of private property which allowed the capitalist to do this was not only unjust but irrational, and he claimed that private economic decision making was responsible for the chaos in production which led to unemployment, periodic depressions, and constant waste. Marx recognized that capitalism had given a tremendous boost to economic growth, but felt that in the long run the inherent irrationality of the system would cause it to become a barrier to further growth. Just as the feudal systems of the Middle Ages had been overthrown to make way for capitalism, so capitalism would be overthrown and replaced by socialism.

Marx believed that his critical economic theories could not be divorced from his radical political theories. He also believed, unlike J. B. Say (see Chapter 16), that the job of the theorist was not simply to explain but to promote change. Marx's historical significance should not be underestimated; no other economic theorist has had so much influence on the policies of so many governments. The variety of economic measures implemented by the many types of socialist and communist countries, however, serves as a reminder that Marx was primarily a critic of capitalism, not the designer of any particular socialist economy.

In the capitalist countries, economists tend to separate Marx's economic analysis from his political views. While *Das Kapital* is recognized as the major alternative explanation of the workings of the market economy, most orthodox economists reject most of Marx's specific arguments. Critics of his theory point to the staying power of capitalism and to the ability it has shown, contrary to Marx's predictions, to solve its problems of instability and to produce the highest standard of living in the world. The persistence of such conditions as poverty, unemployment, inflation, and periodic recession, however, has caused a minority of economists to maintain an interest in Marx's approach. Joan Robinson (see Chapter 26) is an example of a prominent contemporary economist who feels that neoclassical economic theory cannot by itself adequately answer many of the questions Marx posed.

league, Friedrich Engels, wrote the *Communist Manifesto,* in which he argued against and predicted the ultimate downfall of capitalism. Marx later expanded his criticism of capitalism in a three-volume work, *Das Kapital (Capital).*

Marx suggested that all economic value is produced by labor and not by any other factors of production. Yet he was convinced that the price of labor always remains at a subsistence wage level, since business firms will pay only as much as is necessary to ensure a continued supply of labor in the resource market. Marx also thought that, though technology, average workers can produce more than the value of their households' subsistence needs, yet the surplus of value of their labor is ultimately expropriated by business owners as profit.

He pointed out that because accumulated profits allow expansion and the purchase of even more advanced technology, the profits of the owners will continue to grow. Thus, according to Marx, ownership of capital becomes more and more concentrated, and the gap between the few rich owners and the many poor workers becomes wider. Marx predicted that the final result would be mounting ill feelings among the workers, who would eventually lead a revolution in which the capitalist market system would be overthrown.

The impact of Marxist thought on social and economic organization throughout the world has been profound. Since 1917, when the first socialist state was created by the Russian Revolution, Marxism as an ideology has spread to all parts of the world, and serves today as a viable alternative to the capitalist system.

Model

Marx was most concerned with the fall of capitalism, and he did not describe in great detail the economic system that was to replace capitalism.

Nevertheless, he envisioned the basic framework of a socialist command economy: collective ownership of the means of production and a centralized decision-making process. Later theorists have worked out many of the concrete details of the model.

How does a command economy answer the basic production questions? How can this function be performed in the absence of a price mechanism? How are the forces of supply and demand registered?

According to advocates of a command economy, allocations of resources would be measured in physical units, and so would output. Money prices would be used only as a way of measuring aggregates of products that are dissimilar. Prices simply would not serve a guiding function.*

Maurice Dobb, a well-known theorist of the socialist command economy, more or less dismissed the validity of prices as a meaningful guiding force.† Dobb argued that consumer sovereignty had little meaning even in a capitalist society because of the inequality of income distribution and the importance of the producer in deciding practical production matters.

Dobb went on to point out how the economic questions were to be answered in the absence of consumer sovereignty. The question of what and how much to produce would be decided by a central planning board. Dobb suggested that the task of planning an economy was not really as overwhelming as it seemed. A number of necessities must be produced; these are given priority. After these necessities are taken care of, the central planning board will make choices based on production possibilities, which are limited in practice by history, technology, and existing social relationships.

The question of how the output is to be produced is also answered by a central planning board. Again, Dobb suggested that the problem was not as complicated as it might appear on the surface. He suggested that most of the limitations would come from technology. First, there is a minimum scale within which most types of production can take place efficiently. This sets one dimension—the size of the factory—and by implication also helps to answer the question of how much will be produced. Dobb also felt that the combination of inputs was more or less set by the product itself and that there could therefore be very little adjustment in the relative quantities required (although this conclusion is not accepted by many economists). For example, the production of iron requires a certain proportion of inputs (for example, iron ore and coal), which cannot be varied to any great extent. Hence technology has answered the question of how production will take place.

The command economy projects the interaction of all economic factors so that there can be few unforeseen fluctuations. This has important implications for the accomplishment of economic growth. In command systems, all facets of the production process can be geared toward the achievement of planned goals. The achievement of these goals, in fact, usually assumes utmost significance in a command economy.

How does a command economy implement the numerous decisions and directives that determine the production process? In the area of employment of labor, command economies essentially maintain freedom of choice. Because of the downgrading of the price mechanism and the reliance on physical units in measuring output, wages of workers are often tied to their individual productivity. Those workers able to produce more nails than their colleagues will also earn more. Plant managers, apart from receiving higher basic wages than their subordinates, are given additional incentives to achieve and surpass production goals—for example, better housing, an automo-

---

*See Paul M. Sweezy, *Socialism*. New York: McGraw-Hill, 1949.

†Maurice Dobb, "Economic Theory and the Problem of a Socialist Economy," *Economic Journal* 43 (December 1933), pp. 588–598.

bile, and longer vacations. Thus, the incentive system still operates in a command economy —rarely can any economy rely on the altruism of its citizens to get the best job done simply for the good of the nation.

Turnover tax
The central planning authority tries to cope with the absence of a price mechanism and the resultant problem of gauging demand and the relative satisfaction that various goods provide by attempting to manipulate demand. This is done principally thorugh imposition of a **turnover tax,** *a levy applied to each sale through which a commodity passes in the process of production and distribution to the final consumer.* For example, the sale of wheat is taxed when it moves from farmer to miller; the sale of flour is taxed when it moves from miller to baker; and the sale of bread is taxed when it moves from baker to final consumer. As opposed to a value-added tax, a tax which is imposed only on the value added to the commodity since its last sale, the turnover tax is applied to the total value of each transaction which occurs.

Although the turnover tax also has been a recent feature of some capitalist economies, its use differs in a command economy, insofar as its rate varies from product to product. The effect of this variation is to make some goods relatively more expensive than others and to regulate demand to some degree. It is also the principal way by which governments of command economies obtain their revenues. Insofar as it curtails consumption, the turnover tax is actually an enforced kind of saving; the supply of goods to match the reduced demand is then regulated through production quotas. Since the government also pays all wages and in most cases ties them to productivity, it retains tight control over all consumption and assures itself of the resources for capital investment.

Relative success of the command model
How well does the command market model operate? There are many factors to consider. Since all workers are employed by the state, which can create jobs when they are needed, there is little problem with unemployment.

Regarding inflation, however, the situation is more complicated. By employing the entire labor force, the government also controls the overall level of income in the economy. As long as increases in income are accompanied by gains in productivity of equal magnitude, there is no tendency for prices in general to rise, as greater spending is matched by greater output. If, however, income increases faster than productivity, shortages of goods and services in general will appear if total spending exceeds production quotas. In a capitalist market system, under these circumstances, prices increase to eliminate shortages, but in a command economy, a central planning authority sets prices, so shortages persist. Prices do not rise, but consumers are unsatisfied. In terms of stability, therefore, the command economy provides high levels of employment, but the issue of inflation cannot be legitimately addressed since price flexibility does not exist. The system itself does not guarantee economic security, but the fact that anyone who wants to sell labor resources can find some sort of job does provide a certain degree of protection of the individual against economic insecurity.

Contrary to popular belief, the command system does not eliminate inequalities in income distribution. It still allows people to choose their own occupation, so there must be some incentive for people in the labor force to supply the skills that are scarce relative to the demand for them. Hence there must be wage differentials and a resulting inequality of income distribution. The degree of income inequality in command economies, however, tends to be considerably less than that which is found in most capitalist economies.

The command system also necessitates some restrictions on economic freedom. For example, in some cases, certain people are allowed to obtain particular types of education or training. Yet, unlike the United States experience, all of those who get trained get a job in their field. However, a person from Moscow may be required to move to Siberia in order to practice medicine—the freedom for this person to choose to be unemployed in Moscow is not available. Although workers may choose their own jobs and consumers may choose their own purchasing patterns (subject to the limited availability of goods), businesses have very little freedom of enterprise.

On the criterion of efficiency, the command system must also be given a relatively low rating. As an economy becomes more affluent, the decisions about what, how much, and how to produce become more and more complex. The central planning authorities simply cannot know the varying amounts of additional satisfaction that an increasing number of products will provide. As a result, there is often a less than optimal allocation of resources.

Example

In his writings, Marx made an important distinction between socialism and **communism.** *An ideal communist system would be characterized by a classless society in which all goods would be in ample supply so that there would no longer be any need to regulate the economy. As a consequence, the state would wither away.* Socialism, according to Marx, is merely a stage of development toward communism. Russian society has not yet reached this final goal; it is not communistic in the Marxian sense of the word. Under the present system of Russian socialism, the state has not been abolished and there is a need to regulate the economy, because many goods are not in ample supply. According to Marx, in order to accomplish these goals, the dictatorship of the proletariat must pave the way by eliminating classes and by gearing the economy toward the day when everything will be abundant. This requires great sacrifices, but the dictatorship of the proletariat—and we stress the word "dictatorship"—must be entrusted to make the necessary decisions.

How has the Soviet Union implemented the economic theories of Marx in its command economy?

Ownership of productive assets

In the Soviet Union today, the state owns virtually all of the means of production—land, capital, natural resources, and business enterprises. There are, however, some limited exceptions. In retail trade, for example, state-owned stores account for about two-thirds of the value of total sales, with the remaining one-third being derived primarily from rural cooperatives (closely supervised by the state), with a small number of agricultural commodities being sold in unregulated "farmers' markets." Although accounting for only 8.6 percent of aggregate *food* sales in 1968, items sold in unregulated markets are quite important in terms of the supply of certain goods. For instance, in 1970, unregulated market sales of potatoes, eggs, and meat represented 67 percent, 54 percent, and 35 percent, respectively, of all sales of these products.

In the agricultural sector, ownership of land resources has gone through several phases. In the years immediately following the 1917 revolution, agricultural policy departed from the Marxist model of collective ownership, as the new leadership divided the large estates and distributed them among the peasants. The immediate result of the land policy was a drop in production of agricultural products. Then in 1929, Joseph Stalin launched another agricultural revolution—**collectivization.** *Peasant land was confiscated by the state and organized into larger collective farms which were closely regulated by the government. The goal was* *to secure more efficient use of productive resources particularly machinery.* The peasants were allowed to retain only their own dwellings and some land on which they could grow agricultural products for their private use.

The agricultural problem, however, has persisted in the Soviet Union and agriculture is a much less productive industry there than it is in the United States. The question has been how to collectivize and at the same time encourage farmers to increase production. At present, Russia is moving toward the institution of vast state-owned farms and the gradual elimination of subsidiary farming. About one-third of all agricultural output today comes from farms that are owned and operated by the state; about two-fifths from collective farms virtually controlled by the state; and the remainng one-quarter is produced on privately owned farms or on small garden plots given to members of the large collectives.

Organization of production

In the Soviet Union, all decisions concerning production are made by a highly organized bureaucracy. The highest ranking planning agency, the Soviet Planning Committee, or Gosplan, however, does not decide what and how much of *each good* will be produced. It does determine production and distribution plans for about 300 industrial products (known as funded commodities) that are considered critical to the success of Soviet development efforts. In addition, Gosplan, along with two other agencies, devises production and distribution plans for several thousand other industrial goods called planned commodities. Nevertheless, most production decisions are made by lower ranking ministries without the explicit approval of Gosplan.

Regardless of the product under consideration, the individual plant manager eventually receives an output quota to be met during the current year. Since monetary units do not have the meaning of market prices, quotas are given in terms of physical output, and resource allocation is made in units of inputs. One of the disadvantages of this method is the difficulty of specifying physical units. For example, a quota for nails might be stated in terms of weight. The manager receives a directive from above that this year so many thousands of pounds of nails must be produced. The manager is motivated to meet and perhaps exceed the quota. Production is geared for huge nails, as there is less production required per weight for the larger nails. Hence the factory will be able to produce the required weight of nails quickly and easily.

As time goes by, the shortage of smaller nails begins to appear. Builders have to use the huge nails available, and so must anyone who wants to hang a picture. Now the central authority attempts to correct the problem by specifying the quota in terms of number of nails. The manager reevaluates the situation and sees that the production quota can be met most easily by gearing the factory for the production of very small finishing nails. The manager now does not have to worry too much if the amount of iron or steel necessary to produce medium-sized or large nails is unavailable because the quota can still be met with the smaller nails.

The manager often tries to anticipate the problem of quotas by participating to some extent in the plan for the next period of production. In doing so, it is advantageous to estimate that production will be relatively low in the early part of the period. If production is increased too rapidly, the manager might not be able to show an increase during the next time period, and such an increase is crucial to company superiors. Managers also develop informal relationships with one another. As managers operate their businesses they learn who is managing the firms or the distribution of inputs essential for their business. They also may have some service that can be offered to suppliers in return for special consideration when it is time to distribute inputs. Through these informal relationships, they also protect themselves from shortages. Hence, there are other types of competition for resources.

Communication difficulties A difficult general problem for a centrally directed economy is ensuring that the proper and correct information is relayed from the producing unit all the way up to the central authority, and that directives are accurately passed down to the producing units. Volumes of information must somehow be screened and condensed. But each time information is processed there is a possibility of information distortion. Because of the long channels of communication required in a centrally directed system, the chances of developing inefficiencies along the line are greater. In a market system the problem of the channeling of information is somewhat simplified, since the firm must be concerned only with prices in the resource market and in the market for its products.

Response to consumer demand Compared to the situation in the United States, the variety of consumer items available in the Soviet Union is extremely limited. The state establishes production quotas for basic consumer goods, but without a profit motive, little incentive exists for government officials to gauge consumer demand accurately. Besides, the emphasis of Soviet planners has been on developing military and industrial power rather than on catering to the desires of consumers. Consequently, when a shortage of a particular item arises, the government may increase the turnover tax rate, rendering the product expensive relative to other goods. This, it is hoped, will restrict quantity demanded to the available supply. Consumer frustration results at least until the ensuing production period, when the output quota *may* be increased.

Naturally, Soviet consumers do not covet every item on department-store shelves. Since individuals are free to spend their income as they please, the reaction to a generally uninteresting menu of consumer items is often a simple refusal to buy. Thus, surpluses are as likely to occur as shortages.

Under these circumstances, it is no wonder that black markets flourish. Reports abound of foreign students, studying in the USSR, selling blue jeans, stereo components, record albums, and the like for several times the prices paid for these items in Western Europe or the United States.

The government has demonstrated heightened sensitivity to consumer desires in recent years by increasing quotas for items continuously in short supply. Nevertheless, resource allocation to the consumption sector, however improved, ranks far down the list of official Soviet priorities.

Agriculture: the problem child It is commonly known that agriculture is the problem child of Soviet economic planning. A few years after the Bolshevik revolution, 84 percent of Russia's labor force was employed in agriculture. After the first attempts at collectivization in the late 1920s, farm output dropped to the level of 1890. In the years since Stalin, the trend has been toward increased collectivization, but certain compromises have been made with farmers, notably the tolerance of small private plots for satisfying the peasants' personal consumption needs.

Today about 25 percent of Soviet workers are still employed in agriculture, and the persistent inefficiencies of farm production weigh heavily on the economy as a whole.

Distribution of goods
Extreme accumulations of wealth are ruled out in the Soviet Union because of the state ownership of the means of production. There is no maximization of profits and no inheritance of firms or factories. But there is a managerial class that is more privileged than the masses of workers and consumers, and this class also receives a larger

income. The managers also have greater purchasing power, but the recurring shortages of consumer products substantially reduce that advantage. (Those who have the money may, however, buy luxury goods on the black market.)

As we mentioned earlier, the drawback of planned production in an economy that is capable of producing more than the necessities of life is that it cannot accurately predict what consumers will want to buy. Shortages reflect complications in the overall production plan, which is essentially beyond the influence of lower-echelon managers. Thus goods are distributed relatively equitably, but also inefficiently, in regard to variations in consumer demand. Such pitfalls, however, are inevitable in the absence of a real price mechanism to regulate supply and demand.

Growth rate

There is some difference of opinion concerning the actual growth rate the Soviet Union has achieved. The disagreement stems from the difficulty of assigning values on the basis of administered prices rather than market prices. In spite of these problems, most economists agree that the Soviet growth rate in the post–World War II era has been significantly above that achieved by the American economy, although that does not mean that its growth rate has exceeded all capitalist market economies.* One economist, Angus Maddison, estimates that only Japan has approached the overall growth rate of the Soviet Union.

In evaluating the performance of the Soviet economy, economist George Halm observes:

> The success of the Soviet economy is outwardly quite impressive, particularly as seen by poor countries which want to develop their economies in the shortest possible time. Bureaucratic frictions and noneconomic allocations are not as visible as grandiose development schemes, full employment, and a high rate of accumulation.†

OTHER ECONOMIC SYSTEMS

Most modern economies lie somewhere between the two extremes of pure capitalism and pure socialism, combining features of each model. It is generally true that private ownership accompanies a free-market system, and public ownership accompanies a command economy. However, free markets can combine with public ownership, and a high degree of centralization can accompany private ownership. Let us look at these variant combinations.

Socialist market economy: Yugoslavia

The problem that Yugoslavia faced after World War II, when it came under communist control, was similar to that of Russia in 1917—accomplishing an economic transformation and achieving a high rate of growth. But Yugoslavia, under Marshal Tito, found that the model of the Soviet command economy was not entirely applicable to conditions in Yugoslavia. Russia had 30 years of consolidation behind it; Yugoslavia was starting from scratch. In addition, ideological differences developed between Tito and the Soviet leaders.

In 1948, Yugoslavia decided to assert its independence from Soviet influence. To secure its position, rapid progress would be necessary. Tito soon realized that he did not have the pool of trained civil servants required for central decision making. He also knew that the ethnically diverse Yugoslavs were not inclined toward total submission to a central authority. Since he had abolished private ownership of productive means, his solution was to maintain public ownership, while at

---

*A growth rate depends both on the addition to GNP and the level of GNP. Since most capitalist nations were already at a higher level of GNP than the Soviet Union, equal additions to growth would result in a lower growth rate in more prosperous nations.

†George N. Halm, *Economic Systems*. New York: Holt, Rinehart and Winston, 1962, p. 252.

the same time allowing market conditions to exist on the factory level. Workers would manage the plants they worked in, deciding the prices of their products and sharing the profits. They would be guaranteed a basic wage by the central government and would in turn pay taxes to it. But all other activities would be guided by local supply-and-demand factors, much as in a capitalist system. This reduced greatly the bureaucratic burden on the central government, which could then concentrate on long-term growth projects, regulate the overall allocation of resources, and ensure an adequate rate of investment. After initial collectivization in agriculture, farmers were again allowed to work their own land. Most of them still do so today, although some have joined state-run cooperatives.

In the industrial sector, the price mechanism determines the supply of consumer goods. Since wages are partly tied to the profit margins of individual firms, efficiencies in production and market expansion are encouraged. The distribution of goods is uneven to the extent that persons with higher incomes are actually able to buy more goods. But the accumulation of great wealth, as in a capitalist system, is prevented by the joint ownership of the means of production by the employees. Competitive ventures may spring up when there is substantial unemployment in a region, but by and large, new investment is undertaken by the state. The government may also intervene in the market to ensure competitive conditions and the maintenance of overall growth.

Such a combination of market and command features seems to have worked well for Yugoslavia. According to official figures, the country has achieved a growth rate of 8 percent annually since 1949. Although it does not have the full employment of which the Soviet Union can boast, shortages of consumer goods are relatively rare. In addition, Yugoslavs have retained a greater degree of economic freedom than the people living in pure command economies.

Democratic socialism: Great Britain

In the years following World War II, countries such as Germany, France, and Japan vigorously pursued strategies for economic growth. Great Britain, on the other hand, concentrated less on growth than on the redistribution of wealth through taxation, various social welfare measures, and nationalization of industry. The essentially capitalist economy of Britain had produced conditions of income inequality that the British brand of socialism was intended to correct. British socialism is democratic in the sense that the Labor Party, which championed these policies, assumed the reins of government through existing political channels, i.e., elections, rather than through violent revolution.

Although Britain is by no means a command economy, the role of government is prominent since public spending accounts for over one-half of the GNP. The National Health Service provides medical care for 100 percent of the population, while far-reaching subsidized housing and old-age pension programs, among others, also exist.

These social initiatives are expensive, as the British taxpayer is painfully aware. In 1975, for example, most Britons were in the 33 percent marginal tax bracket, but all earnings in excess of $38,000 were taxed at the nearly confiscatory rate of 83 percent. Thus the price tag of social progress has been expensive.

Besides heavy taxation and liberal spending, the state has taken over several ailing industries, such as shipbuilding, and heavily subsidizes others, including coal and steel. There has been reluctance, however, to nationalize more profitable sectors.

Despite good intensions, this social experiment has met with limited success, at best. The heavy tax burden has resulted in the emigration of many wealthy individuals, while those remaining, who are subject to the 83 percent tax rate, have little incentive to work or undertake risky investments. In addition, the performance of supported industries has been unimpressive, and gains in worker productivity and industrial production in general have lagged behind the advances registered by the French, German, and Japanese economies. The inflation picture has also been dismal.

This lackluster record was instrumental in the ouster of the Labor Party in the May 1979 elections. The Conservative victors have pledged to cut income taxes and government spending, reduce industrial subsidies, and generally encourage the free working of a market economy. Whether such promises will be fulfilled remains to be seen, but one thing is clear: if democratic socialism does survive in Great Britain, it will be of a much less ambitious variety than has existed for the past 30 years.

The Chinese command economy

Since the communists gained control of China in 1949, that nation's economy has experienced several periods of significant change. In an attempt to establish self-reliance and to modernize rapidly, the new government inaugurated the Five-Year Plan of 1952–1957, stressed the growth of heavy industry. Real output per capita rose at an annual rate of about 4 or 5 percent during this period, and even greater advances were projected for the ensuing campaign—the Great Leap Forward. This effort, however, due to poor planning and implementation procedures, proved a miserable failure, and was scrapped in short order.

The 1961 plan placed more emphasis on the agricultural sector and less on industrial production. But mediocre economic performance, coupled with the desire of chairman Mao Tse-tung to heighten the political awareness of the populace, led to the Cultural Revolution in 1966. In this quest for egalitarianism, service to the community and self-denial were key elements. Politically, achieving equity had higher priority than achieving economic growth. Hoping to eliminate intellectual elitism, the government downplayed the importance of formal education and assigned millions of teenagers to vocational jobs. In addition, the government attempted to minimize the distinction between urban and rural life through the adoption of labor-intensive, semiskilled technologies that could be implemented in small-scale plants in the countryside as well as in the city. To accommodate this rural emphasis, a massive forced relocation of the population was necessary. In terms of production, agriculture remained in the spotlight and farm output grew at an average annual rate of 2 to 3 percent from 1966 to 1975.

Since Mao's death in 1976, the ideological fervor of the Chinese has slackened somewhat, and economic issues are receiving renewed attention. The new regime has set modernization of agriculture, industry, defense, and science and technology as its goals. Formal education and professional skills are given priority, as intellectual pursuits are again viewed as necessary for the common good. Large-scale production is considered a necessity, as is a much-expanded role for foreign trade. Furthermore, the need to provide at least modest incentives to the labor force has been recognized through the reinstatement of various forms of bonuses, piecework remuneration, and other schemes relating income to productivity.

While this latest plan does not completely abandon the basic tenets of Maoist thought, it does stretch some basic ideological notions for the sake of economic development. Given the rather dramatic changes in strategy that have occurred over the past three decades, however, the permanence of this new direction is by no means assured.

Summary

■ This chapter examines alternative economic systems and compares the performance of the United States, and the USSR and economic systems that combine features of capitalism and socialism.

■ There are several criteria that are useful in comparing different economic systems. (1) Providing plenty (maximizing satisfactions) for the population; this can be determined by measuring real GNP per capita. (2) Economic growth; this can be determined by measuring changes in real GNP over time. (3) Economic stability—the ability to minimize fluctuations in output and prices; this can be determined by measuring real GNP growth rates and price levels. (4) Economic security for individuals; this can be achieved by providing a stable economy. (5) The level of efficiency in resource allocation. (6) The degree of equity in income distribution. (7) The amount and kind of economic freedom enjoyed by individuals and production units in choosing jobs, what to consume, and what to produce.

■ Economic systems can be classified by using two pairs of characteristics. In a market economy, prices determine production decisions; while in a command economy, decisions are made by a central authority. Capitalist economies are defined by private ownership of the means of production, while socialist economies are built on public (government) ownership and control.

■ In a model of a capitalist market economy, the price system answers basic production questions, and consumer decisions are the ultimate authority. This decentralized system gets high marks for efficiency of resource allocation, economic freedom, and the provision of plenty. A capitalist economic system has no automatic guarantee of individual security, economic stability, or growth. In the American capitalist economy, the efficiency of the model has been reduced by imperfect markets, and government regulation has decreased economic freedom. On the other hand, steps have been taken (primarily by government) to ensure greater security, stability, growth, and equity. Nevertheless, these steps have entailed some loss of efficiency and freedom.

■ In his model of a socialist society, Marx envisioned a framework based on collective ownership of the means of production and centralized decision making. The socialist command economic system as it has emerged downplays the role of prices and concentrates instead on the physical measurement of output as the information used by central planners in making decisions. Labor retains some freedom of choice, since wages are often tied to productivity. The use of turnover taxes at each step in the production process allows the planning authority to regulate prices and demand, and it also raises revenues to guarantee capital growth. Socialist economies do a good job of providing security for the individual and stability of income, along with restrictions of economic freedom and a less than optimal allocation of productive resources.

■ In the USSR, most of the means of production are state owned, with private ownership playing a secondary role in agriculture, retail sales, and housing. Agriculture in the Soviet Union has progressed from dividing the prerevolutionary estates into small plots for peasants, through collectivization in the 1930s, to the current trend toward state-owned farms. Production is organized by the state bureaucracy, with extensive delegation of responsibility to regional and local authorities. Difficulties in communicating important information accurately through various levels of authority are a serious problem in such an economy, leading to losses in efficiency. The Soviet government has made some effort to respond to consumer demand in production decisions, but consumer desires still have low priority compared to the attention given to industrial and military development. Substantial private accumulation of wealth is prohibited. The growth rate of the USSR has generally exceeded that of the United States since World War II and is matched among the industrial capitalist countries only by Japan.

■ Most of the world's economies lie somewhere between the poles of the socialist command economy and market capitalism. Yugoslavia, for example, has experimented with worker management of factories and the use of market forces within a socialist system, producing a relatively high growth rate and a greater degree of economic freedom. Democratic socialism in Great Britain since World War II has relied on heavy taxation, liberal spending, and the nationalization of ailing industries. China under Mao emphasized rural over urban development and equity over growth, but since his death the Chinese leadership has stressed production, material incentives, increased trade, and modernization of the economy.

Key Terms

command economies

capitalist economies

socialist economies

consumer sovereignty

turnover tax

communism

collectivization

Review & Discussion

1. What are the most useful measures of comparson between different economic systems? Can any combination of these measures overcome the problem of subjective judgments?

2. What are some major ways of classifying economic systems? What are the principal features of command economies, capitalist economies, and socialist economies?

3. What are some of the problems of a capitalist market economy? What happens to the allocation directed by the price system if the market does not include a measure of all desires? How

close is the United States economy to the model of market capitalism?

4. What are the advantages and disadvantages of the socialist command system? What are the strengths and weaknesses of central planning? What changes have occurred in the economic system of the USSR since the Russian Revolution of 1917?

5. Suppose that there is a demand for paint in both the United States and the Soviet Union. How would the demand for paint be translated into production decisions in each of these economies? What problems would be encountered?

6. What is a socialist market economy? What features of a market system and a socialist command system does the Yugoslavian economy combine?

7. In what sense is the choice of an economic system also a political choice? What are the opportunity costs for various systems of organization? The choice between the economic systems of the United States and the USSR might be summarized as a choice between a system that provides greater efficiency, plenty, and economic freedom and a system that is more successful in providing individual security, stability, growth, and equity. How would you compare these trade-offs?

Chapter 41

Radical Economics: The Old and the New Left

What to look for in this chapter

What are the basic tenets of radical economic analysis?

What is the Marxian economic legacy on which contemporary radical economics is based?

How do radical economists view modern capitalism as an economic system? As a social system?

How do radical and liberal economists differ in their analyses of economic and social problems?

Throughout this text we have presented a "mainstream" view of economics. Traditional theories, problems, and solutions to these problems have been analyzed. Most economists today believe that this so-called mainstream economics is the most accurate representation of the capitalist system. However, in the 1960s and 1970s models of capitalism have emerged that differ sharply from this traditional view of the system. A small group of practitioners of such nonclassical theories has come to be known as the New Left, neo-Marxists, or, simply, radical economists.

What prompted the rise of these thinkers who dissent so vigorously from the mainstream? One answer lies in the unrest on college campuses that occurred during the civil rights and Vietnam eras. America's increasing involvement in Southeast Asia was the chief catalyst for a sudden leftward shift by faculty and students alike at universities from Berkeley to Boston. To some, the accusation of United States imperialism seemed to grow more creditable year by year. A far more important reason, however, was the perception that mainstream economics was not suitable for analyzing why the capitalist system had failed to solve such long-standing problems as racial and sexual discrimination, inequitable distribution of income, deterioration of the environment, exploitation of natural resources both at home and abroad, and the twin pressures of inflation and recession. Indeed, the radicals see orthodox economists as actually being a part of the system. Therefore, they regard the chances for solving these problems as slim since all traditional changes in the economy must come from within. In their view, a fundamental change in the system itself—perpetrated from the outside—is necessary before reform is possible.

The purpose of this chapter, then, is to outline the basic tenets of radical economics today. Let us first examine the philosophy from which the views of the New Left economists have sprung.

MARXISM: THE ROOTS OF RADICAL ECONOMICS

"A specter is haunting Europe—the specter of communism." These are the opening words of the *Communist Manifesto*—the foundation for all future Marxian economics. In the more than 130 years since the publication of this work, communism has become more than a specter or loosely bound alliance of radical intellectuals. It is now the basis for the political economy of more land area in the world than Marx ever envisioned. Moreover, the influence of communism continues to spread to developing countries the world over. To have a good working knowledge of the radical view of the world's economy, therefore, it is essential to become familiar with the fundamental concepts and principles of Marxist theory.

Class struggle

According to Marx, capitalism was characterized by the existence of two opposing social classes: the bourgeoisie—the owners of the means of production—and the proletariat—the workers who were employed by the owners. The bourgeois class possessed the factories, equipment, resources, and other forms of capital; the working class was employed to produce the goods. Marx believed that under the capitalist system the workers had no chance to own any part of the means of production. They could not save enough to purchase capital because their wages barely provided subsistence. The workers were exploited by the owners and were powerless.

Marx was outraged at the extremes of wealth and poverty that were created by the capitalist system's separation of classes. He expressed it this way in the *Communist Manifesto*:

> Modern industry has converted the little workshop of the patriarchal master into the great factory of the industrial capitalist. Masses of laborers crowded into the factory are organized like soldiers. As privates of the industrial army they are placed under the command of a perfect hierarchy of officers and sergeants. Not only are they slaves of the bourgeois class and the bourgeois state; they are daily and hourly enslaved by the machine, by the supervisor, and above all, by the individual bourgeois manufacturer himself. The more openly this despotism proclaims gain to be its end and aim, the more petty, the more hateful and the more embittering it is.

Labor theory of value

In the capitalist system, the price of a commodity is determined by the manufacturer to be that amount at which the product can meet the competition. Marx, however, believed that a commodity should be valued according to the "socially necessary" amount of labor needed to produce it. That is, the amount of time a worker devotes to the production of a particular product determines its "exchange value"; two wholly different items requiring the same labor time would be exchanged for each other.

Marx argued that laborers never received in wages an amount commensurate with the value of the commodity they produced. The working class received only a subsistence level of compensation; all of the surplus value (profits) left over after wages were paid belonged to the capitalists (owners).

> On the one hand, the labor theory of value argued that labor created all the value of the goods sold by the capitalist; on the other hand, an "iron law of wages" kept the laborer's income down to a subsistence minimum; consequently, it must follow that the workers were not receiving the full value of their labor, that there was a large "surplus" kept by the capitalist owner of the means of production.*

The need to accumulate capital

What do the owners do with the surplus value? Marx maintained that the bourgeoisie could not afford to spend the profits on personal luxuries for the following reason. It is in the nature of the capitalist system that the owners, in competition with one another, try to lower their costs by increasing productivity. Therefore, in order to stay in business, the capitalist has to invest most of the profit that has been earned in machinery, and has to keep from falling too far behind technologically. Thus an irreversible trend has begun.

Since the value of a commodity depends solely on the labor time involved, the substitution of machines for workers actually lowers the *rate* of profit. The declining profit rate forces the capitalist to become more and more efficient—more machines are purchased, wages are lowered, workers are laid off. This idle pool of laborers forms Marx's "industrial reserve army," which in turn causes more downward pressure on wages. The market for goods must then decline, generating both extensive overproduction and deepening wretchedness of the working class.

The rise of concentration and imperialism

According to Marx, the workers were not the only ones to feel the effects of the inexorable march of capitalism; the owners were affected as well. As competitive pressures forced the capitalist owners to substitute more and more machines for labor, smaller or less efficient producers gradually would be squeezed out of business and ultimately would join the working class. The wealth and power of each industry would become more concentrated in fewer hands, creating vast technocratic monopolies and widening the gap between extreme wealth and dire poverty. As Marx says in *Das Kapital (Capital)*, competition "always ends in the ruin of many small capitalists, whose capitals partly pass into the hands of their conquerors, partly vanish." But given a falling profit rate and a shrinking domestic mass market, where do the corporate giants sell their goods?

The answer lies in the acquisition of new markets and new sources of raw materials through imperialism. The large capitalist countries must expand their operations, and they do so by means of aggressive domination of the political and economic systems of underdeveloped countries. Imperialism is facilitated by the centralization of production into monopolies and, when necessary, military intervention. Thus, through the imperialism of capitalist countries, workers of *all* countries will eventually be subjected to the inequities of capitalism; the world will become one big capitalist system to the advantage of a few and the toil and misery of many.

---

*From *Essential Works of Marxism*, edited by Arthur P. Mendel, p. 6. Copyright © 1961 by Bantam Books, Inc.

A proletarian revolution

Although the capitalist system gradually becomes international, the condition of the working class does not improve. Labor is reduced to "a mere commodity to be bought if a profit could be made on the purchase. Whether laborers can sell their labor power is completely beyond their control. It depends on the cold and totally impersonal conditions of the market. The product of this labor is likewise totally outside of the laborer's life, being the property of the capitalist."* A revolution is only a matter of time.

As the never-ending cycle of aggressive competition–frantic reinvestment–falling rate of profits produces crisis after crisis, and as economic power becomes concentrated in fewer and fewer hands, the condition of the working class steadily worsens. The strains on capitalism eventually reach a point where the laborers have had enough; they revolt and overthrow the existing system. The proletariat, forms an authoritarian state and creates a new political and economic society with the following characteristics:

- Abolition of private property
- Institution of graduated income tax
- Abolition of inheritance rights
- Centralization of credit by the state
- Centralization of communication and transportation
- Combination of agriculture with manufacturing industries
- Education provided free in public schools

Of the end of capitalism, Marx writes in *Das Kapital:*

> Along with the constantly diminishing number of magnates of capital, who usurp and monopolize all advantages of this process of transformation, grows the mass of misery, oppression, slavery, degradation, exploitation; but with this too grows the revolt of the working class, a class always increasing in numbers, and disciplined, united, organized by the very mechanism of the process of capitalist production itself. The monopoly of capital becomes a fetter upon the mode of production, which has sprung up and flourished along with, and under it. Centralization of the means of production and socialization of labor at last reach a point where they become incompatible with their capitalist integument. This integument is burst asunder. The knell of capitalist private property sounds. The expropriators are expropriated.

The Marxist legacy

Marxists today, especially the young, are almost fanatical in their efforts to follow and implement the ideology of Karl Marx. How can this German journalist-economist-philosopher of over a century ago still inspire such strong emotions in intellectual circles the world over? One explanation is the passionate prose of his works. Turn to any page of *Das Kapital* or the *Communist Manifesto,* and you will be struck by the outrage and indignation Marx expressed toward the capitalist system.

But mere inspirational style would hardly be enough to trigger revolutions in all parts of the world. A far more important reason for the appeal of communism is Marx's carefully reasoned argument which predicted the demise of capitalism. By outlining the eventual—and inevitable—triumph of the communist movement in a rigorously logical manner, Marx's principles encourage young idealists to take risks for the cause because they believe that no sacrifice will be in vain. Some reversals were even built into the theory. Defeats were to be expected now and then, because the revolution would naturally suffer setbacks in the course of its development. But in spite of the rigor of Marx's argument, as history has shown, there are unforeseen consequences associated with an ideology which generates an absolute faith in it-

---

*E. K. Hunt and Howard J. Sherman, *Economics: An Introduction to Traditional and Radical Views.* New York: Harper & Row, 1972, p. 78.

self. Stressing the laws of science as a basis for the coming revolution brought about the rise of an intellectual elite who believed that they alone were able to coordinate the movement. Moreover, Marxists tend to emphasize the role of science as justification for all their actions—actions which more often than not include some form of revolutionary violence. Finally, Marxists generally take a zealous, uncompromising stand against other political and economic systems. Cooperation in reform of existing capitalism is impossible when opposition to Marxism is interpreted as being a part of the class struggle. Thus, in addition to a carefully reasoned economic theory, the legacy of Karl Marx includes the emergence of a guiding elite, justified violence, and an uncompromising stance.

RADICAL ECONOMICS TODAY

The radical versus the liberal view

Before we examine the New Left economics that grew out of Marxian thought, we should distinguish between what is meant today by the terms radical economist and mainstream liberal economist. Liberal economists see little or no relationship between social and economic problems. They believe that economic problems result from past mistakes or miscalculations and that the government is an objective agency ready to help individuals of all classes. In their view, reform comes from within the system when the government steps in to remedy a given inequity.

Radicals, on the other hand, see no chance for effective change from within. Their view of the economy is more complex than the orthodox view; they point out that many factors—political, sociological, technological—interact to form an economic system. In other words, the New Left believes that traditional economists "are obsessed with *marginal changes* within a given economic system—that they study the effect of small parameter shifts, susceptible to analysis by differential calculus, rather than discuss large *qualitative changes* in the economic system."* Social and economic problems are *related* and, according to the New Left, are in fact *caused* by the capitalist system. The fundamental foundations for capitalism—the ownership of private property and the free competitive market—must be eliminated and a completely new socialistic system established before significant reform can even begin to take place.

The radical view of capitalism

Where do the disciples of Karl Marx stand today? In what ways have they changed the philosophical foundation for communism that Marx provided over a century ago? In order to criticize capitalism, the radical economist needs a vantage point from which to view the economy. The current New Left view of capitalism is characterized by the following points.

Monopoly power

The most obvious characteristic of current capitalism as perceived by radical economists is the emergence of the monopoly. The days of free competition, during which small autonomous firms made profits by cutting costs and investing in increased efficiency, are over. From partnerships, to small companies, and even to agriculture, large and prosperous firms have merged with or underpriced and driven out of business their competitors in any given industry. Since the two world wars, the economic power in industries in the United States—the most advanced of the capitalist countries—has been so concentrated in fewer and fewer hands that by 1962 less than 1 percent of all manufacturing corporations controlled almost 60 percent of manufacturing capital.

---

*Assar Lindbeck, *The Political Economy of the New Left*. New York: Harper & Row, 1971, p. 15.

[T]he result is an irresistible drive on the part of the monopolistic firm to move outside of and beyond its historical field of operation, to penetrate new industries and new markets. Thus the typical production unit in modern developed capitalism is a giant corporation, which is both conglomerate (operating in many industries) and multinational (operating in many countries).*

Dependence on government

In the capitalist economy there is the state to contend with as well as the monopoly. Fearing the detrimental effects of the rise of the giant corporations, the public has entrusted the government to watch over and regulate concentrated industries. The regulatory commissions, however, have failed abysmally at controlling or uncovering monopolistic behavior; all they have done is facilitate capitalistic accumulation. "In fact, the line between public and private authority in the industrial system is indistinct and in large measure imaginary, and the abhorrent association of public and private organizations is normal."† Moreover, monopoly capitalism is further aided by government spending. The working class is pacified by the doling out of welfare, and sources for labor and raw material and markets for commodities abroad are provided by aggressive militarism. "Clearly the modern organized economy was designed with a perverse hand. For how, otherwise, could so many needs seeming so inescapable conspire to make a system which still rejoices in the name of free enterprise in truth be so dependent on government?"‡

Imperialism

The last characteristic of capitalism as perceived by radical economists that we will consider is the one that brings the system into worldwide focus—imperialism. When the economy of a capitalist country reaches a "critical mass," the ills of the capitalist system—worker exploitation, social inequalities, and economic irrationalities—begin to spill over into other, less-developed nations. A capitalist economy needs global influence and authority over many nations if it is to obtain the raw materials and labor it needs to produce its goods and if it is to have a large enough market to sell its goods—in short, if it is to continually expand. Thus radical economists would say that "imperialism is the process whereby labor is alienated and (with land) turned into a marketable commodity on an international scale.... It manifests itself most visibly in the flow of private capital from stronger capitalist nations to weaker foreign countries and territories."§

Economic expansion, of course, has by no means been limited to capitalist societies; history provides numerous examples of political empires of many different origins. Capitalist imperialism, however, does bear its own unique stamp. From the explorations and colonializations of the sixteenth century to the height of competitive expansion in the early years of this century, capitalist countries have intervened, controlled, and then exploited less-developed countries. In recent years, imperialism has been embodied in a rapidly growing entity of global industrialization, the multinational corporation. Operating with near autonomy, protected by military intervention, and spreading at an alarming rate, the multinational

---

*Paul W. Sweezy, *Modern Capitalism and Other Essays.* New York: Monthly Review Press, 1972, p. 8. Copyright © 1972 by Monthly Review Press. Reprinted by permission of Monthly Review Press.

†John Kenneth Galbraith, *The New Industrial State.* New York: Mentor Books, New American Library, 1968, p. 305.

‡*Ibid.*, p. 304.

§Herbert Gintis, in Richard C. Edwards, Michael Reich, and Thomas A. Weisskopf (eds.), *The Capitalist System: A Radical Analysis of American Society,* © 1972, p. 408. Prentice-Hall, Inc., Englewood Cliffs, N.J.

corporation dominates less-developed economies and now concentrates the wealth of the *world*, not just that of a single nation, in the hands of the few.

The radical view of social problems

The radicals see the capitalist system as being characterized by a number of distinct social problems. These problems, however, are not just random occurrences that would emerge from time to time in any political economy; rather, they are a part of the system itself. That is, competition, the free market, and private property invariably produce the following phenomena.

Alienation

"A young ex-marine, perched atop a twenty-story University of Texas building with rifle and rangefinder, topples several dozen unknown passersby. . . . A man arrives home from a brutal day's work and sits before the television set watching football, hockey, boxing, baseball; he drinks beer and smokes cigarettes and never engages in sports or physical activity himself. . . . A throng of furious blacks in Watts (or Harlem or Detroit or Baltimore or Washington, D.C., or . . .) riot, loot, and burn, destroying square blocks of ghetto 'property.' They realize their lack of control over their communities and lives."* These are but three examples of a sense of alienation that radical economists see as pervasive in American life today. From the *psychological* alienation of simply disliking school or a job to the deeper *social* alienation of realizing that one has no control over his or her purpose in life, the anguish of being "cut off" is reflected throughout capitalist society. Workers—blue collar and white—face monotonous assembly lines or demeaning tasks dictated by the rules of profit maximization and corporate hierarchy. At home, people become alienated from communities partitioned according to the whims of private developers. Gradually, as people see the purposes of their work becoming meaningless and their communities and family lives disintegrating, a feeling of alienation even from oneself sets in. Working, creating, relating disappear. The individual takes no part in decisions affecting his life, he "does not experience himself as an active agent, as the bearer of human powers. He is alienated from these powers, his aim is to sell himself successfully on the market. . . . The anonymity of [these] social forces is inherent in the structure of the capitalist mode of production."†

Inequality

Inequality is perhaps the most pervasive of the social problems which radicals believe are inherent in the capitalist system. The clearest example is in the distribution of income and wealth. Walking out from the center of virtually any large American city, one passes from the crowded slums of the urban ghetto to the spacious houses of middle- and upper-class suburbia. In a few short hours one can drive from the luxurious coastal resort communities of the Eastern Establishment to the one-roomed, tin-roofed shacks of Appalachia. In 1977 in the United States, the richest 5 percent of all families received as much income as the bottom 40 percent; in 1972 the wealthiest 1 percent of all households owned about 21 percent of total wealth, and the wealthiest .5 percent owned 49 percent of all corporate stock! Thus earnings potential is tied to the proportion of labor and capital a person uses to generate income; the more an individual relies on labor—wage and salary earnings—the less his or her income will be. "The plain fact is that the probabilities of being both a

---

*Edwards, Reich, and Weisskopf, *The Capitalist System*, p. 274.

†From *The Sane Society* by Erich Fromm. Copyright © 1955 by Erich Fromm.

capitalist and poor are slim compared with the opportunities for poverty if labor forms the principal means of acquiring income. And under capitalism, there is no mechanism for sharing the returns from capital—it all goes to the private owners of capital."*

Although they are readily seen and easily measured, income and wealth are not the only inequities of capitalism but they do lay the foundation for other means of keeping the working class under the capitalist's foot. For example, instead of creating an equal opportunity for all, the educational system serves to pass political and economic power to the same few hands generation after generation because the poor, by and large, cannot afford to send their sons and daughters to expensive schools. In addition, their children often must help out the family with their own wages as soon as possible. Progressive tax legislation does little to correct the inequities when loopholes, discovered by high-priced lawyers available only to the wealthy, cause the before- and after-tax income distributions to be almost identical. Wars on poverty are nothing more than frauds when the welfare system continues to have a negligible impact on the income of the poor.

Discrimination The inequalities of income and education are intertwined with racial and sexual discrimination. Racism—whether individual or institutional—has generated gaps between blacks and whites in income, social status, vocational opportunities, mortality rates, and many other factors for hundreds of years. Since 1967, the median income for blacks has hovered near the level of 60 percent of white income. Discrimination against women has been no less pervasive, if slower to come to light. Work traditionally associated with women—child rearing, housework—is not an income-producing commodity sold in the market. In a capitalist system, where wealth is everything, it stands to reason that women hold little leverage. And those women who do work—almost half of the labor force—by and large hold service or clerical jobs which do not pay as well as jobs traditionally held by men. (The labor income of the full-time female work force averages roughly 60 percent of full-time male workers' wages.)

But if capitalism thrives on competition and profit maximization, what difference does a person's race or sex make? Plenty, answer the radicals. By pitting races and, to some degree, sexes against each other, hostility toward capitalism itself is diverted. If there is to be a bourgeoisie, then by definition there must be a proletariat as well, and the capitalist will use any means— including oppression of blacks and discrimination against women—to preserve this separation of classes.

Irrationality
The United States churns out more automobiles, televisions, stereos, and cigarettes annually than any other nation in the world and spends billions of dollars a year to advertise these goods. In that same year, however, many Americans will live without adequate housing, will have to make do with rundown public playgrounds and swimming pools, and go without good medical care. While the government budgets over $105 billion for national defense alone, it spends considerably less than that on such human services as urban redevelopment, health, education, mass transit, and public housing combined. Furthermore, as capitalism expands—as it must in order to thrive—industry befouls the land, sea, and air in ever-increasing intensity.

What is the explanation for such full-scale abuse of natural resources and such gross expenditures on weaponry and nonessential consumer goods? One answer lies in the capitalist society's constant need to expand. As Marx pointed out,

---

*Howard W. Wachtel, in David Mermelstein (ed.), *Economics: Mainstream Readings and Radical Critiques.* New York: Random House, 1970, p. 274.

the accumulation of capital and the drive for profits require the capitalist economy to grow unceasingly. But the more the economy produces, the more natural resources will be used up, the more pollutants will be absorbed by the environment, and the more the government will have to spend money on military hardware or some other wasteful expenditure in order to buy up the excess supply of goods. In addition, this growing flow of goods and services does not spread out evenly among the citizenry. With income distributed so unequally, a relative few dictate the needs and priorities for all. As long as the rich can afford to satisfy their own needs for transportation, education, health care, recreation, and housing, such "externalities" will never be made available to the public.

The radical model of the socialist society

Some of the problems produced by the capitalist society are described above. What alternatives do the radicals propose to take its place? Most radical economists will not commit themselves to outlining the specific means by which a socialist or communist economy should be established. The institutions for developing a new political and economic system would depend on a number of factors: locale, populace, stage of industrialization, etc. But there are certain values common to most radical views of postcapitalist economies.

The cornerstone of any socialist society is absolute equality in the distribution of income and material wealth, in the social decision-making processes, and in the opportunity to fully realize individual creative potential. Alienation from one's job, discrimination of any kind, production for profit instead of for human needs—all would be eliminated. Uniform availability of all materials and resources means that all forms of private ownership of property would be abolished. The citizenry would be governed not by large, impersonal bureaucratic hierarchies, but by a governing body that serves with the day-to-day agreement of the people. It is an egalitarian society in the truest sense: people cooperating with one another and yet recognizing individual differences and respecting individual rights. But it will not come easily.

> These socialist values and process—and the institutions which would encourage and promote them—must grow out of specific struggles against alienation and other forms of oppression. Hence one part of our struggle against concrete problems and forms of oppression that face us now must be to develop institutions which promote equality, nonalienating production, and the other requisites of a decent society.*

Is the end result worth the effort? Can this so-called "decent society" be established? The radicals earnestly, passionately believe it can. But as any one of them readily admits—there is much work to be done.

RESPONSE FROM THE MAINSTREAM

How do traditional economists respond to the radical criticisms of the existing capitalist system? Let us look at some of their rebuttals.

☐ Liberal economists point out that the Marxist labor theory of value does not distinguish between the quantity of labor input (time) and labor quality. One great contribution of the modern theory of human capital is the recognition that the value of labor in production depends on its quality, which in turn depends on education, training, health, innate ability, motivation, and other factors. There is evidence that in modern capitalist economies a worker's pay is dependent, at least in part, on his or her own human capital. Moreover, mechanisms have developed that enable workers to increase their human capital or productive potential. Although the rich in general clearly find it

---

*Hunt and Sherman, *Economics: An Introduction*, p. 520.

easier than the poor to obtain high-quality education, for example, efforts to make available high-quality education for the poor are nonetheless being pursued. Many individuals do rise from low-income backgrounds and obtain the education that permits them to succeed in a wide variety of areas in our society.

☐ Without attempting to deny that discrimination exists in capitalist economies, traditional economists stress the growing evidence that those operating within the system are working to break down prejudice and discrimination by means of laws, affirmative action programs, and incentives. Black/white and male/female wage differentials are narrowing, and wage levels are *not* falling as a result.

☐ Income levels in capitalist economies are rising, not falling, in terms of real purchasing power. Most workers earn considerably more than subsistence, and many are able to save part of their earnings, which they can invest in the accumulation of capital if they choose.

☐ It is simplistic to characterize large corporations in general as antisocial and self-serving. Many valuable social developments owe their existence and continuation to forward-looking and socially aware business organizations. Big business enables Americans to choose from a great variety of products in order to maximize their satisfaction. In addition, while much advertising is nonproductive, some provides valid information enabling consumers to make reasoned choices. Furthermore, big business is subject to regulation by the government and to pressure from the public. Also, small companies and independent proprietors have persisted in capitalist nations.

☐ Mainstream economists remind us that no ideal Marxist state has yet come into being. There is a bourgeoisie in almost all communist countries. Evidence of a privileged class in Russia shows up frequently in reports of Black Sea villas, better housing and greater freedom for party members and political leaders than for the average worker. Communist nations have also found it necessary to provide incentives to workers. The promise of more and better consumer goods has been a motivating factor in encouraging workers to increase their productivity. Material-reward systems seem at least as important as the national good in motivating communist workers.

☐ There is no evidence that communist nations are less imperialistic than capitalist ones. If the United States has attempted to extend its influence in various areas of the world, so too have socialist nations such as the Soviet Union and Cuba.

☐ The development of communism has been accompanied by the withdrawal from the citizenry of many freedoms, such as freedom of movement, worship, press, and expression. The loss of the freedom of movement has perhaps been the most burdensome loss. Despite known deficiencies in the areas of personal and civil rights, the United States has never taken steps to prevent emigration. Anyone who wants to leave can do so—a privilege frequently denied citizens of communist countries. In Russia, for example, when exit visas have been allowed, long lines of applicants have routinely developed.

Clearly, mainstream economists offer some strong rebuttals to the criticisms of the New Left. Nevertheless, it cannot be denied that radical economists have made a significant contribution in emphasizing the problems related to highly developed capitalist societies and in providing an alternative perspective on the ways that economic systems affect the lives of people.

Summary

- This chapter presents the basic outlines of radical economic analysis in the United States.

- The roots of radical or New Left economic analysis lie in the tradition of Marxian economics. Marxian analysis of the capitalist system centers on the class struggle between the bourgeoisie (the owners of the means of production) and the proletariat (the working class). Labor produces all value, and the amount of labor used to produce goods determines their exchange rates. The owners of capital, however, exploit labor by expropriating the surplus value produced as their profits. Because of competition, capitalist enterprises have to expand and develop technologically; the reduction in the ratio of labor to machinery, however, means in the long run that the rate of profit falls, since there is less labor to exploit. Falling profits force the layoff of workers and the creation of a "reserve army of the unemployed" which serves to hold wages down. The inevitable result, according to Marx, was crises of overproduction and general misery for the working class. The scramble for profits also produces a trend toward monopolization, squeezing out smaller firms, and also to imperialism, the expansion of capital overseas in search of cheap labor, cheap raw materials, and new markets. Capitalist expansion on a world scale creates the conditions for a working-class revolutionary movement to overthrow the capitalist system and establish socialism. One of the attractions of the Marxist outlook for today's radicals is its rigorous, logical explanation of the inevitability of the collapse and overthrow of capitalism.

- Liberal economists regard economic and social problems as being basically unrelated to each other, and stress the possibility of change from within the system. Radicals, on the other hand, believe that most social problems are intimately related to the capitalist economic system, and see the elimination of captialism as necessary for the solution to social problems. Contemporary radical economists in the United States point to the continued growth of monopoly power and see the state as supporting, not checking, monopoly control. They argue that regulatory agencies basically serve business interests, that welfare and social service programs serve to calm discontent, and that the state protects imperialist expansion and multinational corporations.

- Radical economists also argue that the capitalist economic system produces profound social problems: widespread alienation; severe inequality in the distribution of income, with resulting high levels of poverty and discrimination; creation of racial and sexual antagonisms that divide people; and irrational production priorities, waste, and environmental destruction, all perpetuated by the constant need for profit and expansion. While radicals argue that it is not possible beforehand to spell out the details of the socialist alternative, they advocate a society based on the equality of income and decision-making power.

- Liberal economists respond to these radical arguments by denying the labor theory of value, pointing to the differences in human capital among workers, and suggesting that the development of human capital provides a means for overcoming inequality. They argue that discrimination is being overcome within the system already, and worker income in the capitalist countries is rising, not falling. There is also evidence that large corporations do produce social benefits for society, and small business does continue to exist. Liberals also point out that the socialist countries have their own elites and their own patterns of intervention in the affairs of other countries, as well as restrictions on the freedom of their own citizens.

Review & Discussion

1. What are some of the reasons for the growth of interest in radical economics? What were some of the historical developments of the 1960s that seem to have fostered such interest?

2. What is the significance of the radical critique of mainstream economics as being "part of the system"?

3. Describe the main features of Marxian economic analysis. What is the role of class conflict? What is the labor theory of value? What is the "reserve army"? Why does capitalism, in this view, inevitably lead to monopoly power and to imperialism? How does the "success" of capitalism produce the conditions for its own downfall?

4. How well does Marxian economic analysis describe contemporary capitalism in the United States?

5. In the view of radical economists, how does capitalism produce alienation, inequality, discrimination, and irrational priorities? How persuasive are these arguments? If these social problems are not produced by capitalism, how are they produced?

6. Distinguish between the major arguments of radical and liberal economists. What are the areas of disagreement? Are there any areas of agreement? How persuasive is the liberal rebuttal to the radical arguments?

7. What values characterize the ideal post-capitalist society envisioned by radicals? How likely is it that these can be achieved in the socialist society? How close can a capitalist society come to achieving them?

Appendix 3

A Review of Formulas Used in Economics

The question "How much?" is a major issue in economics. To measure productivity and economic efficiency, certain mathematical skills are needed, and certain definitions and formulas must be understood.

Aggregate demand (Chapters 11, 12)*

Aggregate demand is the total amount of money expressed in current dollars that all buyers are willing and able to spend on all goods and services at a given time. Aggregate demand is the sum of personal consumption spending, business investment spending, and government spending:

$$D = C + I + G.$$

Average or mean

To find the average, or mean, of several quantities, add the values of the quantities and divide by the number of quantities in the set.

A factory produces 200 cars in January, 250 in February, 350 in March, 350 in April, 300 in May, and 350 in June. To measure the factory's average monthly production over the six-month period, add the monthly totals and divide by the number of months, as follows:

$$\frac{200 + 250 + 350 + 350 + 350}{6} =$$

$$\frac{1800}{6} = 300.$$

The average monthly production is 300 cars.

---

*When applicable, the chapter numbers in parentheses indicate the chapter in which a concept is first presented.

Average propensity to save and average propensity to consume (Chapter 10)

The average propensity to save (APS) is the percentage of a given total income that is saved. It is calculated by dividing savings by disposable income (S/DI = APS). Thus, assuming a disposable income of \$14,000 and savings of \$3,200, APS would be .23,

$$\frac{3,200}{14,000} = .23.$$

The average propensity to consume (APC) is the percentage of a given total income that is consumed. It is calculated by dividing consumption by disposable income (C/DI = APC). If a household spends \$10,800 and its disposable income is \$14,000, APC is .77,

$$\frac{10,800}{14,000} = .77.$$

Balance of payments (Chapter 38)

The balance of payments is the difference between a country's foreign earnings and its foreign expenditures.

If a country imports \$5 million worth of goods, exports \$6 million worth, and earns \$3 million as profit on its foreign investments, its balance of payments is

\$6 million + \$3 million − \$5 million
= \$4 million.

Because the value is positive, there is a balance-of-payments surplus. If the value of imports is greater than the value of exports and profit from foreign investments added together, there is a balance-of-payments deficit; that is, the country loses money in foreign trade.

Cost formulas (Chapter 22)

☐ **Marginal cost (MC).** Marginal cost (MC) is the cost of producing each additional unit of a product. The formula for calculating marginal cost is

$$MC = \frac{\text{change in total costs}}{\text{change in output}}.$$

☐ **Average fixed costs (AFC).** Fixed costs are costs that cannot be increased or decreased in the short run, no matter what the size of the firm's output. Average fixed costs can be calculated by dividing TFC for any level of production by the number of units produced:

$$AFC = \frac{TFC}{Q}.$$

☐ **Average variable costs (AVC).** Variable costs are costs that can be increased or decreased in the short run. Average variable costs can be calculated by dividing TVC for any level of production by the number of units produced:

$$AVC = \frac{TVC}{Q}.$$

☐ **Average total costs (ATC)** the average total cost (ATC) is the total cost to a firm at any level of output divided by the total quantity of output. Average total costs are calculated by dividing total costs at each level of production by number of units produced:

$$ATC = \frac{TC}{Q}.$$

Elasticity (Chapter 20)

Elasticity is the measure in percentage terms of the degree to which a change in price of a good affects the quantity of the good demanded. The formula for elasticity is:

$$E_D = \frac{\Delta Q}{(Q_1 + Q_2)/2} \div \frac{\Delta P}{(P_1 + P_2)/2}.$$

Suppose the price of eggs decreases by 30 percent, from 30¢ to 20¢. If demand for eggs rises 40 percent, from 100 dozen to 140 dozen, the elasticity is:

$$E_D = \frac{40}{(100 + 40)/2} \div \frac{10}{(30 + 20)/2} = 1.425.$$

Exchange rate (Chapter 38)

The exchange rate is the price at which one currency may be traded for another.

If the British pound (£) sells for $2.50, the exchange rate is expressed

$$£1 = \$2.50.$$

With this information, we can also discover that the dollar sells for £0.40, because

$$\$1 = \frac{1}{2.50} = £0.40.$$

Let us first consider an American tourist in England who buys a tweed coat for £25. She can determine the cost in dollars as follows:

$$25 \times 2.50 = \$62.50.$$

Now let us look at what happens when an Englishman buys a leather jacket in the United States for $75. He can calculate the cost of the coat in his own currency either by multiplying or dividing:

$$75 \times 0.40 = £30,$$

or

$$\frac{75}{2.50} = £30.$$

Growth rate (Chapter 18)

The percentage change in value of a nation's output over time constitutes its growth rate. To calculate growth rate, we divide net change in GNP by the earlier GNP figure.

Let us say that a country's 1979 GNP is $4,000,000,000 and its 1980 GNP is $4,150,000,000 (adjusted to the base, 1972 dollars). Net change in GNP is

$$\$4,150,000,000 - 4,000,000,000 = \$150,000,000.$$

The growth rate is then

$$\frac{\$150,000,000}{\$4,000,000,000} = 0.0375, \text{ or } 3.75 \text{ percent}.$$

Inflation rate (Chapter 9)

The inflation rate is the rate of increase in the general level of prices over time. For example, if the weekly cost of feeding a family of four goes from $70 to $90 in a year, we calculate the rate of inflation as

$$\frac{\$90 - \$70}{\$70} = \frac{\$20}{\$70}$$

$$= 0.29, \text{ or } 29 \text{ percent yearly}.$$

Interest rate

The interest rate on a loan is the ratio of the payment required for the use of the borrowed money to the amount of that money.

If a woman borrows $4000 to buy a car at 9 percent interest, the interest payment will be

$$\$4000 \times 0.09 = \$360.$$

Stated in another way, if she borrows $4000 and must pay back an extra $360 in addition to the $4000 loan, the interest rate is

$$\frac{\$360}{\$4000} = 0.09, \text{ or 9 percent.}$$

Marginal physical product (MPP) (Chapter 28)

The marginal physical product (MPP) is the change in total output (total product) contributed by the addition of one more unit of a variable factor of production. Expressed as a ratio,

$$\text{MPP} = \frac{\text{change in total product}}{\text{change in units of a variable factor}}.$$

Suppose three workers in a shop can produce 14 stereo speakers in a day. With a fourth worker hired, production rises to 19 speakers daily. To measure the MPP of the fourth worker, subtract previous output from present output:

$$19 - 14 = 5.$$

The MPP of the additional worker is 5 stereo speakers a day. If two more workers are added and total production rises to 31, the MPP of each of the two new workers is

$$\frac{31 - 19}{2} = \frac{12}{2} = 6 \text{ units per new worker.}$$

Marginal propensity to consume and marginal propensity to save (Chapter 10)

The marginal propensity to consume (MPC) is that fraction of any extra income that a person will spend rather than save. Expressed as a ratio,

$$\text{MPC} = \frac{\text{change in consumption}}{\text{change in income}}.$$

An accountant gets a $200 annual pay raise and spends $150 of it. His MPC is

$$\frac{\$150}{\$200} = \frac{3}{4}.$$

Assuming that whatever money is not spent is saved, we calculate the marginal propensity to save (MPS)—the fraction of new income saved—as

$$\frac{\$200 - \$150}{\$200} = \frac{\$50}{\$200} = \frac{1}{4}.$$

Note that the sum of MPC and MPS is always 1.

Marginal revenue product (MRP) (Chapter 28)

The marginal revenue product (MRP) is the change in total revenue that results from the addition of one unit of a variable factor of production. Expressed as a ratio,

$$\text{MRP} = \frac{\text{change in total revenue}}{\text{change in units of a variable factor}}.$$

Median

The median in a set of values is that value that has the same number of values above and below it in the set.

If five farmers own 10, 13, 16, 12, and 18 cows, respectively, the median is 16 cows, because two farmers own fewer and two farmers own more. Note that the median differs from the mean, or average, which here would be 13.8 cows.

$$(10 + 13 + 16 + 12 + 18) \div 5 = 13.8)$$

Multiplier (Chapter 11)

The multiplier is a ratio that indicates the ultimate change in income that will result from an initial change in investment. The multiplier is the reciprocal of the MPS. Assuming an MPS of ¼, the multiplier is ⁴⁄₁, or 4. We can also calculate the multiplier if we know the MPC. Since the MPS plus the MPC must always equal 1, the multiplier can also be calculated as 1/(1 − MPC); thus, assuming an MPC of ¾, the multiplier can be calculated as follows:

$$\frac{1}{1 - ¾} = \frac{1}{¼} = 4.$$

Percentages

Percentages are used to measure the ratio of one quantity to another.

In a class of 30 students, of which 18 are men and 12 are women, the ratio of men to all students is

$$\frac{18}{30} = 0.60, \text{ or } 60 \text{ percent}.$$

The ratio of women to all students is

$$\frac{12}{30} = 0.40, \text{ or } 40 \text{ percent}.$$

The ratio of men to women is

$$\frac{18}{12} = 1.50, \text{ or } 150 \text{ percent}.$$

The ratio of women to men is

$$\frac{12}{18} = 0.666, \text{ or } 67 \text{ percent}.$$

Price index (Chapter 8)

A price index measures the percentage of increase or decrease in prices from one year to the next. The method used is to calculate price changes of selected goods from one year to another and relate those changes to a base year. At present the United States government uses 1972 as the base year, so the 1972 price index is given as 100. Since 1978 prices were 152.09 percent of prices in 1972, the 1978 price index deflator is 152.09. With 1972 as the base line, the real value of 1978 GNP is its unadjusted GNP ($2107.6 billion) multiplied by the ratio of 1972 prices to 1978 prices.

$$\$2107.6 \text{ billion} \times \frac{100}{152.09} = \$1385.8 \text{ billion}.$$

Quantity theory of money (Chapter 13)

This theory deals with the relationship of price level to money supply, as expressed in the equation $MV = PQ$ (money supply × velocity = average price per unit × quantity of units of output). The equation tells us that changes in the supply of money or the velocity rate must cause corresponding changes in either price levels or quantities of goods produced, or both.

Ratio

The ratio is the size of one quantity expressed in terms of the size of another quantity.

If Jane drinks six cans of beer while Michael drinks eight, the ratio of Jane's drinking to Michael's is ⁶⁄₈, or, reduced ¾. In other words, Jane drinks ¾ as much beer as Michael does. (Ratio is also expressed in the form 3:4.)

Velocity of money (Chapter 13)

Velocity is the term used to indicate the number of times each dollar is spent or turned over during a given period of time. We can also define velocity (V) as the dollar value of GNP divided by the money supply (M), or $V = \frac{GNP}{M}$. Thus, if GNP is $1000 billion and there is $125 billion worth of cash in circulation, the velocity is

$$\frac{\$1{,}000{,}000{,}000{,}000}{\$125{,}000{,}000{,}000} = 8.$$

This means that, in the course of a year, each dollar changes hands an average of eight times.

Appendix 4

Nobel Prize Winning Economists

1969 Ragnar Frisch (Norway) and Jan Tinbergen (Netherlands) for work in econometrics (application of mathematics and statistical methods to economic theories and problems).

1970 Paul A. Samuelson (United States) for efforts to raise the level of scientific analysis in economic theory.

1971 Simon Kuznets (United States) for developing the concept of using a country's gross national product to determine its economic growth.

1972 Kenneth J. Arrow (United States) and Sir John R. Hicks (United Kingdom) for theories that help to assess business risk and government economic and welfare policies.

1973 Wassily Leontief (United States) for devising the input-output technique to determine how different sectors of an economy interact.

1974 Gunnar Myrdal (Sweden) and Friedrich A. von Hayek (Austria) for pioneering analysis of the interdependence of economic, social, and institutional phenomena.

1975 Leonid V. Kantorovich (Union of Soviet Socialist Republics) and Tjalling C. Koopmans (United States) for work on the theory of optimum allocation of resources.

1976 Milton Friedman (United States) for work in consumption analysis and monetary history and theory, and for demonstration of the complexity of stabilization policy.

Source: *Information Please Almanac, Atlas, and Yearbook, 1979* (33rd Edition), Viking Press, New York, 1978, pp. 18 and 521.)

1977 Bertil Ohlin (Sweden) and James E. Meade (United Kingdom) for contributions to the theory of international trade and international capital movements.

1978 Herbert A. Simon (United States) for "his pioneering research into the decision-making process within economic organizations."

1979 Sir Arthur Lewis (United Kingdom) and Theodore W. Schultz (United States) for their work in the field of economic development, particularly on the topics of industrialization and investment in agriculture.

Glossary

Glossary

(Page numbers shown after the definitions provide the primary references for the terms.)

ability-to-pay-principle A principle of taxation that suggests that the amount of taxes an individual pays should be directly related to the individual's income; that is, those people with the most money should pay the highest taxes. [p. 133]

absolute advantage One nation has an absolute advantage over another nation in producing a good or service when it can use fewer resources than the other nation to produce one unit of the good or service. [p. 707]

accelerator theory The concept that investment spending is closely related to changes in consumption. An increase or decrease in consumption spending will induce a change in investment that is proportionally even greater than the change in consumption. [p. 199]

ad valorem tariff A tariff levied according to the value of the goods imported. For example, a tariff might be set at 10 percent of the total value of a shipment of plywood when it arrives in the United States. [p. 724]

aggregate demand The total amount of money (expressed in current dollars) that all buyers are willing and able to spend on all goods and services at a given time. [p. 208]

aggregate supply The total value (in current dollars) of all goods and services produced or available for purchase at a given time. [p. 208]

"all-other-things-equal" assumption The assumption that all factors (except price) that could affect the relationship observed in demand and supply schedules are held constant. [p. 56]

arbitrage Buying any commodity (for example, currency) in one market and simultaneously selling it in another market in order to profit from a price discrepancy. [p. 739]

assets (1) Things of value, such as cash or property, owned by an economic unit such as a household or business firm. (2) In banking, liabilities plus net worth. [p. 267]

average fixed costs The total fixed costs for any level of production divided by the number of units produced. [p. 454]

average product The ratio of total product to the quantity of variable input resources used to produce that product. [p. 448]

average propensity to consume (APC) The percentage of a given total income that is consumed. [p. 190]

$$\frac{C}{DI} = APC$$

average propensity to save (APS) The percentage of a given total income that is saved. [p. 190]

$$\frac{S}{DI} = APS$$

average total cost The total cost to a firm at any level of output divided by the total quantity of output. [p. 455]

average variable costs The total variable costs at each level of production divided by the total number of units produced. [p. 454]

balance-of-payments statement A nation's balance-of-payments statement is an attempt to record all of its monetary transactions with the outside world. [p. 743]

balance sheet Summarizes a firm's financial position at any given time. The term "balance sheet" is used because the two sides—assets and claims—will always be equal, or balanced. [p. 267]

balance of trade The relationship between a nation's merchandise exports and imports. A country with more exports than imports is said to have a trade surplus or a favorable balance of trade; a country importing more than it exports is said to have a trade deficit or an unfavorable balance of trade. [p. 744]

benefits-received principle Pertains to the distribution of the tax burden and states that people who gain most from goods and services provided by the government should pay most in taxes. [p. 132]

black market An illegal market where goods are traded for more than their fixed legal price. [p. 68]

bond A loan from a private individual or an institution. The lender agrees to lend a fixed amount for a specified time period, during which interest is collected. At the end of the loan period, the lender receives exactly the amount lent. [p. 114]

budget constraint See *line of budget constraint*.

budget deficit See *deficit*.

budget surplus See *surplus*.

business cycles Recurrent fluctuations in economic activity that vary in length and severity. In its simplest form a business cycle consists of a period of economic expansion followed by a period of contraction. For descriptive purposes business cycles are divided into four phases: recovery, peak, recession, and trough. [p. 177]

business firm An organization that produces goods and services. [p. 110]

capital Produced (man-made) instruments to be used for further production; that is, goods that are used to produce other goods and services. One of the factors of production along with land, labor, entrepreneurship, and technology. Also includes productive characteristics of people which are referred to as human capital. [p. 36]

capital accounts The original sums of money that commercial banks pay to purchase stock in their regional Federal Reserve bank, plus the accumulated profits that have not yet been returned to the Treasury. [p. 289]

capital consumption allowance A system for charging for depreciation of capital goods, whereby a firm adds a certain percentage of the purchase price of capital goods to its costs of production each year for a specified number of years. [p. 153]

capital/output ratio The concept introduced by post-Keynesian economists which holds that increases in output, and therefore in income, are a function of capital accumulation, or the investment rate. [p. 370]

capitalist economy An economic system in which most resources are privately owned (for example, the United States). [p. 776]

cartel A group of producers (or countries) who formally agree to control price and output of a commodity or commodities. [p. 396]

central bank Comprises the principal banking authorities of a nation. Its primary function is to provide a means of controlling the size of the total money supply. In the United States, the central bank is the Federal Reserve System, which consists of a Board of Governors and 12 regional Federal Reserve banks. [p. 266]

change in demand See *demand curve*.

change in quantity demanded See *demand curve*.

change in quantity supplied See *supply curve*.

change in supply See *supply curve*.

circular flow A model of an economy that shows the interaction between the product and resource markets. Supply and demand in the resource market determine the prices of factors of production. Households offer the use of their resources to businesses in exchange for money incomes. In the product market, supply and demand determine the prices of goods and services. Business firms use the resources they have purchased from households to produce consumer goods. Households in turn use the money incomes they have received from businesses to buy the commodities that the firms offer for sale. [Chs. 5 and 8]

classical school of economics A school of economic thought that originated in England with the writings of Adam Smith and that included the writings of other English economists such as David Ricardo, Thomas Malthus, and John Stuart Mill, as well as the work of the French economist Jean Baptiste Say. The classical economists believed that an economy functions best if left to itself. They further held that competition alone determines prices, wages, profits, and rents, but that some investments that would benefit society as a whole should be undertaken by the government. [p. 328]

closed shop A factory or business in which only union members are accepted for employment. [p. 612]

collective bargaining The process by which union and management arrive at a mutually acceptable contract that spells out the privileges and obligations (such as wages and working conditions) of both parties for an agreed-upon period. [p. 614]

collectivization An agricultural program launched by Joseph Stalin in the Soviet Union in 1929. Peasant land was confiscated by the state and organized into larger collective farms which were closely regulated by the government. The goal was to secure more efficient use of productive resources, particularly machinery. [pp. 783-784]

collusion Secret agreement among firms in an industry to set a single industry-wide price; also referred to as price-rigging. [p. 527]

command economy A centralized economic system in which the economic decisions of what and how much to produce and sometimes for whom to produce are the responsibility of agencies of a central government (for example, the Soviet Union). [p. 776]

commercial bank The primary unit of the United States banking system. It is a business firm chartered by a state government or the federal government to serve a variety of financial functions, the most important of which is creating demand deposits by lending money. [p. 265]

communism An ideal communist system would be characterized by a classless society in which all goods would be in ample supply so that there would no longer be any need to regulate the economy. As a consequence the state would wither away. [p. 783]

comparative advantage A principle that states that if one country can produce each of two goods at a lower opportunity cost than another country and can produce one of these goods at a lower opportunity cost than the other, it should specialize in the production of the good with the lower opportunity cost and should trade with another country to obtain the other good. [p. 707-708]

competition Rivalry among buyers and sellers in the purchase of resources and products. [p. 87]

complements Commodities that can be used with another commodity such as hot dogs and hot dog rolls. When two goods are complements the demand for one is inversely related to the price of the other (cf. *substitutes*). [p. 59]

concentration ratios Ratios measuring the percentage of total output produced by a certain number (usually four) of the largest firms in any particular industry. [p. 546]

conglomerate mergers Mergers between firms that produce unrelated products. [p. 549]

consumer goods and services Anything, material or otherwise, that satisfies a human desire. [p. 34]

consumer price index Measures the price level of the goods and services purchased by an average American household unit. [p. 165]

consumer sovereignty A situation in which the consumer has the freedom to choose between possible purchases, and in which consumer choices in the marketplace have some consequences for production decisions and the allocation of resources. [p. 776]

consumer surplus The extra value that a good has for a consumer in excess of the price of the good. [p. 432]

consumption schedule A schedule showing the amounts a household plans to consume at each possible disposable income level at a specific point in time. [p. 189]

corporate profits The residual accruing to a corporation after all payments of interest, rent, salaries, and wages have been made to the owners of capital, land, and labor. [p. 152]

corporation A form of business enterprise in which the organization is created as a legal entity separate from the persons who established it. It can own property, acquire resources, extend credit, and sue persons or other corporations. It can also outlive its creators. Once it is granted its existence, it continues to operate as long as it can balance costs with revenues over the long run. [p. 113]

cost-push inflation An increase in the general price level due to increased costs of production (increased profits and/or increased resource prices). [p. 166]

constant-costs industry An industry in which the expansion of existing firms and the entry into the market of new firms will have no effect on the prices of input resources. [p. 480]

countervailing power A concept proposed by John Kenneth Galbraith which holds that the existence of concentrated economic power in one group tends to stimulate a counterbalancing reaction by another group. [p. 553]

creeping inflation Usually refers to an annual rate of inflation of less than 5 percent. [p. 168]

cross elasticity of demand A ratio which indicates the effect of price changes of one good on the quantity demanded of another good; calculated by dividing the percentage change in the quantity demanded of a good by the percentage change in the price of another good. [p. 417]

cyclical unemployment Unemployment that is linked to changes in the level of economic activity. [p. 174]

decreasing-costs industry An industry in which the entry of new firms and expansion might result for a time in lower resource prices and therefore lower costs of production. [p. 482]

deficit (budget deficit) An excess of expenditures over revenues. [p. 225]

deflation A drop in the general level of prices of most goods and services in an economy. [p. 163]

deflationary gap The amount by which aggregate demand falls short of the full-employment level of net national product. [p. 219]

demand The quantities of a product that individuals are willing and able to buy at each and every possible price during some specified period of time. (See also *law of demand*.) [p. 54]

demand curve A graphic representation of the inverse relationship between price and quantity demanded. The demand curve always slopes down and to the right. A *change in demand* refers to a shift in the position of the whole demand curve; a *change in quantity demanded* refers to a movement along a given demand curve. [p. 55]

demand deposits Deposits of money in banks against which checks can be written. The bank promises to pay at once (on demand) money in the amount specified by the consumer who owns the deposit. [p. 249]

demand-pull inflation An increase in the general price level caused by an increase in demand at a time when an economy cannot increase production because it is at full employment, or is unable to increase production fast enough to keep pace with the increase in demand. [p. 166]

demand schedule A table that shows the various quantities of any given product that consumers will demand at different price levels during some specified period of time. [p. 55]

derived demand Demand for a resource that is based on the demand for the finished products that can be manufactured with that resource. For example, an electric power company's demand for generators is derived from consumers' demand for electricity. [p. 571]

devaluation Occurs when a nation declares the official value of its currency to be worth less than it was in terms of gold and other currencies. [p. 756]

development See *economic development*.

discount rate The interest that the Federal Reserve banks charge commercial banks on funds they borrow from the Fed. [p. 298]

discretionary fiscal policy The purposeful alteration of the rate of taxation or government spending to help adjust equilibrium NNP to a full-employment level while also maintaining price stability. [p. 227]

discrimination In economic terms, discrimination exists when, between two workers with the same skills and training, one worker is preferred over the other on the basis of some criterion that is not directly related to the worker's ability to perform the job. [p. 672]

diseconomies of scale Reduced efficiency and higher costs that occur when a business grows too large. [p. 47]

disposable personal income The amount of income available to households to spend or save after personal income taxes have been paid. [p. 105]

dissave To spend more than is earned. [p. 104]

domestic exchange ratio The opportunity cost of one good relative to another. [p. 709]

durable goods Goods designed to last a year or more (for example, cars, beds, and refrigerators). [p. 148]

economic development A situation in which economic growth (increase in real GNP) is accompanied by favorable changes in the economic and social structure and institutions of a country such that continuing economic growth is not only possible but also encouraged. [p. 379]

economic externality A situation in which the use of resources by some individuals has unintended side effects on the welfare of others and in which there is no economic mechanism to record the change in welfare. [p. 635]

economic good Any good or service that is both desirable and scarce and for which people are willing to sacrifice some amount of other desirable goods. [p. 11]

economic growth An increase in real gross national product. [p. 356]

economic imperialism Overt or implicit control over the territory, resources, or destiny of a nation by foreigners. [p. 389]

economic profit The payments to a business in excess of its explicit and implicit costs. [p. 117]

economic rent The price paid for the use of land or any other resource that is fixed. [p. 586]

economics The study of the way people may choose among alternative uses of scarce resources. [p. 4]

economies of scale Reductions in a business firm's production costs brought about by increasing the scale of production. [p. 39]

elasticity coefficient A ratio which indicates the degree of elasticity, calculated by dividing the percentage change in quantity demanded by the percentage change in price for any good. [p. 409]

elasticity of demand The responsiveness in percentage terms of the quantity of a good demanded to changes in price. Degrees of price elasticity include the following: (1) Price elastic: the percentage change in quantity is larger than percentage change in price; the elasticity coefficient is greater than one. (2) Price inelastic: the percentage change in quantity is smaller than percentage change in price; the elasticity coefficient is less than one. (3) Unitary price elasticity: the percentage change in quantity is equal to the percentage change in price; the elasticity coefficient is equal to one. (4) Perfectly elastic demand: any given percentage change in price will lead to an infinite change in quantity purchased; the elasticity coefficient is equal to infinity. (5) Perfectly inelastic demand: there is no change in the amount purchased regardless of any percentage change in price; the elasticity coeffcient is zero. [p. 408-411]

elasticity of supply The responsiveness in percentage terms of the quantity of a good supplied to changes in price. If percentage change in quantity supplied is greater than percentage change in price, supply is elastic; if percentage change in quantity is less than percentage change in price, supply is inelastic. [p. 417]

entrepreneurship (business enterprise) A group of skills which include the ability to combine land, labor, and capital in the most efficient way, the willingness to run the risks of business failure, and the creativity required to invent new products and new ways to market them; one of the factors of production along with land, labor, capital, and technology. [p. 36]

equal marginal utility principle The attempt to balance marginal utility per last dollar spent such that a consumer achieves an equilibrium condition in which no changes in the way income is allocated could yield any increase in total utility. [p. 434]

equilibrium price The price at which the quantity supplied is equal to the quantity demanded; that is, the point at which the supply curve intersects the demand curve. [p. 67]

escalator clause Provides for automatic increases in wages and/or other benefits to match any rise that might occur in the cost of living as measured by the consumer price index or another measure. [p. 616]

European Economic Community (EEC) A union of European nations for trade purposes. Originally formed in 1957, the objective of the EEC (often called the Common Market) was the gradual elimination of tariffs and quotas among the members, so that goods and capital could move freely from one country to another. [p. 755]

excess reserves That amount by which a bank's actual reserves exceed its required reserves. [p. 270]

exchange rate The price at which one currency may be traded for another. [p. 738]

exclusion principle The principle which states that those who can pay the price can get the benefits of the product, but those who cannot pay are excluded from the benefits of the product. [p. 126]

explicit costs The costs recorded in a firm's account books. These include various types of taxes, costs of labor and raw materials, costs of acquiring capital, and costs of depreciation of capital. [p. 117]

external diseconomy A situation in which the actions of a producer have a harmful effect on others and in which no compensation is paid to the affected individuals. [p. 635]

external economy A situation in which a producer's actions have a beneficial effect on others and payment cannot be extracted from those who receive benefits. [p. 636]

factor endowments See *theory of factor endowments*.

factors of production (productive inputs) Input resources of an economy, including land, labor, physical and human capital, entrepreneurship, and technology. [p. 35]

fallacy of composition An incorrect assumption that what is true of the part is also true of the whole. [p. 14]

featherbedding The imposing by unions of limits on workloads, production quotas, or kinds of equipment to be used on the job as a means of increasing the demand for labor. [p. 619]

Federal Reserve banks The 12 member banks of the Federal Reserve System; they share the responsibility for implementing monetary policy. [p. 286]

Federal Reserve notes Paper dollars that the Federal Reserve banks print for member banks and their customers on request. [p. 289]

Federal Reserve System The central banking system of the United States, established by the Federal Reserve Act of 1913 and consisting of the Board of Governors, 12 regional reserve banks and their branches, and any commercial banks that have chosen to join the system. [p. 286]

fiat money system A money system in which paper money need not be backed by any set amount of precious metal. [p. 249]

financial capital Loanable funds that businesses can borrow and use to purchase capital goods. [p. 589]

fiscal drag The contractionary effect of increased tax revenues produced by increases in net national product. [p. 225]

fiscal policy Actions taken by the government to alter the level of its taxes and expenditures in order to bring about desired changes in economic activity. [p. 224]

fixed costs Those production costs that cannot be increased or decreased in the short run, no matter what the size of a firm's output is. [p. 451]

fixed inputs Productive inputs that a firm cannot change in the short run; typical examples are capital goods and plant facilities. [p. 444]

floating exchange rates Under this system of exchange, the price of one currency in terms of another is determined simply by supply and demand, as exporters compete in the open market to buy currencies they require. [p. 741]

free good A good available to everyone in unlimited supply without the sacrifice of any other good. [p. 12]

frictional unemployment Unemployment caused by functional imperfections in the labor market, such as the lack of mobility of labor resources and the lack of complete knowledge of all job opportunities. [p. 173]

futures contract A contract under which the seller promises to sell the buyer a given amount of foreign currency (or another commodity) at a stated price some time in the future, regardless of the actual market price of the currency (or commodity) at that future date; businesspeople dealing in international trade use futures contracts to avoid price uncertainties connected with floating exchange rates. [p. 742]

general equilibrium analysis Analysis of the effects of changes in one market on other markets in the determination of a general balance between economic forces. [p. 594]

GNP gap The difference in potential GNP for a year compared with the actual GNP. Reflects the cost of unemployment in terms of production loss. [p. 174]

gold certificates "Warehouse receipts" given by the Treasury to the Fed for gold held by the Treasury. [p. 288]

gold-exchange standard A modified version of the gold-standard mechanism used in international trade: under this system, the exchange value of each currency is fixed in terms of both gold and United States dollars, and every major currency is convertible for foreign trade purposes into the stated amount of gold or dollars. [p. 740]

gold points The upper and lower limits within which the price of currency fluctuates under a gold standard. [p. 738]

gold standard A mechanism whereby each country defines its monetary unit in terms of gold. Under the gold standard every country agrees to convert its paper money to gold on request at a set legal rate and to permit gold to be imported and exported freely. [p. 738]

gross investment The total value of real productive assets produced in one year. [p. 149]

gross national product (GNP) The total market value (expressed in monetary terms) of all goods and services produced for final consumption in the economy during a given year. [p. 142]

growth See *economic growth*.

horizontal integration The purchase by a firm of competing companies in the same industry, or companies that produce substitutable products. By this means a firm is able to consolidate its market power. [p. 548]

household Any person or group of people living under the same roof and functioning as an economic unit. [p. 99]

human capital The productive skills and degree of knowledge possessed by an individual worker. [p. 669]

hyperinflation The most rapid type of inflation in which daily increases in wages and prices are noticeable. Hyperinflation is also characterized by a snow-balling effect—instead of steady increases in prices, the percentage rise in the price level multiplies rapidly. [p. 168]

imperialism See *economic imperialism*.

implicit costs The amount of money that the labor and capital resources owned by the company and employed in its production process could have earned in some alternative employment; the opportunity cost of being in business. [p. 117]

implicit price deflator The price index for gross national product. [p. 166]

income effect The change in the real purchasing power of a consumer produced by a change in prices. [p. 439]

income elasticity The responsiveness in percentage terms of changes in quantity demanded to changes in income. Degrees of income elasticity include the following: (1) Income elastic: the percentage change in the amount of a good demanded is larger than the percentage change in income; the elasticity coefficient is greater than 1. (2) Income inelastic: the percentage change in the amount of a good purchased is smaller than the percentage change in income; the elasticity coefficient is less than 1. [pp. 416–417]

increasing costs When increasing amounts of a product must be sacrificed to get equal additional amounts of another product, the costs are said to be increasing. [p. 45]

increasing-costs industry An industry in which the entry of new firms and the expansion of old ones usually result in increased competition for the factors of production. [p. 481]

indifference curve A graphic representation of the various combinations of two goods which yield the same level of satisfaction to the consumer. [p. 435]

indifference map A set of indifference curves describing the range of consumer preferences; derived by changing the magnitude of the combinations of goods available to a consumer. [p. 437]

indirect business taxes Taxes (primarily sales, excise, and business property taxes) that are often treated by business as part of the costs of manufacturing and therefore added to the price of the products the business sells. [p. 152]

individual proprietorship A business enterprise in which one person, the proprietor, owns all the productive property and legally is solely responsible for the success or failure of the firm; it is the simplest form of legal business organization. [p. 111–112]

industry A group of producers of the same or similar commodities, such as the American automobile industry. [p. 110]

inferior goods Goods whose demand varies inversely with income; that is, as income increases, demand for these goods falls, and as income decreases, demand rises. Typical examples are bread and potatoes. [p. 59]

inflation A rise in the general level of prices of most goods and services in an economy. [p. 163]

inflationary gap The amount by which aggregate demand exceeds the full employment level of net national product. [p. 219]

infrastructure A stock of public goods necessary to facilitate modern production. [p. 388]

input coefficient A ratio measuring the value of each input needed to produce $1 worth of output in an industry. The input coefficient is calculated by dividing each input requirement by the total value of inputs in that industry. [p. 600]

input-output table An economic model that can be used to quantify changes in general equilibrium. The main goal of an input-output table is to show the interrelationships between different industries within a single economy. [p. 597]

interest (1) All payments by businesses to the suppliers of borrowed money capital; payments may be made to banks or to holders of corporate bonds. (2) Payments made to purchase the use of money or loanable funds over a period of time. [p. 152, 589]

interest rate The ratio of the payment for the use of financial capital to the amount borrowed. [p. 589]

International Monetary Fund A world monetary body designed to provide a central pool of currencies on which any member nation could draw when its own reserves of gold or dollars became temporarily inadequate to maintain its currency-support operations. [p. 741]

inventories The amount of finished goods not yet sold, goods in the process of manufacture, and raw materials held for future production. [p. 149]

investment (1) Commonly refers to the purchase of durable goods or financial properties with the intention of receiving income or profit. (2) For national income accounting, it is defined as the amount of current output that adds to or replaces the national stock of real productive assets. [p. 149]

labor The human effort needed to turn raw materials into useful goods and services; one of the factors of production along with labor, capital, entrepreneurship, and technology. [p. 36]

land All raw natural resources that might be used to produce goods and services; one of the factors of production along with labor, capital, entrepreneurship, and technology. [p. 35]

law of demand The principle which states that as the price of any good decreases, the quantity of the good that buyers are willing and able to purchase will increase. As the price increases, a smaller quantity of the good will be demanded. [p. 55]

law of diminishing marginal utility The economic principle proposed by William Stanley Jevons which states that as an individual acquires additional units of an economic good, each unit provides less marginal utility than the previous one. [p. 430]

law of diminishing returns The principle which states that beyond a certain point in the production process, the addition of successive equal amounts of one or two variable factors of production (usually labor and land) to a fixed factor of production (usually capital) will result in a smaller and smaller increase in output. [p. 46]

law of supply The principle which states that as the price of any good rises, the quantity of the good that suppliers are willing and able to offer for sale increases; as the price drops, a smaller quantity of the good will be supplied. [p. 62]

liabilities Things of value, such as cash or property, owed by an economic unit such as a household or a business firm to creditors. [p. 267]

line of budget constraint A price line that indicates the combinations of goods that a consumer may purchase given the price of each good and the consumer's level of income. [p. 437]

liquid assets Those assets—stocks, bonds, bank accounts, etc.—that can be converted relatively easily into cash. [p. 193]

liquidity preference curve A demand curve which shows the relationship between changes in the interest rate and the amount of liquid assets a person is willing to hold. [p. 251]

lockout The closing of a plant by an employer to deprive workers of their salaries; usually imposed in order to dampen enthusiasm for unionization. [p. 611]

long run The period of time sufficient to allow a firm to alter its fixed inputs as well as its variable inputs. [p. 47]

Lorenz curve A diagram that includes curves that illustrate a totally equal distribution of a society's income and the actual distribution of that income; the distance between the two curves indicates the degree of inequality of the distribution of income in a given society. [p. 667]

luxuries Goods or services which are not absolutely necessary but for which people will spend an increasing proportion of their income as income rises. [p. 35]

M_1 Currency (coins and paper money) and demand deposits (checking accounts); the narrowest definition of the money supply. [p. 247]

GLOSSARY

M_2 Money from savings deposits and time accounts in addition to currency and demand deposits. [p. 250]

macroeconomics The level of economic analysis that deals with the activity of the whole economy and with the interaction between the major sectors (aggregates) of the economy. [p. 14]

margin requirements The minimum percentage down payment required from customers to purchase stocks. [p. 299]

marginal cost curve A cost curve showing the additional cost of producing each additional unit of a product. [p. 453]

marginal efficiency of investment (MEI) The relationship between the interest rate and the level of investment. [p. 261]

marginal physical product (MPP) or **marginal product** The change in total output brought about by a change of one unit of a variable factor of production. [p. 46, 446, 567]

marginal product See *marginal physical product*.

marginal propensity to consume (MPC) The proportion of new income devoted to consumption. [p. 190]

$$\text{MPC} = \frac{\text{change in consumption}}{\text{change in income}}$$

marginal propensity to save (MPS) The fraction of new income saved. [p. 190]

$$\text{MPS} = \frac{\text{change in saving}}{\text{change in income}}$$

marginal rate of substitution The number of units of one good that a consumer is willing to sacrifice to obtain an additional unit of another good, with total satisfaction remaining the same. [p. 436]

marginal revenue product (MRP) The change in total revenue that results from the addition of one unit of a variable factor of production. [p. 567]

marginal unit A small amount added to or subtracted from the whole. Since most basic economic decisions involve additions or subtractions of small units, economists use marginal units as a basic analytical tool for studying the smaller, more measurable steps that contribute to a larger process. [p. 13]

marginal utility The additional satisfaction derived from one additional unit of a good. [p. 430]

market demand schedule The sum of all individual demand schedules for any given commodity at each and every price. [p. 60]

market economy An economy in which decisions concerning production, consumption, and resource allocation made by producers and consumers are realized primarily through a system of markets and prices. [p. 52]

market price The price that the buyer and seller agree on for a good or service. [p. 54]

microeconomics The level of economic analysis that deals with the activity of individual agents of the economic system, such as the price of a single product or the behavior of a single business firm. [p. 14]

model A framework for analyzing and predicting the way that a system would work under specified conditions. [p. 13]

monetary theory The study of the way changes in the money supply and the interest rate can affect levels of income, employment and prices. [p. 246]

money Any item that is widely accepted by buyers and sellers as a medium for exchange. [p. 52]

money flow The flow of money income to households and the spending of this income on goods and services. [pp. 76–77]

monopolistic competition A market structure characterized by many small firms selling a differentiated product. [p. 525]

monopoly Hypothesizes a market structure in which only one supplier controls a particular good in the market for which there is no close substitute and thus is able to determine price and production levels for that good. [p. 88]

monopsony A resource market in which there is only one buyer of a good or service. [p. 548]

multiplier A ratio which indicates the ultimate change in income that will result from an initial change in investment. The multiplier is the reciprocal of the MPS. [p. 217]

multiplier effect The ultimate change in income that will result from an initial change in consumption or investment. [p. 217]

national income (NI) The amount paid out by businesses in wages, salaries, interest, rents, and profits to purchase or to rent productive services. [p. 151]

national income and product accounts The device that economists use to measure an economy's performance. These accounts can tell us the exact value of the goods and services purchased by households from businesses in the product market, and the exact value of the goods and services that businesses buy from households in the resource market. [p. 142]

nationalization Assumption by a government of control and ownership of a firm that previously was privately owned. [p. 390]

near-monies Assets that can be converted easily into currency or demand deposits but that unlike money are not widely accepted as a medium of exchange. [p. 249]

negative income tax A system of taxation in which each household would report its total earnings on a tax form, just as it does now. If the total amount was above the level established as the poverty line, the household would have to pay a tax to the government (a progressive tax). But if total income was below the poverty level, the government would pay the household an amount to bring it closer to the minimum income. [p. 679]

neoclassical school of economics A school of economic thought based primarily on the work of English economist Alfred Marshall. The neoclassical economists incorporated the role of technology into the classical growth models, suggesting that technological development could alleviate the problem of scarcity of resources and create more opportunities for profitable investment. They also made other additions to the theory of investment. [p. 367]

net exports The value of goods and services exported from the economy minus the value of those imported (net exports = value of exports − value of imports). [p. 150]

net investment The actual measure of change in the stock of productive assets (net investment = gross investment − depreciation). [p. 149]

net national product (NNP) Measures the value of a year's production after it has been adjusted for the consumption of capital goods during the period. [p. 152]

net worth The value of the capital stock owned by the bank's stockholders (investors). Net worth is equal to assets minus liabilities. [p. 267]

nominal A term used in economics to indicate that a figure has not been adjusted for inflation; it is measured in current dollars.

nondiscretionary fiscal policy (automatic stabilizers) Built-in stabilizers in government economic policies that automatically diminish or cushion any fluctuations in economic activity that occur. [p. 224]

nondurable goods Goods disposed of within a short period of time (for example, paper towels, lettuce, and nylon stockings). [p. 148]

normal goods Goods whose demand varies directly with income; that is, demand for normal goods rises as income rises and falls as income falls. Includes most consumer goods. [p. 58]

normal profit A profit equal to what the same resources would earn if they were employed in any alternative use. [p. 444]

oligopoly A market structure characterized by a few firms selling either a uniform or a differentiated (similar but not identical) product. [p. 525]

OPEC (The Organization of Petroleum Exporting Countries) A cartel formed in 1960 by 13 nations that produce just over half of the world's current daily production of crude oil. [p. 396]

open-market operations The purchase and sale of United States government securities by the Fed in the open market. [p. 293]

opportunity costs The amount of other goods and services that must be sacrificed to obtain more of any one good. [p. 40]

optimum resource mix The best combination of input resources to use in the production of a commodity. A firm achieves the optimum resource mix when the MRP from the last dollar spent to purchase each resource is exactly equal to the MRP per last dollar spent on every other resource. [p. 571]

paradox of thrift A reduction in the actual amount of aggregate savings that follows a period of widespread planned increases in saving. [p. 213]

parity pricing A pricing concept whereby year after year there should be an equivalence between farmers' current purchasing power and their purchasing power at a selected base period. This equivalence is maintained by government support of agricultural commodity prices. [p. 495]

parity value An exchange or equivalency rate. [p. 757]

partial equilibrium analysis The analysis of the economics (price and output determination, supply and demand interactions, etc.) of individual, independent markets for specific goods and services. [p. 593]

partnership An expanded proprietorship, in which two or more people share direct ownership of, and responsibility for, a firm. [p. 113]

patent laws Laws that give a firm the exclusive right to produce, use, transfer, or withhold a product or process for a limited period of time, thus in effect enabling the firm to exercise a temporary monopoly. [p. 509]

peak The phase of a business cycle during which capacity is fully utilized, and full employment is achieved. [p. 178]

per capita GNP The average distribution per individual of the goods and services produced in a given year; calculated by dividing a country's GNP by the number of people in the country. [p. 155]

perfect competition A market model which assumes that there are many suppliers producing a uniform product and many demanders for the product. The model further assumes that no one supplier produces a large enough percentage of the total goods on the market to be able to influence the market price of any good by individual action, that everyone has full and immediate knowledge of changes in production and price, and that when necessary productive resources can be switched instantly to more profitable uses. [p. 88]

permanent income A worker's average income level throughout his or her life. [p. 194]

personal income The total amount of income actually received by households from all sources. It is derived from six basic sources: wages (the largest source of income), rent, interest, proprietors' income, distributed corporate profits, and transfer payments from the government. [p. 101]

petrodollars Dollars accumulated by OPEC nations from the sale of OPEC oil. [p. 763]

Phillips curve A curve that illustrates the relationship between the level of unemployment and the level of inflation. [p. 325]

plant An individual producing unit that contains the physical equipment of production, such as office equipment, machines, land under cultivation, etc. A plant is owned and operated by a business firm. [p. 110]

precautionary demand The need to hold more money than is actually required for everyday transactions as a precaution against unexpected contingencies. [p. 250]

price The amount of other goods an individual is willing to sacrifice to obtain a desired commodity. [p. 52]

price ceilings Enforced maximum prices established by the government that can legally be charged for a good. [p. 419]

price discrimination The practice of charging different prices to the same or to different buyers. [p. 518]

price fixing Secret agreements among business firms in the same industry to maintain artificially high prices or to restrict supply. [pp. 124–125]

price index Measures the percentage increase or decrease in prices from one year to the next. [p. 144]

price leader In an oligopolistic industry, the firm that makes the initial move to set prices, which all other firms in that industry then follow with matching increases or decreases. [p. 530]

price system The mechanism the American economy uses to answer the basic questions of production, including: what goods are to be produced and in what quantities, how the goods are to be produced, and for whom the goods are to be produced. [p. 78]

prime rate The interest charge that commercial banks make on loans to their best customers. [p. 299]

private costs (of production) The costs to the producer incurred in the production process. [p. 636]

private goods All kinds of products and services (milk, bread, cars, clothing) purchased from private producers. Private goods are subject to the exclusion principle, which states that those who can pay the price can get the benefits of the product, but those who cannot pay are excluded from the benefits of the product (cf. *public goods*). [p. 126]

producer price indexes Measures of average changes in prices of goods at various stages of processing. [p. 165]

product market The market for final goods and services. [p. 62]

production possibilities The various combinations of goods that an economy is capable of producing when it is fully and efficiently employing its resources. [p. 41]

profit The excess money received by a producer after production costs have been paid. A broad, long-run definition might be the increase in value of a firm—the amount that a "well-informed and prudent" businessperson would be prepared to pay for ownership of the firm, based on future earning potential—plus the amount of dividends paid out to owners of the company. [p. 62]

progressive tax A tax for which the effective rate of taxation increases as the base amount taxed increases; for example, the income tax. [p. 133]

proportional tax A tax for which the same tax rate is used regardless of the base amount taxed; for example, the property tax. [p. 133]

proprietor's income The income generated by unincorporated business enterprises, including the incomes of all proprietorships and partnerships, and the income of farmers (including the value of the food that the household consumes personally). [p. 151]

protective injunction A court order prohibiting a strike or a boycott. [p. 611]

public debt The money owed by a government to its citizens. The public debt comprises that part of the total of all past budget deficits that has not been eliminated by all past budget surpluses used to retire existing budget deficits. It is incurred when government finances a budget deficit by borrowing money from the public. [p. 236]

public or social goods Goods and services that are not subject to the exclusion principle; that is, people who are unable or unwilling to pay for the use of such goods may not be excluded from using them. Public goods are used in common and their benefits cannot be measured in discrete monetary units. Because the exclusion principle cannot be applied to public goods, most private producers are unable or unwilling to supply them. As a result many public goods are provided by the government. Examples of public goods are police and fire services, military defense, and highways (cf. *private goods*). [p. 126]

quantity theory of money Deals with the relationship of price level to money supply, as expressed in the equation $MV = PQ$ (money supply × velocity = average price per unit × quantity of units of output). This equation tells us that changes in the supply of money or the velocity rate must cause corresponding changes in either price levels, or quantities of goods produced, or both. [pp. 252–253]

real A term used in economics to indicate that a figure has been adjusted for inflation and is measured in constant dollars (e.g., 1972 dollars, 1968 dollars, etc.).

real flow The flow of resources from households to businesses for use in the production process and the resulting output in the form of goods and services flowing from businesses back to households. [p. 76]

recession The phase of a business cycle during which consumption spending slows down and investment shows a sharp decline. [p. 178]

recovery The phase of a business cycle during which employment, income, and profits begin to advance as business activity increases. [p. 177]

regressive tax A tax for which tax rate decreases as the base amount taxed increases; for example, sales taxes. [p. 133]

rent Income earned by persons for the use of real property (houses, stores) or income from royalties received from copyrights, rights to natural resources, and the like. [p. 151]

reserve ratio (reserve requirement) A minimum percentage of monies that member banks of the Federal Reserve System must hold in the form of cash or cash equivalents against deposit liabilities. [p. 268]

resource market The market in which productive resources—for example, an hour of a worker's time or a bushel of wheat to make flour—are sold to producers. [p. 62]

right-to-work laws Laws that make it illegal to require membership in a union as a condition of employment. [p. 617]

saving (1) The sacrifice of current expenditure in order to be able to purchase more in the future. (2) In the context of income analysis, saving refers only to that portion of disposable income that is left over after current expenditures. It includes the cash reserves held by individuals in checking and savings accounts, the amount of insurance equity they own, and the corporate bonds they have purchased. [p. 101, 188]

saving schedule A schedule showing the amounts a household plans to save at each possible disposable income level at a specific point in time. Figured by deducting consumption from disposable income. [p. 189]

Say's law A law of economics attributed to Jean Baptiste Say which states that the act of producing goods generates an income exactly equal to the value of goods produced; therefore supply generates its own demand. [p. 328]

SDR See *Special Drawing Rights.*

services Work or activity of economic value, such as haircuts or medical treatment. [p. 148]

Sherman Antitrust Act An act of Congress passed in 1890 aimed at curbing the power of trusts and monopolies. The act made it illegal to monopolize trade or to conspire to restrain trade. [p. 554]

short run The period of time that is long enough to allow a firm to alter its variable inputs, but insufficient to allow changes in fixed inputs. [p. 147]

shortage An excess of quantity demanded over quantity supplied at existing prices. [p. 68]

social costs (of production) The costs to society incurred in the production process (such as the damage caused by air and water pollution,) in addition to private cost. [p. 636]

socialist economy An economic system in which most productive resources are owned publicly by the government (for example, England). [p. 776]

Special Drawing Rights (SDRs) A form of international reserves credited to the accounts of IMF members that can be used to settle international balances. SDRs can be created in any amount approved by 85 percent of the member nations in amounts roughly proportional to each nation's original DNF contribution. SDRs are listed on the Federal Reserve balance sheet as an asset. [pp. 288-289; 759]

specific tariff A fixed amount charged per unit of goods imported. For example, a $5 tariff might be levied on every 100 lbs of bananas brought into the United States. [p. 724]

speculative demand The tendency of households and businesses during periods of economic unrest to convert assets into money and to hold onto the money until conditions are more predictable. [p. 251]

stagflation The simultaneous occurrence of a maintained unsatisfactory growth rate (stagnation) and a maintained increase in the general level of prices (inflation). [p. 335]

strike An organized work stoppage designed to win or enforce certain conditions of employment. [p. 610]

structural unemployment Unemployment that results from some structural change in the economy, such as a decreased demand for a certain skill or a change in the technology of a certain industry. [p. 173]

substitutes Goods that can be used in the same way as related goods and therefore compete with these related goods for the consumer's dollar. An example is hamburger and chicken. When two goods are substitutes, demand for one is directly related to the price of the other (cf. *complements*). [p. 59]

substitution effect The principle which states that as the price of any commodity declines, consumers turn to that good as a substitute for other similar goods whose prices have remained the same. [p. 439]

supply The various quantities of a product that the supplier is willing and able to offer for sale at each and every possible price during some specified period of time. (See also *law of supply.*) [pp. 61-62]

supply curve A graphic representation of the direct relationship between the price per unit of a good and the quantity of goods offered for sale. The supply curve will always slope upward and to the right, indicating that as price rises, the quantity offered for sale will also increase. A *change in supply* refers to a shift in the position of the whole supply curve; a *change in quantity supplied* refers to movement along a given supply curve. [pp. 63-64]

supply schedule A table that shows the various quantities of any given product that producers are willing and able to offer for sale at each and every possible price during some specified period of time. [p. 62]

surplus (1) An excess of quantity supplied over quantity demanded at existing prices. (2) An excess of revenues over expenditures; a budget surplus. [p. 68, 225]

target prices Government-guaranteed minimum prices on basic agricultural products. [p. 501]

tariff A tax levied on commodities imported into a country. This kind of tax reduces or eliminates a trading partner's comparative advantage. [p. 724]

technology The application of industrial science to production and distribution; often considered one of the factors of production along with land, labor, capital, and entrepreneurship. [p. 37]

terms of trade The number of units of goods that must be given up in exchange for one unit received by each trading party. [p. 711]

terms-of-trade line Represents new, possible combinations of goods that are available to a nation as a result of trade. [p. 712]

theory of factor endowments A theory that explains the supply forces that affect international trade. It states that different domestic exchange ratios exist primarily because (1) the distribution of factor endowments is uneven among nations, and (2) the production of different goods requires the use of varying proportions of the factors of production. [pp. 714-715]

total cost The total sum of a firm's fixed input costs and its variable input costs. [p. 449]

total cost curve A cost curve showing the total dollar costs for each different level of production. [p. 453]

total product curve A curve showing the total amount of output that can be produced from increasing levels of a variable input, holding all other inputs constant. [p. 445]

total revenue The price of each unit of a product multiplied by the number of units sold. [p. 468]

transactions demand The need to keep some money readily available to carry out day-to-day transactions. [p. 250]

transfer payments Payments to an individual by government for any reason other than current productivity; examples are Social Security and welfare payments. [p. 130]

Treasury deposits The funds that the United States Treasury deposits in Federal Reserve banks. [p. 289]

trough The phase of a business cycle during which there is substantial unemployment and unused capacity, little investment spending, low profits, little confidence, and downward pressure on some prices. [p. 178]

trust A combination of firms or corporations under the control of a single individual or group. [p. 554]

turnover tax A levy applied to each sale through which a commodity passes in the process of production and distribution to the final consumer. [p. 782]

underemployment of resources Inefficient methods of production which result in waste of resources. [p. 38]

unemployment rate The fraction of the total civilian labor force that is classified as unemployed. [p. 172]

union shop A factory or business in which every employee must join the union within a specified period after being hired if he or she is not a union member when hired. [p. 612]

utility The ability of a good or service to satisfy a certain want. [p. 430]

value added The increase in value of a good or service added by each step of the manufacturing process; value added is equal to the sum of all income payments made during the production process—wages, rent, interest, and profit. [p. 145]

variable costs All expenses connected with a firm's production that can be increased or decreased in the short run. [p. 449]

variable inputs Productive inputs that a firm can increase or decrease in the short run; typical examples are labor and raw materials. [p. 444]

velocity The number of times each dollar is spent or turned over within a stated period of time. Also defined as the dollar value of GNP divided by the money supply, or

$$V = \frac{GNP}{M}$$ [p. 253].

vertical integration The process through which a firm eventually acquires control over all of the resources necessary to produce and market a particular product. [p. 548]

wage and salary All kinds of compensation paid to any business employee (wages, bonuses, tips, fringe benefits, employer's share of Social Security contributions); a component of GNP. [p. 151]

yellow-dog contract An agreement made by an employee never to join a union, usually as a condition of employment; now illegal in the United States. [p. 611]

Index

Index

Definitions of terms can be found on the pages indicated by boldface type.

Ability-to-pay principle, 133, 134
Absolute advantage, **707**, 710
Accelerator theory of business investment, 198, **199**-200, 204
Administrative lag, 332
Advertising
　critics of, 536-537, 540
　economic value of, 537
　goals of, 506
　and individual freedom of choice, 9
　and nonprice competition, 536-537
Affluence
　and economic decision making, 783
　and environmental issues, 635
AFL-CIO, 613
Age
　and discrimination, 681
　and household trends, 105
　as labor limitation, 38
Agency for International Development (AID), United States, 393
Aggregate demand, 209-210
　defined, **208**
　and economic growth, 365
　excess, 335
　formulas for, 805
　level of, 210
　tabular analysis of, 210
Aggregate supply, **208**
Agricultural Adjustment Act of 1933, 498
Agricultural Extension Service, 491
Agricultural industry, 465, 484
Agricultural products
　demand for, 495, 500
　dumping of, 497
　price inelasticity of demand for, 491, 493, 502

Agricultural sector
　in China, 788
　curtailing planted acreage, 498, 503
　direct income subsidy for, 499-500
　disposal problem, 497-498
　and farm legislation, 501
　farm vs. nonfarm income and, 488, 502
　free markets for, 499
　government purchase of surpluses in, 496-497
　income inelasticity of demand in, 490
　instability in, 489-495
　in 1970s, 500-502
　parity pricing in, 495-498
　as perfectly competitive market, 487
　production assets used in, 491
　production controls in, 498
　in the short run, 493-495
　in Soviet Union, 783-784
　surplus problem in, 489
　target prices in, 501
　uneven effects of technology in, 491-492, 502
Agricultural Trade and Development Assistance Act of 1954, 393
Agriculture and Consumer Protection Act, 502
Aid to Families with Dependent Children (AFDC), 678
Air pollution. *See also* Pollution
　costs of, 636
　and government regulation, 640
Airline industry
　deregulation of, 339, 542-543
　horizontal integration in, 549
Alaska pipeline, 691
Alcoa, 510
Alienation, 799
Allende, Salvador, 390

Allocation of resources
　in capitalist economy, 778
　effect of unions on, 621
All-other-things-equal assumption, **56**, 58
American Agriculture Movement, 501
American Federation of Labor (AFL), 611, 613, 624
American Medical Association, 620
American Telephone and Telegraph Co., and antidiscrimination legislation, 680
Anderson, Robert, 641
Appalachia, 799
Arbitrage, **739**
Arbitration, 618
Arrow, Kenneth J., 811
Assembly line, 90
Attitudes. *See also* Discrimination
　toward big business, 547-548
　as determinant of aggregate consumption schedules, 193-194
　and economic good, 11-12
　toward environmental issues, 635
　toward poverty, 668
Automatic stabilizers, **224**-227, 228
Automobile industry, **110**
　demand for smaller automobiles in, 692
　dominance of, 547
　economies of scale in, 40
　effects on economy, 197
　rebate tactic in, 93-94
Automobile use
　demand curve for, 649
　private and social costs of, 649-652, 661
Average cost curve, 454-457
Average fixed costs, **454**
Average product, **448**
Average propensity to consume, **190**
Average propensity to save, **190**
Averages, 7
　formulas for, 805

Average total cost (ATC), **455**
Average total cost curve, 455–457, 458, 459

Bain, Joe S., 551
Bakke v. The University of California, 681
Balance of payments, 334
  and American dollar, 761
  capital account, 745–746, 747
  formulas for, 806
  and gold reserves, 758
  international, 743
  and invisible trade, 745
  and military transactions, 744
  unilateral-transfers account, 745
  United States, 744, 746–747, 748
Balance-of-payments statement
  defined, **743**
  goods-and-services account, 744–745, 747
Balance sheet, 267–270
  defined, **267**
  of Federal Reserve bank, 287
Balance of trade
  defined, **744**
  and economic policymaking, 334
Banking
  balance sheets, 267–270
  checking account system, 269–270
  loans, 270–274
  reserve requirements, 268–269
Banks. *See also* Commercial banks
  central, 266
  Federal Reserve, **286**, 287
  regulation of, 553, 560–562
Barter system, 52, 53
Becker, Gary S., 673
Benefits-received principle, **132–133**, 134
Bentham, Jeremy, 85
Big business
  competition restrained by, 548–550
  and economies of scale, 551, 558
  future for, 556–557, 558
  legal and political advantages of, 550
  monopsonistic power of, 570
  in 1970s, 555–557

and product improvement, 551–552
public policy and, 553–555
and technological change, 551–552
Bigness
  attitudes toward, 547–548
  defining, 546, 557
  trend toward, 546–547
Birth-control programs, 391
Birthrates, and household composition, 105. *See also* Population growth
Black(s)
  discrimination against, 800. *See also* Discrimination
  unemployment among, 341
Black labor, 159
Black markets, 785
  in coupon rationing, 695
  defined, **68**
  and price ceilings, 420–421
Blackmail, economic, 686
Bonds. *See also* Government bonds
  corporate, 114, 152
  defined, **114**
Boston, transportation in, 652
Boycotts
  beef, 73, 500
  consumer, 500–501, 503
Brannan, Charles F., 499
Brannan plan, 499
Bretton Woods Conference, 756–757, 765
Bretton Woods gold-exchange standard, 753
Brookings Institution, 339
Budget, federal
  acceptance of deficits, 313
  challenge to balanced, 313
  deficits, **235**, 310
  surplus, **235**
Budget committee, of House of Representatives, 318
Budget constraint
  on business, 196
  on government, 130
  on households, 100, 101
  line of, **437**
Business(es). *See also* Big business; Firm
  and accelerator theory of

investment, 198–200, 204
accountability of, 121
banking, 267–270
households vs., 100–101
inventory investment of, 200–201, 204
investment decisions of, 196–250
and money flow, 77
purchases of plant and equipment by, 195–200, 204
Business cycles, 177–180, 181. *See also* Recession; Recovery
  accelerator theory and, 200
  causes of, 179–180
  defined, **177**
  forecasting of, 180
  peak in, 306, 318
  phases of, 177–178
  recession in, 307–308, 318
  recovery in, 306, 318
  seasonal variations in, 178
  theory, 306–308
  trough in, 308
Business enterprise(s). *See also* Corporations
  corporation, 113–116
  defined, **36**
  individual proprietorships, 111–113
  nature of, 109–110
  partnerships, 113
  principal forms of, 111–116
Business firms. *See also* Firms
  defined, **110**
  income sources of, 116
  nature of, 116
  revenues and expenditures of, 116
Business sector, American
  breakdown of, 110, 111
  trends in, 117–118, 119
Business taxes, indirect, 152
Butz, Earl, 501
Buyers. *See also* Sellers
  in competitive market, 464
  government protection of, 124
  number in market, 61
By-products, 40

California
  Proposition 13 in, 136, 339
  reduction in property taxes, 137

INDEX   831

Campaign-financing laws, 550
Canada, as exporter of natural gas, 689
Capital, **36,** 39. *See also* Financial capital; Human capital; Investment
  cost of, 116
  defined, **36**
  and economic growth, 359, 361, 373
  extensive use of, 89–90
  inefficient mix of, 671–672
  and investment decisions, 197
  in less developed countries, 385–387
  under Marxism, 795
Capital account(s)
  defined, **289**
  in international trade, 745–746, 747
Capital consumption allowance, 152–**153**
Capital goods
  accumulating, 391–393
  and economic growth, 363
Capital resources, underemployment of, 39
Capital-intensive good, 715
Capitalism
  alienation in, 799
  decay of, 365
  dependence on government in, 798
  discrimination in, 800
  imperialism, 798
  inequality in, 799–800
  irrationality in, 800–801
  monopoly, 798
  radical view of, 797–799, 803
Capitalist economies, 774, **776**
  evaluating, 777
  example of, 777–778
  model of, 776–777, 789
  modern American, 88–91
Capital/output ratio, **370**
Cartel. *See also* International trade
  defined, **396**
  and less developed nations, 396–398, 399
  long-term stability of, 398
  OPEC, 396–398, 399
Carter administration
  and dollar crisis, 762, 763, 765

energy policy of, 687, 696–697
  wage-price guidelines of, 339
Caveat emptor, 118
Celler-Kefauver Antimerger Act, 555, 558
Central bank, defined, **266**
Chart, surface, 23, 24
Checking accounts, 249, 262, 269–270
Chicago School, 256, 263
Chile, and economic imperialism, 390
China
  command economy of, 788, 790
  economic growth of, 361
Choices, economic, 40–48, 49, 51
Chrysler Corporation, 93–94, 556
Circular flow, 76, 91
  omissions from, 78
  in United States economy, 143
Cities, 654. *See also* Urban problems
  exodus from, 654
  federal aid to, 659
Civil Aeronautics Board (CAB), 125, 542
Civil rights, 802
Civil Rights Act, 680, 683
Civil servants, 128
Class action suit, 550
Class economics
  quantity theory in, 254, 262
  stability in, 328–329, 343
Clayton Antitrust Act, 555, 558
Clean Air Act of 1970, 691
Clearing operations, of Federal Reserve System, 290
Closed shop, **612.** *See also* Unions
Coal, and government policy, 689
Coins, 247–248. *See also* Currencies
Collective action, 8
Collective bargaining, 614–618, 624
  breakdown in, 614–615
  and contract terms, 615–617, 624
  defined, **614**
  role of government in, 617–618
Collectivization. *See also* Command economies
  defined, **783–784**
  results of, 785
Collusion
  defined, **527**
  oligopoly and, 529–530

Command economies, **776**
  background for, 778–780, 789
  Chinese, 788, 790
  example of, 783–786
  model for, 780–783
  Soviet Union, 784–786, 789
  success of, 782–783, 789
Commercial banking system, 265
  components of, 265–266, 277
  currency leakage in, 276–277
  largest members of, 266
  multiple expansion in, 274
Commercial banks
  check clearing of, 269
  defined, **265**
  establishing, 267
  excess reserves of, 270
  Federal Reserve purchases from, 293–294
  government bonds of, 275–276
  prime rate of, 299
  reserve requirements, 268–269, 278
  transactions of, 270–276, 278
Commodity value, **248**
Common Agricultural Policy (CAP), 755
Common Market, 755, 764
Commonwealth v. Hunt, 610
Communism, 753
  defined, **783**
  development of, 802
  production goals of, 128
Communist Manifesto, 780, 794
Comparative advantage, 707–716, 719
  defined, **707–708**
  principle of, 712, 737
Compensation approach, to economic externalities, 641–642, 645
Competition, 463. *See also* Market; Price system
  defined, **87**
  effect of big business on, 548–550
  government maintenance of, 124, 125
  imperfect, 89
  and rate of MRP decline, 573–574

resource allocation under,
538-539, 540
resource demand in, 569-571
monopolistic, 88, 529, 530, 532,
539
defined, **525**
long-run equilibrium in,
534-535
nonprice, 535-538, 540
advertising in, 536-537
through product development,
536
perfect, 88, 125, 463
application of, 465-466
assumptions of, 464-465
benefits of, 482-483, 485
defined, **88**
function of market in, 464, 484
problems with, 483-484, 485
resource demand in, 566
Complements, **59**
Composition, fallacy of, **14**
Comprehensive Employment and
Training Act (CETA), 341
Computer industry. *See also*
Technological advances
effects on economy, 197
IBM's antitrust case, 560-562
Concentration, Marx on, 795
Concentration ratios, **546**-547, 557
Concepts, economic, 11-13
Conglomerate mergers, **549**, 558
Congress, United States
budget committee of, 318
compulsary arbitration decreed
by, 618
Fed and, 290
gold-backing requirements
replaced by, 757
Joint Economic Committee,
227
reserve requirements set by, 268
and tariff, 733
Ways and Means Committee, 230
Congress of Industrial
Organizations (CIO), 612,
613, 624
Conservation, and limits on
resources, 38. *See also*
Environmental issues
Constant-costs industry, **480**-481,
485

Consumer(s)
choices of, 75
desires of, 34
dollar votes of, 81
government protection of, 124
production and, 83
and public interest, 638
revolt, 93
Consumer boycotts, 73, 500-501
Consumer cooperatives, 118
Consumer debt, 280-283
Consumer demand
indifference theory of, 435-438
marginal utility theory of,
430-435
in Soviet Union, 785
theories of, 429-439, 440
Consumer goods, **34**. *See also*
Goods
Consumer price index (CPI),
defined, **165**, 181
and price stability, 325
problems with, 165
Consumer sovereignty, **776**
Consumer surplus, **432**-433
Consumption, 188-195
aggregate, 192
and disposable income, 30
and economic growth, 366
hidden costs of, 634-635, 644
and income levels, 190, 194
and international trade, 709-710
marginal propensity toward, 808
personal, 148
propensity for, 806
during recovery, 306
and saving schedules, 188-190
Consumption schedules
aggregate, 190-194, 204
defined, **189**
Convertibility, free, 757
Cooperatives, 117
Copyright laws, 510
Corporate profits, in national
income, 152. *See also*
Corporations
Corporation(s), 113-116, 119. *See
also* Business enterprise;
Firms
advantages of, 114
competition restrained by,
548-550

and control of distributors,
549-550
defined, **113**
disadvantages of, 114-115
largest in United States, 546
and product improvement,
551-552
role of, 121
statistics on, 112
taxes of, 116
and technological change,
551-552
Correlations
defined, **14**
on scatter diagrams, 31
Cost(s). *See also* Long run; Short run
and decision making, 48
explicit, 117
formulas for, 806
implicit, **117**
increasing, 43-48
marginal, 470-472
opportunity, **12**, **40**, 49, 669, 706
private vs. social, 636
Cost of living. *See also* Standard of
living
in collective bargaining, 615
doubling of, 426
Cost schedule, 450
Cost/benefit analysis, for crime
prevention, 657
Cost-push inflation, **166**-167, 168,
181
Countervailing power, **553**, 558
Coupon rationing, 695
Crandall, Robert, 339
Credit, and consumer debt, 280-283
Credit cards, 361
Credit controls, selective, 299-301
Creeping inflation, **168**-169
Crime, urban, 656-657, 662. *See
also* Urban problems
Crime prevention, cost/benefit
analysis for, 657
Cultural Revolution, 788
Culture. *See also* Attitudes
and agricultural sector, 492-493
as determinant of aggregate
consumption schedules,
193-194
and economic development, 389
and economic good, 11-12

INDEX 833

Curbe, Mike, 638
Currencies, 247-249, 262. *See also*
    Dollar, American
  distribution of, 290
  foreign, 761
  leakage, 276-277
  paper, 248
Cycles, business. *See* Business cycles
Cyclical unemployment, **174**

Day care, need for, 676
Debt. *See also* Public debt
  consumer, 280-283
  as determinant of aggregate
    consumption schedules, 193
Decertification elections, 627
Decision lag, **230**
Decreasing-costs industry, **482**, 485
Deficit, in federal budget, 235-236
Deflation, **163**
Deflationary gap, 218-**219**, 220
DeGaulle, Charles, 755
Demand, 70
  aggregate, 208, 209-210, 805
  for agricultural goods, 491
  change in, 56-59
  defined, **54**
  derived, **571**, 576
  determinants of, 51-52, 54, 71
  and economic growth, 360-361,
    365-366, 374
  effect on wages, 677. *See also*
    Wages
  effects of free trade on, 727
  elasticity of, 408-417, 423
  for energy, 689-690, 694-696, 700
  government actions affecting,
    419-423, 424
  impact of energy conservation
    programs on, 695
  in imperfect competition, 466
  income elastic, **416**, 417
  individual, 58-60
  in international trade, 716, 726
  law of, **55**, 57, 407, 438-440, 441
  and marginal revenue curve, 514
  market, 60-61
  market equilibrium of, 67-68
  in monopoly model, 511-512,
    522
  and necessity, 415

  and number of uses of product,
    415
  in oligopoly, 528
  price elastic, **409**
  price inelastic, **411**
  in price system, 66, 79, 93-94
  and production, 83
  in resource market, 566-571, 576
  in teacher market, 604
  and terms of trade, 711-712
  and unionism, 618-620
Demand curves
  and all-other-things-equal
    assumption, 56, 58
  and change in quantity
    demanded, 57
  defined, **55**
  elastic and inelastic portions
    of, 412-413
  and income effect, 440
  kinked, 528
  market, 61
  for money, 251-252, 262
  in monopolistic competition,
    532-533
  plotting, 20
  for resources, 568-569
  and substitution effects, 440
Demand deposits, **249,** 262. *See also*
    Money
Demand schedule
  defined, **55**
  market, **60**
  market supply and, 66, 67
  of monopolist, 512
  in perfectly competitive market,
    467
Demand-pull inflation, **166,** 181
Deposits, bank, 267-268
Depression. *See also* Business cycles
  economic effects of, 195
  impact lag during, 230
  shortage of capital following, 281
Depression, Great, 319
  and attitudes toward poverty,
    668
  and international trade, 752
  monetary policy during, 308
  unemployment levels during, 174
  and unionism, 611
Deregulation, of airline industry,
    542-543

Derived demand, **571,** 576
Detente, 763. *See also* Soviet Union
Devaluation, 756, 764-765
  defined, **756**
  and international finance, 762
  for long-term imbalances, 757
Developed countries. *See also* Less
    developed countries
  and foreign aid, 393-395, 399
  growth rates in, 392
  health conditions in, 386
  and OPEC, 396
  per capita income in, 387
Developing countries, and
    communism, 794. *See also*
    Less developed countries
Development, economic. *See also*
    Growth
  barriers to, 383-390, 398
  defined, **379**
  in less developed countries,
    390-396
Development programs, 391
Diagrams
  flow, 28
  scatter, 28-31
"Diamond-water paradox,"
    430
Diesel shortage, 697
Diminishing returns
  basis of, 366-367
  in city management, 348
  and cost curves, 453
  law of, **46,** 47
  and marginal revenue product,
    568
  and population, 362
  and poverty, 671
  product curve and, 446
  supply curve and, 473
Discount rate
  changing, 298, 302
  defined, **298**
Discrimination, 800
  defined, **672**
  and dual labor market theory,
    676
  effects on economy, 672-673
  legislation against, 680-681
  and minority groups, 673-674
  quotas for, 681, 683
  "reverse," 681

Diseconomies, external, 635
  possible remedies for, 636–642, 645
  and urban land use, 655
Diseconomies of scale, 47–48, 49
  defined, 47–48
  for federal government, 129
Disposable income (DI)
  decrease in, 160
  defined, **104**
  relation to GNP, 153
  in two-sector economy, 191
Dissave, defined, **104**
Distributors, control of, 549–550
Diversification, of United States economy, 90
Dividends, in household income, 102
Dobb, Maurice, 781
Doctors, income of, 585, 620, 669
Dollar, American
  decline in, 762
  devaluation of, 762. *See also* Devaluation
  fluctuation of, 760–762
  vs. foreign currency, 761
  future of, 764
  "rescue package" for, 762, 763, 765
Dollar votes, 78–79
Domar, L., 370
Domestic exchange ratio, 709–719
  defined, **709**
  difference in, 714–716
Double counting, 145
Dual labor market theory, 676–677, 683
Dumping, 756, 764
  of agricultural products, 497
  and tariff policy, 754
Durable goods
  and business cycles, 178–179
  defined, **148**
  as determinant of aggregate consumption, 192
  radical economists' view of, 800–801

Eastern Establishment, 799
East-West trade, 763
Economic behavior, basic assumptions about, 83–89, 91

Economic choices, 40–48, 49, 76
Economic externalities, **635**–636, 645
Economic goals, 161–163
Economic good, **11**–12
Economic imperialism, **389**–390
Economic performance, measuring, 154–156
Economic profit, defined, **117**. *See also* Profits
Economic rent, 586–587
Economic study
  fundamentals of, 10–15
  goals of, 15
Economic systems
  alternative, 774
  classifying, 776, 789
  evaluating, 774–775, 789
  purpose of, 8
Economic theory
  classical, 366–367
  Keynesian, 187–188, 370
  neoclassical, 367
  nineteenth-century, 179
  post-Keynesian, 370–371
  subjectivity of, 7–10
  twentieth-century, 179–180
  value of, 8–10
Economics
  classical, 254, 262, 328–329, 343
  defined, **4**
  nature of, 4–5, 15
  vs. politics, 9–10
  and problem of scarcity, 3
  radical vs. liberal view of, 797, 803
  scientific method applied to, 6
  and social problems, 7
  as social science, 5–7
Economies of scale
  defined, **39**–40
  and economic growth, 364–365
  in large corporations, 551, 558
  in oligopoly market, 526
  and urban problems, 648, 661
Economists
  conservative, 86
  interpretation of, 5
  liberal, 797, 803
  methods of, 16
  Nobel-prize-winning, 811–812

  radical, 793–794
  tools of, 15
Economy
  barter, 52, 53
  capitalist, 776–778, 789
  command, 788
  democratic socialist, 787–788
  evaluating, 774–775, 789
  external, 636
  market, **52**
  modern American, 89–91
  planning, 395–396
  socialist command, 778–786
  socialist market, 786–787
  underground, 159–160
Education
  in China, 788
  and economic growth, 362–363
  and household trends, 105
  and income, 26, 103
  in less developed countries, 383, 390–391
  and poverty, 677–678
  public, 129, 654
  as public good, 8
Efficiency
  in comparing economic systems, 775, 789
  labor unions and, 621
  in monopolistic market, 515–517
  and price system, 483
Eisenhower administration, fiscal policy of, 312, 315
Elasticity
  defined, **408**
  formulas for, 806–807
  and total revenue, 413
  unitary, 411
Elasticity coefficient, **409**
Elasticity of demand, 408–417
  calculating, 409
  for commuting by automobile, 649
  cross, **417**
  determinants of, 414–416, 423
  income, **416**
  in perfect competition, 467, 484
  and pocket calculator, 426–427
  and price ceilings, 420, 421
  in resource market, 573–575, 576
Elasticity of supply, 417–419, 423
  in constant-costs industry, 481
  defined, **417**

Electronics industry, 731. *See also* Computer industry
Elementary and Secondary Education Act of 1965, 604
Elites, 125
Embargo, 500, 618, 725
Emissions-control devices, 639
Empirical data, **6,** 10
Employment. *See also* Full employment; Unemployment
　farm, 493
　and Federal Reserve monetary policy, 291
　in monopsonistic market, 570
　tariff stimulation of, 730
Employment Act of 1946, 162
Energy
　alternative sources for, 689, 693, 698-699
　demand for, 689-690, 700
　Department of, 697, 698
　future for, 698-699
　and government intervention, 693-698, 700
　government regulation and control of, 688-689
　solar, 698
Energy crisis, 685-686, 699
　causes of, 688-692, 699
　of 1973-1974, 686-687, 699
　since 1974, 687-688
　proposed solutions, 692-698
Energy policy
　federal, 696-698
　geothermal power, 699
　harnessing the sea, 698-699
　price controls, 690-691
　wind, 699
Energy Policy and Conservation Act (EPCA), 696
Energy Security Fund, 697
Engels, Friedrich, 780
Entrepreneurship, 39. *See also* Business enterprise(s)
　defined, **36**
　and economic growth, 361, 365
　risk of, 387
Environmental issues, 634. *See also* Pollution
　and consumer demands for, 556, 558

and energy problems, 691-692
and governmental regulation, 639
programs, 334
quality standards, 644
Environmental Protection Agency (EPA) 70, 636
Environmentalists, and energy crisis, 687
Equal marginal utility principle, **434**
Equal Opportunities Commission, 680
Equal Pay Act of 1963, 680
Equal Rights Amendment (ERA), 681. *See also* Women
Equilibrium. *See also* General equilibrium analysis
　aggregate demand-aggregate supply approach to, 208-211, 220, 233
　effect on planned saving and investment, 213
　and full employment, 218-219
　graphic analysis of, 212
　long-run, 476-479, 485
　market, 208
　in money market, 259
　reaching saving-investment, 213
　saving-and-investment approach to, 232
　saving-equals-investment approach to, 211-212, 220
　short-run, 475-476, 477, 478
Equilibrium price, **67,** 71. *See also* Price system
Equity, in comparing economic systems, 775, 789
Ethnic minorities, and economic growth, 363. *See also* Discrimination; Minority groups
European Economic Community (EEC), 755
European Monetary Unit (EMU), 755, 764
European recovery program, 753, 764
Excess reserves, 278
　defined, **270**
　and open-market operations, 293
Exchange rate
　defined, **738**
　floating, 741-743

formulas for, 807
on international market, 711-712
Exchange transactions, 52-54, 70. *See also* Money
　barter system, 52, 53
　conditions for, 52-54
　interbusiness, 76
　interhousehold, 76
　medium for, 52
　money as medium of, 246
Excise taxes, effect on supply and demand, 422-423
Exclusion principle, **126**
Expectations
　and demand, **59**
　as determinant of aggregate consumption schedule, 193
　and economic policymaking, 333
　inflationary, 336-337
　and investment decisions, 197-198
　and money demand, 252
　and supply, 65
Exports
　Japanese, 763-764
　net, **150**
Externalities, economic, 635-636, 645
　compensation approach to, 641-642, 645
　price-system approach to, 642
Exxon Company, 556

Factor endowments, theory of, 714
Factor market. *See* Resource market
Factor substitution, 572-573
Factor suitability, 45-46
Fair Labor Standards Act of 1938, 69, 612, 622
Fair Packaging and Labeling Act, 125
Farm income
　effect of demand on, 495
　effect of supply on, 493-495
　vs. nonfarm income, 488, 502
Farm policy, government, 495-500, 503
Farm subsidies, 124, 499-500
Farmers. *See also* Agricultural sector
　per capita income of, 501
　traditional problems of, 491-493, 502

Featherbedding, **619**–620, 625
Federal Advisory Council, of Federal Reserve System, 287
Federal aid, to cities, 659
Federal Aviation Agency, 124
Federal Deposit Insurance Corporation (FDIC), 268–269, 307
Federal Farm Board, 495
Federal Government. *See also* Government
  energy policy of, 687, 696–698
  expenditures, 130, 131
  financing of, 130–132
  price ceilings imposed by, 74
  sources of revenue for, 130, 131
  spending of, 27
  transfer payments of, 130
Federal income tax, 104, 134. *See also* Tax(es)
Federal Mediation and Conciliation Service, 618
Federal Reserve Act, 298
Federal Reserve banks, 287
  balance sheet of, 287–289
  board of governors of, 286–287
  defined, **286**
Federal Reserve notes, 289, 301
Federal Reserve System, 266–277
  assets of, 288
  background of, 285–286
  committees of, 287
  and discount rate, 298, 302
  functions of, 290–291, 296, 301, 302
  independence of, 289–290, 301
  installment credit of, 299
  and interest rate, 590
  interest rates on deposits of, 299–301
  liabilities of, 289
  member banks of, 287
  membership in, 267
  monetary policy of, 291–293, 302
    mechanisms for implementing, 293–301, 302
    during 1930s, 309
    from 1945 to 1950, 311–312
    during 1950s, 312
    during 1960s, 314
    during 1970s, 317
    during World War II, 310
  moral suasion of, 301
  organization of, 286, 301
  and recession, 308
  Regulation Q of, 299–301
  reserve requirements of, 268–269, 278, 297–298, 302
  selective credit controls of, 299
  transfers to, 269
Federal Trade Commission (FTC), 555
Federal Trade Commission Act, 555, 558
Fiat money system, **249**
Financial capital
  defined, **589**
  supply of, 588–591, 592
Firms
  accountability of, 118
  competitive
    and long-run equilibrium, 476–477, 482
    minimizing losses of, 473–474
    in short run, 466–474
    and short-run equilibrium, 475–476, 477, 478
    in short run, 466–474
    short-run supply curve for, 473–474
  and control of distributors, 549–550
  defined, **110**
  and determinants of supply, 64–66
  expenditures of, 116
  funds raised by, 196
  insurance, 118
  nation's largest, 546
  optimum resource mix for, 571
  profitability calculations of, 195–196
  in resource markets, 76
  revenues of, 119
  supply curve of, 565
Fiscal drag
  defined, **225**
  of 1959–1960, 315
Fiscal policy, 224–239
  alternatives to, 339–342
  defined, **224**
  discretionary, **227**–231, 239
  effects on equilibrium output and income, 231–235
  and expectations, 333
  during 1930s, 309
  1945–1950, 311–312
  of 1950s, 312
  of 1960s, 315
  during 1970s, 316–317
  nondiscretionary, 224–227, 239
  and public debt, 236–239
Fixed costs
  average, 23, **454**, 455
  defined, **451**
Fixed inputs, of production, **444**, 459
Floating exchange rates, **741**
Food and Agriculture Act of 1977, 501
Food and Agriculture Organization (FAO), 384–385, 394
Food for Peace program, 497
Food stamps, 678–679
Ford administration
  and energy policy, 687
  and grain sales to Soviet Union, 501
  WIN program of, 338–339
Ford, Henry, 360
Ford Motor Company, recall policy of, 121–122
Forecasting
  of business cycles, 180
  and Federal Reserve monetary policy, 292
Foreign aid, 393–395, 399
  agricultural products in, 498
  historical perspective on, 393
  and international agencies, 393–394
  issues in, 394–395
Fort Knox, gold in, 334
Fortune, 555, 558
France, economic growth of, 357
Free convertibility, 757
Free good, **12**
Free market, and agricultural sector, 501
Free trade, barriers to, 723
Freedom, economic, 775, 789
Free-market approach, to energy problems, 692–693, 700
Free-market economy, 48
Frictional unemployment, **173**, 181

INDEX **837**

Friedman, Milton, 86, 115, 256, 340, 811
  biography, 257–258
  on business cycles, 179
  on economic theory, 7
  monetarist views of, 331, 333
Frisch, Ragnar, 811
Fuels. *See also* Energy
  in future, 698–699
  shortages, 686, 687
Full employment, 161, 162, 171, 181, 187
  growth rate for, 371
  limitations to, 38
  and quantity theory, 254
  in socialist economies, 787
  and stable prices, 325
Full Employment and Balanced Growth Act, Humphrey-Hawkins, 161–163, 318, 341–342
Futures contract, **742**

Galbraith, John Kenneth, 8, 552, 553, 558
Gas, interstate vs. intrastate markets for, 689
Gasoline shortages, 686, 687, 698. *See also* Oil prices
  and agricultural sector, 502
  rationing, 695–696, 700
General Agreement on Tariffs and Trade (GATT), 753–754, 764
General equilibrium analysis, 594–601
  defined, **594**
  input-output approach to, 597–599, 600, 602
  product-market/resource-market approach to, 595–597, 598, 600, 602
General Motors Corporation, 547, 556
George, Henry, 587
Geothermal energy, 699
Germany, economic growth of, 357
Ghana, industrialization of, 731
Gold
  drain, 334
  future of, 764
  two-tier system, 758

Gold certificates, **288**, 301
  Bretton Woods, 753, 756
  defined, **740**
Gold points, **738**
Gold reserve, in United States economy, 248–249
Gold standard, 738–740, 743, 747
  advantages of, 739–740
  collapse of, 755–756
  defined, **738**
  disadvantages of, 740
Gold-backing requirements, elimination of, 757, 765
Gold-exchange standard, 743
Gompers, Samuel, 611
Good(s). *See also* Products
  capital, 391–393
  capital vs. consumer, 36
  complement, **59**
  durable, **148**, 192
    and business cycles, 178–179
    radical economists' view of, 800–801
  economic, **11**–12
  free, **12**
  inferior, 59
  nondurable, **148**, 178–179
  normal, **58**
  obtainable profits from competitive, 64–65
  opportunity cost of, 40
  in perfect competition, 465
  personal valuation of, 53
  private, **126**
  public, 8
    defined, **126**
    government inefficiency in producing, 128–130
  social, **126**
  substitute, **59**
  union-made, 619, 625
Goods-and-services account, 744–745, 747
Gosplan (Soviet Planning Committee), 784
Government. *See also* Federal government
  in collective bargaining, 617
  distributive function of, 123
  economic functions of, 130, 134

  effectiveness of, 128–130
  and environmental issues, 639–640
  farm policy of, 495–500, 503
  inefficiency of, 128–130
  and inequities in price system, 125–126
  measuring efficiency of, 128
  military defense spending of, 127
  municipal. *See also* Urban problems
    financing of, 658–661, 662
    revenue sources and expenditures, 132
  public goods and services provided by, 126–127
  revenue sources for, 134
  stabilization function of, 127–128
  stabilizing effect of, 224–231
  state
    and banking laws, 266
    revenue for, 131–132
    spending of, 132
  tax programs of, 133–134
Government bonds
  buying, 275–276
  Federal Reserve sales of, 295
  and public debt, 238
  selling, 276
Government intervention, 9
  costs of, 562
  and demand and supply, 419–423
  in energy problems, 693–698, 700
  farm policy, 499–500
  income redistribution as goal of, 126
  and laws of market, 68
  and monopoly market, 519, 520–521, 523
  need for, 86
  and opportunity costs, 12
  opposition to, 257
  reasons for, 124, 134
  revenue-sharing, 132
  Paul Samuelson on, 215–216
Government spending, 134
  difficulties of reducing, 333
  effect of tax revenues on, 225
  effects on NNP of, 233–235
  in GNP, 150

Graph(s)
  bar, 26-27
  circle, 28
  different forms of, 21
  in economic study, 10-11
  empirical, 20
  interpreting, 19
  kinds of, 19
  multiple-scale arithmetic, 23
  plotting, 18
  semi-logarithmic, 23, 25
  simple arithmetic line, 21
  theoretical, 19
  time trend, 21-22
Great Britain, democratic socialism in, 787-788, 790
Great Leap Forward, 788
Grievance procedures, and collective bargaining, 617
Gross investment, **149**
Gross national product (GNP), 142-147, 157
  avoiding double counting in, 145
  calculating, 147-153
  classification of output, 154
  comparisons of, 156
  concentration on market transactions, 154
  defined, **142**
  deflator, 166
  and economic growth, 355-359, 374
  expenditures approach to, 148-150, 153, 157
  and foreign aid, 395
  gap in, 174
  government expenditures as percent of, 310
  government purchases in, 150
  implicit price deflators for, 144
  income approach to, 148, 150-155, 157
  and international trade, 731
  investment included in, 149
  limitations as measure, 156, 157
  and military demands, 361
  and net exports, 150
  during 1950s, 312
  during 1960s, 313, 314
  in 1970s, 315
  nonincome items in, 152-155
  omission of some goods in, 155
  payments excluded from, 145-147
  per capita, 155
    for countries with populations of 1 million or more, 380-381
    of less developed countries, 382
    and literacy, 384
  real, 146
  role of industries in, 111
  social welfare in, 155-156
  and standard of living, 358
  unadjusted, 146
  underground economy in, 159
  United States, 547
Grossman, Gregory, 774
Growth, economic
  benefits of, 372-373, 375
  classical theory of, 366-367
  in comparing economic systems, 774-775, 789
  costs of, 371-372, 374-375
  defined, **356**
  demand and level of output, 365-366
  in developed countries, 392
  and economies of scale, 364
  and education, 362-363
  factors causing, 359-361
  and investment decisions, 197-198
  and labor, 362-363
  in less developed countries, 380-381, 392
  long-range policy for, 373
  long-term, 358
  measuring, 356
  modern theory of, 370-371, 374
  and natural resources, 362-363
  neoclassical theory of, 367, 370
  noneconomic factors in, 361
  rate, 357, 807
  slowdowns in, 361
  in Soviet Union, 786, 790
  and standard of living, 358-359
  and technology, 363-364, 367, 371, 373, 374
  theories of, 355-356
  and United States economy, 361-366, 374, 379-382
  in world's largest countries, 380-381
  in Yugoslavia, 787

Gulf & Western Industries, Inc., 549

Halm, George, 786
Hand, Learned, 555
Hansen, Alvin, 180
Harrington, Michael, 666
Harrod, R., 370
Hawley-Smoot Tariff, 752
Hawtrey, R. G., 179
Hayek, Friedrich A. von, 811
Health
  as economic good, 11
  indicators of, 386
  in less developed countries, 383-384, 391
  and pollution, 643
Health, Education and Welfare, Department of, 680
Heckscher, 714, 717
Hicks, John R., 811
Hiring, discrimination in, 676, 678. See also Employment; Unemployment
Honeywell, 510
Horizontal integration, **548**-549, 558
Hours, in collective bargaining, 615. See also Wages
Household(s)
  consumption and saving schedule for, 189
  defined, **99, 104**
  as determinant of aggregate consumption, 192
  effect on economic behavior, 105-107
  functions of, 99-100
  headed by women, 666
  importance of, 106-107
  income level determinants for, 102
  and inequalities of income, 103
  in less developed countries, 385, 392
  and money flow, 77
  personal income of, 101-102, 107
  as production unit, 100-101, 103, 107
  in product markets, 76
  regional variation in income of, 102
  and resource market, 579
  saving by, 104-105, 188, 204

self-sufficiency of, 100
source of revenue for, 101–105, 107
spending of, 103
taxes on, 104
trends in, 105–106, 107
urban vs. rural, 105
Housing
and economic development, 388
as public good, 8
urban, 647
Housing construction, cycles in, 200–202
Human capital
developing, 390–391
and discrimination, 673–674
modern theory of, 801
and poverty, 669–670, 682
Human resources, *See also* Education; Labor
developing, 390–391
and economic growth, 362–363, 371, 374
in less developed countries, 383–385
Humphrey-Hawkins Full Employment and Balanced Growth Act, 162–163, 318, 341–342
Hunter, Robert, 665
Hyperinflation, **168**, 181

Illiteracy, 383
Impact lag, **230**
Imperialism
capitalist, 798
capitalist vs. communist, 802
economic, **389**–390
Marx on, 795
Implicit costs, **117**
Implicit price deflator, 166
Imports. *See also* International trade
quotas for, 725
tariffs on, 724
Incentives, in perfect competition, 483
Income
discrepancy between farm and nonfarm, 488, 502
disposable, 30
education and, 26, 103

equilibrium level of, 208, 209
family
advantages and disadvantages of inequality of, 664–665, 682
in metropolitan areas, 653
poverty level for, 664
fixed, 169–170
indifference curve for, 581
and individual demand, 58–59
male vs. female, 675
of minority groups, 673–674
and money demand, 252
nonfarm, 666
permanent, 194
personal
defined, 101
disposition of, 104
sources of, 101
and productivity, 668
proprietors', 101n, 151
real vs. money, 665
regional variations in, 102
Income distribution
in capitalist economy, 777
in command economies, 782
and government intervention, 126
households and, 103
in less developed countries, 385
and market imperfection, 670–672, 682
in 1977, 667
in United States, 666–668, 682
Income effect, **439**
Income level, determinants of, 102–103
Income tax, negative, 679–680. *See also* Tax(es)
Increasing costs, 43–48
defined, **45**
of production, 48
Increasing-costs industry, **481**, 485
Indexing, of taxes, 339–340
India, economy of, 37
Indifference analysis, 580–581
Indifference curve, **435**, 436, 440
Indifference maps, 436–**437**, 580–581, 582
Indifference theory, 435–438
Indirect business tax, **152**
Individual, vs. collective action, 8. *See also* Self-interest

"Industrial reserve army," 795
Industrialization
and environmental issues, 634
and labor movement, 610
Industry
agricultural, 465, 484. *See also* Agricultural sector
airline, 339, 542–543, 549
in American GNP, 111
automobile, 40, 93–94, 110, 197, 547, 692
computer, 197, 560–562
constant-costs, **480**–481, 485
decreasing-costs, 482, 485
defined, 110
electronics, 731
and high set-up costs, 507
increasing-costs, **481**, 485
in less developed countries, 731
in long-run equilibrium, 479
manufacturing, 547
plastic, 197
pollution fee for, 641
railroad, 79
shoe, 173, 547
and short-run equilibrium, 476
steel, 552, 556
supply curve in long run, 480–482
and tariffs, 729, 734
television, 548
Inequality, 799
Inferior goods, **59**
Inflation, 163–169, 181
acceleration of, 336
and capitalist economy, 777
causes of, 166–168
and change in demand, 57
and consumer debt, 280
cost-push, **166**–**167**, 181
costs of, 169–170, 181
creeping, **168**–169
defined, **163**
demand-pull, **166**, 181
double-digit, 315
and economic growth, 372
and energy policy, 693, 697
and expectations, 336–337
government-induced, 167–168
hyperinflation, **168**, 181
"insurance" against, 339
measuring rate of, 168
in 1970s, 315

and productive output, 170
and redistribution of income, 169–170
stagflation, 334–342, 343
and tax system, 160
and unemployment, 325–329
and unions, 621–622
and wage and price controls, 74
wage-push, 167
WIN program, 106n, 338–339
worldwide, 395
Inflation rates, 168–169
formulas for, 807
measuring, 163–168
Inflationary gap, 218–**219**, 220–230
Infrastructure
defined, **388**
in less developed countries, 388–389
Injunction, protective, 611
Innovation, and investment decision, 196. *See also* Technological advances
Input coefficients, 600–601
Input-output table, 602
defined, **597**
example of, 599
Integration
horizontal, 548–558
vertical, 548, 558
Interdependence, and international trade, 706–707
Interest
defined, **152, 589**
in household income, 102
in national income, 152
Interest rate(s), 589, 591
and balance of payments, 746
controls on, 69
and economic growth, 370
formulas for, 807
influence on investment, 202–203
and investment spending, 259–262
and money demand, 251–252
and money supply, 256–259, 263
International agencies, 393–394
International Business Machines Corporation (IBM), 12–13, 560–562
International finance
Bretton Woods Conference, 756
after Bretton Woods, 757–759

collapse of gold standard, 755–756
International Labor Organization (ILO), 394
International Ladies Garment Workers Union, 619
International market, dumping of agricultural products in, 497
International Monetary Fund (IMF), 289, 301
and Bretton Woods Conference, 757
defined, **741**
role of, 740–741
and two-tier gold system, 758, 765
International monetary system
"dirty float," 759
special drawing rights, 759–760
International Telephone and Telegraph (ITT), in Chile, 390
International trade
and absolute advantage, 707, 710
balance of payments in, 743–747. *See also* Balance of payments
barriers to free trade in, 723–725, 733
basis for, 706–707, 719
capital account, 745–746, 747
and comparative advantage, 707–716, 719
distribution of factors, 715
East-West, 763
effects of, 716–719
financing of, 738–743
floating exchange rates in, 741–743
and gold reserves, 757
gold standard in, 738–740, 747
historical developments in, 752–753
model for, 708–711
and national income, 718–719
price equalization in, 717–718, 720
proportion of factors, 715
quotas in, 725
removal of trade barriers, 753–755, 764
tariffs, 724. *See also* Tariff

unilateral-transfers account, 745, 747
after World War II, 751
Inventory
defined, **149**
in GNP, 154
investment, 200–201
Investment, 195–203, 745–746, 748
acceleration theory of, 198–200, 204
business purchases of plant and equipment, 195–200, 204
defined, **149**
effect of open-market transactions on, 296
encouraging, 392–393
factors influencing decisions on, 196–250
in GNP, 149–150
gross, **149**
and intended saving, 213, 220
inventory, 200–201, 204
in less developed countries, 385, 387
and level of income, 203
marginal efficiency of, 196, 261–262
net, 149
in residential construction, 201–202, 204
stabilizing influences in, 202
theory of, 367
Investment schedule, aggregate, 202, 203
"Invisible hand," Adam Smith's concept of, 84, 85, 366
Iran
crisis in, 398
oil export of, 397
political upheaval in, 688
Irrationality, 800
Israel, economy of, 37
Italy, economic growth of, 357

Jamaica agreement, 760
Japan
economic growth of, 357, 372
and international trade, 763–764, 765
Jevons, William Stanley, 430, 431–432

INDEX **841**

Johnson administration
  building projects cuts of, 333
  fiscal policy of, 315
  IBM antitrust case filed during, 561
  and minimum-wage protection, 622
  new economics of, 313
  War on Poverty of, 666
Joint Economic Committee, Congressional 227

Kantorovich, Leonid V., 811
Kapital, Das (Capital), 780, 795, 796
Kenen, Peter B., 732
Kennedy Act, 754, 764
Kennedy administration
  agricultural quotas suggested by, 498
  fiscal policy of, 315
  new economics of, 313
Keynes, John Maynard, 187, 329
  on depression, 369
  on economic growth, 365, 370
  on government intervention, 330
  on money demand, 250
  on permanent income, 194
  on public debt, 237
  on quantity theory, 254–255, 263
  Paul Samuelson on, 215
  on stability policies, 329–331, 343
Keynesian theory, 187
  assumptions of, 209
  fundamental assumptions of, 207
Keynesianism, politics of, 331
Knights of Labor, 610–611, 624
Knowledge, imperfect, 671
Kondratieff, 180
Koopmans, Tjalling C., 811
Korean war, 312
Kuwait, economy of, 36. *See also* Organization of Petroleum Exporting Countries
Kuznets, Simon, 811

Labor, 39. *See also* Union; Wages
  defined, **36**
  division of, 90
  dual market theory of, 676–677, 683
  and economic growth, 362–363
  foreign, 730

  and household income, 102
  indifference analysis of, 581
  inefficient mix of, 671–672
  limitations on full employment of, 38
  market demand curve for, 569
  market supply for, 584
  nonmonetary rewards for, 581, 591
  in resource market, 579–584
  shorter work week for, 363
  supply curve for, 581–584
  unemployment of, 170–171
Labor force. *See also* Employment; Unemployment
  in China, 788
  civilian, 171
  fluctuation in size of, 42
  size of, 580
Labor market
  teachers in, 604–607
  wage determination in, 586–591
Labor movement, 622. *See also* Unionism
  American, 610
  weakening of, 628
Labor theory of value, 793
Labor unions. *See also* Unions
  declining memberships in, 627–629
  functions of, 614
  future of, 622–624, 625
  and resource market, 572
  structure of, 614
Labor-intensive good, 715
Labor-Management Relations Act, 612, 624
Labor-Management Reporting and Disclosure Act, 612
Land, 39. *See also* Resource market
  economic definition of, 35
  limitations on full employment of, 38
  in price system, 588
  supply of, 586–588, 591
  user productivity of, 587–588
Land use, urban, 654–656, 661–662
Land-intensive good, 715
Landrum-Griffin Act, 612
Laws
  of demand, **55**, 57

  of diminishing marginal utility, **430, 432,** 440
  of diminishing returns, **46,** 47
  of supply, **62,** 64
Legislation
  antidiscrimination, 673, 680–681, 683
  antipoverty, 677–678, 683
  antitrust, 554, 555, 557
  child labor, 38
  environmental, 639
  farm, 501, 503
  minimum-wage, 126, 622, 625
  prolabor, 611–612
  right-to-work, 617
Leisure. *See also* Standard of living
  as economic good, 11, 12
  indifference curve for, 581
Leontif, Wassily, 602, 811
Less developed countries
  accumulating capital goods in, 391–393
  barriers to economic development in, 383–390
  and cartels, 396–398, 399
  characteristics of, 398
  defining, 382–383
  economic growth in, 380–381, 389–390
  effect of cartels on, 396–398, 399
  encouraging investment in, 392–393
  and foreign aid, 393–395, 399
  growth rates in, 392
  health conditions in, 386
  and international trade, 763, 765
  lack of supporting infrastructure in, 388
  low capital accumulation in, 385–387
  multinational corporations in, 799
  paths of economic development in, 390–396, 399
  planning in, 395–396
  population growth in, 369
  private foreign investment in, 394
  problems with technology in, 387–388
  tariffs in, 732
Liberal economists, 797, 803
License fees, and urban land use, 656
Line of budget constraint, **437**

Liquid assets
  defined, **193**
  as determinant of aggregate consumption, 193
Liquidity preference curve, 251, 252, 262
Literacy, and per capita GNP, 384
Loan support program, of federal government, 497
Loans
  foreign, 745
  and monetary policy, 294
  private, 270–274
  repayment of, 274–275
  unwillingness to make, 277
Lobbying activity, 550
Local governments, revenue and spending of, 132. See also Government
Lockout, **611**
Long run, 418–419
  defined, **47**
  equilibrium in, 476–479
  monopoly in, 510
  monopoly market in, 515–517, 522
  for production costs, 445, 459
Loopholes, tax, 133
Lorenz curve, **667**–668, 682
Losses, minimizing short-run, 473–474
Lucas, Robert, 333
Luxuries, 49
  defined, **35**
  demand for, 35

Macroeconomics, **14**, 141
Maddison, Angus, 786
Malnutrition, 385
Malthus, Thomas Robert, 367, 368–369, 374
Management
  in less developed countries, 383
  problems of, 648
  Soviet, 785–786
  specialization of, 39, 48
  and unionism, 629
Manufacturing, large acquisitions in, 547
Mao Tse-tung, 788
Margin requirements, **299**, 302
Marginal cost
  and marginal revenue, 470–472
  in monopoly market, 513
  and profits maximizations, 472, 484
Marginal cost curve, **453**–454, 460
Marginal efficiency of investment (MEI), 196, 260, 261–262
Marginal physical product (MPP), 567, 575
  defined, **567**
  formulas for, 808
Marginal product (MP), 46–47, **446**
Marginal propensity to consume (MPC)
  defined, **190**
  formulas, 808
  and income levels, 195
  and NNP, 216
Marginal propensity to save (MPS)
  defined, **190**
  formulas for, 808
  in less developed countries, 385
  and NNP, 216
Marginal rate of substitution, **436**
Marginal revenue
  derivation of, 470
  and marginal cost, 470–472
  in monopoly market, 513
  and profits maximization, 472, 484
Marginal revenue curve, in monopolistic competition, 515, 532–533
Marginal revenue product (MRP), 567, 575
  defined, **567**
  formulas for, 808
  rate of decline of, 573–574
  of worker, 669
Marginal units, **13**
Marginal utility, **430**
Marginal utility analysis, 431, 432
Marginal utility principle, 434
Marginal utility theory, 430–435
Marginality, concept of, 12
Market
  agricultural, 465. See also Agricultural sector
  black, **68**, 420–421, 695, 785
  competitive vs. monopoly, 463
  Thomas Malthus on, 369
  monopoly, 505
  number of buyers, 61
  obligopoly, 526–527
  perfectly competitive. See Competition
  and pricing system, 79–80
  product, **62**, 68–69, 76
  resource, **62**, 69, 76. See also Resource market
Market demand schedule, **60**
Market economy, **52**
  competition in, 87–89
  competitive, 83–89
    assumptions of, 88
    profit motive in, 87
  and self-interest, 83–86
Market equilibrium, in short and long run, 515. See also General equilibrium analysis
Market imperfections and poverty, 670–672, 682
Market period, and elasticity of supply, 417
Market price, **54**, 70. See also Price system
Market supply
  and demand schedules, 66, 67
  determinants of, 66
Marshall, Alfred, 367
Marshall Plan, 753, 762
Marx, Karl, 774, 778, 783
Marxism, 780, 793–797, 803
  class struggle in, 794
  and imperialism, 795
  labor theory of value, 794
  legacy of, 796–797
  and need to accumulate capital, 795
  proletarian revolution, 796
Mass transit systems, 687. See also Transportation
Material-reward systems, 802
Mathematics, in economic study, 10–11
Meade, James E., 812
Mean, formulas for, 805
Meat-packing industry, by-products of, 40
Median, 102n, 808
Medicaid, 334, 679
Medicare, 334, 679
Menger, Karl, 431

Mergers 527, 546
   conglomerate, **549**, 558
   legislation regarding, 555
Mexico
   problems of, 401-402
   as supplier of natural gas, 689
Microeconomics, **14**, 407
   consumer demand, 429-439
   defined, **14**
Middle-class flight, 652-654, 661. *See also* Urban problems
Migration, urban, 652, 653, 661
Military, in GNP, 361
Military aid, 393
Military defense spending, 127
Military transactions, and balance of payments, 744
Mill, John Stuart, 85
Miller, Roger Leroy, 657
Minimum-wage laws, 69, 70
   net effect of, 126
   and unions, 622, 625
Mining, large acquisitions in, 547
Minnesota Mining and Manufacturing Company, 202, 510
Minority groups
   and dual labor market theory, 676
   low incomes among, 673-674
   quotas for, 681, 683
   and unions, 623
Mobility, imperfect, 671
Models, economic, **13**-15
   causation and correlation in, 14
   changing, 8
   fallacy of composition, 14
   relevance of, 13-14
Modernization, in China, 788
Monetarism, 331, 340
Monetary policy. *See also* Federal Reserve System
   alternatives to, 339-342
   and expectations, 333
   Federal Reserve
      contractionary measures of, 300
      expansionary measures of, 300
      mechanisms for implementing, 293-301, 302
      objectives of, 291-293, 302

Monetary system
   Bretton Woods, 756-757
   international, 759-760
Monetary theory, **246**
Money
   checks as, 249, 262
   in commercial bank transactions, 270-276
   defined, **52**
   demand, 250-251
   demand curve for, 251-252, 262
   functions of, 246-247, 262
   in Keynesian model, 256-262, **263**
   kinds of, 247
   paper, 248, 262
   precautionary demand for, 250-251
   quantity theory of, 252-254, 256, 262, 809-810
   speculative demand for, 251
   token, 248
   transactions demand for, 250
   in United States economy, 247-250
   velocity of, 253-254, 262, 809-810
Money demand, 250-251
Money flow, **76-77**
Money supply
   changes in, 259
   defined, **249-250**
   and equilibrium interest rate, 256-262, **263**
   and Federal Reserve System, 291
   limitations on expansion of, 276-277
Money system, fiat, 249
Monopolist
   cost and revenue schedule for, 511
   short-run equilibrium positions for, 516
Monopoly, 88-89, 505
   advertising in, 506
   defects of, 517-518, 522
   defined, **88**
   economic costs of, 517
   evolution of, 507
   inefficiencies of competition in, 534-535

   long-run situation for, 510
   natural, 510
   patent, 509
   and poverty, 671
   price discrimination of, 518-519, 523
   price and output under, 510-515
   pure, 506
   radical view of, 797-798
Monopoly market, 463
   barriers to entry, 507-510, 522
   characteristics of, 506-510, 522
   equilibrium in, 515-517, 522
   indivisibility of product in, 508
   legal restraints on, 509
   maximizing profits in, 512-515
   ownership of essential materials in, 508-509
   regulation of, 519-522, 523
Monopsony power, 548, 557
   defined, **548**
   and poverty, 671
   in resource market, 570
Moonlighting, 159
Moral persuasion, 637-639, 645
Morgan, J. P., 554
Most-favored nation clause, 754
MRP. *See* Marginal revenue product
Multinational corporations, 798-799. *See also* International trade; Less developed countries
Multiplier
   defined, **217**
   formulas for, 808
Multiplier effect, 216-218, 220
   defined, **217**
   graphic analysis of, 217
Multiplier theory, 216-218, 220
Municipal government. *See also* Urban problems
   financing of, 658-661, 662
   revenue sources and expenditures, 132
Myrdal, Gunnar, 811

National Association of Manufacturers, 611

National defense, industries necessary to, 732
National Education Association, 604
National Environmental Protection Act of 1969, 691
National Health Service, British, 787
National income
 components of, 151–152
 defined, **151**
National income and product accounts, **142**
National Labor Relations Act, 611
National Labor Relations Board, 612, 624
Nationalization
 defined, **390**
 of energy sources, 700
Natural gas
 and government policy, 688–689, 699
 liquification of, 689
Natural resources, distribution of, 35
Near money, **249**
Negative income tax, **679**
Neo-Marxists, 793
Net exports, **150**
Net investment, 149
Net national product (NNP)
 aggregate demand-aggregate supply approach to, 208–211
 defined, **152**
 effect of net exports on, 718
 effects of taxation on, 233–235
 equilibrium, 208
 and GNP, 153
 limitations as measure, 157
 savings-equals-investment approach to, 211–212, 220
New Economic Policy (NEP), 335–336
"New" economics, 255
 Kennedy-Johnson, 313–314
 "new," 256
New Left, 793, 797
New School of Social Research, 664
New York Bakers, 610
New York City
 and population shifts, 653
 rent control in, 421
 transportation in, 652

Nixon administration
 and gold reserves, 759
 price controls of, 690
 wage freeze of, 617
 wage-price controls of, 337–338, 343
Nondiscretionary fiscal policy, 224–227, 239
Nondurable goods, **148**. *See also* Goods
Nonprofit organizations, 118
Normal goods, **58**
Normal profit, **444**
Norris-La Guardia Act of 1932, 611
North
 migration from, 622, 625, 629
 unionization in, 622
North, Douglas C., 657
Notes, Federal Reserve, 289
Nuclear power, and government policy, 689, 700
Nuclear Regulatory Commission, 639
Nutrition, and less developed countries, 384–385. *See also* Health

Occupations
 distribution of, 28
 of women, 675. *See also* Women
Office of Economic Opportunity, 680
Ohlin, Bertil, 714, 717, 812
Oil. *See also* Energy
 and agricultural sector, 502
 depletion allowance, 134
 enhanced recovery and conversion to, 698
 and government policy, 688
Oil companies, and energy crisis, 685–686
Oil prices
 and advanced technology, 388
 and American dollar, 762
 and embargo, 500, 618
 and government policy, 688
 1973 crisis, 396–397, 399
 since 1973, 397
Oil producing nations, largest, 687. *See also* Organization of Petroleum Exporting Countries

Oil spills, 691
Old age, survivors, and disability and health insurance (ODASHI), 678
Oligopoly, 526–527, 539
 and collusion, 529–530
 defined, **525**
 and price inflexibility, 527–529
Open Market Committee, of Federal Reserve System, 287, 296
Open-market operations
 defined, **293**
 effect on investment, 296
 and public debt, 297
 purchases, 293–294, 302
 sales 294–296, 302
Opera industry, 509
Operational lag, 332
Opportunity costs, **12, 40, 49**, 669, 706
Optimum resource mix, **571**
Organization of African States, 396
Organization of Petroleum Exporting Countries (OPEC), 326, 394
 nations of, 396
 and 1973 crisis, 396–397
 oil embargo of, 336, 686
 and stagflation, 338
Output
 equilibrium level of, 208, 209
 maximization of, 37–40, 49
 under monopolistic competition, 510, 532–535
 and monopoly market, 520–522
 under oligopoly, 527–530
 in perfectly competitive market, 468
Overhead, 451
Ownership, private, 90

"Paper gold," 759
Paradox of thrift
 defined, **213**–214, 220
 graphic analysis of, 214
Parity equilibrium analysis, 593–594. *See also* General equilibrium analysis
Parity pricing, 495–498
 defined, **495**
 formula for, 496

Parity value, **757**
Partnerships, 119
 advantages of, 113
 defined, **113**
 disadvantages of, 113
 statistics on, 112
Patent laws, **509**, 522
Patronage, 128
Peak, defined, **178**. *See also* Business cycles
Per capita GNP, **155**
Per capita income, worldwide statistics on, 387
Percentages, formulas for, 809
Perfectly elastic demand, **411**
Perfectly inelastic demand, **411**
Permanent income, **194**
Personal income (PI), 153
Personal taste, 52
Petrodollars. *See also* Oil prices
 defined, **763**
 future of, 764
Philadelphia Cordwainers Case, 610
Phillips, A. W., 325
Phillips curve, 325-329, 342
 defined, **325**
 shifts in, 326-328
 trends in, 325-326
Physical necessities, 34, 39
Planning
 influence on investment, 202, 204
 stabilization policy, 341-342
Plant, **110**
Plastics industry, 197
Plenty, in comparing economic systems, 774, 789
Pocket calculator, and elasticity of demand, 426-427
Policymaking, economic
 and balance of trade, 334
 and economic growth, 334
 noneconomic goals of, 334
 problems with, 332-334
Political corruption, and economic development, 389
Political science, economics as, 5
Politics, vs. economics, 9, 229-230
Pollution. *See also* Environmental issues
 automobile, 649
 costs of, 70, 643
 and economic growth, 372

hidden costs of, 634
 price of, 640-642
Pollution control, 642
 cost-benefit analysis for, 643-644, 645
 costs of, 643-644, 645
Poor. *See also* Poverty
 in America, 665
 invisible, 666
 negative income tax for, 679
 welfare programs for, 678-679
Population growth
 and cities, 652-654
 and economic development, 391
 and economic theory, 367, 368-369
 of less developed countries, 382-383
Postal Service, United States, 129
Poverty
 in America, 665-668
 attitudes toward, 663, 668, 682
 causes of, 668-672
 definition of, 664-665, 682
 and discrimination, 672-674, 682
 and dual labor market theory, 676
 and education, 677-678
 and human capital, 669-670
 and inefficient mix of capital and labor, 671-672
 and welfare programs, 678-679
Precautionary demand, 250-251
Price(s)
 in agricultural sector, 501
 in black market, 68
 change in and quantity purchased, 439
 and changes in demand, 66
 and changes in supply, 66, 73-74
 defined, **52**
 and demand, 79
 and demand schedule, 55
 determinants of, 54, 76
 equilibrium, **67**, 71
 equilibrium determination of, 68
 and Federal Reserve monetary policy, 291-293
 and future expectations, 59-60
 market, **54**, 70

as mechanism for rationing scarce resources, 692
 under monopoly, 510, 520-522, 532-535
 during 1950s, 312
 under oligopoly, 527-530, 535
 percent change per year, 163
 and perfectly competitive market, 466-467, 484
 and quantity, 55
 in socialist economies, 781
 stable, 161, 162, 181
Price ceilings, 419-422, 424
 and black markets, 420-421
 defined, **419**
 effects of, 420
 and freely produced commodities, 421-422
Price controls
 effects of, 74
 and energy policy, 690-691
Price determination, 518-519, 523
 conditions necessary for, 518-519
 defined, **518**
Price elasticity
 perfect, 411-412
 types of, 409-412
Price fixing, **124-125**
Price index
 defined, **144**
 formulas for, 809
Price leader, **530**
Price supports, 69, 422, 424
"Price taker," 466
Price system, 78-83, 90
 competition in, 82, 482-484
 consumer in, 83
 correcting inequities of, 125-126
 defined, **78**
 demand in, 93-94
 dollar votes in, 78-79
 externalities in, 640-642, 645
 and government intervention, 124
 land in, 587-588
 and poverty, 668-669
 and production decisions, 81
 role of, 82
 and self-interest, 85
 shortcomings of, 588
Price uncertainty, in international trade, 742-743
Prime rate, **299**

Private costs
  for crime prevention, 657
  vs. social costs, 636
Private goods, **126**
Producers
  choices of, 75
  competition among, 82
Producer Price Indexes (PPI)
  defined, **165**, 181
  limitation of, 165
Product curves, 445-449
  average, 448-449
  marginal, 446-448, 459
  total, **445**-446, 459
Product development, competition through, 536
Product image campaigns, 537. *See also* Advertising
Product improvement, and big business, 551-552
Production
  and capital need, 197
  in China, 788
  costs of, 64
  curtailing, 639
  efficiency of, 38-40
  in existing markets, 79
  factors of, 35, 39, 49, 565
  fixed factor of, 568
  fixed inputs of, **444**, 459
  hidden costs of, 634, 644
  household, 100
  increasing costs of, 43-48
  inefficiency in, 42
  and input resource costs, 82
  inputs, 39
  in international trade, 709-710
  method of, 82-83
  in new markets, 79-81
  outdated facilities for, 359-360
  and price system, 90
  private costs of, 636
  social costs of, 636
  variable inputs of, 444-445
Production costs
  analysis of, 128
  defining, 444-445
  explicit and implicit, 444, 459
  long-run, 457-459, 460
  resource cost as percentage of, 575
  short run, 449-457, 460
  and supply, 64

and supply schedule, 80
  variable, 449-451
Production goals, of government, 128
Production possibilities, 40-43
  concept of, 48, 49
  defined, 41
Production possibilities curve, 40, 43, 359, 708, 709
Productivity, household, 103
Product(s). *See also* Goods
  complementary, 59
  marginal, 46-47
  substitute, 59
  union-made, 619
Product market, 68-69, 76
  defined, **62**
  equilibrium in, 207
  in general equilibrium analysis, 595-597, 598, 600, 602
  perfect competition in, 566, 567
Profit(s)
  and collective bargaining, 616
  corporate, **152**
  defined, **62, 110**
  distributing, 117
  economic, **117**, 469
  and investment decisions, 198
  maximizing short-run, 468-472, 484
  and MC=MR method, 472
  normal, **444**
  "psychological," 117
  in socialist economies, 787
  undistributed, 152
Profit motive, 87, 90
Progressive tax
  defined, **133**, 135
  stabilizing effects of, 226
Property taxes, 136
Proportional taxes
  defined, **133**, 135
  stabilizing effects of, 226
Proposition 13, 136, 339
Proprietors' income, in national income, 151
Proprietorships
  advantages of, 113
  disadvantages of, 112
  income from, 101-102
  individual, **111-112**, 119
  statistics on, 112t

Prosperity, effect of, 34. *See also* Affluence
Protectionism, 752, 764
Psychology, economics in, 5
Public debt
  benefits of, 238-239, 240
  defined, **236**
  effects of, 237-238
  emotional attitudes generated by, 238, 240
  historical theories of, 237
  and open-market transactions, 297
Public goods, 8
  defined, **126**
  government inefficiency in producing, 128-230
Public interest, difficulty in evaluating, 638, 645
Public opinion. *See also* Attitudes
  and big business, 556
  and economic policymaking, 332-333, 343
Pubic policy, and big business, 553, 557
Public schools, functions of, 129. *See also* Education
Public services, measuring value of, 154
Public transportation system, 651. *See also* Transportation
Public Utilities Commission (PUC), 542
Public-works spending programs, and time lag, 230. *See also* Government intervention
Purchase, characteristics of, 83

Quantity
  and change in demand, 56
  and change in supply, 64
  price and, 55
Quantity theory, 252-254, 256, 262
  formulas for, 809
  and full employment, 254
  and "new" economics, 255-256
  and unemployment, 254-255
Quotas
  for discrimination, 681, 683
  and free trade, 723
  in international trade, 725

Racism, 800
Radical economics
  capitalism in, 797–799
  Marxism, 794–797, 803
  response to, 801–802
  for socialist society, 801
Railroad industry, and demand, 79
Rationing, gasoline, 695–696
Ratios, 809
"Razor's edge, the," 371
Real estate taxes, effect on supply and demand, 423. *See also* Tax(es)
Real flow, **76**
Recession, 319. *See also* Business cycles
  consumer demand in, 307
  defined, **178**
  during energy crisis, 687
  investment demand in, 307
  money supply in, 307–308
  1948–1949, 311
  in 1950s, 312
  of 1960–1961, 315
  1970, 335
  in 1974, 316
  and pricing externalities, 641
Reciprocal Trade Agreements Act of 1934, 753
Recognition lag, 332
Recovery
  in business cycle, 306, 318
  defined, **177–178**
  of 1960–1961, 315
Recreation, as public good, 8. *See also* Leisure
Regressive taxes
  defined, **133**, 135
  stabilizing effect of, 226
Regulation, and energy crisis, 688–692, 699. *See also* Government regulation
Regulation Q, interest rates on deposits of, 299
Relevance, problem of, 13–14
Rent
  defined, **151**
  economic, 586–587
  in national income, 151–152
Rent controls, 69, 421

Research and development. *See also* Technological advances
  and big business, 552
  and economic growth, 373
  in energy field, 699, 700
Reserve ratio, **268**
Reserve requirements
  changing, 297–298, 302
  defined, **268**
  purpose of, 268
Residential construction, determinants of, 201. *See also* Housing
Resource demand, and poverty, 669, 682
Resource market, 69, 76
  defined, **62**
  demand in, 566–571
  determinants of demand in, 571–573
  financial capital in, 588–591, 592
  in general equilibrium analysis, 595–597, 598, 600, 602
  labor unions and, 572
  land supply in, 586–588, 591
  monopsonistic power in, 570
  optimum resource mix, 571
  substitutability in, 575, 576
  supply of labor, 579–584
Resources. *See also* Human resources; Labor; Natural resources
  allocation of
    in capitalist economy, 778
    and unions, 621
  and economic growth, 361, 362–363
  input, 82, 116
  labor, 36
  productive, 37–38
  scarcity of, 3, 33, 35–37
  underemployment of, **38**
Revenue
  marginal, 470–472
  total, **468**
Revenue Sharing Act, 132
Revenue-sharing programs, 134, 658–659
Ricardo, David, 366–367, 368, 374
Right-to-work laws, **617**
Robinson, Joan, 531
Robinson-Patman Act, 555

Rockefeller, John D., 554
Roosevelt administration, 309, 330
"Rule of reason," 555

Safety
  demand for, 556, 558
  as economic good, 656
Sales, and business cycles, 178
Sales taxes, 131, 422. *See also* Tax(es)
Sales value, and value added, 147
Samuelson, Paul, 215–216, 730, 811
Sargent, Thomas, 333
Satisfaction, maximization of, 33, 37–40, 49
Saudi Arabia, oil production of, 397. *See also* Organization of Petroleum Exporting Countries
Saving
  average propensity for, 806
  defined, **101**, **101n**, 105
  and economic growth, 363
  by households, 104–105, 188, 204
  in income analysis, 188
  and intended investment, 213, 220
  marginal propensity toward, **190**, 216, 385, 808
  patterns of, 105
Saving schedule, **189–190**
Say, Jean Baptiste, 328, 329
Say's Law, **328**, 343, 365
Scale. *See also* Economies of scale
  diseconomies of scale, 47–48, 49
  problems of, 648
Scarcity
  and economic growth, 366
  fuel, 686, 687. *See also* Energy
  problem of, 3
  of resources, 3, 33, 35–37
Schumpeter, Joseph, 365, 387
Schwartz, Anna, 257
Science
  economics as, 5, 7–10
  social vs. physical, 6
Scientific method
  applied to economics, 6–7
  limitations of, 6–7
  objectivity of, 6
Second-hand goods, sale of, 147
Securities, 114

Security, job
  and collective bargaining, 616. *See also* Collective bargaining
  in comparing economic systems, 775, 789
Security and Exchange Commission, 167
Self-interest
  as assumption in market economy, 83–86
  environmental protection and, 639
  and government intervention, 86
Sellers
  in competitive market, 464
  government protection of, 124
Seniority, and collective bargaining, 616
Services, 118
  defined, **148**
  demand for, 34
  increased position in economy, 629
Sex, as labor limitation, 38. *See also* Discrimination; Women
Sherman Antitrust Act, 554, 558, 611
Shoe industry, 173, 547
Shortage. *See also* Scarcity
  defined, **68**
  in Soviet Union, 786
Short run
  competitive firm in, 466–474
  defined, **47**
  and elasticity of supply, 418
  equilibrium in, 475–476, 477, 478
  minimizing losses in, 473–474
  monopoly market in, 515–517, 522
  for production costs, 445, 459
Simon, Herbert A., 812
Skills, in labor market, 584–585. *See also* Labor
Smith, Adam, 195, 258, 356, 368, 430, 665
  on economic growth, 366, 374
  on self-interest, 85–86
  on specialization, 706
Social attitudes. *See also* Attitudes
  and agricultural sector, 492–493
  and economic development, 389

Social costs
  of crime, 657
  vs. private costs, 636
Social goods, **126**
Social organization, and economic growth, 361
Social problems, radical view of, 799–801, 803
Social programs, 334
Social Security, 678, 778
Social welfare, in GNP, 155–156
Socialist economies, **776**, 778–780, 789
  democratic, 787
  example of, 783–786
  model for, 780–783
  success of, 782–783, 789
  Yugoslavia, 786–787
Socialist society, radical model of, 801
Sociology, economics in, 5
Solar energy, 698. *See also* Energy
South
  and Sun-Belt phenomenon, 629
  unionization in, 622
South Africa, 758
Soviet Union
  agricultural sector in, 783–784, 785
  command economy of, 784–786, 789
  communication difficulties in, 785
  consumer demand in, 785
  distribution of goods in, 785–786
  and economic growth, 361
  growth rate of, 372, 786
  organization of production in, 784–785
  ownership of productive assets in, 783–784
Special Drawing Rights (SDRs), 288–289, **288**, 301, 759–760, 765
  defined, **759–760**
  future of, 764
Specialization
  advantages of, 109
  and international trade, 706–707
  in United States economy, 90–91
Speculative demand, 251
Spending
  business, 116–117

consumption component of, 188–195
deficit, 237–238
and employment levels, 174
equal marginal utility principle and, 435
by households, 104–105
investment component of, 195–203
patterns of, 105
total, 188, 195–203
Staats, Elmer, 125
Stability
  in comparing economic systems, 775, 789
  traditional theory and method, 328–331, 343
Stabilization policies, 323, 324–328, 342
Stagflation, 334–342, 343
  approaches to, 337–342
  defined, **335**
  and WIN program, 338–339
Stalin, Joseph, 789
Standard of living
  and definition of poverty, 664
  in economic theory, 367
  and GNP, 358
  of less developed countries, 382
  and pollution control, 642
  and women in labor force, 674
Standard Metropolitan Statistical Areas (SMSAs), 659
State government(s)
  and banking laws, 266
  and interstate vs. intrastate markets for natural gas, 689
  revenue sources of, 131–132
  spending of, 132
State and Local Fiscal Assistance Act, 132
Status symbols, 5
Steel industry, 552, 556
Stocks, corporate
  in balance-of-payments statement, 746
  household ownership of, 102
  investment in, 113–114
  margin requirements on, 299, 302
Stopler, Wolfgang, 730
Strikes, **610**. *See also* Unions
Structural unemployment, **173**, 181

Subsidies, farm, 124, 499–500. *See also* Agricultural sector
Substitutes
  defined, **59**
  and demand, 59
Substitution, factor, 572–573
Substitution effect, **439**
Sun-Belt phenomenon, 622, 625, 629
Supplementary Security Income (SSI), 678
Suppliers
  in competitive market, 464
  and perfectly competitive market, 467
Supply
  aggregate, 208
  change in, 64
  changes in determinants of, 71
  and changes in price, 66
  defined, **61**
  determinants of, 51–52, 62, 64–66
  and economic growth, 359
  effect on wages, 677
  effects of free trade on, 727
  and future expectations, 65
  government actions affecting, 419–423, 424
  and growth of demand, 366, 374
  in international trade, 726
  law of, **62**, 64, 408
  market equilibrium of, 67–68
  in perfect competition, 466
  and prices, 73–74
  and production, 83
  in teacher market, 604
  and terms of trade, 711–712
  and theory of factor endowments, 714
  and unionism, 620
Supply curve
  backward bending, 582, 591
  defined, **63**
  market, 584
  short-run, 473, 484
Supply schedule
  defined, **62**
  for financial capital, 589
  for individual producer, 63
  and production costs, 80
  and sales taxes, 422
  for worker, 580

Supreme Court
  on big business, 554
  on discrimination, 681
  and industry-wide steel strike, 618
Surplus
  consumer, 432–433
  defined, **68**
  in federal budget, 235–236
  land rent as pure, 587
Surplus revenue, disposing of, 235–236

Taft-Hartley Act, 612, 618, 624
Target prices, **501**
Tariff(s), 724–733
  ad valorem, **724**, 733
  causes of, 729–732
  defined, **724**
  economic effects of, 725–729, 733
  and free trade, 723
  Hawley-Smoot, 752
  imposition of, 728
  inefficiencies caused by, 729, 734
  political uses of, 732–733, 734
  protective, 724
  reduction in, 754, 764
  supporters of, 730
Tariff cuts, "Kennedy Round" of, 754
Tastes, and demand, 60
Taxation
  ability-to-pay principle of, **133**, 134
  altering rates of, 229
  benefits-received principle of, **132–133**, 134
  and discrimination, 673
  effects on NNP, 233–235
  in Great Britain, 787
  and land supply, 587
Tax(es)
  corporation, 116
  excise, 422–423
  on households, 104
  indirect business, **152**, 153
  and inflation, 160
  loopholes in, 133
  for military defense, 127
  negative income, 679–680
  progressive, **133**, 135, 225, 226
  property, 136

  proportional, 133, 135
  regressive, 133, 135, 226
  sales, 131, 442
  turnover, 782
  types of, 133–134, 135
  and urban land use, 656
  user, 660–661
Tax incentives, for efficient energy use, 695
Tax protest, of 1978, 136, 137
Tax rates, and entrepreneurship, 37
Tax Reduction Act of 1975, 316
Tax revenues, effect on government spending, 225
Tax structure, stabilizing effect of, 224, 226
Tax system
  indexing in, 339–340
  and inflation, 160
Teacher market, supply and demand in, 604–607
Teamsters, 613. *See also* Unions
Technological advances, 39
  and big business, 551–552
  and energy conservation, 698–699
  and environmental issues, 634
  and investment decision, 196–197
  and women in labor force, 674
Technology
  and agricultural supply, 491–492, 502
  alternative energy, 693, 698–699
  and consumer demand, 35
  defined, **37**
  and economic growth, 361, 363–364, 367, 371, 373, 374
  and less developed countries, 387–388
  and resource market, 572
Television industry, vertical integration in, 548
Tennessee Valley Authority (TVA), 230
Terms of trade, **711**–712
Terms-of-trade line, **712**
Thompson, Wilbur R., 660
Three-Mile Island Power Generating Facility, 689
Thrift, paradox of, **213**, 213–214, 220
Time, 697
Time lags, **230**, 332, 343

Tinenbergen, Jan, 811
Tito, Marshal, 786
Token money, 248
Total cost
　defined, **449**
　in monopoly market, 512
　and total revenue, 468–469
Total cost curve, **449**–453, 360
Total product curve
　defined, **445**–446, 459
　variable cost curve derived from, 451
Total revenue
　defined, **468**
　in monopoly market, 512
Total spending
　consumption component of, 188, 203
　investment component of, 195–203
Total variable cost (TVC), 451
Tourism, and energy policy, 697
Trade. *See also* International trade
　gains from, 712–714
　invisible, 745
　political barriers to, 507
Trade Expansion Act, 754, 764
Transactions demand, **250**
Transfer payments, 101n, 130–131, 134
　defined, **130**
　exclusion from GNP of, 145
　stabilizing effect of, 226–227
Transportation
　energy use for, 690
　improved public, 651–652, 661
　in less developed countries, 388
　public, 651
　as public good, 8
　urban, 648–652, 661
Transportation forms, dollar votes of, 78–79
Treasury, United States, and Federal Reserve System, 291
Treasury deposits, **289**
Trough, **178**. *See also* Business cycles
Truman administration
　Brannan plan of, 499
　fiscal policy of, 311
Trust
　defined, **554**
　and public policy, 554

Turnover tax, **782**
Two-tier system
　introduction of, 758
　problems with, 758–759

Underemployment, 107, 172
Unemployment, 169–177, 181
　costs of, 175–176
　cyclical, **174**
　and economic growth, 372
　during energy crisis, 687
　frictional, **173**, 181
　and inflation, 325–329
　involuntary, 38
　of labor, 170–171
　level of, 174
　measurement of, 39n, 171–173
　during 1940s, 309
　during 1950s, 312
　in 1970s, 315, 317
　and quantity theory, 254–255
　social costs of, 176–177
　special policies to reduce, 341
　structural, **173**, 181
　types of, 173
　vs. underemployment, 39
　and women, 676
　since World War II, 343
Unemployment compensation, 316, 679, 778
Unemployment rate, 21, 22
　defined, **172**
　and inflation, 327
　for minority youths, 341
　in 1970s, 315
　in United States, 175
Unilateral-transfers account, 745, 747
Unionism
　and antilabor activities, 611
　and demand for labor, 618–620
　effects of, 609
　history of, 610–614
　in postwar period, 612
　trends in, 614
　and supply of labor, 620
Unions
　American Federation of Labor, 611
　and collective bargaining, 617

　Congress of Industrial Organizations (CIO), 612, 624
　contemporary, 624
　critics of, 621–625
　declining memberships in, 627–629
　and demand for labor, 619
　educational functions of, 618
　functions of, 614
　future of, 622–624, 625
　higher wages achieved by, 618–621
　and inflation, 621
　Knights of Labor, 610–611, 624
　membership in, 613
　and minimum-wage law, 622, 625
　and resource allocation, 621
　and resource market, 572
　structure of, 614
　success of, 620
　and supply of labor, 619
　supporters of, 621, 625
　Teamsters, 613
　United Auto Workers (UAW), 613
　United Mine Workers, 613
Union shop, **612**
Unit prices, 125
Unitary price elasticity, **411**
United Auto Workers (UAW), 613
United Federation of Teachers, 619
United Kingdom
　democratic socialism in, 787–788, 790
　and gains from trade, 713–714
　production possibilities curve for, 710–711
United Mine Workers, 613
United Nations, 393, 394
United States economy
　aggregate consumption schedule for, 191–192
　and balance of payments, 746–747, 748
　bigness in, 546–548
　circular flow of, 143
　and declining dollar, 760–761
　division of labor in, 90
　dual labor market theory in, 676–677, 683
　dynamic nature of, 7

effects of discrimination on, 672–673
environmental issues in, 634
extensive use of capital in, 89–90
and gold reserve, 248
and gold-backing requirements, 757
government in, 122–123. *See also* Government intervention
growth in, 361–366, 374
growth rate for, 379–382
imperfect competition in, 89
income distribution in, 666–668, 682
increasing labor force of, 363
in international trade, 708. *See also* International trade
macroeconomic experience of, 305
major characteristics of, 91
median household income in, 102. *See also* Households
money in, 247
in 1930s, 308–309, 319
1940 to 1945, 309–311, 319
1945–1950, 311–312
in 1950s, 312, 319
in 1960s, 312–315, 319
in 1970s, 315–318, 319
poor in, 665–668. *See also* Poverty
private ownership in, 90
shift from manufacturing to service, 629
specialization in, 90
supply and demand in, 70
and tariff policy, 754
unemployment rate in, 175
women in, 674. *See also* Women
United States Steel Pension Fund, 295
United States v. United States Steel Corporation, 554
Urban problems
crime, 656–657
economics of, 647
financing municipal government, 658–661, 662
land use, 654–656, 661–662
of management and scale, 648
transportation, 648–652, 661. *See also* Transportation
shifting population, 652–654, 661

User charge, 652
User taxes, 660–661. *See also* Tax(es)
Utility
and decision making, 48
defined, **430**
marginal, **430**, 440
maximizing, 433–435, 440
total, 430–440

Value
commodity, 248
and decision making, 48
labor theory of, 794
money as standard of, 247
Value added
defined, **145**
vs. sales value, 147
Variable cost
average, 23, **454**–455
defined, **449**
and minimizing losses, 474
Variable cost curve, 451
Variable inputs, **444**–445, 459
Veblen, Thorstein, 194
Velocity, 262
defined, **253**
and Federal Reserve monetary policy, 292
formulas for, 253–254, 809–810
Vertical integration, **548**, 558
Vietnam war, 314, 334, 762
and economic views, 793
and inflation, 316
and stagflation, 335
von Hayek, Friedrich A., 811

Wage(s)
in collective bargaining, 615. *See also* Collective bargaining
determination of, 584–586, 591
discrimination in, 676
effect of supply and demand on, 677
in monopsonistic market, 570
satisfaction with, 582
in socialist economies, 781, 787
and unions, 618–621
women and, 674–676
Wage constraint, line of, 580–581

Wage and price controls, 316–317
alternatives to, 339–342
and stagflation, 337–343
Wage and salaries
defined, **151**
in national income, 151
in personal income, 101
Wage-push inflation, 167
Wagner Act, 611
Wallace, Neil, 333
Wall Street Journal, 562
Walras, Leon, 431, 594
War. *See also specific wars*
farm income during, 488
and inflation, 168
and protective tariffs, 732
"Warehouse receipts," **288**
Waste loads, 635
Water Pollution Control Act, Federal, 70
Wealth, money for storage of, 247
Wealth of Nations, The, 85–86
Welfare, and economic growth, 357
Welfare programs, 678–679, 683
Wheaton Glass Company, and antidiscrimination legislation, 680
Whip Inflation Now program (WIN), 106n, 338–339
Wholesale Price Index, 165
Wind energy, 699
"Wine wars," 755
Women
discrimination against, 800. *See also* Discrimination
and dual labor market theory, 676
and economic growth, 363
in Moslem countries, 389
and need for day care, 676
occupational distribution of, 675
unemployment rate for, 341
unionization of, 623
in United States economy, 674–676, 682
Workers
alienation of, 799
full employment of, 37
and job demands, 585–586
in less developed countries, 388
minority, 623

nonfarm, 628
and poverty, 668–669, 682
in secondary sector, 676
shorter work week for, 363
and skills, 584–585
supply schedule for, 580
tariffs for protection of, 729–730, 733, 734
union, 622
union vs. nonunion, 620
World Bank, 393, 394
World Health Organization (WHO), 394
World War I, and agricultural sector, 496
World War II
 economic effects of, 195
 fiscal policy during, 310
 and international trade, 751
 monetary policy during, 310–311
 United States economy during, 319
 women employed during, 674
Worldwide statistics
 in growth rate, 380–381
 on health conditions, 386
 on per capita GNP, 380–381
 on per capita income, 387

Xerox Corporation, 510

Yellow-dog contracts, **611**
Yugoslavia, socialist market economy of, 786–787

Zoning codes, 655, 656. *See also* Land

Notes Chapter 8

GNP − Capital consumption allowance (Depreciation) = Net National product

GNP − Dep = NNP
NNP − Indirect Business taxes = NI
National Income − Income not recieved by households
+ Income not earned in production of GNP (Transfer payments) =
Personal income − Taxes = Disposable income

POPULATION, EMPLOYMENT, AND WAGES / PRODUCTION AND BUSINESS ACTIVITY / PRICES

Year	Population (Millions of persons)	Civilian labor force (Millions of persons)	Unemployment as percent of civilian labor force (Percent)	Average weekly hours of work Total nonagricultural private sector (Hours)	Average gross hourly earnings Total nonagricultural private sector (Dollars current)	Index of industrial production (1967 = 100)	Business expenditures for new plant and equipment (Billions of dollars)	Consumer Price index (1967 = 100)	Producer price index for total finished goods (formerly wholesale price index) (1967 = 100)
1929	121.8	49.2	3.2%	—	—	21.6	—	51.3	49.1
1930	123.1	49.8	8.7	—	—	—	—	50.0	44.6
1931	124.0	50.4	15.9	—	—	—	—	45.6	37.6
1932	124.8	51.0	23.6	—	—	—	—	40.9	33.6
1933	125.6	51.6	24.9	—	—	13.7	—	38.8	34.0
1934	126.4	52.2	21.7	—	—	—	—	40.1	38.6
1935	127.3	52.9	20.1	—	—	—	—	41.1	41.3
1936	128.1	53.4	16.9	—	—	—	—	41.5	41.7
1937	128.8	54.0	14.3	—	—	—	—	43.0	44.5
1938	129.8	54.6	19.0	—	—	—	—	42.2	40.5
1939	130.9	55.2	17.2	—	—	21.7	—	41.6	39.8
1940	132.1	55.6	14.6	—	—	25.0	—	42.0	40.5
1941	133.4	55.9	9.9	—	—	31.6	—	44.1	45.1
1942	134.9	56.4	4.7	—	—	36.3	—	48.8	50.9
1943	136.7	55.5	1.9	—	—	44.0	—	51.8	53.3
1944	138.4	54.6	1.2	—	—	47.4	—	52.7	53.6
1945	139.9	53.9	1.9	—	—	40.7	—	53.9	54.6
1946	141.4	57.5	3.9	—	—	35.0	—	58.5	62.3
1947	144.1	59.4	3.9	40.3	$1.131	39.4	19.33	66.9	74.0
1948	146.6	60.6	3.8	40.0	1.225	41.1	21.30	72.1	79.9
1949	149.2	61.3	5.9	39.4	1.275	38.8	18.98	71.4	77.6
1950	152.3	62.2	5.3	39.8	1.335	44.9	20.21	72.1	79.0
1951	154.9	62.0	3.3	39.9	1.45	48.7	25.46	77.8	86.5
1952	157.6	62.1	3.0	39.9	1.52	50.6	26.43	79.5	86.0
1953	160.2	63.0	2.9	39.6	1.61	54.8	28.20	80.1	85.1
1954	163.0	63.6	5.5	39.1	1.65	51.9	27.19	80.5	85.3
1955	165.9	65.0	4.4	39.6	1.71	58.5	29.53	80.2	85.5
1956	168.9	66.6	4.1	39.3	1.80	61.1	35.73	81.4	87.9
1957	172.0	66.9	4.3	38.8	1.89	61.9	37.94	84.3	91.1
1958	174.9	67.6	6.8	38.5	1.95	57.9	31.89	86.6	93.2
1959	177.8	68.4	5.5	39.0	2.02	64.8	33.55	87.3	93.0
1960	180.7	69.6	5.5	38.6	2.09	66.2	36.75	88.7	93.7
1961	183.7	70.5	6.7	38.6	2.14	66.7	35.91	89.6	93.7
1962	186.5	70.6	5.5	38.7	2.22	72.2	38.39	90.6	94.0
1963	189.2	71.8	5.7	38.8	2.28	76.5	40.77	91.7	93.7
1964	191.9	73.1	5.2	38.7	2.36	81.7	46.97	92.9	94.1
1965	194.3	74.5	4.5	38.8	2.46	89.8	54.42	94.5	95.7
1966	196.6	75.8	3.8	38.6	2.56	97.8	63.51	97.2	98.8
1967	198.7	77.3	3.8	38.0	2.68	100.0	65.47	100.0	100.0
1968	200.7	78.7	3.6	37.8	2.85	106.3	67.76	104.2	102.9
1969	202.7	80.7	3.5	37.7	3.04	111.1	75.56	109.8	106.6
1970	204.9	82.7	4.9	37.1	3.23	107.8	79.71	116.3	110.3
1971	207.1	84.1	5.9	36.9	3.45	109.6	81.21	121.3	113.7
1972	208.8	86.5	5.6	37.0	3.70	119.7	88.44	125.3	117.2
1973	210.4	88.7	4.9	36.9	3.94	129.8	99.74	133.1	127.9
1974	211.9	91.0	5.6	36.5	4.24	129.3	112.40	147.7	147.5
1975	213.6	92.6	8.5	36.1	4.53	117.8	112.78	161.2	163.4
1976	215.2	94.8	7.7	36.1	4.86	129.8	120.49	170.5	170.3
1977	216.9	97.4	7.0	36.0	5.24	137.1	135.80	181.5	180.6
1978	218.5	100.4	6.0	35.8	5.68	145.2	153.82	195.3	194.6

Details may not add exactly because of rounding.